TEMPEST, FIRE AND FOE

A.H.G.

Tempest, Fire and Foe

TEMPEST, FIRE AND FOE

Destroyer Escorts in World War II

and

The Men Who Manned Them

by

Lewis M. Andrews, Jr.

Narwhal Press
Charleston/Miami

Library of Congress Catalog Card Number: 98-066132

ISBN: 1-886391-31-9 (paperback)
ISBN: 1-886391-30-0 (hardcover)

FIRST EDITION

Front Cover: Skipper R. Wilcox of *Joyce (DE-317)* performing last rites for 1 of 3 German submariners from the sunken *U-550,* 16 April 1944.

Back Cover: Jubilation aboard the *USS Wileman (DE-220)* at news war ended. US Navy Photo

Title Page: Edgar G. Chase launching a depth charge attack.

Cover design and layout by Kris Adams

Printed in the United States of America.

DEDICATION

To all the young men who went down to the sea in small ships
to fight for their country in World War II.

From Rock and tempest, Fire and Foe
Protect Them where so 'ere They Go...

ACKNOWLEDGMENTS

The material for this book has been derived from Naval archives, the *Dictionary of American Naval Fighting Ships*, *DESA NEWS* (Quarterly publication of the Destroyer Escort Sailors Association), numerous publication sources which are listed in Appendix I, and officers and men who were involved and willingly shared their experiences with me. Many men supplied me with cherished personal diaries and photos never before published. I am also indebted to: The staff at the Naval Historical Center, Washington, D.C.; The United States Naval Institute Press, Annapolis, Md.; Rear Admiral E.M. Eller, former Director of Naval History; The staff at DESA NEWS headquarters; Captain James E. Wise Jr., USN (Ret.), my researcher.

CONTENTS

Lewis M. Andrews, Jr.

FOREWARD

I started to accumulate material for this book in the early 1950s when many war diaries, logs, and action reports were still classified and had to be declassified before I could extract material. Rear Admiral E.M. Eller, Director of Naval History, was most helpful in making documents available to me and encouraging me to continue. I had fully intended to write this book at that time, but I had to set it aside to meet the demands of my peacetime occupation.

Actually, this would have been an extremely difficult book to write before the era of personal computers. With about 400 destroyer escorts and fast transports (APD) placed in commission in World War II, a data base control had to be established from the beginning. Word processing enabled me to take data from several action reports in one ship, division, convoy or task group and meld them with personal narratives from officers and men so as to arrive at a single, cohesive product. I tried not to lose sight of the fact that destroyer escorts were great, but the men who manned them were greater.

Now, retired from business, I have again taken up the pen to relate storied deeds and heroism, tears and laughter so that they will be known to our countrymen long after we are gone.

All destroyer escorts had their time of humor and tragedy and rendered their share of dedication and heroism. In general, I eliminated monotonous "boiler plate" such as construction, shakedown, sea trials, yard availability, etc. Three exceptions were *Borum*, *Gendreau* and *Pavlic*, the first in the Atlantic chapter Operations Overlord and Neptune, the second and third in the Pacific DE and APD chapters Iwo Jima to Okinawa. In all three cases, I was fortunate to procure extraordinarily well written and documented diaries that most any destroyer escort officer or enlisted man can relate to. I did not include ship namesake histories because they are available elsewhere. Some operations were obviously more exciting than others. Some DEs simply never crossed the path of a submarine, nor were "lucky" enough to have a *kamikaze* pilot want to introduce them to his ancestors. Others were repeatedly and violently engaged.

The activities of all DEs in World War II are summarized in the final chapter, Destroyer Escort Summary of Operations. Narratives are confined to ships that were engaged with the enemy or involved in other hazards such as convoy collisions and fires, hurricanes and typhoons. Within those narratives, however, other passive or interactive DEs are also named. An example might be an account of the destruction of a submarine by one DE while others remained in the carrier screen or played a minor role. Tribute is paid herein to all the DE men of World War II, from captain to lowest rating, alive and departed.

The DE was the highest combatant ship command that most reserve officers could aspire to in World War II. It was also coveted by Naval Academy graduates, as it was the youngest command for which they could compete.

An association known as DESA (Destroyer Escort Sailors Association) includes thousands of ex DE officers and enlisted men. Another association is known as DECO (Destroyer Escort Commanding Officers).

Together, DESA and DECO are a living, but unfortunately diminishing, reminder of a dynamic period in which we had the privilege of sharing experiences together. Greatness has no rank. Combat against submarines, suicide planes or simply the cruel ocean were time frames recorded aboard small ships on the high seas in time of war.

Except for *Slater* in the Destroyer Escort Museum in Albany, New York, and a few left in some foreign navies, the DEs are gone today, long ago sold for scrap and to make way for their modern successors, frigates and guided missile frigates. If ships have souls, as some believe, then they are still somewhere out there, along with the ships of Jones, Perry and Farragut.

The *Might,* a Canadian built corvette. The author was its executive officer in 1943.

LCDR Lewis M. Andrews Jr.

Lewis M. Andrews, Jr.

PREFACE

On graduating from Connecticut Wesleyan University in June, 1939, my immediate plans were to take a trip around the world on freighters that would take the better part of a year.

In spite of the threatening European situation, I decided to go ahead with my plans. Crises and threats of war had been weathered over the past few years and might do so again. Besides, I didn't have plans to go to Europe. At the end of the first week in July, I took a train from New York to New Orleans where I boarded *Silverpalm*, a British freighter belonging to the Silver Java Steamship Lines. She headed nonstop to Cape Town, South Africa, a three week journey.

I saw a world that would never be seen again, a world of Empire that some dreamed would last forever. There was no Third World. Virtually all of Africa and large parts of Asia belonged to the European powers. The politics and economics of most of the global land mass were the politics and economics of the colonial masters. Indigenous people rarely made the front page of a newspaper.

There had been a lot of upsetting news the first few weeks after departing from New Orleans. Hitler was demanding that Poland cede back to Germany Danzig and the Polish Corridor which had been established by the Treaty of Versailles. England, starting to awaken from the Czech fiasco, warned that it would fight if Germany attacked Poland. Nonetheless, Hitler sent his *panzer* divisions crashing across the Polish frontier. A few of us were invited to Captain Wilson's cabin at night to listen to the latest news from the British Broadcasting Corporation on short wave.

We listened to Chamberlain's mournful and uninspiring request to Parliament to declare war on Germany. Although expected, the older ship's officers such as the captain and the chief engineer were downcast. They had both been through the First World War, only 20 years before, and had never expected to see a second one. Although we were far from what we erroneously thought to be the area of combat and German submarine capability, I slowly realized that I was on a ship belonging to a combatant. Passengers became more subdued, a trifle anxious, as war became the main topic of discussion.

After South and East Africa, we arrived in Singapore without mishap. *Silverpalm* went into dry dock for periodic maintenance, and all 12 passengers had to live ashore for a month. The captain recommended Raffles Hotel so I simply took a cab there with my luggage and checked in; there was no need for reservations then. I had no inkling of the fame and nostalgia that would surround that Empire bastion in later years. Raffles was the headquarters for the local social register and the preferred watering hole for administrators, military officers and visiting dignitaries.

British officers in their gleaming uniforms and their ladies in their finery danced the night away, completely secure in their powerful fortress with its huge shore batteries commanding the sea approaches, but never a thought to the land approaches. After all, who could possibly think of marching south through the IndoChinese and Malayan jungles to attack Singapore? The very idea was laughable except, in the end, the only ones who laughed were the Japanese.

After a month, *Silverpalm* had been floated and was ready to sail. Something new had been added to the freighter, paravanes attached to serrated cables for cutting mine moorings and a 4.1" gun mounted on her stern. As soon as we cleared the harbor, the new ordnance was tested. A Royal Navy team came aboard to instruct the crew in operations. The paravanes were streamed, one on each bow. In my days on a U.S. minesweeper, to follow only one and a half years later, we used paravanes to cut the cables of moored mines, ie. mines submerged a few feet below the surface and anchored to the bottom. When they popped to the surface after being cut loose, they could be sunk by gun fire. In my five years in the navy, I never again saw paravanes on any vessel other than a minesweeper. In retrospect, it may have been a good idea to have merchantmen sweeping a channel as they entered it, providing they didn't cut the channel markers free as well.

An elevated platform was constructed on the fantail to support the gun. A gun crew was formed from the cadets and engineers with one ship's officer in charge. Several rounds were fired at different elevations and angles. The British did not use a naval armed guard to handle the weaponry on merchant ships as we did after Pearl Harbor. Merchant seamen manned their own guns. I believe their system made more sense. The chances of a merchant vessel sinking a submarine or raider were so insignificant that they did not warrant tying up naval personnel. Of course, merchant seamen were technically civilians or noncombatants, but that didn't make sense when they were also the prime targets of enemy submarines. The gun was good for personnel morale and could deter a submarine from surfacing and using her deck gun to conserve torpedoes.

I did get a kick out of British naval instructors, in their impeccable white uniforms, looking askance at the *Silverpalm* gun crew in grease spotted coveralls and worn out fedoras.

I felt as though I ought to do something within my neutrality parameters, and I asked the first officer for a suggestion. The lifeboats on *Silverpalm* had masts and sails. Knowing that I was familiar with sails, he told me I could check the standing and running rigging, blocks, cleats and other items to be sure the boats could be sailed if it ever came to that. I enjoyed the job even though the pay was zero.

I would say that the British did an outstanding job in acting promptly from the outset to protect their merchant marine. Convoys were quickly formed in sensitive areas. Regrettably, their experience was lost on the U.S. Navy with disastrous results on the Atlantic seaboard, in the Gulf of Mexico and the Caribbean in the early months of our entry into the war.

Underway from Singapore to Telok Beton, Sumatra, the captain received orders from the Admiralty to blacken ship henceforth. I asked for a few minutes delay to take a last shot of *Silverpalm* with her night lights still on. Then we were plunged into darkness. The lights on deck, under which we joined so often at cocktail hour in animated discussion of shore experiences, went out. Our running lights, internationally designed to avoid collision, were turned off. Black bunting was draped across cabin portholes. I suddenly recalled a passage in English history. The day England declared war on Germany in World War I, Prime Minister Sir Herbert Asquith looked vacantly out of the window after an all night cabinet session at 10 Downing Street as the area gas lights were being doused. He mumbled only half aloud, "The lights are going out all over Europe, and I fear they will not be lit again in our time."

I wondered the same thing, not only about Europe, but about the world.

The blackout was a considerable strain on the captain. He was called to the bridge more often, was frequently absent at meal time, and we no longer played bridge in his cabin. This was something I would be able to identify with later on. I do not believe that radar ever was made available to merchant ships in World War II except perhaps to the huge converted troop ships. The Java Sea was heavily travelled by ocean borne commerce. "Flying blind," as it were, was hazardous and demanding in the extreme. Lookouts were doubled.

After Java and Bali, I left *Silverpalm* in Manila and toured the Philippine Archipelago on an inter-island steamer, *Legaspi*. I then shipped out on a Danish freighter, *Peter Maersk* of the Isbrandtsen Moeller Line. It was a very modern ship, gleaming and clean from stem to stern. We had a smorgasbord lunch every day, and the captain was most generous with his wine, aquavits and brandy. At this point in time, Denmark was a neutral.

In a Hong Kong bar, I got into a conversation with some soldiers dressed in British style uniforms and I was surprised to discover that they were not British. The Dominion troops had taken over. Mostly, they were glad to be where they were rather than facing the hazards of war in Europe, or so they thought. The year was 1940. At the end of another year, survivors among them would be in Japanese POW camps.

In Shanghai, I saw the results of the senseless Japanese naval bombardment of the Chinese sector, little children sitting on mounds of rubble with dirty bandages, unattended, staring blankly, some whimpering.

In the port cities of Japan, the skies over the waterfront sectors were lit throughout the night with welding arc flashes, something we would come to learn more about soon enough. I spent two weeks in that country, followed continuously. Incredibly, he wore a bowler and a cutaway. He stood out in every crowd.

The main interest across the broad Pacific to Los Angeles, listening to short wave every day, was the battle between the German battleship *Graf Spee* and the British cruisers *Exeter*, *Ajax* and *Achilles*. It was a naval classic. Captain Nielsen produced a chart of the area so that we could follow the retirement of *Graf Spee* into La Plata between Argentina and Uruguay, where she was scuttled. An officer of the old school, Captain Hans Lamsdorff wrapped himself in the banner of Imperial Germany and shot himself. He despised Hitler.

I came home with the feeling that the whole world would soon become unravelled and that the so-called "phony war" in Europe was only the tip of the iceberg.

I became a "Ninety Day Wonder." I joined one of the first V7 classes in July 1940. Any man with a college degree and who could pass the physical was eligible to become an apprentice seaman for 30 days on a battlewagon. After that, if recommended by his division officer, he went to a midshipman school for a 90 day course to be awarded, if successful, a commission as Ensign, USNR. I served my thirty days as apprentice seaman on the battleship *New York (BB-34)*. Subsequently, I got my commission on the *Prairie State*, then known as the *Illinois (BB-7)*, a Spanish American War era battleship fitted out as a school on the Hudson River, New York City.

Early in 1941, I was assigned to *Mockingbird (AMc-28)*, then being converted from a Maine fishing trawler to a minesweeper at the Charlestown Navy Yard, Boston. She was 90 feet long and carried a crew of two officers and ten men. Lieutenant (jg) Frank Steel, a Yale NROTC graduate, was the captain and I was the executive officer.

On that weathered wooden hull, the yard placed a steel superstructure, enclosing a foc's'l forward for the crew, a steel wardroom aft, a steel bridge amidships, and all the gear necessary for the sweeping of moored, magnetic and acoustic mines. To keep her from rolling over, several tons of lead were bolted to the keel. We had special generators, a bank of about 200 storage batteries, and were finally left with 18 inches of freeboard. Even when the weather was ideal, wavelets spattered onto the deck.

When alterations were completed, we sailed in miserable weather from Boston to the Navy School of Mine Warfare at Yorktown, Virginia. There we became a school ship for officers taking the course in mines. We showed them how to stream the paravane cutters for moored mines and the 1800-foot, 2000-amp, double magnetic tail for blowing up magnetic mines. There was also an "A" frame on the bow with an air hammer inside a watertight drum for detonating acoustic mines. Lastly, we gave lessons in handling ships going alongside the dock.

For me, this was wonderful seamanship experience. The old single Cooper Bessemer diesel kept breaking down, and we had to improvise with hand machined parts because the navy didn't have any spares. The man who performed these miracles was a Machinist Mate, First Class. One day, workmen from the Virginia Power Company left a hatch on the dock open. Coming back from a liberty with shipmates, he walked into the void and disappeared in the York River in spite of frantic efforts by his buddies. His body was located two days later. That was my first lesson that my occupation was dangerous even without a war.

This ship had movements to it that were never anticipated by *Knight's Modern Seamanship* nor the *Bluejacket's Manual*. *Mockingbird's* high superstructure blew like a sail, and getting alongside a dock in a cross wind was an experience all by itself.

I had begun to wonder if our country might not go to war after all and that year would follow year with me still executive officer of the *Mockingbird*. In the summer of 1941, however, Frank Steel was relieved to take command of a new minesweeper of the YMS class. I was given command of the *Mockingbird*. Although only an ensign, I was now being addressed, "Captain," by the crew. I liked it.

I got up earlier than usual on the morning of Sunday, 7 December 1941, because I had a brunch date with a girl in Williamsburg. I turned on the radio while I was shaving, and it suddenly went dead. Then an announcer came on to say that, since dawn, Pacific time, unidentified planes, presumably Japanese, had been attacking Pearl Harbor! The razor fell out of my hand.

Chief Boatswain's Mate Thompson asked me, "When do we start fightin', Cap'n?" "Probably sooner than you think," I replied. I went into the wardroom and sat at my desk, figuring I'd better get all my paperwork caught up. A messenger came down the dock and delivered a message to me from the Commander in Chief Atlantic Fleet which read, "Execute War Plan Love (L) immediately." If I knew what War Plan Love was, I would have been only too glad to comply, but I never did find out.

I looked at the bright single gold stripe on my sleeve, surmounted by a gold star symbolizing a line (combat) officer. I stared thoughtfully at the porthole and said to myself, "Lewis my boy, life is going to be different from here on in."

Lewis M. Andrews, Jr.

I did not keep the lady waiting. We made the brunch on time.

I was 23 years old and had already successfully acquitted a command. However, I was enamored of those 110 foot subchasers being built, and urged Captain Ashbrook, the Base Commander, to recommend me to the Bureau of Naval Personnel to command one. I was sent to the Fleet Sound School in Key West to learn how to echo range on subs. After Key West, in April 1942, I proceeded to Luders Marine Works, nowadays known as Yacht Haven West, Stamford, Connecticut, where *SC-532* was nearing completion. I met my executive officer, Harold (Pete) Peterson, a huge man from Minnesota, with an enviable football record.

From Stamford, we took *SC-532* to the Brooklyn Navy Yard where we loaded up with everything from mattresses to light bulbs to screws to small arms. The next day, with wardroom box springs and general mess equipment lying about, the crew was called to quarters and the Admiral's representative put us through the commissioning ceremony. I made a speech that was apparently stirring, something to the effect that we on *SC-532* would not rest until the enemy U-boat fleet was utterly smashed. Now, all I had to do was to smash it.

Leaving Brooklyn, we took the *SC-532* to Key West via Cape May, Norfolk, Charleston and Jacksonville. I'll never forget the look of dismay on the crew as we passed Miami without stopping.

A subchaser was not a highly effective antisubmarine weapon. It did, however, look smart and racy. I am not aware of any subchaser having definitely sunk a U-boat all on its own. Some subs were possibly damaged, and many merchant ships in convoy were spared when subs turned away from depth charge attacks. We had an old 3"/23 caliber gun on the bow, two 50 caliber machine guns amidships, depth charge racks on the stern and a "K" gun mortar on each side to throw depth charges outward from the ship. The depth charges, of course, were a lethal threat to any submerged sub, but our accuracy of delivery was insufficient. We had echo ranging sound gear but, without a gyro compass, contact bearings obtained were relative, not true. The absence of a trained sonarman was a distinct handicap, but I trained a couple of men as best I could.

Shortly after leaving Charleston, we had a beautiful sound contact replete with propeller noises. We made two attacks, each a four depth charge pattern and then lost it. In retrospect, we could not have made a kill except with the greatest luck. I should have held contact until a destroyer could arrive on the scene and taken over. Admittedly, it was lack of training. The Key West solution to a contact was to rush in, holding a stop watch to time depth charge releases while observing the relative bearing sound gear, and translating its results to magnetic compass headings. The Subchaser Training Center in Miami had not yet been born. If nothing else, I'm sure we upset the submariners' breakfast.

At Key West, we were promptly assigned to nonstop, eight knot convoys from Key West to Trinidad. We refueled en route. When we came in from the first trip with our tongues hanging out, we learned on subsequent trips to manage the water supply and to take along 50 gallon drums of water lashed to the deck.

There were side trips on smaller escort tasks to Guantanamo, Willemstad, San Juan, Barbados, Saint Lucia, Saint Vincent, and I guess we got around the whole Caribbean in one way or another. Lest this sound like a pleasant winter vacation, it must be recalled that 1942 was a year of carnage for merchant shipping and their crews in the Caribbean, and we didn't have much more than subchasers and a handful of "four pipers," World War I type destroyers. German subs would dart in on the surface at night, launch their torpedoes, and race away before they were barely detected. Subchasers did not have radar, and visual contact was the only means of interception unless a "four piper" was in the convoy.

Somehow, it was always the convoy before us or the one after us that had losses. It was a vital area for the enemy. Convoys from Gulf ports such as Houston, Galveston or New Orleans were loaded with materiel for General Montgomery's Army in Egypt. Trinidad was the first leg. From there, freighters were escorted to Recife in Brazil, then across the South Atlantic to Cape Town and North to the Red Sea. Obviously, it was to the enemy's advantage to destroy ships in the close confines of the Gulf of Mexico and the Caribbean before they broke out into the relative obscurity of the South Atlantic. My subchaser division did its best. Our escort command ship was a "four piper," *Upshur*, always quick to commend us for a good job at refueling in heavy weather, always encouraging us when depth charging sonar contacts, which we did on almost every convoy. Nobody knew for sure if we were attacking submarines or whales, but we never lost a ship, something to be proud of. I had been promoted to Lieutenant (jg) on this tour of duty.

On one convoy to Trinidad, off the Netherlands West Indies, we had a strong echo-ranging contact and went in on the attack with four depth charges set shallow. I don't know if we did the sub any harm, but the explosions knocked out both our engines and opened a seam in the hull. Apprised of our situation, the Commodore replied "Good luck"! We got the leak under control but not the engines. The next morning, a Dutch tug came out and towed us to Curacao. It took a couple of days at the dock to get the engines going again and to continue to Trinidad.

In January 1943, now a senior grade lieutenant, I was transferred to Quebec and assigned as executive officer on a corvette, *Might (PG-54)*, a 200 foot vessel manned by seven officers and a hundred men. The temperature was below zero when I arrived at quarters in the Chateau Frontenac, an unwelcome change from the Caribbean.

In a familiar snafu, the ship had departed two days before I arrived, headed for Boston. It took over a week to receive new orders for me to proceed to Boston, during which time I made the best of it in my quarters in the Chateau Frontenac. The local girls came up there every night to meet new acquaintances, and I was surprised how well I recalled my school French. The only time I stuck my nose out the front door was when I went to the train station to leave.

Arriving at the Charlestown Navy Yard, Boston, I learned that *Might* had been locked in the ice in the St. Lawrence for three days before being "liberated" by a Canadian icebreaker. The corvette astern of *Might* was liberated too rapidly and put a three foot deep hole in the stern of *Might*. When I boarded her in Boston, my much bedraggled skipper, Lieutenant Kenneth J. Hartley Jr., welcomed me with open arms. On top of the ice problem, his temporary exec didn't know how to navigate.

The Canadians had built *Might* for the British Admiralty, but the U.S. Navy was desperately short of escorts. That's how I wound up on a corvette. Our right hand screws and bolts didn't jibe with the British left hand ones; our light bulbs didn't fit their sockets; we did not have 4.1" ammunition for their 4.1" gun.

Tempest, Fire and Foe

When Boston got through with us, we were practically remade. We still had the original single screw steam reciprocating engine, and Warrant Officer Jackson knew how to make it work; such men were at a premium unless they had prior ferry boat experience. We had two 3"/50 caliber guns, six 20mm guns, a hedgehog, depth charge racks and "K" guns. We had British radar and sonar, otherwise known as Asdic. Both of the latter were very early models, moderately useful.

This was my first venture out of the "spit kit" class. Compared to *Mockingbird* and *SC-532*, this was a big ship. The corvette was an excellent boat in a seaway, a good thing because our New York to Guantanamo convoys made about one pass a week off Cape Hatteras. Ken was one of the ablest officers I had ever met or worked with. He was in his early thirties, had graduated from the Naval Academy during the bottom of the depression and left a seemingly static service to go into his own business in Jamestown, New York. As a reservist, he was recalled at about the same time I got my commission.

Ken was the most tireless man I ever knew. He would stay up all night showing me fine points on navigation, instructing the chief radioman how to operate his equipment, exploring an engine failure with the chief engineer, or lecturing the wardroom on a gunnery problem. He didn't seem to need sleep or rest and deserved full credit for turning a green crew into an outstanding fighting team in short order. We had a contact off the Florida Keys one day, used up a lot of our hedgehogs and depth charges on it but got nothing except some oil.

The best thing in Guantanamo was the ship's store which sold Corona Corona cigars, genuine alligator purses and other items which made the home folks happy. The officers' club had wall to wall slot machines set 49% to 51%. You could play all night before losing your money. The 2% went for rest and recreation, baseball bats, gloves, and other athletic equipment.

I never did get command of *Might*. In September 1943, we had a severe gale while heading north off the Virginia Capes. A huge wave slammed against the hull. I wasn't holding onto anything at the moment and wrenched my body to grab almost anything to keep from being knocked off the flying bridge. I was conscious of acute pain. On arrival in New York, I ended up in surgery for internal injuries at the Brooklyn Navy Hospital. I stayed for a month plus another month at the Navy and Marine Corps officers' recuperation facility on the Harriman Estate, Harriman, New York. That ended my corvette career. The Navy transferred *Might* to the Coast Guard and Ken was given command of a new destroyer escort. I never saw him again; he was killed in an accident at sea.

Of all the disciplines learned as a midshipman, celestial navigation made the most profound impression on me. I practiced it daily on my sub-chaser, *Might,* and as executive officer on the DE to which I was subsequently assigned. I had never before realized that there existed a compact between earth and the stars, billions of light years away. Celestial observation of the heavenly bodies, with reference to certain tabular publications, enables the navigator to determine latitude and longitude, to check the time, to correct the compass.

Celestial navigation has been handed down from the ages and improved along the way. Mitchener's book, *Hawaii*, tells how Polynesians in the first century A.D. navigated thousand mile round trips from Bora Bora to Hawaii by observing the "Three Little Eyes." The early Arab and European explorers used an astrolabe, the forerunner of the sextant. They learned how to determine latitude from the north star (Polaris) and, in later years, the relationship of time to longitude.

I am, of course, aware of the split second accuracy of modern day electronic devices such as Loran and GPS (satellite) navigation, but they lack the ethereal, the awe of contact with eternity experienced by the celestial navigator.

When I was discharged from Harriman, I was assigned to the Submarine Chaser School at Miami. Serving and learning under the famed Captain McDaniels was a gratifying experience. In October 1943, I was ordered to report to *Sims (DE-154)* as executive officer, relieving Lieutenant Robert Newcomb, whose fate on the *Underhill* is related in the chapter *Pacific Antisubmarine Warfare*. Our complement consisted of 11 officers and 200 men.

We ran convoys from New York to Londonderry, Northern Ireland. During the time I was executive officer, and later as commanding officer, my crew experienced about everything convoys had to offer. We weathered a storm of hurricane proportions. We had two submarine attacks, losing a tanker in one and one DE in our division in another. See chapter *Convoys to the United Kingdom.*

Sims was named after Admiral William S. Sims who commanded the U.S. Naval Squadron in Europe in World War I. We were the second to bear that name in World War II, the first being a destroyer sunk in the Battle of the Coral Sea. We were christened by the Admiral's widow.

Achieving command of a destroyer escort was certainly one of the proud moments of my life. The assignment carried a promotion to Lieutenant Commander in due course. I was 25 years old, but I do believe that war made me a good deal older than my years. The men looked to their captain for leadership, their lives, and a good deal more. I felt far more strain when asked in privacy by a seaman to advise him what to do about a marital problem than I experienced in attacking a U-boat. At that time, I wasn't even married.

We were in the Brooklyn Navy Yard the day I took command. The crew was at quarters. Jim Moffett rendered a magnificent farewell address, and I did the best I could with an acceptance of command speech. I went home to dine with a very proud family and returned to *Sims* rather late. When I reached the dock, I noticed another DE on the other side. Curiosity led me to look at her bow numerals, and I was delighted to find this was none other than Ken Hartley's ship. I bounded up the gangway with visions of telling him how his protege had made good; I now had a DE command of my own. In the wardroom of *Brough (DE-148),* I heard the final story of Ken Hartley.

En route from Bermuda to New York, *Brough* had run into a bad storm. The number one 3" gun shield was torn loose, and a volunteer party was sent forward to secure it. Hartley, impatient and conscious of the ship's battle readiness, went forward to supervise the operation. A sea came over the bow and threw him against the breech of the gun. The men carried him into the wardroom unconscious, and he died within ten minutes of a broken neck. One of the officers in the wardroom handed an unopened letter back to me which I had sent to Ken about two weeks before. When I reached *Sims* gangway, I tore it up and threw the scraps in the water, one by one.

As the war with Germany began to subside, I was transferred to the Naval Operating Base, Norfolk, Va. as executive officer of the *MerryGoRound*, a highly technical training facility. My C.O.

was Lieutenant Commander Hoaglund, an ex DE skipper like myself. The *MerryGoRound* was in fact a DE bridge inside of a dome which could be completely blacked out. It had everything, including echo ranging gear, radar, gyro repeaters, all the dials, a combat information center. Its name was derived from its 360 degree turning capability.

The realism was extraordinary. We could set up problems involving submarine attacks, antiaircraft, torpedo runs and shore bombardment. We even had all the sound effects. DEs and APDs going from the Atlantic to the Pacific stopped off in Norfolk for our training courses. I spoke to some skippers after the war, and they told me that these exercises were invaluable when they got into the real show.

In some ways, I was sorry to leave my ship. However, this was my first shore assignment in nearly four years aside from a few weeks of schooling and the hospital. Without attempting to calculate the number of convoys in which I had participated and the average number of ships convoyed while on *SC-532*, *Might* and *Sims*, I would guess a figure of 2000 tankers, freighters and troopships. Of that number, I only saw one go down, *Seakay* in the North Atlantic. I thought that was a reasonable record which was largely due to our aggressive attacks when opportunities presented themselves.

I have presented my story in the navy because it was so similar to that of thousands of young men who made the transition from civilian life to the ways of the sea. It was an extraordinary phase of my life. I recall it as though it were a dream. It was a time that is slowly slipping from our hands and minds as our numbers diminish. It was a time, we hope, that subsequent generations may also want to remember.

Author takes command of *SC532*.

Sub Chaser underway

Author as captain of the *Mockingbird*

Silverpalm test fires stern gun.

View from bow of *USS Sims (DE–154)*, typical of most DE's with three 3"/50 caliber main battery guns. The *Rudderow* and *John C. Butler* classes had two 5"/38 caliber guns. US Navy Photo

Chapter I - The Destroyer Escort

The production of destroyer escorts was first seriously considered by the United States Navy in the spring of 1939 when war clouds were gathering in Europe. Even then, it was suspected that, in the event of war, there would be a need for a mass produced destroyer type capable of transoceanic convoy and antisubmarine warfare. A number of designs were produced and rejected since production was not yet considered a matter of urgency. However, by the spring of 1941, a design was approved by the General Board, an assemblage of senior officers with authority to approve or disapprove new construction.

At about the same time, the need for escorts demanded immediate attention. The British had their backs to the wall fighting a foe under the sea as dangerous as the one in the air. Royal Navy Rear Admiral J.W.S. Dorling, Senior Officer of the British Supply Council in North America, impressed American Navy Secretary Knox with their urgent need for destroyer escorts, using Lend-Lease funds to defray the cost. Because of commitments for other types of craft, it was not until February 1943 when the first DE was delivered.

The capability of submarines to interdict their enemy's supply lines and to destroy his ability to wage war was the single reason for the inception of the destroyer escort. Since the destroyer was the only surface fleet unit that could effectively locate, attack and destroy a submarine, it was logical that we should develop a destroyer type that would concentrate on the submarine and thereby release destroyers for fleet assignment. Hence, the destroyer escort.

The first two DEs went to the Royal Navy. They, and the ones that followed, were to be known in that Navy as the "Captain Class." The next two DEs went to the U.S. Navy, i.e. *Doherty (DE-14)* and *Austin (DE-15)*, and they were followed by twelve more in short order. By July of 1943, the program was going full blast. No less than sixteen U.S. yards were involved in building DEs. Between February 1943 and the end of the war in September 1945, 563 DEs were built. Of these, 37 were manned by the U.S. Coast Guard, 78 went to the Royal Navy, eight to the Brazilian Navy and six to the Free French. In 1944, 95 destroyer escorts were converted to APDs, high speed transports. Like destroyers, all DEs and APDs commissioned in the U.S. Navy and Coast Guard were named after Navy, Marine or Coast Guard heroes.

Destroyer escorts varied from 1140 to 1450 tons unloaded displacement, 300 tons more when fully loaded, and 290 to 308 feet in length. Complements ranged from 180 to 220 officers and men. They did not have the offensive armament and fire control of destroyers, nor the speed. They were, however, vastly more maneuverable than destroyers and had a much smaller turning circle.

They also had the latest and best equipment in antisubmarine warfare (ASW), including sonar echo ranging gear with a maximum underwater detection range of 4000 yards (two miles). This was an electronic apparatus that obtained accurate ranges and bearings on submerged objects through supersonic sound transmission. Supersonic sound, unlike audible sound, travels in a straight line like a light beam. When it strikes a solid, metallic object, such as a submarine, it bounces back on the same bearing to the source. Instrumentation at the source (the DE) heterodynes supersonic sound to audible "pings" and indicates true compass bearing and range or distance to the target, enabling the destroyer escort to attack.

In addition to sonar and surface search radar, air search radar was installed on DEs operating in areas where air attack was probable.

There were two depth charge racks on the stern and four "K" guns on each side to fire depth charges outward, and an ahead thrown weapon called a "hedgehog." The latter fired a batch of twenty-four bombs which would take off from the bow like a flock of geese, land in the water in an elliptical pattern measuring fifty yards in diameter, and explode on contact with a solid underwater object. Developed by the British, it was an excellent ASW weapon.

The depth charge, with its 300 to 600 pounds of TNT, was the traditional antisubmarine weapon. However, a depth charge barrage required a high degree of accuracy to score, particularly against the double-hulled German U-boats. The "water hammer" effect of a 300 pound depth charge required an explosion within 30 yards of the submarine hull for damage and 10 yards for a kill. The 600 pound depth charge lethal area was considerably enlarged. They had a "teardrop" shape with tail fins, like aerial bombs, to make them sink faster. Depth charges were detonated by hydrostatic pressure, and depth was set before firing. Later models also had magnetic impulse detonators which would fire when in proximity to a submarine. Japanese submarines, lacking the hull strength and depth tolerance of their German counterparts, were more vulnerable to destruction by this weapon. A DE carried about 100 depth charges.

DEs were classified in two types, distinguished from each other by main battery armament. The earlier type had three 3"/50 caliber dual purpose (surface or air) guns mounted inside circular gun shields. Later types had two 5"/38 caliber dual purpose destroyer type guns in enclosed movable gun mounts. Both types could be fired individually or by director fire control. The 3" guns were frequently criticized as lacking in penetration power against double-hulled U-boats. The 5" type was far more effective. Most DEs were of the 3" type.

In addition to the above weapons, a DE had a secondary battery of about eight 20mm machine gun cannon and one quadruple 1.1" or one twin 40mm machine gun cannon. Although designed primarily for antiaircraft, these guns were quite often effective antipersonnel weapons. They could quickly sweep an enemy gun crew off the deck of a submarine or keep men pinned down inside the conning tower of a damaged submarine on the surface. The advent of *kamikazes* in the Pacific induced a hurried and massive addition of 40mm, 20mm, 50 caliber and even 30 caliber machine guns.

All 5" and most 3" DEs had a battery of three torpedo tubes. The *Evarts* class, diesel powered and with shorter hulls, did not have torpedoes. Some experts thought that torpedoes were superfluous. As will be seen in chapter *The Battle off Samar*, torpedo batteries were among the main reasons for the destroyer escorts' hour of glory.

Both the 3" and the 5" DEs had a highly developed tactical

control system known as a combat information center (CIC). This was an area abaft the bridge and under the flying bridge that received, evaluated and plotted on a universal drafting machine (DRT) all information from sonar, radar, bridge, lookouts, radio, semaphore flags or signal lights, and anything else pertinent. It then fed data and recommendations to the captain on the flying bridge to assist him in his decisions. The CIC was generally, but not always, under the immediate supervision of the executive officer. The value of the CIC in the destruction of enemy submarines was considerable.

A number of different power plants were used. The navy contracted where it could. There were DEs with diesel geared engines, diesel electric, steam turbo geared and steam turbo electric engines. In general, DEs with similar main engine plants were kept in the same operational divisions to simplify problems such as fuel type, speed, maneuvering capabilities and spare parts.

Two DEs in every division had high frequency direction finders (HF/DF), replete with the latest editions of compromised German, Italian or Japanese submarine codes. HF/DF was casually referred to as "Huff-Duff." The two DEs were stationed far enough apart so that cross bearings could be obtained when submarines surfaced to transmit messages to headquarters or to each other. This was one of the most important electronic tools aboard the DEs. The data produced was vital. Unfortunately, it was an incredibly boring station to man. Days might pass without a signal being received. Frequently, this transmission lasted only a minute or so, and considerable skill was required to get an accurate fix on the surfaced submarine.

All DEs had radio telephone. All tuned in on at least three long range coded frequencies, ie. the Navy Department in Washington, the Commander in Chief Atlantic (or Pacific) Fleet, and one other such as the Admiralty in London. All had navigation radio direction finders. Some had the newly developed Loran. All had one officer who spent a large part of his time encoding or decoding classified messages.

The great majority of officers and men were reserves. With the exception of the earliest DEs, when some regular Navy officers were placed in command to train their juniors, DEs were commanded by reserve officers with ranks of senior grade lieutenant or lieutenant commander. Practically all commanding officers had prior command experience on subchasers, patrol craft or minesweepers.

Extreme youth characterized the men and, to a lesser degree, the officers. On most DEs, except for the senior petty officers, the average age of the enlisted personnel was under 20. The commanding and executive officers were both generally under 30 and were often the only officers aboard with seagoing experience. On the first few ocean crossings, these two officers frequently stood "watch and watch" on the bridge under way because there were no others qualified to stand "Officer of the Deck Underway" watches. This allowed for very little sleep. Both senior officers had undergone intensive courses in antisubmarine warfare at a training facility at Miami, the Subchaser Training Center (SCTC). The school commandant, Captain MacDaniel, was extraordinary. Later on, if a skipper had an under-performing officer on his ship, he could quickly be removed by a word to "Captain Mac."

The enlisted men were not only young but often "fresh off the farm." Only a few chief and first class petty officers were sent aboard at commissioning. They formed a nucleus from which to build a crew capable of operating and fighting the new ship. They were the key personnel who could make or break a ship and upon whom officers heavily relied. Many of them came from large ships and had extensive sea going experience in wartime. They were tolerant of some of the obvious mistakes made by the officers, and their loyalty was unquestioned. They maintained the ship's readiness and trained and educated the youthful seamen put in their charge.

Fueling at sea was a necessity. Whereas DEs had the capacity to cross the Atlantic or run from the west coast to Hawaii without refueling en route, this presupposed steady steering on a great circle course at the most economic speed. In convoy, however, DEs zigzagged, followed devious routes to avoid submarines, and ran at speeds about three knots faster than the merchant ships. Fueling at sea was a tense operation that tested the mettle of the skipper and helmsman alike.

Destroyer escorts customarily went alongside a designated merchant marine or navy tanker in the convoy to fuel, although some preferred to fuel astern of the tanker. This author initially did it both ways, finally settling on the alongside procedure as the faster. Escorts took their fuel through a heavy hose. The black bunker oil came across heated to about 250 degrees Fahrenheit and at 100 pounds per square inch pressure. Once hooked up, a DE could take about 95,000 gallons of fuel in 50 minutes. However, coming alongside the tanker and getting the hose across in rough weather could be nerve wracking.

Both ships had to be steaming at exactly the same speed, and the escort had to maintain a precise position relative to the oiler. It was necessary to bring the two ships in close proximity, (about 100 feet) get heaving lines across, follow with heavy lines, haul the 6" diameter hose over to the escort, and commence pumping fuel. This was usually carried out at nine to ten knots, out of the main formation, sometimes with an escort fueling from the other side of the same tanker. Astern waited another escort ready to move into the fueling position as soon as it was clear and also to act as a rescue ship in case of a man overboard during this hazardous evolution. Of course, all this had to be carried out with alacrity as the escorts being fueled weakened the antisubmarine screen. It was customary to fuel each escort twice on each transatlantic passage so that their bunkers remained at least 40% full in case an emergency or extended bad weather made fueling impossible. Unlike navy tankers, merchant marine tankers had little or no prior experience in fueling other ships at sea. Yet, this author never fueled from one that did not handle the procedure professionally and expeditiously.

I remember an incident on *Sims (DE-154)* when our men did not secure our end of the hose properly before signalling the tanker for pressure. In a shot, the hose backed out from the fill pipe with a dedicated coxswain hanging onto it. The hose stood straight up in the air, pouring gallons from its spout, and the coxswain looking like an oriental fakir who climbed a rope after miraculously straightening it. The tanker quickly closed the valve, slamming our seaman to the steel deck, still holding the now limp end. He was pretty tough though; all he needed was a shower.

Fueling from an aircraft carrier was not one of my accomplishments. I am told, however, that it was one of the prime destroyer escort experiences. George Scarborough from Knoxville, Tennessee, was aboard *Snowden*, one of the DEs in the *Croatan (CVE-25)* Hunter-Killer Group. He remembers what it was like:

> "There were some hairy times refueling from the carrier. The natural shape of the vessels and the physics of the situation would draw the two ships together. I've seen full opposite rudder and the ships still closing. The closing sometimes becomes inevitable; you can see it happening before the correction command is given. Keeping an eye on the carrier's flight deck, immediately opposite the DE's flying bridge, crew members were adept and ready to evacuate the vertical height of the superstructure in a single bound. You can see the ships closing, you can feel the tension, you can sense the screw guards about to catch the sides of the carrier. You mentally strain with the man on the helm. That is a memory you retain!"

The destroyer escort was classified as a major combat vessel. In general, DEs were deployed in four types of operations. The first consisted of escort divisions of six or more DEs each, escorting merchant marine convoys, navy supply vessels, or troop transports. Convoy escort was a defensive operation designed to ward off enemy submarine and aircraft attacks on ships carrying men and equipment for the overseas war effort.

The second grouping operated as part of "hunter-killer" (HUK) teams in task forces, each consisting of a small aircraft carrier (CVE) and five or six DEs that went to sea for the specific purpose of locating and destroying submarines.

A third operation, more common in the Pacific than the Atlantic, was antisubmarine and antiaircraft screening of capital ships as they bombarded enemy shore installations prior to amphibious assaults.

The fourth assignment developed in the Pacific in the later stages of the war. The DEs manned "picket" stations on the outer perimeter of fleet and landing operations to engage *kamikazes* and to warn inner perimeter vessels of their approach. This was very hazardous duty, and DEs suffered severe personnel and material casualties.

In fact, there were few tasks DEs could not perform. They engaged shore batteries, suicide manned torpedoes and suicide speed boats. They guarded minesweepers while they performed their dangerous tasks. They even delivered personal mail to other fleet units, a highly important morale function.

The High Speed Transports (APD)

APDs were destroyer escorts and World War I type (four piper) destroyers altered to have light troop transport capabilities. They were created by two opposite but complementary situations. The first was a need for light transports with relatively shallow drafts and a capacity to move light army or marine units rapidly to myriads of Pacific islands. The second was a growing excess of destroyer escorts in the Atlantic, permitting several to be converted.

Another deck was added along with troop berthing and messing accommodations for about 10 officers and 150 men. A very large davit was installed on either side, each of which could launch and recover two 36 foot assault landing craft (LCVP). It could carry underwater demolition teams (UDT) or move troops, supplies, light trucks and jeeps to and from the staging areas. The 3"/50 caliber main battery was replaced with a more efficient destroyer type 5"/38 caliber gun forward in a movable mount. Torpedoes, hedgehogs and Kguns were removed. The sound gear and depth charges in stern racks remained to leave the APD with a reduced antisubmarine capability. Additional 40mm and 20mm guns were installed to increase the ship's close-in antiaircraft armament.

The destroyer escorts played a major role in breaking the back of the German and Japanese submarine fleets and, together with APDs, contributed heavily to the defense against the *kamikaze* corps. From North Africa to Anzio to Normandy, across the broad reaches of the Atlantic and Pacific Oceans, from Leyte to Iwo Jima to Okinawa to Tokyo Bay, their crews cheered, laughed, fought, bled and died.

Ernie Pyle Takes a Short Trip on a Destroyer Escort

Ernie Pyle was unquestionably the best known American journalist of World War II. He made a celebrity of "G.I. Joe," the slogging, battle-weary infantryman. He went where the action was, recording his experiences on ships, at the fronts, everywhere. He was a journalist who felt his job to be the building of morale in the fighting forces and on the home front as well as the gathering of news. In 1945, Pyle was killed by Japanese machine gun fire during the Okinawa campaign, but he left a legacy of outstanding news stories. One of these described a short cruise on a destroyer escort.

> "In the Western Pacific so now I'm a DE sailor. Full-fledged one. Drenched from head to foot with salt water. Sleep with a leg crooked around your sack so you won't fall out. Put wet bread under your dinner tray to keep it from sliding.
>
> And you don't know what a DE sailor is? A DE, my friends, is a destroyer escort. It's a ship, long and narrow and sleek, along the lines of a destroyer. But it's much smaller. It's a baby destroyer. It is the answer to the problems of colossal amounts of convoying; amounts so huge that we simply hadn't the time to build full fledged destroyers to escort them all. The DE is the result.
>
> They are rough-and-tumble little ships. Their after decks are laden with depth charges. They can turn in half the space of destroyers. Their forward guns sometimes can't be used because of waves breaking over them. They roll and they plunge. They buck and they twist. They shudder and they fall through space. Their sailors say they should have flight pay and sub pay both because they're in the air half the time, under the water the other half.
>
> I came back from the northern waters on a DE. When a wave comes over and you get soaked, a sailor laughs and says, "Now you're a DE sailor." It makes you feel kind of proud. And I did not get seasick! I better have my stomach examined.
>
> My ship formed part of the escort of a convoy returning to a southern base island for more planes and supplies, to be hurried back north to the battle. We mothered ships that were big and slow. We were tiny in comparison. We ran way out ahead, and to the side. We and DEs like us formed the

'screen', and there was nothing bigger than us in it. We felt like strutting.

A DE carries about 200 men and a dozen officers. That's small enough so that those who serve on her know almost everybody else personally. Sailors always seem to be proud of their DE. So proud that they often get in a fight with crews from other DEs if they go ashore together.

In the Western Pacific, the boys on a DE are very friendly and glad to have you aboard, for it's seldom they have a visitor. I've spent three days aboard two different DEs. Both had been out there quite a while, but neither had very much contact with the enemy.

It might be an illusion, but it seemed to me the men on these little DEs were happier than the sailors on big ships. They had been out for 15 months and, true they talk a lot of wanting to go home, but they didn't seem as sorry for themselves as the other boys on larger ships.

My DE got credit for helping to sink two subs. They only got credit for an assist. It burns them up, for it was they who discovered the subs. The boys say 'We dig em up', and then they order some other DE to sink them. Our skipper got so mad about it he threatened to have a protest painted on the stack.

The boys talk mostly about the storms they've been through, for when you've been through a storm on a DE, you've been somewhere. They toss off angles of rolling that are incredible. They tell of times when the ship rolled all the way from 65 to 75 degrees, which is almost lying flat on the side.

There are little things all over the ship to indicate how rough she is. Fiber rugs are fastened to the steel decks of cabins with scotch tape so they won't slide. Ash trays are tied to stanchions with wire. There are hand railings the entire length of the narrow decks. (My ship never had a man washed overboard.)

The boys have trouble airing their bedding on deck, even on the bright warm days, for there is almost always some spray coming over the side. It gets so rough they can't cook on board. The boys in the bakeshop say that, during bad storms, the bread dough all runs to one end of the pans, and the loaves come out only half as long as usual, all jammed up at one end. So now they keep three days supply of bread baked ahead, thus outwitting the storms.

My crew really was the best-natured bunch I've run into in a long time. They enjoyed telling stories on themselves, even about seasickness. And speaking of meals, we ate well on my DE, but the boys laughed and said they wished I'd stay on here permanently because the chow has been twice as good since I came aboard."

The forty-third reunion of Destroyer Escort Commanding Officers (DECO) took place in Honolulu in April, 1990. Admiral David E. Jeremiah, Vice Chairman of The Joint Chiefs of Staff, was our guest speaker. He delivered a message from the Secretary of The Navy which, in a few words, summarized our mission over fifty years before:

"On behalf of the Department of The Navy, I take great pleasure in extending warm greetings and deep appreciation to the Destroyer Escort Commanding Officers from World War II who have gathered in Pearl Harbor, Hawaii, for your forty-third annual reunion. It is indeed fitting that you hold your reunion in Pearl Harbor, the site of the most devastating naval attack the United States has ever suffered. While the first destroyer escorts had been championed by Commander Robert D. Carney, based on British designs and built for the vitally important Lend-Lease Program, Pearl Harbor ensured a major national commitment to construct a large fleet of these highly maneuverable, extremely effective escort ships.

Besides the critical mission of providing inexpensive escorts for allied convoys, these stouthearted warriors were excellent antisubmarine platforms. In the Atlantic, destroyer escorts helped to end the scourge of 'Wolf Packs' and to reopen the sea lanes to shipping traffic critical to our war effort. And in the Pacific, the destroyer escorts became famous for their unparalleled bravery in staving off Japanese forces at Leyte Gulf during the largest naval action of all time. Our destroyer escorts battled a fleet of Japanese battleships and cruisers at point blank range and caused the superior enemy forces to retreat. The numerous stories tell of the bravery, the sacrifice and the glory that the courageous destroyer escorts tallied while protecting vital wartime convoys, sinking submarines, battling *kamikazes*, and rescuing our sailors.

I congratulate each of you, including those present only in spirit, for your gallant service and invaluable leadership in the cause of freedom and the defense of our nation. Best wishes for a most memorable reunion and every continued success."

H. Lawrence Garrett, III
Secretary of the Navy

A few pages from a crewman's diary on *Neal A. Scott (DE-769)* relate an introduction to destroyer escorts on the high seas in wartime and will be easily recognized by those who served:

"On 9 December 1944, *Scott* departed from Hampton Roads, Virginia, with Task Force 63, composed of 98 merchant cargo ships and tankers with eight destroyer escorts in the screen. Encountering extremely rough seas, the convoy was badly scattered, one ship almost ramming into the fantail of *Scott*.

We officially entered the European war theater on 22 December, passing south of the Azores. The count of men washed overboard from ships in the convoy now numbered five. What a way to spend Christmas! In spite of the sea, our cooks turned out a traditional turkey dinner for all hands.

On 28 December, Task Force 63 arrived in Mers el Kebir, Algeria, and *Scott* went on to Oran, where we had liberty. There was a great shortage of food, glassware and pottery and people were using necks of bottles, embedded in concrete, as wine glasses. The cognac on New Years Eve wasn't the best but it was potable.

We departed from North Africa on 2 January 1945, convoying 78 merchant ships for the homebound run. At 1504, a scraping noise was heard in the crew's quarters, followed by two muffled explosions. The merchant ship, Henry Miller, in position 51 and Norman Mack in position 61 were both struck by torpedoes just off the Rock of Gibraltar.

The sound of the alarm sent the *Scott's* crew to their fifty-first General Quarters since starting convoy duty. At 1731, *Scott* made the first contact on the U-boat. Her depth charges rolled off the racks and flew out from her Kguns 11 minutes later and again nine minutes after the first. Two hedgehog attacks followed. Three underwater explosions were heard during the four attacks, and some lookouts claimed to see oil and some debris in the ship's wake.

On 7 January, the radio shack received a report of a tanker sunk 200 miles ahead and on the convoy track. A few days later, the DE's high frequency direction finder located a submarine in the vicinity but none of the escorts gained contact.

And so it went, convoy after convoy."

In chapter *Twilight of The U-boats*, *Neal A. Scott* and *Carter (DE-112)* send a U-boat on her final dive.

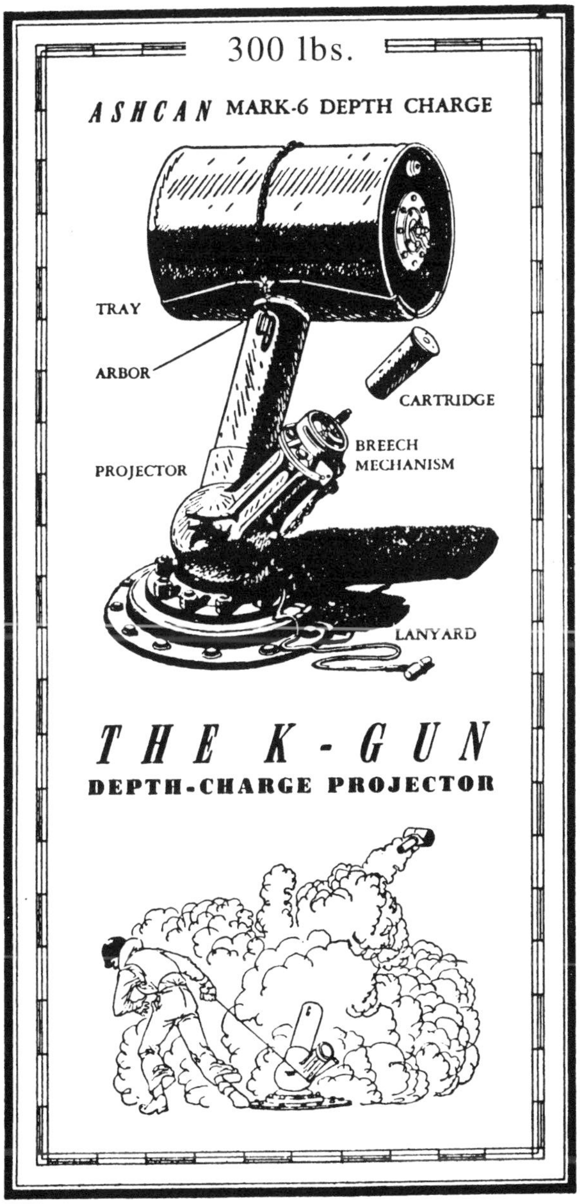

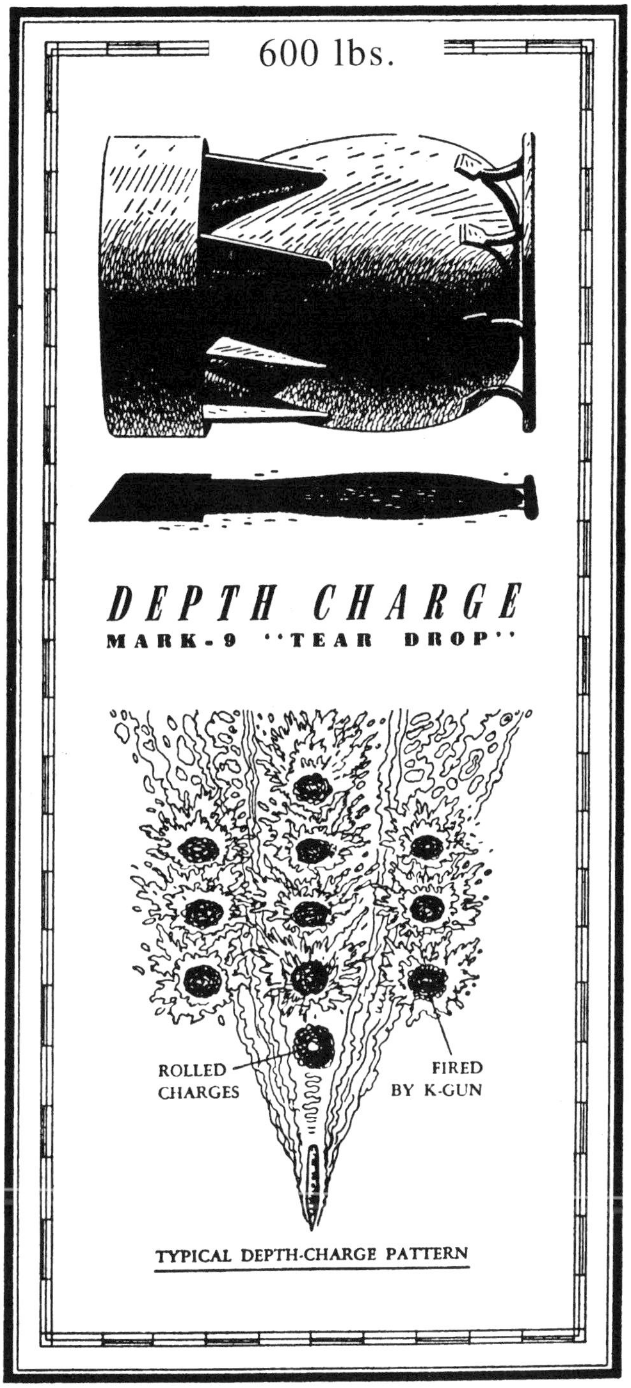

Above: The Depth–Charge release pattern
Left: The K-Gun Depth-Charge Projector

Charts on Pages 5-7 are from *Destroyer Operations in World War II* - Courtesy Naval Institute Press.

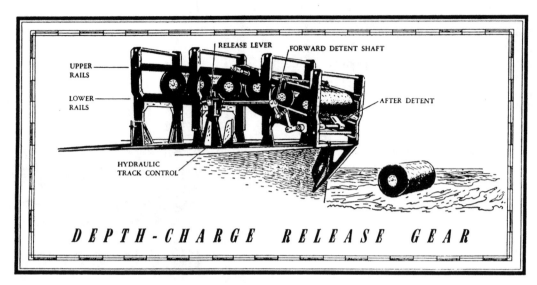

DEPTH-CHARGE RELEASE GEAR

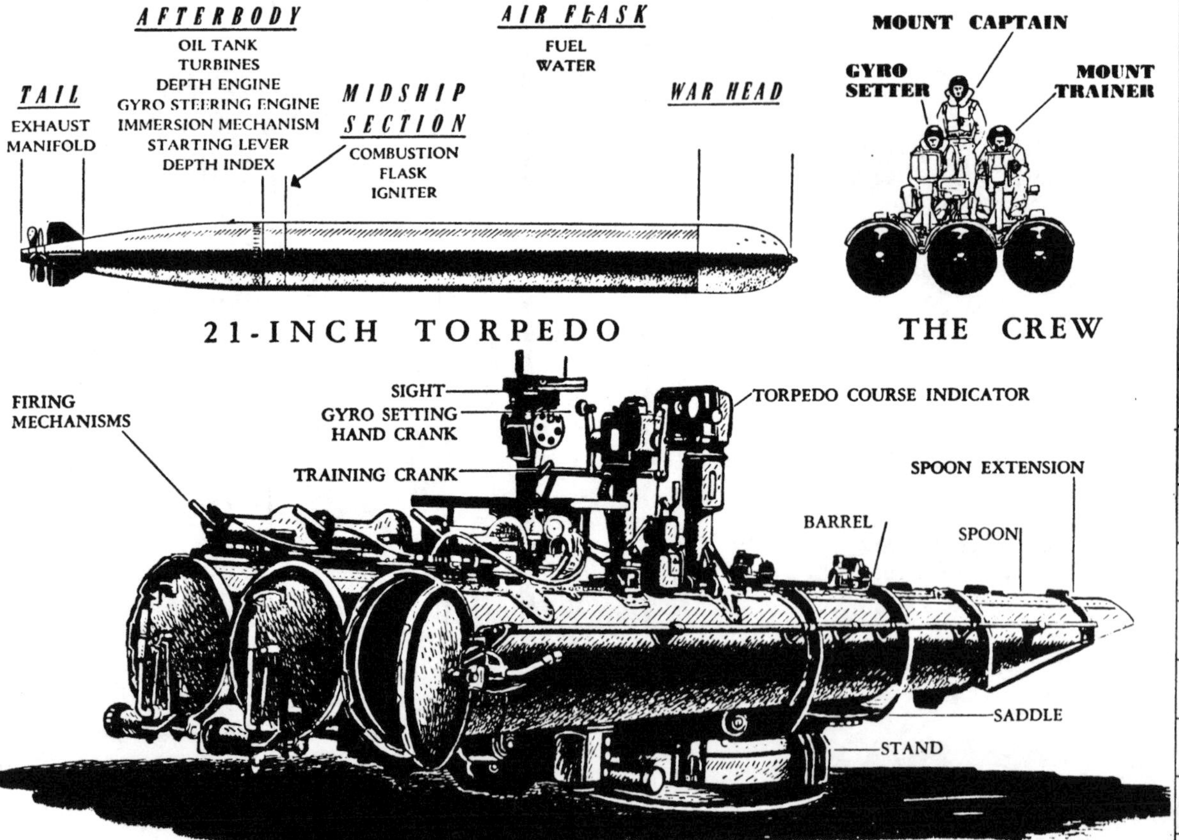

TORPEDO, TUBES AND MOUNT
TYPICAL WORLD WAR II DESTROYER MOUNT

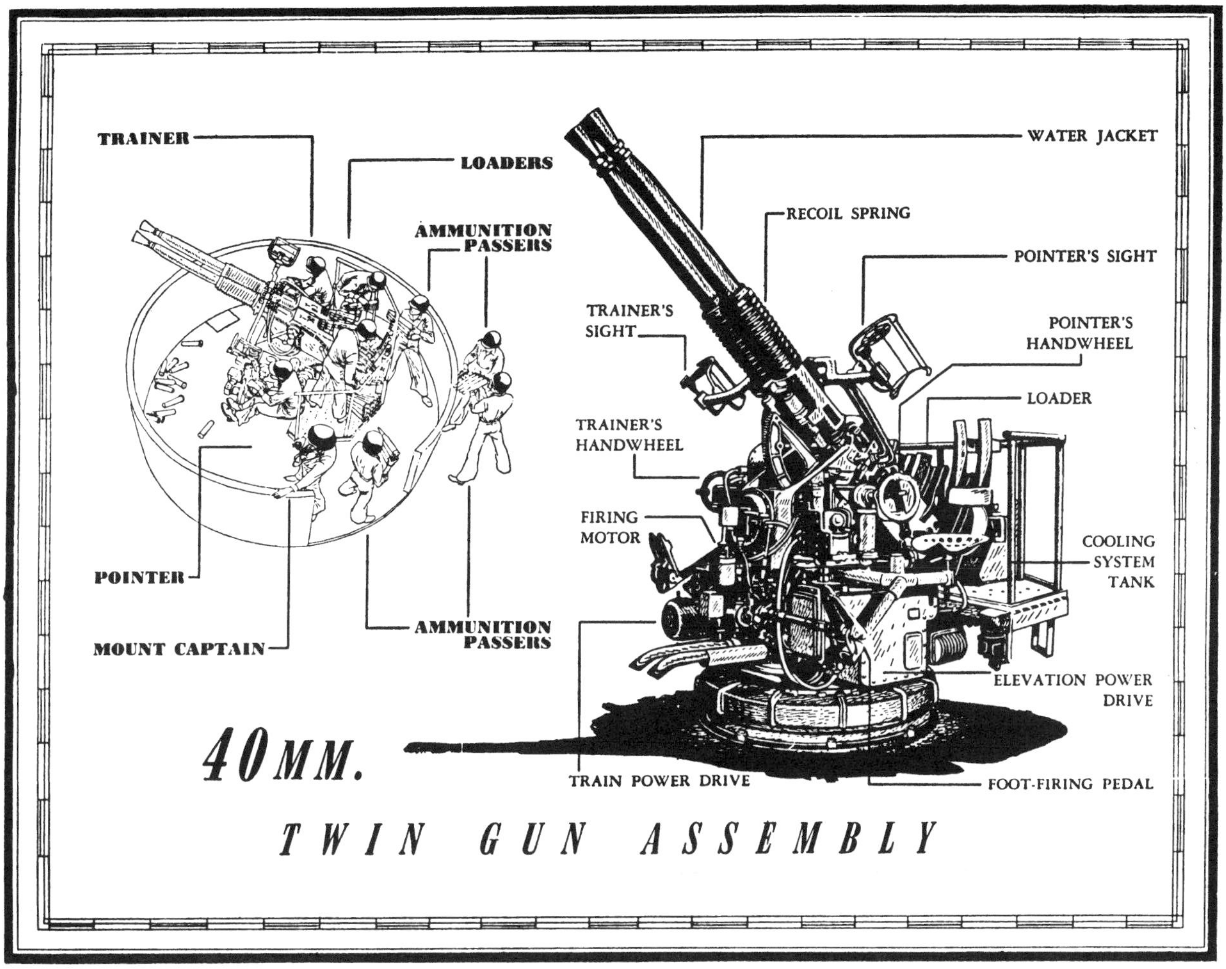

Above: 40mm Twin Gun Assembly and crew
Bottom right: 20mm Gun and crew

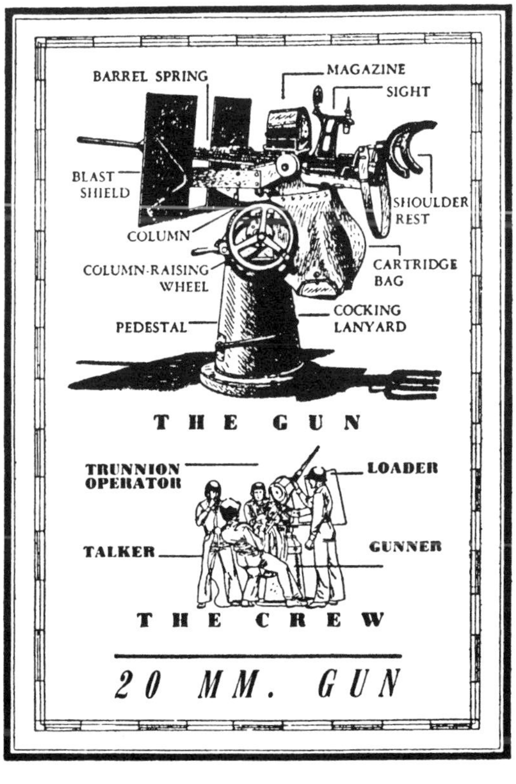

Top opposite page: Depth-Charge Release Gear
Bottom opposite page: Torpedo Tubes and Mount.
The destroyer had triple torpedo tubes.

All the above from *Destroyer Operations in World War II* - Courtesy Naval Institute Press

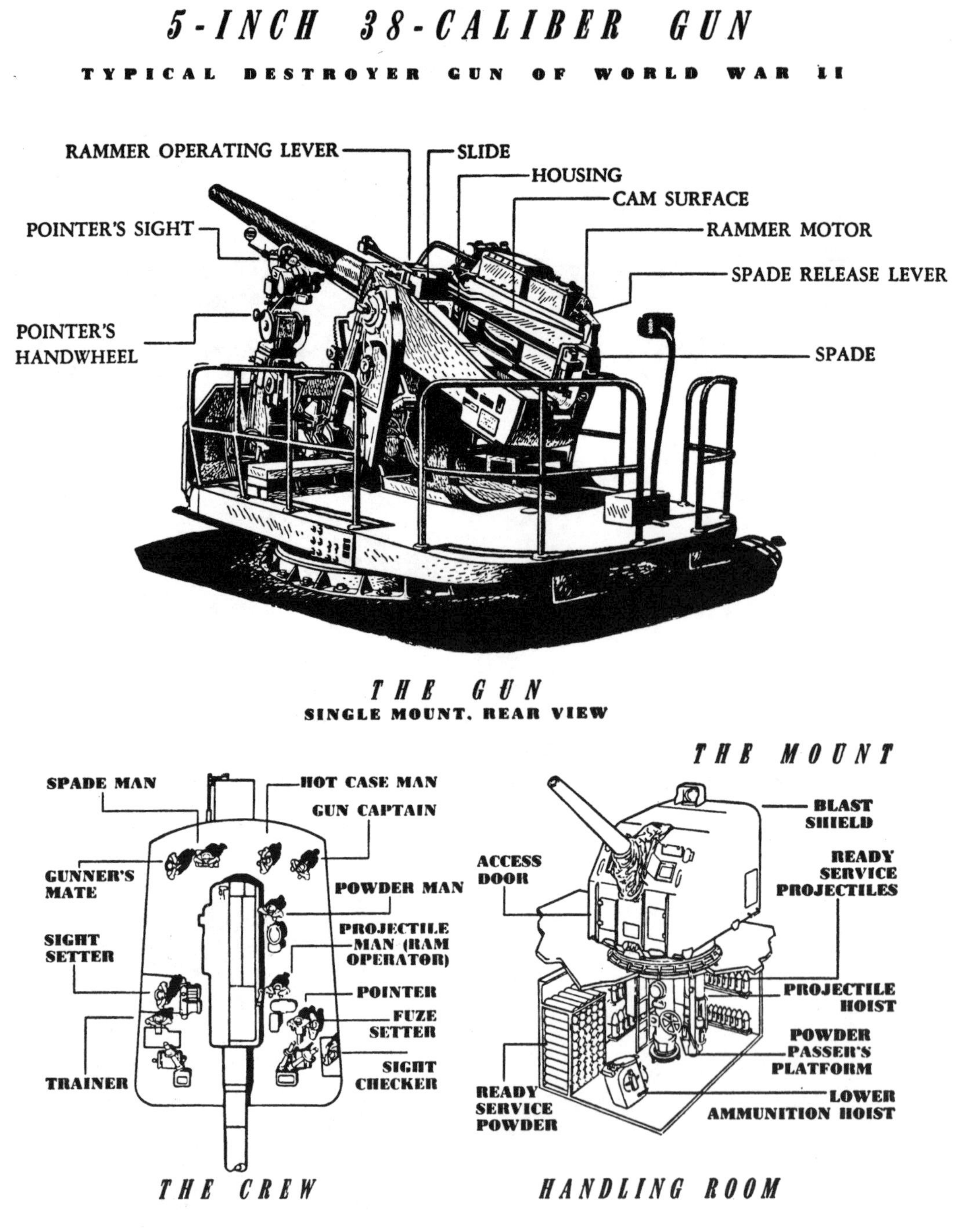

The earliest destroyer escort main batteries consisted of three 3"/50 caliber guns in fixed circular mounts. Later classes, *Rudderow* and *John C. Butler,* were armed with two destroyer type 5"/38 caliber guns in movable mounts. *Buckley* class ships that were converted to fast transports were equipped with single 5" guns. Had the war continued, all *Buckley* class ships would have been armed with 5" guns instead of 3" guns. Both guns were designed for surface and antiaircraft fire.

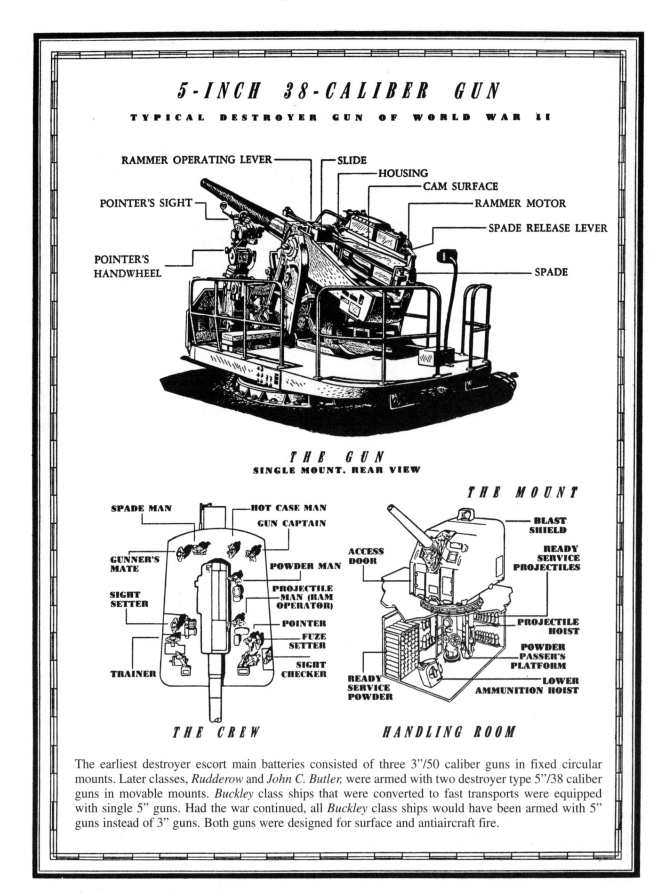

5-Inch 38 - Caliber Gun. From *Destroyer Operations in World War II* - Courtesy Naval Institute Press

USS Sims underway – US Navy Photo

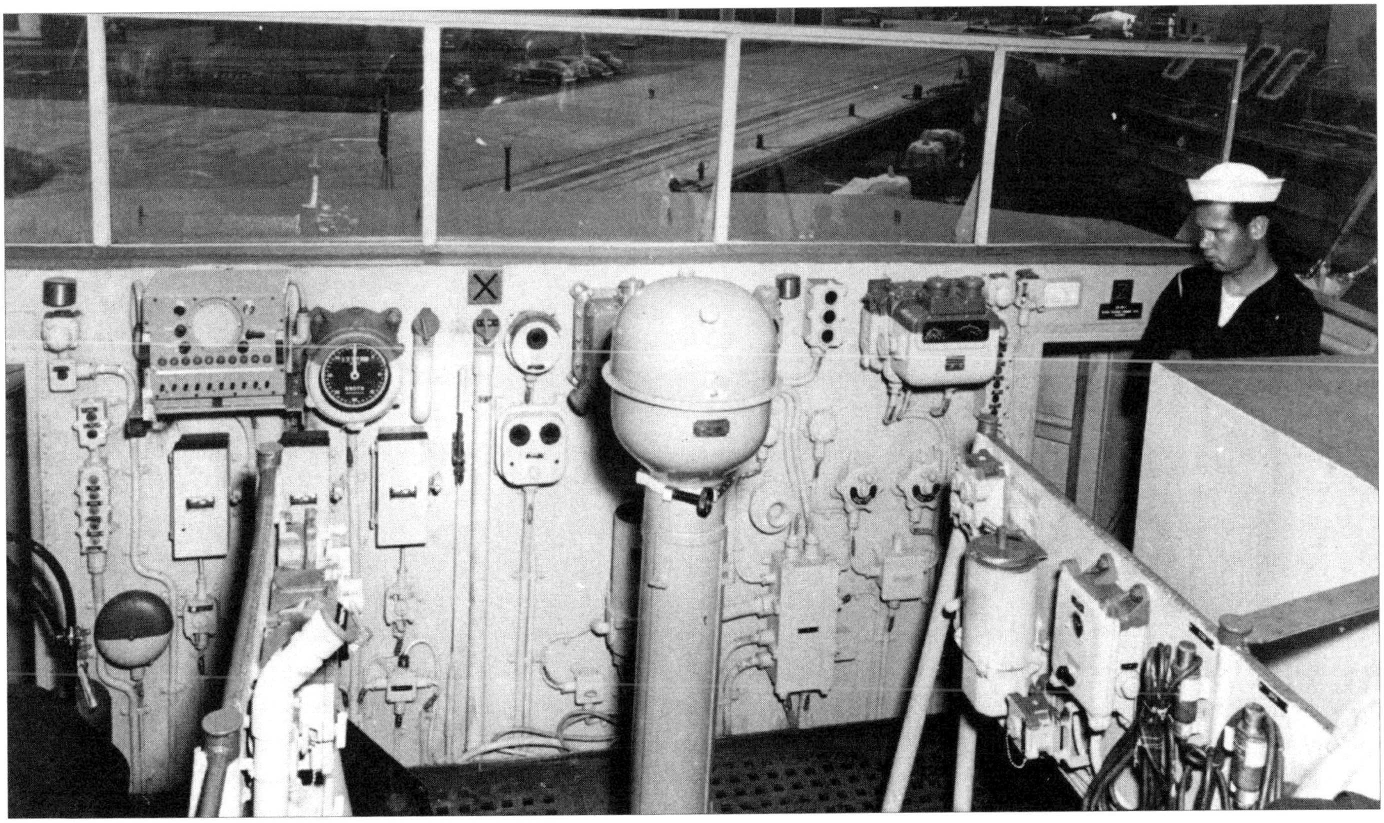

USS Sims flying bridge – US Navy Photo

Above and lower left: "Cruising" the North Atlantic — Photos supplied by L.E. Racicot, crewman on *Bostwick (DE-103)* near Iceland, winter 1944-1945.

Ernie Pyle boarding *USS Reynolds (DE-42)* in a breeches buoy.
US Navy Photo

From *Destroyer Operations in World War II* - Courtesy Naval Institute Press

USS Sims amidship showing torpedo tubes. US Navy Photo

Chapter II - The U-boat and the Battle of the Atlantic

That Other Pearl Harbor

It has often been said that those who do not learn from history are destined to repeat it. Nowhere could that wisdom be more aptly applied than to the sorry state of defense against the German U-boats at the outset of American entry into World War II. We were totally unprepared for the worst submarine onslaught in history, despite the fact that we were witness to similar operations against Great Britain for two and a half years before we entered the war.

That other Pearl Harbor," described in *Torpedo Junction* by Homer H. Hickam Jr., illustrates the decimation of Allied merchant shipping along the Atlantic Coast. Within six months, more tonnage went to the bottom in that area, the Caribbean, and the Gulf of Mexico than the Japanese had sunk in the Pacific within the same time frame, Pearl Harbor to Midway! Whereas the Japanese deployed the most powerful fleet in the world, the Western Atlantic carnage was accomplished by a couple of dozen German U-boats in its original offensive!

At the outset of war in Europe in 1939, Admiral Karl Doenitz, Commander of the German Submarine Fleet, had exactly twenty-two submarines capable of operating on the high seas. Doenitz was a studious man. In the years before the war, he had spent most of his time studying U-boat operations and tactics. It was his belief that, if war should come, Great Britain could be brought to its knees through starvation and interdiction of combat materiel. With the British out of the picture, the *Wehrmacht* could over-run the continent without British or American interference. Fortunately, the British had an unlikely ally in Adolph Hitler and the German High Command. Hitler wanted the *Kriegsmarine* to have battleships, cruisers and destroyers. In his mind, they gave Germany grandeur, visible power and prestige. Neither Hitler nor the High Command understood sea power. Doenitz' pleas for a crash program to build more submarines fell on deaf ears.

As things turned out, the Nazi investment in powerful surface units was wiped out by the Royal Navy. It was fortunate for the allies that the enemy shipbuilding program did not emphasize submarines at an earlier date. At the outset, the Germans worked pretty much with their old World War I design, type VII U-boats. The type IX were just beginning to come on stream; thirty-three were under construction.

Doenitz was ordered to blockade the British Isles and to bottle up the Royal Navy, very fancy orders for twenty-two U-boats. However, his shortage in numbers was largely balanced by commanding officers who were fiercely loyal, audacious and courageous. The Germans wasted no time in assaulting merchant shipping to or from the United Kingdom.

The Royal Navy reacted promptly. Convoys had been very effective in the First World War and were soon reinstated, making isolated U-boat attacks hazardous for the U-boats. In addition, ASDIC or echo ranging "pinging" equipment was installed on destroyers, limiting the surprise factor that the submerged submarines had enjoyed. Doenitz, however, developed another tactic, namely wolf packs attacking at night. Echo ranging equipment was far less effective on surfaced submarines than on submerged ones. Surfaced submarines, moving at 18 knots, could dart into a convoy undetected, launch their torpedoes and retire before the escorts could engage them. The results were horrendous. Between June and October of 1940, the U-boats dispatched 1,400,000 tons of merchant shipping to the bottom. The British were losing tonnage far faster than it could be replaced.

German submarine crews referred to that time frame as the "Happy Time," tremendous successes and few losses. By the winter of 1940/1941, however, the Royal Navy had installed radar on many of their escorts, robbing the wolf packs of their best weapon, surprise. Rates of sinkings were cut to less than half, and U-boat losses sharply increased. Also, the British discovered that their North Sea fishing trawlers made effective antisubmarine vessels when equipped with the necessary arms and electronics. They were not nearly as good as destroyers, of course, but they were easy to build in the United Kingdom and in Canada. The situation remained bad but not disastrous.

In World War I, the American Navy had bottled up the German U-boat Fleet with the North Sea mine barrage. In World War II, however, the collapse of French resistance in the autumn of 1940 created a very serious problem for the Royal Navy. German U-boat pens, concrete shelters, were established at such Atlantic ports as Brest, Lorient and St. Nazaire, insuring access to the entire Atlantic.

Doenitz' response to the latest British antisubmarine measures was to plead with the German government for larger and faster submarines to knock Britain out of the war. His request again fell on deaf ears. The German submarine offensive was further blunted by the participation of U.S. Navy destroyers in convoys, known as "Mr. Roosevelt's Private War." Also, fifty American World War I-type destroyers were given to the Royal Navy in exchange for bases in the Caribbean.

That was the situation when the Japanese attacked Pearl Harbor, plunging America into war with Germany and Italy as well as with Japan. Doenitz made an in depth study of American logistics on the Atlantic Seaboard, in the Caribbean and the Gulf of Mexico. It was obvious that the northern states relied on heating fuel brought in from Venezuela, the Dutch West Indies, Texas and Louisiana. By this time, Germany had slightly over ninety operational U-boats. Doenitz asked the High Command for permission to send twelve IX types across the Atlantic to cut the American jugular. He got permission to send five. These, however, were commanded by five of his very best aces. The operation would be called *Paukenschlag* (drumbeat).

The arrival of the five U-boats off the Atlantic Coast was not a surprise. British agents in France had passed that information on to London which then promptly informed Washington. Admiral Adolphus Andrews had been placed in command of Atlantic coastal defenses. He was a highly capable and experienced officer. His problem was that he had little to command except for a few Coast Guard cutters, converted yachts and a couple of Army patrol bombers with no recognition training. One such bomber, having sighted the submarines approaching, reported a fleet of destroyers and cruisers!

Admiral Andrews warned the Chief of Naval Operations, Admiral Ernest J. King, that the situation would get out of control very shortly. He didn't have a vessel that couldn't be outrun and outgunned by the U-boats. This has been a matter of considerable censure by historians. For one reason or another, Admiral

King refused to place Atlantic Fleet destroyers under Andrews' command.

"That other Pearl Harbor" was about to unfold. Off Boston, New York, Philadelphia, Hampton Roads, Cape Hatteras, freighter after freighter, tanker after tanker would meet their fates. The sickening sight of merchant seamen caught in cauldrons of burning oil floating on the surface became commonplace. Bloated corpses washed up on beaches. Spectators watched in humiliation as surfaced submarines sank merchant ships with gunfire, without fear of retribution. Lights remained lit along the coastline at night providing a silhouette of merchant ships for stalking U-boats. Former Secretary of The Navy John F. Lehman Jr. has noted that:

> "The U.S. very nearly lost World War II because we lost 238 ships in the first nine months of 1942 almost half the ships we have in the entire American Merchant Marine today!"

This author can heartily support Secretary Lehman's observation. I spent 1942 and 1943 convoying merchant vessels along the Atlantic Coast of the U.S. and in the Caribbean on *Subchaser-532* as commanding officer and the corvette *Might* as executive officer.

When death and U-boats lurked beneath the waves
by Tom Infield Dateline: January 14, 1992
Reproduced with permission from the
Philadelphia Inquirer

Reinhard Hardegan is the last living captain of the five *unterseeboote* that arrived nearly simultaneously off the coast in January, 1942. In his eighties and a retired marine businessman living in Bremen, Germany, he recalls:

> "It was incredible to me. I thought that the United States Navy learned from the experience the British had for years with submarine warfare. And they did nothing . .The destroyers were in their harbors. There was no blackout on the coast and no blackout on the ships. They were all lit up".

The blow fell mainly on the civilian U.S. Merchant Marine which, in the first year of the war, had a far higher casualty rate than any of the armed services. Nearly 6,000 mariners perished in World War II.

In April 1942, U-boats sank 69 ships off the Atlantic shore. In May, it was 111. In June, the losses topped out at 121 ships. Then, very slowly, the havoc began to subside as the Navy made headway with improved defenses and, at last, blackouts and regular convoys. Sinkings would persist, of course. By war's end, more than 700 American merchant ships would go to the bottom in all four oceans. But losses would never again approach the levels of what the elated Germans had dubbed "the American shooting season."

Michael Gannon, a University of Florida professor and author of the book *Operation Drumbeat* noted:

> "The U-boat offensive during the first six months of 1942 constituted a far greater disaster for the Allied war effort than did the Japanese attack on Pearl Harbor. The assault took about two and a half times more lives than Pearl Harbor and cost more in materiel. That's how history has come to view a nearly forgotten battle of World War II that began off the East Coast over 50 years ago."

General Eisenhower was enraged. He warned President Roosevelt that the entire Allied effort could collapse unless a convoy system were established to cut the losses in fuel and materiel destined for war theaters. Roosevelt did intercede with King who promptly ordered the establishment of convoys which radically reduced losses. In the spring of 1942, subchasers began to come out of yacht yards. Then came larger patrol craft. We were by no means ready to reduce the enemy forces that opposed us but we successfully guarded convoys. Approaching U-boats lost much of their prior audacity when faced with the probability of depth charges close aboard, the dimming lights, flying chunks of insulation from the bulkheads, the violent lurch, the fear of a submarine turned into a steel coffin.

German Admiral Karl Doenitz wrote:

> "With the introduction of the convoy system along the East Coast of the United States and its subsequent extension to the Caribbean, the situation in these waters became less favorable for the conduct of U-boat warfare."

By this time, many American merchant seamen had made numerous Atlantic crossings at great personal risk. Similarly, the American and British escorts in the convoy screens had fought their overworked ships and near exhausted navy crews on this North Atlantic run. The winter months provided a test often greater than that of enemy submarines. The merchant seamen were on the receiving end of German torpedoes. During the war's earlier months, navy crews made do with escort vessels unequal to the task. Indeed, before gaining command of a long awaited destroyer escort, this author had ridden some woefully inadequate escorts that frequently were obliged to concentrate more on survival in tumultuous seas rather than on their charges. Such was the price of unpreparedness.

Let us then examine the scenario played out by the destroyer escorts and their crews in their effort to prevent the Germans from winning the war through winning the Battle of The Atlantic.

The increasingly inexperienced U-boat crews grew younger and younger as they were sent forth to do battle in the North Atlantic. This situation is well described by Lothar Gunther Bucheim in his excellent word and picture record of German submarine warfare in World War II, entitled *U-boat War*, Alfred Knopf, May, 1978. He made several war cruises in German submarines and lived to tell his story. He writes:

> "Every submarine mirrored at once both the greater strategy of war and its every day horror. Anyone who nowadays wants to find out what the military realities were which governed World War II could do worse than study the history of submarines. Anyone who at that time was confronted with the phenomenon of the submarine was afforded an insight into the very essence and aberration of the entire war, if only he had the will to see.
>
> The Chiefs of Staff must know why they are sending such children out on the submarines. At that age, they don't yet have anything to lose. 'A boy knows nothing of love,

knows not what it is to die.' That was one of the songs we used to sing as Hitler Youths. Whenever someone went around the bend during a depth charge attack, it was usually one of the older men, a bosun or a mate, someone with a family. These overgrown children are carried as human spare parts, muscle machines trained to react instantly".

Of course, when it finally became clear to the German High Command that Doenitz was right, that massive quantities of U-boats could sever the Anglo-American lifeline, could actually bring victory, a huge building endeavor was initiated. But it was too late. The destroyer escorts were rolling off production lines in 1943 with the electronics and weaponry that would be more than a match for the U-boats. Air/sea allied combat tactics were heaping destruction on the enemy. Whereas the beginning of the war saw a ratio of as many as 20 merchant ships sunk for every submarine destroyed, the end of the war saw a reversed ratio of two subs sunk for every merchantman sent to the bottom.

The Third Reich placed about 830 submarines in operations against the Allies. Of these, a staggering 784 were lost, mostly in action, some by scuttling or surrender when the war ended. Of the nearly 50,000 German officers and men who went to sea in submarines, about three quarters made their final dive to the ocean floor.

Portions of the above by B.D. Hyde, former Commanding Officer of *Bunch (DE-694)*

THE TENTH FLEET

By Ladislas Farago
Courtesy DESA News

The "Fleet" in Being

The Tenth Fleet was not a combat organization per se, and whatever glamour it had was subtle. It never came in for the familiar ballyhoo treatment by public relations. This was welcome to Admiral Low who had a genuine passion for anonymity.

From the captured files of the *Kriegsmarine*, we now know that the Germans, although somewhat intrigued by this phantom "force," had but the haziest notion of the Tenth Fleet and never fathomed its unique concept. In his postwar memoirs, Admiral Doenitz ignored it completely. Such neglect was not confined to him. Even American historians of the war at sea dealt sparingly with it, a reflection of their failure to grasp its implications and enduring influence, and to recognize the genius that created and managed it.

As fleets go, the Tenth was a fleet in being at best that operated around the clock. There was something urgent and vibrant about it that filled its crammed premises occupying part of a single wing on the third floor of the Navy Department with the close-hauled air of a fleet organization afloat. Its "lookouts" scanned the ocean. Its operations officers moved the ships and the planes assigned to antisubmarine work. The Battle of the Atlantic was a full time enterprise and the men delegated to conduct it by remote control had to adapt their hours to those of the opposing forces at sea.

The organization was relatively small. The charter was patterned after the COMINCH (Commander in Chief) Headquarters Organization, adding the Convoy and Routing Division, a scientific advisory council, and with close liaison to two major antisubmarine (ASW) organizations left intact in the Atlantic Fleet. The COMINCH Headquarters Organization consisted of four major divisions: Plans (Fl), Combat Intelligence (F2), Readiness (F3), and Operation (F4). F1 had no division status because planning was done by Low and his top level associates in close, almost daily, consultation with Admiral King.

Similarly, the Tenth Fleet did not have an intelligence service strictly of its own but utilized F2, the Combat Intelligence Division of COMINCH, to take care of its own crucial and enormous intelligence requirements. However, the Atlantic Section of F2 soon became a part of the Tenth Fleet and also operated its situation plot.

Within the Tenth Fleet, the functions and responsibilities of the COMINCH Readiness Division were assigned to the Antisubmarine Measures Division that was thus charged with research, material development and training. It further included units engaged in statistical and analytical work, indispensable for operational calculations in the development of doctrines. The Tenth Fleet also maintained its own Operations Division whose function was to move the ships into action. It kept a constant check on the fleet organization, the allocation of ships, the adequacy of ships to carry out given ASW operations, and the capabilities of all types of ships suited for ASW. But it left to Admiral Ingersoll's Atlantic Fleet to implement its "recommendations" by alerting and assigning the vessels and planes needed for the physical phase of operations.

This basic function, in which the Tenth Fleet became operational, was an immensely delicate task, requiring as much savvy in tact as in tactics. In the course of the war, the Tenth Fleet's messages to Admiral Ingersoll employed an impressive variety of semantic artifices to avoid the impression that the Tenth Fleet was giving orders to CINCLANT. Thus the messages usually began with "Suggest that you..." or "It is recommended that you...," or were expressed in question form such as "Would it be possible for you...?" or "Would you concur in...?" Of course, the only answer Ingersoll was expected to give to these politely formulated questions was affirmative.

This strict adherence to etiquette, and the urbane ingenuity and modesty with which Admiral Low practiced it, proved an important element in the Tenth Fleet's effectiveness. The fighting men of the Navy naturally resented any kibitzing, especially by people who were hundreds of miles from the hot breath of war. Much sooner than they cared to concede, those fighting men came to depend on prompting by the Tenth Fleet and to cherish its counsel. But they were loath to admit that any of their successes had originated in the brain of some chairborne Washington meddler.

Captain Dan Gallery, in his book *Clear The Decks*, never gave credit to the Tenth Fleet for guiding him to *U-505* which his gallant escort group captured. In private, however, he was quite lavish with his acknowledgment and even sent a picture of the captured German submarine, with an appropriate inscription, to Commander Knowles whose accurate and timely plotting had made the coup possible.

The Antisubmarine Measures Division was the "egghead" of the Tenth Fleet, not merely because it harbored the civilian scientists and actuaries who analyzed the U-boat war, but especially because it published the "Yellow Peril." That was the Navywide nickname of the secret U.S. Fleet Antisubmarine

Warfare Bulletin, a superb periodical published once a month from June, 1942, to June, 1945, in which the Tenth Fleet disseminated its ideas, conclusions, doctrines, as well as information about weapon developments, the tactics and capabilities of U-boats, simply everything even remotely connected with antisubmarine warfare. The "Yellow Peril" was the Tenth Fleet's major means of direct communication with the skippers of the escort carriers, destroyers and destroyer escorts, and the pilots, whose job was the actual destruction of the enemy.

Another series of its publications was called Tenth Fleet Incidents, of which several thousands were issued during the war. They reconstructed actions and operations in a graphic manner to stimulate their readers to original ideas and to teach them how to benefit from the experience of others. Admiral Low used both media most considerately, proffering advice in the circumspect and inspiring manner of the self-effacing educator.

The outer layer of the Tenth Fleet consisted of the Convoy and Routing Division, functioning as its integral part but with a great deal of autonomy; and the group of some seventy civilian scientists, known as the ASWORGS. Beyond that, the Tenth Fleet maintained close liaison with the Operational Training Command and the Antisubmarine Development Detachment of the Atlantic Fleet.

Convoy and Routing (C&R) was grafted on the Tenth Fleet. It long predated the Tenth Fleet as it was one of the first agencies the Navy had organized specifically for the impending war. It was established in 1941, as a section in the Ship Movement Division of OpNav. The Chop Line, a longitudinal line in mid Atlantic dividing Allied responsibility between CincLant on the west and the Admiralty on the East, was drawn. The United States Navy became responsible for the routing and diverting of convoys and troop movements in the western half of the Atlantic. Often, DE skippers knew which side of the Chop Line they were on by simply listening to directives, ie., " Change course to – degrees immediately (US) or "Change course to – degrees forthwith. (UK)Later, King incorporated C&R into COMINCH Headquarters. Finally, he moved it into the Tenth Fleet.

One of the reasons for this was a dilemma presented by the director of C&R. From its inception, a retired captain (later rear admiral) named Martin Kellog Metcalf, headed C&R. He earned the Navy Cross for chasing U-boats, escorting troop convoys and conducting rescue operations in World War I. Now in World War II, he ran C&R with well oiled efficiency. Two reserve officers, Everett Alexander Rhodes and Charles E. Ames, with know – how gained in the Merchant Marine, proved extremely useful in the management of the section.

Convoy and Routing had to work closely with the Admiralty but, unfortunately, Metcalf belonged to a faction who viewed the British with jaundiced eyes. His anglophobia resulted in several lively breezes and squalls where smooth sailing was a condition *sine qua non*. Largely to accommodate the British by curbing Metcalf's "anti-Limey" regime, King decided to throw C&R in with the rest of the Tenth Fleet. Low, on his part, was a past master of inter–allied cooperation and maintained the friendliest relations with his opposite numbers of the Royal Navy.

There now remained only two organizations outside the Tenth Fleet with exclusive responsibilities in ASW, the Operational Training Command under Rear Admiral Donald Bradford Beary, USN, and the Asdevlant of Captain Aurelius B. ("Abe") Vosseler, a pioneer naval aviator, developer of the high-altitude oxygen mask, and charter member of the first antisubmarine fraternity under Captain Baker in Boston.

Beary's command operated as an "antisubmarine university" on the Oxford pattern, with independent "colleges," several sound schools and fifteen antisubmarine training and refresher centers. The alumni were expected to spread the know-how they had gained in the rough-and-tumble world of the Atlantic.

Vosseler's Antisubmarine Development Detachment Atlantic Fleet, brought together in yet another "college" naval pilots and crewmen, technicians and scientists, to explore and improve the air aspects of antisubmarine warfare. They tested equipment, developed their optimum operational use, and worked out coordinated ASW tactics and communication procedures between aircraft and surface vessels, in accordance with the Navy doctrine that "aircraft and ships should operate as one team."

Though not an integral part of the Tenth Fleet, it worked in exceptionally close association with it. It consisted of a handful of Navy planes. Low recognized the great value of the Detachment and recommended several improvements to Captain Kilpatrick, Admiral Ingersoll's Chief of Staff. Among others, he recommended that Asdevlant be given its own surface vessel section to make it self-contained in its experiments.

Afterward, when the Tenth Fleet sought to develop new air/surface cooperation tactics, and wanted to test them, Low would call Kilpatrick and ask him to initiate the tests. They were then carried out immediately, often on the basis of telephoned instructions.

Time was of the essence and the Tenth Fleet had none to lose. It was the urgency of the problem and the immediacy of its solution that dominated all considerations and motivated all decisions. Once when Low was offered a device that looked promising for excellent effects against U-boats, he turned it down when told that it would take two years to produce it.

It was the formulation of King's dictum, "Do the best you can with what you have." But Low was tireless in cutting red tape and using his influence to get the best to do his best. This principle was applied to the Tenth Fleet and especially to its human equation.

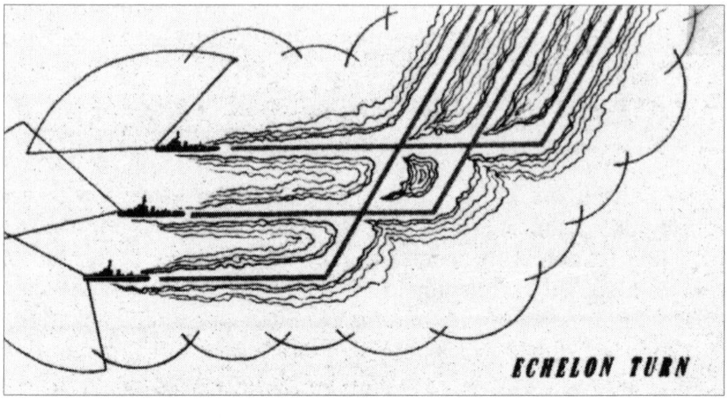

Three Ship Retiring Search. From *Destroyer Operations in World War II* - Courtesy Naval Institute Press

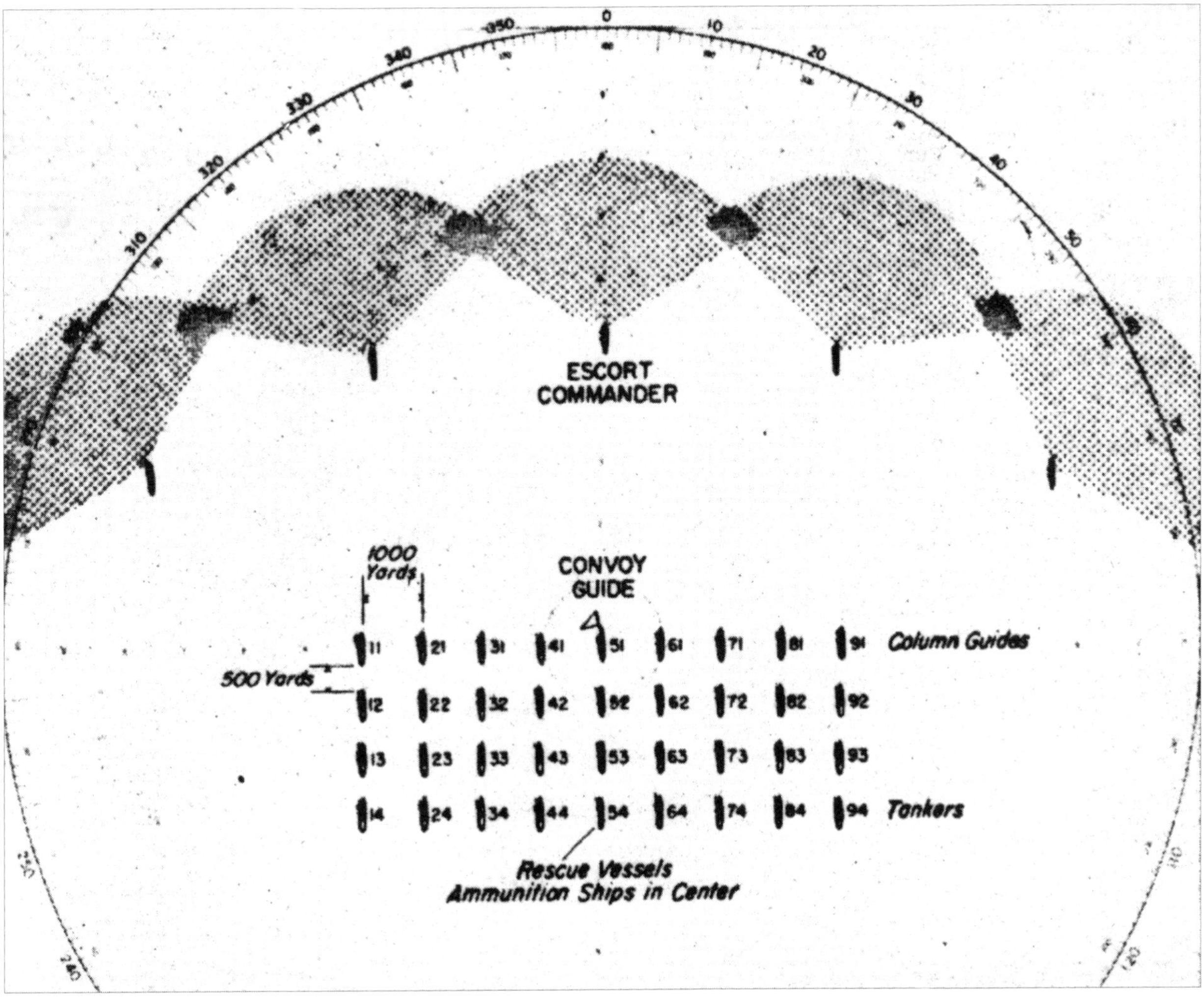

Typical Merchant Ship Convoy

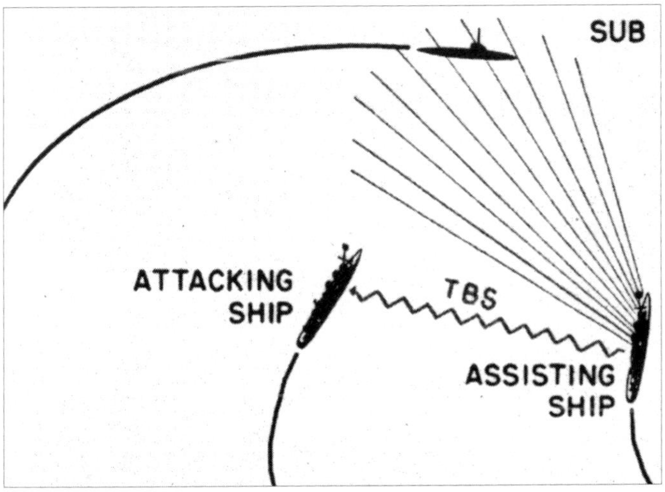

Two Ship Co-ordinated Attack

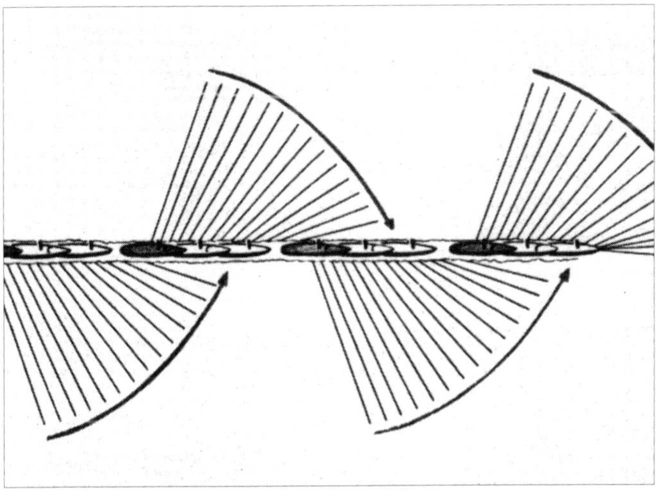

Anti-Submarine Speed Search

All images on this page from *Destroyer Operations in World War II* - Courtesy Naval Institute Press

USS Donnell being prepared to receive a new stern. US Navy Photo

Chapter III - Convoys to the United Kingdom

The North Atlantic : Wild, Cold, Desolate and U-boats

Lieutenant Commander B.D. Hyde, commanding officer of *Bunch (DE-694)* gives us an abridged account recalling his six transatlantic round trip convoys:

> "The arrival of the DEs was timely for there were some important submarine innovations which threatened to become operational soon. Indeed, one of these, the snorkel, was being deployed in increasing numbers, permitting U-boats to run submerged on their diesels instead of battery powered electric motors with vastly enhanced speeds up to 19 knots. Their ability to go to greater depths and the general use of acoustic torpedoes were serious threats.
>
> A convoy might consist of 45 to 50 vessels with a front four to six miles wide. Although the ships in the convoy had a faster capability, the convoy's actual steaming speed seldom exceeded 12 knots. Weather more often than not set the formations speed. Also, the proximity of these large ships to each other, the frequent need to make emergency turns on short notice, as well as the use of zigzag patterns limited their speed of advance".

This book author wishes to add the hazards of collision between merchant ships whose officers had little or no navy training in station keeping or coordinated maneuvers. In addition, convoyed ships were of varied design and tonnage, with dissimilar propulsion plants, resulting in different rudder angles and turning circle diameters. It is remarkable that there were not more accidents than occurred. In the "Christmas Hurricane" of 1943, my convoy was simply blown away and never re-formed. Ships straggled into port from all directions and days apart, all fortunately accounted for! Continuing Lieutenant Commander Hyde's recollections:

> "Since the escorts had to actively patrol their assigned sectors in order to preserve the integrity of their sound search patterns, they usually had to zigzag at about 15 knots. In heavy weather, this speed could put escorts and their people through considerable punishment. A typical east bound trip would last 10 days.
>
> At the eastern terminus, the main convoy would make its landfall on the rocky island of Inishtrahull in the Northern Approaches. It would then run down off Orsay Island and the Mull of Oa near Islay. There, the formation would be broken down into subgroups according to their final destinations in the UK. Upon arrival off the north coast of Ireland, the weary escorts were relieved and ordered to proceed to some nearby port where the calm of a well sheltered harbor was to be found at last. Upon arrival of the escorts at Gourock or Greenock in the Clyde or at Londonderry in Northern Ireland, about a four day layover was customary. These days were used for catching up on sleep, preventative maintenance, officer antisubmarine training, and sightseeing. Our hosts were always hospitable and often supplied buses and guides to take the ship's company on memorable tours of their beautiful country, gasoline shortage notwithstanding. The winter months were most remembered. Convoy speed dropped to 10 knots or less, slowing as necessary in the frequent winter gales. This was latitude 56 degrees north or higher, and it could truly blow in winter. Of course, it made a world of difference whether we were bound east or west. In the former, the gales which follow each other in endless succession during a North Atlantic winter frequently had their own speed of advance, closely approximating that of the convoy. Therefore, a storm picked up off New York, Boston or Halifax would often remain with the convoy until it made its landfall on Scotland or Ireland. These storms built up heavy seas, resulting from a 2,000 mile "fetch," and made it difficult for the merchant ships to maintain their assigned stations. The much smaller escorts were hard to steer and suffered severe discomfort while patrolling stations with these seas under their quarters. Such conditions implied reduced effectiveness for escort sonars and their ability to carry out attacks on suspected submarine contacts.
>
> In westward bound convoys, there was the endless slamming of the merchantmen into the head seas, often at painfully low speeds. These empty ships were steaming light and rolled and pitched in extraordinary fashion. Sometimes, the formations speed would fall to four knots, virtually hove to. Thus, these empty ships returning to the USA became prime targets for submarine torpedoes. When possible, air cover was supplied to convoys by long range Liberators and Flying Fortresses. Both often flew at the outer limits of their ranges and thus could only remain with the convoys for two hours or even less before having to return to their bases to refuel. Communications between aircraft and the convoys were often very difficult because of low ceilings and rolling escorts, such that exchanges by flashing light were nearly impossible.
>
> Without communications, the effectiveness of the patrolling aircraft was greatly reduced. (Voice communications were not permitted except in the case of a submarine contact or the need for an evasive course change.) Finally, there was a period of three to four days where no air cover could be furnished because of distances from air bases. As might be expected, this was the zone of greatest submarine activity. Later in the war, escort aircraft carriers became available on these runs, and thus air cover could extend further out. However, they too were subject to their worst enemy, the weather."

ESCORT DIVISION TWELVE

The Enemy Struck a Heavy Blow

By September 1944, *Fogg (DE-57)* was a true veteran of the Atlantic, having escorted convoys to the Caribbean, Algiers and Londonderry, the latter logging six round trips. Task Group 27.4, a special towing convoy, departed westbound from Plymouth, England, in December. This eight knot convoy was composed of twenty-one vessels, and the screen included four DEs of Escort Division 12, zigzagging at 12 knots.

Tempest, Fire and Foe

All appeared well in the convoy. *Fogg* was in position on the starboard bow of the formation, 3500 yards from the convoy center. *Ira Jeffery (DE-63)* was on the starboard side of the convoy, astern of *Fogg*, same distance from the convoy. *George W. Ingram (DE-62)* was in the opposite position of *Fogg* on the port bow, and *Lee Fox (DE-65)* was in the same position as *Ira Jeffery* but to port.

Submarine position and situation reports from both Commander in Chief Atlantic Fleet (CincLant) and the Admiralty were kept plotted and up to date. On the previous evening, Commander Task Group (CTG) 27.4 had warned all ships present that there was a submarine within striking distance and for all ships to be alert. The dawn of 20 December approached on the 0400–0800 watch, and soon bleary-eyed sailors would be roused by the bosun piping "turn to."

Ingram, *Ira Jeffery*, and *Lee Fox*, the High Frequency Direction Finder (HF/DF) equipped ships, intercepted a U-boat transmission. A triangulation of the composite bearings determined that the reported signals were sky waves coming from the starboard side of the convoy course. This placed the signal as originating in the northwest at an inexact distance exceeding 30 miles. Everett N. Schrader was Soundman First Class on the Ira Jeffrey and supplied a considerable amount of detail in his book on the history of *Fogg*. He also supplied a short course in interpreting "Huff-Duff" signals:

> Radio waves can be "ground waves", in which case they are considered nearby, or 'sky waves' that bounce off the atmosphere and are considered to be more distant. Ground waves usually extend 30 miles or less. Sky waves usually exceed 30 miles. The HF/DF operator could determine the type of wave by looking at his scope. Ground waves formed a figure eight on the screen and maintained an almost constant reciprocal bearing. Sky waves also formed this pattern but would frequently change bearing. Also, the strength of the signal sometimes would help define either type wave.

This signal reoccurred later on the same frequency and from the same general area. The weather was good with a 15 mile visibility. Sonar conditions were measured by a bathythermograph on *Fogg* and were classified good. Once again, Soundman Schrader wanted his readers to know the technical details:

> A bathythermograph is a device reeled over the side which measures temperature variation with depth. From this and related tables, sonar conditions could be determined. One of the interesting properties of a supersonic sound wave in sea water is it's ability to be bent or refracted when encountering a layer of water of different temperature or salinity. This effect could be exploited by a submarine, allowing it to hide from a searching sonar beam.

The assured sound range was 1700 yards. The calm sea, after the storms the convoy had gone through and the excellent sonar conditions now prevailing, augured well if a sub contact were made. At midmorning the convoy position was 370 miles from Sao Miguel, Azores, from where air coverage was being furnished. A plane was sighted by *Fogg*, on a sweep ahead of the convoy. But the aircraft missed one important detail immediately below it – peering through his periscope, *Korvettenkapitän* Ernst Hechler, Commander of *U-870*, had just given the order to fire a torpedo!

Lookouts and the Officer of The Deck on *Fogg* observed an explosion on the port side of the tank landing ship *LST-359*, then being towed by the tug *Farallon*. The general and chemical alarms were sounded, the latter alarm being used as a submarine contact or alert aboard this vessel. The commanding officer, Lieutenant Commander F.H. Martin, and Commander Task Group 27.4, Commander Harry T. Chase, were on the bridge within thirty seconds. The skipper turned the ship toward *LST-359* and increased speed. Although equipped with voice radio, no message was received from the *LST*, nor was any signal or hoist displayed. *Fogg* went to flank speed.

The FXR gear was streamed. Soundman Schrader wanted to be certain that all our readers understood the function of the FXR:

> The FXR gear consisted of two metal rods separated and parallel at the end of a long wire cable streamed in the water off the stern and paid out for some distance in the wake of the ship. The clattering of the metal rods generated a loud noise of high intensity that was designed to attract and foil (out fox) German acoustic torpedoes in use at the time. It generated a noise source louder than the ship's propellers which the torpedo would normally home on. German U-boat personnel called it the "buzz saw," coined from the noise it made. *Ira Jeffery* had earlier acted as a target ship in tests at Quonset Point, Rhode Island, during the development of this device.

Continuing his almost inexhaustible supply of ASW knowledge, Soundman Schrader resumed his discourse on the FXR:

> Recently, I had a long conversation with Charles Francis Adams Jr., the first commanding officer of *Fogg*. He related a story of Carlo Colosi, an Italian physicist with a brother in the Italian Navy. He became interested in and developed a torpedo aiming device that operated on the principle of detecting a ship's propeller noises, converting them to directions to the torpedo's steering mechanism and thereby causing the missile to proceed directly to the noise source and explode. This was the design of the first acoustic torpedo.
>
> Having no love for the Germans who were pouring into Italy, he was persuaded by the OSS to leave for the USA. He was spirited away by boat to America for debriefing of the device. After proving his sincerity and approbation for the allied cause, he was put to work at the prestigious Massachusetts Institute of Technology. The Germans by now had the acoustic torpedo, but Colosi was able to develop a countermeasure, labeled the "foxer," to decoy the torpedo away from an escort's propellers. His work saved many ships, notwithstanding the unfortunate experience of *Fogg*.

Ira Jeffery commenced searching the starboard quarter of the convoy. *Fogg* still had not determined the cause of the explosion on the *LST*. The DE's FXR gear was determined by sonar to have a low noise level, so a second FXR was ordered streamed. *Farallon* was still towing *LST-359* but began to lose speed and drop back. *Fogg* was ordered to close her to determine the cause of the explosion. The DE was now moving into the convoy on a reverse course between columns four and five intent on approaching *LST-359* and to pass her about 500 yards on *Fogg's* port hand.

Suddenly, the tug *Moose Peak* was observed crossing from the rear to the starboard of the *LST* and blowing repeated blasts on her whistle. Simultaneously, a TBS radio message crackled: "Convoy Commodore from *Moose Peak*. Periscope to my starboard!"

Ira Jeffery was ordered to search the tug's starboard area. At the same time, *Fogg* made a wide turn to port to the rear of the tug to approach the same area and aid in the sonar search. The ASW officer on *Fogg* ordered setting a shallow depth charge pattern to be ready for an urgent attack but, unfortunately, the bridge was not so notified. *Fogg* came out of her turn, steadied on a westerly course astern of *Moose Peak*, and started a sonar search.

An explosion blasted the stern of *Fogg*, followed by two more explosions! *Fogg* abruptly and urgently radioed over TBS: "We have been torpedoed!"

The two explosions that followed the torpedo detonation were a result of at least two of the depth charges being blown over the side, close aboard. These charges were the Mark 8 type that would explode when they perceived a magnetic influence, as from a submarine, at the arming depth of 50 feet. In this case, it was determined that *Fogg's* hull created this influence and the preset charges exploded.

The above situation presented a very hazardous condition due to the remaining charges still aboard, some on the damaged stern, difficult to reach and set on safe so they could be jettisoned. After a very hazardous effort by the *Fogg* crew, all charges were thought to be set on safe and dropped over the side. But three had escaped resetting and detonated. One wounded survivor was in the water at the time of these explosions and received additional injuries.

The DE lost way and stopped dead in the water. She began to settle by the stern, and it was noted that the fantail had been knocked approximately four feet above normal level. Communication to all interior stations were determined to be intact with the exception of Repair III, the after steering and depth charge stations.

Repair II was ordered to investigate the extent of damage and to take counter measures. At word that the ship was not making way, and evidently the propellers were gone, the main engines were secured.

Except for a few minutes after the torpedo hit, power to the forward part of the ship was maintained. All exterior communications, radio and radar, continued to function. From the bridge of *Fogg*, Commander Harris directed the movements of the convoy against further attack. He stayed aboard until evening, then transferred his pennant to *Lee Fox*. The net laying ship *Chinaberry (AN-61)* stood by to take *Fogg* in tow. Light displacement ship *LT-643* and infantry landing ships *LCI-419* and *LCI-420* were directed to stand by.

The convoy was ordered to clear the area at best possible speed. *LST-359* was abandoned, and fleet ocean tug *ATF-101* was ordered to stand by and sink her by gunfire if necessary. The *LST* was reported to be broken in two and in sinking condition.

Ingram was ordered to cover and protect the convoy. *Ira Jeffrey* and *Lee Fox* were directed to execute a retiring search plan from the scene of torpedoing. Later, *Lee Fox* stopped the search, joined *Fogg* which had been taken in tow by *Chinaberry*, and then proceeded along the convoy route while transferring Commander Harris. After the transfer, *Lee Fox* took station ahead of *Fogg* and acted as escort. *Ira Jeffrey* continued the search.

Sonarman Schrader's station on *Ira Jeffrey* was the sonar attack recorder in the sonar "shack," just forward of the flying bridge. He again offered an explanation of the workings of sonar electronics:

> "The attack recorder registered the echoes sent to it by the sonar equipment we called the 'stack', a name I never understood. These echoes were registered on thermal sensitive paper, and the recorder then acted as a mechanical computer, determining when the depth charges were to be dropped. The attack recorder operator, on approval from the bridge, gave the order to fire or drop depth charges at the appropriate time via sound powered telephone and a hand operated firing signal. Both were received by the crews on the stern who were responsible for firing "K" guns or releasing charges or both. Charges would be dropped to form a pattern around the suspected U-boat, usually held to a maximum of 13 in one attack. Smaller patterns were also used for urgent situations."

Ira Jeffery was 3500 yards from *Fogg* and proceeding toward her when *Fogg* was torpedoed. During the course of her approach, she obtained a contact evaluated as positive submarine due to the moderate closing doppler of the echoes received and target width as determined from "cut on" bearings. This contact was detected at 1400 yards but was lost at 1200 yards because of an attack recorder failure, the recorder stylus hanging up on it's extreme right end of travel. Schrader relayed the problem to the sonar operator, John Ludwig, and asked that he change to normal stack operation. This was necessary as the stack was "slaved" to the recorder when in use. Disappointingly, contact was not regained. Soundman Schrader explained:

> "Doppler was named for Johann Christian Doppler, an Austrian physicist who, during his lifetime of 1803–1853, discovered the effect. We can think of it using an analogy of the higher pitch sound we hear from an approaching train and, after it passes, the sound changing to a lower pitch. Likewise, a submarine approaching a sonar beam will reflect the sound and return an echo whose pitch is higher than the pitch of the transmitted signal. Conversely, a submarine moving away from a sonar beam will reflect a sound lower than the transmitted signal. This effect allows a sonarman to evaluate the movement of a target, its direction and to establish it as a positive submarine. Bearings to the contact, relayed by the sonarman to the conning officer, detect target movement relative to the attacking ship's course, allowing this officer to direct the ship to a successful depth charge or hedgehog run".

In this situation, training called for the recorder operator to proceed with the echoes obtained and, as the ship moved at 15 knots, drop the pattern as indicated by the mechanical settings on the recorder. This is appropriately known as an embarrassing attack and can be used whenever contact is lost on a sonar run. Obviously, submarine evasive maneuvers could take place in the interim as the U-boat sonar operator below assesses what is happening above.

The attack proceeded as described; a 13 charge pattern was set up on the attack recorder and preparations were made to fire. At the appropriate time, the order to fire charges was given in the normal sequence of "rolling" a charge off the fantail or "firing" a charge from a Kgun. After two charges were dropped, the sound team received an order from the captain, Lieutenant Commander William H. Doheny, to cease firing. Concerned, Schrader went up the two steps to the flying bridge and immediately saw the reason; a *Fogg* crewman was in the water holding on to a mattress and would have been right in the middle of the pattern. Attempts were being made by others to rescue him so *Ira Jefferey* continued on the run and dropped a seven charge pattern in the suspected area of the U-boat to convince him his presence was not desired and to deter any further attacks.

Obviously, at this time, the convoy was very vulnerable, and the loss of another destroyer escort or convoyed ship was the last thing anybody wanted to happen. At noon, another five charge pattern was dropped with the same game plan. *Ira Jeffery* then went into a retiring search, wherein the escort ship searches in ever widening squares from the last contact in an attempt to locate the submarine. *Ira Jeffery* was joined by *Lee Fox* and commenced a special sonar procedure called a "sleeper" or "creeping" attack. As eloquently explained by Soundman Schrader:

> "In this method, one ship echo ranges and directs the other by radar and radio to the contact; the CIC plot is essential. Since the directed ship is not echo ranging, the U-boat only hears the directing ship at a great distance and sees no need to take evasive maneuvers when, in fact, it is about to be attacked."

The search was in vain as no contacts were made. It began to appear that the U-boat had made a clean getaway. *Ingram* was directed by Commander Harris to radio the Azores operational authorities and request surface vessels to relieve TG 27.4 of its searching duties. Several hours later, relief by Task Group 27.5 appeared, began searching, and relieved *Ira Jeffery* to rejoin *Fogg* and *Lee Fox*.

Sometime during the attack, two Liberator bombers out of the Azores flew very low over the attack area, swung around where the U-boat might be and commenced dropping sonobuoys in an attempt to pick up submarine screw noises. Once again, Soundman Schrader came to the rescue of the non-ASW readers:

> "The sonobuoy was a passive listening device that could radio it's findings back to the aircraft. If a submarine were located, the plane would either drop depth charges or, if well out of the area of friendly ships, could drop an aerial acoustic torpedo named "Fido" or direct escorts to the area."

However, no contact was made by the aircraft. During the attack on *Fogg*, Commander Harris had directed *G. W. Ingram* to protect the convoy and to clear the area at the best possible speed.

At mid afternoon, *LCI-420* came alongside *Fogg* and received a number of crewmen. Transferred were four injured and 61 uninjured, all of whom were taken aboard the oiler *Mattole (AO-17)*. *LCI-542* then joined *LCI-419* in standing by *Fogg* in case additional personnel needed to be removed.

As soon as *LST-359* was torpedoed, *Moose Peak* proceeded to her assistance. At the request of the *LST* commanding officer, *Moose Peak* went alongside and removed seven officers and 98 enlisted men, 16 of whom were injured. They were then transferred to *Mattole*. The *LST* had two fatalities. *Fogg* lost four men. Later in the afternoon, the *LST* broke in two and sank.

Thus ends the story of the tank landing ship *LST-359*. She participated in some of the hardest fought landings in Europe at Sicily, Salerno, Anzio, Nettuno and finally Normandy, only to suffer almost humiliating destruction at the hands of a U-boat while being towed in the Atlantic. A fighting ship that earned five battle stars must have been the source of great pride for the crew.

After nightfall, *Ira Jeffery* was ordered to cease searching and to return to *Fogg*. The search for the U-boat continued by ships from TG 27.5 as mentioned above. *Ira Jeffery* and *Lee Fox* assumed positions as escorts for *Fogg*, now in tow by *Chinaberry* to port and *LT-643* to starboard, resulting in more stability, control and reduced yawing.

In the early afternoon of 21 December, *Chinaberry's* tow line to *Fogg* parted. A few hours later, *Chinaberry* put another line over, and the tandem tow was resumed. Speed was maintained until within five miles of Bahia Praia, Azores. All possible efforts were exerted to lighten the *Fogg's* stern and to assume maximum watertight integrity.

By 2100, the force of wind and sea increased slightly, and action waves on *Fogg's* counter became a matter of concern. The fantail was working slightly and settling. The next 17 hours were spent in severing and discarding gun mounts, depth charge racks and other heavy fixtures. Nonetheless, the stern section continued to settle, and tears and cracks were observed increasing in width and length.

Two and a half hours later, 35 men were transferred from *Fogg* to *LCI-419* to lighten ship and to remove excess personnel from danger. Their effectiveness in damage control was at an end, and a strong possibility existed of the stern shearing off with unpredictable consequences. The stern was reported to be cracking up with seas breaking three or four feet over the fantail.

Just before midnight, tearing noises were heard in the after end, and the entire stern section sheared off. The ship took a ten degree list to starboard, and the remaining after part of the ship lifted to the normal level above water. The fresh water and all material were shifted to balance the list, and the course and speed were resumed.

On the morning of 23 December, a careful inspection showed that the ship was riding well and could have every expectation of making the Azores safely. In addition, the stern had sheared clear in such a manner that little work would be necessary to make *Fogg* seaworthy for continuing to a U.S. port which she did.

Soundman Schrader paid his respects to *Fogg*:

> "It was getting dark now, the sea was calm, the wind just a breeze and we should have been happy to be on our way to the Azores, a new land we had never seen before. Instead, at our stations or in our bunks, we could not help thinking of the families of six brave sailors who would never see their loved ones again. Even for those of us not knowing them personally, it was a great loss. I, for one, will never forget that day. May they rest in peace."

Lewis M. Andrews, Jr.

ESCORT DIVISION SIX

The Tempest and the Foe

This narrative is one of the few opportunities this author has had to write in the first person.

In October 1943, I reported to *Sims (DE-154)* as executive officer, relieving Lieutenant Robert Newcomb, whose fate on the *Underhill* is related in the *Midgets* narrative in chapter *Pacific Antisubmarine Warfare*. As executive officer, I was also navigator.

We convoyed fifty or more tankers and freighters across at a time, New York to Londonderry, Northern Ireland. Some ships also carried aircraft and army ordnance, such as artillery and tanks, lashed to their decks. *CortDiv 6* consisted of six DEs, all with turbo-electric main engines. Whenever troop ships were added, a "jeep" aircraft carrier was usually assigned to our division.

The other DEs in *CortDiv 6* were the flagship *Charles Lawrence (DE-53)*, *Reeves (DE-156)*, *Daniel T. Griffin (DE-54)*, *Hopping (DE-155)* and *Donnell (DE-56)*.

Bridge was the favorite wardroom relaxation for one tenth of a cent per point. We were assigned a station astern of a British aircraft carrier one evening when she was recovering her planes. The engine of the last one to come in suddenly cut out, and we saw it splash just short of the flight deck. Our captain, Lieutenant James A. Moffett, proceeded at flank speed to the area of the crash, and we were happy to see the pilot swimming and unhurt in the midst of a huge green dye. A rope ladder was dropped over the side, and the young New Zealand Lieutenant scrambled up. Somebody remarked: "Hope he plays Blackwood."

Between convoys, we went on training maneuvers in Casco Bay, Maine, as cold a place in winter as I'd seen since Quebec. It was good training though. If we could keep our guns and depth charges from freezing up in Casco Bay, we'd have no trouble on that score in the North Atlantic. On anchoring in the base at sunset, lobster fishermen would come alongside with lobsters for the wardroom at 25 cents apiece. Having gotten underway at 0500 in the midst of Maine's winter to conduct firing and ASW exercises all the freezing day, those crustaceans were a delight for the soul and palate alike.

While I was exec, we had a bout with the sea that we'll all remember. We had departed from Lough Foyle, Northern Ireland, at 0600 on 19 December 1943. The sea and sky were gray and mean as we headed into a miserable Atlantic Ocean. It was bitterly cold and wet. The storm would come to be known in naval annals as the "Christmas Hurricane."

On 20 December, *Sims* recorded a 35 knot wind and a convoy speed of only six knots into the sea. On 21 December, we logged the wind at 45 knots with seas increasingly turbulent, and convoy speed slowed to a crawl. A storm of hurricane proportions was approaching from the southeast, and the convoy was rerouted to the north in the hope that the eye of the storm would pass us to the south. We did not have the kind of weather information that is available today. Weather "surprises" were commonplace.

The 22, 23 and 24 December brought no change. We ate a Christmas Eve turkey dinner, preoccupied with keeping the plates and silver on the table. The captain did find the very necessary time to go back to the crew's quarters and compliment the men on their two foot high Christmas tree lashed to a stanchion.

The morning of Christmas Day was an eerie, too-quiet calm, dark and foreboding. In the afternoon, just after lunch, it hit. Winds suddenly rose to gale force, 50 knots, then 60 knots. By nightfall, we were heading into a 65 knot wind, making steerageway (going backward) while heading one third speed into the sea. The convoy was dispersed over a wide area. None of us on the *Sims* will ever forget that Christmas night as the wind velocity continued to increase.

The captain and I took turns with the Officer of The Deck on the bridge. When the night closed in, the sea was fitful. We'd take off from the top of a comber and slam down into a valley with the wave tops almost as high as the mast. Green water broke over the main deck and boiled back to the stern. All deck watches were secured. The howling wind was such that one had to shout into a man's ear to be heard. We rolled and pitched violently with our screws coming out of the water, wrenching *Sims* from stem to stern. We were an eerie lot on the flying bridge, what with heavy clothes, wool helmets and face masks covering everything but eyes and mouth. The only mark of rank or distinction was on the forehead, "Capt," "Exec," "1st. Lt." etc.

The commodore announced on voice radio that a freighter near us had engine failure, and was dead in the water. He directed *Sims* to go about to stand by or render assistance. Coming about was nothing to relish. Captain Moffett said to me: "All you have to do is count three big ones, then turn."

Three huge waves were surmounted, and he roared into the voice tube, "Left full rudder! Port engine back full! Starboard engine ahead full!"

Sims turned off the sea, and more than one of us held his breath when we were parallel to the trough. Our stern would now come up into the sea as we reversed course, or else.... Later on, I learned that, as opposed to a destroyer, it was almost impossible to capsize a DE because of her stability. But we didn't know it, then.

We found the freighter, and the skipper again took us about, this time bringing the bow into the sea. We stood by that hapless vessel for about an hour as she gyrated through every pitch and roll imaginable while lying in the trough. There were times when we could actually see her keel. Apparently, however, she was well stabilized with ballast because she always managed to come back up again. Then her engineers got her going, and she turned into the sea. We returned to our best estimate of our station, very inexact because the convoy formation had become disorganized. The time was about 2200.

At about 2300, I took over the bridge, and the captain went down to the wardroom for a cup of coffee. There was nothing to be seen, just huge black mountains of sea to cross. Atop one mountain ahead of us, I thought I saw another shape with a silhouette similar to a DE. Then suddenly I knew it was a DE, crossing our bow from port to starboard. "Left full rudder!" I shouted into the voice tube.

The vision of *Griffin* landing keel first on our foredeck was nothing to look forward to. We straightened out before reaching the trough, and I guess we passed about 50 yards under the stern of the other DE.

At midnight, we confronted a problem that could have wreaked havoc. The captain and myself were both on the bridge. The storm was at its crescendo, a screaming, crazy sea, white with foam against a black night. We suddenly thought we could hear a rumbling, bumping noise from the port main deck but, with the dark and main deck awash, we couldn't see a thing. Somebody called the bridge from the after crew's quarters to say that there was the damnedest noise from outside, like a giant's bowling alley. It was a real puzzler.

The skipper was watching the sea ahead, so I walked to the after railing of the flying bridge and strained my eyes down in hopes of finding the cause of the disturbance. The ship rolled hard to starboard, the water sloshing off the port deck. I thought I saw some objects rumbling about, like big drums or ash cans.

"Ash cans!" I felt a lump in my throat. Ash cans, of course, depth charges free and rolling up and down the afterdeck! I walked over to a phone and spoke to the depth charge watch who had been secured inside the after companionway. I told him to exercise caution but to step outside, take a quick look at the port depth charge rack and tell me what he saw. After some seconds, I heard his strained voice over the sound-powered phone: "Mr. Andrews, the inboard safety bar is dislodged. There appear to be three charges loose on the main deck!"

I took a deep breath and walked up to the windshield where the skipper was peering into the night. "Captain, those rumbling noises..." Jim looked at me, and I could see he was not expecting glad tidings. "Inboard safety bar dislodged. About three depth charges rolling free on the port side afterdeck!"

I was shouting above the wind, but I knew by the way he looked at me and compressed his lips that he had heard. Neither of us was under any delusions about our predicament. Three depth charges, each containing 300 pounds of TNT, were rolling to and fro on the deck, smashing into bulkheads, stanchions and fittings. If one went off, it could conceivably have countermined the other two with untold consequences to the ship and crew.

The captain turned over the conn to me and went aft to the carpenter shop via the below deck passageway. The carpenter shop was in the midship structure and opened onto the main deck, port side. He had to work fast. The two toughest men on the *Sims* were a coxswain, known as "JuJu" because of his proficiency at that sport, and a hardy gunner's mate, Milligan. The word was passed for both to report to the skipper in the carpenter shop.

The captain explained he needed two "volunteers," and they would make outstanding "volunteers." This was the plan. Each time the ship rolled to starboard and the water momentarily drained off the port deck, they would undog a port door, dart out onto the deck, grab a depth charge, check for safe setting and deep six it. They would then jump back into the carpenter shop and dog the door before the ship rolled back under water on the port side. The "volunteers" stared at each other. Most mortals would have blanched at such an assignment. "We'll give it a try, Cap'n."

At the first favorable moment, they leaped outside, wrestled a depth charge, checked it for safe, threw it over and got back safely inside before the port main deck was deluged. *Sims* rolled to starboard again, and the two men repeated the performance. A telephone talker kept all watch stations apprised, and all began to breathe a sigh of relief. Two depth charges were dispatched, only one to go.

But what a one!

Both men had repeated the routine. They grabbed the depth charge and started to check the depth setting, but *Sims* did not cooperate and began to settle rapidly on the port side. Faced with the imminent probability of being washed overboard, they signalled glances: "Heave the son-of-a-bitch!"

The depth charge went over the rail without being checked, and the pair made it back into the carpenter shop, dogging the door just as the water started to rush into the doorway.

We were heading into the sea at our slowest speed, virtually standing still relative to the ground so the depth charge went straight down under the keel. On the flying bridge, I lurched sharply as the surrounding water lit up in explosion! There was no panic, but there was consternation throughout the ship. The engine room, where the percussion effect was strongest, temporarily lost circuit breakers, plunging interior spaces into darkness. After closing the circuit breakers, they called the bridge to ask where the torpedo hit!

We were pretty lucky. A shallow setting of 50 feet could have had serious consequences. We'll never know for sure what the setting was. My best guess would be in the vicinity of 100 feet. The carnage we had been saving for a U-boat very nearly turned on us.

It was my second trip across as commanding officer. At 1000 on 18 March 1944, *Kapitänleutnant* Joachim Zander, commander of *U-311*, had the lead vessel in the outboard starboard column of our convoy in his periscope sight. He had managed to get inside our sound screen without being noticed. Just as our sound operator announced "contact," an ugly orange-red plume burst out of the tanker's starboard bow. Her name was *Seakay* of Esso registry. She was lucky. Loaded with aviation fuel and with a deck super-cargo of fighter aircraft, her bow went down so fast that the fire was snuffed out before it could ravage the crew. All hands, with one exception, were saved, 83 out of 84; one of the lifeboats had capsized, trapping one man underneath. In spite of a hardened mind set acquired as one became adjusted to the vistas and sounds of war, the sight of a fine ship sinking beneath the waves was a traumatic experience.

We saw the periscope and conning tower almost immediately after *Griffin* had made an effective depth charge attack, blowing the U-boat up from the depths. On orders from the escort commander, we proceeded to attack. We gained contact and attacked with a depth charge pattern at shallow setting but it was a hasty attack designed to drive the sub down and prevent it from getting off another torpedo.

Reeves was assigned to rescue survivors. *Sims* was detached from the convoy, along with *Griffin*, to attempt to destroy the sub. This we did through most of the day, conducting standing search patterns.

Throughout the search and destroy operation, *Griffin* was SOPA, Lieutenant Eastwood being senior to myself. Although his report varies somewhat from my own, I believe his should be given primary credence. The following is an abbreviation:

> "On the first contact, doppler had been reported as up. The bearing remained steady until about 400 yards when it started dropping aft. No change in doppler was evident. The skipper ordered firing on the recorder, a full pattern of medium-set depth charges. Contact was lost at 150 yards, about normal.
>
> This was believed to be an accurate attack. The submarine's conning tower broke the surface just outside the depth charge disturbance with very little way on, then lay dead in the water with no visually apparent forward motion at an approximate range of 700 yards. The conning tower steadied about half way out of water for a short time, then came slow-

ly up again until the bow broke about two feet above the surface. *Sims* reported hydrophone effect at this time which may have been the sub blowing tanks. *Griffin* went to flank speed.

The total time the submarine remained on the surface was estimated at slightly over 60 seconds. It then settled. Oil was noted in the area but was later completely covered by the sinking tanker's oil and wreckage. Several observers reported that the conning tower was damaged but, due to the excitement at the time, this is not accepted as fact. All agreed that both periscopes were in the down position and undamaged.

The second attack was also made on the recorder. It was believed to be an accurate attack, but unfortunately only five shallow and three medium charges exploded. Due to the excitement from sighting the submarine and imperfect (short) chains on the arbors (one was thrown over the side with disgust), three of the eight K-guns were not reloaded in time for firing. Personnel failure resulted in rolling three medium set charges from the port rack before realizing that a shallow pattern had been ordered. In the resulting confusion, no more charges were rolled.

Contact was not regained. The convoy was executing an emergency left turn at the time the tanker was torpedoed which created many water knuckles and a heavy wake throughout the area. *Griffin* went into a retiring search, ordering *Sims* to join for Operation Observant. Observant was continually interrupted by investigation of false contacts.

Griffin then ordered *Sims* to join an "unwinding" box search of the area. *Sims* took a position 3000 yards on *Griffin's* port beam. No false contacts were reported on this sweep. Later sound conditions were excellent and the sweep continued uninterrupted until *Sims* reported a contact at 1227. *Griffin* closed the area while *Sims* attacked two minutes later. (This author-skipper recalls a large bubble surfacing , but no debris was sighted.)

Sims was unable to regain contact so *Griffin* headed in, gaining contact at 1500 yards. *Griffin* came to a center bearing and commenced her run. At this time, *Sims* reported that two of her lookouts had sighted a periscope and both agreed that it came up about two feet for about two seconds, went down and came up again about four seconds later for another two seconds. After the attack, both of these lookouts agreed they had seen the periscope near the position where *Griffin* dropped her pattern.

Captain Eastwood remained convinced that the sub had been sunk or seriously damaged, but I was unable to concur in my action report. Contact was not regained, and both DEs were ordered to return to convoy stations."

About a year before this book was completed, I bumped into Ray Sileo, a former crew member of the *Seakay*. He had done some research on *U-311*. The torpedoing of the tanker was her first after 13 months of operation, hardly up to Admiral Doenitz' expectations. A month after our encounter, a submarine was reported to have been sunk in the same area by Canadian Air Force planes. It could have been *U-311*, but she was lost with all hands and her logs.

On one midwinter crossing, while patrolling our station, we sighted about twelve life rafts with four or five men on each. I instinctively gave the order to bear down on them and, at the same time, heard the commodore telling us not to waste too much time because they were all dead. As we approached the rafts, however, some of the men appeared to be waving their arms. I brought the ship to full speed to get into the area as fast as possible and braked for one raft where the occupants seemed to be waving.

When we came alongside, I could see the gray of death in the faces of men frozen from life, still lashed together in sitting positions, some with lifeless frozen arms still waving. It was the same with the rest of the rafts. The animation was caused by the rolling rafts in the sea. Our commodore knew this from prior experience but let us learn for ourselves lest we fret that we had abandoned castaways. It was a moving sight. Sometime after the war, I was interested to read about a similar experience in Montserrat's *Cruel Sea*.

One day, *CortDiv 6* was wounded. *Donnell* was hit! The date was 3 May 1944, the Division's fifth convoy to Londonderry. It was a beautiful spring day. The sun sparkled on the water, and the sea was calm. I was on the bridge when the TBS suddenly sprang to life. *Donnell* was reporting to the commodore that she had a positive sub contact and was going in on the attack. I immediately ordered condition affirm, a partial manning of battle stations. I focused my glasses on *Donnell*.

Her captain was Lieutenant Commander Gordon Street. I had known Gordon for some years, going back to subchaser days when a few of us convoyed merchantmen in the Caribbean, hopefully guarding them from U-boats. *Donnell* was preparing a depth charge attack. The commodore had already ordered the convoyed ships to turn 45 degrees to starboard to avoid torpedoes that could already be on their way.

The series of events that preceded the attack involved a coincidence that could almost be called bizarre. *Donnell* was conducting an antisubmarine exercise. A sonar echo was feigned to originate in the sound gear. The dummy submarine attack commenced, its purpose being to exercise the second watch section plotting team, conning officers and sonar personnel in attack procedure. One officer had the conn, another stood by the chemical recorder, and a third was reading ranges, cut-ons, and doppler effect from a prepared sheet. Soundman Second Class Krupa was calculating center bearings and passing them to plot with ranges. Soundman third class Newton continued regular sound search. The bridge talker and bridge messenger were at station on the remote control depth charge firing and release mechanisms. The depth charge watch on the fantail was ordered to set a medium depth pattern. Because this was only a drill, the FXR was not streamed.

When the problem was nearly over, distinct echoes were heard over the sonar loud speaker by all present in the Asdic hut. The bearing of this sudden new contact was on the starboard bow whereas the practice contact had been on the port bow. The contact and bearing were reported to conn for checking, and the conclusion was positive submarine. The attack began.

Depth charges were set at medium pattern, about 250 feet, because the order to set on safe that would follow a drill, was not given. All personnel were at stations. Lieutenant Schauffhauser began the attack. Lieutenant Bell cut in the recorder, the first range to the real sub showing 2500 yards. Ensign Boone immediately notified the OTC over voice radio. The black pennant, signifying "I am going in on the attack" was two blocked. Ensign

Stewart and Quartermaster Striker Sorenson began a new plot on the Dead Reckoning Tracer (DRT). The commanding officer came up to the bridge from the CIC where he had been observing the mock attack. He stood by at conn. All stations were told, "This is not a drill," repeated several times. Soundman Third class Newton took over the sound stack and Soundman Second Class Krupa continued as standby, passing information to plot in the CIC. The general alarm was not sounded, in line with ship's policy to avoid confusion in changing stations, phones, etc. during an urgent attack.

The conning officer brought the ship around to the bearing of the target and followed its movement, which was slowly to the right. The recorder reported an initial range rate of 12 knots. Doppler was indicated as moderately low. The captain stood by, watching the picture develop. At about 1200 yards, he took over the conn. Throughout the attack, the target bearing never varied more than 10 degrees. At about 600 yards, the range rate decreased to 11 knots and a periscope was sighted a few degrees on the port bow. Bridge lookouts Ensign Boone, Signalman Third Class Rowe and the crew of number two 3" gun saw it simultaneously. No feather (wake) was noticeable, indicating that the sub was moving slowly.

Upon the periscope sighting, depth charges were ordered set shallow. Racks and port K-guns acknowledged changed settings with the range down to 200 yards. As the captain rang the alarm for GQ, the periscope disappeared. At about that time, the ASW Officer reported that the target seemed to be turning away.

The next development was a water slug at 250 yards, resembling the slug released by our own subs during ASW exercises. (An air slug from one of our subs came from a torpedo tube and indicated to the DE how close it came to scoring with depth charges had they been used in actual combat.) Gun number two fired a round at the air slug at 100 yards. The slug was perfectly round and without motion. It was presumed to be evidence of a torpedo fired at the DE or at the convoy. At this close range, the bearings of the target were dropping rapidly down the port side. Echoes became instantaneous.

The recorder plotter bar was lined up for firing on a 10 knot range rate. (Ed. Range rate = combined speed of both vessels.) About 10 seconds before the time of the first firing order, a torpedo hit astern, blowing both depth charge tracks, K-guns 6, 7, and 8, off the ship, along with the fantail, 20mm guns 9 and 10, and number three 3" gun! The depth charge watch and the number three 3" gun crew disappeared. A few seconds later, the explosions of the depth charges that were flung into the sea knocked out all power on the ship and sealed the fate of many men in the water.

We've been hit!" That transmission from the stricken *Donnell* came like a lightning bolt from the blue. Unfortunately, the bridge never issued an order to stream the FXR, and no report was received from the fantail indicating that it was streamed. The reason was that, during the early stages of the practice run, streaming the FXR was either assumed or simulated. The order to stream the FXR was obviously overlooked in changing from a drill to the real thing.

It was a great pity and the rarest of happenstances that a DE, conducting an antisubmarine exercise, had to abort abruptly, and mentalities had to change from a perfunctory "This is a drill" to an urgent "This is not a drill." Had the ship not been conducting a drill, there is a good chance that contact with the U-boat might have been made sooner, at a greater range and without "This is a drill" handicap. Most likely, the FXR would have been streamed. Some of the crew must have been momentarily confused. Recalling one of Murphy's immutable laws, "If it can happen, it will happen."

From messages that filled the air, it was apparent that *Donnell* would not sink, but most of her stern had been blown away, and all propulsion had been lost. Twenty-five percent of the crew were casualties, 29 killed and 25 wounded. The commodore ordered *Hopping* to take the stricken DE in tow and *Reeves* to act as escort. The remaining four DE's, including mine, re–formed our screen to continue coverage of the convoy. I have to admit that I was downcast, as was our crew and the crews of the other DEs in *CortDiv 6*. It could have just as well been us. "There, but for the Grace of God, go I"!

We were on the eastern side of "chop," that half of the North Atlantic where the Admiralty had charge of all allied convoys. We couldn't have known it at the time, but we were only a month away from Operation Overlord, the invasion of Normandy. After some discussion between the Admiralty and Cinclant as to whether the hulk should be sunk or salvaged, the latter view prevailed, and the British seagoing tug, *HMS Samsonia*, was dispatched to the scene to relieve *Hopping*. The latter had been making a valiant effort to tow her sister ship, but a tug was obviously better suited to the job.

The *Donnell* was towed to Lisaholly, Northern Ireland, and thence to Plymouth, England. The following August, American troops had pushed the Germans out of Cherbourg, but not before the enemy blew up the local power plant. This left the city without power for emergency services, even hospitals. Somebody remembered *Donnell*, and she was towed across the English Channel to Cherbourg. Her turbo-electric propulsion plant remained undamaged. Tied to the dock, she was able to pour electricity into vital areas of the city. In a sense, one could say that *Donnell* remained undefeated.

In ten round trips across an Atlantic infested with U-boats, *CortDiv 6* successfully delivered thousands of troops and hundreds of thousands of tons of war materiel to the fighting fronts. The loss of a tanker, the crippling of a DE and no hard evidence to claim sinking a U-boat were a small price to pay. We were a convoy escort division, not a hunter-killer group. Division commanders could not spare DEs to concentrate on search and destroy missions which could consume many hours, even days. Escorts in convoys operated defensively, their main responsibility being to deliver their charges safely to port. That we did and earned our "Well Done" from the Commander in Chief Atlantic Fleet on completion of hostilities.

Shortly thereafter, *CortDiv 6* DEs were converted to APDs, high speed attack transports. The Japanese *kamikazes* were waiting to give them a warm welcome at Okinawa. See chapter *Iwo Jima to Okinawa – The Fast Transports*.

ESCORT DIVISION TWENTY-TWO

The Coast Guard Goes to War... An Eye for an Eye...

On 2 December 1943, Convoy GUS26, comprising 81 ships and 14 escorts, was westbound to New York from Casablanca.

Lewis M. Andrews, Jr.

The voyage was one of misery for *Peterson (DE-152)* and *Joyce (DE-317)* even without enemy action. The slow convoy was tossed and smashed about by howling gales and high seas in some of the worst winter weather of the season. Some days, the convoy failed to make any distance good, in one case losing four miles in a 24 hour period. Most merchant ships ran out of food, and the Navy vessels almost did the same. It was a badly pounded but infinitely wiser group entering port in late January 1944, sailors all! They believed they weathered the worst the Atlantic had to offer, and came out on top. However, the sea knows no limits; a storm worse than the last was in their crystal ball.

In late February 1944, after yard availability and lengthy training at Casco Bay, Maine, the two ships joined the other destroyer escorts making up Coast Guard Escort Division 22. With one exception, the ships they would be with until the end of the war were *Poole (DE-151)*, *Harveson (DE-316)*, and *Kirkpatrick (DE-318)*. *Leopold (DE-319)* was the exception. Captain W.W. Kenner was Division Commander with his pennant in *Poole*.

On 1 March, *CortDiv 22* began its first combat operation, screening convoy CU16, 27 fast tankers bound for Londonderry, Northern Ireland. The first few days were uneventful except for a merchant seaman lost overboard in the fog. Submarines reported in force along the track lead to several course diversions as ordered by the Admiralty.

Leopold, the only ship in the division equipped with a high frequency direction finder (Huff-Duff), had been monitoring German submarine radio traffic. On the evening of 9 March, the convoy was 500 miles south of Iceland, making good 14.5 knots, only two days from its destination. A freezing wind kicked up choppy seas. The sky was ominous with bright moonlight, partly overcast with heavy cloud patches. As *Leopold* began to close her night patrol station, her radar made a contact five miles due south of the convoy.

Ordered by *ComCortDiv 22* to investigate, the captain, Lieutenant Commander Kenneth C. Phillips, called for full speed toward the contact. Chances were that the target was a U-boat; there were no other Allied vessels in the vicinity. At 2,000 yards, the lookouts saw something off the port bow. Phillips' voice was heard over the voice radio (TBS) exclaiming, "This looks like the real thing."

The Escort Commander was faced with a dilemma. He had sent *Joyce* to assist *Leopold*, leaving only four escorts with the convoy. If a wolf pack were preparing to attack, all remaining escorts would be vitally needed on their stations. His available intelligence favored that probability, but *U-255* was alone, probably charging batteries on the surface.

Leopold fired two star shells to illuminate the target. As they burst in the night sky, bridge personnel could see the darkhulled U-boat silhouetted by the flares. Surprised German sailors scrambled back into the submarine. Skipper Phillips quickly ordered flank speed and rapid fire as the target closed rapidly. The sub fired a spread of torpedoes and, before *Leopold* could turn to comb the torpedo tracks, two of the deadly fish hit the DE on the port side.

The detonations lifted the ship out of the water and knocked every man off his feet. The *Leopold* staggered to a halt midst the deadly ripping of metal and the screeching and groaning of the buckling hull. The back of the DE was broken! The captain, seeing his vessel was doomed, calmly gave the order to abandon ship. Seaman First Class Troy S. Gowers was at his gun station:

> "I was blown right out of my shoes and into a life net a dozen feet away. I crawled back to my station and, without power, tried to work the gun manually, but it was jammed. Then came the order to abandon ship. I helped release a life raft on the starboard side and jumped into the sea. The water was almost freezing, and the wind felt even colder. When I pulled myself aboard the raft, there were 18 or 19 of us. When we were finally picked up, there were only three or four."

Joyce, commanded by Lieutenant Commander Robert Wilcox, proceeded at full speed, arriving 2,000 yards from *Leopold* at 2005. *Joyce's* crew had seen the star shell bursts and noted that, after *Leopold* initially opened fire, it ceased abruptly. Skipper Wilcox reported to Captain Kenner that *Leopold* failed to answer TBS or signal lights. At 1,500 yards, *Leopold* was seen dead in the water with a massive hole in the port side. She had no power and her back was jackknifed with bow and stern pointing skyward. She was being abandoned.

Seaman Warren Young on *Leopold* stood by a 25-man raft when an officer approached and said a man had been trapped in the galley and a knife was needed to open the door. Young recalled:

> "I had a knife, so the officer and I worked our way back. We got the door open and went in. There was a stove on top of the trapped man, and his leg was hanging by a piece of skin. He was screaming, begging the officer to shoot him. When the officer refused, he pleaded with him to leave a gun by his side so that he could shoot himself. We got him out and I put a life jacket on him. The chief machinist's mate went into the water and caught him as we dropped him down. We never saw him again."

The ship settled deeper as the tempo of the storm increased. An officer went below to fetch whiskey and blankets to help everyone keep warm in the 22 degree (fahrenheit) air. Then they saw *Joyce* and signalled with a flashlight.

As *Joyce* approached, she began a sound sweep in the vicinity, attempting to pick up a sub echo, but without success. About the same time, *Leopold* broke in two. The icy water was filled with survivors as *Joyce* maneuvered to pick them up. Spirits had soared when *Joyce* hove into view and then plummeted in despair as the DE had to abandon them to stave off an attack. While some *Leopold* men were on cargo nets and various lines slung over the side, *Joyce's* sonar picked up an approaching torpedo, necessitating a surge to flank speed and hard over rudder. Skipper Wilcox shouted through a megaphone: "We're dodging torpedoes! God bless you. We'll be back."

Many men were lost, some caught in the churning screws. *Joyce* returned but again departed precipitously to avoid a torpedo. Further sweeps failed to locate the U-boat. The unendurably cold water claimed an increasing toll of life as *Leopold* continued to sink.

A storm was blowing, and waves broke over the small life rafts. On one of them, Seamen Gowers and Haynes crawled about, trying to keep the men awake so that they would not freeze or be washed away. Hypothermia set in quickly, numbing limbs and dulling the senses.

"Those who were freezing knew it," Gowers recalled. One boy said 'I'm dying, I can't hold any longer'. In a minute, he was gone."

Joyce slipped away into the night. While she maneuvered with radical turns to avoid the fate of *Leopold* , the men in the water were freezing to death. In a little while, the stern of *Leopold* rolled to port, and a lot of men were thrown off. Those who managed to climb back lasted for another one and a half hours. The hulk settled lower in the water. The waves were extremely high and, one by one, the men were washed off. Seaman William G. O'Brien remembered:

"I'd see a big wave coming and I'd close my eyes and hold my breath until the stern raised out of it. In one of these, the water didn't go down, and I realized the stern had finally settled for good. So I let go, and my life jacket carried me to the surface. After a while, I saw a life raft and struck out for it."

Some, including O'Brien, managed to climb into close by rafts which were now almost empty as their prior occupants had already frozen to death. O'Brien said:

"The captain was one of them, and I didn't see him again."

There were about 20 men aboard this raft; only three lived to be rescued. All of *Leopold's* 13 officers and 158 of her enlisted complement of 186 men were lost. It was most regrettable that *Joyce*, twice on the verge of rescue, had to depart to avoid being torpedoed herself.

Fire Controlman Warren Young, mentioned above as the man who helped to rescue a seaman trapped under a stove in the galley, was interviewed by The *Eagle Times* of Reading, Pennsylvania on Veteran's Day, 11 November 1990, the 200th anniversary of the Coast Guard.

" Even after all these years, it keeps me awake. When I sleep, I dream of it. Maybe I kept it inside me too long. This is the first time I've told the whole story."

Young spent six hours in the icy waters before he was rescued:

"Everything on the ship went dead. A geyser of water blew a man beside me overboard. The deck had buckled, and I had to crawl to my raft at the abandon ship station. There was no panic. No fire. It was quiet. All I had was a life preserver. I crawled down a cargo net hanging off the port side and let the water come up gradually. Then I just let go and dropped into the sea. I thought 'The ship is sinking; I better get away from it'. I started swimming. Didn't even notice how cold it was. I wasn't really worried and felt as though I was going to be rescued. I swam a piece. Then I looked around and saw the wind was pushing the ship right after me. I wasn't getting away from it.

Both of the *Leopold* 's propellers were clear out of the water. Beneath them was a raft holding two men. As Young swam toward it, the propellers dipped and knocked one seaman off.

I figured I was getting in that raft one way or another, so I got in. Just at that time, the wind caught either the ship or the raft, and we drifted away from the hulk. In the darkness, I could hear guys calling for help; some were blowing whistles.

We kept pulling men into the raft until we had so many we wouldn't let any more on. They were sitting on the edge and inside. Some were hanging to the sides, dying of cold and exposure. I saw men on my raft foaming at the mouth. They were going out of their heads. Their buddies were slapping them in the face trying to keep them conscious. Every once in a while, we knew someone had died. We pushed him off to make room for another one. I was sitting inside the raft and the water was up to my chin! By now, it must have been after midnight; I had lost track of time. The moment I hit the water my wristwatch stopped.

The hands of the watch, a prized memento in the Young home, points to 20 minutes after 8. As *Joyce* advanced and retreated, some of the seamen took up a chant.

Once more, *Joyce* returned. Lines were tossed to the survivors.

The water was so rough the ship sideswiped the raft, tipping it over. Only two of us were able to get back in. They threw a line down. I tied it around my waist. They hauled me up the cargo net, upside down. I was the last one they pulled in from that raft.

When they dragged me on board, they had one guy on each side of me. I said, 'I can walk. Let me go.' They wouldn't let me go. They just dragged me in. I don't know if I could have walked or not. I still don't have good circulation in my legs. They don't bother me, but they're always cold. They took me and another guy up to the officers' quarters and put us on the mess table. They stripped us, put hot towels all over us, and gave us whiskey. That helped. We were shivering so bad we kept moving off the table; they kept pushing us back on.

Young remembers the seaman who, when the call came to abandon ship, didn't want to get wet. The man jumped overboard, aiming for a raft. When he hit, he crashed through the latticework and into the water, the only humorous incident he could remember.

Every year, about the beginning of March, it comes back to me. Maybe because it was inside me. No one ever talked to me about it until now."

Richard Novotny

Richard R. Novotny, one of the survivors, recalls that four of the rescued men subsequently died on the *Joyce*, reducing the actual number of survivors to 25. The highest rank among them was Cleveland Parker, a chief steward's mate. Novotny's remarkable story (abridged):

22 August, 1993
Dear Mr. Andrews:

It is painful for me to recall that night of 9 March,

1944, but I want to do what I can to perpetuate the memory of my departed officers and shipmates.

I was getting ready to 'hit the sack' because I had the 0000 to 0400 watch in the after steering station. I was almost asleep when GQ was sounded. With all our drilling, I reacted spontaneously, and raced to my battle station. I was trunnion operator on a 20mm gun on the starboard side, and we were given our firing orders. Ensign William Tillman was our fire director officer.

About the time I reached my station, the forward 3" gun fired a star shell. I turned around and saw the conning tower of a surfaced submarine about 10 degrees off the port bow. It appeared that we were running at flank speed, approaching the sub bow on, and about to smash into the conning tower.

A second star shell was fired. Immediately after, it seemed to me that 'the lights went out'. I didn't even hear the explosion or anything connected with the torpedoing. From then on, I was in and out of a conscious state; I recall events like a series of short movie reels, detached from each other.

When I regained consciousness, I found myself in the water, swimming with one arm toward a raft some 15 yards away. I could still see the splinter shield of my gun and that it was protruded and cantilevered over the deck in line with the gunwhale.

The only way I can understand how I got into the water was that I must have been blown over the starboard side clear of the ship. There was a huge 20mm ammunition locker immediately behind our gun; It exploded and caused a lot of casualties. I remember having use of my right arm only in swimming toward the raft. I cannot recall having any use of my left arm or legs to propel me through the water. When I reached the raft, consciousness faded. When I again came to, I realized there were about 14 men, a sea of faces, in and hanging onto the sides of this seven man life raft.

In another scene, I saw a man half inside and half outside the raft and me hanging on with my right hand. In various time intervals, I would awake and find myself losing hold of the raft because of the height and roughness of the sea. I can also recall feeling the frigid temperature of the water and the air, me being clad solely in shredded dungarees. I sensed that I had no shoes and that my wristwatch was gone.

I can recall the raft turning so that I could see *Leopold* split in two from bow to stern with the full moon lighting up this horrible scene. I could see the ship breaking more and more in the middle. After a while, I can't remember how long, I saw our Chief Quartermaster, William E. Graham, hanging by his foot on the starboard anchor's fluke. I knew it was he because he was my immediate superior. I was a Quartermaster Striker and was to receive my Third Class rate on our return from this crossing.

I saw heads and shoulders in life jackets in a 360 degree circle from my life raft; they faded out and returned periodically. Later, I learned that we were an ideal set up for the U-boat that fired the fateful torpedoes. Our ship made a beautiful silhouette with the full moon behind us. What a turkey shoot! [Note in the *Buckley* narrative in chapter *The Hunter-Killers* how her skipper used the full moon to his advantage.]

I can recall, on and off, shipmates having fallen asleep, releasing their hold on the raft and drifting away. Others tried to restrain them, but being so exhausted themselves, they were unable to hang on to their comrades.

In one scenario, I vividly remember one of the cooks holding the raft in a position next to me. He was in terrible pain. He kept saying his legs hurt, or his legs were gone, or something that gave him frightful pain in spite of the water temperature. In one of his rantings, he started swinging his fists as though he were in a fight, and I caught a punch in the eye, and another on the nose. Added to my wounds were a real shiner and an unbelievably swollen nose. Expired or passed out, he started to drift away. I tried to grab him, but my left arm had no power. I couldn't hold him and the raft at the same time.

It was after this incident that I experienced a remarkably lucid apparition. I saw, in animated life size, my loving wife of eight months, my wonderful mother and father, smiling together and looking down at me. The three figures of those I loved the most stood in a hazy background, framed in a perfect square, seemingly suspended about five feet above the crest of the waves. The seas were running at 10–12 feet in height. Transfixed by this splendor, pain was replaced by a very satisfying sensation. There are times when I think I must have crossed to the other side and then came back. Up to this writing (1993) at age 70, I do not have any fear of death if what I saw was similar to it.

I remember seeing the profile of *Joyce* approaching our raft. I could hear Captain Robert Wilcox telling us on the bullhorn that he had been dodging torpedoes. He also promised us that he would be back to pick us up 'as soon as I can'. Although only half conscious, I cannot describe the sinking sensation and thoughts as I watched that ship pull away with their crew members lining the deck and shouting, 'we'll be back'.

There were now only two other shipmates with me, namely Seaman First Class Robert Chandler and Fireman William Smith. We exchanged a few words to keep up morale such as 'They will be back to pick us up' and how G.D. cold we all were. I do not remember the time, but I can vividly remember that the aft end of *Leopold* was gone, and the bow half was afloat in a vertical position.

Time had no meaning for me but I did remember the sequence of events. I saw *Joyce* approaching again, the three of us hollering and waving as hard as we could with nearly paralyzed arms. The DE came alongside the raft on her port side, rolling sharply to starboard, exposing to our view the steadying keels or fixed keel stabilizers and parts of her port propeller and rudder. Not being sucked under the hull when she righted must have been God's Will! Never having seen the bottom of the *Leopold* , I saw all I needed to know from *Joyce's* bottom.

Dozens of crewmen lined the rail, standing by to rescue us. A boarding net was rigged over the side. Several men were making their way down the net to help us. Bob Chandler and 'Red' Smith were closest to the hull and, therefore, were rescued first. My turn came, and I tried to change my position from the far side of the raft to the opposite side. I couldn't even move. There was no power in my legs from the hips down, and I could scarcely keep my face out of the water.

The motion of the sea caused the life raft to drift away a foot or two; it was sloshing back and forth. A *Joyce* seaman, with a manila line around his shoulders, flew down the net and grabbed me, damn near falling into the sea himself! He tied a bowline under my arms and around my shoulders, and then the crewmen on deck pulled me up and aboard. They held me in a standing position, removing the rope. They then figured I was OK on my own and let me go. With that, I crumpled to the deck like a sack of potatoes.

I could hardly express my feelings about Chuck Friend, the crewman who fastened the line around me at considerable risk to his own life. I will never stop appreciating the heroism and the great all out effort of Captain Robert Wilcox, his officers and men. Were it not for these people, I would not be telling my story today, 49 years later.

My memory of so many terrible things, shipmates dying in the water, getting lambasted by a half crazed man, so many around the raft falling asleep and drifting away, my chief quartermaster hanging by one leg from an anchor fluke lead me to believe that other things I witnessed just blanked out. Maybe it is nature's way of reducing an overloaded circuit before it blows a fuse.

I was thawed out from a nearly frozen state and put in the custody of some very caring people. I was taken below and placed in the bottom sack of three tiers of pipe beds. The bunk was close to the ship's infirmary and the pharmacist mate's facilities. I remember the sensation of warming up and becoming a little more comfortable in one sense. In another, freed from the anesthetic effect of icy water, I was visited by horrendous pain. The more I warmed up, the more painful it became lying only on my back.

The first class pharmacist mate was a very understanding and qualified man about 25 years old. I wish I could recall his name. In the past 20 years at *Joyce/Leopold* reunions, I have inquired, but without success. The only pain drug available to injured combatants at that time was morphine. An injection, however, was good for only four hours. I can tell you right here up front, a man in my kind of pain did not need a clock to tell him when he had his last ministration! The pharmacist mate did an excellent job of closing two shrapnel wounds, a one and a half inch gash in my forehead and a small hole through the left thigh.

Best Regards,
Richard Novotny

A period of three days elapsed with Novotny in and out of a conscious state while *Joyce* rejoined the convoy to Londonderry. He was transferred to the base hospital, the worst injured of all the survivors. The medical report indicated severe damage to three spinal vertebrae and pleurisy in both lungs in addition to the head and thigh wounds. He was flown back to the USA for further hospital treatment. Happily, the pleurisy was cleared up and, in due time, he regained use of his limbs. On 12 January 1945, he was honorably discharged from the U.S. Coast Guard. It is doubted if they make men anywhere tougher or more resilient than Quartermaster Striker Richard Novotny.

The death toll staggered the men of *CortDiv 22*, but soon their sorrow gave way to anger against the enemy. Soon the men of the other DEs were to get their opportunity for revenge, and repay in part this debt of blood.

Commendations from Commander in Chief, Atlantic Fleet, were presented to Lieutenant Commander Robert Wilcox, Soundman Nelson W. Allen and Soundman Winston T. Coburn for their efforts to rescue the crew of *Leopold* while holding a hostile submarine at bay. Eleven other men received the Navy and Marine Corps Medal.

On 15 April 1944, *CortDiv 22* with a *Leopold* replacement, *Gandy (DE-764)*, a navy manned ship skippered by Lieutenant Commander W.A. Sessions, stood down Ambrose Channel with Convoy CU21, again bound for Londonderry. The day before, Lieutenant Commander Sidney M. Hay, assumed command of *Peterson*.

An unannounced observer watched the vessels as they maneuvered into their convoy positions. *U-550* was on its first patrol and had lain in ambush outside New York harbor for an opportunity. Its young Captain, *Kapitänleutnant* Klaus Hanert, peered through his periscope. He ignored the escorts milling about their charges and lined up on a large tanker riding low in the water. Every U-boat commander knew that a fully loaded tanker was a valuable target. He also felt that the confusion caused by a torpedo's explosion within the convoy as it formed up would provide him with an opportunity to escape safely.

0800. Hanert checked the range and bearing to the target and ordered, "*Feuer*!" A TBS transmission announced that *Pan Pennsylvania*, the largest tanker in the world at that time, had been torpedoed. She carried a highly combustible cargo of 140,000 barrels of 80 octane gasoline, a fact not lost on its 50-man crew or its 31 navy gunners. Many men panicked and leaped into the frigid water while others attempted to launch a lifeboat without awaiting the abandon ship order. The lifeboat capsized, flinging its occupants into the sea. Luckily, the cargo did not immediately ignite, but bridge-to-engine-room communications were cut. The tanker's master sent the chief engineer to check on the engine room while he informed the Convoy Commander of his predicament. He then searched the ship to make sure no remaining crewmen were trapped as the huge tanker began to sink.

Captain Kenner, immediately ordered *Joyce* to retrieve the survivors and *Peterson* and *Gandy* to screen the rescue effort. The *Pan Pennsylvania* situation worsened. The chief engineer discovered what the men feared most; a fire had broken out and was spreading. With that report, the master ordered the ship abandoned. The tanker continued to settle and developed a list to port, but the crew managed to launch two lifeboats and three life rafts before the ocean's surface washed over the foredeck.

As the escorts joined, the area was searched for the sub. No chances were taken; every contact was methodically worked over. *Joyce* hove to near the sinking ship, and her crew quickly went to work retrieving survivors, so many that *Peterson* had to lend a hand. It was a nervewracking business as the survivors were unable to help themselves. They were sick from the tanker's gasoline fumes, and there were many injuries as well. Coming to a full stop in order to pick them up, was dangerous with the marauder's location unknown.

Chief Boatswain's Mate Stuart B. Goodwin and Motor Machinist Mate David J. Stephenson of *Peterson*, without a thought for their safety and ignoring the hazard that other escorts might drop charges nearby, went over the side to help survivors aboard. Both were subsequently decorated. *Joyce's* crew pulled 31 men from their lifeboats and rafts, and the *Peterson*'s crew recovered 25, but 25 more were unaccounted for. Later on, the tanker capsized and sank.

Joyce had just gotten underway when her sonar operator obtained a contact at 1,800 yards. She urgently announced over the TBS for the *Peterson* to hurry; a "hot" contact had been made! *Gandy* formed up astern of *Joyce* to aid as directed. Goodwin and Stephenson were still rescuing survivors when the order crackled down, "Make all possible speed, *Joyce* is about to attack." The two men scrambled aboard as all engines went ahead flank and *Peterson* raced to the contact area. *Joyce* had launched one 13 depth charge attack at a shallow setting. Perfectly timed and executed, the depth charges bracketed the target and literally blew the *U-550* out of the water in the midst of three DEs, girded for the kill!

As the U-boat's bow broke the surface, both the *Gandy* and *Peterson* captains gave the order to ram. The three DEs opened fire on the sub, but two ceased fire as *Gandy* sailed between them and the submarine, closing with the U-boat. From the action report of *Gandy*:

It was my intention to ram at the sub's after antiaircraftgun mount, but her movement caused us to hit about 25 or 30 feet from her stern. Gunfire continued as we swung left along the starboard side of the sub. About this time, a voice shouting something in a Germanic accent was heard on TBS. Supposing it to be an offer to surrender, I ordered cease fire. Almost immediately, the U-boat manned a machine gun battery and commenced firing on us. We swung left to bring guns to bear and resumed fire.

Gandy had only struck the sub a glancing blow, and the U-boat, spitting fire, was closed and taken under fire by *Peterson*. The sub was passed close abeam to starboard, and her conning tower was laid open by the withering fire. As a parting gesture, two depth charges set shallow were fired from the starboard K-guns. Shortly after, the Germans began to abandon ship, and the *U-550* started to settle by the stern and head for the bottom. A great cheer went up from the men of the three DEs. When the 12 survivors of the sub, including their captain, had been collected by *Joyce*, the destroyer escorts steamed proudly ahead to rejoin the convoy. (Twelve survivors out of an average U-boat crew of 40 to 60 was not many. The apparent attempt to surrender the sub, if it were a ruse, was a grievous mistake. War is a killing game with few rules, surrender being one of them. Treachery is likely to be repaid in kind.) Several years later, *Joyce* skipper Wilcox stated in a newspaper interview that the submarine had fired a white flare at the same time it spoke on the TBS and that "I took it as a sign they were surrendering."

Although the Navy Department gave *Gandy* the major credit for sinking *U-550*, *Gandy's* captain noted in his action report, "The pattern dropped by *Joyce* was accurate. Beyond doubt, it threw the sub out of control and caused it to surface." For this action, Lieutenant Commander Wilcox of *Joyce* was not only awarded the Legion of Merit, but also the USSR Order of the Fatherland War, First Class!

In early July, Commander R.J. Roberts relieved Captain Kenner as Division Commander.

On 19 August 1944, *CortDiv 22*, with Convoy CU 36, began its last trip to Londonderry. On 30 August, the Division, having arrived off Loch Foyle, prepared to depart from the convoy. The ships were to go on alone because the British considered these confined (and defensively mined) waters to be free of submarines. Incoming convoys were joined there by British escorts for the trips to ports on the Irish sea.

As the escorts were leaving, four ships were being detached to go under escort northward to Loch Ewe in Scotland. Suddenly, the last ship, the *Jacksonville*, carrying a full load of aviation gasoline, went up in a roaring hell of flames and exploding fuel; only two men survived the disaster. Of immediate urgency was the imminent arrival of a huge but slow convoy, including Doenitz' elusive prize, *Queen Mary*. A dispatch flashed to the Commander of the Western Approaches brought quick action. *Queen Mary* and the convoy were diverted. CU 36 merchantmen began to maneuver at top speed, and escorts and aircraft rushed to the area.

By evening, nearly thirty escorts were searching for the audacious invader. For several days, the hunt went on with further casualties when a cargo ship and a British escort were also sunk. This was a tough submarine and was later believed to be one of the first German *schnorkel* subs in operation. So, the great allied advantage over the U-boats, that they could only move at slow speed and for a short time when submerged, was eliminated. Very bad news!

On 3 September 1944, *CortDiv 22* went through the North Channel to Belfast to pick up a westward bound convoy. The following day, all ships were under way down the Irish Sea, through the St. George Channel to the Atlantic. The convoy headed for New York and what was probably the biggest storm anyone sailing in that formation had seen.

In the CIC, the *Peterson*'s navigator was studying his charts and the track of a hurricane moving up the East Coast of the United States. To him and to routing officers ashore, it appeared that the convoy was headed for trouble. It didn't take long. On 14 September, the full fury of the 100 knot tempest exploded on the convoy. Headway between the mountainous battering seas was impossible, and the screeching wind enveloped the ship in a blinding sheet of water. As it darkened, communications between ships grew weak, then died away completely. At the worst of the storm, *Peterson*'s radar ceased operations. All that night, convoy crews fought to stay afloat and remain together, but gradually the convoy was driven helplessly apart.

When morning and calm arrived, the men of *Peterson* looked about and blinked. There was not a ship to be seen! Some 40 ships and five escorts had vanished into thin air. The sun was hidden behind clouds, precluding use of the sextant. Nonetheless, the navigator's best estimated position turned out to be correct. The next day, a weary and sorely battered *Peterson* limped into New York, tired but all in one piece. The other ships also began to show up until all were accounted for.

VE day found *CortDiv 22* sailing home with its last convoy. The long, arduous days of North Atlantic duty were over. Some of the division ships were ordered to the Pacific to join in the war against Japan, but that conflict ended by the time they reached Pearl Harbor.

CONVOY CU FIFTEEN

A Convoy in Great Trouble

Accidents in Atlantic convoys were sometimes as tragic as

adverse enemy encounters. In this narrative, we are fortunate in procuring eye witness, gripping descriptions from two articulate former coast guard sailors, Sonarman Len Spinner from *Marchand*, and Fireman First Class Alfred E. Schreiber from *Rickets*.

Len Spinner, Marchand

"The sea saga, as closely as I can recollect, began on 22 February 1944 with Convoy CU 15, bound from New York to Northern Ireland. Coast Guard Escort Division 20 consisted of the flagship *Marchand (DE-249)*, *Hurst (DE-250)*, *Camp (DE-251)*, *Crow (DE-252)*, *Pettit (DE-253)*, and *Ricketts (DE-254)*. *Marchand* was in the lead, and *Rickets* remained behind the convoy as the rear shadow. The other four were evenly distributed in stations port and starboard of the merchant marine columns.

Late in the evening of the 25th, the battle station alarm was sounded. As I approached the open door of the sonar shack, the voice radio (TBS) was blaring emotion filled voices. Two ships had collided. One was an ammunition ship *SS El Coston*, the other a tanker, *SS Murfreesboro*, loaded with aviation gasoline.

From my vantage point on the flying bridge, looking aft, the scene was awesome as fire consumed the two ships. Decisive action was needed! Commodore Roundtree was on the 'horn' with orders to the convoy vessels for emergency turns to avoid further disaster. *Rickets* and *Marchand* were directed to proceed with rescue operations, the other four escorts to spread the sonar canopy, filling the gaps left by the detachment of two DEs.

Activity on the *Marchand*'s bridge shifted into high gear. Even as our captain, Lieutenant Commander Lynch, spoke, the ship heeled as she turned sharply to the area of the collision. Upon arrival, it was evident that the vessel in greatest distress was *Murfreesboro* and that high seas would hamper the rescue of survivors. The spreading gasoline fire was an awesome sight, threatening to consume the lifeboats as the crew abandoned ship. As we closed the distance to the men in the water, *Rickets* was seen doing a yeoman's job of pulling others from lifeboats and the flaming sea."

Alfred Schreiber, Ricketts

"On the night of the collision of the two ships, I was at my battle station, repair one. It was biting cold and rough, with the ship rolling to 40 degrees in the trough of the sea when she lost way to recover survivors. As the ship rolled, she exposed the bilge keel, which proved deadly to the seamen in the water and lifeboats.

Our sailors ran frantically up and down the starboard side, trying to recover men in the water and in the lifeboats. We broke off several times due to possible submarine alarms with *Murfreesboro* illuminating the background. We managed to drop a boarding net over the side, and some crewmen climbed down to pull oil-covered and burned survivors up to the deck. I particularly remember Bill Bible rescuing a man by dangling over the side to grasp him and dragging him up and over the rail while our ship was rolling wildly. We were aghast when *Rickets* rolled and the bilge keel caught a lifeboat underneath, smothering it and its occupants as the ship stood upright. None of them resurfaced.

There was a lot of shouting and cursing about the deck, especially when the gun crews joined to help. A burly boatswain's mate ordered me inside because, I must admit, I was just gawking."

Len Spinner, Marchand

"The spread of fire inside the tanker was heating up her entire midsection plating, precluding a boarding attempt. Rescue operations were accelerated as *Marchand* crew members helped those survivors who could no longer help themselves up the side of our ship, burned but grateful to be alive.

The gaping hole in the side of *Murfreesboro* was huge and, with each roll to port, flaming gasoline flowed out like lava down a steep slope. By this time, I believed it wouldn't be too long before she would blow like a volcano.

At the peak of this flurry of activity, either the dying tanker was still moving under its own power or the wind had turned her bow into the sea. The gap between the tanker and *Marchand* closed rapidly at an angle about 35 degrees relative off the starboard bow. With this miserable development, the captain called for all ahead flank, hoping thereby to cut across the tanker's bow. *Marchand*'s wheels dug in, but not enough to clear the rapidly closing tanker. The bow of *Murfreesboro* caught us just forward of the main deck weather door and raked the starboard side, crunching everything in its path. The tanker then cleared beyond the fantail.

A highlight to the urgency of the moment while the two ships were in contact was an outstanding gymnastic performance. The tanker's Chinese cook, standing on the bow of the dying ship, jumped in a 25 foot free fall to *Marchand*'s boat deck, landing on his feet without injury, and shouting 'Me lucky, me lucky'!

The scenario then changed to the damaged *El Coston*. With a crushed bow, she was still under way, her harassed crew doing its best in damage control. For several hours, there was a continuing dialogue between the flagship and *El Coston*, attempting to ascertain the most effective means of maintaining the vessel's watertight integrity to reach Bermuda, the nearest port. All things considered, weather permitting, she might make it. Commodore Roundtree transferred his flag to *Rickets*, and *Marchand* took her station to escort *El Coston* southwest to Bermuda at daybreak. Our ship was damaged but seaworthy. *El Coston*, her bow a tangled mass of steel, was open to the sea and forward movement was very slow."

Alfred Schreiber, Ricketts

"The next day, we put a boarding party on *Murfreesboro* and transferred our survivors to *Marchand*. The fire was largely out on the tanker, only burning forward, leaving the after crews quarters and engine room intact. We found a cat aboard and brought it back to *Rickets*. Neither ship had sunk thus far. *El Coston* went with *Marchand* toward Bermuda, and *Murfreesboro* was towed back to the United States. Several of our crew received medals and promotions for their efforts. *Marchand* was awarded a plaque from the merchant seamen for her part in the rescue."

Len Spinner, Marchand

"All went well during that day, as both ships plodded along with *El Coston* trying to shore up its forward bulkhead. Her only chance of survival lay in the strength of that bulwark. As darkness fell, sonar showed her position as slightly abaft our starboard beam, just out of visual range, speed less than six knots. However, later that night, the situation deteriorated. The silence was shattered by a high pitched, frantic voice: "We're going down *Marchand*. Where the hell are you? We can't see a thing, we're going down!"

The TBS slave set was located near my station. Rescue procedures were promptly summoned. Because of the frantic emotion in the operators's voice, I tried to calm his fears until help arrived.

The forward bulkhead was breached. Water was pouring in, and the ship was already foundering when our searchlights picked her up. Men over the side in rafts and boats strove to save themselves and to abandon *El Coston* to her doom. The sea and wind were kind in this instance because, as the crew moved away from the doomed hull, the drift brought the men directly to us. Eager hands on *Marchand* assisted them to safety.

There being no further need to go to Bermuda, we were ordered to New York for repairs. *El Coston* slid beneath the foaming sea. As the cold water reached her boilers, they exploded, leaving an aftershock felt throughout *Marchand*. Searchlights were extinguished, and the quiet darkness enveloped the history behind us.

CortDiv 20 made nine more round trips from New York or Boston to United Kingdom ports. With the war in Europe drawing to a close, the division was ordered to the Pacific, arriving in Pearl Harbor at about the time Japan surrendered."

Unfortunately, after 50 years, so many of the men contacted by this author simply couldn't remember those glory days nor the number of merchant seamen who perished in the disaster. Alfred Schreiber gives us an insight into life aboard a DE, much of which was probably duplicated in destroyer escorts at war all over the world."

Alfred Schreiber, Ricketts

"On one of our early convoys out of New York, while heading down Ambrose Channel, we sighted the *SS Queen Mary*, also putting to sea. She passed a request to nearby vessels for a needed radio part. Our captain, Lieutenant Commander Glen Rollins, informed her that we had it. He conned Ricketts onto *Mary's* port quarter, looking like a skyscraper towering over us. Her wake action pulled us in, and we collided, tearing out one of her portholes. The *Mary's* captain on the bridge wing wildly waved us off. With our torn off railing and 20mm mount, we quickly obliged. That was the end of the spare part; Mary disappeared over the horizon. Later, over the PA system, Captain Rollins apologized to the crew for his poor ship handling, which deeply impressed the men. He was very well liked and respected by most of us.

When we moored in Casablanca, the skipper decided we should wear flat hats to show we were a Coast Guard crew. The MPs didn't know what to make of them. We had a great time; the locals thought we were Russian sailors. We managed to unload our T-shirts, Parker pens and mattress covers for hard American cash. We didn't know where they got the money, and they were secretive about it.

The machine shop was located amidships on the main deck, starboard side. It was the domain of Chief Machinist Mate Fenton, an expert at making emergency parts. He claimed to have constructed the first towed FXR to thwart acoustic torpedoes. Whenever we lost one, he would promptly make another. It was also our hobby shop, and we spent many an hour making "shark" knives, converting 40mm shell casings into ashtrays and lamps (officers' requests, an enlisted man couldn't get a shell casing without stealing it). Many a dime or quarter was converted into rings for girl friends and wives.

Four hour watches in the engine room were boring, and some read books (forbidden). Some exercised, paced, drowsed, some actually worked. When the seas were rough, the engine room was the best place to be. Warm, with coffee at hand, one could watch the bilge water run up the bulkhead as the DE rolled. Many an off duty snipe would sleep on the mat adjacent to the switchboard when we rocked and pitched. *Ricketts* was rough riding, but she saw us through many a North Atlantic storm. Looking out on some mornings after storms, we noticed that deck cargoes of tanks, planes and vehicles on some liberty ships and tankers were wiped out.

We were continually looking for alcoholic beverages to drink, be it torpedo juice (wood alcohol, poisonous) or liquor smuggled on board. While waiting for convoys to assemble, we anchored outside the mouth of the river. Often, locals would row out to the ship and sell us "Irish whiskey" for a pack of cigarettes; it was homemade rotgut, but a pack of cigarettes only cost us a nickel.

Our favorite spot to partake of this booze was the battery compartment, port side forward, near the wardroom. No bigger than a closet, it was accessed from the main deck. There were several racks for batteries on charge and for distilled water, a perfect place to store the booze and drink unobserved. We could also eavesdrop on loud conversation in the wardroom. Deck apes generally used the storage under number three 3" gun mount. You could only lie prone there, but you were mostly prone after drinking that stuff anyway. Another place was the muffler space, accessed from the main deck, port side. It was quite spacious. In the North Atlantic, it was cozy and warm, but very noisy. In the Pacific, it was unbearably hot and not used. I now think of all the asbestos insulation that would foul the air from the vibration of the mufflers and wonder how I made it this far.

Not all times were happy times. There were arguments, fights, and men who hated or were frightened to sail on the *Ricketts*, some going AWOL. We had bed wetters, malingerers, people with self inflicted wounds and acting crazy to try to get off the ship.

Gambling was rampant with card games, dice, and anchor mooring pools. The officers tried to break them up but to no avail. Sometimes, you couldn't use the head forward late at night because of the crowd shooting dice. One time, I came off watch and went to wash up; the head was crowded with gamblers. I took off my engraved gold Coast Guard ring my mother gave me and left without it. After hitting the sack I remembered it and went back; it was gone, and no one knew anything. So much for shipmates. Most men were in cliques, usually from the same department that made liberty together. There was a 'caste' system where certain departments thought they were better than others.

We lost one man overboard in bad weather. He was swept off while on watch on the stern. The ship's dog was killed when a gunner's mate accidentally dropped a 40mm gun barrel on him while cleaning the gun. Another dog we had jumped ship after one trip; he sighted shore from a couple of miles out and went overboard.

Toward the end of my tour on *Ricketts*, I was made 'oil king' when the previous man in that job overfilled the tanks under the engineers' quarters. All their clothes were oil soaked. It was a good job with no watches to stand. I was on call 24 hours to keep the tanks full of clean fuel oil. I cleaned the oil purifiers, transferred oil to keep the vessel trim, sounded all tanks for the daily fuel report to the captain. I supervised the boiler and evaporator watch. I ran the at sea fueling station. Whenever the black flag was run up (a sub contact), I would hustle to the engine rooms and purify enough fuel to meet calls for flank speed; at times, it was touch and go whether I could keep up. The captain had a clinometer in his cabin and frequently called for me to trim ship. I wondered if he knew that moving ammunition also disturbed the trim and not always my fuel in the wrong place! I took particular delight in sounding fuel tanks under the mess deck during chow when certain people from the deck department were eating.

During bad weather, we lined up for chow in the inside passageway. The line passed the open hatch to the galley. For a joke, I dumped a pound of rice in the spaghetti steam kettle.

When it was served it looked like a commotion of maggots in the spaghetti. I sat down and ate it, saying that was the best spaghetti I ever ate. There was such a stir that the Officer of The Deck ordered the cooks to throw out the spaghetti and serve sandwiches. Had I been found out, I could have gone to Captain's Mast for it. Many pranks were played on board, but that was the only one I concocted.

Ricketts was a well constructed ship. For the 31 months of her life, she never suffered an engine or machinery casualty, never ran aground, never sustained any hull fractures. When we took possession of her in Houston, her builders were mostly women. Inspection tags on equipment had lipstick kisses, some with telephone numbers, some with 'good luck' on them. They did an excellent job of constructing her, and for that I'm eternally grateful. From the North Atlantic, South Atlantic, to the far islands of the Pacific, she got us there and back. When I left her in Green Cove Springs, Florida, for me, it was a sad day."

CONVOY NY 119

The Sea is Unforgiving

The following account of ill-fated Convoy NY 119 was written some years ago by the late Lieutenant Commander Russ V. Bradley, third commanding officer of *Edgar G. Chase (DE-16)*. Convoy NY 119 departed from New York on 19 September 1944 and arrived at Falmouth, England on 20 October. Escort Division 80 consisted of *Bermingham (DE-530)*, *Edgar G. Chase*, *Mason (DE-529)*, *O'Toole (DE-527)* and *Powers (DE-528)*. They were assisted by the fleet ocean tug *Abnaki (ATF-96)* and the fleet oiler *Maumee (AO-2)*. Captain Bradley:

> "Much has been written about The Battle of The Atlantic. Our understanding of its events is colored by the fact that our side won the war, though you may wonder how after reading this story.
>
> Drawing on my memory and a small book published by The South Street Seaport Museum in New York and titled *The Ordeal of Convoy NY 119*, I will describe a month in the lives of about 1500 men that may have contributed little to the war effort but loomed large in the experiences of those who were there.
>
> In August 1944, we were withdrawn from the South Atlantic to New York City for a special assignment. Our division had been ordered to deliver a convoy of army vessels to a staging area on the coast of England. We took their word for it that the army had ships but we could not believe what they intended to float across the North Atlantic in the midst of the hurricane season:
>
> 14 steel railroad car floats
> 12 wood cargo lighters
> 12 large tugs with seakeeping ability
> 15 small tugs with no business outside the harbor
> 1 Panamanian tramp ship with a Greek crew
> 2 British net tenders
>
> The plan was to steam in twelve columns with a large tug at the head of each, pulling one or two car floats with cargo lighters strapped on top and small tugs towed behind to conserve their fuel. The oilers and taggers-along would follow under their own steam since they had enough fuel for the crossing. It took a few weeks of hectic scrambling to get all the little tugboats outfitted with even the minimum gear for getting underway. They were manned by twelve civilians each, hired by the Army Transport Service.
>
> The Task Group was headed by Commander A. L. Lind. He did an extraordinary amount of putting his foot down and firing urgent appeals to higher authority in order to get three extra large tugs with trained Navy artificer rates aboard. There obviously had to be some ships to act as utility vessels and help out where needed. Our one big, beautiful, competent, sturdy fleet tug *Abnaki (ATF-96)* and the navy tanker *Maumee (AO-2)* were assigned as guide and supply ships.
>
> On 19 September, we finally got underway, trying to keep the five DEs steaming slowly enough to stay back with our seventy five charges as they bravely sortied into the

unfamiliar territory of open ocean. The sea that day was mirror calm; it gave no hint of what was to come. The job was to form up in an unwieldy convoy covering an area that seemed about half the size of Rhode Island. I remember feeling serious anxiety about how this mess could be maneuvered in any kind of sea, and I also felt a sort of despair that we might be stuck out there forever. How could this group, straining to advance at 4.5 knots, ever get to England?

The first two weeks were a constant scramble to maintain formation. Even modestly bad weather broke up the convoy. There was a series of equipment failures, sick crew members or plain inability to perform. The first week out saw the first serious casualty. One column consisted of a large tug towing four small tugs in tandem; the front one, *ST-719*, lost her bilge pumps, developing a bad list.

Before the problem could be addressed, a combination of waves and heavy strain on the fore and aft tow lines of this little vessel, plus a sudden course change, turned him right over. In the night and rough sea, there was no time for life rafts. The Navy signalman on board contacted a DE with an SOS from his flashlight. After hours of ticklish maneuvering, 10 of the 12 man crew were rescued. The small tug astern of *ST-719* cut itself loose before it too was pulled under. The sinking vessel wrecked the large tug's towing engine before the line parted."

Lieutenant Commander E. Allen Loew was commanding officer of *John J. Powers*. Having only been commissioned the prior February, she had made two crossings to the UK before being assigned to this memorable convoy. Captain Loew described that fateful night when the tug *ST-719* was lost:

"At 0201 the night of 25–26 September, the Officer of The Deck, Ensign A.J.F. McCarthy, observed a flashing SOS signal well forward in the convoy. He immediately headed for it at maximum speed. I was in combat information center at the time and took over the conn from there to direct the ship through the oilers and tows as we set course for the distress signals. Moments later, when we were reporting our actions to the Commander Task Group 27.5, reports came in from both CTG 27.5 and *Maumee* indicating that they were aware of the SOS signals.

We went to GQ and piped survivor rescue. Due to close maneuvering while threading through the convoy, it was not possible to maintain maximum speed or direct course. Consequently, it took 35 minutes to reach the swimmers. Searchlights played on the scene by the three adrift ST tugs guided us to the area. There was little night visibility with no moon or stars, and the sea was rough and choppy, wind northeast about force 7.

The survivors had already become considerably scattered. The largest group, five men, was picked out. The ship worked to bring them alongside where they could reach lines thrown to them or the two survivor nets put over on each side or the rubber boat which had been launched and manned and was being tended from the ship on a long line. One 24 inch light was kept trained on the group of five. Another one was trained on a group some 200 yards away and to whom the recently arrived *Abnaki* was directed. We had a hair raiser when the *LT-537*, with column nine in tow, steamed directly through the scene of our operations. Only four of the five survivors were recovered by *Powers*. The fifth was the navy signalman. He was panic stricken, missed our lines, and drifted down toward *Abnaki* where he was picked up.

From 0303 until 0915, *Powers* and *Bermingham* continued to search the area for survivors, but without success. Reports from other rescue ships and interviews with survivors determined that only two men were missing. Out of the inquiries, there came a harrowing tale about First Mate Malone and Able Bodied Seaman Thebus being trapped in the forward living quarters with water rushing in. Since the towing ship was unaware of the calamity, the pressure of forward motion was too great to permit opening the hatch. The seaman lived to tell by forcing himself through a 15" porthole on the down side. After twice getting stuck in the port and then struggling back in for a breath of trapped air in the cabin, he made it on the third try. Malone never made it.

The cook, Thomas Janos, had been severely seasick and had become very weak. He did, however, make his way out of the ship. When last seen by any of the rescued men, he was lying on the side of the overturned tug and wearing a life jacket. He was not seen again after the ship sank.

Instructions and encouragement spoken to the swimmers over the *Powers*' bull horn had stopped panic in some, thereby conserving their strength and helping them to gain the ship's side. One of the survivors on *Powers*, Captain Swartwout, was suffering from exhaustion and had swallowed a considerable amount of salt water. Chief Engineer Dorwart had cut his feet on broken glass, one quite deeply. The two AB seamen, John A. Thebus and Ridgeway C. Leonard, were unhurt, even though neither had a life jacket."

Back to Captain Bradley on *Edgar G. Chase*:

"After that emergency, we devoted our time to running a standard ASW (antisubmarine) patrol, though we all considered our charges a very unlikely target for a discriminating U-boat commander. Also, there were constant errands, most involving the supply ship/tanker and the utility tugs. The latter had to repeatedly pick up dropped hawsers and pass them back to the towed tugs. Occasionally, at great risk to personnel, they put salvage crews in open rubber boats onto the car floats to repair towing bridles or pump out compartments. Mere subsistence became a problem. None of the small tugs had usable fresh water tanks or refrigeration. The water had to be passed in five gallon cans by other ships, and great quantities of fresh food had to be thrown away since it spoiled after three or four days.

The next phase of the journey entailed a decision to detach one DE with the big navy tug and one of the towing units that had a car float in sinking condition. They were to seek calm water in the lee of Flores Island, Azores, and fix the float.

On 10 October, the final phase of the ordeal took shape. The wind began a gradual and intermittent buildup. Breakdowns in equipment and spirit increased. All of our tug crews refused to go further and had to be replaced by volunteers from the navy tanker. (If there had been time, it could have been treated as a mutiny.)

The barge repaired at the Azores was in sight of rejoining when it suddenly developed a heavy list. After hours of risky work by a boarding party, it had to be abandoned. The ultimate humiliation came when no amount of 3" bombarding could sink the wooden lighter. It was left floating as a hazard to navigation.

Later that day, the other float in that group took a notion to sink as well. The remaining ships, consisting of the DE and tugs in company, tried to rejoin the main convoy, but the small tug could not manage the extreme sea conditions that were developing. Running down into the trough of a 45 foot wave, she broached and tumbled right over. Though it was still before dawn, *Powers* saw it happen and spotted the survivors in the water, by now too cold for men to survive very long.

Maneuvering the ship took full power with the attendant risk of drawing floating men into the propeller turbulence. For this reason, *Chase* had to stop and drift down on the survivors, working a rescue attempt from a deck rolling 55 degrees. (We didn't know at the time that destroyer escorts were the only major warships that could handle such an angle from the vertical without fear of capsizing.) Even so, *Powers* later discovered eight broken frames and four broken longitudinal beams.

It only takes a few words to cover what seemed like a lifetime of exhausting effort to rescue the tug crew. They were already numb and helpless. The only way to effect a rescue was for two men of the DE crew to go over the side with life lines on and play the violent roll in such a way that they could grab a survivor and snag him in a cargo net rigged on the side. In this way, they flipped four men up onto the reeling deck to relative safety. Eight had apparently drowned because there were no further signs of swimmers when *Powers* called off the search.

And so, back at the main convoy – one more small tug capsized, this time with the loss of all hands but one, in spite of the concerted rescue efforts of DE *O'Toole* and a large tug. By now, the meteorologist had no good news at all for us. What was later known as the 'Great Storm' one of the worst in the annals of the Atlantic War was steadily building. The wind reached a velocity of 90 mph. The great sea swells peaked as they came from the deep trenches of the Atlantic and into the shallow bottom of the Western Approaches. The result was awesome as the waves crested in a great crash from heights of 60 to 80 feet. The *U.S. Coast Pilot* reads: 'In a westerly blow, do not come inside the 100 fathom curve'. We understood what we were reading, but there was no way to avoid doing just that. The poor little tugs and oilers could do nothing but run with the waves and try to survive.

Fortunately, before conditions had reached their worst, one of our DEs with tugs astern was detached to run for Lizard Head at the best speed the little fellows could make. This group, which included the remaining small tugs, oil barges and miscellany, all made it without further loss.

It is interesting to note that the DE on this assignment, *Mason* the only major warship in the Navy at that time with an all black crew turned right around to come back and help the rest of us, some more than 100 miles away. She did this despite a 17 foot crack in her deck plates causing her to take on water.

The two British destroyers assigned by the Admiralty to help our outfit keep track of the barges, by now drifting all over that part of the ocean, would not proceed beyond the headland, and they were probably right. Any heavily armed warships of that size, including our own USN destroyers, with less than the extraordinary stability of the remarkable DEs, might not have made it.

We were learning what a sturdy ship we did have. The angry crests would tower over our bridge, itself 40 feet above the waterline, and lift the stern sky high. The slide down into the trough was unnerving with dark and heaving water all around, and it seemed most likely that the ship would break up or else dive right under. After a night and day of this, however, through a sort of numb fatigue, we thought perhaps we would make it.

There was always the necessity to keep track of somebody else. Two of the larger tugs were staying with us. At one point, we could not see one of them nor hear him on TBS radio. After about ten minutes, he came back on the circuit to say he had taken water down the stack and shorted the board; it had taken a while to repair it. Our navigator was somehow able to find out where we were. Since the seas were driving us toward the Scilly Isles, our commodore decided to run in behind one of them to look for a little safety and possibly some rest. The tugs willingly followed and, late one afternoon, we dropped anchor in smooth water, though we could still see the terrible seas breaking on the other side of the island. I was given a message to send to two tugs to wait for better weather and head for Falmouth. To our utter surprise, we learned they had no charts and no idea how to get there. We gave them courses and distances. We wished them luck because we felt bound to get back out there with the rest (having paused long enough to serve the first hot meal in a week).

Now, going into the huge seas, we had to hang on with both hands as *Chase* skidded and twisted and dropped like a stone each time a crest passed under. This all night struggle was not rewarded by any success in making contact with other units, but early morning brought a sudden end to the high winds and a dramatic drop in the wave heights. All day, we steamed around the scene, rounded up what we could and, by nightfall, had our anchor down in Falmouth outer harbor. For most of us, it had been a lost month. There was no feeling left. I believe we were the last one in, and it was 20 October 33 days out of New York!

The DEs with major damage (*Chase* was actually the only one without) were tended by skilled hands in the Devonport Dockyard. With some new tugs rounded up in the area, we went out to salvage what barges we were able to find with the help of the Royal Air Force. After two or three days of this, we ended the comedy by towing a tug which had disabled itself by wrapping its own towing hawser around its propeller. We towed it all the way into Plymouth Harbor at 15 knots. It is likely that he had an exciting 20 hour ride bouncing around back there in the rough water, but it bothered us little because we were so annoyed at his inept performance. We cut him loose at the harbor entrance in stony silence.

The final losses added up to three small tugs, eight steel car floats and five wooden cargo lighters. The rest were salvaged and, whatever became of them, we never heard. When

Commander Lind had tried to report our arrival to the Army Transportation Corps, Falmouth, he could not find the Officer in Charge to take over the remnants of our convoy. The young Lieutenant he did find at headquarters could only reply,

'What convoy?'
Nineteen men lost their lives!"

Edgar G. Chase

This author would not like to leave the impression that DE life consisted solely of battle and storms, relentless from day to day. On the contrary, there were hearty laughs, even if in retrospect. Some people have a capacity for seeing the bright side of dark clouds. One such man is Elmo Allen, former radioman first class on *Edgar G. Chase*, one of the escorts in Convoy NY 119. He supplied a large part of the information for that narrative. He also remembers:

"It was a very dark night in mid-1943, and *Edgar G. Chase* was proceeding south along the Atlantic Coast, running fairly close to the shoreline. She was operating in company with two navy patrol craft (PC) vessels, searching for enemy submarines.

Suddenly, a very bright light stabbed through the dark night off the starboard bow. Moving quickly from right to left, it would disappear, only to reappear intermittently. The captain of the DE, suspecting the very worst, immediately detached one of the PCs with orders to proceed dead ahead at full speed, investigate this very suspicious light and report his sightings promptly.

Off into the night went this little ship, quickly disappearing from view. After what seemed to be an unusually long time, a signal light began to flash in our direction

W-E H-A-V-E I-N-V-E-S-T-I-G-A-T-E-D T-H-E L-I-G-H-T I-T I-S A-N A-U-T-O-M-O-B-I-L-E A-N-D W-E A-R-E A-G-R-O-U-N-D "

No comment needed!

The Big Red Button

After standing those long, hot, monotonous watches in *Edgar G. Chase* engine room for some months, all this time eyeballing a large red button which had a very large plaque above it reading something to the effect 'DO NOT UNDER ANY CIRCUMSTANCES TOUCH, PRESS, EVEN THINK ABOUT PUSHING THIS BIG RED BUTTON', Motor Machinist Mate Third Class John Bowman, couldn't stand it any more. Curiosity got the best of him.

Putting down his ever present cup of coffee, he walked over to that big red button, gritted his teeth and pushed hard.

Immediately, it became very quiet and very dark all over the ship. Luckily for Bowman, an alert shipmate pushed all the right buttons and operations quickly returned to normal. A very frightened Bowman looked up to see his engineering officer, Lieutenant Felix Fortin and a very irate skipper, Russ V. Bradley, descending the ladder in great haste. Bowman, by now so scared he was reduced to speaking fluent Babylonian, could only mutter something that sounded like 'The Devil Made Me Do It'. Fortunately for Bowman, nothing came of the incident."

SS Seakay going down. Photo by Lou Grasek, *Reeves* crew

Survivors coming alongside *Reeves*.
Photo by Lou Grasek, *Reeves* crew

Armed guard sailor didn't make it. Photo from *Sims* crew

Hissem (DE–400) after bout with North Atlantic tempest. Note damage to 20mm gun sponsons stove in by heavy sea. Courtesy ex–crew member Joseph Carinci.

Crew of *U-550* abandon ship, only a few minutes after being hit by rapid fire of 3" 50 from *USS Joyce (DE-317).* Twelve German seamen were rescued by *Joyce*, 16 April 1944. Courtesy National Archives

Five survivors of *SS Pan Pennsylvania* approaching *Joyce (DE-317)*.
The DE recovered a total of 35 survivors from the tanker.

Mason crew manning a 40mm quadruple anti-aircraft gun.

The abandoned U-boat sinks.

Last of the *U-550*.

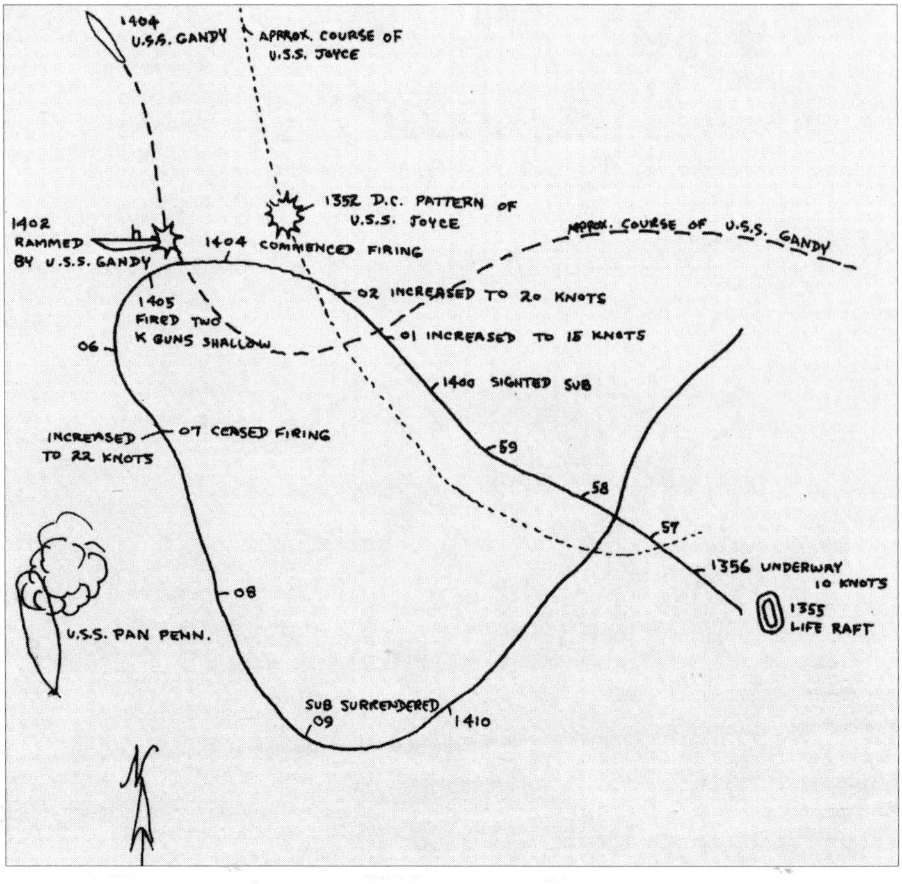

USS Peterson track lines. Scale 500 yds – 1”

Crew of *Edgar G. Chase* relaxing in Havana.

Proud of their ship.

Menges under tow; note wrecked stern. Photo by Art Green, USCG. US Navy Photo

Chapter IV - Convoys to the Mediterranean

The Cradle of Civilization Under Fire

Regaining control of the Mediterranean was of primary importance to the Allies, partly accomplished by the British victory at El Alamein and "Operation Torch," the invasion of Algeria by American, British and Free French Forces on 2 November, 1942.

North Africa fell under Allied control, but Southern Europe remained Axis-dominated. Thus the Mediterranean remained contested. Ahead lay the campaigns in Sicily, mainland Italy and Southern France. The supply of troops and materiel to the North African staging areas required massive convoys, guarded by destroyers. Early in 1943, destroyer escorts began to arrive on the scene, relieving destroyers for fleet duty elsewhere. Ultimately, the majority of convoys on these routes were guarded solely by DEs, routes that remained vulnerable to vicious air and undersea attacks almost to the end of the war.

East bound convoys were code named UGS, and west bound convoys were code named GUS. Each letter designation was followed by a number, ie. UGS 36 or GUS 36.

CONVOY UGS THIRTY-SIX

Battle in the Night

In the black and misty morning of 1 April 1944, Convoy UGS 36 was making its way along the North African coast en route to Bizerte. Task Force 64 included Coast Guard Escort Division 23, Destroyer Division 57, plus *Tomich (DE-242)* and *Sloat (DE-245)*. A British contribution to the force consisted of four or five assorted ships plus two antiaircraft sloops and one small antiaircraft cruiser.

0358. Just prior to the enemy raid, the convoy was about 50 miles from Algiers, base speed 8.5 knots. "Mersigs pennant 6," code for imminent action, was given over the TBS by the Task Force Commander.

Minutes later, a heavy explosion was heard in the direction of the convoy, immediately followed by heavy antiaircraft fire from the ships. Enemy bombers were picked up by escorts almost immediately on their SL (surface search) radars as they increased speed and began steering erratic courses while closing the convoy flanks.

On board *Savage (DE-386)*, radar reported planes close at hand. Her commanding officer, Lieutenant Commander O.C. Rohnke, promptly sent his crew to GQ, but the planes were almost immediately lost on radar as they flew low over the convoy, the main area of enemy fire concentration. They could be heard overhead but none were sighted. Bridge personnel noticed three bright flares and tracer fire on the starboard side of the convoy, the side opposite to *Savage*. The DE continued to close the forward port flank and commenced firing in the direction of the main enemy echelon. During this time, it was noted that several ships had directed their fire at the aircraft flares in the hope of dousing them. The exhaust of a plane was seen by one of the gun crews, and fire was immediately shifted in that direction. Ensign Rollins W. Coakley scanned his memory back to that morning:

"My personal recollection of the attack came from my station as the captain's talker on the flying bridge. I remember the flares dropped in our vicinity, our exposure to their light, and our gunners directing their fire at them. The presence of enemy planes was eerie in the darkness. Motor Machinist's Mate Third Class James Searcy, stationed at the K guns aft, was struck in the ankle by part of a 20mm projectile."

War appeared to be all about *Savage* but did not come to grips with her. Things were somewhat different elsewhere.

The log of *Mills (DE-383)* recorded that the convoy was attacked by a squadron of low level German torpedo bombers. Also, the sonar operators were getting many contacts. What with the diesels at flank speed, antiaircraft fire, and exploding depth charges, the din was deafening. In the melee, it was not known exactly which ships actually shot down enemy aircraft. At daybreak, *Mills* was ordered to the assistance of *SS Jarard Ingersoll*, a liberty ship seriously damaged by an aerial torpedo and slowly sinking. After picking up the survivors, *Mills* tied up alongside the burning vessel so the fire pumps could be utilized and a fire fighting party put aboard her. After courageous and long hours of exhausting work, the fire party extinguished the flames. *HM* Tug *Mindful* and *Mills* then took the *Ingersoll* in tow and beached her in Algiers Harbor.

Rhodes (DE-384) had her hands full. Immediately closing to her antiaircraft station, she joined the battle and, for the next 15 minutes, engaged 18 Junkers 88 and Dornier 217 planes. Twice in succession, her mast was nearly destroyed by low diving German attackers, but her stubborn fire turned the enemy away.

Sellstrom (DE-255), Flagship of Escort Division 23 with Commander F.P. Vetterick *(ComCortDiv 23)* aboard, was heavily engaged. The war diary of her captain, Lieutenant Commander William L. Maloney, reported a plane suddenly coming in over the port quarter, altitude 600 feet, circling to the left and returning over the starboard beam. Flares appeared at the same time. The GQ alarm activated all stations manned and ready to fight in a little over one minute.

Five planes passed within 2000 yards. The first two approached from the starboard beam at an altitude of 600 feet and passed overhead. *Sellstrom's* AA fire caused the third plane to sheer off well to starboard. The fourth plane came in from ahead, passed along the port side, distance 1000 yards, also 600 feet high, then retired to avoid AA fire. The fifth plane approached from the port quarter; AA fire caused it to break off promptly. Sporadic fire was maintained thereafter in various sectors, based on radar information. During the action, red and white flares, tracers, shell bursts, and loud explosions were seen and heard surrounding the nearby ships.

Of all escorts, *Ramsden (DE-382)*, commanded by Lieutenant Commander S.T. Baketal, appeared to be the most heavily engaged. A Dornier 217 crossed ahead from port to starboard, close aboard, speed 200 knots and 100 feet high. This aircraft was not sighted until at a range of 1000 yards. However, friendly aircraft were identified on SA radar, coming in from the same direction, tracked to 4000 yards where they swerved across the bow. Presumably, these friendlies had been pursuing the enemy plane and had come within dangerous ship AA range before breaking off. Thus, bandit and friendlies showed as one pip, causing the radar operator to follow friendlies only. The guns were unable to bear before the target disappeared into the convoy's flak.

Five minutes later, *Ramsden's* radar reported enemy aircraft on the port beam of the convoy, initial range 12,000 yards. When the plane closed to 6000 yards, *Ramsden* fired a star shell spread and turned toward the target. The enemy aircraft immediately banked to a course reciprocal to the convoy before entering the illuminated area. From the ship's log:

> 0415. The vessel was brought back to her base course when lookouts reported the sound of motors approaching from the convoy's starboard quarter. Immediately, the plane was seen to be approaching from astern. As all guns that could bear were directed aft, a twin-motor, twin-tail Dornier 217 roared into sight, banking slightly to pass up our starboard side.
>
> All batteries opened up simultaneously when the plane was just abaft the starboard beam, range 500 yards, altitude 200 feet, speed 200 knots. The first round from the after 3" gun burst on the starboard motor of the plane which immediately exploded into searing white flames. Many 20mm and 40mm shells also struck the target. Fire continued from all forward guns until 'cease fire' when the target was 2000 yards dead ahead. The plane lost altitude in a long glide as it passed out of range, finally crashing in a red burst of flames at a distance of about 7000 yards!

Gunner's Mate First Class Walter Palmer was in the thick of it:

> "This German bomber came at us flying low. It was silhouetted by our flares behind it so that it looked like a big black box car. Our 20mm and 40mm opened fire, and you could see the tracers go in but not come out. The badly hit plane belly landed. As it went down, our ordnance officer, Mr. Welton, was so elated that he yelled over the PA system, 'Amen Brother'. The men below decks, hearing all the gunfire and then hearing 'Amen Brother' over the PA system, thought the worst and came piling onto the top decks."

Upon arriving in the area where the enemy plane was seen to crash, a gasoline slick was noted, and cries of help in German and English were heard from four men in the water. Lighted life rings were thrown overboard, and attempts were made to rescue them. However, because their obvious injuries prevented them from securing themselves to heaving lines and the necessity for keeping the ship underway in view of continuing danger, rescue attempts were temporarily abandoned.

Gunner's Mate Palmer was close to the scene:

> "Meanwhile, the Germans who had escaped from the plane and onto a rubber raft, began shooting off their flare pistols. Our captain had a man on the bridge who could speak German, Seaman Hockstedder. He shouted in German 'In the water stop shooting the flare pistols, and we will pick you up when the all clear is sounded.'
>
> The all clear sounded at daybreak, and we proceeded to try to pick them up. All the Germans were now gone except one man who was lying half on the rubber raft. Our chief boatswain's mate climbed out on the propeller guard rail to reach down and grab him, but the ship was gliding forward too much, and the order was given to back down. The churning screws sucked the remaining German off the raft and chopped him up in the screws. Of course, this scared the hell out of the chief boatswain!"

0420. The raid appeared to be over. Firing was intermittent and enemy aircraft were departing to a rendezvous about 22 miles distant from *Ramsden*. The SL radar reported friendly planes in the same vicinity, presumably allied fighter escorts giving chase.

Ten minutes later, the DEs secured from battle stations and proceeded to return to convoy patrol stations. In 15 minutes, 0405 to 0420, the *Luftwaffe* had damaged one merchantman and lost five aircraft, one to *Ramsden*'s guns.

CortDiv 23 made another convoy to Bizerte, then shifted to the North Atlantic shipping lanes, escorting seven convoys to the United Kingdom and France. With the collapse of Germany, the division was transferred to the Aleutians. *Ramsden* operated from Attu on plane guard duty; *Savage* screened oilers in Task Force 92's bombardment of shore installations in the Kuril Islands; *Mills* served as a weather ship in Adak; *Sloat* and *Tomich* operated with hunter-killer groups in the North Atlantic and Caribbean until reassigned to the Pacific; *Rhodes* and *Sellstrom* headed for the South Pacific. Cessation of combat with the surrender of Japan was welcome news to *CortDiv 23*.

CONVOY UGS THIRTY-SEVEN

One Down but Not Out

Task Force 65 was assigned the protection of Convoy UGS 37, consisting of 60 merchant ships and six *LST*s (Tank landing ships), bound from Norfolk, Virginia to Bizerte, Tunisia, on 31 March 1944. TF 65 was composed of *Escort Division 58*, and *Destroyer Division 66*.

CortDiv 58 included *Price (DE-332)*, flying the command pennant of Commander E.E. Garcia; *Strickland (DE-333)*; *Forster (DE-334)*; *Stockdale (DE-399)*; *Hissem (DE-400)*; *Holder (DE-401)*; *Swasey (DE-248)*; *Lansdale (DD-101)*; and *Stanton (DE-247)*, flying the flag of *CTF 65*, Captain W.R. Headden. Escorts of *CortDiv 58* were in the forward echelon.

Also reporting to *ComCortDiv 58* were the AA cruiser *HMS Delhi*, escort vessels *HMS Jonquil* and *HMS Nadder* and rescue tug *HMS Mindful*. *DesDiv 66* included five old "four pipers," assigned the rear echelon and not under attack.

The trip to Gibraltar was uneventful. Once the convoy passed through the straits, however, it was continually trailed by German planes on reconnaissance. All escorts were put on alert. On the night of 10 April, the convoy went to GQ three times, but no attack came. The dawn of 11 April brought mounting anxiety as the North African shore loomed ahead. An hour before midnight, attack was a certainty. Some men were sleeping in their bunks; most were pretending to sleep.

Sailing through the Straits of Gibraltar into the Mediterranean was like walking into a hornet's nest. The German

Air Force had been fighting for five years. They were veterans of the Battle of Britain and campaigns in the Soviet Union. And less than 20% of the destroyer escort crews had been to sea before! The previous convoy, UGS 36, was attacked by some 20 *Luftwaffe* dive bombers and torpedo planes on 1 April and fought them off with only one merchant ship suffering a hit. Now, 10 days later, Convoy UGS 37 was entering the same area, with the same enemy lying in wait. It seemed as if the attack on Convoy UGS 36 was only a dress rehearsal for Convoy UGS 37. The *Luftwaffe* bided its time until the evening of 11 April when the convoy arrived off Cape Bengut, Algeria.

It was a beautiful Mediterranean night, a clear sky with multitudes of stars, calm sea, and a moon in its third quarter. However, this was a war, not a cruise. Given a choice, UGS 37 would have opted for cloudy skies and no moon. Given a choice, the enemy liked it the way it was. The old proverb: A beauty to one can be a beast to another.

Prior to the assault, *CTF 65* had issued a directive to expect attack by glider controlled bombs as well as torpedoes and to fire on any air target that came within sight. (Destroyer *Lansdale* was included in *CortDiv 58* because of her guided missile-jamming capability).

About seven miles off Cape Bengut, the attackers were gathering. At 2245, one enemy aircraft was spotted by radar approaching the convoy, and soon 10 planes were dotting the green phosphor of the radar screens. A white flare was seen about five miles ahead of *Holder* who, with *Forster*, was in the van of the convoy. Suddenly, additional flares broke the darkness, lighting up the entire area.

CTF 65 heard German words on one of the voice circuits he was guarding and immediately called the convoy to GQ. Escorts on the starboard flank of the convoy, less than two miles from the North African shore as the attack began, had little maneuvering room. The escorts put up a tremendous barrage, but the enemy had sent out his best. The onslaught was delivered with cool determination by 26 Junker 88 and Dornier 217 aircraft arrayed against the convoy. *CTF 65* ordered the escorts to lay smoke screens to hide their charges from the attackers.

Holder's radar operator reported to the captain, Lieutenant Commander W.P. Buck, a contact at 16 miles. There were now about a dozen planes in the immediate vicinity. The fight was on. A low flying torpedo bomber made an approach on the bow of *Stanton* at a distance of 1000 yards, altitude 200 feet. As it was fired on by *Stanton*, it veered and approached *Holder*. Sighted off *Holder's* port beam, that DE opened fire with all guns that could bear. The crew went into battle like veterans.

The plane roared in like the growl of doom from the darkness. It was flying very close to the surface, and *Holder* personnel could easily see the torpedo drop into the water at a distance of 250 yards. The torpedo was clearly visible in the phosphorescent water, and the sound hut reported hearing strong propeller noises. "All engines ahead full! Left full rudder!"

Only one minute after the plane was sighted, barely time for the DE to respond effectively, the torpedo struck on the port side amidships and blasted open three of the four engine rooms slightly below the waterline. A fraction of a second later, another explosion erupted with a blinding yellow flash. *Holder* began to settle deep into the water as the sea poured into the ruptured compartments. An oil-fed fire broke out in the fourth engine room.

Strickland's radar showed the enemy closing the range rapidly, and the captain, Lieutenant Commander A.J. Hopkins, ordered zigzagging at high speed to spoil the aim of a torpedo or dive bomber. During this maneuver, all hands topside saw a brilliant flash and felt a tremendous explosion as the lead escort ship in the formation (*Holder*), received a torpedo hit. Just after this explosion, one of the JU 88s coming up from astern of the convoy on the shore side (*Strickland's* side), opened up with his machine guns. The flash of his guns gave the *Strickland's* gunners a perfect point of aim. Every gun that could bear opened up on the aircraft. The plane's starboard motor caught fire. Nonetheless, it kept coming as the gunners kept firing. Finally, just before the plane reached *Strickland*, the sweating gunners swallowed throat lumps and had the satisfaction of seeing it swerve and crash in flames on the shore!

Four minutes later, *Swasey's* guns opened up on a torpedo plane approaching her port bow. The torpedo passed down the port side, only 15 feet from the ship! Ten minutes after commencing fire, her gunners splashed an enemy bomber over the fantail from a height of 50 feet! Just past midnight, an aircraft launched a torpedo 200 yards off *Swasey's* bow, prompting radical maneuvers to avoid it.

Continuing to settle, *Holder* listed to starboard. Lights and power were lost, severing bridge communication with repair parties. Captain Buck attempted to contact *ComCortDiv 58* via TBS. Somehow, the transmitter seemed to be alive, but the receiver was dead. *Holder* couldn't know that the message was indeed received. The assistant engineering officer, Lieutenant (jg) Edward A. Maki, was largely responsible for the salvaging of the ship and recalls that weary day:

> "I was sitting topside, admiring the weather and the convoy, and proud that we were lead ship in the formation. I was also thinking about my wife who was about to bring our child into the world. (While preparing for delivery in the hospital, she received notice from the Navy Department that *Holder* had been torpedoed. A lovely little girl was promptly born.) My GQ station was in the after control room. Flank speed was ordered, and then we were torpedoed. I was knocked out. On recovering, I ordered a man to go topside and bring a report. When he returned with the news, I put the electrician in charge to keep our electric circuits on line if possible. I then went up and took control of all those available to save our ship."

His citation for a Bronze Star Medal, quoted in part, tells about the meritorious conduct of this officer:

> "Lieutenant (jg) Maki skillfully, courageously and tirelessly devoted himself to saving the ship. He was largely responsible for restoration of auxiliary power to pump out flooded compartments, fight fires and to localize the flooding and trim. He aided promptly and fearlessly in the rescue of a wounded man blown overboard and in immediate danger of drowning."

The first lieutenant dispatched a messenger to the bridge to advise the flooding of three compartments and a fire in another. Water pressure was not yet available but, after flaring up twice, chemical foam subdued the blaze. Fortunately, the generator functioned, and emergency power lines were rigged. The repair party shored up the bulkhead abaft the flooded compartments; It was intact and held against the sea. Depth charges were set on safe.

All through hull fittings were found to be tight. One bulkhead forward of the damaged compartments was slightly broken above the water line, a condition remedied by caulking. A watch was posted nearby to avoid unpleasant surprises if the stressed bulkhead should weaken further. Considering the lack of experience the crew had with the ship and the few drills conducted, the performance of damage control parties was truly outstanding.

Meanwhile, *Holder* was dead in the water with no possibility of regaining propulsion. Having been stationed at the head of the convoy, merchant ships were now weaving past her on both sides. Men not involved in damage control remained at GQ, firing at nearby targets. The 40mm crew claimed a direct hit on one plane seen to spiral down and crash into the sea! The number three 3" gun also claimed a direct hit on another plane crossing *Holder's* stern. Unfortunately, neither hit was observed on the bridge because of preoccupations. Consequently, the gunners did not get official recognition of their claims. Nonetheless, it was a valiant show, firing all guns while without propulsion, while trying to save the ship and tending the dead and wounded.

0010. *Swasey*, stationed astern of *Stanton*, reported a torpedo passing to starboard. *Stanton* was turning to bring her guns to bear on an approaching plane when the same torpedo wake was seen heading her way. A hard turn avoided disaster. The plane that dropped this torpedo turned toward shore when abeam of *Stanton* and increased altitude. Trailing fire, it crashed on a mountain! Several attackers employed low level bombing, using antipersonnel (fragmentation) bombs. A plane approaching *Stanton* released a stick of five bombs which exploded at about 200 feet; there were no casualties. High level bombing was also employed after the release of parachute flares.

Aboard *Price*, planes were tracked nearing the convoy. Except for barrage firing, gun crews were ordered to fire only upon sighting the targets because of escorts nearby and the convoy beyond them. *Price* then moved directly ahead of the convoy center, covering an area vacated by *Holder* and *Forster*. At 2348, she commenced firing with all guns on an air target racing in at mast height. The plane burst into flames, crashed and exploded! The captain of *Price*, Lieutenant Commander J.W. Higgins Jr., noting that other ships also fired, modestly declined sole credit. (*The Dictionary of American Naval Fighting Ships* credits *Price* with downing the plane.)

Hissem had been patrolling off the convoy's port quarter, astern of Stockdale. All her 3" guns commenced firing on a radar bearing from the combat information center. A barrage was maintained at any target within 3,000 to 4,000 yards and closing.

Hissem's 40mm and 20mm guns opened up on a plane roaring through the barrage. At least three 20mm guns obtained hits. Smoke and sparks were seen, but no indication that the plane had crashed. A second plane came up the starboard side, close aboard, very low, and was fired on by the entire starboard battery of 20mm and number one 3" gun. At least three 20mm guns were believed to have scored hits,. The plane turned off through the smoke screen, and toward the convoy. Two bombs had been dropped by this attacker, one close aboard on the starboard beam and one just off the stern of *Stockdale* while she was laying a smoke screen. The next three planes came in on *Hissem's* port beam but disappeared in the direction of the convoy. All planes were flying very low, and gunners invariably opened up at close range. Another plane approached *Hissem's* port side and passed astern. Barrage fire was maintained until early the next morning. Joe Carinci remembers it well:

> "I was gun captain of number one 3" gun. There were so many shell cases on the deck around my gun that I had to order the empties thrown overboard. I remember Chief Gunner's Mate Wyatt who stood just behind me howling 'Joe, Joe look at that German sneaking into the convoy to drop his torpedoes'. I can see that pilot just as plain today as I could then with his cockpit light on. He wasn't ten feet above the water."

Hissem expended 2600 rounds of all types of ammunition. Lieutenant Commander W.W. Low, captain of *Hissem*, and his crew were gratified later on to learn they were credited with shooting down one enemy plane and damaging another. Two *Luftwaffe* aviators were picked up from a raft by one of the escorts.

The attack steadily diminished and finally stopped as the enemy retired. The only damage suffered was on *Holder*; all merchant ships were reported unharmed. *Forster* had previously received orders to stand by *Holder*. With the enemy gone, she came alongside to assist in damage control and to receive the 13 wounded. The engineering officer and 15 other men were killed or missing. Most of the dead and wounded were from the engineering spaces.

ComCortDiv 58 in *Price* returned to *Holder* to cover her return to port. *Price* went alongside *Forster* and transferred her doctor and supplies to treat injured crewmen taken aboard. By mid-afternoon on 12 April, *Holder* had stabilized and was no longer in danger of sinking. A bit later, both assisting DEs cast off, and *Forster* returned to the convoy. *HM* Tug *Mindful* secured a tow line aboard the disabled DE and, eight hours later, brought her safely into Algiers harbor, escorted by *Price*.

On 24 May, after temporary repairs, *Holder* was taken under tow of the oceangoing tug *Choctaw (AT-70)* in a westbound convoy. On 9 June, at the New York Navy Shipyard, an evaluation by expert repair and salvage crews concluded that *Holder* was beyond repair. Her first taste of battle became her last. But her spirit went on to live in the rejuvenated *Menges*. See the following narrative, *UGS/GUS 38*.

After two more convoys to Bizerte, *CortDiv 58* was reassigned to the punishing North Atlantic with seven convoys to France and the UK, then finally to the South Pacific and another enemy.

A pensive seaman on *Strickland* wrote a suitable finis to UGS 37:

> "One thing we now knew for sure. We had all become sailors and veterans. Somehow, we had less to fear."

CONVOYS UGS/GUS THIRTY-EIGHT

Battle Scarred Coming and Going

As UGS 38 approached Cape Bengut, French West Africa on the evening of 20 April 1944, it was greeted by three successive waves of hostile aircraft. For many of the escorts in Task Force 66, this would be their baptism of fire. It was a huge convoy, 85 merchant vessels guarded by two escort divisions with the flag of TF 66 on Coast Guard cutter *Taney (CGC-68)*.

Joseph E. Campbell (DE-70) flew the pennant of *Commander Escort Division 21 (ComCortDiv 21)* and included *Laning (DE-159), Fechteler (DE-157), Fiske (DE-143), Mosley (DE-321), Pride (DE-323), Falgout (DE-324),* and *Lowe (DE-325)*. The first two listed were Navy, the remaining four were Coast Guard.

Menges (DE-320) flew the pennant of *Escort Division 46 (ComCortDiv 46)* and included *Newell (DE-322), Chase (DE-158), Fessenden (DE-142), Lansdale (DD-426), HNMS Heemskerk* (Dutch escort), *HMS Delphi* (British AA cruiser), *HMS Speed* (British minesweeper), *HMT Vagrant* (British tug), *Sustain (AM-119)* (U.S. minesweeper), *L'Alcyon* (Free French destroyer), *Senegalais* (Free French destroyer escort), and *HMS Blankney* (British subchaser). The first two DEs listed were Coast Guard; the second two were Navy. The British and Free French escorts were not in the eastbound (UGS) crossing; they were added in North Africa for the return (GUS) trip.

The Germans were using the lessons learned from the previous assaults on the UGS 36 and UGS 37 convoys and were refining their attack techniques. The TF 66 name for the approaching enemy was "Whoopie," and several "Whoopies" were received during daylight hours of the 20th. At dusk, as the convoy passed three miles offshore, it was attacked by 25 to 30 German bombers and torpedo planes.

2053. A Red Three warning from *Lansdale*. Five planes were reported ahead by *Lowe*) on the starboard side of the outer screen. Ten minutes later, they were reported by *Campbell* coming in about six miles dead ahead of the convoy.

The enemy planes approached the convoy almost undetected, flying at near wave-height altitude. The first after-dark alarm was not given until the planes were almost on top of the convoy. At 2103, *Lowe* suddenly sighted five incoming bandits (Code name for enemy aircraft), and then it was "Whoopie" without question. During the engagement, escorts zigzagged at 15 knots, it being deemed inadvisable to use higher speed due to the proximity of other vessels.

The first two raids consisted of *Junker 88s (JU 88s)* and the third by *Heinkel 111s (HE 111s)*. The first wave struck from dead ahead with torpedoes, hitting *SS Paul Hamilton* as well as the merchant cargo vessel *SS Samite*. This unexpected attack did its work so fast that most of the escorts were unable to fire on the leading *JU 88s*, finally opening up an effective barrage on the trailing planes.

From her station on the starboard side of the convoy, *Fessenden* saw tracer fire beyond the convoy's port side, followed by the explosion of *Paul Hamilton*. The latter was loaded with high explosives as well as troops, an unfortunate combination costing the lives of 500 men. George D. Simon bore the unlikely coast guard rate of torpedoman third class. He displayed pride and pleasure at having been one of the only group of torpedomen the coast guard had and most likely ever will have. He was on deck when the German planes hit:

> "The air attack on UGS 38 was disastrous. I saw two British Beaufighters overhead at about 900 feet, headed for the coast as the German planes passed the outer screen at 30 feet off the water. Nobody fired, not even the lead merchant ship in column one! A plane passed over her beam, dropped a "fish" and zoomed over her king posts. Not a shot! Possibly the IFF (coded identification) from the Beaufighters was mistakenly applied to the attackers. Nonetheless, doctrine forbade allowing any planes to fly unmolested into a convoy already alerted by an air raid warning. The *Paul Hamilton* went up with a 'Whoop-Boom-Boom'. CTF 66 called an escort in the van, *'Pheasant,* (*Lansdale*) are you picking up survivors?' Reply 'There is nothing left to save'. Along with destroyer *Lansdale*, who put up a gallant fight before sinking, other merchant ships were damaged or sunk in what Samuel Elliot Morrison calls 'The high water mark of the *Luftwaffe* in Mediterranean convoys."

Three planes screamed in at about 40 feet above the water along *Newell's* starboard side, cutting between herself and *Lansdale*. All starboard 20mm and the 40mm guns opened fire. Four of the guns were hitting the after plane repeatedly and it was seen swerving to port. Later questioning revealed that a member of the 40mm gun crew saw a plane explode on the port hand, probably the same one fired upon. The probability of that plane being downed was later verified by two German aviators picked up in the same vicinity along with survivors of *Lansdale*.

The gun captain of number three 3" gun on *Newell* saw them coming in aft, apparently not seen by other guns. He opened fire, followed by the 40mm, and drove the planes off. Four minutes later, another raid tracked by radar was approaching from ahead. All guns were cautioned not to open fire until planes were sighted visually. At 2114, planes came into view dead ahead. Both number one and number two 3" guns opened fire along with the forward 20mm guns. Fire from these forward guns blanketed two incoming planes, and they turned off sharply.

Mosley laid covering smoke and opened up with intensive antiaircraft fire throughout the three attacks. She was credited with splashing one JU 88 and damaging another bomber during the first strike. Seaman First Class Alexander Greenspan recalled:

> "I was in the ammunition party when we were ordered to bring ammo to the 20mm guns on the fantail. We accomplished that in quick order. When I turned around to go back, Rivers on 20mm gun number 30 was firing at a plane on our port quarter. Then the other 20mm guns aft commenced firing, and I saw the plane swerve and hit the water immediately abaft the stern. It bounced, and then I could see the tail sticking up. I hollered 'There goes one plane!"

The second wave of JU 88s was right behind the first. However, ignoring the convoy center, it split up, hitting a column on the starboard flank and succeeding in putting torpedoes into *SS Stephen T. Austin* and *SS Royal Star*. The third wave, HE 111s, hit the convoy's port bow. During this attack the *Heemskerk* lookouts spotted three torpedo wakes. Ships swerved, with *Lowe* and *Taney* doing the tango to avoid the "fish" close aboard. *Menges* shot down one of the attacking planes and found the time to rescue its pilot and radioman. *Fechteler's* gunners also splashed a bomber. *Fessenden* sent up an intensive antiaircraft barrage, damaging several planes, for which the ship received a compliment from the Escort Commander.

Lansdale blasted away at the barely visible enemy planes on both the starboard and port sides and was credited with one plane destroyed and two "probables." Then, with a fiery roar like a demon from hell, a torpedo crashed into *Lansdale's* forward fire room, breaking her back. Her crew fought a valiant but losing battle to save the ship. Settling rapidly, the destroyer wallowed helplessly in the sea, steam and smoke pouring from the vast hole in her side. The *Lansdale's* captain, Lieutenant Commander D.M. Swift, fearing that the danger of capsizing was imminent, gave the order to abandon ship.

Newell came upon *Lansdale* dead ahead, breaking in two and sinking. A closer approach showed an area saturated with a great number of men in the water and on floats. *Menges* rescued 111 men, while *Newell* saved 119. Two of those plucked from the sea subsequently died, and 47 were missing. Had it not been for volunteer swimmers from *Newell* and *Menges*, the toll would have been much higher.

When the battle was over, the Germans, with five planes shot down and five planes damaged, had scored heavily. *Chase*, also occupied in recovering survivors of sunken ships, rescued 65 men and transferred them to *Menges* during the night. Repair parties, led by Chief Boatswain's Mate Cavender and Chief Torpedoman Stanley Gaines, gave an outstanding account of themselves. Swimmers from *Chase* saved many exhausted men who might otherwise have perished.

At dawn, *Chase* went alongside *Royal Star*. An inspection was made of the torpedoed ship by Lieutenant Blake Hughes, first lieutenant of *Chase*. The *Royal Star* captain and Lieutenant Hughes concluded that the damage was such that she could not remain afloat long enough for a tow to Algiers. Nonetheless, the flagship ordered a tow, and the tug *HMS Athlete*, arrived to pass a line to *Royal Star*. As predicted, however, the vessel sank, and *Chase* returned to the convoy. In the early hours of 21 April, *Newell* and *Menges* increased to full speed to Algiers to disembark *Lansdale* survivors.

Convoy UGS 38 had four merchant ships torpedoed, two sunk and two others severely damaged. On 22 April, that portion of the convoy continuing east of Bizerte was turned over to British escorts. With the *Lansdale* now resting on the floor of the Mediterranean, Task Force 66 limped into Bizerte, licking its wounds.

On 1 May, the return convoy, GUS 38, sortied from Algiers. It was an even larger convoy, consisting of 107 merchant ships, the reason for adding additional escorts to the westbound run. Whereas the eastbound convoy had to contend with attacking aircraft, the homebound convoy had to deal with U-boats lurking in the narrow waters between Spain and North Africa. The Task Force was approaching the southeast coast of Spain early in the morning of 3 May.

Shortly before midnight, *Menges* was patrolling astern of the convoy when her radar detected a U-boat on the surface, range six miles. The DE headed for the target at maximum speed. Just under two miles, the pip disappeared from the radar screen, indicating a submerging submarine. With the crew at battle stations, *Menges* began to zigzag. At 0115, speed was slowed to 15 knots to allow the sonarmen to conduct a more efficient search for the U-boat.The skipper, Lieutenant Commander Frank M. McCabe, ordered the FXR streamed astern. (Many DE commanders were beginning to doubt its effectiveness.) Shortly after *Menges* advised she was commencing a sound search, a thundering explosion ripped open her stern and after compartments. *Menges* notified *ComCortDiv 46*, Commander L.M. Markham Jr., that she had been torpedoed. *U-371* struck hard.

The blast carried away the propellers, rudders, after emergency steering station, ship's laundry and carpenter shop and main after crew's quarters. Jagged deck plates on the fantail were blown skyward. A washing machine was lobbed from below decks 150 feet into an antiaircraft gun position on the upper deck. The explosion was so violent that all depth charges were flung into the sea, creating further explosions that killed many of those who were blown overboard. Two officers and 29 men died instantly and another 25 were severely wounded.

Heroic crewmen prevented further destruction by leaping astride torpedoes torn from their cradles with their motors started and rolling uncontrollably on the deck. Fireman First Class Gaylen E. Doak and Water Tender Second Class John D. Lawless hacked their way into a wrecked compartment to rescue two trapped shipmates. Stanley G. Putzke, Radioman Second Class, lowered a small boat in the dark and retrieved two men blown overboard. In the absence of a doctor, Harold Levy, Chief Pharmacist Mate, labored in the sick bay single handed. The rest of the crew was busy with damage control.

Menges, taking on water, listed badly to port, but Captain McCabe would not abandon ship. A party led by Lieutenant (jg) James A. Mackay risked death in flooded and oil soaked compartments to secure broken water lines and to shut off electricity. The injured DE wallowed heavily in the sea, virtually paralyzed and defenseless.

Menges damage control crew, like the one on *Holder* in the previous Convoy UGS 37, waged a valiant and successful battle to keep her afloat. After an hour and a half, a tug dispatched from Algiers arrived to tow *Menges* into that port where the dead and wounded were transferred ashore. As with *Holder*, temporary repairs were made to render the ship seaworthy enough to withstand a transatlantic crossing at the end of a seagoing tug's tow line.

The victory celebration on *U-371* was short lived. The sub escaped only to be hunted down and destroyed by escorts two days later. Seaman John Redler on *Lowe* recalls a fate he barely missed:

> "My skipper was Commander R.H. French. We took the straggler position astern of the convoy but changed positions with *Menges* only a few minutes before she was hit. A deep sigh of thanks was tempered by sorrow for the *Menges* crew. When DE history is finally written, I know it will say, 'Destroyer Escorts were trim but deadly'. Each was a ship with a heart and soul only because of the gallant, brave and never-say-die men who graced their decks. I was proud then, I am proud now to have been a U.S. Coast Guardsman and especially, a DE sailor."

Arriving in New York, *Menges* was eased into a dry dock at the Brooklyn Navy Yard and positioned next to *Holder*. Workers streamed onto both ships, cutting away the rear 94 feet of *Menges'* stern while welding torches cleanly cut off the undamaged 94 feet of the *Holder's* stern. Powerful cranes and hydraulic jacks tugged and pushed the *Holder's* stern along the greased skids until it was positioned directly behind *Menges*. Although built in different shipyards at different times, when the keels were aligned, there was not more than an inch-and-a-half difference in the mating of the two hulls. A slight push here and a little pull there and the ships came together in perfect harmony. Soon thereafter, following a short shakedown of the new *Menges*, she rejoined the fleet.

On 11 February, 1945, the new *Menges* was assigned to the first all Coast Guard Hunter-Killer Group. On 6 March, *Menges*, *Pride* and *Lowe* destroyed *U-866*. The *Menges* group subsequently combined with two other carrier groups to sink three more submarines. See chapter *The Hunter-Killers*. *Holder* and *Menges* were avenged.

Returning to GUS 38 – *Oberleutnant* Horst Fenski, Knight of the Iron Cross and Commander of *U-371*, was typical of the German submarine commander eulogized and idolized by the Nazis. He was young, only 26, strikingly good looking, courageous and determined. With a veteran crew, he sortied from a French base on four North Atlantic and four Mediterranean cruises. He sank a number of ships, but his greatest prize was the Royal Navy cruiser *HMS Penelope*. Now, he lay in wait for Convoy *Gus* 38 off the coast of Algiers, blasted *Menges* with an acoustic torpedo, and hit yet another escort before *U-371* met her end.

Pride, under command of Commander Ralph R. Currey, was ordered by CTF 66 to the assistance of *Menges*. *Joseph E. Campbell*, with Lieutenant J.M. Robertson commanding, was directed to proceed to the same area and to act as OTC (Officer in Tactical Command) to search out and destroy the enemy submarine. *Menges* had previously passed all accumulated data on the submarine contact to *Campbell* and *Pride*. In the early hours of 4 May, *Pride* gained submarine contact near *Menges*, and the two DE skippers closed in to avenge the attack. It was soon apparent that the U-boat captain was not a beginner and that they were up against a seasoned veteran. The battle would last for the next 30 hours.

In view of *ComCortDiv 46's* advice and knowledge of acoustic torpedoes, discussed in some detail en route to the probable encounter, *Pride* proceeded with exceptional caution. She streamed two sets of FXR gear, one on each side of the stern. This didn't help one bit. When the FXR gears were later recovered, they were smashed out of shape and hopelessly entangled; one set would have given greater protection.

Campbell caught up with *Pride*, and both went into a prescribed search pattern. *Pride* zigzagged in a wide circle in the hope of keeping out of the moon wake. While approaching the area, about two miles from *Menges*, *Pride* dropped two depth charges set for a depth of 100 feet at intervals of one minute so as to disconcert the submarine and to "deafen" any torpedo that might already be en route.

Shortly after midnight, *Pride* gained sonar contact at 1000 yards and went in on the attack. The order was given to fire hedgehogs, but, great embarrassment, they failed to leave the rack!. The DE passed directly over the submarine area with its depth recorder indicating turbulence all over the dial. An electrical check was ordered to determine the cause of failure of the hedgehog switches to close. If it is true that certain verbiage can turn the air blue, then bank on that transient hue present even in the dark. The report quickly established that there was nothing wrong with the circuits. Sound contact had held down to 300 horizontal feet, indicating a submarine depth of only about 100 feet.

Pride's radar showed a small pip within 700 yards but it disappeared quickly. Apparently, the sub had come up for a quick look and then submerged. It was interesting to note that this U-boat was not taking defensive escape maneuvers but rather appeared more interested in torpedoing another DE. But *Pride* was not going to let that happen if at all possible. She rolled another shallow depth charge, then regained contact at a distance of 2200 yards.

A speed of 10 knots was set on an intersection course with the submarine in preparation for another hedgehog attack. The contact was held down to 150 feet when the order was given to fire hedgehogs. The embarrassment and frustration to the captain, sound team and hedgehog crew could be felt as well as heard as the hedgehogs again failed to fire. It would be interesting to know what the U-boat captain and crew made of this as they braced for each attack. Perhaps they thought it to be a new form of psychological warfare. This time, however, Captain Curry took a wide lead ahead of the projected sub course and rolled a pattern of five depth charges set for medium depth.

Pride regained contact at 1200 yards and commenced an approach for another depth charge attack. Contact was lost at 800 yards, an indication that the U-boat had gone deep, but was regained at 200 yards. The target was tracked moving away and slightly to the right of *Pride*. OTC on *Campbell* then ordered *Pride* to join *Campbell* in a coordinated two-ship creeping attack, *Pride* to continue echo ranging and to guide *Campbell* over the sub.

0210. The creeping attack commenced. A plot of the submarine movements in *Pride's* combat information center (CIC) showed the U-boat to be "fishtailing" or violently zigzagging. Apparently, *Oberleutnant* Fenski had abandoned his earlier indifference. *Pride* maintained a range of about 1300 yards and, at this moment, told *Campbell* to drop her depth charges. The Mark 8 proximity charges would fire on magnetic impulse, taking some of the guesswork out of depth settings. *Pride* regained contact and again directed *Campbell* onto an attack course but aborted the dropping of depth charges because of insufficient information in the last critical stage of the run. *Pride* regained contact at about 1500 yards.

The OTC directed *Campbell* to activate her sonar and assume the contact, the DEs to swap positions, *Campbell*'s CIC doing the plotting and *Pride* doing the attacking. *Campbell* made sonar contact at 2700 yards, and *Pride* maneuvered to attack. *Pride* and *Campbell* conducted two more creeping attacks, again exchanging positions, but without any visible effect.

The CIC on *Pride* indicated that the sub was again "fishtailing" and making erratic turns. The echo appeared mushy, lacking the solid ping expected from a steel hull. (When pursued while submerged, German submarines often released through a torpedo tube a *pillenwerfer*, a canister of highly compressed air. It would burst and create a "hard" bubble that could return a sonar echo of sorts, hopefully to divert the sound operator on the pursuing vessel. However, an experienced operator could usually tell the difference between a *pillenwerfer* and the real article.) *Campbell* was ordered to break off the attack. *Pride* regained a good, solid contact at a range of 2000 yards and once more directed the *Campbell* to go in on the attack. *Campbell* again dropped a full pattern of 13 depth charges.

Daybreak. Except for evasive maneuvers, the submarine had been edging toward the shallow coastal North African waters. It had now gotten so close to the rugged shore that return echoes to the *Pride's* sonar from undersea peaks and valleys became hopelessly intertwined with echoes from the submarine.

It became evident that the submarine was going to sit on the bottom, marked on the chart as *Parc des Kabyles*, until dark when it would have a better chance of escape. Both DEs stopped and listened. They had more waiting time than their deadly enemy below. The situation on *Pride* and *Campbell* could best be described as weary anxiety. They had been at GQ for over nine hours, not daring to let down their guard. All hands remembered *Menges* and were not anxious for a repeat performance. They also understood that the unseen men below the surface were still dangerous as long as they were alive. One way or another, they had to be killed!

The situation on *Unterseeboot 371* was considerably more grim than on the DEs. Fenski knew this was the tightest situation he had ever been in, and the chances of escape were narrowing by the hour. The oxygen supply was becoming thin and stale, mixed with the stench of engine fuel and the sweat of unwashed bodies. They couldn't use the head because the sound of the expulsion pump would give them away Consequently, feces accumulated in the toilet, and men urinated in sloshing cans tied to stanchions, all adding to the pervasive stink. Dozens of depth charges had been dumped on them, some from afar, some close enough to throw them off their feet, to cause gauge needles to gyrate crazily, insulation to crack, water to back up in pumps. Captain Fenski knew he had to do something sooner than later.

0810. *Pride* picked up strong vibrations on her sound gear. Initially, the noise was like a throb, then a clicking sound. Captain Curry wrote in his action report that he analyzed the sounds to be from main engines and a pump. He opined that the sub had put its nose into the sand and was now trying to back out. This estimate proved to be correct when prisoners taken later confirmed that their submarine had indeed been stuck in the sand for several hours.

Pride remained in the area until 1100, but no further sounds were heard. Wearily, the captain recorded an admission that contact had been lost after having attacked the U-boat intermittently since the previous evening. It had not been easy. The hedgehog hangup had forced them to rely on depth charges, and echoes from water disturbances caused by explosions were invariably intermingled with echoes from the sub. As a result, renewed contact was generally effected only at a considerable distance, slowing the attack frequency.

OTC in *Campbell*, however, was not to be distracted by second guessing. He initiated a wide ranging and systematic sound search by *Pride*, and *Campbell*, now also joined by *HMS Sustain*, *HMS Subchaser Blankney*, the Free French destroyer *L'Alcyon*, and the Free French DE *Senegalais*, all of the latter temporarily detached from Convoy GUS 38. *Senegalais* was assigned to search close inshore near the last contact. *Blankney* and *Senegalais* both depth charged sound contacts during the afternoon but without results.

0120 on 5 May. *Senegalais* reported a surfaced submarine at a distance of two miles. She illuminated the target with star shells and opened fire. *Pride* and *Campbell* went to flank speed to cut off an escape to the north of the area and to get into firing position. *Blankney* and *Sustain* cut off escape to the west. *Senegalais* shifted to rapid fire, and it was becoming apparent that the submarine was being cornered. Odds were on *Senegalais* to make the kill.

But not so fast. *Senegalais* reported she had been torpedoed! *Oberleutnant* Fenski scored again. *Senegalais* was in a floating but disabled condition. The submarine submerged as approaching escorts came into firing range very quickly.

A sound contact was reported by *Blankney*; she dropped a depth charge pattern. Minutes later, sound contact was made by *Sustain*. She dropped a pattern and started to circle around to get into position for another attack when her lookouts sighted many people in the water. She immediately hove to and started rescue procedures. They were German! By the count, it appeared that the entire crew of *U-371* had abandoned the submarine. Other escorts participated in the rescue operation, but all prisoners were transferred to *Campbell*. *Oberleutnant* Fenski had chalked up his final score. *Campbell* was directed to return to Algiers with the prisoners. Captain Curry on *Pride* recapped the exhausting hunt for *U-371*:

> "Thus ended a chase which had lasted more than 30 hours, through two nights, during which there was little sleep for anyone. After having been on the bridge for several hours with no sleep while patrolling and waiting for the sub to come up, I was very tired. However, the stimulation of the hunt was overpowering; I just couldn't fall asleep. At about 2200, *Campbell* had a surface contact inshore, and we were ordered to cover her. The target turned out to be a fishing vessel. Somehow, I had to get some sleep. Finally, at the pharmacist mate's prescription, a small potion of brandy was consumed, and I fell fast asleep. When the sub surfaced, I had about three hours of sleep and felt fresh and ready for another chase, or come what may."

Investigation of the hedgehog circuit revealed that a fuse in the AC circuit was blown. There was a backup DC circuit, but the gun captain did not have the presence of mind to shift over.

A Salty Commentary

> "I served aboard *Joseph E. Campbell* with *ComCortDiv 21*. The story of how *Menges* got one up the kilt, towed home, and a butt transplant courtesy of the navy is history.
>
> We gathered in 41 men and seven officers; the rattiest, stinkiest bunch I have ever seen. Germans had no bathing facilities on board their subs; these men had been out for some time and were quite ripe. They were made to strip as they came over the side (concealed weapons) and run down to the showers. We of the crew donated clothes as theirs were not fit for rags.
>
> I and several other six footers were furnished .45 automatics and posted in the officers wardroom as guards while the seven officers were cleaned, clothed and fed. We did a slow boil as each of the enemy officers was asked what he would like for breakfast and all were ordering and receiving eggs, bacon, pancakes, etc. We were not far from where the *Menges* men were lying on the bottom, and we felt it was not right!! Those who served on the Mediterranean convoys may remember that we had to carry food for the round trip, and the last 1000–2000 miles were a steady diet of baloney. We felt "horse cock" was good enough for prisoners too, especially those who ordered "Fire!" on our ships.

All the Germans were quite happy as they thought we were westward bound to the States, and they could picture a cushy camp in America. They did not realize until we docked that we had returned to port, brought them topside and turned them over to a detail of those big, black, tough looking Senegalese troops with three foot bayonets. Such bellowing and weeping, most enjoyable! The captain was dragged down the gangplank screaming and cursing, someone had stolen his cap and boots. We cheered!

The boots were beautiful, a Wellington style of fine soft leather and just my size. They had a 1" felt lining, however, and I could not get that dirty bastard's foot stink out no matter how I tried. That odor came through my locker lid, cleared the compartment, ruined my clothes and some pogy bait I was saving. ('Pogy bait' was a name applied to canned food, cosmetics, costume jewelry, candy, nylon stockings, under garments or other items known to be valuable barter for feminine favors in war-starved areas). I finally sold those boots to a stateside coast guard officer from a down wind position. I've often wondered of his reception at home with his 'souvenir'.

All in all, I was most pleased with the outcome (of the battle). We avenged our fellow DE sailors, and I even turned a small profit.

For God's sake, though, don't anyone tell Captain Robertson or Lieutenant Bolton. I always seemed to be on their list."

Dean J. Miles, Soundman, Third Class

One would think that GUS 38 had suffered enough, but the enemy had one more blow to land before it was finished. *Fechteler*, skippered by Lieutenant C.B. Gill, was singled out for that dubious honor as the convoy passed Oran on a westerly heading. The convoy was within sight of the tiny Island of Alboran in the center of the narrow passage between Spain and Morocco.

The action developed in the early dark hours on 5 May when *Chase* reported a surface radar contact ahead of the convoy, distance 16 miles, moving at a speed of 18 knots. Shortly afterward, *Laning's* radar operator reported to the captain, Lieutenant Commander E.A. Shuman Jr., that he had a "pip" on a vessel at a distance of 13 miles which subsequently disappeared from the screen, obviously a submarine. CTF 66 ordered the merchantmen to make the first of a series of emergency turns away from the location of the contact.

Laning was directed by CTF 66 to investigate the target and to keep it clear of the convoy. She reported that the target was positive submarine, was sighted by several men prior to submerging and had disappeared from her radar screen. *Laning* did not close the point of submergence of the submarine, nor did she conduct a box search. Some confusion of intent was unrecorded. CTF 66 directed *Lowe*, *Fessenden*, and *Fechteler* to cover the forward port corner of the convoy, the earliest target the submarine could reach.

An explosion was heard by all escorts, but the direction was not determined. No depth charges had as yet been dropped. *Steady (AM-118)*, patrolling astern of the convoy, reported that the explosion was near her. CTF 66 redirected *Lowe* and *Steady* to join the search for the submarine. One minute later, there was another explosion, and it was reported that *Fechteler* had been torpedoed.

Fechteler had been patrolling her assigned sector, roughly between the convoy and the reported contact. At that moment, she was in a turn to conform to zigzag procedure. The DE never had a contact nor any indication that a submarine was close at hand other than the *Laning* report. The ship was suddenly brought to a stop by an horrendous explosion that jarred and tossed the DE, virtually ripping it to shreds. The FXR gear was streamed and had just been tested satisfactorily by the soundman. Almost the entire crew was thrown to the deck, even those on the bridge, the area furthest from the epicenter of the blast. Unhurt men went immediately to the aid of their wounded comrades. They dived into compartments flooded with oil and water to rescue those who couldn't help themselves. Lieutenant (jg) William Hunter Bowman, was Officer of The Deck with the 2400 to 0400 watch when the torpedo hit. He related:

> "I obtained reports from the forward and after repair parties where the talkers remained at their phones until ordered to abandon ship. They said that there was plenty of freeboard in the forward and after portions of the ship but that the vessel was sinking amidships where the explosion had occurred. At this point, all hands were ordered not to abandon ship, but several of them jumped into the water before the floating and organizing of nets, rafts and the ship's boat.
>
> Almost immediately after the explosion, the captain ordered the boat lowered. Although he did not give the order to abandon ship, he made certain that the rafts, nets and boat were ready to go. At that time, it seemed that the ship might still be saved, and we continued to get reports from the forward and aft repair parties. We also continued to try to contact CTF 66 over the TBS in the chart house and radio shack, but without success.
>
> I then secured permission from the captain to lay below and destroy communication devices and publications. Classified publications were thrown overboard in weighted bags. All of the encoding wheels were thrown over the side. The ECM (encoding/decoding) machine was pounded into uselessness. I went back to the bridge where the captain, Lieutenant Calver B. Gill, decided after a damage survey that it would be best to abandon ship; her keel was broken.
>
> In the meantime, distress signals had been fired from a Very pistol. At the time the order to abandon ship was given, things appeared to be better organized than at the beginning. The men went over the side in orderly fashion to nets and rafts, and the captain supervised the loading of the ship's boat. He ordered the uninjured to swim to the rafts to make way for the wounded. He requested me to make a final tour of the ship to make certain that no men were trapped below decks. I was accompanied by Chief Boatswain's Mate Read. Calling out loudly, we directed our flashlights into the forward messing compartments, officers' country, then into the engine spaces, but nobody replied.
>
> We went back aft and heard someone calling from the machine shop. The passageway into that compartment was blocked with machinery. We then went out on deck, waded through the water amidships, and climbed to the upper deck and to the after entrance to the machine shop. There we discovered a small space leading into the machine shop. There were two wounded men inside, both unable to move.

Read immediately crawled through the small aperture and handed out one man with great difficulty. At this point, Signalman First Class McLaughlin arrived on the scene and went back for a second man, Electrician's Mate Miller. I asked them to help Read to get the other injured man out. They crawled into the machine shop, removed weights pinioning the injured man and, with considerable difficulty, handed him through the hole to me. We carried him down the side to the ship's boat.

Read then informed me that there was somebody down in the 20mm ammunition stowage space forward of the machine shop. Read was unable to get through the doorway. However, Miller descended from the deck hatch into that compartment and discovered an injured man buried under several 20mm magazines and with water up to his chin. He refused aid at first. Read obtained two lines. Miller tied one onto one of the magazines; we hauled it out and passed the line down the second time. O'Gorman, Read, McLaughlin, Miller, and Kootz helped to pass up three more, and Miller shifted the rest of the magazines within the space. They fastened a rope around the man's shoulders and hauled him out.

Another man was discovered face down in the water amidships. I put him in the boat and ordered artificial respiration be given to him. I went back and told Kootz to take the light around and make certain no one was trapped in any other section of the ship. Kootz deserves special commendation for his actions in the after part of the ship. He reported back that nobody was left behind.

The boat was crowded, and the captain shoved us off before jumping about three feet into the boat. He took charge, discovered that the tiller had been blown off the boat, and guided the rudder by hand. He directed the rowing and also had the water cask opened for the wounded men who were in considerable pain. He ordered Chief Pinkert to break out the morphine and give injections to the wounded. Uninjured men gave their coats to the wounded. The boat moved away from the ship which was buckling amidships.

There were men clinging to the sides of a raft. We passed life belts to them, but it was difficult to keep them fastened. They came loose and were lost during strenuous bodily movement. Seaman First Class Simon helped a great deal. While swimming in the water, he took a line from the boat to the raft and assisted the men who were hanging on.

About 0417, the midships section of the ship disappeared below the water. Both bow and stern pointed skyward at a 90 degree angle to the surface. The noise of falling material was heard from within the ship. Very slowly, both sections sank.

Laning came alongside and let down the life net. The uninjured men clambered aboard, and then suddenly there was a terrific explosion. We thought that *Laning* had been torpedoed, and everybody cursed the bastards (enemy). We shoved off, thinking that *Laning* was going to sink. Orders had been issued to check depth charges at least four times before abandoning *Fechteler*. Nonetheless, one or more of the depth charges had detonated. *Laning* was unharmed and lowered stretchers for the injured. Finally, all hands were on board.

Laning was most cooperative. She launched her boat to help rescue some men. At the time she thought she was torpedoed, her men ran back to get blankets for our injured men. The doctor treated the injured promptly. Their officers and men brought out everything they had; clothes, food, cigarettes, etc."

CTF 66 directed *Lowe* to take charge of the submarine hunt. Escorts were ordered to drop charges between the estimated position of the submarine and number one column of the convoy. *Fessenden* immediately moved between the convoy and the estimated position of the submarine and dropped a pattern of seven depth charges as an harassment tactic. *Mosley* was immediately made available to *Lowe*, and *Laning* was already hunting. A dispatch was sent to Gibraltar advising the loss of *Fechteler* and requesting a sea tug and planes at daylight for the submarine hunt. Torpedoman George D. Simon recalled an incident on *Mosley* while proceeding to join *Lowe*:

> "The clear, moonlit night left me hoping that the sailor who yelled from the oily waters to *Mosley* 'How about a lift', as we proceeded among the wreckage at dead slow, did get a lift, but not from us. The guys on our bridge asked the captain for permission to tie lines to themselves and try to retrieve some of the men in the water. We couldn't stop. We dropped all but one life raft and some of our floater nets and moved on."

Escorts were directed to give first priority to hunting the submarine. About this time, *Steady* joined in the hunt. Planes arrived and were directed by CTF 66 to report to *Lowe*.

At dawn, the search for survivors was completed. *Laning* recovered 124 men, one dead man, and ten officers, including Captain Gill. The tug *Hengist* recovered 52 survivors. The doctor from *Taney* was transferred to *Laning* along with additional blood plasma. Between them, *Laning* and *HMS Nimble* collected all survivors from other vessels, then proceeded directly to Gibraltar where assistance was awaiting the injured.

The report of CTF 66, Captain Duvall, summarized:

> "Prior to the torpedoing of *Fechteler* and thereafter, no sound contact was obtained by *Laning*, *Fechteler* or any ship of the screen. Bathythermograph readings taken prior to and after the attack indicated that sound conditions were very poor, with maximum surface ranges from 400 to 700 yards.
>
> It is believed to be quite probable that the first explosion heard at 0313 was a torpedo, perhaps a "gnat," which was fired at *Laning* and detonated at the end of its run. The dropping of depth charges by flank escorts between the probable position of the submarine and port flank of the convoy may have prevented torpedoing of ships in convoy.
>
> There is no particular credit or censure due any unit of this Task Force. The ease and rapidity with which the one hundred and seven ships in the convoy performed emergency turns is considered remarkable. *Laning* performed sterling work in recovering survivors and administering to them en route to Gibraltar."

It is not known if the submarine that fired the torpedo was the same one that had been detected in *Laning's* radar or if it had been another lying in ambush and well positioned ahead of the convoy. There was also the possibility that the torpedo was a long shot, fired beyond sonar range, designated for the merchant convoy and inadvertently intercepted by *Fechteler*. Nobody had a sound contact, and *Fechteler* was a poor target in a zigzag turn. Also, the intensity of the explosion would appear to have been caused by a conventional rather than an acoustic torpedo.

UGS 38/GUS 38 had paid a heavy price. Four merchantmen were torpedoed, two of which sank. Four escorts were torpedoed, two of which went to the bottom. The Allies fully intended to win this war, but it was not going to happen the day after tomorrow!

CONVOY UGS FORTY

Victorious Beyond Doubt

On 23 April 1944, Task Force 61 sortied from Hampton Roads, Virginia, to form the screen of Convoy UGS 40, 65 merchantmen headed for North Africa. The Commander of Task Force 61 (CTF 61) was in Coast Guard cutter *Campbell (WPG-32)*, not to be confused with *Joseph E. Campbell (DE-70)* in UGS 38. All other U.S. ships were navy:

Destroyer Division 60: Three flush deck (four-pipe) destroyers, *Dallas (DD-199)*, *Ellis (DD-154)*, *Bernadou (DD-153)*.

Destroyer Escort Division 5: Six DEs, *Evarts (DE-5)*, *Decker (DE-47)*, *Dobler (DE-48)*, *Smartt (DE-257)*, *Walter S. Brown (DE-258)*.

Two French DEs were included: *FNS Cimeterre*, *FNS Tunisien*.

The savaging of UGS 38 by the *Luftwaffe* motivated CTF 61, Commander Jesse C. Sowell, to devise an improved air defense plan. Practiced in Hampton Roads and while crossing the Atlantic, these tactics were designed to counter attacks by German aircraft carrying a variety of weapons from bombs to torpedoes to radio-controlled glider bombs.

Off Gibraltar, additional escorts joined the British AA cruiser *HMS Caledon*, *Wilhoite (DE-397)*, and *Benson (DD-421)*. Two American minesweepers, *Steady (AM-118)* and *Sustain (AM-119)* also joined with electronics to jam glider bomb radio transmissions. A British salvage tug, *HMT Hengist*, brought up the rear of the reinforcements.

Two days after entering the Straits of Gibraltar, German "snoopers" began trailing the convoy. Successive shorebased interception sorties by British radar-equipped Bristol Beaufighters failed to drive off enemy reconnaissance aircraft. The escort screen went to GQ shortly after noon on 11 May, the first of five sequential alerts. CTF 61 enjoined his escorts to be especially vigilant; a dusk attack was quite possible. The merchant ships were formed into nine columns, 500 yards apart beam to beam, about seven ships per column, separated 1000 yards (1/2 mile) from stern to bow.

When the enemy was reported 70 miles off the African coast, UGS 40 was steering due east through a glassy sea past Cape Bengut. Eleven minutes after sunset, beneath a dark and overcast sky, escorts were ordered to lay a smoke screen. Action commenced when the convoy was attacked five miles from the shore.

Campbell was in the van. From front to rear on the starboard side of the convoy, *Dobler* was in number two position off the bow of ship 91. *Walter S. Brown* was 4000 yards off *Dobler*'s starboard quarter. *Ellis* was 5000 yards on *Brown*'s starboard quarter. The nearest convoy ship was two miles from the escorts.

Forty enemy planes approached the convoy from seaward and, after proceeding ahead of the ship formation, broke up into several waves to attack from different angles and at staggered timing. The assault was a low level torpedo attack, engaging the convoy for 40 minutes with few lulls.

The first indication of the scope of the attack came at 2056 when CTF 61 reported 25 enemy planes crossing four miles ahead of the escort front, port to starboard. Barrage gunfire was promptly initiated by escorts whose guns had a field of fire. Escorts in the starboard bow sector commenced laying a barrage against about ten enemy torpedo bombers heading across the screen front. Apparently, they were searching for a soft spot to break through to the convoy, necessitating intrusion into the starboard sectors covered by *Brown*, *Dobler* and *Ellis*. The closest plane to *Dobler* was about 1200 yards away. In the face of heavy fire from that ship, *Campbell*, and *Brown*, the pilot banked and was lost from view in the smoke. *Dobler* was engaged with that target for about 30 seconds.

Two planes were sighted on *Brown*'s port bow at about half a mile. At this point, *Brown* was heading out from the convoy, having previously been ordered by CTF 61 to act independently. Fire was opened immediately by all guns in the firing sector, following the two planes out of sight. At this time, the convoy was executing an emergency turn of 45 degrees to port.

Almost immediately after the first few planes were out of range, two more appeared dead ahead of *Brown* on a course to pass her starboard side at a range of 800 yards. All guns on the bearing opened up. Many hits were scored on both planes. As the second plane passed *Brown*'s starboard quarter, it went up in a vertical bank and then splashed between *Brown* and the starboard bow of the convoy!

Three enemy planes crossed *Brown*'s bow under her fire, turning between *Brown* and *Dobler* and heading directly for the convoy. They were immediately taken under fire by *Dobler*'s entire starboard battery. Two pilots decided the heat was too great, pulled up and turned away. Within a few seconds, the third plane launched a torpedo in the middle of its turn. This torpedo had the *Dobler* name on it. However, her captain, Lieutenant Commander E.F. Butler, avoided it with a quick starboard turn to parallel the torpedo track. Likewise, the skipper of *Brown*, Lieutenant Commander L.C. Burdett Jr., ordered full right rudder, continuing to fire as the plane retired. However, a murderous cross fire of 20mm and 1.1" guns of the two ships resulted in many hits. Personnel on *Brown* saw this plane hit the water and disappear. The action report of *Dobler* was more emphatic:

> "It passed abeam at a range of 700 yards and crashed in flames half a mile off the starboard quarter and about a mile in front of the leading merchant vessel in the ninth column! Lookouts claimed that this plane broke in two before splashing and one section, a mass of flame, skidded along the water a considerable distance."

This engagement lasted about 20 seconds. A total elapsed time of seven minutes was spent in continual firing as one target after another crossed the screen to the starboard escort sectors.

Prior to the time of action, port side escorts were arrayed from the port bow of the convoy to its port quarter, each one on the port quarter of the escort ahead. *Campbell* was still in the van, followed at two mile intervals by *Decker*, *Smartt*, *Wilhoite*,

Benson, *Wyffels*, and *Evarts*. However, once action began and escorts turned to unmask batteries or avoid torpedoes, this nicely arranged pattern was considerably altered. (There were fewer escorts on the starboard side than on the port side because the proximity of shore on the starboard side reduced maneuvering capability.)

2115. A plane headed in, either attempting a torpedo run on *Dobler* or a breakthrough to the convoy between that ship and *Campbell*. All guns on *Dobler*'s starboard side that could bear immediately took this target under fire. *Campbell* had already opened up. AA bursts were seen close to the aircraft and appeared to rock it violently, whereupon it turned abruptly and passed out of view. On *Brown*, all forward guns were tracking the same target and opened fire as the plane attempted to launch a torpedo at *Campbell*. Despite the fact that the gunners could not hear the bearings being called from the bridge over the sound powered phones, the men manning the *Oelikons* (20mm) kept up a withering fire, forcing the last attacker away.

Lookouts, bridge officers and forward gun crews on *Decker* sighted numerous enemy planes dead ahead. Three minutes later, the *Smartt* CIC reported bogies at 10 o'clock, distance 18 miles. Almost simultaneously, a brief but vigorous tracer fire erupted in the enemy area, and it was presumed that they were being engaged by our fighters. Wishful thinking. They were recognized as JU 88 fighter-bombers. FXR gears were streamed, and all escorts were ordered to full speed.

Wilhoite picked up bandits on her SL radar, range 18 miles on the port bow of the convoy, and the port screen commenced its barrage. From the observation of her captain, Lieutenant Commander Eli Roth, the attacking planes sheered away from the barrage, flew aft outside the port screen, then cut across the stern of the convoy in a circling movement. This DE laid several barrages in front of enemy planes as they came around to the stern of the convoy. Former Lieutenant Robert Q. Whitely of *Wilhoite* tells us what it was like:

> "The engagement with JU 88s took place almost 52 years ago. I was the Officer of The Deck during GQ on *Wilhoite*. I can recall the excitement of the attack at dusk as we were making smoke to camouflage the convoy. From my vantage point, the sky in every direction took on the appearance of a giant 4th of July fireworks display; guns of the convoy escorts were firing in every direction. Our quadruple 40mm shot down at least one bomber."

The *Smartt* plot had tracked the targets accurately as the first wave came into visible range. *Benson*, *Evarts*, and *Wyffels* promptly initiated a barrage. The three ships maneuvered at high speed into the direction of the attack. Hard right rudder was ordered on *Evarts* by her skipper, Lieutenant Commander T.G. Bremer, as one plane dropped two torpedoes on her starboard side. It was believed that one of the planes on her port side was damaged. Two torpedo wakes crossed her bow.

The main force of enemy planes broke into several groups, one with five planes raced out on the port bow of the convoy toward the convoy flank, range 3000 yards, altitude 50 feet. The headings of several DEs were turned quickly to unmask their antiaircraft batteries. The planes attempted to pass from the port to the starboard sides of the escorts, searching for a thin spot in the smoke screen to break through to the convoy. They made their attack on the port beam of *Decker*. All her guns trained on the oncoming planes and laid a barrage at 2000 yards, as three planes passed down her port beam.

2110. The leading plane dropped a torpedo 800 yards from *Decker*, then crossed the bow of the DE with its starboard engine nacelle in flames and German markings clearly visible. The *Smartt's* skipper, Lieutenant Commander E.R. Wepman, recorded:

> "This plane came into *Smartt's* range aflame with *Decker's* men still hot on her tail. We gave *Decker* a hand, and the cross fire was going at full blast when the plane splashed into the water about a mile off our port beam!"

Almost at the same time, two planes came in broad on the starboard bow of *Decker*, crossed over, then each dropped a torpedo on her port side about half a mile from the ship. The *Decker's* commanding officer, Lieutenant Commander H.S. Cody, ordered the helm brought hard left, combing the torpedo tracks port and starboard and close aboard. Other planes, racing along her port side, were engaged by the after guns. One 3" shell exploded in the after fuselage of one plane. It turned sharply and disappeared into the smoke screen astern. *Smartt* witnessed the action and reported:

> "One of the planes in the group that passed over the stern of *Decker* after being engaged by her after gun crews, fell off on the ship's starboard quarter and crashed astern, about a mile in front of column one!"

Smartt, meanwhile, had her first breather in the few hectic minutes before *Decker* was attacked. Nonetheless, her lookouts were sharply scanning their sector. At 2117, the *Smartt* CIC reported two targets moving up on her starboard side. Her guns trained to the radar beam, waiting for the planes to come through the smoke screen. She tagged her target 1500 yards just abaft the beam and kept it in her line of fire. She turned left with it so as to keep all guns firing on the target until it was seen to splash 11/2 miles off her port bow!

Smartt's after guns had just ceased firing on this target when it started on another coming out of a blinding smoke screen less than 1/2 mile away. This plane banked and crossed over 500 yards in front of her bow. The 20mm and 1.1" guns poured a blistering fire into this close target, smoking profusely as it flew out of range. Two bridge observers claimed this plane crashed into the sea; it was listed as probably destroyed.

2123. A JU 88 made a torpedo attack on *Wilhoite*, approaching from her starboard quarter. As soon as the plane appeared, all guns were on target. Fire was very accurate, tracers having entered the aircraft's fuselage and causing the pilot to drop his torpedo at too great a range for accuracy. He banked sharply and disappeared in *Wilhoite's* smoke screen, then flew across the stern of *FNS Cimeterre*, astern of convoy column two. His flight seemed erratic but he was not seen to crash anywhere in the vicinity.

Wilhoite laid down a barrage at a range of three miles to intercept a plane approaching rapidly but ceased firing when the plane's IFF identified itself as friendly. She sighted and fired on two others that were circling astern before the end of the action. She also laid several barrages on radar bearings. A large splash was noted during an attack on this ship 500 yards to starboard immediately after her radar tracked a bandit overhead. Apparently, this was a dud bomb.

2124. A JU 88 approached *Wyffels* from the direction of the convoy on her starboard bow, flying directly toward her. Her captain, Lieutenant Commander S.N. Gleis, conned his ship into a position to unmask the maximum number of guns. The aircraft was clearly visible through the smoke at one mile, altitude 100 feet, when the starboard guns opened up. At less than 1/2 mile, the plane banked sharply toward the DE, just forward of amidships. Several hits were recorded as it flew through the 20mm fire. When directly overhead, it leveled and continued over *Wyffels*' port quarter, receiving fire from her 1.1" and port 20mm guns. Before it could escape, another DE, probably *Evarts*, joined *Wyffels* in a heavy crossfire. A streak of black smoke poured out of the port side of the plane; it lost altitude and fell off sharply. At 3500 yards, a large burst of black smoke was seen in the water; believed to be the same plane that crashed.

A plane came through a heavy barrage from other ships ahead and was picked up on *Wyffels*' port bow at about 1/2 mile and at an altitude of 300 feet. The forward 20mm guns opened up when the aircraft closed to 800 yards. It passed directly over the forecastle and along the starboard side where it was fired upon by the starboard midships 20mm and 1.1" guns. Although several hits were recorded, it flew off steady in flight with no visible serious damage.

Evarts ordered right rudder at 2125 as two planes dropped two torpedoes. It was believed that one of the planes was damaged by *Evarts*' fire. Two torpedo wakes passed across her bow close aboard.

There then seemed to be a temporary lull of about 15 minutes in the attacks on *Decker*. Several single planes approached the ship and were driven off by her fire. Another plane screamed in from the dark, range only 600 yards when first observed. At about 1/4 mile, it dropped a torpedo which broached once and then disappeared. The plane was engaged as it flew over the bow, but it was not believed any damage was inflicted. Seconds later, a torpedo passed under the ship, coming from broad on the starboard quarter!

2133. The convoy returned to course, due east, and a few minutes later the order was given by CTF 61 to cease making smoke. The master plotting ships reported the sky was clear of bandits, and the screen was ordered to resume patrol stations as weary crews stood down from battle stations. *Brown, Evarts, Hengist* and *Cimeterre* were then ordered to proceed astern of the convoy to check for possible casualties; there were none.

The aggressive action of escorts against the enemy, coordinated with other forces present, broke up the attack and disrupted his plans with no allied losses. On the contrary, the enemy suffered a heavy loss in planes. The Task Force Commander commended the commanding officers, their officers and crews for their splendid and effective action under fire. This was an extraordinary victory, an air-sea battle with aircraft suffering severe losses compared to surface forces emerging intact. Former Lieutenant William T. Morris Jr., *Wilhoite* gunnery officer, tells us some of the reasons why:

> "On the trip across the Atlantic, CTF 61, Commander Sowell, drilled us constantly. For example, the *Campbell* ready gun crew would fire an unannounced AA burst and call to one of the escorts on TBS 'Eli, that is yours!' Then the chosen ship would fire three AA shells at the target (burst) from her ready gun. By the time we reached Gibraltar, we were as fast as Wyatt Earp!
>
> Before the Germans arrived, all escorts accelerated to 20 knots and laid smoke. With the convoy at eight knots, astute ship handling was a requisite. The smoke thoroughly confused the enemy, causing planes to scatter. Meanwhile, the escorts fired barrages as the planes approached. Shell fuses were set to burst just above the surface at two miles throughout the attack. When a plane was actually sighted, we opened up with our 40mm or 1.1" and 20mm batteries.
>
> In his book *The Atlantic Battle Won*, Samuel E. Morison said of this convoy that enemy planes crashing and burning caused the Germans to believe they were making hits, but there was another factor. Each escort had recently acquired a new smoke screen generator, located in the after steering engine room with the nozzle between the two depth charge racks on the fantail. In the final seconds of the attack, these generators overheated, and about six of them flared up, shooting flames 10 feet into the air. The German pilots, seeing this phenomenon, thought they were having a field day, when in fact they had hit nothing.
>
> At the end of the attack, we found that we had expended every round of our 3" shells in ready service boxes. Our crew and all the other escort crews performed superbly.
>
> I have enjoyed reliving some 52 year old memories as I discussed these experiences with Bob Whitely, who corroborates it all. Good luck with your book."

It would be unfair to leave the impression that the DEs accounted for all the 19 downed enemy planes. A large number were splashed by the British antiaircraft cruiser, the three destroyers and allied fighter aircraft. They are hereby acknowledged but have not been covered in detail because this is a book about destroyer escorts. It is obvious from the above narrative that DEs did extremely well.

CONVOY UGS FORTY-EIGHT

Running the Gauntlet with High Marks

Convoy UGS 48 was escorted by DE divisions 15 and 66, with Commander of Task Force 62 in destroyer *Moffett (DD-362)*. Antiaircraft (AA) cruiser *HMS Delhi* joined the Task Force at Gibraltar. On 1 August 1944, 10–15 bombers attacked the convoy six miles off the North Coast of Algeria, between Algiers and Bougie. Poor visibility prevented accurate plane recognition, but they probably were JU 88s. The engagement lasted 48 minutes, like hours to the participants, and is seen through the eyes of *Reuben James (DE-153)*, commanded by Lieutenant Commander Grant Cowherd.

> "Starting at three minutes after midnight, bogies were spotted on radar at various ranges by navy escorts *Reuben James, Moffett, Atherton (DE-169), William T. Powell (DE-213), Buckley (DE-51), Amick (DE-168)* and *HMS Delhi. Reuben James*' radar revealed an aircraft echelon seven miles on the convoy's port bow.
>
> 0101. Delhi opened fire. Minutes later, *Reuben James*

repelled the first of six sequential attacks. The first came in three miles on her port bow. All batteries that could bear fired on a radar bearing. The target closed to two miles and then turned away. After a three-minute respite, this DE faced a second attack consisting of two planes, one of which made its approach 5,500 yards miles broad on the port bow. The second came in from astern of *Moffett*. The first one was turned away, but the second plane closed rapidly and dropped something at 500 yards with a large splash. Soon afterward, a torpedo wake was seen 40 yards astern. An explosion, from a torpedo at a distance of 500 yards was probably a self-destruct at the end of its run. The detonation was intensive but not damaging. The plane retired under fire.

Two minutes after cease fire from the second attack, *Reuben James* faced up to the third. It could have been the same plane that launched the torpedo, circling and returning to strafe. The plane was picked up on the starboard bow, distance 5000 yards, and the ship's batteries commenced firing almost immediately. This plane was identified by the recognition officer as a JU 88 when it passed about 200 feet ahead of the port bow. Captain Cowherd indicated in his action report that there was a definite attempt to strafe the ship. A line of splashes was noted close aboard, and spray showered the deck. Dents up to 1/4" deep in the port bow, three feet above the waterline with paint freshly chipped off, confirmed the strafing, probably .50 caliber ricochets. The plane then turned toward the convoy and dropped two objects in the water, about 200 feet from the DE, possibly torpedoes or bombs.

A series of six explosions erupted at 0122. Lacking any distress signals, they were again presumed to be torpedoes self-destructing.

The fourth attack was picked up by radar three miles abaft the port beam. Once the target was sighted, firing was director controlled. About 45 seconds later, a red glow was observed trailing smoke and followed by a short-lived bright flash. *Moffett* and *Atherton* also fired on the target. The radar contact disappeared at two miles. This action was classified as a probable hit.

0125. The fifth attack plane was picked up by radar three miles on the port bow. *Reuben James* commenced firing, and the aircraft turned away 30 seconds after closing to 3000 yards. This plane was probably hit; it was also fired upon by *Moffett* and *Atherton*.

The SA (air search) radar operator reported nine bogies operating in a 90 degree sector from due north to due east. The attacking planes commenced an approach from a distance of six miles. However, there was a lull in the attack until 0139, at which time one plane was tracked approaching *Reuben James*. The sixth attack never materialized beyond the approach stage. It turned away at two miles, and all bogies retired from the area.

Four more explosions were heard together in the distance. Like the previous explosions, they probably emanated from self-destructing torpedoes at the end of their runs."

The failure of enemy planes to press home assaults on the convoy was atypical of German pilots. Captain Cowherd attributed this behavior to the use of smoke promptly, efficiently, and in sufficient volume to hide the convoy almost completely during attacks. The smoke was impenetrable when combined with both white chemical and black stack emissions in spite of bright moonlight. Flares dropped by the aircraft early in the attack showed dull yellow through the smoke without brilliance or illumination. The failure of the enemy to press home ship attacks was due to inability to identify individual targets as well as the effectiveness of the barrages. The latter was demonstrated by the torpedo and strafing attacks made on *Reuben James* when not obscured by smoke. The ship was well silhouetted as the attacks came from down moon.

The *Reuben James* captain's action report concluded that the only detrimental effect of smoke noticed was the inability of the merchant ships in the convoy to maintain good station due to the lack of visibility.

The initial opening fire consisted of heavy barrages in the ship defensive sectors when the plane tracks were closing at a range of 5500 - 6000 yards. Three inch gun fire was rapid, without a major casualty, and was very effective. The 40mm fire was coordinated with the 3" guns to take advantage of self-destructive bursts at 4000 yards during barrages. Individual targets were fired on whenever sighted. Automatic fire (20mm) was only used when firing at sighted targets. Firing was frequently inaccurate due to poor visibility and the blinding effect of flashes and tracers.

The overall effect seemed commendable, however, as planes were turned back at ranges of 3000 to 4000 yards. All firing information from radar was transmitted to guns in relative bearings. Violent maneuvering at maximum speed while laying smoke greatly complicated gunnery problems. Nonetheless, performances were outstanding. John Lampe, radioman third class, kindly obliged us to tell something of his experiences on *Reuben James*:

Dear Mr Andrews:

" I served aboard *Reuben James* from April 1944 until the war in the Atlantic was over and I then was transferred to the Pacific. When I came aboard in Norfolk, I was 17 and soon made seaman first class radioman striker. It was a rough crossing, and we weren't properly prepared to handle it. The trays and utensils were flying all over the messing compartment, making it ankle deep in cold coffee, soup, and slop water. Until the carpenters secured places for trays on the tables by adding wooden strips, we were fed "horse cock" sandwiches and coffee at our watch stations. In the radio shack, we would be at the radio transmitter, typing away with our ear phones plugged in. The next minute, we were slamming against the opposite bulkhead, chair and all, with the ear phones attached to nothing. The shipfitters finally welded our chairs in front of the radio transmitters to keep us in place.

I remember the August air raid off Algeria quite well. Early that morning, a German observation plane was noted flying overhead out of gun range. Late that afternoon, I was on watch in the radio shack copying my five letter, coded, word groups sent out of Washington. All of a sudden, the transmissions became 'herky jerky'. I didn't realize that what I was copying was plain language. I was still trying to put it all into five letter word groups. Since it made no sense to me, I asked Second Class Radioman Sam Trowbridge to take over.

He immediately copied the message correctly and sent me to the captain with it. All I can remember of it was something about 'red tambourines' and 'bandits at 0040'. We were immediately called to battle stations. Mine was as a messenger in the radio shack. At dusk, a squadron of JU 88 torpedo bombers attacked the convoy. Then all hell broke loose as ships commenced firing. I was sent from the radio shack to the bridge to deliver a message. While there, I saw a plane drop a torpedo which missed our ship by a fairly wide margin. There was a great deal of confusion because of the noise and because all of the DEs laid a smoke screen. I heard a 'hit the deck' order as the ships were firing almost point blank over one another when the planes dived between them. One crew member was wounded in his rear end by shrapnel from one of our sister ships. He didn't duck low enough.

When I was secured from my battle station, I went below to take a shower and wash the soot from my hair and face. First Class Radioman Armstrong came to the shower room looking for me. He ordered me to my cleaning station immediately. I told him what he could do with his order (as only a smart ass seventeen year old can). For this, I was put on report for negligence of duty and insolence to a leading petty officer. I spent my eighteenth birthday on the fantail scrubbing garbage cans and never did get ashore in North Africa."

CONVOY GUS SEVENTY-FOUR

Did a Procedural Error on Fowler Result in Victory?

Between 1 February and 16 March 1945, Convoy UGS/GUS 74 was harassed by U-boats in both directions. Near Gibraltar on 17 February, two of the merchantmen in the eastbound convoy were torpedoed but brought safely into Gibraltar. Westbound from Oran on 28 February, *Fowler (DE-222)* picked up a sound contact and made an urgent attack.

This DE, one of a five-ship screen in Task Force 60.9, escorting convoy GUS 74, was patrolling on the port beam of the formation. A chilly winter's dawn saw the coast of Morocco falling away astern as the Casablanca section of the convoy was in sight and maneuvering to join. The *Fowler's* Officer of The Deck, Lieutenant (jg) Gordon Numitz, could hear the steady "pings" from the sound shack where the operator, Soundman Second Class M.A. Kurzynski, was echo ranging.

0648. "Contact! Starboard bow, range 2900 yards!" The soundman was suddenly alert as his instruments flashed a U-boat warning. After first suspecting the contact to be the wake of *Francis M. Robinson (DE-220)*, the evaluation quickly changed to possible submarine. The O.O.D. ordered the depth charges set for magnetic firing. The captain was called, and he promptly ordered Lieutenant (jg) Numitz to attack.

As the range closed to 600 yards, the sound stack indicated a sharp metallic echo and slight down doppler, changing the evaluation to submarine. Orders were given to fire on the recorder as the O.O.D. sought to cross the bow of the U-boat, causing her to enter the deadly explosion pattern in an urgent attack. The captain took the conn.

A magnetic pattern was fired in accordance with prior instructions from the O.O.D. Use of magnetic depth settings in an "embarrassing" attack was contrary to standard ship procedure as well as prescribed doctrine. The purpose of an "embarrassing" attack was to unnerve the submarine captain and rattle his aim with depth charges exploding about him. Magnetic impulse settings might not cause detonation at all if not in close proximity to the submarine. The commanding officer, Lieutenant Commander S.F. Morris, was upset.

Nonetheless, four explosions occurred at intervals after dropping of the first charge. Following the first two explosions, debris rose to the surface. The captain conned the ship so as to stand between the convoy and a possible submarine. Contact was regained at 300 yards. Opening the range to 1000 yards, the ship turned for a second attack. However, as the echo showed no doppler and there was no movement of the target, the contact was evaluated as turbulence from previous explosions, and no charges were dropped.

0702. *Robinson* reported a sound contact and dropped a shallow pattern but without results. *Fowler* dropped another pattern in the middle of the debris, then spreading over a widening area, with no results. A towel was dragged through the debris to obtain lumps of heavy oil sludge, but no samples were recovered.

CTF 60.9, Captain N.E. Dennett, ordered the French escorts, *PC Le Resolu* and *PC L'Indiscret*, to join in the hunt and for *Robinson* to rejoin the convoy. This made *ComCortDiv 30* in the frigate *Knoxville (PF-64)* the OTC in charge of *Fowler* plus the two French PCs. *ComCortDiv 30* was ordered to rejoin the convoy after four hours unless positive evidence of a submarine was obtained.

An Observant search for the next four hours failed to regain contact. U.S. ships returned to the convoy. Subsequently, the Task Group Commander intercepted radio traffic between the *L'Indiscret* and the Commander of the Moroccan Sea Frontier as follows:

> "Made attack on very good sound contact which caused a large black object to break surface and immediately sink. Object unidentified and no further debris sighted. No more contacts made."

In his action report, Captain Morris praised the performance of duty by all personnel except one O.O.D. He was given a verbal reprimand.

The report from CTG 60.9 to the Flag Officer of Gibraltar and the Mediterranean Approaches stated that the original attack was made on a "possible submarine." It was considered that the first explosions were premature, and the debris could not be accounted for. Finally, the much browbeaten Lieutenant (jg) Numitz was again mentioned:

> "The actions of the Officer of The Deck in ordering a magnetic pattern fired are inexcusable."

This could be the end but for a postwar perusal of German U-boat records indicating that *U-869* was lost that day in the area of the debris! The first attack was probably a lethal one. The question: Are medals awarded for sinking enemy vessels with the wrong weapons?

COLLISION AT SEA

Roaring Flames in the Night

On 2 October 1944, *Holton (DE-703)* departed from Norfolk on her second convoy to the Mediterranean. About 400 miles from her destination, routine was suddenly and violently interrupted.

While patrolling her night station astern of the starboard outboard column of the convoy on 14 October, the dark was illuminated bright as day when two of the convoyed vessels closest to *Holton* burst into flames. The DE immediately proceeded at full speed to investigate the cause of the conflagration. Upon arrival, it was apparent that a liberty ship, *SS Howard L. Gibson*, had collided with a British tanker, *SS George W. McKnight*.

Roaring flames covered *Gibson's* forward section, from the bow aft to the bridge, and were being fought by her crew amidships. The stricken ship was rolling in the trough. The seas were moderate, though a fairly heavy ground swell was building up. Four hoses were rigged to the forecastle of *Holton* with the intention of maneuvering as close as possible to *Gibson* and directing water on the fire. The DE approached downwind to a position close aboard the port bow of the *Gibson* and poured water onto the fire. Carried dangerously close to the burning ship, *Holton* backed away and maneuvered to close *Gibson's* port side amidship.

Once alongside, the DE had five hoses playing on the well deck. She again had to stand clear to avoid damaging her lifeboats which had been swung out ready for lowering. While backing away, a heavy swell threw the bow of the *Holton* against the side of *Gibson*, fouling her anchor. The kenter shackle parted under the strain, and the anchor was lost overboard.

While maneuvering for another approach, *Gibson's* crew was lowering lifeboats to abandon ship. The DE promptly maneuvered to pick up survivors, rescuing three merchant marine crewmen, including the master, and twenty five members of the Armed Guard crew. The master and three of the Armed Guard men were badly burned about the face and hands and were suffering from shock. The *Holton's* skipper, Lieutenant Commander J.B. Boy, directed an intensive search of the area for two Armed Guard members still missing.

As the lifeboats cleared the port side of *Gibson*, *Holton* rounded her stern and made fast to her starboard quarter. It was decided to go alongside to place men and equipment on the freighter to more readily direct water from the DE's fire mains. A small group of volunteers from the merchant marine crew, led by the first mate, and some of the *Holton's* repair party, led by the executive officer, Lieutenant Commander Laurence C. Arpin, boarded *Gibson*. Fireman Ernest L. Hughes remembers it well:

> "As a young 18 year old fireman on the *Holton* and a member of the damage control party, I volunteered to board *Gibson*.
>
> We did that by jumping from our port bow to *Gibson's* midsection. As the captain approached the blazing ship, we were running in huge swells. While we were climbing a swell, *Gibson* was running down and rolling in the opposite direction from us. We had to time our leaps to be level or a foot above or below *Gibson*. If one missed, he would have been crushed between the ships. Only two could make the jump at the same time. The captain would back away and come in again for the next two to jump until all the repair party was aboard *Gibson*. When it was all over, we were happy that none of us 'missed' the boarding."

The remainder of *Holton's* repair party, under the first lieutenant, Lieutenant Milton Knight, rigged hoses to hand to the boarding party. It was reported that engine room spaces on *Gibson* were undamaged and capable of propulsion. Several hoses and two portable gasoline pumps with hoses and attachments were carried aboard *Gibson*. At the same time, *Ahrens (DE-575)* approached to render assistance, stood in close to the port bow of the *Gibson* and played streams of water on the blaze in the forward section of the freighter.

By 2300, volunteers from the merchant marine crew, the Armed Guard and repair parties from *Holton*, fifty-seven in all, were aboard *Gibson* and fighting the blaze. Uninjured members of the Armed Guard, under the leadership of their officer, Lieutenant Frank Baicerzak, returned aboard *Gibson* to jettison ammunition from the ready lockers amidship which had become dangerously hot. Fireman Hughes added:

> "As we moved forward and the flames and steam were clearing, I spotted an Armed Guardsman's body, charred and face down on the red hot boat deck. I notified the Officer in Charge that I had located one of the two known to be aboard, but it was hours before we could retrieve the body. By this time, we had the fire out and, for the first time, I realized my feet were HOT! And with good reason half the double soles on my shoes were melted away."

Throughout the night, the ground swell increased, doing considerable damage to the port side of *Holton* as she rolled against *Gibson*. All fenders were carried away and all but two mooring lines parted. When it was reported that the fires aboard *Gibson* were sufficiently under control, *Holton* backed off and stood by. By 0500, the fire was reported under control, allowing the transfer of the remainder of the merchant marine crew back to their ship and to pick up *Holton's* men. The executive officer and four men from *Holton* remained with *Gibson* until she reached port. Fireman Hughes concluded:

> "We didn't have to jump back onto *Holton* but returned first class on a boatswain's chair the crew did a tremendous job in retrieving us. To counter the swells and rolls, the men had to control tension lines to keep us out of the sea. However, they relaxed on my turn, and I got my feet wet and cooled."

A burial service was held for two Armed Guardsmen, one dead and the other missing.

The French *L'Eveille (PC-471)* supplied a pharmacist mate and screened *Gibson* to Casablanca. It was later learned that, during that night, division escorts had gained radar contact on two enemy submarines not more than 40 miles away. They must have seen the sky lit up. For whatever reason, they decided not to attack.

The other ship, *SS McKnight*, was temporarily abandoned, her crew rescued by one of the other DEs. Her fire spent itself and the crew returned aboard the following day. She was brought safely into port, minus part of her precious cargo of high octane gasoline and fighter aircraft which had been lashed to her weather decks.

It was estimated that the two salvaging jobs saved the U.S. government upward of three million dollars, a stupendous sum in 1944. For the salvage operation, the *Holton* received a "Well done" from the Commander in Chief of the Atlantic Fleet. The following *Holton* personnel received commendations:

> Lieutenant Commander J.B. Boy, captain; Lieutenant Milton Knight, first lieutenant and damage control officer; J.E. Ross, Seaman First Class; C.N. Petty, Shipfitter First Class; R.G. Beach, Metalsmith Second Class. Lieutenant Commander L.C. Arpin, executive officer, received the Navy and Marine Corps medal.

Ordered to the Pacific a few months later, *Holton* arrived at Manus, Admiralty Islands in February 1945. She conducted escort of convoys within the Philippine Sea Frontier, to Okinawa and finally to Tokyo.

THE ELECTRONICS WAR

Herbert C. Jones and Frederick C. Davis on a Top Secret Mission

At the Washington Navy Yard in September 1943, *Herbert C. Jones (DE-137)* and *Frederick C. Davis (DE-136)* acquired equipment from naval research engineers for investigation of German rocket-propelled, radio-controlled glider bombs. This early guided missile proved to be devastatingly accurate. (This author recalls a British Indian cruiser in Londonderry that, hit by one such bomb, displayed a 10 foot diameter hole through her bow.) In early October, the two DEs sailed for the Mediterranean to test its equipment under fire.

Motor Machinist Mate William F. Placzek wrote of his experiences on *Jones* and the remarkable adventures of both DEs:

> "With land falling away astern, the captain called the crew topside to discuss our mission. He told us about the enemy radio-controlled bomb that was raising havoc with Allied shipping and that our new equipment was a jamming device to counter it. The radiomen were to intercept the frequencies of radio-controlled bombs and jam them so they would fly off on erratic courses and miss their targets. The operation was code-named *Shingle*."

On 16 October, while lying to in the harbor of Algiers and awaiting a berth assignment, *Jones* was accidentally rammed by a British submarine with a steering failure. She punched a hole about 9'X3' in *Jones*' hull, delaying operations four days to repair the damage.

Jones and *Davis* were formed into Task Group 80.2, of which Lieutenant Commander Alfred W. Gardes, captain of *Jones*, was Task Group Commander. Based in Gibraltar and the Mediterranean, the Task Group would meet east bound convoys in the Atlantic, just beyond the operational range of enemy aircraft. The two ships would take station on opposite sides of the convoy, waiting for a glider bomb attack. On the evening of 6 November, *Jones* participated in her first action. The convoy was attacked by German torpedo bombers. Three radio signals were intercepted, permitting *Jones* to jam them. Her gunners also accounted for one plane. Placzek had a more earthy description:

> "I'd only been in the navy four months and I never even heard a 22 caliber rifle fired. I was an unloader on a 20mm amidships, starboard side. At dusk, we were at battle stations and knew that enemy aircraft were nearby. Suddenly, like out of a John Wayne movie, here comes a torpedo plane and, of all places, starboard side, amidships. This being my first taste of war, when our guns opened up, I froze up. The gunner kicked my butt so that I would take the empty magazine off. With the kick, a veteran was born. The pilot dropped his fish, but our captain maneuvered out of its path. The plane banked sharply and was seen to crash in the distance! Numerous glider bombs were launched in this raid, and *Davis* and *Jones* jammed most of them."

The second engagement was on 26 November while protecting a vitally needed convoy, including eight British troop ships. The engagement lasted two hours in one of the most concentrated attacks against a Mediterranean convoy. A German bomber sneaked in low and dropped a bomb, narrowly missing a transport. The 40mm gun crew on *Jones* opened fire as the plane crossed her stern. Its engine began smoking and was suddenly enveloped in crackling flame as it dived beneath the waves! This attack was followed by two waves of planes carrying glider bombs. The two DEs were able to jam the control frequencies and make recordings of the signals. Only one ship was hit.

The bombing attack was followed by a torpedo attack at dusk with one German choosing *Jones* for special attention. The forward 20mm guns opened fire as soon as the attacker became visible. As the plane came down her starboard side, the after 20mm and 40mm guns opened fire and continued firing until the plane passed out of range on the starboard quarter. Riddled with hits, the aircraft splashed after releasing its torpedo which was successfully evaded! The attack ended about 1900. Placzek filled in some data on this "electronics war."

> "After the November 26 raid, we went to Oran. Two officers on board, who had been supervising the jamming operation, flew back to the states to report. The mission was very successful. We also had two army radiomen aboard who translated conversations between German pilots and gave that information to the skipper."

Early in December, more powerful jamming sets were installed in *Jones* and *Davis*. This marked the beginning of serial production and the end of experiments, the mission now being to jam control signals on a larger scale in virtually all operations.

On 7 December, Lieutenant Commander Alfred W. Gardes Jr. was relieved of command of *Jones* by Lieutenant Commander Rufus A. Soule III, the then executive officer. Most of December was spent in training with LCT and *LST* landing craft for an amphibious operation.

Arriving at Naples on 13 January 1944, Task Group (TG) 80.2 assisted amphibious forces in establishing a beachhead for the Anzio operation. *Jones* and *Davis* sailed from Naples at 0430 on 21 January at the head of a column of *LST*s. At dawn the next day, the two DEs were part of the outer antisubmarine and glider bomb screen, moving to the transport and fire support areas as troops stormed the beaches.

It was a bloody campaign. The lack of initial resistance didn't last long. After a month or so, the Allies had crowded the beach with antiaircraft guns. The shore batteries would cover the harbor area with a blanket of flak. The sky was almost solid with red tracers and deafening 90mm shells exploding overhead. Raids were continuous day and night, lit by flares and moonlight. Ships supporting the invasion were forced daily to run the gamut of low level and dive bombing planes, glider bombs, and torpedo attacks. *Davis* came under fire from shore batteries, wounding one man. Placzek continued:

> "In Anzio, we were introduced to the German Stuka dive bombers with their screaming sirens. Usually, they were preceded by planes dropping flares which lighted up the harbor brighter than Yankee stadium. In our first attack, the skipper tried to turn away from the flares, and the phosphorous in the water lit up the ship's wake like a neon light. A German pilot knew there had to be a ship in front of the wake and dropped his bombs ahead in a straddle. For some strange reason, all our engines stopped without being ordered to do so. Had we kept moving at full speed, we would likely have been hit because the bombs exploded just a few feet in front of us. It had to be a miracle how else can you explain it?
>
> The first two months at Anzio were my 'Hell on Earth' as far as I was concerned. The only bright spots in the Anzio campaign were our occasional visits to the Isle of Capri for a little relaxation."

Jones and *Davis* were in the area for a total of forty out of the first sixty four days. For their superb conduct under fire at Anzio, they each received a Navy Unit Commendation:

> "tenaciously defended vital allied shipping concentrated off Anzio, battling with unremitting vigilance and fury in the face of repeated hostile air attacks and the destructive power of guided missiles, shooting down many aircraft and consistently intercepting enemy radio messages to supply ample warning of impending air strikes. Pioneering in the field of electronics warfare, *Jones* (and *Davis*) rendered outstanding service to the Task Force in jamming a great majority of the radio-controlled enemy bombs directed at the ship-packed anchorage, thereby preventing incalculable damage and casualties to shipping and men. She (*Jones* and *Davis*) was a contributing factor in maintaining the security of the all-important bridgehead."

Although their primary mission was antisubmarine and glider bomb protection, they provided another very valuable service. Until the army was firmly established and able to set up its radar stations, the warnings of air attacks were given by the ships, mainly British fighter director cruisers. Because of the proximity of hills and German airfields, many raids were not detected until the actual attack developed. By utilizing their special equipment, the two DEs were able to accurately predict raids and even types of raids. During the period through 29 February, *Davis* participated in eight guided missile attacks. Thereafter, the missiles were discontinued in the Anzio area. As most missile attacks occurred when it was too dark to see, no jamming operation could be claimed as a success. However, it stands to reason that, had the enemy perceived their guided bomb deployment as successful, it would not have been discontinued.

Davis underwent ninety-eight air attacks wherein bombs fell either in the anchorage or along the waterfront. The action report filed by the captain of *Davis*, Lieutenant Commander R.C. Robbins, Jr., stated that, during the entire period, *Davis*' station was very close to the port of Anzio. The ship never patrolled more than three miles off the shore and usually was within a mile. Whenever an air raid sounded, it was the policy of *Davis* to get close to the beach and to position herself between the attacking planes and the waterfront.

Davis broke up attacks before "bombs away" and claimed six planes shot down. Because of her location, she was able to score many hits. However, since she was firing in competition with shore batteries, it was not possible to compute "possibles" or "probables." The six claimed were only those seen to be splashed by *Davis*' guns. Most attacks were reviewed with the army antiaircraft unit, and credits were allocated accordingly. During operation "*Shingle*," *Davis* expended 12,618 rounds of all types of antiaircraft ammunition!

On the lighter side, the skipper stated that, apropos of those flares, one of his officers displayed a previously unsuspected streak of Tin Pan Alley in his makeup. He composed a ditty to be sung to the tune of Deep in The Heart of Texas which began: "The flares at night burn long and bright down in the bay at Anzio."

One night, *Davis* and another vessel brought down two Italian torpedo planes, and a prisoner recovered from one of them described *Davis*' fire as multo buono. He also stated that the Germans had briefed them not to expect fire from ships in the anchorage.

On 31 March, *Jones* and *Davis* received a fifteen day availability at Oran, Algeria, their first since leaving the U.S. They had been underway seventy percent of the time. While in Oran, Lieutenant Commander Rufus A. Soule III, the captain of *Jones*, was presented with the Legion of Merit.

The Task Group was returned to duty during the period from 5 May to 13 June, convoying among Anzio, Naples and Civitavecchia, Italy, the latter being the first convoy to move north of Anzio following the breakthrough and advance of the Fifth Army.

July and the first week in August were occupied with escorting, mostly between Oran and Naples, the "buildup" period for the invasion of Southern France. The Task Group sailed from Taranto, Italy, on 13 August with a convoy of ten troop transports and six assorted French destroyers and destroyer escorts, arriving in the assault area on 16 August, D-Day plus one. On the previous day, one radio controlled bomb signal was received and jammed by *Davis*, and the alarm was sounded over the TBS. It was reported that an *LST* was struck by a controlled missile at about this time. Twice on 16 August, a radio-controlled bomb signal was received and jammed, and warnings of the attacks were also broadcast over the TBS. Four minutes after the second attack, the DEs commenced firing at enemy aircraft overhead.

Jones and *Davis* parted company when *Jones* was next assigned to Escort Division 9, operating with a carrier hunter-killer group in December 1944. The *Herbert C. Jones* was then ordered to the Pacific, but the war ended when she reached Pearl

Harbor. Placzek had a final tribute to his old ship:

> "Where the *USS Herbert C. Jones* is now, I don't know. Wherever she is may she rest in peace. She earned it; well done!"

Unfortunately, the war ended for *Frederick C. Davis* in a scene of blazing violence. This valiant ship went down with heavy loss of life and a large number of casualties. (See chapter *Twilight of the U-boats*) Motor Machinist Mate Placzek on *Jones* had a suitable epitaph for their sister ship when the sad news reached them:

> "The war with Germany would end in about three more weeks. What a shame that this gallant ship and crew had to meet such a fate, just when victory was in our grasp."

Above: U-boat crewmen in North Atlantic
Left: Oberleutnant Horst Fenski

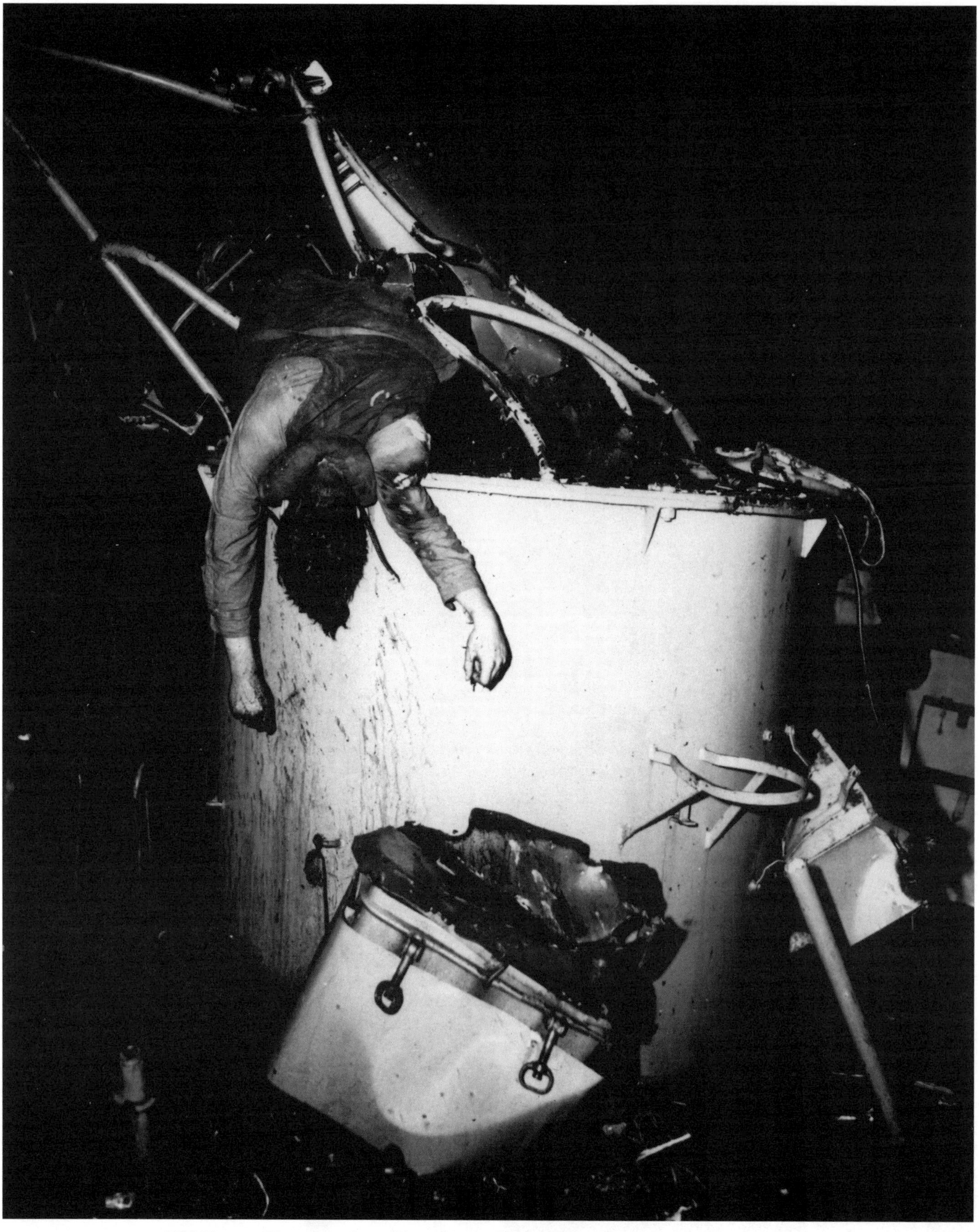

USS Menges. The price of war. Photo by Art Green, USCG. Courtesy National Archives

SMARTT (DE-257) fighting off German torpedo–bombers off the coast of North Africa. Artist's conception
Painting by Sam L. Massette © American Naval Art

A young *Menges* sailor dead almost before he has a chance to live. US Navy Photo

U-boat prisoners on *Inch.* US Navy Photo

Lewis M. Andrews, Jr.

Chapter V - The Hunter-Killers

Hunter-killer (HUK) groups were very bad news for U-boats. Unlike convoys which operated defensively to deliver men and materiel to the fighting fronts, HUK forces operated offensively, hunting and killing subs.

The heart of a HUK group was an escort carrier with fighter bombers which could attack, conduct extended reconnaissance, or vector DEs to U-boat sightings. Escort carriers (CVEs) were inexpensive to build and they relieved large carriers for fleet duty. Whereas surface radar is line of sight transmission, good only from the top of a ship's mast to the horizon, aircraft could maintain surveillance of hundreds of square miles around the task force. Previously, U-boats felt safe from air attack when beyond the operating range of shore-based aircraft. That security was shattered as HUK forces radically altered antisubmarine warfare.

By the summer of 1944, the *Kriegsmarine* faced unacceptable submarine losses, largely attributed to the aggressive HUK tactics. U-boat Commandant Admiral Karl Doenitz introduced two counter measures. The first was the *schnorkel*, a device that allowed submerged submarines to force air into their hulls, supporting diesel speeds up to 19 knots. Heretofore, the best speed on battery-operated motors was seven knots in short bursts, and Allied ASW doctrine was formulated accordingly. Fortunately, *schnorkels* had a number of technical problems, not fully resolved before the war ended. The second development was the acoustic torpedo, which homed on the noise of an attacking ship's propellers and sank or damaged a number of DEs.

THE BLOCK ISLAND HUNTER-KILLERS

Phase I: The First Group

On 13 December 1943, *Bronstein (DE-189)*, under the command of Lieutenant Sheldon H. Kinney, with a green crew, fresh from shakedown, sailed for Norfolk, Virginia, to join HUK Task Group 21.16. Included were the flagship, escort carrier *Block Island (CVE-21)*; destroyer *Corry (DD-463)*; and destroyer escorts *Bronstein, Thomas (DE-102), Breeman (DE-104)*, and *Bostwick (DE-103)*.

The task group sailed for the North Atlantic antisubmarine patrol on 16 February 1944. Heavy weather cancelled plane operations in a storm so violent that it ripped loose *Block Island's* flight deck. Nevertheless, the group was redirected to a pack of about sixteen German submarines. Sonarman First Class Clinton L. Gantt Sr., a former crew member of *Bronstein*, remembers the stormy North Atlantic:

> "The seas were mountainous. Several times, we rolled so far we feared the ship would capsize. The number one gun shield was flattened like a tin can. A refrigerator welded to the deck in the Chief's area was torn loose and thrown onto the starboard side at the waterline, creating a breach open to the sea. The damage control party closed the rupture with 4"X4" timber shoring and mattresses. The weather decks were declared off limits, but one sonarman didn't get the word and ventured onto the main deck. A huge wave picked him up about midships and slammed him onto the port depth charge rack aft. Badly hurt, he was transferred to the carrier via a breeches buoy."

(The splinter shield around number one 3" gun was a weak spot on many DEs in heavy weather. The profile of this author at the beginning of this book refers to a former skipper, Lieutenant Commander Kenneth J. Hartley Jr., killed at sea on *Brough (DE-148)* while contending with the same problem.) The war diary of *Thomas'* captain relates:

> "23 February 1944. Barometer falling rapidly in early morning. Seas and wind picking up. Full gale now blowing. Seas tearing two bad holes in deck from shield at number one 3" gun, flooding forward compartments. Two Mark 10 hedgehog ready boxes full of ammo carried away and adrift about the foc'sle. Ship slowed to 1/3 speed while making temporary repairs. Starboard life net carried away with large sea. Effected temporary repairs and resumed station. Gyro is out. TG hove to for remainder of day."

Early evening, 29 February. Aircraft returning to *Block Island* from patrol reported sighting a submarine. *Corry* was detached from the main force and ordered to locate and attack the marauder. The carrier and DEs steamed toward the last reported position of the submarine. Star shell and tracer fire suddenly lit up the night!

It was *Corry* opening rapid fire with her main battery. The U-boat, however, managed to submerge. Meanwhile, the Task Group Commander, Captain Logan C. Ramsey, ordered a group course change with the objective of circling *Corry* to prevent escape of the sub and without fouling *Corry's* guns. At 2216, *Thomas* obtained a sound contact, and *Bostwick* was ordered to assist her. The target echo was sharp and clear as *Thomas* went in on the attack. The DE dropped an urgent five charge shallow pattern to thwart an attack on *Block Island*. A night marker (lighted) was released in the center of the pattern. Regain contact procedure was immediately initiated.

2222. A radar contact at 8-1/2 miles, closing rapidly on a collision course, was picked up by *Thomas*. All guns were trained to the radar bearing while attempting to regain sound contact. The U-boat submerged and eluded *Thomas*. Together with *Bostwick*, she commenced a retiring search from the point of the prior depth charge attack, finally making contact after a one hour search.

The lethal cat and mouse game was on: it invariably started with a sound contact, followed by closing of the target, lost contact just before firing hedgehogs or depth charges. A search was made to regain contact, then contact all over again. There were variables. In this case, two-ship creeping attacks were employed with the attackers rotating between the conning and firing positions. The game could be rudely interrupted by a torpedo to the DE or a depth charge detonation close aboard the sub. The first of March arrived with the two DEs and the U-boat having played out the dance of death twelve times.

On the eighth attack, virtually everybody on board reported an explosion half a minute after the hedgehogs were fired. On hedgehog runs five and eight, the recorder traces indicated hits. The twelfth attack involved the firing of 13 deep–set depth charges by *Thomas* and *Bronstein*. The entire crew heard a distinct detonation one minute after all depth charges had exploded. This explosion clearly showed on the recorder trace. Unable to regain contact after an eight hour search, the DEs were recalled by the carrier. Postwar German records acknowledged the loss of *U-709* with all hands, the majority credit going to *Thomas* and her captain, Lieutenant Commander David M. Kellogg.

Turning the clock back to *Bronstein*, eight bells announced midnight on the dark and cold morning of 1 March 1944. What happened was later described by Admiral Robert B. Carney (Chief of Naval Operations 1953-55) as "the most concentrated and successful antisubmarine action by a U.S. ship during World War II."

The force commander warned *Thomas* and *Bostwick* of a radar contact three miles from them, probably a submarine. *Bronstein* was ordered to investigate. Captain Kinney rang up full speed. *Bronstein* did not gain immediate radar contact, but the proximity of the enemy warranted GQ. This was a winter midnight in the freezing wastes of the North Atlantic. Sleep on *Bronstein* was a scarce commodity, and hearts skipped a beat and adrenaline flowed at the first bong of the alarm, the bosun's whistle, and the ship's intercom blaring "General Quarters, this is NOT a drill, repeat NOT a drill"

Only three minutes after acting on orders from CTG in *Block Island*, radar contact was made dead ahead, range 6500 yards (3-1/4 miles). *Thomas* and *Bostwick* were silhouetted by the light of a night depth charge marker that had been dropped by one of them in the course of a depth charge attack. The DEs were obviously in a nest of submarines. The contact obtained by *Bronstein* was most likely a U-boat heading for *Thomas* or *Bostwick* with the intention of torpedoing one or the other. The probability was that the quick decision of CTG to send *Bronstein* to intercept the radar contact near *Thomas* and *Bostwick* saved one or the other from a torpedo attack.

Lieutenant Kinney was confronted with a major ASW action. Six surface ships were dashing about in the dark in pursuit of at least two deadly U-boats. Flares fired from *Thomas* and *Bostwick* illuminated themselves as well as the prowling U-boats. The exact location of the enemy was unknown although he certainly was there in force. Avoiding collision while hunting subs at the same time was an exercise in seamanship. The problem was compounded by the sea, still restless after the stiff gale the ships had weathered.

The *Bronstein* radar operator reported: "It can't be a submarine; it's pip is larger than a DE's," which meant to the combat team that they were approaching a sub high out of the water. The captain ordered full speed to the target. Ranges and deflections were fed to the guns, all trained on the bearing of the anticipated submarine.

At the command, three salvos of star shells from each of the three 3" guns were to be fired at a range beyond the sub to silhouette it for subsequent rounds. Guns number 1 and 3 would then shift into rapid fire with armor-piercing (AP) shells while gun number 2 maintained illumination of the target. At the command, 40mm and 20mm fire would begin immediately.

Range 3700 yards. "Illuminate!" Immediately, three star shells leaped from their muzzles, soared over the target, and turned night into embarrassing day. Deck hands were treated to the sight of a 300-foot-long U-boat with decks well out of the water. The night was turned into a demoniac roar. The 40mm fire was very accurate, and hits with AP shells could be seen as they straddled the submarine. Discussing the action later, Lieutenant Kinney said:

> "We fired an illuminating spread and saw the sub preparing to make attacks on *Thomas* and *Bostwick*, who were well within its range. How our gunnery officer, Lieutenant Richard Roe, ever did it, I'll never know. At over 3000 yards, he smacked the conning tower of *U-441*, on the first salvo from our 3" guns!"

This was a special sub. Grand Admiral Doenitz wrote in his memoirs:

> "On 22 May 1943, *U-441*, was the first boat to be converted into an 'aircraft trap'. Her task was not to drive aircraft off but to shoot them down. We hoped that once they were severely handled by this type of antiaircraft submarine, enemy aircraft would lose their zest for attacking U-boats on the surface."

Lieutenant Roe called out "Range 1500," and *Bronstein* lunged toward the sub at top speed, intent on ramming the enemy. *U-441* quickly reacted to the charge and first fired a bow and then a stern torpedo at the DE before crash diving to avoid the ramming.

> "We could hear the propeller whine of the torpedoes on the sonar," said Captain Kinney. All we could do was take standard evasive action and hope we were lucky. We all breathed a sigh of relief as the diminishing sound told us they had passed."

The U-boat broached once, and the radar operator reported to the combat information center, it's fading from the screen, [pause] no, there it is, [pause] now it's gone." The sub was completely submerged only 90 seconds after the first star shell spread, a tribute to the alertness of the *Bronstein* crew in illuminating and scoring hits within that tiny time frame. Even the torpedo personnel had received target speed and angle from the CIC plot and were ready to launch their torpedoes upon command. The launch order was not given because the torpedo track was too close to the other two destroyer escorts.

Bronstein's aggressive attack on *U-441* had probably saved *Thomas* or *Bostwick*. The thwarted submarine escaped but was so severely damaged that she lay in the yard several months before returning to the sea. She was subsequently sunk on another war patrol.

At this stage in the narrative, we need to sort out some conflicting data. The time of *Bronstein's* contact on *U-441*, 0008 on 1 March, is taken from her action report. However, *Thomas'* action report indicates that this engagement took place after her sound contact at 2216, 1 hour and 52 minutes before the events following her second contact at 2350. The timing is not important enough to warrant investigation except to point out that two submarines were involved rather than one as was assumed by Admiral Morison who was denied access to confidential intelligence at time of writing.

Lewis M. Andrews, Jr.

Bronstein now prepared for an underwater attack with depth charges on *U-709*, thinking it was *U-441*. We now know that both of the foregoing numbers were confused. *U-441* was damaged by *Bronstein's* gunfire but escaped. *U-709* was sunk largely by *Thomas*. (This has been confirmed to this author by copies of correspondence between the two ex DE skippers after the war.)

Bronstein again gained contact. Return echoes were poor with mushy right and left cutons, making it difficult to estimate the sub's evasive tactics. This sub skipper was no amateur. He used bursts of speed and sharp turns to confound his attackers. Hedgehogs were fired. The sound officer on *Bronstein* noted a sharp course change by the sub just after firing, too late for a correction maneuver with the missiles on their way. The U-boat captain displayed an ability and courage to go to the last second when he expected his pursuer to fire his weapons before making an evasive maneuver.

Even under the best of circumstances it was not easy to regain contact. In the process of making a hedgehog or depth charge attack, contact was lost when the range narrowed down to a few yards. After the attack, the ship's own wake acted as a sonic barrier. In this case, the problem was magnified by the unclear echoes from the sub. However, contact was regained at 800 yards.

In spite of difficulties, a second attack was pressed home. Within the short time span between contact regained and the second firing of hedgehogs, it was apparent that the submarine was moving away. In the final stage of this attack, the sub turned sharply right. Her course change was made just before firing and loss of contact, when the CIC plotters might know what the sub was up to. This information was fed into the firing mechanism to give the missile flight a right bias. Nonetheless, there was no explosion to signal a hit. The U-boat had outwitted her attacker a second time.

A short time later, *Block Island* signalled *Bronstein* to return. Steaming toward her assigned station, *Bronstein* sonarmen picked up yet another contact (*U-603*) at 1900 yards from the carrier. The U-boat was almost directly beneath *Bronstein*, apparently about to torpedo the carrier. Lieutenant Kinney ordered depth charges dropped and opined to his executive officer, Lieutenant Robert Coe, "A depth charge has a magnificent laxative effect on a submariner."

Bronstein laid an 18 charge pattern. Just before the last of the explosions, a U-boat torpedo detonated under her stern. Although the ship's hull had not been pierced, her electrical system was knocked out, stopping the diesel electric engines. The force of the explosion was such that it lifted the alidade from its stand on the bridge, sailed it over Kinney's head and landed it on the forecastle. *Bronstein* was dead in the water, and Lieutenant Walker P. Youngblood's engineers scrambled to make repairs. Fifteen minutes dragged on like hours. *Bronstein*, the target of U-boat attacks, lay rolling defenseless in the seaway.

> "I've never heard anything as sweet as the sound of those diesels when they finally started," said Kinney. "Why we weren't attacked during that time, I'll never know. It was a fatal error on the part of the skipper of *U-603*, because, as soon as we were underway again, we made contact and sank him."

Bronstein crisscrossed the area, tracking and attacking with hedgehogs and depth charges. As *Thomas* and *Bostwick* continued their search, *Bronstein* repeatedly attacked. Finally, a *Bronstein* sonarman reported that the sounds of the submarine's screws were fading as the U-boat sank to the bottom. After the war, German records confirmed the kill.

The Task Group steamed into Casablanca on 8 March for refueling and a few days rest before sailing to hunt a fueler submarine reported to be operating with several others off the Cape Verde Islands.

16 March. Aircraft from *Block Island* attacked a sub which promptly submerged, then followed up with several disappearing contacts. At sundown, CTG directed *Corry* to proceed to the target area, 23 miles distant. Other escorts stayed in the *Block Island* screen, trailing *Corry*. From the action report of *Bronstein*:

> "Frequent countermarches were necessary in order to recover or launch aircraft, and little progress was made in the direction of the contact. Flying operations were conducted throughout the night. It was later learned that aircraft had killed two men on the U-boat and put her periscope out of commission. By the time *Corry* reached the position, the submarine had again submerged, and *Corry* searched throughout the night."

0717 on 17 March. CTG ordered *Bronstein* to assist *Corry* in her search. *Bronstein* promptly headed for the destroyer, taking a position 2500 yards on her port beam. *Corry*, being senior, was in tactical command. The two vessels conducted a box search, a series of ever widening squares moving out from the center. An airplane seven miles to the north was seen circling continuously. Fifty minutes later, the same plane dropped smoke flares and requested the ships to investigate an oil slick marked by the flares. The two ships proceeded to the head of the streak, thence on a course along its track.

1042. *Bronstein* established sonar contact and promptly closed the target. The contact was identified as a submarine by the target width on the sonar recorder screen, nature of the echo, recorder traces, range rate of seven knots and moderate down doppler. The submarine was turning left. Constant information as to target course and speed and recommended courses kept flowing from the executive officer at CIC to the conning station. *Corry* stood by.

Bronstein fired a full hedgehog pattern but without effect. Contact was lost, then regained on the port quarter. The return sonar echoes were sharp and clear. The skipper opened the range to 1000 yards for maneuvering room and another attack. Pursuer and pursued approached each other rapidly, confirmed by up doppler. A hedgehog pattern was fired. The depth recorder indicated 360 feet. Since the depth of the ocean floor was 2600 fathoms, the 360 foot reading could only have been the sub. They missed.

Bronstein regained contact on her starboard quarter. She circled slowly to open the range and attack again. Submarine propeller noises could be heard by their hydrophone effect in the sonar. The hedgehog attack missed. As before, the DE had passed directly over the sub with fathometer running and pointing to 240 feet. This decreasing depth of the sub indicated that it was slowly rising. With this acquired knowledge, the captain felt that a depth charge attack might be more effective.

1106. Contact was regained on the starboard quarter. *Bronstein* circled slowly, opening the range to 1200 yards, and preparing a depth charge attack. Speed was increased to 15 knots, a prescribed depth charge attack speed to get the DE beyond the damaging range of its own depth charge explosions. Eighteen depth charges were dropped. Boils rose to the surface and exploded water and black smoke into the air. Down below a German crew felt the compression and vibrations, saw instrument needles go awry, insulation crack off the bulkheads, lights dim or go out. Some cursed; others prayed.

A huge air slug came to the surface in the vicinity of two depth charge explosions. It was considerably larger than the depth charge disturbances and very turbulent, so much so that it excited a spontaneous cheer from topside personnel. It stood out in green very clearly against the black-brown color of the depth charge boils and the blue of the ocean. A later examination of the plot showed this attack to be extremely accurate and must have jarred the submarine considerably. Some oil in the water was noticed.

Bronstein opened out to reattack. Contact was regained but it was in the depth charge disturbance area, casting doubt on whether it was the sub or the turbulence. Two sweeps were made through the area. No patterns were dropped because the echo was doubtful and it was desired to keep the area clear of depth charge disturbances. *Bronstein* did not want to give the sub the opportunity to escape behind the resultant sound interference. Later results indicated that the sub was actually in the disturbance and creeping away at minimal speed. The contact probably was the submarine after all.

1131. *Corry* moved in to take up the search. *Bronstein* moved out to circle the area. *Corry* gained sound contact and attacked with depth charges. *Corry* and *Bronstein* commenced an "unwinding clock" search with *Corry* in tactical command. *Corry* made two more depth charge attacks without result and lost contact. Her attempt to regain contact was unsuccessful, and *Bronstein* joined the search. This went on for almost one anxious hour, but patience and perseverance together were the name of the game in antisubmarine warfare.

1315. *Corry* gained contact and went in on the attack, dropped a full pattern of depth charges, then opened the range for a second attack. *Bronstein* paralleled *Corry* on her starboard quarter. What about the crews of both ships that had been at battle stations over three hours since first gaining contact? Waiting for something to happen is one of the most trying aspects of war. Gun crews remained silent; they were constantly informed. There was a sub in the depths nearby.

They saw hedgehogs fly into the air and dive on their prey. They knew the submarine could surface at any time, and they had to be ready. Gunners looked down their sights in anticipation. Would they ever get to squeeze the firing keys? They also knew that other destroyers and destroyer escorts had been literally blown out of the water by torpedoes. It could go either way. But now they didn't have to wait longer; the adrenaline suddenly began to flow.

1318. The bow of the submarine broke water astern of *Corry*! All guns on *Bronstein* that could bear opened up immediately as she turned to avoid fouling *Corry's* range. (Fouling another ship's range is a naval expression for getting in the way or moving between the target and the firing ship.)

The conning tower came into view and then the decks. Underwater, a sub was always at a great advantage oversurface vessels. It operated in three dimensions as compared to the surface vessel's two. It was an electronic war, visually blind and with detection instruments limited in effectiveness. Once forced to surface, however, a submarine was out of its element. It was overwhelmed by superior fire power. This was the position of the U-boat when she was forced to abandon her sanctuary of the deep.

Bronstein scored hits with her main 3" battery on the third salvo and continued throughout the engagement in a rapid pointer fire mode. (Gun captains fired at will rather than centralized control). *Corry's* fire was excellent too, and it was assumed that the majority of damage was caused by her larger guns. Captain Kinney stated in his action report that both ships were consistently on the target. It was impossible to state the exact number of hits because they couldn't distinguish between those scored by one ship or the other. Most hits were on the conning tower which was enveloped in smoke.

The 40mm fire was not as accurate as the 3" but it made up with many hits. 20mm fire was short at first, but the gunners soon elevated sufficiently to come on target. The submarine began to settle by the stern, dead in the water. The conning tower disappeared, but the bow twisted around as though the ship had turned turtle and then disappeared beneath the waves. The *Kriegsmarine* would have no further contact with *Unterseeboot 801*.

Thirty-seven prisoners were taken aboard *Bronstein* and several were rescued by *Corry*. Brought aboard *Bronstein* were an officer who appeared to be the captain and two chief petty officers. They were separated from the men. All were searched on coming aboard and then marched forward to the forecastle under guard. They were not allowed to converse with each other.

A wheel, part of a coding machine, was found upon the officer. He had supported and towed a wounded man to the ship's side, and the wheel was taken from him as soon as he reached the rail. Probably, he put the wheel in his pocket before abandoning the submarine and, in the excitement, neglected to get rid of it in the water. The wheel was slightly bent and the wiring broken, implying that it had been wrenched from the encoding/decoding machine; it was transferred to *Block Island*. (This discovery caused all action reports to be classified as secret instead of simply confidential).

Bronstein transferred prisoners to *Corry* for further transfer to *Block Island*. Two stretcher cases were moved after treatment by pharmacist mates, one badly burned, and the other with severe shrapnel wounds. *Bronstein* rejoined *Block Island* and resumed her station in the ASW screen. Sonarman Gantt remembered that famous cruise:

> "We would be at battle stations for hours. We knew the submarine was there. We knew we would get him, hopefully before he got us. We were exercising our training in technology of the weapons at hand. We were fortunate to have sunk the enemy before he gave us a torpedo. We are credited with involvement in four U-boat sinkings with survivors from one. We had been stalking the last sub for five hours. Finally, he broke the surface. We had a turkey shoot!"

For the actions on the night of 29 February, 1 March 1944, and on 16-17 March 1944, Lieutenant Kinney received the Navy Cross, and his crew received the Presidential Unit Citation.

Lieutenant Kinney was barely into his 25th year when he commissioned *Bronstein*. He had served as engineer, first lieutenant and gunnery officer in the *Sturtevant (DD-240)* until sunk, earned the Navy and Marine Corps Medal for heroism in lifesaving, and then commissioned and commanded *Edsall (DE-129)* before taking command of *Bronstein*.

THE SECOND BLOCK ISLAND HUNTER-KILLER GROUP

In the first week of operations of the second *Block Island* Group, two submarines were sunk. The first U-boat was killed by a carrier pilot who spotted it lying on the surface with its crew enjoying a swim! The other U-boat dispatched was by *Buckley (DE-51)*. The release of classified documents surrounding the *Block Island* and a division of valiant little destroyer escorts unfolded a history of one of the most stirring epics of the *Battle of the Atlantic*.

The new escorts were *Ahrens (DE-575)*, *Eugene E. Elmore (DE-686)*, *Barr (DE-576)*, *Robert I. Paine (DE-578)* and *Buckley*. (*Robert I. Paine* had relieved *Buckley* after the damage sustained by the latter in battle with *U-66*.)

The story is a drama in two acts. In act one, *Buckley* sank a submarine in a knock down, drag out fight not seen since President Jefferson's war with the Barbary pirates. In another act, *Block Island* was sunk by a U-boat, *Barr* torpedoed and crippled, and *Ahrens* simultaneously directing the sinking of a submarine while rescuing some 700 of the *Block Island* survivors.

The Destroyer Escort Buckley

> "The night was brilliantly moonlit, with the moon 25 degrees above the horizon to the west. The sea was calm with a gentle breeze blowing from the northwest," from the action report filed by Lieutenant Commander Brent M. Abel, commanding officer of *Buckley*."

The sea has known many such nights and days of high adventure, mizzen tops, grappling irons, boarding parties. Destroyer escorts in 1944 were replete with radar, sonar, remote control gadgets, and a myriad of ways to kill an enemy without seeing him. Firing a pistol point blank into his face, braining him with an empty shell case, bashing his teeth out with one's fist could hardly be an action report of a destroyer escort captain in the twentieth century. But it was!

Perhaps this is the profound, symbolic way of the sea. Perhaps, amid the arts of war, it is inevitable that there must be a time when electronics and ballistics are replaced by raw combat. When this does happen, the lonely captain walks with his antecedents, the shades of Jones, Perry and Decatur. A great sea tradition was a challenge to uphold in a short but fateful time frame for the captain, officers and men of *Buckley*. Sixteen minutes saw the DE victor over the German submarine *U-66* in an action that involved main battery, automatic weapons, tommy guns, rifles, pistols, hand grenades, crockery, fists and knees on a beautiful, calm, moonlit night.

Block Island (CVE-21) and the escorts in Hunter-Killer Task Group 21.11, commanded by Captain F.M. Hughes, departed from Norfolk on 22 April 1944 with orders to relieve the *Croatan* Hunter-Killer Group west of the Cape Verde Islands and to operate offensively against enemy submarines in that area. German U-boat activity in this location indicated the presence of a fueler.

29 April. TG 21.11, arrived in the prescribed area and commenced search operations. Two days later, intelligence reported a submarine within 150 miles of the Task Group and, about midnight, a plane made radar contact on the U-boat, now only 60 miles from them. Thus began the lethal hide and seek game of antisubmarine warfare. Persistent scouting brought intermittent sightings of the sub by aircraft during the next four days and nights, whenever she surfaced to charge her batteries.

On the night of 5 May, after a lost contact, a plane reported a U-boat 20 miles from the HUK formation, maneuvering evasively and not attempting to submerge. Perhaps her batteries were exhausted, and she was charging them by running on the surface under diesel power. Captain Hughes on *Block Island* ordered *Buckley* to investigate. The plane, being on a reconnaissance patrol, was unarmed. However, the pilot, with the sub and DE in his radar at once, fed a stream of information to *Buckley*, keeping her CIC plotters advised of course or speed changes. *Buckley* raced toward her mortal enemy.

A ship of war is without a peep of light at night. On the flying bridge, the captain glanced at his luminous dials, faintly green enough to be read only right there. A few orders went down the brass voice tubes to the helmsman, to the combat information center (CIC), and acknowledgements wound their soft way up the tubes to the flying bridge. The crew was kept informed; the short time before battle is for very personal reflection.

There is an uneasy feeling near a submarine in the moonlight, very much in the captain's thoughts. The moon could alter the outcome. There formed in his mind an observation drawn from experience in the ways of the sea. *Buckley* would approach from down moon, seeking a silhouetted submarine, while remaining obscure!

Listening to the TBS on the flying bridge was like a voice from another world. But the voice was very near, and the occasional drone of an engine proved the plane's proximity, a lone pilot who would soon have to find a small, unlit flight deck on a great sea.

Once accustomed to the distant throb of the engines and the soft sigh of sea and wind, one can hear a pin drop on the flying bridge. In this silence, a pattern formed in the captain's mind. At times, the U-boat lay to, at times it roamed in circles or proceeded on a steady course. This surely was either the fueler awaiting a rendezvous or a U-boat awaiting the fueler. The Officer of The Deck could see the radar antenna rotating, probing, and he knew it saw what he could not yet see. Instinctively, he looked at the alarm lever so that there would be no fumbling when the order came "General Quarters!"

Throughout the ship, the urgent bongbong brought every man to his feet who was not already on them. Radar contact due north, range seven miles. The Boatswain's Mate of the Watch stepped up to the address speaker and boomed: "Man your battle stations! This is NOT a drill!"

As *Buckley* raced through the night, the skipper weighed his options. When should he open fire? If he fired at long range, the sub might submerge and escape. If he waited for close range, his shots would likely be true if the sub waited for that to happen. Even if located on sonar after going under, the chances were markedly less for a kill than if she were caught on the surface close aboard. He opted for the latter, delayed fire. He would see the sub before she saw him. She was likely waiting for another sub and was unaware of *Buckley's* approach. The luck factor - he crossed his fingers.

0300. Range 9000 yards. *Buckley* streamed her FXR. Gunners gasped as the U-boat fired three red flares, a prearranged recognition signal for another U-boat. The speed came from the motor and boiler rooms beneath the waterline where sweating and now silent men watched gauges, levers, rheostats and thermostats. Torpedo talk was taboo. To hear fighting without participating, to feel the impact of steel against steel without seeing, to sense the acrid gunpowder without smelling, that was a brand of stoicism unknown to the rest.

0317. Range 4000 yards. The sub came into full view. Its long, low cigar shape with conning tower was unmistakable. As *Buckley* men saw the sub, they also saw a white streak of foam on the starboard bow. "Torpedo off the starboard bow!"

An evasive maneuver let the white wake pass down the starboard side. Shocked and aware that *Buckley* was not a companion U-boat, the submarine fired the torpedo and opened a scattered but inaccurate 20mm burst against the hull of the oncoming DE.

0320. Range, point blank, 2100 yards. "Commence fire!"

Three 3" shells leaped from *Buckley* with tails of red orange flame, and one of them struck the foc's'l of the sub just forward of the deck gun, disabling the gun momentarily. *Buckley* immediately shifted into rapid fire with her 3" main battery, 40mm and 20mm guns. The gunnery officer sped ranges and deflections to all gun stations. Pointer (local, not centralized) firing was permitted to individual gun captains throughout the engagement. From *Buckley* to *Block Island*, "Attacking U-boat!"

0322. Recovered from the initial surprise, and maneuvering rapidly, the U-boat slipped out of the moon wake, *Buckley* thereby losing her greatest initial advantage. The sub's deck gun was now back in action and firing rapidly together with her 20mm guns. The sub's aim, at first, was high. A shell went through *Buckley's* smoke stack, then there were splashes all around, as close as 25 yards.

A quick turn by *Buckley* had the dual effect of confounding the sub's ranges and putting her back up moon on *Buckley's* starboard bow, range 1500 yards. After their first taste of powder, *Buckley's* gunners were extremely accurate. Hits from her 20mm and 40mm guns splattered the conning tower. The U-boat, turning her stern tubes to the DE, fired another torpedo. Again, the wake was seen in the phosphorescent sea, and a fast maneuver outwitted the torpedo. A fire burned on the sub's bridge until snuffed out by a 3" hit.

Range 500 yards. The gun flashes were blinding and deafening, an earsplitting roar. The blasts of the 3," 40mm, and 20mm blended into something unreal, as though all the demons of hell had been released simultaneously. Above the roar, the shouts of gun captains exhorted their crews to load and reload ever faster and faster. Blood was drawn. The quarry was at bay. The hunter was out to kill and to keep from being killed. The *U-66* was buried under a hail of withering point blank fire.

0328. The U-boat was 20 yards to starboard, zigzagging violently at 19 knots. Skipper Abel had to make a decision, one that could cost him his ship, his crew, his life. The U-boat was badly hurt. *Buckley* might have stood off and pounded it to bits. But, supposing the sub did aim a torpedo into *Buckley* and get away to be repaired and fight again? *Buckley* was expendable; transatlantic shipping was not. A DE captain had to know what to do at a time of decision. He decided to ram the U-boat!

0329. "Right full rudder!"

Hundreds of tons of steel clashed, twisted and ripped as *Buckley* rode up on the foc's'l of *U-66*!

There then occurred one of the most remarkable incidents of the Atlantic War as attributable to an extraordinary courage on the part of the enemy as to the valor of the *Buckley* crew. Men began swarming out of the conning tower and forward hatch of the submarine and up onto the foc's'l of *Buckley*. Because the sub was now below the maximum depression of the DE's guns, a bitter fight had suddenly become man-to-man for the possession of *Buckley*!

Surprised at first, the *Buckley* men rallied quickly. Forward gun crews met the boarders with a formidable hail of general mess coffee mugs. Empty shell cases were highly effective, as were fists, knees and feet. One boarder had his brains bashed out with a 3" shell case. From the bridge, the captain saw a man smash a boarder in the face with his fist, sending him spinning headlong into the sea. The boatswain's mate in charge of the forward ammunition party fired his .45 into a German's teeth as he vainly tried to board the DE.

Men of the midships repair party, having equipped themselves from the small arms locker, manned the starboard life lines with rifles and shot down several of the sub crew as they tried to board. The chief fire controlman mounted to the bridge with his tommy gun and wreaked havoc with a group attempting to come over the side.

0330. The enemy persisted in boarding. Men on the foc's'l were locked in combat, some rolling on the deck, grappling, pummeling, kicking. Captain Abel had to make another decision. If too many boarders got on, they might reach the bridge or engine room. Better to break it up and attack again. Engines were reversed as *Buckley* backed away from the sub. The remainder of the boarders, now only five, disheartened and cut off from reinforcement, surrendered their arms and went aft under guard.

0331. "All engines ahead full!" Now, the guns could bear again. Gun crews who, only a moment before, were grappling with the enemy, were back at gun stations and pouring a living hell of fire into *U-66*. Hits rained on her bridge, conning tower and deck. It seemed a miracle that a ship could take that much punishment and float, let alone move at 19 knots. Alongside the U-boat to starboard, range 25 yards, Captain Abel fully intended to ram again, but he didn't.

The sub rammed the DE!

U-66 veered sharply to port and struck under the after engine room of *Buckley*. In a vain effort to save the starboard shaft, Captain Abel stopped the starboard engine, but the shaft and propeller were sheared clean off. The *Buckley's* deck crew could look right into the conning tower which was a flaming shambles. Yet, even with *Buckley* sitting on the sub, a German crewman ran toward his deck gun and attempted to man it; he disintegrated when hit by a 40mm shell. The torpedomen threw a couple of hand grenades, one of which went through the conning tower hatch and exploded inside!

U-66 was a blaze of death and horror; her decks were wet with blood. With a twisting, scraping and groaning of steel plates, the sub drew aft and cleared under *Buckley's* stern. She popped up right under number three 3" gun which scored three hits on the conning tower.

0336. Raked fore and aft by a merciless fire, with towers of flame and smoke belching from her open conning tower and forward hatch, *U-66* rode under the sea to her end. Violent underwater explosions marked her disintegration!

Buckley's casualties: Several bruises and a few bloody noses! Ammunition expenditure in 16 minutes of combat, all types, except nonqualifying coffee mugs: 3585 rounds. For the next three hours, *Buckley* steamed about the area and recovered thirty-six prisoners, including four officers. The captain of the submarine did not survive, but the executive officer, *Oberleutnant* Klaus Herbig, was taken prisoner. Years later, Herbig set down his version of the boarding (abridged):

> "As I came up onto the bridge, our commander was again standing, but the destroyer (DE *Buckley*) was on our port side, with its crew preparing to board and capture our ship (not so). The commander ordered me to take all the men on the bridge and jump over to the destroyer to prevent a boarding by the Americans. Boarding would have meant scuttling our boat with part of the crew still below decks, destroying classified equipment. Our sub now rammed the destroyer in the propeller on her starboard side.
>
> The chief engineer, Olschewski, was the last person on board our sub. Many must have been killed while abandoning. The engineer left with the waves foaming over the bridge. Now the destroyer ceased firing and began picking men out of the water. This action by the American commander was very commendable, a deed we appreciated very much. We were badly shaken when we surveyed our small group of survivors and realized how many of our comrades, with whom we had made many dangerous voyages, no longer lived."

Vincenz Nosch, an Austrian Seaman First Class, wrote a good deal about his sub's encounter with *Buckley* (abridged):

> "A grenade exploded in our boat. The lights went off. There was a smell of powder, you could hear water pouring in. There was a command, "Everyone out of the boat." It was chaotic everybody ran to the same exit, all trying to get out of the tower and overboard whenever there was a pause in the firing. As I entered the tower, Seamen Jahn and Sundermann, badly injured and lying on the deck, asked to be taken along. The first one had his arm blown off. My comrade Ronge and I climbed up on the bridge; We saw our dead comrades lying around next to the 3.7 centimeter cannon.
>
> During a pause in the fire, Ronge yelled I should jump overboard and swim with him to the destroyer. Unfortunately, he mistimed his jump and fell between the approaching destroyer and our boat. I jumped away on the starboard side. While swimming, I saw our boat sink tail first. Since I knew there were no ship routes in the area, I wanted to surrender. I prayed. I hoped I would be saved. At daylight, I suddenly saw an airplane and a flare. After swimming in the Atlantic for almost four hours, I saw a mast on the horizon, and I was picked up by a destroyer *(DE Buckley)*."

In the morning, *Buckley* rejoined *Block Island* and fueled. It was a tremendous triumphal experience for Captain Abel, his officers and men when the crew of the carrier lined the rail to give *Buckley* the rousing cheer she so richly deserved. What a show! What a fight!

With her starboard shaft gone, flooded compartments and widespread damage, the Commander-in-Chief Atlantic Fleet ordered *Buckley* detached from the Task Group and to proceed to the New York Navy Shipyard, a trip which she made on her port screw without incident.

End of the Block Island

One of the sensational stories of the Battle of the Atlantic is that of *Ahrens* on her first war patrol. Commander Morgan H. Harris, renowned Boston yachtsman, was her captain on 29 May 1944. Previously, he had been awarded the Legion of Merit for outstanding services as skipper of a minesweeper during the invasion of Sicily. He was now to be awarded a Gold Star by Admiral Ingersoll, Commander in Chief Atlantic Fleet, for commendable conduct immediately following the sinking of *Block Island* and the damaging of *Barr*.

Ahrens was patrolling off the port bow of *Block Island* when two torpedoes struck the carrier, one in the bow and the other in the stern. As the carrier lost headway, her four destroyer escorts concentrated on a search for the underwater attacker. *Block Island* ordered *Elmore* to attack but, before *Elmore* could do so, a third torpedo hit *Block Island*, leaving her dead in the water.

Upon finding communication severed with the stricken carrier, Commander Harris, as senior DE escort officer, assumed tactical command and directed an attack on the U-boat while conducting rescue of the carrier's survivors. Less than 15 minutes after the first torpedo hit the carrier, an acoustic "fish" slammed into the stern of *Barr*, rendering that vessel inoperative.

The commanding officer of *Barr*, Lieutenant Commander H.H. Love, was in his cabin writing his night orders when General Quarters were sounded by the Officer of The Deck after witnessing two explosions on the port side of *Block Island*. The skipper recalled:

> "Proceeding immediately to the bridge, I looked at the carrier through my glasses. All I noticed were two planes which appeared to have slid from the flight deck into the net aft. My first reaction was that there had been an explosion on her deck."

The carrier commenced to settle. Realizing that she had been torpedoed, Captain Love ordered full speed toward the port quarter of the carrier from where he assumed the torpedoes had been fired.

Elmore evidently had the same idea as both DEs were proceeding in the same general direction. When the distance to the carrier was down to 2000 yards, *Elmore* claimed sighting the submarine's periscope approximately 800 yards on the starboard quarter of the carrier. She immediately altered course to lay an embarrassing barrage. However, Captain Love on *Barr* held to his original estimate, namely that the submarine was still ahead and roughly on his course.

Barr reduced speed in order to permit operation of the sound gear. Eight minutes went by without having gained contact. Suddenly, there was a terrific explosion on the stern which either blew away or flooded the after section of the DE. *Barr* was brought to a dead stop with the water around her covered with debris and bodies! Her FXR had not been streamed. The captain's action report explained:

> "As soon as it (FXR) was received in inventory, its streaming was part of our battle bill and the automatic function of repair party three. However, in the type of HUK action that we normally expected, we could not use our FXR. When interacting with planes, the noise interfered with their sono buoys. Therefore, the automatic feature of FXR streaming was deleted. In the excitement of the carrier being torpedoed and the intense anxiety to get the submarine, the command to stream the FXR was never given."

Seaman Andrew C. Soucy recalled the trials of *Barr*:

> "While fueling earlier that day, maple walnut ice cream and the carrier's newspaper were sent over to our ship, and the crew settled down for the long trip back home. Suddenly, two explosions and smoke came from the side of the carrier. The *Barr* crew knew that the carrier had taken hits and the men were at their battle stations in a matter of seconds after the sounding of GQ. *Barr*, being in the most distant station from the Task Group, was able to estimate the sub's position in little time. She maneuvered to launch a full depth charge attack when she was suddenly hit in the stern by an acoustic torpedo."

Adding to the problem, the ship's whistle was jolted to the open position and, amid escaping steam and exploding depth charges, caused great confusion. The captain was unable to give orders, even by screaming in the ears of his talkers. Some thought the whistle was being blown as a signal to abandon. Nobody left the ship, however, although someone cut loose one of her life rafts. After a minute or so, the executive officer, Lieutenant Commander P.T. Dickie, calmly climbed the smokestack and shut off the steam.

The first lieutenant could not immediately assess damage but he did not consider the ship in immediate danger of sinking. Internal electric communication circuits were restored. The captain then cautioned the crew that, because the ship was dead in the water, it was possible that the submarine might take another shot at the ship. He urged all hands to remain at their battle stations and not to succumb to panic. All flying bridge and most of the CIC personnel, no longer needed at their stations, were sent aft to assist the doctor in caring for the dead and wounded and to help control the damage.

In record time, the first lieutenant made a detailed report to the effect that two compartments were flooded and everything aft was either completely blown off or raised up out of the water. Fires on the main deck aft and in number two engine room were extinguished.

The executive officer, the first lieutenant and the captain sized up the situation. Areas up to the after bulkhead of number two engine room were flooded. If the ship were to remain afloat, buoyancy had to be maintained forward of the engine room bulkhead, and the dead weight astern had to be removed. All available hands were engaged throughout the night in jettisoning depth charges, K guns, number three 3" gun and anything else removable, lightening the stern by approximately 35,000 pounds. Fuel oil adrift negated use a cutting torch.

All available submersible pumps, handy billies and fire and bilge pumps were used to pump out the flooded compartments. Leaks were stuffed to a point where the water could be controlled by the bilge pump in number two engine room alone.

As *Elmore* and *Paine* continued their search for the sub, *Ahrens* concentrated on rescuing *Block Island* survivors. The carrier's stern was down and she was broken amidships. All hands were abandoning her, and the planes aloft were directed to the nearest island. Survivors were taken aboard *Ahrens* from floater nets, cargo nets and sea ladders. While conducting rescue operations, she made contact on the sub. Because *Elmore* was nearer to the U-boat, Commander Harris held his ship immobile and directed *Elmore* to attack. *Paine* was ordered to stand by the two damaged ships.

Lieutenant Commander G.L. Conkey, captain of the *Eugene E. Elmore*, conned his ship so as to locate the sub in record time. *Elmore* delivered an accurate and lethal hedgehog assault on the enemy, subsequently identified as *U-549*. Three detonations were followed by a tremendous fourth explosion, marking the destruction of the U-boat.

Debris was clogging *Ahrens'* circulating pumps, making it urgent to get underway. Commander Harris ordered *Paine* to rescue the remaining *Block Island* survivors (over 250). The count aboard *Ahrens* was 73 officers and 601 men in addition to the DE crew of 200. A full complement on a warship normally occupied all berthing space. Increasing the complement by 350 percent was a huge burden on all facilities. Nonetheless, the survivors were happy to be alive, and the *Ahrens* crew cheerfully accepted their sacrifices.

Captain F. Massie Hughes, resumed command of the Task Group in the extremely crowded quarters of *Ahrens*. About 1-1/2 hours after she was first hit, *Block Island* went to the bottom. *Elmore* was directed to stand by *Barr* and take her in tow in the morning.

Daylight checkup revealed that five of the *Block Island's* crew had been killed in torpedo explosions, and only one of the entire ship's company was missing. Of the six fighter pilots who were directed to the nearest island, two made water landings and were picked up, but the other four failed to reach safety.

The search for survivors concluded in the morning, 30 May, and the voyage to Casablanca got underway. With nearly 900 aboard *Ahrens*, there was barely room to move; some survivors hardly left one spot over the entire three day period. As many as five rescued men were stretched across a single bunk, while others took turns sleeping on the decks. Although only two meals a day could be provided, nobody complained. The crew supplied dry clothes for the survivors.

Throughout the night, the *Barr* crew remained at GQ, mostly concerned with damage control and care of the wounded, with *Elmore* circling for their protection. The stricken DE had suffered severe personnel casualties: four dead, 12 missing, and 14 injured.

At first light, *Elmore* came close aboard *Barr* to receive her injured plus 91 uninjured, leaving on board only those needed for damage control. *Barr* was taken in tow by *Elmore* and headed for Casablanca at four or five knots, accompanied by *Ahrens* and *Paine*. During the towing, lost shipmates, were buried at sea with full military honors on this Memorial Day.

At 1910, *Evarts (DE-5)* and *Wilhoite (DE-397)* joined *Barr*, relieving *Ahrens* and *Paine* to proceed to Casablanca with *Block Island* survivors. (*Evarts* and *Wilhoite* had just reached port after a heavy engagement with the *Luftwaffe* in convoy UGS 40; see chapter *Convoys to the Mediterranean*. They were rushed to the scene of the *Block Island, Barr* disasters. A short time later, the seaplane tender *Humboldt (AVP-21)* joined the formation.

Barr suddenly developed a marked list to port, caused by a crack in the skin of the ship from the effect of the sea on her damaged stern. The crack permitted water to enter a compartment which had previously been ballasted to an elevated position above the waterline. Pumps quickly dried it out and the cracks were stuffed with mattresses.

On 1 June, *Elmore* passed the tow to *Wilhoite*. *Barr* was slowly losing her fight to control the water aft. *Humboldt* came alongside with some additional pumps, enabling the crew to maintain buoyancy. Exhibiting superb seamanship, the men fastened the stern overhang with mooring lines, thereby stopping the leaks. An hour later, the Netherlands tug *Amtic* relieved *Wilhoite* of the tow. Tug and DE proceeded into Casablanca on 5 June without further incident. Captain Love summarized his action report:

> "The performance of personnel of this ship was highly satisfactory. With every man doing his duty so well, it is difficult to single out individuals deserving special mention. The commanding officer would like to list some who, by their utter disregard for their own safety in entering flooded compartments to remove dead and injured, by handling live ammunition and by their tireless efforts to keep the ship afloat, are deserving of special mention: Lieutenant Commander Porter T. Dickie, Lieutenant (jg) Franklin R. Navarro, Chief Boatswain's Mate Robert Franklin Payne, Sr., Seaman First Class Chester Roberts, Quartermaster Third Class William Rufus Armstrong, Fireman First Class James Robert Mack."

After undergoing emergency repairs at Casablanca, *Barr* was towed to the United States and entered a dry dock in the Charlestown Navy Yard, Boston, to be converted to a high speed transport and reclassified *APD-39* on 31 July 1944. Her adventures with launching underwater demolition teams in Pacific combat zones were accomplished without casualties. Prior to her last trip to the United States, she participated in evacuating Allied prisoners of war from Japan. See chapter *Iwo Jima to Okinawa – The High Speed Transports.*

THE CROATAN HUNTER-KILLERS

Phase I: Four U-boats Dispatched to the Bottom

On 24 March 1944, the escort aircraft carrier *Croatan (CVE-25)* stood out to sea from Norfolk, Virginia, accompanied by destroyer *Champlin (DD-601)* and destroyer escorts *Huse (DE-145), Frost (DE-144), Inch (DE-146), Snowden (DE-246), Barber (DE-161), Swasey (DE-248)* and *Stanton (DE-247)*. All were veterans of transatlantic convoys to the Mediterranean.

While undergoing training at Casco Bay, Maine, on 7 April 1944, an alarm indicated a submarine in the vicinity. *Champlin* and *Huse* were ordered to sea to intercept a suspected U-boat. Late that afternoon, the destroyer made sonar contact and dropped a pattern of deep–set depth charges, forcing the sub to the surface. *Champlin* and *Huse* opened fire, starting a furious blaze on her conning tower. *Champlin* dashed in for the kill, ramming her in the stern. With her hull ripped open to the sea, *U-856* plunged to the bottom just 1-1/2 hours after initial contact. The cost, however, included the commanding officer, Commander John J. Shaffer III, wounded by shrapnel from the sub during the attack. Despite emergency surgery, he died the next morning. Other ships arrived on the scene to assist in rescuing enemy survivors as *Huse* screened the rescuers against the possibility of another U-boat in the area.

On the same evening, *Huse* rejoined the Task Group and proceeded to Bermuda with a highly elated crew, having tasted their first enemy action. Although *Champlin* bore the brunt and got most of the credit for sinking the sub, it was nonetheless a first for *Huse*. On 12 April, Task Group 21.15 stood out to sea on another mission, to hunt submarines off the Cape Verde Islands. Action was not long in coming.

25 April. *Huse* and *Frost*, were detached from the screen to investigate a report by aircraft due west of the Cape Verde Islands. Just before dawn the next day, *Frost* gained a sonar contact and made a hedgehog attack, followed by three underwater explosions. *Huse* fired a hedgehog pattern 20 minutes later with no apparent results. *Inch* then joined the hunt. All three ships conducted a retiring search until recalled to the *Croatan* screen. Two days later, aircraft spotted a large oil slick rising to the surface. *Frost* and two other DEs proceeded to the area to make several depth charge attacks, obtaining a violent underwater explosion. Post war German naval records identified *U-488*, lost with all hands.

9 June. *Frost* and *Huse* were detached to investigate a contact. After an extensive search, the contact was classified as "possible but unlikely," and both vessels rejoined the screen. On the same evening, the duty radioman on *Inch* picked up a German message to her home base. Third Class Sonarman O.A. "Rocky" Schoenrock recalls:

> "The radio direction finder indicated a signal from the northeast. Contact with the Navy Department in Washington (Tenth Fleet) corroborated the same message. It was also received by a ship in the Mediterranean and another ship off Greenland. All bearings were accurate within five degrees. The Task Group now had a crossfix on the U-boat's position and proceeded at full speed toward the suspected submarine location. We arrived at a point southeast of England just after midnight on 11 June."

Minutes later, *Huse* intercepted a morse code transmission in German. She was detached from the screen to make a radar sweep 12 miles from the *Croatan* Group. After about eight hours, *Frost* gained a sonar contact, classified as definitely submarine. *Huse* was ordered to join *Frost* as an assisting ship. *Frost* fired a hedgehog pattern, obtaining three underwater explosions. Two minutes later, *Huse* gained a sonar contact and, after target evaluation, fired a full depth charge pattern. Throughout the long day, until dark, *Huse* and *Frost* carried out extensive, well coordinated depth charge and hedgehog attacks on the submarine. All sound contacts were good and sharp. Twelve hours had elapsed since *Frost* made her first attack, and the crews of both

DEs, still alert, awaited a surfaced sub, ready to battle it out. Their crews did not have to be reminded of the fate of the captain of the *Champlin*.

The loner, now cornered between Flores and Flemish Cap, was the 1600 ton *U-490*, outward bound for Penang, Sumatra, with supplies for the Indian Ocean raiders, a conclusion established by the Tenth Fleet. But *Oberleutnant* Wilhelm Gerlach, in command of *U-490*, had taken his big boat to a depth believed to be exceeding its designed maximum.

If the tension on the DEs was debilitating, it was mild by comparison with the crew of *U-490*, with their twisting, evasive maneuvers, trying to keep their undersea home from turning into their undersea coffin. They were damaged, the air was foul and deteriorating. There was no chance of finding a thermal gradient to hide under this day with the echo ranging "pings" bouncing back to the surface ships clear as a bell. Contact was maintained the whole day with the crew of *U-490* nearing the limit of endurance They began to panic as they listened helplessly to the recurrent explosions of depth charges, the continuous pinging of sonar, and the buzzing noise of the escorts' FXR that penetrated to them. A dozen guinea pigs which their surgeon had on board for some experiments panicked even more. They started squealing so loud that Gerlach ordered them killed for fear their shrill clamor might be picked up by American sound gear.

Huse had fired a total of six full depth charge and two hedgehog patterns. All attacks were considered excellent. An earlier attack at 1314 had brought up a large, persistent air bubble. Two creeping attacks were made, one by each ship with the other directing. At 1955, *Inch* relieved *Huse* because of the latter's heavy expenditure of depth charges. Midnight arrived without evidence of a kill, and the escorts decided to feign a withdrawal from the area, hoping the submarine would surface. Without hesitation, the sub popped up into the dark night. Seconds later, both DEs had radar contacts and promptly retraced their steps. Within half an hour, they had the U-boat in sight and took it under fire. "Rocky" recalls:

> "Star shells were fired, and we saw a huge tanker U-boat, obviously damaged, trying to escape on the surface. We scored several 3" and 40mm hits on her hull. Suddenly, her stern went down, and her bow pointed straight up as she slowly sank."

(The Tenth Fleet report indicated that the U-boat had signalled a surrender request, or something like it, which was not understood or not reported to Captain Vest, Task Force Commander). *Frost*, *Inch* and *Snowden* picked up survivors. Rocky says he never would forget:

> "It was a weird scene. The immediate area was filled with flickering, tiny lights, pinned to survivors' life jackets. Sixty members of the U-boat crew were rescued by three DEs, including my ship. One man refused to come aboard for whatever reason. After several attempts to reach him, we abandoned him to his fate. It was quite crowded with the addition of that many passengers. They were housed in the head and were given cots to sleep on. Armed guards covered both exits."

As the only American aboard who could speak German, Rocky was ordered by the captain to interrogate each of the prisoners. Much information about the U-boat was revealed by her crew. Especially interesting was the claimed ability of the U-boat to dive to the incredible depth of 1300 feet! (This was either a gross exaggeration or shocking news to our ASW experts.) She was on her maiden voyage out of Hamburg. The POWs were aboard about three days until the weather calmed. They were then put aboard the carrier by way of a breeches buoy.

On 14 June, one of *Croatan's* planes crashed into the sea while attempting to land. *Huse* proceeded at full speed to the scene of the accident and picked up the three-man crew.

In the dawn of 17 June, *Huse* made another HFDF (High Frequency Direction Finder) contact, identified as a ground wave from an enemy submarine radio transmission. The contact was investigated, but nothing further could be found. The following day, a torpedo bomber from *Croatan*, crashed, and *Inch* rescued its crew.

Arriving in Casablanca, French Morocco, on 26 June, the POWs from *U-490* were put ashore; many appeared pleased that their war was over. Uncharacteristically, the German captain, who had been on *Inch*, wished her crew God speed on its voyage.

Steaming on a westerly course on 3 July, *Inch* reported a sound contact classified as probable submarine. What happened thereafter is graphically described by Rocky Schoenrock on *Inch*:

> "The chance engagement with a U-boat occurred off the African coast, somewhere near the Azores. We were cruising, waiting for Washington to advise the location of a submarine. However, we had no indication that there was one under our noses. Our sound operator picked up an echo, sending us to GQ. I took over the sound stack (my GQ station). As soon as I heard the echoes, I realized the sub was only about 100 feet deep, and the doppler indicated it was headed directly toward us. I only got a few echoes before I heard the hissing sound of a torpedo. I announced that fact to the bridge and simultaneously lost contact due to the proximity of the submarine. We were headed directly toward the U-boat. It being no longer necessary for me to stay at the stack, I ran out on the bridge to prepare for an explosion I looked over the side in time to see the torpedo streak on by about 10 feet away from the hull! An order had been given to stream FXR, and sure enough the torpedo headed for it and blew up well astern! Our hedgehogs were fired dead ahead when we lost contact, followed by k-guns and depth charges from the stern.
>
> We returned to the area and echo ranged again when we saw debris floating all about. A motor whale boat was lowered, and evidence retrieved indicated the sub could not have survived. We searched and echo ranged the entire area but could not pick up anything. Later, we learned that we had destroyed *U-154*."

On 22 August, another torpedo bomber from *Croatan* crashed into the sea. *Huse* proceeded at top speed to the scene, but all attempts to recover the pilot were unsuccessful.

On 1 September, still another torpedo bomber from *Croatan* crashed into the sea while taking off. The aerial torpedo (acoustic) from the crashed aircraft was seen in the water, making an erratic run on the surface. Engines were stopped and guns were manned to fire on the torpedo if necessary. It passed 150 yards ahead of *Huse* and headed toward *Croatan*, sending the carrier to flank speed to avoid it while opening fire with her 20mm and 40mm guns to destroy it. *Huse* rescued one survivor from the aircraft; the other two were lost.

Again, on 3 September, *Huse* was ordered to effect rescue of a crashed plane crew. This time, fortunately, she was able to rescue all three from a raft.

Underway from Bermuda on 11 September, the Task Group was ordered to rescue the crew of the destroyer *Warrington (DD-383)*, capsized and foundered in a furious Caribbean hurricane. *Huse* was ordered to transfer the division medical officer to the refrigerator ship *Hyades (AF-28)* to assist a number of injured survivors on board. *Huse* then lowered a whaleboat to recover six survivors from a raft, all suffering from exposure, shock, immersion, and minor abrasions. *Swasey* and *Frost* also lowered their whaleboats, recovering between them nine swimmers and 57 fatalities; the latter were buried at sea.

The first day of October found the Task Group again heading for the New York Navy Yard, marking the end of Phase I of the operations of the *Croatan* HUK Group. Four U-boats would never again prey on Allied shipping, but this was not the end. Three more would be dispatched to the bottom by this group; see chapter *Twilight of the U-boats*.

THE GUADALCANAL HUNTER-KILLERS

Phase I: The Sinking of U-515

Escort Division 4 was formed in January 1944 and included *Chatelain (DE-149)*, *Pope (DE-134)*, *Neunzer (DE-150)*, *Flaherty (DE-135)* and *Pillsbury (DE-133)* with the pennant of Commander F.S. Hall.

Homeward bound from the Mediterranean, *CortDiv 4* escorted five surrendered Italian submarines. En route, the DEs held ASW exercises with them after sending American sailors of Italian background to the submarines as interpreters. Joe Abbato from *Chatelain* typically recalled "family" Italian, but neither naval nomenclature nor jargon. After a few near collisions, the practice was discontinued.

On 7 March, *CortDiv 4* was assigned to the HUK (Hunter-Killer) Task Group 21.12, centered on *Guadalcanal (CVE-60)*, commanded by Captain Dan Gallery. Their orders: "Hunt and destroy German submarines anywhere in the Atlantic Ocean."

Twice in the early morning of 9 April, planes from *Guadalcanal* attacked a surfaced sub. She dived both times after returning fire from the aircraft. *Pillsbury* and *Flaherty* arrived at the scene 45 minutes later. *Pillsbury* gained sonar contact and made two hedgehog attacks while *Flaherty* conducted a circular search around her. Contact was lost after the second attack. *Chatelain* joined the two DEs, and the three initiated a retiring search.

Pope also joined and made a contact at 1130. During the next several hours, she made numerous depth charge attacks. *Chatelain* was ordered to assist *Pope*, with *Pillsbury* and *Flaherty* searching a perimeter around the other two DEs. By midafternoon, *Pope* reported contact lost, and all DEs joined the search until *Chatelain* got a firm contact on the sub. Lieutenant Dawson Molyneus, the *Chatelain's* first lieutenant, related what followed:

> "Lieutenant Commander James L. Foley, our skipper, relieved me of the conn early that Easter Sunday afternoon. Commander Hall ordered *Chatelain* to guide *Pope* in a creeping attack."

Lieutenant Goodglass coached the CIC with great skill. He directed the sonar silent *Pope* over *U-515* where she dumped charges right on the target. *Chatelain* then delivered two accurate and destructive depth charge attacks. Lieutenant Molyneus continued:

> "The sub was badly hurt. She broached so close aboard *Chatelain* that the DE's K-gun depth charges landed on her deck. The U-boat and the surprised *Chatelain* opened up simultaneously. *Flaherty* could not assist immediately because *Chatelain* fouled her range. Meanwhile, I had gone to my battle station, repair I forward, and was getting bits of the engagement from our talker. Suddenly alarmed, the talker warned that Germans were manning their big deck gun. All hell broke out on *Chatelain*. All guns, including the gunnery officer with a tommy gun, were blasting the sub."

Chatelain was on a course opposite to that of the U-boat, which was either dead in the water or moving very slowly. At 3000 yards, when the angle between the sub and *Chatelain* opened, *Flaherty* commenced fire with her main battery. The angle was still too small to use the 20mm or 40mm guns which relied on multiple wide straddles, the shotgun rather than the rifle approach. *Flaherty's* guns were accurate; the sub was crossed twice, and hits were scored.

At 1200 yards, *Flaherty* launched a torpedo which passed about 30 yards ahead of the U-boat. A spread of three was not launched because of the proximity of our ships. During the engagement, the sub fired several rounds at *Flaherty* with its forward deck gun; two shells splashed close aboard. When *Flaherty* was abeam of *Chatelain* and the U-boat, *Chatelain* reported that the submarine was sinking and all DEs ceased fire.

1512. The submarine sank. *ComCortDiv 4* directed *Flaherty* and *Pillsbury* to sound-search the area while *Pope* and *Chatelain* recovered survivors. Six officers and 37 men were rescued. Although DEs worked as a team, there was keen rivalry for major credit. Joe Villanella offered his illicit diary as proof that *Chatelain* was most responsible. Excerpt:

> "*Chatelain* was the main ship involved in the sinking of the *U-515*. We blasted her out of the water with depth charges. All our guns opened fire, making direct hits as sailors rushed from hatches and the conning tower. One German running toward the deck gun was cut down. After that, most of them jumped overboard. Our men lined the deck and cheered when *U-515* went down bow first. A blinker message from *Pope* to *Chatelain* stated 'beautiful job, we envy you. [Joe has a copy of the message.]"

Without commenting on the discrepancy between Joe Villanella's diary and the *Flaherty* skipper's action report, it is arguable that *Chatelain* had the most eloquent spokesman.

Joe stated that Captain Jim Foley was a great commander, and every man aboard respected and admired him. The excellent morale of the officers and crew was due to their confidence in him. Joe recalled:

"I carved a model of a German sub out of a piece of wood I got from "Chips" (ship's carpenter), inscribed the date we sank *U-515*, and presented it to Captain Foley. I'll never forget the expression on his face when he accepted it."

The crew gave the prisoners dry clothes, coffee and sandwiches and took the sub commander to the wardroom. *Kapitanleutnant* Werner Henke spoke English fluently. Our captain and executive officer, Lieutenant D.S. Knox, had just sat down with Henke when the German said "You didn't have to kill so many of my men; we would have surrendered." Captain Foley replied: "Your men were making for the gun; we couldn't take chances." (The U-boat had fired on *Flaherty*). Henke identified his boat and talked about her exploits, that he was awarded the Knights Cross of the Iron Cross for sinking a troop ship but later learned that it was the British passenger ship, *Ceramic*. That was his undoing. Captain Gallery on the *Guadalcanal* knew something more than what Henke told Foley.

Ceramic was en route to the United States, apparently under safe passage, with English women and children fleeing the Blitz. Upon learning the ship's identity, Henke realized that, if he were taken to England, he would be tried as a war criminal and hanged, something the *Chatelain* officers were not aware of. He had a slight cut on his forehead. We learned that Seaman First Class Coleman, cox'n of the rescue raft, hit Henke on the head with a paddle because he was crowding the German sailors trying to climb onto the raft. Coleman yelled "Get back Mac, give the other guys a chance!" The exec asked Henke who was going to win the war. For an unreconstructed Nazi, his surprisingly frank reply was "You have already won it!"

With the conversation ended, Henke and his crew were passed to *Guadalcanal* via breeches buoy. Captain Dan Gallery received him curtly and locked him up in the brig. Admiral Gallery's book, "*U-505*," gives an interesting account of his conversations with Henke and the events leading to his incarceration.

Sent to a Canadian POW camp, Henke awaited shipment to England to face a hearing concerning the sinking of *Ceramic*. *U-515* was also charged with machine gunning survivors, which Henke denied. Another account states that he was being deported for failure to cooperate with British Naval Intelligence as he had earlier promised to do. Whichever was correct, Henke made his decision. In broad daylight, he set out to climb over the compound fence, ignoring repeated warnings from a guard. A burst of automatic fire sent *Kapitanleutnant* Henke to the ground dead. A failed escape attempt… or suicide?

Phase II: The Capture of U-505

The Task Group, now designated 22.3, sailed from Norfolk, Virginia on 15 May 1944. *Jenks (DE-665)* replaced *Neunzer*, the only change in composition. On the forenoon of 4 June 1944, TG 22.3, on its third ASW cruise, was steaming on antisubmarine patrol in the vicinity of the Cape Verde Islands. The group was about to engage in one of the most dramatic actions of the Atlantic War.

The capture of a sub was inspired by the previous sinking of *U-515*. A simultaneous thought occurred to several officers that a capture would have been possible if the Task Group had been so prepared. Lieutenant Commander Means Johnston, captain of *Flaherty*, was obsessed with the idea. He broached the notion to the Escort Commodore, Commander Hall, aboard *Pillsbury*. Hall pointed out that the British had tried that before and failed. Nonetheless, with some misgivings, *Pillsbury* was to create a boarding party composed of men with previous sub duty plus additional personnel as needed.

There were no guidelines for boarding a contemporary enemy submarine. It could entail a fire fight in close, unlit quarters. There could be demolition charges and other scuttling actions to contend with. Once secured, the sub would have to be kept afloat, a risky undertaking. *Pillsbury's* boarding party would be both a marine salvage and a combat operation. It required weapons personnel to wrest control, engineering ratings to handle machinery and neutralize scuttling, deck hands to rig a tow, and communications personnel.

Word was passed for volunteers. Instructions and a diagram of a sub's control room were drawn, specifying each man's duties upon boarding. Torpedoman Second Class Arthur Knispel, armed with a submachine gun, would go down the conning tower hatch first and wipe out enemy personnel. Signalman Second Class "Fritz" Hohne and Radioman Second Class Stan Wdowiak would provide communications. Hohne was to remain in the conning tower for semaphore communication with the ship. His parents were German immigrants, and he was fluent in the language. Wdowiak was to seize classified information.

Electrician's Mate William Rideau stepped forward. So did little Machinist's Mate Zenon Lukosius, whose brother had served aboard the first *Pillsbury*, a destroyer sunk by Japanese cruisers in 1942. First Class Gunner's Mate Chester Mocarski, who had worked in Great Lakes steamers, volunteered, as did Bosun's Mate Wayne Pickels. He was to take along a 30 foot chain, lash one end to the conning tower rail and drop the other end down the hatch to prevent trapping the boarding party below. Chief George Jacobson was senior among the enlisted men, a big, cheerful and popular man. He was to take an assortment of wrenches to ensure that the U-boat's ballast tank vents were closed and pressurized. This meant entering the control room to identify 14 unfamiliar controls and operate them in correct sequence. Any mistake could send the sub to the bottom with all aboard!

Pillsbury's assistant engineer, Lieutenant (jg) Albert L. David was designated officer in charge in light of his training at the Submarine Repair School. The boarders' whaleboat would be manned by Philip Trusheim, a young coxswain who survived the Pearl Harbor attack, Seaman First Class E.J. Beaver and Machinist's Mate R.R. Jenkins.

Commander Knowles of the Tenth Fleet (See narrative in chapter *Battle of The Atlantic*) was preoccupied with a U-boat moving in and out of his noose, identified by the unique touch of her wireless operator. Her story began in late March when first sighted as she departed from Brest on *Feindfahrt* (scouting for a target). She was tracked down the Ivory Coast to Freetown, then to Cape Palms, Liberia, searching in vain for victims. Knowles had her number! From the telltale HF/DF evidence, he recognized one of the older boats with a 90 day fuel capacity. So, he figured that she would have to begin her homeward journey toward the end of May. Sure enough, on 27 May, a transmission identified by several HF/DF stations, located her about 750 miles north of Cape Palms. On 30 May, she was plotted along the French West African Coast. Her position and course were supplied to Admiral Ingersoll who immediately instructed Captain Dan Gallery to run down the U-boat, 300 miles from the Task Group.

The elusive German was *U-505* with *Oberleutnant* Harald Lange in command. On her first three war cruises, *Kapitanleutnant* Axel Loewe commanding, she had sunk more than 50,000 tons. Suddenly, she became a hardluck boat with recurring mechanical problems. On *Feindfahrt* in November 1943, beset by troubles and Allied attacks, her second skipper, *Kapitanleutnant* Zschech broke down. During a depth charge attack, he put a bullet into his temple. The stigma of suicide rested heavily on *U-505*. Lange tried his best to erase it.

Cruising to Cape Town, South Africa, Lange found nothing. Although the Tenth Fleet tracked him, he managed to elude it. He ran at periscope depth in daytime and on the surface at night. He crash dived only nine times in a whole month. Three times, his lookouts sighted aircraft. At least once, aircraft from *Guadalcanal* had sighted him. Six times, his Naxos gear gave early warning of hostile planes. Lange had a keen sense of the enemy's presence.

24 May. The sub headed home, but Captain Gallery had different plans for *U-505*. The boat bound for Brest in France would wind up in Chicago, Illinois. On 31 May, *U-505* was off Marsa in French West Africa while the *Guadalcanal* Group was well out at sea. But it was moving up fast, fix after fix reaching Gallery from Knowles. Then, on 2 June, "Captain Dan's" own HF/DF reported that the U-boat was nearby.

There were sporadic radar blips at night. Search pilots reported hearing the distant propeller noises of a U-boat on their sonobuoys. Lange was aware that someone was breathing down his neck. From 30 May on, his Naxos search receiver warned him of aircraft. Following those warnings, he kept crash diving. Each time, he surfaced and continued his course at high speed until his Naxos picked up more and more radars that sent him crash diving again and again.

Lange knew he was being followed by a HUK group. He decided to make an 84-mile jog due east, but Gallery was on his trail, catching up on 3 June, only 175 miles apart. By the morning of 4 June, it appeared that the Task Group would be putting into port empty-handed. Fuel was running low. Commander Earl Trosino, chief engineer of *Guadalcanal*, warned Gallery that he had reached the end of the chase and he would have to abandon his quarry:

> "Captain," Trosino said, "we've got to quit fooling here! I'm getting down near the safe limit of my fuel!"

Gallery argued with Trosino all day about the fuel, but next day being Sunday, he prayed at mass along those same lines. It was a beautiful, clear day, but Gallery was downcast because he feared he had lost the sub. Actually, the submarine was approaching at less than periscope depth, apparently attempting to fire a torpedo at *Guadalcanal*! Then, at 1100 sharp, the squawk box on his bridge came alive.

> "Frenchy (*Chatelain*) to Bluejay, (*Guadalcanal*). I have possible sound contact!"

Radarman Second Class Joe Villanella on *Chatelain* still had his faithful (and unauthorized) diary, recording every word:

> "The carrier gave full left rudder, and DEs to starboard had to go like the hammers of hell to catch up. While coming around at flank speed, we got a contact. Soundman Second Class Priddy and Soundman Second Class Underhill were on watch and notified Captain Knox who called Captain Gallery."

Chatelain reported her contact as definite sub and she was going to attack. Captain Gallery ordered Commander Hall to take two DEs and assist *Chatelain*. *Guadalcanal* would stay clear. Commander Hall, on the verge of combat, pondered this last message:

> "An aircraft carrier right smack in the scene of a sound contact is like an old lady in the middle of a barroom brawl. She has no business there, can contribute little to the work at hand, and should get the hell out of there!"

Hall broke off from the screen with *Pillsbury* and *Jenks*. Two Wildcats circled overhead, sent by Gallery to lend a hand if needed, but warned the pilots: "Use no big stuff. If he surfaces, chase the crew overboard with 50 caliber fire!"

The range, however, was too close to attack. The sub headed toward *Chatelain* on the same course but from the opposite direction. The sub tried to break off the sound contact by going under the DE. It worked, but *Chatelain* regained contact without assistance at 200 yards, then proceeded to open to 700 yards. Captain Knox would have liked to open out more, but the sub was trying to get a torpedo into the carrier; speed was of the essence. *Chatelain* fired a full set of hedgehogs without result. Contact was lost at 50 yards, indicating a relatively shallow target. *Chatelain* changed course to regain contact, which she did almost immediately at 100 yards. She lost it as the sub went under her again even as the skipper was preparing to make another attack. At that moment, a fighter aircraft piloted by Ensign John Cable, sent an urgent message to *Chatelain*: "Ship that just fired hedgehogs, reverse course!" Joe Villanella continued:

> "The excitement aboard ship was indescribable with all hands manning battle stations, CIC shouting information to the bridge, soundman yelling range and bearing to the sub. As the sub rose slowly toward the surface, an aircraft kept repeating 'Frenchy do you read me?' Nobody answered the pilot, so I grabbed the TBS mike and answered. The pilot replied, 'I will fire over spot where sub is'. I gave him a 'Roger'. Rushing to the voice tube, I yelled the information to the bridge."

The plane then fired its machine guns at the water, just forward of the starboard beam of *Chatelain*, and at the same time said: "I am firing at spot where submarine is." *Chatelain* made contact on the sub at 500 yards and turned onto an attack course. The DE closed the submarine, noting slight down doppler without hydrophone effects, an indication that the sub was virtually standing still.

1121. *Chatelain* dropped a full pattern of depth charges. Each was set to fire at shallow depth or magnetically, whichever tripped the firing mechanism first. All but one depth charge detonated at depth setting, but one fired out of sequence, probably by magnetic influence. There was a huge explosion, giving

Chatelain a severe jolt. A great geyser of water shot into the air, followed by a large and rapidly spreading oil slick. From the pilot to *Chatelain*: "You struck oil! Sub is surfacing!"

The submarine broke the surface bow first, 700 yards on the starboard quarter of *Chatelain*. "Action starboard!" was passed to the three 3" caliber guns, the 40mm and the starboard 20mm guns. The forward number one 3" gun crew also manned the hedgehogs when the sub was submerged and had to race from the hedgehogs to their 3" gun. All guns opened fire. Joe Villanella continued:

> "We threw everything at that sub. The noise of guns was deafening, and the ship shook with each 3" round fired. When I looked out from the radar shack, I saw this gray monster so close I could see the insignia on the conning tower."

Several hits on the U-boat were scored. In accordance with the capture plan, anti-personnel (shrapnel) instead of armor piercing shells were to be used. *Pillsbury*, racing toward the combat area at flank speed, opened fire with all guns. *Chatelain* ceased fire and set up a torpedo attack plot, and Lieutenant (jg) Snodgrass ordered a torpedo fired at the U-boat. It missed by 75 yards across the sub's bow. Joe Villanella thumbed through his diary:

> "We didn't know how much damage we had done, and we were sure the Germans would come out shooting if given a chance. They didn't come out, and skipper Knox called 'cease fire'. There was a deadly silence about the whole area. For several minutes, we spoke in whispers, not knowing what to expect as the sub lay still, facing us beam to beam. Finally, *U-505* came to life and turned slowly, her bow starting to point menacingly at *Chatelain*.
>
> As the bow passed, there were sighs of relief, but *U-505* was running in a tight circle, her rudder jammed by the depth charge attack. Captain Lange and other officers had been wounded, and I suppose the crew was glad it was over for them."

Pillsbury ceased fire. Enemy personnel were abandoning ship. According to the chief radarman observing the action on *Flaherty*:

> "The German captain, *Oberleutnant* Zur See Harald Lange, was the first man up into the conning tower and was knocked off the U-boat by a 20mm round. The crew piled out almost in panic, leaving the sub unmanned and still underway."

Lange had received a leg wound which would eventually lead to amputation. Later, on board the *Guadalcanal*, he stated:

> "I received two bombs (hedgehogs) and then two heavy crashes, perhaps from depth charges. Water broke in, lights and all machinery went off, and the rudders jammed. Not knowing exactly the entire damage or why they continued bombing me, I gave the order to bring the boat to the surface, scuttle and abandon her."

The submarine continued to swing toward *Chatelain*. Engines were ordered ahead, just in time for the sub to pass close aboard under the DE's stern. *Jenks* observed men on the deck of the submarine with their arms upraised and others jumping overboard. Together, the DEs had smothered the sub with all types of fire, negating any possibility of its crew manning their guns. *Pillsbury* ordered its boarding and salvage party to assemble on deck.

1131. *Jenks* was instructed to assist *Chatelain* by lowering her boat in the water to pick up survivors and interesting flotsam. The first rescued was a lone survivor on an inflated raft. He gave his name as *Oberleutnant* Meyer, second in command of the U-boat.

Once the whaleboat had cleared *Pillsbury*, Cox'n Trusheim set a course to bring the boarders onto the U-boat's starboard quarter, inside her turning circle. He expected the pressure of the submarine bearing to the right could help him butt his boat against the conning tower rail. *U-505* was so far down at the stern that the rail was level with the boat's gunwales. He edged his boat up the submarine's starboard side, timing the motion of the waves, alternately speeding and slowing until he reached the shattered conning tower.

Knispel and Wdowiak were the first aboard, scrambling for footholds as they swung over the rail. Wdowiak slipped and nearly went overboard. They found themselves on the bridge with the body of Hans Fisher, the action's only fatality. Forward of the periscopes was the open conning tower hatch, a dark invitation into the bowels of a half-sunk enemy warship. Heedless of what awaited them, the torpedoman and the radioman dropped below. It took three tries to get the party aboard. When his turn came, Mocarski missed his hold, fell, and was crushed between the heavy whaleboat and the conning tower. Badly injured, he was pulled out by Lukosius and Pickels. In the urgency of rescuing his shipmate, Pickels dropped the chain which went "deep six." Back aboard *Pillsbury*, Mocarski was treated by pharmacist's mates with instructions radioed from *Guadalcanal's* doctor. Under their care, he would recover.

Most of the boarders were below now. Knispel had gone forward, Wdowiak aft. The Germans had left no one behind. On his way down the ladder, Lukosius tore open his inflatable life jacket. When he reached the control room and stepped onto the deck, he heard a gurgling noise. Following the sound, he found water coming in through a strainer with its cover beside it on the deck. Working feverishly, he replaced the cover and dogged down the wing nuts that sealed it in place. With his life jacket deflated, he had a special interest in buoyancy control; he couldn't swim! The submarine's interior was dimly lit, odorous, eerie. Later, Hohne recalled hastily abandoned meals of partly eaten liverwurst and pumpernickel bread, food that was familiar to him from childhood.

As Jacobson, Lukosius and Riendeau labored at the maze of controls and gauges to kill the submarine's engines and keep her afloat, the rest of the party began hustling documents topside. The whaleboat soon became a jumble of papers, pistols, binoculars, flags, submachine guns, even Lange's pen. Wdowiak had nearly a dozen pair of Zeiss binoculars hanging from his neck. Lukosius resembled a modern day pirate with two submachine guns hanging from his shoulders and pistols stuck in his belt. Laws governing prizes taken at sea have not changed. Bosun's Mate Wayne Pickels recalled:

"Since I had lost the chain, and Mocarski couldn't make it down, I went below into the control room. I was with Wdowiak and Knispel, gathering logs, maps, books, documents, etc. and passing them up the hatch to topside. I went into the captain's cabin, pulled out drawers, opened cabinets (smashed open the locked ones), to see what was worth taking.

Lieutenant David, who was topside, kept hollering to us down below, 'The sub is sinking, everybody get topside!' We knew the sea cock valve was secured, so we kept on looking. I confiscated five pair of binoculars, a Belgian Mauser revolver, a leather officer's coat and other items. In the crew's quarters, there were lots of tinned food items, 'foofoo' water (cologne) and even brandy."

Shortly after noon, the sub's stern continued to settle as water surged from aft into the conning tower hatch. David ordered his men to close the hatch, turning the U-boat into a floating tank. By some caprice of fate, Wdowiak and Knispel were left below, sealed with their prize because, once closed, the hatch refused to open again. The *Jenks'* whaleboat, commanded by Lieutenant J.D. Lannon, came alongside *U-505* to offer assistance. Two prisoners picked up nearby told Lannon that, on surfacing, the crew did not change from battery to diesel power. Consequently, the weakened batteries were slowing the submarine. Apprised of the hatch problem, Lannon picked up two more survivors; one of them with the intimidating title of *Maschinenoberbergefreiter* (Chief Machinist's Mate) Heinrich Bran, who obligingly reopened the hatch.

The boarding and salvage party had given a superb exhibition of seamanship by overtaking and boarding the submarine while it was underway in a tight turn. Only 40 minutes after *Chatelain* had gained her first contact on *U-505*, the submarine was in the possession of the boarding party! There were cheers from all ships. Lieutenant David and his men had prevented scuttling. Eight preset demolition charges were resting against the hull, awaiting a time signal to blast the sub to the bottom. They yanked off the wires with their hands without any assurance that this would not cause a detonation. With the sub close to negative buoyancy, they stayed below deck, seizing everything of a classified nature. Captain Casselman of *Pillsbury* noted in his action report:

"For his outstanding accomplishments, his actions beyond the call of duty, and with utter disregard for his own life, I recommend the award of the Navy Cross to Lieutenant (jg) A.L. David and the award of the Bronze Star to each member of his boarding party."

On orders from *ComCortDiv 4*, *Chatelain* lowered her motor whale boat to pick up anything of interest as well as 48 prisoners, including the captain, and transferred them to *Guadalcanal*. *Pillsbury* picked up the remaining 12 survivors.

Now came the daunting task of towing the sub, still turning in a tight circle at 4.5 knots. Alongside, *Pillsbury* passed a line which was secured to the sub's bow. A minor collision flooded a compartment in *Pillsbury's* hull. With the sub's rudder jammed hard right, the tow parted. In spite of the possibility of further damage, *Pillsbury* again came alongside the sub and passed two lines. The sub again collided with *Pillsbury*, her diving planes slicing the DE's hull like a can opener. This time, damage was serious and compartments were flooded below the water line, including a motor room.

Lieutenant David finally cut off power and stopped the sub. At about this time, the boarding and salvage party from *Guadalcanal* with Commander Trosino, her engineering officer, arrived to assist the beleaguered *Pillsbury* party. A survey by the new arrivals determined that the sub could be salvaged. *Pillsbury* cast off lines when her serious damage was examined. All hands were required to assist in damage control. *Pillsbury's* boat returned, almost filled to the gunwhale with all manner of confidential publications, materiel and equipment to be sent to *Guadalcanal*. Bosun Pickels related:

"I was on the sub's bow when her diving vanes ripped the DE's hull below the waterline. It was late afternoon when we returned to *Pillsbury*. There was no power due to flooding. Mattresses and shoring had been placed against the ripped hull. They were waiting for me to rig a collision mat. With that accomplished and power resumed, we had our first chow since breakfast. It was the next day before we caught up with the carrier to transfer prisoners."

Guadalcanal managed to put a towing line on the U-boat, now dead in the water. The boarding party continued pumping out flooded areas until the sub was seaworthy. Shrouded in secrecy, so that the enemy would think the sub was lost, the U-boat was towed to Bermuda, albeit with considerable difficulty. The towline continued to part. When it broke at night, escorts had to go back and find the sub. On nearing their destination, a seagoing tug with the proper gear rendezvoused with the Task Group and took the tow safely to the American Naval Base in Bermuda. Bosun Pickels concluded:

"We were warned that the capture of the sub must be kept secret and were ordered to turn in all souvenirs, promising we would get them back after the war. I complied but I 'forgot' to turn in the captain's fountain pen, Nazi submarine insignia and two snapshots of the captain and crew. Just before pulling into Bermuda, we (the boarding party) were transferred back to *U-505*, getting to ride into Bermuda on the deck of the sub."

The submarine was informally identified as *USS-505* as it approached port. A detachment of marines awaited its arrival on the dock, one explaining they were suspicious because there was no submarine *USS-505*. Lieutenant David told him: "Son, there is now."

All but one of the sub crew had been taken. Aside from a great yarn, the capture of *U-505* was an intelligence bonanza. Our side could analyze her classified publications. Our ability to operate the sub, to know her characteristics, strengths and vulnerability would create important modifications to ASW manuals and training.

If John Paul Jones witnessed the action from somewhere, he must have been mightily pleased.

Portions of this narrative were researched by Richard Brust Jr. of Rock Springs, Wyoming. The Tenth Fleet reference was abridged from an article by Ladislas Farago in *DESA NEWS* issue of July/August 1983.

ESCORT DIVISION 62

Terminating the Aerographers

Lieutenant Edward J. Keyes, on *Hayter (DE-212)*, described an event, a bit squeamish, but a good yarn.

> "Ed McKay was the division doctor on *Hayter*. On another ship in the convoy, a POW, Heinrich Schaefer, developed appendicitis. Our captain asked the Escort Commander if the patient could be operated on aboard our ship because our doctor needed the practice.
>
> Schaefer was scared to death, as anybody might be with his enemy about to wield the knife. Fire Controlman Arthur Brown broadcast a cut by slice account of the operation over the sound powered phone system. All was well until the anesthetic ran out and the patient began to cough before the sutures were applied. Brown described how the guts were squeezing out while Doc was stuffing them back in. At least two men on the bridge turned green and relinquished their head sets. I believe that Brown later became a mortician! Schaefer survived and got along nicely with the crew."

General Von Rundstedt's 1944-1945 winter counter offensive, the "Battle of the Bulge," produced a major effort on the part of the U.S. Army to contain the threat. The weather was carefully monitored by the Germans, picking a time of fog and snow when Allied planes would be grounded and mechanized forces immobilized by icy roads. Weather reports were vital for the enemy. Accordingly, *U-248* sortied from her Norwegian base to take up station between France and Newfoundland as an advance aerographer for the *Wehrmacht*. She arrived about mid-January and began transmitting meteorologic data. However, an interceptor of her coded data was Escort Division 62, well equipped with HF/DF and with orders to locate and destroy the U-boat.

Under Commander J.F. Bowling, with his pennant in *Otter (DE-210)*, the Division consisted of the destroyer escorts *Otter*, (Lieutenant Commander J.M. Irvine); *Hayter (DE-212)*, (Lieutenant Commander Fred Huey); *Varian (DE-798)*, (Lieutenant Commander L.A. Myhre) and *Hubbard (DE-211)*, (Lieutenant Commander L.C. Mabley). On 16 January, the four ships, without air cover, obtained bearings on the U-boat's transmissions and plotted her position.

CortDiv 62 proceeded toward the radio fix in Formation Delta, a four ship search deployment, maintaining all DEs in visual contact with each other, thereby avoiding voice conversation. At 0500 the same day, *Otter*, *Hubbard* and *Hayter* obtained HF/DF bearings on coded U-boat transmissions, distance approximately 10 miles. At best speed, course was set for the submarine.

Hayter made the first sound contact and attacked with depth charges. *Otter* was next. First one DE, then another, gunned across the submerged U-boat's position while sowing lethal depth charges. The dull reverberations of exploding TNT rolled across the sea. With her sonar gear out of commission, *Hubbard* dropped out, but the others fired a sufficiently punishing barrage upon the target. John Shovan was a crewman on *Otter* who was kind enough to share a meticulous diary with us:

> "Tuesday, 16 January 1945. At sea. Today was the big day the crew of the *Otter* had been hoping for. In commission for almost 11 months, we finally felt that we were fighting a war. At 0910 on this bright and sunny morn, the alarm bell summoned us to GQ. *Hayter* had picked up a sub contact, and we were making full speed to her position. On arriving in the area, our sound operator announced a contact. We made the second attack."

1108. *Hayter's* turn. She started an approach, but the sub's maneuvers caused the conning officer to belay the run and open the range for a new attack. Contact was lost, however, and Operation Observant was begun with contact regained almost immediately. On the second run, a stern chase resulted in ideal conditions for a hedgehog bracket. A CIC evaluation of the submarine speed at 12 knots necessitated an attack speed of 15 knots instead of the usual 10. (Although the *Hayter* action report did not comment on the underwater speed of the U-boat, it must be assumed that the sub was equipped with a snorkel.) Upon ordering "Fire," the hedgehogs did not respond, apparently an electrical failure. (The gun captain had neglected to activate the selector switch.) Accordingly, a new course was plotted with the object of crossing the sub's bow to drop depth charges. Sound contact was suddenly lost, negating a depth charge attack. It was believed that the sub had reversed engines, causing the DE to over-run its target. Seaman Shovan continued:

> "Immediately, we went in and dropped a pattern of magnetic impulse charges. A few of them went off rather quickly, and the commander said that they assuredly damaged the submarine."

Varian made an unsuccessful attack with hedgehogs, their fathometer showing the depth of the submarine to be 45 fathoms. After regaining contact 46 minutes later, *Varian* made a depth charge attack, followed by a similar attack by *Hayter*. Shovan's diary recalled:

> "Then the *Hayter* came in and dropped a pattern. As I watched her going in on the attack, I knew it was something I shall always remember. Her sleek, new camouflage paint job looked beautiful as I saw the black flag hoisted to the yardarm when starting her run. Then I counted the flashes as she fired her "K" guns to port and starboard; two, four, six, eight flashes. A moment later, I could feel the cans go off. The concussion was terrific. Three runs had been made by us on the sub. Now, it was our turn again."

The traces and echoes were clear and sharp. On the attack described by Shovan, *Hayter* fired a pattern of 13 magnetic impulse depth charges. There were two explosions 40 seconds after the first depth charge was dropped. Two large air bubbles were reported. *Otter*'s fourth attack commenced at 1300. Due to the various wakes and explosion disturbances, contact was hard to maintain but was helped by the modulation control. Thirteen magnetic charges were fired, resulting in four explosions; one was premature because of the failure of an arbor to detach itself from the charge. *Otter* then made another run, finding oil slicks and air bubbles. Shovan recalled:

> "The DEs formed a triangle, keeping the U-boat in the middle so that she couldn't escape. Each ship had sound con-

tact on the sub. We went in and, as we approached the spot where the sub was submerged, there was a water disturbance, bubbles coming to the surface. *Otter* dropped her pattern right on the bubbles."

Varian delivered a telling blow with explosions indicating that her magnetic impulse charges had found their mark. A few minutes later, water boiled up as the sub apparently blew her tanks in an effort to surface. A black ball, evidently from the hull of the U-boat, bounced up from the deep. Men scanned the surface, grimly following the turmoil of the exploding charges and now the churning sea was tinged with spreading black as *Otter* raced to drop another pattern. There were heavy explosions in the depths as all manner of debris floated to the surface. Finally, there was a violent explosion that may have been the collapse of the main pressure hull of the submarine. *Otter* lowered a boat to recover debris. Men fishing over the side with buckets and grappling hooks picked up a garrison cap, gloves, a black leather helmet, a pipe bowl, an instruction book in Norwegian on guitar playing, and some human remains. Shovan was a little more specific about the human remains:

"I saw a piece of a brain floating by the port side. Pieces of flesh floated to the surface. The small boat picked up a large piece of a male part containing the lower part of the back, buttocks, penis and some intestines; it weighed about 20 pounds. All items were retrieved for delivery to the evaluators as proof of the sinking. Three hours later, oil gushed to the surface"

Reconstructing the battle later, Commander Bowling believed that the first depth charges dropped by *Otter* exploded close enough to damage the submarine and reduce her maneuverability. The damage was increased by subsequent attacks. Then the sub tried to surface and was knocked down again, probably with her conning tower destroyed. After a brief period of control, she began to sink inexorably until, far down, her hull collapsed from the pressure. All escorts commenced a retiring search, continuing until noon the next day when they secured from the operation and headed for the Azores.

The *Wehrmacht* would receive no further weather reports from the aerographers of *U-248*.

THE CARD HUNTER-KILLERS

A Hard Act to Follow

On 5 July 1944, Task Group 22.10 HUK Group was patrolling 200 miles from the Sable Islands in the North Atlantic. Captain R.C. Young was Group Commander as well as commanding officer of the aircraft carrier *Card (ACV-11)*. This was the first antisubmarine patrol in which the carrier was escorted solely by destroyer escorts. It was a hard act to follow with *Card's* aircraft and destroyers having previously sunk six U-boats. In the inner screen about *Card* were *Thomas (DE-102)*, *Bostwick (DE-103)* and *Breeman (DE-104)*. In the outer screen, ten miles distant, *Baker (DE-190)* and *Bronstein (DE-189)* patrolled the left and right flanks of the Group.

1907 that day was a fateful moment for *Kapitanleutnant* Hans Steen, commander of *U-233*. The sub was at a shallow depth of only 30 meters, required to reduce pressure on a torpedo tube being repaired by the torpedomen. Suddenly, a high, whining sound was heard in the U-boat, soon followed by screw noises. At that moment, *Baker* had gained sound contact at a distance of 2200 yards. Lieutenant Commander Norman C. Hoffman, captain of *Baker*, promptly ordered the FXR streamed and sounded GQ. Lieutenant Howard D. Edwards was *Baker's* ASW officer and remembers the series of events:

"My GQ station was in the sound hut. Soundman Nicholson was on duty and was doing an outstanding job. As we closed the contact, we developed a clear image of a sub moving toward us very rapidly and in a sharp right turn. Hard left rudder was applied to cross the sub's bow."

The sound team reported the sub to be somewhere between medium and shallow depths. Hoffman ordered the depth charges set at medium because, if the sub were shallow, the charges could fire on magnetic impulse, if they were close to the sub. The range closed rapidly.

Baker dropped her first depth charge pattern without visual result but with unobserved severe damage. Depth charges burst around the U-boat; glass was smashed and loose gear flew through the spaces. Steen ordered rapid descent to 100 meters where the after compartment flooded so rapidly that the sub became stern heavy. A torpedo on the loading rails in that space suddenly slid into the tube with such speed that it disemboweled a torpedoman standing in the way.

Baker regained sound contact. There then befell an agonizing happenstance to sound team and skipper alike. The remote training unit from the sound hut on the bridge to the sound dome under the keel went out of commission. However, there were no cheers in the submarine. Not a single man escaped from the stern compartment, electric motor room nor diesel room. The submarine continued to sink by the stern, out of control, with chlorine gas spreading throughout the boat. (Batteries in salt water create chlorine gas.) The door between the control room and the diesel room was sealed off.

The crew of *Baker* did a monumental job in effecting quick repairs with a jury rig, enabling the sound team to continue functioning, albeit with severe limitation. A second full pattern was dropped, and all hands in open spaces saw a huge geyser mixed with oil as the second charge detonated. The ASW officer added:

"Having completed our run, I looked aft out of the sound hut door and noticed the usual white geysers as each depth charge exploded, but then one black one stood out in stark contrast to the others."

Meanwhile, Captain Young had ordered *Thomas* to go to the assistance of *Baker*, an assignment accepted with relish by the skipper of *Thomas*, Lieutenant Commander David M. Kellogg. (Same DE and skipper as in *Block Island Hunter-Killers.*) *Thomas* sped toward *Baker* at flank speed, arriving just after the second attack.

Baker had regained sound contact, followed by a radar blip on the same target. The bow of the U-boat broke water at a sharp angle, apparently out of control, only 1200 yards from *Baker*. Unable to contain his damage, Steen surfaced from certain death to the next best (or worst) alternative. All guns on *Baker* had been loaded and torpedoes were readied. The U-boat also came into view on *Thomas*.

"Action starboard! Commence fire!" Main and secondary batteries on *Baker* opened up at once, hitting *U-233* accurately and repeatedly. Hoffman had long felt that it would be an exciting twist of fate if a DE could torpedo a submarine, a momentous turn of the tables that would make ASW history. The assistant gunnery officer was sent amidships to fire a torpedo salvo at an opportune moment.

1935. The torpedo officer decided that the opportunity was at hand and fired two torpedoes. They splashed into the water and raced to their prey. A new ASW doctrine hung in the balance, but *Baker* was too close to the U-boat. The torpedoes never got a chance to arm. Both actually hit the sub, but neither one detonated. *Thomas*, meanwhile, had opened fire but quickly ceased because *Baker* fouled her range. A U-boat survivor recalled:

> "On the sub, the order was given to blow all tanks, and the U-boat broke water rapidly, regaining an even keel. On reaching the surface, we were immediately brought under a very accurate fire by the attacking destroyer escorts. The chief engineer opened the conning tower hatch, and the top of his head was blown off. Successive crew members who attempted to leave the boat by this hatch were no more fortunate, and the conning tower was littered with dead and dying."

Baker then passed 75 yards across the bow of the sub, firing her port "K" guns with shallow set depth charges. The charges straddled both bows of the sub and detonated close aboard. *Baker* came about and again opened rapid fire with all guns as she crossed the bow of the sub, laying a full pattern of 13 depth charges. The sub was caught in the midst of the detonations and boils and sustained tremendous damage. At this point, a few of the sub's crew could be seen swimming in the water astern, apparently having abandoned ship. Others, having just jumped into the sea, had their insides pounded to shreds by the "water hammer" effect of the explosions.

1940. *Thomas* was in a position to end the fight by ramming. Kellogg ordered the sound dome to be retracted into its housing and then he charged in. *Thomas'* two forward 3" guns opened fire at a range of 4500 yards and kept firing until the flare of her bow obscured the U-boat from the guns. There was some automatic return fire from the sub, but no damage was inflicted on *Thomas*. Even in the tense seconds that followed, Captain Kellogg had time to observe:

> "The submarine was of the 740 ton class, without identifying numerals or insignia. Her armament appeared to consist of one 3" or 4" gun on the main deck abaft the conning tower and three mounts of twin automatic weapons located on the step or bandstand at the after end of the conning tower."

Thomas slowed to 15 knots. As she approached to ram, it was observed that the conning tower was smashed, twisted and holed by many shells The grating forward of the conning tower was crushed in such a way as to indicate that one 3" shell had hit there also.

1946. "Back emergency full!" The reason for backing down just before impact was to bring the bow of the DE out of the water and down on the U-boat. *Thomas* rammed into the starboard side of the submarine 20 feet abaft the conning tower! Just prior to the ramming, a sub crewman attempted to train one of the guns on *Thomas'* bridge. The impact of the collision threw the man over the port side or down the conning tower hatch. Kellogg stopped both engines. The U-boat appeared to be cut about one third of the way through and rolled to port approximately 65 degrees as *Thomas* rode up on her hull. The sub split wide open and her stern went down almost immediately. Men began jumping from the conning tower and hatches into the sea. A POW described the last moments of his submarine:

> "The survivors left the boat by the forward hatch and cowered behind the conning tower while shells and bullets tore through the plating around it. One shell penetrated the pressure hull and exploded in the petty officers' living quarters, killing everyone in there and filling the compartment with acrid fumes. The survivors jumped overboard, and the bow of *U-233* rose high in the air. She sank almost vertically."

1947. Captain Hoffman on *Baker* noted in his log, "*Unterseeboot U-233* dove to 2450 fathoms" (the bottom). The battle was ended.

Assisted by *Breeman*, the DEs picked up 31 prisoners from a crew of 69, including the commanding officer and three other commissioned officers. Each man was searched, stripped, placed under a shower, and issued a complete kit of survivor's clothing. All were given hot soup, coffee, cigarettes and alcoholic stimulants where necessary.

Two survivors on *Thomas* were injured. The captain, a stretcher case, was the most seriously wounded with several bad lacerations and shrapnel wounds. The other injured man was a petty officer with a badly damaged hand. Both were given prompt medical attention by the division medical officer who was on *Thomas*. The sub captain, under the influence of morphine, volunteered in English his name, the sub number and the size of his crew. He had resided in America for several years and had commanded this sub for five years. The injured petty officer told of a brother in the German infantry, now in a POW camp in Oklahoma. His home was in Konigsberg but his wife left after the Americans bombed it; he no longer had a home.

In searching the prisoners, two coding wheels from an electric coding machine were found on a communications man, Ludwig Engelmann, a real find at any price. In the excitement of abandoning ship, he had also kept two code books, of which he was duly relieved by his captors. The knowledge that our side had obtained these codes was classified as top secret. The deciphered data was printed and distributed to all Allied antisubmarine units.

Prisoners and their personal gear were transferred to *Card* by breeches buoy. Despite all available medical efforts, the submarine captain died. *Kapitanleutnant* Hans Steen, Knight of the Iron Cross, was buried at sea with full military honors.

There were no personnel casualties on either *Baker* or *Thomas*. The latter, of course, was damaged, but not critically. There were some ruptured tanks, flooded compartments, and engineering malfunctions. The destruction of *U-233* was an outstanding example of the type of teamwork and coordination developed to combat the submarine menace. The aim was to kill the U-boat. The DE crews threw everything they had at her, even one of their ships as a last resort. The clicking of the operator's key was sweet music to Kellogg and Hoffman when the *Card* broke radio silence to report to the Commander, Atlantic Fleet:

> "*U-233* sunk by *Baker* and *Thomas* X latitude 42 degrees 16 minutes north X longitude 59 degrees 49 minutes west X 5 July X 31 prisoners."

Two DEs had demonstrated that they could indeed follow the "hard act" of their predecessor DDs. See chapter *Twilight of the U-boats* for the final massacre of enemy submarines by the *Card* Hunter-Killers.

One final note of interest. When *Thomas* went into dry dock for repairs in the Charlestown Navy Yard, Boston, a small portion of the *U-233* hull was discovered wedged into the ship's prow. It was mounted on a plaque with suitable comment and posted in *Thomas'* midship passageway. It now has a permanent resting place as an exhibit at the Naval Academy in Annapolis.

THE WAKE ISLAND HUNTER-KILLERS

A Clap of Thunder and Terrible Destruction

Fiske (DE-143), commanded by Lieutenant J.A. Comly, was attached to Destroyer Escort Division 9, operating with Task Group 22.6 HUK Group centered on the escort carrier *Wake Island (CVE-65)*. The Group was sweeping a sector of the North Atlantic between the United Kingdom and Newfoundland. The simple directive to the Task Force was to locate and destroy enemy U-boats. Submarines with *snorkeling* capabilities had been seen in the area.

The carrier was screened by *Fiske*, *Farquhar (DE-139)*, *J.R.Y. Blakely (DE-140)*, *Hill (DE-141)* and *Howard (DE-138)*, flying the pennant of *ComCortDiv 9*.

On 2 August 1944, the Task Group was attempting to locate a German submarine, last sighted approximately 400 miles east of Newfoundland. Since the intelligence positioning of this U-boat had been derived from weather broadcasts, it was presumed that its primary responsibility was of a meteorological nature.

1157 the same day. *Howard* and *Fiske* sighted a white puff of smoke similar to that emitted by a diesel engine when subjected to sharply increased acceleration. The smoke was concentrated enough that it showed as a blip nine miles ahead on the surface search radar. The sighting could hardly have been classified as a U-boat, but the fact that it was only sighted on the PPI (radar) scope and visually for about three minutes before disappearing made it highly suspicious.

ComCortDiv 9 felt that there was enough evidence of a submarine to warrant investigation and for *Howard* and *Fiske* to head for the contact at full speed. *Fiske* took a position 4000 yards on *Howard's* starboard beam so as to gain the maximum sonar sweep area.

1218. Speed was reduced to 15 knots. Based on both ships' estimates of the last known contact point, it should have been reached somewhere between them. They continued to exchange information as to the probable location of the last contact. Both realized they were close. Captain Comly ordered condition "Affirm," a partial manning of battle stations and the setting of watertight integrity throughout the ship, except for the mess halls. The FXR gear was not streamed but was readied to go on short notice. This could have been a fatal omission. The bright noon sun had already created some "afternoon effect," ie. thermal gradients that could often cause difficulty in sonar function. Frequent bathythermograph readings were taken. The sound range recorder had been in a standby condition and was turned on. A weak contact was made by *Fiske* at a distance of 2000 yards, roughly midway between the two ships.

The contact was classified as definite submarine. At 1223, *Fiske* reported to *Howard* that she had a submarine in her sound gear and was proceeding to attack. Now at GQ, she prepared to make a depth charge run. The hedgehogs were also made ready in the event the skipper decided to change the mode of assault. When the range had closed to about 1500 yards, the echo had a characteristic metallic ring with unmistakable down doppler. At 1300 yards, *Fiske* reported that movement of the target was slight. At 1200 yards, Captain Comly, sensing a kill at hand, reported that his attack was a stern chase and that the target was moving toward *Howard*, then about 2500 yards distant. The last reported range to the U-boat was 1075 yards. The CIC reported to the bridge, with some pride, that the first sonar contact had been obtained only 500 yards from the dead reckoning position. *Fiske* was closing with her mortal enemy, preparing a murderous assault. But it didn't happen.

1235. *Fiske* was jolted by a terrific underwater explosion! *U-804* had scored a complete surprise. Nobody had seen a wake. Sonar had not heard propeller noises. The best speculation was that the ship had been hit by a battery-operated, wakeless torpedo. Traditional torpedoes were powered with alcohol fueled motors which were very effective but necessarily left a bubbly exhaust wake. This one, however, was a silent killer.

The damage was fatal. The center of the ship rose into the air while both bow and stern headed down. Her back was broken; the keel had snapped in two. The center section then dropped, and the ship rolled about twenty degrees to port with the midsection below the surface and freeboard rapidly diminishing. Water washed over the stern in such quantity as to float men off the ship. Communications and power were lost. The engineering spaces had blown out port and starboard, creating immediate flooding. The main deck on the port side was torn asunder, held together by a few jagged pieces of steel. On the starboard side, the main deck was buckled and tearing apart. The port and starboard bulkheads to the deck house and the deck forward of the torpedo tubes were blown outward. Several 20mm platforms crumpled.

In spite of such crippling damage, Captain Comly did what he could in a desperate effort to save the ship. Emergency sound powered phones were ordered rigged to reestablish internal communications and command. Clear headed thinking set the depth charges on safe, thereby preventing an ugly addition to casualties already suffered. The hedgehogs, were also secured.

1240. There was a blinding flash and a muffled but violent explosion in the forward part of the ship, followed by dense, acrid smoke and steam, making it almost impossible to determine its source. Choking men groped their way up ladders to avoid asphyxiation. This was an internal explosion, the only fire on board. The initial detonation had blown some hatches off the deck and sprung others. The second blast blew off another. There were two holes, each four feet square, approximately five feet above the keel and abaft the sonar dome.

Most of the crew were concentrated on the after end of the ship which appeared to have more buoyancy than the forward section, although both were settling. Nets and life rafts were put over with swimmers to pull them clear of the ship. The truncated forward part of the hull was listing about 25 degrees and was breaking away.

The ship broke in two, and the order was given to abandon. The process was orderly, a source of pride and great satisfaction to Captain Comly. Eleven months of continuous, organized and disciplined training was saving lives when the chips were down. The forward section was torn loose, increasing its list to about 60 degrees and continuing to settle by its after end.

The captain then climbed over the bridge rail and stood on the starboard side of the hull which was approaching the horizontal. He saw that the after section, though further down by its forward end, still maintained its trim, creating second thoughts about the wisdom of having abandoned so soon. But he needn't have; the ship was doomed. From where he was standing on the hull, he could see that the after section was clear of personnel. Just 19 minutes after the torpedo hit, convinced that he was the last man aboard, the skipper abandoned ship, a true commanding officer to the very end.

Two minutes later, the bow section pointed straight up and headed to the bottom. In another five minutes, the stern turned vertical with its propellers pointing up and out of the water. A menace to navigation, the stern section was sunk by gun fire from *Howard* later in the day.

All survivors were picked up by *Farquhar*. The losses were painful, 33 dead or missing and 55 injured on the first count. In his action report, the captain made special mention of Ensign Eugene L. Swearingen, Supply Corps, and Pharmacist Mate Andrew for the work they performed in caring for so many wounded and seeing to it that they were safely transferred to rafts. He also expressed his thanks to Lieutenant Commander D.E. Walter, commanding officer of *Farquhar*, and his officers for their efficiency in rescuing survivors and handling the wounded. Special mention was made for Lieutenant (jg) Frank R. Keith, Medical Corps, for untiring efforts in ministering to the wounded and saving lives. Single handed, he tended to twenty fractures plus several internal injuries and severe lacerations.

A good many years later, Chief Hospital Corpsman George W. Brodie recalled the casualties on the *Fiske* and how they were handled:

> "We did not have a doctor aboard. The hospital corps personnel assigned to *Fiske* consisted of a chief hospital corpsman (myself), one first class and one third class hospital corpsman. (Early in World War II, a medical petty officer was referred to as a pharmacist's mate. Some time later, the designation was changed to hospital corpsman.)
>
> My battle station as chief hospital corpsman was in the mess hall. Immediately upon the impact, I was thrown to the deck. All lights went out, and the ship lurched toward the port side which was listing badly. I promptly made my way in the darkness to the starboard ladder leading up to the main deck. Fortunately, there had not been time to close the hatch, and I had no trouble getting out onto the deck. The time lapse between the torpedo hit and the two halves of the ship separating was only 15 minutes. There was a certain deathlike quietness prevalent on deck. I noticed that uninjured men were walking around stunned.
>
> My first reaction was to reach for my knife, which I always kept attached to my life belt, and cut the line on the forward starboard life raft. However, this raft did not do the expected thing, and it hit the water. I believe the failure was due to dried paint which kept the raft secured to its rack until someone later yanked it loose. With the aid of a fireman, I set up an emergency dressing station forward on the main deck, starboard forecastle.
>
> My materials were acquired quickly from the first aid box at the number one gun mount. Two injured seamen were helped by their shipmates to my improvised dressing station. One suffered from a back injury and the other sustained a leg injury. Under the existing conditions, the exact degree of injury to either casualty was impossible to ascertain. However, first aid measures were instituted as best we could. Both men were in great pain and each was given the contents of a morphine syringe. The man with the leg injury had a deep laceration, and a sulfanilamide dressing was applied to the wound. All this time, the ship was listing more to port, creating an obvious danger of capsizing and taking most of the crew under with it.
>
> The captain ordered abandonment of the ship which the able bodied men did with surprising calm. With the aid of a few crew members, my two charges were put into the water. Although incapacitated, they were helped and saved by concerned shipmates.
>
> Hospital Corpsmen Third Class C.H. Andrew and First Class H.E. Cornell, who sustained a nasty head laceration himself, were both in the aft part of the ship taking care of casualties, more numerous than the ones forward. Mention should be made at this point of the gallant and professional way in which both corpsmen handled the wounded. This applies particularly to Cornell who worked untiringly to aid others; the laceration at the top of his head required six sutures later aboard the rescue ship.
>
> The time spent in the water until rescued varied from one to five hours. In my case, the lapse was approximately two hours. The water was very cold. The men's teeth were chattering, and their color was almost blue from the freezing North Atlantic. There were about 20 men on my raft. One man with a possible leg fracture was helped onto the raft; the rest of us hung on via the hand lines. Generally, the men's attitude after the first half hour in the water until we were picked up was one of despondency. Given the uncertainty of rescue, this was not unusual.
>
> Happily, the rescue ship carried a doctor in addition to my ship's hospital corps complement and those on *Farquhar*. Among the casualties, there were about eighteen leg fractures of varying degrees. In addition, there were arm fractures and head and body lacerations. For the first 19 hours aboard the rescue ship, all the corpsmen worked without sleep, food or drink until all possible emergency treatment was ministered to the casualties.
>
> The supply of splints was soon exhausted, and the *Farquhar* ship's carpenter promptly went to work to improvise more. The supply of morphine and dressings was soon used up as well. A sea bag full of medical supplies was dropped to us from an aircraft based on *Wake Island*. The

casualties were kept aboard for three days until we reached an east coast port where 55 of the worse cases were hospitalized. Two badly injured men died during the first night aboard *Farquhar* and, along with four bodies recovered from the water, were buried at sea the following morning. The final count was 35 men lost, killed or missing and presumed dead."

Now, Captain Comly had to carry out the hardest task of all; writing to the next of kin in a manner that might somehow relieve their sorrow, perhaps also add to their pride.

Subsequent rain and fog prevented the *Wake Island* Group from exacting revenge, and operations were placed in limbo. Two days later, Task Group 22.6 was dissolved as the carrier was ordered into a yard for modifications and transfer to the Pacific Theater.

THE BOGUE HUNTER-KILLERS

Three U-boats Withdrawn from Circulation

Three destroyer escorts and one destroyer reported to the Commander of *Bogue (CVE-9)* and Task Group 21.11, Captain J.B. Dunn. The Group departed from Norfolk on 26 February 1944 on a mission to destroy U-boats along the U.S.-U.K. convoy routes.

At 15 minutes prior to the end of the forenoon watch on 13 March, a carrier plane dropped sonobuoys on an oil slick 35 miles from the formation. The weather was clear with a gentle breeze and smooth sea. *Haverfield (DE-393)*, commanded by Lieutenant Commander Jerry A. Mathews, was ordered to proceed to the scene at full power. Nothing further was heard from the plane; it was not yet known that *U-575* had shot it down. Another aircraft, 15 miles ahead, was challenged and recognized as a B-17 type Royal Air Force plane (Liberator). Moments later, a plane from *Bogue* came into view. *Kapitanleutnant* Wolfgang Boehmer, commanding officer of *U-575*, on her tenth war patrol, was also nearby and on the hunt:

> "We had surfaced in order to fix our position and to air out the boat. Suddenly, a four engine Liberator dropped out of the clouds to attack us. Being too late to dive, we gave the boat full speed ahead and just managed to escape the bombs and strafing. With a brief radio message, we signaled headquarters that we were being attacked. That was our last transmission. We dived to 40 meters We did not know that an oil slick had betrayed our location."

Haverfield's lookouts detected a strong odor of diesel oil and spotted a sonobuoy in its midst. Captain Mathews slowed *Haverfield* to 15 knots, and started a search. Assistance was rendered by voice communication from the *Bogue* aircraft.

1409. "Contact!" Loud and clear from the sound operator, William J. Ladlock. He had obtained a contact at 1700 yards, medium depth, with slight down doppler and classified as positive submarine. As the contact was maintained down to 300 yards on the first run, a hedgehog attack was fired on the recorder without visible results. Two more hedgehog attacks followed. In each case, contact was retained and the range opened to 1200 yards before coming to a new attack course. The Canadian Navy corvette *HMCS Prince Rupert (K-324)* reached the scene. As hedgehog attacks had been ineffective, *Haverfield* fired a full medium set depth charge pattern, resulting in a large black oil bubble spreading into a wide slick.

Comment from the plane pilot: "That shook him up." Following this attack, the sub headed into the depth charge disturbance, and contact was lost for 13 minutes, then regained at 2400 yards. As the DE started another attack, *Prince Rupert* gained contact and crossed the DE's bow on a firing run with depth charges, then circled and fired a hedgehog pattern into the depth charge disturbance with no results.

For the next two hours, the DE and the corvette hammered the U-boat with magnetic impulse depth charges and hedgehogs in single ship and creeping attacks. The submarine had apparently submerged to the limit of her depth endurance. The destroyer *Hobson (DD-464)*, commanded by Lieutenant Commander K. Loveland, arrived to assist the two ships. *Hobson* fired a full pattern of depth charges without visual result. *Haverfield* regained contact and lay to about 1300 yards from the sub to direct *Hobson* in a creeper attack. When the DD was in position, *Haverfield* signalled "fire." *Hobson* dropped a full pattern set very deep. From her vantage point, the corvette described the pattern as "excellent." Boehmer's situation was hopeless:

> "We attempted escape by diving to 180 and then to 200 meters. With valiant efforts of my crew, we escaped many of the bomb clusters (hedgehogs), but damage made it more and more difficult to control the boat. Finally, the electric engines stopped. I ordered the donning of life belts and rescue equipment. The engine room reported a bad leak, and the boat sank to 240 meters. That was the end. I gave the order to blow the tanks."

The submarine broached in the center of three surface ships disposed in a triangular formation. Ranges from the escorts to the submarine were about 1500 yards. *Haverfield's* number two 3" gun opened fire immediately, the first projectile striking the sub at the waterline under the conning tower. As the DE turned to ram, *Prince Rupert* opened fire with her 20mm. The DE abandoned ramming and backed two thirds speed to avoid the corvette's fire. As the sub turned and pointed her bow at the DE, the latter quickly maneuvered from that hazardous position to a course parallel with the submarine. All guns that could bear were unmasked, and firing was very effective. A plane from *Bogue* dived on the sub and dropped two depth bombs, circled and fired rockets into the port side of the sub. *Hobson* was firing her forward guns. A violent explosion erupted on the aft end of the U-boat, presumably from her battery compartment.

1843. With foc'sle and conning tower aflame, the sub settled slowly on an even keel until almost submerged, then sank stern first with her bow projecting skyward. Boehmer described the end:

> "Our U-boat rushed to the surface, right in among the three destroyers. They opened fire on us at once, and some planes (actually one) also joined in to attack us with aerial bombs and guns. As captain, I gave my last order, to scuttle and then leave the boat. Seven minutes after surfacing, my

boat sank stern first below the waves in the light of the setting sun. Seventeen crew members who did not leave the boat, went down with it. Some of us in the water were wounded by firing, but then we were rescued."

Information was pieced together from direct conversation with survivors and interpreters eavesdropping on talk among prisoners.

The U-boat, built in Hamburg in 1941, was of the 750 ton class with a crew of four officers and 50 men. She had a quadruple 20mm mount and two single 20mm guns abaft the conning tower. She sortied from a French port on 29 February 1944. On 9 March, about sunset, she had a carrier (*Bogue*) in her periscope and was about to attack when an escort fired depth charges, forcing her down. At dusk on 10 March, a plane strafed her. She returned fire and believed she scored a hit (Shot it down). At 0500 On 13 March, the U-boat was attacked on the surface by the RAF B-17 reported by *Haverfield*. The U-boat submerged with oil tanks damaged. At 1400, they heard a surface ship. The depth charge attack (by *Haverfield*) extinguished their lights, damaged their rudder and started a slow leak aft.

The sub remained at 140 meters throughout the early attacks. Some later attacks were very close, some far off, but damage grew steadily worse until, just before the last attack, the crew blew all tanks and started to the surface. The last depth charge pattern exploded well below her as she was already half way up. On surfacing, the first shell sprung the conning tower hatch, preventing access to the gun mount. All men who could get clear abandoned in a hail of gun fire.

Of the original submarine crew, 37 were rescued. Medical treatment was administered to wounded prisoners. The Task Group then proceeded to Casablanca where the prisoners were turned over to the Commander of the Moroccan Sea Frontier. *Kapitanleutnant* Boehmer's leg was badly damaged in the battle and had to be amputated in a military hospital.

We are indebted to Leonard Roberts, former crewman on *Haverfield*, for his interview with ex U-boat Commander Boehmer in Germany several years after the war.

After a period of escorting along the East Coast, *Francis M. Robinson (DE-220)* arrived at Norfolk on 2 May 1944 to join the *Bogue* HUK Group, in whose Presidential Unit Citation she was about to share. Designated Task Group 22.2, the Commander (CTG) was Captain A.B. Vosseller, the new commanding officer of *Bogue*. The Group was composed of the carrier and four escorts from *Escort Division 51*: *Janssen (DE-396)*, *Swenning (DE-394) Willis (DE-395)* and *Haverfield*, flying the pennant of commander of *Escort Division 51*, Commander T.S. Lank.

Francis M. Robinson, the fifth escort, flew the pennant of the commander of *Escort Division 54*, Commander M. E. Dennett, who was ordered to the *Bogue* screen as an observer for the cruise. Prior to sailing, Lieutenant (jg) R. L. Rather reported on board *Robinson* for temporary duty as an antisubmarine specialist. His knowledge and frank criticisms were extremely valuable during his stay on board. The Group's second combat cruise departed from Norfolk on 5 May 1944.

On 13 May, the Task Group made contact with *Block Island (CVE-21)* HUK group and plans were made to establish the position of two Japanese submarines operating in that area. Actually, they were German U-boats transferred to the Japanese who desperately needed the superior German submarine technology. The cruise was marked by fair weather and two attacks on U-boats.

Evening of the same day. Near the Cape Verde Islands, *Robinson* established a contact with a submarine at 825 yards. The sub was almost abeam when the DE swung to port and headed for the contact. The sound officer, sound operator and ASW specialist classified the echo as a submarine with slight down doppler. Recorder traces, definite doppler, and target movement gave undeniable proof of the presence of a submarine. A preliminary run was made from 700 yards for the express purpose of delivering an urgent attack between *Bogue* and the submarine. Accuracy was sacrificed for speed but, when a firing position was reached, *Bogue* was positioned stern to the contact and heading away at full speed. Therefore, an urgent attack was no longer necessary.

Contact was readily maintained as the range was opened during the final attack. A combination of hedgehogs and Mark 8 depth charges, set on full magnetic, was delivered. They produced two distinct hedgehog explosions seven seconds after entering the water and three depth charge explosions at close intervals up to three minutes after the hedgehog explosions. Several minutes after the last depth charge detonation, a loud underwater explosion was heard, followed a minute later by a much louder one. These two explosions were clearly heard and felt on *Bogue* five miles away and, according to Captain Vosseller and others on board *Bogue*, they greatly exceeded in force any of the previous explosions. A standard search procedure was employed. However, the target had disappeared.

Malcolm B. Fraser was a junior officer on *Robinson*. He was the only one aboard who had completed a course in aircraft recognition and, consequently, had a battle station on the bridge. He repeated the captain's orders to internal stations or on the TBS. His story about the attack on the submarine:

> "When we got the two hedgehog hits, I grabbed the TBS ship to ship voice radio instead of the interior communications phone in the excitement and yelled, 'We got the "sonofabitch", we got him!' Thus went out the report to the Task Group Commander! I only wanted the crew below to know. After we secured and were going over the whole thing in the wardroom, Paul Campbell, executive officer and our next captain, wanted to know who it was on the TBS. Captain Johansen was sitting in his place at the end of the table. He said, 'What was that?' I blushed and admitted I got too excited and grabbed the TBS by mistake. The skipper said, 'I want that in the log'. He thought it was great."

A box search of the area was commenced but abandoned 3-1/2 hours later by order from *ComCortDiv 51*. It was believed that no sub could have survived this attack, and the Group continued in pursuit of other U-boats reported by CincLant.

One of the most interesting results of this attack in postwar analysis was that *Robinson* had sunk the Japanese submarine *RO-501*, the former German *U-1224*. An article in *DESA News*, January 1986, (abridged) elucidated the background of this encounter:

> German Vice Admiral Paul H. Weneker arranged the deal in Tokyo. He was in charge of the submarine block-

ade running between Japan and Germany. A number of U-boats reached the Java Sea and Singapore and several made it to Japan. One or two Japanese submarines managed to run from Japan to Germany. Weneker thought little of Japanese submarines. 'They were too big for easy handling when under attack', he asserted, 'and consequently not hard to sink.' However, Weneker cooperated with Admiral Miwa and arranged for a Japanese crew to be sent to Germany for training.

(This possibly explains the loud explosions from the submarine. It was commonplace in the Pacific and was believed by some to be a form of *hara kiri* to avoid "dishonorable" capture when damaged beyond repair.)

Failing to make further sub contacts, the Group proceeded to Casablanca. Just before midnight on 29 May, *Haverfield* was ordered out on an emergency mission to render assistance to *Block Island (CVE-21)* and *Barr (DE-576)*, both of which had been torpedoed. (See narrative *The Block Island Hunter-Killers*.) Her orders were subsequently altered to the Canary Islands to search for six fighter pilots who were aloft when the carrier was sunk. A sweep recovered two survivors from a raft. The remaining pilots were lost.

The group departed from Casablanca on 2 June. After leaving, efforts were directed toward several submarines west and north of Casablanca, including a possible rendezvous of a northbound Japanese sub and a southbound U-boat. Their estimated tracks were swept over and over and followed with continuous day and night air search until the Group's northeast limit was reached. The course was then set for northeast Azores. Here, the most determined efforts were rewarded only with numerous attacks on large schools of fish.

At long last, the Task Group started home (with a wistful eye on the Normandy invasion area and the large number of U-boats reported there). During flight operations on the dark night of 20 June, two planes went down; crews were rescued by *Haverfield* and *Robinson*.

All ships have special moments, and Malcolm Fraser of *Robinson* remembered one in particular:

> "I have already told you I was on the bridge, manning the voice tubes for the captain. Whenever an aircraft had a contact, we were sent out to inspect the area. One night, while investigating a contact, a pilot dropped a flare on us. It was like Times Square in the middle of the Atlantic. Skipper Johansen got on the radio and asked 'What in the hell is going on?' Response from the *Bogue*, 'Sorry, Captain, I can brief my pilots, but I cannot be held responsible for their mental processes."

En route to Norfolk, the escorts were detached from the carrier and sent on to the New York Navy Yard for availability. *Haverfield* had been underway continuously for 60 days with the exception of two 12 hour periods in Casablanca and a 24 hour stop in Bermuda, all three periods to refuel and provision.

This report would not be complete without mentioning the efficient manner in which *Bogue* fueled its escorts at sea. Alongside the carrier six times, *Robinson* received 300,647 gallons of fuel oil in a total overall time of seven hours.

The *Robinson*'s commanding officer, Lieutenan Commander J.E. Johansen, noted in his war diary:

> "The cruise has been a definite boon to this vessel; both officers and crew have benefited considerably from the training received during long periods at sea. Officers in particular have become adept at ship handling during day and night evolutions of the screen. The commanding officer agrees with nearly everyone on board that this type of duty is to be preferred over any other type of present destroyer escort operations (convoys)."

Haverfield, as part of the Task Group composed of five escorts and the carrier, departed from Norfolk on 25 July 1944. The second day out, *Haverfield* rescued three men who had been knocked overboard from *Bogue* by a plane crashing on the flight deck.

In April 1945, *Bogue* put to sea, forming part of Captain G.J. Dufek's Barrier Force. Her destroyer escorts brought her final war tally to 13 submarines. See chapter *Twilight of the U-boats*.

Francis M. Robinson was detached from the *Bogue* Group to screen five successive convoys to North African ports.

Late morning on 17 February 1945, the fourth voyage. As the convoy passed eastward through the Straits of Gibraltar, two merchantmen were torpedoed by *U-300*. One made port under her own power. One of the torpedoes passed underneath *Robinson* and hit the merchant ship *Regent Lion*, right next to her. This was obviously an acoustic torpedo as it hit the propeller of the merchant ship.

Parky Howe, who had extensive experience with torpedoes, said that the only reason the torpedo did not go for the DE's propellers was that it had not yet armed when it passed under her. *Robinson* remained with *Regent Lion*, sending a damage control party on board to assist in stopping the flooding. It was a harrowing experience, related by her commanding officer, Paul Campbell, executive officer at the time of sinking of *RO-501*:

> "At the time, Carmine Forzono and Jim Deal, both of our engine room gang, were in the after crew's quarters. Both were up and getting ready to go on watch when they heard the torpedo go right under them and promptly headed for their battle stations. Neither of them had ever heard a noise like that. There was also a card game going on in the compartment; everybody threw their cards in the air and headed for their battle stations. When they heard the general alarm, they were way ahead of it!
>
> We then ran back alongside the convoy at full speed and dropped an embarrassing barrage near the tanker to drive the U-boat down. The explosion of our depth charges countermined a second torpedo that was apparently headed for us only a few yards away. Thus, we missed a second attack by a matter of seconds. This torpedo was fired about five to ten minutes after the first one.
>
> We went alongside the torpedoed tanker, which was awash at the stern, and got pumps and hoses aboard to keep her afloat. It was a hairy maneuver in a choppy sea. We put fenders over to avoid sparks from the two ships rubbing each other and igniting her cargo of aviation gasoline. We could see fumes rising in the air. When Charlie Krull got his damage control party aboard, the tanker captain came aft, offered

Charlie a cigar, and lit both of them with all the fumes rising around us! I was horrified, but the captain was just trying to show Charlie his appreciation for our saving his ship. While alongside the tanker, I told our engine room to keep up steam and have the men stand by the throttles. If the tanker caught fire or exploded, they were to back full without further orders, our only chance of saving the ship. A British tug came out from Gibraltar and took over a few hours later.

The *Robinson* crew will never forget that experience. But we accomplished our mission, and several commendations were issued later by the Commander in Chief of the Atlantic Fleet. The "Rockin Robbie" was a lucky ship.

When I went below from the bridge later that evening, our ship's medical officer, Dr. Kuber, motioned me into his cabin, broke out a couple of small bottles of Scotch, poured one into a glass and handed it to me. It was the only drink I ever had aboard a Navy ship. My only criticism is that he should have done it for every man aboard because each did such a magnificent job. And I'm sure they were all just as pooped as I was."

Completing her convoy duty on 15 May 1945, *Francis M. Robinson* aided submarines training out of New London and was a school ship at the Naval Training Center at Miami to the end of the war.

THE MISSION BAY HUNTER-KILLERS

Fessenden is the Star

Fessenden (DE-142) was a veteran of the harrowing Convoy UGS/GUS-38 (See chapter *Convoys to the Mediterranean*). On 8 September 1944, she sailed from Norfolk with *Mission Bay (CVE-59)*, whose captain, John R. Ruhsenberger, was also Task Group Commander. The Screen Commodore was Commander E.W. Yancey, *ComCortDiv 9*. Other escorts were *Farquhar (DE-139)*, commanded by Lieutenant Commander D.E. Walter; *J.R.Y. Blakely (DE-140)*, commanded by Lieutenant A.S. Archie; *Douglas L. Howard (DE-138)*, commanded by Lieutenant J.T. Pratt and *Hill (DE-141)*.

On 20 September, The Task Group was ordered by CincLant, Admiral Ingersoll, to join *Tripoli (CVE-64)* HUK Group and to break up a scheduled rendezvous of two German submarines west of the Cape Verde Islands. Grossadmiral Doenitz had tracked the 'milk cow' *U-1062*, inbound from Penang, Malaya, laden with a valuable cargo of petroleum products for Germany and the U-boats. At the same time, *U-219* was trying to run the blockade and get to Japan. *U-1062* was directed to refuel *U-219*, then about 600 miles west south west of Fogo Islands in the Cape Verde Archipelago. The *Mission Bay* and *Tripoli* Groups joined up on 28 September. That same day, planes from *Tripoli* attacked a submarine, probably *U-219*, without success and lost one plane and its crew. That plane's pilot had made contact and radioed: "I've got him! He's shooting at me and I'm going in to make a run!"

The rest was silence. Two other planes attacked the boat but without success. There was no further contact on that day or the next.

The carriers alternated in maintaining constant air surveillance until the last day of September when a *Mission Bay* plane dropped a smoke flare at a point of visual contact. Finally, early on the first dog watch on 30 September, *Fessenden*, *Douglas L. Howard*, and *J.R.Y. Blakely* were detached to investigate a sonobuoy indication of a submarine. Arriving in the area in midafternoon, *Fessenden* made sonar contact. One minute later, her skipper, Lieutenant Commander W.A. Dobbs, began an attack run. When the range had closed to 600 yards, the contact was established as positive submarine. The DE fired a pattern of 24 hedgehogs. Four undersea explosions sent up a large geyser of water and, two minutes later, *Fessenden* dropped a 17 depth charge pattern over the explosion point. Gurgling and cracking noises were heard. Contact was lost and never regained.

Two hours later, two more depth charge patterns were dropped. At nightfall, a plane reported an oil slick near the point of attack. By the next morning, the slick was 1000 yards wide and two miles long. The position of the oil slick never changed and, by 6 October, it covered 25 square miles. *Fessenden* was credited with destroying *U-1062*. It is interesting to note that this sinking took place only 15 miles from the position indicated by the Tenth Fleet estimate of the U-boat rendezvous. "Huff-Duff" interpretation, Navy Intelligence and combat efficiency spelled the end of another sub.

After serving as a school ship at the Subchaser Training Center in Miami, *Fessenden* returned to the *Mission Bay* Task Group 22.1. The Group departed from Guantanamo Navy Base on 15 February 1945 to supply antiaircraft and antisubmarine coverage for President Franklin Roosevelt and his party, returning from the Yalta Conference.

In company with the *Mission Bay* Group, *Fessenden* left Norfolk to participate in the final North Atlantic sweeps and destruction of still another enemy sub. The objective was the protection of the eastern seaboard of North America from "Operation Seawolf," snorkel U-boats attacking in wolf packs. (See chapter *Twilight of the U-boats* for final actions of the *Mission Bay* HUK.

Some of the above was taken from *Fessenden* ship's chronicles, compiled by Mitchell E. Sapp, as part of a family history and in honor of his father, Fireman First Class James H. Sapp Sr., a crew member.

Both photographs were taken aboard *Bronstein* while patrolling off Iceland in WWII.

Bronstein underway in the North Atlantic in WWII.

Lieutenant Sheldon H. Kinney, Commanding Officer *USS Bronstein*, being congratulated by Vice Admiral Royal E. Ingersoll, Commander–in–Chief U.S. Atlantic Fleet. April 15, 1943. Courtesy US Naval Historical Center

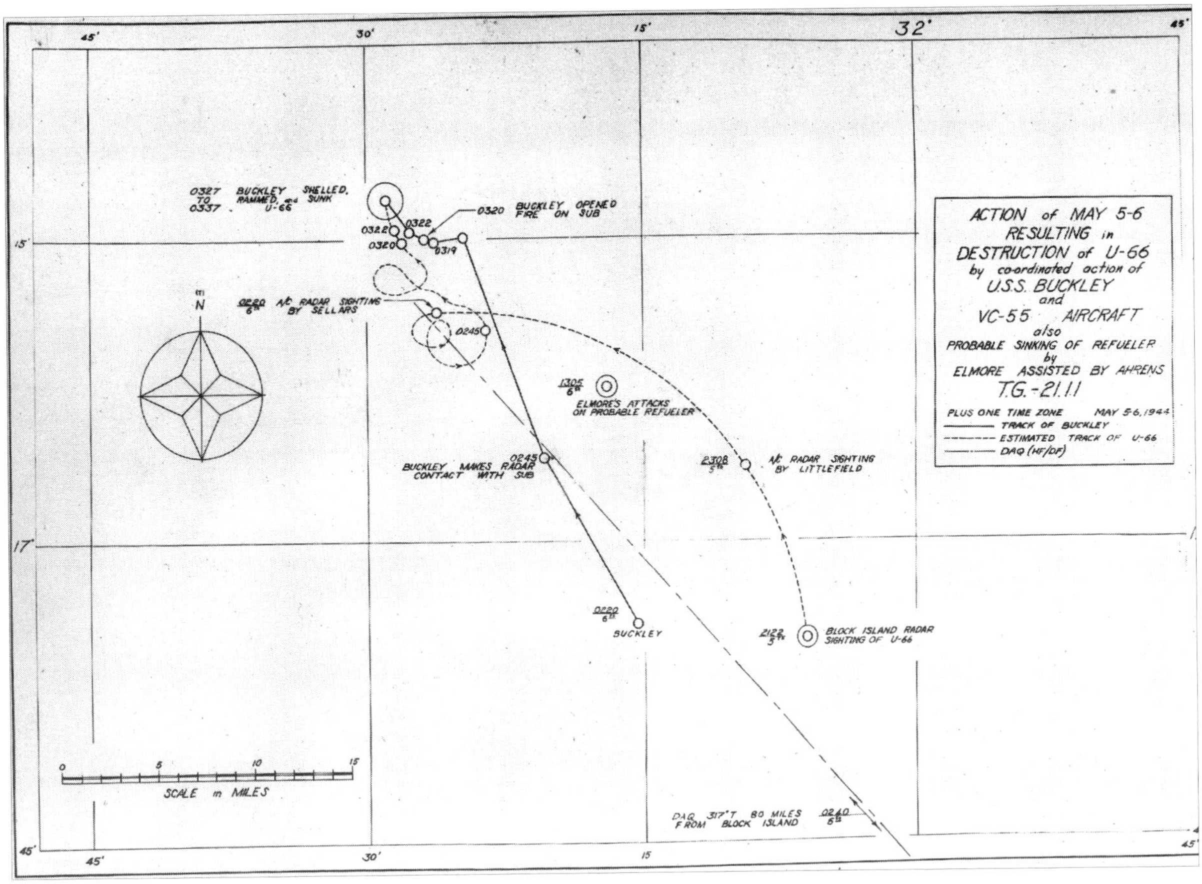

Action of May 5–6 resulting in the destruction of *U–66.* Courtesy Naval History Division

Taken from the deck of *Bronstein* while *Bronstein* and *Corry* sink *U-801* with gunfire.

Survivors of *U-66* – US Navy Photo

Surviving officers of *U-66* – US Navy Photo

Lewis M. Andrews, Jr.

USS Buckley – US Navy Photo

U-515 surfacing after depth charge attack

U-515 makes final dive after engagement

USS Baker (Taken from carrier, *USS Card*) – US Navy Photo

Aerial view of sinking *U-515* – Courtesy National Archives

Survivors of *U-515* boarding *Chatelain* – Courtesy National Archives

Boarding party chasing *U-505* – Courtesy National Archives

Pillsbury coming alongside *U–505* – Courtesy National Archives

Old Glory flies over captured *U-505* as boarding party secures tow line. US Navy Photo

Captain Daniel V. Gallery, task force commander, and Lieutenant (jg) Albert L. David, boarding party commander, on *USS Guadalcanal*. US Navy Photo

Thomas ramming and sinking *U-233*. Enlargements from motion picture frames, taken by Lt. Ed Sherman on bridge and given to author by David M. Kellog, who was C.O. at time of attack.

USS Fiske broken in half, going to the bottom – US Navy Photo

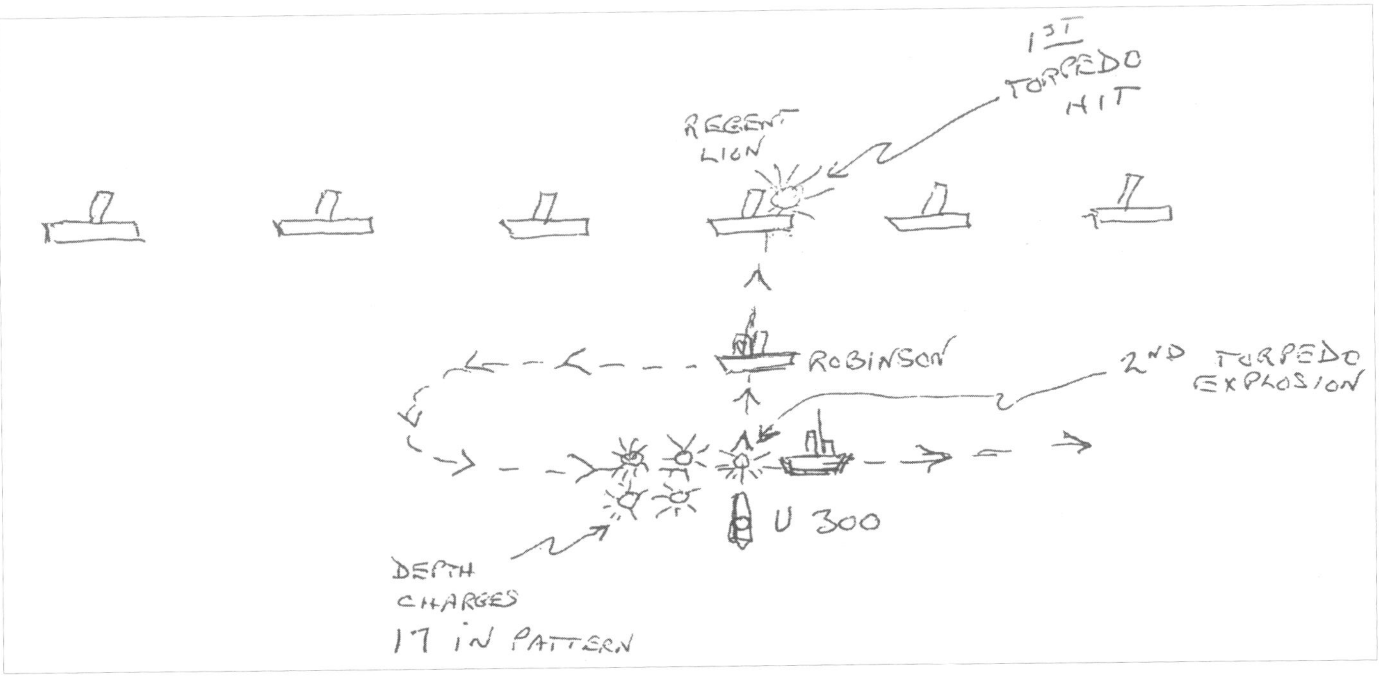

Convoy of about 100 ships including escorts, headed eastward through the Straits of Gibraltar. 17 February 1945.

Chapter VI - Saga Of The Polish Gold

In a matter of days following the German attack on Poland, 1 September 1939, the Nazi military machine had crushed all resistance. On 17 September, Russia entered Poland from the east, and both invaders partitioned the conquered country. By 30 September, all that remained of Polish independence was a provisional government in Paris.

Unlike men o'war, which prepare in advance an abandon ship bill, few nations are prepared to deliver their essentials to safety if the state must be abandoned. The lack of an "abandon nation" bill is manifested in the chaotic attempts of an invaded state to rescue its treasury, without which its currency is void, its foreign credit nil, and ability to fight back crippled. The weight of the precious metal in the face of confusion and panic renders its transport difficult under the best of conditions.

Navy vessels aided many of Europe's governments to carry their gold to safety. A British destroyer raced to Crete to secure that island's gold before capture. French gold was transported by French cruisers from Bordeaux to America, Dakar and Martinique. Norway's gold was rescued by three British cruisers.

German *panzer* forces reached the outskirts of Warsaw so swiftly that the gold of the *Bank Polski* still lay in its vaults far below the now shattered city. Faced with imminent capture, the bank directors commandeered and loaded 15 Polish army heavy trucks amid constant bombing and started south for the Rumanian border. The Nazis knew the gold's location; its capture was a campaign objective. Hitler wanted the gold to buy badly needed raw materials; German military commanders were directed to take pains to block its escape.

Ignace Matuszewski, former Polish Finance Minister; Zygmunt Karpinski, a director of the bank, and six other officials joined the stream of refugees pouring out of Warsaw. Children and women sat atop the trucks to divert suspicion. Going across Rumania, a squadron of German planes, informed of the ruse, attacked. Men died, and their comrades worked to exhaustion salvaging bullion from the debris wrought by aerial bombs. Some gold was lost in the attack, but the bulk of the cargo reached the Rumanian Black Sea port of Constanta. It was loaded aboard a tanker which sailed immediately. A few hours later, the government of Rumania, at German direction, acted to seize the ship, only to learn that it had slipped through their fingers.

The cargo reached Lebanon. French cruisers loaded and shipped it to the south coast of France. The gold was then sent north by rail and placed with that of the Bank of France. Security evaporated with the Battle of France and the advancing enemy. Polish officials agonized as decision replaced decision. It had been agreed that, in an emergency, shipment was to be made to America. French gold was being sent to the U.S. by every ship available, some in American warships. Yet, the Polish gold was sent by the French to a hiding place near Bordeaux. With Belgium and Northern France occupied, the gold then traveled northwest to Lorient as France surrendered.

On the day following the surrender, the gold escaped from Lorient in a French vessel. German mines were planted by aircraft in the harbor entrance as the ship sought escape. Both the ship ahead and the ship astern of her hit mines, but the floating bank got clear. The first day at sea, three successive dispatches directed her to return to Lorient, but the captain distrusted the messages. Though the coding was correct, he detected a phrasing more German than French, and proceeded to Casablanca. Later, it was proved that the Germans had obtained the French naval codes and were originating the dispatches.

Casablanca was only a temporary halt. The next stop was Dakar and a jungle hiding place. Only one Polish Bank official was in Dakar and he was kept in the dark. Rumor was rife. Some said the Germans had discovered it. Others claimed the hiding place was so good that even the French couldn't remember it.

But none of this was known to *Block Island (CVE-21)* and her five escorts, operating in the vicinity of the Cape Verde Islands when, on 20 February 1944, orders were received to detach two escorts, *Breeman (DE-104)* and *Bronstein (DE-189)*, and send them to Dakar. (These were the same two ships that were heavily involved with U-boats as per chapter *The Hunter-Killers*.) Scuttlebutt ran wild, but nobody had any idea of what the actual assignment would be.

The Germans knew the approximate location of the gold. Dispatching a large vessel to transport it, would have been an invitation to a torpedo. What better ships for the job than destroyer escorts whose business was sub hunting and who obviously would not be entrusted with large quantities of gold?

On 25 March, orders from Vice Admiral William A. Glassford were received by the commanding officer of *Breeman (DE-104)*, Lieutenant Commander E.N.W. Hunter. (The *Breeman* skipper was senior of the two ships. The contributor to much of this article, Lieutenant Sheldon Kinney, was captain of *Bronstein*.) The DEs were to receive a cargo of gold from Mr. Stephan Michalski, Director of the Bank of Poland, then proceed to New York City without delay.

By the time the ships reached Dakar, the gold had been brought from the interior and lay in the French fort overlooking the harbor; the same fort that, not too long before, had felt the weight of British guns when General De Gaulle had made an unsuccessful attempt to take the city. The Polish Bank Director was on hand to see this shipment en route to the United States. In all fairness, it must be noted that the French had exerted considerable expense and effort to maintain the treasury intact since received in Lebanon five years before. But for French assistance, it would have long ago fallen into German hands.

As soon as the working day was over in the French Naval Base, the yard was cleared of all but responsible military personnel. French army trucks commenced a series of trips from fort to pier. Senegalese soldiers with fixed bayonets guarded the trucks. Aboard the ships, ammunition was shifted to make space for the heavy load. While the bulk was not large for a cargo ship, it was daunting to those faced with its stowage in a DE. Stability and security seemed best achieved by employing magazines near the keel and as close as possible to the machinery spaces. The weight was huge in proportion to the displacement of the ships. Munitions in those areas were removed and squeezed into comparable stowage in other parts of the ship.

It was agreed that possession passed out of French hands upon delivery to the main deck. The trucks were unloaded and the boxes carried aboard by Senegalese sailors of the Free French Navy. Each box was about 12" X 24" X 10." Within each, four gold bars were packed in sawdust. The boxes were bound in iron bands and sealed with "BP" (*Bank Polski*). They were numbered and checked as they came aboard.

The black sailors who did the carrying were short, about 5'6" in height, but of extremely powerful build. The Senegalese stacked a pile of boxes on deck, their line slowly moving from truck to hatch as they shouldered each box and walked it aboard. As the Senegalese carried the first boxes aboard and set them on the deck, the crew formed a line to carry them below. A seaman leaned over to lift the first box, but it didn't budge. Embarrassed, he stepped aside to let another try. After several attempts by the huskies of the deck and black gang, the crew admitted defeat and rigged a block and tackle to the hatch davit. First Class Sonarman Clinton L. Gantt Sr. of the *Bronstein* added a metaphor to the above:

> "You remember in the movies where the robbers say, 'Throw down the gold chest'. The stage coach driver complies with the demand and heaves the gold down. One of the robbers dismounts, easily picks up the chest, throws it on his saddle and rides off. Let me assure you that the weight of the gold negates this comedy. Gold is one of the heaviest metals and cannot be handled so easily. You can forget about the action in movies."

The DE skippers had presumed that some official of the Bank of Poland would take passage in each ship as custodian. To their surprise and dismay, a receipt was requested of each for the gold, and it became clear that this was strictly a bank messenger job, with each captain "holding the sack" for the heavy treasure stowed in the magazines.

The spaces which held the gold were put under lock and key. An officer was assigned duty at the entry to the magazine and the ladders leading to the spaces below deck. This security was maintained all during the voyage right up to the time that the gold was offloaded. No "souvenirs" would be taken from this cargo.

The vessels cleared the harbor at midnight. Passage through the mine fields was made by following the lead of a French subchaser. The course to New York was to be a great circle, speed 18 knots. A slight deviation avoided the Cape Verde Islands, from which reports of passing naval vessels had a way of falling into the wrong hands.

Shortly after dusk of the third day, *Bronstein* made contact, classified as probable submarine. In accordance with orders, a depth charge pattern was dropped, speed increased to full, and the vessels continued on, sending position data to a nearby HUK Group. Heartbreaking as it was for a destroyer escort to pass up a U-boat contact, too much was at stake to risk being torpedoed while attacking.

The loading of the cargo contrasted with the offloading. There were units of the Marines, FBI, New York Police, Naval Intelligence, and the Navy Yard Police. To complicate matters, the vessels arrived in the yard after "banking hours." The Federal Reserve Bank announced that it would be impossible to accept it until the next day. Strict isolation was ordered for the ships until the gold was removed. Sonarman Gantt recalled the scene in the Brooklyn Navy Yard:

> "Only the captain was allowed off the ship. Yard workers attempting to board us to perform maintenance and repairs were turned away. The next morning, an army of Brinks Armored Trucks and yard security forces appeared. Cranes unloaded the cargo."

Armored trucks of the Federal Reserve shuttled the boxes to the vault of the New York Branch under Liberty street in downtown Manhattan. Two commanding officers wiped the sweat from their brows and, with a sigh of relief, inspected their receipts from the government for a cargo of boxes, "stated to contain gold." Down in those damp, robber-proof, bomb-proof vaults, lay $4,000,000,000* in gold from various nations for protection. The Polish gold, $65,000,000*, joined the greatest and most abrupt mass movement of gold in history.

Unfortunately, the Russian sponsored Polish government was the de facto controlling body in Poland. When the United States formally recognized that government of Poland, the last hope of the Bank of Poland faded. It was a bitter blow to the men who had devoted a large part of their lives to keeping the treasure intact. For them, there would be no triumphant return.

In France, a final $285,000,000 had been rushed aboard the carrier *Bearne* to Fort de France in Martinique as Marshall Petain was signing the armistice. When it arrived, the military Governor, Admiral Georges Robert, disobeyed orders to sink the gold and scuttle the warships in case the United States intervened in the islands. After the bloodless seizure of Martinique in July, 1943, several American and French officials traveled to Fort de France and found all the gold packed in 8,766 "shoe boxes" in the Fort Desaix casemates.

This author was skipper of a subchaser in the Caribbean during 1942 and recalls occasional small convoys from Trinidad to St. Lucia, then a British colony, immediately south of Martinique. The U.S. Army had about 1800 troops stationed there for the purpose of seizing Martinique when and if the order came. Admiral Robert had under his command the aircraft carrier *Bearne* and the cruiser *Richelieu*, on which we kept a close surveillance. As the war progressed, however, those ships were gradually weakened by French sailors deserting to the Free French Navy. When American Admiral Hoover, Commander of The Caribbean Sea Frontier in San Juan, Puerto Rico, threatened invasion, Admiral Robert surrendered peacefully.

The above was largely derived from *Naval Institute Proceedings* with permission, copyright 1948 U.S.N.I. and an article by Ms Sylvia Porter, *The Great Nazi Gold Rush*, Colliers, September 1945.

* Monetary figures are based on the mandated gold price of $35.00 per ounce which prevailed from the Roosevelt to the Nixon Administrations. Today, the values are 11 to 12 times those amounts on the world market for the gold bars plus an undetermined amount for the seigniorage and numismatic values of coins that were also included!

Survivors of *USS Rich* being rescued by *PT-504* and *HMS ML-116*. Courtesy US Naval Historical Center

Lewis M. Andrews, Jr.

Chapter VII - Overlord/Neptune. Channel Islands

ESCORT DIVISION NINETEEN

AMESBURY

While awaiting the formation of a return convoy from Londonderry, Northern Ireland, orders suddenly arrived for *ComCortDiv 19*, Commander H.W. Howe, on his flagship, *Amesbury (DE-66)*, to join the 12th Fleet at Belfast without delay. Other escorts in *CortDiv 19* were *Bates (DE-68)*, *Blessman (DE-69)*, *Bunch (DE-694)* and *Rich (DE-695)*. Speculation ran high after joining the huge, assembled battle force. *CortDiv 19* was to be a part of "*Operation Neptune*," the naval phase of "*Operation Overlord*," the invasion of Normandy.

She departed from Belfast on 3 June 1944 in the screen of Bombardment Group "Oboe," Task Force 124, comprising battleships, cruisers and destroyers of the American, British and Free French Navies. Signalman Third Class Walter Z. Sanker remembers the feverish preparations:

> "All hands were given instruction in first aid, fire and rescue, man overboard, and general repair; each division went through drills in its own specialized area. All hands were told to rest up and be in tip top shape, because we weren't going to a picnic. To many of us, this was to be the first live combat we'd seen. So, to say the least, we were pretty scared. One quartermaster said he had nibbled down to his knuckles and wondered what would be left of his fingers after it was all over.
>
> Besides all the drills, we were given orders to stow unnecessary gear, 'clearing the decks for action'. On the day before departure, all hands were called to GQ in order that the officers might correct any weak points that could arise. The executive officer then told the men to gather around the loud speakers; the captain wanted to speak to us. Within five minutes, everyone was so close to the loud speakers that one would have thought the captain was going to whisper his message to us.
>
> He told us why we had such rigorous training the past week, that we were about to participate in a very dangerous mission, what the world has been waiting to hear The invasion of France! He also wanted to relay the message issued by General Eisenhower."

Supreme Headquarters, Allied Expedition Forces Soldiers Sailors Airmen of the Allied Expeditionary Force.

> "You are about to embark upon the greatest crusade, toward which we have striven these many months. The eyes of the world are upon you. We will bring about the destruction of the German war machine and the elimination of Nazi tyranny The tide has turned! The free men of the world are marching together to victory.
>
> Good luck! And let us all beseech the Blessings of Almighty God upon this great and noble undertaking. We should feel proud and honored to be given a position on the first team. Let us all show them that they chose wisely in picking us. Good luck to you all and may God bless you."

Dwight D. Eisenhower
Supreme Commander

Signalman Sanker continued:

> "It took 15 minutes before anyone could speak. That was the best speech most of the men had ever heard or ever hoped to hear. That evening, Chaplain Kelly came aboard. With little equipment, a crude altar, barely space for the congregation, services were held in an after compartment. We set sail bright and early on the morning of 4 June. During the ride down the Irish Sea, no one was wisecracking or talking as usual. Some were off to themselves, contemplating what lay in store for them. Others, were huddled in little groups, chancing words now and then."

D-Day at Normandy had been scheduled for the morning of 5 June but, upon arrival in the English Channel on the afternoon of the 4th, the big show had been postponed 24 hours due to poor weather. With the arrival of the assault force on 6 June, after a nightmare (rough) crossing of the Channel, *Amesbury* was assigned to picket duty off Omaha Beach, Normandy. During the next week, she took part in several antiaircraft actions. Signalman Sanker put it with more emphasis:

> "We had just stopped our engines when the roar of airplane motors could be heard far behind us, drawing louder and clearer by the minute. Shortly after they passed over us, all hell broke loose."

Both air forces suffered heavy casualties that night. The DE men, watching the fracas on the open deck, alternated cheering with sorrow, depending on whose plane was being shot out of the air, resembling a cheering section at a football game. It was a chilling sight when a friendly plane, hit by antiaircraft fire from the beach, burst into a fireball and plunged to the ground.

At dawn, the air was almost clear of bombers, and the navy began its shelling. While battleships and cruisers offshore were blasting away, the landing craft and Higgins boats were edging their way toward the beach. Ships and landing craft alike quickly became targets of German gun emplacements that had survived the air bombardment. Before a smoke screen could be laid, the enemy scored hits on numerous landing craft and blew away the after part of a British cruiser; the forward section was still fighting back despite the damage.

Ten hours at GQ every night for a week in the picket area became an imprint on the minds of the men. They wearied of the frequent night air attacks and the daily sight of vessels crippled or sunk by mines.

0200 on D plus 3. *Amesbury* was ordered to dash out through the mine fields and bring in a British convoy of small merchantmen that was under air attack. Upon sighting the convoy, she was greeted with the scream of a radio-controlled glider bomb from a JU 88, passing 15 yards down her starboard side, followed by an attempted strafing attack. The plane was beaten off by a nearby destroyer while *Amesbury* led the convoy to safety.

2112 on 11 June, D plus 6. *LST-496*, loaded with tanks and troops, struck a mine while proceeding to the assault area, 1000 yards from *Amesbury*. The DE immediately made her way to the side of the stricken vessel. Three smaller craft also arrived on the scene and were picking up survivors from the water. *Amesbury's* skipper, Lieutenant Commander A.B. Wilber, skillfully maneuvered his DE alongside the *LST*, and her boarding party carried off the dead and wounded as the vessel settled into the sea. Captain Wilber summoned a doctor from *LCI-530* to treat the injured men taken on board.

Meanwhile, the tug *ATA-125* arrived on the scene and, with the assistance of *Amesbury's* men still on board the *LST*, secured a tow line to the crippled ship. However, when barely underway, the landing ship began to capsize to port, catching *Amesbury's* starboard side and pulling her over. Axes were quickly broken out as *Amesbury* cut her lines to clear, and her men aboard the doomed ship were ordered to jump off. Lieutenant H.J. Riley, in charge of the boarding detail, made certain that all of his men were safely away before diving in the water himself. All of the DE's sailors were picked up uninjured, but the ship they had attempted to salvage soon sank.

RICH

In Londonderry, Northern Ireland, the windows at the officers' club were blacked out with opaque drapes. The air was heavy with smoke. Americans, Canadians, Britishers stood at the bar, drinking Irish whiskey as a rule, Scotch if they were lucky. There were rumors. Were they going to convoy back to New York or something else?

The word came to the skipper of *Rich*, Lieutenant Commander Edward A. Michel, Jr. The Division Commander received orders to detail four of his ships to forces afloat in European waters for "other duties." Michel and his officers perked up at the news.

The crew became excited when ammunition was loaded in quantity. It was also a great letdown when four of the division steamed out without *Rich*. It began to read like another transatlantic convoy. Michel returned aboard and stomped up to his cabin, Out of six destroyer escorts to go, why should *Rich* be left behind? He was still musing restlessly when the quartermaster on watch knocked on the door: "Telephone, Captain, Operations Londonderry."

That was all the skipper needed to hear as he raced past the startled petty officer to the quarterdeck and took up the temporary phone installed at dockside. The orders were loud and clear: "Get under way as soon as possible for Plymouth, England!"

The only problem was the liberty party and some officers ashore. Michel exerted all his efforts on the shore patrol, and it was a tribute to that detail that the officers and men on shore were back on board within an hour. A few of the situations that were interrupted might have made good stories in themselves, had they been recorded.

> "Ireland isn't Australia," Water Tender D.J. Lawrence was saying to Torpedoman Mizes and Boatswain's Mate Russo as they stood on a street corner and watched the colleens pass. "Now, in Australia, the girls were... well, something pretty special." A veteran of the destroyer *Patterson* at Pearl Harbor on 7 December 1941 and with considerable liberty in Australia, he was acknowledged to be an expert in such matters. Before the conversation could be pursued, two shore patrol men, with urgent stride, hauled up before the three Lotharios.
>
> 'You guys from the *Rich*?'
> 'That's right.'
> 'Then, back to the ship on the double.'
> 'Why? We haven't done anything.'
> 'I know, Mac, but we just take orders. So, back to the ship!'"

Captain Michel wasted no time. *Rich* dropped down the dark Lough Foyle, turned northeast between Ireland and Scotland, then south into the Irish Sea. The captain ran her at full power through the black, unlit and unmarked waters until off Plymouth early in the morning of 1 June. There they received orders covering their mission.

The next five days were spent in evaluating the orders, preparing guns and ammunition, drilling all hands for all contingencies. To assure security, there was no liberty. Morale was extremely high, and the crew looked forward to the part it was about to play in the attack on "Fortress Europe." The men of *Rich* knew that a great many lives depended on how well they were to perform their assigned mission.

Rich departed from Plymouth in company with other destroyers, destroyer escorts and the transport *Bayfield (APA-33)*, flagship of Admiral Moon, Commander of the Utah Beach landing. Michel then decided to address the crew via the intercom and explain their purpose in the English Channel: "This vessel will form a close screen for the battleship *Nevada* and other heavy ships of the bombardment group shelling Utah Beach!"

The weather was frightful. *Rich* plowed through tons of water boiling over the foc's'l and spray sweeping her full length. The sea was grisly, gray and angry. It almost appeared as though the elements had combined to defeat this incredible armada.

Rich rendezvoused with *Nevada (BB-36)* and proceeded in the vanguard toward the invasion area. As they closed Utah Beach that night, the buoys that had previously been anchored by small craft to guide the force were somewhat out of position. *Nevada* directed *Rich* to proceed ahead and locate a particular buoy, which *Rich* was able to do, enabling *Nevada* and other heavy ships (battleships and cruisers) to reach their assigned positions. At daybreak, the bombardment force trained on targets and commenced its shelling of the enemy shore batteries. The DE was directed to seaward of *Nevada* as an antisubmarine and anti-E-boat patrol. (German E-boats were similar to U.S. motor torpedo boats.) Water Tender Lawrence recalled:

> "There was nothing tame about the morning of the 6th of June when the *Rich* moved in through the sharp swells of the channel. As far as the eye could see, the display of invasion craft moved through the gloom. Inland, a dull roar of bombs could be plainly heard as the air force softened up the opposition. Then the battlewagons and cruisers opened up.
>
> The enemy was coming back hot and heavy. Splashes were keeping the cruiser *Quincy (CA-71)* moving around as she laid her own salvos on the beach. As a precaution, a

smoke screen was laid between the bombarding force and the shore. However, the destroyer *Corry (DD-463)* was so far in that she was denied this protection and, in a few seconds, the entire weight of the defending batteries was on her. Big shells found their mark and broke the back of the DD.

All of 6 and 7 June, the story was the same for *Rich*. GQ all night, steady steaming, and watchful eyes turned toward the skies. The *Luftwaffe* made an appearance on the night of the seventh when the antiaircraft guns on *Rich* suddenly jarred into life for the first time. The deck crew noted that the bomber was dropping a string of blue lights, trailing out like Christmas tree bulbs, purpose unknown. Gunner's Mate Third Class Fox, on number three 3" gun, thought he should have had the Nazi and was still cursing his luck the next day. The bomber swooped low, dropped a bomb that exploded close astern of the DE, then dropped another on a 2100 ton French destroyer with a square hit. The Frenchman went up in one crashing, blinding flash. "

Counterbattery fire from enemy shore emplacements lobbed a few shells over, but none very close to *Rich*. With *Bates* she cruised back and forth, watching *Nevada* shell the beach with her big guns. When night came, the formation moved out from the beach, making it easier to avoid prowling E-boats. In the morning, the ships returned, and *Nevada* was joined by *Tuscaloosa (CA-37)* and two other cruisers in the bombardment of German fortifications. When night again came on, Michel secured from GQ and let all hands not on watch turn in with their clothes on except himself. He did manage to fall asleep in his chair on the flying bridge.

0200. Michel awakened to the sound and flash of considerable gunfire to seaward as well as over the beach. Planes came in, and *Rich* opened fire. Looking down at the water, Michel saw a torpedo wake closing the ship, too late for evasive action. The wake went right under her, the setting was too deep. However, it was close enough to be heard and to unsettle the engine room watch. Seconds later, a new destroyer, *Meredith (DD-434)*, close to *Rich*, exploded with a terrific blast as the same torpedo ripped out her innards. Almost immediately, the flag ordered a smoke screen about the heavy units. *Rich* raced at full speed to lay a smoke screen from both chemical generators and boilers. She circled the entire group of heavy ships, blocking them from visual sighting near or far.

8 June. *Rich* again secured from GQ, and Michel went down to the wardroom for breakfast. Only then did it occur to him that this was the first time he had been in the wardroom since leaving Plymouth. It felt so good he stopped by the his cabin and shaved off a growth of beard. He had scarcely wiped the residual lather off his face when an urgent visual dispatch was received from Admiral Deyer, Group Commander. Orders were to proceed to the aid of the destroyer *Glennon (DD-620)*; she hit a mine in the inner support lane.

The skipper consulted briefly with the navigator as to the swept channels down to *Glennon*. He ordered engines to full speed. The commander of the bombardment group on *Tuscaloosa* told *Rich* to follow two minesweepers into the area. This they did but they failed to overtake the sweepers. When *Rich* hove to near *Glennon*, the destroyer was down by the stern with her crew gathered on the bow. A sweeper had already gone alongside the starboard bow of the vessel while another was backing into position to tow her clear. *Rich* put a motor whaleboat over the side, but *Glennon* advised she had all the assistance needed, and the boat was recalled.

0920. *Rich* started back to the bombardment group. While still in proximity to *Glennon*, there was a terrific explosion 50 yards off the starboard bow. *Rich* was deluged with water. Interior telephone communications were temporarily disrupted, and there was some superficial damage in the engine room. However, the ship was not making any water, was in full operation, and there were no injuries. Water Tender Lawrence remembers:

> "I was at GQ in the fire room. The Jo pot (coffee) was going as usual. I had just made an entry in the engine room log when an explosion rocked the ship, like we were picked out of the water and then thrown violently back again. The coffee pot flew across the room. Buckets crashed around our heads, and the floor plates came loose; the one in the engine room was ripped up and hurled into the condenser. Then the lights went out and, as I picked myself up, I could hear the hiss of superheated steam."

A man in the black gang (engineering) knows the fear that envelopes him when, suddenly plunged into darkness, he hears a thin, stabbing finger of steam, so hot it can sear the flesh from the bones. Lawrence found a flashlight and soon discovered that the port gauge glass was shattered. The fire room crew cut the glass out of the steam line, then lit off number two boiler to raise the steam pressure which had fallen sharply. The lights came back on, the explosion having only tripped the generators. *Rich* had hardly recovered from that explosion when the second one occurred about two minutes later, closer and far more violent. The skipper recalled:

> "I was thrown to the deck. When regaining my feet, I looked aft through the weird green-yellow haze of smoke and water. I could see a large section of the ship's stern floating away."

The explosion severed the ship along a bulkhead between the after 3" gun and the 1.1" gun. Michel clutched a stanchion and saw his men in the water and others drifting away on the after section. On the main part of the ship, men were lying about, stunned from the concussion. Michel promptly gave orders to whoever could obey to remind the men on the after section to set depth charges on safe.

The main section was still afloat and not taking much water. As a security precaution, the communications officer, radio technician, and signalmen were ordered to destroy classified publications, radar and sound gear. *Rich* had survived two mines, but she was not about to survive the third and worst blast only three minutes after the second and five minutes after the first. It hit just forward of the bridge with a violent impact. Said the captain:

> "I was blown into the air. I remember going up but can't recall coming down. I heard the assistant gunnery officer calling me. Upon standing, I saw that he and I were the only ones on our feet. The mast had fallen across the bridge. The place was a shambles of mast, halyards, antennae and various other gear. Most of the men forward were either unconscious or unable to help themselves."

Water Tender Lawrence was in the engine spaces:

"We didn't have time to think about damage because, no sooner had the lights come on, when we were thrown to the deck by the second explosion. Again, we were plunged into darkness and again that hissing of steam in the inky black told us a steam line had ruptured. It was the starboard gauge glass this time, and the crew set about rectifying damage as swiftly as possible. The chief engineer groped his way into the fire room to check the damage, then ordered the men to get topside."

They needed no urging, feeling the ship taking on a list even as they climbed. It was then that the third and heaviest blow struck. *Rich* had evidently entered a mine field, perhaps one that had been planted the night before by the plane whose "blue lights" had caused the crew so much debate. Lawrence relates:

"Bateman was just climbing through the hatch when the explosion threw him up to the overhead, leaving a nasty gash across his head. Balack had secured the evaporators before heading up; he was hurled across the deck and badly bruised. We climbed up in the dark and into the shambles of the machine shop. It was like going through tangled barbed wire blindfolded; the spare boiler tubing had come down from the overhead and was twisted like spider webbing. Ammo from the 20mm clipping room was askew. Tools, boxes, pipes, and spare parts dangled, and leaned in crazy and dangerous positions. But we got through the tangle and out to the deck.

For the first time, we engineers could see the carnage. The entire stern was blown off. There was no smoke or fire, just the low, deadly hiss of steam from number one fire room and the broken body of the twisted ship. No doubt about it, we were finished. The starboard side had been thrust up a good three feet. The mast had come down across the flying bridge, trapping several men."

Rich began to settle by the bow, and the uppermost thought penetrating Michel's reeling mind was how to get the crew off, particularly the wounded. At *Rich's* worst moment, it was her fortune to be within call of a PT squadron under Lieutenant Commander John Bulkeley, the very same one who took General MacArthur off Corregidor. His PTs came alongside and boarded with blankets and stretchers. The majority of the crew were dead, wounded or missing. Those at least able to walk assisted the PTs in the transfer of the wounded, working against the imminent drowning of prostrate men. Water Tender Lawrence continued:

"There was no sign of panic as the crew worked to care for the wounded while the ship was going down under their feet. Every man did something. Some went about the ship administering morphine to the more painful cases. Others were carried to waiting PTs. When they ran out of stretchers, volunteers descended to the wardroom to bring up mattresses on which the wounded could be transferred."

As Lawrence went about the deck, assisting where he could, he was hailed by the gunnery officer, Lieutenant Fraser, who had a bad blow on his head. "Go up and see if the captain is all right."

When he got to the bridge, he found that the range finder had been blown off its mount and, with the fallen mast, had inflicted injuries on a great many men. The skipper was alive but had a bad leg. The executive officer, Lieutenant Commander Pearson, was also severely injured but, when efforts were made to move him, he refused. "There are others hurt worse than I am, I'll be all right." Ensign Cunningham, the assistant gunnery officer, had a broken leg but, in spite of it, he helped others down from the shattered bridge. And so it went, a quiet heroism that pervaded the entire crew.

Lawrence reported back to the gunnery officer and found the water had now almost covered the main deck. Lieutenant Fraser made sure that the depth charges were set on safe. Almost all the wounded had been transferred. A few could not be moved, and others were trapped by the mast and range finder on the bridge. Now, however, the ship began to roll slowly. The rescue craft cast off so as not to be caught as the ship turned over. At the last moment, a few men on the flying bridge dove into the water that was rising up to meet them.

The executive officer, who had refused to be taken off ahead of other members of the crew, went down with the ship; it was too late to help him. Those in the water turned on their backs to watch the ship as they swam. Their DE went down slowly and gracefully with her colors still flying. The rescue craft swiftly swarmed back to pick up the last few to get off. Among the few swimmers when the ship disappeared was her commanding officer, rescued and ultimately restored to duty.

Watertender Lawrence paid his final tribute:

"The survivors were returned to the States shortly afterward. There was nothing in the short span of the DE's life that will emblazon her name across the history books for future generations to read. The name of her skipper, the names of the men who made up her crew, the very name of the ship itself will be recorded only in the official records of the Navy Department." (This author hopes this book has modified that prediction.)

From a nearby PT boat, United Press War Correspondent, Robert Miller, wrote the following eye witness account of *Rich*. Announcement of the allied naval losses in the invasion of France permitted him to release the following dispatch.

Aboard an American PT Boat off Normandy, France (United Press by Robert Miller):

"Only a few hours ago, *USS Rich* was a proud American destroyer escort, loaded with hundreds of men. She had just moved in alongside the destroyer *USS Glennon*, slowly sinking from a mine contact, when a series of explosions sent the DE to the bottom in a matter of minutes.

We were about a quarter of a mile away when the violent explosions sank the stricken ship. Lieutenant Commander John D. Bulkeley of the expendables, a hero of PT boat fame, ordered his PT boat alongside *Rich* to offer assistance. However, at the time, the *Rich's* bridge replied that none was needed. Then came a muffled roar as another explosion ripped the ship, shooting into the sky a fountain of salt water mixed with oil, bodies, fragments of freshly killed men and pieces of steel. We were only fifty yards away, and the tremendous explosion hurled our frail PT boat as if slapped by a mighty hand. As the great green wall of water fell backward, like a giant theatrical curtain, it revealed *Rich* torn in half behind her stack.

The PT boat had not moved 50 feet away when the third and final blast ripped what was left of the sinking hull. One figure was draped over the side, motionless like a rag doll. Even the ship gave off weird sighs as the steam from her boilers escaped.

Another PT boat arrived and began removing what few survivors were left. The skipper was Lieutenant (jg) Calvin Whorton, former Los Angeles Times sports reporter. He dived into the oily water and rescued two men who were blasted from the ship. We came alongside and began taking men aboard from *Rich*. They mostly were mangled messes, dying from injuries. A few had miraculously escaped death and were attempting to carry their mates onto blood soaked decks. After depositing a few wounded on a hospital ship, our PT boat returned to the sinking area. There was nothing left of *Rich*, only a large oil spot and a few pieces of debris."

Seaman Ed Black from Pinehurst, North Carolina, wrote these final words in his diary shortly before his ship was mined.

"We all thank God that we survived the night without a mishap. In the time since the invasion started, we have slept only a few hours and eaten very little food. All of us are nervous and jumpy. At the present time, *Nevada* is shelling a town on the coast with her large guns. If we come through this OK, we will be lucky. However, our trust is in God to take us through safely."

He then put the diary back in his pocket. The last explosion blew Black up and into an overhanging metal signal flag container. His skull was fractured, his jaw was broken in five places, and his leg was broken. He received numerous shrapnel wounds in his face; half of the upper lip was blown off, and a deep gash on the right side of his face caused partial paralysis. He was a bloody mess on a dying ship. Ed Black remembers the nightmare:

"My best friend was Carlie Black (coincidental, not a relation) was beside me. I said, 'Carlie we've got to get out of here', but then I knew I couldn't make it. Carlie locked arms with me and said 'Come on, Ed', and we jumped into the water. Carlie pulled me to a life raft with six of us hanging on when I passed out."

The injured men on the raft were picked up by a rescue boat. Four of them, including Carlie Black, died. Ed Black, unconscious for 31 days, recovered and went home to North Carolina. He never thought of his diary again. He assumed it had been lost at sea.

Now we jump ahead to 6 June 1984, the fortieth anniversary of the Normandy invasion. Black, now retired, was standing on Utah Beach, looking out at the waters where his ship and his friends died. On the back of his jacket he has written, "Ed Black, *USS Rich*."

"Suddenly, a guy called my name. He said, 'I got you out of the water more dead than alive. I can't believe you are here'. He was very upset, and he almost fainted on seeing me. I just got his address and told him I'd get in touch with him later."

Ed went to Connecticut to meet Frank Calvo, the man who had saved his life. They had dinner, and then Calvo told Black he had something that belonged to him, and he handed Ed the 40 year old diary.

"He handed me that diary, and I liked to have passed out. I cried. The diary had fallen out of my pocket when Frank cut my clothes off. He'd kept it all these years because he thought I was dead."

Calvo had written one final entry in the diary he picked up from the bloody deck of his rescue boat that day:

"*USS Rich (DE-695)*. Two PT boats picked up survivors and brought them to *LST-57*. It is a miracle how any of them lived after being blown up so bad. We worked like mad taking care of them, but four passed away. We done all we could for them."

The rest of the pages are blank.

"I never thought I'd see the man who saved my life so I could thank him and hug his neck," Black said. "I'm getting ready to send him a country ham. It would take a better mathematician than me to figure the chances of two men finding themselves on the same beach 40 years later, thousands of miles from their homes, at the same moment and with my back turned so Frank could read my jacket."

The diary, its pages still stained by the bloody waters of Normandy, has been placed in a French museum, dedicated to the men who came to France in June 1944.

BATES

The officers on *Bates (DE-68)*, aware of their ship's historic mission at Utah Beach, contributed their observations to a consensus record. This author was privileged to come into possession of that unpublished document and has arranged excerpts in the original first person plural with certain technical modifications.

26 May 1944. For *Bates*, tied up in Londonderry, Northern Ireland, the invasion started when the captain, Lieutenant Henry A. Wilmerding Jr., returned from a briefing with the Division Commodore and announced to his officers that we probably would be a part of the Normandy invasion task force. On 27 May 1944, we stood out from Londonderry in company with *Blessman* and *ComCortDiv 19* on *Amesbury* and proceeded with them to Belfast. *Bunch* was en route to Plymouth, England, and *Rich* remained in Londonderry for the time being.

We anchored in Belfast Lough that evening, and one glance at the huge assembly of capital ships told us the invasion was imminent. The next morning, the captain took the communications and gunnery officers to the flagship and, upon return, he called a meeting of all officers in the wardroom to brief us on the situation. We were to screen the battleship *Nevada (BB-36)* while she bombarded enemy shore batteries.

On the afternoon of 30 May, *Bates* was ordered to depart immediately for Plymouth, England. We proceeded through the North Channel and the Irish Sea, tricky piloting as the British had planted large mine fields in these waters, close to our course line. The next morning, about 10 miles off the coast of Cornwall, *Bunch* approached from the opposite direction and sent a message: "I have left all information for you with the flag aboard *Bayfield (APA-33)* (attack transport) in Plymouth. Good Luck." That left us wondering two things: why was *Bunch* standing up the coast and why the "Good Luck?" We found the answer to both when we arrived in Plymouth that afternoon.

The invasion would consist of three main parts: a heavy aerial bombardment for five hours preceding H-hour; shelling of the shore defenses by battleships, cruisers, and destroyers; and finally the landings made by various assault craft. About three hours before H-hour, 15,000 paratroopers are to be landed behind the enemy lines facing the assault beach. On her way from Londonderry to Plymouth, *Bunch* had hit a floating log, damaging a propeller. Consequently, the Admiral at Plymouth ordered her to return to Belfast to be drydocked, and we were to take her place in the invasion.

The St. Marcouf Islands lie off Utah beachhead. Reconnaissance photos indicated a blockhouse on the Isle de Terre and a French fort on Isle du Large. The mission of *Bates* was to lend fire support while *PC-484*, with five landing craft, would debark troops and secure the islands. These islands controlled the area through which the main invasion force would pass, and it was imperative that they be secured prior to the arrival of the Allied force. Therefore, at H-hour minus 2 hours and 20 minutes, *Bates* was to proceed ahead of the main body and, at H-hour minus 1 hour and 40 minutes, she was to be in fire support position off the islands. This meant proceeding through an area that had not been cleared of enemy mines and standing close to the coastal batteries containing guns of major caliber!

4 June. Until two days prior to departing from Plymouth, the crew had no knowledge of their assigned task. In spite of the ship being sealed and liberty cancelled, the men soon became aware of our mission. Army personnel came aboard to install two-way radios for communication with troops assaulting the islands. As the soldiers had already been briefed, they passed the information to the crew. When the captain found out, he gave division officers permission to brief the men. The news was received with mixed feelings. The 24 hour delay provided an opportunity for a chaplain to come aboard and hold services.

5 June. *Bates* was assigned to screen 500 yards on the starboard beam of *Bayfield*, the flagship of Admiral Moon, commander of the Utah beachhead. In late afternoon, the formation passed through two very large groups of tank landing ships, each towing a barrage balloon from her stern to protect against lowflying, strafing planes. We received the following message from the Admiral:

> "To all ships and troops. The greatest invasion in history is underway. We are about to be an essential part of it. Soon we will meet the enemy in the most vital battle in modern times and we will defeat him. History awaits us on the other side of the Channel. God speed and God bless all of you!"

A late evening meal of steak and eggs was served to the officers and crew, and everyone ate heartily in the realization it would be the last cooked meal we would have for some time.

We were fortunate in having the division doctor. With two enlisted assistants, he turned the wardroom into a battle dressing station, complete with sterilizer, operation lamp, and dressings. Seaman L.R. Frost was asked by an officer if he were ready for the battle; his reply could have voiced the opinion of all hands: "I'm as ready as I ever will be and that isn't very ready." Although tension was high, everybody wanted to get to it and get it over with.

6 June. After midnight, heavy enemy antiaircraft fire was clearly visible. Tracer shells marked the path of fire. When a plane was hit, there would be a ball of flame, resembling ancient Greek fire, then the crash, leaving a pillar of flame up to 1000 feet in the air.

From the explosion of the heavy bombs, the beach resembled a blast furnace. It seemed impossible that anything could live through such a bombardment. About this time, the paratroop planes, having discharged their cargoes, were returning to British bases by the shortest route, directly over our striking force. It was weird to see these huge planes, 25 to 50 feet above the water, and banking in and out to miss the ships. Some damaged planes made water landings while others, with engines shot out and holes in the wings, were limping along. One plane was having a difficult time, slowly losing altitude while heading for us. Then, almost crashing, it gradually gained altitude, and the gun crews of *Bates* sounded like the home team hitting one out of the park in the bottom of the ninth inning.

0130. *Bates* was detached from the main body and proceeded toward the islands. None of us knew what to expect: mines, shore based bombardments, air attack, or enemy destroyers and E-boats. The Germans had giant radar stations located along the entire coastline of the Cherbourg Peninsula, and it would have been easy for them to track us and transmit the data to shore batteries.

The islands were clearly visible, outlined against the horizon by fires from the burning beach. We could see and hear the explosions of the bombs from aircraft as they pounded the shore emplacements. The Germans were jamming radio circuits and detecting devices with some degree of success. Proceeding slowly, we reached our fire support position off the St. Marcouf Islands and waited for the landing craft to make their assault. *PC-484* arrived 1/2 half hour late, which didn't help to calm our nerves. Finally, in the first light of dawn, the PC and the landing craft approached the island beaches and, aside from one star shell fired over a landing craft, we had no indication that they were aware of us. Our main striking force was then about three miles from us and proceeding into position to bombard the beach.

0530. Suddenly, flashes of light were seen on the beach, and shore batteries opened up on us! It was unsettling to see a flash of light in the distance, to hear a noise like an express train, and then a terrific concussion when the shell exploded in the water. Although several shells were close, there were no hits or shrapnel wounds. After a few ranging salvos, the shore batteries came right on with a perfect straddle, some shots over and some short, and we knew the next ones would get us. Then, for some unknown reason, the guns shifted their fire to the striking force. Instead of being a target, we now could cruise slowly and listen to the enemy shells passing overhead. Battleships, cruisers and destroyers moved into position. The 5" secondary guns of *Quincy* (CA-71) sent the first salvo toward the shore.

As though this were a signal, the guns from all ships opened up, and the noise was music to our ears. Until then, we had not received a word about the assault on the islands so, in accordance with the prearranged plan, we left our fire support position, proceeded to screen *Nevada* and moved out of the line of fire of her guns. The most remarkable thing about the invasion to this point was our complete mastery of the air. Our Spitfires, Lightnings, and Mustangs flew overhead at will. One German plane approached the beach and was immediately shot down by a Spitfire. By this time, it was almost light, and the shoreline stood out in clear, bold relief.

0545. H-hour minus 45 minutes. The transports discharged their hundreds of small landing craft which headed for the beach.

0615. The 14" guns of *Nevada* and the 8" guns of the cruisers opened up on a wall along the beach where troops would land.

Within a few minutes, the wall was a mass of dust. The landing was covered by every gun that the ships could bring to bear, and the noise resembled ten Fourths of July rolled into one. Speedy attack bombers swept down over the beach and laid a smoke screen between the landing troops and enemy artillery. The beach was completely obscured from sight, but without affecting the radar-controlled gunfire from the ships. Evidently, the Germans had a similar system because shells penetrated the smoke screen and landed among the assault craft. One infantry landing craft (LCI) received a direct hit from a heavy gun, and boat and soldiers alike flew high into the air. It all seemed like a dream or a movie that such an operation was taking place and we were part of it.

0620. H-hour. The first landing craft hit the beach. The guns on the ships now increased their elevation and were firing over the heads of troops on the beach. The smoke screen drifted away, and we could see the explosions of shells as they hit enemy ammunition and fuel dumps; they caused great glee on the part of all hands. It was not so much a sentimental expression as a choice of kill or be killed, and we preferred to do the killing.

0700. *PC-1261*, which was lying about 1000 yards from us and assisting in the screening, received a direct hit and, when the smoke cleared away, there was no trace of the ship!

After another hour's bombardment by the ships, the return fire from the beach appeared to slacken, and fewer shell bursts were seen. By this time, the shore fire control parties had landed and were transmitting their data back to the firing ships by two-way radio. Results were apparent as one enemy battery after another was silenced.

0730. We received a signal from *PC-484*, asking permission to come alongside and transfer casualties from the capture of the islands. At the same time, a British landing craft came along our other side and gave us additional casualties she had picked up from the islands. We received a total of two officers and six enlisted men. They told us that both islands were evacuated by the Germans but they had sown large fields of land mines and booby traps; our troops had landed in the middle of one of them. One private had received five wounds; his major regret was that there was no way of shooting back at a mine.

During the remainder of the first day, we steamed slowly back and forth, screening *Nevada*. There were reports of enemy mines in the vicinity so the Admiral ordered two divisions of high speed minesweepers to sweep the area east and west of the beachhead. The sweepers steamed in column until two miles from the beach, then turned 90 degrees to a course parallel to the beach and to each other. After proceeding three miles, a shore battery opened up and straddled the first sweeper. The second salvo scored several hits and, after burning fiercely for fifteen minutes, the sweeper turned over and sank. The cruiser *Tuscaloosa (CA-37)*, let go her big guns at that shore battery and, after three salvos, the guns were knocked out.

7 June. 0412. This morning, we had our first air attack, but all reports of enemy planes came from radar. A glider bomb exploded 300 yards off the starboard quarter of *Bates* but did no damage. This was the first time this DE had come under air attack. None of the other ships received hits. For two hours, the sky was filled with tow planes pulling troop-filled gliders and heading directly behind the beach. Within 30 minutes, we counted 104 of them.

1530. Destroyer *Jeffers (DD-621)*, sister ship of *Corry* sunk the previous day, received a hit in number two engine room and was forced to retire. She had been in a fire support area, exchanging salvos with a shore battery in back of the beachhead. She steamed out of the area with a collision mat over her port side.

During the entire day, battleships, cruisers and destroyers continued to shell the beach and directly behind it. Word was received from shore parties that the landings were satisfactory and on schedule. At nightfall, *Bates* proceeded to the inner destroyer screen to guard *Nevada* and *Quincy*.

8 June. 0512. *Meredith (DD-434)*, a new destroyer of the 2200 ton class, suffered a huge explosion and started listing to starboard. *Bates*, about 1000 yards away, headed to the stricken DD. We placed our port quarter against her starboard bow to take off her crew. Several life jacket lights could be seen blinking in the water, also three life floats which the destroyer had launched. Our whaleboat was put in the water to rescue those men. A PC reached *Meredith's* port side and assisted in taking off personnel. Within 30 minutes, all survivors had been removed, and we cleared with alacrity, expecting the destroyer to founder momentarily.

Our doctor was easily the busiest man aboard because, in addition to the army wounded, he now had injured men from the destroyer, some in serious condition. Survivors were suffering from severe stress. We learned that the explosion was underwater and that the ship had been mined. (In the prior narrative on *Rich*, it was claimed that a torpedo passing under her keel had struck *Meredith*. The difference is not easy to discern.) Contrary to earlier anticipations, the destroyer remained buoyant. We remained in the vicinity until dawn when we were joined by *Jeffers*. She went alongside *Meredith* with a salvage party, and we returned some key *Meredith* personnel.

0800. Two rescue tugs arrived, and it appeared there was a chance that the ship could be saved. In spite of huge efforts, however, the *Meredith* sank shortly afterward. We received orders from *Bayfield* to transfer survivors to an *LST*, which was going back to England. By taking a muster of the survivors as they left the ship and checking it against the crew list of the *Meredith*, it was determined that she had lost two officers and 60 men. While we were unloading survivors, the destroyer *Glennon (DD-620)* was lying off the beach in one of the fire support areas and firing at targets of opportunity.

0900. While moving toward a new target area, *Glennon* was rocked by a severe underwater explosion and she began to settle.

We were watching *Rich* closely and, while she was still in the vicinity of *Glennon*, there were three explosions. She rolled over and sank.

As she had been in our division since inception, most of us had very good friends on board her and it hit us hard. The Admiral immediately ordered the minesweepers into operation and, no sooner had they commenced sweeping, when they started exploding mines in the area.

1015. Two *LSTs*, proceeding up the boat lane from the beach to the transports, struck mines and started to sink. One sank within 15 minutes, but the second was beached and saved for repairs.

1330. Captain Tompkins, the Admiral's chief of staff, came aboard. The transports, commanded by merchant marine officers, were heaving round on their anchor chains, getting underway for the unloading area. As that sector had become overcrowded with ships, it was necessary to delay further arrivals until more unloaded ships had cleared. The transports could not (or would not) respond to blinker light or radio messages, so it was necessary to pass the word orally. *Bates* was selected to ride herd. While racing at 20 knots, Captain Tompkins shouted through the PA speaking system to the merchant ships: "Danger! Stay anchored!" It worked. They stayed anchored.

We proceeded near the beachhead to give a mine warning to a British gunboat anchored nearby. We were returning to our station when suddenly: "Whish! Wham!," and a shell exploded about 100 yards off our port quarter! A few seconds later, another one exploded a little closer. We promptly bent on turns (RPM) to bug out of the area.

A small ammunition ship, 400 yards on our starboard beam, also observed the threatening shell fire and was steaming along with us. In a flash, she hit a mine and went down with all hands! The luck of *Bates* still held as we raced out with the German shells making neat patterns around us. As we were approaching the flagship, we noticed two British planes at an altitude of about 1000 feet. When the first was slightly ahead of us, a black object detached itself from the plane, and a parachute blossomed out of it. The plane dropped over on one wing, went into a steep dive and crashed a few yards from a transport laden with soldiers. The other plane went into a vertical dive, but the crew didn't have time to clear it until about fifty feet from the water; their parachutes didn't open. We later passed close by the wreckage of the plane, and two bodies were floating, supported by life jackets which inflated when they crashed.

This place was beginning to be called a blood bath. We saw the navy ships go down, but now the army wounded were beginning to come out to the hospital ships and their casualties were heavy. Throughout all this, our crew reacted like veterans. Even though they saw friends going down, they never shrank from their duty. We arrived near the flagship, discharged the chief of staff in a small boat, and proceeded to our screening station near *Nevada*. A lookout reported that the chief of staff's boat was returning; Seaman Crabb then made his classic remark: "Just let him go by. We done made our Paul Revere ride today, and that's enough."

1520. A small coastal transport ship struck a mine and sank rapidly. The minesweepers had been in constant operation and were exploding a mine every few minutes.

9 June. 0029. Enemy aircraft attacked and lit up the anchorage with flares. In the midst of the air raid, German E-boats made a foray, but it was repulsed, and one boat was sunk by our destroyers. As yet, we had no air strip on the beachhead to accommodate night fighter planes, so all night coverage came from England. Although we saw thousands of our planes during the day, there were very few at night. During this day, we maintained our screening position on *Nevada*, and all hands got a little sleep. In the evening, there was another air raid alert, and we witnessed the largest volume of antiaircraft fire we had seen thus far. Three enemy aircraft were destroyed, and one pilot was killed. *HMS Warspite* stood in to provide heavy shore bombardment while *Nevada* returned to England for ammunition.

10 June. The customary night air raid alert was sounded at 0345, and the flares lit up the sky. Although there was some firing, no enemy planes were brought down. The army had completed the installation of antiaircraft batteries on the beach, supplementing the fire from the ships. About midmorning, several minesweepers were targets for a heavy enemy battery on the beach. After receiving a few salvos from *Quincy*, the battery was silenced. We stayed at battle stations throughout the night, expecting another enemy combined air and E-boat attack. They came, but there were no hits from either.

12 June. 0110. Red air alert. Two transports were hit by rocket bombs. E-boats torpedoed the 2200 ton destroyer *Nelson (DD-623)*, the same class as *Meredith*. Most of her stern was blown away but, thanks to excellent damage control, she remained afloat. Heavy fire from screening destroyers beat off both air and E-boat attacks with no further losses.

By this time, virtually all enemy shore batteries had been knocked out, and the inland installations were being reduced by major caliber guns of the capital ships. At 0900, we were joined by *Amesbury* and *Blessman*, who had been screening at Omaha Beach. Upon receiving departure orders, we set out for Plymouth.

BLESSMAN

Blessman (DE-69) entered Belfast Harbor on 27 May 1944 to join her sister ships, *Rich*, *Bates*, and *Amesbury*. Radarman Joseph L. Young recalled:

> "We knew something was up because of the many ships in the harbor. We were assembled and told where we were going and that there would be no liberty. Gunners were also warned that all allied aircraft would have two distinct stripes painted on the underside of their wings to assist in avoiding friendly fire."

On 3 June, *Blessman* departed for Baie de la Seine, France, as escort for the Bombardment Group of the European Assault Force. Off Portsmouth, *Blessman* was assigned to screen the transport *Ancon (AP-66)*, on which were embarked several high ranking officers who were directing the invasion. The DE then proceeded to the Normandy beaches. The surrounding waters swarmed with hundreds of ships, large and small, loaded with troops. Overhead, there droned flight after flight of bombers on their way to soften up the enemy. The dawn of D-Day, 6 June, found the invasion successfully begun and *Blessman* assigned to the antisubmarine, E-Boat screen to seaward of the main force. Radarman Joe Young continued:

> "I was on and off radar watch. Most of us, when off watch, would only go down below to the head or to grab

something to eat. Nobody wanted to be below decks any longer than necessary. We slept inside the gun shields, using our life preservers as pillows. That way, we could relieve gunners to go below for the same reasons. I remember seeing the bombers and fighter planes going over us, seemingly by the thousands, and sure enough you could see the stripes under their wings.

Mostly, they were B 26 and DC 3 planes pulling the gliders. From that time on, I have always admired the old B 26s because at least a third of them coming back had an engine out. It seemed that the German planes would only come out at night, and you could recognize them by ear. It had something to do with piston firing sequence.

We heard that the *Rich (DE-695)* had gone down after hitting three mines, but we didn't know until later how many men were lost."

While the army was struggling for a foothold, the navy so completely dominated the Channel that the *Blessman's* task was comparatively easy. Only the vast German-laid mine fields presented a considerable hazard, sending a good many ships to the bottom. On 7 June, the DE was directed to go alongside the transport *Susan B. Anthony (AP-72)*, mined and afire. Although she was sinking rapidly, *Blessman* stayed alongside to remove six officers and 38 enlisted men. As the transport became engulfed in flames, her captain ordered *Blessman* away, the last ship to leave as the stricken *Anthony* sank beneath the surface. Joe Young related a heroic incident relative to this episode:

"We went alongside with nets and fender guards out. As the transport men started climbing across, a young seaman fell into the water between the two ships. The sea was quite rough, and both vessels bobbed and bumped together. We were sure that he would be crushed. He was about to drown when coxswain Bob Burdett kicked off his shoes, jumped into the water between the ships, grabbed the man, got him on the rope cargo net and helped him over the life line. Both would have been killed had the ships at that moment banged together. For whatever reason, that didn't happen.

Bob Burdett was a very nice person, quiet, soft spoken, and interesting to talk to. He was an old salt, although not more than two or three years older than most of us. I was quite impressed with Bob as a leader of men and his bravery. As a previous armed guard gunner, he had a ship torpedoed from under him and was a castaway in a small boat for a long time.

As for *Susan B. Anthony*, it was a sobering sight to see such a large ship sink. I had never seen such destruction close up."

In less than an hour, *Blessman* was on another errand of mercy. This time, she came alongside the transport *SS Francis C. Harrington*, also damaged by a mine. The crippled ship was in no danger of sinking but had 26 seriously wounded men in urgent need of medical attention. *Blessman* quickly delivered them to a hospital-equipped *LST* for treatment. This ended her active participation in the invasion. Several days and several enemy air attacks and E-Boat attacks later, the *Blessman* was detached and returned to Plymouth on 12 June.

A parting radio dispatch:

From: ComNavEu (Commander Naval Operations Europe)
To: ComCortDiv 19 (Commander Howe on *Amesbury*)

"Congratulations to all hands in Escort Division Nineteen for your splendid work and assistance in the assault on the continent, Well Done. My deep regrets over the loss of *Rich*."

The following morning, a dispatch was received ordering the remnants of *CortDiv 19*, *Amesbury*, *Bates* and *Blessman* to proceed at best speed to New York for their sixth and last transatlantic convoy. On her final return to the United States, *CortDiv 19* was dissolved.

With the end of the Atlantic War, *Amesbury* was converted to an APD. She headed for the Pacific and another foe, but Japan had surrendered by the time she reached Okinawa. *Bunch*, also converted to an APD, emerged unscathed from the fury of Okinawa.

Unfortunately, this was by no means the last action for *Bates* and *Blessman*. Both were converted to APDs and sailed to the Pacific to join in the last but bloodiest naval battles of the war. *Blessman* suffered in the carnage at Iwo Jima with a well aimed aerial bomb that took a huge toll. Three successive *kamikaze* crashes sent *Bates* to the bottom at Okinawa with severe casualties. See chapter *Iwo Jima to Okinawa – The High Speed Transports*.

MALOY AND BORUM

Maloy (DE-791) was flagship of most operations in which she and *Borum (DE-790)* were involved. In this narrative, we see some of the same actions involving both ships but from a very different perspective. In early March 1944, they crossed the Atlantic to Northern Ireland and, until June, conducted amphibious training along the English coast in preparation for the invasion of France.

On D-Day, 6 June, the two DEs supported operations off Omaha Beach where naval gunfire support played a decisive role. Long after other ships in "*Operation Neptune*" had been assigned elsewhere, they continued to patrol off the Normandy coast and among the Channel Islands for the remainder of the war.

MALOY

Joe Mahoney was engineering officer on *Maloy* with an outstanding memory for details and with a tinge of good humor. For example, he remembers the first meeting of officers, called by the captain, Lieutenant Commander F.D. Kellogg, the day after commissioning:

"There were many jobs to be assigned. One enthusiastic young ensign, just out of Princeton, volunteered to be sonar officer, assistant communications officer, assistant first lieutenant and, of course, a Junior Officer of The Watch, later qualifying as a Watch Officer. For the next two years, he tried to shed some of these duties but without success. Once a senior officer had an assistant to do the work, he wasn't about to let him go."

On 8 March, *Maloy* and *Borum* sailed for Londonderry, Northern Ireland. After a fuel stop at the Azores, they arrived in Plymouth, England on 3 April. The construction of a radio shack on the port weather deck and the arrival of flag communication personnel confirmed the future duty of *Maloy*.

On 1 June, the ship was "sealed" and, on the night of the fifth, she left Plymouth to join the invasion forces gathering for the assault on the beaches of France. *Maloy* was assigned to the second wave of the force attacking Omaha Beach. Joe Mahoney remembers the details:

> "On 4 June, while still berthed in Plymouth, two dignitaries came aboard. The first was Brigadier General Charles H. Gearhart, Commander of the 29th Infantry Division. The other was Commodore Edgar, whose presence would make *Maloy* the auxiliary flagship of the invasion at Omaha beachhead. Our communications officer and the captain went ashore to a meeting. The former, on his return, whispered the lowdown as all ears bent forward. The *Luftwaffe* had 8000 planes waiting for us, blocking out the light of day with all their aircraft overhead! A little bizarre but amusing
>
> That evening and the next day, General Gearhart joined in our regular game of poker with officers off watch. Usually, there were seven or eight players."

5-6 June. *Maloy* was underway at 0007 as a convoy escort. At 1647, she entered the transport area. Joe Mahoney continued:

> "It was dark when *Maloy* dropped her hook in Bay de la Seine, off Omaha Beach. Since 6 June was the General's birthday, we had a birthday cake for him in the wee hours of the morning. After the party, a card game got underway with the General back in the game. We were playing with all kinds of money, dollars, pounds, francs, and military script. Everybody was expert in the values."
>
> *Maloy* swung on her anchor parallel to the waves. As she rolled, all hands at the wardroom table playing poker would hang on to it. A little before daybreak, I just won my first pot of the game, a huge pile of money. I leaned forward to scoop in my winnings as the ship rolled. Then, with all hands hanging onto the table, it broke loose and everybody ended up in a pile against the bulkhead. My pot flew about the wardroom, never to be retrieved as GQ called all hands to battle stations.
>
> A destroyer astern of us commenced firing her 5" guns at enemy emplacements on the cliffs overlooking Omaha Beach, followed by the battleships and cruisers offshore. The first wave of LCIs passed us, headed for the beach, and the Germans opened up. We saw many LCIs, fully loaded with troops, take direct hits, killing all occupants. Fortunately, their guns never ranged on us. At low tide, we were as close to shore as our 14 foot draft would allow.
>
> Later in the morning, an LCI came alongside to pick up General Gearhart. I was there to wish him a happy birthday as he departed to join the second wave heading for the beach. As he climbed down the Jacob's ladder to board the LCI, he appeared cheerful and unworried. He did comment that he looked forward to a more relaxed birthday next year. I admired him as he rode off in the LCI to join his troops heading for Omaha Beach. I watched his craft all the way to the shore and saw shells from enemy batteries splash near his landing craft en route, but I knew he made it to the beach. I guess he was about 38 years old then. I was 23."

2230. Air alert. An hour later, the DE commenced firing at low altitude enemy aircraft. Fire spurted from her 20mm and 1.1" guns and scored hits on a JU 88, sending the plane burning and splashing ahead of the ship. Three minutes later, a parachute from the crashed plane landed 100 yards off the port side. The parachutist was dead and his parachute fouled in the struts and shafting on the port side. The men were unable to recover the body. Minutes later, cries of help were heard from dead ahead. A man was sighted in the water, and Captain Kellogg ordered a small craft to pick him up. The survivor was a German officer, Walter Kollmer, the pilot of the crashed plane. He was placed under guard and given first aid and dry clothing.

9 June. After dark, German aircraft again bombed the ships lying offshore. The DE commenced firing on enemy planes. A near miss was scored by enemy aircraft 300 yards on the starboard quarter. Four men received shrapnel wounds: Coxswain E.J. Van Diver, Torpedoman Third Class G.A. Pizzini, Seaman First Class J. Futchko, Seaman Second Class P.E. Lockhart Joe Mahoney described his ship's radio jamming capabilities:

> "When the allies made their landings at *Anzio* and Salerno Beaches, the ships were attacked by radio-guided missiles from German aircraft. (See narrative *The Electronics War* in chapter *Convoys to the Mediterranean.)* Since it was assumed that guided missiles would be used by the Germans in this invasion, counter measures were taken. A couple of weeks before D-Day, *Maloy* was fitted out with a radio control room on the weather deck. I was assigned as the officer in charge of six radio and electronic personnel. We had attended a course in Exeter, England, to learn about the anti-bomb jamming equipment. On the morning of D-Day, we were getting all sorts of indications that radio-guided missiles were in operation. The crew effectively jammed them with their transmitters. The operators were kept at a high state of alert, knowing that missiles were in midair, headed for the fleet."

11 June. *Maloy* proceeded to Portland, England, where the Commodore and his flag personnel departed. The next day, the ship returned to the assault area in France and was assigned to escort the destroyer *Nelson (DD-623)* back to Portland; she had been torpedoed by an E-boat and her fantail had been blown away. *Maloy* took aboard about 130 of the surviving crew, escorted *Nelson* and her tow back to Portsmouth, and then returned to the assault area.

During the remainder of June and all of July, *Maloy* was on duty in the battle vicinity, screening the battleships at night, escorting ships from the beachhead to English and Northern Irish ports, escorting troop ships to the beaches, and patrolling off Cherbourg, France. Eventually, *Maloy*, *Borum*, and a number of PTs were assigned to patrol the Channel Islands, still controlled by the Germans and located a few miles off the coast of France.

A couple of months after D-Day, *Maloy* was assigned an engineering job. She went to Cherbourg alongside a dock at a power plant. Her job was to supply light and power to the city because its power plant had been destroyed. Being a turbo-electric vessel, the *Maloy* was highly suited for such a project. One main turbine operated at half speed produced 2600 Volts, 3 phase, from the generator. The amp load ashore was small in contrast to the potential the ship could provide. She carried out this assignment for about three weeks until relieved by *Donnell (DE-56)*, another turbo-electric DE that had its stern blasted away. (Donnell was in this author's division when hit by an acoustic torpedo while attacking a U-boat.) After the war, *Maloy* performed an identical task for the Town of Bath, Maine, when a local power plant was destroyed by fire. Today, the navy has no turbo-electric vessels that could perform a similar task.

1745 on 6-7 August. *Maloy* was underway from Cherbourg, en route to the Channel Islands, north of the Brittany peninsula, for a night attack on enemy shipping. This group was composed of *Maloy* as flagship and vectoring vessel for four PT boats. Lieutenant Commander Peter Scott of the Royal Navy, advisor and liaison officer, and U.S. Navy Lieutenant H.J. Scheretz, Commander of PT Squadron 34, were both on board *Maloy*. The first part of the trip being in daylight hours, this force skirted well outside of the Channel Islands, out of range of the heavy gun emplacements.

2325. *Maloy* slowed and began a patrol four miles north of St. Malo harbor channel. The patrol was maintained off Ile de C'ezembre, a small island just north of St. Malo Harbor. This group was challenged by an enemy signal station on a small island west of C'ezembre. With visibility in favor of the ships, no reply was made because it would have revealed their presence. The moon silhouetted St. Malo and the small islands. In addition, huge fires were burning in St. Malo, following a raid by Allied aircraft.

The group was challenged again before dawn, ignored by *Maloy*. Thirteen minutes later, the shore battery on C'ezembre fired two star shells. The range was correct but the deflection was off 3000 yards, failing to silhouette the ships. *Maloy* increased her speed and retired to Cherbourg. It was considered unwise to remain within range of the shore batteries with daylight about to break.

8-9 August, night action. The group sortied from the Cherbourg anchorage toward the Channel Islands, this time with the object of a night attack on enemy shipping. The PT boats, under the direction of *Maloy*, had two additions. Fog reduced visibility to 1000 yards. Twenty minutes from the sortie, *PT-506* was obliged to return to Cherbourg with a damaged propeller. Visibility dropped under 400 yards. *Maloy* and her PTs slowed speed and began patrolling a station between Guernsey and Jersey Islands.

0320. Visibility was less than 200 yards. An hour and a half later, radar contact was made at a distance of 12 miles from La Corbiere, Jersey Island. The CIC plot indicated enemy shipping approaching and moving at 14 knots. Three PTs were vectored to the enemy ships by *Maloy*. Torpedoes were fired by all PTs without results. The firings were made entirely on radar information because of the low visibility. Two PTs were then vectored to intercept the enemy southeast of La Corbiere. Plotting of the PTs by *Maloy* was impossible due to their small size and distance from the DE. The maximum range for radar contact on the PTs was six miles.

Both PTs fired torpedoes, and the sound of gunfire was heard. The PTs reported that an enemy force consisting of six ships was firing at them. *PT-509* reported: "I am right in the middle of them!"

From 0619 until 0700, futile attempts were made to contact *PT-509* by radio. *Maloy* closed to within three miles of the Jersey coastline but could not locate *PT-509* on radar. Ten minutes later, the PTs made a rendezvous with the DE near La Corbiere, but *509* was not among them. The apparent loss was reported to the Commander of Task Force 125.

Lieutenant Scheretz embarked in *PT-503* and, with *PT-507*, was dispatched to search for PT- *509* along the southern coastline of Jersey. *Maloy* commenced a search three miles south of Jersey with two other PTs. About 30 minutes later, *PT-503* reported enemy contact and fired one torpedo as the fog suddenly lifted to 400 yards ahead. A running fire fight ensued with PTs *503* and *507* vigorously engaging the enemy with their guns and retiring under a smoke screen. *Maloy* heard the gun fire during the battle, and one loud explosion blasted through the fog, probably a torpedoed enemy vessel.

0820. PTs *503* and *507* rejoined this group. *PT-503* reported six casualties and came alongside. *Maloy's* pharmacist's mates rendered first aid. *PT-507* reported one slight casualty: Ensign Koenen- small fragment in his back; Gunner's Mate Third Class Drumm - dead multiple wounds; Motor Machinist's Mate Second Class Albright -chest wound, scalp and face wounds, very weak pulse; Motor Machinist's Mate Second Class Albie- lacerated leg and fingers; Motor Machinist's Mate Second Class Peppel - large shell fragment in left side of back; Quartermaster Third Class Lang - light fragment in shoulder blade.

0926. Visibility increased rapidly and course was set for Cherbourg, speed 23 knots. En route, *Maloy's* skipper reported to CTF 125 and suggested that an air search be started for *PT-509*. Contact was made with a Sunderland flying boat to conduct a surveillance of an area south of Jersey. Later that morning, Machinist Mate Albright died after repeated attempts by *Maloy's* pharmacist mates to administer blood plasma. The PTs were ordered to proceed to base independently as the DE headed back to Cherbourg. *Maloy* hove to as *PT-501* came alongside to transfer Lieutenant (jg) Kurrie, Navy Medical Corps, and a few hospital corpsmen. After an examination, Machinist's Mate Albright and Gunner's Mate Brumm were pronounced dead. Upon anchoring in Cherbourg, casualties were transferred to *PT-503* for delivery to the U.S. Naval Hospital, Cherbourg, completing the night's operation.

1942 on 9 August saw *Maloy* underway from Cherbourg en route to the Channel Islands with orders to conduct night attacks on enemy shipping with six PT boats. Lieutenant Commander Peter Scott, Lieutenants Scheretz and J.J. Weiberg, and the medical Lieutenant (jg) Kurrie were on board *Maloy*. Visibility being excellent, this group skirted around the islands, just outside of gun range, then commenced a slow speed patrol between Guernsey and Jersey Islands. However, there was no sign of the enemy. At dawn, the PT's were ordered to rendezvous with *Maloy* for the return to Cherbourg.

1 September. *Maloy* captured an unregistered German hospital ship, a converted seagoing tug, being used to transport a German General attempting to escape from the Channel Islands.

6 September. *Maloy* and *Borum* closed to 6 1/2 miles off Guernsey to prevent German ships from leaving. Shore batteries opened fire on both vessels. In spite of evasive maneuvering,

there were a number of near misses, and one of the *Maloy* gun crew on the fantail was hit by shrapnel. *Borum* also had a man wounded from a near miss.

1430 on 9 September. While on patrol off Guernsey and Jersey, *Maloy* sighted smoke three miles from La Corbiere, Jersey Island, and immediately altered course to close it. Five German armed trawlers and three unidentified vessels were sighted proceeding out of St. Helier Harbor. Her radar made contact at eight miles, and a plot tracked the enemy on a northerly course at nine knots. Six minutes later, *Maloy* reversed course as a shore battery north of La Corbiere opened fire with a three round salvo; one shell splashed within five feet of the starboard quarter and another 30 yards off the port quarter. Speed was increased as *Maloy* maneuvered to avoid salvos. The second salvo fell short 400 yards. Her radar lost contact at 15 miles.

1500. *Maloy* observed gun fire from Guernsey Island emplacements firing at *Borum* while she was attempting to join the action. *Borum* reported that she was unable to join up due to the accuracy of enemy batteries. Smoke was sighted four miles from La Corbiere, and a report to CTF 125 brought aircraft to attack the enemy shipping. *Maloy* did not open fire due to the target being beyond the extreme range of 3"/50 caliber guns and also the fact that she was repulsed by the superiority and accuracy of German shore batteries. *Maloy* remained in the area, out of range of the big guns until the arrival of friendly planes at about 1800.

Six rounds were fired by the shore batteries, and one man, Torpedoman Second Class Vincent Scalise, sustained injuries from a shell fragment that pierced the right side of his back, just above a kidney. The hull on the starboard side aft was showered with shrapnel, resulting in five small holes which were plugged by damage control parties. Seven depth charges in the starboard racks were pitted.

Maloy continued routine patrol of the Channel Islands until the German surrender. On 8 May 1945, she escorted the first convoy into the Channel Islands, entering St. Peter Port, Guernsey Island.

BORUM

The Diary of Frederic Shelby Brooks

This was an extraordinary man. A Marine Corps veteran of World War I, he enlisted in the Navy in World War II at the age of 43, well beyond the reach of the draft. Why? We suspect from his meticulous chronicle that love of country and distaste for the enemy played a large part in his decision, as did a desire to recapture the fleeting joys of early youth. We also recognize an overpowering desire to be in the midst of his time and to record what he believed to be the most decisive war in history.

He was a sensitive man, quick to notice a beautiful sunrise in the tropics, a lush green shore, a graceful cathedral rising above the ruins of bombardment. They became mental snapshots that he would never forget. His poetry came from within, and his ability to write about horseplay or the exhaustion and strain of battle was truly a talent. In addition, he displayed a subtle sense of humor.

We get the impression of rolling drums, barely audible in the dawn of war, gradually increasing to a crescendo in the high noon of war, the invasion of Normandy and the Channel Islands. The drums did not just stop; they faded away as battle slowly ceased in the twilight of war.

Some passages have been abridged or modified because they were unrelated to the ship and the war or to improve sentence structure and clarity without altering the impressions of the diarist.

FRINGE of WAR

Cruise of the USS Borum (DE-790)

The following chronicle concerns the activities of *Borum*, a destroyer escort, as seen through my eyes as a radarman aboard this vessel.

Not being an objective account, but a very personal one, I shall start with a brief outline leading up to the day I went aboard. Enlisting on 25 July, 1943, in El Paso, Texas, I was sent to the San Diego Naval Station for boot training, after which I completed a course in radar at Point Loma. Upon graduation, I reported to the Naval Station, Orange, Texas, where *Borum* was under construction at the Consolidated Shipbuilding Corporation.

I paint a small picture of a nation at war, a thumbnail sketch laced with comments, musings and reflections. Please bear with my notes, unaltered and often made during times of stress. *Borum* was to take us to the lush tropical splendor of Panama, to Bermuda, the Azores, Northern Ireland, England, Wales, the beaches of Normandy on D-Day, the Channel Islands, the ports of France and eventually home.

We were a happy ship. There were days of monotony and days of rare excitement. There were liberties and leaves to be remembered for the span of years allotted to us. So, I give greetings to my former comrades-at-arms and, with a distant handshake, "Welcome aboard."

Underway at last on *Borum*. I am proud of my ship and wonder what is in store for us. For the most part, we are landlubbers. However, we have some experienced officers and men aboard. My bunk is in the after crew's quarters at the foot of the fantail hatch. I am now a member of "C" Division, and my immediate superior officer is Lieutenant (jg) William Harrison. He will have direct supervision over radio, sonar, radar, encoding and decoding messages. He will also be responsible for the amendment of codes and secret or restricted publications, and I will assist him.

8 December 1943. Somewhere in the Gulf of Mexico, en route to Galveston. It is warm and the Gulf Stream is a lovely blue. We are just getting our sea legs. At midafternoon we anchored and piped a swimming party. There is speculation as to when we will make the shakedown cruise. Thus begins the "scuttlebutt" (rumors), and they will be with us from now on.

9 December. The SL (surface search) and SA (air search) radar gear are operating well. Picked up a large convoy on collision course with us. Our radar watch should have spotted it sooner. Passed through the convoy without incident.

Christmas Day. We had departed from Galveston on the 22nd, en route to Bermuda for shakedown. Seas are rough, and the mess hall is a shambles. I ate Christmas dinner on deck, a sandwich and a piece of mince pie, while braced against a bulkhead. I know now that I will never be seasick. I feel that I am a part of ship and sea.

1 January 1944, New Years Day, Bermuda. A brand new

year! No fanfare to welcome it. We had arrived on 28 December with an enchanting shore line to greet us. The hills are of emerald green with, here and there, white houses, white even to their roof tops. They stand out like jewels in this semi-tropical setting.

The shakedown and maneuvers have been grueling for both officers and men. I went ashore on the 13th day of our stay and got drenched by rain and spray. Bought a few souvenirs. Missed the *Borum's* whaleboat and returned to ship by thumbing a ride in another ship's boat, barely making it before expiration of liberty. The weather remained good during our stay. We now learn that we are to go to Boston for availability. We are issued foul weather gear, long underwear and fleece-lined jackets.

22 January. Very cold on the flying bridge this morning as we near Boston. Bunker Hill Monument stands out against a leaden skyline.

25 January. The people are quite hospitable.It was 13 degrees below zero one night when I had shore patrol in the Chinatown district. However, our post was a chop suey place, and all we had to do was maintain order and eat chop suey on the house. Not a bad assignment. While here, I got a 72 hour leave and took the train to Washington, D.C. and Fort Belvoir, Virginia, where my son Jean is stationed as a Second Lieutenant. We had a grand weekend together. Upon return to Boston, I went aboard the new cruiser *Quincy (CA-71)* and was shown their new fire control radar gear.

4-10 February. We are underway again and, as usual, speculation is rife as to our destination. Entered East River, New York, on the morning of the 5th, remaining several hours. We are to convoy a ship or ships south. The following day, we arrived at Norfolk, Virginia, after one of the roughest passages yet experienced. It was hang on and cuss. Anchor aweigh on the 10th, destination Panama. We are elated at the prospect of going to the Pacific theater. We are to convoy a troop ship with marines.

14 February. Haiti and her 5000 foot peaks are a purple line on the horizon at sun up. This is the Windward Passage, referred to as "Torpedo Junction". Nazi submarines have had a field day here. It is warm on deck, and we strip to our shorts. Some of the men turned lobster red, and the skipper has ordered no more sunbathing.

16 February. Panama! After sleepless nights and tension at battle stations, it looks heavenly. We rescued two navy flyers from their rubber life raft just before entering Coco Solo Sub Base. Gosh, I'm tired tonight, and the sack looks good to me, but then when doesn't it? Never seem to get enough sleep. During this cruise, I have spent much time amending code publications. We are now moored at a dock alongside a beautiful lagoon. What a swimming hole!

17 February, Coco Solo Sub Base. Sunrise in Panama! Mists dimming the distant lavender hills and mountains, palm fronds stirring in the morning's first whisper of a breeze, a frigate bird wheeling lazily above the blue lagoon, seas break against the distant coral reef. 1100, morning swim call. Harmon Mulbar and I race for the water.

18 February. We are enjoying liberty in Colon. Cash Street is something to remember. The cribs are clean and well furnished. They should be, with a steady influx of the "Yankee Dollar" and sailors ready and willing to spend them. Word has been passed that we are to change the color of the ship from Pacific blue back to Atlantic gray. This means we are not going to join the Pacific Fleet and will return to the states and enter convoy service. I am disappointed.

8 March. Arrived New York again to rendezvous with an *LST* repair ship and, with *Maloy*, will escort her to Europe via the Azores.

10 March At Sea. It is rough and squally today with scattered snow flakes. Our charge has slowed to four knots, and we roll and pitch in our own slow speed to match hers. A lone, half grown sea gull alighted on our fantail, and Coxswain Lane put the little black and white bird in a cardboard box and presented it to Chief Durab. Maybe our feathered friend is a good omen. Our ETA Azores, is sometime on the 17th. The allies were permitted bases there last year.

18 March. Ponta Delgado, San Miguel, Azores. The island of San Miguel presents from the sea a picture of quaint beauty. The hills are of many shades of green, a patchwork of terraced vineyards. The houses are of pastel shades pale greens, pink and lavender. Many of the buildings are camouflaged in surreal designs, making them stand out too prominently. Lateen rigged boats, laden with fresh fruits, bananas, pineapples, etc., swarm out to meet us. They are also loaded down with other items such as Swiss wrist watches, baskets, hats and colorful scarves. The fishing vessels have colorful red, blue and yellow sails. We are moored alongside a Portuguese destroyer of ancient British vintage. An English liaison officer is aboard.

Neither the Portuguese sailors nor ourselves speak each other's language, but sign language suffices. When our OD is not looking, bottles of wine are spirited across to our fantail in exchange for soap, cigarettes, tooth brushes and toothpaste. A run on the latter (and most popular) item in our ship's store was cut off from further purchase. However, the trading goes on with a new medium of exchange. One of the boys had the brilliant idea of getting tubes of prophylactic (a venereal disease preventive) from sick bay and passing them off as toothpaste. This worked well for a time until that English officer wised them up. The next bottle to come over the stern contained urine. That broke off the trading operations.

We are to get underway for Londonderry, Northern Ireland, in the morning. Mr. Landreth has just made a trip through the crew's quarters, shaking his head. Half the crew is under the weather, but some have passed out completely. As Mr. Landreth passed one tier of bunks, the topside occupant let fly with wine and yesterday's chow. The exec departed in a hurry after instructing a detail to get swabs and clean ship. Mr. Landreth never mentioned this incident, and he stands tall in the saddle as far as we are concerned. We only hope that, when the sea detail is set in the morning, there will be enough of us able to stay in a vertical position. I have had experience with wine before, so did not drink too much of it. But the others have the advantage of youth, and can snap out of it in no time.

I review the past several weeks in verse, of a sort:

New York again but no time to stay.
Just long enough to see the sights;
The lights were dim, but still were lights.
Stage Door Canteen, a show and a dance,
And a bunch of girls in sailor pants.
Norfolk found us a seasick bunch,
Even the skipper lost his lunch.
Three days later we set out to sea,
We didn't know where, this time we'd be.

Well, the Azore Island, next port of call;
No liberties here to prevent a brawl.
The Azores are neutral and open to all.
Moored here 'longside the "Portuguese Fleet."
Two tin cans but what a treat!
Alongside one, secured with lines,
We swapped cigarettes and toothpaste
For "escudos" and wines.
The Quarterdeck winked as we bargained and swapped,
We had a swell time till the trading was stopped.
Some guys swapped prophylactic in tubes;
They said it was toothpaste and took them for rubes.
So wine they returned and said it was bliss,
But turned out to be nothing but Portuguese piss.
A limey officer had queered the whole deal;
So here's to an S.O.B. and heel!

21 March, Londonderry, Northern Ireland. We arrived today after 13 days at sea. We are moored at a dock in the River Lough Foyle, and the green hills beyond are of breathtaking grandeur. Sheep graze contentedly on their grassy slopes, and there is an air of age-old peace and quietude; the war seems so far away. Port watches have been set and liberty will be granted. It will be welcome.

One morning, while on the fantail, Lieutenant Atwood called my attention to a flock of wild swans in flight; they made a beautiful and rare picture. Mr. Atwood, a former game preserve officer with the Louisiana State Wild Life Commission, was particularly interested. Food ashore isn't great and, leaving *Borum* and its excellent chow for "fish and chips," is rather foolish, at best a novelty. Have been to several dances at the Corinthian Dance Hall. Its manager, a red headed Irishman and a nice guy, gave me two dollars in Irish Free State money as souvenirs. I met a nice girl, Daphne Jane, and her mother. The father is off with the fighting forces somewhere in Africa. One day, a young Irish lad of about 12 came aboard and entertained us with some fine tenor singing. The skipper put a stop to his visits after the disappearance of some small personal items. The girls here, for the most part, are leery of sailors and, from the outward appearance of some of them, I can understand why. It's the same everywhere, can't change nature.

4 April, Plymouth, England. We sight England at last. This is the land of my forefathers, generations ago. Perhaps racial memories stir in me; I don't know. Maybe it is just the sight of a land I am seeing for the first time. There is a certain undefinable thrill in it for me. Upon entering Jenny Bay, Chief Durab has this to say:

> "Well boys, you are now about to enter Plymouth, England, situated on Rock Candy Mountain, by Marshmallow Lake, where every girl is beautiful and an heiress in her own right, with a cellar full of good whiskey waiting for you at Tamar Quay, and ready to make immediate bundling arrangements."

Plymouth is noted for its unavailability of women, for warm beer and no whiskey. The navy has been Durab's life for so many years. To me, he typifies the navy, and somehow I cannot visualize him shore-bound. He has traveled all over the world and can spin many a yarn of foreign ports and their environs. As he is "deck" I do not see as much of him as I should like. He was patient in the teaching of green hands; this I liked about him, an amicable trait not found in all Chiefs.

5 April, Plymouth. Another morning, mist on the harbor and scattered nimbus clouds. I counted 68 barrage balloons, like so many sky cows tugging at their moorings. Mr. Harrison has just returned to the ship and says he is awed by the havoc created by the incessant bombings. The stately old churches and cathedrals have suffered greatly. From the ship, I can see one lone spire etched against the sky. We are anchored about a quarter of a mile from a high railroad trestle, over which freight, passenger and troop trains constantly run. The Germans have repeatedly attempted to bomb this bridge, but without success. Blackened ruins and roofless houses of stone lie at one bridgehead. Across the harbor is a scene of serenity. A castle is perched on a distant knoll amid pristine green, plowed fields, stone fences and hedgerows a gentle, undulating countryside. A formation of four-engine bombers is now circling high above us and gaining altitude. Contrails make ribbon patterns at 20,000 feet. They rendezvous and head southeast, 30 minutes from the French coast. It doesn't seem possible that we are only 50 miles from enemy-held country, just a narrow channel separating us.

6 April. I had the deck watch from 1600 to 2000 hours. We are having a surprise inspection, dress blues and flat hats, the uniform of the day. An Admiral came aboard and chatted briefly with me when he noticed my World War I ribbons. I suppose he wondered what an old goat like me is doing in uniform. Well, he's not so young either, the difference a "small" gap in rank.

7 April. I have been ashore. The wanton destruction everywhere is appalling and numbs the senses. A chill wind was blowing; It seemed to me a dirge of a sort; a requiem of fire and ruin. Plymouth comes alive when the pubs and dance halls open at 1800. Almost everyone is in uniform. All of the Allied nations are represented here, and few girls are in mufti. The alphabetical nuances are multitudinous (WAAF, WREN, etc.) I find Plymouth far from being a happy place. It shows a false surface and, beneath, life must be going on as normal as one would expect in a town subject to bombing attacks almost nightly. I went into a small restaurant for a bite to eat and was told I would have to put up a deposit in advance on the silverware. The knives and forks were of very cheap make, but I see their point.

10 April. Made convoy trip to Falmouth. This is getting to be a "milkrun."

0200 Battle Stations, Condition Yellow, Enemy planes detected by British Radar.

0205 Condition Red. antiaircraft fire plainly discernible.

0206 First bombs fall.

0209 Raiders split into several groups, apparently by interceptors.

0210 Fires can be seen approximately 15 miles to the south.

0212 Concentrated A.A. fire and Rocket A.A.

0213 Near miss on south shore.

0214 Near miss off port quarter.

0215 Bridge reports barrage balloon afire off starboard quarter.

0219 Bombs fall in harbor south of us.

0223 All clear signal. Condition Green, our sector.

The above is the way I logged it, cooped up in the chart house. I didn't see any of it, just the fires after we had secured. Fisher and his boys in the radio shack had a good running description of this 23 minutes of action; the bridge had box seats. Later, I talked with some of the men who witnessed the raid and received a dozen different versions. The ship's log will probably be less graphic than my own description. Logs are like that.

11 April. We picked up a formation of planes, range 53 miles, and plot indicated they would intersect our course. They were coming from the direction of the French coast and changed course about the time our radar became inoperative. Repaired, we easily determined their friendly status. We are safely back in Plymouth outer harbor, within the antisubmarine and mine nets, standing off the Hoe. With the anchor down and gun watches set, movies were shown.

12 April. I was Petty Officer of the Watch from 0400 till 0800. It was cold, and a moon swam in a cloudless sky. Mr Spratley, Officer of The Deck, and I talked for several hours about the possibilities of a raid, of home, of our sons and of the fortunes of war. My notes were interrupted at 2100 by GQ. Condition Red, a few tense moments as spitfires roared out to intercept.

14 April. A wicked sea ran all night with closing fog and rain; great waves broke with an echoing hollow thunder on the Welsh coast which we could occasionally see through the fog banks. Low-flying planes came in for a close look. They were Sunderland flying boats and soon disappeared in the fog. We challenge and receive recognition from a group of bombers with fighter escort ranging some 60 miles to the south. These DEs were not made for Sunday cruising, especially in weather like this. However, after watching the sea behavior of some of the smaller and amphibious craft such as PCs, LCIs, LSTs and LCMs, we should thank our lucky stars for a "luxury" can.

23 April. The afternoon turned out clear and fairly warm, considering this is England. I walked from Tamar Quay, Devenport, to Plymouth, stopping on the way to wander through an old churchyard cemetery. Some of the 17th and 18th century epitaphs are interesting; some quite amusing. I went to Plymouth Rock, at the foot of the Hoe where some of the Pilgrims embarked. Despite the fog now drifting back in, there are many people in swimming. The water is icy!

A skylark sang in Devon,
A wave kissed Tamar Quay,
A flower bloomed in Devon,
A ship stood out to sea.

1800. There was an alert, but the planes bypassed Plymouth. It is Sunday, and the chimes of St. Andrews could be heard as usual, calling the faithful to services. The belfry stands proudly.

29 April. A beautiful day, and I took my liberty walking for miles through the countryside. Even here, there is the stamp of ruin being erased gradually by nature's gentle hand. The trees, hedgerows and flowers are beautiful. Returning to Plymouth, I went shopping, but the shops have little to sell, and I came away empty handed.

I don't know the flowers and trees by name,
But the grass is just as green,
As the grass that grows in your own kept yards,
Soft, with a satiny sheen.
These rivers and hills are but marks on a chart,
In this censored, unmentionable land,
It could as well be Mt. Franklin,
And the river, the Rio Grande.
There's the same old sun and moon and stars,
The same old sky of blue,
The same old theme runs through it all,
Telling my love, you.

30 April, Plymouth. Battle stations at 0310. A formation of enemy planes came over. Flak was heavy and kept them high. However, flares were dropped and incendiaries fell near the Hoe. I saw the action from the flying bridge. Rocket barrages were repeatedly sent up, much flak. Shore batteries of search lights kept the targets bracketed. It was quite a pyrotechnic display. One plane came over the harbor, dropping flares and, possibly, magnetic or delayed action mines. We did not get underway until noon, waiting for the minesweepers to clear the channel. Departed Plymouth at 0200 for Portland.

3 May, Portland. We lie at the harbor entrance, just outside the submarine and anti-torpedo nets, standing war cruising watches. There is a castle standing on a promontory at the harbor mouth. I wonder as to its antiquity and ponder upon those days when it must have guarded this harbor against raiders, perhaps Norsemen or Normans. I doubt if ever it looked down upon stranger craft than now ply its waters.

7 May, Milford Haven. I find myself exclaiming, as ever, over the beauties of the landscape. From the harbor, Milford Haven is a picture to be retained in my memory for all time. A flight of bombers, leaving miles long vapor trails, the only flaw in an otherwise faultless sky.

10 May, Torquay. Weighed anchor for Plymouth after leaving our amphibious craft charges. Heavy gunfire to port across the channel all morning. Some survivors were picked up from a badly damaged four-motor bomber by an air-sea rescue vessel. The plane did not quite make it back across the Channel and had to ditch. Huge formations of bombers have been crossing the Channel all morning. None of us have been ashore in days and are on edge.

I have no rendezvous with death; I've come unscathed
through latitudes of war;
I've heard a skylark sing in Devon's Fields; have heard
The coast of France, heard cannon roar.
I have a rendezvous with love, where purple shadows fall
On desert sands.
My heart alone must keep this tryst, while I remain in
Far off foreign lands.

12 May, Portland. We had an air raid warning at 0900. Saw a dog fight on radar, but could not arrive at definite conclusions. The P38s would not answer our IFF; probably didn't have the d'things turned on. "D-Day" should be soon we hope.

15 May, Portland. Air raid at 0300 14 planes came over, and we hear night fighters shot down seven, one piloted by a German Ace with 28 Allied planes to his credit. *Borum* could not fire due to restrictions put upon American ships by the British while in their harbors. Shore batteries blazed away but, as far as we could tell, failed to score any hits. One plane fell in flames near Weymouth.

0115 on 28 May, Weymouth. A German heavy bomber came in below mast height. Evidently, the pilot did not see us and pulled up sharply, narrowly missing our mast and stack. There had been no warning, and we assumed he was one of ours. Immediately afterward, the plane dropped flares across the harbor entrance to guide the other bombers which followed him in. We went to GQ, and all hell broke loose. Bombs narrowly missed us, and the sky was full of flak from the British shore batteries. Red, blue, green, yellow and orange tracers crisscrossed above us. One bomber was pinned by searchlights and crashed into a hill across the Bay. I raced for my battle station. At the pilot house hatch, I paused for a moment and caught a piece of flak in the collar of my foul weather jacket; an inch higher and I would have had my throat cut. Ironic indeed, had I been killed or wounded in an English harbor by English flak. One bomb fell close to one of our destroyers, throwing a shaft out of line. A few English sailors on a nearby destroyer were wounded by flak.

0600. Upon being relieved, I went to the bridge for a look. While talking with Mr. Harrison and Lieutenant Joe Davis, a delayed action bomb or mine exploded in the antisubmarine net at the harbor entrance, throwing up a great column of water. A few minutes later, another one exploded near the cargo vessel *Ancon (AP-66)* where we were anchored yesterday. While we were eating chow, another exploded near ships in the inner harbor.

1400 on 30 May. A violent explosion occurred less than 1000 yards off our starboard bow. I was in the code room, and the concussion was terrific. I went out on the torpedo deck in time to see the column of water descending on another delayed action device.

2 June, Weymouth. There has been a steady build up of ships with many amphibious craft in the harbor. Mr. Turnbull, gunnery officer, added a note to the "plan of the day":

> "When a shipload of good looking WACs goes by, the ordnance department doesn't blame you for wanting to get a better look at them through use of the gun telescopes. But, please, please replace the telescope covers! Generally, the best policy for you to follow with regard to ordnance gear is to 'leave it alone', unless your duties require that you handle it."

4-5 June, Weymouth. On the 4th, the Bay was filled with landing ships and transports. We are alongside a small troop ship loaded with Rangers, and we swap banter with them. All shore leaves had been cancelled the night before, and we were told that personal items of value should be left for safe keeping ashore. This was not mandatory. I only had a few English pound notes and my indispensable watch.

All day, small craft with bull horns plied the harbor area, admonishing us to observe the white diamond markings painted on the bows of landing craft and all small craft. Planes roared overhead with zebra stripes newly painted on wings and fuselages. The skipper and Mr. Harrison had been ashore and now returned with large envelopes marked "Most Secret." It was my great privilege to read these historical charts and documents as I assisted Mr. Harrison. The grid pattern of the English Channel was now designated "Main Street."

6 June, D-Day. As I write these lines, the bombardment by battleships, cruisers and destroyers has been blasting the enemy since 0530, "H" hour. An hour later, LCIs and other amphibious units landed their troops on Omaha and Utah beaches. We lie offshore at St. Lorient and Asigny, spearheading the first assault wave. We followed the minesweepers and were, in turn, followed by landing craft.

We stood on deck until midnight, watching the tremendous and awesome sight of antiaircraft fire and rocket barrages thrown up against our planes. I witnessed the destruction of three of our bombers. P 38s, Spitfires and fleets of bombers come over constantly.

We now lie in our predetermined "grid" position. The outer Baie de la Seine is marked off on the charts, like a football field. We see countless landing craft, circling, awaiting their turns to hit the beaches. The skipper has bloodshot eyes; Mr. Landreth appears calm, but he cannot hide his inner excitement. It shows on all the faces of the officers and men.

All code books, the encoding and decoding machine and other classified papers have been made ready for jettisoning, should it be necessary. *Dinard*, a hospital ship, was sunk within sight of us; we watched her go down. The destroyer *Jeffers* was hit by shell fire about 1600. Understand we lost *Rich* and the destroyer *Glennon*.

7 June, D-Day plus one. Landing boats took the men in; many were lost before they could reach Omaha beach. We are now guarding three voice radio circuits and what little news we have is confined to local operations. From the beach:

> "This is Ranger One. We have ten casualties and urgently need replacements. Our position is becoming untenable!"
>
> Reply from "Letterbox": "Sorry, all rangers are ashore. There are no troops available."
>
> Reply from beach: "I understand the situation perfectly; shall try to hold on."

The only thing real about this invasion is its fantastic unreality. It is a newsreel one senses he has seen before and watches again and yet again. It becomes impersonal and remote. But this is real! It dawned on me at last that I am actually a participant in all this. This is a time, too, for personal soul searching. The radarscope mesmerizes me until the awareness of the presence of death jolts me back to the real world. Bodies of men in the water are so much flotsam and jetsam; a grim harvest to be reaped by scores of small vessels. One looks on without emotion.

8 June, D-Day plus two off Omaha Beach. The same ordered confusion.

> Message to "Letterbox": "We have fifteen casualties and request that you take us off."
>
> A destroyer sent a whaleboat, but it was lost.
>
> "The LST you sent can't come in close enough. Send an LCM. If you can't take us off, urgently request ten thousand rounds 30 caliber and mortar ammo. We are out of food and water too. Send gas in an alligator for tanks. We have the tanks but no gasoline!"

I never did learn what happened to those men trapped in a murderous crossfire at the foot of the cliffs. As I look back, I can remember many such intercepted messages plain language, no code. In war, as in other events, tension, excitement, weariness all merge into one great gray dream so that, when it is over, it is hard to remember the simplest episodes.

0800-1200 on 8 June. Mines were laid by enemy planes last night. On this watch, the destroyers *Fitch (DD-462)* and *Glennon* and the DE *Rich* struck mines and sank within minutes of each other. The destroyer *Meredith* has also gone down.

8 June, D-Day Plus Two, Baie de la Seine.

The tide came in and spewed ashore
The retchings of amphibious war,
And all the while, twixt ebb and flow
More Devil's broth eddied, swirled below.
Life belts, gas tanks, husks of men,
The tide came in, went out again.

Can't figure why I am impelled to write verse at a time like this. It doesn't seem possible that, only two days ago, we hit the beaches in Normandy. I get what sleep I can at intervals near my station. Looks like a permanent GQ. The skipper goes to the sea cabin occasionally for a few minutes rest, but he is as weary as we and shows it. Must rest my eyes now as much as possible as I find myself seeing things on the radar scope that are not there and have to look twice.

Rough again today and lowering cloud banks permit a bleak and reluctant sun, fleeting glances. Even the shadows seem to stumble haltingly. We are all too weary to even bitch about the chow. I was sleepily awake at GQ and stumbled groggily to my battle station. Mr. Landreth was in the chart house and read bearings and ranges of approaching aircraft. *Maloy's* guns downed it before coming within our range. *Maloy* will now paint a plane on her stack.

1400. We now know about the hospital ship *Dinard*. She struck a mine and sank as she was outward bound for the U.K. with wounded evacuated from Omaha Beach. She went down fast, and we understand there were few survivors.

9 June. Admiral Bryant, aboard the battleship *Texas (BB-35)*, is directing naval gunfire. From his voice messages, which we read, he is a sleepless fireball. *Texas* leaves at 0900 tomorrow. GQ at 0130. Subs or E-boats got some of our *LST*s.

13 June, Baie de la Seine. Events are crowding themselves. Day is night; night is day. We stand continuous night watches in addition to war cruising. GQ usually occurs at 0100 to 0300. The Bay is infested with E-boats. Submarine activity also reported. This morning, the destroyer *Plunkett (DD-431)* opened fire on a merchant vessel and a DE, off course and standing in 3000 yards abaft our port beam. The targeted ships reached the DD with a message. She ceased fire, leaving *Mulogh* (Name not identified) in sinking condition.

15 June. Parachute flares and paramines were dropped by the enemy, and one of their planes was shot down. Bombs came close aboard. At 0600, an LCT inbound struck a mine and went down. We now have nine newly sunken ships off the beaches. At dawn, *Texas* and *Arkansas* again bombarded the still unsecured beach areas and targets farther inland. We are five miles off West Beach. Wish I could record some of the messages coming over the phone circuits. We sure have some salty brass with us. A recording would be priceless someday.

16 June. Baie de la Seine is littered with the junk of war. Life belts, khaki clothing, blankets and other things not so nice. There are schools of fish, belly up, victims of exploding mines. Cases of canned goods come floating by; pictures, letters, gasoline cans, refuse, garbage, soiled linens from the sunken hospital ship.

19 June. To add to our discomfort, the bay is a tumultuous mass of seething water. The air raid last night was punitive. Bombs were dropped, and several torpedoes were tossed into the Utah sector. "Vermin" (radio-controlled missiles) were also detected. The planes were JU 88s. We had some difficulty in picking them up on the SA radar because they dropped "window" (strips of aluminum foil) to confuse us. The Germans inland are still shelling Omaha and Utah beachheads. Yesterday, we stood on deck, fascinated as towering pillars of black smoke denoted the high explosive shells when they landed. The concussion was terrific.

We are now standing 2-1/2 miles offshore as the shelling was too close for comfort. I believe that we on *Borum* have seen much more of the struggle ashore than the warships which stand far offshore and lob in the heavies. Today, *Texas*, *Arkansas*, *Nevada*, *Quincy* and possibly *Tuscaloosa*, stood out to sea. Apparently, their job here is finished. The enemy is now out of range of their batteries. The hospital ships continue to come and go. The LSTs, the transports and lesser craft continue to land thousands of men a day.

20-21 June. Heavy lashing seas. An ML (British motor torpedo boat) capsized and sank 2000 yards off our port bow. We rescued two sailors by heaving lines to them. Another boat picked up an additional three. Later, an English LCT broke in half, and we rescued 13 men, causing superficial damage to our hull. Four English officers and men elected to remain aboard the stern section of the LCT, and the last we saw of them they were drifting toward the beach. An LST also capsized; many more of our craft are being damaged by the mountainous seas. Sleep is virtually impossible. Have had my clothes on since June 5th weather is still very cold not a real warm day since reaching Europe. Our English "guests" extol the merits of our mess and are openly exuberant over the prospect of remaining with us for several days. The captain intends to put them ashore in the British assault area as soon as permission is granted. We have practically denuded them of souvenirs.

Musings in the chart house
Mamselle lived in Normandy,
In a white chateau beside the sea.
With an ageless wisdom in her eyes
She learned to kiss in Paradise.
Golden mists were in her hair.
A vision? Yes, *C'est la Guerre*.

22 June. Anchored a half mile off Omaha Beach. The wreckage is awesome. However, many of these ships were purposely scuttled to create a harbor breakwater on D-Day. The storm is over, thank God, and the sun is shining, although the air is chill and raw. Huge fires are burning in and about Cherbourg. We are closing in on that city and understand the place is a shambles. Our "wagons" (BBs) and cruisers left last night to assist in opening up the area from seaward positions.

2000 hours. Anchored a quarter of a mile off the British beachhead, near Manvieux. A B 24 has just come spiraling down and crashed, throwing up a huge pillar of fire and smoke. Naval gunfire and enemy flak are heavy. On the 2000-2400 watch, a German JU 77 was shot down, and its two pilots were rescued by a PC.

23 June, 0800-1200 Watch. Sultry overcast skies, restless ground swells delivering up the bodies of our soldier dead. A PT boat is working between us and *Augusta (CA-31)*; she has recovered a number of bodies this morning. The Peninsula is flaming today. There is a great smoke pall, and livid flashes break through. We were raided tonight, but did not go to GQ as we lie between *Augusta* and *Ancon*; firing would have revealed their positions.

Our bombers are over again in force. The *Luftwaffe* attempts to give their troops air coverage but with little success. We are losing some planes as they wade through flak. It is cold again today. Bombs were dropped, an empty LST the only casualty. What we took to be a B 24 which crashed yesterday with one parachute opening, now appears to have been a "bandit," and we all feel better about it. The storm has caused severe damage to our ships, and beach forces were badly hampered by our inability to land reinforcements. There was a limited evacuation of wounded by air and sea.

24 June. Warm and balmy the first real good weather we have had. The bay is smooth. There continues a steady traffic between sea and shore. It seems so peaceful here, yet the fighting is only some 10 or 12 miles away. I scribble the following:

I'd tell a tale of stormy seas,
Of oceans green and blue,
Of submarines and sinking ships,
Of boys turned men; the *Borum's* crew.
I'd tell a tale of foreign shores,
From Panama to France,
Of reefs and shoals and still lagoons,
Where carefree moonbeams dance.
(unfinished)

25 June, 1944. I believe we are returning to some state of normalcy after the strain and tension of the past 20 days. I took my clothes off for the first time tonight to shower, dress and go topside to watch the buzzbombs go over. Mail from home is a big morale booster.

Weighed anchor for Portsmouth this afternoon, having aboard three high ranking generals, including General Bradley; two war correspondents; a commodore and other navy officers. On arrival, all hell broke loose, continuing until midnight, rocket (buzz) bombs launched from German shore installations. They plastered this area. This new weapon is nightmarish in appearance and sound. It can be sighted over the Channel, leaving a red exhaust trail and a noise like a banshee. The harbor defense guns and ships' batteries knocked one down.

27 June, 0400-0800. At anchor off Grandcamp, France. According to BBC, Cherbourg has been taken. Street fighting was in progress last night., and the dock areas have been secured. *Tuscaloosa* has moved in close, shelling gun positions holding up the main advance.

27-28 June. Escorting *Ancon* from Omaha Beach to Portland. Moored alongside *Nevada*. She has just returned from shelling Cherbourg. We will return to the combat area later in the day. Visited the CIC on *Nevada*, a sweet setup and enough to make any radarman envious.

0700 on 29 June. Underway to Belfast, with *Nevada* and a destroyer group. We suffered damage to a propeller while pulling away from *Nevada*; Lieutenant Davis is disturbed. We have been joined by the cruisers *Quincy* and *Tuscaloosa*, an imposing array of ships. We are in inner screen protection for the battleships and cruisers.

Lands End, England. *Maloy* is also "inner screen." Air coverage is heavy. Sea is calm, and the skies have been clear since leaving Portland. The big ships have accomplished their mission here and will go stateside, but not us. There's too much cleanup work to do here. However, morale is high despite the rough sea and tough duty.

2 July. We departed from Belfast last night. We are escorting, along with *Maloy*, destroyers *Jonet* (unidentified), *Jeffers*, *Somers (DD-381)*, and *Murphy (DD-603)*, four infantry transports bound for France, steaming through raw, impenetrable fog. We made several contact runs and brought up "the bottom of the channel."

0200 on 4 July. Anchored off the Omaha Beach assault area. A plane has just been shot down over the beach and exploded. A parachute opened and descended into the water. Howie Jung and I take turns on the flying bridge, watching the "fireworks." Antiaircraft fire is desultory; bomb flashes are continuous, and artillery fire is quite heavy. We are to depart at 0600 to Plymouth for much needed repairs.

15 July, 1944. For three days, we have been patrolling from Cherbourg to Port de Barfleur. Yesterday, we saw a German shell strike an ammunition dump on the beach, sending a huge pile of debris high into the air. The concussion was terrific. The initial excitement of the Normandy invasion is over.

Midnight on 26 July, still daylight in these latitudes. Attacked by two torpedo planes. Howie and I recognized low-flying planes and tracked them successfully on SL radar as they closed the ship. They made three runs on us. Our 20mm guns may have scored hits. Our 1.1" guns were ineffective, and the 3" guns could not be trained fast enough. Two torpedoes were launched, one passing across our bow, the other missing our stern section by a scant few yards.

29 July, Cherbourg. Arrived in Cherbourg this morning from our PT boat patrol. A harbor mine exploded, sending up a column of water. We are to patrol off Cape Leng tonight with *HMS Serapis*, code name "Green Horn." As Mr. Turnbull would say, "Some watermelon patrol!"

Evening of 11-12 August, Cherbourg. We are at anchor with four PT boats moored on our starboard side and two others to port. A doctor and a British Commander have come aboard. A conference of officers is taking place and have just learned that we have a target for tonight. Time is 2000 hours, and we are making 24 knots. The PTs are following in our wake, a beautiful picture. We patrol between Jersey and Guernsey and are subjected to occasional coastal battery fire.

Two British ships, along with our PTs, have engaged seven small enemy vessels, sinking four. Casualties aboard *HMS Samurez*, five officers and one rating; aboard *HMS Onslaught*, five ratings. Later, PTs or the British have set one enemy craft afire. Nine miles off Le Corbier, Jersey, we were shelled by shore batteries. Four casualties on a PT. One PT was badly damaged, and we are towing her. The action was fast and furious for a few minutes. I vividly remember one plain language message from a PT: "Let's get the fucking Hell out of here."

16-17 August. Another fruitless patrol between Jersey and Guernsey. We are standing out beyond effective range of the shore batteries ten miles from Fort Albert. At nine miles, their gunnery is excellent. We have now been on patrol three days and nights without returning to Cherbourg, getting little sleep. Two PT boats, *Katie*, and *Mairzie Doats*, brought mail tonight.

21 August, Cherbourg. I went ashore last night. This first liberty in France was an event, one I had looked forward to for many months. The area is still a jumble of debris. "Ducks" ply back and forth unloading supplies. Guards are overseeing some 1000 sullen-faced German prisoners who are stacking supplies. The cafes had little to sell, and the shops were closed, Against the advice of army MPs, I wandered out into the uncleared open area looking for German helmets found one with a hole in it. The Army has beat us to the "loot."

23-24 August. Monotonous patrol between Jersey and Guernsey broken by the discovery of *PT-509* which failed to return from night patrol. She had been shot in half, her bow section still afloat. We think she lost out in a fire fight with an enemy mine layer. Judging from her riddled hulk, we doubt if there were survivors. (A sequel to *PT-509*, related in prior narrative on *Maloy*).

24 August. The Germans on these islands are trying to break out. Our PTs have stopped them so far without more casualties. Tonight, we were the target for the 74th salvo fired at us from the Jersey shore batteries. Closest fell some 500 yards astern. Jersey and Guernsey have been declared target areas, and expect some bombing by the RAF.

Evening of 25 August. On patrol, we saw two A 20s shot down midway between Jersey and Guernsey. We spotted the survivors on SL radar, and the captain decided to risk a rescue attempt by sending the whale boat in, *Borum* remaining ten miles out. When the boat returned, there was just enough time to get the American airmen aboard before shore batteries opened up, missing us by a scant 400 yards. We drew out of range at flank speed, leaving the whale boat with Chief Durab in charge; they caught up with us later. Eight airmen were lost and four were rescued. Not recognizing the islands as enemy territory, they attempted a landing. One craft was shot down and collided with the other. They said it was so cold in their rubber raft they would have welcomed any kind of a rescue, even by the Germans.

30 August, Plymouth. Arrived here today from the Channel Islands. We were given 72 hours leave, and I have decided to go to Exeter. Mr. Harrison has been there and has told me enough about it to intrigue me. I also picked up a German HQ sign of the Elite Corps.

We left the Channel Islands just in time to miss a "show." Shore batteries and armed trawlers mauled our relief ships. The *PT-505* lead us into the inner harbor at Cherbourg on the 20th. The PT boys think it great sport to pull the pins on German hand grenades and drop them over the side. Some of our crew have taken up this practice. Below decks, the grenade explosions sound like someone had thrown a handful of nails against the hull. Mr. Harrison said he saw some sailors playing "ball" with grenades as they stood on a cliff by the sea. One above would pull the pin and toss it to his companion standing below him who would, in turn, toss it into the sea. Great sport!

1 September. In Exeter, I found lodging in a private home, a two story house with a beautiful flower garden in the back yard and within walking distance to the main part of town. My room was large and comfortable but without hot water. There was a bath at the end of the hall, also without water. When I inquired, the serving girl heated several kettles and brought them to me. My gracious hostess said that plumbing was a luxury few middle class English could afford. They hoped one day to have hot and cold running water. I asked my host where I could see some of the old Roman ruins in the vicinity. I didn't have an answer to that one. I also asked him about the River Avon, and he replied, "Don't you sailors see enough water?"

6 September. Tonight we are again patrolling off Aldernay. On all the war maps, the Channel Islands have been taken by us, and how we wish that were true. Our PTs lie in ambush in Great Russell and, to the south, is *Maloy* with other PTs and English destroyers. We will try to sneak in tonight, but the shore batteries on Aldernay outrange us by eight miles. We are bombing Jersey and Guernsey, but our planes are high and the flak is heavy. There is some bombing over Isle de C'ezembre. The enemy is still holding out on the mainland, including St. Nazaire and Brest. The English papers had us in Brest weeks ago, but radio reports indicate heavy fighting still going on.

To recap, *Borum* has had a checkered career thus far, having played nursemaid to everything from PTs to BBs. First, we had a convoy with a marine brigade, then a convoy for an LST Tender, then a convoy for LSTs and LCIs. We screened for cruisers and battleships, then radar ship and screen during the invasion, island attack unit, control ship for PT operations and Coastal patrol. And now *Borum* and *Maloy* are the only DEs left for permanent duty.

Afternoon of 9 September. We got clobbered while patrolling in the Channel Islands, four rounds from Guernsey within 50 yards of *Borum*.

1535 14.5 miles four hits.

1537 Port quarter, port bow damage, range opening.

1541 Hit on port bow estimated range 16.5 miles.

Numerous holes in stack, deck houses, hull and ready ammunition boxes. A searchlight broken. Radar equipment and range finder on flying bridge hit by large chunks of shrapnel. Captain's cabin and adjoining ship's office had four holes. Shrapnel and fire damage in Chief's quarters and wardroom. Three radio aerials down. We suffered three casualties; one hospitalized; two minor wounded remained aboard.

26 September, Plymouth. We arrived on the 24th, and leaves were granted. I have just returned from Bristol, the trip having been influenced by my recent reading of "The Sun Is My Undoing" which, in part, concerns Bristol as one of the original slave trading ports.

I trod the cobbled streets that Matthew trod;
I saw the docks where Matthew put to sea;
Stood down in Bristol Channel, sails unfurled,
A slave ship his, the sun his destiny.
I stood upon the spot where slaves were sold;
Envisioned haggling barter, the flesh of men;
Left England bound for great and distant lands,
With black ivory and gold, sailed home again.

Bristol was heavily damaged by bombing, the worst raids being carried out in 1940. It was from Bristol that John and Sebastian Cabot set sail about 1497 for the new world. The Church of St. Mary Radcliffe, one of the most beautiful parish churches in all England, is here.

September status. Cherbourg is still subject to an occasional attack. Supply ships come and go. Subs were reported in the area, also E-boats. We sighted an E-boat, a fugitive from C'ezembre or Brest, now in our hands. She was fast and avoided an encounter. Crosby, pharmacist striker, went over the hill (deserted) with about $600 of Doc's money from the sick bay safe. Chief Durab was transferred at Plymouth. Ireland and Mulbar are now in the states. Fire Controlman Quinlan has taken Ireland's billet. Dady and Monus were taken to London to serve 30 days each in the brig as the Plymouth brig was overcrowded. Ensign Bob Gardner was promoted to Lieutenant (JG), and John Stensrud is our only Ensign aboard.

3 October. We received notice authorizing us to wear a battle star on our campaign ribbons for our part (quote) "In the assault and bombardment of the French coast on D-Day, for screening patrol duties, and E-boat attack prevention 6-25 June 1944."

7 October. Today the Channel is rougher than ever, and we are on a five mile patrol off Jersey and Guernsey. When we move closer in than 13 miles, their batteries open up. On the west side of Guernsey, the shore batteries are massive. Understand these batteries were captured in France (Probably from the Maginot Line) and moved to the islands during the early days of the war.

11 October. GQ at 0550. Unidentified ship north of the swept channel near Cape Frenel and C'ezembre. Our challenge went unanswered, so we illuminated the target with star shells and placed a shot across her bow. Coming within bullhorn hailing distance, she identified herself as a British coastal vessel standing out of Malo, France.

Her skipper hailed us: "What the bloody hell you think you're doing?"

Our captain replied: "You may proceed."

The Germans continue to lay mines hereabouts, and we are a part of the anti-mine laying group. Our assigned patrol is 11 miles north of C. Frenel and C'ezembre.

14 October. Very rough gale warnings. The PTs have "headed for the barn." We have five injured men, taking them to Molaix, France.

22 October. The PTs, *Maloy* and *Borum* are keeping the enemy mine layers inside, and they refuse to come out and fight. Enemy aircraft occasionally arrive and depart from Jersey, and we are helpless except to report our observations to Cherbourg. Submarines are in the vicinity, and E-boats are in the island anchorages, but they will not approach within our gun range. They are too fast for us anyway. Hope the PTs get them tonight.

2240 Hours. *Perch 1* to *Perch 2*:

"Let's get the hell out of here".

Perch 2 to *Perch 1*:

"Okay Pal, but I have a steering casualty. Don't believe I need a tow. I can make it. It's hotter than hell. They're using rocket cannon on me. You get the fuck out of here. I'll make it."

2320 Hours We are unable to raise *Perch 2*, and *Perch 1* is returning to scene of action. The beach is sending support aircraft.

9 November. Returned to the ship this morning from a three day leave in London. I set out on my own to see as much as 72 hours would allow. Visited the Dunhill pipe factory, Westminster Abbey, Houses of Parliament, the Admiralty, St. Paul's Cathedral, The Trocadero, Claridge, Buckingham Palace. I walked along Bond Street, Leicester Square, Scotland Yard, the Bank of England, Fleet Street, the Crypt, St. James Palace and two London Bridges. The better class hotels are off limits to non-commissioned officers, but I breezed in anyway amid cold stares (from the British). I visited a number of pubs, and wound up meeting one of the most beautiful girls I have ever seen. Vicki is a WAAF but has been working at the American Red Cross. She was an artists' model in civilian life, is well educated and has more animation than any girl I've met thus far in England. Too bad I had to meet her just before departure, but I will see her again if I should get another chance to visit London.

17 December. Another London leave ended tragically. Upon arrival at Paddington Station, I caught a cab for Picadilly and met Vicki. We decided to go to Convent Gardens to dance that evening. I took her to her home in Kensington so that she could change into mufti. Later on, I caught a cab to pick her up but, on the way, the V2s started coming over, and I had to abandon the cab for an air raid shelter. After the all clear, I went on to Kensington but, when I reached her area, there wasn't anything to see. The entire block had been blown out of existence. There were some survivors, but I could not find her. She was such a sweet and pretty young thing. I can't yet believe she's gone. I will be a long time getting over this.

17 December, London Leave. I really didn't have the heart for it. I saw one V2 the last night I was there. It hit close to Paddington Station and caused a large fire. I was caught in a residential section near the underground (subway) and went there for shelter. There were thousands of civilians with blankets, food, etc. Wandering around after dark is something to remember, especially in the vicinity of Picadilly. Servicemen are accosted by "ladies of the evening" in droves. Have never seen anything quite like it, not even in a Texas oil field boom town. Five pounds seems to be the current tariff.

18 December. Departing Portland for C. de la Hague, arriving same date. With the approach of Christmas, the boys are pretty homesick. Some of us in "C" Division, as a gag, had previously written a letter to Santa Claus, c/o Wannamaker, New York. It was written in verse and ended by wishing them the kind of a Christmas "we once remembered."

The reply we received was a work of art. It also was in verse and beautifully illustrated water colors of us on the *Borum* dreaming of beautiful girls, Santa rowing out to meet us, Santa climbing down the ship's stack, pictures of twelve real beauties. Wannamaker's' advertising department apparently handled it, and it is superb:

T'was the night before Christmas, when all through the ship,
Not a creature was stirring; not even the Skip.
The boys were all nestled so snug in their beds,
While visions of damsels, danced in their heads.
The socks were all hung by the hammocks with care,
In hopes that St. Nicholas soon would be there.
And sure enough Santa was then on his way
To cheer the brave seamen at dawn Christmas Day.
He rowed to the ship, and he climbed down the stack,
And guess what St. Nicholas had in his pack!
He's heard about pleas that were fervent terrific!

From all of those boys, maybe the far South Pacific?
And so, for each sailor he had a surprise,
The gift each one wanted, a sight for sore eyes.
First, emerged Betty, a joy to behold,
The fairest of damsels, with hair of pure gold.
Then Nancy and Mary and Janie and Belle,
With angel-like look, but ah, human as well.
Then Helen and Peg, both redheads you see,
And Dottie and Ruth, as fair as can be.
And Ginny and Florence with dark raven tresses,
And Patty and Kay in their prettiest dresses,
And beautiful Jeannie and oh, sakes alive,
There's one for you all to the age forty-five.
To show you how Santa, and all folks at home,
Are thinking of you, though on oceans you roam.
And hoping, next year, when it comes to December,
You will have the Christmases you used to remember.
Signed Santa Claus

24 December, 1944. We received the following message this afternoon:

Borum and all ships on screen: "Maintain especially vigilant watch tonight. Enemy may take advantage of Christmas Eve celebrations and make attack. Merry Christmas!"

1700. An American transport was torpedoed and sunk while approaching the harbor, a great loss of life, soldiers, doctors, WACS and nurses. Small boats are scouring the area for survivors and bodies and ply back and forth between the outer harbor and the docks. All available navy and army ambulances were called to the dock area. Survivors are being picked up but, in these frigid waters, hypothermia sets in quickly. We are maintaining our station, a helpless feeling.

9-20 January 1945, Le Havre, France. Arrived for yard availability. It is cold, and snowing. Le Havre and its residential districts are a shambles from air, artillery and infantry attack. We moored in Basin de la Citadel, near the main part of the city. A carton of cigarettes brings 500 francs ($10.00 U.S. with the invasion franc valued at 2 cents. Although we are trying to peg the franc at 2 cents, the French have applied a more realistic valuation, about 1/4 to 1/2 cent.

We have had to turn in all English and US currency to remove the temptation to further abet this inflationary situation. We have also had candy and cigarettes rationed. What people won't do for a candy bar, a tube of toothpaste, a pack of cigarettes or a bar of soap!

Where souls are sold, but not for gold,
  I know I hadn't oughter,
But I'm going ashore with a Hershey bar
  And seduce the Mayor's daughter.

16 January, Le Havre, graveyard of 337 ships! Jack Knox and I went on liberty, and heard that a cafe owner had a German Luger and holster. The Frenchman and his wife were delightful people, but we couldn't make a deal. As we looked out the window, we saw a long line of fresh American troops, just disembarked and on their way to the railroad station, bound for the front. Jack and I bought several bottles of calvados and cognac and went out to talk with them. I asked a young lieutenant if it would be all right to give some of the men a drink, and he said, "Ask the sergeant." The sergeant gave a nod so, for a few minutes, we had one hilarious time.

1 March, Le Havre, France. To the Officers and Crew:

> "We've been plank owners for fifteen months. During that time, we've sailed thousands of miles, some smooth, many rough. Sometimes, the duty was monotonous but often exciting. With it all, *Borum* has indeed been a lucky ship. Here's wishing you more of that luck until you're safely home again.
>
> So long and smooth sailing."
>
> Joseph E. Davis
> Lieutenant USNR

Mr. Davis is the first officer to leave us, and it is with much regret. I admired him greatly. An attorney in civilian life, he resides in Miami, Florida. Hope I can see him down there some day.

6 March 1945, Paris. We were transported to the Grand Central Hotel where each of us was assigned a private room with bath! The rooms are large and luxuriously appointed complete with maid service. There is also a prophylactic station (Navy of course). My room also had a mirrored ceiling. Saw the Eiffel Tower, the Arc de Triomphe, Napoleon's tomb, Notre Dame, and the Sorbonne.

I attended a matinee at the Folies Bergere with Abbot; it was quite elaborate although the theater had no heat. How those gals stood it *sans* clothing beats me. We were cold in our pea coats. We went to a swanky little cafe across the street after the show. Some of the girls came over and, one in particular, latched on to us. She sang several request songs, ending with "The Eyes of Texas"! The French civilians insisted on paying for the drinks.

Some of the girls here are fabulous. I found a set of little French dolls dressed in provincial costumes to send to little Lucy. The prices are very high for almost everything. Champagne is 1000 francs a bottle. As I write this, some of the boys have just come into my room waving a bottle of it. Well, here's to Paris and all that's beautiful. I drink to you in champagne!

11-12 March. Departed for Dieppe today. Bitterly cold night, and Jack Knox and I have the duty. Jack was POD (Petty Officer of the Deck) and came down to my bunk to ask me if I wanted to go ashore with him and pick up some of our boys being held in the stockade by the army. We finally found Military Police HQ where a very young Second Lieutenant was in charge of the night patrol. He exploded:

> "It's about time the navy took these bums back; take them and good riddance, and don't come back. We never have any trouble with our own men, just the *Borum* crew, the only navy men in Dieppe."

So we took our prisoners, but liberty did not expire till 2400, and it was only 2200. Therefore, we turned them loose in town for another round of drinks when they promised to make it back to the ship by 2400. Jack and I returned to the ship and Lieutenant Turnbull informed us that they had been picked up again. So back we went and, after some abuse by the Second "Louie," went back to the ship with the prisoners. We barely made the 2400 deadline. Captain Knox Turnbull only laughed when we told him the story.

We have moved our ship to facing No. 10 Granville St., a rather swank brothel. Since the army has moved in, replacing the Canadians, the place is off-limits to the military. The girls wave to us with their panties and scanties from the upstairs windows. The British ship *Daffodil*, carrying locomotives and other rail equipment has been sunk by a submarine at the harbor entrance, bottling up this port.

We are finding Dieppe a wonderful liberty port. We are the first American navy vessel here since World War I. The box of toilet soap Aunt Elizabeth sent me for Christmas is "legal tender plus!"

22 March, Dieppe. We are still penned up here, and we do not know just when the French will declare an open port. Demolition teams are at work on *Daffodil*. Last night, I walked from the harbor entrance to the western cliffs along Boulevard Verdun. Our army, fresh from the states, has practically taken over the once beautiful waterfront. Many hotels are on this boulevard facing the English Channel and have been heavily damaged. The entire beach area is booby-trapped, and we walk at our own risk.

30 March. On patrol off Cherbourg, weather brisk and a moderate sea running. The bridge sighted a small boat with a makeshift sail, and we took aboard two alleged Russians who profess to be prisoners of war and escapees from Aldernay. Some of our boys can converse a little with them in Polish and German. They claim to have been at sea for five days, fighting wind, sea and current in a vain attempt to reach Cherbourg. The current is extremely fast in this area, creating a question as to the veracity of their story. They are suffering from hunger and exposure. These alleged Russians say they killed a German guard on Aldernay when they made their escape.

They claim they stole his shoes and coat, a pocket watch as well as other personal items. According to their story, there were originally three of them, but a companion was killed by German rifle fire. They also claim that shore batteries fired on them. Those shore batteries have earned our respect, and I seriously doubt they escaped. The captain is not satisfied with their story and believes them to be German. An ML is coming out from the beach to pick them up.

1530, Double British summer time, Cherbourg. We have just heard Mr. Churchill's speech. The war is over; whistles are blowing on the beach and from the ships in the harbor. We are moored alongside *Maloy*; an English MTB is moored to our port side. Small French sailing craft ply the harbor; flying boats are overhead patrol craft, ours and the British. A British sailor on the bridge of the MTB is doing an impromptu flag dance to the tune of "Don't Fence Me In," which we are playing over the 21 MC circuit (loud speakers). We hear that the Channel Islands are to be liberated today! Thank the Good Lord for that; we weary of the very name. Scuttlebutt is rife.

21 May. Last night, we had a ship's party, inviting as many French girls, Navy nurses and WAACs as would or could come. An invitation, decorated with the crossed flags of both nations, was distributed:

> *Veuiller honorer de votre presence la soiree dansante sera donee, par les Americains, le 20 Mai 1945. Rendezvous a 19 Heures, Place Napoleon.*
>
> J. L. Landreth,
> Lieutenant, USN
> Welfare Officer

Some crew members slipped copies of this invitation under the doors of a few places off limits to us. These girls, I'm sorry to say, didn't show up. But the party was a huge success and was even attended by the Mayor's daughter. She was a beautiful and buxom lass of sixteen. We managed to get a few auxiliaries and nurses as well as French mademoiselles. Plenty of good food, cognac and calvados. We made a good impression on our guests who enjoyed the chow. Renee, my date for the evening, told me that she didn't know sailors could behave so well. She was impressed, and so was I, with her.

> *To all hands:*
>
> "Over a year and a half ago, 200 men from every part of the United States gathered in Orange, Texas, as the crew of *Borum*. They went through seasickness, homesickness, shakedown, convoy duty, the invasion of Europe, enemy bombardment, and the heartfelt loneliness of month after month away from native soil and loved ones. As we have worked together for the accomplishment of our purpose, the bond between us has grown strong and, now as I leave you, it is with the natural emotion of parting from close associates and good friends in this common experience.
>
> To one and all, well done, pleasant sailing, and the hope that you will soon get that well-deserved stateside leave."
>
> J. L. Landreth, Lt., USN

Mr. Spratley will make a good exec. Yet I deeply regret Mr. Landreth leaving us.

4 June, Cherbourg. It is certain that we shall join a small fleet of vessels which will steam past the Normandy beachheads day after tomorrow. At long last, we are going home. I have finished correcting some code books and find time to scribble:

> I kissed a girl in Derry, beside the River Foyle,
> When the escorts lay at anchor; her name was Molly Doyle.
> I kissed a girl in Plymouth, near the docks of Tamar Quay,
> With our ship again at anchor, inland from the sea.
> I kissed M'm'selle in Cherbourg, there was moonlight in her hair
> She was both sweet and lovely, her name Marie St. Claire.
> And I kissed and kissed in every port, Juanita, Jeanette, Marie
> And we wept a bit at parting when *Borum* put to sea.

6 June. We are standing out to sea. *Maloy*, *Borum* and 19 PCs left France. The group steamed past Omaha Beach and fired a salute in remembrance of the first anniversary of D-Day. The PCs will have to be fueled and watered en route, and this is to be our job.

19 June, Off New York. Her skyline is most impressive. We, who have seen it often, realize that we have never really looked

at it before. We are getting quite an ovation from the fire boats and other craft in the harbor. We have been long gone for 469 days. The sight of automobiles in such great numbers awes us. We had forgotten!

The scene is difficult to describe. For some aboard *Borum*, New York is home and the sight must be one of reverence, home and loved ones just minutes away. I understand a directive has come through authorizing discharge of men who have attained the age of 45, and it is quite possible I will be in that category. Frankly, I do not relish the thought of leaving *Borum* until the war is over in the Pacific. The war certainly can't last much longer, and I should like to see it through. But this I know, the past two years have been a wonderful interlude in my life, never to be repeated.

I bid my shipmates farewell and bid you to remember that you are as young as your faith, as old as your doubt, as young as your self confidence, as old as your fears, as young as your hopes, as old as your despair.

Frederic Shelby Brooks

Rich strikes third mine after her stern is blown off by second mine. Courtesy US Naval Historical Center

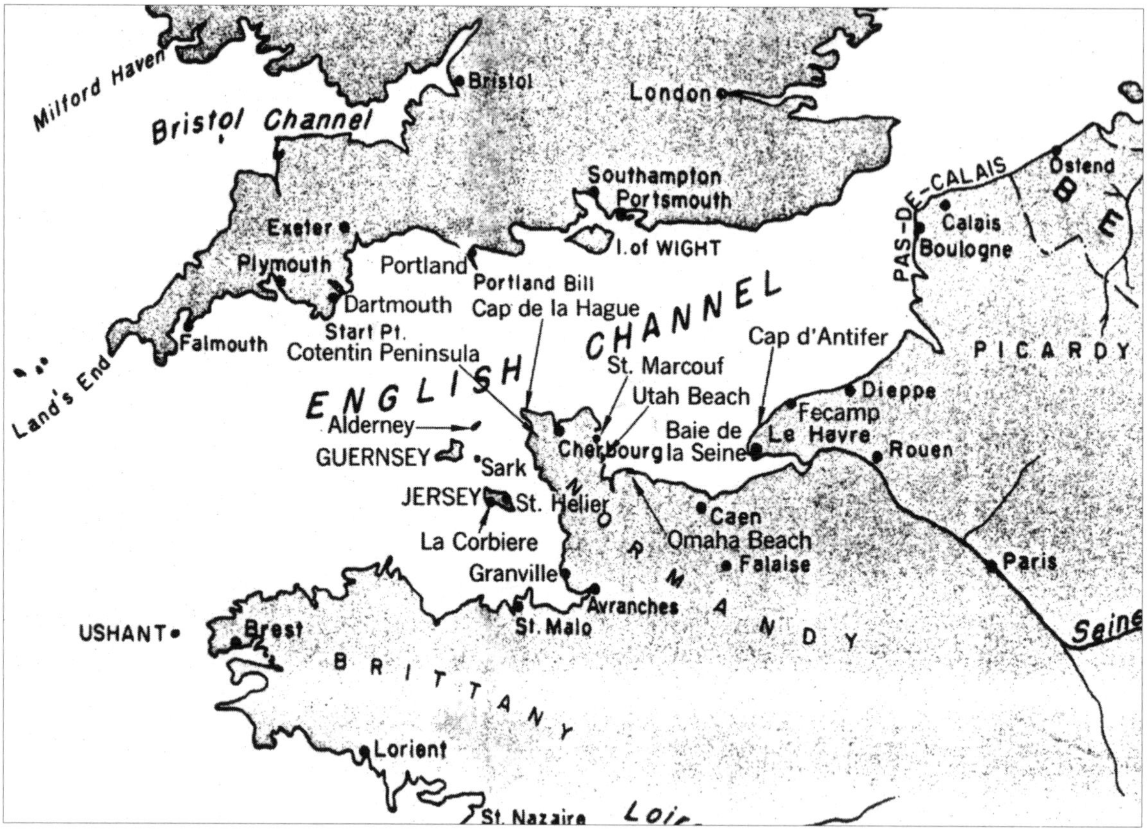

Area of operations in Overlord/Neptune and Channel Islands. *USS Borum, USS Rich.*
Photocopied from P.T. Book "At Close Quarters."

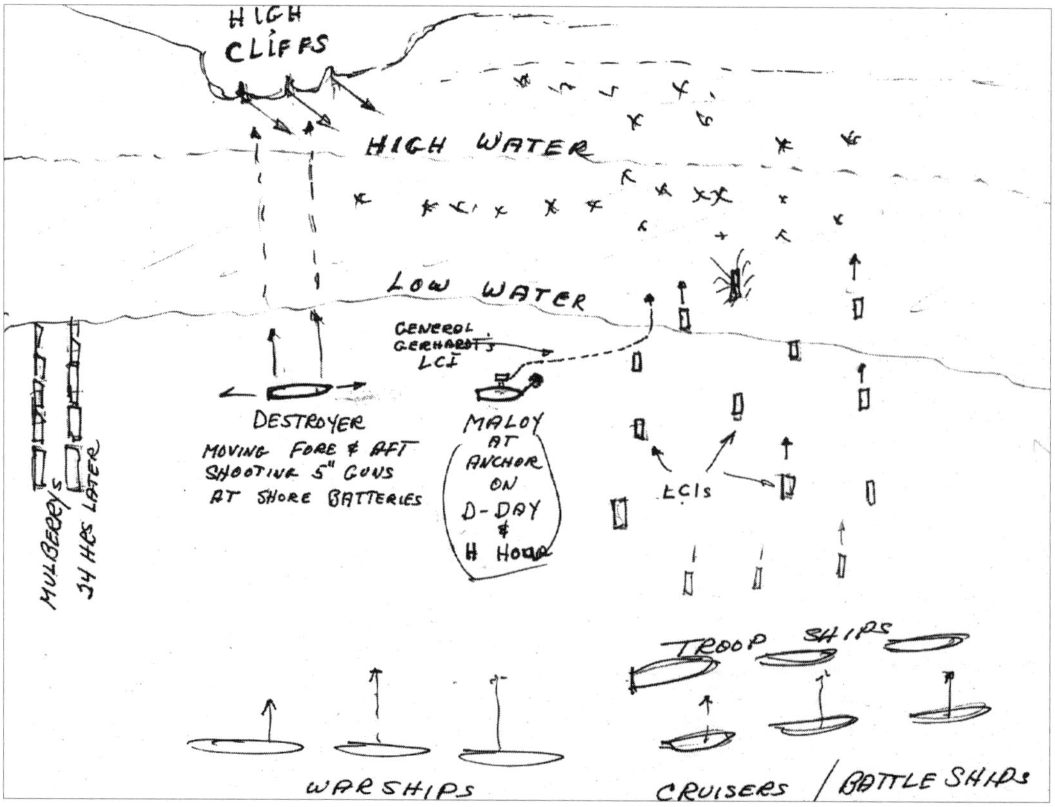

Disposition of *Maloy* and other ships at Omaha Beach, "H" hour 6 June 1944. Drawn by Joseph M. Mahoney

FRINGE OF WAR

SMALL SHIP - LARGE WAR

CRUISE OF THE USS BORUM - DE-790

1943 - 1945

BY

FREDERIC SHELBY BROOKS JR.

RdM. 2C.

Original fly leaf of *Borum* diary.

U-66 and crew in German home port. Photo taken from captured crewman. US Navy Photo

Lewis M. Andrews, Jr.

Chapter VIII - Twilight of the U-boats

As the Allied armies thundered into Germany in the spring of 1945, the *Kriegsmarine* exhorted its U-boats to redouble efforts to interdict the seemingly endless supply of troops and materiel that were reducing German armies. However, this was not 1942 when submarine commanders could choose targets with impunity. The ratios had been reversed. More submarines than Allied vessels were dispatched to the bottom of the Atlantic in the closing months of World War II.

Nonetheless, the U-boats were still dangerous, particularly the new ones. Their snorkels enabled them to go as fast submerged as on the surface, about 19 knots. Their acoustic torpedoes threatened pursuing destroyer escorts. They continued to exact a price up to the moment of surrender even though they were being overwhelmed by sheer numbers.

Another enemy, the North Atlantic, continued to dog the DEs to the bitter end. Lieutenant William S. Adams of the *Keith (DE-241)* recalled in his history of that ship:

[The Task Group was roughly between the Faeroe Islands and Iceland.]

An unceasing high wind generated very rough seas, making life miserable. There were a few brief sonar contacts, but the weather made it impossible to launch a reasonable depth charge attack. A man was swept overboard from one of the other DEs. Although the next wave returned his body, he was dead from drowning and exposure to the frigid water. A plane from the carrier crashed in the sea, but the search for the pilot had to be abandoned as hopeless.

On 21 February 1945, the steady wind from the north had increased until it reached 120 miles per hour, creating enormous wave crests about 100 yards apart. Their heights above troughs were sufficient to completely hide the carrier, including her radar dome, 135 feet above her water line. As the crest of a wave passed under a ship's hull, the bow would first rise high in the air, then plunge into the water as the fantail flew up and the propellers raced free. Going downwind at a speed slower than the crests of the waves made steering control tenuous, raising fear of broaching in the trough.

All the ships in Escort Division 7 reported structural damage and personnel injuries. While executing a course change, Keith fell off a huge crest and was trapped in the trough, pushed over on her starboard side by wind and sea until water poured into her air intakes. The clinometer showed 90 degrees, and the hydraulic steering system failed. After what seemed an eternity, but only a few seconds, she slowly returned to the upright position.

Desperately, the crew rigged the manual emergency steering gear and manned the pumps to bail destabilizing, sloshing water from the engineering spaces. Herculean efforts by the crew achieved control. 'Helpfully', the *Core (CVE-13)* radioed a rebuke to the *Keith* for being 'off station'. Our reply was tacitly restrained.

Fuel was running low on the DEs. At 0500 on the 26th, there was a loud crash followed by scraping noises down the sides of *Keith's* hull. She had slammed into a field of pack ice. Fortunately, the ice was thin so the ramming bow sliced it neatly and harmlessly.

There is no doubt about the roll inflicted on Keith. In talking to DE sailors, however, this author quickly learned that a good deal of "one-upmanship" existed as the yarns were perpetuated. The degrees of roll invariably increased.

ESCORT DIVISION FORTY-SIX

The Coast Guard Scored Again

Lowe (DE-325), the principal ship in this narrative, had seen action on 20 April 1944 when her convoy came under a tenacious enemy air attack off the North African coast (see chapter *Convoys to the Mediterranean*). On 5 March 1945, she joined an exclusively Coast Guard Hunter-Killer Group operating due east of Newfoundland.

Menges (DE-320) was a "retread" destroyer escort. We previously described how the after end of *Holder (DE-401)* was attached to the surviving forward end of *Menges*, the latter name prevailing. She joined *Pride (DE-323)*, *Mosley (DE-321)*, and *Lowe* late in February 1945 to form the four hunter-killer Coast Guard ships in TG 22.14, *Escort Division 46* (CortDiv 46). Commander Reginald H. French was Division Commander (ComCortDiv) as well as Commander of Task Force 22.14 (CTG 22.14).

Mission: Commander French opened his secret dispatch from CinClant, directing him to – "Find and destroy an enemy submarine, approximate location on 4 March 1945, 49 degrees-30 minutes north latitude, 39 degrees-30 minutes west longitude."

The ships proceeded south of Cape Sable, Nova Scotia, and Sable Island, to a point south of Flemish Cap, where the estimates placed the submarine on 9 March. Search areas were adjusted to scout along the track of the U-boat as estimated by the Tenth Fleet daily submarine reports. On 17 March, CTG 22.14 ordered a search plan around an area in which *Mosley* had reported a sonar contact.

1317 on 13 March 1945. *Menges*, commanded by Lieutenant Commander F.M. McCabe, made sonar contact with an underwater target at a range of 650 yards. The assured range, per the bathythermograph readings, was only 600 yards. For the next 2-1/2 hours, *Menges* made three hedgehog attacks and two depth charge attacks, set to fire on magnetic impulse. Both types of attack produced negative results but may have caused minor damage to the target.

Sound conditions were very poor. Accordingly, it was impossible to evaluate the target and to make accurate attacks. However, the last attack (depth charge) was considered to be fairly accurate. From the trace, the target seemed to be zigzagging at about three knots. However, the miserable sound conditions prevailed, and the target was lost.

0843 on 18 March. *Menges* again made a good sonar contact at a range of 1200 yards. Fifteen minutes later, she echo-ranged on a different target at 1800 yards but, since the first one was believed to be the real one, *Menges* continued to search for the original contact. Two hedgehog attacks were fired with negative results. *Menges* continued to search but got several false contacts, most of them from the bottom. According to a note on the chart, the soundings in the area were very inaccurate. Having failed to regain contact and believing previous contacts may have been on pinnacles, *Menges* rejoined other ships to continue the search.

1018. *Lowe* reported making a sonar contact. It may possibly have been one of those previously picked up by *Menges*. It is very probable that the submarine about to be attacked by *Lowe* was the same one that was attacked by *Menges*. If the U-boat had proceeded in a straight line from the position of the attack on 13 March to the position of the attack on the 18th, its average speed would have been 2.3 knots, average for submarine war cruising.

1027. *Menges* made another attack with hedgehogs, all exploding 10 seconds after hitting the water. Since the sinking time agreed with the sounding, it was thought that the attack was made on a rock on the bottom. Twenty minutes later, *Lowe* attacked a target successfully with hedgehogs and began a search of the area for evidence. Diesel oil from the point of the attack was spreading rapidly and later covered several square miles. In quick succession, *Menges* made contact with the damaged submarine and was directed by CTG 22.14 to take charge, coordinate with *Lowe* and drop full patterns of Mark 8 charges (magnetic setting) on the target.

At the time of the next contact, the units of the Task Group were in a formation, code termed "Icy," a scouting line, speed 12 knots, with all DEs conducting a sound search from 80 degrees on one bow to the same on the other bow. The distance between ships was 3000 yards, and the surface radars probed 360 degrees around the horizon. *Menges* was approximately five miles astern of the line investigating a sonar contact. The maximum sonar range of the day was calculated at 2200 yards, based on bathythermograph and other sea water recording instruments. Visibility was 300 yards. The sea was calm with a slight swell. Wind was from the southwest, force five knots. The depth of water varied from 45 to 75 fathoms with a sandy, even bottom.

1419. The commanding officer of *Lowe*, Lieutenant Commander Herbert Feldman, reported a contact at 1800 yards.

The ship slowed to seven knots to investigate the contact. The FXR gear was promptly streamed. Initial contact was lost but regained and evaluated as possible submarine. The DE's speed was increased to 12 knots and an approach was begun. The contact had slight down doppler and bearing movement. The dead reckoning tracer (DRT) and attack plotter recorded the submarine's course and speed of three knots.

1442. A full pattern of hedgehogs was fired. About 25 seconds after firing, a series of explosions was heard. At about the same time, fathometer readings were obtained on the sub for about six recordings, indicating 45 fathoms. The depth of water at the time was 72 fathoms. The detonations were believed to be on the bottom. The sonar gear was inoperative after the explosions because interlock switches in the receiver had opened; these were quickly closed. Contact was regained with a little down doppler, and another approach was started. The bearing movement was slight, and doppler changed to zero during the approach.

1459. *Lowe* fired a full pattern of hedgehogs, obtaining two explosions, followed by a tremendous explosion a fraction of a second thereafter! The apparent slowing of the target during the approach was assumed to be due to the submarine stopping on the bottom. Oil and air bubbled to the surface at the point of the last attack. Quantities of debris were sighted in the area. Samples of oil were obtained by dragging waste over the side. Contact was regained and held. The plot and the lack of doppler indicated a sub stationary on the bottom. Fathometer traces displayed a bump on the bottom while the ship was maneuvering in the oil slick. This was assumed to be the submarine.

Menges obtained sonar contact on the bottomed submarine at 1600. *Lowe* lowered the ship's boat and spent the next hour retrieving samples of debris. During that time, the ship maneuvered at various speeds in the area of the oil slick, and sound contact was maintained intermittently.

1720. *Lowe* approached the submarine to start a drop of magnetic depth charges. The target had a sharp echo with no doppler. A pattern of thirteen depth charges was laid on the submarine, resulting in four violent explosions. No fresh debris was sighted, but this may have been because of poor visibility, only 300 to 500 yards. Casualties were inflicted on the sound gear, the fire control radar, the surface search radar, the DRT plotter, and machinery in the engineering compartments. The DRT sustained several gears out of line.

1735. *Menges* dropped a pattern of Mark 8 depth charges and obtained several explosions. A second depth charge approach was made. The echo was not as sharp as on previous attacks. The target still had no doppler. Over the next two hours, three more attacks were delivered by *Menges*. On the second attack, a series of explosions were felt which seemed more violent than previous ones. *Menges* sonar gear stopped operating; the key relay was found to have completely jumped out of its sockets. On the third attack, a standard thirteen charge pattern was dropped in the same manner as before, and a series of explosions was obtained which seemed to increase in violence.

2023. A heavy underwater explosion rocked the attacking DE.

Lowe was about one mile away. Just prior to the last explosion, a sound was heard on the sonar gear resembling what would be heard if the beat frequency oscillator were moved from 0 to 600 while the receiver was picking up initial reverberations. *Lowe* and *Menges* held sonar contact intermittently until the Task Group left the area on 19 March 1945. At this time, it was considered that the submarine had been destroyed, and TG 22.14 departed for Halifax in accordance with previous orders. However, that procedure was aborted by CinClant at 0700 the same morning when he ordered the task group to return to the area of the attack in the hope of obtaining further evidence and to make sure of the kill.

1700. *Menges* obtained sonar contact on the same target, attacked, and reported bringing up fresh oil. The *Menges* confirmed the position with a three-line fix, using Loran. The task group departed from the area and was allowed to proceed to Casco Bay, Maine, in the belief that the submarine was destroyed and the possibility of obtaining any fresh evidence was remote.

Postwar investigation verified the destruction of *U-866* by this group. The major credit was awarded to *Lowe*.

On 30 May, *Menges* escorted her last convoy to Europe, then spent the remainder of the war as a training ship for the U.S. Coast Guard Academy in New London, Connecticut.

While still attached to TG 22.14 on 3 May, *Lowe* rescued the crew of the foundered Newfoundland schooner *Mary Duffit*, and her guns sank the hull to eradicate a menace to navigation. Commencing 6 July, the ship assumed duties as a training vessel at Norfolk, Virginia.

Lewis M. Andrews, Jr.

THE BARRIER PATROL

Phase II of the Croatan Hunter Killers

In the narrative *The Hunter-Killers*, we witnessed the sinking of four U-boats by the *Croatan* Hunter-Killer Group. Now, in the final days of the Atlantic War, three more were added to its laurels.

25 March 1945. Four hunter-killer groups took up their assigned North Central Atlantic sectors, extending from just south of Iceland to well south of Newfoundland. This was a massive combined operation, including *Croatan (CVE-25)*, *Mission Bay (CVE-59)*, *Bogue (CVE-9)*, and *Core (CVE-13)* HUK Groups, code-named "Teardrop." They were to intercept a wolfpack of six U-boats, approaching the east coast of the United States in a last but foolhardy attempt to turn the tide.

Coverage of the Barrier Force was published in *History of U.S. Naval Operations in World War II* by Admiral Samuel Eliot Morison under the heading of "Teardrop vs *Seawolf*." His story relates the weather suffered by the *Croatan* and Task Group 22.5.

> "...On one occasion, planes could not be recovered and had to fly 360 miles to land at Argentia, Newfoundland. Wind and sea continued very heavy. One lurch at dinner hour on 5 April rolled tables, benches, mess furniture and food in *Croatan's* mess halls into a heap on the port side, then hurled the whole conglomeration to starboard, injuring over a hundred men..."

That occurrence was on a 10,000 ton escort aircraft carrier. Imagine the discomfort on the 1700 ton destroyer escorts!

Croatan Task Group 22.5 included VC (air) squadron 55, *Frost (DE-144)* with the Commander of Escort Division 13, Commander F.D. Giambatista embarked; *Huse (DE-145)*; *Inch (DE-146)*; *Snowden (DE-246)*; *Stanton (DE-247)* and *Swasey (DE-248)*.

TG 22.5 was ordered to support the Barrier Patrol, maintained from 5 to 22 April, with *Mission Bay* in tactical command. The tally: three submarines destroyed, two by *Stanton* and *Frost* and one by *Neil A. Scott (DE-769)* and *Carter (DE-112)* (DE-112), the latter as flagship of *CortDiv 79*, attached to *Croatan* at the time of the action.

Croatan HUK Group had been searching for a westbound submarine south of Newfoundland. As the *Mission Bay* Group had been ordered to the same area, *Croatan* moved to another locale to intercept a U-boat heading southwest. Searches were unproductive, and CTG 22.5 was ordered to rendezvous with CTG 22.1 in *Mission Bay* plus Task Group 22.13 (The *Bogue* HUK) plus *Muir (DE-770)* and *Sutton (DE-771)* plus Task Group 22.14 which included *Menges (DE-320)*, *Mosley (DE-321)*, and *Pride (DE-323)* with *ComCortDiv 46* aboard, and *Lowe (DE-325)* to establish a Barrier Patrol beginning about half way between England and Newfoundland.

The Task Forces were in position at daylight on the 9th with TG 22.1, and DEs *Herbert C. Jones (DE-137)*, *Douglas L. Howard (DE-138)*, *Farquhar (DE-139)*, and *Fessenden (DE-142)*, plus Task Group 22.14, itemized above, plus *Hill (DE-141)* and *J.R.Y. Blakely (DE-140)*. They initiated a patrol on a north-south line from latitude 48-30N. The carriers, *Mission Bay* and *Croatan*, with four DEs each as escorts, were stationed 40 miles west of the Barrier. Two DEs from each screen were assigned to TG 22.13 and 22.14 on the Barrier Patrol, making twelve DE's in all on the Barrier. Air searches covered the area east to the Barrier and 40 miles to the west. *Croatan* also searched 60 miles south of the Barrier to prevent any "end runs" by U-boats.

This ship muster is not meant to confuse the reader but to impress you with the massive antisubmarine power in the final months of the war.

At 1916 on 9 April, a pilot picked up a small blip at two miles. *Swasey* was immediately ordered to the contact area, a position about five miles from where *Frost* and *Inch* were investigating an oil slick sighted at 1335. *Swasey* made a good sound contact and, on her third run, made an accurate depth charge attack. About 27 seconds after dropping the depth charges, there were two explosions with two more shortly afterward. Surface and air search that night and the next day disclosed no evidence of damage, nor was the contact regained.

All ten DEs of Escort Divisions 13 and 79 were fueled on 14 and 15 April. Those from the Barrier were being replaced by DEs from *Croatan's* screen to avoid a hole in the Barrier. Fueling the escorts used the last of *Croatan's* diesel oil. Each DE was allotted 50,000 gallons and reduced patrolling speed to 13 knots.

ESCORT DIVISION THIRTEEN

Stanton (DE-247) had escorted convoys to North Africa, including the embattled UGS-37 on 11 April 1944 when twenty-four enemy planes attacked and torpedoed *Holder*. See chapter *Mediterranean Convoys*.

Frost (DE-144) was an old hand with the *Croatan* Hunter-Killers. On 26 April 1944, she and three other escorts of the group joined in sinking *U-488*. See chapter The *Hunter-Killers*.

Shortly before midnight on 15 April 1945. While zigzagging on station off the starboard bow of *Croatan*, Radarman First Class Joseph C. Labedis of *Stanton* announced a radar contact 5000 yards from the Task Group. The skipper flashed a warning to *Croatan*, the carrier usually being the target of a U-boat. The distance was great enough, however, to give the carrier time to maneuver and not require urgent attacks by escorts.

Stanton attempted to open the range and evaluate the target. Heavy seas made it difficult to bring the ship on an attack heading, but the helmsman managed to hold his course. The radar held the target down to about 400 yards. The captain, Lieutenant Commander John C. Kiley Jr., and the Officer of The Deck saw a submarine crash dive, range 300 yards.

The target was estimated to be making eight to ten knots on the surface and on a collision course with *Stanton*, a constant bearing from 2500 yards down to 500 yards. A plot of the submarine's track after it submerged showed it had changed course immediately upon diving. At 2340, the range was opened to 1000 yards, and *Stanton* made a hedgehog attack, as directed by ComCortDiv 13, firing on an excellent recorder trace. No detonations were seen from the bridge nor heard on the sonar. Personnel on the fantail, however, reported detonations as the ship passed by the hedgehog splash area.

The DE was rocked by an extremely heavy explosion six minutes after the attack, and another two minutes later!

Stanton was so badly shaken that she reported being torpedoed and listing. Fortunately, that was not correct. When contact was regained, she started another run with the target 1250 yards distant. Firing was belayed as *Frost* appeared to foul the range. When the attack was resumed, the captain believed that he narrowly missed due to a sudden roll in heavy seas. The projector (hedgehog) trainer reported difficulty in keeping up with the roll of the ship.

Stanton regained contact two minutes after the second attack and held it out to 2500 yards while *Frost* made her first attack. There was a constant exchange of information between ships, checking their DRT plots. When one ship lost contact, the CIC in the other ship would coach it back on target. Sonar information was clear and detailed. At 550 yards, the skipper asked sonar for left cuts to assure that the ship would not be lagging the target in the final stages. (Left or right cuts identified the bow or stern of the target. The bow required the most attention for sub movement analysis.)

0032. Thirteen seconds after firing, the first projectile exploded!

It illuminated a large area of water, was heard on sonar and felt throughout the ship. The detonation was not nearly as loud as the explosion following the first attack, nor the two explosions that would follow after the fourth and fifth attacks. Smaller explosions followed six seconds later. ComCortDiv 13 reported a strong odor of diesel oil. The sub was undoubtedly damaged by this attack.

Stanton then crossed a short distance astern of the target and opened the range while *Frost* gained contact. Topside personnel on *Stanton* reported a heavy odor of diesel oil. Men on the fantail said they could taste oil in the spray breaking over the stern. At 0045, *Frost* reported that she was preparing for another attack. Her ranges and bearings checked with *Stanton's* dead reckoning plot.

Four minutes later, *Stanton* regained contact at a range of 1600 yards. *Frost* started in for another attack but soon lost it. ComCortDiv 13 then ordered *Stanton* to attack. With the target range at 1500 yards, she started to close. Initially, the sub showed a beam aspect (approximately a right angle to the attacker), changing to a slight bow bearing. *Stanton* lost contact at a range of 1200 yards, and ComCortDiv 13 ordered Operation Observant.

It was believed by both ships that the submarine had gone very deep after the last attack. Thirteen minutes after Observant was commenced, the ships felt terrific explosions. This time, both DEs thought they had been torpedoed! Another two minutes brought explosions of less intensity and deeper. ComCortDiv Giambatista announced: "That is the end of the sub! The explosions jarred us completely off the deck!"

The contact was lost, and so was a U-boat with all hands.

0155, 16 April. A surface radar contact at 500 yards was reported by *Frost* while still conducting Observant. She fired star shells to no avail, but her searchlight illuminated a U-boat. *Frost* opened fire with all guns that could bear with superb marksmanship, scoring several hits on the conning tower. However, the forward 3"/50 caliber guns, capable of firing armor-piercing projectiles, were silent because of heavy seas breaking over the forecastle. *Stanton* closed *Frost* to lend support, but the target submerged before she could open fire. *Stanton* obtained sonar contact at 2000 yards, shortly after *Frost* lost the radar target and ceased firing. The sound contact disappeared less than a minute later.

Huse then joined and, with *Stanton*, was ordered to run Operation Observant around *Frost* as she waited in the center for the submarine to surface again. At 0254, *Frost* reported that she had regained radar contact, and ships were ordered to close. However, the contact quickly faded. *Frost* then made a sonar contact. *Stanton* was in the center, *Frost* to the south and *Huse* to the north of the area. *Frost* attacked this target, now believed to be a second submarine. When *Frost* made her first contact, it was thought to be the previous sub they had been attacking right along. It now was obvious that the first had been sunk and they were now engaged with a second. *Frost* attacked again at 0353 and then coached both other ships onto the target in "creeping" attacks. *Stanton* started her approach on the sub at a range of 1750 yards with down doppler (sub moving away).

0406. *Stanton* fired hedgehogs and heard and saw four projectiles detonate under the surface 11 seconds after firing!

The detonations were similar to those seen when attacking the first U-boat. A reading of 110 feet was obtained on the fathometer. There was a heavy explosion, followed seconds later by an even heavier one!

Croatan, 15 miles away, was rocked by the blast.

0417. *Frost* closed the target for her last attack. She fired one more pattern which produced three deep explosions! Diesel fuel gushed to the surface!.

Only minutes following the severe explosions, the contact slowly faded until it disappeared completely. *Stanton* regained contact, range 2200 yards, two minutes after the attack by *Frost*. On approaching the sub, the recorder indicated it to be dead in the water from 1200 yards on. The only deduction was that, down in the depths, a U-boat's propulsion machinery had been hammered or flooded into paralysis. A submarine has to maneuver to outwit an attacker. Dead in the water – her desperate crew must have known – signaled dead indeed!

Stanton was conned into position on the right cut, intending to add five degrees left projector train to the pattern if there were still no motion in the final stages. The projector misfired due to the electric plug not being properly seated in its socket. At the same time, the ship passed through a large and heavy oil slick.

0435. *Stanton* regained contact and opened the range. Indications showed the sub still dead in the water. A planned attack, combining hedgehogs and depth charges, was belayed as the U-boat disappeared from the screen. Echoes had been getting steadily weaker for the last few minutes. ComCortDiv 13 ordered Operation Observant, then a modified search plan, using four ships. (*Swasey* had previously joined the group). After making another thorough sweep of the area of lost contact, the search was discontinued.

The above actions were carried out under the most unfavorable weather conditions, 40-50 knot winds, state six seas, 500-1000 yard visibility and a 500 foot ceiling with haze and intermittent squalls. Personnel performance aboard *Stanton* was excellent. The two forward 3"/50 gun crews alternately shared the burden of firing the hedgehog projector. Both endured considerable danger and discomfort on the forecastle because of heavy seas. Repair parties re-fused several rounds of hedgehogs and, under the supervision of one gunner's mate, twice re-fused 24 rounds in less than 10 minutes. Gun crews readily reloaded a full pattern of hedgehogs in less than five minutes despite the weather and darkness. Repair parties also provided abundant sandwiches and coffee during the 6 1/2 hours the ship was at GQ.

Conclusions drawn from all obtainable sources lead the Division Commander to conclude that two submarines sustained severe damage, leading to their probable sinking. He was correct beyond a doubt. *U-1235* and *U-880* were identified after the war as the two subs sunk by Escort Division 13.

2000 on 16 April. A CinCLant top secret dispatch ordered the *Croatan* Group to retire to westward at 100 miles a day from the barrier center, all forces maintaining their same relative positions. *Croatan* and her ten DE's were detached from the barrier on 22 April.

ESCORT DIVISION SEVENTY-NINE

0050 on 22 April, while *Croatan* was awaiting the picket DEs to join up and head for Argentia, Newfoundland, *Carter* picked up a return ping which developed into a positive submarine evaluation. *Neil A. Scott* was ordered to join in the attack.

0056. *Scott* captain, Lieutenant Commander P.D. Holden directed a hedgehog attack and was rewarded by several explosions!

0109. Lieutenant Commander F.J.T. Baker, commanding officer of *Carter*, ordered hedgehogs fired and obtained three hits!

0111. Only 95 seconds after the hedgehog hits, there was a tremendous explosion that so shook *Carter* that her engineering officer ordered the auxiliary boiler evaporator and all steam lines secured in the belief that the ship was hit!

The concussion was felt and heard by ships three miles away. Contact was lost. However, while passing through the area of the attack after daybreak, *Carter* sighted a large oil slick and quantities of debris, including scraps of paper and wood and battered boxes. Three large sharks were swimming through the debris. Because of the severe rolling of the ship, *Carter* was unable to recover any evidence. A subsequent review of enemy records indicated that *Carter* and *Neil A. Scott* had sunk *U-518* beyond doubt.

At 1300 on 22 April, Task Groups 22.5 and 22.13 departed for Argentia and passed through the barrier being maintained by Task Group 22.2, including ten DEs, *Otter (DE-210)*, *Hubbard (DE-211)*, *Hayter (DE-212)*, *Haverfield (DE-393)*, *Swenning (DE-394)*, *Willis (DE-395)*, *Janssen (DE-396)*, *Wilhoite (DE-397)*, *Cockrill (DE-398)*, *Varian (DE-798)* and the *Core (CVE-13)* and Task Group 22.4 with twelve DEs, *Pillsbury (DE-227)*, *Pope (DE-134)*, *Flaherty (DE-135)*, *Frederick C. Davis (DE-136)*, *Chatelain (DE-149)*, *Neunzer (DE-150)*, *Moore (DE-240)*, *Keith (DE-241)*, *Tomich (DE-242)*, *J. Richard Ward (DE-243)*, *Otterstetter (DE-244)* and *Sloat (DE-245)*. These ships comprised the Second Barrier Force, sent to relieve the *Croatan* and *Bogue* Groups. The above listing demonstrates the overwhelming force that had been brought to bear on German U-boats in this late stage of the Atlantic War and the utter uselessness of their continuing resistance.

28 April. CinCLant directed Task Groups 22.5 and 22.13 to depart from Argentia and to sweep an area further west. Continual fog prevented air operations but, on 2 May, ten DEs from the *Bogue* Group and two from *Croatan's* screen were sent to intercept two U-boats, one approaching from the northeast and one homebound from the southwest. *Croatan* and her remaining DEs were to operate to the north of this new barrier.

As no contact was obtained before darkness on 3 May, the Task Groups departed from the assigned sector to hunt for three U-boats nearby.

At 1127 on 4 May, about 15 miles from the daily estimated position of a U-boat, *Stanton* made sonar contact but could not hold it closer than 1000 yards, indicating a very deep submarine. The other five DEs of *CortDiv 13* were sent to assist. Contact was regained, then lost. About the same time, three DEs had contacts in three different places. A disappearing radar blip was picked up by a plane at 0626 on 5 May, but the contact evaluation was uncertain. In view of the fruitless 48 hour air and surface search, a sub presence was doubtful.

The Task Groups then started a search for U-boats estimated in the vicinity of Flemish Cap. On 7 May, by CinCLant dispatch, the Task Groups were ordered to form another barrier to be in a position to meet U-boats indicating a desire to surrender. The Nazi military machine had collapsed, and Germany sued for peace. Surviving U-boats surfaced and surrendered to Allied naval forces. On 9 May, *Scott* and *Sutton* were detached to intercept *U-1228* and to escort the submarine. *Carter* and *Muir* were also detached to intercept *U-858* in her given position and to escort the sub until relieved by *Pillsbury* and *Pope* on 11 May, when *Carter* and *Muir* returned to the barrier being maintained by TG 22.5.

On 12 May, complying with a CinCLant dispatch, Task Group 22.5 departed from the barrier for replenishment in New York.

The *Croatan* Group received the Presidential Unit Citation, and small wonder. Including the submarines sunk the year before, the roll call of victories sounded like the drumbeat of enemy disaster. *U-856*, *U-488*, *U-490*, *U-154*, *U-518*, *U-1235* and *U-880* sunk with hundreds of their crew against the loss of only a few men to accident and enemy action. The DEs fulfilled their mission. Together with carrier aircraft, they crushed the enemy grand design to interdict men and materiel bound for the United Kingdom and the European continent. Reassigned to the Pacific, the war ended before the *Croatan* DEs could see action against the Japanese enemy. However, most will agree, they contributed more than their fair share to winning the war.

A considerable portion of the above was supplied by the former Commander Task Group 22.5 in *Croatan*, Captain K. Craig.

TASK GROUP 22.10

Buckley and Reuben James Do It Again

Reuben James (DE-153) escorted two convoys to the Mediterranean. On her first eastbound voyage, off Algeria on 1 August 1944, nine German bombers attacked her convoy. *Reuben James* shot down one of them. See chapter *Mediterranean Convoys*. Returning to Boston she joined Task Group 22.10, a hunter-killer formation.

On 22 April 1944, *Buckley (DE-51)* joined the Hunter-Killer Task Group 21.11 (*Block Island*) for a sweep of the North Atlantic convoy routes. In the early hours of 6 May 1944, this DE emblazoned the annals of Navy history in a hand to hand fire fight with a U-boat. See chapter The *Hunter-Killers*.

Eleven months later, a German submarine, then believed to

be *U-369* from markings on recovered debris, was attacked and sunk by *Buckley* with the assistance of *Reuben James* at 0734 on 19 April 1945 while operating with the inner Barrier Patrol south of Nova Scotia.

Buckley was attached to Task Group 22.10, then proceeding from Halifax, Nova Scotia, to New York, making a wide sweep for enemy submarines while en route. The ships were formed in a scouting line normal to the base course, from left to right, *Jack W. Wilke (DE-800)*, *Reuben James*, *Buckley*, and *Scroggins (DE-799)*. Distance between ships was 4000 yards, zigzagging at 15.5 knots. The sea was moderate; visibility was 500 yards with heavy fog and rain.

0648 on 19 April. A sonar contact was established by *Buckley*, range 1500 yards. The sound stack operator reported excellent echoes with moderate down doppler. The Officer Of the Deck promptly reduced speed to five knots and dropped out of the formation to investigate. Other escorts in the formation were advised of the sonar contact and were ordered to slow to five knots while holding the base course.

Buckley sounded GQ at 0654 and notified the Task Group that the contact was classified as probable submarine. A firm sonar contact was maintained until after a hedgehog attack at 0729. At this time, *ComCortDiv 22.10* ordered Lieutenant Commander Grant Cowherd, commanding officer of *Reuben James*, to act as assisting ship and *Wilke* and *Scroggins* to conduct a four square mile search around the point of contact. The submarine speed was plotted at four knots.

While awaiting the arrival of *Reuben James*, *Buckley* moved from the starboard quarter of the submarine to forward of her starboard beam. It was thought possible that the submarine did not hear the *Buckley's* slow approach from astern due to the noise of her own screws. During this entire period, a continual flow of valuable information was given by the sound team and accurately plotted and interpreted by the Combat Information Center. No evasive action was taken by the submarine, although she gradually altered her course. The actual range to the submarine was kept between 550 and 900 yards.

While *Buckley* was on the starboard beam of the submarine, the latter commenced a turn to the right in what was thought to be a maneuver to gain a position for a torpedo attack with her bow tubes. Shortly thereafter, *Reuben James* arrived and made a firm sonar contact; her plot checked with that of *Buckley*. At 0721, *Buckley* increased her speed to 10 knots, opened the range to 1050 yards and commenced an approach for a hedgehog attack.

The approach was made from astern with the submarine moving at a speed of about 2-1/2 knots. Echoes remained clear and sharp throughout the entire run, having unmistakable metallic qualities. Doppler was slightly down, and the plot showed slow movement to the right. At 1050 yards, the target width was 15 degrees (determined by the distance from "right cut" to "left cut") and increased to 20 degrees at 550 yards. At a range of 400 yards, a false echo was noted by the sound stack operator who momentarily trained 10 degrees to the right of the actual contact, but he was immediately coached back onto the U-boat by the alert recorder operator. The course was never altered due to the false contact.

A full pattern of hedgehogs was fired and, 20 seconds later, three to six detonations were heard, indicating a target depth of 250 feet. *Buckley* changed course to the left, still maintaining sonar contact.

0731. A loud underwater explosion was heard and felt by *Buckley* and other ships of the task group, followed by another even more violent underwater explosion!

A minute later, no further contact with the submarine could be made. It was believed that the U-boat disintegrated and sank after the last violent explosion.

The point of contact was illuminated by searchlights. Shortly thereafter, an oil slick was observed on the starboard bow, followed by a considerable quantity of debris. At first glance, this consisted of hundreds of pieces of splintered wood of various sizes and several cushions. The motor whaleboat from this ship and the one from *Reuben James* were lowered to recover evidence.

Some of the more important evidence to substantiate the destruction of the submarine was submitted by *Buckley*: A large quantity of diesel oil was still rising eight hours after the attack and covered an area two miles long and one mile wide when last seen. An enormous amount of debris was recovered, including three pieces of human flesh and hair, a chronometer case with a swastika emblem, a tube of Unguentine (a sunburn salve) with German characters, a yo-yo and several pieces of wood, one bearing the marking *U-369*.

There was no battle damage to *Buckley*. Comments by Lieutenant Commander R.R. Crutchfield, commanding officer:

> "When contact was first made and the ship slowed to five knots, the pitometer log (a device that records ship's speed through the water) became inoperative. This was due to the instrument becoming air-bound from the heavy rolling earlier in the night. The casualty caused the dead reckoning tracer (DRT) to stop and render plotting impossible with that instrument. The difficulty was temporarily overcome by the combat team falling back on the "Halifax plot," a manual substitute procedure. A shift was then made to manual speed control by the interior communications room personnel. This input caused the DRT to operate in such a fashion that an accurate plot was possible during the entire operation. The speed input, while satisfactory for the most part, did introduce some slight inaccuracies in the plot when the course and speed changes were made. This inaccuracy was evidenced by the unnaturally sharp turn of the submarine near the end of its run.
>
> All hands performed in a most satisfactory and commendable fashion. The value of a well trained combat team was strongly demonstrated in this action. A consistent flow of accurate information was furnished to the conning officer throughout the entire operation and was passed to other ships, enabling them to keep an accurate plot of the contact and thereby render all possible assistance."

The major credit for sinking the submarine was awarded to *Buckley* for fatally damaging the U-boat with only one hedgehog attack. The role of *Reuben James* was confined to maintaining sonar contact on the U-boat for guidance assistance to *Buckley*. Soundman First Class Raymond Sargent Kaiser on the *Reuben James* did an outstanding job.

In spite of the piece of wood bearing the letters *U-369*, the sunken submarine was identified as *U-879*.

Buckley escorted one more convoy to Algeria during June-

July 1945 and, upon her return to the east coast, commenced her conversion to a picket ship. She operated in the Atlantic and the Caribbean to the end of the war.

ESCORT DIVISION FOUR

The Last Performance of a Very Gallant Ship and Her Retribution

The Central Barrier Force, Task Group 22.3, was based on two hunter-killer air/sea commands, escort carriers *Bogue (CVE-9)* and, 100 miles distant, *Core (CVE-13)*. Between the two were 14 destroyer escorts, designated Escort Division 4. The Task Group was commanded by Captain G.F. Dufek, with his flag in *Bogue*.

Commander F.S. Hall was *ComCortDiv 4* with his pennant in *Pillsbury (DE-133)* and 13 other DEs: *Keith (DE-241)*, *Otterstetter (DE-244)*, *Pope (DE-134)*, *Flaherty (DE-135)*, *Chatelain (DE-149)*, *Frederick C. Davis (DE-136)*, *Neunzer (DE-150)*, Joseph C. *Hubbard (DE-211)*, *Varian (DE-798)*, *Otter (DE-210)*, *Hayter (DE-212)*, *Janssen (DE-396)* and *Cockrill (DE-398)*.

Frederick C. Davis was a veteran of many campaigns. In the autumn of 1943, she ran the gauntlet of air attacks on two Mediterranean convoys, splashing at least two planes and taking part in the sinking of *U-73*. She won the Navy Unit Citation for air and submarine actions while supporting the bloody Anzio operations in Italy and for jamming the control frequencies of German radio air-launched glider bombs. In the invasion of Southern France, she again was deployed to use her jamming gear. See chapter *Convoys to the Mediterranean*. Her final operation, however, met with disaster.

On the morning of 24 April 1945, less than three weeks before the surrender of Germany, the scouting line of *ComCortDiv 4*, was seeking a U-boat reported by aircraft. *Davis* was steaming on a line of bearing normal to the base course with *Hayter* on the starboard beam, distance 3500 yards, and *Neunzer* the same distance on the port beam.

0830. The duty soundman reported a contact on the starboard beam, range 2000 yards. The contact looked good, sharp, metallic, with a clear doppler effect and closing rapidly. The Officer of The Deck, Lieutenant (jg) McWhorter, called the captain. At the same time, he turned the bow toward the contact and advised *ComCortDiv 4* that *Davis* had a sub contact and was proceeding to attack it.

The Junior Officer of The Deck went to the CIC to start up a plot and passed Captain J.R. Crosby who was racing to the bridge. McWhorter had ordered the crew of number two 3" gun to man the hedgehogs, pull the safety pins, and stand by to fire. Lieutenant (jg) Downing arrived on the foredeck in preparation to fire hedgehogs. Lieutenant (jg) Astrin, the CIC officer, took charge of the plot, and Lieutenant F.S. Bombauer, executive officer, appeared at the same time. The sound contact was sharp and strong as the skipper took the conn. Possibly, he told the Officer of The Deck to sound GQ, but!!!

0840. Everybody on the bridge and practically everybody forward was suddenly, violently and grotesquely dead!

Davis was struck by a torpedo on the port side, amidship. The following description of the ship after the hit is based on accounts given by those survivors who actually saw conditions as they existed in the several compartments and deck spaces:

The passageway and the crew's and chief petty officers' quarters filled with smoke. The fume-tight door to the CPO quarters was jammed so that exit had to be made via the escape scuttle. The ladder was red hot as was the gun crew shelter just above. The after mess hall suffered severe damage; tables were tossed on top of each other, and all lights went out. The after bulkhead and the deck were so ruptured that compartments below were exposed to view. Oil gushed out of the overflow pipes, and fires were raging. The engine room area was seen from a deck hatch to be a roaring furnace. Two men escaped from that compartment but both were badly burned and did not survive.

Gratings were blown out of place; the emergency switchboard caught fire as did fuel oil filters near the engines. Number four engine was bent over. The bulkhead on the port side was caved in but apparently was watertight. Water entered on the starboard side through a split seam and poured on the service generators, shorting them out and cutting pressure to fire and bilge pumps after three minutes of operation. Paint blistered on the bulkheads. Engineering spaces flooded rapidly up to the topside escape hatches.

The berthing compartment and sick bay apparently suffered little damage and occupants were able to get topside safely. The steam line broke on the port side. The hatch leading topside to a passageway was jammed and could not be properly dogged down. An observer on the fantail reported a huge gush of flame and smoke on the starboard side amidship at the time of the torpedo hit. One man, having exited the galley, proceeded down the port quarter deck and was blown forward about ten feet, in time to witness the buckling of the weather deck.

Flames issued from the starboard side of the athwartship passageway. The deck was hot and buckled. The ship's galley was ablaze, and its equipment overturned. The mast broke near the yardarm, the upper part falling aft and dangling from the lower part by the rigging. A yeoman, after extricating himself from beneath an upset filing cabinet, got out of the ship's office. He noticed as he left that there was smoke and fire in the passageway and that the door to the radio shack was closed. The Junior Officer of The Deck, Ensign R.E. Minerd, reported dense smoke and fumes in the CIC and the pilot house, and several doors were jammed. One occupant of the pilot house had badly broken legs and another was lying on the deck unconscious. The starboard lookout was seen hanging inboard from a belaying pin on the signal bridge. The executive officer was seen to jump off the bridge without a life jacket and probably drowned. The bridge messenger was last seen swimming from the ship without a life jacket.

Some of the crew began to abandon ship on their own initiative soon after the explosion. Many tried but were unable to man their battle stations. No word was passed after the explosion. Life rafts, life nets, and shores (wood timber) were thrown over the port side, which appeared favorable for abandoning ship. Cool heads checked the depth charges to see if they were on safe. Two survivors later recalled that two charges were in such a position that they couldn't be set on safe. At least one depth charge did explode after submerging.

The expansion joint amidship appeared to be the point at which the ship finally broke in two and began to settle. A port list developed, and about 17 minutes after the explosion, the *Davis* was entirely beneath the waves. That the fantail stayed afloat as long as it did was probably due to the fact that personnel aft were able to dog down and secure most major water tight fittings.

From the bridge of *Hayter*, billows of smoke could be seen rising from *Davis* as she crumbled amidships, and *Hayter* reported to *ComCortDiv 4* that *Davis* was torpedoed. With the other ships in the scouting line, *Hayter* was ordered to gain contact on the submarine, and *Flaherty* was ordered to recover survivors. *Hayter* commenced an Observant around the stricken *Davis*. At approximately 15 minutes after *Davis* was torpedoed, *Flaherty* picked up contact on the submarine, resulting in *Hayter* being ordered to replace *Flaherty* in the rescue of survivors.

Ensign Lundeberg:

"I was the assistant first lieutenant and damage control officer on the *Frederick C. Davis*. It's my regret that we couldn't do more in the way of damage control than we did. Those of us who slept back aft always feared a hit between our propellers by an acoustic torpedo and usually offered up a short prayer for ourselves before going to sleep. Naturally, we were surprised that the torpedo hit just forward of the midship line.

Mr. Kip, Mr. Anderson and myself were asleep. We woke up, ran out to the passageway and started to dog down doors for watertight integrity. We didn't know exactly where the damage was but, from the list of the ship, we knew she was going down quickly. We went topside, and my first impression was disbelief. The ship had caved down right in the middle, was going, sinking, fast. Nobody reported seeing the torpedo. The sound gear was trained right on the submarine at a range of 650 yards. The soundman, who would have reported noises, didn't hear any. He survived with a considerable loss of memory but he was clear on that point.

Apparently, the torpedo was a large one because the blast effect was terrific. It blew the Officer of The Deck off the bridge, up in the air, over the sound shack, and down to number 2 gun. We don't know what happened to the captain; he may have been blown into the water. Mr. Minerd, down in CIC, was the only man who got out of there alive. He was leaning over the DRT at the time and possibly didn't go up the way everybody must have to hit the overhead. He was knocked out and barely came to in time to get off the ship. The water was up to the level of the signal bridge, normally 25 feet above the surface, when he got off.

Very few men escaped from the forward part of the ship. Led by Mr. Downing, the hedgehog men were standing by to fire when the torpedo hit; they were able to rescue others from the forward part of the first platform deck. Unfortunately, Mr. Downing didn't survive the experience in the water. The same crew tried to flood one of the magazines with controls near the wardroom and noted that the wardroom was aflame. Apparently, everybody in there was killed instantly. Carpenter's Mate Golay looked in through the smoke and noticed that the deck was blown halfway up to the overhead.

Boatswain's Mate Hancock, the most rugged man aboard, was the most severely injured of all the survivors. He was down in the mess hall, only one compartment away from where the torpedo struck. He was miraculously blown up through the hatch, got out somehow and over the side. He was able to swim with the aid of Epstein who did not survive and was picked up by *Flaherty*.

Hancock remembered a number of details. He said that the bulkheads to the forward engine room were blown open and that he could see right in there and could also see the deck that had been blown up and down in the interior communications room. He saw oil pouring out of the diesel overflow pipes. There were fires. He saw a number of the mess cooks trying to go up the port hatch, but they were apparently killed right there.

Most of our injuries were legs and heads. A man would have his legs rather severely compressed and broken, then go up and hit the overhead. For that reason, I'm afraid a lot of men never came to, literally never knew what hit them. All the officers on the bridge were apparently killed. Those in the after spaces got out almost unharmed. We tried to organize things a little bit back aft, but the ship was going down so fast we weren't able to accomplish anything more than a hasty setting of watertight integrity aft and a checking of the depth charges.

We had no survivors from the forward living compartments. The center compartments flooded very quickly. One of the men, cleaning up the forward crew's head, had closed the door. The door was blasted off its hinges, and he managed to get out. As you can see, the blast was terrific throughout the ship. I think the reason it didn't affect us too much back aft was that we had expansion joints at frames 61 and 90 which took up quite a bit of the shock. The men in the after living compartments, some thrown out of their sacks, were able to reach topside without difficulty.

Finally, after, oh I'd say about nine minutes, the water had come up to the deck house, and it was necessary for us to go over the side. I stepped into the water, now only two feet below the deck where I stood and swam out to one of the life rafts. It was rather crowded. We had to take turns holding onto the raft and, when one's turn came, it wasn't easy to keep a grasp.

Finally, one of the depth charges went off, and I had a rather severe pain in my stomach. It felt as though my insides were being twisted around. I'm afraid some of the men close to the explosion were killed by it. A number of others had minor internal injuries.

We were a little further away. The men on my raft were calm and not upset by the depth charge explosion. We had one injured man, Williams. Some on other rafts got hysterical, overturning their rafts and losing some men. All were in rather weakened condition. There were periods when they'd lose consciousness and float away. Sharks were in the vicinity. We were confident we'd be picked up soon by a nearby DE. We just prayed she wouldn't be obliged to drop any depth charges near us.

We just hung on for dear life and were rescued in about half an hour. When rescue was near, I fainted, something that happened to a lot of men when they knew safety was at hand. The next thing I knew I was in a bunk on *Hayter*."

Lieutenant Kip added:

"I was the Division radio specialist officer. I'd just been sent to *Davis* from the flagship to fix some radar gear. I'd barely become acquainted with the ship, and you can imagine it was quite a surprise to me when we got torpedoed. The morning of the 24th, I was asleep back aft near Mr. Lundeberg and Mr. Anderson. We had a long watch the night before, and nobody came to wake us up.

When the torpedo hit, drawers jumped out of the cabinets, and there was a great deal of broken glass about. All lights were out, and it was difficult to orient myself. Fortunately, Mr. Lundeberg knew where the door was, and he made a bee line for it. Out in the passageway, I saw Mr. Lundeberg and other members of the repair party dogging down hatches. I was just dressed in my skivvy shirt and shorts and decided to go back and put on something warmer.

I went topside, and there didn't seem to be any chance of saving the ship. There was very little panic on the fantail. A few badly wounded men came by, their faces blackened by burns, but they had their life jackets on and were being helped by other crewmen. I was afraid that the ship would turn over on top of us, so I went over the side. I swam to a raft and found Mr. Lundeberg on it with several other men. Some were wounded, and it was crowded, so I moved onto a floater net, on which there was only one other man.

We were on the floater net about 15 minutes when one of the ships in the division came toward us, intending to pick us up (*Flaherty*). They fired empty depth charge cases to which lines were attached for men to grab and be pulled to the ship. However, they gained a sound contact on the U-boat and had to go on the attack

The next ship that came to the rescue was *Hayter*. She hove to and drifted down on us. When she got close, I swam for it, and they threw me a life ring. I put my arm through it, was hoisted to the deck, and that's all I remembered until I woke up in a bunk in the wardroom, shaking from shock but otherwise feeling fine. (We wonder how one shakes from shock and feels fine at the same time!) The *Hayter's* crew was very hospitable, doing everything possible and cheering us up with an occasional dose of brandy.

The *Hayter* gave up two whole compartments of the crew's quarters to the survivors, some of them quite badly wounded. I remember some of the *Hayter* crew who had no previous experience in first aid but who were doing an excellent job in administering blood plasma to the wounded. I also have to give a great deal of credit to Doctor McKay who worked to the limit of his capacity to save men who were badly wounded and who were dying."

The captain of *Flaherty*, Lieutenant Commander H.C. Duff, related in his action report:

"At 0918, when rescue operations were belayed, two *Davis* survivors had been rescued, and a lifeline was thrown to a third, Motor Machinist Mate Gent, William Thomas, who was being drawn into the current of the starboard propeller. He was very weak and his situation was critical. At considerable peril to himself, Chief Commissary Steward George Martin climbed out onto the starboard propeller guard, reached down and helped him to the survivor's net. Martin is being recommended for citation and award."

Hayter commenced a circular sweep around the outside of the area, stopping often where survivors were located. They were first brought to the side of the *Hayter* by members of the crew who, disregarding their own safety, jumped from the ship into rough and shark infested waters. Survivors were then brought by rescuers to the side of the ship where lines were secured about them from the deck.

Davis' men were hauled aboard, most of them being unable to assist themselves. Heaving lines were thrown to rafts and life nets to pull them alongside so that occupants could be brought up to the deck. *Hayter* crew members went onto the rafts to assist the survivors aboard. Once, *Hayter* was forced to leave a raft with three of her own crew and an unconscious survivor who they were trying to assist aboard. These men were not picked up until 1-1/2 hours later.

Hayter also fired empty depth charge cases with buoy lines attached. Survivors clung to the lines, making it possible to pull them alongside and bring them aboard. After the life rafts and nets had been emptied, the ship's boat was put over with a volunteer crew to pick up remaining survivors. Because of the ship rolling in rough seas, the launching was perilous. It often seemed that the boat would be swamped while pulling men aboard. On returning with 11 survivors, only six inches of freeboard remained in the boat.

Hayter searched the area for several hours, during which she had rescued 66 survivors and 11 dead; subsequently, one of the survivors died. All who could be spared from GQ stations took part in the rescue and in the ministration of first aid. Some men were revived with artificial respiration by *Hayter* crew members.

Over a drink at the St. Petersburg (Florida) Yacht Club, former Radarman First Class John Shovan of the *Otter* lent this author some photos as well and his 50 year old diary which so eloquently and sadly describes a side of war that many DE veterans remember:

"We were 30 miles south of *Davis* and were ordered to proceed to her vicinity at flank speed, arriving 1-1/4 hours later. About eight DEs were already there. Two had contact on the sub. Another was busy picking up survivors. Four DEs, including us, assisted in the rescue. I was in the CIC and couldn't see what was going on so I stepped out on the signal bridge and looked down in the water.

Right along our starboard side, one of our men was swimming while towing an unconscious man by the collar. Off our starboard bow was a floater net with a man in it too weak to help himself; one of our boys was swimming out to pull him alongside. Ahead of us, there were quite a few men in a life raft. Planes would spot survivors and drop smoke markers or circle the area to guide ships to them. I won't write about some of the things, but it was an experience I shall not ever forget. I saw the faces of the water-soaked men who were dead. They had died for their country after spending hours in the frigid North Atlantic.

We picked up 26 survivors, of whom six were pronounced dead when brought aboard. Two of the dead were killed by sharks, an ugly sight. One man was but 200 feet from the ship when attacked by one. A man on the fantail had a Thompson submachine gun. He cut loose at the sharks, killed one and routed another.

There were 15 men who were practically dead when brought aboard. They were given four to five hours of artificial respiration, but only one or two regained consciousness.

Of our 26 rescued, only eight lived. The other 18 were the dead we had on board. We were ordered to transfer all living and dead to the carrier *Core*. We transferred the living but, as the sea was quite rough, we buried the dead from our ship. We brought a chaplain aboard to conduct the services at sea the following morning. The dead were all lying on the starboard side, There wasn't much to see when you looked at the blankets on the deck. Here and there, was a curly head, a stiff hand, or a bare foot sticking out from under the blankets.

25 April 1945. At 0530, everyone was up for the burial at sea. Some of the men had been up all night taking the dead men's fingerprints and sewing them up in canvas bags. A dummy hedgehog was placed inside with the body to weight it down. As I came out on the signal bridge to watch, the first four bodies were on the slides and covered with the ensign. As each slide was tilted, the bodies slipped beneath the waves. When the last went over, the bugler blew taps at the same time. I had goose pimples all over. Eighteen sailors made their last liberty port, the deep blue."

Survivors from *Hayter* were also transferred to *Bogue* where appropriate burial services were held for eight more dead.

SWIFT VENGEANCE

The explosions from *Davis*' depth charges caused sonar problems on *Flaherty*, with all power relays going out. With the replacement of a some fuses, the sound gear commenced operating. Subsequent depth charge explosions, however, caused even more damage. Survivor recovery was halted when Chief Sonarman Roger W. Cozens on the sound stack reported: "Probable submarine, 2000 yards, down doppler!"

0920. Cozens quickly reclassified the contact. "Positive submarine, very deep, down doppler." *Flaherty* skipper requested Commander Hall to provide an assisting ship, and *Pillsbury* (with Hall on board) was designated. Chief Cozens reported the sub was throwing "knuckles" (water compressed by radical turns or torpedo tube air blasts, giving return echoes to confuse the DE sound operator). While *Flaherty* was waiting for *Pillsbury* to establish contact, the U-boat started evasive tactics and headed for *Flaherty*.

0940 to 1017. *Flaherty* and *Pillsbury* alternated creeping hedgehog positions, four attacks without result. Contact conditions were good with strong doppler, but *Flaherty* continued to be plagued by damage from *Davis*' depth charges. However, Soundman Second Class Warren C. Middleton managed to effect repairs on short notice.

Almost immediately after regaining contact at 1017, *Flaherty's* sonar clearly indicated a noise like a torpedo being fired. The release of air was plainly heard, followed by a high propeller beat. The sub was on her starboard quarter, and It was a very tense moment as word was passed: "All ahead full, right full rudder, stream the FXR!" No torpedo was sighted, and it was decided that the sub must have been making a knuckle and was speeding up. Another attack by *Flaherty* at 1022 was unproductive but did indicate that the sub was coming up.

Flaherty CIC reported the ship to be in an excellent position for a depth charge attack to drive the sub back down. Between the sinking of *Davis* and the reported torpedo fired at his ship, the skipper wanted to keep the U-boat down. A full magnetic depth charge pattern was dropped when the DE crossed the sub's track. At "Fire 3," two simultaneous explosions were felt. Contact was lost as usual.

1058. *Pillsbury* and *Flaherty* started Observant. They formed a scouting line with a 3000 yard ship interval. *Flaherty* now had *Varian* on the starboard beam and *Janssen* on the port beam. At 1152, the ships closed to 2000 yard intervals. Four minutes later, Middleton, who had previously relieved Cozens on *Flaherty* sound stack, picked up a good sonar contact, distance 1700 yards and, immediately thereafter, the sonar gear failed. The plague from the *Davis*' depth charges still haunted *Flaherty*

However, the contact had been reported to the OTC as being immediately ahead of *Varian*. That DE promptly picked it up as it passed down her port beam and dropped back to investigate, assisted by *Janssen*. The sonar casualty on *Flaherty* was a broken relay which Cozens located and repaired. From 1218 to 1804, creeping attacks with two and three ships continued without letup as DEs alternated guiding and attack positions. *Flaherty*, *Pillsbury*, *Neunzer*, *Varian*, *Keith* and *Hubbard* literally poured hedgehog missiles on the hapless U-boat, fighting for its life with *pillenwerfers* and radical maneuvers.

The plot showed that the sub had been making an "S" turn and was now turning to port, steadying up on a course as *Flaherty* came in on the same heading. All indications were for a deep water and stern chase. Sonar pings echoed through a *pillenwerfer*, clearly shown on the recorder; there was virtually no bearing movement. The recorder was set at a 150 foot depth on the assumption that the sub's rise, as indicated by *Keith*, would continue.

1813. *Flaherty* fired a hedgehog pattern and turned with full right rudder. Seconds later, there was an underwater explosion. Large air bubbles and oil came to surface. She closed in for another attack and established contact on her starboard beam, range 2000 yards. She reported this contact to *Varian* who said it did not agree with hers and was now deep on *Flaherty's* quarter. Accordingly, *Flaherty* shifted to *Varian's* target.

1831. *Flaherty* made a second hedgehog attack, delivered with a clear echo but with a wide trace and no doppler. Results were negative although the pattern was right into the oil slick from the previous explosion. She turned left with full rudder, and finally as though it might never happen the sub surfaced on her starboard quarter, range about 2300 yards!

"She's surfacing, stand by your guns!"

In the same breath, the command, "commence fire," went to *Flaherty's* own guns. She rang up ahead full speed with right full rudder to head for the U-boat. The sub's surfacing was met by a large volume of enthusiastic fire by all ships. The sub was seen to flash its signal light repeatedly, furnishing a convenient point of aim.

Flaherty's track was bringing her into the line of fire from the *Neunzer*, and the latter was requested to cease fire. Torpedo tubes were ordered trained to port, using a visual estimation of the target. A turn was made to the right to unmask the port guns and to clear the *Neunzer's* line of fire. *Flaherty* fired two torpedoes; the runs were straight and normal. It was then seen that the sub was sinking rapidly by the stern. The right hand torpedo passed just ahead of the sub, and the other passed over the submerged stern of the target.

1844. The sub sank!

Flaherty maneuvered to rescue crewmen from *U-546*, including the captain, *Kapitanleutnant* Paul Just. Other destroyer escorts picked up the remaining survivors. The hunt for the killer of F.C. *Davis* was requited. "An eye for an eye, a tooth for a tooth."

Varian, commanded by Lieutenant Commander L.A. Lyhre, took the submarine prisoners to the U.S. base at Argentia, Newfoundland. En route, *Kapitanleutnant* Just described his part in the fray: He said that he saw three DEs coming at him and he thought they were screening a larger ship. He had been sitting there, intending to throw a fish at the carrier, but the *Davis* picked up contact on him, and he had to fire his torpedoes at her. He said he then went down to 600 feet, and the other DEs started dropping charges on him.

He slipped away several times, but they kept picking him up again. He said she was pretty well damaged by then. His two forward compartments were flooded. He was leaking badly, and almost all his instruments were out. After quite a spell, he thought he had eluded his pursuers, so he came up to 200 feet. Then, one of the DE's picked him up and made a hedgehog attack. One hit him, and he started leaking badly.

Finally, he had to bring her up. As the conning tower broke the surface, the DEs poured 3" and small stuff into it. He said that the conning tower hatch was so battered by depth charges and gunfire that it wouldn't open. The crew had to abandon through an escape hatch on the deck, and the sub sank six minutes after surfacing.

The *Flaherty* skipper had some pertinent observations to add to his action report:

> "With the exception of 20mm guns numbers 9 and 10, whose personnel also man the depth charges in a sub attack, every fixed weapon on the ship was fired during the engagement. They included both 30 caliber machine guns, all 20mm, the 40mm, all 3"/50, the torpedoes, the hedgehogs and the depth charges. It was as close as possible an 'all hands' affair.
>
> I desire to pay tribute to the exceptional performance of Chief Sonarman Cozens, whose services on the sound stack during the day, plus his alert and rapid repairs of battle damage, were invaluable. The CIC team also functioned perfectly. Through a day-long engagement, requiring frequent DRT scale changes, CIC never failed to supply the captain with quick and accurate information.
>
> The first lieutenant, Lieutenant W.B. Rose, also made an important contribution to the day's success. The ship was at GQ from 0840 to 1918. His repair parties were called upon in rapid succession to rescue *Davis* survivors, to prepare for attack, to provide two meals on stations for the crew, to replace large quantities of every type of ammunition, and finally to put the prisoner of war bill into effect. Every task was accomplished smoothly and expeditiously.
>
> During the surface engagement, the fantail sent word that a torpedo was passing 10 feet astern from port to starboard. The sub captain laid that to rest. He said the only torpedoes he fired were at *Frederick C. Davis*.
>
> The CIC Team of *Varian* did an excellent job in furnishing assistance and coaching the attacking ships in damaging creeper attacks. Her information enabled us to keep a continuous plot of the sub when our sonar was secured. We had gained so much confidence in *Varian's* information that we did not question her evaluation of a contact that furnished a good echo.
>
> Because of sonar casualties caused by explosions and gunfire, it was subsequently found necessary to completely retune the radar and sonar gear. All told, however, the performance of equipment was excellent. It worked 'just like the salesman said it would'.
>
> The men cheered like a group of Dodger fans when the enemy surfaced and they opened fire with deck guns, but after all, it was a great occasion in our lives. We had a chance to avenge the *Davis*."

Keith, commanded by Lieutenant W.W. Patrick, had scored two 3" hits on the sub before it headed for the bottom, but Lieutenant William S. Adams was mostly impressed with the four survivors they recovered. To him, they lent credibility to the title of this chapter *Twilight of the U-boats*, a euphemism for the death rattle of the Third Reich:

> "Whereas there had been some trepidation about trying to control giants of Hitler's 'super race', the actual appearance of these prisoners was quite a surprise. They were trembling, pale, skinny, small, and obviously terrified. They were quickly wrapped in dry blankets and bundled into warm bunks next to the sick bay. Hot soup and brandy brought them around, and they all survived."

Chief Sonarman Roger W. Cozens also made an interesting observation of one special prisoner taken on the *Flaherty*:

> "Approximately 29 survivors of the sub, from a crew of 65, were recovered by the DEs. Among others, *Kapitanleutnant* Paul Just was taken aboard *Flaherty*. In a book by Just after the war, he stated that this episode was a day of hell aboard *U-546*, starting with the first depth charge from *Flaherty*. He also reported that he was too weak to climb the cargo net on *Flaherty* and almost relinquished his hold when a powerful black American sailor picked him up with one hand and placed him right on the deck."

Chief Cozens was awarded the Bronze Star Medal for his faultless operation and interpretations of the sound gear input.

Following the surrender of Germany in May, Escort Division Four was dissolved. Some remained in the Atlantic in a training capacity until the end of the war. Others went to the Pacific, too late for enemy action, but were engaged in various occupation duties.

GUSTAFSON

A Heavily Travelled DE and a U-boat Killer

Gustafson (DE-182) (Gus) could very well claim to be one of the most highly travelled destroyer escorts in the Navy.

20 February 1944. She was assigned to the Fourth Fleet en route to Recife, Brazil, in company with the carrier *Mission Bay (CVE-59)* and destroyer escorts *Trumpeter (DE-180)* and *Straub (DE-181)*. The next port was Capetown, South Africa, guarding a

load of army planes and personnel headed for the Burma Front. While returning to Recife, command was turned over to Lieutenant Commander A.E. Chambers. Lieutenant Fred T. Mayes, Jr. became executive officer

13 March. The three DE's were ordered into Rio de Janeiro, Brazil, where they joined the cruiser *Memphis (CL-13)* and the destroyer *Winslow (DD-357)* enroute to Montevideo, Uruguay. The Task Force anchored in Rio Grande do Sul, Brazil. During the three day stopover in this small city, holiday routine was declared by the Mayor, and the DEs got their first taste of Brazilian hospitality.

The next port was Salvador, Bahia, Brazil's fourth largest city, halfway between Rio de Janeiro and Recife. During a 10 day upkeep layover in that port, the crew spent time buying up huge quantities of imitation Chanel #5 and arguing with taxi drivers. Next to the incomparable Rio, it became *Gus'* favorite city.

28 March. *Straub*, *Trumpeter* and *Gustafson* rendezvoused in mid-ocean with the carrier *Solomons (CVE-67)*. For the next eight months, they assisted other DEs of Escort Divisions 18 and 24 in escorting CVEs. Other escorts were *Christopher (DE-100)*, *Alger (DE-101)*, *Marts (DE-174)* and *Mika (DE-176)*. This Hunter-Killer Group paraded back and forth over the entire South Atlantic, Uruguay to Capetown, north to Dakar, and Trinidad — once achieving the doubtful distinction of crossing the Equator seven times in 24 hours searching for U-boats. On 23 April, *Gustafson* made an unsuccessful attack on a submarine, believed to be *U-196*.

15 June. Task Group aircraft caught an enemy supply sub on the surface in the middle of the South Atlantic, just south of St. Helena, a most unwelcome surprise for the U-boat crew. The attack resulted in the kill of *U-860*. However, the price was high, four planes lost with 10 men; victory does not come cheap. Submarine survivors were recovered, and the group proceeded homeward.

On another occasion, *Gus* was instrumental in saving the lives of two airmen whose plane crashed in a night take-off. Alert ship handling, and the daring of crew members who went into the water when enemy subs were known to be about, saved the two airmen. The pilot could not extricate himself and went down with the plane.

Solomons was replaced by *Tripoli (CVE-64)* on 22 August. About the end of September, *Gus* made a good contact on an enemy sub, resulting in a probable kill. No survivors were taken, nor was the enemy ever seen, but the indications were that he broke up under water.

22 November. *Gus* set sail for a rendezvous with the light cruiser *Omaha (CL-4)*, the transport *General M.C. Meigs (AP-116)*, one Brazilian cruiser and two Brazilian destroyers. The group transported Brazilian Expeditionary Forces to join the allies in Italy. The rendezvous was effected, but in passing the orders ship-to-ship, *Gus* was caught in the cruiser's stern, and the *Omaha's* screw hacked a great tear in the *Gus'* bow. There also was serious damage to the port shaft of the cruiser. Both ships carried out their respective missions, and the *Gus* went into dry dock at Bahia. The Board of Investigation ruled that, in view of the construction of the two ships and the high speed of the maneuver, (20 knots), a collision was inevitable. At the time, orders forbade reducing the speed of the task force. Both skippers were commended on their ship-handling ability in avoiding further damage and carrying out their assigned tasks in spite of the damage incurred. On 21 December, *Gus* was ordered to the New York Navy Yard for additional repairs, just in time for Christmas.

Gus was now an old hand. She had made an enviable record with the Fourth Fleet. The leaves were well earned especially at Christmas. For a month, the *Gus* remained in the navy yard while her crew caught up on life at home and in New York City.

Orders were received to report back to the Commander of the Fourth Fleet. On 17 February, she picked up a slow convoy from Trinidad to Recife, arriving in time to see her division steaming happily toward Rio on a tour of large South American ports. But *Gus* was ordered back to New York to be detached from the Fourth Fleet.

She proceeded to Casco Bay, Maine, for an intensive refresher training period. It was a month before the training was completed. The delay was due to a sub scare off Boston, during which *Gus* in company with *Micka* and two Coast Guard frigates joined the search. *U-857* had announced her presence by torpedoing the American tanker *Atlantic States*. The fact that an enemy submarine was searching for prey only 20 miles off Cape Cod was known to only a few informed officers in the First Naval District in Boston.

The Tenth Fleet in Washington was advised of the U-boat presence, and the word was flashed by Admiral *Ingram* to all his forces afloat. All ships in the vicinity were apprised of the fact that a U-boat was on the prowl virtually within sight of Boston Light!

There then followed a sub hunt off Cape Hatteras, during which two subs were sunk in areas adjacent to that in which *Gustafson* was engaged with the rest of CortDiv 24, (*Micka*, *Straub*, *Trumpeter*). The Task Force Commander, Coast Guard Captain Ralph R. Curry, wrote of the action sometime after the war.

> "The following account of a search for an enemy submarine during early April 1945 off Cape Cod, Massachusetts, is according to the best of my recollection since I do not have a diary or a copy of my action report. At the time in question, I was Commander of Escort Division 30 in the frigate *Knoxville (PF-64)*. My flagship, together with one other ship of my division, was in Casco Bay undergoing refresher training when a tanker was torpedoed off Cape Cod on or about 6 April 1945. I was immediately ordered to depart from Casco Bay in command of a Killer Group to search for the enemy submarine. Two vessels of my own division, together with four destroyer escorts of another division (24), including *Gustafson*, were assigned to the HUK."

This hastily formed Task Force immediately departed from Casco Bay and proceeded to the probable area of the U-boat. It was deployed in a search formation and commenced a diligent coverage of the area assigned. In the early hours of 7 April, contact was made and reported by *Gus* and she was promptly directed to attack. Meanwhile, a cordon was thrown around the area with the remainder of the group to prevent an escape by the submarine. From the information supplied by *Gus'* skipper, and the area of the contact, Captain Curry was convinced that the contact was a strong probable sub. Accordingly, *Gus* was directed to make repeated attacks while all the other vessels of the HUK Group were ordered to continue intensive search around the point of contact. Skipper Chambers had decided that the situation called for a hedgehog attack.

0226. The projectiles leaped from their racks with trails of orange flame and plunged into the dark water. An extended moment of silence indicated a miss. The captain turned off to open the range and close it again for another attack. Once more, the hedgehogs soared. This time, a rumbling explosion was felt by all hands!

Gus turned off and waited, expecting all manner of debris to come to the surface, but that did not happen. Between 0409 and 0503, she delivered four hedgehog attacks but none produced the desired results. Apparently, their only hit was the one at 0231. In spite of a large oil slick, the skipper and the sound team were disappointed. It was estimated that the attacks and the searches following the attacks covered a period of approximately six to 10 hours, at which time standard search measures were resumed without gaining contact. Captain Curry noted:

> "As the Hunter-Killer Group Commander, I reviewed the action report of the *Gustafson*. As will be seen from my endorsement thereon, I classified it as a strong contact on a probable submarine and estimated the heavy probability of serious damage having been inflicted.
>
> I later discussed this action with Commander Chambers upon our return to Casco Bay. He did not share my optimistic point on the probable damage to the submarine. However, I attributed this to his comparative inexperience. Although it is true that no log books or bits of the submarine were brought to the surface in the vicinity of this attack, there was considerable oil in the area, observed during daylight hours. Several other attacks were made on possible contacts during the week's search. However, the one made by the *Gustafson* was by far the most likely to have been the submarine. I remember the dates only vaguely. Nonetheless, there is one clear date which stands out in my mind, that we were still patrolling this area in search of the submarine when President Franklin D. Roosevelt died on 12 April 1945."

After the war, when the Navy had the opportunity to examine the records of the German U-boat operations, it was revealed that *U-857* had been lost with all hands. Her demise was credited to the *Gustafson*.

The war in the Atlantic ended in May, and the *Gustafson* was outfitted for the combat then raging at Okinawa, on the doorstep of Japan. She headed through the Canal to the Pacific, but that war ended well before she could again sail in harm's way.

ESCORT DIVISION 48

A U-boat Overwhelmed

Escort Division 48 was attached to the inner screen of the Barrier Patrol off the east coast of the United States. Composed of three DEs and one frigate, it was designated Task Group 02.10:

Thomas (DE-102) commanded by Lieutenant Commander D.M. Kellogg. *Coffman (DE-191)* commanded by Lieutenant Commander J.C. Crocker. *Bostwick (DE-103)* commanded by Lieutenant J.R. Davidson. *Natchez (PF-2)* commanded by Lieutenant J.H. Stafford. Captain G.A. Parkinson was CTG 02.10 and *ComCortDiv 48* in *Thomas*.

Thomas had been with the *Block Island (CVE-21)* HUK when that DE sank *U-709*. Assigned to the *Card* (CVE-11) HUK, she and *Baker (DE-190)* destroyed *U-233*. See chapter *The Hunter Killers*.

Coffman was also assigned to the *Card*. After several convoys to North Africa and the United Kingdom, she joined a group searching in stormy and icy waters for a German weather submarine south of Iceland.

Bostwick had participated in transatlantic convoys and had been with the *Block Island* and *Card* HUK Groups in a support mode with the carrier while other escorts were engaged with the U-boats.

Natchez was a Canadian built vessel of the *Asheville* class, designed for the Canadian Navy. Acquired by the U.S. Navy in July 1942, she convoyed between New York and Guantanamo Bay, Cuba.

The mission of TG 02.10 was to search for enemy submarines in the vicinity of Cape Henry, Virginia. *Natchez* had been operating in the screen of a coastal convoy close to the Task Group.

In the dark of 29 April 1945, *Natchez* was patrolling her night station when the duty soundman, V.E. Ross, sang out a sonar contact at 2000 yards! *Natchez* immediately altered course to bring the contact on her bow. The echo was evaluated as probable submarine as the captain took the conn with the intention to ram or, at least, to drop an embarrassing depth charge pattern and deflect the submarine from sending a torpedo into the convoy. It was not at first realized that the U-boat was traveling at a very high speed until the schnorkel and periscope were sighted dead ahead with a noticeable feather.

By that time, it was impossible to alter course fast enough to ram. The sub went down close aboard the frigate's port side and submerged. A shallow pattern of charges was dropped, and the frigate's course was altered to regain contact. Unfortunately, the convoy passed over the area of the last contact as the merchant ships were executing an emergency turn to starboard. *Natchez* had to change course to avoid collision and to search astern of the passing ships.

After clearing the rear of the convoy, contact was regained and speed reduced to 10 knots, preparatory to a hedgehog attack. During the approach, the submarine engaged in evasive maneuvers and released a *pillenwerfer* about the time of firing. After the ahead thrown attack with negative results, the range was opened, part of the time from the *pillenwerfer*. However, definite contact was regained at 1400 yards. Speed was increased to 15 knots and *Natchez*' course was set to deliver a depth charge attack with magnetic impulse settings. There were four detonations, two about 15 to 20 seconds after firing and two much later, probably due to the water pressure at great depth.

By coincidence, while on patrol, *Thomas*, *Coffman* and *Bostwick* had crossed ahead of the convoy a few minutes prior to the contact. CTG Parkinson offered assistance and stood toward the contact area. When *Natchez* requested support, all three DEs raced toward her position.

The search was turned over to CTG 02.10. *Natchez* was detached from the convoy and attached to the Task Group. At 0115 on 30 April, a creeping attack was begun, the frigate being the attacking ship. She began closing the target, as directed by

Coffman, whose Soundman Second Class J.W. Rogers had a strong contact as well as hydrophone effects. *Natchez* fired a depth charge pattern, followed by 10 detonations, one of which was premature. Three were much delayed, probably due to heavy pressure at great depth. She returned through the pattern area, and illumination with her searchlight produced a spreading circle of oil. *Natchez* then cleared the area.

In view of the several explosions of depth charges set with magnetic impulse detonators immediately following the drop, a moderate depth of the submarine was recorded. However, there was no definite indication of serious damage or destruction. Premature explosions were probable. At the time *Natchez* had loaded Mark 8 depth charges, she had been unable to secure a full allowance of new arbors. It was believed that some premature detonations were caused by failure of the old arbors to break away from the charges. However, during the previous attack, two charges with separated arbors detonated at a very shallow depth in vicinity to the target, causing moderate damage to the submarine.

Two depth charges had inadvertently fallen overboard and exploded at 50 feet. As a result, a steam drain line from the steering engine ruptured at a junction, the SL surface radar was damaged with a fractured relay and the dead reckoning tracer (DRT) became inoperative. Consequently, an accurate plot was not available. In addition, an unlocated hull leak developed in the aftermost compartment beneath the deck plates which could not very well be removed at sea.

Sonar personnel were outstanding in evaluating, holding and regaining contact. The 3"/50 guns numbers two and three opened fire on the schnorkel at maximum depression, narrowly missing hits, probably causing the U-boat to submerge without firing a torpedo. The depth charge crew changed pistols in record time. (The pistol explodes a depth charge at a preset depth or by magnetic influence) The damage control parties and radio technicians demonstrated speed and efficiency in repairing material casualties.

0235. *Thomas* dropped three successive sonobuoys and started Observant with *Coffman* assisting. *Bostwick* was conducting a box search outside of the Observant area when ordered to proceed to the point of the first attack by *Natchez* and illuminate, reporting any debris. In the process of rejoining, *Bostwick* picked up a strong sonar contact and commenced evaluation and plot. Doppler, recorded traces, CIC plot and echo all indicated a submarine. She started a hedgehog attack but belayed firing when the plot indicated too much lead. The contact was lost at 350 yards, and the fathometer recorded a target at 70 fathoms as the ship passed over the sub. By accident, the recording was thrown away. *Bostwick* illuminated; results negative.

Coffman followed through with three hedgehog attacks without result. CTG ordered *Coffman* to assist *Thomas*, *Bostwick*, and *Natchez* in creeping attacks (in that order). *Coffman* promptly positioned herself as the directing vessel. *Thomas* then began a creeping attack with a depth charge pattern. She reported several premature detonations but also a number of explosions 18 seconds after firing.

0449. *Coffman* coached *Bostwick* as she fired 22 charges. A pattern of 24 had been ordered, but there was a communications failure at two K-guns. Her fathometer recorded a metallic target at 95 fathoms. *Bostwick* heard two muffled explosions on her sound gear. The target was located directly under her when the number two depth charge was fired. The K-guns blanketed the area by hurling depth charges from both sides of the attacking ship. Delayed, muffled explosions, indicated that *Bostwick* dealt damage to the U-boat. She was never in sonar contact with the target, such being the responsibility of the directing DE, *Coffman*. Contact was lost but regained shortly, and *Coffman* directed *Natchez* onto a creeping attack.

0608. *Natchez* fired a magnetic pattern which knocked all her radars out of commission. Five minutes later, she reported an object on the surface. *Coffman* was directed to illuminate while *Natchez* closed, but the object disappeared. Contact was lost again, and *Coffman* and *Thomas* commenced Observant, regaining contact half an hour later.

Coffman reported to CTG in *Thomas*:

> "The last run looked excellent right up to the time of firing the first charges, after which we lost contact, regained it momentarily and lost it again. We are now trying to regain it. So far, on our three runs and creeping attacks, the submarine has consistently moved in an area to the right of north, ie. 010 to 060 degrees."

0635. *Thomas* gained contact and commenced guiding *Coffman* in a creeping attack with a full pattern of magnetic depth charges. Apparently, this was the *coup de grace*. *Coffman* reported that the explosion from the firing of K-gun number 7 was far more violent than a depth charge would normally produce, even considering the distancing of the attacking ship from the detonation. Shortly after, cracking noises were reported from the sound hut.

The last attack was hampered by two minor material casualties, but otherwise all other equipment gave excellent performance. The entire pattern detonated at depths ranging from 930 to 1200 feet. An exception was the charge fired from number seven projector, which detonated in 50 seconds, indicating a sub depth of about 530 feet.

Following this attack, *Thomas* lost contact, and none of the ships were able to regain it. Captain Parkinson ordered *Coffman* to remain in the area to look for debris while the other three ships started a search. Twenty minutes later, *Coffman* passed through an oil slick which quickly developed into an extremely concentrated cover on the surface of the sea. No other evidence was recovered.

The final evaluation by Captain Parkinson:

> "This was a definite submarine which submerged after being first sighted by *Natchez* and went deeper after the first attack. Sonar conditions at that depth were very good, and neither *Coffman* nor *Thomas* experienced any difficulty in maintaining contact once it was made. The cumulative effect of all indications — doppler, recorder traces, quality of echo, fathometer, explosions and the failure to obtain any contact or indications except oil after the last attack caused me to believe that we either sank the sub then and there or so seriously injured her that she subsequently sank.
>
> The creeping attacks were conducted by the CIC teams in a manner that left little to be desired. The commanding officers acted as safety officers and attempted to keep their

ships in positions with respect to the target and the attacking ships so that maximum information could be obtained from sonar.

The performance of personnel was well up to required standards in all respects except the reloading of K-guns. It is felt this deficiency was caused by the impossibility to practice with actual firing and the inordinately short time allowed by standing procedures for the reloading of the Mark 8 depth charges."

After the war, German sources confirmed that *U-548* had evaded the mid-Atlantic Barrier Patrol with the intention of inflicting losses on convoys exiting Hampton Roads. Its fate was to be sent to the bottom by Escort Division 48 and a frigate, together comprising Task Group 02.10, off the Virginia Capes on 30 April 1945 two weeks before Germany surrendered.

Like other DEs at the termination of the Atlantic war, those involved in this episode were either retained in the Atlantic for training purposes or sent to the Pacific for the last stages of that war. *Natchez* remained as a cutter in the Coast Guard service.

THE LAST GASP OF THE U-BOATS

The Atlantic War Ends in a Disaster for Friend and Foe Alike

The Providence Journal of 13 November 1990 reported a gathering of over 100 people at Point Judith, Rhode Island to pay tribute to the last U.S. ship sunk by a German submarine on 5 May 1945. Buttoning his collar against the icy wind and spray from huge breakers crashing ashore, Alcester R. Colella said this was something he had to do for shipmates sleeping on the ocean floor.

He was in the Armed Guard on the freighter *Black Point*, en route from Newport News to Boston, torpedoed 2-1/2 miles off Point Judith two days before the Atlantic war ended. Twelve men from that ship went to a watery grave. He thought it was an incredibly irrational attack, being so close to a major naval base and with numerous antisubmarine units in the area. The ship's SOS was received simultaneously by Navy, Coast Guard, and Army Air Force units in New London, Mystic, Montauk, Newport, Providence and a home-bound Atlantic convoy only a few miles away. The submarine had virtually committed suicide. Said Colella: "It was only a waste of his crew, and we lost 12 men."

One of the dead was Lonnie Wilson Lloyd of the Armed Guard crew. His two brothers brought a beautiful red, white and blue wreath to throw upon the spot where *Black Point* sank. Because of a high wind and stormy sea, the ceremony was enacted ashore with a plaque placed in front of the Point Judith Coast Guard Station. Petty Officer Glenn Fogg climbed over the boulders and hurled the wreath into the waves.

THE FINAL HOURS OF U-853

by David Arnold. Reprinted courtesy of the *Boston Globe.*

"The fog had lifted, unveiling the antiquated steamer *Black Point*, chugging in the late afternoon sun along the Rhode Island coastline. On 5 May 1945, She was just off Point Judith and the Newport Naval Base, en route to the Edison plant in South Boston with a full load of coal. Most of the 46 crew members were finishing their regular Saturday meal when *Oberleutnant* Helmut Froemsdorf, at periscope depth 1000 yards away, took aim.

The commander of *U-853* was a tall, 24-year-old child of a war about to end. If he was dutiful by nature, he was also the ambitious, confident new commander of a submarine that had never sunk a ship. To him, *Black Point* must have seemed something like an unhurried duck paddling along. If the Americans couldn't be beaten, Froemsdorf possibly figured, perhaps he could throw a spiteful last punch.

He probably checked his escape route from the shoal waters inside Block Island. What he didn't know was that, by coincidence, four American warships were racing one another from New York to Boston and were behind Block Island, shielded from the submarine's periscope and electronic ears. Convinced that he was at the safe end of a shooting gallery, Froemsdorf probably barked, *Torpedo los*, sending 800 pounds of explosives toward *Black Point*.

Captain Prior of *Black Point* never saw what hit the ship. He had been standing on the steamer's bridge, an unlit cigarette in his mouth and a flaming match in hand. To this day, Prior doesn't remember whether he lit the cigarette or swallowed it. The warships, on the far side of Block Island, never heard or saw the explosion. Not until after the lead ship was well past the site did the ships reverse course, return to Rhode Island, locate the submarine and then spend 16 hours hammering it to death with depth charges and hedgehogs. Twelve Americans died on *Black Point*, and all 55 Germans in *U-853* were entombed.

Black Point was the last American ship torpedoed by the Germans in the war. It was the only American ship sunk by a foreign navy this close to the mainland since the War of 1812. Today, *U-853* and the skeletons of its crew rest 130 feet deep, beneath waters where sailors now spar with racing yachts. Modern nautical charts note "unexploded depth charges" in the area - an understatement.

The attack is not well known today, partly because the navy censored reports of it until after the German surrender. By then, V-E Day dominated the headlines, and a submarine attack off Newport received but modest mention. The incident is vivid, however, for the sport recreational scuba divers willing to descend 130 feet to gawk at the stilled, giant submarine and the bones of its crew.

Last fall, several scuba divers and I dived to *U-853*. In the murky undersea silence, the remains scream – of panic, last-minute flailing, attempts to swim for the surface, of suicide. The last hours of *U-853* tell an unromantic story of World War II in detail, threatened only by a crust of encroaching sea growth.

The day was uncharacteristically sunny for the western Norwegian coast when Froemsdorf sailed from Stavanger Fjord on February 23, 1945. His mission, according to later correspondence between his sister, Helga Deisting, and his Flotilla Commander, Guenther Kuhnke, was to join five other submarines dispatched to the western Atlantic to hamper American shipping. It was thought this might improve Germany's bargaining position, should Hitler seek a conditional surrender.

Kuhnke never heard from Froemsdorf again. Contrary to normal operating procedure, *U-853* never radioed back to headquarters. It probably was his radio silence that kept Froemsdorf and his crew alive into May. The flotilla's other four submarines, all reporting in regularly, had been detected and sunk by the end of April.

The submarines could listen to American radio broadcasts, according to Hans Goebler, who now lives in Indiana and who served four years on the *U-505*, the sub captured at sea by the *Guadalcanal* Hunter-Killer Group. (See chapter The Hunter-Killers.) By monitoring American radio, Goebler says, Froemsdorf must have known of the impending surrender, but it remains a mystery whether he received the message Grand Admiral Karl Doenitz sent to the entire German fleet one day before Froemsdorf fired on the *Black Point*:

'ALL U-BOATS. ATTENTION ALL U-BOATS. CEASE FIRE IMMEDIATELY. STOP ALL HOSTILE ACTION AGAINST ALLIED SHIPPING. DOENITZ.'

I talked recently with Helga Deisting at her home in Rothenburg, Germany. In discussing her brother, she told me that he was neither a fanatic nor even a member of the Nazi party. She is a tall woman of 67 whose sturdy voice wavered when she started paging through a scrapbook of old family photographs. Before her was Froemsdorf the skier, the accordion player, the dancer.

She had three brothers but was closest to Helmut. It disturbs her greatly that divers penetrated his tomb. I tell her that, in diving to *U-853* and *Black Point*, I choose to remain outside. A few divers who enter the *U-853* abuse its sanctity by disturbing the bones, but many others respect the remains of the dead and emerge from the wreck awed by the sacrifices of war. To these divers, the *U-853* is a memorial that hasn't been cast in marble and cleansed of death.

Her brother was six feet, 10 inches tall. One photograph of the crew, taken just after the submarine narrowly escaped an attack on an earlier mission, shows him with a radiant smile. He may not have been a party member, but the self-esteem in the photograph portrayed a man who believed in himself, his country, and his mission to defend it.

It was not until U-boat Ace Guenther Prien penetrated the British Naval Base at Scapa Flow in *U-47*, sank the battleship *Royal Oak*, and returned to a hero's welcome, that Froemsdorf decided for the submarine service. He was not alone. More than 39,000 Germans joined this service during the next six years; only 7000 would survive. Even into the spring of 1945, with chances of survival less than one in five, the submarine service remained the only over-subscribed branch of the German war effort, largely due to the heroics of Guenther Prien.

Deisting last saw her brother while he was on leave in September 1944. By then, her father had died at sea, her husband had died in the siege of Stalingrad, and another brother had been crippled in France. The Russians were entering Poland, and the Western Allies were at the Rhine. Both she and her brother knew that the war was over. She remembered the family 150-year-old standing clock that only her tall brother could reach to wind without a chair. As Froemsdorf and his sister started to leave for the train station, he remembered to wind the clock. She recalls him saying, as he gave the key a last turn, 'Who knows, maybe this will even suffice until I return.'

The spring snapped. They drove to the station in silence.

Froemsdorf officially took command of *U-853* on 1 November 1944. He had performed well on the previous mission, in which the submarine's skipper, Helmut Sommer, had been severely wounded. Sommer had been stalking the *Queen Mary*, loaded with American troops destined for the D-Day invasion, when British planes attacked his submarine.

In Froemsdorf's last letter to his parents, he wrote:

> 'I am lucky in these difficult days of my Fatherland to have the honor of commanding this submarine, and it is my duty to accept. I'm not very good at last words, so goodbye for now and give my sister my love.'

Reading that farewell 40 years later, Frau Deisting fights back tears. She pauses, staring at the letter through glazed eyes, and says, 'So young, this handwriting'. She folds the letter into quarters and returns it to an old envelope.

Prior, now 79, resembles a trim Colonel Sanders with a closely cropped mustache. That was a foggy day along the eastern seaboard, and merchant ships were not yet equipped with radar. Twice, during his steam up Long Island Sound, Prior lost sight of his own bow and had to anchor - first off Eatons Neck Point, Long Island, and then off Watch Hill, Rhode Island. He was not in convoy because the U-boat threat to coastal traffic by then was considered minimal. Even so, Prior recalls, the coast guard still required coastal steamers to thread through the East River and Long Island Sound. Prior remembers,

> 'Because you just never could be sure about those German critters'.

By the spring of 1945, merchant marine losses had slowed to a trickle. It is not surprising then that U-boats were far from Prior's mind when he returned to the bridge after dinner on 5 May. The seas were calm, and the fog had lifted. There were two hours of sunlight left at 1739. Third Mate Homer Small stood at the helm, keeping *Black Point* on course for the Cape Cod Canal. The only traffic in sight, far off to starboard, was a tug pulling lazily at three barges and the Yugoslavian freighter *Kamen*.

Stephen Svetz was a gunner on the 3"/50 caliber deck gun mounted on *Black Point*'s stern. He was writing a letter in his quarters, located just forward of the gun, while Gunner Lonnie Lloyd was absorbed in a comic book nearby. In the crew's quarters below them were 11 off-duty merchant seamen who had just finished dinner. The other 34 men were throughout the ship. The American flag fluttered over the gunners' quarters. Froemsdorf would have seen it in the cross hairs of his periscope.

And he would have determined: Target's speed, eight knots. Length, 368 feet. Gross tonnage, 12,000. Froemsdorf saw no threat of American warships, neither through the East Passage into Narragansett Bay nor toward the open ocean, to either side of Block Island.

The crew slid a 1-1/2 ton, electrically powered torpedo that had been stowed between their bunks down a greased track, and winched it into a bow launching tube. "Sonya" remains painted on the door to one tube; "Hannelora" is on another. Goebler of *U-505* thinks that Froemsdorf chose a conventional torpedo over the newer acoustic models because of the shallow water. (If the acoustic torpedo malfunctioned, it might turn and attack the submarine by homing on her engines. In the shallow waters off Newport, *U-853* would be unable to dive for safety.) Goebler estimates the torpedo range to the *Black Point* for this shot would have been 1000 yards, speed about 30 knots.

Froemsdorf had six teenagers in his crew. He must have known that Hitler was dead, Berlin had fallen, it was the end. If, during the next 16 hours of utter hell, Froemsdorf did not regret his command to fire, he must have had a sensational sense of duty.

As glass shattered around him, Prior's first thought was: 'Jesus, we've hit a mine!'

Doors splintered. Instruments cascaded from the bulkheads. The smell of explosives was everywhere. Forty feet of the *Black Point*'s stern had been blown off. The blast catapulted a 1/4-ton section of the after gun's mount onto the bow. Gunner Svetz was thrown to amidships and survived. The captain recalls prying the hands of the panicked helmsman free of the wheel, then running for the ship's records while the radio operator started tapping out an SOS. The ship was sinking fast, stern first. Men jumped from the rails, others tangled in the lifeboat lines. At 1805, *Black Point* rolled hard to port, paused, belched trapped air and gurgled out of sight. Prior considers it a miracle that everyone lived except the 12 men astern.

Prior has saved the six letters he received from families and loved ones of sailors who died. A letter from a young woman, Julie Macejka, asks about crewman Richard Shepson who, she said, knew nothing of war:

> "I didn't know him for too long, but long enough to know that I must learn what happened. All the letters I sent to Boston after he departed have come back. Does this mean he's not coming back?"

Shepson and his mates died instantly, Prior believes. It was a death the Germans would have envied.

Froemsdorf headed straight for open water. Perhaps he was aware that, had he done the unexpected and hidden closer to shore, he would have tripped an alarm as his submarine crossed magnetic coils laid on the ocean floor outside Narragansett Bay.

U-853 had been fitted with a snorkel to allow its diesel engines to "breathe" at periscope depth. Under diesel power, Froemsdorf's peak speed was almost 18 knots. Below snorkeling depth, the submarine switched to electric motors, driven by batteries that propelled the submarine at a paltry three to four knots. He must have been at periscope depth when he received a severe shock. He would have seen a small flotilla of American destroyers and destroyer escorts emerging from behind Block Island and cleaving through the calm seas at top speed.

It was the destroyer *Ericsson (DD-440)*, the flotilla flagship. The coast guard frigate *Moberly (PF-63)* and destroyer escort *Atherton (DE-169)* were close behind, and destroyer escort *Amick (DE-168)* several miles astern. They had just escorted a convoy of 80 ships to New York and were racing for the Charlestown Naval Base (Boston) and home because the war was over.

Froemsdorf the predator had become the prey. With her dive horn wailing, *U-853* started down. To get a 252-foot vessel down fast, the crew had to dash forward, through an obstacle course of machinery and hatches in each of the sub's six watertight compartments. It was done with well rehearsed acrobatics.

Froemsdorf apparently hoped he could hide by lying still on the shallow bottom. Perhaps enemy sonar would mistake the *U-853* for a rock or a wreck. Probably no sooner had the submarine settled than some unbelievably good news came to Froemsdorf in a whisper. Wearing earphones, radio technician Schanz would probably have reported that propellers were not approaching but were passing several miles ahead. The waiting continued in silence. Crew members lay on their bellies in darkness to conserve oxygen and batteries.

Inside the submarine, dank air, laced with the odor of battery acid, began to cool from the 40-degree water outside the hull. Space heaters, wasteful of power, were out of the question. With the chill, came condensation; clothing got soggy; skin that was 10 weeks without a shower became clammy; metal surfaces turned slippery; water dripping from the overhead mixed with the diesel soot that coated the sub's interior. Schanz might have whispered that the propeller noise was fading. The crew of *U-853* probably believed they would live.

The flagship let almost an hour slip by before heading toward the submarine. Why the ships didn't alter course immediately remains a mystery. The flotilla was still behind Block Island, when it learned of the torpedoing, according to Lewis Iselin, the *Atherton's* commander and King Upton, executive officer.

Shortly before 1800, word was received from the Yugoslavian freighter *Kamen*, which was picking up survivors. Iselin remembers forwarding the message via light signals to Task Force Commander Francis McCune on *Ericsson*, but he ordered all ships to stay on course for Boston. McCune does not remember that aspect of the battle. It was not until *Atherton* was well east of the attack site that orders were changed to reverse course and search for the U-boat.

Also aboard was a German prisoner of war who was recovering from an emergency appendectomy that a medic had performed by following diagrams in a book as Executive Officer Upton turned the pages. The prisoner survived with the blood donated by crew members who would later pummel 55 of his countrymen below.

U-853 probably hadn't budged when Schanz once again picked up approaching propellers, this time with sonar pings. At 2014, the *Atherton's* sonar returned the metallic echo of a submarine. Iselin recalls, 'We had a soundman who was an ace trombone player and had perfect pitch'.

By then, the Germans had been breathing the same air for over two hours. When below periscope depth, the oxygen supply depended on how many men were aboard to share it. By mid-1944, the Germans were losing so many U-boats that submarines went to sea with 15 extra men just to man deck guns. *U-853*, designed to carry 40 men, had 55. Less than 24 hours of breathable air remained when *Atherton* began to pound them.

Atherton's log begins with the following entries:

> "2030. Fired magnetic pattern of depth charges. One explosion observed."

Goebler likened the experience below to sitting in a 55-gallon drum while it was pounded with sledgehammers.

"2046. Fired hedgehogs. Unable to reestablish contact due to extremely disturbed condition of water."

More than 2-1/2 hours of silence followed as *Atherton*, joined by seven other escorts, tried to locate the quaking submarine. The air in the submarine was deteriorating. If the crew followed procedure, it would have organized into groups, each with a leader assigned to watch his mates' eyes with a flashlight. At the first sign of sleepiness, a result of carbon dioxide poisoning, the leader would jab the victim awake. Occasionally, the leader might find himself getting jabbed.

With time, came the need to urinate. The pressure at 130 feet would have overpowered the flushing mechanism, and quiet was of utmost importance, so men used buckets scented with diesel fuel.

'2337: Reestablished contact.
2341: Attacked with hedgehogs. Large quantities of oil, lifejackets, pieces of wood and other debris, and air bubbles, coming to the surface.'

Shooting debris out the torpedo tubes was a ploy that submarine skippers often used to feign destruction, so the attacks continued. Soon oil was rising like a well head. At 0105 the next morning, *Atherton* reported that it had finished the sub. But orders came back to continue the deluge. Iselin recalled:

'There was no doubt that, by this time, we knew we had it, but it seemed that everyone wanted to get into the act. "I don't think there's a hull that took a bigger beating during the entire war.'

In the late 1950s, when the wreck of *U-853* was discovered, divers found an opened cognac bottle, emergency ascent vests, and a skull punctured by a single bullet through the mouth.

Today, divers can see that the most damage to the submarine occurred at its stern. The path of the crew, based on the location of the bones, apparently had been forward, from one cracked compartment to the next, each airtight door dogged shut to hold back the flood. The forward torpedo room remained dry until 1960, when a diver who had hoped to raise *U-853* for profit blew off the hatch. The German government quashed his plan, pleading that the remains of its war dead be allowed to rest in peace.

According to divers who have been inside the submarine, dogs (clamps) still lock shut a torpedo tube door and the airtight entrance to this compartment. A live torpedo and the bones of several men lie on the floor. The dogs tell of a struggle to hold back water. A greater struggle, however, appears to have taken place just aft of this compartment. Most of the bones in *U-853* are piled up against the same airtight door that had been dogged shut on the other side. These men died in a frenzy, scratching for a few more seconds of life as they fought against a door locked shut by their mates.

More from the *Atherton* log:

'1710. Picked up items of wreckage.
1840. Fired hedgehogs, all of which exploded.
1841. Fired full pattern of depth charges.'

Three blimps arrived from Lakehurst, New Jersey and started dropping bombs. At 0901, the *Atherton* again reported: 'Have definite proof we have submarine'. But orders were to keep up the bombardments. *Ericsson* made a depth charge attack.

'2138. Fired 13 depth charges.
2327. Fired hedgehogs with positive results.
2337. Fired hedgehogs with positive results.'

By then, ships with experimental sonar gear were entering the fray to test their equipment; others were dropping charges just for the practice. A blimp commander even insisted the *Atherton* make an attack run so he could get a photograph.

It is entirely possible, Goebler believes, that several Germans in the airtight forward compartment would have survived all the practice runs and were still alive when the attack stopped at 1224. By then, the men may have gone insane. Their deaths would have come from suffocation, as the world above prepared to celebrate peace. Before the bombing stopped, however, sonar picked up a final, unexplained rhythmic hammering on a metal surface that was interrupted periodically in *U-853*. This was followed by a long, shrill shriek. And then there was silence."

Atherton and *Moberly* alone were credited for the destruction of the submarine. Both sailed into Boston Harbor with brooms at the mastheads, "Clean Sweep."

The precise date of the above article is not known but was probably 1986. References to the present should be considered as of that approximate date.

U-853, however, was not the last U-boat to be sunk. *Farquhar (DE-139)* claimed one more only hours later on 6 May and just before the end of the Atlantic War.

THE MISSION BAY HUNTER-KILLERS

Farquhar Sends the Last U-boat to Its Last Dive

Farquhar (DE-139) was one of the earlier transatlantic escorts, beginning operations in early October 1943. On 3 April 1944, she sailed for Casablanca in a hunter-killer group formed around *Core (CVE-13)*, guarding the passage of a convoy while hunting submarines in the general area through which the convoy sailed. Homeward bound on 2 August, she went to the rescue of the torpedoed *Fiske (DE-143)*, arriving in time to rescue 186 survivors. (See chapter *The Hunter-Killers*.)

In September 1944, *Farquhar* began patrols and convoy escort duty in the South Atlantic with the *Mission Bay (CVE-59)* Hunter-Killer Group. She voyaged from Bahia, Brazil, to Dakar, French West Africa, and Capetown, Union of South Africa. During a submarine hunt off the Cape Verde Islands on 30 September, *Farquhar* made a sound contact on which she and her sister DEs attacked over a period of six days, finally sighting a large oil slick, but no other evidence of a kill.

During training exercises off Cuba in December 1944, *Farquhar*, commanded by Lieutenant D.E. Walter, rescued 10 aviators from life rafts after their patrol bomber ditched in the sea. Again, while in Florida waters as plane guard for carriers conducting operations to qualify aviators, she rescued a downed pilot on 3 February 1945.

Operation Teardrop" was formed in early 1945 to protect the eastern seaboard of Canada and the United States against the new schnorkel U-boats operating as a group, code-named "*Seawolf*." As the Northern Force, the *Mission Bay* I Hunter-Killer Task Group 22.1 established a barrier patrol north of latitude 48 degrees 30 minutes north.

The Task Group Commander and skipper of *Mission Bay (CVE-59)* was Captain John R. Ruhsenberger. Commander E.W. Yancey was Escort Screen Commander (*ComCortDiv 9*) in *Douglas W. Howard (DE-138)*, Lieutenant J.T. Pratt commanding. Other DEs and their commanding officers were: *J.R.Y. Blakely (DE-140)*, Lieutenant A.S. Archie; *Hill (DE-141)*, Lieutenant A.G. Borden; *Fessenden (DE-142)*, Lieutenant Commander W.A. Dobbs. Also present were Coast Guard DEs *Pride (DE-323)*, Lieutenant W.H. Buxton with *ComCortDiv 46* Commander R.H. French aboard; *Menges* (*DE-320*), Lieutenant Commander F.M. McCabe; *Mosley (DE-321)*, Lieutenant Commander E.P. MacBryde. *Pride*, *Menges*, *Mosley* and ComCort Div were Coast Guard; others were Navy.

18 April 1945. The Northern Force, *Mission Bay* II HUK, had just set up its barrier when a submarine was detected but escaped. On the 24th, a plane crash-landed on the flight deck of *Mission Bay* and went over the side, taking another plane and crew with it. During the *Fessenden's* rescue of four survivors, Chief Motor Machinist's Mate Robert E. Jewell, plunged into the freezing water, risking his life to support one of the survivors until rescued. He received the Navy and Marine Corps medal for his heroism. However, hypothermia had taken its toll, and the rescued pilot could not be revived.

0322 on 6 May. While bound for New York in a convoy screen, *Farquhar* made a sonar contact at a range of 1300 yards. The Officer of The Deck had no time for evaluation; an embarrassing barrage was urgent to prevent a torpedo from finding its way into the merchant ship columns. Just five minutes after the contact was reported, the DE delivered an urgent attack with 13 depth charges, set shallow, and then dropped a night marker sonobuoy 1800 yards from the pattern. Following the explosions of the depth charges, seven separate and clear detonations were heard from the sonobuoy. Six minutes later, two final explosions were heard, and there was no further contact.

Operation Observant, together with *Douglas L. Howard*, for almost 13 hours failed to regain contact. Although Captain Walter and Commander Yancey strongly suspected that a kill had been achieved, there was nothing floating on the surface to corroborate their assumptions. If *Farquhar* had indeed sunk a U-boat with a single well placed pattern of 13 depth charges, she had scored a remarkable victory. The Atlantic war ended the next day, and the crew was obliged to wait several years for confirmation. Post-war evaluation revealed that she had been the last American ship to sink a submarine in the Atlantic in World War II, sending *U-881* to the bottom.

Lieutenant Casucci told this writer what he knew of the sinking of the U-boat:

> "Regarding the skipper's action report relative to the sinking of *U-881* on 6 May 1945, I didn't think he sent one in, probably because there was no evidence of a sinking. Usually, when we participated in an attack and if we dropped many depth charges, we sometimes were fooled by the U-boat skipper. He would release an oil slick, perhaps some rags or clothing, or maybe we would see a large air bubble or two. These tricks were intended to throw us off our continued attack.
>
> The day we attacked *U-881* we stayed in the vicinity for quite some time. We criss-crossed the area, hoping to catch him moving under our depth charge patterns. Evidently, our strategy worked. We must have hit him in a critical spot in order to sink him. The strange thing is we never saw any evidence of a sinking. I was the first lieutenant; it would have been my job to recover debris. There was none!
>
> When I was advised of the sinking only last year, I had a feeling of sadness and dismay. Had we known that we had sunk the *U-881* on the day of the attack, I suppose we would all have cheered. That was our mind set during the war. When I got the report last year, I could only feel sadness for 57 young Germans who gave up their lives needlessly with just one day to go before Germany capitulated. A great shame."

Farquhar prepared for duty in the Pacific and arrived at Pearl Harbor on 8 August 1945. Post-war escort duty took her to Eniwetok on 5 September and, on 10 September, she sailed in company with *Hyman (DD-732)* to receive the surrender of Ponape. There she served as station ship for several months, then sailed from Kwajalein early in January 1946 for the east coast of the United States.

This narrative on the sinking of *U-881* is uncommonly brief. As Lieutenant Casucci indicates, there is no record of an action report at the Navy Historical Center in Washington and there is no way of knowing if one ever existed. Under the circumstances, this is all the information that could be supplied.

Some of the above was taken from the *Fessenden* ship's chronicles, compiled by Mitchell E. Sapp, as part of a family history and in honor of his father, Fireman First Class James Henry Sapp Sr., a crew member.

As we complete the history of destroyer escorts in the Atlantic, we marvel at the number of DEs blasting U-boats to the bottom. What a contrast to only three prior years when German submarines were massacring merchant ships and threatening the Atlantic lifelines! This author recalls the six knot convoys across the Caribbean which we guarded with wooden subchasers shortly after Pearl Harbor! First, we stand in awe of the productive capacity of the United States to turn out huge quantities of destroyer escorts and trained crews in so short a time. Secondly, we take pride in the destroyer escorts and their crews who, with escort carriers, broke the back of the U-boat fleet and safely escorted to Europe the men and weapons needed to win the war.

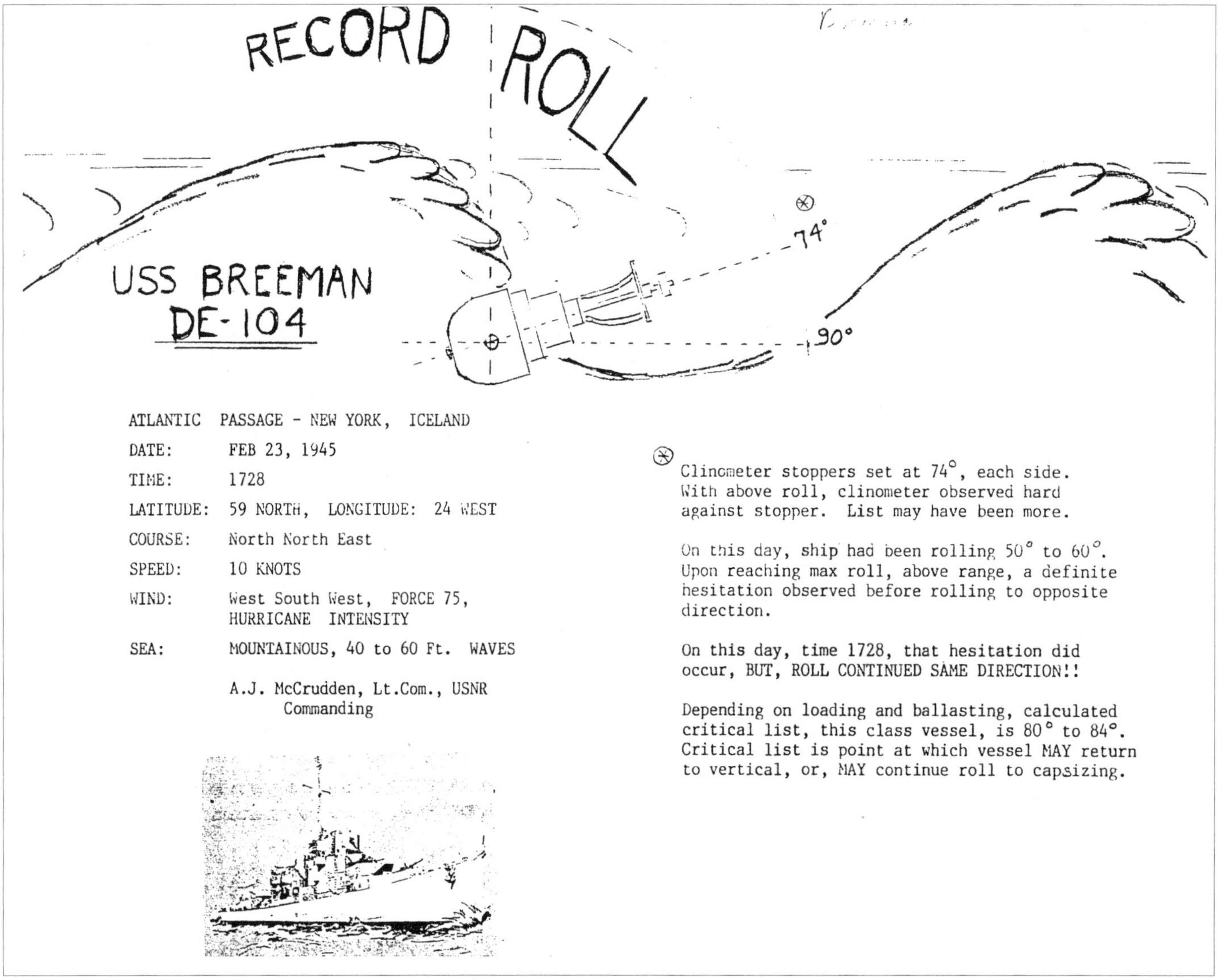

ATLANTIC PASSAGE - NEW YORK, ICELAND

DATE: FEB 23, 1945

TIME: 1728

LATITUDE: 59 NORTH, LONGITUDE: 24 WEST

COURSE: North North East

SPEED: 10 KNOTS

WIND: West South West, FORCE 75, HURRICANE INTENSITY

SEA: MOUNTAINOUS, 40 to 60 Ft. WAVES

A.J. McCrudden, Lt.Com., USNR
Commanding

⊛ Clinometer stoppers set at 74°, each side. With above roll, clinometer observed hard against stopper. List may have been more.

On this day, ship had been rolling 50° to 60°. Upon reaching max roll, above range, a definite hesitation observed before rolling to opposite direction.

On this day, time 1728, that hesitation did occur, BUT, ROLL CONTINUED SAME DIRECTION!!

Depending on loading and ballasting, calculated critical list, this class vessel, is 80° to 84°. Critical list is point at which vessel MAY return to vertical, or, MAY continue roll to capsizing.

USS Breeman (DE-104) record roll

USS Davis plunges to the bottom, survivors in water. Photo taken from *USS Neunzer.* US Navy Photo

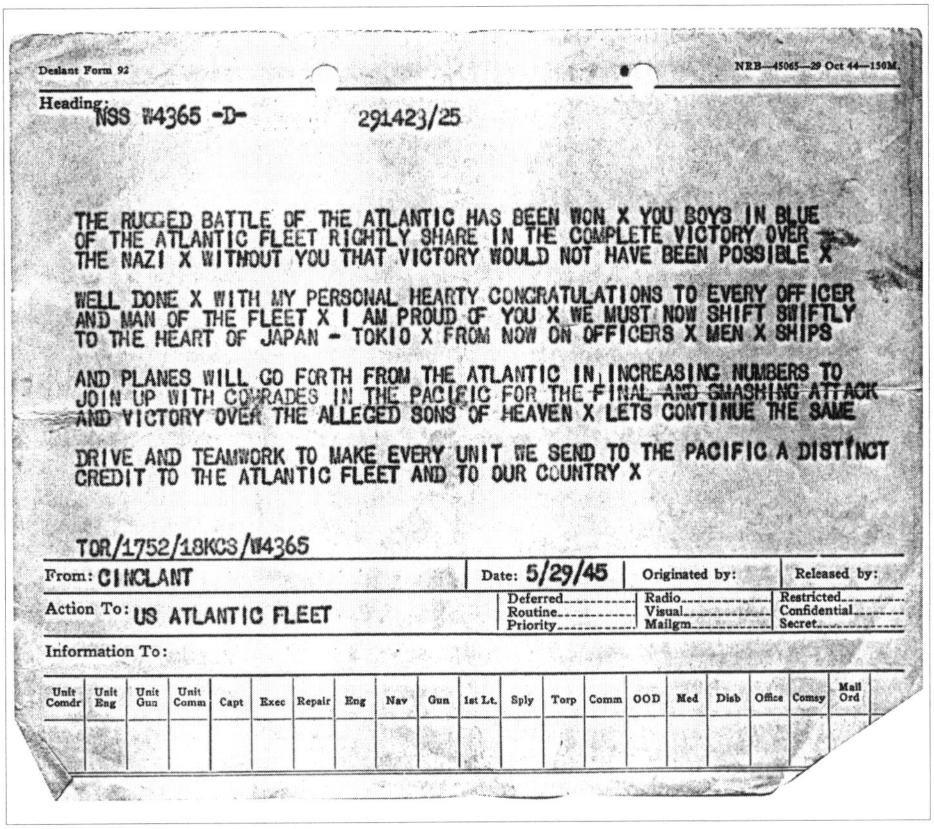

Deslant Form 92 NRB—45065—29 Oct 44—150M.

Heading: NSS W4365 -D- 291423/25

THE RUGGED BATTLE OF THE ATLANTIC HAS BEEN WON X YOU BOYS IN BLUE OF THE ATLANTIC FLEET RIGHTLY SHARE IN THE COMPLETE VICTORY OVER THE NAZI X WITHOUT YOU THAT VICTORY WOULD NOT HAVE BEEN POSSIBLE X

WELL DONE X WITH MY PERSONAL HEARTY CONGRATULATIONS TO EVERY OFFICER AND MAN OF THE FLEET X I AM PROUD OF YOU X WE MUST NOW SHIFT SWIFTLY TO THE HEART OF JAPAN - TOKIO X FROM NOW ON OFFICERS X MEN X SHIPS

AND PLANES WILL GO FORTH FROM THE ATLANTIC IN INCREASING NUMBERS TO JOIN UP WITH COMRADES IN THE PACIFIC FOR THE FINAL AND SMASHING ATTACK AND VICTORY OVER THE ALLEGED SONS OF HEAVEN X LETS CONTINUE THE SAME

DRIVE AND TEAMWORK TO MAKE EVERY UNIT WE SEND TO THE PACIFIC A DISTINCT CREDIT TO THE ATLANTIC FLEET AND TO OUR COUNTRY X

TOR/1752/18KCS/W4365

From: CINCLANT | Date: 5/29/45 | Originated by: | Released by:

Action To: US ATLANTIC FLEET | Deferred / Routine / Priority | Radio / Visual / Mailgm | Restricted / Confidential / Secret

Information To:

Unit Comdr	Unit Eng	Unit Gun	Unit Comm	Capt	Exec	Repair	Eng	Nav	Gun	1st Lt.	Sply	Torp	Comm	OOD	Med	Disb	Office	Comsy	Mail Ord

ALNAV, a dispatch from Commander-in-Chief U.S.
Atlantic fleet to all ships at sea upon conclusion of hostilities with Germany.

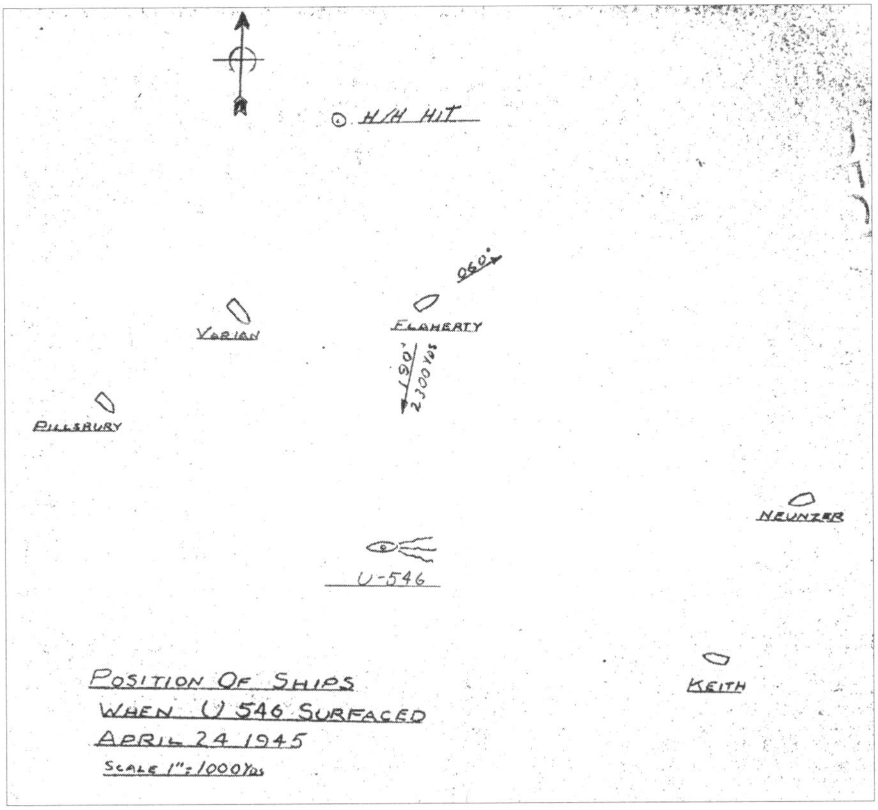

Position of ships when *U–546* surfaced April 24 1945.

Chapter IX - American Sailors Decorated By The U.S.S.R

By Commander Sheldon H. Kinney, U.S. Navy

Reprinted from *Proceedings* with permission.

In 1948, the same Lieutenant Kinney of *Bronstein* fame, by that time a full Commander, recalled decorations received by himself and other American Navy men from the U.S.S.R.

Decree #222-46 of the Presidium of the Supreme Soviet of the U.S.S.R. was probably a top secret document within their borders for, in this decree, the communist leaders refuted their own claim that the Russian people, and they alone, defeated Nazi Germany.

The decree awarded one-hundred-and-twenty orders and seventy medals of the U.S.S.R. to men of the United States Navy and Coast Guard, for "outstanding military activities aiding the delivery to northern ports of the Soviet Union during the war against the common enemy of the U.S.S.R. and the United States — Hitlerite Germany — of transports with military cargo and for valor and courage displayed while performing this duty. Recognition by Russia of the role of United States sea power in the Atlantic in World War II was completely at odds with the party stand that the Soviet Union crushed Germany unaided by the United States or any other nation."

The Orders and Medals presented to American Navy and Coast Guard personnel run the scale of Russian decorations. They include, in order of precedence, the Order of the Patriotic War, Order of the Red Star, Order of Glory, Medal of Shakov, Medal of Nakhimov, Medal of Valor, Medal for Distinguished Service and the Medal for Bravery. The elaborate nature of these decorations, together with the benefits which they carry are astonishing.

The author received the Order of the Patriotic War, First Class. The Order resembles in size the Department of the Army General Staff emblem. It has no suspension ribbon of the type normal to the decorations of our nation. On the back of the order is a heavy stem, to which a large threaded nut attaches. It cost one American officer a hole in his number one uniform coat on the occasion of presentation, to learn that the Russian method calls for attaching the nut from inside the coat. He received first the "punch hole" treatment, then the decoration.

The Order of Patriotic War leaves little doubt as to its nation of origin. It consists of a gold sunburst background, on which is mounted a large red star. Projecting between sunburst and star are a rifle and sword, crossed upon each other. Superimposed on the star is a white disc on which are pyramided a gold hammer and sickle.

Accompanying the decoration are two booklets, one an identity book, the other a book of chits. A translation reveals the amazing benefits which accrue to recipients of the award.

Twenty rubles per month, for life, is to be paid to the holder of the award. He is entitled to free passage on the railroads and water transportation of the Soviet Union. All city street cars were his to ride free, including the Moscow subway system. The Government will pay part of the person's rent, and certain tax exemption is granted. The booklet concludes with the statement that the family of the recipient will inherit the award, and its privileges upon his death.

The second booklet is a book of chits, which the frontal page informs the recipient he is to surrender upon receipt of his monthly pay. This pay is far from idle promise. On the 27th of May, 1946 a letter was received by the author in Destroyers Atlantic from the Embassy of the Union of Soviet Socialist Republics in Washington, D.C. It contained a check drawn on the Riggs National Bank in the sum of $165.28. The letter stated that this amount represented the payment for the months August, 1945, through May, 1946, as a holder of the Order of the Patriotic War. In considerable haste, the check was sent to the Secretary of the Navy, and returned to the Soviets. The Constitution prohibits an officer of the United States from accepting any present emolument, office, or title from a foreign state without the consent of Congress. The Congress had authorized the acceptance of the decorations and directed their presentation to the members of the Navy and Coast Guard recognized by Russia but certainly had no intent of authorizing such payment.

The incident is not without its humorous side, however. There is considerable pleasure in contemplating the prospect of the Soviet Government officially subsidizing our Navy and Coast Guard.

In awarding these decorations, the Russian government disclosed the type of American assistance for which they were grateful. An analysis of the types of duty and achievement of the officers listed in the Decree gives a clear pattern.

Names of the men who fought the convoys through to Murmansk first strike the eye, men who, in the endless daylight of far northern latitudes, beat off the relentless waves of *Luftwaffe* aircraft which harassed the plodding merchantmen with bombs, machine guns, and torpedoes.

Then there are names that speak of the hunter-killer groups that pitted themselves against the German submarines and turned the tide of battle from defensive to offensive, that made the hunter the hunted. These groups led by such men as Captains (now rear admirals) Dan Gallery, Massey Hughes, Logan Ramsey, and screen commanders with such outstanding records as Captains Frank Giambattista and George Parkinson performed under the command of Admiral Royal Ingersoll, Commander in Chief, U.S. Atlantic Fleet. They brought to bear upon the enemy a new concept of search and attack weapons, combining air and surface power.

Many of the men recognized by awards in the list are the naval aviators who flew from the decks of the CVEs *Bogue*, *Card*, *Block Island*, *Casablanca*, *Croatan*. In some of the dirtiest operational conditions of the war, they proved to the U-boat commanders from Iceland to the Cape Verdes and Gibraltar to the Virginia Capes that no square mile of Atlantic was free from carrier air attack.

Other names reveal the personnel of the destroyers and destroyer escorts that formed the surface attack units of these killer groups and teamed with the carrier pilots to break the morale and shatter the vessels of Admiral Doenitz's undersea fleet. Since much of the hunter-killer work was in support of the pre-invasion convoys, the awards are in indirect acknowledgment of the necessity of invasion in the west. The order of the Presidium is a tribute to maintenance of control of the seas by the allies, without which victory would have been impossible.

Lewis M. Andrews, Jr.

The orders and medals recognize every facet of war against the enemy submarines. Captain (then lieutenant commander) John Corbus, commanding the United States Submarine Herring, fought a duel with an enemy submarine under conditions which gave the initial tactical advantage to the enemy. By skillful conning, he gained the upper hand and torpedoed the enemy. The German was met in his own medium and defeated. Seaman Francis P. Perret was a member of an armed guard crew aboard the SS Bellingham that drove off a submarine that had placed a torpedo (which did not explode) into the ship. During the nerve-wracking days that followed, the crew shot down one of a flight of Focke-Wolf raiders that attacked them. Commander (then lieutenant) Doug Hodson led his squadron from CVE decks in attacks against enemy submarines that took an impressive toll. Destroyer and destroyer escort skippers Charles Hutchins, Norman Hoffman, Bob Baughn, and Dave Kellogg made dogged attacks that ended in destruction of U-boats.

The significant contribution of the United States Coast Guard to the destruction of enemy submarines is typified by the award made to officers of that service. Commander (then lieutenant commander) Robert Wilcox, U.S. Coast Guard, sought out a submarine that had torpedoed a tanker in convoy. With accuracy, he straddled the sub with depth charges causing the undersea craft to lose control and surface, where the destroyer escort under Wilcox's command and others of the escort group destroyed it. Lieutenant Commander Sidney Hay, U.S. Coast Guard Reserve, commanding a DE, contributed to this feat which sent another U-boat to the bottom. Perhaps the most striking performance for which the Russians recognized the work of the Coast Guard was that of the attack in which Lieutenant Commander Francis Pollard, U.S. Coast Guard, succeeded in sinking a U-boat off Iceland with the ice breaker *Northland*. Despite limited equipment and a scant number of depth charges, he skillfully executed attacks that sent the submarine into its final plunge.

The list is no respecter of rank. Names such as those of Seaman Grandey, Gunners Mate Houghton, Aviation Machinist's Mate Haycroft, Coxswain Schwartz, Machinist's Mate Pagnotta, meet the eye as quickly as names preceded by Lieutenant or Ensign.

From Decree #222-46, Presidium

of The Supreme Soviet of The U.S.S.R.

For Outstanding Military Activities Which Facilitated the Sailing of Transports with War Supplies to Ports of the Soviet Union During the War Against the common Enemy of the U.S.S.R. and the U.S.A. — Hitlerite Germany — and for the Valor and Gallantry They Displayed, the Presidium of the Supreme Soviet of the U.S.S.R. Awards Decorations to the Following Servicemen of the Navy, Naval Reserve, Coast Guard and Coast Guard Reserve of the United States of America:

(Slightly less than 200 Navy and Coast Guard personnel received Soviet awards. Destroyer escort personnel were:)

Order of The Patriotic War, First Class

Sheldon H. Kinney, Lieutenant USN
David M. Kellogg, Lieutenant Commander USNR
William Sessions, Lieutenant Commander USNR
Robert H. Wanless, Lieutenant Commander USNR
Norman C. Hoffman, Lieutenant Commander USNR
Francis C. Pollard, Lieutenant Commander, USCG

Order of The Patriotic War, Second Class

Robert I. Baughan, Lieutenant USN
John A. Church Jr., Lieutenant Commander USNR

USS England – US Navy Photo

Lewis M. Andrews, Jr.

Chapter X- Pacific Antisubmarine Warfare

ENGLAND

Six Japanese Submarines Destroyed

The record written by *England (DE-635)* is unsurpassed in the annals of antisubmarine warfare. In the last two weeks of May, 1944, that vessel, under the guidance of her talented young executive officer, Lieutenant John A. Williamson, destroyed six Japanese submarines.

Why the executive officer? An outstanding quality of command, or any other high executive position for that matter, is the ability to recognize and employ an outstanding talent in a subordinate. The commanding officer, Lieutenant Commander W.B. Pendleton, was highly competent in all phases of his office, but he did not begin to have the antisubmarine experience of his executive officer who had been an ASW instructor before being assigned to *England*. The skipper had decided beforehand that, should *England* gain contact on a submarine, the conn would be turned over to Williamson.Behind this amazing exploit lay a vast network of Navy Intelligence, a team dedicated to deciphering Japanese operations. By May 1944, the Japanese Naval code had been cracked. We knew where their ships were going and why. On 18 May, for example, Escort Division 39 knew that a Japanese submarine was en route to Buin off the southeast tip of Bougainville, New Georgia.

Five days before, in Truk Harbor, Caroline Islands, Lieutenant Commander Yoshitaka Takeuchi, commanding officer of Japanese submarine *I-16*, urged his men on as they loaded 75-pound sacks of rice in water resistant bags. *I-16* was one of the largest subs built by the Japanese, able to accommodate a seaplane with retractable wings. She departed on 14 May with orders to supply an isolated and starving garrison on Bougainville. The captain had radioed the Commander Submarine Squadron 7 on Saipan that his estimated time of arrival would be 2000 on 22 May. Unfortunately for Takeuchi, his radio audience also included CincPac (Commander in Chief Pacific Fleet) Intelligence.

From Admiral Halsey to the Commander of Escort Division 39 went the order to intercept. *ComCortDiv 39,* Commander H. Hains, on *Raby (DE 698)*, included that vessel under his command plus *George (DE 697)* and *England*. On 19 May, the three DEs arrived in the designated area and commenced search operations. It was a beautiful day with an almost cloudless blue sky, a gentle east wind and an indigo blue sea. They were formed on a 90 to 270 degree relative line of bearing. That is to say, they were all on the same course, even with each other, and 4000 yards apart, a scouting front of 8000 yards, (four miles).

On any ship, decisions were up to the conning officer, but behind him lay a complex war machine of men and electronics. His failure or success must necessarily have hinged upon the training and efficiency of personnel as well as on performance of equipment. Everything had to be ready to go at the right time. The helmsman had to handle the ship as though it were part of him, when and how and immediately as the conning officer desired. The engineers had to give or take speed with precision and without hesitation. And, when the word was given to fire, buck fever had nothing in common with victory. It took a whole ship to kill a sub, and *England* was that ship.

The illusion of a South Sea cruise was rudely interrupted when Soundman John D. Prock sang out, "Contact! Bearing 305 degrees, range 1800 yards". The Officer of The Deck sounded the alarm, and Williamson raced to the CIC to start a plot going before heading for the bridge. The recorder was turned over to Ensign Gus Daily. As the ship turned toward the sub, the contact was lost, then regained at 1800 yards. *England* closed the range to the point of firing, but Williamson had a hunter's intuition that he didn't "feel" a kill; he sheered off on his first run without firing the hedgehogs. This was an evaluation run, the conning officer of the DE feeling out the skipper of the sub, how he maneuvered, what he did when the chips were down. Neither captain, nor executive officer nor crew nor ship had killed a sub before. They were going according to the book, and the book said a hunter shouldn't shoot if he couldn't "feel" the target.

Sheering off from a contact was risky. The DE couldn't echo range back through the propellers. The water turbulence from the propellers destroyed sound waves and could cause permanent loss of contact, particularly if the sound or CIC crews were inexperienced or ruffled. But whereas the people on *England* were inexperienced, they were not ruffled. Williamson headed *England* into the contact again with more confidence than the first time. It felt right. The sound officer turned knobs and moved coordinates on the recorder. The run looked good. He recommended a firing run, and the exec concurred. The push of a button closed an electric circuit, and 24 missiles leaped from the bow to the sound of a July 4 string of 2-inch firecrackers. High in the air, they formed an elliptical pattern 50 yards across and then plunged straight down into the sea ahead. There was no sound or indication of a hit. However, contact was retained. A spot analysis of the attack indicated that *England* had not lead the target sufficiently and should have been further to port. Another attack produced an explosion at a depth of 130 feet, but no debris rose to the surface. Captain Takeuchi maneuvered to hide in *England's* wake, thereby causing the DE to lose contact, but only momentarily. Contact was regained at 1410, and a third hedgehog attack was launched on a center bearing (between the right and left "cut-ons"). The fathometer registered the sub depth at 325 feet.

By this time, *England* had acquired a sense of the sub's evasive tactics. Williamson opened the range to gain maneuvering room for the fifth run. The salvo took off and plummeted into the water, scoring several hits. A moment later, there occurred an explosion so violent that most of *England's* crew was thrown to the deck. The ship shuddered from stem to stern, and the immediate thought was that she had been torpedoed.

But *England* was unharmed. It was the sub that had blown up. Oil poured to the surface as the submarine settled into 950 fathoms (5700 feet) of water, many times over her hull resistance to pressure. All manner of debris came to the surface. *England* remained in the general area until daylight, picking up pieces of flotsam – a 75 pound bag of rice, pieces of finished wood, a prayer mat, a chopstick, splotches of human blood. By the following day, an oil slick three miles wide and six miles long had spread over the tranquil sea.

Even while *England* was racking up her first momentous victory, Navy Intelligence passed on to the Admiral's staff the tidy bit of news that a scouting line of seven enemy subs was proceeding from Manus in the Admiralty Islands to Truk, in the Micronesia Group, maintaining a distance of 30 miles from each other on a line of bearing approximately 200 miles wide. On 20 May, Admiral Soemu Toyada, Commander of the Combined Fleet, issued an order labeled, *A-Go*, designed to block and annihilate American surface units as they moved westward. Captain Ryonosuka Kato was placed in command of seven submarines for the assigned task. *RO-105*, *RO-104*, *RO-109*, *RO-112*, *RO-116* comprised Submarine Squadron 7 and was reinforced by *RO-108* and *RO-106* moving out from Truk. The latter two were on the "other side" of a line that separated Admiral Chester W. Nimitz' Pacific Fleet from General MacArthur's Southwest Pacific Command. Hence, they were excluded from attack, and the DEs were specifically ordered not to cross the line. Since U.S. forces were on both sides, such a restriction seemed a little bizarre.

But the five that remained were fair game and represented a good hunt. Built during the war, these were the most modern of enemy submarines, about 200 feet long, 20 feet in the beam, and displacing 525 tons. They carried crews of 40 or more and were armed with four 21" torpedo tubes, two twin 25mm automatic antiaircraft guns, a radar detection device and sound gear. As rated, they could withstand maximum pressure at 250 feet, but this was readily exceeded.

This information was radioed to *ComCortDiv 39* on 20 May with appropriate orders to search, intercept and destroy. On 22 May, *Raby*, *George* and *England* arrived ahead of the estimated track of submarine number one of the force of seven and proceeded to search for her with sound gear and radar. *George* was in the center, *Raby* to port, *England* to starboard. At 0350, *George* reported a radar contact seven miles ahead, almost immediately corroborated by the other two ships. *George*, being somewhat the closest, raced through the darkness to close the range with the apparently unsuspecting sub.

0410. Almost on top of the target, *George* illuminated the sub with her searchlights, preparing to open fire with her deck guns. The ships were so close that, upon illumination, personnel on all three DEs saw the sub at once. *George* never got a chance to open fire, however, because Lieutenant Shigehiro Uda, Submarine Commander, lost no time in taking the *R-106* down.

Sound contact was gained almost immediately by *George*, and she started a hedgehog firing run. She missed and reported contact lost. *England* was requested to assist. When asked by Commander Hains if she knew where the sub was, *England* replied, "Affirmative", which was somewhat at variance with the facts. However, their plot was so good that they quickly turned a little fib into a big fact.

0425. The sonar operator on *England* reported to Williamson that he had a contact on the sub at 2500 yards. *England* began an attack run. It looked good. She fired hedgehogs but missed. Contact was retained, however, and Williamson guided his ship in again. Under the pitch black sky on the flying bridge, he could hear the outgoing and returning "ping" signals from the sonar, could hear them getting louder, more metallic, and clearer as they approached the submarine. To the sound officer went a now familiar order, "Fire on the recorder!" A command to fire when instruments so indicated.

England's bow turned bright as day as the blinding flashes of hedgehogs turned into thin streaks of red light in the air above and ahead of them. The missiles disappeared into the night and churned the water phosphorous white seconds later when they dived on their prey.

There were three explosions; the submarine was hit!

Williamson maneuvered his ship into position for a third run, but he never completed it because, exactly two minutes after the hedgehog hits, the sub blew up! The water shock and concussion were similar to their experience with the first sub sunk a couple of days before.

England remained in the general area until noon the next day, recording large slicks of oil on the surface and picking up such telltale evidence as insulating cork and deck planking. It was most interesting to note that this submarine was only 10 miles from the position estimated by intelligence.

Number one Japanese submarine silhouette was painted on the bridge of *England*, the number one sub of Scouting Force 7. At this stage, one DE in a force of three had destroyed two subs, and the other two had destroyed nothing. A pale shade of green could almost be observed in the navy gray of *George* and *Raby*. One can only guess the exact text of pep talks given by captains to officers and men of the two non-scoring DEs — and worse was yet to come!

23 May. The day was spent running up and down the estimated Japanese scouting line, ie. a course perpendicular to, and ahead of, the predicted course of the enemy. DEs were on their usual line of bearing, this time in daylight formation, 15,000 yards apart abeam, *Raby* to port, *George* in the center, *England* to starboard.

0604. *Raby* reported a radar contact ahead, distance four miles. Called to the bridge by the Officer of The Deck, Williamson promptly ordered *England's* course changed so as to close *Raby*.

Raby held the radar contact for only six minutes when the alerted submarine submerged. Lieutenant Suseme Idebuchi, skipper of *RO-104* was warned by his radar detector and crash dived before being sighted. Fifteen minutes after radar contact, *Raby* gained sound contact and closed the distance to the sub. Her first run was a miss. By this time, *George* and *England* were circling *Raby* at a distance of 2000 yards. *Raby* must have felt like a lesser gladiator warming up the lion for the champ. The second firing run was a miss. The third firing run was a miss. The fourth firing run was a miss.

Williamson was holding his breath. Then, half an hour after first gaining sound contact, *Raby* lost the sub. Her sound dome probed to port and starboard, through wake and bubble, but the sub was gone.

ComCortDiv 39, had two important tasks at hand. The first was to seek out and destroy the enemy. The second was to keep one DE from hurting the morale of two others. *George*, therefore, was obviously the next DE directed to proceed to the last sub contact area. *George* gained sound contact on the sub and attacked. Contact was regained. She made three additional hedgehog runs on the sub between 0730 and 0810, but no hits. Idebuchi was well trained in evasion tactics.

OTC then had little choice but to call off *George* and direct *England* to try her luck. Hains' voice tone was a mixture of resignation and exasperation. *George* still had contact, so it was a matter of *England* moving into position and taking it over. *George* then retired to the outer circle. The champ was in the arena. The DE that had sunk the last two subs now faced up to her third. Idebuchi, meanwhile, had turned off his echo ranging gear and started to slip away. He almost succeeded, but not quite.

The first run looked fairly good, but not on the cutting edge. Nevertheless, *England* fired hedgehogs, and missed. She turned off, keeping the sub broad on the bow, opened the range and closed in again. This time things looked brighter. No matter how experienced the crew, it took at least one run to sharpen wits. One sub captain might not react the same as another. The sub took evasive maneuvers. There was a point when the hedgehogs would be fired when the sub could have made her most effective maneuver, and also when the DE could have anticipated that maneuver and was guided accordingly. Here were two ships and two crews who labored mightily against each other without ever seeing their opponents. Here were two officers, each reacting to his own intuition, split seconds apart, one Japanese, one American, one guessing right, one ultimately guessing wrong.

The second firing run at 0804 scored something between 10 and 12 hits!

The submarine depth had been estimated at about 300 feet. *England* opened the range to prepare for a third attack. But the submarine blew up with a tremendous force three minutes after the hits. To make certain, *England* crossed the explosion area and dropped a full pattern of deep set charges. Again, oil and debris poured to the surface from the stricken submarine. A boat was lowered to pick up oil samples and evidence of the kill.

Williamson went below to the wardroom for a cup of coffee. On the way, he was approached by a young seaman with a troubled countenance. He wanted to know how many men were in the crew of a Japanese submarine. Williamson replied that, depending on the submarine size, there would be between 40 and 80. Then came the question Williamson feared, "Sir, how do you feel about killing all those men?"

Williamson hesitated, ruminating in his own conscience, then recalled General Sherman's admonition that "War is Hell". However, once in a war, there is no quarter, ie. kill or be killed. Further judgments would have to come from a Higher Authority than us mortals. The teen age sailor seemed to be satisfied with the explanation, but the exec recalled that the coffee didn't taste so good after all.

This was the third sub sunk and initially thought to be the second of the Japanese scouting line. This sub, however, was not exactly in the position she was estimated to be in. It was actually the third submarine in the scouting line rather than the second. However, a message came through from one of our planes that it had sunk a Japanese submarine in the position where the second one of the scouting force ought to be. The first three of the seven submarines comprising the Japanese scouting force were sunk!

The violent explosions of the first three submarines sunk by *England* shortly after being hit, as well as Japanese submarines sunk by other DEs, have been a matter of some speculation. An evaluation of the cause of detonation, when damaged beyond hope of escape, it was suggested that the Japanese commanding officer may have detonated a torpedo warhead to avoid any possibility of ship or personnel falling into the hands of the "Yankee devil", a mass hara-kiri. Unlike German U-boat sailors, there is no record of a single Japanese submarine crewman taken alive after his ship was damaged beyond repair by a destroyer escort.

0120 on 24 May. *George* had a radar contact seven miles ahead and, with the other two DEs, raced toward the target. The radar detector on *RO-116* gave warning, and the skipper, Lieutenant Commander Takeshi Okabe, submerged at a distance of 9000 yards from *George*. *England* was then about eight miles on the port beam of *George*, and Williamson sent his ship to flank speed to close the gap. *George* was searching for sound contact.

0150. *England* had sound contact, range 3000 yards, slowed to 10 knots and prepared to attack. The first run was dry; Williamson decided not to fire. He did not feel as though he was on target, nor did the sound officer. Commander Okabe pulled out all the tricks in the book. He "fish tailed", echo ranged in a manner to interrupt the DE "pinging" and even tried to hide in *England's* wake.

England did not turn off but passed right over the sub to get a fathometer reading, 168 feet from the surface to the sub. Passing over a sub meant probable loss of contact, but a calmly functioning sound and CIC team could lead the DE back to contact. *England* could take all manner of chances with the fourth. She was a winner, no matter what!

The second run was dry too because of violent evasive maneuvers by the sub. A Japanese submarine was trying to outwit *England*, waiting for the right moment to throw her off contact and slip away. When his sound gear detected that persistent sub-hunter echo ranging on him for a third time, it must have felt like the ping of doom. The Japanese captain had played his whole bag of tricks. He could only repeat his performance and hope the American captain would make a mistake.

0214. *England* scored three hedgehog hits on her third run!

Rumbling, breaking-up noises, like collapsing airtight compartments, could be felt on *England*. Giant air bubbles, fuel oil and debris shot to the surface, including the wood box in which a sextant had been stored. This sub did not blow up, probably because the damage from three simultaneous hits was so enormous that all hands were immediately killed or incapacitated. *England* continued to circle the area until 0700 to obtain final confirmation of the sinking. A great many excited sharks were in the vicinity, apparently in a feeding frenzy. *England* assumed her normal night patrol but in the morning returned to the area to recover debris, including a pair of oil soaked gloves, a chopstick and other flotsam. In the wee hours of the night, before retiring, Williamson noted as a condescending eulogy to the sub captain that he had been the most elusive sub of all.

Including the one sub sunk by aircraft, numbers one, two, three and four of the scouting line were accounted for, and *England's* log showed four subs sunk, *I-16* and three *ROs*.

22 May. Admiral Halsey had formed a new Hunter-Killer Group composed of the carrier *Hoggatt Bay (CVE-75)* as flagship and destroyers *McCord (DD-534)*, *Hazelwood (DD-531)*, *Heerman (DD-532)* and *Hoel (DD-533)*. Captain W.V. Saunders, OTC and Commander of *Hoggatt Bay*, was directed to the vicinity of the sacrosanct "NA" line to join up with the three DEs and locate and destroy the enemy subs. Captain Saunders, however, had no knowledge of the successes of *England* because Commander Hains had been under orders to maintain radio silence lest Japanese Admiral Owada intercept the messages. *England* was, therefore, detached to intercept the Hoggatt force and to relay by flashing light what had transpired and that *ComCortDiv 39* had been ordered back to base to replenish fuel and ammunition.

George and *Raby* were no longer on intimate speaking terms with *England*, but things appeared to have taken a turn for the better on 25 May, when Admiral Halsey ordered *ComCortDiv 39* to repair to Manus for fuel and hedgehogs. Since two of the remaining subs of the scouting force lay between the DEs and Manus, it looked as though Halsey ordered them to Manus, sinking subs en route. By this time, Halsey had obtained permission from General MacArthur to cross the "NA" line in pursuit of the enemy. (This is not a joke.)

With this acquired permission to cross the forbidden line, Commander Hains decided to make the most of it. The DEs were on their usual line of bearing, this time *England* to port, *Raby* in the center, and *George* on the starboard wing. Between Manus and the DEs, lay two enemy subs, and two DE's were determined that they would sink them and that a third DE would not be allowed to enter the contest.

2304 on 26 May. *Raby* and *England* obtained surface radar contact simultaneously, eight miles dead ahead of their sonar search line. The contact was exactly equidistant from both vessels. When the captain of *RO-108*, Lieutenant Kanichi Kohari, got the radar warning, he crash-dived 4000 yards from *England*.

Meanwhile, *Raby* was heading for the sub. However, unfortunately for herself, the submarine chose to cooperate with *England* rather than with *Raby* by moving toward *England*. As the sub submerged, Williamson frankly noted in the log: "*England* beat him (*Raby* skipper) to the contact."

2318. Range 1700 yards, *England* got sound contact on the submarine. However, there was an ammunition problem; exactly two patterns of hedgehogs, two firing passes to make at the sub, and that was all. Supposing then, if Williamson made two attack runs and missed — lost contact for good — and nobody else regained it? The scuttlebutt (gossip) at the officers' club would surely run to one vein. "If Williamson hadn't been so greedy and let *Raby* have the contact, we'd have gotten another Jap sub. He knew his ammo was about gone!"

The crew of *England* knew the consequences as their ship headed in on the first firing run. But victory tends to perpetuate itself, creating a mind-set which reflects on the conquest at hand and with never a thought to the possibility of defeat.

England made one firing run. The hedgehogs soared, then down 250 feet below the surface — and several of them hit the submarine at once! The explosions were simultaneous and violent. Several seconds later, there followed a series of small explosions and rumbling — or breaking up noises! Again, oil and debris poured to the surface, including the Japanese captain's paraphernalia from the conning tower. What a performance!

Number six of the Japanese scouting line of seven was sunk, and *England* had destroyed four of them plus the original stray sub, totalling five. Williamson made a grateful observation at this time in favor of Navy Intelligence. Every sub sunk so far had been destroyed within 50 miles of the position in which Intelligence had estimated it to be! *England* remained in the area until daylight of 27 May, picking up debris for proof of the kill.

Subs number five and seven of the Japanese scouting force remained thus far unaccounted for. Aside from the first stray sub, *England* had accounted for numbers one, three, four, and six of the Japanese scouting force, and number two had been sunk by one of our planes.

Spangler (DE 696) had departed from Purvis Bay on urgent orders with enough hedgehogs to supply a hunter-killer division. She arrived at Manus at almost the same time *CortDiv 39* entered the harbor. All DE's took on fuel, provisions and precious hedgehogs as expeditiously as possible and all four, now including *Spangler*, returned to the remainder of the Japanese scouting line.

ComCortDiv 39 formed his usual front on a line of bearing 4000 yards abeam by day and 16,000 yards at night. In daylight, subs were submerged, requiring antisubmarine vessels to maintain a distance permitting the overlap of echo ranging sound search equipment. It was expected that, at night, subs would be surfaced to charge their batteries while running on diesel power. DEs would, therefore, open out to maximum radar, rather than sonar, range.

Life on *George* and *Raby* was grim. *England* had actually sunk five subs to their none. This was going to make one helluva action report, and something had to be done about it. *Spangler*, a relative newcomer, was not as deeply concerned. But *George* and *Raby* had a common problem, deep and gnawing, bigger than the subs and Japs, bigger than the whole damn war in fact!

0156 on 30 May. Destroyer *Hazelwood* of the Hoggatt Group established a radar contact at a distance of 10,000 yards (five miles). On board submarine *RO-105*, instruments quickly warned Lieutenant Junichi Knoue, commanding officer, and Captain Ryonosuka Kato, Commander Submarine Division 51, that they were being targeted by radar. The sub dived immediately. *Hazelwood* gained sound contact, made a depth charge attack and missed.

England was on the starboard wing, about 16 miles from *George* on the port wing. *George* and *Raby* were the closest and were directed by *ComCortDiv 39* to take over the submarine contact from the destroyer. *England* and *Spangler* were ordered to the extreme southern end of the scouting line, beyond sight and sound of *George* and *Raby*. No doubt this was designed to cover the last of the Japanese subs, but it was also effective in getting *England* as far as possible from her sister ships. Starting at 0400, and for the next six hours, attack after attack was made by *George*, *Raby* and *Hazelwood* to no avail. Division Commander Captain Kato was apparently conning the Japanese sub with great skill.

1300. *England* reached the southern limit of the line of search 12 hours after leaving the formation, then turned around and started back, searching up the line. As Williamson got closer to *George* and *Raby*, he could hear their intermittent voice radio, indicating that those ships still had contact on the sub and were working her over.

0324. Twenty-five hours after *George* and *Raby* first attacked the sub, *England* was within 20 miles of her sister ships. *Spangler* was about eight miles to port. *England* could now clearly hear conversation between *George* and *Raby*.

Williamson couldn't resist the temptation. He picked up the radio telephone, took a deep breath, asked *George* and *Raby* for their position and could he, perhaps, be of some small assistance? *England* was still over the horizon, consequently beyond radar range, and could not exactly pinpoint the position of the two attacking DEs.

Most of the officers and men on those two ships hadn't slept in over 24 hours. They were tired, but sleep was unimportant compared to that super DE breathing down their necks 20 miles away. They had fired hedgehog patterns galore, but the enemy sub was still alive and operational. Nonetheless, they had determined this would be their kill — if it killed them to do it.

England's request was answered loud and clear:

"1. Assistance not needed, thanks!
2. They had a possibly damaged submarine at bay.
3. Their position was none of *England's* damn business.
4. Unprintable and unauthorized verbiage.
5. Stay clear!"

Five minutes later, with Williamson beginning to fret over having sunk only five subs, the sixth gave him just the cooperation he needed. She surfaced almost exactly between *George* and *Raby*. Commander Hains ordered *George* and *Raby* to illuminate and open fire. One searchlight, however, pointed straight up momentarily, putting a pencil of light on the horizon for *England's* bridge personnel to see, even at 20 miles. Within seconds, the Officer of The Deck on *England* lined up the pelorus on the flying bridge gyroscope compass repeater and advised Williamson that he had a bearing on the two DEs.

That was all Williamson needed to know. Captain Pendleton hesitated but recalled that Admiral Lord Nelson had once disregarded an unwise order, thereby prevailing over the enemy. *England* went to flank speed. This was difficult information to put into the log. The Captain was not about to admit that he left his assigned patrol or violated orders or anything of the sort. His log entry was a masterpiece: "We got rendezvoused with *George* and *Raby* at 0500."

ComCortDiv 39 was genuinely concerned with the morale of two DEs. He ordered *George* and *Raby* to hold contact and make no more attacks until daylight, and further, he ordered *England* not to come in closer than 5000 yards. He'd had enough experience with that DE to know how she could just sneak in and sink somebody else's sub. This would be a *George* and *Raby* sinking or bust! After all, he had to write the report of this operation, and he didn't want to write *England* over and over to the monotonous eclipse of his other two ships.

At daybreak, *George* attacked and missed. *Spangler* did the same.

Wrote the "mutinous" Williamson in the log: "In the meantime, we had edged into position 2000 yards from the submarine."

ComCortDiv 39, in despair and weariness, could no longer delay his inevitable decision. As hard as it would be to record that one DE got all and the other DE's got none, it would be harder still to report to Admiral Halsey that he let a Japanese sub escape because he wanted to deflate the ego of a bright young officer. He groaned and moaned and ordered *England* to attack.

The champ circled in slowly, feeling out the Japanese captain, like a bird dog creeping up wind. The three DEs stood off and watched *England*. Those other three DEs were manned by stalwart, patriotic Americans, but it would be testing credulity to assume that they wished hunting luck to their colleagues on *England*.

On *England*, the sound team felt like the master of their target, and they acted like it. The CIC fed information to the conning officer as laconically as a news announcer. What happened is best described in Williamson's log entry:

"When directed to do so, we attacked and fired one salvo (hedgehogs). After the expected time interval five minutes and 43 seconds, we heard the usual WHAM! The explosion was violent and very deep. At first, not even a swirl of water came to the surface. Then, as we continued to comb the area, a fountain of oil bubbled up 500 yards from the point of attack. Debris gradually followed. Once more, we lowered the boat and recovered oil samples, deck planking, shreds of insulating cork, a fragment of interior wood, bottle stoppers (one with a Japanese label) and a bar of soap. Once more, we saw dozens of excited sharks. In the next two or three hours, we had conclusive evidence that we had sunk our sixth submarine."

RO-105, after withstanding 21 attacks over a period of 30 agonizing hours, had gone to her final port of call, defiant to the last.

ComCortDiv 39 picked up the voice radio phone and, in a tone mixing weariness and wonderment, asked the question of the day, "God damn it, how do you do it?"

And a lot of other DE skippers in the Atlantic and Pacific oceans would have liked an answer to that question. Williamson was much too modest to say it, but the obvious answer was that *England* had an officer on board by the name of John Williamson, their secret weapon.

The epitaph for Submarine Division 51, and the final comment on the twelve days of *England*, was provided on 13 June 1944. As the U.S. forces moved in for the invasion of Saipan, Vice Admiral Takeo Takagi sent an urgent appeal to Admiral Owada. All the available strength of Submarine Squadron 7 was to be immediately stationed east of Saipan to "intercept and destroy the American carriers and transports at any cost". admiral Owada replied, "This squadron has no submarines to station east of Saipan".

The remarkable record of *England* in being able to paint six submarine silhouettes on her bridge in two weeks was a record for all navies in both World Wars and an astounding feat of arms. There is no doubt that such an accomplishment would have been vastly more difficult against the double hulled, deep diving and highly skilled German U-boats with their homing acoustic torpedoes and their snorkels that permitted 18 knot speeds at periscope depth.

Nonetheless, this was a great victory. The performance of *England* must be credited to superior ability, outstanding leadership, inspired training of personnel, and superb maintenance of equipment. Those are the qualities of a top fighting ship, and *England* had all of it.

Advised of this cascade of enemy submarines by one DE, Admiral of The Fleet Ernest J. King, Chief of Naval Operations, announced, "There'll always be an *England* in the United States Navy."

Had the war ended at this juncture, the crew of *England* would have had nothing but pride to recall. Somewhere in their crystal ball, however, there lay in waiting a *kamikaze* aircraft to exact revenge. See narrative, *Iwo Jima to Okinawa – The Destroyer Escorts*.

A word for *George* and *Raby*. They were good, average DEs competing with a former ASW instructor who had spent months "sinking" simulated submarines or friendly ones in practice at sea. As will be seen later in this chapter, a single kill was generally accomplished after many long hours and many attacks. *Raby* took part in a sub sinking in a subsequent narrative.

Most of the foregoing was derived from *England's*

action reports, with some paragraphs from Proceedings by permission: Copyright U.S. Naval Institute, Annapolis, Md.

GRISWOLD

A Tenacious Hunt Paid Off with a Kill

After reaching Bora Bora in the Society Islands on 23 July 1943, *Griswold (DE-7)* escorted convoys through the South Pacific. On 12 September 1943, she conducted a four hour attack on a Japanese submarine off Guadalcanal and, although debris and an oil slick rose to the surface, she was not credited with a kill.

Undaunted, *Griswold* struck again three months later. On the night of 23 December 1943, while patrolling near Koli Point, Guadalcanal, Solomon Islands, a visual dispatch, received from the signal tower, warned that a submarine periscope had been sighted off Koli Point. The commander of the Guadalcanal screen in the destroyer minelayer *Breese* ordered *Griswold* to investigate.

Search was quickly rewarded with a sound contact, distance 900 yards. The range was opened to 1600 yards and an approach was started on the contact. The sea was smooth with a light southeast wind, and the average sound range of the day was 2500 yards. During the approach, range recorder traces indicated a range rate of 13 knots, which dropped to 11.5 knots as a hedgehog firing range was reached. (Range rate is a combination of speeds of attacker and submarine, similar to relative speed.) Traces were sharp and clear.

Hedgehogs were fired on the recorder at 2228. Thirteen seconds after firing, three explosions were seen and felt dead ahead. In the absence of any apparent target motion, the attack was continued and a 13 depth charge pattern was fired, depth setting 100 feet, centered on the point of the prior hedgehog explosions. The fathometer indicated a 165 foot bottom. All depth charges exploded. While circling the area in an attempt to regain contact, considerable oil and air bubbles were observed rising to the surface in and around the disturbed water.

Five minutes past midnight, sound contact was regained, and the ship was maneuvered to run over the target twice. The fathometer and the frequency sweep modulator setting of the sound equipment were used to identify the target as a possible submarine or wreck lying on the bottom. However, the Guadalcanal Base Commander advised that no wrecks were located in the attack area.

Upon receipt of this information, the captain, Lieutenant Commander Charles M. Lyons, decided to make a series of attacks, using depth charges that would explode after reaching the bottom. Charges were fired to fall in a straddle 10 yards ahead of and 10 yards behind the target, using the dead reckoning trace plot and sound stack data to determine firing time. All but two charges exploded. As the ship passed over the target, the fathometer located it on the bottom. Except for short intervals, the sound contact was continually maintained with the DE circling the attack area at a distance of 1000 to 1500 yards from the day marker that was dropped during the first attack. Oil and air bubbles continued to rise.

After waiting 30 minutes for the last two delayed action charges to explode, another attack was delivered at 0210, firing a five depth charge pattern with a depth setting of 150 feet. All charges detonated and, while circling the area and attempting to regain sound contact, a heavy explosion was felt in the attack vicinity. This explosion may have been caused by the two unexploded depth charges referred to above. Oil and air bubbles continued to rise to the surface.

Three minutes later, a periscope was sighted on the edge of the disturbed area, broad on the starboard bow, distance 800 yards. A distinct feather (small wake) was trailing the periscope, which remained visible for 30 to 45 seconds. Captain Lyons ordered the *Griswold* turned toward the target with intent to ram. Sound contact was obtained almost immediately on the same bearing as the sighting, range 600 yards. The sub submerged, and an 11 depth charge pattern was fired, using a 100 foot depth setting. Large air and oil bubbles rose in the disturbed area as before.

0240. Sound contact was regained at approximately 400 yards. The ship was turned toward the target and commenced an attack. The recorder showed a target width of 10 degrees and a range rate of 11 knots. *Griswold* went to attack speed, 10 knots, and fired hedgehogs. Six explosions were seen and felt ahead 14 seconds after firing. A 13 depth charge pattern was fired, using a depth setting of 150 feet. Oil and air bubbles again surfaced in the vicinity.

After circling for about 15 minutes, 1200 yards from the position of the last contact, sonar contact was regained, range 1300 yards. A range rate of 15 knots, matching the DE's speed of 15 knots indicated a motionless target. *Griswold* fired hedgehogs with the target dead ahead. Fifteen seconds later, at least eight hedgehog explosions were observed and felt. The DE then fired a 12 depth charge pattern, using a depth setting of 150 feet.

Large oil and air bubbles were seen by *Breese* and aircraft to be rising from the area . A retiring search plan was carried out for the next four hours without regaining contact. During the night, several other ships were ordered to the area to patrol and search. A strong odor of diesel oil was present in the attack area and was also reported by *HMNZS Matai* (His Majesty's New Zealand Ship).

Griswold was ordered to continue a retiring search. At 0400 on 25 December 1943 (Christmas), 25 hours after the last attack, large amounts of floating debris, including pieces of planking, a wooden grating, and human remains were observed five miles from the position of the last attack. Large oil slicks were seen to extend from the attack position to six miles in a strong northwesterly current.

A small boat was put over the side for the purpose of examining the debris. The Medical Officer of Escort Division 8, Lieutenant (jg) William G. Donald Jr., was in the boat and certified human remains. One consisted of ribs and flesh with skin attached. Another was a large and small intestine containing some feces and with an appendix attached. Donald stated that these remains had not been in the water very long and that they had been torn and scorched, as if by blasting.

A visual dispatch received via *Matai*:

"FROM COMFLOT 25 (Flotilla Commander) X MY OPINION IS THAT YOU MADE A CLEAN KILL YESTERDAY AND THE DEBRIS HAD DRIFTED TO ITS PRESENT LOCATION. I SHOULD NOT BE SURPRISED IF A CAREFUL SOUND SEARCH INSIDE THE 100 FATHOM CURVE

MIGHT REVEAL ONE OR MORE PIECES OF WRECK ON THE BOTTOM X CONGRATULATIONS ON A GOOD CHRISTMAS PRESENT"

A postwar evaluation confirmed that *Griswold* had sunk Japanese submarine *I-39*.

Griswold also turned out to be bad news for the *kamikazes* at Okinawa. See narrative *Iwo Jima to Okinawa-The Destroyer Escorts*.

FAIR

Not "Fair" to I-21

Late on 4 February 1944, while *Fair (DE-35)* was operating in a screen with Task Group 58.3, the battleship *New Jersey (BB-62)*, reported a radar contact without recognition, distance 21 miles. The Task Group was centered around the aircraft carriers *Monterey (CVL-26)*, *Cowpens (CV-25)* and *Bunker Hill (CV-17)*. *Fair* received orders from the Task Group Commander to join the destroyer *Charrette (DD-581)* and to act as a killer group.

Charrette made a surface radar contact 11 miles from the Task Group, disappearing when within five miles. *Fair*, under the command of Lieutenant D.S. Crocker, joined up shortly after the destroyer had dropped a full depth charge pattern. *Charrette* coached *Fair* into position for a hedgehog attack. The submarine apparently had been expecting another depth charge attack and took too long to turn away at the last moment. The echoes were distinct, and excellent doppler was noted during the attack.

Four detonations were heard 15 seconds after firing the hedgehogs. The evidence from all available sources of information, depth of water (2800 fathoms), loss of contact at 250 yards, and recorder depth settings, proved conclusively that the 15 second interval between firing and detonation could only have been caused by the hedgehog projectiles striking an object at a depth of 200 to 300 feet. Four minutes after firing, two heavy underwater detonations were felt.

While conducting a retiring search, *Charrette* called *Fair's* attention to a heavy odor of diesel oil, a slick covering 1500 by 500 yards and spreading rapidly over the surface. Eight hours later, when the search was abandoned, the bubbling of oil and air was still apparent to the two ships in the location of the explosions. The slick increased in size until it was two miles wide and four miles long.

The *Fair* skipper noted in his action report that he felt that his ship had made a successful attack and that the enemy submarine was sunk, corroborated by the commanding officer of *Charrette*.

The Navy agreed with that assessment after the war, and *Fair* was credited with the destruction of Japanese submarine *I-21* in the early hours of 5 February 1944. The post-war review also brought to light some very interesting data about this hapless submarine. It was a unit in forward elements of the Japanese striking force at Pearl Harbor and it was also identified as the submarine that sank the destroyer *Porter* at the Battle of The Santa Cruz Islands.

After serving in the assault and capture of Saipan in the spring of 1945, *Fair* had another encounter — with the *kamikazes*. See chapter *Iwo Jima to Okinawa — The Destroyer Escorts*.

GILMORE

A Sub is Destroyed in The Frozen Arctic

The capture of Attu and Kiska in the Aleutians early in the war gave the Japanese more prestige than strategic real estate. Ultimately, it cost their army thousands of men, and their navy lost twenty surface ships and six submarines with nothing to show for their efforts. They thought that the American counteroffensive against Japan would come via the Aleutians because those islands are very close to Japan. The Americans found it expedient to encourage the enemy's distraction. Actually, U.S. forces were slowly withdrawn from that area to the Central Pacific to support the seizure of enemy-held islands.

Submarine *I-180* was a unit in a Japanese scouting force, spying on activities in Dutch Harbor. On the evening of 25 April 1944, this sub surfaced to charge batteries about 120 miles south of Kodiak Island. Its timing could not have been less opportune – for itself.

Gilmore (DE-18), under the command of Lieutenant W.D. Jenckes, had completed eleven escort missions between Alaskan and Aleutian ports until 20 January 1944 and nine escort missions between Bremerton Harbor, Washington, and Attu by 20 April 1944. She departed from Dutch Harbor on 23 April to assist *Edward C. Daly (DE-17)* in the escort of merchantmen bound for Kodiak.

Near midnight of 25 April, *Gilmore's* SL radar picked up a small target, presumed to be a surfaced submarine, distance four miles. *ComCortDiv 14*, Commander L.F. Sugnet, in *Daly* was notified. The course was changed toward the target which was promptly challenged by light. The target failed to reply, prompting Captain Jenckes to order General Quarters, followed by the shrill whistle of the Boatswain's Mate of The Watch, "Man your battle stations!". Off duty men jumped from their bunks, pens fell onto unfinished letters, books went face down and playing cards dropped abruptly as all hands raced to appointed stations, donning life vests and helmets as they ran.

The dead reckoning tracer (DRT) plot indicated the target course and speed, 15 knots. As the DE turned to head for the contact, the sub disappeared from the PPI scope at two miles. *Gilmore* proceeded to the last surface position of the sub, went into a search pattern, and shortly gained sound contact. Having become more accustomed to Arctic gales and storms as the enemy rather than the Japanese, the astonished radar operator let out a yell:

"Holy cow, I think that's a diving submarine!"

Contact was made at 2600 yards. *Gilmore* commenced an attack run with hedgehogs, and the submarine maneuvered radically as the range closed. The captain of *I-180* would do his best to outsmart the captain of *Gilmore*. Down to the wire, however, the sub didn't look like a winner. *Gilmore* held fire and reopened the range to get a better shot and commence a new run. Three hedgehog attacks failed to produce a hit.

Contact was lost but regained 20 minutes later, and *Gilmore* commenced a depth charge run, dropping 13 charges set at medium depth without results.

0055 on 26 April. The DE commenced a run directly over the target while operating the fathometer. As the target was crossed, the depth sounder indicated 47 fathoms (282 feet). A second run was commenced.

0127. Thirteen depth charges, medium depth, were dropped on the submarine. A violent underwater explosion occurred but without visible surface indications due to extreme darkness. The explosion caused minor damage in the after motor room of *Gilmore*. The sound of the explosion was somewhat greater than that of a depth charge but the concussion was very intense. Contact was lost and not regained. Sound operators on both ships reported that the explosion was immediately followed by a series of five or six short blasts.

The area was searched with both sound and radar with negative results. A retiring search was then initiated and continued until after daybreak when the search was changed to sweep the area of the attacks and to look for oil or debris.

1255. A message was received that a Kingfisher aircraft operating from the Naval Air Station at Kodiak had found a heavy oil slick about 50 miles south of Chirikof Island. A later report by the pilot indicated the slick to be one mile square and sufficiently thick to prevent white caps breaking through in a 35 knot wind.

Gilmore proceeded to search about her best estimate of the position of the last attack without results. The weather became increasingly worse and, by sunset, the wind was force six, and the seas were very high. Visibility was extremely poor. An extended search during the night and again in the early afternoon of 27 April were joined by *Daly* On orders from the squadron commander, search was abandoned at 0030 on 28 April, and both ships proceeded to Kodiak.

Subsequent information after the war confirmed that *Gilmore* had destroyed the 1630 ton Japanese submarine *I-180*.

MANLOVE and PC-1135

Tireless Persistence Paid Off

On 24 March 1944, on her first HUK assignment, *Manlove (DE-36)*, commanded by Lieutenant Commander J.P. Ingle, departed from Majuro Atoll in company with *PC-1135* with orders to rendezvous with destroyers *Halsey Powell (DD-686)* and *Hull (DD-350)*. Contact with the two destroyers was made 45 miles southeast of the entrance to Erikub lagoon, Wotje. *Manlove* was instructed by *Halsey Powell* (OTC) to join in a search for an enemy submarine nearby.

0145. *PC-1135*, dutifully following *Manlove*, was well astern. Her crew could not yet know that they were about to glorify the nameless PCs by taking part in a victorious ASW action. (A PC was something between a sub chaser and a DE, about 175 feet. It did not have the sophisticated electronics nor the armament of a DE).

0421. OTC directed *Manlove* to investigate a radar contact. She altered course promptly, followed by *PC-1135*. A few minutes later, *Manlove* made a radar contact, distance 12,000 yards. However, the target faded from the radar scope at 2950 yards.

The DE made a sonar contact, distance 2600 yards. The contact had very slight movement to the left, then appeared dead in the water. No doppler was discerned during the entire run. Contact was lost at about 550 yards. *Manlove* did not fire. A DRT plot was not made on this run because the plotter was changing the scale from 2000 yards =1" to 1000 yards =1" to accommodate the close-in ranges of sonar as opposed to the long ranges of radar.

The sonar operator regained sound contact at 1700 yards. The PC was making a run on the same contact at the same time and fired her depth charges at 0512 without result. *Manlove* then began a direct approach to the target which showed neither apparent movement nor beam traces throughout the run. Contact was lost at about 500 yards, and an attack was made on the center bearing. Depth charges were fired at a 300 foot depth setting without apparent effect.

0520. The PC regained contact and made an attack, firing mousetraps (A smaller and but less effective version of hedgehogs). Results were negative. Two minutes later, *Manlove* made a sound contact at 1900 yards. The target indicated a pronounced movement to the right, but the big puzzle — no doppler effect.

0527. *Manlove* again fired hedgehogs but without result. She then initiated a search pattern and located the target after about 10 minutes. There was still no doppler. The target was moving rapidly to the left, and *Manlove* made numerous course changes to maintain a lead. The DE fired depth charges at a 450 foot depth setting. Again, there was no apparent effect from the barrage. Just before dawn, another hedgehog attack by the DE and another mousetrap attempt by the PC failed to score.

It was apparent that the submarine was quite deep, more so than most Japanese submarines encountered were able or willing to go. In addition, this captain was wily; he seemed to be able to turn inside the DE or PC turning circles after he estimated when their contact would be lost. At considerable depths, hedgehogs or mouse traps were less effective than depth charges because of time lag for the bombs to reach the desired level, giving the sub captain more room for maneuver at the critical time. Depth charges did not have to be so precise.

0624. *Manlove* resumed contact at 2900 yards, this time with a marked doppler effect. The pitch was moderately down, indicating that the target was moving away at an angle to its attacker. The DE changed to a speed of 10 knots and the course was changed so as to keep a lead ahead of the sub. Preparation was made for an attack with ultra-deep settings. (The standard attack speed was 15 knots for firing of depth charges, giving the attacker enough time to get away from her own explosions. However, in cases of extreme submarine depths and the resultant longer sinking time of depth charges, a slower speed could be used.)

Initially, the target had indicated moderate down doppler with very little motion. At 900 yards, doppler decreased to slight down, then to no doppler. (No doppler would have indicated the submarine to be at or near a 90 degree angle to the attacker or was stationary.) At the end of the run, the target motion was definitely to the left. The contact was lost at 550 yards.

Contact was regained at 2550 yards. The PC also had contact and was permitted to go in on the attack. The target appeared to be moving left, and quarter traces were noted with slight down doppler, quickly changing to moderately down. The PC again fired mousetraps, but with negative results. *Manlove*, after taking some time to evaluate submarine movements, observed a moderately down doppler with a slight movement to the left of her course.

0656. The DE went in on the attack with hedgehogs, and contact was lost at about 550 yards, just after exhibiting stern traces. Six minutes later, she fired a 13 depth charge pattern with an ultra deep setting at a 6.5 knot range rate. (The foregoing may be confusing to a non-ASW person, but it isn't that complicated. Stern traces meant that the sub was showing its stern to the attacker, indicated on the recorder printout. This DE was attacking at a speed of 10 knots. With the DE making 10 knots and the range rate 6.5 knots, the sub was probably doing 3.5 knots in a stern chase. In a quarter chase, the range rate would be greater, depending on the angle at which the sub was moving away.) There were no apparent results from this last attack. *Manlove* regained contact fairly close to the explosion area. The target appeared to have moved but very slightly from the explosion vicinity. No doppler was indicated. The PC had a firm contact and went in on the attack.

0722. The PC fired mousetraps. Explosions were heard through the sound equipment on the DE and by ear, followed a moment later by an unaccountable underwater explosion!

0725. A very heavy underwater explosion followed the first one. It was believed to be near *Manlove* because the explosive effect was strong. The DE stopped to investigate small pieces of wood floating on the surface. Contact was not regained by either surface vessel and both started a retiring search.

1550. Three DEs arrived in the area to join in the hunt. They were *Bangust (DE-739)*, *Canfield (DE-262)* and *Burden R. Hastings (DE-19)*. The five vessels formed up for a box search. After two hours, oil with a distinctive diesel odor had surfaced. The new OTC in *Bangust* directed *Manlove* and the PC to investigate. At 1800, they discovered an oil slick approximately five miles long and 3000 yards wide. They stopped to retrieve some oil samples. *Manlove* and *PC-1135* searched until 0500 in the slick area, then left on another mission. The other DEs conducted a box search for the next two days.

25 March 1944. *Manlove* was advised by *Bangust* that the oil slick from the point of attack had increased to a length of 14 miles. Whereas *Manlove* was credited with an "assist", the major credit had to go to a very proud *PC-1135* which actually scored the killer blow. It may very well have been the only PC in the Navy to have received credit for the leading role in destroying an enemy submarine.

Manlove departed for Saipan to join a unit of the Fifth Fleet assembling for the Okinawa campaign. There she assisted in repelling enemy air attacks until damaged on 11 April by a kamikaze. See narrative *Iwo Jima to Okinawa — The Destroyer Escorts*.

BANGUST

A Chance Meeting with a Happy Ending

Between February 1944 and August 1945, *Bangust (DE-739)* escorted various logistic groups in support of the Central and Southern Pacific offensives. As Flagship of Escort Division 32, she flew the pennant of Commander Rowland H. Groff.

Shortly before midnight on 10 June 1944. While steaming independently from Pearl Harbor to Roi, 60 miles from her destination, a radar contact at 12 miles was tracked in Bangust's Combat Information Center. Seventeen minutes later, the commanding officer, Lieutenant Commander Charles Fraser MacNish and the Officer of The Deck saw a craft proceeding out of a rain squall. Visibility was so poor that immediate identification was not possible but, when the range closed to 3000 yards, it appeared to be a small surface craft or submarine. Upon being challenged visually, it turned away and submerged. Bridge Talker Daryl Dugan was in a position to see and hear it all and rendered his own recollection of the chance contact:

> "As the bridge talker to the 40mm gun crew, I was out in the open and able to see the action. The CIC plotted the sub continually, found she was dogging our trail and moving in closer. Undoubtedly, she took us for a cargo ship or tanker and got within 3000 yards before discovering the mistake and dived. We were after him like a hound after a rabbit. It was exciting, but I wasn't scared."

Soundman First Class John F. Hansen remembered that night:

> "I have located the papers in my file relating to the action. I was not on the radar at the time the surface contact was made but I did relieve that station at 2330 and continued to give ranges and bearings so the sub could continue to be plotted. I gave the last range, 3000 yards; then the contact disappeared from the screen. At GQ, I went to my battle station in the sound hut.

At the same time the alarm sounded, star shell illumination was fired by the ready 3" main battery. Almost at the same time the submarine submerged, the hedgehog projector was placed in readiness. A sound contact was obtained, and an underwater challenge was made without response. The enemy was attacked at once, then a second and third time without obvious result. A fourth attack, however, produced a series of hedgehog explosions.

Soundman Harold A. Lapham Jr. reflected on that night:

> "I was in a sound sleep when the GQ alarm went off. Upon arrival at my station in the CIC, I went to the surface recorder and, when contact with the target was made by the sonar gear, I entered the data on the surface recorder. Then, with the ranges and bearings taken from the sonar operator's continual reports, I plotted a course and speed of the target.
>
> The telephone circuit connecting my station with the sound hut also had a number of other stations about the ship with lookouts and fire control stations on the same line. After we completed the first hedgehog firing, I remember hearing comments from various stations that those 'ping-happy' soundmen had picked up a school of fish or a whale. Gradually, the word got around amongst those who were in the sack until GQ was sounded that there was a target, that it was an unfriendly submarine, and this was no drill.
>
> After two more non-productive runs, I again began to hear comments as to the abilities of the soundmen, etc. The fourth run started, the hedgehogs were fired, and then a few seconds later there was a powerful 'whupp', then a 'whupp-whupp', almost running together. Then the feelings of elation began in the CIC, and I could hear comments and cheering on the telephone line."

Soundman Hansen filled in more of the details:

"At GQ, my station was the sound gear, with Zeke on the range recorder. Callahan was on the device that directed the degree of tilt to the hedgehogs, and Percy Claflin was the standby sound operator. The first contact (sonar) was made one minute after midnight at 2700 yards. I was ordered to challenge the submarine IFF via morse code, which I did with no reply. The chase continued until I lost contact at 350 yards; the hedgehogs were then fired without results. During this run, as with each of the other runs, I was giving doppler effect and target angles.

On the second run, contact was regained at 0033 at a range of 700 yards. I again lost contact at about 300 yards. The hedgehogs were fired a third time with negative results. Contact was regained at 2700 yards, lost at about 300 yards, and the hedgehogs were fired once more with no effect.

On the fourth run, contact was regained at 1700 yards. There was some confusion at the start of this run. The range recorder was giving indications that it was a non-sub. Captain MacNish asked me if I thought it was the sub, and I answered in the affirmative. CIC had also informed the conn that there was wake at the bearing of the contact. With this information, the fourth run was started, and the hedgehogs were fired, resulting in the destruction of the Japanese submarine *RO-42*."

About 90 seconds after the hedgehog hits, there was a tremendous explosion under or nearly under *Bangust*. The shock was so terrific that all hands first thought that their ship had been torpedoed. Pieces of equipment such as the ventilator in the sound hut, the azimuth circle on the bridge gyro repeater, and other articles were tossed in the air. Soundman Harold Lapham recalled:

"The ear phones were knocked off my head; other men were slammed to the deck. I remember that, were it not for the surface plotter supporting me, I probably would have fallen too. The first thing I thought of was that we had been hit by a torpedo. I remember hearing the Captain asking for damage reports over the ship's loud speaker and calling for depth charges to be set on safe. Most everyone in CIC was checking out his life belt One of the lookouts stated that it looked like the whole stern of the ship came out of the water. It seemed like forever before the damage reports started trickling in. Between reports from various stations on my line, I finally heard the Captain making an announcment that we were not torpedoed. All hands let out a cheer! The report that a seam was leaking in one of the engine rooms kind of made us nervous but gradually we all settled down. Since there were no ranges or bearings coming in, I had no plotting to do. At the same time, I wondered if I had damaged the plotter gear when I was sprawled over it. A close look showed that it was still working."

Fire Controlman Bob Esheim related his experience with the hedgehogs.

"I was asleep when GQ was sounded. By the time I reached my station, we had fired the forward 3" gun, and the sub had submerged. We were tracking by sonar and fired hedgehog salvos. When the first salvo was fired, the vibrations shattered the jeweled bearings in the hedgehog aiming device. There was a backup system but it was hard to follow if one were not familiar with its use. I was sent down to see what had happened and took over the trainer's job after the second salvo, which missed. (As with a main battery gun, the trainer moved the firing device in azimuth or right or left.) You followed a bubble in a curved tube, much like in a carpenter's level. The bubble was supposed to indicate a stable vertical as the ship rolled but it would drift somewhat even when the roll stopped. You had to feel the ship movement and compensate for it.

It was on the fourth salvo when we hit the sub. I was thrown against the port rails. We were right on top of the sub when it blew up. If the netting hadn't been there, I would have gone over the side and so would the rest of the hedgehog loaders."

The damage control parties rapidly checked all lower deck compartments but found no hull damage except a small leak in the forward engine room where a welded seam had been split. The captain noted that the closest comparison he could make to the nature of that blast was that it resembled a torpedo hit without flame or the simultaneous explosion of about four or five depth charges set at a depth of about 100 feet. With the thought that some of Bangust's depth charges might have been fired accidentally, her K-guns and racks were checked but found complete. The blast must have been within the submarine.

The skipper also noted how pleased he was that, in spite of the sudden and violent nature of this explosion, there was no sign of panic or confusion. Although this was the first combat experience for the DE, all officers and men performed their duties with the coolness and efficiency of veterans, demonstrating the results of intensive training and drills.

Sonar Operator Hansen reported two additional rather weak explosions, also some hissing like escaping air and gurgling noises. There was a strong odor of diesel oil in the vicinity of the final attack.

On the early morning of 11 June, the surface of the sea was covered with a heavy oil slick about two miles long and 1/2 mile wide. In this same area, numerous small particles of cork were seen. Specimens were recovered to be forwarded to the Commander in Chief, Pacific Fleet with the action report. Oil was bubbling to the surface in the vicinity of the explosion. About two dozen large sharks were seen hunting in the flotsam. Soundman Hansen had some feelings about that:

"The ship remained at GQ the rest of the night, and Claflin and I alternated on the sound gear. At daylight, I went out on the bridge to get some air. I looked over the side and saw the sharks surrounding the ship. At no time during the four attacks on the submarine did I have any fear as I was very busy. But, when I saw the sharks, I felt a jab in my stomach. My first thought — It could have been us instead of them.

The sound gear performed very well through all of this, and the BDI scope (bearing deviation indicator) that had just been installed at Pearl Harbor was a tremendous help in maintaining contact and mid-bearing on the target."

Storekeeper Daryl Dugan's GQ station was bridge talker and also had some recollections about the sharks:

> "The water was thick with sharks. Ensign Andrews, who was in charge of the work party retrieving oil samples and cork insulation, lost his officer's hat over the side. A big shark grabbed it as it hit the water. That was frightening, thinking what would happen to a man overboard."

By late afternoon, the oil had spread to cover an area about 10 miles in diameter and was still bubbling to the surface at about the same spot. The depth of water in this locality was about 86 fathoms (516 feet). A search was carried out without regaining contact.

The Escort Division Commander recommended several citations relative to outstanding performance in darkness, adverse weather and poor visibility:

> "That all hands but one be awarded an engagement star to be worn on the Asiatic-Pacific Area Service Ribbon. That Lieutenant Frederick Augustus Lind, Jr., executive officer and chief evaluator in the CIC, be awarded a letter of commendation for outstanding performance in maintaining a continual flow of essential information to the bridge.
>
> That Gunner's Mate Second Class James Francis McKeon be awarded a letter of commendation. As gun captain of the hedgehog projector, he displayed outstanding efficiency in handling his men, ordnance and ammunition.
>
> That Lieutenant (jg) Robert Adrian Zuercher be awarded the Bronze Star Medal in recognition of exceptionally meritorious performance of his duties as antisubmarine warfare officer against the enemy submarine who demonstrated an unusual degree of skill in the employment of evasive tactics.
>
> That Soundman First Class John Francis Hansen be awarded the Bronze Star Medal in recognition of his exceptionally meritorious performance of duties as operator of the sound gear against the enemy submarine captain who continuously and efficiently tried to throw his attacker off his trail.
>
> Finally, but foremost, he recommended the commanding officer, Lieutenant Commander Charles Fraser MacNish for the award of the Legion of Merit for the exceptionally meritorious service in conning and commanding his ship so well that he succeeded in destroying an enemy submarine with promptness and precision."

Soundman Lapham referred to an entry in his diary:

> "12 June 1944. Arrived at Roi about 0900 with two brooms, one on each yard arm for 'Clean Sweep'. A Japanese flag was painted on the bridge for sinking a sub. That's it!"

This author would like to cite Harold Lapham for his efforts in procuring letters from all the petty officers quoted above in addition to his own.

Some months later, *Bangust* was caught in the iron grip of the historic "Typhoon Cobra". See her skipper's eloquent account in chapter *The Pacific Typhoons*.

BURDEN R. HASTINGS

Two Hedgehog Attacks Sufficed

Highlights of the activities of *Burden R. Hastings (DE-19)* included a passage to Tarawa, Gilbert Islands, on 12 November 1943, where she carried out pre-invasion bombardments of Japanese positions until the 20th, when the troops stormed ashore. She departed from Pearl Harbor on 28 January 1944 and proceeded to the Marshall Islands where she supported the occupation of Kwajalein on 5-6 February. She took part in the Palau-Yap-Ulithi-Woleai raids from 30 March until 1 April.

0250 on 16 June 1944. *Hastings* was about 120 miles east of Eniwetok, Marshall Islands, en route to Pearl Harbor. A surface contact was reported by SL Radar at a distance of 20,000 yards, and showing no IFF. The initial range and size of the "pip" seemed very similar to contacts on American submarines during recent training operations, although it could also be a patrol craft or subchaser. The commanding officer, Lieutenant Commander E.B. Fay, decided to close the range to 5000 yards, challenge visually with an Aldis lamp, and open fire if a proper reply were not made. The sea was moderate and visibility fair except for thunderheads and low lying clouds about 15 miles in the east, obscuring the rising moon.

The CIC estimated the target moving at 18 knots. Condition I (partial manning of battle stations) was set. Upon closing to 5000 yards at 0337, the course was altered to unmask the main battery. Three visual challenges were made at 15 second intervals. Not receiving a reply, the DE fired four star shells from two of her 3" caliber main battery guns to illuminate the target. After the second star shell burst, the target submerged.

0344. The CIC estimated the range at 2500 yards, and speed was reduced to 10 knots to prevent over-running the submarine. Ten minutes later, sonar contact was made dead ahead at 1700 yards. *Hastings* continued her course to make a hedgehog attack on the submarine's port quarter. No hits were recorded on this run.

The ship turned sharply and increased speed to 15 knots to open the range as quickly as possible. Contact was regained at 1500 yards; the DE turned toward the target and slowed to a hedgehog attack speed of 10 knots. The submarine depth was estimated at 240 feet. Echoes were strong. There was no doppler, and the target was drifting slowly to the left. *Hastings* made a second hedgehog run by firing on the recorder and on the leading cut of the bearing. Nine seconds after the pattern struck the water, a hit was indicated by a heavy explosion felt throughout the entire ship and by a phosphorescent flash in the water. The ship then proceeded over the spot of the explosion and rolled two depth charges set at 200 feet and two at 300 feet; markers were dropped simultaneously.

Five seconds after all of the dropped charges were thought to have detonated, a tremendous explosion was felt, throwing out the circuit breaker on the forward main motor and the lube oil circulating pump. In addition, gyroscope power was lost for about 15 minutes. The explosion was believed to be internal, occurring about 2-1/2 minutes after the hedgehog hit. Use of the dead reckoning tracer was lost without its gyro repeater but, fortunately, guiding flares had been dropped. Although a thorough search was made of the area in a retiring search plan, no further sonar contact was made.

At sunrise, oil was rising and a moderate slick was seen in the area of the flares and markers. Debris started to surface, and the boat was put over to recover as much of it as possible. The vicinity was heavily infested with sharks, and an increase in the wind created enough sea to make recovery of flotsam difficult. However, by 1042 when the boat was taken aboard, its crew had collected a considerable amount of deck planking up to eight feet; internal, lacquered and colored wood scraps with Japanese characters; all manner of crew possessions, a few with human flesh attached.

Throughout the day, the ship searched the area as oil continued to rise at the original point of the explosion. Later in the afternoon, the slick increased in size to about one by four miles and became progressively heavier. The quantity of oil rising from the bottom was sufficiently heavy to color the bow waves dark brown. In response to radio dispatched orders from the Commander of Task Force 57 at 1900, *Hastings* resumed her course for Pearl Harbor.

Upon arrival on 23 June, an officer from Intelligence translated the Japanese inscriptions and markings. The writing on an oak box top identified the submarine as *RO-44*, and an aluminum plate listed electrical parts. A stainless steel deck plate was part of a main vent valve. All writing was identified as Japanese, the translations being "do not open," or referenced to religious papers, etc. The flesh samples were thought to be human by the Division Medical Officer. In accordance with his recommendation, however, the remains were delivered to the hospital for positive identification. The destroyed Japanese sub was subsequently identified as *RO-44*

During the remainder of the war, *Burden R. Hastings* operated as a convoy escort, plane guard and a unit in various hunter-killer groups in the area of the Marshall, Gilbert, and Western Caroline Islands.

RIDDLE and DAVID W. TAYLOR

Depth Charges Completed the Deadly Assault

In June 1944, after serving as an escort between Majuro Atoll and Manus Island, *Riddle (DE-185)* was active in the Marshall and Marianas Islands.

Late afternoon on 4 July. The DE was screening fueling operations with Task Group 50.17, ahead of the main body of six oil tankers and one escort carrier. Soundman Second Class W.H. Hundley Jr. was echo ranging. He didn't expect anything out of the ordinary, just carrying out his sound sweep and remain alert until relieved of his watch. It was a sunny and clear day with a smooth sea and a balmy, tropical breeze, perfect for this national holiday. Suddenly, he stiffened. A ping bounced back at him clear as a bell!

"Contact! Bearing 250 degrees, range 1900 yards!"

The Officer of The Deck lost no time. All ASW stations were manned on three blasts of the chemical alarm. Soundman Second Class E.L. Hite, whose battle station was on the sound stack, relieved Hundley. On report of contact by TBS, the Task Group Commander ordered the formation to execute an "Emergency Six Turn" (sixty degree turn to port). Echoes were sharp and metallic with marked down doppler. The recorder showed a stern aspect and a 10 knot range rate. By this time, the commanding officer, Lieutenant Commander Roland H. Cramer, was on the bridge and in control.

A standard five charge urgent barrage was ordered and set. A target course was established by the CIC during the approach with firing time slightly ahead of the recorder. Excellent metallic echoes with clear doppler indications of the target aspect (angle to the DE) were experienced on this and all subsequent approaches. A search started after firing to avoid ships in the convoy, but the wily sub captain had turned into the ship formation wakes. After circling the attack point at a radius of 1000 yards, a search was commenced.

Contact was regained at 1250 yards, 18 minutes after the urgent attack. Speed was reduced to 10 knots, and an approach commenced for a hedgehog run with a deep setting and to be fired on the recorder. Steady sonar data with moderate to sharp down doppler was obtained. The dead reckoning tracer (DRT) had run off the board while on the 200 yard scale and was reset at 2000 yards per inch in preparation for search, too small for an attack. The attempt to run a plot on this scale was unsuccessful, and no information from CIC was available during this approach. Contact was lost at 350 yards, confirming the estimate of a deep target. The recorder operator complained of difficulty in selecting firing time from the trace (because of sub's depth). A pattern was fired on the best available traces between 700 and 350 yards. The last left cut-on was not heard by the conning officer, possibly because of TBS transmission then coming in. It was felt that the pattern missed astern of the submarine. The destroyer *David W. Taylor (DD-551)*, assigned as assisting ship, was requested to stand clear while the range was opened for a second hedgehog attack.

Contact was regained at 600 yards. The approach commenced after opening out to 1400 yards on the target's starboard quarter. This aspect was maintained throughout the run with bearings drawing steadily to the right. Contact was lost at 350 yards, and the pattern was fired with a deep recorder setting. This was thought to be a good run but no detonation followed. There was a hang-fire on one of the missiles which fired 30 seconds late. The CIC provided continuous information throughout the run, confirming target movement. The CIC also obtained sonar data by voice tube from the sound hut and relayed it to the conn over an interior telephone circuit.

Contact was regained at 750 yards. The ship's heading steadied on the target at 1000 yards off. The aspect appeared almost bow-on. Slight up-doppler was reported, and a slow bearing drift to the right was also noted. Sonar information on target movement was confirmed by the CIC. Again, no detonation followed what appeared to be a good attack. It was now thought that the great depth of the submarine relative to hedgehog runs was the problem. With the good sound conditions then prevailing and the established ability to regain contact, it was decided to attack with deep-set depth charges.

Contact was regained at 1000 yards and opened to 1400 yards for the approach. During the run, the target appeared deep with a quarter or stern aspect and with strong down-doppler. The bearing at first drifted left, changing to right at about 750 yards.

Just prior to loss of contact, the left cut steadied and reversed slightly. This may have been a normal broadening of the target but, in the light of the submarine's previous tactics, it was thought possible that it indicated the beginning of a fish-tail maneuver. A full pattern set deep was fired just inside the last reported right cut. The CIC confirmed the target movement throughout the approach, and it was felt that this pattern was correctly placed.

The estimated range, bearing, and target course of the submarine were passed to *Taylor* as she made contact close to the green marker of the prior attack and dropped her charges. Two minutes later, *Riddle* was again headed for the attack point and was approaching when a heavy underwater explosion occurred directly ahead in the vicinity of attack. The approach was continued through the area, but no contacts were obtained. By sundown, oil and debris had broken the surface. *Riddle* screened *Taylor* while the latter recovered debris.

A box search of the area, two ships abreast on 15 mile legs, commenced at 1944, but no further contacts were made. The following day, an oil slick was observed to stretch about nine miles down wind from the point of attack, from which samples were obtained. The search was abandoned in early afternoon in the belief that the depth charge attacks had succeeded in causing destruction of the enemy submarine. On passing through the area five days later, a slick with some fresh oil patches in it was observed extending roughly 12 miles from the attack point. A post-war review of Japanese naval records confirmed that submarine *I-10* had been sunk by the two American vessels.

On 4 October, *Riddle* got underway with an escort group to screen the sortie of a carrier and fueling group from Seeadler Harbor for the Philippine Invasion. In the Iwo Jima area in February 1945, she acted as antiaircraft and antisubmarine patrol and escorted various fleet units in their operations in that bloody battle area.

On 12 April, the DE was on a picket station off Okinawa when attacked by two *kamikazes*. She splashed the first but was crashed by the second. See chapter *Iwo Jima to Okinawa — The Destroyer Escorts*.

WILLIAM C. MILLER

Too Many Depth Charges for this Sub

As a unit of Task Group 54.9, Fifth Fleet, *William C. Miller (DE-259)* screened the ships of the Tarawa garrison group and patrolled in area "Longsuit" off the invasion beaches into early December 1943.

1944 proved to be a busy year for *Miller*. She earned six of her seven battle stars supporting the capture and occupation of Kwajalein and Majuro, Eniwetok and Tinian. During the Saipan screening operations, the ship claimed her fame in antisubmarine warfare.

2120 on 13 July 1944, *Miller* was participating in a submarine search as part of a hunter-killer group, of which the commanding officer of the High Speed Transport *Gilmer (APD-11)* was OTC (Officer in Tactical Command). *Miller* launched an attack on a Japanese submarine in an action that lasted eight hours.

A patrol plane sighted a Japanese submarine submerging 78 miles from Rorogattan Point, Saipan. Accordingly, *Miller* and *Gilmer* raced to the area of the sighting. Shortly after midnight, the DE and APD arrived at the point of submergence and commenced searching. *Gilmer* kept station 4500 yards on the port beam of *Miller*. Although *Gilmer* flew the OTC pennant, its ASW capability was limited, and the primary engagement responsibility was passed to the DE.

Seven hours later, contact was first obtained by *Miller*, range 1700 yards. The skipper, Lieutenant Commander D.F. Francis, made his attack at 15 knots, and a 13 depth charge pattern, medium setting, was dropped without apparent damage to the sub. The range was opened, and contact was regained at 1500 yards, followed by a second depth charge pattern of 13, but with a deep setting. The dead reckoning trace showed that the submarine had been moving at about 1.5 knots.

That pattern appeared to have proved disastrous to the submarine. Nonetheless, the range was once more opened for attack. Contact was regained at a range of 2600 yards. An approach was made for the third attack, but it was interrupted when sighting pieces of wood popping to the surface about 500 yards distant, one point off the starboard bow. One minute later, a very heavy and prolonged underwater explosion was heard and felt close aboard. The recorder trace showed this explosion to last about five times as long as a depth charge explosion, and the "water hammer" effect on *Miller* was at least twice as severe. It was also recorded by *Gilmer*, whose skipper stated he felt it to be three times the shock of a depth charge.

Immediately afterward, a large boil, approximately 50 yards in diameter and well above the surface, was seen slightly forward of the starboard beam. The third 13 depth charge pattern, deep set, was laid over the explosion. The range to the sub at the time of the explosion was 350 yards. At this time, sonar indicated the sub to be dead in the water. The recorder trace showed that the depth charges in the third pattern were dropped directly over the sub, completing whatever devastation had been wrought by the second salvo.

Contact was never regained after the third attack. The depth charge barrage had literally torn the submarine apart. The destroyer escort closed the oil slick and debris and lowered a boat to investigate. The boat soon recovered small pieces of cork insulating material, fractured wooden decking with Japanese characters, and a fur-lined Japanese seaman's cap (quoting the action report) "...the owner presumably no longer having need of same". Additional objects also recovered were: One fur-lined cap with metal Japanese naval insignia, one long woolen undershirt, one long woolen underdrawers.

There was almost no chance of survivors even if the enemy wanted to survive, which they usually didn't. There were samples of pieces of flesh that the pharmacist mate believed to be were human lung tissue. He noted that the blood was fresh and the odor unspoiled. This may appear to be a bit bizarre, but DEs wanted credit for their kills and no details were overlooked in gathering proof!

While *Miller* was picking up samples of debris, *Gilmer* circled the area without making contact. *Miller* resumed a retiring search plan at the direction of the OTC. The oil was still gushing to the surface while the small boat was investigating and, just before noon, the slick had extended to 3-1/2 miles long and 3/4 mile wide.

The depth of water was approximately 2000 fathoms. The sea was smooth with a slight swell. The sky was overcast with heavy rain squalls throughout the area during the time of the antisubmarine attacks. Visibility varied from 10,000 down to 400 yards at various times during the action. The executive officer, Lieutenant Richard Small, in charge of the Combat Information Center, was of great assistance in regaining contact when rain squalls blotted from view the green dye markers of previous attacks. Soundman Second Class Harold C. Wilson was alert in picking up initial contact. He and sonar officer, Lieutenant (jg) Arthur G. Keywan, were skillful in regaining and holding contact through wakes and depth charge knuckles.

The retiring search was abandoned late in the afternoon. It was based on the opinion of both *Gilmer* and *Miller* that, had this submarine survived, contact would have been regained; all evidence pointed to the fact that the enemy submarine was destroyed.

In due course, *William C. Miller* was credited with the sinking of Japanese submarine *I-6*.

After a number of convoys, *Miller* sortied from Pearl Harbor on 6 February 1945 to participate in the assault on Iwo Jima. After that action was completed, she participated in more convoys and then joined the Third Fleet in its attack on the Japanese home islands until the enemy surrendered on 2 September 1945.

With a twinkle in his eye, former Seaman Bob Meyer related to this author the next serious encounter by the *William C. Miller*. It might have been dubbed "Operation Laundry", where Meyers was stationed. After being away from American shores for 18 months, the word was passed to the crew that they were homeward bound. Expecting to look their very best, practically all of the men broke out their blues for washing and pressing. With such heavy demand, it was hard to exercise normal care, and a lot of the blues were shrunk. On approaching San Francisco, the word was passed over the loud speaker that the uniform of the day would be undress blues. Said Meyer:

> "That was when all hell broke loose!"

A lot of the men couldn't button their pants; others looked at sleeve cuffs terminating somewhere between elbows and wrists or pant legs falling several inches above the ankles. When the outraged crew descended upon the laundry for explanation, they were told that they probably ate too much and had grown a few inches while the ship was in the far Pacific!

Fortunately, the ship was not scheduled for immediate admiral's inspection.

WYMAN

Two Submarines Painted on the Bridge

While with Task Group 12.2, with the OTC in *Hoggatt Bay (CVE-75)*, *Wyman (DE-38)* departed from Eniwetok on 5 July 1944 and headed for the antisubmarine operating area. En route, she investigated a submarine contact which had been depth-charged by *Lake (DE-301)*. *Wyman* fired one hedgehog barrage but without success. Other escorts in the Task Group were *Reynolds (DE-42)* and *Donaldson (DE-44)*

While patrolling her station just past midnight on 19 July, *Wyman* was ordered to investigate a surface radar contact. She closed the range until contact was lost, then commenced a sonar search.

After missing a kill the previous month, *Wyman's* skipper, Lieutenant Commander E.P. Parker, and his crew were more than anxious to make up for it. *Wyman* picked up a strong metallic echo and fired a full pattern of hedgehogs with negative results. She opened the range to start a second attack as *Reynolds (DE-42)* arrived on the scene.

0116. *Wyman* regained contact at 2850 yards and immediately turned to the bearing. The first echoes had pronounced up doppler, although the plot did not bear this out. As the approach started, doppler dropped to zero. The bearing which had been steady began to drift slowly right, indicating that the sub was turning away. The echo was clear and strong, and there was no doubt at any time but that they were making an attack on a submarine.

Wyman launched a second full pattern of 24 bombs at a range rate of 9.5 knots – dead on the target! Fifteen seconds after firing and 5 seconds after the bombs hit the water, a series of violent explosions rocked the DE as the depth bombs blew the submarine apart!

The explosions were so close together that it was impossible to count the exact number; estimates ranged from three to ten. The sequence and timing of the explosions agreed with observations made by *Reynolds*. *Wyman* officially recorded the explosion of five projectiles, causing a phosphorescent flash in the water. The violent underwater explosions produced a shock in *Reynolds*, 2500 yards away.

Wyman opened the range, attempting to regain contact. Meanwhile, almost continuous light explosions were noted but could not be identified. Five minutes later, a very violent one took place, followed in 30 seconds by another of similar intensity. They were heavier than those made by depth charges and shook the ship severely. It was first thought that she was struck by a torpedo, and repair parties were ordered to check for damage. They reported the ship to be secure except for two broken light bulbs.

Wyman then circled sharply and passed through the firing point in an attempt to regain contact. A mushy echo was heard, believed to be from an explosion knuckle, but no solid contact was obtained. *Reynolds* took station 3000 yards on *Wyman's* starboard beam, and a box search was immediately started and continued throughout the night. The area was scoured without pause for 31 hours with no further contacts, indicating that the target had been destroyed.

The oil slick was first seen by planes from *Hoggatt Bay* which signaled the two surface vessels to return to the vicinity of the firing position. On arrival that evening, an oil slick was found extending 1-1/2 miles in length and 200 yards wide. Oil was steadily rising to the surface, and the slick grew rapidly until it covered an area 10 miles long and 2 miles wide. Oil was still rising in large quantities when the search was later abandoned. There was considerable debris, and the ship's boat was lowered to collect samples, including some oil cans, teakwood, a candle, many with Japanese characters.

Unfortunately, before the operation could be completed, the ship's boat was mistaken for a surfacing submarine by an aircraft from the carrier and was strafed. Two men were injured, forcing *Wyman* to abort the debris hunt and transfer the wounded to *Hoggatt Bay* for medical attention. However, *Reynolds* remained in the vicinity.

Additional kill evidence was recovered. The water depth in the area where the attack took place is approximately 19,000 feet, probably the reason oil and debris were so late in surfacing in quantity. An object which appeared to be the top of a human skull, including the hair, was seen, but it drifted past and was lost before it could be positively identified. There was little doubt but what *Wyman* carried out a successful and wholly destructive attack.

Oil from the sunken submarine, identified by a postwar examination of Japanese records as *RO-48*, continued to bubble up in copious quantities for 31 hours into the next day. Satisfied that the kill was definite, *Wyman* rejoined TG 12.2.

Daybreak on 28 July. *Hoggatt Bay* sighted a submarine, identified as a Japanese I Class, surfacing 15,000 yards from the formation. The sub apparently saw the Task Group concurrently because it immediately submerged. Also, at the same time on board *Wyman*, a lookout reported an unidentified object in approximately the same position seen by the *Hoggatt Bay* lookouts. Two minutes later, *Wyman* and *Reynolds* were ordered to the vicinity to conduct a search.

On approaching the area of the sighting, both ships reduced speed to the standard 15 knots to commence searching. The screen commander on *Reynolds* took over direction of the search, and *Wyman* was ordered to take station on the port beam of *Reynolds*, distance 3000 yards. Before she could gain her station, however, *Wyman* obtained a sound contact at 2500 yards. Her course was altered and speed was reduced to 10 knots. The hedgehog projector was made ready for firing.

The echo was sharp, clear and metallic. No doppler was detected and the bearing, steady at first, moved slowly to the left in the latter stages of the attack. The DRT plot showed a target movement of only 300 yards throughout the entire run. Screw noises were not heard at any time. It seemed reasonable to believe that the submarine was attempting to run silent, moving only enough to maintain stability.

Using the chemical recorder to obtain firing time, a full pattern of 24 charges was fired. Seventeen seconds later, a number of explosions occurred, causing a concussion similar to a deep set depth charge!

It was followed by water turbulence at the point of attack. Although these explosions were too close together to be counted accurately, their number was estimated at 10. As *Wyman* opened the range, two additional minor explosions were noted, followed by an extremely violent one. At the time of the final explosion, *Wyman* was approximately 1600 yards from the point of attack.

In the meantime, *Reynolds*, commanded by Lieutenant Commander E.P. Adams, had also gained contact and kept her position well clear on the starboard beam of *Wyman*. She commenced an approach as soon as *Wyman* was clear and closed to about 600 yards from the attack point when the final explosion took place. She continued to close and fired a full pattern of 24 hedgehogs, but without results. *Wyman* again approached the explosion point, crossing it but was unable to regain contact. However, a strong wake echo with a smaller fading echo in the background was noted. At this time, the start of an oil slick with a strong diesel odor was seen, along with a large piece of deck planking. The latter was recovered by *Reynolds*.

Reynolds crossed the explosion point again without regaining contact. Immediately afterward, a box search with both vessels participating was commenced by the Escort Commander. The search was pursued throughout the night without results.

By morning, the oil slick had expanded to a length of seven miles down wind from the explosion area and a width of one mile with scattered patches covering a larger area, later increasing to 15 by three miles. Since the oil cover was so thick, *Wyman* obtained samples by lowering buckets over the side and skimming the oil from the tops with ladles. Numerous small pieces of cork were floating in the oil. *Reynolds*, at the leeward end of the slick, recovered pieces of deck planking and wood remnants, some with Japanese characters. Samples were forwarded to the Engineering Research Laboratory at Annapolis, Maryland.

Search of the area continued throughout the day and night of 29 July and the afternoon of the 30th. The odor of diesel oil was prevalent throughout the search, the oil coming from the ill-fated Japanese submarine I-55.

The violent explosion five minutes after the hitting salvo was believed to be a from a self-destructive mechanism in the submarine.

In his report, *ComCortDiv 49*, Commander R.E. Lockwood, pointed out that *Wyman* had two sound contacts, fired a total of only three hedgehog salvos, and destroyed two submarines. Such a record reflects great credit upon the commanding officer and the ship. However, the *Wyman* captain was quick to recognize two external factors for his victory; one was the accuracy of *Hoggatt Bay* lookouts in designating the area of visual contacts; the second was the skill and dedication of the *Reynolds* CIC in supplying extremely accurate plots.

With the dissolution of TG 12.2 on 9 August, *Wyman* continued in escort operations between the Marshalls and Marianas and subsequently to support the Philippine, Iwo Jima and Okinawa invasions.

SAMUEL S. MILES

Bad News for the Enemy in the Air or under the Sea

The first fleet operation in which *Samuel S. Miles* participated commenced on 29 March 1944. In company with five other DEs, *Miles* escorted six fleet oilers in support of the Fifth Fleet's carrier raids on Palau, Yap, Ulithi, and Woleai. After a few days of patrol duty off Majuro, *Miles* escorted an oiler group to fuel Task Force 58 near New Guinea in support of landing operations at Hollandia.

Miles got under way from Eniwetok on 13 June in company with two other escorts, convoying three fleet oilers to a fueling rendezvous off Saipan. The fueling group spent three days in the area east of Saipan during the assaults and landings being carried out by American forces on that island. On the evening of 17 June, off the southeast coast of Saipan, *Miles* had her first action with the enemy, opening fire on five torpedo planes attacking the fueling group. The planes turned away, and none were seen to be hit.

On the afternoon of the next day, while this DE was fueling from the oiler *Neshanic (AO-71)*, about ten enemy aircraft, Zekes and Haps, attacked the formation with dive bombing and low level bombing runs. *Miles* was in a very disadvantageous position. Lines and the hose were quickly cast off with oil unavoidably spilling into the pristine waters. She tried to get clear of the heavier ships so that more effective gunfire protection could be offered to the oilers.

The planes split in two groups, understandably concentrating their attack on the most valuable targets, the oilers. *Saranac (AO-74)* and *Neshanic* were both hit aft, three men being lost over the side of *Neshanic*. *Saugatuck (AO-75)* sustained some damage and casualties from a near miss. *Miles* was ordered to pick up the men lost by *Neshanic*. Only two were recovered.

Three planes were seen by the *Miles'* crew to have splashed. She took five planes under fire and downed two of them. A patrol was maintained by her around *Saranac*, which was dead in the water, until after midnight. The oiler was then able to proceed to Eniwetok with *Miles* and another DE as escorts. On 20 June, a Japanese patrol plane was taken under fire, but it remained just out of range.

21 August. *Miles* joined Hunter-Killer Task Group 30.7, comprising in addition to herself *Hoggatt Bay (CVE-75)*, *Bebas (DE-10)*, *Steele (DE-8)*, and *Seid (DE-256)*. The Task Group Commander was Captain W.V. Saunders, commanding officer of the *Hoggatt Bay*. The Screen Commander was in *Bebas*, Commander T. F. Fowler, *ComCortDiv 8*. *Miles* was zigzagging in station on the port bow of the carrier.

The Task Group took station as an advance HUK, screening from 45 miles ahead of Task Force 38 as it entered the Philippine Sea for the first pre-invasion air strikes about 6 September. During the invasion of Palau, the HUK performed antisubmarine search and patrol duties among the Philippines, Palau and Saipan from 15 September until 3 October.

The weather was poor, – wind force and sea condition five to six. There was a high overcast with intermittent light rain. However, with a full moon, the visibility was about 8000 yards. *Miles* was pitching and rolling 30 to 40 degrees. The sonar conditions were good - assured range 1900 yards with 2000 to 3000 yards possible. There was considerable quenching due to the sound head coming out of the water during the rolling and pitching. The depth was 3000 fathoms.

On 3 October, TG 30.7 was searching the area where a submarine was reported sighted on the previous day. At 0320, the *Miles* radar operator reported a surface contact, range 16,900 yards; a plot was started immediately.

0337. The forward starboard lookout reported an object on the surface dead ahead. Three minutes later, a surfaced submarine was seen moving slowly from starboard to port, classified by the recognition officer as an I-class Japanese submarine. The radar range was 6000 yards. Immediately after the sighting, the contact submerged. *Miles* began a search and made sonar contact at 1900 yards.

The DE's speed was slowed to 10 knots for a hedgehog attack. Good contact was held until about 450 yards when the echo became mushy. However, the attack was carried out with negative results. It was determined that the submarine had made a sharp turn to port, and *Miles* had finished the run on a water knuckle. (Compressed water from a sharp turn by a sub will return an echo of sorts.) *Steele* was detached to assist, arriving as *Miles* was regaining contact.

0412. Contact was regained at 700 yards and was opened to 1500 yards for a second attack. The sea was still quite rough. A muffled complaint was heard from the sound shack:

> "If you can keep the sound head in the water once in a while, we might be able to regain contact."

Echoes were excellent during the approach. The second hedgehog attack was followed 15 seconds later by two exploding projectiles, indicating a submarine depth of about 150 feet.

After another 25 seconds, there was a terrific underwater explosion close aboard on the starboard quarter! Like many of her previously successful sister ships, the first impression was that the ship had been torpedoed. The violence of this explosion was such that it was heard and felt by the remainder of the Task Group 12 miles distant. It gave *Miles* a severe shaking up and caused some damage. Sonar, radar, and TBS were temporarily disabled, a result of power loss. One antenna was snapped off at the mast and crashed to the bridge. Light bulbs and glass fittings were broken throughout the entire ship. Impulsively, the recognition officer shouted, "who has my helmet?"

As the sonar gear was temporarily out, *Steele* was ordered to take up the attack. Three runs were made through the area without regaining contact. At 0455, *Miles* secured from GQ. A generous captain, Lieutenant Commander Brousseau, announced over the PA system, "secure from general quarters, set war cruising. We'll have late reveille this morning at 0630!"

Operation Observant was started and completed with negative results. Several small pieces of wood were seen, but rough seas made it difficult and dangerous to pick them up. By 1350, an oil slick was sighted, four to six miles long and one to two miles wide. Many attempts were made to get oil samples but were frustrated by the state of the sea and wind. Her sonar gear now restored, *Miles* and *Steele* made a thorough search of the entire area, especially upwind from the slick, without contact. The two ships rejoined the Task Group.

The enemy submarine had undoubtedly been destroyed as a result of being hit by two projectiles, leading to its demolition as evidenced by the secondary underwater explosion. On the afternoon of 5 October, planes from *Hoggatt Bay* reported oil was still bubbling up at the scene of attack. From the commanding officer's report:

> "The performance of all hands was so excellent that it is almost impossible to pick out any individual or group for special praise. The sinking of the submarine was a result of perfect teamwork by all departments. The speed with which the hedgehogs were reloaded was exceptionally praiseworthy, considering the rolling and pitching of the ship. The "black gang" (engineers with oil-stained faces) did particularly well in maintaining power and repairing damage in the engine room. The work of the ASW officer, the CIC personnel, and sonar operators in feeding a stream of information left nothing to be desired."

A class "B" assessment was awarded in the antisubmarine action, an example of the unbending Navy requirements before a definite kill could be acknowledged. Post-war examination of Japanese records, however, confirmed the destruction of submarine *I-177* by *Miles*. In fact, much more may have been accomplished. A key officer, a specialist in *kaiten* or suicide submarines was on board and was lost with the submarine.

The HUK Group was ordered to patrol an area east of Luzon, Philippine Islands to give antisubmarine assistance to the carrier groups attacking Luzon in support of the Leyte Operation. On 20 October, the Killer Group was given a special assignment to furnish air, surface and antisubmarine protection to the cruisers *Canberra (CA-70)* and *Houston (CL-81)*, both of which had been damaged in action off Formosa (Taiwan) and were under tow to Ulithi.

From 4 November 1944 until 27 January 1945, *Miles* was assigned to duty with fleet oilers and spent the majority of her time in the fueling areas east of the Philippines in support of the Leyte and Luzon operations. During February 1945, she was engaged in the operation for the invasion of Iwo Jima, escorting transports in the Marine landing forces. *Samuel S. Miles* now had to prepare for her gravest trial in the war. See chapter *Iwo Jima to Okinawa — The Destroyer Escorts.*

DISASTER AT MOROTAI

Shelton and Rowell in Their Tragic Hour

Until now, readers could be lulled into believing that anti-submarine warfare in the Pacific was a "high tech" shooting gallery with DEs knocking off enemy submarines in comparative safety to themselves. This narrative should allay such comforting misconceptions.

Shelton (DE-407) and *Richard M. Rowell (DE-403)* had been occupied with convoy activities from Eniwetok to Seeadler Harbor, Admiralty Islands, until mid-September 1944 when both were transferred to Task Force 77, a segment of the Seventh Fleet. They were assigned to protect an air support group during the landings on Morotai, Dutch East Indies. *Rowell* rescued two downed pilots en route.

Rear Admiral T.L. Sprague was in overall command. There were six escort carriers in the force, code-named "Taffy 3", destined to fight for their lives three weeks later at the Battle off Samar. The same fate awaited three of the six destroyer escorts in the screen, *Dennis (DE-405)*, *John C. Butler (DE-339)*, and *Raymond (DE-341)*.

Ray Sullivan was Third Class Sonarman on the *Richard M. Rowell*:

> "The troops went ashore on 15 September 1944, and there was practically no opposition. We had numerous calls to battle stations, but nothing happened. This was our first operation and, other than rescuing pilots in the water and routine chores, we were lulled into a period of boredom."

0745 On 17 September. *Rowell* made a possible sound contact but lost it before it could be developed. At noon the following day, seven men parachuted from a B-24 Liberator which had been circling overhead with one engine out of commission. One chute failed to open. The Liberator crash-landed just off the beach in shallow water. Three men, apparently uninjured, were seen standing on the wing when the spray subsided. Small boats were standing by. The pilot and the injured were transferred by *Rowell* to a nearby carrier.

0808 on 3 October, off the coast of Morotai. A considerable sea was running, a result of unsettled weather conditions during the preceding three days. Visibility was excellent. Lieutenant Ejlif Schmidt was well positioned to know what happened:

> "I was CIC officer and assistant gunnery officer of *Shelton* and had just taken over the watch that morning. A TBS message came from the carrier *Midway (CVE-63)*. — 'A torpedo just missed us and is coming your way!' I sounded GQ and ordered all ahead full but, before I could give the helm an order, the captain was on the bridge and took over. I was headed to my battle station in CIC when I looked out and saw the torpedo wake. I thought it was going to pass astern when it seemed to veer toward us, and the explosion followed, leaving us dead in the water. With the high probability of abandoning ship, I busied myself with the disposal of the coding machine, classified documents, code books, etc. With the above accomplished, I was able to go back to the stern to look at the damage. I could see that the stateroom where I would have been asleep if I had not been on watch was obliterated!"

Shelton was taken completely by surprise. She did not have sonar or any other type of contact. The torpedo wake was sighted only a few seconds before it hit and before the conn could take evasive measures. Soundman Third Class Sullivan on *Rowell* wrote in his diary:

> "I had just got off the 0400-0800 watch as sonarman and was eating breakfast in the forward mess when GQ sounded. A message over the PA system stated '*Shelton* has just been torpedoed!' The stricken DE was about 500 yards off our starboard quarter, and we were dispatched to assist her while the rest of the force took off."

Lieutenant C.R. Disharoon was first lieutenant and damage control officer on *Shelton* and gave this account of his damage survey:

> "I was in Combat (CIC) at the moment of the explosion, and there was very little shock or noise in that vicinity. As soon as the hedgehog missiles that had been blown high in the air had all dropped, I immediately ran aft to survey the damage.
>
> The main deck aft had been blasted upward about 45-50 degrees. The main deck forward was mostly intact. At midship, the main deck was inclined forward and terminated in a large buckled frame (130), particularly noticeable on the port side. The after bulkhead of the deck house had been inclined forward at an angle of about five degrees to the vertical.
>
> The first below deck compartment I entered was the forward of two living compartments aft. I called for sounding rods and emergency flood lights. There was approximately a foot of oil sloshing over from the adjacent after living compartment. I shut the door between the compartments, thereby cutting off leakage from one compartment to another.
>
> We started sounding an underwater compartment where we believed that flooding could be stopped. Access to that compartment was made through a hatch. A quick survey showed the after end of the space to be dry, but a sharp decline in the deck forward terminated in a foot deep buckle. There was about 2-1/2 feet of pure oil in the forward port end of this compartment.
>
> About this time, a fire main cutout valve carried away, and considerable water entered the compartment until the engine room closed the valve. Soundings were then com-

menced in a number of areas. One magazine had no sounding tube and, with about three feet of oil above the scuttle access, no effort was made to enter that compartment. It was believed to be dry though because it was a centerline tank.

One could proceed no further aft as wreckage was piled high at that point. Soundings were again made, and we found one stores compartment to be dry and another flooded full. The provisions compartment and two magazines were flooded full.

The after end of the ship was a mass of twisted wreckage open to the sea and, for all practical purposes, not a part of the ship except for the weight of the metal. The port shaft alley sounded three feet of oil and the starboard shaft alley sounded three feet of water. In the meantime, all gasoline handy-billy pumps were broken out to start pumping flooding compartments. However, the handy-billies would not handle the oil and had to be secured. An electric submersible pump was then rigged. At first, it took a good suction but, upon striking pure oil, petered out.

About this time, I went to the bridge to report the soundings and general condition of the ship and that I believed she would stay afloat long enough to be towed a reasonable distance. The ship had about a three degree port list, was rolling in a running sea with a good, quick roll, indicating no danger of capsizing. There was about seven feet of freeboard at the lowest point, customarily about 10 feet. The ship appeared to be in a stable condition.

The captain passed the word to commence jettisoning topside weight, and a bucket brigade was started in the flooded compartments. Upon returning aft, I inspected the outside port side skin of the ship. The hull was opened below the waterline, evidently forcing the oil up through a rupture in the deck. Accordingly, the bucket brigade continued with hopes we could remove all oil and attempt to patch up decks by welding. No progress was made in reducing the liquid level below but no increase was noted relative to a mark previously made on a bulkhead.

In the meantime, the handy-billies were being rigged to pump out other compartments through the sounding tubes. Also, at this time, the fire room personnel tried unsuccessfully to take a suction on fuel tanks. However, the engine room did take a good suction on both shaft alleys.

I went forward to check on rigging for being towed at sea. When work started, the word was passed, 'Fire in the handling room aft'. I rushed to the scene, passing orders en route to bring two fire hoses aft. However, the fire hoses were not needed because the problem was the after heating system steam line, carried away and creating quite a noise and a lot of vapor resembling smoke. The steam line was secured and work continued once more. Quite a lot of difficulty was encountered in rigging the handy-billies to the sounding tubes due to inaccessibility of the tubes. In fact, a suction was never started as orders were then received from the Task Unit Commander to abandon ship.

So, while the crew was transferring to another ship, the Chief Bosun's Mate, the Chief Machinist's Mate and myself went forward and opened up below deck hatches to facilitate the sinking of the ship. We were aft as far as possible when we were ordered to evacuate. Naturally, before abandoning, fires were secured in the boilers, and I was informed the after engine room was leaking through the hull to the extent of 50 gallons per minute. Under such conditions, the compartment would soon fill to the waterline."

The above outstanding report by the first lieutenant was submitted in the action report as a numerical list and was converted into simplified prose by this author. Lieutenant Disharoon was cited for outstanding performance of duty under the most trying conditions.

Lieutenant J. P. Wolfe, on his own initiative, entered the damaged and rapidly filling compartments to determine if all surviving personnel had been evacuated. His work in directing the removal of the wounded and their subsequent transfer to the rescuing vessel made possible the successful completion of this difficult operation without further loss of life. When the wounded had been removed and cared for, Lieutenant Wolfe led a damage control party into the flooded compartments and materially aided the first lieutenant in controlling damage.

0925. Subsequent to the torpedoing, *Shelton* made a sonar contact with the enemy submarine, range 1000 yards. As submarine screw noises were distinctly audible and her underwater position defined, it was concluded that the enemy was maneuvering to conduct a second torpedo attack against the vessel. *Richard M. Rowell*, at that time conducting Operation Observant for the submarine, was requested to return to the immediate area in order to intercept *Shelton's* contact. When *Rowell* had closed to within 500 yards of the submarine position and had not made sound contact, pinging by *Shelton* indicated the range was down to 900 yards. This position was transmitted to *Rowell* by voice radio.

Rowell dropped three depth charges exactly on the bearing indicated by *Shelton*, then turned about and dropped three more charges approximately between the known position of the enemy submarine and *Shelton*. Immediately following this action, *Shelton* lost sound and radio power and no further sound contact could be established.

By means of visual signals, *Rowell* was contacted and stood close by to receive the wounded survivors as they were being loaded into the ship's whale boat. Due to the critical condition of the wounded and the agitated condition of the sea, transfer by boat took longer to accomplish than was anticipated.

To facilitate the transfer of the remaining personnel, *Rowell* came alongside *Shelton*. As a result, *Rowell* sustained some slight damage because of the rolling sea, but the abandonment of *Shelton* was considerably hastened. Captain Salomon was the last to leave his ship for *Rowell*. Total survivors numbered 210 plus the ship's cat. Three men were seriously wounded and 19 others were wounded in varying degrees. *Rowell* cleared *Shelton* and began circling her, looking for additional survivors who might have been thrown clear by the explosion; there were none.

After completing the rescue of survivors, *Rowell's* skipper, Lieutenant Commander H.A. Barnard Jr., directed resumption of an ASW search of the area. At 1225, almost immediately after abandoning the search for more survivors, an antisubmarine patrol plane reported a sub on the surface about seven miles away. The plane attacked and dropped a dye marker, but results of the attack were negative and the submarine submerged. *Rowell* raced to the location, marked by a dye. She made sound contact, and attacked with hedgehogs.

The submarine attempted to jam *Rowell's* sonar with a continuous dash on her own sound gear from 300 yards on in and was highly evasive, fish-tailing all the time. Soundman W.W. Hussong reported one explosion, but it was not noted on the bridge. The second attack, 12 minutes after the first, was followed by three to five underwater explosions, heard or felt on the bridge. Debris was blown to the surface and sank at once, indicating it was metal or some heavy material. No oil slick was noticed for the total time *Rowell* remained in the area.

A large bubble of air surfaced shortly after the debris. One piece, looking like the end of a periscope, was seen to come up vertically out of the water about two feet, tilt over to an angle of about 70 degrees, and then sink.

1340. *Rowell* made a third hedgehog attack but with negative results. The area was now full of wakes and explosion boils, and it was doubtful that any of the remaining attacks were made on the submarine itself, although they were close. The DE made a fourth hedgehog attack, again with negative results. She then fired a 13 depth charge pattern, set very deep, where the sub was thought to be. About two minutes after explosions of the charges, a more distinct underwater explosion was heard on the bridge, coming from the general direction of the submarine.

1403. *Rowell* made her fifth hedgehog attack, again with negative results in poor sound conditions. During all early attacks, the submarine was estimated to be making three knots and was conducting highly evasive course changes during all attacks. It was thought possible that the embarrassing attacks made earlier by aircraft may have shaken her up, causing her to surface when planes and surface craft were nearby and that her speed was reduced somewhat. This would account for her low speed during attacks. *Rowell* commenced a retiring search curve, attempting to regain contact.

1508. An antisubmarine patrol plane reported a sub on the surface, 10 miles from *Rowell* and identified her as friendly. *Rowell* proceeded at best speed to investigate regardless of the friendly report by the plane because no friendly subs were known to be in the area. She challenged and exchanged calls with *Darter (SS-227)* which was not included in any submarine notices to date. Considering the sub they attacked undoubtedly sunk, *Rowell* returned to the vicinity of *Shelton*, arriving about 1600.

Medical aid for the *Shelton's* seriously wounded was imperative. The commander of Destroyer Squadron 4, with *Stevens (DD-479)* and *Lang (DD-399)*, was at the scene and had the hulk in tow of *Lang*. The Task Force Commander ordered *Rowell* to proceed with the wounded to Morotai at best speed. That evening, at the harbor entrance, she met a crash boat with a pilot and doctor aboard. Inside the harbor, she went alongside seaplane tender *Tangier (AV-8)* to transfer the wounded, delayed by a red alert and GQ until the all clear sounded. Underway the next morning, *Rowell* was ordered to Manus with the other *Shelton* survivors.

The captain of *Rowell* took the opportunity to point out the great credit due to Captain Salomon of *Shelton*. The sinking DE was abandoned without confusion, all records intact, and all confidential and secret material destroyed. Several of his officers praised him for his courage and coolness and the example he set for all hands.

An abbreviated account of the *Rowell* action which lead to gaining underwater contact with a submarine and the tragic sinking of the *Seawolf (SS-197)* was pieced together. A reconstruction indicated that two planes were sent from the carrier *Midway (CVE-63)* to assist in the search. One of the planes sighted a submarine submerging and dropped two bombs on it even though it was in a safety zone for American submarines.

An examination of the DE's action report elaborates on the submarine transmissions during the first and second attacks:

> "When the range was opened to approximately 700 yards, the target sent the letter "M" twice with its own sonar oscillator, followed by the letter "K". After a second letter "K", the target varied its frequency about two kilocycles and attempted to seek *Rowell's*'s frequency. The target transmitted continually with no break, varying frequency and succeeding in jamming the DE's frequency so that no echoes could be heard by *Rowell*. The target continued to transmit until the range opened to approximately 2500 yards, final transmissions being in the form of letter "A", varying frequency all the time. At about 2500 yards, the target ceased transmitting until *Rowell* had closed to 400 yards on her second attack."

It is possible that the sub was trying to send an IFF. If so, it was using the wrong signal. Combined with the lack of notice that a friendly sub was in the area and the attack on *Shelton* by an enemy submarine, a deadly scenario for tragedy was in place. On 28 December, six weeks after *Rowell's* attack, *Seawolf* was announced overdue from patrol and presumed lost. As accumulated data revealed the lost submarine and *Rowell's* attacks to be in the same area, the chill of reality replaced the exuberance of victory. Needless to say, it was agonizing news for *Rowell* whose crew had been under the impression that their ship had destroyed an enemy submarine. It was a confused situation but a hard one to live with just the same. "Killed by friendly fire" is an all too frequent communique issued in any war, this one being no exception.

It is interesting to note that a *Rowell* contact took place the day before *Shelton* was hit and that her captain worried about possible confusion in the safety lanes even before his ship was torpedoed and the resultant *Seawolf* tragedy. It is not known if the submarine that attacked *Shelton* was the same one on which *Rowell* gained contact the day before. Post-war Japanese records indicated that the submarine that torpedoed *Shelton* was *RO-141*.

The skipper of *Rowell*, by exercising an extremely high degree of skill and seamanship under adverse conditions, expeditiously completed the rescue of all hands from the sinking *Shelton* without injury to any person, and without serious damage to his own ship.

Shelton's executive officer, Lieutenant James S. Dowdell, made the observation in his report that the entire complement of *Shelton* performed its assigned duties coolly and efficiently in the traditional manner of the naval service during the entire action, and some were entitled to special awards:

> "Between the sounding of the General Alarm and the torpedo hit immediately following, all physically capable men reported promptly to their stations and remained thereon until ordered to leave.
>
> During the three hours prior to abandoning, every effort was made to save the ship. This was primary and all action was directed toward this end and to the rescue, treatment and transfer of the wounded. At no time was there any sign of panic or confusion. Outstanding acts of merit were numerous. The men listed below represent my own observation and

those subsequently brought to my notice:

Fireman First Class Dean H.H. Skinner - As a member of the repair party, with complete disregard for his personal safety, he reentered a flooded magazine upon the report of a fire to determine its location and to extinguish it.

Baker Third Class Thomas E. Robinson Jr. - Though wounded by the explosion, took his place in the bucket brigade, working in a water-filled compartment without reporting his injuries until his weakened condition caused his collapse.

Machinist's Mate Third Class Paul Raymond Shurtleff volunteered to accompany the first lieutenant into the damaged compartments and magazines to determine the extent of the damage with complete disregard for his own personal safety.

Boatswain's Mate Second Class Quinton Edmund George - Without waiting for orders, organized and directed a repair party in an effort to control the rapidly rising water in flooded compartments.

Pharmacist's Mate Second Class Myron Bernard Levine, Pharmacist's Mate Second Class Charles Henry Caires, Seaman First Class Robert James Agnes - for especially meritorious conduct in rescuing, treating and transferring injured members of the crew."

Lieutenant Commander Lewis G. Salomon was cited for gallantry and intrepidity in action against the enemy while in the profession of his duty as commanding officer of the *Shelton*. He set a high example of efficiency, calm and courage during the entire action that was an inspiration to all hands.

At the start of the Battle off Samar on 25 October, *Rowell* operated in Group Taffy 1 off Surigao Island, about 130 miles south of Task Force 3 (Taffy 3), which engaged the main Japanese force. Taffy one had just launched planes to attack Japanese ships, retiring from their crushing defeat at the Battle of Surigao Strait, when it was attacked by six enemy planes from Davao. Responding to this emergency, *Rowell* rescued one survivor from *Santee (CVE-29)*. She fought off a *kamikaze* attack on the 26th as she was attacking an enemy submarine.

Rowell joined air and antisubmarine patrols for the landings at Lingayan Gulf, Luzon. She guarded transports to Iwo Jima and supported air units during the landings on Okinawa. She spent the remainder of the war in convoy screening actions and patrols among Leyte Gulf, Ulithi, San Pedro Bay and Okinawa.

LAWRENCE C. TAYLOR

Two Submarines to the Bottom

16 October 1944. *Lawrence C. Taylor (DE-415)* sortied from Pearl Harbor, flying the pennant of Commander A. Jackson Jr., *ComCortDiv 72*. The Division was assigned to ComTaskGroup 30.7, Captain P.W. Watson, commanding officer of the carrier *Anzio (CVE-57)* as a Hunter-Killer Group. In *CortDiv 72* with *Taylor*, were *Melvin R. Nawman (DE-416)*, *Oliver Mitchell (DE-417)*, *Tabberer (DE-418)* and *Robert F. Keller (DE-419)*. The Leyte, Philippines invasion was just getting underway.

18 November. *Taylor* drew first blood for the Division after arrival off Leyte. The Task Group was steaming under orders of the Commander Third Fleet (Admiral Halsey) to patrol the perimeter of a tanker refueling group. The Task Group Commander ordered *Taylor* to investigate a radar contact by an aircraft seven miles from the formation, and *Melvin R. Nawman* was directed to assist in the search.

0417. Lookouts reported flares dropped by aircraft. *Nawman* took a position abeam of *Taylor*, speed 15 knots, and the two ships in tandem instituted a sound search of the immediate area. An hour and a half later, *Taylor's* skipper, Lieutenant Commander R. Cullinan Jr., reported a sonar contact. She made one run with her hedgehogs but without result. However, contact was retained and *Taylor* stood in for a second hedgehog attack which produced no more than the first.

0616. *Nawman*, under command of Lieutenant Commander F.W. Kinsley, followed *Taylor* and made her first attack with hedgehogs, also with negative results. *Taylor* made her third attack while *Nawman* opened range...Hits!

Directly after this last pattern of hedgehogs hit the water, three minor explosions were heard on the sound gear of both vessels, followed by a very heavy underwater explosion which felt as if it had occurred directly beneath the ships. *Taylor* and *Nawman* each made two more hedgehog attacks without further result.

Although another four attacks were made on a doubtful contact, no further positive indications of a submarine were observed until a pilot in one of *Anzio's* planes reported oil rising from the point of *Taylor's* successful attack. Shortly thereafter, debris, including cork, deck planking and small pieces of red lacquered wood rose to the surface. *Taylor* lowered her motor whale boat to recover tell-tale evidence. After 24 hours, a three-mile long oil slick emanated from the point of attack. Both ships commenced Operation Observant.

0945. *Taylor* heard definite propeller noises in the sound gear, but the crew was unable to secure from debris recovery and echo-range on the contact. Assisting aircraft dropped sono-buoys at the outer limits of the area being searched. A half hour later, screw noises were lost. *Nawman* then took station 3500 yards on the starboard beam of *Taylor* and both DEs instituted a box search.

1125. An aircraft reported an excellent contact, dropped markers on the spot, and Operation Observant was moved to the immediate area. All engines on both ships were stopped while they listened for five minutes but heard nothing. They continued their retiring box search without incident for the next two hours when they were recalled by ComTaskGroup to previous positions in the screen. Captain Watson expressed the opinion that the submarine was definitely sunk. The sinking was awarded an official "B" assessment, and *Taylor* painted her first little submarine flag on the side of the bridge.

And post-war research proved the captain to be absolutely correct. *Taylor* had sunk Japanese submarine *I-41*.

The Legion of Merit medal was later presented to the *Taylor's* captain. The executive officer, Lieutenant Commander D.A. DeCoudres, and the antisubmarine officer, Lieutenant (jg) D.S. Wolfrom, got Bronze Star Medals and letters of commendation. Citation ribbons were presented to Chief Gunner's Mate J.L. Temples, Sonarman Second Class J.J. Smith and Sonarman First Class P. Cerbus.

Many months passed before *Taylor* would engage another submarine. In the interim, she saw actions of another nature.

After Leyte was secured, *CortDiv 72* survived the wrath of Typhoon Cobra, 17-19 December, damaging some of the destroyer escorts in the Division. Others, like *Tabberer*, were cited for bravery in rescue operations. See chapter *The Pacific Typhoons*.

Taylor saw fast action with the famed Task Force 38 in supporting Luzon landings and strikes at Formosa. Then there was unforgettable Iwo Jima, massive *kamikaze* attacks, the sinking of *Bismarck (CVE-95)* and the bravery of the *Taylor* crew in effecting rescues. Okinawa was a replay of Iwo Jima – only worse!

At 2350 on 15 July 1945, ComTaskGroup 30.6 (The revised designation of the *Anzio* group) reported that a plane from the carrier had sighted a surfaced Japanese submarine approximately 67 miles from the formation. At 0737 on 16 July, an Avenger pilot from *Anzio* spotted a surfaced submarine and made three depth bomb and rocket attacks as the sub dived for cover. An oil slick remained on the surface.

The Task Group Commander directed *ComCortDiv 72* on *Taylor* to proceed with one other escort and develop a contact or render assistance to aircraft as might be required. This vessel rang up 24 knots and, accompanied with *Robert F. Keller*, proceeded on a line of bearing normal to the base course, distance 2500 yards between the two ships. The sky was overcast with occasional drizzle; visibility was six miles; the sea was moderate; the wind was from the northwest at about eight knots. The assured sonar range of the day was 1000 yards as indicated by a previous bathythermograph recording.

The two DEs arrived in the area of the original aircraft contact in the early afternoon. The plane had dropped a smoke marker about four miles ahead of the escorts. Speed was reduced to 13 knots as they proceeded in the direction indicated by the smoke marker. The sono-buoy receiver in *Taylor* had been continuously monitored since leaving the task group. The planes had repeatedly dropped sono-buoy patterns to maintain contact with the sub.

0238. *Taylor* gained a sound contact on her port bow at a distance of about 1200 yards and reduced her speed to 10 knots. Definitely identifiable screw noises started up just as *Taylor* commenced the first attack run. She fired a full pattern of 24 hedgehogs.

Almost immediately, the screw noises speeded up markedly. No doppler or target movement was noted when *Taylor* attacked although, just before contact was lost at 200 yards, there was a slight indication of movement away from the ship. Personnel throughout the DE felt two small explosions, followed by two more blasts seconds later.

Flank speed was immediately rung up in order to clear the area. Before this change of speed could take appreciable effect, a violent detonation knocked out both switchboards in the engine room, causing a temporary loss of the electric load. Another powerful explosion rocked the DE, knocking out all power to the sonar gear and stopping the fuel oil pumps in the after fire room.

Engineering personnel corrected the two malfunctions in quick time and the ship was able to keep moving away. The first lieutenant and other personnel from the midship repair party station proceeded to check compartment soundings. That final and most violent explosion at the last submarine location boiled up and was black with oil. The plane pilot reported on VHF that he felt the concussion at 1000 feet.

0245. *Keller* fired a full pattern of hedgehogs with no explosions observed or felt. *Taylor* obtained a very wide and mushy contact and turbulence which disintegrated upon investigation. The submarine appeared to have been destroyed. Debris was seen to be rising from the point of *Taylor's* attack. For 10 minutes, the sono-buoy receiver in *Taylor* recorded numerous small explosions and breaking up noises, culminating in three large explosions.

The motor whaleboat was lowered to recover debris. Items retrieved consisted of a large quantity of deck planking, some containing bolts with fresh breaks; sponge rubber; corking; one bundle of Japanese newspapers which had not been opened; a picture of a Japanese family; several bundles of evidently personal letters bound together with string, indicating the submarine might have been carrying mail for other units or bases; several candles; and some small pieces of polished wood. Only representative samples of debris were recovered, and the area was still cluttered with flotsam upon departure. To the task group came warm words from Admiral Halsey:

> "Violent explosions emanating from Nip subs are music to all ears. Well done."

The performance of ordnance material in *Taylor* was highly satisfactory. The first run was considered to be eminently successful, even though the assured sonar range was only 1000 yards and no preliminary approach maneuvers were used.

The engineering personnel received much praise. It was the opinion of the captain that his vessel could have sustained damage from the last of the explosions had the ship lost headway with resultant inability to keep moving away from the blast epicenters.

Also, high compliments were directed to the hard working and efficient TBM pilots from the *Anzio*. Their cooperation and the assistance rendered was poetic in its perfection. They were intensely alert on the VHF, reporting probable movements of the sub, location of debris, movement of the oil slick, etc. Their reports always came in at just the right time in order for the CIC on *Taylor* to keep an accurate picture and plot of the situation.

The bundles of letters (estimate 100) and other printed matter which might be of possible intelligence value were assembled for forwarding to proper authorities. In one magazine, there was a map of the United States, showing all American oil producing centers. Lines were noted in a position approximate to that of the 'Big Inch' pipeline. Twin engine bombers were also shown to be approaching the United States from the southern tip of Florida and others were winging in from the Pacific. This map also contained a table of figures, seeming to indicate American petroleum production 1920 to 1940.

It seemed plausible that this sub was carrying mines, three were destroyed between the Task Group and the point of contact and destruction.

Upon departure from the area, the oil slick covered five square miles. At a later date, the submarine was identified as *I-13*.

It was another "B" assessment for *Taylor*, another little red silhouette flag on the bridge and again the awards for the action. Recommendations this time included the Legion of Merit for the new Captain Grey; the Bronze Star Medal for the Engineering Officer, Lieutenant (jg) Donald J. Vlasnik; and Letters of Commendation for Sonarman First Class Robert J. Riede, Sonarman Second Class John E. Cook, Chief Gunner's Mate Thomas P. Wyra and Gunner's Mate Third Class Robert K. Grove. Captain G.C. Montgomery, Task Group Commander (also new), addressed the following to the Commander-in-Chief Pacific Fleet (abridged):

"The series of attacks on 16 July 1945 which culminated in the certain destruction of the Japanese submarine is an outstanding example of the splendid cooperation and teamwork between air and surface forces. Throughout this period, the *Commander Escort Division 72* has displayed a very high standard of leadership and efficiency in training and directing ships of his division. The commanding officer of *Taylor* demonstrated his courage and effectiveness by the precision in which his ship made the kill."

Taylor and other ships of *Escort Division 72* were ordered to accompany the Third Fleet into Tokyo Bay for the official surrender ceremonies, a fitting finale to an outstanding combat record.

EVERSOLE –WHITEHURST–BULL

Disaster and Victory

9 August 1944. *Eversole (DE-404)* put to sea, screening carriers for the attack on Morotai. She continued serving with escort carriers in the initial assaults in Leyte Gulf on 20 October. *Eversole's* orders on 27 October were to rendezvous at daybreak the following morning with Rear Admiral Sprague's battered Task Force (Taffy 3), returning from the Battle off Samar.

0210 on 28 October. The DE made a radar contact at 5-1/2 miles that then disappeared. Within eight minutes, the sonar watch advised the conn that they were echo ranging on a contact at 2800 yards. A half minute later, a torpedo crashed into the ship, causing immediate loss of power and a 15 degree list. Within seconds, another torpedo found its mark through the same gaping hole ripped by the first one. The explosions wreaked havoc below decks, mortally damaging the ship and rapidly increasing her list to 30 degrees. Dead and wounded were everywhere. With damage control unable to cope with the immensity of the destruction, the commanding officer, Lieutenant Commander George Marix, ordered the ship abandoned. Within 15 minutes, Eversole plunged to the bottom. Captain Marix recalled:

"I was on my way to the bridge when the first torpedo hit. A second torpedo hit shortly afterward, but no panic was noticed in the abandon ship procedure. I made a personal inspection of the ship as far as I could. Three men were frozen to the rail, afraid to move. I beat their fingers until they dropped into the water below. On my final check, I found a man with a broken leg. I lowered him into the water with a line attached and then followed him in because the ship was flat on her side and I thought it was time to leave. After stepping into the water, I towed the injured man to a floater net about 100 yards away. On the way, I picked up a life preserver as I had given mine to the wounded man."

The men scrambled over the side as best they could, taking the injured with them. The captain continued:

"There was another floater net about a hundred yards away. I ordered them lashed together so as to concentrate the men. Officers were placed around nets 10 yards out to pick up any who might slip off and drift away.

0300. A submarine surfaced near a group of men hanging on to a raft some 200 yards away from myself. Some of the survivors, unable to identify the sub through the predawn gloom and believing that a friendly ship had come to their rescue, shouted loudly. Their pleas were answered by a murderous and ruthless hail of 20mm fire from the Jap sub that lasted for 20 minutes. Fortunately, it was so dark and raining that their gunner couldn't see us, and nobody was hit. The men were ordered to keep quiet as the sub circled us about 150 yards away.

After 20 minutes in our area, the sub submerged, followed five minutes later by a terrific underwater explosion that killed or injured many survivors in the water. My communications officer, about five feet from me, was killed instantly. I was seized with very bad cramps and lost all control of my bowels. Unconscious men began drifting from the floater net. My officers, aided by some slightly injured men and myself, swam them back to the net and put them aboard. I estimate that this explosion killed about 30 men. The detonation was believed to have been caused by a time-set anti-personnel bomb. It could not possibly have been one of our depth charges because they had been set on safe and because a half hour had elapsed since our ship went down."

Bull (DE-402) had arrived in an area of heavy oil slicks and survivors in the early morning of the 29th. Quartermaster Third Class Robert L. Smock had unforgettable recollections of the rescue:

"It was very late at night when we lost the *Eversole* from our radar screen. Needless to say, we came across the crew in the water. I can vividly remember the smell of the fuel and hear those cries for help. It is a cry like none other in the world!"

Captain Marix concluded:

"At about 0400, we sighted *Bull* and attracted her attention by means of flashlights. She circled us for about an hour until *Whitehurst (DE-634)* arrived on the scene to act as covering ship. While circling the area, *Bull* frequently stopped to pick up survivors. By 0630, all survivors had been taken aboard.

I wish to commend all my officers and men for the fine work they did in spite of their own injuries.

The torpedoing and the bomb created unusually high casualties. Out of a roster of 213 officers and men, 77 were dead and 136 were rescued, all injured. Of the latter number, three subsequently died, bringing the death toll to 80. Had it not been for the arrival of *Bull* and *Whitehurst* shortly after sinking, the death toll would have been total. The efforts of the officers and men of *Bull* in recovering and caring for my crew were exemplary. The doctor on board, Lieutenant Hartley, from the oiler *Sangamon (AO-28)*, undoubtedly saved the lives of some 30 to 40 men by his untiring efforts and skill. He worked without rest for 36 hours, treating the critically wounded."

Having exhausted her supply of blood plasma, *Bull* acquired an additional supply from *Whitehurst*. The officers and crew worked day and night trying to relieve the sufferings and save the lives of many of the badly burned members of *Eversole*.

Prior to the submarine attack, and after fighting off two attacking planes on 27 October, *Whitehurst* proceeded to a rendezvous east of Leyte Gulf. She had been acting as escort for Task Unit 77.7.1 during fueling operations at sea and in Leyte Gulf. During the night of 28-29 October, the Task Unit had been steaming slowly to await daylight and to continue fueling ships. Submarines had been reported in the area, and it could be presumed that the Japanese were by this time aware of the routes used from Hollandia to Leyte Gulf.

0325. A strong underwater explosion had been heard on *Whitehurst*, judged to be several miles away. The weather was cloudy, obscuring the moon, and with occasional rain squalls reducing visibility. The breeze was light and variable with calm seas and a long, low swell.

Word was received from *Bull* that *Eversole* had just been sunk and *Bull* was requesting an escort to act as antisubmarine screen while she was rescuing survivors. The Screen Commander on *Bowers (DE-637)* detailed *Whitehurst* to be the screening vessel.

The DE's speed was increased to full and a course was set for *Bull*. CTU 7.7.1 ordered the convoy on an emergency turn to reverse course and to clear the danger area. Eleven minutes later, *Whitehurst* had closed the range to *Bull* to three miles.

The range and bearing to the center of the survivor area from the *Bull* was determined and plotted on *Whitehurst*'s DRT. Because of poor visibility and on the advice of *Bull*, speed was reduced to 10 knots in order not to run down any survivors. Operation Observant was begun, using beam to beam sonar search. At 0515, visibility had improved, and speed was increased to 18 knots, then considered to be the maximum speed at which a good search could be made.

0545. After nearly completing an entire search around the area, *Whitehurst* made a good sound contact and slowed to 10 knots for attacking with hedgehogs. Three attacks were made over the next 90 minutes without result. The fourth run, however, was a different story. A few seconds after the bombs hit the water, six minor explosions were heard in quick succession. In true form, there was a violent underwater detonation, followed by heavy rumbling noises!

The echo ranging gear on *Whitehurst* was knocked out by the blast. Accordingly, *Bull* was asked to continue the search and to attack. *Bull* made a contact at the point of explosion and searched the area. However, she reported her echo was only from the water disturbed by the explosion. *Bull* commented to *Whitehurst* over the TBS:

> "From the sound of the explosion where I was three miles away, I don't think there is any chance that there is anything left of the sub."

0720. The *Whitehurst* sound gear was repaired, leaving *Bull* to continue the rescue of survivors. Considerable oil on the surface was noted, along with pieces of wood and other debris, but *Whitehurst* launched Operation Observant as a precaution. She lowered her boat in the center of the oil slick to retrieve debris. An hour later, her motor whaleboat retrieved numerous pieces of deck planking, a damage control plug with Japanese marking, other pieces of wood painted red and oil samples soaked up in rags. At 1215, the search was abandoned.

The heavy underwater explosion had been of such violence that, at first, it was thought the ship had been torpedoed. All departments reported, and the only damage was to the sound gear which was temporarily out of action, fuses having blown in the three phase power supply. The after engine room reported a lube oil pump stopped, caused by the concussion tripping a solenoid valve. The sound gear was checked out by the leading soundman and the electrician's mate, and the trouble was quickly located and repaired.

The submarine was credited by her attacker for excellent evasive tactics and maneuverability. She would invariably try to turn away from the attack, presenting her stern and wake. At her depth of 225 feet at the time of losing contact, this was the best maneuver; a salvo could not be fired until after the contact was lost, giving the sub additional time for evasion.

At a later date, it was confirmed that *Whitehurst* had sunk Japanese submarine *I-45*, the same one that sank *Eversole*.

Further actions with Japanese aircraft by both *Bull* and *Whitehurst* are described in chapters *The Philippine Campaign* and *Iwo Jima to Okinawa — The Destroyer Escorts*.

McCOY REYNOLDS AND CONKLIN

Two More Submarines to the Bottom

20-24 September 1944. *McCoy Reynolds (DE-440)* screened shore bombardment ships as they covered the marines in their assault on Peleliu.

In the early dark hours, while en route to join Task Force 57 out of Guam, *Reynolds* picked up a target on surface radar at about 9000 yards. Five minutes later, it disappeared but was quickly located by her sonar at 2500 yards. She launched seven vigorous and intensive attacks on the target with hedgehogs and depth charges. Four hours after the first attack, a violent underwater explosion was felt, and her lookouts spotted an oil slick, subsequently covering an area of two square miles. Although no other data was collected, the attacks were later determined to have destroyed Japanese submarine *RO-47*.

For the next few months, *Reynolds* served on convoy and escort duty, screening oilers as they refueled hard-hitting carriers of the fast carrier task force.

Conklin (DE-439) was engaged in convoy escort duty between Kwajalein and Eniwetok until 3 October, when she arrived at Guam to serve as a plane guard. She then patrolled on antisubmarine duty off Saipan until 6 November, when she headed for Ulithi and Leyte, guarding a convoy of reinforcement troops and supplies.

0858 on 19 November. While the net-laying ship *Winterberry (AN-56)* was laying a torpedo net across the west entrance of Kossol Passage, she sighted a surfaced submarine, distance 2500 yards, lasting about one minute. A contact message was sent by her commanding officer, Lieutenant Commander S.E. Aarens, to the Port Director of Kossol Passage and also to the *YMS-33*, then on listening watch at the west entrance. The minesweeper was ordered to investigate the submarine.

Twenty seconds later, the sub again surfaced in approximately the same position, repeating the same diving and surfacing twice in succession, the last time around mid-morning. The last two times, she came up at quite a steep angle with her bow approaching the vertical and seemed to have shot up out of the ocean quite fast. The YMS did not get contact on the submarine.

While anchored in Kossol Passage, a message relative to the sub sighting was received by *McCoy Reynolds* and *Conklin* from the Commander of Task Group 57.6. The two DEs were ordered to the scene. The commanding officer of *Reynolds*, Lieutenant Commander E.K. Winn, was designated Officer in Tactical Command (OTC). Lieutenant Commander E.L. McGibbon was captain of *Conklin*. The ships raced out of the entrance at flank speed. A retiring box search was started with the two ships parallel and spaced 3000 yards apart, speed 15 knots, pinging a 180 degree arc beam to beam.

Upon arrival at the point of sighting, both ships were directed to sweep the perimeter of the immediate area which was being searched by navy planes. The proximity of the assigned area to shore and reefs made it necessary to modify somewhat the prescribed search procedures. The ships' hunt commenced about two hours after the submarine was reported. This time span, together with the speed factors, were used to determine probable hourly arcs of advance of the enemy submarine. Doctrinal search tactics were selected and modified by Captain Winn as to which would best meet the unusual tactical situation.

1500. *Reynolds* obtained a sonar contact at 1600 yards. She headed toward the target and notified the *Conklin* to stand clear. Shortly before the dispatch from *Reynolds*, *Conklin* had picked up a solid contact in the same area, range 2700 yards. The black pennant was two-blocked and *Reynolds* was so informed by TBS. Evidently, this transmission was not received for no "Roger" was given and, about a minute later, *Reynolds* two blocked her black pennant. As the two ships were obviously converging toward the same contact, *Conklin* broke off the attack and turned to stand clear. *Reynolds* closed the range to approximately 800 yards while classifying the contact as probable submarine. She opened the range in order to commence the first attack and speed was reduced to 10 knots. During the run, the target was moving at moderate speed with slightly down doppler. Its movement was to the right.

A full pattern of hedgehogs was fired without results, and the same held for a second attack. The range at lost contact during the first two attacks indicated the submarine's depth was about 350 feet and going deeper. Accordingly, depth charges replaced hedgehogs and speed was increased to 15 knots. *Reynolds* opened the range to 1200 yards.

The third run was begun. The target movement was slightly to the right, and the doppler was moderately high, indicating a bow-on target. The range was closed to 700 yards, and the left to right movements of the submarine became much more marked, indicating that it was turning away. Accordingly, the rudder was put over hard right, and the recorder operator was ordered to fire five seconds late. A 13 depth charge pattern, deep setting, was fired. Contact was lost at 350 yards with no apparent results.

During all this time, *Conklin* was standing clear and was able to maintain contact intermittently. When *Reynolds* lost contact after her depth charge attack, *Conklin* regained it at 2500 yards. The black pennant was two-blocked, indicating that *Conklin* was attacking. *Reynolds* informed *Conklin* that the target depth was at least 400 feet. Nonetheless, a hedgehog run was made. Target movement was to the right with down doppler and gave every evidence of maneuvering. The echo was sharp and clear.

1615. Hedgehogs were fired by recorder on the leading right cut of the contact — A hit!

Twenty-five seconds after firing, a single pronounced underwater explosion was heard and felt by everyone aboard *Conklin*. Deducting eight seconds of time from the air flight of the projectiles, the time of the explosion indicated a target depth of approximately 400 feet, corroborating prior information from *Reynolds*.

Conklin immediately turned away and increased speed to open the range. The pattern area was dead astern, and there was insufficient opportunity to make an examination for evidence of damage. Contact was regained at 1300 yards. On the next hedgehog attack, target movement was again to the right, but no maneuvering was noticed.

1625. The second pattern was fired slightly inside the leading right cut of the target. Twenty-eight seconds after firing, the ASW Officer and personnel aft reported a detonation but, since it was not detected on the bridge, this hit was classified as probable but not certain.

Conklin again turned away to open the range to 1400 yards. On this run, target inclination was at first closing with the bearing movement to the right. Doppler then changed from none to slightly low, indicating that the target was in a slow turn with left rudder. It was believed that too much right turn was applied by the DE and that the target turned inside the pattern. No hits were recorded.

As the range was being opened for the next attack, *Conklin* was directed by *Reynolds* to cease pinging and stand clear; she had contact and would deliver a depth charge attack. Throughout all foregoing attacks, the target movement was along the same base course. The target now appeared to have made a major course change. *Reynolds* had developed the contact at a range of 1700 yards. After a slow turn to the right, the ship proceeded on an attack course. The target movement was also slightly to the right with moderately low doppler. The target aspect was between deep quarter and direct stern. Contact was lost at 450 yards, and the ship came to a firing course.

1645. She fired 12 deep set, depth charges. The DE made a slow circle to the right to regain contact. A very large air bubble arose at the point where the depth charges were dropped, about 500 yards dead astern. The skipper noted in his action report:

> "This bubble, about 25 feet in diameter, rose about five feet above the surface, was darker in color than the surrounding sea, and appeared to remain in a mushroomed elevated position for several seconds. Nothing more conclusively indicated a tremendous internal underwater explosion than was ever observed by this command in over two years of frequent dropping of depth charges."

While still turning to the right, contact was regained at 1300 yards, and *Reynolds* came to an attack course. From the time the contact was regained, the echoes and recorder traces were such that it was doubtful as to whether or not this contact was on the submarine. The stack operator, however, pointed out that there was discernible,within these mushy echoes, a typical submarine echo. Apparently, the submarine was surrounded by considerable underwater disturbances, and it was decided to continue the attack.

1700. When the range to the target was approximately 800 yards, a terrific underwater explosion emanating from the submarine was felt throughout the ship!

This eruption shook the ship violently, knocking the sound gear out of tune. A very severe underwater explosion was also felt close aboard by all hands on *Conklin* at the same instant. Although the target probably blew up, *Reynolds* decided to fire her pattern nonetheless. The course was continued and, in about one minute, a huge air bubble arose about 20 degrees on the starboard bow of the ship. Since the sound gear was unusable as a result of the violent explosion, it was decided to drop very deep-set charges from the stern racks and starboard "K" guns over the point of the disturbance.

Sonar contact was never regained after the first underwater explosion. *Reynolds* continued across the area and circled to return to where the last charges were dropped. Separate and distinct, deep, dull explosions of lesser character were felt, like the prior underwater explosion from the submarine. *Reynolds'* sound gear was quickly tuned, and both ships continued to search the immediate area. Because of the series of underwater explosions, particularly the violence of the first one, and the failure of either ship to establish further sonar contacts in the area, it was concluded that the enemy submarine had been destroyed. It was recalled from a prior successful attack by *Reynolds* on 26 September that evidence of destruction would not appear on the surface for a considerable time after the sinking of the submarine. Considering the 450 foot depth of the submarine at the time of the last attack, it was considered that it would be at least 30 to 45 minutes before evidence came into view. Accordingly, the ships continued to search for further sonar contacts and to keep a sharp lookout for oil and debris.

1723. *Reynolds* put over her whaleboat to search the area for evidence of damage and ordered the *Conklin* to assist.

Sudden gushes of debris and oil emerged in a large area around the ship. The pieces of debris, appearing in ever increasing amounts, were of all descriptions and included fragments of wood, chunks of cork, and many unidentified objects. At about the same time, the odor of oil was noticed and increased in intensity to an obnoxious degree, especially when the ship moved downwind of the area. The fragments and floating debris almost instantaneously covered a large sector. The oil was not only extremely noticeable from its odor, but the surface of the water over an increasing area became covered with a dense slick, increasing in size in large globular masses.

Sundown. In the short time the boat was out, much flotsam was recovered, including some wood pieces with stenciled Japanese characters. Some of the items collected were highly polished and appeared to be from cabin furniture or instrument cases. Deck planking with counter-sunk bolts were profuse. By darkness, the oil slick had expanded to an area of several square miles, and new debris continued to appear until dusk precluded further searching. It was determined beyond a doubt that the submarine had been destroyed. Among the items picked up was a piece of flesh with black hair, identified by the ship's Chief Pharmacist Mate after a microscopic examination as being human flesh with bits of steel embedded in it. The ship's boat party reported several sharks near the surface in the area where the flesh was retrieved.

23 November. The piece of flesh was taken to the Chief Pathological Medical Officer on board *Bountiful (AH-9)* for further examination. The report of this officer was that the flesh was definitely not that of a fish and, in his best opinion, was that of a human being.

The above detail is not meant to satisfy a ghoulish mania. It merely illustrates the tough "show me" attitude of the Navy Evaluation Board and the desire of DE crews to achieve appropriate recognition.

On 15 November, prior to the sortie of this two-ship Hunter-Killer group from Kossol Passage, Lieutenant Chauncey R. Goodwin had reported aboard *Reynolds* in his official capacity as an Antisubmarine Staff Representative. He was aboard *Reynolds* during the period covered in this narrative. His very willing and helpful assistance was an important factor in the successful conclusion of this operation.

After the war, it was revealed that the destroyed submarine, *I-177*, was returning from a unique mission. The sub had been involved in ferrying Japanese General Hatazo Adachi to an isolated garrison of 12,000 troops at Sio, New Guinea. They had been cut off by the Australians and were in need of leadership. They got the leadership but that was about all. They just withered and died from starvation, thirst or disease.

Through 19 March 1945, *McCoy Reynolds* escorted convoys in the Marianas and Marshalls and conducted antisubmarine patrols. She departed from Ulithi on 26 March to screen the Logistics Support Group of the Fifth Fleet's Fast Carrier Task Force during the Okinawa campaign. During her third escort mission on 12 May, *Reynolds* went to the aid of the carrier *Bunker Hill (CV-17)*, struck by two *kamikazes* with heavy losses and serious damage. With the same Logistics Group, she experienced the Okinawa typhoon of 6 June.

On 12 July, she captured two enemy soldiers attempting to escape from an island in a dugout canoe. On 9 September, she rescued two survivors of an army fighter which had flamed out over Hagushi.

Conklin returned to escort duty in convoys to Eniwetok, Ulithi, and Guam. On 21 January 1945, she joined another hunter-killer group patrolling near Ulithi. Two days later, she headed a team of three destroyer escorts in the sinking of another submarine. See the next action report.

CONKLIN, RABY AND CORBESIER

A Second Silhouette on the Flying Bridge

Two months after sinking a submarine with *McCoy Reynolds*, *Conklin* was senior ship in a special Hunter-Killer Group, operating between Ulithi and Yap during the third week of January 1945.

The HUK Group consisted of *Conklin*, *Raby (DE-698)*, and *Corbesier (DE-438)*. The Officer in Tactical Command (OTC) was the commanding officer of *Conklin*, Lieutenant Commander E. L. McGibbon. This unit was operating under the next higher operational command of Commander D.C. Brown, Commander of Escort Division 65 at Ulithi, and was augmented by air coverage from the same base.

Corbesier had served on patrol and escort off Saipan from 12 October to 11 November 1944. She departed from San Pedro Bay on 19 November for Ulithi where she carried out antisubmarine and escort missions, calling at Guam, Saipan, Kossol Roads and

Manus.

Raby had engaged in hunter-killer operations in the Solomons during the early spring of 1944. She resumed convoy escort missions at the end of June, remaining in the Solomons until 26 October when she got underway for Manus to perform similar duties in the Admiralties. *Raby* had been in the same task group with *England (DE-635)* when that ship destroyed six Japanese submarines.

2030 on 21 January 1945. Upon receipt of a report from the Ulithi Atoll Commander that a plane had sighted a surfaced submarine 18 miles offshore, the HUK Group was ordered to rendezvous in that area.

In formulating his original search plan, the OTC assumed that, after the sub had been sighted, she would probably seek to return to Yap, the nearest base, and that she would likely abandon the original mission because of extensive air coverage and the probability of surface ships being sent out to destroy her. Also, the air cover would very likely force the submarine to make its escape submerged as long as possible until near Yap.

The OTC plan would be an expanding search, starting from the point of the original sighting. The expansion of the search plan was conceived on the basis of a three knot submerged submarine for the first night and day. The first night, an interval of 5000 yards between ships on line abeam was directed. Thereafter, ships were at 3000 yard intervals in the daytime and 9000 yard intervals at night. Searching speed was 15 knots. On the night of 22-23 January, it was determined to sweep the route from Ulithi all the way to Yap, passing close to that enemy-held island just prior to dawn.

Throughout the period of the search and the action, the weather was good. The wind varied from northeast to east, force three to four. The sea was moderate. It was bright and clear. Sonar conditions were excellent. The search was begun at daybreak on the 22nd.

0310 on 23 January. Radar contact was made about 9800 yards on the port bow of *Corbesier*. Her CIC plotted the target moving at 18 knots and with no response to the IFF. *Corbesier* being the closest, was ordered to investigate. Five minutes later, she reported the target had disappeared.

Conklin and *Raby* turned to join *Corbesier*. The latter was ordered to drop a flare marker at the point of submergence. However, *Corbesier* reported that good sound contact had been obtained, and she started her first run, firing hedgehogs. First attack - results negative. *Corbesier* regained contact at 750 yards, and commenced a second run. *Conklin* and *Raby* maneuvered to gain positions broad on each bow of *Corbesier* to act as assisting ships.

0402 and for the next hour, four more hedgehog attacks fired by *Corbesier* produced nothing, and contact was lost.

Conklin commenced Operation Observant, an expanding box search with three ships abeam, distance 3000 yards. There followed a nine box turn (90 degrees to the left) executed to due east, then to due north, then to due west.

0902. *Corbesier* made a sound contact and turned to investigate. It looked good, and she commenced a run for a hedgehog attack. *Conklin* and *Raby* executed maneuvers independently to gain positions on each beam of *Corbesier*. She fired. Results negative.

0912. *Conklin* made contact, range 2800 yards. *Corbesier* was asked if she had contact and, if not, to draw clear. *Corbesier* reported she had temporarily lost contact and *Conklin* commenced a run. The target showed down doppler and was moving slowly left. At 550 yards, a range rate of seven knots was computed by the CIC.

Conklin fired a hedgehog salvo with a lead of 10 degrees inside the left cut-on. Seventeen seconds after firing, at least four or five hedgehog explosions were heard and felt by all hands! Deducting eight seconds for time of flight, a target depth of 175 feet was indicated.

0936. As *Conklin* was abeam and close aboard the pattern area, an extremely violent explosion occurred underneath which seemed to lift the ship out of the water. Huge air bubbles came up alongside, and a boil covering a large area started to spread. Engines, steering gear, power and all equipment went out on *Conklin*. As an example of the violence of the explosion, a 1400 pound safe in the ship's office was lifted from its welded base and moved eight feet over on the deck!

Conklin hoisted the five flag (I am disabled), and *Raby* and *Corbesier* commenced to screen her. Shortly thereafter, electric power was restored on *Conklin*, followed by reactivation of the equipment; the five flag was hauled down. Another but lesser explosion occurred, followed by loud grinding noises, heard on the sound gear.

Oil and debris began rising. *Conklin* passed directly over the pattern area and took a sounding of 1200 fathoms. She put over her motor whaleboat and commenced a slow circling of the immediate vicinity. *Raby* and *Corbesier* continued searching around the entire perimeter while *Conklin*'s whaleboat was in the water.

Oil began bubbling to the surface. Large quantities of human remains were sighted all about the ship. The commanding officer observed a shoulder joint with part of an arm. Several sharks were seen. Planking and cork were on all sides. A report was made to *ComCortDiv 65* that a definite kill had been obtained.

1044. The motor whaleboat reported it had recovered all manner of human remains and debris. A bucketful of remains was subsequently taken to the hospital ship *Samaritan (AH-10)* for a pathological examination and was identified as human. Remains included a piece containing pubic hair, a section of intestine, and other recognizable parts. All manner of planking, splintered wood, cork, interior woodwork with varnished surfaces, a sleeve of a knitted navy blue sweater containing flesh, condoms, chopsticks, and a Japanese Seaman's Manual.

Damage to *Conklin* from the violence of the explosion included communications equipment, hull fittings, and ordnance gear throughout the ship. However, no structural damage to the ship's shell plating or strength members was discovered.

The attitude of the commanding officer of *Conklin* concerning the other ships in the group is reflected in the following message sent to *Raby* and *Corbesier* upon returning to Ulithi:

> "Many thanks. This was a three ship job. Your cooperation and performance contributed materially to the successful result"

That was very generous, but we can be sure that ninety percent of the exhilaration in the Hunter-Killer force was on *Conklin* as another submarine silhouette was painted on both sides of the ship. The destroyed submarine was identified after the war as *I-48*.

Corbesier sailed from Ulithi with the logistics group on 18

March, supporting the fast carrier striking force in the Okinawa campaign. Sailing from Saipan for Okinawa on 28 June, she performed antisubmarine screening, protecting the island operations. She underwent the hazards of *kamikaze* attacks and typhoons. At the end of hostilities, she engaged in support of the Japanese occupation.

In January 1945, *Raby* shifted operations to Guam where she served as escort and patrol ship into June. Between 22 June and 31 August, she completed two slow tows to Okinawa. With the war with Japan concluded, she sailed for the United States on 13 September.

27 February. *Conklin* joined the screen for the logistics group supporting the mighty carrier Task Force 58. From 20 March to 5 June, she was almost constantly at sea with this group for the Okinawa operation. On 5 June, she was heavily damaged in a typhoon off Okinawa, during which one of her men was killed, many were injured, and two were washed overboard. See chapter *Pacific Typhoons*.

FLEMING

Sharks Provided the Evidence

2316 on 13 January 1945. While guarding two tankers enroute from Ulithi to Eniwetok, the surface search radar operator on *Fleming (DE-32)* reported a very indistinct "pip" at 14,000 yards. *Fleming* turned to the contact. When the range was reduced to 10,500 yards, a blinker light challenge was correctly responded to. Nonetheless the Task Unit Commander in *Carlson (DE-9)*, agreed that the contact still merited further investigation.

It suddenly dawned on *Fleming* CIC personnel that ranges to the contact and to the *Carlson* were the same, that the challenge was actually from *Carlson* and not from the contact. The plot indicated the target course to be the same as that of the convoy, speed eight knots. However, the target suddenly changed course, probably because she spotted the DE's approach.

A challenge was flashed at 4000 yards. It seemed unlikely that it could be anything but a subchaser or a submarine. No answer was received, but the contact slowed to four knots at a range of 2800 yards and then to two knots at 2100 yards. Suddenly, it faded from the radar scope at 1900 yards. Sonar, which had picked up a faint echo at 3225 yards, obtained clear echoes at the same range and bearing as the radar. Lieutenant James T. Krause, gunnery officer, recalled:

> "The sound conditions were almost unbelievable with hardly any thermal gradient in the water. Before the contact submerged, we unsuccessfully attempted to illuminate at about 4000 yards with star shells from our forward 3" mount. As we closed the contact, which we now knew was a sub just submerged, our first objective was to drive her down deep with a spread of depth charges. Having prevented an attack on the tankers we were escorting, we then methodically began our hedgehog runs."

Fleming proceeded with five sequential hedgehog attacks. On the first one, firing was five seconds early due to an error in relaying the order, "Stand by to fire", by the bridge talker. This attack was also complicated by attempts on the part of the submarine captain to jam the *Fleming's* sonar equipment. The ASW Officer reported hearing underwater keying, like a radio operator's transmitter. This officer and everyone in the CIC, sonar hut and on the bridge heard severe grating noises in the receiver. It made communication among these three stations inaudible and the echoes almost impossible to hear. In 2-1/2 years of constant contact with sonar equipment, the captain, Lieutenant Commander K.F. Burgess, had never heard comparable noises.

The next two runs were uneventful except for another brief attempt at jamming in the early stages of the first run. On the fourth and final attack, the best remembered by its success, the ASW Officer suspected another miss in a beam situation. However, the sonar operator picked up a last minute turn to port by the submarine at almost zero speed, which evidently prevented the hedgehog pattern from falling astern.

0057 on 14 January. On that fourth attack, three distinct, sharp explosions were felt and heard and seen 20.5 seconds after the order to fire. Lookouts saw reddish colored flashes in the water on the three explosions, and all personnel forward saw considerable boiling of the water's surface. Four seconds later, another explosion of far greater intensity than our hedgehog hits was heard and felt and which caused the echo ranging equipment to cut out for approximately one minute. It also cracked the salt water intake line from the sea chest suction to number three auxiliary engine and number three fire and bilge pump. This last explosion was of an entirely different tone than the other three and seemed comparatively muffled and deep. Lieutenant Krause admitted to having mixed feelings:

> "To me, it felt strange knowing that we were responsible for the deaths of many men even though they were our enemy."

In an article in the *Oregonian*, dated 23 September 1945, former Quartermaster Second Class Robert A. Campbell Jr. related:

> "The men danced about the decks, jumped up and down, clapped their hands and whistled. In an instant, they returned to a vigilant watch for a possible surfacing of the sub. There was no such luck. A careful search was made and no traces were found."

Contact was regained, however, and preparations were made for a medium depth charge attack on the premise that the submarine was badly damaged and that depth charges would finish her off. Unfortunately, the turn toward the contact was made too soon when steadied up on an attack course, only 1000 yards away. In view of the continuing clear echo, a turn was made away from the target to open the range for a deliberate attack. Just as a new attacking course at 1500 yards was reached, all hands heard and felt two successive explosions. The contact faded in the middle of the attack run and was never regained.

Evidence thus far could not claim a kill. More was needed, and *Fleming* set out to find it. Operation Observant was commenced at 0124. After completing a full-sweep and returning to the location of the explosions, debris was sighted by men on deck, and the very obvious strong odor of diesel oil was noted by every one topside. The DE began a retiring search, continued for four hours. With daybreak *Fleming* returned to the scene of the explosions and found a decided oil slick, but the previously reported debris had disappeared. A general sweep was conducted through the area, and the ship passed through the windward end of the oil slick, 500 yards wide with evident bubbling up of fresh oil. The line of demarcation on the windward edge between the slick and the rough water was very distinct. *Fleming* proceeded on a course directly with the wind and continued to find the same light diesel oil after traveling 14 miles. To check the position, she returned to the head of the slick for the noon fix which was four miles north of the dead reckoning position which they had reported in their contact amplifying dispatch. As this was the first fix obtained since noon the previous day, it was believed that the attack and observed positions were pretty much the same.

Fleming continued a search of the area as originally ordered by the Task Force Commander in Ulithi. The ship's boat was used at 1430 to collect an oil sample. At this time, a brownish residue material was bubbling to the surface along with the diesel oil. It appeared to be either lubricating oil or very low grade diesel. The quantity of rising oil had decidedly increased, and photographs were taken to accompany Captain Burgess' action report. Quartermaster Campbell went on to relate in the *Oregonian*:

> "The crewmen of the *Fleming* were certain that they had destroyed the Japanese submarine, but they needed something in the way of tangible evidence to bolster their claim. Yankee ingenuity solved their problem. At first, the schools of sharks were ignored until one of the more abstract minds thought there might be evidence in the sleek, gray bellies of the man eaters. Grappling hooks and lines were broken out."

Lieutenant Krause remembers:

> "We put chunks of meat on grappling hooks and threw them over the side. Each hook was attached to a line which was reeved through a wheel at the top of a davit. About twenty men would then haul a shark up and onto the fantail. I shot each shark through the back of the head with a rifle as it was hauled on board."

In less than two hours, six sharks out of twelve spotted at the head of the oil slick had been pulled aboard, none of them less than five feet in length. Their stomachs were removed and, upon examination, were found to contain fists full of partially digested flesh, some with small particles of metal. One palm-sized piece of matted black hair with sections of flesh or scalp attached was also recovered.

Lieutenant Krause also noted:

> "The fantail was a bloody mess from cutting their stomachs open and removing their teeth. Every crew member who wanted a shark's tooth got one as a souvenir."

Photos of this evidence were taken. In the opinion of the Escort Division 31 Medical Officer, the hair in particular might very probably have been human. This assumption seemed highly probable in view of the fact that no land was within 313 miles of the ship, and the captain could not recall ever having seen black haired fish in the sea. With the unusual concentration of sharks and the partially digested samples, it did not seem beyond possibility that human remains may have come to the surface and been seized by the sharks during the six hours of darkness after the explosions.

(A friend of this author who read this section of the manuscript asked me a pointed question. "What was the difference between primitive warriors who brought back from tribal wars, scalps, heads, hearts or genitalia as proof of their bravery against defeated enemies and, on the other hand, DE sailors who gladdened at the acquisition of bodily parts for the same reason? After some hesitation, I could only think of Winston Churchill's reputed remark in viewing reconnaissance photos of Allied bombing of a German city, "Alas for poor humanity".)

The Navigator obtained star fixes at the head of the oil slick at dusk and again at dawn on 15 January. The positions were identical with the previous fix. Since the head of the oil slick remained constant, its source must also have been constant, ie. a Japanese submarine on the bottom.

As *Fleming* departed from the area, oil was still rising to the surface in undiminished quantities. Thirty-one hours after the explosions, the slick was 600 yards wide at the very head, expanding to three miles in width and extending at least seven miles to leeward. The wind had increased to approximately 23 knots, and the seas were breaking except in the area of the concentrated slick. The light oil was rising to the surface in heavy enough quantities to have a calming effect at the point of origin. Beyond doubt, an enemy submarine rested in the fathometer indication of 3200 fathoms.

The practice of the ASW Officer to get his officers and men to an attack teacher at every opportunity proved its value. In the previous four months, 27 hours of practice had been logged. (An attack teacher was a machine that simulated submarine attack problems.)

It was believed that the primary evasive maneuvers of the submarine involved speed changes. In the early stages of the attacks, she resorted to "fishtailing" on several occasions. From her movements in the last attack, it was assumed that she had no idea of how to avoid a hedgehog attack and seemed schooled only in evading depth charges. In closing his action report, Captain Burgess related:

> "After 12 months in the forward area, this action came as a considerable relief to all hands. Every officer and man acted according to the finest traditions of the Navy. This officer is proud to be a member of such a group."

At a later date, it was confirmed that *Fleming* had sunk Japanese submarine *I-362*

15 January 1944. Upon returning to Tarawa, an officer from shore command came aboard to announce that it was necessary to place a portable radar station on one of the smaller Southern Marshall Islands. *Fleming* was to take the gear and operators to the island, and Ensign William P. Clark became very involved in the procedure:

> "I was assistant gunnery officer, and our watch bill stated that the Second Class Gunner's Mate and myself would lead the landing party. We were also told that Navy Intelligence had determined there were only a couple of

Japanese families living on the island.

I immediately met with my gunner's mate to review the names on the watch bill. We were to have ten men. In a muster of the landing crew, I found that most had not even fired a rifle in training. Somewhat appalled, I put out a call for volunteers who knew which end of a rifle the bullets came out of. The next day was spent in target practice on cans thrown off the fantail.

Just as *Fleming* exited through the coral reef, we received a blinker message to stand by. An LCVP arrived, and we took aboard a number of marines. With the LCVP in tow, we resumed our trip.

The Marine Lieutenant had orders to go ashore with the radar. Further intelligence had revealed there was a small number of Japanese troops on the island. Our captain volunteered our landing party, but the Marine Lieutenant stated that we would only get in the way, to which I heartily concurred.

The next morning, we arrived in the Marshalls and the marines went ashore. As soon as they landed, all hell broke loose. The marines were pinned down on the beach and radioed for assistance. We contacted Tarawa, and they replied that the earliest they could get reinforcements to the area would be the next morning.

The marines held out all night. At dawn, an LST arrived with more marines. After two days of sharp fighting, they secured the island that had an estimated 200 Japanese soldiers on it. This was an island invasion I was lucky not to have led."

Some Japanese pilots would have liked to avenge their undersea comrades. See the hair raising experiences of *Fleming* in chapter *Iwo Jima to Okinawa – The Destroyer Escorts*.

ULVERT M. MOORE

Adding a Submarine to Her Laurels

Fresh from a series of splashed *kamikazes* in Lingayan Gulf under the most trying circumstances, *Ulvert M. Moore (DE-442)* and her captain, Commander Franklin Delano Roosevelt Jr., son of the President, were now called upon to exercise their antisubmarine talents.

1230 on 30 January 1944. *Moore*, in company with *Goss (DE-444)*, *Jenkins (DD-447)*, and *Lavalette (DD-448)* (OTC), was ordered to carry out hunter-killer operations against an enemy submarine sighted by aircraft west of Manila Bay. The operations were unsuccessful, and the group rejoined their Seventh Fleet Task Groups.

2000 the next night. the group intercepted a TBS transmission from the cruiser *Boise (CL-47)* that she had a radar contact. The destroyers *Bell (DD-587)* and *O'Bannon (DD-450)* left the screen to investigate. When *Bell* had closed to four miles, the radar pip disappeared from her screen but, shortly thereafter, she obtained a sonar contact and proceeded with a depth charge attack. The target was classified as definite submarine. Results were negative for this as well as another depth charge attack by *O'Bannon*.

2049. *Bell* again attacked. She reported the opinion that the submarine was damaged on her second depth charge attack because an extra large explosion, separate from the depth charge detonations, was heard, and an oil slick was seen. Five minutes later, *Moore* made a run through the point of last contact with no results, and all ships commenced Operation Observant. As *Jenkins* joined the group and took charge of the operation, *Moore* obtained a sonar contact, classified as positive submarine.

As the range was opened from the original contact, the echo became progressively weaker, and contact was lost. The ship was immediately turned to close the range and regained contact at 1000 yards. Echoes were not of sufficient intensity for good evaluation until down to 900 yards. As these limiting sound conditions were repeated on the second run, it was decided to reduce the opening ranges during subsequent regain contact procedures to 1000 yards.

Twenty seconds after firing hedgehogs on the third run, three explosions were heard on the sonar gear and seen on the fathometer. A few seconds later, an explosion heard on sonar gear was also felt by all hands, and men on the fantail also saw a large bubble break the surface just astern.

Twenty-two seconds after firing on the fifth run, a sharp crack was heard on the sonar gear, followed by distinct hissing and bubbling noises, also heard close aboard by men on the fantail. Sonar then reported two distinct explosions.

Four minutes after the sixth run, two marked explosions were heard on sonar gear and felt by engine room personnel.

While opening the range on the seventh run, shortly after midnight on 1 February, a very loud hissing sound was heard on sonar, completely drowning out the transmission.

Eighteen seconds after the eighth and last non-firing run, three violent explosions in rapid succession were felt by sonar, seen by all topside personnel and on the three assisting vessels. The crew was thoroughly jarred. The water ahead and on both bows appeared to rise about one foot over an area about 100 yards in diameter, displaying a bluish light similar to a flash of burning gas. As the ship passed through the explosion point, the water became more disturbed.

About four minutes after the above explosions, another and even more violent blast was felt and reported by all ships. Personnel on *Moore* saw a blinding flash and disturbance in the water about 800-1000 yards astern. Retired Coast Guard Commander, William A. Powers, was Chief Gunner's Mate on *Moore* at the time and recalls:

> "I had a problem rearming the hedgehog battery so often. The projectiles and fuses could not be stowed together, so I had to set up an assembly line, using torpedomen and a damage control party. The telephone talker reported that engineering people had heard small explosions under our ship. The 'tear drop' depth charges had become canted in the stern racks as a result of the disturbances. I went aft the ship with a crow bar to clear the stoppage. (With hedgehogs located near the bow and depth charges located on the fantail, the chief must have hustled!)
>
> While struggling with the depth charge, I heard a tremendous explosion. The whole ship was raised out of the water, almost throwing me overboard. I felt airborne! Later, Sonarman Reichert, who had experience with German U-boats, said this Jap skipper was very good at his job. The

Dead Reckoning Tracer plot showed that, when under attack, he used all the evasive tactics, fish-tailing, change of speeds, continuous turns, and a shrewd use of wakes. At no time, did the sub go to a depth of over 300 feet."

A few minutes after this last explosion, *Jenkins* passed through the vicinity of the blast and reported a large area of disturbed water and a strong burnt powder smell. For two hours after this explosion, *Moore* thoroughly searched the surroundings but without another sound contact. Deck personnel on *Moore* noted a strong odor of diesel oil and oil slicks, a clothing article, a box, planks, wood objects and scraps of paper.

Throughout the entire series of attacks, wakes caused considerable difficulty. They had a tendency to "hang" and remain persistent for long periods. They proved difficult to echo range through and produced weak, mushy echoes.

Float lights were dropped on all firing attacks. These proved of invaluable assistance to the conn in checking the CIC's estimated bearing of the sub during regained contact periods.

The success of the action was attributed largely to the high degree of coordination achieved among conn, sonar and CIC crews. During attacks, the CIC evaluator was frequently able to confirm the sonar officer's information on target movement, range rates, estimates of sub's speed, target aspect and identification of wakes encountered. During regained contact periods, the remarkably accurate CIC was able to give the estimated range and bearing of the submarine, verified by the recorder. With one exception, contact was immediately regained on the expected range and bearing. This one exception was due to the submarine's utilization of the DE's wake. Even then, after 23 minutes of lost contact, *Moore* picked it up only 10 degrees and 50 yards off the bearing and range furnished by the CIC. As a result of this effective coordination, the commanding officer at the conn never had any doubt as to the ability of his CIC and sonar teams to regain contact even though sound conditions were far from ideal.

Captain Roosevelt entered his opinion in the log that the submarine was destroyed with all hands. Post-war analysis proved him to be absolutely correct. The DE had sunk Japanese submarine *RO-115*.

Moore departed with other ships from Ulithi on 18 February to provide antisubmarine protection for the carriers furnishing close air support for the forces attacking Iwo Jima. The ship thus began her most grueling period, steaming continuously for 78 days to support this operation and the subsequent one against Okinawa. The destroyer escort operated with the carriers *Tulagi (CVE-72)* and *Anzio (CVE-57)* southeast of Okinawa. During the Okinawa operation, President Roosevelt died on 12 April, a loss felt not only by the nation and the fleet, but particularly by Captain Roosevelt.

On 19 June, *Moore* put to sea with a Task Group providing logistic support for Admiral William F. Halsey's air strikes against the Japanese home islands. On 2 September, the escort vessel entered Tokyo Bay, in the words of her ship's historian, as "a fitting culmination to approximately 14 months of strenuous operation".

THOMASON

A Submarine Handily Dispatched

In June 1944, *Thomason (DE-203)* was involved in heavy enemy action with the Seventh Fleet off the Coast of New Guinea. Near Wadke on 13 June, her gunners helped army antiaircraft units repel an enemy air attack. On the 19th, she took army artillery observers along the coast to Sarmi where she shelled enemy emplacements and an air strip. On 8 November, *Thomason* and *Neuendorf (DE-200)* bombarded Sarmi and targets along the bay. The two ships set fire to enemy storehouses and several other buildings. On 28 December, the DE sailed for Luzon with the San Fabian Attack Force.

One month later, both ships began patrol duty off the west coast of Luzon with the commanding officer of *Thomason*, Lieutenant Commander Charles B. Henriques, as Task Unit Commander. The two vessels were engaged in hunter-killer operations, searching on a 90 degree relative line of bearing (abreast of each other), distance 4,000 yards.

2222 on 7 February 1945. *Thomason's* surface radar operator, Third Class Radarman Paul E. Worsham, made a contact, range 14 miles. The pip was small and erratic at first and did not appear at every sweep of the radar scope. When contact was first reported to the captain by the Officer of The Deck, Lieutenant (jg) Robert M. Denike, the target was believed to be a small surface vessel as it was not thought possible to pick up the low profile of a surfaced sub at that range. Nonetheless, the radarman and the OOD deserved credit for finding the contact and plotting it at the original long ranges. The DE closed the distance and challenged the craft with a flashing light. There was no answer, and surface radar lost contact.

Sonar soon made an underwater contact. After the attacking DE closed the submarine range to 1000 yards on the firing run, the tactics of *Thomason* called for a simple, direct attack. The escort made a hedgehog run but did not fire because she was going too fast. She made another run and fired a hedgehog pattern. From Captain Henriques' war diary:

> "After the range was closed to 300 yards, a white luminous outline of a large submerged mass was seen. At firing range, the water had taken a long, oval shape and was definitely the appearance of a submarine which could not have been more than 25 to 50 feet deep or at periscope depth."

Considering the crippling attrition that was visited on the Japanese undersea vessels by the end of 1944, it was remarkable that this sub would choose to carry out its patrol at or near periscope depth.

Five of the hedgehogs detonated almost simultaneously, and the target was lost. The range was opened for another run. However, the only contact obtained was on the water disturbed by the explosions. As the target area was approached, a heavy diesel oil slick about 250 yards in diameter arose in the disturbed water. A flare night marker was dropped at the windward edge of the slick.

From the explosions and the heavy amount of oil that gushed up from the depths and the failure of both DEs to regain contact in very good sound conditions, it was believed that the submarine was destroyed.

Subsequent search through and around the target area by both ships failed to produce contact other than an explosion disturbance which diminished gradually and disappeared after about 45 minutes. Shortly after midnight, an expanding search pattern was started and continued for nine hours with neither ship regaining contact.

In the morning, an attempt was made to obtain an oil sample. However, the wind and sea had increased to force four. Waves breaking on the side of the ship disturbed the slick and made it very difficult to obtain a sample. The little that was recovered was not considered satisfactory for analysis but was retained on board for future examination.

A post-war disclosure of Japanese naval records, confirmed the presumption of a destroyed submarine beyond a doubt. *RO-55* had been sunk in over 800 fathoms of water.

The attack team functioned efficiently throughout the operation. The flow of information to conn – ranges, center bearings, cut-ons, range rates, doppler and target drift – all were given in an orderly manner and were thoroughly reliable in making the firing runs. Throughout the action, Soundman First Class William A. Hendricks was on the sound stack and Soundman Second Class Eugene G. Zachary was on the sonar range recorder. Lieutenant Commander Charles F. Wiedman jr., ASW Officer, gave interpretations of the tracings and advice to the conn regarding movements of the submarine.

Thomason returned to Mangarin Bay to resume antisubmarine patrols, rescuing four airmen who had bailed out of their burning Liberator. From March 1945 through the end of the war, the ship continued patrols and escort duty among various Philippine ports, Palau, and Hollandia.

FINNEGAN

The Japanese Submarine Fleet Reduced by One

15 February 1945. *Finnegan (DE-307)* sailed from Saipan for the assault on Iwo Jima. On arrival four days later, she screened transports as they launched their initial invasion boats onto the bloody sands of that enemy stronghold.

Early morning of 26 February. This vessel was proceeding from Iwo Jima to Saipan and acting in a screen with destroyer mine layer *Shannon (DM-25)* and *William C. Miller (DE-529).* The convoyed vessels consisted of nine large transports.

0555. Suddenly, a radar surface contact was reported by *Finnegan's* CIC at 17,600 yards. A plot was immediately started and the contact tracked on the dead reckoning tracer. The target was reported to be moving at five knots in a left turn.

0612. *Finnegan*, commanded by Lieutenant Commander H. Huffman, left the screening formation to steer an interception course at 17.5 knots with the range to the contact now shortened to 10,000 yards. Eight minutes later, the contact disappeared from the radar scope at 6700 yards. The DE passed over the point where the target had disappeared and commenced Operation Observant.

0642. The sound team made initial contact with the submarine at 1500 yards. Speed was reduced to 10 knots in order to take a fathometer reading and to classify the contact as a submarine. The target was lost when passing over the sub but was quickly regained, and the range was opened to enable an attack run. The sub speed was three knots.

The DE fired a hedgehog pattern with negative results. Contact was lost and regained at 400 yards. The second and third hedgehog attacks were equally disappointing. Unfortunately, on the latter attack, the operator inadvertently tripped the power switch, allowing only two projectiles to be fired at the proper instant. The remainder of the pattern was fired after a delay of from three to five seconds. Antisubmarine operations were fought in seconds and fractions of seconds. An error of three seconds invariably meant a sure miss.

In opening the range, the operator was distracted by a wake echo. Once corrected, however, the sonar found the correct target. After opening to 1350 yards, the DE commenced its fourth hedgehog attack.

Somewhere down in the depths, a Japanese skipper was being watched anxiously by his crew as he changed courses and speeds. Unlike depth charges, hedgehogs were silent — until they hit, cracking holes in the hull and bringing certain death by drowning or crushing from pressure. All the men could do was to obey orders, hope and wait.

The fourth pattern fared no better than the others, nor the fifth as well. It was now about two hours since *Finnegan* had first made a radar contact and since her crew had gone to GQ, hoping that each successive attack would produce a cheer. So far, nothing to cheer.

It was now apparent that the submarine had reached a very considerable depth, and a depth charge pattern with deep setting was indicated. Speed was increased to 15 knots, range was opened out to 1100 yards, and a dry run was made to obtain a fathometer reading. Contact was lost, then regained after passing over the submarine's position.

0811. Captain Huffman, with renewed determination, commenced the first depth charge attack, starting from 1650 yards. *Finnegan* fired a 13 depth charge pattern with deep setting. No results.

0838. The DE started a run for another depth charge attack with nothing to show for the effort. The plot revealed the submarine to be maneuvering radically during the approach. Power was lost in the sound gear for two minutes following the explosions, but contact was quickly regained at 750 yards. The range was opened to 1000 yards, and the ship passed over the submarine to obtain depth readings. Soundings between 120 and 180 feet were obtained, indicating that the submarine was varying its depth, hoping to confuse its attacker.

0913. The ship reduced her speed to 10 knots, opening the range to 1500 yards for a hedgehog attack. She fired a full pattern. One projectile detonated one to three seconds after striking the surface. However, there was no supporting evidence of a hit, and it was believed to have been from faulty ammunition. Contact was lost at 325 yards on weak recorder traces, indicating that the submarine was now very deep. Accordingly, it was decided to make the next attack with a depth charge pattern on deep setting. Contact was regained at about 600 yards, and the range was opened to 1900 yards.

0947. *Finnegan* commenced her third depth charge attack. The submarine was now believed to be considerably nearer to the surface, but there was not sufficient time to change the pattern setting from deep to shallow, and the attack was broken off. Contact was regained at 700 yards, and the range was opened to 1700 yards.

The ship restarted the aborted third depth charge attack. A medium pattern was set on the assumption that, since the submarine was apparently changing depth and had been fairly near the surface at last estimate, he would now have submerged somewhat. A full pattern of depth charges was fired at a medium setting. Contact was held down to 200 yards. Four minutes and 51 seconds after rolling the first depth charge, a terrific underwater explosion was felt. It was preceded and followed by rumbling noises which soon turned into bubbling noises, both clearly audible on the sound gear. Contact was lost.

1008. Floating debris and oil were observed in the water, discolored by the dye marker used by the DE to help regain contact. The motor whaleboat was lowered to search the area and recover wreckage and samples of oil.

Operation Observant was conducted despite the time interval since the last contact because it was believed that the submarine had been heavily damaged and could have sufficient power to propel itself from the area searched by the DEs. Observant was followed by a retiring search, but no further contact was obtained.

The heavy explosion felt after the final depth charge attack was evidently at great depth because no surface turbulence was observed. The water depth was 1300 fathoms. Oil and debris continued to rise over the same spot during the remainder of the day and, by 1800, the oil slick covered an area two miles wide and four miles long. Strong diesel oil fumes, increasing in intensity during the day, was fairly heavy by late afternoon. The fumes were also plainly noticeable by all hands until their departure from the area.

The debris collected consisted of numerous and varied pieces of timber in assorted sizes. One of the smaller pieces was covered with red lacquer or veneer and bore a single painted Japanese character. One of the larger pieces bore Japanese characters written in pencil.

A floating mine near the plotted position of the submarine, identified as a Japanese horn type, was sunk by rifle fire before *Finnegan* departed from the area.

Debris and oil samples remained on board until they could be shipped to examination authorities in Pearl Harbor. *Finnegan* was subsequently credited with having sunk Japanese submarine *I-370*.

Arriving at Okinawa in April, *Finnegan* participated in numerous antisubmarine operations and screening of assault vessels. On 28 May, she drove off a would-be suicide aircraft. With the war ended, she sailed on 15 September for a lengthy and final voyage to Charleston, South Carolina.

HORACE A. BASS

An APD Demonstrates Its Antisubmarine Capability

High speed transports started their careers with DE hulls. Some were converted after they had been in service as DEs whereas others were modified while still on the ways. In the process of conversion, the APD retained much of its antisubmarine abilities, becoming a dual purpose vessel. At times, when ferrying troops, it would be convoyed by DEs. At other times, it could revert to its original DE role and convoy large vessels. It was in this latter role that *Horace A. Bass (APD-124)* was about to show her mettle as an antisubmarine vessel.

During the nerve shattering picket duty at Okinawa, *Bass* fought off *kamikazes* and splashed at least one. A welcome reprieve came on 10 April 1945 when she sailed with a convoy to Guam for a short period of rest and recreation. After a week in Guam, she was ordered back to Okinawa as escort for another convoy. *Bass* was one of four ships in an antisubmarine screen protecting a convoy of seventeen ships.

Allen Hodges, a 19 year old ensign, was Officer of The Deck at 1804 on 25 April 1945 when the ensuing action developed. This author expressed surprise to Hodges that a 19 year old could be an ensign. He stated in no uncertain terms that there were a good many ensigns around that age from the V-12 officer training program if they had completed three years of college, were at least 18 years old, could pass the physical, and had completed the required courses in navigation, seamanship, ordnance, etc. He also had trained as an attack amphibious officer and was assigned to *Bass* with a 16 man UDT crew. Furthermore, in his short stint on the *Bass*, he had become a fully qualified OOD and watch officer at sea. Lastly, he wanted me to know that graduates of the V-12 program included John Cameron Swazey, Senator Pat Moynahan, Johnny Carson and Jack Lennon among many other notables. I said nothing more.

The sonar operator announced that he had a good, solid echo, distance 1250 yards. Ensign Hodges promptly notified the captain, Lieutenant Commander F.W. Kuhn, who instructed him to proceed to the CIC and to start a plot. The contact was classified as authentic. Captain Kuhn related in his action report:

> "After evaluating the contact as a submarine because of very sharp echoes and slightly down doppler, we started our approach. The doppler continued moderately down with a sharp echo and, when we had steadied our course on the center bearing, the submarine moved to the right. The range rate was 13 knots. We took our lead to the right and dropped five depth charges, firing on the recorder. We then opened the range and circled back toward the area of attack but we were unable to regain a good contact because of the residual water disturbance from depth charge detonations.
>
> We made a quick swing again to the right and cut off the recorder to enable us to examine the recorder traces. We restarted the recorder and regained sound contact at about 900 yards. The submarine returned a very sharp echo and revealed slight up doppler, increasing to moderately up. There were two echoes, but the second one was sharp, and the sub again moved to the right. We took our lead in the same direction. Near the end of this run, the bearings moved sharply to the right. We applied hard right rudder and dropped five depth charges, again firing on the recorder.
>
> After the second attack, the sub dived deep. We made several more runs on her, but each time we lost contact at such a great distance that it was not considered worth-while to drop more charges without better close-in data. The traces seemed to indicate that the sub was using *pillenwerfers* and knuckles. Underwater transmissions six times in succession attempted to distract our approach. As we only had six depth charges left, we wanted to make them count. Two hours after the last contact, we were able to make two attacks. All manner of debris and oil came to the surface. We were still trying to get another shot at the sub when we reached the end of our time limit set by the Task Unit Commander. Shortly

after 2000, we abandoned the attack and set our course to rejoin the convoy."

Sometime after the cessation of hostilities, it was learned that *Bass* had sunk the Japanese submarine *R-109*.

At the end of this convoy, *Bass* returned to the fiery hell of Okinawa, from which she did not emerge unscathed. See narrative *Iwo Jima to Okinawa — The Fast Transports*.

EARL V. JOHNSON

Score One – Hopefully

7 August 1945. *Earl V. Johnson (DE-702)* was acting as escort in company with *Knox (DE-580)*, *Major (DE-796)*, and *PCE-849*, forming an ASW screen for a convoy of 25 LSTs, en route from Okinawa to Leyte. *Johnson* was the senior escort, designated as Commander Task Unit and was patrolling ahead of the formation.

1223. *Johnson's* sonar stack operator, Soundman Second Class William Joseph Archibald, announced a sound contact at 800 yards. The convoy was promptly signalled "45 turn" (Turn 45 degrees to port).

Lieutenant Commander J.J. Jordy, commanding officer of *Johnson*, immediately set about the launching of an urgent depth charge attack, 14 charges in a shallow pattern with negative results. The ship then established procedure to regain contact but soon shifted to Operation Observant. After 25 minutes, she made contact at 1300 yards, but it widened strangely at the end, suggesting the sub captain's use of a German-style *pillenwerfer*.

1255. *Johnson* followed up with a nine depth charge attack at a medium setting. Results, however, were nil. Because of certain odd characteristics of the contact and excessive wake effect, the attacking ship again opted for Operation Observant instead of regain contact procedure. When completed an hour later, contact had not been regained. Because she was scheduled to be detached the next morning and did not wish to make the convoy vulnerable to attack, an order was sent to *PCE-849* to relieve *Johnson*.

While awaiting the *PCE*, *Johnson* prepared to execute a new search procedure and started on the first leg. About 25 minutes later, *PCE-849* arrived with orders to relieve *Johnson* and to carry out the new search plan. However, before the DE could depart, she made a good sonar contact at 2200 yards and went in on the attack.

A nine charge medium depth pattern was dropped. Shortly thereafter, a loud underwater explosion was heard on the DE. Once again, *Johnson* started Observant after failing to regain contact in normal procedure. Twenty minutes after this barrage, *PCE 849* made contact and attacked with hedgehogs without apparent result.

0235. A torpedo wake crossed *Johnson's* bow about ten yards ahead! At that particular moment, the captain was talking on the TBS with *PCE 849* and did not see the torpedo wake. The first report was erroneous, that the torpedo came from starboard and passed aft. To meet the threat, he gave the order for right full rudder to run down the track and then was told that the torpedo had actually come from the port side forward. He shifted the rudder in order to run down the indicated track from the port side. Of course, the dead time between the two commands created a dangerous hiatus, broadside to the torpedo; Fortunately, the torpedo was slightly off target.

0245. Two more torpedoes came from the port beam, the track angle normal to the ship's course!

The skipper ordered left full rudder to comb the torpedo tracks. The first one passed less than 10 yards ahead; the second passed beneath the DE amidships. The submarine range was about 1000 yards, and a large cloud of very black smoke rose from the water. Seaman Dan Senoff remembers the torpedoes and likely will not forget them:

> "We were two days out of Okinawa, heading for Leyte. Knowing the waters were notorious for enemy submarines, we were all on edge, especially after spending restless days and nights trying to dodge Japanese suicide planes.
>
> The alarm sounded at 2410, designating a submarine contact. It didn't take too much deliberation on my part to get to my battle station on the double. After spending a few minutes on the alert, word came to secure from battle stations. I decided not to go below deck and to stay topside for a while. I don't recall the time lapse before the second alarm had sounded. By now, I got the feeling that no sleep would be had by any of us this night.
>
> My usual GQ station was located inside in the aft part of the ship. I wanted to see what was happening so I made my way in the blackness to the boat deck. It couldn't have been more than a few minutes of searching when we started dropping depth charges. After the roar of our charges had died down, I heard the blood-curdling cry, 'Torpedo wake coming at us off the port side!' By now, my eyes had become accustomed to the dark, and I knew the situation was very dangerous. I guess I didn't know what to do, and everybody near me was in the same stupor.
>
> I tightened my life jacket a bit and tried to think how high I'd be blown when it hit. Before I knew it, the surging messenger of death went past our ship by 10 feet! —- I was damn scared! Men in the area were discussing how close we were to our ancestors. I started to relax, meaning I started to breathe again. All was quiet in a few minutes, but we knew this Jap was playing for keeps.
>
> Again, out of the night a lookout screamed, 'Torpedo wake coming in amidship'! Knowing I didn't have time to run, all I did was to brace myself for the explosion that would surely blow us to eternity. The seconds seemed like hours. Finally, I looked over the side and saw the wake of the fish zooming away from us. From all indications, the missile was set at the wrong depth because it went under us, or the way I saw it, God was watching over us!"

Because of the many wakes in the area, resulting in constant echoes, the situation was considered dangerous in not knowing the precise location of the sub. The difficulty of sound gear in distinguishing water knuckles from the real thing prompted the skipper's decision to clear the area temporarily and let the water settle. The PCE was ordered to do the same.

0256. The PCE reported a good contact and went in on the attack with her hedgehogs.

Results were negative, and *Johnson* reversed course two minutes later to assist the PCE. At the same time, Soundman Archibald received possible hydrophone effects. The DE proceeded down the bearing to investigate but found nothing. Minutes later, possible hydrophone effects were received on her starboard beam. A run down that bearing was unrewarding for the effort. She again proceeded to assist the PCE. En route, the *Johnson* radarman announced a small radar contact, range 1400 yards. Captain Jordy proceeded to investigate but without any better luck than before.

0326. *Johnson* made a good sonar contact at 1700 yards and fired a 14 depth charge pattern. Fifty seconds after the last charge detonated, a loud underwater explosion was heard. At the same time, there was a prolonged rumbling, crumbling noise in the sound gear, followed by a high column of white smoke above the explosion point.

The bridge lost steering control and shifted to emergency steering aft. The selsyn motor was on fire and burned out. Power was lost on the number one main motor. The ship proceeded on one motor and emergency steering aft to clear the area. The former engineer officer has a more detailed account of damage sustained:

> "My name is James E. Stockton and I was engineer officer on *Earl V. Johnson* at the time. The following is an account of this action as best I can recall it.The damage to *Johnson* was self-inflicted. Here's what happened:
>
> My battle station was in number one engine room. The ship took a terrible beating from the depth charges. Sometime in the midst of all this, I was called to number two engine room. Our port propulsion motor (electric) had two large slip rings, and the forward one had become almost red hot. The brushes were arcing due to the ship's bouncing from the concussion of the depth charges. I reasoned that, if we could make 410 turns per minute (flank speed) on two slip-rings, we should be able to make 200 (RPMs) on one slip ring. We removed the brushes from the forward ring and, for the remainder of the encounter, we made 200 turns on the port screw.
>
> Meanwhile, the concussion from the depth charges had so damaged our selsyn motors which controlled the rudder that part of the crew was back there steering with block and tackle on the rudder control."

Because the convoy was inadequately protected with only two escorts, and since it would be futile and dangerous to remain in the area with inadequate steering and one engine, Captain Jordy felt that it would be best for *Johnson* to clear the area and rejoin the convoy. Repairs were effected en route. Captain Jordy wrote an interesting analysis of the engagement:

> "The DRT track showed that it was physically impossible for all contacts to have been made on one submarine. Hydrophone effects, which were not definite, and radar indications, all in the southerly part of the track, suggested the possible presence of another submarine.
>
> High speed was used to avoid torpedoing. High speed (tear drop) depth charges were used on all attacks primarily because hedgehogs had been stowed below when Typhoon Condition II was set a few days earlier. Weather had been too rough until darkness set in to bring up, re-fuse, and reload hedgehogs. As it turned out, this was extremely fortunate because there is no doubt in the commanding officer's mind that we would have been hit by torpedoes had we been steaming at 10 knots, hedgehog attack speed.
>
> It was felt that the Japanese were using *pillenwerfers* or something similar. Several of the contacts ended up peculiarly at close range with echoes suggesting wake effects, although earlier echoes indicated a solid target, a positive range rate and definite target movement. Several contact echoes, classified as definite wake, subsequently indicated that they were possibly submarine.
>
> At the time of the torpedo firings, the submarine was well within the sound search area. During this time, several contacts were made and hydrophone effects were heard, but inasmuch as *PCE-849* was directly in the line of bearing and at the approximate range, it was judged that the target was the PCE. The PCE was asked to keep clear but did not do so, probably because of the speed and radical maneuvers of *Johnson*.
>
> With this in mind, the commanding officer has decided to try conning the next submarine attack from CIC, putting the executive officer on the bridge to act as safety officer to conn ship in the event of an emergency such as sudden appearance of torpedo wakes, mines, etc. (Captain Jordy was ahead of his time. This is the manner in which commanding and executive officers are positioned today on destroyers and frigates, not only at General Quarters, but for other drills and entering or leaving harbor.)
>
> It is felt that attack number four was successful and resulted in the destruction of the submarine. It is a certainty that the submarine was just about in the middle of the pattern. A shallow pattern (alternating 50 and 100 foot depths) was used and, since contact was lost at about 125 yards, it is fairfairly certain that the submarine was also shallow."

Commander E.E. Hull, Commander of Escort Division 60, stated (In part) in his report to The Commander-in-Chief U.S.Fleet:

> "It is concurred by this command, from both the description of the action and subsequent conversation with the commanding officer, as well as from a study of the track chart, that the attack made at 0330 was effective and must have resulted in serious damage or destruction of the submarine. It is unfortunate that further search could not have been undertaken, although the commanding officer's decision to clear the *Johnson* from the area is considered well advised.."

Unfortunately, the inability of *Johnson* to reinforce her claim with debris, oil or Japanese post-war confirmation has denied her an award for a kill.

With hostilities ended, *Earl V. Johnson* arrived at Okinawa on 4 September and a week later began the occupation of Jinsen and Taku. She departed from Buckner Bay, Okinawa, in November and arrived at Boston on 15 December 1945.

THE MIDGETS

Kaiten, the Undersea Kamikazes

Like the airborne *kamikazes*, the one or two man submarines called *kaiten* were suicide vehicles. These bizarre weapons were really torpedoes driven by their occupants to certain death. In fact, many were retrained aircraft fighter pilots. If the pilots reached their targets, which only a few did, they were blown to bits. If they were sunk by antisubmarine vessels, they were finished as well. If nothing happened, they died of asphyxiation or lack of oxygen as their vessels became slowly sinking coffins. Like the suicide aircraft, they were part of the desperate Japanese attempt to stem the inexorable advance of the U.S. Fleet onto their home islands.

The midgets were about 54 feet long, a few as long as 80 feet, and the warheads in their bows carried 3000 pounds of high explosive. They could attain a maximum speed of 40 knots submerged.

The first midgets to introduce themselves to the U.S. Navy paid a call only a couple of hours before flights of *Zeros* came screaming over Diamond Head, Oahu, Hawaii to pounce on a sleepy fleet at anchor in Pearl Harbor, 7 December 1941. An old flush deck (four piper) destroyer, *Ward (DD-139)* was patrolling her assigned sector outside of the anchorage. This was a first command for Lieutenant W.W. Outerbridge. He had relieved the previous captain two days before the attack. A couple of weeks prior to *Ward's* patrol, Washington had flashed a "war warning" to all forces. Accordingly, the Commander in Chief Pacific Fleet, Admiral Husband E. Kimmel, placed his sea patrols on a war footing with orders to promptly fire on or depth charge any submarine contacted and to do so without further orders.

0408 on 7 December 1941. *Ward* was advised by minesweeper *Condor (AMc-14)* that she had sighted a periscope close by. The DD scoured the area until her lookouts spotted a periscope and partial conning tower astern of the minesweeper. That ruined the submarine's plan to follow the minesweeper unobtrusively through the boom net defenses as she returned to base. General quarters was promptly sounded as Outerbridge raced to the bridge, clad in a rather unmilitary kimono over pajamas and an old style helmet on his head.

Ward fired the first shot of the Pacific War at 0605. It missed, but subsequent shots were true and smashed into the sub. Four depth charges followed, and the oil pouring to the surface marked the sub's watery grave.

Captain Outerbridge radioed a terse action report to the Commandant 14th Naval District Headquarters and, to distinguish his message from numerous questionable sightings by local patrol forces, stated that he had sighted, fired upon and sunk an unidentified submarine in the defensive sea area. Delays in seeking confirmation and a reluctance to heed the warning resulted in the message's transmission through tortuously slow communication channels. In the interim, *Ward* echo ranged for further contacts and soon latched on to another one. She dropped a depth charge pattern but without noticeable result.

Nearing the harbor entrance around 0800, those on *Ward's* deck heard the sound of gunfire and explosions as smoke began to engulf Pearl Harbor. Soon, a strafing plane with "meatballs" painted on the wings dispelled any doubt that a war was in progress.

Dwelling on hindsight may be a useless occupation, but one does have to recall the approximate hour and 15 minutes between *Ward's* urgent radio report and the Japanese attack. Within that time, fighters and bombers might have scrambled in sufficient force to change the course of history. What a pity! The loss of thousands of American and Allied lives and a huge outpouring of treasure might have been avoided.

Destroyer escorts had not yet been built, but *Ward* was the nearest thing to one. Later on, refitted and reclassified as *APD-16*, she conducted numerous escort operations and met her end in furious action at Ormoc Bay. See chapter *The Philippine Campaign*.

Five *kaiten*, each with a crew of two, were transported by a mother sub(s) and released in the Pearl Harbor area. One was sunk by *Ward*, one was sunk inside the harbor, and one was beached on the shore. The one that *Ward* sank was 80 feet long. She was discovered on an offshore coral reef by a diving instructor many years after the war. She was raised and sent to Japan, where it is a memorial.

In retrospect, we wonder why the Japanese sent the midgets into the target area before the main attack. Their discovery could have wrecked the whole operation. The Japanese could not have known that our communications would be so badly handled. In spite of the failure of the Pearl Harbor *kaiten* to accomplish anything of importance, the Japanese constructed a large number of them.

In February 1944, the design of a prototype *kaiten* was approved by the Japanese Navy. After nearly 20 months of fruitless proposals through the chain of command, Lieutenant (Jg) Kuroki and Ensign Nishina got permission to build a few *kaiten*.

The Japanese Model 93 torpedo, used by surface warships, was called "Long Lance" because of its great range. Its warhead was nearly 1000 pounds and it could make up to 49 knots, faster than American torpedoes. It also had a range of 20 miles. Kuroki and Nishina wanted to take a Model 93, cut it in two, then insert a passenger compartment with controls and a periscope at the center. At first, the *kaiten* was not intended to be a suicide weapon; it became one about the same time as the formation of the *kamikaze* corps. The finished product ended up much thicker than the Model 93's original 24 inch diameter. Its length was extended from 30 to 54 feet and its warhead increased to 3000 pounds.

The *I-366* was one of eleven supply submarines of the I Type. They were built for the Japanese Navy as undersea transport vessels to run supplies past allied ships to their blockaded island garrisons. The submarines in this class had the greatest submerged and surfaced range of any Japanese submarines and had an endurance of 60 days. They could descend to 245 feet and could carry five *kaiten* suicide subs.

When interviewed at the end of the war, Japanese officers were under the impression that they had sunk about forty allied combat and service vessels. Their over-estimates were probably a result of the inability of a midget to radio its accomplishments or failures because it was doomed on launching from the mother sub. Our best estimates of ships having been hit by midgets included two Navy ships, the fueler *Mississinewa (AO-59)* and the destroyer escort *Underhill (DE-682)*, and one merchant ship, *SS Canada Victory* . These seem to be meager returns for eight carrying submarines and 900 lives expended in the midget program. Both navy ship losses are described in this chapter under headings of *Rall* and *Underhill*.

Tempest, Fire and Foe

RALL

A Kaiten Strikes and Another Is Struck in Return

In the early weeks of November 1944, *Rall (DE-304)* served in an escort group, protecting the oilers of Task Group 30.8, which in turn supported the assault ships at the Leyte Gulf landings. During this assignment, she rode out heavy weather from a typhoon with no serious damage but with many pale faces and protesting stomachs.

To Japanese Admiral Miwa, commander of midget submarines, the heavy units anchored in Ulithi looked like tempting targets. The midgets were alluded to by American sailors as "seagoing sewer pipes". This new torpedo-sub differed from prior ones in that the operator could abandon it, but only in the event of an operational failure. The Germans used something similar against allied forces in the Mediterranean, but the occupant was expected to abandon after the torpedo was on course but before it found its mark. Not so, the gung-ho Japanese; it was *banzai*-boom - goodbye!

Eight of the *kaiten* were transported piggy-back on two I-boats to an area near the channel leading to the Ulithi Lagoon. They were detached from their carriers during the late hours of 19 November. At dawn on the 20th, a ship's lookout reported a periscope near the sea buoy at the bottom of the channel. *Case (DD-370)* was close by and destroyed the midget by ramming. Two others, however, made it inside the lagoon.

The gangway watch Petty Officer on *Rall* reported to the Officer of The Deck an explosion on one of the ships anchored near the southern end of the anchorage and close to the Mugai Channel entrance. The commanding officer of *Rall*, Lieutenant Commander C.B. *Taylor*, ordered preparations to get underway.

The explosion was a torpedo hit by a *kaiten* on tanker *Mississinewa (AO-59)*. The blast and resultant flame lit up the area brighter than the developing dawn. *Rall* and *Halloran (DE-305)* of Escort Division 61 and *Weaver (DE-741)* responded to a general TBS summons from *Cotten (DD-669)* for any destroyers types underway to investigate in the vicinity of the cruiser *Mobile (CL-63)*.

Weaving among ships at anchor, *Rall* raced across the crowded anchorage. As the DE approached the moored cruisers *Mobile* and *Biloxi (CL-80)*, *Mobile* reported that she had sighted a swirl in the water between *Biloxi* and herself. *Rall* maneuvered to run between the two cruisers, avoiding a destroyer and two other destroyer escorts in the immediate vicinity, all moving at high speed.

When first sighted, the water disturbance was about 200 yards ahead of *Rall*. The swirl was very distinct, with continuous, agitated air bubbles rising through it, apparently caused by a circular motion. The swirl was abreast of the bow of *Mobile* and somewhat closer to that ship than to *Biloxi*. The depth of water was 20 fathoms.

Because of the close quarters between the big cruisers, use of the "K" guns or a full depth charge pattern was ruled out. As the *Rall*'s stern passed through the swirl, one charge set at 50 feet was dropped. The *Mobile* reported by TBS that the charge landed about 50 feet past the swirl. The DE was brought around sharply and headed back through the swirl. The depth charges were reset to 75 feet.

This time, the captain timed his first depth charge drop after the bow of *Rall* cut the swirl. The approach was made with the current parallel to the direction in which the cruisers were tailing; it was felt that the enemy sub was located up-current from the swirl. The water disturbance was still apparent on the second run. As the bow passed through it, two charges were dropped five seconds apart. Speed during both attacks was 10 knots with no sonar contact on either run.

ComCortDiv 61, Commander H. Reich, was embarked in *Rall* during this action and noted that this was the first time a depth charge had been dropped in Ulithi Lagoon and that the captain of *Rall* exhibited initiative and quick thinking in making the two limited attacks.

Immediately following the second attack, *Mobile* reported two men in the center of the turbulent water, agitated by the exploding charges. *Rall* hastened to return to the area, but *Halloran (DE-305)*, being closer to the water disturbance, moved in rapidly, hoping to pick up survivors. *Rall* then cruised slowly, well off the bows of *Mobile* and *Biloxi*, watching the activities of *Halloran* and continuing sonar search. This continued until *Rall* was ordered by the Task Unit Commander to join the inner harbor patrol. After *Halloran* had retired from the scene, *Mobile* sent out a small boat to search the area and buoy the spot of the attacks.

Mid-morning, same day. *Halloran* signalled *Rall* that, following her second attack, two Japanese men bobbed up in the water right where the depth charges were dropped. One was swimming for a while and then went under. There were no apparent signs of life in the other one; his body went down alongside *Halloran's* fantail before recovery could be made. A few hours later, Commander Cruiser Division 13 reported that the boat sent out by *Mobile* had picked up a block of wood, a wooden seat with Japanese markings, a brightly colored pillow with Japanese writing on it. Some oil and bubbles were seen by the boat crew. The search was continued for more debris.

Rall subsequently received credit for destroying a Japanese midget submarine. Somewhat later, at Okinawa, this DE would receive a far greater challenge to her existence. Could the ghosts of the *kaiten* have been resurrected in a suicide aircraft seeking a bloody revenge?

See narrative *Iwo Jima to Okinawa – The Destroyer Escorts*.

UNDERHILL

An Unhappy Prediction Came True

As related in the early part of this book, I (the author) reported aboard *Sims (DE-154)* in late 1943 as executive officer, relieving Lieutenant Robert Newcomb.

Since two executive officers are not needed aboard one ship, and since Bob was anxious to get to his new assignment, it took us just half a day to report to the captain that Bob was ready to go and that I was ready to take over. But one day in a war is like many days in peace, and I recall Bob Newcomb as though it were yesterday. A Princeton graduate and NROTC Navy reservist, I placed Bob in his early thirties, about eight years older than I. He was a strikingly good looking man, tall and erect, with dark hair and mustache, and a tinge of gray on both temples. Bob was about to be promoted to Lieutenant Commander with a DE command of his own.

I sat with him in the executive officer's stateroom that day, going over his paper work, the ship's routine, navigational instruments and publications and what the captain liked and didn't like. With business completed, we chatted for a while. It was quitting time in the Brooklyn Navy Yard, and the clatter of tools suddenly ceased. He was packed and ready to go when he mentioned something about a premonition that he would not survive the war.

I didn't take it seriously. I was about to say something of not much consequence, like I'd see him in the Emperor's palace in Tokyo after the war. Fortunately, I was spared the necessity of saying anything because a mess attendant knocked at the door to advise that the captain would like to see us both in his cabin.

On a dark, stormy night in mid-Atlantic, some weeks later, I was chatting over a cup of coffee with our first lieutenant, Keith Urmy. Somehow, the subject of my predecessor came up, and I was surprised to learn that he and other officers were aware of Bob Newcomb's acceptance of imminent demise in World War II. I was also apprised that he had even told close relatives and friends to prepare for the certainty of his fate.

It was almost two years later, August 1945, when I suddenly had occasion to remember him. Germany had surrendered in May, and Japan was not far from doing the same. In the last months of the war, in the vicinity of Nansei Shoto, Okinawa, there were nests of camouflaged or concealed *kamikazes*, suicide torpedo boats, and midget submarines. They posed a threat to supply and warship traffic between Formosa (now Taiwan) and Southern Japan. Consequently, picket ships and organized convoys were still in operation. The last Japanese naval offensive of World War II was waged by Submarine Division 15, commanded by Captain K. Ageta. The division was composed of six I-boats, each of which carried six *kaiten* as described in the preceding *Rall* narrative. However, there was little success for them until *I-53* made a big score.

SORRY, NO ICE CREAM

Lieutenant Nathaniel Benchley was commanding officer of *PC-125* in a convoy with *Underhill (DE-682)* and recalled the traumatic events of 24 July 1945.

> "My ship was part of a convoy from Okinawa to the Philippines. It was a strange convoy because the escorts outnumbered the ships being convoyed. We had eight ships, screened by nine escorts, mostly PCs and the smaller 110 foot sub chasers. The escort commander was the destroyer escort *Underhill*. This unbalance, plus leaving the combat zone for a rear area, made us all feel unusually relaxed as we filed out of Okinawa one sunny afternoon.
>
> *Underhill*, our immediate superior, was a happy and well run ship with high morale. A few days before, we had gone alongside to deliver some charts and noticed that she was clean and efficiently run. We also observed a good deal of light hearted clowning among the off-duty crew.
>
> One morning, when we had been out about a week, *Underhill* picked up an unidentified aircraft on her radar and all the escorts closed smartly into their antiaircraft stations. However, the plane remained more than seven miles distant and, after a while, it disappeared, permitting us to return to our normal screening stations. It was a brilliant, fire-hot day and the glassy sea sparkled in the sun. I turned the ship over to the Officer of The Deck and went down to the comparative coolness of the wardroom. Gunnery Officer Howard Tampke was playing solitaire at the wardroom table, while Wallace Roth, the executive officer was manicuring his nails with a hunting knife.
>
> Tampke finished his solitaire, and he and I started a game of double solitaire. We played quietly, lulled by the engine vibrations and the gentle, almost imperceptible rocking of the ship. There was a knock at the door, and the signalman handed me a message from *Underhill*, 'It occurs to me that you people might like some ice cream. I will give five gallons of ice cream to three ships a day in the following order of rotation.' We were second on the list to go alongside. The signalman left, smiling.
>
> 'That's pretty damned nice', I said, 'He (Bob Newcomb, *Underhill* skipper) didn't have to do a thing like that.' I sent for the cook. 'It seems that *Underhill* is going to give us five gallons of ice cream if we come alongside with a container to take it. Just break out some kind of can. We won't be alongside for a half hour or more.'
>
> 'Aye, aye, sir!' The cook jammed on his hat and disappeared. As he ran down the deck, we could hear him shouting, 'Ice cream, you bastards! Ice cream!'
>
> Tampke and I had just started back to our cribbage when the intercom opened up with a crackle:
>
> 'Bridge to wardroom', is the captain there?'
>
> 'Go ahead.'
>
> 'Captain, the DE says hold off on the ice cream deal. deal. He's spotted a mine and he's going to sink it.'
>
> 'O. K.'
>
> I had just got my hand arranged when the intercom opened up again. 'Captain, the convoy is changing course. The mine is just ahead of them. The whole convoy is coming over this way.' I put my hand face down on the table. To Tampke, I said, 'No fair peeking' and then went out and up to the flying bridge.
>
> The sun was hotter than before, and the bridge railing burned to the touch. The sea and sky were a blazing, brilliant blue and, far off, astern of the convoy, was a small cluster of puffy cumulus clouds. The ships had turned and were heading in our direction, all except *Underhill*. Through the binoculars, I could see a small black dot in the water ahead of her with little dashes of spray spurting up around it from the DE's 20mm guns. I steered our ship out to leave more room for the convoy and then watched *Underhill* become smaller as we drew away from her.
>
> Tampke came up on the bridge, squinting in the glare of the sun:
>
> 'Ain't he sunk it yet?'
>
> 'I guess not', I replied.
>
> 'I was about to call you anyway, Captain, the O.D. said we were next in line for the ice cream.'
>
> The intercom on the bridge sputtered, and the voice of the radioman came on. 'Tell the Captain that the DE has a sub contact. He's leaving the mine to chase the contact.'
>
> Through the glasses, I could see that *Underhill* had changed course. She was rapidly becoming smaller. 'DE says he's making a run now', said the intercom
>
> By this time, *Underhill* was about three miles astern of

the convoy, but I could see the small puffs of smoke as depth charges were launched from the side throwers, and then the fountains of gray water as the charges went off. At that distance, there was no noise and no perceptible movement. On our ship, the word of *Underhill*'s chase had spread quickly, and members of the crew began to appear on deck in various stages of undress, all looking back at the slowly disappearing speck on the horizon.

'DE says he's got a sub on the surface', came the radioman's voice. 'He's chasing it and is going to ram.'

I strained my eyes looking through the glasses, but *Underhill* was beginning to shimmer in the horizon heat waves and, for a moment, I lost sight of her. Then I saw a small burst of smoke and thought excitedly that she might have exploded the sub, but the smoke turned into a boil of orange flame that started to rise straight upward; it bubbled and churned in a curdling of orange and black until it got up to about 10,000 feet. Then the smoke flattened out and mushroomed, soiling the base of the white cumulus clouds. *Underhill* disappeared from sight. Around me, I heard the comments of the crew:

'That was the DE that blew up.'
'Christ, did she go!'
'That was the DE.'
'There ain't no survivors there. Where's the DE?'
'She blew up'.
'Jesus, look at the smoke. That's the DE, all right.'
'There's nobody getting off that ship. That son- of bitch certainly blew up.'
'You can't see nothing but smoke.'

The smoke lifted a bit from the horizon, and underneath it was a tiny spot that seemed to be spurting steam. It disappeared as I watched. A lonely, hollow feeling came over me, and I lowered the glasses and looked at Tampke. His face was without expression, and his eyes were fixed on the horizon. The intercom opened up, and we both jumped.

'*PC-804* is going back to look for survivors.'

For a long while, nobody said anything. Then the radio began to chatter with reports from several ships, and it appeared that the water astern of the convoy was swarming with small submarines. (We learned later that they were manned torpedoes, run by suicide pilots. They were launched from a mother sub, guided into our path by the aircraft that had tailed us that morning.)

I remember the rest of the afternoon indistinctly, and the sunset came upon us quite fast. I do recall, however, that the dark mushroom of smoke from *Underhill* hung in the sky until the last pink streaks of afterglow were blocked out by the oncoming night."

A major warship had been sunk with all logs and notes and without an action report. The disaster had to be laid to rest, and the events are described by Lieutenants E.M. Rich and Joseph M. Timberlake, the two senior surviving officers as related to the Division of Naval History:

Lieutenant Porter (into a tape recorder):

"Mr. Rich, I understand you were doing convoy work at the time. Just tell us what you were doing in the Pacific area."

Lieutenant Rich:

"We reported to Commander Philippine Sea Frontier and were doing escort work among the Philippines, New Guinea and the Admiralty Islands. The time was about 1400 on 24 July 1945. We had just changed course, preparing to start a new escort patrol plan when we got a sound contact. Depth charges were ready to roll, but the contact didn't look too good. The ASW officer said it was mushy with no doppler effect or movement. He advised the captain not to drop depth charges.

The captain agreed and changed course to regain position ahead of the convoy. Upon arriving on station, we sighted a mine about 25 yards off the port bow. The convoy was ordered to change course. We opened fire on the mine in an effort to sink it. Meanwhile, we retained sound contact on the possible sub. The contact began to indicate some movement with down doppler, and it showed up a little stronger than before.

We sent one of the PCs over to see if he could pick up contact while we were firing on the mine. We lost contact at a range of 2300 yards, but the PC had gained contact and made a depth charge attack. Immediately afterward, we saw a periscope come up just abaft the area of depth charge explosions. The GQ alarm was sounded, and I proceeded to my position down in the log room as damage control officer.

Although I was unable to observe the action that followed, I knew pretty much what was going on by listening to sound powered telephone conversations. I heard the lookouts give the bearing of the periscope. The word was passed over the phones and PA system to stand by to ram, but this was belayed to drop a shallow depth charge pattern. We heard and felt the depth charges explode, then heard the captain report via the PA system:

'We got one Jap midget submarine. We can see oil and debris on the surface!'

The skipper apparently began to circle to return to the area when we sighted another periscope. Of course, we immediately started for it. I also heard that the range was only 700 yards. Then the word was passed to stand by to ram. I heard one talker say, 'He's looking right at us'!

I braced myself for the collision. When it came, there were two sharp jars. We had apparently hit something and gone right over the top of it. Immediately, there was a terrific explosion. I lost my phone. Everything went dark in the log room. In feeling around trying to find my headphones, I felt water coming in. I believed the ship was sinking and decided to go topside.

As soon as I got outside on deck, I tried to contact control. Mr. Timberlake came out right behind me and informed me that engine spaces had lost all power. I went aft to the fantail to find a set of phones. I found a pair and tried to raise control, but somebody cut in to tell me we didn't have any control. It was only then that I realized that the whole front end of the ship had been blown off up to the forward fire room bulkhead. All forward of that was gone. All the bridge area, the bridge structure, and the mast — all had been blown away. We sank very quickly.

The PC we had previously sent out after the contact returned to pick up survivors. She put a small boat over. Another PC was detached from the convoy, picked up a doctor from one of the LSTs, and came back for us. We could see her 5000 or 6000 yards away where she evidently had some kind of contact. The PC skipper later told me that lookouts could see two periscopes at the same time, one on either bow, and they were going to ram when the PC near us advised them not to. That was the mistake our DE made, and there was no sense repeating it.

PC-803 and *PC-804* were trying to pick up survivors, but they'd no sooner come alongside than they'd get a sound contact and have to go out after it. Finally, we were taken aboard one of them with our wounded. The time was about 1800. Between the two PCs, all survivors were picked up.

As for the submarines, there evidently was no attempt on their part to take any action against us or any of the other ships. To the best of our knowledge, they never fired torpedoes. They seemed to be just kind of teasing us on, trying to lure us to ram them, which our DE unfortunately did. I'd call one of those contraptions more a manned mine than a submarine. We lost 10 officers and 102 men, including the captain!"

Lieutenant Porter:

"Suppose you put on record here the name of the captain of the *Underhill* and anything you care to say about him."

Lieutenant Rich:

"Our commanding officer's name was Lieutenant Commander Robert Newcomb. He – was a very fine man, indeed – He had been on board since commissioning had taken command about the end of August, 1944."

Lieutenant Porter:

"Mr. Timberlake, please tell us whatever you feel will add to our records of the disaster."

Lieutenant Timberlake:

"Of the four surviving officers left from the sinking of *Underhill*, three of us had battle stations below deck. Ensign Kearny, assistant engineer, was in number two engine room. Lieutenant Rich was in the log room, and I was in number one engine room. Ensign Davis, the assistant first lieutenant, was topside at his battle station on the 1.1" guns. Even though he had on his helmet at the time, he suffered major wounds of the head. Guns from the forward part of the ship were blown aft and there were a number of casualties among after gun crews, caused by flying debris from forward guns, the mark 51 director and other bow gear."

Paul Adams, then an Electrician's Mate Second Class on *Underhill*, recalled the disaster:

"We were in the process of sinking a mine when we went to GQ. I was on the starboard forward K-Gun. A great cheer went up from the men on the port side. I saw oil and much debris which I assumed to be from the mother sub. We started to take a sharp turn to starboard. Then I could see what I believed at the time was a midget sub periscope and part of the forward hull. We loaded the guns and stood by. Again from the bridge: 'Stand by to ram!'

This time, there was an explosion with flames shooting up to the heavens. My thoughts were, if this flame engulfs me, I will have to dive into the sea. I therefore proceeded aft to go between the smoke screen tanks and depth charge racks, away from the forward position where I could end up in the screws. When another explosion shot flames further into the sky, the concussion knocked me flat onto the deck. Water, oil, and debris commenced to fall on me. I thought we were sunk and I was under water. I crouched to jump for the surface when there was a break in the cloud that covered the ship.

I straightened up, looked forward, saw brightness I did not recognize at first. I saw the bow off the starboard side. At first I thought we got the son-of-a-bitch. Then I realized the reason for the brightness – no mast, no bridge. That was our bow afloat in the sea. I looked around and I tried to see if I could be of help and to prepare for any attack by the enemy. *Underhill* was dead in the water. We were finished."

Several years after the war, this author read a reprint of a story in the Springfield (Massachusetts) Daily News by Harry Steinberg, a crew member of *Underhill*. He recalled a lot of memories, some unhappy ones. In reminiscing on lost comrades, he carried the thought that it could just as well have been him. Although a husband and father, and superintendent of a textile plant in Canton, Massachusetts, Steinberg was drafted in 1944. *Underhill* was his only ship, and he saw no combat except one apocalyptic instant.

Swabbing his eyes with a handkerchief, staring out his office window at the distant past, Harry Steinberg remembered the confusion and anguish wrought by one suicide submarine that hit *Underhill*. Steinberg was a gunner's mate on the DE when it exploded and sank near Okinawa, in the deepest part of the Pacific.

"We heard that we should stand by for ramming a small submarine. There was a tremendous explosion. I found myself washed helplessly from port to starboard until the water subsided and I could look around. One guy from Rhode Island was crying, 'Help me!' His bones were sticking out. I got a hole in my head, but it wasn't serious. A gun from above landed on an ensign.— 'Tell my mother I'm OK', were his last words.

The orders were to sink the other half of the ship, because it was in our shipping lanes. The compartments were closed, and it could have floated forever. It took two hours of firing to sink it. Toward noon, we were taken to the Philippines."

Reading the article by Steinberg reminded me of that afternoon when I relieved Bob Newcomb as executive officer of *Sims*. Only five weeks before the end, his prophecy had come true.

Tempest, Fire and Foe

JOHNNIE HUTCHINS

A Bad Day for the Kaiten

Bo Keally was a plank owner on *Johnnie Hutchins (DE-360)*. Fresh from the Great Lakes boot camp and gunnery school, he recalls duty in the Caribbean when his new ship plowed through huge waves to rescue survivors of the destroyer *Warrington*, capsized in a hurricane.

"It was very exciting for a 17 year old on my first cruise. A hurricane, huge waves, a ship sinking, survivors, etc. I was really impressed and wondered what lay ahead."

23 January 1945. In the Pacific.

"We left Humboldt Bay, Hollandia, New Guinea, for antiaircraft exercises. My battle station was in the forward 5" gun mount as hot shellman. My job was to catch the expended shell cases after the gun fired and throw them into a small hatch at the rear of the gun mount. One day, with the entry hatches of the mount closed, having fired several rounds, there was a terrific explosion inside the mount. The concussion was painful on our ears. My face was only about two feet from the blast.

It knocked me back against the mount bulkhead. There was a hard rubber spade that rammed the projectile into the chamber. The rubber had disintegrated, and many small pieces flew into my face with one piece embedded in my eyeball. I could not see or hear for several minutes. Our gun captain, John Kline, had his head sticking out of a small hatch in the top of the mount. He thought we were all killed in the explosion and that the magazines were blowing up. He jumped up on top of the mount and dove into the sea. Another man, named Hearne, not connected with or even near the gun, also jumped over the side.

The mount was full of smoke. Someone finally got a hatch open and pushed me out, and another man lead me around to the starboard side of the ship. Although still dazed, I could see 20 or 25 men lined up at the rail near a life raft. Bos'n. Arsnault, was cutting the straps that held the raft; the release would not work. At the same time, I could hear our captain on the PA system saying we should man the life rafts.

Not knowing that two men were in the water, seeing others lined up on the rail at the raft being jettisoned, along with the captain saying, 'man the life rafts', I assumed the ship was sinking and he was telling us to take to the rafts. In my condition, I didn't realize we were to take man overboard stations, not abandon ship stations. I said, 'lets go men', and jumped over!" (No wonder commanding officers get prematurely gray!)

"Imagine my surprise when I surfaced and saw the ship heading for the horizon. I swam to the raft, climbed aboard, cut a paddle loose and picked up the other two men. As I pulled Hearne aboard, he said, 'Keally your face is covered with blood', but I didn't feel anything. I lost track of time; we couldn't see a ship anywhere. I later learned that our ship had to get relieved from her screening station before she could come back for us.

After being picked up, I was taken to sick bay for the corpsman to remove the fragments of rubber from my face, about 70 pieces. He could not get the piece from my eyeball and planned to send me to a hospital ship when we got to Leyte. He gave me a patch to wear. About three days later, the particle came out all by itself. While I was in sick bay, the captain came in and asked me if I had gone overboard to man the raft and rescue the other two men. Had I thought fast enough and agreed, I think he would have gotten me a medal. Instead, I said, 'No sir, I thought we were sinking and I was just getting off'. Nothing further was ever said.

Three volunteers were needed to go in the gun mount to test fire the gun after repairs were made. The gunnery officer had no choice and occupied the most dangerous position. He picked me and one other to go with him. I had the phones on and made sure I had a lot of metal between me and the breech. While awaiting the order to fire, sweat was running off the gunnery officer like a spigot. We finally got the word to fire and everything went OK."

1 August 1945. *I-366*, the prototype *kaiten* mother ship described above under *The Midgets*, commanded by Lieutenant Takami Tokioka, departed from Hikari, Japan. His orders were to search and destroy enemy ships in the convoy lanes between Okinawa and the Philippines. Five *kaiten* were carried on the submarine's deck.

9 August. Lieutenant Tokioka detected a large group of warships off Okinawa and prepared to launch his midgets. He succeeded with only three, however, for two were found to be inoperative. Aboard the ones that were launched were Lieutenant (Jg.) Kenji Naruse, Petty Officer Tokuei Uenishi, and Petty Officer Hajime Sano. As soon as the three *kaiten* were safely away, Lieutenant Tokioka departed for Hikari, arriving on 16 August to report that his *kaiten* had sunk three large transports. (It is not clear why he filed such an erroneous account; perhaps he mistook the explosions of depth charges from the attacking destroyer escort to be torpedo hits.)

Hutchins joined Task Group 75.19 on hunter-killer operations in the same convoy lanes as *I-366*, near where *Underhill* and the cruiser *Indianapolis* had recently been lost to enemy undersea operations. She was assigned picket duty 12 miles from the escort carrier formation guide. With her were two other DEs, *Rolf (DE-362)*, and *Douglas A. Munro (DE-422)*. On the inner screen with the carrier, were the DEs *William Seiverling (DE-441)*, *Ulvert M. Moore (DE-442)*, *Kendall C. Campbell (DE-443)*, and *Goss (DE-444)*.

9 August 1945. On joining the Task Group, lookouts on *Hutchins* sighted an enemy aircraft flying out of gun range in much the same manner as an aircraft that was sighted by crew members of *Underhill*.

1143. Lookouts on *Hutchins* reported what at first glance resembled a whale breaking water 2000 yards ahead but was quickly recognized as a small submarine. Battle stations was sounded as Lieutenant Commander Hugh M. Godsey, the *Hutchins* skipper, headed his ship toward the sub. At 1500 yards, the forward gun crews opened fire, and *Hutchins* closed to 300 yards. From the skipper's war diary:

"At that distance, the target looked like a floating iron boiler. It was about 45 feet long and similar in appearance to Jap midget subs with the exception of the conning tower which extended six or eight inches above the hull, apparently an escape hatch. A small periscope stuck up from the conning tower."

The DE gunners opened fire as the skipper turned his ship away, refusing to ram. He was was not taking a chance in having another *Underhill* disaster. *Hutchins* maneuvered to bring her guns to bear as she made another approach to the target:

"The queer little submarine passed down the port side at about two knots. It appeared to be trying to keep its bow pointed at us."

Then a new peril was encountered, continuing the war diary:

"As the submarine was being closed again, noises were heard over the sound gear and, at the same time, a periscope was sighted on the port bow beyond the surfaced submarine. Sonar contact was obtained at 700 yards and a run was begun on this contact while the first submarine was under fire."

As the first submarine, still surfaced, passed abeam of this DE on the port side about 100 yards away, a direct hit from the after 5" gun holed her and she sank immediately.

"Meanwhile, the periscope of the second submarine had disappeared, and a torpedo wake was seen passing down the starboard side of *Hutchins*. A pattern of magnetic impulse depth charges was dropped on the contact, and three explosions were heard. The range was quickly opened and another depth charge attack was made."

At this point, *Kendall C. Campbell*, *Douglas A. Munro*, and *Rolf* moved in to assist in the hunt. The flagship of *ComCortDiv 70*, *William Seiverling*, took charge of the attack. The three DEs linked up with *Hutchins*, forming a scouting line, and began a search for other submarines in the area.

Some eight miles from the area of the first two contacts, lookouts on *Hutchins* sighted a periscope, and the DE launched a depth charge pattern, producing a prodigious explosion and a water geyser 30 feet in the air! The concussion shook the flagship over a mile away.

The four destroyer escorts continued the hunt and, at 1830, were joined by *George A. Johnson (DE-583)*, *Connolly (DE-306)*, *Metivier (DE-582)*, and *Kenneth M. Willett (DE-354)*. The ships ran the legs of standard search plans until 1400 the next day but failed to turn up any more submarines. Of course, they had no way of knowing that only three suicide subs were launched from the mother submarine.

The crew of *Hutchins* was awarded the Navy Unit Commendation for its performance in the sinking of three *kaiten* submarines.

Somehow, it wouldn't be right to end this narrative without recording the experience of Bo Keally in the storied typhoon at Okinawa, 16-18 September 1945.

"As we left Buckner Bay harbor, Okinawa, the waves were getting increasingly larger. There was a carrier ahead of us and one astern, and their flight decks were taking water over their bows.

Our little DE was tossed around like a cork. I was on watch on the after 5" gun and was sitting on top of the mount, enjoying the ride like a roller coaster, but that didn't last long. The sky got darker and the waves got taller. All the other ships were now out of sight. One minute we would be down in a valley, looking up at a 60 foot wave; the next minute, we'd be on top, looking down.

The waves reached new heights and were breaking over the ship. The captain, fearing that the gun crews might get washed overboard, ordered us to stand the watch inside the deck house. We were trying to think of the best way out if the ship should capsize.

This was the only time during the entire war and many dangerous situations that I was ever frightened and thought this might be it. We had been in other hurricanes and typhoons but nothing like this. Sometimes the ship would roll over so far that I had to stand with one foot on the deck and the other on the bulkhead. Most of the time, we sat because it was almost impossible to stand. The ship would roll to one side and hesitate for a moment, and I would think it was never going to right itself. I would guess we took some 60 to 70 degree rolls. I said a little prayer: 'Lord, get me out of this one, and I will go to church every Sunday and never miss mass again.' Well, we did survive, and I go to church every Sunday.

We rode out this typhoon for three days and returned to Buckner Bay on the afternoon of the third day. The island was levelled. There was not a building standing. Ships and buoys were scattered everywhere. One of my friends was on an LST that was unable to get underway when the warning sounded; it was now up on the beach a quarter of a mile from the shore. The same was true of other small ships and boats."

THOMAS F. NICKEL

The Last Act of the Kaiten Story

Thomas F. Nickel (DE-587) had seen considerable action in the Philippine Campaign. In December 1944, she screened the San Fabian Attack Force, transporting the 43d Infantry Division to the initial assault on Luzon. She entered Lingayan Gulf to rescue men from the attack transport *Dupage (APA-41)*, sinking after a *kamikaze* hit.

Nickel reported to Captain C.A. Peterson, commanding officer of the Landing Ship Dock *Oak Hill (LSD-7)* on 11 August 1945, for escort duty from Okinawa to Leyte, Philippines. Both ships were zigzagging at the time because of the possibility of submarine attack, especially from midget submarines in the area. The first atom bomb had been dropped on Hiroshima, and all the world was waiting to see if Japan would throw in the towel. So far, it had not.

1829 on 12 August 1945. *Oak Hill* reported a periscope on her port quarter. The Officer of The Deck on *Nickel* ordered engines ahead full, turned the ship toward the periscope and sounded GQ at the same time. Lieutenant Paul M. Hickox, former communications officer on the *Nickel*, filled in a few details:

"I take it you would like some comment on our manned Japanese torpedo experience. Please forgive me for any failings in precise recollection as I am reaching back more than

51 years. at age 79."

We were in the Philippine Sea, northeast of Luzon in the early evening. I was on the bridge when the TBS speaker blared from the LSD in a very calm and deliberate voice 'Ginger (*Nickel's* code name), we have a torpedo track on our port quarter'.

Within a minute or so, the captain, Lieutenant Commander Claude S. Farmer, climbed the few steps to the bridge and took over the conn. All of us were searching for a torpedo track in hope of getting some idea of where a submarine might be lying; our sonar had not reported a contact."

From the captain's action report:

"When I got to the bridge, the ship was traveling in a direction opposite to *Oak Hill*. Just forward of our port bow, I saw a spray of water. It disappeared and then reappeared several times, later passing down and away from our port side."

1830. *Oak Hill* reported a torpedo breaking the surface astern of her. Immediately afterward, a wake of an apparently broaching torpedo was sighted by lookouts on the *Nickel*. In the initial belief that the torpedo had come from a conventional submarine, the escort had proceeded to the torpedo track, took a course in the direction opposite to that of the torpedo, toward what she thought to be the source rather than toward the intended target. *Nickel* fired an embarrassing depth charge barrage. One rack jammed, clearing only one charge. However, the "K" gun projectors performed properly.

1835. DE to LSD: "I do not have a contact. I dropped a shallow pattern for distracting purposes. I have not seen any object or periscope since last reported."

1837. LSD to DE: "The wake is coming up parallel with us and into our own wake! Put on all your speed and follow my wake!"

The DE utilized her best speed and full rudder to come about in the direction of a submarine, which could be seen breaking the surface in the wake of *Oak Hill*. As described by Lieutenant Hickox:

"Within a minute or two, a periscope was sighted off our bow. In hot pursuit, with black smoke pouring from our funnel and engines at full speed, we gained on the submarine, expecting to ram it."

The captain wrote:

"I saw that there was a small, triangular-shaped, black object which seemed to move through the water. Its motion reminded me of a small high-speed motor boat traveling through the wake of another craft. It would bob to the surface, skitter across the wake and then disappear. It seemed to be cutting across and following the direction created by the wake of *Oak Hill*. About this time, it was realized that what was first believed to be a broaching normal torpedo must have been a piloted torpedo or midget submarine.

About 1840, the forward and after fire rooms and the after engine room reported scraping along the port side of the bilge as though there were a metal to metal contact. The best guess on *Nickel* was that their ship had brushed a human torpedo which had its eyes on *Oak Hill*. Some quick "thanks" were offered with eyes rolled skyward.

1842. LSD to DE: "The object is still following us. It is about 2000 yards astern and making a wake itself."

1843. DE to LSD: "I think I have sighted it and am heading in that direction now."

Captain Farmer:

"The object appeared again directly in the wake of *Oak Hill* and, although it was moving noticeably slower, seemed to have gained on the LSD. Then it was observed on the surface with very little spray showing, seemingly almost stopped. It hung there a few moments and, accompanied by a bright flash, it exploded, sending smoke and water about 200 feet into the air. Particles of wreckage and debris could be seen falling into the water around the explosion area."

The reason for the explosion of this *kaiten* has never been pin-pointed. However, there was a fair assumption. The pilot was sealed inside the capsule with no means of escape if his mission failed. Had he the ability to detonate the warhead, it would have been preferable to a slower death by asphyxiation. Hickox pretty much confirmed this supposition:

"We never did ram what we earlier thought was a submarine. All of a sudden, it exploded with a thunderous repercussion right before us. It was then that we realized we had been pursuing a manned torpedo — not a submarine — and had been saved from ourselves!

Apparently, the Japanese torpedoman recognized that he had missed his intended target and was not even aware that we were behind him, with us unknowingly trying to blow ourselves up. It is my belief that the Japanese Navy made no effort to rescue their men on such missions, and so their only recourse was to follow the fanatic *kamikaze* aircraft pilots. He pulled the cord, and that was it."

Oak Hill had made two or three course changes from the time of sighting the torpedo to seeing the torpedo changing course as it pursued that ship. She also observed the explosion.

1854. DE to LSD: "After considering our little occurrence, I am convinced that we had a piloted torpedo. In that case, it is my opinion that there is a large submarine controlling the attack, and a recurrence must be expected."

LSD to DE: "I agree. I am making some radical changes."

Still making 20 knots, *Nickel* continued to head for *Oak Hill*. In the belief that another *kaiten* attack was probable, a sharp lookout was maintained visually, on radar and on sonar, looking for wakes or periscopes. The after 40mm control officer, Ensign

Eugene T. Darden, reported sighting a periscope in the wake about 1500 yards astern of the *Oak Hill* which was on the port bow of *Nickel*, about 1000 to 1500 yards distant. A periscope was also reported to the 20mm control officer at gun number 28, having been sighted by First Class Steward's Mate, H. Drummond.

1905. DE to LSD: "Periscope sighted dead astern of you."

On receipt of this report, *Oak Hill* came hard right, and the DE came hard left to cross the LSD's track. When steadying up, the forward 40mm control officer, Lieutenant John J. Deasy, reported sighting a periscope on the starboard bow. *Nickel* changed course to the right to cross ahead of the *kaiten*. The last sighting was dead ahead at a reported 500 yards. When in a position ahead of the projected course of the periscope, the DE fired a shallow depth charge pattern. On this second attack, only four cleared the rack, but the depth charge projectors operated normally as on the first attack.

After the explosion of the first charge from the starboard projector, a secondary explosion 50 feet outside the pattern limits was observed by the executive officer, Lieutenant Commander Robert Berry, Ensign Eugene T. Darden, and others. The periscope was not seen again. The reported secondary explosion was of greater intensity and caused greater water disturbance than normal depth charge explosions. In addition, the executive officer reported seeing debris falling on the outside of the water disturbance. Captain Farmer wrote:

> "In the second attack, a periscope sighting was reported to the bridge. We immediately turned in that direction to impose an interdict between the periscope and the *Oak Hill*. After firing, I looked aft and noted the first charge from the side throwers on the starboard side hitting the water. As the bubble from its explosion came to the surface, another larger bubble was seen adjacent to the first. The water pushed up was very black and thrown about 50 feet in the air. I noticed around the explosion area little particles as of wreckage splashing into the water. Shortly afterward, *Nickel* proceeded to the target area and observed a long wake of oil slick extending from abaft the port beam to broad on the starboard bow.
>
> I believe from the evidence presented that our second pattern either scored a direct hit or a near enough miss to countermine a manned torpedo."

This was the last brush the Navy had with the *kaiten*. The dropping of the second atom bomb precipitated the end of the war, sparing the lives of the *kaiten* zealots along with their *kamikaze*, *bukha*, and explosive motor boat colleagues. Nonetheless, after reviewing the *Nickel-kaiten* incident, Admiral Oldendorf noted:

> "An excellent example of a comparatively new type of attack which threatened to become of major importance had the war continued."

S2/C Charles K. Gilmore on *USS Miles (DE-183)* 1945

Emblem of *Samuel S. Miles (DE-183)*

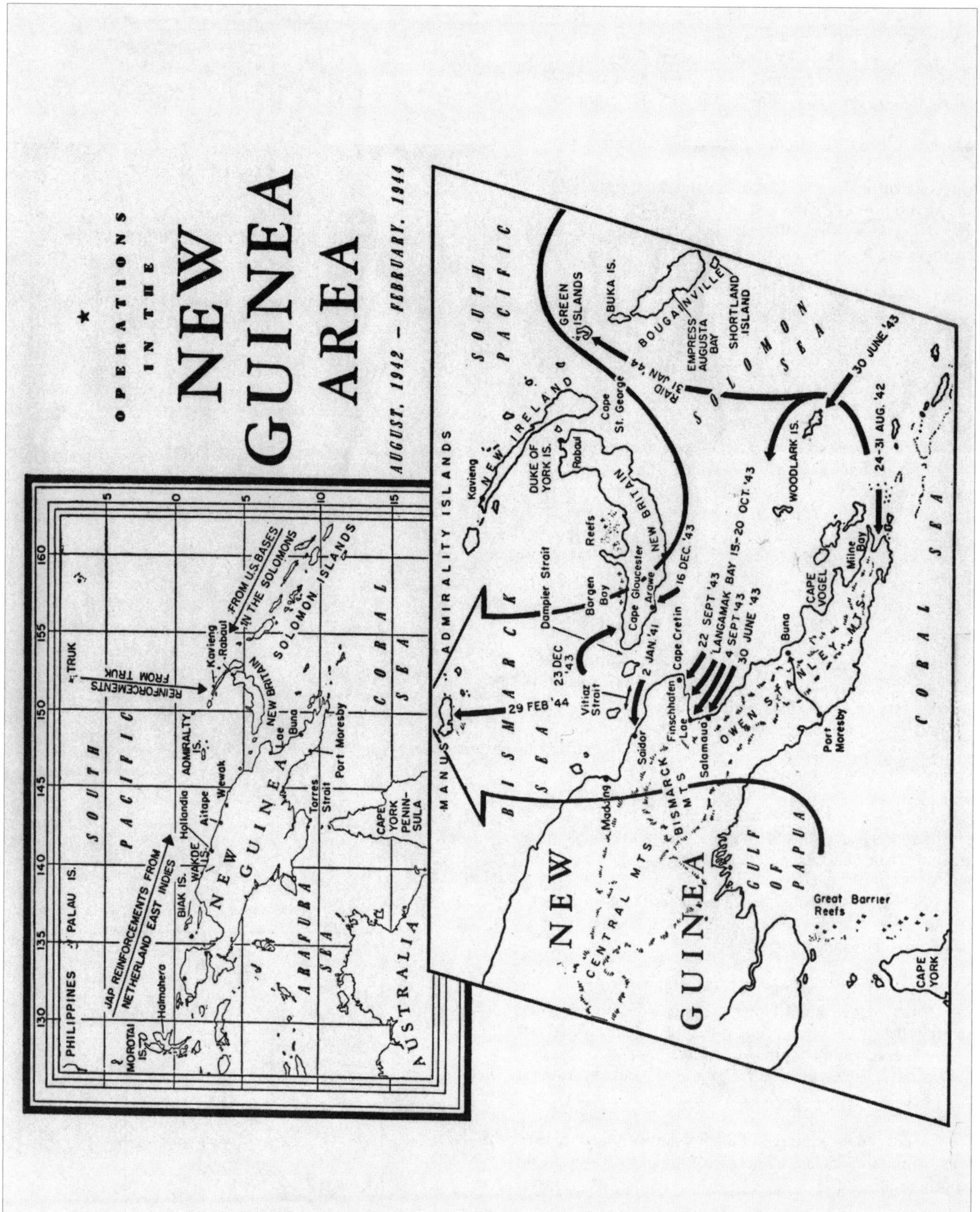

Operations in the New Guinea Area 1942-1944. From *Destroyer Operations in World War II* - Courtesy Naval Institute Press

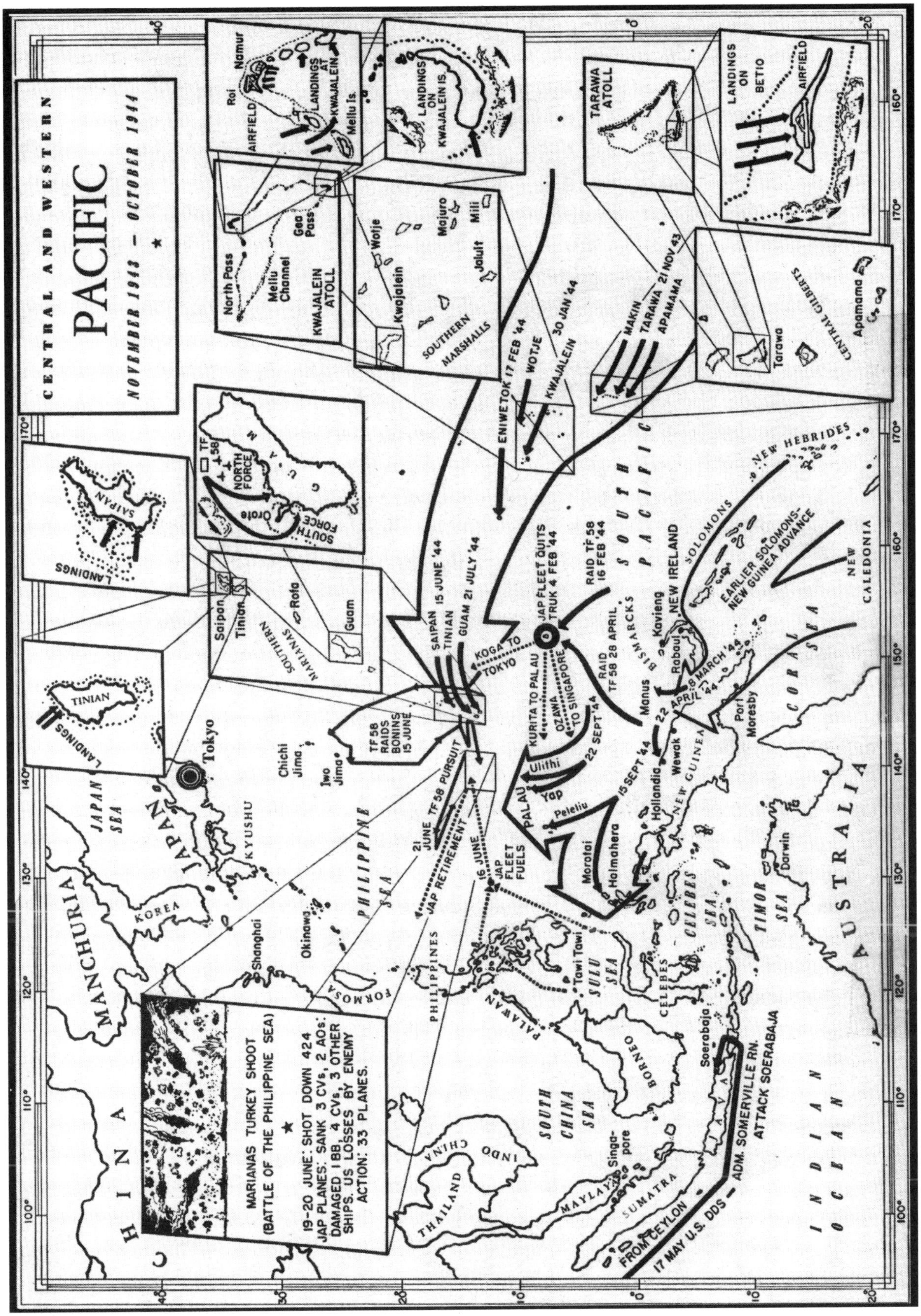

Central and Western Pacific 1943-1944. From *Destroyer Operations in World War II* - Courtesy Naval Institute Press

USS England. Note shrapnel and fire damage. Submarine and anticraft victories displayed. US Navy Photo

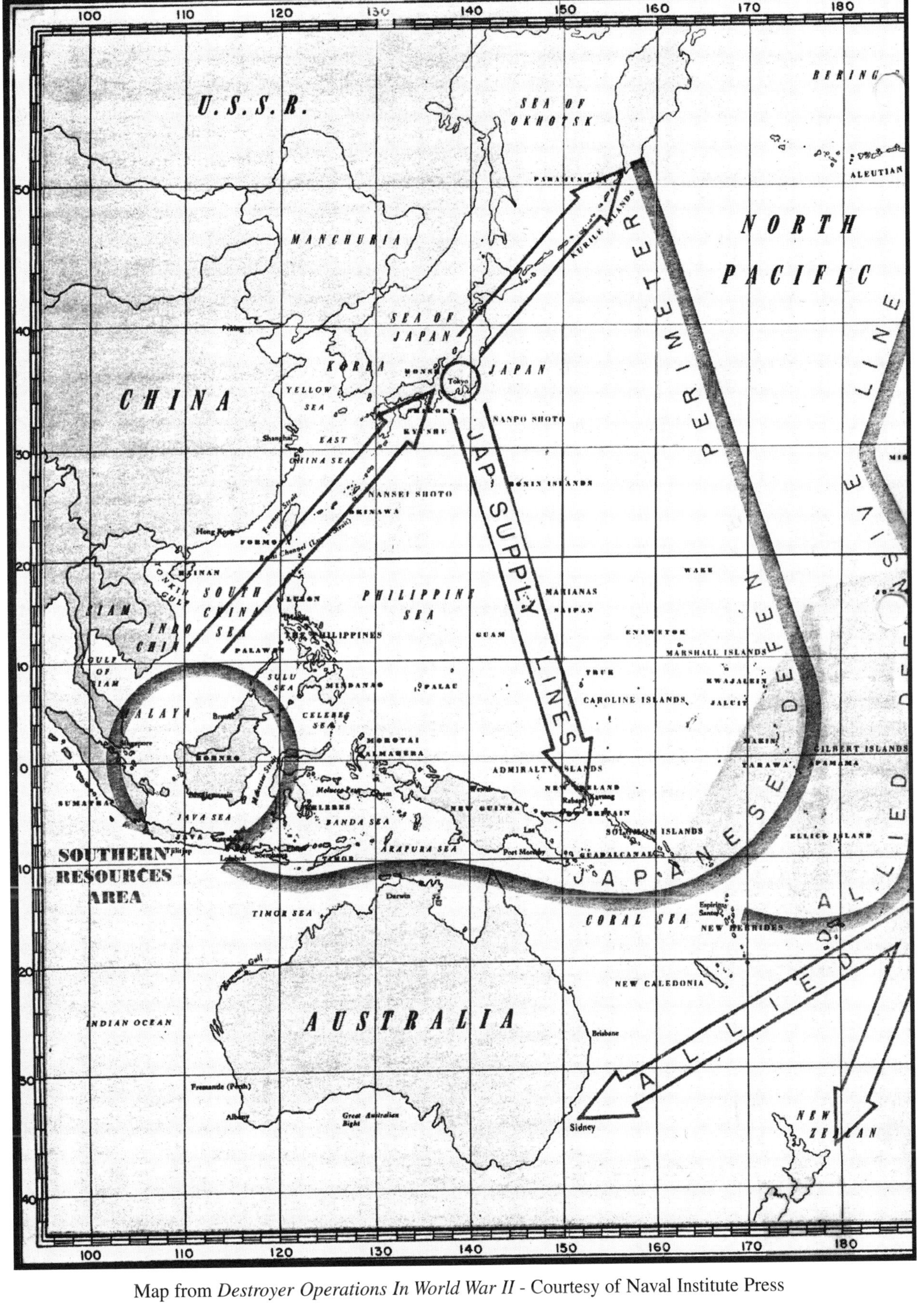

Map from *Destroyer Operations In World War II* - Courtesy of Naval Institute Press

USS Underhill (DE–682) – US Navy Photo

Chapter XI - South Central Pacific

Destroyer escorts began operations early in 1943. They were active in many island hopping campaigns, the Gilberts, Marshalls, Solomons, Marianas, Ellice and peripheral islands. They screened the train of the fast carrier strike forces, guarding vital replenishment, without which the heavy capital ships could not operate. They had begun to display their antisubmarine capabilities without peer, sending one Japanese submarine after another to the bottom. Prior to the Philippine Campaign, some were involved in other matters as per the following narratives.

INCIDENT AT GUADALCANAL

Introducing a very Resourceful Ensign

Upon arriving at Espiritu Santo, New Hebrides Islands, early in October 1943, *Osterhaus (DE-164)* made repeated escort missions from New Hebrides and New Caledonia advanced bases to various fighting fronts in the Solomons.

11 October. The sky was clear and an almost full moon lit up the sea and islands surrounding *Osterhaus* as she screened two anchored ships a mile off Lunga Beach, Guadalcanal. They were discharging their cargo to lighters, flooded in light, ideal targets for enemy aircraft.

In the dark pre-dawn, the Officer of The Deck heard the sound of low-flying aircraft. Two planes made a short run down the island with landing lights on, flew over Henderson Field and circled as if to set down. Instead, the pilots made attack runs over the two cargo ships and one then pulled up into a climbing turn directly over the stern of *Osterhaus*, exposing the plane's belly to the after 40mm crew. Evidently, the pilot didn't see her.

The Officer of The Deck, Lieutenant Al Slessinger, called the captain, Lieutenant Hart. He must have used a particularly anxious tone. Al said later that, as the last letter of the word "Captain" left his mouth, the skipper was there beside him. At GQ, her guns were silent, per orders from the shore command that ships were not to fire on any target during the night. The shore installation and ships were caught by surprise; condition red was only given after the attack.

The first ship, *SS George Bliss*, was struck by a torpedo on the starboard side aft. She settled but was towed and beached for further unloading and repair. The second ship, *SS John R. Couch*, was hit by a delayed action bomb and burst into flames. Her cargo was diesel oil, lube oil, gasoline, jeeps and mail. It was later discovered that her engine rooms were flooded because an engineer, in his haste to depart, had failed to dog down a hatch leading from those spaces.

Osterhaus shoved off her Fire and Rescue party under the leadership of Lieutenant Charlie Buck. The rescue party boarded the blazing ship to help fight the fire but, on arrival, found the ship largely abandoned. Buck noted a very unenthusiastic attempt on the part of the remaining merchant crew to fight the fire. There was pressure on the mains, but only one hose was lead forward to the scene of the explosion. Soon after boarding, Charlie Buck was ordered by a shore Navy Commander, who had come out in a lighter, to get off the ship. There were high explosives, TNT and nitroglycerine, aboard which might go off any minute.

The high explosives story was subsequently labeled as grossly incorrect, promulgated by the merchant crew to cover the considerably less than heroic action of officers and seamen in not staying with the ship to fight the fire. Buck's party then departed from *Couch* and lay to in the small boat until later when the *Osterhaus* skipper decided to take matters into his own hands and, without permission, came alongside to fight the fire.

As *Osterhaus* was approaching *Couch*, the DE's ammunition in 20mm ready boxes and clipping rooms began to explode from the terrific heat. Captain Hart decided to back off until all apparent signs of damaging heat ceased and then went on in. .

0845. *Osterhaus* came alongside the blazing ship, starboard side to the port side of *Couch*, to help the *Bebas (DE-10)*, secured on the opposite side of the burning ship. Ensign John F. Cykler, who supplied most of the information for this narrative, related:

> "When we first went aboard the burning ship, the flames were going up into the sky at least 300 to 400 feet. Gasoline and diesel oil drums were constantly blowing up in the hold, causing the whole ship to shake. A mountain of flame and smoke swirled over our heads. The wind was blowing the smoke, flames, and steam back toward us, making it difficult to see what we were doing. I took charge of five men near me to receive the first hose over to the burning ship and to play the stream into number 3 hold.
>
> The smoke was getting so bad that one couldn't stay near the blaze without fear of passing out, so I asked one of the men who had on a rescue breather if he didn't have another for me. Off came his like a flash of lightning and he installed it on my face, so excited that he fastened the straps around the hose along with my face. Then he cleared out like a flash. Soon, a couple of 20mm rounds went off, and two more men disappeared from view.
>
> `Just after that, some barrels of oil and gasoline blew up, and the remaining two men departed. This left me with the hose, and at times I was all over the deck, having been pushed around by a combination of the force of the water, a slippery footing and a starboard list. Mr. Dunn kept the flames from coming out of the ventilator near me by turning his hose into it periodically. He also played water on both me and the bulkhead to keep us cool as the ship was getting hotter all the time."

Both destroyer escorts placed their hoses into holds one, two, and three but finally gave up from what appeared to be a useless endeavor; they were unable to get the conflagration under control. It was decided to cast off so that *Bebas* could shell the number three 3 hold with her 3" battery and flood that compartment. However, *Couch* showed no signs of losing freeboard forward.

In late afternoon, *Osterhaus* also shelled *Couch*, but again no apparent results were noticed, although shell holes were seen above the waterline. During the night, the fire was visible through the shell holes. *Couch* blazed away until morning when *Couch* showed signs that the fire was abating and might be controlled and extinguished. The blaze was still confined to the forward part of the ship. The superstructure and the bridge were burned out.

Mid-morning on 12 October. Another hand-picked group made up a Fire and Rescue party and boarded the burning ship. They fought the fire and salvaged gunnery, engineering equipment, and tools. About an hour after boarding, the hoses had cooled the engine room bulkheads sufficiently to permit personnel below the main deck. Even so, the smoke and steam were so dense that, unless one had a rescue breather, it was impossible to stay below. They probably could have salvaged more engineering parts, but the list of the freighter was so bad that the men feared getting caught in the hold if she went over.

The Ordnance Division under Lieutenant Vic Blurton, Chief Rogers, and a working party, stripped down three 20mm guns, a 3" gun, plus thousands of rounds and ammunition. The *Osterhaus* crew fought the remaining fires and salvaged whatever could be useful until early afternoon when a tug arrived to tow the derelict to the beach.

Many discouraging stories can be told of this episode. First, the *Couch's* crew made no effort to save the ship and would not assist the Fire and Rescue party as it boarded the freighter. Second, the shore establishment didn't show any interest in fighting the fire or salvaging any of the badly needed supplies. Their only effort was to beach the ship and play hoses into the forward holds, but then the ship capsized and the unburned and undamaged supplies were never removed. Ensign Cykler noted in his memoirs:

> "This salvage work could have been going on for two days, using salvage tugs to lift the cargo out of the after holds. There were steel beams, wooden piling, and drums of 80 octane gas and 50 octane diesel fuel. The only salvaging done by the shore base was a treasure hunt for small articles adrift about the deck and after living quarters. The ship could have easily been saved by quick action by the merchant crew plus our efforts.
>
> I turned around to look for Charlie Buck and found him on the deck holding his eyes. He had been caught in the face with a fire hose spouting 100 pounds of pressure. The water cut his eyes, but this injury, although painful, was temporary and did not permanently impair his vision. Two of us lead him over to *Bebas* for medical attention. Half an hour later, he was back on the job with a patch over one eye, reminiscent of a buccaneer on a plundering raid rather than a salvaging effort!"

Ensign Cykler had a few good stories: One concerned Sebastian, the ship's laundryman, who hooked up a hose to the diesel oil outlet on deck instead of salt water and started to play fuel on the fire. Fortunately, there was little pressure, and the error was caught in time before the stream caused havoc.

Ensign Cykler remembers his days on his first ship assignment:

> "I took the whaleboat and a few men ashore at Guadalcanal and, between the fighter airstrip at Henderson Field and the Army, we procured .45 caliber sidearms, sub machine-guns, two air cooled .30 caliber machine guns, two .50 caliber machine guns with tripods, and two boxes of ammo. We mounted the .30 caliber machine guns on the fantail for depth charge talkers to use at GQ and the .50 machine guns on the wings of the bridge. We were getting ready for close-in Japanese small boat attacks.
>
> At the same time, I picked a large roll of aluminum foil and insulating paper from Henderson Field maintenance. A condenser in our surface radar had gone sour, and we decided to make one, using our engineering handbooks as reference. We laid the material out on the main deck and made a tight roll of foil and paper. It was a large condenser but somehow it worked.
>
> We had no diving gear on the ship, so I made a helmet from a 20mm ammunition can. I put in a plexiglass face plate, padded the shoulder areas, and inserted a globe valve for the air hose and air control. A few weeks later, we sliced up a whale with the screws, and the skipper ordered me over the side to inspect the propeller struts. It was necessary to straddle the prop shafts and inch my way to the struts to see if their connection to the ship was sound. The ocean current was strong, and the fish didn't help. The screws were not damaged and the struts were OK."

Remarks: A jury rig expert without peer!

Osterhaus departed Kwajalein Lagoon on 16 September 1945, bound with *CortDiv 11* for Pearl Harbor and onward routing to San Diego.

THE MARIANAS

Elden Barks Her Guns at Tinian

Elden (DE-264) sailed from Pearl Harbor on 1 June 1944 with a convoy for Eniwetok, then saw action in the capture and occupation of the Marianas. She patrolled off Tinian to prevent enemy troops from landing behind American lines on Saipan.

25 June. The destroyer *Bancroft (DD-598)*, *Elden (DE-264)*, and *Wileman (DE-22)* screened a task group from Eniwetok to Saipan. Upon arrival, Commander Destroyer Squadron 56 assigned all three vessels to patrol stations in the transport area screen. In early evening, *Bancroft* relayed orders from *ComDesRon 56*, directing her and *Elden* to patrol the west coast of Tinian during the night to prevent movement of troops toward Saipan and to conduct harassing fire into Tinian town and harbor.

The major mission of the two ships was to prevent embarkation and movement of enemy troops from Tinian and in Tinian Channel. *Bancroft* ordered *Elden* to fire several rounds of illuminating and ten rounds of antiaircraft service ammunition from her main battery of three 3" guns on each run past the town and harbor. *Elden* was to space fire at intervals after *Bancroft* salvos. It was assumed that return fire might be expected from shore batteries.

The two ships steamed in column, interval 2000 yards. In due course, they encountered 12 to 20 enemy barges and fishing vessels. The number was uncertain because they were first sighted under the short duration of star shell illumination. The sea was calm with a slight ground swell. Visibility was high until moonset at 2225.

The DD and the DE proceeded from their screening stations at 13 knots and established a patrol line about 4700 yards from Tinian. *Elden* commenced firing at 2015 and repeated her salvos on each run at intervals of about half an hour. While *Bancroft* was firing star shell illumination, *Elden* spotted a group of barges, apparently moving near the shore. She reported them to *Bancroft* who could not see them immediately.

Elden opened fire with her two forward 3" and her 1."1 guns, the after 3" gun firing illuminating ammunition. The DE closed to 300 yards with fire continuing under illumination by both ships. Within two hours of firing, the ships ran out of star shells, sharply curtailing the operation. *Bancroft* tried searchlight illumination for a short period but with meager results. It was decided to wait about an hour until daylight to continue the action.

Bancroft remained in the vicinity and sent *Elden* south into Tinian Channel to prevent the escape of the barges in that direction. At dawn, both ships converged on Tinian Harbor, where approximately 12 barges and fishing vessels were moored and took them under fire. When *Elden* had closed the range to 2500 yards, small caliber splashes were seen a few hundred yards off her bow. Shortly thereafter, larger splashes appeared near *Bancroft* who then ordered a retirement to open the range because neither ship could see the location of the shore batteries to take them under fire. While making the turn to seaward, *Bancroft* advised that orders were received for both vessels to resume patrol stations in the transport screening area.

During the shore bombardment phase, numerous fires were started by direct hits on a factory and within the town. The exact number of barges sunk could not be determined, although one was definitely seen to break up under fire from *Bancroft's* main battery. Both *Bancroft* and *Elden* registered hits with gratifying regularity. It is not believed that any personnel were in the barges.

Before the action commenced, a grid chart of Tinian had been set up on *Elden's* dead reckoning table (DRT) for the purpose of obtaining ranges. The DRT was not sufficiently accurate, however, requiring constant scale resetting, so this was abandoned in favor of straight ranges from the SL radar. The radar screen showed an almost perfect reproduction of the coast line, and it was relatively simple to pick off the range to the desired target area. The CIC also furnished target bearings on those runs during which no fires remained to provide a visible point of aim.

This was *Elden's* first attempt at night shore bombardment. There were no personnel casualties. After antisubmarine patrol off Eniwetok in early July, she returned to screening transports at Saipan and delivered harassing fire on Tinian. During the invasion of Guam, she escorted convoys from Eniwetok.

Elden operated out of Manus from 26 August 1944, screening oilers to refueling rendezvous with ships invading the Palaus and Leyte. She arrived off Iwo Jima on 7 March 1945 to patrol the transport area until 20 March. The DE operated from Ulithi beginning 21 July as escort for oilers refueling fleet units in the final massive raids on Japan. *Elden* served in the Far East on occupation duty, then returned to San Francisco on 25 November.

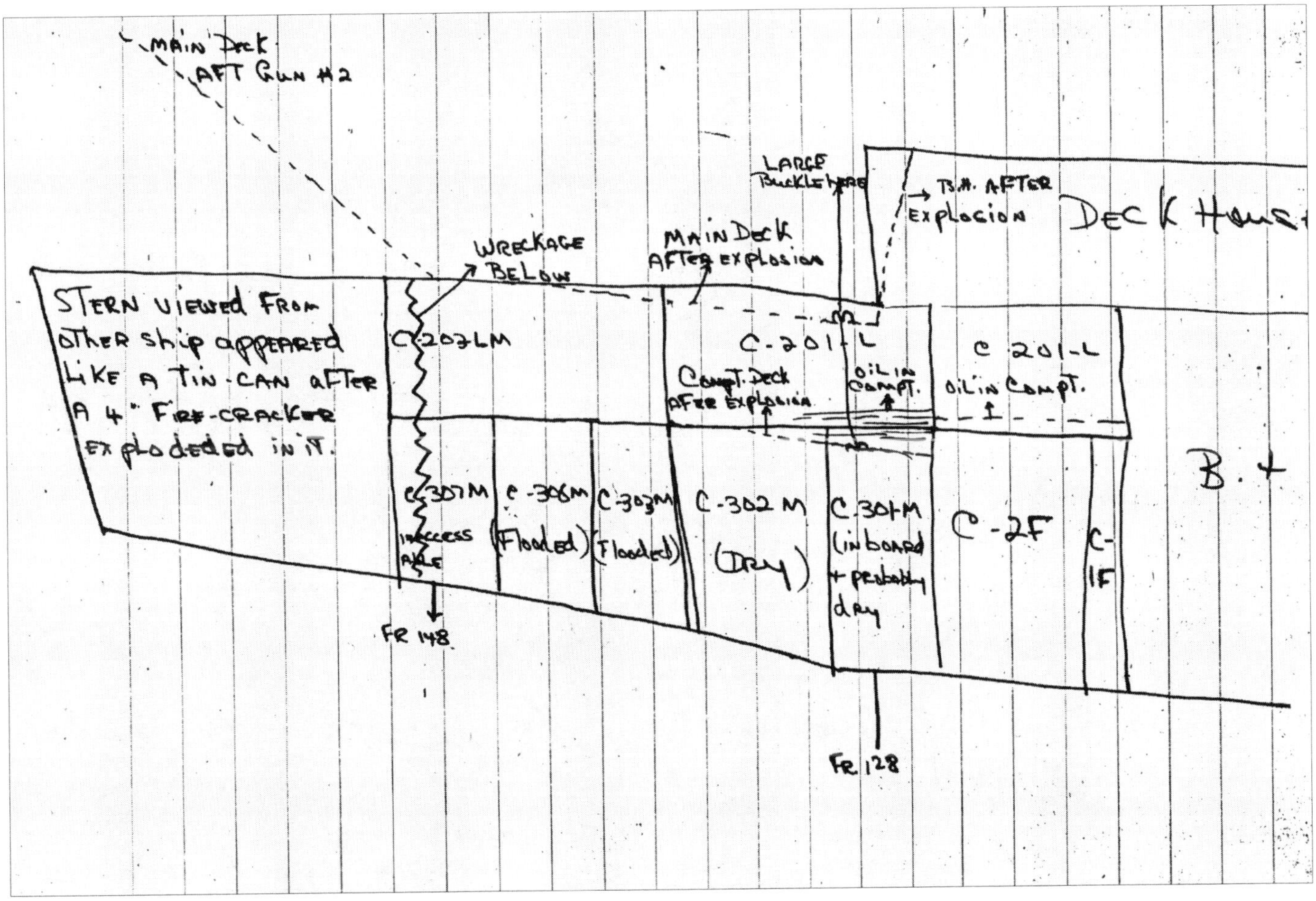

Drawing of *Shelton's* damage.

Survivors from *Samuel B. Roberts.* Courtesy National Archives

Lewis M. Andrews, Jr.

Chapter XII - The Battle off Samar

"Small Boys" Avert a Disaster at Leyte

THE SECRETARY OF THE NAVY
Washington

The President of the United States takes pleasure in presenting the PRESIDENTIAL UNIT CITATION to TASK UNIT SEVENTY-SEVEN POINT FOUR POINT THREE, consisting of *Fanshaw Bay (CVE-70)* and *VC-68*; *Gambier Bay (CVE-73)* and *VC-10*; *Kalinin Bay (CVE-68)* and *VC-3*; *Kitkun Bay (CVE-71)* and *VC-5*; *Saint Lo (CVE-63)* and *VC-65*; *White Plains (CVE-66)* and *VC-4*; *Hoel (DD-533)*, *Johnston (DD-557)*, *Heerman (DD-532)*, *Samuel B. Roberts (DE-413)*, *Raymond (DE-341)*, *Dennis (DE-405)* and *John C. Butler (DE-339)* for service set forth in the following CITATION:

"For extraordinary heroism in action against powerful units of the Japanese Fleet during the Battle off Samar, Philippines, 25 October 1944. Silhouetted against the dawn as the Central Japanese Force steamed through San Bernardino Strait toward Leyte Gulf, Task Unit 77.4.3 was suddenly taken under attack by hostile cruisers on its port hand, destroyers on the starboard and battleships from the rear. Quickly laying down a heavy smoke screen, the gallant ships of the Task Unit waged battle fiercely against the superior speed and fire power of the advancing enemy, swiftly launching and rearming aircraft and violently zigzagging in protection of vessels stricken by hostile armor-piercing shells, anti-personnel projectiles and suicide bombers. With two carriers of the group sunk, others badly damaged, unarmed squadron aircraft valiantly simulated attacks by making dry runs over the enemy fleet. As the Japanese relentlessly closed in for the kill, three of the Unit's valiant destroyers and four destroyer escorts charged the battleships point-blank and, expending their last in desperate defense of the entire group, three went down under the enemy's heavy shells, a climax to 2-1/2 hours of sustained and furious combat. The courageous determination and superb teamwork of the officers and men who fought in planes or manned the ships of the Task Unit were instrumental in effecting the retirement of the hostile force threatening our Leyte invasion operations. They were in keeping with the highest traditions of the United States Naval Service."

For the President
/s/ James Forrestal
Secretary of the Navy

Vice Admiral Kurita, Commander of the Japanese Second Fleet, sortied from Brunei, Borneo, with orders to execute war plan *Sho-Go,* the destruction of American forces attempting to seize Leyte, the initial toehold in the Philippines. Although his fleet had suffered losses from American carrier aircraft attacks in the Sibuyan Sea, it was still a first class armada, enough power to accomplish its mission. Kurita's orders: "Advance, counting on Divine assistance."

About midnight, the Japanese big guns reached the Pacific end of San Bernardino Strait, bound for Leyte Gulf. By 0600 in the morning of 25 October, the ships were about halfway between the San Bernardino exit and the Gulf of Leyte. Had Kurita known the composition of the force that lay ahead, he could indeed have thanked Providence for permitting his advance. He could also have thanked Admirals Ozawa and Halsey.

Ozawa in the north had been wandering around with "decoy ducks" in the most attractive fashion, breaking radio silence, making smoke, and doing everything possible to invite attention. Halsey needed no engraved invitation. He was, of course, unaware that the enemy carriers off Cape Engano were deliberate lures. Convinced that the Japanese flat-tops had to be kept away from Leyte at all cost, he had drawn off the task groups of Admirals Bogan and Davison and sent them on a top-speed run to intercept.

Halsey's move left the San Bernadino gateway open at the very time Kurita was hoping to slip through. For this reason, the departure of the Third Fleet from the Samar area was subjected to considerable post-war criticism. Halsey's answer was the destruction of Ozawa's Carrier Force with a series of aerial hammer-blows, at that date unparalleled in the history of naval warfare. It seems, however, that he failed to inform Admiral Kinkaid of the Third Fleet's northward run. Consequently, Kinkaid did not know that the Samar approaches to Leyte Gulf were left wide open. His first intimation of this dangerous gap came when Rear Admiral C.A.F. Sprague's Northern Carrier Group called for help from the waters off southern Samar.

0645 on 25 October 1944. Kurita's force detected the American ships about the same time his ships were detected by American aircraft.

ENEMY SURFACE FORCE OF FOUR BATTLESHIPS SEVEN CRUISERS AND 11 DESTROYERS SIGHTED 20 MILES NORTH OF YOUR TASK GROUP AND CLOSING AT 30 KNOTS!

Shouted down from the sullen, gray clouds, this message from reconnaissance pilot Ensign W.C. Brooks stunned its recipients on *Fanshaw Bay*. Unable to believe this unwanted intelligence, Admiral Sprague demanded verification. He was informed that the ships had pagoda masts. A smattering of AA fire above the horizon to the north dissipated all doubt. At once, he ordered a course change at flank speed and the launching of all aircraft.

A moment later, the enemy opened fire at a range of 17 miles. As Sprague's ships began laying a smoke screen, planes buzzed away from the "jeep" carriers to strike at the oncoming Japanese battleships and cruisers. Justifiably alarmed, Sprague reported the situation in plain language, urgently requesting help.

Help was not immediately available. Halsey's Third Fleet was far to the north. In Leyte Gulf, Rear Admiral Oldendorf's force was low on fuel, weary from its stunning victory in Surigao Straits, and almost out of ammunition. In any event, it could not reach Sprague before afternoon. Southeast of Sprague's group, Rear Admiral F. B. Stump's escort carrier group was stationed. Only he could be counted on for ready aid, and the two escort carrier groups were the only American naval forces standing between Kurita's ships and General MacArthur's invasion troops at Leyte Gulf.

The immediate burden fell like an avalanche on Sprague's escort carriers. On them too, would fall shellfire from the Japanese heavy ships, including *Kongo*, *Haruna*, *Nagato*, and the monster *Yamato*, sister-ship of the dead *Mushashi*. The giantess was out for revenge, and no American baby flat-top would be able to endure her 18-inch salvos. American destroyers were never made to withstand battleship fire, much less the shells of a super BB. Such shots, of course, would burst a DE as a pistol shot would burst an egg.

Sprague could only run hell-bent-for-leather. With most of his planes in the air, he turned his ships southward for a lengthy sprint and then shifted the course southwestward toward Leyte Gulf. A friendly rain squall offered a few minutes' cover. But the same cloudburst gave the pursuing Japs a measure of protection from air assault.

Kurita himself provided the desperate Americans with a break. Instead of sending his ships south to cut off the approach to Leyte Gulf, he split his force three ways in an effort to box Sprague's formation on three sides. Piling on best speed, the enemy cruisers raced across the rear of the American formation and then closed in from the east. The Japanese destroyers swung westward to take the Americans from that direction. Down through the center, boomed the imperial battlewagons.

Kurita's tricky maneuvering gave Sprague a momentary breathing spell. But the cruiser threat from the east proved mortally dangerous. It prevented the carriers from turning into the wind to launch planes. As the Japanese cruisers gained, the threat of a "box" compelled drastic counteraction. The burden was assumed by Sprague's destroyers and destroyer escorts, an epic in the drama of destroyer warfare. Never before had American DDs rushed in to trade blows with such a force of heavies. And never anywhere had little DEs presumed to exchange blows with cruisers and battleships, particularly such a mastodon as the 63,000-ton *Yamato*.

USS Dennis laying a smoke screen Battle off Samar, Philippines. Courtesy US Naval Historical Center

0720. The first destroyer to attack the closing enemy was *Johnston* (Commander E. E. Evans); she peeled off to rush a heavy cruiser. Evans fired a full torpedo salvo. A cyclone of shells hit *Johnston*, and she reeled through the water with her speed reduced to 17 knots. Then, taking one hit after another, she maintained fire on the Japanese cruisers, shooting at ranges as short as 5000 yards.

Meanwhile, Sprague ordered the DDs and DEs to spread smoke, and his flat-tops were soon covered by a thick screen. As the Japanese fire slackened, Sprague ordered the screening ships to form up for two torpedo attacks.

0727. Destroyer *Hoel* (Commander L. S. Kintberger) rushed out of the smoke to launch a half-salvo at a battleship 9000 yards distant. She was hammered by shells but managed to get off another half-salvo that apparently damaged a heavy cruiser. And the fight was just beginning.

0754. Destroyer *Heerman* (Commander A. T. Hathaway) made her attack. Racing out of the smoke-fog, she flung seven torpedoes at a heavy cruiser. Six minutes later, she threw three torpedoes at a battleship. Then, bold as brass, she exchanged gunfire with a pair of heavy cruisers. Lucky *Heerman*! With tons of projectiles crashing in the sea around her, she came through the action only slightly damaged.

The relatively slow destroyer escorts had been instructed to launch their torpedo attacks after the three destroyers stepped out. Another rain squall swept the seascape as the DEs turned to tackle the enraged enemy. Maneuvering in sheeting rain and dense smoke, the DEs at first had difficulty in coordinating their torpedo strikes. Blinded, some nearly collided. But they threw the enemy off stride.

Closing to within 4000 yards of a heavy cruiser, destroyer escort *Samuel B. Roberts* (Lieutenant Commander R. W. Copeland) unloosed a spread of torpedoes at the enemy. Between 0805 and 0855, the *Roberts* engaged the Japanese heavies, firing point-blank at ranges as short as 6000 yards. She was hit at 0851, the beginning of the end.

0759. Destroyer escort *Dennis* (Lieutenant Commander S. Hansen) closed the enemy and fired three torpedoes at a range of 8000 yards, after a gun-battle begun at 10740. She then blazed away for almost two hours when she reeled out of the action, savagely mauled.

Destroyer escort *John C. Butler* (Lieutenant Commander J. E. Pace) did not launch a torpedo attack. After engaging a heavy cruiser and a destroyer with gunfire, she was ordered ahead of the carriers to lay smoke. *Dennis* retired behind *John C. Butler's* smoke screen.

0730. Destroyer escort *Raymond* (Lieutenant Commander A. F. Beyer), closed the Jap cruiser column to within 5700 yards. She slammed 16 shells into the superstructure of one vessel and then threw three torpedoes at the enemy. Hers was a charmed life. In the thick of battle for two hours and 20 minutes, she emerged without a scratch.

Johnston, Hoel, Heerman, Samuel B. Roberts, Dennis, John C. Butler, Raymond — the names of these warships were indelibly written that morning in the Navy's Log of Fame. The history of naval warfare contains few actions which match the battle fought by these DDs and DEs against the heavyweight men-of-war of the Imperial Navy.

"Small boys," Admiral Sprague had called them, ordering them to cover his carriers. "Small boys form for our second attack!"

They pitched in, literally no bigger than midgets against the giants of the Japanese Navy. Five-inch guns against 8-16- and 18-inchers. Unarmored ships against capital vessels clad in coats of steel.

Despite their courageous efforts, they were unable to save all the carriers. The Japanese landed four 8" shells on *Fanshaw Bay*. *Kalinin Bay* was hit by 15 shells. *Gambier Bay*, hit below the waterline, was disabled, torn apart and sunk by cruisers. However, these blows only served to indicate what could have happened to Sprague's force if the DDs and DEs had not intervened.

That intervention blunted Kurita's force and gave Admiral Stump's aircraft time to arrive on the scene. It gave Sprague's aircraft time to reload and refuel on Leyte and fly back into the battle. It also gave Seventh Fleet bombers from the waters off Mindanao a chance to reach the battle area in time. By 1130, these air reinforcements had convinced Kurita that the American flat tops were not worth the risk of further pursuit, and the way into Leyte Gulf was barred. Their defense had been so magnificent that he thought he had encountered Essex class carriers with cruiser escorts! With victory almost in his grasp, he ordered a general retirement northward. If the "small boys" were not entirely responsible for Kurita's frustration, they were to be credited with a large share of that responsibility.

But, as we expected, the DDs and DEs took a frightful beating. *Dennis* limped out of battle with her superstructure a shambles, six of her crew slain, and 19 wounded. *Heerman's* damage was light, but the term meant little to her five dead and nine wounded. The ships that suffered untold agony were destroyers *Johnston* and *Hoel*, and destroyer escort *Samuel B. Roberts*. All three were riddled by the enemy's fire and went down, fighting undaunted to the end.

The above from *United States Destroyer Operations in World War II* by Theodore Roscoe. Copyright 1953, U.S. Naval Institute. Annapolis, Maryland.

Naval historian Samuel Eliot Morison described the Battle off Samar, "The most gallant naval action in our history and the most bloody – 1130 killed, 913 wounded."

SAMUEL B. ROBERTS

The Destroyer Escort That Fought Like a Battleship

We ex-destroyer escort skippers, returned to our civilian careers, had a reunion dinner at the New York Yacht Club in 1952. Bob Copeland, former captain of the *Samuel B. Roberts*, was our guest speaker. Bob had, by that time, established a successful law practice in Los Angeles, and he flew to New York to recount the amazing narrative of the action off Samar. Bob was most impressive with his articulate account of a battle that has become legendary. We were all in high spirits when Bob started to talk. As the story unfolded, a great hush fell upon the audience. For the next 45 minutes, we relived the engagement with him. I never saw Bob again. He stayed in the Naval Reserves and ultimately became a rear admiral as well as an outstanding attorney. He passed away on 25 August 1973.

Perhaps a hush will fall over our readers too as you peruse this account with wonder and humility. This is a story about which all Americans may be proud and which all seafarers will remember. It has become a small part of our history, and it ranks with the greatest. This is a recount of heroism and gallantry unsurpassed.

Roberts, in company with other vessels in her task unit, was engaged with an overwhelmingly superior Japanese force for two hours and 15 minutes, when the word was passed to abandon ship. When that order was given, all power had been destroyed on the vessel, her after section was a roaring blaze, she was listing to starboard, was down four feet by the stern and settling rapidly. One 5" gun was smashed and the other unable to bear on any target, and all but 42 rounds of the ship's 5" ammunition of all types had been expended.

Abandonment, delayed somewhat because of care and handling of the wounded, was completed about 0935. The ship continued to list to starboard, about 80 degrees off center, where she hung for some time. Finally, twisting stern down, bow high, her ensign still snapping defiantly from her twisted and broken mast, she plunged to the bottom. In the few hours between the beginning of the engagement and the end, *Roberts* laid heavy and effective smoke screens that contributed to the escape from destruction of several escort auxiliary aircraft carriers. She brazenly, and without regard for her own safety, launched a torpedo attack against the leader of a Japanese cruiser column and possibly scored one hit from a spread of three. She fired 608 damaging rounds of 5"/38 caliber ammunition from her two 5" guns. In the words of her Captain:

> "We succeeded, largely through the Providence of God, the chasing of salvos, the smallness of the Japanese patterns, and the inaccuracy of enemy fire, in escaping damage for almost two hours before the first hit was recorded."

All logs, records and notes were sunk. This account has been reconstructed from the memories of three surviving officers, Lieutenant Commander Robert W. Copeland, Lieutenant William S. Burton and Lieutenant (jg) Thomas S. Stevenson Jr.

There were men in this auxiliary force who fretted at not being with Halsey's ships and, in a way, you could hardly blame them. The Third Fleet consisted of the best seagoing machines men had devised. Great carriers, battleships, cruisers and destroyers churned the sea at fabulous speeds, daring the enemy to come to grips. They fought real battles, not the occasional plane or sub that this task unit might take on. "Yes indeed," a man might grumble to himself, "the Third Fleet would corner and destroy the enemy in a smashing sea victory while I would sit it out in a DE not far away, never seeing, hearing or joining what would soon be one of the greatest naval battles since the dawn of history, maybe the greatest."

But, at sea and in war, nothing is sure.

That man could not know that Halsey was searching for an enemy fleet far to the north and that, just over the horizon and dead ahead, closing on an opposite and collision course at a relative (combined) speed of 40 knots or more, was an enemy force comprising:

four battleships
eight heavy cruisers
one light cruiser
twelve destroyers

Their mission, was to wipe out the transports and beachhead at Leyte. That man could not know that he was about to engage the pride of the Japanese Grand Fleet, including the 63,000 ton mammoth, *Yamoto*, and her 18" guns!

0650. *Samuel B. Roberts* went to GQ just as heavy caliber shells were falling all about the carriers, destroyers and destroyer escorts. Great geysers shot up into the air as Japanese fire controlmen sought to obliterate this force that stood in their path to destroy General MacArthur's invading force.

Commander Thomas, in *Hoel*, promptly ordered *Johnston* and *Roberts* to join him in laying a smoke screen astern of the retiring carriers. Surely, this was one of the most useful smoke screens ever laid, and it was tremendously effective. The air humidity was heavy, and the smoke lay close on the water, obscuring everything. To catch the urgency of the moment, one must envision five "jeep" aircraft carriers "racing" away at maximum speed, (only 19 knots), their deck crews and pilots working frantically to prepare the planes for flight. Across the sterns of the carriers streaked the two destroyers and one destroyer escort with black smoke pouring from their funnels and white smoke streaming from chemical containers on their fantails.

0735. Commander Thomas ordered his destroyers to attack the Japanese battle line with torpedoes. Traditionally, this was a destroyer's finest hour. A destroyer that could dart in toward an enemy fleet and launch a successful torpedo attack had fulfilled her mission in life — even if she were sunk in the process. Although no match for cruisers or battleships, a destroyer was a powerful and, yes, beautiful ship of war. It was the fastest of all fleet units, and its five 5" guns could lay a deadly fire. Its salvo from two quintuple torpedo mounts was a threat of extinction from the sea.

But not so a DE with two 5" guns and three torpedoes. When Thomas gave the order for the torpedo attack, therefore, Copeland asked whether he meant both destroyers and destroyer escorts, or just the former. Thomas replied that the destroyers should make the first attack and that the DEs should then make a coordinated second torpedo run. That might have been the pattern of action except there appeared to be a communications failure. None of the other DEs acknowledged the order. They apparently had not heard it, with the exception of Copeland on the bridge of *Roberts*.

This was a time for decision. The commanding officer of a destroyer escort had been told that he would attack in a second wave but, if the destroyer escorts did not know of the order, how would they attack? Copeland came to one conclusion. In time of war, with the enemy at hand, with his position favorable for attack, lacking clear and concise instructions, there remained only one course of action...Close with the enemy!

Fifty years later, gunnery officer William S. Burton, recalled:

> "I was on the bridge beside the captain. He looked in the book and saw that the skippers in the other DEs were senior to him, and he waited for them to attack. He looked around, and nothing happened, and he said, "Burton, we're going in ourselves."

The skipper asked his combat information center for a torpedo attack course and, on his own initiative, without being specifically ordered to do so, Lieutenant Commander Robert W. Copeland turned through his own smoke screen to attack the Japanese fleet!

Neither captain nor officers nor crew suffered any misapprehension as to the danger of the task to which they were now dedicated. The average member of the crew had been in service for less than one year. Copeland took the interior communications microphone in his hand and, in a calm and serious voice, he told the crew his estimate of the situation. He told them precisely what the force had gotten into and what they were going to do about it. Further, he told them that they were going into a fight against tremendous odds, from which survival could not be expected, but during which they would bring down upon the enemy all the damage that *Roberts* was capable of inflicting!

Roberts made her approach on the starboard bow of the Japanese cruiser squadron. Almost head on, the range closed at a relative (combined) speed of 47 knots. Amazing as it may seem, their own smoke screen had been so effective that they were now doubling back through it almost undetected. The intention was to fire torpedoes at 5000 yards on a high speed setting. This plan was upset by a stray enemy shell which knocked over the radio antennae on top of the torpedo tubes. Although the tubes were not damaged, the speed setting wrench was dislodged, and there was no way to change from intermediate setting, 4000 yards.

At that range, *Roberts* fired a spread of three torpedoes at an *Aoba* class cruiser heading the Japanese column. The helm was then put full over to turn 180 degrees. The ship heeled sharply to starboard, the water astern appeared to boil as in a cauldron, shell splashes about them reached higher than the mast.

Imagine the elation and cheering of the tense, hard-breathing deck crew of *Roberts* when a column of water shot up into the air immediately abaft the midships line of the *Aoba*, followed by flames and coal black smoke. The Destroyer Escort *Samuel B. Roberts* had apparently torpedoed a Japanese cruiser, herself remaining relatively unharmed and streaking back into her own smoke screen! (Although Copeland and topside personnel with a clear view of the action claimed a definite torpedo hit, naval history does not confirm it.)

Radioman John F. Keefe, now a retired postmaster in Dracut, Massachusetts, remembers running to his battle station in the CIC.

> "I was inside and could only see on radar, and what they had was unbelievable, all the blips. We knew we were in trouble. I also recalled the firing bearing I relayed from the radar operator to the torpedo men: 'Torpedo bearing 050 degrees."

The mouse had bloodied the cat's nose, the sparrow wounded the hawk, the gazelle kicked the lion. When last seen, the *Aoba* was no longer in column, and the lead had been taken by a *Tone* class heavy cruiser.

In retiring from the torpedo attack, Copeland recorded an interesting sidelight representing man's mastery over machinery. During trial runs after being commissioned, *Roberts* had registered a flank (maximum) speed of 24 knots. In the withdrawal from her torpedo run toward her smoke screen, however, the pitometer log was claimed to have registered 28 knots. If so, it was a real tribute to the engineers who understood without urging the chances of a DE 4000 yards from a Japanese cruiser column!

0805. *Roberts* opened fire for the first time with her main battery of two 5" guns at a range of 10,500 yards. Singling out the *Tone* column leader as her principal target, *Roberts* closed the range to 8500 yards. There was exhilaration and there were wild cheers on deck and on the bridge as 5" shells could clearly be seen exploding all over the Japanese cruiser.

Between 0815 and 0840, the range varied between 6000 and 7500 yards. At 0855, the range had closed to 5300 yards, and *Roberts* was slamming shells right into the Japanese cruiser! Upon the *Tone* was delivered the fastest and most accurate fire of which the *Roberts* was capable with her limited fire control system. Copeland's strategy was to hit without being hit for as long as possible. Unbelievably, he got away with it for some time. As enemy fire got too close, he broke off to change the range and bearing, and then raced in again, like a dog on the heels of a bear, snapping but never grappling.

During such brief intermissions, when *Roberts* broke off from the *Tone* to confound the latter's fire, she opened fire on targets of opportunity, i.e. enemy cruisers and destroyers! All destroyers and destroyer escorts were laying smoke, standing between the carriers and the Japanese fleet, and firing for all they were worth. Thus far, *Roberts* had been ducking in and out of the splashes of heavy caliber shells, escaping salvos, scoring hits. On this day, off Samar, heroism was the order of the day, and nowhere was the flag more splendidly borne than on *Samuel B. Roberts*. But luck was running out.

0851. *Roberts* received her first hit. An 8" shell put a hole below the water line in the forward fire room, rupturing the main steam line and releasing live steam throughout the area. With one of her two fire rooms out of commission, her best speed was reduced to 17 knots. *Roberts* was wounded

0900. The range had closed to 4000 yards, with *Roberts* continuing to pour shells into the *Tone* cruiser. But she now began to receive successive hits. Her forward engine room was hit and knocked out of commission. A shell, possibly from one of the battleships, landed on the 40mm gun mount. The gun and gun shield, director and gun crew disappeared — obliterated. The odds were catching up. Bravery and audacity could no longer outwit or outmatch such one-sided power. The heroes were dying.

0910. There was a frightful explosion when three heavy caliber shells smashed into the port side at the waterline. The after engine room was blasted into silence, leaving *Roberts* without power, motionless in the water. The after fuel tanks were ruptured by the explosion, and a blaze started on the fantail. Her hour of greatness had been lived; *Roberts* was mortally hurt. She had become a ghastly, inert mass of battered metal, incapable of propulsion or combat. This was doom, expected but terrible.

Gunner's Mate Third Class Paul Henry Carr was gun captain of number two 5" gun. The rapid and continuous fire from that gun was an inspiration to every man on the ship. Within a period of 50 minutes, his gun had expended over 300 rounds, including illuminating star shells when everything else ran out. After all power, compressed air and communications had been lost, and before the word had been passed to abandon ship, the crew of number three gun, under the immediate supervision of Carr, loaded, rammed and fired six rounds entirely by hand and with certain knowledge of the hazards involved. The failure of the compressed air gas ejection system made it sheer suicide to continue firing that gun, and the inevitable happened. While attempting to get off the seventh round in this condition, there was an internal explosion in the gun, killing all but three members of the gun crew, two of whom subsequently died in the sea.

After the explosion, the first man to enter the gun mount saw Carr with a 5" projectile in his hands. His body was ripped open, and his intestines were splattered throughout the mount. Nonetheless, he held the shell above his head and begged the petty officer who had entered to help him get that round into the gun. Of course, he could not see that the breech of the gun had been blown into a shapeless mass of steel. But Carr would not be dissuaded or restrained. For the next five minutes, he kept trying to get back to his gun to deal one last blow to the enemy. Then, death mercifully relieved him of his irreparably shattered body. Somewhere, we would like to believe, Gunner's Mate Paul Henry Carr wears his posthumously awarded medals with pride and composed dignity.

The number three turret of the *Tone* appeared to be knocked out of commission. The bridge of the cruiser was badly holed and set on fire. There were also observed several small fires immediately abaft the bridge.

Lieutenant Burton filed a report after the battle and said of Gunners Mate Paul Henry Carr:

> "We had to maneuver radically in order to avoid the oncoming salvos. Nevertheless, Carr was able to obtain confirmed hits, numbering possibly 40, upon the Japanese heavy cruiser. We positively knocked out their number three 8" gun turret, demolished their bridge, and started fires."
>
> Today, Burton says he was wrong about knocking out the 8" gun. He saw the Japanese gun pointed up at a peculiar angle and thought Carr's gunnery had knocked it out. Later on, having seen the Japanese armor plate and "upon sober reflection", he says:
>
> "I'm not sure we did it. It was probably a 500-pound bomb from one of our planes. But we were making hits all the time".

Keefe, hearing the order to abandon ship, was glad enough to leave the smoke and fire inside the combat information center and ran to the bridge:

> "I was barefoot and the deck was boiling. I heard the captain say, 'Let's try to beach it on the Samar Island', but we had no power to get to the beach. I can remember jumping into the oil and calling to swimmers to join hands and stay in a circle to keep together. We did that but, after a while, we broke the circle and swam through the oil for rafts. I recollect one other thing. When I was first in the water, one Jap ship came toward us, and I took off my life jacket to go under (to drown) because I didn't want to be captured. I figured they would kill us, anyway. I can remember trying to get to one of the rafts and the swimming getting easier because finally I got out of the fuel oil. I was alone in the water, and right beside me were two large sharks. One grazed my leg. I kicked like hell, and they slapped their tails and swam away. I hung on to the outside of the net. Inside the raft were the wounded. Those of us hanging on the outside had water up to our chins. We got into the rafts in spells to rest. Some of the men were horribly wounded, and the sun beat on them all day. What saved us (from the sun) was the fuel oil."

The oil probably saved them from the sharks, too. Gunnery

Officer Burton, now a lawyer in Cleveland and the son of former U.S. Senator and Supreme Court Justice Harold H. Burton, noted in his report:

> "We had been in and out of large patches of fuel oil and everyone, of course, was covered with oil. This no doubt accounted for the fact that, whereas they were continuously in sight, no sharks bothered our group, although they did bother other groups or survivors whose ships had been lost in the same action."

Burton tells of Pharmacist Mate Oscar M. King*, who distinguished himself by tending to the wounded in his raft. King was fastidious:

> "When it came time to defecate, as is necessary during a period of some 50 hours, he would leave the group and swim by himself to perform this function. It seems that once he had removed his trousers, the lower portion of his body, not having been covered with oil, was entirely white and attracted a shark. The shark came up and nudged him gently. He replaced his trousers, returned to the group and did not even say anything about the incident until we were picked up some 30 hours later."

Wilfred J. Labbe of Jay, Maine, remembers he had to scrape the oil off when he was rescued: "Salt water and oil just won't wash." Labbe was injured before the order to abandon ship:

> "I was standing looking at the gauges, and we got hit. There was a railing around the bilge plates and a shell-hit knocked me right through the railing."

When Labbe got back on deck, an officer asked him to go back down and open the sea valves to scuttle the ship.

> "I knew where one valve was in the back of the aft fire room and opened that. I went to the forward fire room – there was no one left there. Two had been killed right in that room. And I opened the valve there."

There were other valves he could not find, not that it was necessary. *Roberts* was sinking quickly. Labbe recalls:

> "I went over the side. I had a life belt on and swam to a net. It was all snarled up, and I asked the boys to help me, anyone able to, those without broken arms, and we unsnarled the net and rode on that for two days."

Labbe was more comfortable sitting in the water in the net than he had been on the ship because of his back injury. He was not discouraged, as he remembers it, and was hopeful of rescue. "The only thing was seeing those boys suffer. Some really hurt bad." He does not think much now about the *Roberts* or about the battle: "I forgot a lot, which I wanted to do."

Seaman Yusen was in the water that day but was uninjured. He had tied himself to the life raft as had the others who bobbed in the water, since there was no room for them inside the raft. On the first night, he fell asleep, became untied from the raft, and floated away. But, he remembers, "Bud Comet woke up and yelled, 'Where's Yusen?' And he cut himself free from the raft and swam and got me. He saved my life."

Fifty hours in the water is a frightfully long time, even if one is healthy and sound. Two days and two nights of salt water will rot the skin off of anybody. But when that salt goes deep into a goring wound, the pain cannot be described. A man can groan and clutch a line as long as he can — or as long as he feels that life is worth saving. After that, he can become resigned to the water closing over his face, the light of day fading away, the bells of the depths calling the sailor to final peace from his agony.

This was the lot of the survivors of *Roberts*. There was no question of any of their hard pressed sister ships turning back to help them. Shortly after abandoning, they all expected a brutal death. A *Katori* class cruiser and two destroyers bore down on them. The Japanese, at that time, had hardly earned a reputation for mercy or respect for the living soul. The survivors prayed and braced themselves for what surely would be a hail of machine gun fire on and about the rafts to eliminate for good this small band of men who had dared to strike the best of the enemy fleet. This was bound to be the final lash of vengeance. The thoughts that go through minds at such times are numerous. Is wound to be added to wound, or is one to die now outright? Was one to watch his own blood run out into the sea?

But let this be said for the Japanese. The cruiser and destroyers passed by our men, like a salute, and never a shot was fired. Characteristically, they were taking pictures.

Fifty hours later, a PC happened upon the survivors. The battle was over. The ship was gone. The deeds were done. A small chapter in American history had been written by a small ship that would come to be known in later years as "The DE that fought like a battleship". Copeland took stock of what he had left, and it was not too much. Sadly, and with the lonely, heavy heart of a great captain who has seen his men fight for all they were worth, yet torn asunder, he jotted down his casualty report:

> Killed in action: 16 men.
> Died of wounds: seven men.
> Missing in action and presumed dead: three officers and 63 men.
> Wounded in action: two officers, 47 men – and the commanding officer.
> About seventy-five per cent of the crew of *Roberts* was on the casualty list!

What we will all remember about the Battle off Samar was that one of the first blows struck, by the *Samuel B. Roberts*, although incomparable to the destruction wrought by the heavy American units shortly after, was among the bravest. Many tall ships and many gallant crews have fought the bitter fight, but no record can surpass what happened off Samar. On that day, a United States destroyer escort, on her own initiative, and without being ordered to do so, attacked and damaged an enemy cruiser squadron. This is a story for our children, and our children's, children.

To emphasize the honors awarded to that action, three destroyer type vessels constructed in recent years have borne the names of: *USS Samuel B. Roberts*; *USS Robert W. Copeland*; *USS Paul Henry Carr*.

•Data relative to Lieutenant Burton, Radioman Keefe,

Lewis M. Andrews, Jr.

Water Tender Labbe, Pharmacist Mate Oscar M. King and Seaman Yusen courtesy of "Against All Odds", by Peter Anderson, The Boston Globe Magazine, January 27, 1985.

DENNIS

> "Our main objective was to extricate the carrier group from its precarious position and to inflict as much damage on the enemy as possible."
>
> Lieutenant Commander S. Hansen
> Commanding Officer

0650 on 25 October 1944. *Dennis* heard the report from the pilot whose eyes suddenly bulged in disbelief. It is interesting to note that *Samuel B. Roberts* did not record such a message, saying instead that her first indication of impending battle was the sight of enemy shell splashes near the Task Force. This could have been a TBS malfunction, quite probable because *Roberts* believed that other DEs had not acknowledged torpedo attack orders when in fact they had.

Lieutenant O. Carroll Arnold, now a retired Protestant minister, was CIC Officer on *Dennis* and in a position to observe the entire engagement. Aside from official records, his is the best individual account of the action reviewed by this author:

> "Wednesday, 25 October 1944, dawned dull and overcast for Taffy 3, stationed off the island of Samar in the Philippines, just north of Leyte Gulf. Our job, along with Taffys 1 and 2, was to conduct antisubmarine patrols and to furnish close air support for General MacArthur's Sixth Army which disembarked at Leyte on 20 October.
>
> After the carriers launched planes for the morning, we prepared to make a routine day of it, chipping paint and bitching about MacArthur's having called us 'his' Seventh Fleet.
>
> But the day was not scheduled to go that way at all. Having stood the midwatch that morning, I had gone below to log some sack time when the horns began to howl, and I stumbled wearily out of my bunk and to my battle station in CIC. As I went up the ladder, I heard the roar of mighty guns and, as I glanced out, I saw giant splashes bracketing our carriers. Great geysers tinted in garish shades of red, purple, and yellow rose up around the flattops. (The Japanese dyed their shells so gunners could determine accuracy.) The nightmarish color display lent an air of unreality to a scene that was already too bizarre and dreadful to be believed.
>
> As I came into the radar room, I was met with the startling words, 'It's the whole damned Japanese fleet!' Every radio transmission, every frightened face, and the raucous yells coming down the voice tube from the bridge of our little DE confirmed the riveting fact.
>
> There were four battleships, six or eight cruisers, and a dozen or so destroyers. The air was heavy with the din of their giant guns. And Taffy 3, the northernmost Task Group of the three, was their target! Baby flattops and DEs against battleships and cruisers?
>
> I remember how secure and smug we had felt the afternoon before. We were standing off Samar with our carriers, enjoying the late evening breezes and exchanging scuttlebutt. Suddenly, a mammoth fleet had blipped our radar screens and soon appeared on the horizon. From our little 'spitkit' we gazed in awe and wondered at Admiral Halsey's highly touted Third Fleet. How safe we felt to know that those fast carriers of the *Essex* and *Independence* classes, those immense battleships - *New Jersey*, *Massachusetts*, *North Carolina*, *South Dakota*, and others - were on our side. The sleek and deadly cruisers bristled with 6" and 8" guns. Around the periphery were destroyers, fast, impudent, and sleek. They were heading north at full speed, or so we thought, to guard San Bernardino Strait and thus protect MacArthur's flank.
>
> On the other end of San Bernardino was a powerful Japanese battle fleet under the command of Admiral Kurita. Halsey knew the force was there, for his planes had attacked it just the day before, and his torpedo bombers had sunk the mighty battleship *Musashi*, which purportedly carried 18-inch rifles, as did her sister, *Yamato*. We were content as we watched Halsey's behemoths heading north. We were certain we'd be sailing under the Golden Gate Bridge by Christmas!
>
> The next morning, when Admiral Kurita, minus *Musashi*, but having successfully negotiated San Bernardino Straits during the night, opened fire on us with his 18-inch rifles at 14,000 yards (which for battleships is like shooting cans in the backyard), we had no time to wonder what had happened to Halsey and his Third Fleet.
>
> Taffy 3's commander, Rear Admiral Clifton Sprague on *Fanshaw Bay*, quickly ordered a southeasterly course. His tactic was simple - to run away from the big guns, although at a flank speed of 19 knots there was a certain grim comedy about our prospects of escape.
>
> The screen began to form a ragged battle line astern of the carriers. Crisp orders came over the TBS: "Small boys, make smoke!" And make smoke we did, with all the enthusiasm born of desperation. On our ship, Chief Gunner's Mate Blackburn carried two smoke flasks weighing 300 pounds each from their stowage point amidships to the fantail dispensing position. It was our only protection from the Japanese fire.
>
> The smoke was effective in hiding the carriers, although an occasional hole would open up, and when it did we could see the multicolored splashes as enemy gunners lobbed in their salvos. Our communicator, Lieutenant Raymond Carlson, Officer of The Deck, was conning the ship, headed for the splashes when he saw them, on the sound theory that the next salvo wouldn't splash in the same place (A tactic known as the chasing of salvos. As long as you could see the splashes, you were still in the war.)"

Shortly after the beginning of the engagement, the three destroyers, *Heerman*, *Johnston* and *Hoel* with the Escort Commander, Commander W. D. Thomas in *Hoel*, were ordered to make a torpedo attack on the enemy battle line. At 0750, the destroyer escorts, *Dennis*, *Raymond* and *John C. Butler* were ordered to make a second torpedo attack, and the destroyers (if any survived) to make a third attack. The carrier planes, meanwhile, carried out sporadic attacks on the enemy formation with considerable losses to intensive Japanese antiaircraft fire. Arnold recalls the commands distinctly:

"I remember the Screen Commander's calm voice on the radio asking Admiral Sprague, 'Do you want the destroyer escorts to go in too?' 'No', said the Admiral, 'let them wait for the second attack'. I remember how fervently my instinct for self-preservation applauded the Admiral for what seemed to me a wise decision.

ComScreen's order was brief, instant, and to the point: 'Come on, boys, let's get 'em!' The words were unmilitary but clear and gallant beyond measure. They were the last words we ever heard from him as the destroyers turned toward the Japanese guns and began their incredible, hopeless and altogether splendid attack.

With their five-inchers popping, their tubes extended and at the ready, they went down that long and terrible road that all destroyer skippers train for and dream about, but from which few ever return. Later, we pieced together the furious fight that the three gallant destroyers made at incredibly short distances, destroyers against battleships at point-blank range.

Heerman alone emerged from the fray to tell the tale, and her decks were awash. A part of the account she related was that, at one point in the melee, surrounded by battleships and cruisers, her 5" ammunition gone, her tubes empty, one indefatigable gunner on a 40mm gun arose and shouted at the skipper, 'Don't worry, Captain, we're sucking 'em into my 40mm range!'

As Admiral Sprague continued his flight to save his carriers, he ordered the DEs to go in for a second torpedo attack. I remember seeing our coordinates on the radar screen in CIC widen out as two Japanese cruisers at incredible speed (our plot showed 38 knots) broke out of the main attacking force and began to encircle us. We picked out one of these cruisers and prepared to attack it.

If we had gotten any time off from being frightened and amazed, we might have contemplated the comedy of the situation. A destroyer escort with three torpedoes and a flank speed of 24 knots was preparing to attack a cruiser with eight-inch guns and capable of 38 knots. It had to be the unlikeliest engagement since David and Goliath. But nobody was amused."

Rain squalls were heavy and intermittent, and the humidity combined with the smoke to hang a curtain above the surface of the water, giving excellent protection to carriers and escorts alike. *Dennis* raced in at flank speed to the nearest cruiser with her two 5" guns in rapid fire. At one point, she had to alter course to avoid torpedoes launched by the enemy. *Dennis* fired her torpedoes at 8000 yards, then turned and raced back toward the carriers. During the torpedo run, *Dennis* recorded several 5" hits from her battery on a Japanese cruiser. Because of the rain and the smoke, she could not see the results of her torpedo attack.

The surviving escorts, including *Dennis*, interposed themselves between the enemy and the retiring carriers and conducted a running gun duel against opposing battleships, cruisers and destroyers, meanwhile laying a smoke screen to protect the carriers! *Dennis* observed that two destroyers and one destroyer escort were missing, i.e. *Hoel*, *Johnston* and, of course, *Samuel B. Roberts*. Some items from the log of *Dennis*:

"0819. *Gambier Bay* reported that her engine room was flooded. She dropped out of formation.

0843. *Dennis* personnel observed a definite hit on a Japanese cruiser from the ship's 5" battery.

0846. Observed an aerial bomb hit on another cruiser.

0847. Eight enemy destroyers were reported closing in on the starboard quarter. Enemy salvos had become more accurate. Splashes were observed close aboard.

0850. An enemy salvo bracketed *Dennis*. She received a direct hit on the port side, three feet above the first platform deck. The shell passed through the deck and out the starboard side, three feet above the water line, flooding the ordnance and dry stores storerooms and fatally injuring one man in Repair I. It exploded after it exited the ship, causing considerable damage with shell fragments that pierced the hull."

Arnold was not certain if this were reality or a nightmare:

"Down to effective range we went. The torpedoes were launched, and immediately we began that hallowed naval maneuver called, 'Getting the hell out of there'. While turning, as we showed our profile to the cruiser, we took the broadside - four eight-inchers all at once! The ship shuddered, but maintained speed. We completed the turn and dodged into the smoke.

We all wondered why the ship didn't blow up. It had no right to survive an eight-inch salvo. The damage control parties began to report to CIC: 'Forward gun knocked out. One hole forward through both skins of the ship.' Actually, the shell went through the chief's quarters (right over the forward magazine), through the chief's icebox, and out into the water. Damage aft was similar, a hole through both skins of the engine room and a direct hit in the aft fire-control tower. That was the reason the ship had lived. Two shots had been a little high. The direct hits had 'holed' us, that is to say they had gone through the ship and exploded in the water. How lucky can you get? Later we learned that Admiral Kurita thought we were cruisers and had fired armor-piercing projectiles. Blessed myopia!"

It should be noted that the logical use of armor piercing (A/P) shells by the Japanese forces against our DEs was a paradox that quite possibly saved *Dennis* from destruction and enabled the *Samuel B. Roberts* to fight as long as she did. An A/P had a delay mechanism that permitted the shell to pierce heavy steel plating before exploding. DEs were budget priced vessels and covered with a lighter plating than was applied to DDs. Consequently, an A/P hit could go right through a DE, exploding after it exited the ship. There could still have been extensive shrapnel damage to personnel and materiel, but much less when compared to what would have been sustained with an internal explosion. Many photos of DEs exhibit a "tired old horse" appearance with the skin pressed in against the ribs from encounters with heavy seas. In this case, a bit of skimping in construction actually saved lives.

0900. *Dennis* sustained a direct hit on the after 40mm director. The shell then passed through the superstructure deck and into another compartment. Two men were killed outright, two were fatally injured.

Up to this time, the two 5" guns comprising this DE's main

battery were engaged in rapid fire on targets of opportunity, the ship still laying smoke to cover the retirement of the carriers.

0901. A glancing hit was received atop the forward 5" gun mount. Personnel casualties were light but serious enough to render the gun inoperative because of personnel incapacitation. At the same time, the after 5" mount went out of action because of a broken breach spring. Momentarily, *Dennis* appeared to be out of the fight.

0903. The after 5" gun crew was transferred to the forward 5" gun to relieve the injured and put the gun back in action. At the same time, gun repair went to work on the after 5" gun. Ammunition had to be brought forward by hand from the after magazines because of the flooding of the ordnance storeroom and access passageways. Marveling that life and limb were still intact, Arnold continued:

> "The Japanese cruisers continued to close in on our carriers. Taffy 3's situation had changed from normal desperate to double indemnity desperate. The fate of the carriers was in the balance. Admiral Sprague gave the orders in plain language: 'Small boys, small boys, interpose; I say again, interpose, interpose!' It was the final irony. Destroyer escorts, which were meant to fight submarines, not only were required to make torpedo attacks on men-of-war in this battle, but now they were to be target practice for the Imperial Japanese Fleet. We were to draw the fire away from the carriers. We started back down that road. We were tardy to the funeral, but we went. The fight moved southward, cruisers and destroyers still pursuing. The carriers fired their foolish little popguns from their sterns, dodging into this rain squall and that patch of smoke. Escorts *Dennis*, *Raymond*, and *Butler* straggled behind the carriers toward the enemy, firing everything in their magazines, even star shells."

0907. Captain Hansen now had to consider the possibility of losing his ship. A weighted sack of classified material was thrown overboard to avoid any possibility of falling into the hands of the enemy.

0910. A Japanese cruiser 7500 yards astern opened fire on *Dennis*. We altered course so that the forward gun could be aimed.

0920. The after gun crew returned to the now repaired after gun so as to more effectively duel with the attacking cruiser. A new gun crew had been reorganized from other stations to man the forward 5" gun.

Dennis was back in action, blasting away at the foe as fast as the guns could be loaded, sighted and fired!

Suddenly, after two hours of steady fighting, Kurita gathered his forces and retired toward San Bernardino. *Dennis* reduced speed to 17 knots and resumed patrol of her assigned station. The skipper secured the ship from GQ as peace returned to the embattled DE. Smoke and the acrid smell of burned black powder faded away. *Dennis* was operative but savaged. Six of her crew were dead, 19 were wounded, and her superstructure was shattered. The crew that was embattled moments before was now tending to damage, pumping flooded compartments, caring for the wounded — mourning the dead. Tension retreated and was replaced by a mild exhilaration; they were alive and victorious. Relax? Maybe.

The battered leftovers of Taffy 3 were allowed a few minutes' respite to lick their wounds and count their dead before the air attack began.

1050. "General Quarters, man your battle stations!"

1052. *Dennis* opened fire with her after 40mm gun on a plane broad off the starboard bow, and it splashed into the sea!

1055. Japanese land-based planes from Manila suddenly appeared overhead; one of them broke through the defense and pounced on the flight deck of *St. Lo*. Violent explosions and fire erupted from the stricken carrier. It was the first American experience with *kamikazes*, the suiciders, from Leyte to Luzon to Iwo Jima and Okinawa. They aimed themselves, trading one plane and one pilot for a carrier and 600 men which, from our viewpoint, was a bad bargain. *Dennis* was ordered into the area, along with the other escorts to recover survivors as the crew of the carrier began to abandon ship.

1101. The remaining carriers were zigzagging away from the attack area. *St. Lo* was covered by a roaring blaze from stem to stern with explosions continuing to arch skyward. Another enemy plane dove on the stricken carrier. Three Japanese planes were observed shot down in the main carrier formation. Arnold continued:

> "The attack was over almost before it began, but the *St. Lo's* wound was mortal. The bomb on the plane had penetrated to and exploded in the hangar deck, and its initial blast began a chain of other explosions - torpedoes, depth charges, and gasoline in the heart of the beleaguered carrier. She blew up and split to pieces. As she went down, she left the crew floating in the water, clinging to life rafts and debris:
>
> Our first lieutenant, Frank Tyrell, and his Chief Bos'n's Mate, Joe Barry, seaman par excellence from Boston, organized the rescue operation, draping the ship with cargo nets. Our captain, a first class ship handler, carefully maneuvered our little craft among the survivors to effect their rescue. As we approached the men, many of whom were desperately wounded, one burly sailor arose from a nest of greasy, bloody bodies in a life raft, shouting, 'Hey, what's for chow?' And another yelled, 'What's the movie tonight?'
>
> Some of the survivors were in pitiful condition. We lined them up on the fantail and gave them shots of morphine. One happy moment occurred in the midst of a generally grim maneuver when we pulled aboard a two-stripe doctor, together with his warrant officer assistant, both in good health, and they immediately assumed command of our hospital operations.
>
> After picking up the survivors of *St. Lo*, we broadened our rescue search to pick up stranded pilots whose planes had been shot down or had simply run out of fuel. One cautious pilot, fearing we were the enemy, hid under his yellow life jacket until he was sure we were friendly. As we hauled him aboard, he shook himself like the airedale he was, took a look around, and then inquired bluntly, 'Where the hell is haul-ass Halsey?' Altogether, we picked up 400 men from *St. Lo* and 35 pilots. On a ship with a crew of 235, we were, to say the least, happily overloaded.
>
> We buried our dead, made emergency repairs to engine and hull, and set course for Kossol Passage where we delivered our wounded to the hospital ship *Hope (AH-7)*. The Battle off Samar slipped into the hands of history."

The fight did not come again to *Dennis* or to the Task Force, what was left of it. *Dennis* had been at General Quarters, with one brief interruption, for eight hours. The physical and emotional drain was enormous, and 25 October 1944 would be implanted in every man's mind for the rest of his days.

Forty-seven years later, Chief Gunner's Mate LeRoy Blackburn recalled the fight and the urgency to put the after 5" gun back into action. He also remembered one man in particular, a living symbol of courage and devotion. His name was Tony Manzi. The chief wrote an open letter to his shipmates:

> "Manzi was a shipfitter by rating, an expert welder, but also a helper in every section of the ship. Wherever any work was being done, he lent a hand. But it was during the Battle off Samar where he distinguished himself. When I was notified of a problem in the number two 5" gun mount, in which Manzi was projectile loader, I was apprised that the spring closing the breech block was broken. A projectile was in the almost red hot barrel, and it could 'cook-off' at any second. All recommended procedures had been employed to close the breech, but failed.
>
> We tried to drive the projectile back with a ramrod, but it was in too tight. I was afraid to strike it too hard for fear it would explode. So, I told the men to run the fire hose into the barrel, hoping to cool the projectile. Then I asked for three volunteers to assist me. Since the hot projectile was a life threatening missile, I could not detail anyone to remain in the gun mount with me. It was my responsibility to remove the projectile. Tony, not being in ordinance personnel, was not obligated to remain, but he said, 'I'll stay'. Whitiak, the mount captain, then volunteered as did the gun captain. That gave me three men besides myself.
>
> I told the remaining men to clear the area because the mount would be ripped apart and the barrel blown off if the projectile exploded. We then put a 2"X4" plank under the block and elevated the barrel, but that would not work either. The water seeping past the projectile was steaming hot. I then decided the only possible solution was to remove the broken spring and replace it. All this time, we fully understood the danger we were exposing ourselves to. I guess we figured 'what the hell', the Jap cruisers posed as much risk also. I got a new spring from the ordnance room and a 3" or 4" piece of round stock from the machine shop. I was just picking it up when an enemy shell hit aft, killing four.
>
> Then, with a crow bar that Tony Manzi got, we were able to repair the gun. When they fired the hot projectile, it only went about 200 yards and then exploded!
>
> Manzi also stood knee deep in water to weld a deck plate over the hole in the starboard hull where an 8" Jap shell left the *Dennis* at the water line. Otherwise, we would have had a lot of problems in keeping the water out of that compartment.
>
> I just thought that my shipmates who were not aware of Manzi's bravery and contribution might appreciate the man even more. The others who volunteered were gunner's mates and perhaps it was their duty to remain. Tony was one of a rare breed, also a member of a wonderful group of men who made the *Dennis* a real fighting ship.
>
> In the Battle off Samar Island, you all performed superbly. To have gone into the Valley of Death, of fire and steel, and to have come out of it, was nothing short of a miracle. By all military odds, we were not supposed to have survived. You created history that day. I'm proud to have served with such a group of men, and I feel it is a great honor to be called "SHIPMATE" by you. I cannot think of another term that carries more pride and appreciation."
>
> Your Shipmate, "Blackie"

RAYMOND

Miraculously Shielded from Harm While Blasting the Enemy

Infrequently, an action report by an officer with a singular writing style of his own was complete and to the point. Such was the case with the commanding officer of *Raymond*, Lieutenant Commander A. F. Beyer. Accordingly, with some deletions and clarifications, the following action report will stand as the history of *St. Lo* in the Battle off Samar.

> "0700. A patrol plane reported an enemy fleet 15 miles distant. Battle stations were promptly manned and, upon orders from the Task Unit Commander, we commenced making smoke. Shells began falling astern of and within the formation. The Task Group Commander ordered our three destroyers to make a torpedo attack, launched all available planes and changed course to the southwest."

Raymond abandoned her patrol sector and was now racing in to engage an enemy cruiser. It must have seemed like a bad dream,

> "0730. We commenced systematic firing on an enemy cruiser at a rapidly closing range. At this time, there was a moderate and intermittent heavy rain squall with leaden cumulus clouds settling low overhead. This and the fact that all ships were making smoke reduced our visibility considerably. A torpedo wake approached and passed 20 yards to port. We continued to make smoke, using both chemical generators and funnel. (Funnel smoke is created by increasing the fuel flow to the boilers while simultaneously reducing the amount of oxygen. Compare it to a poorly adjusted carburetor in a car.)
>
> 0743. The Task Unit Commander ordered us to make a torpedo attack on an enemy cruiser. We put our helm over and came to a northerly course to close the range and place the target dead ahead. We then commenced firing with our forward 5" gun. As the range decreased rapidly to 10,000 yards or less, nine enemy destroyers deployed in a torpedo attack. Their torpedo wakes came toward us, one passing close to port and another passed under our bottom, heading for the carriers. None of them scored hits.
>
> 0756. We fired a spread of three torpedoes at an enemy cruiser at a range of 10,000 yards and closing fast. The target was making an effort to close our formation and outflank it on the port side. The DRT tracing machine in the CIC indicated that, after we fired our torpedoes, evasive action was

taken by the cruiser, closing the range an additional 1000 yards. This made conditions more favorable for our torpedo tracks. Several observers stated that we hit the target. However, visibility was so reduced that there is uncertainty as to who may have actually scored.

On the run in for this torpedo attack, we were under fire from the cruiser, and numerous straddles were obtained by them on us. Just after we fired our torpedoes and before we changed course to return to the formation, I observed *Roberts* on our starboard beam under heavy fire from the enemy. She was firing rapidly from her 5" guns while taking direct hits. A curtain of flashes surrounded her and, when we changed course to return to the formation, we could no longer locate *Roberts*.

While returning to formation at our flank speed of 24 knots, we maintained a continuous fire on the enemy cruiser. The 5" guns were in automatic director control. Radar was used and a computer solution was applied to the gun order corrector. The target was crossed four times, and five direct hits were obtained.

0828. The Task Unit Commander ordered *Raymond* to intercept an enemy cruiser approaching the formation on the port quarter. This target appeared to be the one we were firing at all this time, and we immediately changed course to intercept her. At this time, the smoke supply was exhausted, and we had no torpedoes left. At the start of the run, I considered that changing course toward the cruiser saved this vessel because most of their salvos at that time were overs rather than shorts. However, they did manage to straddle us at least once on the way in. It was simply a miracle that we weren't hit.

The radar indicated a range of 12,600 yards, decreasing rapidly to 5,700 yards. Target speed was 24 knots. After the range decreased sharply, the target changed course and the range increased markedly. A casualty occurred to the director computer at a range of 16,000 yards, at which time the guns were ordered to shift to local control with spotting. Ranges continued to be obtained by radar and spots were applied to them. The firing was continued until the range exceeded 18,000 yards. The enemy cruiser retired at 25 knots. Observers and the gunnery officer reported that during this phase of the action, the enemy cruiser was crossed a minimum of five times and at least fifteen hits were obtained.

Raymond expended 414 rounds of 5" ammunition, including antiaircraft shells. The latter were brought up from the lower handling room of number two gun by mistake when three of the men in that space became prostrate with the heat and were relieved by Repair Party 3. There were only two premature bursts of these projectiles; the remaining appeared to be short, over and on target. There were no casualties at either gun, and the gun crews functioned magnificently.

The enemy fire was not too accurate. Their salvos landed with no dispersion although with beautiful patterns. The colored dye-loaded projectiles used in almost all instances were brilliant, consisting of patterns of five rounds each. Enemy cruisers either did not open up rapid fire or were not capable of maintaining it. The cruiser did not maintain a continuous barrage against this vessel, but shifted fire from time to time to other vessels, then back to us apparently only when they were bothered by our fire. The enemy ships did not take advantage of the several opportunities to close the range and finish us with their superior fire power.

No damage was sustained by this ship during this action. In several instances, this vessel was able to maneuver successfully to avoid systematic ranging salvos on the part of enemy cruisers.

1050. At the conclusion of the action, and while *Raymond* was still at GQ, enemy planes, identified as Vals, approached the formation, and five planes were seen to make suicide dives on our carriers. Unfortunately, this happened so suddenly that this vessel was unable to take a position where our antiaircraft fire could be effective.

1105. We were ordered by CTU to assist in rescuing survivors from *St. Lo*. We commenced picking up swimmers. Our whaleboat was lowered to expedite rescue work, and we picked up 109 survivors. We continued the search until 1700 when we were ordered by *Heerman* to proceed in company with *John C. Butler* at best possible speed to rejoin the formation. We secured from GQ, having been continuously at battle stations since 0700.

All hands on *Raymond* exulted in pride at their spectacular performance in the face of overwhelming odds. At the same time, they were humbly grateful for the fact that they returned from the fray with barely a scratch and with all personnel relatively unharmed."

JOHN C. BUTLER

No Enemy Shell Had Her Name on It

The following is from the action report of the captain of *John C. Butler*, Lieutenant Commander J. E. Pace.

"From the morning of 20 October until the evening of the 24th, the mission of our Task Group was to provide air support for the landings and inland advance of the Army Northern Attack Force in the Tacloban area on Leyte. The mission of our ship was to protect the aircraft carriers from submarine, air and surface attack.

0647 on 25 October. The Officer of The Deck sighted AA fire on the horizon and called me to the bridge. This ship maneuvered to interpose an effective smoke screen between our force and the enemy who were closing at a relative speed of 40 knots. Salvos landed within 300 to 400 yards of *Butler*. With the first shells coming from 15 miles, we realized that they must have originated from heavy ships, probably battleships."

Boiler Tender C. Bruno described what smoke meant to those who have to make it:

"I wonder if you know the story behind that black smoke? My battle station was the forward fire room; my particular job was burners. A burner man is one who lights off the burners of a boiler in order to maintain steam pressure. He also has control of the air supply to the boilers. He increases the air supply to minimize the smoke coming out of the stack. With me in the fire room, were Chief Telesco,

H. Mullis, I. Mollica, and one other. Unbeknown to me, when ordered to make smoke, the chemical smoke cylinders topside were not performing. When the executive officer, Mr. Huntingdon, yelled 'Make smoke, make smoke!', we thought he meant we weren't making enough. I looked at Chief Telesco, who was at my side. He looked at me. I spun the wheel that controlled the air to the boilers and cut off the air supply - you guessed it - black smoke. Well, let me tell you, that boiler started huffing and puffing like a dying person gasping for his last breath. I jumped back a foot. I opened the air valves to minimize the danger of it's blowing apart, but still maintained the black smoke. Well, eventually our chemical smoke cylinders were started, and the exec ordered us to stop making smoke."

Boiler Tender Jim Foust added:

"When the skipper asked for more smoke, we responded with gusto. We took it to the max. We used the regular smoke burner without the regular tip; this gave us a steady stream of oil and gave out smoke so thick you could cut it with a knife. Yep, 'Smoky' did it again. We did not know until much later that we almost set the stack on fire, and later we had to re-brick the boiler. It had a glaze like an Easter ham."

Back to Captain Pace:

"0718. We entered a rain squall and emerged from it 20 minutes later. We couldn't see any enemy ships because we had run out on the starboard beam of the formation to lay smoke. Realizing we were out too far, we came about and headed back in to renew the smoke curtain. The DD/DE screen was ordered to deliver a torpedo attack. For the next 2-1/2 hours, the Task Unit retired at best speed with the enemy force in hot pursuit.

Captain Pace ordered preparation for a torpedo attack, and the ship was turned to join up with the three destroyers. However, the command was clarified for the DDs to make the first torpedo attack. Several minutes later, an order came for the destroyer escorts to form up for the second attack. *Butler*, then constantly in heavy smoke screens, came about and searched for the senior destroyer escort in order to form up. Her surface radar was being used solely for gunnery at the time, and CIC could give no help in determining the location of any of the destroyer escorts. Back to the log:

"0753. We spotted an enemy destroyer on the starboard quarter and opened fire at 18,000 yards. When range closed to 16,000 yards, one hit was recorded.

After about 15 minutes, *Butler* came out of the smoke into fair visibility, located *Dennis* and tried to form up. Just prior to forming, an order was received from the Admiral for the two DEs on the starboard quarter of the formation to interpose between the formation and an enemy cruiser on his port quarter. *Butler* and *Dennis* proceeded in company through the formation, laying a smoke screen en route. At this time, *Butler* learned that all other screening vessels had already launched their torpedoes, and the order was again given to prepare for a torpedo attack. However, the enemy cruiser was drawing up to the beam of the formation at speeds in excess of *Butler's* best speed, and it was determined that she could not close the range for a torpedo attack unless the enemy cruiser headed for the formation. Heavy firing was exchanged between the cruiser and *Dennis* and *Butler* at ranges of from 16,000 to 13,000 yards.

0844.2 We opened fire on a heavy cruiser at about 17,000 yards. *Dennis* and *Butler* were approximately 700 yards apart, on a course converging with the enemy cruiser, and were under steady enemy fire. *Dennis* was just forward of *Butler's* port beam toward the enemy. Several salvos fell between the two ships.

0842.4 The leading enemy cruiser and a destroyer turned away at a range of 14,000 yards, but another enemy cruiser and destroyer, astern of the first two, maintained their course and kept up their fire. We shifted fire to the cruiser. Both destroyer escorts were laying smoke during this engagement.

0900. Just after the two destroyer escorts had reached the port beam of the formation, *Dennis* was badly hit and retired behind the *Butler's* smoke screen. Orders were then received from the Admiral to move up on his bow, and the *Butler* promptly complied. At this time, the *Butler* was the only ship capable of laying an effective smoke screen on the port side of the formation. At about 0930, the enemy light forces on our port side unaccountably turned away and retired after closing to about 13,200 yards."

This respite from battle was not the end. Scarcely had the Japanese Center Force retired when Japanese suicide planes made their appearance at 1050. *Butler* shot down one of the planes attacking the *St. Lo*, but another managed to crash the carrier! *Butler* took aboard 130 *St. Lo* survivors. Captain Pace continued:

"1113. All screening vessels were ordered to stand by the badly damaged *St. Lo*. The four surviving screening ships proceeded with the rescue of survivors while the remaining carriers retired. While rescuing survivors from *St. Lo*, Lieutenant R. Throop Jr., in charge of rescue operations on *Butler's* deck, twice entered the water to assist exhausted survivors while organizing and directing his men to rescue the most personnel in the shortest time. Seaman First Class R. J. Turner, on seeing an officer too tired to reach the side of the ship, jumped overboard, swam to the officer, towed him back within reach of a heaving line and assisted him on board."

Raymond and *John C. Butler* were the only ships in the entire group to emerge without personnel or materiel damage.

Butler, accompanied by *Raymond*, steamed for Leyte Gulf where she transferred stretcher cases, thence to Seeadler Harbor in Manus, Admiralty Islands, where the remaining patients were transferred to hospitals ashore. She escorted the surviving escort carriers of "Taffy 3" from Manus to Pearl Harbor, then returned to Seeadler Harbor in preparation for the forthcoming liberation of Luzon, Philippine Islands. She became a unit of Rear Admiral Richard A. Ofstie's Lingayen Protective Group.

The war was still very much in progress, and *John C. Butler* would fight again at Iwo Jima and deliver a stunning blow to the *kamikazes* in the picket line at Okinawa. See the narratives *The Philippine Campaign* and *Iwo Jima to Okinawa — The Destroyer Escorts*.

CONCLUSION

Perhaps the greatest compliment to our force was unwittingly paid by Admiral Kurita, commander of the Japanese Fleet, who wrote in his action report that he had been engaged with *Essex* class fleet carriers and numerous cruisers!

The range to enemy ships began to open and distance itself from the American ships. Shell splashes tapered off astern. The Japanese Fleet was turning away, abandoning the fight. As startled as this task force was to find itself engaging an overwhelmingly superior enemy force, the Japanese were equally distressed to have their secret mission compromised. By now, the whole Pacific was alerted. In addition, the enemy had not anticipated the wounds they would receive by the ferocity of the defense offered by this small auxiliary force. In Admiral Sprague's own words:

> "At 0925 my mind was occupied with dodging torpedoes when, near the bridge, I heard one of the signalmen yell 'God damn it, boys, they're getting away!' I could not believe my eyes, but it looked as if the whole Japanese fleet was indeed retiring. However, it took a whole series of reports from circling planes to convince me. And still I could not get the fact to soak into my battle-numbed brain. At best, I had expected to be swimming by this time."

The six escort carriers and their screen of three destroyers and four destroyer escorts which formed "Taffy 3", aided by planes from "Taffy 2", had stopped the powerful Center Force and inflicted a greater loss than they suffered. Two enemy cruisers were at the bottom of the sea while four out of the six escort carriers brought under gunfire had escaped. The successful retirement of the Japanese Center Force off Samar was small consolation for the complete failure of its mission to break up the amphibious shipping in Leyte Gulf. The defeat of the most powerful surface fleet sent to sea by Japan since the Battle of Midway was due to the indomitable spirit of the "Taffys".

Two of the carriers, *St. Lo*, and *Gambier Bay*, were sunk; *Fanshaw Bay* and *Kalinin Bay* were heavily damaged. Destroyers *Johnston* and *Hoel* went down in a rain of heavy caliber shells. *Samuel B. Roberts* went down after one of the most brilliant and courageous actions in American navy history. *Dennis* reeled from the fray with her superstructure battered to scrap and 25 dead and wounded. *Heerman* survived but counted 14 dead and wounded. After blasting a Jap cruiser with 5" shells and launching her three torpedoes, *Raymond* emerged unscathed. *John C. Butler*, ordered to break off her engagement with an enemy cruiser and destroyer to lay smoke ahead of the carriers, also avoided damage or casualties. In spite of the blood and tears, it was a great victory. To quote from the official analysis of this engagement:

> "It is not too difficult to surmise with some accuracy the contributory reasons why the Japanese OTC made the very poor decision of breaking off the action and withdrawing the same way he came. From our viewpoint, this decision seems to be the only sure factor which made the difference between success and failure for the Japanese. Had this decision not been made, the Japanese main body could have waded through and completed the destruction of this Task Unit and, continuing to the south, would have found our naval opposition very low on ammunition following their night action (Surigao Straits). In Leyte Gulf, they could have successfully accomplished their mission and retired as was originally intended. During this time, they would have been exposed to only minor damage from weakened air attacks (whose largest bomb was 500 pounds) plus belated air strikes from Taffy 2."

There were two serious faults, one by our side at the onset and one by the enemy at its conclusion. Ours was a failure by intelligence and reconnaissance units to locate the enemy fleet before it collided head on with our vastly inferior force. The other was the decision of the Japanese Admiral to reverse course and retire in the mistaken belief that the American ships encountered were an advance scouting unit of a powerful fleet; he let slip from the palm of his hand his mission to attack and destroy the anchored transports and the staging area at Leyte. A military disaster of that magnitude to our side would have been a severe blow. The first (Leyte, not Luzon) photo of General MacArthur and his aides sloshing through the surf toward the beach, "I have returned", might have required a retake at a later date — assuming they survived.

The four destroyer escorts can take a lot of the credit that a disaster to the Leyte operation was averted, albeit at heavy cost to themselves. The Battle off Samar is indelibly written as one of the greatest in American naval history, and DE men recall it with pride.

Taken together, Leyte, Samar, Surigao Strait, Sibuyan Sea and San Bernardino, comprised the Second Battle of The Philippine Sea. It has been judged by the chronicles to be the biggest sea fight of all time and the last surface battle of World War II. Midway and Coral Sea are not comparable in terms of men and ships and planes.

Lest any feathers be ruffled, this author would like to note that details of the heroic actions of destroyers *Hoel*, *Johnston*, and *Heerman* were not ignored. They were omitted because this is a book about destroyer escorts. The destroyer details are well covered in *Destroyer Operations in World War II*, published by the U.S. Naval Institute, Annapolis, Md.

Samuel B. Roberts –
Courtesy US Naval Historical Center

RADM David M. LeBreton presents the Navy Cross to LCDR Robert W. Copeland, commanding officer *USS Samuel B. Roberts.* Courtesy US Naval Historical Center

Samuel B. Roberts (DE–413) racing through heavy caliber shell splashes to launch torpedo attack on a Japanese cruiser, at the same time making smoke to screen American carriers. Painting by Sam L. Massette © American Naval Art

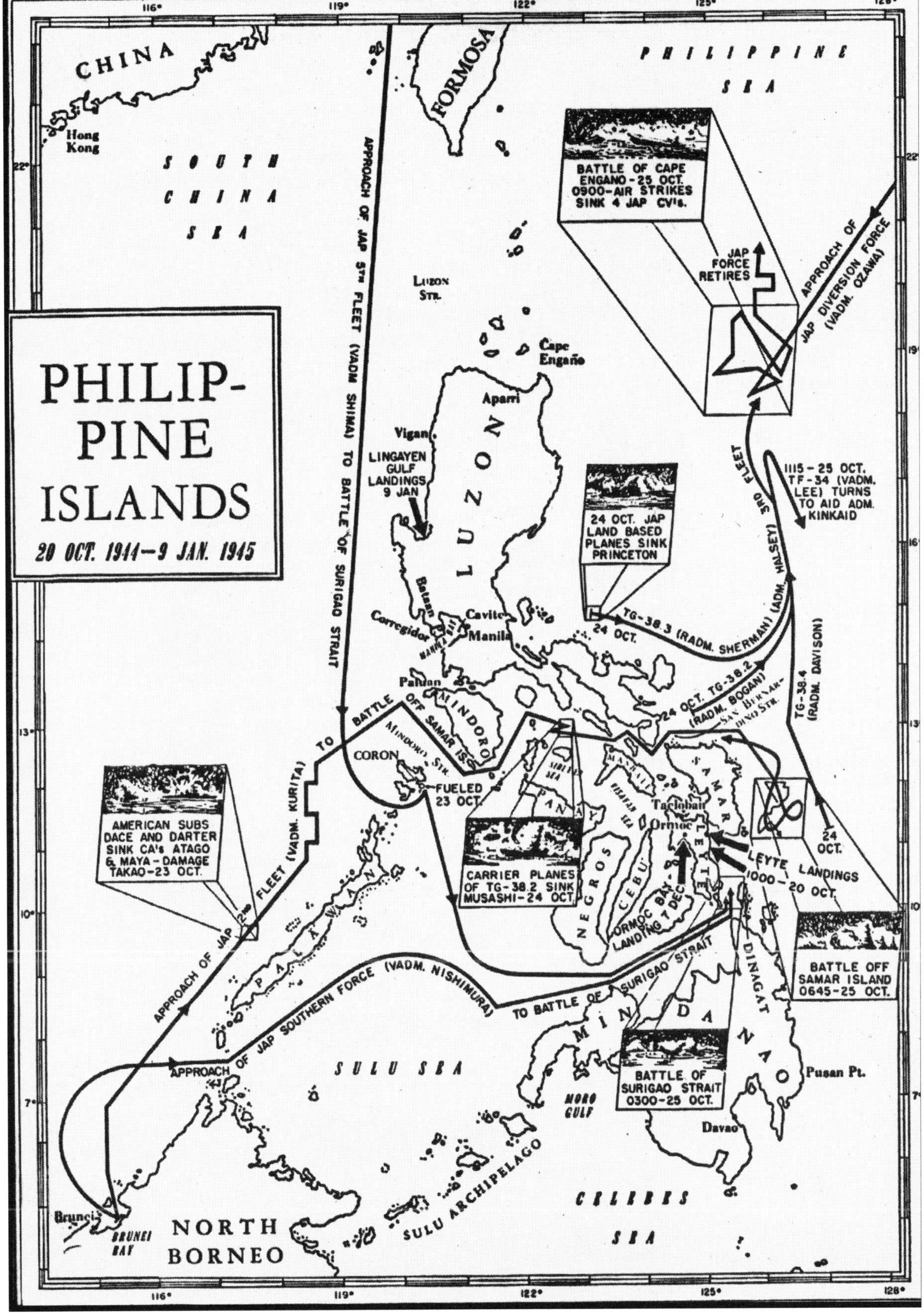

Map from *Destroyer Operations In World War II* - Courtesy of Naval Institute Press

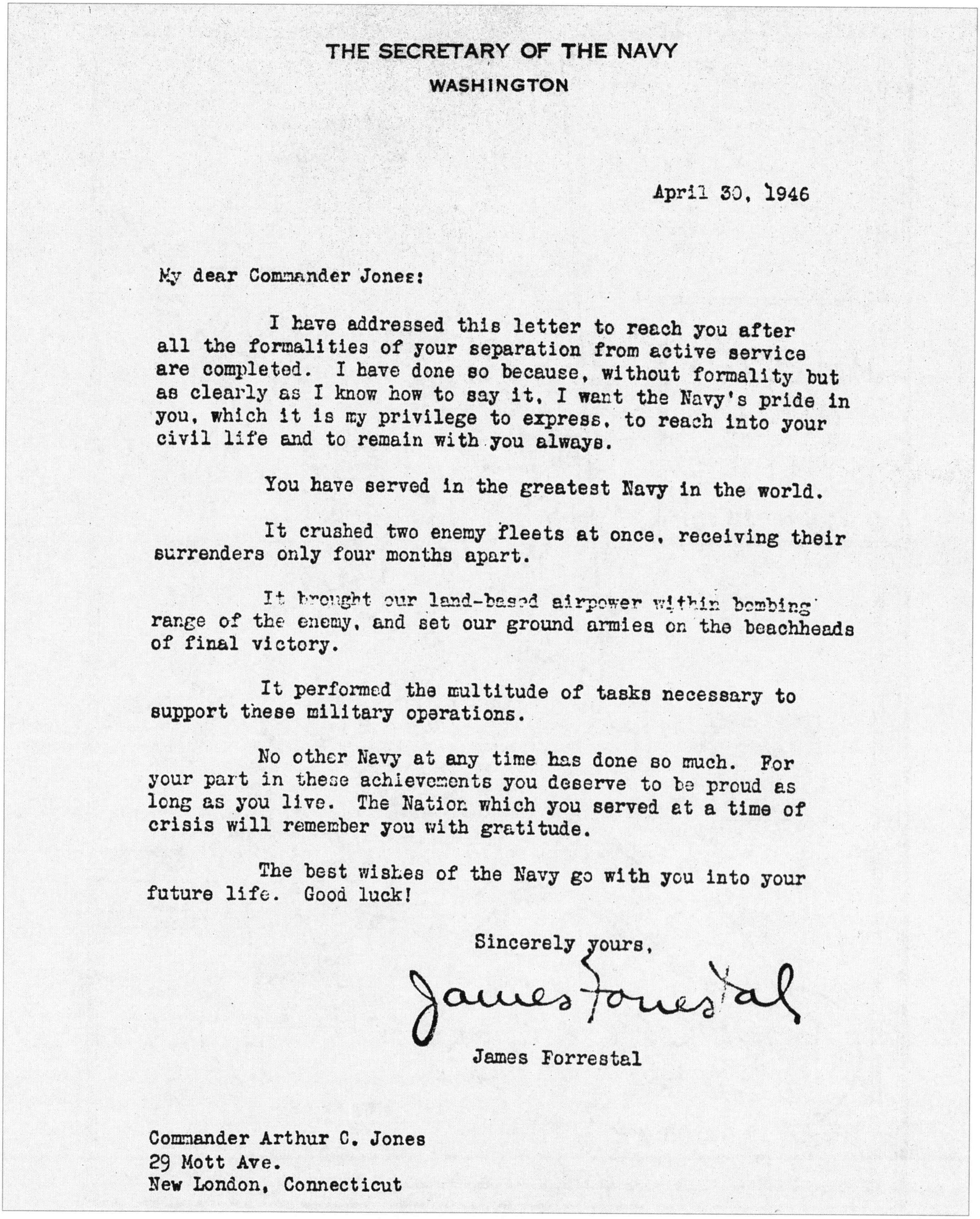

THE SECRETARY OF THE NAVY
WASHINGTON

April 30, 1946

My dear Commander Jones:

I have addressed this letter to reach you after all the formalities of your separation from active service are completed. I have done so because, without formality but as clearly as I know how to say it, I want the Navy's pride in you, which it is my privilege to express, to reach into your civil life and to remain with you always.

You have served in the greatest Navy in the world.

It crushed two enemy fleets at once, receiving their surrenders only four months apart.

It brought our land-based airpower within bombing range of the enemy, and set our ground armies on the beachheads of final victory.

It performed the multitude of tasks necessary to support these military operations.

No other Navy at any time has done so much. For your part in these achievements you deserve to be proud as long as you live. The Nation which you served at a time of crisis will remember you with gratitude.

The best wishes of the Navy go with you into your future life. Good luck!

Sincerely yours,

James Forrestal

James Forrestal

Commander Arthur C. Jones
29 Mott Ave.
New London, Connecticut

Letter from the Secretary of the Navy.

Lewis M. Andrews, Jr.

Chapter XIII - The Philippine Campaign

The bloody and ferocious campaigns across the vast Pacific; Truk, Guam, Saipan, Tinian, and others were stepping stones to redeem an obligation – the recapture and liberation of the Philippines. Next to Japan itself, this was our most important goal. As important as it was to retake that former colony, it was imperative to the Japanese that we fail in our endeavor. They suffered no illusions as to the consequences of defeat; their revered and fanatically loved home islands would be open to invasion.

PACIFIC ANTIAIRCRAFT WARFARE

In the *Battle of The Atlantic*, antiaircraft warfare was pretty much confined to the earlier Mediterranean convoys. Submarines always were the major threat in the entire North Atlantic. The German U-boats were the principal reason for building destroyer escorts in the first place. The situation in the Pacific was very different. Japanese submarines, of course, had to be guarded against and destroyed wherever possible. Their subs did achieve some notable successes. However, they never attained the threatening level in the Pacific as did the U-boats in the Atlantic. The air situation, on the other hand, was a different challenge. Even as their aircraft carriers and surface vessels were being annihilated, Japanese air attacks increased in intensity as our naval forces moved closer to their airfields. Their conventional bombers and torpedo planes were augmented by amazing new aerial missiles, the *kamikazes*. They were suicide planes, armed with 250 or 500 pound bombs, and flown right into our ships by incredibly dedicated pilots. The DEs and APDs, of course, were in the thick of it.

In addition to aircraft, the Japanese also deployed manned torpedoes, suicide speedboats with impact bombs, explosive laden swimmers and manned rocket or jet propelled aircraft called *Oka*. (Americans labeled the latter *Baka*, a Japanese word meaning insane.) They scored some successes, as with the "Midgets" in chapter *Pacific Antisubmarine Warfare*, but none compared to the destruction wrought by *kamikazes*.

THE KAMIKAZES

From the Philippines to Iwo Jima to Okinawa A Carnage Worse than Pearl Harbor

Kamikaze is a Japanese word meaning Divine Wind. In 1274 and 1281, the Kublai Khan, who presided over an Empire stretching from the Pacific coast of China west to the European Balkans, sent his invasion fleets against the Japanese Islands. Both times, they were struck by disastrous typhoons that wrought the total destruction of the Khan's ships and men before they could reach their destination. The grateful Japanese referred to those storms as *kamikazes*. Hence, that was the name they gave to the suicide corps. A volunteer went through an elaborate Shinto ritual, *kare no mizu Sakazuki*, before becoming a living god on his mission to join all the other heroes in Japanese history. The pilot left with enough fuel for a one way trip, anticipating a far more glorious destination than he had ever known.

Vice Admiral Takijoro Onishi was the organizer of the *kamikaze* corps when he was in command of naval forces in the Philippines at the time of General MacArthur's return. His initial successes in scoring hits on carriers, battleships, cruisers, transports, destroyers, and destroyer escorts so impressed the High Command that he was given the job to create a major suicide corps. The deeper our fleet penetrated the Philippines, the more intensive were enemy attacks, hitting more ships at Iwo Jima and building to a crescendo at Okinawa. Pilots from all services with all manner of planes, anything that could fly and be fitted with an explosive, joined the fray and became *kamikazes*.

MOROTAI to LEYTE GULF

Seventh Fleet (TF-77) Leads the Way Back to the Philippines

GOLDSBOROUGH

In March 1944, *Goldsborough (APD-32)* emerged from the Charleston Navy Yard as a conversion from a "four-piper" to an APD or fast transport. Since both this destroyer class and destroyer escorts were converted to APDs and operated side by side, both are covered in the Pacific portion of this book.

She sailed on 29 May to a rendezvous with a transport force proceeding via Ulithi to arrive off the invasion beaches of Saipan on 15 June. As she assisted in repelling a dive bomb raid, an aerial bomb exploded 400 yards to starboard, close but not close enough to do damage. The following day, she landed the Second Company, First Battalion of the Second Marine Division just south of Charon Kanoa. During the next five weeks, she escorted supply and troop convoys between the Marshalls and Saipan, taking time out for direct gunfire support of troops on Saipan on the nights of 29 June and 7 July. With Lieutenant Commander W.J. Meehan in command, she departed from Saipan on 28 July to train Underwater Demolition Team 4 (UDT 4).

In accordance with the Commander, Southwest Pacific (General Douglas MacArthur) Operation Plan, Task Group 77.2 was ordered to destroy enemy personnel, installations and facilities along the east coast of Leyte. Targets were the landing beaches and the entrance islands to Leyte Gulf by gunfire, aerial bombardment, mine sweeping and underwater demolition. The purpose was to assist in the seizure and occupation of the Leyte Area by the Central Philippine Attack Force. Underwater Demolition Team 4, under the immediate command of Lieutenant Carterry, was embarked in *Goldsborough*.

0900 On 18 October. The Task Group commenced a slow and cautious entry into Leyte Gulf because of the danger of enemy mines. Minesweepers had exploded many mines the previous day, but the sweepers were still clearing more of them ahead of the group. Single attacks were made on some of the minesweepers by Japanese aircraft.

1400. *Goldsborough* took station and made preparations to launch the UDT. All hands went to GQ, and UDT 4 disembarked in the LCP(R)s (landing boats). The team stood in toward the beaches near Dulag along with teams from other APDs, but as yet no enemy shore fire was encountered. By 1515, however, the Japanese had opened up with machine gun, mortar and 75mm fire. Moving in to a range of approximately 1500 yards from the shore, *Goldsborough* opened fire on the enemy beach emplacements.

Due to the range and foliage on the beach, no accurate estimate could be made of the enemy positions. Nonetheless, all destroyers and high speed transports lying to off the beach poured a withering fire into concealed enemy positions, covering underwater demolition teams headed for the shore. Several of the boats from other ships were taken under heavy fire, and a boat from Team 8 came alongside to transfer a wounded man. *Goldsborough's* number two boat was struck by mortar fire and sank. All the men were picked up, but several were suffering from serious injuries. The fact that the swimmers were away from the boat at the time of sinking probably precluded any loss of life.

A 75mm shell landed 200 yards short of this ship, just a few minutes after the hit on her number two boat. This was quickly followed by a second shell, long about 150 yards on the port beam. Minutes later, the forward or number one stack received a direct hit by a 75mm shell, inflicting two deaths, and another 16 wounded. Some members of the gun crews on the galley deckhouse were severely wounded by shrapnel, and one was killed. Another man, standing on the main deck near the stack, was also killed. Shrapnel was everywhere at once. Minor damage was caused to radio antennae and radar transmission lines. Shrapnel was thrust down the intake trunk of a forced draft blower, hitting the fan while operating and causing excessive vibration.

Maximum speed was reduced to 20 knots, but the operating efficiency of the ship was not affected. All men of the galley deckhouse gun crews who were not injured by shrapnel gallantly stood by their stations; firing was only interrupted for a short time. The boats returned to the ship, their operation having been satisfactorily completed.

Firing ceased and GQ was secured. A doctor, Lieutenant J.C. Kay, and one pharmacist mate from *Talbot (APD-7)* came aboard to assist with the wounded. As daylight faded, the Task Group retired in the gulf for the night; it had not been an easy day.

With the assigned duties of the APDs completed, they reported for screening duty as the battleships and cruisers of the Task Group carried out a relentless bombardment throughout the next night, 19 October. At sun down, enemy planes attacked the group but were driven off with a minimum of antiaircraft fire. Transports and landing craft of the attack force arrived on the morning of the 20th, and supporting troops launched the invasion.

The inner and outer casings of the number one stack had numerous small shrapnel holes. The damage to the stack and the radio antennae were remedied by a repair ship at Hollandia. However, this APD was never able to replace the lost landing boat.

At 1825 on 21 October, *Goldsborough* was detached from the Dulag invasion area and took her departure to embark troops at Noemfoor, Schouten Islands, Netherlands East Indies, landing them on the Leyte beaches on 18 November. She again arrived off Noemfoor on 19 December for transport of troops to Mios Woendi, Padiados Islands, thence via Morotai, escorting six merchant ships into Leyte Gulf on 6 January 1945.

Goldsborough saw little respite until the end of the war. In the dual role of escort and transport, she was involved in actions at Lingayan Gulf on Luzon, Iwo Jima, and Okinawa. The surrender of Japan saw *Goldsborough* en route to San Pedro, California.

ESCORT DIVISION 37

WILLMARTH

Willmarth (DE-638) sortied from Dutch New Guinea on 12 October 1944 with Task Unit 77.7.1 which included oilers *Ashtabula (AO-51)*, *Saranac (AO-74)*, *Chepachet (AO-78)*, *Salamonie (AO-26)*, ammunition carrier *Mazama (AE-9)*, and merchant ship *SS Pueblo*. Other escorts were *Witter (DE-636)*, *Bowers (DE-637)*, and *Whitehurst (DE-634)*.

Willmarth proceeded north with her convoy, while American troops splashed ashore on the beaches of Leyte, commencing the liberation of the Philippines. On the 23rd, three days after the main landing began, the DE anchored off Leyte while her oilers refueled ships in the attack force.

24 October. Underway off Homonhon Island early in the morning, she received a report of enemy aircraft orbiting over the northern transport area. As she steamed along the convoy's flank, she commenced making black smoke to lay a protective screen in anticipation of the enemy's arrival. While the radio crackled with reports of ships under attack, it was not until late afternoon when a "flash red" sent *Willmarth* to GQ.

Three Jills roared in low from the east in a surprise attack, picked up with binoculars at a range of only 2000 yards, height about 50 feet, speed 180 knots. Torpedoes were slung menacingly beneath their bellies. *Willmarth* opened fire with ten 20mm and one quadruple 1.1" guns on two planes just before they released their "fish." The commanding officer, Lieutenant Commander J.G. Thorburn Jr., noted in his action report that only 10 seconds of firing time elapsed before the planes passed out of range.

One torpedo holed *Ashtabula*, leaving her dead in the water. While the oiler's repair parties controlled the flooding and patched the hole, the convoy passed out of Leyte Gulf and reformed in the wake of the attack. Eventually, *Ashtabula* effected repairs and rejoined the formation late that night.

Willmarth and the convoy remained underway throughout the evening, maneuvering in Leyte Gulf until the first rays of sunlight, marking the dawn of 25 October, streaked the eastern skies. After going to GQ at 0458, the destroyer escort remained at battle stations throughout the day. Less than an hour after her crew first went to battle stations, two Jills attacked the convoy. *Willmarth* promptly opened up with her 3" and 1.1" batteries. As one Jill roared across the stern of the convoy, it was caught by gunfire from *Willmarth* and other ships of the convoy and crashed in flames far astern!

While maneuvering and making smoke, the DE sank a floating mine with gunfire. Soon thereafter, another Jill passed through the area and drew fire from *Willmarth*, but the plane escaped. Just before noon, the oilers anchored in the fueling area as the escorts provided a screen around the valuable auxiliaries.

Later that afternoon, *Willmarth* repulsed an attack made by two Jills coming out of the sun in a glide-bombing attack. The bogies were picked up on SA radar at a distance of 10 miles, altitude 100 feet, speed 180 knots. The angle of fire permitted the use of eight 20mm, the quad 1.1" and one 3" gun. This time, because of an early alert, the guns had four minutes of tracking time, making for better accuracy. The planes attempted to attack the convoy, flying in on the port quarter of *Willmarth* and directly into heavy antiaircraft fire from that ship. One turned sharply across her fantail, flying away from the convoy and was believed to have been damaged. The other turned down the DE's port side and across the rear of the convoy. *Willmarth's* gunfire scored hits, splashing the plane into the water about five miles away!

The convoy departed from the fueling area at mid-afternoon. Frequent alerts and enemy planes enlivened the evening hours as the group maneuvered throughout the night in retirement formation. The *Willmarth* log noted that the Japanese planes seemed loathe to attack ships in the fueling area during daylight, probably because of the concentration of antiaircraft fire that could be directed at an attacker.

Dawn the next day, 26 October, saw a repetition of the same routine that had kept the destroyer escort active since her arrival in Leyte Gulf three days earlier. After maneuvering on screening duties through the night, the warship spotted a lone Val dive bomber making an attack. *Willmarth* opened fire from 6,000 yards but failed to score any hits. Within minutes, she and her sister escorts were laying smoke to cover the convoy, providing antisubmarine screening protection while the oilers conducted fueling operations.

On the following day, *Willmarth* departed from Leyte and headed for the Palaus to take part in the relentless drive to recapture the Philippines.

MANNING

Manning (DE-199), under the command of Lieutenant Commander John I. Mingay, spent the months of January, February and March 1944 operating with the Third Fleet in the South Pacific, escorting among Noumea, Guadalcanal, New Caledonia, Espiritu Santo and Pago Pago.

The first major operation for *Escort Division 37*, with Commander M.W. Firth as commodore, was the Tanah Merah Bay – Hollandia – Aitape invasion. Night air attacks were encountered, and the crew received its baptism of fire. The next operation was at Wakde Island where the DE screened attack transports while troops were disembarked on the morning of 17 May.

In early October 1944, *CortDiv 37* was transferred to the Seventh Fleet at Manus, where the invasion ships for the Philippines were assembling (also in New Guinea). She then joined a service group, consisting of oilers and ammunition ships, to support and supply the major combatant units entering Leyte Gulf.

20 October. The Service Group steamed from Kossols Roads and arrived outside Leyte Gulf on the 23rd after dusk, anchoring off Homonhon Island. The following morning, the Group steamed into the gulf to service the battleships and cruisers, but the course was reversed when air action became imminent. All escorts made smoke to screen their charges. Several large fleet units were serviced during the afternoon and, just before dark, the group headed for the anchorage off southern Samar.

As the oilers and ammunition ships were about to anchor, the Task Group was attacked by at least three enemy torpedo planes which came in over the hills and directly into the center of the formation. One aircraft came out of the center of the convoy, approached *Manning's* port bow, and was immediately taken under fire by the DE's forward 20mm guns. The plane then veered sharply across her bow and passed down the starboard side, absorbing fire from all the 20mm guns which could bear plus the 1.1" quad mount. Countless hits were scored, and the plane was burning in both the engine and fuselage. Less than a minute later, it crashed in a flaming explosion! After the attack, all ships of the group remained underway in the gulf during the night, and continued to do so each night of operation in the gulf.

25-27 October. The oilers and ammunition ships serviced the heavy ships with fuel and ammunition while the destroyer escorts circled the San Pedro Bay anchorage, acting as an antiaircraft screen. Sporadic raids were frequent. The most active times of the day were at dawn and dusk. *Manning* did not score any more kills during this period but she fired each morning and evening to drive off attackers who turned away when taken under heavy fire. On the late afternoon of 27 October, the oilers left the gulf. *Manning* and *Lovelace (DE-198)* remained as escorts for the ammunition ships, *Mazama (AE-9)* and *SS Durham Victory*, still heavily laden with ammunition.

From 27 October to 1 November, firing at closely approaching Japanese aircraft had become routine, and long range planes were fired upon for director tracking practice. The ammunition ships serviced the battleships which were low on ammunition after the Battle of Surigao Strait, an event which *Manning* witnessed while steaming in the gulf.

1 November. After completion of servicing, the ammunition detachment left the gulf and proceeded to Kossols Passage. There the escorts were ordered to Hollandia for a short period of tender availability and repairs. The availability was abruptly shortened on the afternoon of 14 November when *Manning* was ordered to clear the side of destroyer tender *Dobbin (AD-3)* and to screen the sortie of a reinforcement echelon of LSTs, bound for Leyte via Biak.

Rendezvous was made with two separate groups of LSTs at Biak, a total echelon of seventy-three ships with a screen of four APDs, two DEs, two frigates and a PC, formed up for the transit to Leyte.

The journey was slow, monotonous, and uneventful until 23 November, the night before entering the gulf. During the day, snoopers followed the convoy but were always driven off by friendly aircraft before they could close to visual range. The protecting air support departed at sunset, and there was no activity until the end of twilight.

As *Manning* was about to secure from another routine dusk GQ and ease into Leyte under the cover of darkness, radar contact was made on several unidentified planes closing low and fast from eight miles on the port quarter of the convoy. At this time, *Manning* was screening across the stern of the formation, and it was immediately apparent that the planes could not possibly be friendly. Two minutes later, about eight planes were sighted in the dusk, very low and heading directly toward the center of the Task Group. Firing commenced immediately, but no hits were recorded. The planes split up and were temporarily lost in the glare of gun flashes. During the next few minutes, at least six Jills and three twin engine bombers made passes at the screen and the main formation. *Manning* employed evasive maneuvers at flank speed and full rudder to elude simultaneous passes by two torpedo planes, one on each bow. Because of reduced visibility, it was impossible to tell if torpedoes were launched.

The evening's activities concluded at 1835 when a single torpedo plane closed from the starboard quarter and turned sharply toward *Manning* from 4000 yards on a beam run. All guns that could bear fired an intensive barrage, and the plane was lost to sight at 3000 yards. Radar information later indicated that the plane had turned sharply at 2500 yards and escaped by flying low over the water. It was assumed that the planes had come from Mindanao because the convoy was about 75 miles from that coast at the time of the attack.

During the melee, the frigate *El Paso (PF-41)* splashed one plane with 40mm gun fire, and it exploded with its bombs! Although torpedo wakes were observed by other vessels, and bomb explosions were heard, the formation sustained no damage.

On the afternoon of the next day, while preparing to return to Hollandia, *Manning* was fueling during an alert. A Judy came in astern from over the hills surrounding San Pedro Bay, dropped a light bomb about 300 yards directly astern, and then passed overhead. As fuel hoses and lines were cast off, all 20mm guns opened fire and sprayed the plane until it smoked. It was still smoking when lost to view but appeared to be under control.

The ship was ready to return to Hollandia that evening, but a plane attempted to sneak into the center of the LSTs as they formed up for the return trip. Radar information was relayed by *Manning* to the LST guide and, as the plane came in over the center of the formation, an LST gunner brought it down with a six round burst of 40mm fire!

This last flurry of action temporarily brought to a close *Manning's* first operations in the Philippines. The ship arrived at Humboldt Bay on 30 November and, on 1 December, Commander William H. Putnam relieved Commander Firth as *ComCortDiv 37* aboard *Thomason (DE-203)*, then shifted his pennant to *Manning*. More action remained in store for *Manning*. See narrative in this chapter *Return to Luzon*.

JAMES E. CRAIG

On 31 March 1944, *James E. Craig (DE-201)* departed from Espiritu Santo in company with Escort Division 37, including *Lovelace (DE-108)*, *Manning (DE-199)*, *Neuendorf (DD-200)* and *Eichenberger (DD-202)*. Stopping at Tulagi in the Solomons from 2 to 4 April, the division sailed for New Guinea, where *Craig* was to see all the action she needed to see for a long time.

Craig, under the command of Lieutenant Commander Edward F. Andrews, steamed to Humboldt Bay. Arriving on the 17th, she immediately joined an attack convoy bound for Wakde-Sarmi, west of Hollandia. The DE bombarded enemy troop concentrations at Wakde-Sarmi on the 27th and returned to Cape Cretin.

Arriving at Humboldt Bay on 6 June, she prepared for the bitter conquest of Biak Island. With six other escorts, she accompanied the convoy and supported the landing operations on 12 June. While on ASW operations off Wakde, she conducted prolonged and successful bombardments of enemy supply depots at Samar on 11-12 July.

Back at Humboldt Bay on 14 November, she joined a large convoy of transports, amphibious craft, and escorts underway for the Philippine Islands to support the vital allied foothold on Leyte, The convoy of seventy-five ships and nine escorts steamed northwestward and, by dusk of the 23rd, approached Leyte Gulf.

Craig made radar contact with six low-flying unidentified planes approaching from the south at approximately 190 knots. Soon, her spotters observed several Jill torpedo planes seven miles out, closing at high speed. As the enemy planes broke into three groups in an attempt to "box the target," *Craig* turned left with full rudder to meet the attackers; and all guns which could bear commenced firing at the planes, still more than two miles out. Four of the attackers began a run and launched their torpedoes at a range of 1200 yards on her port side. As the ship turned, three torpedoes passed close aboard to port and almost parallel to her. Meanwhile, two planes commenced a run from the starboard side. Approaching almost directly from out of the sunset, a plane dropped a torpedo within 1000 yards which broached once before settling down on its run. As *Craig* turned hard to starboard, the torpedo crossed within five yards astern!

The convoy stood into San Pedro Bay, Leyte, the following morning and remained at battle stations a greater part of that day to repel enemy aircraft which attempted to bomb the convoy. *Lovelace* splashed a suicider! That night, the convoy and escorts reformed and departed for Humboldt Bay via the Palaus. The formation was heavily attacked all the way to its destination but fought its way through.

At the end of December, after a lengthy overhaul, Escort Division 37 departed from Humboldt Bay with a convoy of tankers and merchant ships bound for Leyte, arriving on 1 January 1945.

The following day, *Craig* stood out for Mindoro Island to join Task Group 77.2, ordered to support landing operations on Northern Luzon. Enemy reconnaissance planes maintained close surveillance. Late in the afternoon of 4 January, a *kamikaze* penetrated defenses and struck the carrier *Ommaney Bay (CVE-79)*, causing her to burst into flames. After the conflagration got out of hand. the escort carrier's commander ordered abandon ship. Three men from a sister DE, *Eichenberger (DE-202)*, who had volunteered to man a raft and assist with rescuing men in the water were killed in subsequent explosions. *Craig* assisted in rescue operations and, later that evening, proceeded with other escorts and tankers to Mindoro. See narrative *Return to Luzon* in this chapter.

An impending typhoon disrupted a convoy on 1 September 1945; high seas and 70-knot winds scattered the ships and separated tugs from their tows. As the storm abated on 2 September, *Craig* began search and rescue operations which continued to the 9th. Further typhoon warnings caused the ships to return to Subic Bay, Luzon, where the convoy anchored the following day. See chapter *Pacific Typhoons*.

James E. Craig operated at Subic Bay until 1 October 1945, when she steamed for the United States via Eniwetok and Pearl Harbor.

ORMOC BAY

APDs in a Kamikaze Frenzy

The capture of Leyte was only the beginning of the reconquest of the Philippines. Manila, the capital, is on Luzon, and it was expected that the Japanese would have the largest number of troops concentrated in the defense of Luzon, the nerve center of the archipelago. Only two weeks prior to the attack on Leyte, American strategists were still debating whether the Philippines should be by-passed in favor of an invasion of Formosa (Taiwan). General MacArthur, had strong feelings in favor of the Philippine campaign whereas Admiral Nimitz felt as strongly that those islands could be by-passed. Early in October, the Joint Chiefs gave their approval to the Philippine Campaign, and the invasion of Leyte was set in motion.

Before a Luzon invasion could begin, airfields closer to that island had to be seized in order to bomb Japanese airfields on Luzon and to supply close air support for ground troops. The pause, while debate was in process, gave the enemy time to run reinforcement convoys to Yamashita's command. U.S. submarines and destroyers worked around the clock to intercept Japanese transports, but many slipped through.

The Island of Mindoro, close to Luzon and lightly defended, seemed ideal for the purpose. However, Ormoc Bay, on the west side of Leyte, could be used by the Japanese to attack north-south convoys, and it had to be taken before Mindoro could be occupied. Hazardous destroyer raids were launched through Surigao Strait to interdict and destroy enemy shipping in Ormoc Bay, but Japanese air activity inflicted casualties and sent a destroyer to the bottom. The 77th Army division under General A.D. Bruce was designated for the invasion of Ormoc Bay. Rear Admiral A.D. Struble was to command the amphibious force, comprising eight APDs and 43 landing craft, screened by 12 destroyers.

Transport Division 103 came into being on 5 July 1944.

From March to June 1944, *Kephart (DE-207)* had made four trips to North Africa and the United Kingdom before her conversion to *APD-61*.

Liddle (DE-206) paralleled the *Kephart* experience with three trips to North Africa and the U.K. prior to modification as *APD-60*.

Cofer (DE-208) had made two transatlantic crossings, one to Gibraltar and one to Bizerte. She underwent conversion to *APD-62*.

Newman (DE-205) had made six transatlantic trips and was reclassified *APD-59* 10 days later than the others. Accordingly, she skipped the Ormoc invasion but operated at Mindoro several days later.

Lloyd (DE-200) flew the pennant of *ComTransDiv 103*. She had made one transatlantic crossing to Bizerte before conversion to *APD-63*. A previous commanding officer, Lieutenant Commander Edgar H. Forrest, spun a yarn relative to her conversion to an APD:

> "I wondered why there was a piano in the troop compartment. It seems that, while undergoing conversion, the ship was moored in Norfolk, across the pier from a carrier which was going into commission and suffering from the pangs of getting organized. One of *Lloyd's* chief petty officers was promoted to Warrant Officer and ordered to serve on the carrier. He is reputed to have told his fellow APD chiefs that the carrier was so fouled up that anyone could go aboard and steal the piano. No sooner said than done.
>
> A working party was organized and sent to the carrier's wardroom where the steward's mates were told that they had been sent to repair the piano. The Officer of The Deck of the carrier provided the manpower to move the piano and place it in a tarpaulin covered truck on the pier. Late that night, the piano found its way into the troop compartment of *Lloyd*.
>
> The next morning, *Lloyd* sailed from Hampton Roads. An ALL SHIPS message was received the following Saturday after the captain of the carrier had ascertained at his inspection that the piano was missing from the wardroom. The message requested the return of a piano that was removed without authority. Since the message was sent to all ships, no single ship, it remained unanswered."

This author would not have liked to trade places with the hapless OOD who unwittingly organized a work party at the behest of the "piano repairmen."

26 September 1944. *TransDiv 103* sailed from Norfolk, Virginia. The destination was Hollandia, Dutch New Guinea, stopping only at fueling stations, including the Galapagos Islands, Bora Bora and Espiritu Santo. *ComTransDiv 103*, Captain W.S. Parsons, flew his pennant on *Lloyd* for the entire time the division was in the Pacific.

Arriving off the beaches of Leyte with an LST supply convoy, *TransDiv 103* got its first look at the Imperial Japanese Air Force. Off Mindanao, about dusk, the convoy was attacked by six torpedo bombers without sustaining damage. One of the planes was shot down, and the other five fled. *TransDiv 103* APDs had each embarked between 140 and 160 Army troops and steamed on 6 December with Task Group 78.3 for a surprise amphibious assault on Ormoc Bay.

The landing forces consisted of LSTs and smaller craft in addition to the APDs. Destroyers made up the escort group. Commander TG 78.3 was in *Hughes (DD-410)*. *Kephart* transported 141 Army troops and three officers, a regimental combat team (RCT), to the amphibious area in a flanking movement. Other APDs in *TransDiv 103* were similarly disposed. *Cofer's* radioman second class, Leigh H. Welcome, kept a secret but highly informative diary. His 6 December entry:

> "The skipper, Lieutenant Commander Alvin P. Chester, just gave us a speech and said we were going to make a landing for sure. We can expect attacks from aircraft, destroyers and motor torpedo boats, not counting the numerous shore batteries. Something to look forward to!"

7 December. D-Day for the APDs' first amphibious landing, and the Japanese Air Force made it a day that would live long in the memories of their crews. The invasion fleet would be under continuous attack by the *kamikaze* corps for approximately seven hours, ending only when darkness fell. A tally of 82 enemy planes were shot down that day by the invasion fleet and the Army Air Force.

0542. The APDs commenced preparations for disembarking the troops as the transports entered the landing area and took up assigned positions. The shore bombardment by destroyers commenced at 0630, followed by rockets from LCIs, and continued until the first wave reached the beach. The movements on *Kephart* were typical of the other APDs. By 0643, she had disembarked all troops, and landing craft were moving to the line of departure. The APD was hove to.

0707. The troops stormed the beach that morning, three years to the time and date of the attack on Pearl Harbor. Resistance was negligible, but not for the navy. After the troops landed and the boats withdrew, Japanese suicide aircraft swarmed down on the destroyers and APDs.

The initial defense was less than auspicious. Aircraft were observed flying over the landing area at 0702. Without orders to the contrary, numerous ships opened intensive fire on the first aircraft to appear in spite of their friendly identification broadcast on TBS. Luckily, none were shot down. *Kephart* had fired about 30 rounds at the friendlies. At 0812, all her landing craft had returned to the ship and had been hoisted inboard.

On 6 December, *Lloyd* had taken aboard troops of the 307th Infantry of the 77th Division for transportation to Ormoc. The moon rose at 0030 on 7 December as she approached the landing beach. Everything was quiet except once, just before dawn, when a plane flew overhead and dropped flares. On reaching her assigned area, she loaded the troops in the boats and ordered them toward the beach which had been peppered by bombardment. Her boats were in the first wave to hit the beach, and they returned with a report of no opposition.

Radarman Second Class Robert D. Hemenway on *Lloyd* kept one of those "forbidden" and detailed diaries, to the everlasting gratitude of this author. He went on watch at 2000, was relieved at 2400 and was up again one hour later for battle stations and a long and stressful day.

> "Today is the third anniversary of Pearl Harbor. What a celebration we had here! Troops were sent ashore at 0745. We expected mines and Jap PT boats but didn't run into any. The troops were reported ashore without casualties, but Jap planes began to attack us about 0930.
>
> One suicider was shot down by us 10 minutes later! More Jap "Happy Divers" (suicide) are diving in on us. So far, 18 Japanese planes have been shot down by surrounding ships, all of them *kamikazes*. One Jap dived right in on us, and we kept shooting and shooting. Finally, we shot him up so bad he couldn't maneuver any more. He just soared over the 40mm gun crew's heads by a foot and splashed 20 feet off the bow! The whole ship was covered with gasoline, oil, parts of the plane and. . . the pilot's teeth! I picked up some pieces to send them home for souvenirs. Later on, some of the men converted the bric-a-brac into bracelets."

Lloyd was in the midst of diving planes. Lieutenant Commander William R. Taylor, commanding officer of *Lloyd*, recalls in his memoirs:

> "About noon, we started the return trip, and by this time the Japs were back at us again. We were on the starboard quarter of the convoy, which was the sunny side and the side that all the attacking planes came from. In the early afternoon, one made a run on our stern, but our 40mm guns chopped him to pieces! After the experience of the morning, we shot at anything within range, whether it was coming or going, and all the other ships in the convoy were doing the same. During the afternoon, we saw the same sight repeated with sickening frequency; a plane would make a run on a ship, circle and then crash into it, and those ships hit were all on our side of the convoy. We shot down three planes, possibly four; there were others who also claimed the last one."

Radarman Hemenway on *Lloyd* continued:

> "So far, the Japs managed to make good their suicide dives on four ships, including three destroyers. A Jap plane flew over an LST on the beach and dropped three bombs. They all missed so the plane just gained some altitude and then dove straight down into the LST. I guess those fellows never knew what hit them!
>
> Another plane was making a dive on *Lloyd* and somehow managed to get between an LST and us. The LST broke loose with its 40mm and was firing so low that they hit us on the signal bridge. Three of our signalmen, who ran from the starboard to the port side to gain protection from the plane, ran right into that 40mm fire. Handa, Miller and a Chief Signalman attached to *ComTransDiv 103's* staff were badly wounded. Several other men on the ship received minor shrapnel wounds. Doctor Wicks operated on Handa immediately. His guts were falling out of him because of a large piece of shrapnel that had ripped open his abdomen. He did not survive.
>
> When we started back, Admiral Strubble commended and congratulated the *Lloyd* on its outstanding shooting and on the number of planes shot down. Everyone thinks we will get a group citation for this action today. Boy, we were never so close to death in all of our lives. God blessed us today; everyone was praying hard enough. Every time we see a plane we dive for cover. To the end of our lives, this crew will never forget the Battle of Ormoc Bay."

Radarman Welcome on *Cofer* recorded:

> "We're about two hours from our landing point. So far, we had one air raid alert but the planes changed course before they got to us. Zero hour is at 0650. I've got my fingers crossed. One of our destroyers had contact with a sub and is dropping depth charges now. The Japs are starting to fire at us from the beach. We are firing now. Our troops are going in the second wave. So far, very little enemy resistance on the beach. This operation, if it goes as planned, will be the end for the Japs on Leyte. There's some barges coming down the Bay. They are believed to be Japs. Our landing craft returned without any casualties. Jap convoy sighted. Destroyers, combined with aircraft, are out to take proper action, and a sub attack sinks two ships. We are going after the sub with another of our class. Lost contact with the sub."

During the afternoon, until 1630, the convoy was attacked repeatedly by enemy aircraft flying from aft forward on the starboard side, range about 4200 yards. They were fired upon by *Kephart's* 5" gun and by numbers one and three-40mm guns. A single enemy aircraft came within range of her guns. Number four 40mm opened fire, followed by number one 40mm and the main battery, and finally numbers four and six 20mm guns. Bursts from the 40mm were definitely on target. The second round from the main battery burst directly on the plane, scoring a sure kill. This was the last time an enemy aircraft came within gun range of this APD.

By 1700, all enemy attacks had ceased and there was no further action during *Kephart's* return trip. During landing operations on 7 December, *Kephart's* guns splashed two Japanese planes. The next morning, *Kephart*, in company with Task Unit 78.3, returned to Leyte.

The same, however, could not be said for *Liddle* and *Cofer*.

1400. *Liddle* had assumed her assigned station in convoy and proceeded via Surigao Strait and Canigo Channel to Ormoc Bay, arriving at the transport area without special incident en route. She disembarked her invasion force and made a successful landing, suffering no casualties or material damage except four bent propellers on the LCVPs (small amphibious vessels).

While the *Liddle* boats were en route to the beach, three planes flew over the transport area, identified by Lieutenant (jg) G.J. Leshok, recognition officer, as P-40's. One was fired upon by vessels assembled in the transport area. *Liddle* did not fire because of its belief that the plane was friendly. Undoubtedly, this attack on U.S. planes was the same as reported above by *Kephart*.

0806 on 7 December. Having picked up landing boats, *Liddle* and *Cofer* proceeded to their assigned stations, screening the retraction of other units in the task group. Twenty unidentified planes were reported by SL radar. The APDs received a report on TBS of a Japanese convoy of fourteen ships, 43 miles to the west. Shortly thereafter, word was received from SOPA (Senior Officer Present Afloat) in Leyte Gulf that he would take care of the enemy convoy.

0957. Four Japanese twin-engine bombers, identified as Bettys, were reported at 15,000 feet altitude, west of the strait between Ponson Island and the peninsula on the west side of Ormoc Bay. Shortly thereafter, the screening vessels witnessed four P-38 fighters attacking Japanese planes and four of the latter on fire and falling. Two damaged planes were observed to crash dive two screening ships in the strait, identified as *Ward (APD-16)* and *Mahan (DD-364)*. Destroyer *Mahan* was hit by three *kamikazes*. She could not be saved and was sunk by another destroyer after rescuing survivors.

1010. A message was received on TBS that *Ward* was burning out of control and being abandoned. Minesweepers *Saunter (AM-295)* and *Scout (AM-296)* were seen to head to and stand by *Ward*, along with *O'Brien (DD-725)* and *Crosby (APD-17)*.

Ward and *Crosby* were among the APDs that were originally flush deck "four piper" destroyers. As a destroyer, this was the same *Ward* that sank a midget submarine outside of Pearl Harbor on 7 December 1941, one hour before the Zeros came screaming in to blast the U.S. Fleet. Now, this vessel lay stricken with raging and uncontrolled fires. She had downed a plane before being hit and splashed two others after the crash. Paradoxically, the destroyer *O'Brien*, who went to her aid, was commanded by Commander Outerbridge, the same officer who commanded the *Ward* at Pearl Harbor, and was now trying to help control her fires. It was hopeless, and *O'Brien* was obliged to carry out a traumatic order to sink *Ward* by gunfire after abandonment.

1113. *Liddle* commenced maneuvering at 20 knots on erratic courses to avoid an attack by enemy fighter planes, identified as Zekes, as P-38s were pouncing on them. One Zeke, recorded by assistant gunnery officer Lieutenant Seabrook, went into a tight spin and commenced a suicide dive at *Hughes*. *Hughes* opened fire, and the plane crashed approximately 50 yards on her port bow.

Almost simultaneously, a second Zeke was observed diving on *Cofer*, which opened fire along with *Liddle*. Several hits from *Liddle's* number three 40mm gun were observed by the *Liddle* assistant gunnery officer. The plane exploded in the air approximately 500 yards astern of *Cofer*, probably destroyed by fire from both APDs.

A third Zeke came in on the port beam of *Liddle* in a low, fast attack. The APD opened fire with forward guns and port side batteries. The plane exploded 30 feet from the port side of the ship, and the port and weather decks were showered with fragments of plane and shrapnel, causing several injuries!

Still another *kamikaze* peeled off and headed for the embattled *Liddle* which commenced firing dead ahead with all forward batteries. In a matter of seconds, the Zeke crashed into the flying bridge and exploded, demolishing the bridge, CIC, radio room and the captain's sea cabin!

It was a carnage of senior officers and ratings. Dead or missing were the commanding officer, Lieutenant Commander L.C. Brogger; executive officer, Lieutenant Commander S. Cunningham; gunnery officer, Lieutenant T.E. McAlpine; medical officer, Lieutenant (jg) J.W. Greenbaum; communications officer, Lieutenant (jg) J.A. Murphy; assistant engineering officer, Lieutenant (jg) C.A. Bassett and eleven petty officers.

Two seriously wounded men on the bridge survived. Remarkably, the sound hut was intact, and both soundmen were uninjured. All personnel in the CIC, on the signal bridge and in the radio room were killed with two exceptions: Lieutenant (jg) G.J. Leshok, recognition officer; and Ensign B.H. Behrens, boat officer. Two men in the sea cabin survived.

During this action, *Cofer* had been close by, firing on *kamikazes* as fast as guns could be reloaded. She scored a hit on the plane that crashed *Liddle*, but the smoking aircraft kept going to its target. Captain Chester noted in his book, *A Sailor's Odyssey*, that throughout the action, he was concerned with the number of personnel on the bridge of his ship because that area was the primary *kamikaze* goal. Accordingly, he stripped his bridge structure of all but the most essential personnel and dispersed them so that they could quickly take control of the ship at Sky II or secondary aft. Chester, now a retired shipping magnate as well as a retired navy Captain, also noted that his anxiety for a sister ship was well founded.

Following the crash, the chief engineer of *Liddle* was in the troop quarters just aft of repair number 1 locker, his battle station. He was returning from the fantail where he had gone to inspect possible damage from the explosion of the earlier plane close aboard on the port side. The chief engineer supplied most of the information on *Liddle* until that ship returned to Leyte. His action report on the crash in the bridge structure:

> "I was not immediately impressed by the severity of the damage although realizing we had been hit. I saw smoke and soot forward in the direction of the wardroom passage where I found several wounded and one dying man. Believing we were hit forward, I started below to look for fire and was told all was well below forward. Rushing to the flying bridge, I discovered the extent of the casualty and that the ship was not under control."

Lieutenant (jg) F.H. Stunt had organized control in after steering, with Ensign B.H. Behrens aiding in conning the ship by hand signals from the top of the tripod mast. This was discontinued after emergency sound powered phones had been rigged from the signal bridge to after steering and the engine room. The chief engineer took the conn and maneuvered to keep clear of other ships. Lieutenant Seabrook ordered boats lowered to avoid damage from fire and received permission from the conning officer to try to obtain medical assistance from the flagship. The 24" searchlight on the starboard side was operable and manned by Chief Quartermaster Bailey who signaled *Cofer* for aid.

In his book, Al Chester, *Cofer's* skipper, recorded the harrowing chase of the *Liddle* while it was moving erratically and not under control. Once it was steadied, *Cofer* lowered a boat with Lieutenant Cleland, the doctor, two pharmacist mates and a signalman to assist the stricken vessel.

Liddle's voice radio had been wiped out, but blinker light communications were established with *Cofer*, which in turn relayed damage and casualty reports to the flagship. In response to a call, destroyer *Edwards (DD-619)* came alongside to transfer wounded.

1412. Air attack! No transfer took place because *Edwards* had to cast off and make full speed with radical maneuvers to avoid this new air attack and to catch up with the convoy. *Cofer* and *Liddle* witnessed two planes diving on *Edwards* and saw both destroyed in the air by the destroyer's gunfire. They also saw P-38s shoot down two planes, one of which managed to crash on the bridge of the destroyer *Lamson (DD-367)*, setting her afire. *Liddle* assumed a new position in the convoy center rear, heading south at a speed of 10 knots.

1530. Air attack! A plane was shot down by an unknown surface vessel's gunfire.

1550. Air attack! Another plane was shot down by surface vessel gunfire.

1625. Air attack! The APDs witnessed two planes diving, one of which dropped bombs on the forecastle of *LST-737* on *Liddle's* starboard quarter. This plane was destroyed in the air by gunfire from *Liddle's* number three-40mm gun but it just kept going to its target. Another plane dived on *Cofer* and was destroyed by her gunfire!

1705. Air attack! *Liddle* sighted a plane diving on *LST-734*. She took it under fire and shot it down with her number three-40mm gun. The plane exploded in the water 20 feet from the bow of *LST-737*!

As the furious battle died away with the night, Radarman Welcome jotted an entry in his diary:

> "I took a message to Captain Chester just a little while ago, and he remarked wearily but thoughtfully — 'You know, this was the most vicious battle that has ever been fought in the Southwest Pacific. It will go down in history as The Battle of Ormoc Bay.'
>
> This is the first time that they have used suicide planes on a large scale. Well, I guess this finishes up the day as we just secured from GQ, a day that I will never forget and hope I never go through again. In all, today we were at our GQ stations for exactly 13 1/2 hours, except for about 15 minutes we managed to get off for noon chow. By the way, the troops that we landed are really cleaning up the nips."

0854 on 8 December. *Liddle* went alongside hospital ship *Mercy (AH-8)*, in San Pedro Bay, Leyte, and transferred casualties. Her damage was too severe to attempt repairs locally, and she was directed to return to San Francisco for repairs. While she was being refitted, a sign on her quarterdeck read:

> "This ship lost 38 officers and men. She is anxious to get back into action."

On 22 February 1945, *Liddle* rejoined her division in liberating the Philippines and, later on, transported Australian troops to landings at Brunei and Balikpapan, Borneo.

The next few days in Ormoc Bay brought little respite as Radarman Welcome wrote:

> "10 December. On leaving Ormoc Bay, Our DDs caught a Japanese tanker trying to get away and set it afire. We are heading back to Leyte Gulf (home sweet home to us out here). I witnessed a dog-fight this afternoon, and before they went out of sight, the P38s had three of the Jap planes smoking. It was a pleasant sight.
>
> Well, we are going on another operation very soon. I hope the luck holds out. 'Tokyo Rose' said the Japanese are going to trade plane for ship, meaning their tactics from now on are going to be suicide dives; nothing to look forward to. Seven Jap planes attacked a convoy on its way in, losing a plane and damaging one ship.
>
> 11 December. We picked up more troops today and also refueled.
>
> 12 Decenber. A destroyer squadron was attacked just outside the Bay. We are getting underway in approximately two hours, destination Mindoro. The convoy is much bigger than the one we had before, 35,000 troops compared to 15,000 troops.
>
> 13 December. We are under attack. One of our cruisers was just hit by a *kamikaze*. The fighters took care of the enemy tonight, shooting down seven; the one that hit the cruiser makes eight."

Cofer continued in her role in the return to the Philippines, landing reinforcements at Lingayan Gulf in January 1945, then a series of landings on Luzon and assaults on Palawan in February. In March, it was Zamboanga and then Cebu under heavy mortar fire from the beach. In succeeding months, she was flagship for minesweepers clearing the waters off Tarakan, Borneo, prior to invasion, destroying shore batteries and rescuing minesweeper survivors.

On 17 December, *Lloyd* took part in the daring strike at Mindoro, then debarked troops for the assault on Lingayen Gulf. See the next narrative in this chapter, *Return to Luzon*.

Kephart's war also continued unabated. Returning to Leyte on 8 December, she embarked soldiers of the 19th Infantry, sailed for Mindoro and landed assault troops under heavy enemy air attack.

Carrying 158 men of an RCT, *Kephart* steamed to Lingayan Gulf and landed reinforcements despite aircraft attacks and emerged unscathed. In May, she embarked Australian troops for an amphibious assault at Brunei Bay, North Borneo. She then carried the "Aussies" for the final major amphibious operation of the war at Balikpapan.

For further detail on the East Indies operations, see the final narrative in this chapter, *Mopping Up*.

Lewis M. Andrews, Jr.

RETURN TO LUZON

Violent Resistance at the Back Door to Manila

The Japanese expected a major thrust into Manila Bay to effect landings on Eastern Luzon and were surprised at the enormity of the attack at Lingayan Bay on the west coast. Vice Admiral Shigeru Fukudome's title of Commander Imperial Second Air Fleet was somewhat misleading; Commander of the "suiciders" was more relevant. The Japanese navy was history, but the enemy was increasingly unleashing hordes of *kamikaze* pilots to wreak havoc on allied vessels in this battle and the ones that lay ahead, the Philippines to Okinawa.

The American force at Lingayan Gulf included 200,000 Sixth Army troops and over 800 ships. Heavy capital ships under Rear Admiral Oldendorf supplied support fire, and carriers under Rear Admiral Durgin supplied air power. Admiral Kinkaid was in overall command. Two main task forces of the Seventh Fleet converged on Lingayan Gulf, TG 77 from Leyte and TG 79 (San Fabian) from Manus on 28 December. Destroyer escorts were attached to both forces.

A little over a month prior to the sortie of TG 79, and while it was still being assembled in Manus, a catastrophic event fixed the minds of all who beheld it. It is described in a personal memoir by Raymond Doolan, Signalman Third Class on *Charles J. Kimmel (DE-584)*:

"Looking back over 50 years, I remember an unhappy wartime experience. We were anchored in Manus, Admiralty Islands, a forward supply base. There were many amphibian and cargo ships in the anchorage waiting to provision for an invasion of New Guinea and the Philippines. My ship was scheduled for ammunition replenishment in the early hours of 10 November, 1944. The day before, our captain, Lieutenant Commander Frederick G. Storey, ordered me to signal our loading confirmation to ammunition supply ship *Mount Hood (AE-11)*, that we would come alongside at 0900 hours the next morning to load ammo. I had the 0400-0800 watch on 10 November and was on the bridge, watching for visual light messages. About 0500, I noticed my ship's call sign letters were flashing and I manned my signal light to intercept traffic from *Mount Hood*. The message was personal, merely a fellow signalman on early watch like myself who wanted to 'shoot the breeze'. So I settled down to exchange flashing light messages to help pass the time in the quiet hours before sun up.

We both had graduated from the same Naval Signal and Radio School at the University of Chicago. He was subsequently posted to the ammunition ship while I was transferred to a destroyer escort. He talked about his growing up years, high school, family and a special girl friend. After his 17th birthday, he enlisted in the navy. He loved football and the outdoor life in the northern lakes of New York State. We exchanged growing up memories and futures after the war. He wanted to be an engineer, while I talked about finishing high school and going to college for legal training.

As we continued our signal light conversation, thoughts of oncoming Christmas, the end of the war, and the loneliness of being away from family helped both of us to pass away the early morning watch. At dawn, we exchanged final messages and he signed off with a "God Bless." I raised my binoculars to look at him. He was tall, blonde, with his white hat jauntily cocked on the back of his head. He raised his hand and waved goodbye.

After breakfast, I returned to the signal bridge as the crew prepared to go alongside *Mount Hood*. As the red 'Baker' danger signal flag for handling ammo was raised to the yardarm, I expected that I would now meet with my newly found friend.

Suddenly, I felt a shock impact, throwing me to the deck, and then I heard a tremendous explosion. Large pieces of steel plate and all kinds of debris were flying through the air and falling all around my ship. Unexploded bomb casings crashed into other ships nearby. I hung onto the starboard rail, looking for the source as GQ was sounded. I thought we were under air attack. Amid the shock and confusion, I saw a huge black cloud arising from the anchorage, 2000 yards away, where *Mount Hood* had been positioned. She was totally gone! She had blown up and plunged under the sea with hundreds of her officers and crew. Then I felt what I thought were raindrops but were only oil droplets from the doomed ship. I thought about my friend, the young signalman who just an hour before talked to me about his life and future.

Our ship's whaleboat, which was underway to another command ship, was passing *Mount Hood* at about 1000 feet from the explosion center. The crew was blown overboard but survived due to their position under the arc of the explosion. Other ships in the anchorage suffered, many killed and injured, and the water was filled with remnants of crewmen and debris. Had this explosion taken place 15 minutes later, my ship would also have been lost as we prepared to come alongside *Mount Hood.*

We'll never know why *Mount Hood* exploded. An onboard accident? A suicide swimmer? A torpedo from an enemy submarine? Afterward, I sadly remembered I never asked my lost friend his name!"

In a discussion with Carl Jensen, an officer on *Lough (DE-586)*, about his adventure at Nasugbu beaches, narrated later in this chapter, he told this author that his DE had been the nearest one to *Mount Hood*.

"Although heavy missiles fell all around my ship, she was not hit. As soon as objects stopped falling, *Lough* manned her whaleboat and sent it into the smoke, the first boat on the scene. There was no sign of *Mount Hood* nor any survivors. The complement of that ship was 22 officers and 296 men. Her surviving officer was Lieutenant Lester A. Wallace who had just reached the shore in a boat to pick up some charts. With him were 17 men with dental appointments on the base or assigned to pick up the ship's mail. While walking up the beach, they were knocked flat by the force of two quick explosions. Scrambling to their feet, they got back in the boat and headed toward their ship to find nothing but debris all about. They were the only survivors of *Mount Hood*."

Whereas the voyage from Manus to Lingayan was uneventful for TG 79.2 before reaching its destination, the opposite held true for TG 77.2 and TG 76.6, both of which had departed from Leyte and were headed to Lingayan from the south via Surigao Straits. Air alerts were called from the second day out, and snooping Japanese planes showed up on the third day. They approached the formation but kept just out of range. *HMAS Australia* reported splashing a plane close aboard, but the *kamikazes* did not succeed in crashing a ship until late on 4 January 1945 when one hit the carrier *Ommaney Bay (CVE-79).*

JOBB

Jobb (DE-707), under the command of Lieutenant Commander Herbert M. Jones, sailed for Humboldt Bay, New Guinea, via Bora Bora, arriving on 21 November 1944. The taking of Mindoro was a requisite before the extensive operations at Lingayen Gulf. *Jobb* was involved in convoying replenishment for the operation, screening a slow-tow convoy from Leyte to Mindoro on 12 December. The next morning, enemy snooper aircraft appeared, followed by bombers.

1458 on 13 December. A plane was sighted by a lookout on the same bearing as the sun, a common Japanese pilot maneuver to blind antiaircraft gunners. At the same time, *Radford (DD-446)* reported an enemy plane over the formation. She opened fire but ceased as the plane turned away. A minute later, a second plane was sighted, identified as a Betty or Sally.

Jobb opened fire on the aircraft. Almost immediately, 40mm and 20mm hits on its port wing were reported, and the port engine commenced smoking. Her gunfire had been highly effective. Some of the main battery magnetic impulse antiaircraft shells fired prematurely, but several were seen to burst near the target. Firing ceased two minutes after starting. The plane began to trail black smoke from the port engine and crashed about nine miles from the DE!

0805 on 14 December. Enemy planes approached. One minute later, a Betty passed along the port bow of the convoy and dived on *Halford (DD-480)* which opened fire and then, just as suddenly, ceased fire as the plane disappeared while smoking slightly from one engine.

1050 on 15 December. An approaching enemy plane was reported by radar. Again the alarm, the shrill of the bosun's pipe, General Quarters. The guns had barely swung onto the target when the command came to open fire. The plane dived on a destroyer and dropped a bomb close aboard her starboard quarter. The bomb missed, and so did the Sally type plane that dropped it, crashing into the water 1500 yards on *Jobb's* starboard quarter and 200 yards on the DD's port quarter!

0817 on 16 December. A flight of possible enemy planes was reported in the vicinity, sending the bleary-eyed sailors back to battle stations. A plane was picked up close aboard on *Jobb's* radar. However, she was unable to take it under fire due to its low approach and danger bearings on *Halford* and *Holt (DE-706).* The aircraft, recognized as a Zeke, crashed near the convoy, slightly damaging the fuel oil barge *YO-14*!

18 December. After seeing the tows safely in Mindoro, *Jobb* next sailed to Hollandia. There, she joined a convoy for newly assaulted Lingayen Gulf on 8 January 1945. After striking a reef, she retired to Leyte Gulf for repairs. *Jobb* returned to duty in February to escort troop and supply convoys to Palawan, Mindoro and Mindanao as the conquest of the Philippines proceeded apace.

Jobb departed from Morotai on 4 June to take part in the landing at Brunei Bay, Borneo. She patrolled as troops went ashore on 10 June and captured the strategic bay without opposition. Later in the month, she screened a resupply convoy from Morotai. She arrived at Leyte on 8 July for repairs before conducting antisubmarine patrol between the Philippines and Ulithi until the close of hostilities.

LINGAYEN GULF

At the end of December 1944, *Escort Division 37,* attached to the Service Force Commander, Seventh Fleet, convoyed to Leyte Gulf with oilers *Cowanesque (AO-79), Pecos (AO-6), Salamonie (AO-26)* and *Suamico (AO-49).*

2 January 1945. *Cowanesque* and *Pecos* were escorted to lower Leyte Gulf where they joined the Lingayen Gulf Minesweeper Group and then transited Surigao Straits. With *Manning (DE-199)* and *Neuendorff (DE-200)* as escorts, the oilers were to fuel the sweeper group en route to Mindoro, then act in support of the Lingayen forces by supplying fuel and ammunition. On leaving Surigao Straits, the Task Group (76.6) consisted of seventy-six ships, including minesweepers, ammunition ships and oilers. A circular antisubmarine/antiaircraft screen contained twenty ships comprising *CortDiv 37,* high speed transports (APDs in their DE role) and destroyer minesweepers.

On entering the Mindanao Sea, the formation did not have long to wait for action. At late twilight, *Manning* contacted enemy planes making their approach from dead ahead at 10 miles, and the Task Group was alerted. At medium altitude, the planes closed directly over *Manning's* station on the starboard bow of the formation. Firing commenced as soon as the planes came within visual range. The lead planes veered right, and the next two veered left, dropping bombs as they broke formation. One bomb landed between *Manning* and *Neuendorff,* about 300 yards distant, but caused no damage. Other bombs were dropped, but no hits were recorded, and the planes were lost in the darkness over land. Throughout the night, snoopers tagged along with the formation, tracking its course and speed.

0700 on 3 January. Japanese planes appeared in considerable strength and attacked the Task Group. All planes came in from astern of the formation, diving directly into the center of the group. The obvious targets were the oilers. The first plane in, a Val, dived close to *Cowanesque*, scoring a near miss, but was badly mauled and flew erratically out of the formation, low over the water, attempting to escape. As the plane approached the port quarter of *Manning*, heavy fire commenced from all guns and continued as the limping duck skidded past her stern. As it passed out of 40mm range to starboard, the plane was bracketed with 3" gunfire and splashed!

After the first plane's attack, others continued to dive out of the sun, and at least six single engine and two twin engine bombers were sighted. All planes dropped bombs but caused only minor damage. Intensive antiaircraft fire, combined with an alert Combat Air Patrol, stopped all but one plane, a *kamikaze*, from breaking through. That plane dived directly at *Cowanesque* but luckily caused only minor damage. During the remainder of the day, minesweepers were fueled and red alerts became the rule rather than the exception.

As the Task Group approached Mindoro at noon on 4 January, the oilers proceeded into Mangarin Bay, Mindoro, while *Manning* and *Neuendorff* patrolled. Prospects for a pleasant evening were abruptly interrupted about 1700 when enemy planes were reported in the area, and the escort crews once more staggered to GQ. Sleep was now a forbidden luxury. The DEs flanked *Cowanesque* as she stood out, but *Pecos* remained in the anchorage and continued dispensing fuel to the Army Air Force.

Shortly after clearing the anchorage, a Val *kamikaze* dived on the anchored ships. A P-61 Black Widow was on his tail all the way down, but the chase and ship antiaircraft fire were futile. The Val leveled off low, skip-bombed *Pecos*, and crashed into a Liberty ship loaded with aircraft bombs. The ship disintegrated. *Pecos* sustained a near miss from the plane and shrapnel from the explosion of the nearby Liberty ship. She proceeded out of the anchorage and joined *Cowanesque*. The night was spent underway outside of the anchorage, and a series of red alerts again reduced sleep to a minimum.

The next morning, the ships returned to Mangarin Bay and were joined by oilers *Salamonie*, *Suamico* and *Winooski (AO-39)*, escorted by other ships of *Escort Division 37*. During the next few days, the ships were underway near the anchorage, standing ready for air attacks. There were three fueling missions with Seventh Fleet Forces en route to Lingayen Gulf with the largest group of ships ever used in a Pacific operation. A steady stream of traffic passed Mindoro. On 8 January, tankers *Chepachet (AO-78)*, *Schuylkill (AO-76)* and *Tallulah (AO-50)* joined the Service Group. On the 9th, the *SS Durham Victory* and *SS Bluefield Victory* arrived, filled to capacity with ammunition. The Mindoro-Lingayen Service Group was now complete. TG 76.6 would be the principal filling station for combat and transport ships en route to the subjugation of Lingayen.

The Japanese had determined that Task Force 77 was headed for Lingayen, and they intensified their attacks accordingly. Late that afternoon, the Task Force came under moderately heavy *kamikaze* attacks about 100 miles off Corregidor. Sixteen *kamikazes* with four escorts broke through Combat Air Patrol (CAP) to dive at the ships.

The group consisted of fourteen CVE carriers under the command of Rear Admiral Felix B. Stump and several screening destroyer escorts. Its mission was to give close support to the infantry about to storm the beach and to provide air protection to Admiral Oldendorf's bombardment battleships, the force that had wiped out a Japanese battleship formation in Surigao Straits, capping it with a classical "T."

GOSS, STAFFORD and ULVERT M. MOORE

As units of Vice Admiral Oldendorf's Bombardment and Fire Support Group, *Goss (DE-444)*, *Stafford (DE-411)* and *Ulvert M. Moore (DE-142)* had sortied from Kossol Roads on 1 January 1945. Passage was made from the Pacific Ocean to the South China sea via the Surigao and Mindanao Straits. Antiaircraft training was conducted underway by firing on towed sleeves and by repelling simulated strafing attacks.

5 January. As Admiral Oldendorf's heavy ships steamed within 150 miles of Japanese airfields on Luzon, they were spotted by scout planes. At 0325, a plane flew over *Stafford* and passed up the port side of *Ulvert M. Moore*, distance 300 yards, then turned sharply toward the port bow of *Moore*. For no apparent reason, this plane, apparently out of control, crashed into the sea in close proximity to the two DEs and burned severely for three minutes before sinking. Two underwater explosions were felt shortly afterward. Another plane dived out of the dark side of the ships at morning twilight and made a strafing run on the tug *Quapaw (AT-12)*, about 1000 yards on the port quarter of *Stafford*. Although ship and plane exchanged fire, neither was hit.

0758. The combat air patrol intercepted 15 to 20 enemy planes 35 miles from the formation, shot down nine and turned back the others. At noon, another raid was intercepted and turned back about 45 miles from the ships. *Ulvert M. Moore* had just finished fueling from the tanker *Suamico* when bogies appeared . The DE went to General Quarters and remained there until 0205. She went to GQ three more times that day, twice for enemy aircraft and once for a submarine contact which turned out to be friendly.

During the early afternoon, *Ulvert M. Moore* had been assigned the task of mail delivery. While alongside the cruiser *Minneapolis (CA-36)* and delivering the mail, the DE's lookouts spotted a twin-engined Frances coming through the screen, entering the flight path of the carrier planes and heading for *Ommaney Bay (CVE-79)*. Before the carrier's crew could react, the plane nicked the superstructure and crashed her starboard side. Two bombs from the suicider ignited aviation gasoline fires and ruptured the carrier's fire main lines.

Retired Coast Guard Commander William Powers was chief gunner's mate on *Moore* and vividly remembers the tribulations in Lingayan Gulf:

> "Bogeys were reported in the area, and we went to GQ. My battle station was ordnance repair, aft of amidships on the torpedo deck, which gave a clear view of both port and starboard. A Japanese plane came down almost vertically on *Ommaney Bay*, and fires and explosions started at once. We tried to rescue survivors but had to cease as the force was under attack. Escorts could not reach her because of explosions and intense heat, and she had to be abandoned. The blazing hulk was sent to the bottom by a torpedo from *Burns (DD-588)*. Casualties were heavy."

Ulvert M. Moore had promptly cast off from *Minneapolis* and rushed to the scene. She spotted and rescued four swimmers from the carrier, one of whom expired before he could be brought on board. This DE was commanded by Lieutenant Commander Franklin D. Roosevelt Jr.

Three DEs concerned with action in the outer screen off the port bow of the main body were *Goss*, *Stafford* and *Ulvert M. Moore*, attached to *Escort Division 70*. The commanding officer of *Goss*, Lieutenant Commander C.S. Kirkpatrick, was *ComCortDiv 70*. The division was assigned to a Hunter-Killer Task Unit under Captain J.C. Cronin in the carrier *Tulagi (CVE-72)*.

1747. The rear echelon of the Fire Support Group and Escort Carrier Group of the Luzon Assault Force was attacked from out of the sun by sixteen *kamikazes* with four escorts. These planes were flying very low and fast and had apparently evaded most of the Combat Air Patrol. Several of the group broke off and struck the outer screen further aft, but the main force of about eight planes attacked the area between *Goss* and *Ulvert M. Moore*.

Four of the enemy peeled off to the right and bore down on the carrier and her escorts. In the fierce fight to repel this deadly threat, *Goss shot down two planes, and Captain Kirkpatrick was quick to affix credit where it was due:

"Seaman Second Class Charles Myrle Dunn is the director operator of the after twin 40mm gun, and hits from his guns destroyed the two enemy planes. The testimony of the witnesses and the results obtained show him to be an outstanding gunner in action."

According to the action report of *ComCortDiv 70*, *Stafford* and *Moore* each downed a suicide plane with their guns. **Goss* shot down her second aircraft when the fourth crashed into *Stafford's* starboard side!

The other four planes got through and crashed into the cruisers *HMAS Australia* and *Louisville (CL-28)*, the escort carrier *Manila Bay (CVE-61)*, and one crashed astern of the *Natoma Bay (CVE-62)*! Two other planes made suicide attacks on other large ships without causing a great deal of damage. Lieutenant Charles W. Jenkins, executive officer of *Stafford* vividly recalls the fateful day:

"Late that afternoon, our Task Force was sailing northward through waters outside and west of Manila Bay. We were alert; our battle stations were fully manned. Our radars picked up the bogey and initially reported four planes with no IFF and closing. The DEs in our sector opened antiaircraft fire at targets judged to be 8000 yards on our port side, low on the water, coming out of the setting sun. The original bogey developed into eight planes. Within a few seconds, the plane formation split and four planes peeled off to their right to cross *Stafford's* bow and the *Moore's* stern. The other four planes appeared to pick the carrier as their target."

Stafford's commanding officer, Lieutenant Commander Volney H. Craig Jr., reported that his DE had opened fire about the same time the four planes banked off to the right and headed about 4,000 yards astern; the others continued on their course across the bow of his ship. Lieutenant Jenkins continued:

"The din and deafening clamor of *Stafford's* AA fire was unprecedented in our Combat Information Center (CIC). To that was added the bedlam of important high priority voice communications. Each of our three DE's was given credit for splashing one plane. As I recall, *Stafford* wanted to claim a second splash, but it was awarded to *Ulvert M. Moore*."

Stafford's antiaircraft fire splashed one Zeke 1,500 yards on the port bow! Shortly thereafter, a second plane was hit by her fire. This plane continued about 500 yards across *Stafford's* bow and then made a sharp right turn, heading for her bridge. Being unable to gain altitude, The *kamikaze* made a suicide crash into the starboard hull of the ship amidships, just abaft the stack, between the after engine and fire rooms, putting her out of commission! At this time, another attacking plane was claimed to have been splashed by her antiaircraft fire about 1500 yards on her starboard bow. The fourth plane of the group was reported by lookouts to have crashed into *HMAS Australia*. No one on board needed an explanation or definition of this newly used Japanese tactical weapon, the *kamikaze*!

The larger ships hit by *kamikazes* survived and could maintain course and speed, but *Stafford* was in trouble. Fortunately, the crew's casualties were light in spite of the heavy material damage; two fatalities and twelve wounded.

Personnel performance on *Stafford* was exemplary, both before and after the action. This was her first engagement with the enemy. Forty seconds after opening fire, two enemy planes had been destroyed and the ship was severely damaged. Of the fatalities, one was killed outright; the other died of wounds on an assisting ship. One man was seriously wounded by shrapnel; The remaining casualties were stationed at the after 40mm gun and were injured by shrapnel and flash burns.

The crash ruptured number one fire room and number two engine room and made a large hole in the starboard side about at the water line, flooding the area and destroying the evaporator. Lieutenant Jenkins:

"The stricken DE lost way rapidly and began taking on water. She was losing freeboard, and the stern was virtually awash. Power was limited to the port boiler/main engine combination. Now we needed that damage control training that many of the crew had been exposed to during training sessions and shakedown exercises. It was paramount that the undamaged bulkheads to flooded engineering spaces be shored up. Several shipmates subsequently told me of the heroic and herculean performance of our black wardroom steward, Henry Beasley, who demonstrated his extraordinary strength in the movement and placement of heavy 4"X4" timbers to prevent bulkhead collapse. The captain directed dumping of all topside depth charges and the jettisoning of K-guns and the loading machine to improve stability. Meanwhile, the ship's damaged condition was relayed to our screen commander who directed *Moore* and *Halligan* to maneuver alongside *Stafford* and remove all hands except for a nucleus crew. The executive officer (me) was permitted to stay with the ship and with the captain despite the wording of the save-the-ship bill."

At first sight, she appeared lost as fire broke out on board. *Moore* closed to port and took off 53 men and three officers while destroyer *Halligan (DD-584)* nudged alongside to starboard and took off the wounded and about 50 others. She donated some of her shoring lumber and sent aboard her engineer officer to confer with *Stafford's* Ltjg. Smith about reinforcing bulkheads and confining the water in flooded spaces. *Moore* and *Halligan* received orders to stand by *Stafford* through the night, and the fleet tug *Quapaw (AT-12)* arrived to take the severely damaged DE in tow.

The *Moore* action report of the same engagement states that, at 1744 on 5 January, her CIC reported bogies picked up by surface search radar at 8.5 miles and closing. The ship was at GQ, and all guns were brought to bear immediately. As the planes were in the sun, they were not spotted visually until approximately six miles distant, at which time they were identified as six Oscars. They were closing at an extremely low level and high speed in what appeared to be a torpedo attack heading for *Stafford*, just ahead of *Moore*.

Moore reported that, at about 4.5 miles, the flight split in half, three planes in each. "Commence firing" was ordered. The left hand or southern group appeared headed well astern of this ship but was taken under fire by the after 40mm mount. The main battery and forward 40mm took the northern group, which was closest, under fire, and sharp rudder action was maintained to keep the main battery bearing on this group. One plane was believed to be damaged. Fire was checked when the target approached *Stafford* ahead but was immediately restarted when the trailing plane was observed to be turning toward *Moore*. This plane was shot down about 1000 yards off the port bow of *Moore*!

Continuing the *Moore* report, one plane from the forward group passed through the screen and crash-dived into the Number two stack of *HMAS Shropshire*. One plane, believed to have been damaged by fire from *Moore* after passing ahead of *Stafford*, turned sharply and crashed into the starboard side of *Stafford* at the water line amidships. Chief Powers reported his version:

> "At dusk GQ, six enemy planes were spotted coming in on our port side. We opened fire with our 5" guns at 9,000 yards, the 40mm guns at 4,000 yards, 20mm guns at 2,000 yards. We could see our tracers hitting the Jap, but he didn't splash until about 50 feet off our port side. Later, the black gang said they were cool when the 5" opened up, concerned when the 40mm guns opened up, but started moving toward the ladders when the 20mm guns started firing! As a matter of fact, my knees started to knock when we kept hitting the enemy aircraft without success (I should not have been using binoculars to watch it come in)."

The foregoing was taken from three separate reports of the same action at about 1747 on 5 January 1945. They were somewhat similar but by no means duplicates of each other. *Goss* reported four *kamikazes* in each of two groups, that the escorts were attacked by one group and the other flew off to attack ships in the inner support area. It further stated that *Goss* had downed two, another was splashed by *Moore* and the fourth crashed into *Stafford*. *Stafford* reported two groups of three planes each, of which one group attacked her, that she shot down two and was crashed by the third. *Moore* also stated that three planes attacked, that she splashed one, that another crashed *HMAS Shropshire*, and that the third crashed *Stafford*. It is possible that *Moore* was referring to *HMAS Australia* rather than to *HMAS Shropshire*. Both *Stafford* and *Moore* claimed to have damaged the plane that crashed *Stafford*. The obvious explanation is that, in the heat and excitement of battle, the same situation can appear dissimilar to different participants. Actually, the *Goss* and *Moore* reports were not too far apart. Two or three DEs could have easily been firing on the same plane at the same time, giving each ship the impression that she alone had shot it down. As for *Stafford*, the experience of being crashed by an airplane – the gasoline inferno – a 500 pound bomb explosion – must have been one of deep trauma, compounded by a degree of confusion, smoke, flames, and interrupted communications, leading to inaccuracies. This was confirmed by Captain Craig's statement:

> "All sound powered gunnery telephone, cease firing, salvo signal, and director firing circuits were damaged and became inoperative when the ship was hit. Communications, target designation, and gun control became extremely difficult."

Captain Craig of *Stafford* also recalled:

> "Shortly after we were hit and not knowing what was ahead, I had the word passed 'prepare to abandon ship'. Well, the 'C' Division (eager beavers all), without waiting for an 'execute', did it by themselves! Overboard in the lead-weighted bags went our TBS radio crystals, code books, wheels for the encoding machine, a magnetron for the SL radar, and other confidential gear as specified in the 'Abandon Ship Bill'. So there we were, unable to see, talk, listen, or much of anything else! Capt. Cronin of *Tulagi* (next day) sent us a message by light, saying 'I wish I could do something to help you'. I came back with a list of our needs, and he scrounged up and delivered it all within 24 hours! He was a great guy, thought *Stafford* was tops, always two-blocked flag signals before the others.
>
> Further investigation disclosed that, although one engine room and one fire room were flooded, the remaining engine and fire rooms were in satisfactory condition, and the ship could proceed under her own power with reasonable safety.
>
> When we finally got underway again, we could only make six to seven knots and were obviously sitting ducks. We finally limped into Lingayen Gulf the next day after a couple of nighttime brushes with Japanese aircraft. High winds and rough seas prevailed with the ship working heavily. I thought we might ease the strain by taking a tow from the tug, but it didn't seem to help, so we cast off.
>
> While at anchor in Lingayen Gulf awaiting a returning convoy, a Jap air raid developed, and we were hit by friendly AA fire, igniting the gasoline supply tank for our emergency de-watering pump close to our torpedo tubes. That night, the 'mouse' (officer's name deleted) had the deck for some eight hours and, about 0200, said 'Captain, I am not cut out for this! Please can I go below?'
>
> The second night after the 'incident', I had a mattress sent to the flying bridge so I could catch a few 'z's'. Another air action developed nearby, and I just couldn't wake up! Leaning on the bridge windshield, I fell asleep standing for about forty minutes. I sent for the exec and fell back to sleep still standing."

As this was the first action in which *Moore* and a large percentage of her ship's company had taken part, the commanding officer stated that all hands performed their duties in the finest traditions of the Naval Service. Although no individual performed an outstanding act to deserve special mention, it was felt that much credit for the effectiveness of the ship must be given to prior training programs.

Following the enemy air attack, *Moore* and *Halligan* were ordered by the Commander Battleship Division 3 in *New Mexico (BB-40)* to standby *Stafford* and escort her to the Lingayen Gulf Area. *Stafford* got underway; *Moore* was assigned a screening station ahead, and *Halligan* took up screening station astern. Back on *Stafford* with Lieutenant Jenkins:

> "We advanced slowly toward Lingayen, accompanied by *Halligan* and *Moore*. It was a harrowing night, albeit a quiet one. With only a minimum crew and nearly devoid of antiaircraft gun defense, we were heckled by an unfriendly

bogey. He knew we were down there but he couldn't see us clearly. In moonlight, it was CIC's job to help the captain on the open bridge to avoid being silhouetted.

It worked except for one pass when the plane came in but was not properly aligned. One of our eager gunners opened up without authority, as though our ship wanted to assist the plane pilot. In CIC, we genuflected and prayed that this would not recur. After all, we were playing for keeps! The plane nearly disappeared from the scope as it got set for another run. Things were tense. In a few minutes, its position on the screen indicated it was closing for another run. This time, it dropped its bomb off our port bow. It missed! Some supreme power upstairs was looking after the *Stafford*. Our tormenter must have returned to his base for fuel or ammo or a new flight plan.

It had been a long night when at first light the captain had a difficult duty to perform, one fatality had to be buried at sea. The skipper conducted the military service gracefully on the fantail."

Early on 6 January. Enemy aircraft were picked up by air search radar within 20 miles of the formation. From this time, until the attack at 0707, the ships were continually snooped by anywhere from four to nine planes. They were disposed evenly on a circle about nine to 12 miles from the formation, orbiting the ships in a counter-clockwise direction. At frequent intervals, two or more planes would make a run into the formation from opposite sides. They would either pass directly over at an altitude of 400 to 500 feet, or change course when about two miles distant and continue to circle the formation.

One plane passed close over *Moore* and dropped a bomb in the wake of *Stafford* (Probably the one reported by *Stafford* as being off her port bow). This plane was taken under fire by *Halligan*. Again, at 0645, *Halligan* opened fire with unobserved results. As *Moore* was not equipped with fire control radar, night antiaircraft firing was limited to visual targets. The moon had risen at 0030, and visibility was much improved.

Although ships in the formation could easily be seen, only one plane was briefly sighted by *Moore*. When aircraft were within four miles, she used evasive tactics, conning the ship with the wake always up-moon (astern) so that a plane attacking up the wake could not find the ship silhouetted by the moon. It was noted that, even at 10 knots, the wake was clearly visible, due both to the bright moonlight and the phosphorescent quality of the water. However, Captain Roosevelt considered that the added maneuverability of the ship at 15 knots outweighed the increased wake effect. Although two aircraft runs were made up of the wake of this ship, no bombs were dropped.

0700 on 6 January. Dawn attack. *Moore* had been at GQ since 0030. The CIC tracked six planes within 20 miles of the formation. One was reported closing rapidly, distance seven miles, speed 275 knots. The next nearest plane was 10 miles away, also closing. Right full rudder was ordered and *Moore* steadied on her course.

0706. The CIC reported the nearest plane only two miles away and closing rapidly. Almost immediately, it was sighted at an elevation angle of 40 degrees, diving out of a dark cloud and strafing - ineffectively - the burst landing 50 yards short off the port beam. All guns on *Moore* commenced firing immediately, and several 20mm and 40mm hits were noted. The plane passed about 100 feet over the ship's bow and splashed at a distance of 5000 yards!

0711. The second plane was reported 2 miles off and racing toward the starboard side of the DE. As it passed over the aft end of the ship, the stern guns fired upon it with unobserved results.

1849. *Halligan* was relieved by the destroyer *Ralph Talbot (DD-390)* as senior escort. There was some snooper activity during the night and, at 0500, one plane closed to about five miles. *Moore* went to GQ for dawn alert, still patrolling astern of *Stafford* and *Quapaw*. Task Units in the area were conducting flight operations about 10 miles from *Moore's* position. There were many friendly planes in the area, but enemy aircraft were reported in the immediate vicinity at various ranges and bearings.

0717 on 7 January. Dawn attack. *Moore's* CIC reported a bogey 10 miles away and closing. Another was picked up at seven miles on a course directly toward the formation, speed 240 knots. About two minutes later, it was sighted attacking in a shallow glide from the starboard beam of the formation. It passed directly over *Quapaw*, about 2500 yards ahead of *Moore*, dropping a bomb off the starboard beam of the tug. The plane was not taken under fire by *Moore* during the approach because it was too close to the ships ahead when sighted. However, both main battery and 40mm fired briefly and without results while it was retiring. CIC reported it six miles away, at which point it turned about and commenced an attack on *Moore*, closing rapidly. As the *kamikaze* came in from astern, left full rudder was ordered to unmask all port side batteries.

The plane was sighted visually off the port quarter, range three miles, position angle 30 degrees. Almost immediately, all guns commenced firing. The aircraft dropped a bomb 100 yards off the DE's port quarter, and continued close aboard up the port side.

When directly abeam to port, direct hits by 20mm shells were observed at the base of the plane's starboard wing. A large flash of flames about six feet in diameter engulfed the base of the starboard wing and cockpit. The plane circled away off the bow, and the fire went out. It looked like it was preparing to make another run, and the ship's rudder was brought full right to keep the port 20mm battery trained on the target.

The Oscar splashed at a distance of three to four miles! It disappeared from the radar scope almost instantaneously. Chief Gunner's Mate Powell had some interesting "off the log" comments, varying somewhat from the action report.

"Some enemy bombers eluded our Combat Air Patrol and appeared overhead. A Betty bomber made a run on us, but Captain Roosevelt went hard aport to bring our guns to bear, and two 500 bombs exploded in our wake. The aft 40mm was tracking as were the 20mm guns, but it was too close for the after 5" to get on it. Between the swing of the ship and the momentum of the bomber, the director operator could not get a lead on the target. (Getting a lead on a moving target in the air is an electronic version of leading game birds or clay pigeons in trap or skeet shooting.) However, the bearings coincided for a moment and the aft 40mm shot a wing off the bomber, and she splashed! I had a problem with that aft 40mm it oscillated when on a steady bearing under director control - like a facial tic. The manufacturer, York Safe and Lock Company, previously had a technician try to help me as well as three other Chiefs (Electric, Radio and

Machinist) to no avail. At this time, electric hydraulics were far from perfect. The veer and yaw of the aft 40mm had knocked the wing off the Betty bomber!

After securing from action, I went to the bridge to report expenditure of ammo and armament condition. The captain had his battle helmet on backwards - no one had the audacity to mention it. Altogether, about twelve Japs were downed in our area."

During the next half hour, three more bogies were picked up by radar, the closest six miles from the formation. None were taken under fire. Chief Powers remembers an incident in typhoon weather on 10 January:

"Most of the crew was seasick, including men with prior experience on destroyers and minesweepers. Five inch projectiles with base fuses broke loose from ready service stowage in the forward handling room. Partly because of our super-abundance of ammo passers from the *Stafford*, projectiles were all over the place. They bounced off each other and the bulkhead. Two other gunner's mates and myself, using mattresses, captured the loose ammo and re-stowed it while nauseous and falling all over the place."

Goss departed from the Lingayen area on 20 January to take part in the Iwo Jima and Okinawa operations. In July, she screened the replenishment group for Admiral Mitscher's Carrier Task Force 38 as it struck the main islands of Japan with carrier planes and battleship guns. She served in hunter-killer groups to the end of the war, covering landing units of the 8th Army in Tokyo Bay on 2 September.

Lieutenant Jenkins talked about added *Stafford* woes:

"Compounding our problems as we approached Lingayen Gulf was that, with the loss of our starboard fire room, we had also lost our capability for making fresh water. We had no operating evaporator plant, and we had a thirsty boiler requiring fresh water to supply steam for the operating main engine. Fresh water became a serious logistic matter. We could not operate independently, beyond reach of another ship to transfer water for our needs. This called for prompt action that would not 'endear' the exec with the crew. The edict was published: 'Coffee pots will be temporarily abandoned, no showers will be taken and personal needs are limited to one pint/man/day for dental use and lavatory basin.' The operational boiler had the priority. Salt water was used in the laundry. After we retired from the action area, the Officer of The Deck would announce on the P.A. whenever a rain squall came up, and all hands would strip on deck and have a fresh water shower!"

Stafford remained in the vicinity of Lingayen until 11 January when, after receiving the rest of her crew minus casualties, she departed with a slow convoy for Leyte. After receiving emergency repairs at San Pedro Bay and Manus, she headed for the United States.

Ulvert M. Moore resumed antisubmarine patrols in the vicinity of Mindoro Island. While thus engaged, she received orders to assist two destroyers in contact with a submarine and became the principal actor in the drama. See chapter *Pacific Antisubmarine Warfare*.

HOWARD F. CLARK

Howard F. Clark (DE-533) arrived at Manus on 22 December 1944 and joined Admiral Stump's escort carrier group, forming up for the Lingayen Gulf invasion. *Clark* was in the same Task Force as *Goss*, *Stafford* and *Ulvert M. Moore*, but assigned to the Carrier Air Support Group which sortied on 5 January from Kossol Roads.

Several enemy aircraft had been picked up during the day by radar, but about 1641 it appeared that a concentrated attack against this force by Japanese planes was imminent, whereupon *Clark* went to GQ.

The mission of the Task Group was to provide air support and antisubmarine air patrols for the combined fleet of Task Force 77, engaged in the invasion of the Lingayen Beach area of Luzon. American forces at the time of the attack were off the west coast of Central Luzon, on a northerly course, destined to arrive at the area of the landing on the morning of 6 January.

The entire Task Force was composed of carriers, battleships, cruisers, two destroyer escort divisions and two transport divisions, the largest amphibious attack force the war had seen to date. The fleet was in cruising formation at the time of the attack, with half of the battleships, cruisers, destroyers and destroyer escorts making up a van group and the remainder a rear group. *Clark* was on station with the rear group.

1640. Japanese bombing and torpedo planes were encountered. They appeared to approach from bases on Luzon, and several groups pressed home attacks on our forces. The three planes that attacked *Clark's* sector were flying in a very close "V" formation and approaching at a low altitude. There was a gentle northeasterly five knot wind. The sea was calm, and the ship was not rolling enough to make an unsteady gun platform. The sun was shining, visibility was excellent, broken only by occasional large cumulus clouds.

Commander Task Unit 77.4.2 reported over the Fighter Director Warning Net that there were four to eight bogies 38 miles from the formation. Accordingly, he ordered "Flash Red," "Control Green," indicating that enemy aircraft were about to attack. Two formations of bogies were closing, one just forward of the starboard beam, range 22 miles, the other abaft the starboard beam, range 18 miles. The CTU ordered "Control Yellow," indicating that the planes might be fired on when identified.

The local combat air patrols were in all sectors, and it was difficult for *Clark* to definitely identify the bogies on the radar scope. However, the attackers were picked up at 10 miles. The planes were sighted broad off the starboard bow, approaching from below a large, low cumulus cloud, 4500 yards distant and moving at 200 knots. They were thought for a moment to be friendly but were identified as bogies when seen to launch torpedoes at the heart of the formation.

During the time when the identity of the planes was in question, all guns on *Clark* had been tracking them and, when torpedoes were launched, the order "Commence firing" was given. The planes were at a range of about 4000 yards, having turned toward the middle of the formation with the evident purpose of strafing or suicide diving.

1650. Having tracked the planes for at least one minute, the guns were right on, and tracers from the forward 40mm gun were seen to strike one of the three Jills that were in a very low, close formation. The aircraft burst into flames and splashed!

A shell from the number one 5" gun burst between the remaining two planes, one of which dove headlong into the sea! The third plane was seen to break out in flames at the time of the burst and to turn toward *Maury (DD-401)*, with the apparent intent of crash diving, but it fell in flames on the destroyer's port quarter, about 100 yards short of crashing her! During the firing, *Clark* was maneuvered to unmask all possible guns as the planes approached the starboard bow. *Maury* and *Clemson (APD-31)* were also firing at the planes. It was felt that *Clark* contributed materially to the destruction of two and possibly three enemy aircraft. The commanding officer of *Clark*, Lieutenant Commander D.C. Miller commented:

> "All ordnance equipment functioned. The result of continuous training aboard ship and at Bermuda, San Diego and Pearl Harbor were apparent. This, combined with the unusually great amount of firing conducted by this vessel on towed speed targets, has made the director operators and gunners smooth trackers and deadly.
>
> Whereas *Clark* did not sustain damage or personnel casualties, four vessels in the Task Group were not so fortunate; one was badly damaged."

The troops stormed ashore at Lingayen on 6 January. During the landing and the battle which followed, *Clark* screened the escort carriers as they furnished air support to soldiers ashore and flew combat missions to keep the skies clear of enemy aircraft. The destroyer escort had occasion on both 8 and 9 January to rescue downed aviators from the water and was detached soon afterward to return to Ulithi with Admiral Durgin's carriers.

The ships again got underway on 1 February for the next major step in the campaign - Iwo Jima. *Clark* became part of an underway resupply group and protected the refueling operations of ships in support of the invasion. She joined with ammunition-laden LSTs at Ulithi and departed on 21 March for Okinawa. Reaching Kerama Retto with her precious convoy on 28 March, she screened fueling operations for the Third Fleet strikes on the Japanese homeland as well as for Admiral Beary's Fifth Fleet replenishment group. She departed for the United States on 5 November 1945.

EDMONDS

Escort Division 63 was the first complete division of "5-inch DEs" to report for duty in the Pacific Theater. (So named because they mounted two-5" guns in rotating mounts instead of three 3"guns in fixed mounts.) At Morotai, these DEs proved themselves to be highly capable of the task and were selected to operate with escort carriers throughout the Pacific War.

On the morning of 10 September 1944, *Edmonds(DE-406)* with *ComCortDiv 63* aboard as screen commander, sortied from Seeadler Harbor, Manus Island, with the other ships of *CortDiv 63*, plus *John C. Butler (DE-339)* and *Raymond (DE-341)*. Their assignment was to provide protection against air, surface, and submarine attack for an air support group composed of *Carrier Division 22* and two other CVEs.

Edmonds was underway in this campaign for 28 days. On 3 October, *Shelton (DE-407)* was torpedoed and sunk. (See chapter *Pacific Antisubmarine Warfare*.) *Edmonds* returned to Manus where, on 9 October, Lieutenant Commander John S. Burrows Jr. relieved Commander Christopher S. Barker Jr. as commanding officer. The latter was awarded the Legion of Merit for services in the Morotai operation.

One week after returning from Morotai, *Edmonds* was underway again to participate in the Leyte Gulf invasion, escorting General MacArthur's flagship en route to the landings. On 28 October, she entered Leyte Gulf for fueling, encountering several air attacks. The bodies of many Japanese victims of the American offensive were floating on the surface of the water, the ugly flotsam of amphibious war. On the same night, *Eversole (DE-404)* was torpedoed and sunk while proceeding out of the gulf, also covered in *Pacific Antisubmarine Warfare*.

Edmonds was one of forty DDs and DEs protecting battleships and carriers after the battles of Surigao Strait and Samar. Lieutenant Commander Burrows was awarded the Legion of Merit, the second time this honor had been conferred on a commanding officer of *Edmonds*. On 20 November, *ComCortDiv 63* shifted his pennant to *Dennis (DE-405)*. On 11 December, while steaming in the vicinity of Majuro in the Marshall Islands, *Edmonds* made a sound contact and attacked a submarine which fired at the formation. The wake of a torpedo passed harmlessly under her bow.

As part of the screen of Task Unit 77.2.23, en route to Lingayen Gulf, *Edmonds* screened heavy units in the first force to enter the Japanese-controlled China Sea off Luzon. The escort task unit was commanded by Captain Martin, Commander Destroyer Squadron 51, with his pennant in *Hall (DD-583)*. As in prior narratives, Vice Admiral Oldendorf's battleships and Rear Admiral Durgin's carriers were central to the Force.

1610 on 5 January. The formation was under air attack by Japanese suicide planes. Three torpedo bombers came in on the Edmonds' side, approaching the formation low over the water, apparently on a suicide mission after launching their torpedoes. They were shot down by her gunners, along with those of *Maury (DD-401)* and *Clemson (APD-31)*, none of the planes getting more than 200 yards inside of the screen before splashing. The action report of *Howard F. Clark* in station 13 had not mentioned *Edmonds* in station 7, nor the other way around, and both made the same claims along with the destroyer and the APD. As far as this author is concerned, a number of enemy planes were destroyed by four escort vessels — which is what war is all about.

1745. Five planes came in from the other side of the formation, broke through the fire of the screen and reached the center of the force, attempting to crash dive on the larger ships. One plunged onto the deck of *Manila Bay (CVE-61)* causing minor damage and temporarily cutting off her communications. Another hit the mast of *Savo Island (CVE-78)* and splashed into the water. A third plane was believed to have hit the cruiser, *Minneapolis (CA-36)*, damage undetermined. Captain Burrows action report also stated that one of the planes dropped a bomb on *Stafford (DE-411)*. This, of course, was incorrect because that DE was crashed by a *kamikaze*. This is just another example of the confusion or that can arise in the heat of battle.

On 6 January, *Edmonds* arrived in her designated area and was assigned to the carrier screen. This unit launched aircraft which destroyed enemy personnel, installations, and facilities along the coast of Lingayen Gulf and provided air coverage for all U.S. units in the operation from 6 January until relieved by the Army Air Force on 17 January.

Edmonds left the carrier screen to rejoin the destroyers. On 17 January, she departed from the Lingayen Gulf area and, five days later, reported to the Fifth Fleet. A month later, she would embark on her most perilous assignment. See chapter *Iwo Jima to Okinawa*.

BLESSMAN

In earlier days, before conversion from a DE to a transport, *(APD-48)*, *Blessman* had seen service in Operation Overlord, screening heavy ships as they bombarded German fortifications on the French Coast. She arrived in Palau on New Year's Day, 1945, to witness a harbor loaded with battleships, cruisers, carriers, destroyers, destroyer escorts, and destroyer transports.

4 January. En route to Lingayen, air raid alerts commenced at 0045 and continued during the night. At first light, *Blessman* fueled from the oiler *Winooski (AO-38)*. An air raid at 1130 was followed by receipt of mail from the destroyer *Izard (DD-589)*. This may seem like a superfluous chore in the midst of furious combat. However, mail from home was such a great morale booster that all Navy formations assigned the highest priority to its distribution, even in hours of great danger.

1715. The ships were attacked by an unidentified number of planes. A near miss on the battleship *California (BB-44)* was observed from the bridge of *Blessman*. An escort carrier in the rear echelon was hit by a *kamikaze* and was burning furiously. The CVE, damaged beyond repair, was sunk by her own forces.

0330 on 5 January. The carriers began launching aircraft at dawn. The Task Group fought off four separate enemy aircraft raids between 1600 and 2000.

1647. "Flash red." One enemy suicide plane was shot down!

6 January. As the task force entered Lingayen Gulf, it was met by a large flight of *kamikaze* planes attacking from all directions. When the smoke of battle had cleared, several ships had been hit and 21 enemy planes were destroyed. *Blessman* had been credited with assisting in the destruction of two of them. It was a long day.

0300. Evidence of radar jamming was noted on the *Blessman* SL radar. Major units formed up for the bombardment of Santiago Island and adjoining targets. All APDs took screening stations to seaward of the battle line.

1155. Air attack. One suicider was shot down, another crashed into a screening destroyer! *Blessman* had taken that aircraft under fire but did not score any hits.

1437. Another *kamikaze* was shot down. The transports entered Lingayen Gulf; *Blessman* was stationed 500 yards from the interval between the cruisers *Louisville* and *Portland (CA-33)*. All ships were under sporadic air attack.

1622. One suicider was shot down off *Blessman's* starboard bow!

1720. A *kamikaze* was splashed as still another crashed into Sky II, the secondary control station on *California (BB-44)*, killing 44 of her crew and wounding 155 others!

1723. Another plane smashed into the starboard side of the cruiser *Portland (CA-33)*!

1800. A plane coming in on the APD's port quarter crashed into the *Louisville*, her second hit!

At the same time, a plane believed to be an Irving was observed off the *Blessman's* port bow, low on the water, with the obvious intention of attacking the formation. Her commanding officer, Lieutenant Commander Philip LeBoutellier Jr., noted in his action report:

> "The range was clear, and we fired across the formation with our 5" and number one 40mm guns. Our 40mm tracers were seen to hit. When major units opened up, the plane was engulfed in fire and crashed into the water. It is felt that, since this vessel was the first to take the plane under fire, we should be given credit for at least an assist." (They were.)

1828. Another suicide plane was shot down on *Blessman's* port bow! The formation cleared Lingayen as *Blessman* took her station in the outer screen after dark.

0643 on 7 January. The formation commenced firing at a friendly F4F and shot it down, but fortunately the pilot was recovered.

The APDs were deployed in a screening line to seaward of the bombardment ships. At 1245, they formed up and proceeded to the area assigned to lower boats for underwater demolition operations. Two hours later, *Blessman's* boats were lowered and then loaded at the fantail. The boats subsequently started in to their assigned beaches, 2500 yards from the APD. The covering bombardment opened up midway between the green and yellow beaches.

Blessman commenced fire in support of her Underwater Demolition Team number 15 with two after 40mm guns. Her 5" and forward 40mm guns opened up as she closed to within 1700 yards to the beach. There was no return fire on the APD or her UDT Team. The team went to work under cover of the intense bombardment provided by the heavy ships. In addition, *Blessman* covered her swimmers by making the beaches too hot for an enemy bent on bothering the team in its work. At mid-afternoon, all guns ceased firing as boats returned to the ship, having completed their reconnaissance without casualty. An hour later, the boats were aboard, and the ship was underway to rendezvous with *Transport Division 102*. That evening, the commander of her UDT put off in a boat to deliver beach information to the flag aboard *Humphreys (APD-12)*, and the formation proceeded out of the Gulf for night retirement. So successfully was the job completed that the Army suffered not a single casualty in this APD's sector when their troops went ashore on 9 January.

The following day, the *Blessman* was detached to escort the now empty transports back to Ulithi via Leyte Gulf. There she rested, took on provisions and trained for the next operation, a trial by fire at Iwo Jima, her unexpectedly last duel with the enemy.

ESCORT DIVISION SIXTY-NINE

31 December 1944. DE escorts departed from Manus for Lingayen as part of Task Force 79. The commanding officer of *Richard W. Suesens (DE-342)*, Lieutenant Commander R.W. Graham, recorded the deployment. His ship was in the screen of

Task Group 79.2 and she flew the pennant of *ComCortDiv 69*, Commander T.C. Phifer. Upon arrival at Lingayen on 9 January 1945, *CortDiv 69* was stationed in the antisubmarine screen for the Luzon Attack Force. It commenced patrolling east and west across Lingayen Gulf with *Suesens*, *Oberrender (DE-344)*, *Leray Wilson (DE-414)*, and *Gilligan (DE-508)*.

Evening of 6 January 1945. As The Task Group transited Surigao Strait, a Zeke was shot down by the Combat Air Patrol on the port bow of the convoy. During the night, the formation was constantly shadowed by bogies.

Evening of 8 January. Two enemy aircraft attempting to attack the group were shot down by the CAP about two miles astern of *Leray Wilson*. An enemy dive bomber crashed into the carrier *Kitkun Bay (CVE-71)* which, with *Shamrock Bay (CVE-84)*, constituted the core of Task Unit 77.4.3. At the time of the crash, that Task Unit was about five miles on the port bow of *Leray Wilson's* Transport Group and a few miles on *Suesens*' port quarter, close to *John C. Butler (DE-339)*.

1900. A Val closed the Transport Group on its port quarter. The plane was taken under fire by *Wilson's* main battery and heavy machine guns, and the aircraft crashed in flames 1700 yards off her port quarter! Other vessels were also firing at this plane, and only partial credit for its destruction could be claimed by this DE.

The morning of 9 January. The task force entered Lingayen Gulf. Two bombs were dropped on the formation by a Lilly which exploded harmlessly in the water 2500 yards ahead of *Wilson*. *Abercrombie (DE-343)*, was the first to steam in near the beach in the early light and to anchor only 4500 yards off the main assault beaches. She lay there quietly all morning, her crew at GQ, her guns trained out and ready. Battleships, cruisers and destroyers opened up with a thunderous barrage, with the battleship *California (BB-44)* firing pointblank over *Abercrombie's* mast and the cruiser *Columbia (CL-56)* blasting away only a few hundred yards to starboard.

A Japanese plane dived out of the sky ahead and *Abercrombie's* guns blazed in anger for the first time. Five-inch bursts puffed thick and fast around the *kamikaze*, streams of tracers arched up from the *Columbia*, but he kept coming and smashed in a long, searing tongue of flame into the cruiser's foremast and beyond into the sea.

Meanwhile, the landing craft circled, formed lines abreast of *Abercrombie* and, on her signal, churned off toward the beach which still smoldered and glowed under the finishing touches applied by rocket-firing LCIs. Wave after wave of landing craft formed and disappeared into the smoke with their loads of grim-faced soldiers. By 1100, the big attack transports started in for the beaches and anchored, surrounded by their own swarms of loaded boats which began plying back and forth to the shore.

At 1130, *Abercrombie* steamed out a few miles and lay to as part of an antiaircraft screen for the still loaded or empty transports. At 1230, the radio reported the town of San Fabian in American hands. But evening brought threatening clouds and more air attacks. Under a black sky, torn with streaks of red tracers and dark bursts of flak, *Abercrombie* and other escorts led the empty transports out toward the sunset and into the South China Sea.

The *Suesens* Group also left for its position in the ASW screening line with *Oberrender*, *LeRay Wilson*, *Gilligan*, and *CortDiv 69* embarked in *Suesens*. The transport area came under air attack during evening twilight. At dawn on 10 January, the transport area was again under air attack.

LERAY WILSON

On 7 January, the Commander Task Group 79.1, Rear Admiral Kiland, addressed a message to the ships of his command which read in part:

> "In the event of suicide or other direct attack on any ship of this group, it is expected that all gun crewmen will stand to their guns..."

How well the gunners of *LeRay Wilson* kept faith with Admiral Kiland is related in the ensuing paragraphs, based on the action report of Lieutenant Commander M.V. Carson Jr., her commanding officer:

> "The patrol stations were extra hazardous inasmuch as the DEs were spaced at an average interval of 2.25 miles, there by preventing adequate mutual fire support when attacked. Also, the patrol line was too far away from the transport area to receive fire support from the transports or the DEs assigned to them. Furthermore, isolated as it was, the patrol line seemingly never received the attention of the Combat Air Patrol."

0709 on 10 January. A Betty dived out of a low hanging cloud over the land on the port quarter of *Suesens* passed along her port beam 2000 off and was taken under fire by her 40mm gun. She ceased fire as the *kamikaze* raced toward *LeRay Wilson*.

The CIC on *Wilson* reported to the bridge that a bogey was on a course directly to the ship. Although the rising sun illuminated the mountains on the eastern side of the Gulf, the visibility to the west was still very dark. *Suesens*, 2.5 miles west of *Wilson*, could barely be recognized. A twin engine Nell was observed broad on *Wilson's* port beam in the west, distance 1000 yards, low on the water and heading directly for the bridge. It was immediately taken under fire by one 40mm and four of the port 20mm guns.

About 200 yards from the ship, the port engine and wing were set afire. However, the plane struck the port flag bag, 20mm guns six and eight, the stack, the torpedo tubes and, in crossing the hull, also hit 20mm guns five and seven on the starboard side. Part of the plane fell in the water and the rest was strewn over the superstructure and torpedo deck. At the moment of impact, there was an explosion, followed by flames that engulfed 20mm guns five and eight, the stack, and torpedo tubes.

Since it seemed that the bridge would be covered by burning gasoline, Skipper Carson gave the order to clear the structure, but it became apparent that the fire was all aft of that area, and this order was belayed. It was believed that the bombs carried by the plane did not explode and must have been duds. The fire was quickly brought under control by the use of fog nozzles, and injured personnel were removed from their gun stations to receive first aid treatment. Casualties claimed six dead and seven wounded.

All hands had been given a minimum of 3 1/2 hours of first aid instruction per week under the chief pharmacist's mate, enabling members of the crew to render first aid. *Suesens* and *Stembel (DD-644)* tendered assistance. A doctor and a pharmacist's mate from *Stembel* came on board to help in the treatment of the injured. Casualties were transferred to the Coast Guard attack transport *Cambria (APA-36). Wilson* then resumed her station in the patrol line until evening when she proceeded to Leyte with her Task Unit.

The damage control organization showed the result of many months of training under the able leadership of Lieutenant Howard S. Peterson, first lieutenant. Immediately after the crash, repair parties lead four fire hoses to the scene of the fire and extinguished the flames by the use of fog spray, thereby preventing the spread of fire to other parts of the ship. (This report was especially gratifying to this author because "Pete" Peterson was my executive officer when I was skipper of the subchaser 532 in the opening days of the war.)

Immediately after the crash and explosion, the number 1 engine room became filled with gas and fumes, rendering it almost untenable. The chief engineer, Lieutenant (jg) James H. Jacobs, ordered the engine room cleared, and he remained at his post with Second Class Machinist Mate Tarlington J. Carpenter. Though almost overcome by the fumes and smoke, they kept power on the ship and the fire pumps operating, making it possible for the repair parties to combat the flames.

During the entire operation, the CIC functioned extremely well. On occasion, air plots included as many as 10 planes at a time. The communication department jury-rigged antennae so that the ship never lost communication facilities for a period of more than 20 minutes.

How well the gunners of *LeRay Wilson* kept the faith with Admiral Kiland and with their shipmates can now be told. Boreo, Ellison, Jodoin, Kimble, Bryant and White manned guns numbers five and seven on the starboard or unengaged side. Of these, Boreo, Ellison, and Kimble were missing in action. Jodoin was severely burned and was later picked up by *Suesens*. Bryant was killed instantly. White suffered agonizing third degree burns, had his left hand amputated, and suffered internal injuries. Koapke and Boggess died at their posts and Vehorn, Haney, Humbert and Cottingham were so critically injured that their recovery seemed tenuous at best. Phillips, who was on the torpedo tubes, was less critically injured and apparently had a good chance for recovery. As so eloquently described by the captain:

> "In the face of almost certain death, they unflinchingly stood by their guns until they were relieved at their posts by the Angel of Death or the veil of unconsciousness. May Admiral Kiland know, when he reads this report, that they kept his faith in them. They were my shipmates, and I am proud of them."

Haney, although critically injured with third degree burns from his head to below his waist and suffering from several lacerations, gave first aid to his injured shipmates, refusing aid for himself until so ordered by his commanding officer.

The crews of number one 40mm and of numbers two and four 20mm performed excellently and showed the benefit of training given them by the gunnery officer, Lieutenant Donald D. Ewing and the assistant gunnery officer, Lieutenant Roy Stuart Armstrong, Jr.

The executive officer, Lieutenant Commander Felix L. Englander, was of invaluable assistance to the commanding officer during the entire seven day operation. His coolness throughout the many long nerve-wracking hours were an example to the men under him.

During evening twilight, the transport area again came under air attack. A plane crashed the attack transport *DuPage (APA-41). LeRay Wilson* left the screen.

After the damage was repaired, the ship's new commanding officer was the former executive officer, Lieutenant Commander Felix L. Englander. At Okinawa, *LeRay Wilson* did patrol duty for a period of 50 consecutive days, subject to airplane attacks more frequent and more violent than at any other time in the whole war, but she remained unscathed. One enemy fighter, making a surprise attack over the Hagushi Beach anchorage, was splashed by *Wilson*.

GILLIGAN and RICHARD W. SUESENS

11 January. The transport area was under attack during morning and evening twilight. *J. Douglas Blackwood (DE-219)* and *Goldsboro (APD-32)* joined the screen.

Gilligan departed from Manus on 31 December to escort troopships to Lingayen Gulf, arriving in time for D-Day on 9 January. In constant danger from enemy air attacks, the destroyer escort supported the assault, screened for Attack Group A of Vice Admiral Wilkinson's Task Force 79, and laid smoke screens as necessary.

This author asked retired Rear Admiral Carl E. Bull, at the time a Lieutenant Commander and commanding officer of *Gilligan*, to fill me in on both the Lingayen and Okinawa episodes. Taken together, *Gilligan* was certainly one of the most embattled DEs of WW II. As the saying goes, "Some served more than others."

0620 on 12 January 1945. In anticipation of the usual morning air attack by the Japanese, all hands on *Gilligan* manned their battle stations. The depth charges were checked to be sure they were set on safe, propeller locks were placed on all torpedoes, and torpedo tubes were trained outboard. All 20mm and 40mm guns were cocked and with magazines loaded. Breeches were open on the 5" guns with projectiles in the loading trays, fuses set to two seconds. All hands were checked for complete clothing, sleeves rolled down, shirts buttoned and helmets on. Antiaircraft firing was observed in the direction of the transport area which was covered by a smoke screen.

0645. Combat Information Center reported a bogey on SA radar, distance 12 miles. Five minutes later, it closed to eight miles. Engines were ordered ahead full. The ship was turned to bring the bogey onto the starboard beam and allow the maximum number of guns to bear.

0656. Bogey distance four miles, low altitude.

From then on, the plane was tracked by SL surface radar, and control was informed it was coming in low and fast. Relative bearings were constantly relayed to gun control, and all guns were trained on the bearing, ready to open fire on sight. The last radar range reported before sighting the plane was only 1000 yards.

0658. The target was sighted, a twin engine Betty broad off the starboard bow. All guns opened fire instantly as the plane headed straight for the DE. The *kamikaze* was in a horizontal approach with it's machine guns strafing as it screamed in. *Gilligan's* gunners opened up with everything they had, setting the right wing afire and partly shot off. At an estimated 100 yards from the ship, the plane burst into flame.

According to *The Dictionary of American Naval Fighting Ships*, a seaman under machine gun fire from the attacking plane had leaped from his post onto the main battery director, throwing it off target. This unfortunate and unpredictable panic prevented the 5" guns from getting off more than 14 rounds. Captain Bull noted in his action report:

> "0658.8. The damaged wing caused the plane to veer aft and crash just abaft the stack. No avoidance maneuver would have been effective due to the short interval between sighting and crashing. It hit the torpedo tubes and 40mm director squarely. Everything topside between the stack and the stern was sheared off. Even the after gun mount hatch and the depth charge racks were split and on fire along with the after ammunition handling room. There instantly erupted a tremendous explosion of gasoline, enveloping the ship with flames and blazing wreckage from the nearby torpedo tubes aft to the fantail.
>
> Almost at the same time, a second plane roared in to deliver the final blow, but we were lucky enough to shoot it down!
>
> The huge fire was immediately attacked by the damage control party which did a great job in extinguishing it before it spread to other areas, thereby maintaining our seaworthy condition.
>
> A TBS call was transmitted for medical aid and for rescue of survivors knocked overboard; other ships in the screen picked up some of our casualties. *ComCortDiv 69* in *Suesens*, without waiting for this transmission, had already started toward us.
>
> 0715. The fire was under control and wreckage was cleared from the main deck, making it possible to estimate ship and personnel casualties. There was extensive damage aft above the main deck where the 40mm battery and director had been. The battery had continued to fire up until the time the plane crashed directly into the muzzles of the guns. When the resultant flame and smoke cleared away, there was not the slightest sign of gun, director, mount or ammunition stowage left.
>
> We sustained 12 killed and 12 wounded.
>
> Because of the limited capabilities of Manus to handle such extensive repairs, we were ordered to return to Pearl Harbor."

0729. While searching for *Gilligan* survivors, *Suesens*' radar picked up a bogey coming in from over the land. Emergency full speed was rung up and full rudder applied. This maneuver kept the plane under fire by the entire starboard battery plus three 20mm guns on the port side, shooting across the center line of the ship. Because of the ship's high speed, violent turn and the probability that the pilot was killed by AA fire, the plane passed about five feet over the after 40mm gun and 5" loading machine. It splashed so close aboard that, after the explosion, the wash of the ship extinguished the flames and the fantail passed over the wreckage!

The recognition officer, stationed at the after 40mm director, estimated the plane speed at over 400 miles per hour in its steep, full power dive. *Suesens* guns repeatedly hit the plane when close aboard, and the recognition officer claimed its engine was stopped before passing over the hull. When it exploded, fragments tore into the port side of the ship, causing minor hull damage. Eleven men were injured by shrapnel. At least three lives were saved because all topside personnel wore helmets and kapok life jackets.

The wounded from both ships were treated by the medical officer of the *Schley (APD-14)*. The screen was ordered by the Task Force Commander to return to the transport area, where *Suesens* and *Gilligan* conveyed the wounded to a transport departing from Lingayen that date. The most severely wounded were transferred to the Amphibious Force Flagship *Appalachian (AGC-1)*.

Other ships hit by *kamikazes* that day were *HMAS Arunta*, *Helm (DD-388)*, *Walke (DD-723)* and *Richard P. Leary (DD-664)*.

Gilligan sailed again, arriving off Okinawa on 17 April to commence antiaircraft screening around the transport anchorage, where she splashed at least five *kamikazes* and manhandled a torpedo.

Suesens also arrived at Kerama Retto, Okinawa, to screen the transports. Employed as a picket ship around the Island, she survived the nightly air raids and numerous suicide attacks, splashing four planes and assisting in the destruction of two others.

See chapter *Iwo Jima to Okinawa* for both ships.

HOLT

Holt (DE-706), with *Escort Division 74*, transited the Panama Canal and arrived at Hollandia, New Guinea, via the Galapagos and Society Islands on 21 November 1944.

Bill Morgan was a quartermaster on board with a remarkable talent for recording the lighter side of shipboard life, perhaps more amusing in retrospect than in its time, but an antidote for the grim face of war.

> "I'm reminded of an incident that occurred aboard *Holt* during her short career in World War II.
>
> En route to the Western Pacific, *Holt* fueled at Bora Bora. This otherwise tranquil island had been transformed into a navy fueling station for small ships transiting the Pacific. The fueling dock was of limited capacity, requiring each DE in the Division to take its turn alongside while the others anchored in the lagoon. The refueling operation took a couple of hours. Accordingly, two of our officers decided to hit the 'O' club for a couple of shots.
>
> It was easy to catch a ride from the dock to the club, a couple of miles down a dusty road. Time flew by and, realizing that they had to return to the ship right away, they looked around for a ride back, but none was to be found. Since we had been at sea for a while, their couple of drinks had them feeling bold. The only transportation available was a navy dump truck which neither officer had the slightest idea how to operate. However, the keys were in the switch, and they got it started. With all the levers in the cab to operate the dump bed, they naturally pulled the wrong one and

the bed assumed the 'dump' position.

As they drove away in a low gear, marine MPs spotted them weaving down the road and gave chase. What a sight as the dump truck with bed up came roaring around the bend onto the fueling dock with two MPs in a Jeep in hot pursuit, firing .45 caliber automatics, whose bullets ricocheted off the raised dump bed. All hands topside witnessed the scene as the two officers were accosted by the MPs, then turned over to the ship's captain, who immediately put them 'in hack' confined for two weeks to their staterooms.

The captain, Lieutenant Commander Victor Blue, was seething as we had delayed leaving the dock for some 30 minutes while trying to locate the two officers. Our Division Commander (a full captain), on a sister ship was also irritated at us for not leaving the dock on time. Less than two days later, when the other officers complained about having to do double time, our skipper restored them to duty. (Footnote: While the skipper was mad as hell with the breach in regulations, he was somewhat envious that he did not have the time to get ashore for couple of drinks himself)."

As a unit of the 7th Fleet, *Holt* departed on 28 November to join carrier forces in Leyte Gulf, protecting the vital military operations ashore. She completed this duty on 11 December, and steamed with a convoy to Mindoro for the establishment of a PT base. During this invasion, *Holt's* gunfire protected her supply convoy by driving off a number of aircraft attempting to attack the formation.

1503 on 13 December. The first action commenced when a fighter suddenly appeared over the formation without prior warning from radar. Immediately afterward, a twin-engine bomber approached from the port bow at an altitude of 2500 feet. This plane released two bombs, straddling *Holt's* projected track and hitting close aboard a nearby ship in the convoy.

The target was first taken under fire by *Radford (DE-446)*, stationed 1500 yards ahead of *Holt* in the screen. Within 10 seconds, *Holt* also joined the fray. Her 40mm fire was observed continuously hitting after the target had crossed from her port bow to her starboard bow. Before turning abeam, the airplane began smoking and commenced a gradual descent until it splashed into the sea several miles astern!

0805 on 14 December. About six planes attacked from different directions, several being shot down by the combat air patrol. One bomber suddenly came in from ahead of the convoy on *Holt's* starboard quarter, already having been taken under fire and apparently hit heavily by *Halford (DD-480)* and *Jobb (DE-707)*. *Holt* fired several bursts from the after 40mm gun with unobserved results. This plane may have crashed afterward because it appeared to be out of control in a downward spiral when fired on by *Holt*, although that was not confirmed.

In the third action, a bomber was picked up by *Holt's* radar and plotted at 15 miles from the convoy. This aircraft was first taken under fire by *Bush (DD-166)* and *Radford*, and was tracked by *Holt* as the pilot approached from ahead of the echelon and made his bombing run toward the rear of the convoy. *Holt* then opened fire. As the target passed from broad off her starboard to just abaft the starboard beam, *Holt's* 40mm fire, together with the fire from other ships, was observed to be continuously hitting the target. The aircraft began to smoke and made a gradual descent until it splashed near *Halford* shortly after releasing its bombs at a low altitude!

On the morning of 16 December, within a few minutes of one another, a dive bomber and a group of three twin-engine bombers suddenly appeared over the convoy without radar warning. *Holt* joined other ships of the screen by engaging the dive bomber and later singly engaged the horizontal bombers with her 5" guns. Although 24 rounds were expended, none of the *Holt's* bursts were observed to have hit the target. The planes appeared to be returning from a strike against one of our task groups and, having previously dropped their bombs, did not attack the convoy.

A short time later, *Holt's* SA radar made contact on a fast moving bogey closing the convoy. All guns were trained on the bearing when another fighter plane appeared at a range of 6000 yards, speed 300 knots, making a suicide run on the port beam of *Holt*. Skipper Blue changed course with full rudder, and the plane, finding the *Holt's* target angle unfavorable, chose instead to try to crash the small fuel oil barge *YO-14*.

The target was taken under fire by *Holt* at 6000 yards. As the ship turned right across the head of the convoy, she put her stern toward the target to unmask additional starboard 20mm guns. Those, together with the after 40mm guns, continuously and heavily hit the *kamikaze* as it crossed into the convoy close aboard, showing a fire in the cockpit and emitting smoke. The target quickly lost altitude, splashed and exploded just short of the *YO-14*!

Escort Division 74 (CortDiv 74) comprised six *Rudderow* class DEs. *Rudderow (DE-224)*, *Day (DE-225)*, *Chaffee (DE-230)*, *Hodges (DE-231)*, *Holt* and *Jobb*. Of these, *Holt*, *Hodges* and *Chaffee* were in the thick of things at Lingayen Gulf, out of contact with others, because ships were split into various commands. Within a couple of days, *Hodges* was dismasted by a *kamikaze*, and *Chaffee* took a torpedo through her peak tank, described separately in this narrative.

Sundown on the night of 23 January, Lingayen Gulf. Ships of the inner patrol left their stations and moved to the transport area to gain the protection of the smoke screen laid down during the dusk alert and to offer additional fire support in that area. As darkness fell, the "stop smoke" signal was executed. *Chaffee*, *Rudderow* and *Holt*, were assigned adjacent stations one, two, and three in that order and returned to the patrol line. A half hour later, unidentified aircraft were detected six miles from *Holt*, alerting the entire area. Visibility was high with a bright moon. One of the planes closed *Holt* to within two miles and then disappeared from the radar scope. Ship speed was increased to 20 knots as she commenced vigorous zigzagging. A twin-engine bomber passed directly overhead from the starboard quarter to the port bow, altitude not over 200 feet.

This high-speed aircraft disappeared from sight almost instantly after dropping two bombs. One bomb hit the water 150 yards off the port quarter and the second close aboard the bridge on the port hand. At the same instant, there was a large splash and explosion bursting into flame, a near miss on the port bow. It was determined later that this was caused by a suicide plane, approaching undetected under cover of the twin-engine bomber and attempting to crash-dive the ship. (*Kamikazes* often attacked in pairs, one immediately abaft the other, so as to appear to be a single blip on the radar screen.) *Holt* increased speed to 24 knots and continued vigorous zigzagging to ward off any subsequent air attack. Fortunately, *Holt* did not suffer materiel or personnel casualties from the explosion. From the captain's action report:

> "Returning to the vicinity of the attack, the fire was still burning on the water, and ship's personnel proceeded to extinguish it with fire hoses. In the illumination of the burning debris and our 12" signal searchlight, an inflated pneumatic raft with two adjacent bodies were seen in the water. *Holt* was maneuvered to keep the nearest man illuminated, apparently a Japanese aviator, still alive and swimming sporadically but feigning unconsciousness. The motor whale boat was lowered with instructions to pick up the aviator. However, the Japanese was swimming in such a way as to conceal something under the surface of the water while simulating an unconscious state. Since his actions were threatening (possibly a gun or hand grenade), the boat officer was instructed not to endanger the lives of the boat personnel, but to shoot the Japanese and recover the body. The body was taken aboard in a search for possible intelligence material. An examination of the wrecked plane did not reveal anything of interest, and patrol was resumed at 0025 on the morning of 24 January.
>
> Upon completion of the examination of the body by the chief pharmacist's mate, and in compliance with voice radio instructions from the Commander Task Group 78.1, the Japanese naval aviator was buried at sea. All military honors were dispensed with in accordance with navy regulations then current. A report of the examination, along with all articles removed from the aviator's person, was delivered to the Task Group intelligence officer during the forenoon of the same day."

1 April. *Holt* aided in one of the final operations for the securing of Luzon. Arriving off Legaspi, she provided fire support during the landing that day and then returned to Subic Bay to convoy supporting forces back to Legaspi for the landings on 7-8 April.

Returning to San Pedro Bay, *Holt* next steamed to Morotai to join a convoy in support of the assault on Taraken Island, Borneo. The first target in the series of Borneo landings, Taraken was taken by Australian forces under marine and navy air support on 1 May, and *Holt* arrived with supply ships five days later. The ship was forced to remain constantly on the alert for suicide swimmers and limpet mines while in the roads.

After repairs in a floating dry dock, *Holt* was assigned to weather patrol and cruised the eastern South China Sea, sending reports to help guide movements of the vast fleets then operating in the Pacific.

Quartermaster Bill Morgan related one more of his yarns:

> "Just after the surrender of Japan, we were operating with our submarines in drills off Subic Bay. We were relaxed as we killed time waiting for orders to go home. Several officers and crew had already left, and we were getting replacements fresh out of boot camp and officer candidate school. One young ensign was Junior Officer of The Deck. At that time, I was still a quartermaster. My friend, Hoyt, a first class Signalman and I spotted an object hull down on the horizon.
>
> As we watched. it came closer. Using the high powered long glass, we made out the Japanese ensign. We called this to the attention of the young JOD, who got all excited and hit the general alarm, sounding GQ. This was right in the middle of lunch, so all hands forfeited their meal as they scrambled to their battle stations, all the time wondering what's going on the war was over, was it not? We maneuvered to intercept the Japanese ship, which was a newer class of destroyer and much faster than us. The Japanese captain appeared to ignore our signals (he did not understand them), so we fired a round of 5" well ahead and over his bow.
>
> This got his attention, so he hove to while we prepared a boarding party, complete with steel helmets, bulky life jackets and small arms. The motor whaleboat came alongside the defeated enemy and rode wildly in the four foot seas. The Japanese lowered a rope ladder for our people to board, but it was impossible to climb from a pitching boat while burdened down with a sub-machine gun. So, our gunnery officer in charge of the boarding party, handed his weapon to the waiting Japanese, then climbed aboard. The Japanese very graciously bowed and returned the weapon to our officer.
>
> The ship was en route to Manila to surrender as per radio instructions that had gone out to all enemy ships at sea. They had complied strictly with the orders; thrown overboard all small arms, removed the breech blocks from their guns, and dropped all depth charges. We escorted them to Corregidor. I'll never forget the sight of our gunnery officer handing his weapon to the enemy so he could come aboard to take him prisoner!"

Holt departed for San Francisco on 18 December 1945.

HODGES

Following antisubmarine operations along the Atlantic Coast, *Hodges (DE-231)* departed for the Pacific, reaching New Guinea on 20 November 1944. Subsequently, she was assigned to the Philippines for antisubmarine patrol and escort duty.

In early January 1945, *Hodges* sailed with Vice Admiral Barbey's San Fabian Attack Force for the landings at Lingayen Gulf. Shortly after 0700 on 9 January, a *kamikaze* started a dive on her. Misjudging the target angle, the plane knocked down the ship's foremast and antennas and splashed without inflicting a single personnel casualty!

Motor Machinist's Mate John Miller, currently residing in Lexington, Kentucky, recalled his ship's close brush with disaster:

> "It's January 9, 1945. *Hodges* is lying off the beach at Lingayen Gulf, Luzon, in support of the invasion. We are at General Quarters, and I am at my station in the forward engine room. The hatches are closed, and our only communication with the outside world is the phone talker who is connected to the bridge.
>
> We know that Japanese planes are attacking the beach and the ships. We hear two rounds fired from one of our 5" guns, followed by a heavy thud. The ship rocks and shudders and then all is quiet. We know we have been hit but we don't know by what, where or how. Our talker tries to contact the bridge, but there is only silence. We try to call the bridge on the engine room phone; there is no answer. The other engi-

neering spaces report the same problem.

Time goes by, and each minute seems like an hour. Finally, I suggest to the Chief that I take a peek out of the forward hatch that opens up on the outside deck. With watertight integrity in mind, he says 'no'.

The agonizing quiet continues with still no word from any outside source. Then, we hear footsteps running up above, and the Chief says 'Take a look'. I open the hatch slowly and I'm told that a Betty Bomber has hit our mast which passed like a knife between the fuselage and one of the engines. The plane then splashed and sank. If the plane had been just a little lower, the wing span and resulting crash and probable explosion would have destroyed the superstructure and wiped out a lot of the crew topside.

The pilot had hopped over a destroyer between us and the beach and covered the distance so quickly that only two rounds were fired from the 5." The smaller guns were firing, and perhaps he was hit. For some reason, he pulled up slightly before he hit us. The captain saw the plane and thought everyone on the bridge was dead. Some of the crew topside were in a temporary state of shock after the crash, and this is why we were unable to contact the bridge.

The mast is broken from its mounting and is held by only a couple of the support cables. Since we have no way of remounting it, and it could come crashing down on the deck in any direction, the decision is made to cut it loose. Our repair gang does the job and the mast disappears over the side. Without it, we are now the most streamlined DE in the fleet but we have no radar, IFF, VHF or other navigational and communication gear.

That evening, we leave for Leyte with a group of empty transports and other damaged ships. Later that night, we are joined by more ships, including a heavy cruiser. Without our mast and with our low profile, they thought we were an enemy submarine following the convoy. Since we had no way of knowing we were being challenged, they were preparing to blow us out of the water when another ship identified us. Happily, we didn't know about this until later."

Hodges quickly made emergency repairs and continued to provide screening - thus playing a key role in the successful landing of the 6th Infantry Division and General Wing's 43d Division.

"On 18 January, we leave Leyte and proceed to Manus in the Admiralty Islands. We go alongside a floating dry dock while the mast is removed from *Leray Wilson (DE-414)*, which had other damage, and is installed on the *Hodges*. This work is done by the crew of the destroyer tender *Sierra (AD-18)*. That puts a swift end to the scuttlebutt that said we would have to go back to the States to get this kind of repair done.

By the Grace of God and the skill of all who worked on the repair, this tough little ship is back on duty, rejoining the rest of the destroyer escorts that carry on beyond their expectations."

During the last days of March, she was assigned patrol and escort duty with convoys supplying the Philippines. On 11 April, *Hodges* conducted shore bombardment on enemy gun emplacements in the vicinity of Legaspi, Luzon. For the remaining months of the war, she operated from Manila Bay, training with submarines, then as plane guard between Ulithi and Okinawa.

Departing from Samar, *Hodges*, arrived at San Francisco on 9 January 1946 via Eniwetok and Pearl Harbor.

CHAFFEE

A Rendezvous with Gentle Torpedoes

The Battles at Samar, Leyte Gulf, Ormoc Bay, Mindoro and Luzon were bloody ones for the navy and with little to cheer about except the fact that they were victories. On occasion, however, this author received recollections from DE veterans that concentrated more on the theme that "Boys will be boys" rather than counting the casualties. Such incidents were looked upon by harassed and tired officers as serious infractions of the rules. Now, looking back over a span of 50 odd years from the mellowed autumn of our lives, having raised children and grandchildren, we see those infractions as having been antics of young men in their late teens or early twenties.

The history of a DE as narrated by former Seaman Frank Reynolds:

Chaffee (DE-230) was assigned to *Escort Division 74* with Commander Charles F. Hooper, as Escort Commander. Lieutenant Commander A.C. Jones was in command of *Chaffee*

During shakedown at Bermuda in June 1944, while *Chaffee* was practice-firing all her guns, a man was missing from his battle station. The executive officer was dispatched to locate him, and he was found — asleep in his bunk! It took the officer about 10 minutes to wake him, scarcely believing that anyone could sleep through that racket. After the drill was secured, all personnel in that sleeping compartment were assembled and advised that, if anyone were ever left sleeping at the sound of GQ, everyone would suffer. Needless to say, the offending person was never again the last one to his station. He was dubbed with a new name, ie. "Sleepy Howell."

Shakedown training included antiaircraft exercises. While firing at a target sleeve towed by a plane, one of the *Chaffee* gunners failed to distinguish between the towing plane and the towed target and found the range of the plane. Bracketed by flak, the pilot dropped the sleeve, hit the throttle, and unleashed a stream of invective over the TBS, unprintable even in today's liberal publishing environment.

Prior to leaving Bermuda, we were assigned to pick up a captured German torpedo and lash it down on deck for delivery to the States. After plowing through dirty weather and rough seas off Cape Hatteras, *Chaffee* arrived at the Navy Mine Warfare Training Station at Solomons, Maryland, where she delivered a German acoustic torpedo. Perhaps this was an advance notice of other torpedoes to enter the life of *Chaffee*.

The 15th of July found *Chaffee* in New London, Connecticut, a supplement to a submarine training program, undersea exercises involving torpedo problems. In other words, we were to be a target ship for simulated torpedo attacks. One day, some members of a work force were in the forward paint locker, located below the water line. A "swish" was heard, and one man asked, "What was that?" Someone called down and said it was a torpedo that went under the ship. The area was evacuated in record time, hatches closed and locked. All hands went topside and said a silent prayer. Of course, this was a practice torpedo without a warhead, released by an overly eager submariner. Enemy torpedoes were more business-like, as we would discover later on.

Early evening on 14 October found *Chaffee* underway from New York City with *CortDiv 74* . As we left the harbor, all hands topside viewed the Statue of Liberty and many of us had lumps in our throats; it would be a long time before we would see it again – and many wondered if we would -- ever. The *Chaffee's* tour of Pacific duty began with the lonely rocks of the Pacific Galapagos Islands where the division fueled. The second stopover was Bora Bora in the lovely Societies, then west on the final leg to Hollandia, Dutch New Guinea.

The monotony of the long, three-week cruise took its toll on one crew member. At breakfast, after a long night at his sonar station, the soundman announced that he had enough and was going home. Since he did have a habit of kidding, no one paid any attention to him. On topside, he took off his clothes and, to our stunned disbelief, jumped overboard and started to swim in the general direction of home. After a short "Man Overboard" exercise, he was returned and put in sick bay for a few days. On recovering, he wanted to know what he was doing in sick bay without the vaguest recollection of what happened.

During the stay in Hollandia in December, one of our shipmates brought a monkey on board. He was kept below decks for about a month, when he managed to slip away. While looking for him, we heard a considerable commotion adjacent to the galley. Monkey tracks were all over the wardroom and straight up to the captain's cabin where he made a mess. Bye, bye monkey.

On the morning 8 January 1945, prior to sailing, supplies had to be loaded, including beer. No one knew, or appeared to know, why half of the beer never made it to the storeroom. Somehow, substantial quantities were stored under rags in the engine room, in bunks and even in the anchor ball that was hoisted while we were at anchor. When the pilferage was discovered, all hell broke loose. The captain and the officers demanded that the beer be returned as soon as possible, and it was only then that the crew realized how much had disappeared. After a search of the ship by officers and men, they did find some, but far from all of it. Restrictions were applied to all hands, but no one cared because we were about to shove off anyway.

That night, after everyone supposedly had turned in, the "missing" beer was stacked on the fantail and sprayed with fire extinguishers to get the bottles cold. Everyone off duty had some to drink, and the ones that were on duty were relieved by other shipmates so they could also have some. The next day, one of the officers discovered that one fire extinguisher was empty, and the order immediately was passed to check all extinguishers. All hands were asked who did it, but of course nobody knew, and again we all got chewed out by the officers.

On the morning of 16 January, the convoy reformed for the dangerous run to Luzon via Surigao Straits and the South China Sea. After being detached from the formation, *Chaffee* was assigned to a barrier patrol between Cape Verde and Point Lulu in Lingayen Gulf.

On the night of 23 January, two unidentified aircraft were reported by radar to be approaching the anchorage. *Chaffee* closed toward the mooring area to take advantage of the smoke screen being laid in the ship-filled harbor. One aircraft was seen plunging into the water north of *Chaffee*. Another was tracked flying away from the harbor.

During the early part of the raid, *Chaffee* had three bogies on her radar screen, although the third plane was not reported by any other ship. In spite of the "all clear," our captain knew of the third bogey and ordered all hands to stay at battle stations. At about this time, the moon emerged from the clouds, silhouetting the *Chaffee* between itself and the enemy aircraft. Radar suddenly picked up the bogey on the starboard beam, range four miles, closing rapidly. The captain ordered an immediate full rudder to head for the target. The few seconds warning from radar gave the ship enough time to effect the turn, which probably saved us. The maneuver interrupted the firing run of a Betty, forcing it to alter course. When the plane was again in firing position, she dropped her torpedo which struck the starboard bow, passing completely through the ship without exploding!

The Japanese pilot, in adjusting his firing position, had arrived at a point so close to *Chaffee* that the torpedo did not have a chance to arm. The dropping of the torpedo was so close to the ship that water came over the bridge when it hit the sea. The forward 5" gun was not allowed to fire on the target since the trajectory of its shell would have caused it to land in the harbor among the anchored ships. Despite the limited visibility and the suddenness of the attack, two 20mm guns and the forward 40mm were brought to bear on the 240 knot target. Wing hits were observed, but the plane was not sufficiently damaged to impede its flight.

It is difficult to describe the feelings of the crew when they realized what had happened. First there was incredulity. Then there was reality; they had really been hit by a "fish" that didn't explode! Finally, there were thanks, each in his own way, mumbling a silent prayer of gratitude for this deliverance. This had been their third rendezvous with a gentle torpedo.

During the night, *Chaffee* had been heavy in the bow and hard to keep on course because of the amount of water she had shipped in the forward area. The lowering of the bow raised the stern and reduced the effectiveness of the rudders. The Force Commander in the harbor came out in person to inspect our damage because of the unusual manner in which it had been inflicted. (This incident and the one narrated by the *Gilligan* in the chapter, *Iwo Jima to Okinawa* were the only two recorded instances in the DE navy wherein ships were penetrated by torpedoes that failed to explode.)

We anchored in the bay to make temporary repairs. As the saying goes, "There isn't an ill wind that doesn't blow some good." The next day, we sent two officers to the battleship *Pennsylvania (BB-38)* for spare parts, and they were greeted like royalty. They heard that *Chaffee*, courageously and deliberately, had stationed herself between them and the Jap Betty, thereby taking the torpedo hit to spare the battleship. Needless to say, our officers did not contradict the rumor and just wore that "Aw shucks, it was nothing, fellas" look. As a result, they ended up with all the parts and ice cream they could carry. Ice cream was important to us as we were the only ship in our division that had to crank it by hand. Consequently, we very seldom had any.

Repairs of a temporary nature were started on the damaged compartment by the crew of the salvage ship *Cable (ARS-19)* in Lingayen Gulf and were completed on 2 February. With the other ships of *CortDiv 74*, we participated in the Borneo operation and then returned to San Francisco early in 1946.

TINSMAN

6 January 1945. *Tinsman (DE-589)* departed from Leyte to screen a convoy bound for Lingayen Gulf. Six days later, as *Tinsman* escorted a slow-moving convoy, suicide planes attacked the formation. During the long day, the American ships fought off four Japanese attackers, splashing two enemy planes.

0740 on 13 January. *Tinsman* was 125 miles northwest of Manila and heading due north at a speed of five knots in company with an echelon consisting of two army oilers and 14 miscellaneous tugs and tows. The screen commander was in *Day (DE-225)*, patrolling ahead of the formation. The convoy was disposed in three columns, length seven miles. Visibility was poor, with low clouds and overcast sky. A mild breeze blew on the starboard bow at force one, and the sea was calm.

0744. *Tinsman* picked up a bogey on the starboard side at a range of 12 miles. The radar officer was at the SA radar scope and tracked the approaching plane from 12 down to four miles. He stated that the target definitely showed an imitation of the current IFF code but with an erratic pulse rate, varying from one to four seconds. When sighted, it was diving through the clouds, repeated about a minute later. This did not appear to be an attack dive but apparently it was for the purpose of initial convoy reconnaissance before committing itself. The plane was not in sight long enough to open fire but was recognized as enemy.

0750. The plane, finally designated a Hamp, was sighted in level flight, approaching the starboard beam of the convoy and was immediately taken under fire by *Tinsman's* 5" main battery and 40mm guns. Bursts from the 5" appeared very close to the target, which commenced diving immediately. Fire from *Tinsman* continued until the position angle and bearing endangered the convoy. The target appeared to be diving in a suicide attack at a small army oiler near the rear of the center column. The pilot made a beam approach, diving from a low altitude at an angle of about 25 to 30 degrees, overshot his target and splashed!

A number of observers were of the opinion that it was on fire when it splashed. The commanding officer of *Tinsman*, Lieutenant Commander K.E. Read, noted that ordnance performance was excellent. *Tinsman* had been hampered by erratic air search radar performance due to failure of parts which could not be replaced from repair facilities.

There was no personnel or equipment damage. Nor was any damage incurred by any vessel in the convoy. The next excitement for this DE would be with the Japanese suicide motorboats, described in the following narrative, *Lough and the Q-Boats*.

Tinsman departed from Luzon on 2 February in a convoy bound for Mindoro. Throughout February, she shuttled between Mangarin Bay and Nasugbu Bay on escort duty. Early in March, she left Leyte Gulf, returned to Manila and resumed escort duty until the end of the war.

She arrived at San Pedro, California, on 18 December 1945.

LOUGH and the Q-BOATS

5 January 1945. Joining Vice Admiral Barbey's Luzon Attack Task Force, TF 78, *Lough (DE-586)* and two other DEs escorted two LCT groups heading for Mindoro. At dawn the following morning, an aircraft dropped a bomb close to the port side of the echelon without damage. In the twilight of the same day, an enemy bomber positioned itself so closely behind two friendly aircraft that it was first assumed to be one of the group. This smart enemy left the other aircraft when astern of *Lough* and, protected by a background of dark clouds and land, made a strafing run on the DE without inflicting damage. The aircraft made a second strafing run, but *Lough's* gunners were ready for him this time. The plane exploded in the air, close to the ship's bridge, and splashed about 50 feet off *Lough's* port bow!

During the invasion of Lingayen, the Japanese deployed suicide boats, piloted by sea-going *kamikazes*, that exploded on impact when they rammed other vessels. They were hard to see on dark nights, and they succeeded in blowing up two landing craft, seriously damaging an LST and a transport, and damaging destroyer *Robinson (DD-562)*. A few of the suicide boats were blown out of the water by *Philip (DD-498)*.

31 January. Amphibious Group 8 arrived at Nasugbu Bay, Batangas Province, Luzon, where troops of the 11th Airborne Division landed, supported by gunfire from the Task Group. The real threat came that night as a large number of Japanese Q-boats, small, sinister craft, swarmed out of the darkness to ambush American ships.

In addition to *Lough*, Task Unit 78.2.8 included *Presley (DE-371) Richard W. Suesens (DE-342), Tinsman, PC-1129, PC-623, Clayton (DD-571), Russell (DD-414), Conyngham (DD-371), Shaw (DD-373)* and *Flusser (DD-368)* with the Officer in Tactical Command.

LSIs and LSTs were on the beach or anchored nearby. Patrol sectors were established by several ships between Fuego Point, Fortune Island, and Talin Point off the Nasugbu beachhead. *Lough* was in the south sector, near *Conyngham. PC-1129* was the inshore end of the line patrolled by *Lough* off Talin Point. The area near the beach was partially shadowed by mountains. There were few clouds, a peaceful setting, the silver moonbeams sparkling on a gentle sea, a refreshingly cool and balmy breeze, hardly a war theater. Gunner's Mate Paul H. Smith on *Lough* was there:

> "After over 50 years, it seems like yesterday. We had been at GQ all day while patrolling the outer perimeter of Nasugbu Bay. Both my watch and GQ station were on the after twin 40mm.
>
> In the early evening, we secured from GQ, and I stood my regular watch, 2000 to 2400. We were cautioned to keep a sharp lookout because there might be some small suicide boats out there. When we asked where they would be coming from, we were told that the enemy brought them down

from the mountains on trailers.

2300. As the moon rose over the mountains, we could see about six or eight small boats, at the same time that our radar picked them up. Five minutes later, we made our approach from down moon and opened fire with 20mm and 40mm on the nearest boat to port, enfilading the entire line. The boats scattered, and gun smoke obscured results. We attempted illumination by searchlight."

The chronology of January 31 from the action report by Lieutenant Commander Blaney C. Turner, commanding officer of *Lough*:

> "We saw in the moonlight, about 1000 yards ahead, a line of small boats extending as far as the eye could see, dead in the water or moving so slowly that no wake was visible. Realizing that we were running into an ambush, we turned, increased speed to 20 knots and notified the nearest ship, *PC-1129*. As the full moon rose, the PC skipper, about three miles south of us, reported some small boats nearby and he was going to investigate. Before that ship could do anything, she was surrounded by boats and one blew a six foot hole in her engine room. She rolled over and sank as *Lough* went after the swarm of 'waterbugs' in the moonlight. The boats showed no wake and did not register on the radar screen."

Between 20 and 30 small boats, about 15 feet long, were encountered off Talin Point. When fired upon, they dispersed. The executive officer of *Lough* counted 16 nearby, and the captain of *PC-1129* had previously counted 13. Others not seen at first made their appearance later. *Lough* was using a radical zigzag, approaching to within 5000 yards of Fortune Island and 2,500 yards off Talin Point. Remembering the fracas, Smith recalls:

> "We ran to action stations and opened a rapid fire. The 40mm on my station fired hundreds of rounds before the action was over."

2308. *Lough* suddenly found herself firing at small craft racing out of dark coves. *Tinsman* increased speed and stood toward *Lough* to assist. *Clayton* was also ordered to lend help. *Flusser* commenced firing star shells to illuminate the area; she and *Clayton* continued to illuminate intermittently throughout the action.

2320. A flashing light near *Lough*, was identified as an "S-O-S" from survivors of *PC-1129*. Subsequent reports by both *Clayton* and *Lough* indicated that they had sighted *PC-1129* in a sinking condition, and survivors were in the water. *Lough* continued firing and, despite the extreme difficulty in sighting targets, scored hits on several suicide craft which were assumed to have been sunk. As the remaining Q-boats retired toward Talin Bay, she sent a boat to rescue the PC survivors.

2322. *Tinsman* had been patrolling 2500-3500 yards from *Lough* and reported a small radar blip at 1700 yards. This contact was very difficult to distinguish from minor lobing but was confirmed by sighting the wake of the small craft. *Tinsman* commenced firing star shells which failed to reveal the target to her guns. She then maneuvered to place the Q-boats up moon, during which time the target was distinctly seen by several bridge personnel equipped with glasses. However, they could not be seen by the gun stations, even when the range was closed to 550 yards. At this time, the target was lost to sight and contact was never reestablished. She searched the area for several minutes and then changed course, fearing that the target had outmaneuvered her and would enter the transport area.

Doctor Richard L. Hanna, currently with the Hanna Clinic in Coushatta, Louisiana, was on the *Lough* during her trials and tribulations:

> "I will try to recall all of the events on the night of 31 January 1945. We were in a group of ships screening the beachhead at Nasugbu. I well remember the sight; the moon was full. At approximately 2300, we got a message from another DE that one of the ships (*PC-1129*) had disappeared from the radar screen, and there were numerous pips all around us.
>
> We opened fire on them with 20mm and 40mm guns, small arms and hand grenades. We felt trapped with boats trying to encircle us. The din from the guns was incredible and the sight was like the *Lough* was on fire. Some of the suicide boats got so close you could see the occupants. It was like a lion trapped by 40 dogs. We used most of the ammunition we had on board. When it quieted down, I believe we had sunk 17 of the craft. We moved over to where the PC went down, stopped dead in the water and picked up survivors. After rendering first aid and providing clothing, we transferred them to an LST. We had recovered seven officers and 56 enlisted men."

Lough destroyed six at first count, and probably most were destroyed within the next two hours in a general melee between the ship and the boats attempting to surround her as they did to *PC-1129*. However, *Lough* was too nimble for their clutches, and the surviving sea-borne *kamikazes* retired without penetrating to the LCIs. The Japanese commander of these midget craft notified Tokyo that he had sunk eight enemy ships! Gunner's Mate Smith had his own problem:

> "While all the action was going on, the bridge called down for me to go up to a 20mm on the port side by the stack because it had jammed. Try as I might, I couldn't do any good. I called the bridge and told them that I couldn't unjam it. The gunnery officer, Mr. Anderson, said if we got out of this tonight, it better be jammed come daylight. Well, being I had just made my third class gunner's mate rating, I could see the little bird (eagle emblem) flying away, but we had an awful time the next morning getting it apart, so no problem for me."

A ship, whose name was not recognized, reported torpedoes. None were seen or heard on *Lough*, but one target being closed by her was seen to submerge at a distance of about 1000 yards. This might have been a midget submarine or a boat sinking from previous damage.

0500 *Lough* sank the last Q-boat on 1 February. The starboard lookout reported a small boat about 1000 yards off and heading across the bow. *Lough* illuminated the boat with the 24" searchlight and opened fire with all automatic weapons. Smoke and the flashes of gun fire obscured the target which was lost as it turned toward the stern. *Lough* again closed and illuminated the boat, destroying it with the 40mm and starboard 20mm guns. Wide sweeps of the area, aided by illumination from other ships, revealed nothing more. *Lough* remained on patrol with the same force the night of 1-2 February, being under orders to destroy suspicious craft not making appropriate signals.

PT-77 and *PT-79* were also hunting for the Q-boats. Regrettably, they encountered *Lough* and *Conyngham.*

2245 on 1 February 1945. *Lough's* radar showed faint indications at 7000 yards, and the DE turned in that direction to determine if it were genuine or phantom. The target looked fuzzy, like a cloud, no IFF. Three minutes later, however, a pip appeared clear on the radar screen. *Conyngham* also reported unidentified targets, and *Lough* advised that she was investigating. She steered a course to close the target and, at same time, keep it up moon. Two faint radar pips now appeared, about the size for PTs, and were reported to the Task Unit Commander. Again no IFF. CTU ordered *Lough* to take them under fire and *Conyngham* to assist. Speed was increased to 23 knots.

2300. With the pips broad on her port bow, range 4000 yards, *Lough* changed course to avoid possible torpedoes and to uncork 5" gun number two. A salvo of illuminating projectiles identified PT boats, but still no IFF response. *Lough* continued illumination, closing the range with the object of getting close enough for her 40mm guns. The PT boats laid a smoke screen and changed course toward the shore. The distance opened to 5000 yards, out of visual range. *Lough* changed course to again close the range. A further course modification placed the targets in the path of the moon, close to land, range 3500 yards.

The DE fired on the targets with her main battery, controlled by radar ranges and bearings. The boats were moving slowly along the shore and appeared to join a large group of small boats similar to those which attacked the previous night. Since all could be seen in moonlight, *Lough* opened fire with automatic weapons. The two PTs appeared to join a third. Later, it was decided that the small boats were rocks sticking out of the water at a point seven miles off Talin Point and what appeared to be a third PT was a wreck on the reef. *Lough* reported small boats under fire as well as PTs. The PTs turned and started running along the shore. As they appeared in the moonlight, *Lough* fired on them periodically with 20mm and 40mm guns. She changed course frequently and radically in anticipation of torpedoes.

2315. The PT boats separated, one going north, the other going south and were lost to sight. The situation appeared to be a concerted attack on *Lough.* It appeared that the only way to prevent a successful torpedo attack was to close one of the boats until it could be seen, and the one to the north appeared to represent the best target as well as being the one which offered a hazard to the other ships. This boat was closed at maximum speed. When the DE was about 2000 yards from the target, the letters "PT" were flashed at the DE by a small light. Captain Blaney recalled:

> "On first contact, I felt a little uncertain about the boat identities. It was soon dispelled by the lack of IFF, the orders from the Task Unit Commander to fire, the failure of the boats to withdraw at high speed when first taken under fire and the knowledge that a dispatch intercepted had assigned our PT boats a patrol area much to the south. CTU transmitted on the PT boat frequency and his failure to get an answer further confirmed the opinion that we had some relatively slow enemy boats rather than our own fast PTs.
>
> Since the letters 'PT' could have easily been sent by a Jap, I was not impressed and concluded it was a trap. I ordered the gunnery officer to resume fire as soon as the guns would bear and the target could be seen. The PT maneuvered radically and, at a range of about 1200 yards, we fired with 5" and 40mm guns, and the target immediately burst into flame.
>
> We passed close to the burning PT, which I did not observe closely because of my preoccupation with locating the other boat, which was still a source of danger. However, several others on the bridge announced that the burning PT was one of ours. I attributed that to a mistake in recognition in the excitement of the action.
>
> I asked CTU if there were any of our PTs in the neighborhood. His reply in the negative confirmed my belief in the identity of the boats, and several people recalled that Dutch PTs had been captured early in the war and probably very much resembled ours. We again turned south and sought the second boat."

Lough fired toward shore on radar information at what appeared to be a second PT in vicinity of a wreck. She ceased fire, searched for the PT and fired several more salvos of 5" on what was apparently the second PT boat, stopped or moving slowly. While radar indicated splashes around the target, there were no hits, and so *Lough* ceased fire. Captain Turner:

> "We suggested to *Conyngham* nearby that, since we weren't doing much good, they take over and we would illuminate for them. We fired star shells, and *Conyngham* opened fire with her main battery. The PT boat near the beach exploded.
>
> 0010. *Conyngham*, passing close to the wreckage of the first PT, said a lookout thought he saw someone swimming. Being astern of *Conyngham*, we stopped beside the debris and, for about 10 minutes, searched with lights but found no survivors. We resumed our patrol station."

Skipper Turner of *Lough* summarized:

> "Two of our own PT boats were destroyed, both by 5"/38 fire, killing her squadron commander, Lieutenant J.H. Stillman on *PT-77* and Lieutenant (jg) M.A. Haughian and two petty officers on *PT-79.*
>
> After we illuminated the PT boats and obtained no recognition from them, I had no doubt about their hostility. In the light of later knowledge, it seems almost certain that they must have sent some message other than 'PT' by light, but the smoke and glare from gunfire makes small lights undistinguishable, even if you happen to be looking in the right direction and the light is properly directed."

Thirty men, survivors of both boats, swam ashore, evaded seizure by the Japanese with the aid of guerrillas, and were picked up by PTs from Mindoro on 3 February.

This author has no knowledge as to the fixing of blame for the destruction of two of our PTs. Loss of life by friendly fire once again raised its ugly head. It would appear, however, that *Lough* was not responsible after the events of the previous night and her assurance that there were no friendly PTs in the area. The presence of those PTs in the sectors assigned to other ships must have been an error by the PTs or the authority that directed them to the wrong sector. Carl Jensen, who supplied a considerable amount of the above action data, was an officer on *Lough* and made the observation:

> "The two PT boats we sank were out of their assignment area. When we commenced taking them under fire, they were abandoned except for two men in each boat who volunteered to try to escape. They were killed while the 30 who had abandoned were later picked up."

Skipper Turner continued:

> "It is not known how many of the enemy small boats were destroyed, probably most of them. There was a general melee, and unquestionably some were taken under fire more than once.
>
> Against the enemy suicide boats, our tactic was to approach from the flank to prevent being surrounded, keeping the boats in the light of the moon as much as possible. Some of the men in Repair I obtained small arms and hand grenades and were stationed in the bow and the stern. Men in Repair II also manned the main deck with small arms.
>
> The boats seen close aboard clearly had two-man crews. The craft had a maximum speed of 10 knots. No return fire was observed. The boat encountered at 0500 seemed much larger, about 20 feet long, also with a two-man crew, and had the general appearance of our LCVP. At first, it appeared to be trying to escape but, when the ranges closed, it headed for us.
>
> Because of our inability to obtain replacement for defective parts, the performance of our SL radar had been below standard, despite the diligent efforts of the division radar officer. Initial contact with the small boats was visual. After their presence was established, some were found by radar as far as 1200 yards away from faint indications which would normally have been overlooked.
>
> The attack by the suicide boats would have been very difficult to detect and repel on a dark night. Even in the good light we had, we were outflanked several times when I thought we had attained the desirable position."

After hostilities ceased, *Lough* left Manila on 24 August for the first of a series of escort missions to Okinawa which continued until 28 November, when she left for San Diego, California, arriving on 18 December 1945.

KENNETH M. WILLETT

In compiling the narrative on *Kenneth M. Willett (DE-354)*, this author was stymied because neither the commanding officer's action report, nor his log nor his war diary could be located at the Navy Historical Center in Washington. It would have been a complete washout had I not located two former crewmen, Shirley Phipps and Thomas L. Kidd, who came forward with their diaries. Starting with the former, we'll let them tell it in their own way, subject to mild abridgment and occasional clarification. Shirley has a unique and interesting writing style.

> "Rough, cold seas induced seasickness which left its haunting scent about the ship. Then came 'marching orders', sooner than expected. 'Report to the Commander of the 7th Fleet in Hollandia, New Guinea.' It was too far to imagine, but we all felt that another door had closed behind us. On 21 October 1944, we set out on a long journey with *Escort Division 82*.
>
> It is a memory of long periods at sea, short stops along the way. Cristobal in the Canal Zone, 'Blue Moon joints', tropical luxuriance and squalor; the transit of the Canal, somnolent beneath the brooding mountains at its Pacific terminus; the Galapagos Islands, volcanic cinders in the Humboldt current; Bora Bora, Society Islands; an Eden of stalwart, pleasant people with whom we traded for beads; Espiritu Santo, dull, about to 'fold' as the front moved west, and finally on 28 November, Humboldt Bay, Hollandia, where we settled among the myriad of ships of resupply that choked the anchorage, and reported to the Seventh Fleet. Tension and uncertainty gripped the crew. Rumors flew, and men wrote home more affectionately than before.
>
> *Willett* was assigned to CTF 75, the newly formed Philippine Sea Frontier for escort of convoy duty from 13 December until 25 February 1945. A drab, tedious business it was for the most part, lightened only by the trivia of rounding up stragglers or sinking obstacles to navigation. By the end of this time, *Willett* was manned by a crew lulled into a feeling of security with the certainty that the war had passed them by.
>
> Japanese planes still sneaked into Leyte nightly to bomb shipping. Flash Red was commonplace, and the LCI 'smoke boats' trailed their streamers around the harbor. More than once, we went to GQ and watched the tracers streak the sky. But if action at Leyte was remote, with only the stink of Tacloban's mud to remind us that death had been there, closer action occurred during the return to Hollandia."

Radarman Third Class Thomas L. Kidd recalls the New Years celebration.

> "We had arrived in Leyte Gulf on 31 December to refuel and take on provisions, then stood out to sea late the same afternoon. A slow, seven knot convoy of 12 merchant ships was formed up for a return trip to Hollandia. We were accompanied by three other DEs, *Doyle C. Barnes (DE-353)*, flying the *CortDiv 82* pennant; *Jaccard (DE-355)*; and *George E. Davis (DE-357)*. By the next afternoon, we were steaming south along the coast of Mindanao, close enough to see the coastline and mountains in the background. It being New Years Day, all hands off watch were enjoying holiday routine. We were zigzagging on station, maintaining ASW surveillance.
>
> The escort flagship *Barnes* had the point; the *Davis* was maintaining station on the port side of the three-column convoy; *Willett* was maintaining a similar station on the starboard side; and the *Jaccard* was bringing up the rear.

Lewis M. Andrews, Jr.

It was a lazy afternoon. I was aft on the fantail, reading a paperback novel, when the after lookout spotted two aircraft approaching the convoy from astern. They were coming in low, no more than 100 feet off the water. At the same time, the alarm called us to GQ.

At that time, my battle station was in aircraft plotting along with another radarman in the Combat Information Center. Our captain, Lieutenant Commander Walter T. Flynn, took the conn on the bridge, and our executive officer, Lieutenant Commander John O. Phillips, took control of CIC operations.

One attacking plane quickly dropped a torpedo, which missed by a wide margin, and the pilot immediately headed back toward the coast to minimize any possible antiaircraft fire being directed his way.

The second torpedo plane continued on its course toward one of the forward merchant ships, just aft of the lead escort, *Barnes*. The *Willett*'s 5" main battery was brought to bear on the target, and gunnery officer Lieutenant W.B. Braman gave the order to commence firing. The third round fired struck and demolished the aircraft with pieces of the plane splashing into the sea!

Our plotting team in the CIC followed the action topside, listening to the messages being relayed to us via sound powered phones and voice communications between our bridge and other escorts over the TBS radio telephone system."

Reverting to a very different version by Shirley Phipps:

"With the crew alerted, *Willett*, went to flank speed. Three radar pips to the south, 10 miles out, targets invisible. One pip detaches; plane becomes visible at six miles, dropping from low ceiling. *Willett* opens up at five miles with 5" guns. Plane 50 yards up, heading for *Willett*, is deflected by two close shell bursts. Other ships open up. How slow the plane comes in. Now you can identify it as it enlarges, a Betty, torpedo under her belly. With smoke of shell bursts all around it, still it comes slow, inexorable. The convoy itself now opens up with 40mm guns. It's so close now you can see the pilot as his plane passes astern of us, as two more *Willett* bursts come close. Then a sudden realization strikes us, 'It's through; it can't be stopped now.' Fear of strafing surrenders to disgust. 'Cease firing' rings out. Almost on ship in convoy, the Betty launches her torpedo. A poor shot; the torpedo broaches. Then, on top of the freighter the plane comes, it wings over; she's going to crash the deck. The crash; geysers of flame and smoke conceal the ship, the ship is done, we think. The others will attack now. But, and it seems to us, at a snail pace, the ship pulls past the conflagration. Her side is smudged but without a dent. Our dismay changes to elation. An underwater explosion shakes the convoy: best guess; the torpedo exploded harmlessly (Probably at the end of its run).

For this action *Willett* received an "assist" with DE *Doyle C. Barnes* and two merchant ships. Planes came into a range of five miles in cloud cover the next day but no attack was made."

Willett spent the remainder of the war in convoy escort and as practice target ship for our submarines.

This author apologizes for two very different observations of the destruction of a single *kamikaze*. Lacking a log, action report or war diary, it's the best I can do. One thing more. Anticipating questions relative to Phipps' first name, Shirley, it is bona fide, selected by his parents. I don't know why.

Willett remained after the war. With five other destroyer escorts, she commenced operations from the Yellow Sea to Shanghai in support of Chinese Nationalists' efforts to wrest control of the Northern Chinese mainland from the communists. She departed from Tsingtao and arrived in San Pedro, California on 11 May 1946.

By this time, it became painfully evident that the annihilation of the Japanese navy did not signal the end of the war. The fanatical enemy had no fear of dying. The road to Japan would be violently opposed every step of the way.

MOPPING UP

The Philippine Out Islands and the East Indies

The rapid movements of American forces in seizing key points in the Philippines and the East Indies left many by-passed Japanese garrisons isolated but stubborn. Until the time of surrender, they had to be dealt with in order to restore hegemony and communications to local governments. For some DEs or APDs involved, mopping up by-passed garrisons were relatively easy assignments compared to the next major thrusts, Iwo Jima and Okinawa. For others, the fighting and blood-letting in these minor engagements were as intense as ever.

KEPHART

Kephart (APD-61) was a veteran of the bruising Battle of Ormoc Bay, previously narrated in this chapter. Upon the landing at San Antonio, Luzon, on 29 January 1945, the invasion forces were pleasantly surprised to be met on the beach by guerrilla troops who reported no opposition whatsoever. A revised plan removed a portion of the troops from San Antonio and an overnight movement to Grande Island in Subic Bay, just south of San Antonio and slightly north of Manila.

Kephart and *Transport Division 103* screened the movement. Upon arrival at Subic, the invaders found that both Grande Island and the Olongapo Navy Base, had been evacuated by the enemy. The success of the strategy for the recapture of the Philippines was becoming more evident as each day passed. Aside from scattered activity, the Japanese Fleet and Air Force were wiped out.

Conversion to an APD did not strip *Kephart* of most of her capabilities as an escort vessel. Not only was she employed as a troop carrier, but also as a DE. Her invasions were separated by at least one escort assignment, generally among the Philippine Islands. A landing took place at Puerto Princess on 28 February and was preceded by a very heavy sea and air bombardment, against which the Japanese offered a very feeble resistance. On the next morning, *Kephart* retired from her sixth invasion.

10 March. She joined the ships that were to carry troops for the first assault against Zamboanga, Mindanao. At dawn, the fire support ships commenced the heaviest bombardment *Kephart* had ever witnessed. Again, opposition was overestimated, and

Kephart's seventh landing operation was successful and without casualty.

The second largest city of the Philippines was to be next in the U.S. plan of reconquest. Cebu City, long an enemy strong point, felt the sting of American power on 26 March. This time, *Kephart's* "cargo" was a part of the famous 24th Army Division and, like so many times in the past, she put them ashore safely and according to plan.

Earlier that day, a submarine had surfaced in the midst of the invasion fleet and quickly submerged again. Because of the many coral reefs in the harbor, its detection by sound gear was extremely difficult, and *Kephart*, along with three other ships, was detailed to destroy it. Long hours of searching bore no fruit until late that afternoon when the sub made the fatal mistake of coming to the surface again. By that time, *Kephart* was already underway for Leyte Gulf, and the sub was sunk by another ship.

As *Kephart* lay at anchor off Cebu within visual distance of the ground fighting, orders gave promise of big things to come. She again loaded troops of the Army's 24th division. Her ninth assault landing was in the offing.

13 April. Another strike on Mindanao was scheduled at Cotabato in Polloc Harbor, and the invasion fleet with *Kephart* got underway from Mindoro. This was her last invasion in the Philippines. Upon returning to Leyte, orders were received sending *TransDiv 103* to Morotai in the Dutch East Indies.

May was spent at Morotai in preparation for the coming assault. Australian troops were to be put ashore at Brunei Bay on the northwest side of Borneo. On 10 June, the "Aussies" landed after a heavy day-long bombardment by U.S. cruisers and destroyers. Again, enemy resistance was negligible. None of the ships were damaged. General Douglas MacArthur was present and went ashore with the troops.

Kephart returned to Morotai and began preparations for the next assault. During this interlude, there was a change of command. Commander Cammarn turned over command of *Kephart* to Lieutenant Commander Robert M. Matthews, Jr. of Thomaston, Georgia, veteran of many major Pacific engagements in the early days of the war.

This invasion, like the last, was to be directed against Borneo, and again Australian troops were embarked. On the opposite side of the island from Brunei Bay, at Balikpapan, they would go ashore on D-Day, 1 July. A landing at Balikpapan involved steaming through the Macassar Straits, a particularly dangerous and narrow stretch of water with enemy-held Celebes on one side and an important section of Borneo on the other. The trip was made without casualty, however, and except for a few nuisance raids, no opposition was offered.

The advance mine sweeping units did not enjoy the comparatively easy success of D-Day. The Straits had been heavily mined, and many light units of the fleet were sunk or damaged. The ships involved in the "D-minus" operations met with the most active enemy resistance since the first landing on Luzon. There were frequent air attacks, and the ships were taken under fire by shore batteries time and time again as will be seen in the next narrative on *Cofer*. *Kephart* retired to Leyte Gulf, an unscarred veteran of eleven assault landings. At this point, her boat officer, Lieutenant (jg) Robert J. Quist of Ames, Iowa, received a commendation from Admiral Barbey, Commander Seventh Amphibious Force, for safely conducting his four landing boats to and from many enemy beaches.

In the midst of rehearsals for the twelfth and largest invasion, the war ended. So, after two years of faithful service, *Kephart* was homeward bound. She had spent 15 months in the Pacific, during which time she participated in 11 assault landings, shot down one Japanese plane, destroyed five mines, carried army troops of occupation to Korea, returned Japanese troops to Japan and safely conducted countless convoys to their destinations. Now, she could look back on an illustrious record and forward to a well-deserved rest.

COFER

After the Battle of Ormoc Bay, *Cofer (APD-62)* landed reinforcements at Lingayan Gulf on 11 and 12 January 1945. Then followed a series of unopposed landings on Luzon, assaults on Palawan on 28 February, Zamboanga on 10 March, and Cebu on 26 March, the last under heavy fire from the beach.

Radarman Second Class Leigh H. Welcome, whose secretive diary illuminated many of the events in the narrative on Ormoc Bay, was still recording the life of *Cofer*, including the assault on Cebu:

> 24 March. We are underway to make a landing. I believe it's going to be Cebu but won't know for certain until tomorrow. Our force isn't very big, but we're not expecting very much opposition. (Famous last words in military campaigns since time immemorial.)
>
> 25 March. We will be landing just outside of Cebu City at 0830. To put the Japanese off guard this evening, we steamed past tomorrow's troop disembarkation area as though we were headed elsewhere. We will return to the same place in the morning.
>
> 0700 on 26 March. When we arrived at the landing area, cruisers and destroyers were bombarding the beach. We launched our landing craft and thought everything was going along fine but learned otherwise when our boats returned. The crews said that very few of the men we landed made the beach alive. One cox'n reported that the men in his craft had barely gotten off the ramp when a mortar shell landed square in their midst, killing most of them and badly wounding the rest. One of the boats had to return to the shore with a jeep and, when it returned, the cox'n said the beach was littered with our dead. As soon as our forces had landed, the Japs set fire to the city. We were supposed to leave this afternoon but, because of the outcome, we are ordered to stay until things either improve or reinforcements arrive.
>
> While at anchor, the captain ordered all men on or off watch to be topside and supplied with small arms and hand grenades. The reason was that this is the home base for midget subs and Q-boats. One submarine periscope was sighted already, but no contact was made.
>
> 28 March. We had quite an exciting evening last night. *Newman (APD-59)* made a surface contact with a sub around midnight. She fired a few rounds of 40mm into the conning tower before the sub submerged and then dropped depth charges. They think that they got it, but I guess we will never know." (No record of a sinking.)

Between 27 April and 8 May, *Cofer* operated as flagship and covering vessel for minesweepers clearing the waters off Tarakan, Borneo, in support of the invasion of 1 May. The commanding officer, Lieutenant Commander H.C. McClees, opened his orders:

> "To transport, protect, firmly land, establish, and support the 26th Australian Reinforced Infantry Brigade of the Ninth Australian Division on beaches on the South Coast of Tarakan Island."

There were mine fields covering the approaches. While part of the enemy forces had been removed, there was still a substantial number on the island. There was a possibility of attack by suicide crash boats and suicide planes. Enemy shore batteries could be expected to defend the coast in the objective area.

0810 on 26 April. Lookouts sighted four rafts 10 miles northwest of Sanga Island, Tawi Tawi. Three landing craft and *YMS-73* were detailed by *Cofer* to investigate. Moments later, the raft occupants were identified as Japanese soldiers. On being ordered to surrender, some began to commit suicide with hand grenades; others refused to surrender. Consequently, they were killed by the investigating ships - Japanese casualties 32 - there were no survivors.

27 April. At dawn, the formation arrived in the designated area off the east coast of Tarakan. Minesweepers streamed their gear and began a sweep of the approaches. At mid-morning, *Cofer* anchored in the cleared area, and the minesweepers began to sweep the inner approaches At the same time, *Cofer* lowered her LCVPs for sweeping operations in shallow water. The APD acted as navigational guide and control ship for the operations. At sundown, all ships withdrew from the area for night retirement.

0900 on 28 April. *Cofer* dropped anchor in the same sector as the day before and again lowered her LCVPs for continuation of sweeping operations. Suddenly, a mine explosion seriously damaged *YMS-329*! With her operational capability destroyed, she had to be withdrawn. As the sun dipped to the horizon, the formation got underway for night retirement and repeated the same operations the following day.

0800 on 30 April. *Cofer* returned to the same anchorage to lower her boats and begin the day's sweeping operations. Suddenly, an explosion erupted near *YMS-51*! Her damage, however, was not disabling. An hour later, nearby destroyer *Jenkins (DD-447)* was badly damaged by striking a contact mine! Radarman Welcome had more news for this day:

> "The LCIs with us landed on a small island in back of the island where the main force of 20,000 Aussie troops are going to land. *Jenkins* is under her own power but down four feet at the bow."

1 May (D-Day). *Cofer* anchored off the invasion area. The first wave of "Aussie" troops landed on the beaches under a protective curtain of naval gunfire from the cruisers and destroyers.

2 May. A long day to be remembered, starting at 0700. *Cofer* was underway for mine sweeping operations. About mid-morning, shortly before anchoring in Sesajap Strait, two natives were sighted in a small boat and were brought aboard for questioning about Japanese dispositions. At 1130, the LCVPs left the ship for sweeping operations. Documents received from the natives were forwarded to the Intelligence Officer on board the Amphibious Force Flagship *Rocky Mount (AGC-3)*. Shortly after noon, *Cofer's* anchorage was shifted to westward to cover sweeping operations. The anchor was kept at short stay in six fathoms of water to be ready for a quick departure if necessary. Boats numbers one and three returned from mine sweeping operations and were hoisted aboard. Boat number two remained with the YMS group for a magnetic mine sweep around Tarakan Island.

1530. The magnetic sweepers were taken under fire at close range from hidden batteries on Cape Djoeata, Tarakan. All vessels were ordered to clear the area at best speed. Five minutes after the Japanese opened fire, *YMS- 481* was hit repeatedly, and suddenly there was an ugly explosion from her 3" ready box! *YMS-334*, *364*, *68* and *313* were also under fire!

1545. *Cofer* was unable to fire because the YMS and LCS craft were in her line of fire, fouling her range. She immediately got underway to close the enemy shore batteries and to clear her line of fire. She opened counter-battery fire on the shore emplacements with her 5"/38 gun at a range of 9200 yards. Two minutes later, the APD was taken under fire by four shore batteries, straddling her at 9200 yards. One shot fell short 100 yards off the port bow. Five shots splashed over her starboard quarter, 100 to 300 yards away.

1555. *Cofer* hit the batteries with three rounds, then ordered rapid fire. Numerous hits were witnessed in the target area as she closed to 8200 yards. Two mines exploded close aboard as several of the YMS sweepers cleared the area, still trailing sweeping gear.

1605. *Cofer* checked fire to allow friendly planes to come in for a strafing run. Boats numbers one and three left the ship to rescue survivors from *YMS-481* which, by this time, was on fire from stem to stern!

All batteries on the northeastern side of Cape Djoeata, extending to the water's edge, were silenced. Desultory fire from the batteries on the other side of the Cape continued. Eighty rounds of 5" ammunition were fired by *Cofer* at the rate of 20 per minute during rapid fire. After three spotting shots, all rounds fell in the target area. Two gun emplacements were destroyed. Survivors from the water off the target area stated that a third gun emplacement was also destroyed and that *Cofer's* fire knocked out all guns on the eastern side of the ridge!

1700. The battered *YMS-481* exploded violently and drifted out to shoal water while burning fiercely!

On the morning of 5 May, one *YMS-481* survivor, drifting out to sea on a raft, was picked up by *Cofer's* boat. No damage was inflicted on *Cofer*. However, the burning YMS sank, and *YMS-334* and *YMS-364* were each hit by several shells, causing damage and casualties. Captain McClees had this to say about *Cofer's* gunnery:

> "Performance of personnel during the entire operation was in every way exemplary during the May 2 shore bombardment and subsequent rescue operations. All personnel who distinguished themselves by meritorious achievement have been recommended for appropriate commendation and award."

An excerpt from Radarman Welcome's diary:

> "8 June. Returned to Brunei Bay at sun up. During morning alert, I saw a Jap plane but he didn't bother us.

About 1500, a minesweeper was blown up by a mine right next to us. We picked up all the survivors, including 12 stretcher cases and three dead. One more died while on board. Most all of the 100 in the crew were wounded. At nightfall, we transferred the seriously wounded men to the cruiser *Phoenix (CL-46).*

9 June. Went back into Brunei Bay about dawn. The total of mines destroyed so far is 68. Our boats returned from sweeping and reported that they got three more mines and possibly a fourth one."

Once again, Skipper McClees read his orders:

"–To transport, protect, land and support elements of the First Australian Corps (Seventh Australian Division and supporting forces) in the Manggar - Balikpapan Area of East Borneo, clear the approaches and waters near the beaches of enemy mines, protect resupply convoys, and provide naval support for the operation in order to effect the reoccupation of the Balikpapan Area."

The captain also evaluated the hazards. There were known enemy mine fields as well as "unsterilized" allied mines covering the beaches and approaches. There was a considerable number of enemy troops, naval defense forces and labor forces in the area. There was a possibility of attack by enemy suicide planes, boats and bombers. Enemy shore batteries were expected to defend the coast. Radarman Welcome recorded a tragedy:

"13 June We had some bad luck today. One of our davits fell into the ocean, killing one man and seriously injuring another. I've mentioned him once or twice in my letters. The davit also sank one of our boats and killed two natives who were trading with us at the time. Around 1900, we held taps for Red and buried him at sea."

15 June. *Cofer* arrived off the objective area. Rear Admiral Riggs, in *Montpelier (CL-57)*, was commander of the cruiser covering force and OTC of the entire operation. The minesweepers commenced a sweep of the outer approaches. *Cofer* anchored at point "Oakland" to act as navigational guide and control ship for sweeping operations. At dusk, she was underway for night retirement.

17 June. There was a brief flurry late in the day when snooper planes were picked up and all ships went to GQ. They soon disappeared, and *Cofer* proceeded to her night retirement. Less than an hour later, however, the signal came, "Flash Red"-"Control Yellow," with bogies coming in from the south. The covering force opened fire on the enemy planes, and bombs were dropped in the vicinity of the cruisers, 4000 yards ahead of *Cofer*. There were no hits or casualties.

18 June. The APD anchored in the northwest corner of an area labeled the "*Card*inals." "Baseball" was the code of the day. During the afternoon watch, *YMS-50* struck a mine in the western boundary of an area designated "Phillies." She was dead in the water and taking enemy fire from the beach. Boats numbers two and four, with rescue parties, were dispatched to the scene by *Cofer*.

1453. "Flash Red" was signalled in the area as a twin engined Japanese bomber was sighted at a high altitude. *Cofer* heaved 'round on the anchor. However, "Flash white" terminated GQ 45 minutes later. The two rescue boats returned from *YMS-50* with three officers and 20 enlisted men after first having off-loaded three officers and 10 enlisted men onto *Montpelier* for treatment of injuries. *Cofer* took station 1000 yards ahead of the convoy for night retirement. The latter word was not to be taken literally.

1850. General quarters. Bogey in the area. *Cofer* opened fire on an enemy float plane at extreme range but ceased fire after only firing seven rounds from her 5" gun as the plane passed out of range. No hits were observed.

20 June. *Cofer* anchored three miles west of point "Oakland." A bogey in the area at 1310 sent all ships to GQ. However, it proved to be a PBY friendly aircraft that hadn't responded to IFF.

1322. *YMS-368* detonated a mine close aboard, sustaining severe hull damage, and *Cofer* went alongside to assist. The YMS was flooding rapidly, and quick action was needed to keep her afloat. *Cofer's* repair party took equipment aboard the minesweeper, pumped out water, and repaired leaks. Three wounded men were taken aboard the APD and given first aid; they were then transferred via an LCVP to the cruiser *Denver (CL-58)* for hospitalization.

Late afternoon of 21 June found *Cofer* in the northeast corner of "Braves." It did not take the Japanese long to greet the minesweepers. *YMS-335* came under fire from enemy shore batteries and sustained a shell hit! A boat shoved off from *Cofer* with a repair and salvage party to render assistance. After seeing to the seaworthiness of the minesweeper, the boat headed for *Montpelier* with four dead and six wounded from the YMS, then returned to *Cofer*.

Another day ended, and *Cofer* proceeded to her retirement station. It became apparent to all hands that the Borneo assignment was turning into a bloody one, and the end was not in sight.

0745 on 22 June. *Cofer* anchored in the northwest corner of area "Cardinals." Two and a half hours later, the enemy reminded the mine sweeping formation of its determined presence. *YMS-10* sustained a hit on her bow from Japanese shore batteries! No casualties. The minesweeper came alongside *Cofer* for repairs.

1658. *YMS-58* came under enemy fire from the beach – no hits. Her damage repaired, *YMS-10* shoved off. With the sun dropping behind the horizon in the night retirement area, the crews in the task force couldn't help dwelling on what the morrow - and succeeding morrows - would bring.

2000 on 25 June appeared to be another normal day until proceeding to *Cofer's* new screening station to seaward of the anchorage. Seven minutes later - "Flash Red" - Bogeys racing in from overland. General Quarters! The crew had barely reached their stations when the planes came screaming in. Action starboard! *Cofer* opened fire with her 40mm and 20mm guns!

They were torpedo bombers, probably Bettys. One plane was set on fire by the APD's 20mm and passed over the ship at an altitude of about 50 feet with its starboard engine engulfed in flames. It splashed in the sea and exploded on *Cofer's* port quarter! Seconds later, another plane raced in on her starboard quarter and was taken under fire by *Cofer's* gunners as well as by numerous small craft in the area. It followed the first attacker, splashing into the water! Almost at the same time, a third plane passed ahead of the starboard bow, but no damage was observed to have been inflicted. Cease fire! The time frame for this action was one minute, within which *Cofer* had expended 64 rounds of 40mm and 266 rounds of 20mm ammunition.

Three torpedoes passed close aboard! One was very close, going under the stern from starboard to port, believed to have been launched by the first plane shot down. The other two torpedoes missed ahead, passing from starboard to port. The skipper had ordered the helm put hard over when the torpedoes were sighted broaching.

2032. It was discovered that one man was missing, believed to have fallen overboard when the first flaming plane passed overhead. A muster found Carpenter's Mate First Class Lewis to be missing. All hands secured from GQ, and a systematic search was begun to find the missing man in the darkness. The beginning of a partial eclipse of the moon did not help. However, a few minutes later, *YMS-364* reported hearing a voice in the water. A boat was lowered and Lewis was spotted swimming; he was returned to the ship unhurt.

26 June. After patrolling in area "Braves" since midnight, *Cofer* anchored in the northwest corner of "Bears" at 0800, to continue this somewhat bizarre reference to baseball.

1430. *YMS-365* struck a mine in area "Giants"!

Of course, in an explosion of that magnitude, there were almost always casualties. Survivors were picked up by *YMS-364*, *YMS-196* and boats from *Schmidt (APD-76)* and transferred to the cruiser *Columbia (CL-56)*. *YMS-365* was damaged beyond salvage, and nearby ships shelled her till she sank.

28 June. Midnight found *Cofer* patrolling a 15 mile sector along the coast of Balikpapan. At 0740, boat number two was shoved off to act as standby rescue boat in the event it was needed by the sweepers. Bogeys in the area sent the APD to GQ. An enemy plane 70 miles distant was being chased away by a Combat Air Patrol (CAP) plane in pursuit. The ready boat didn't have long to wait —-.

1415. *YMS-47* struck a mine, sustaining casualties and heavy damage!

Boat number four shoved off from *Cofer* with salvage and rescue parties to render assistance. *YMS-49* took *YMS-47* in tow. Boat number four returned to the ship with two stretcher cases. Fifteen other survivors were picked up from the water by the APD's boat and were transferred to *YMS-366*.

1250 on 29 June. All seemed quiet in the mine sweeping area, but an air force B-25 crashed in the water, close to the beach! Boat number four was dispatched to the rescue. Two survivors were picked up and transferred to the *Montpelier*.

Radarman Welcome made his last diary entry in the Balikpapan assault:

> "1 July. The Australian 7th division made their landing at 0900, and so far there has been very little ground action. Our CAP says the Japs are moving back. P-38's came in and strafed a Jap truck convoy; it was like seeing a movie, only this being for real.
>
> 2-6 July. Just routine days, a Jap float plane came in and dropped a couple of bombs on the ground forces. One of our night fighters caught up with him and shot him down about 40 miles from us. A report on ground action said the Aussies had 232 casualties."

There was no further action on this assignment. The war ended the following month, and *Cofer* was called upon to aid in evacuation of prisoners of war and other occupation duties.

All was quiet on the Borneo front.

CHARLES J. KIMMEL

Brooklyn born Raymond Doolan now lives in Guam. He left high school to enlist in the navy on 14 October 1943, went through boot camp at Sampson, N.Y., and was assigned to *Charles J. Kimmel (DE-584)* when that ship was commissioned at Bethlehem Shipyard, Hingham, Mass. He remained aboard until decommissioning in January 1946.

> "There are many stories of sacrifice and heroism that are now part of history for the many veterans who participated in military combat to regain the Philippines. However, I would like to acquaint you with one incident, a story of personal heroism that resulted in the saving of 22 U.S. Army Air Force officers and enlisted men. They were survivors of a crashed C47 aircraft in enemy held territory on 2 June 1945 off Auqui Island, Philippines.
>
> My ship was on patrol southeast of Leyte when we received an urgent message from the Commander Naval Operations Base on Leyte. We were to attempt the rescue of a downed aircraft, located in the general vicinity of Auqui Island, south of Leyte Gulf. At that time, our military headquarters considered that island as bypassed hostile territory and with unconfirmed guerrilla activity. Faint radio signals from the crashed aircraft were weak but identifiable by our radio shack personnel.
>
> My DE arrived in the Auqui Island beach area after sunset, and all hands went to General Quarters. After a diversionary barrage of covering fire from the ship's guns, we illuminated with star shells and colored flares to confuse the enemy in the surrounding beach area. We also hoped to indicate to any survivors that we were friendly. A volunteer landing party was called to man the ship's only 21 foot motor whaleboat. The mission was to land on the beach under cover of darkness and attempt to rescue any surviving air crew and passengers. I was a 19 year old signalman, third class.
>
> I assisted the rescue whaleboat with searchlight communications for our boat commander, Lieutenant (J.G.) Edward J. Powers. The boat crew consisted of the lieutenant, a coxswain, boat engineer, signalman, and two seamen. The total armament consisted of 3-.45 caliber submachine guns and one sidearm. The boat signalman's only "weapon" was a portable battery powered aldis signal light! We had no ship-to-shore radio equipment. At the time of the beach landing in total darkness, no one knew the size of enemy strength. We did not know if our rescue team would encounter an ambush or possibly be sunk or damaged by an uncharted reef or an enemy mine field. Considering the risks involved, the potential hazards were many, and the possibility of death or capture by the enemy in such a remote location was a definite possibility.
>
> I recall that our DE's draft was 13 feet, and our final depth sounding from the bow was 15 feet as we anchored 1500 yards off the beach. The skipper was really taking chances. Nevertheless, the whaleboat landing took place.

The 22 surviving air crew and military passengers were located in the jungle and on the beach near the downed aircraft. During the initial landing and subsequent departure, our ship was visually contacted by signal light for continued fire and illumination support as the whaleboat attempted to retrieve survivors. These visible exchanges of light signals illuminated the rescue party and the survivors, adding to the boat crew's personal danger on the beach and during offshore transit to our ship. The boat was dangerously overloaded on both trips and within easy range of small arms fire from enemy infantry forces. After two trips to the beach landing area, all 22 airmen were successfully rescued.

Later, it was learned that this area had been mined. Surely, had these unarmed aviators and army passengers survived the night on the beach without rescue, they would have been located, attacked and killed by enemy forces in the early daylight hours. The surviving senior officer said one army officer and an enlisted man had left the group early on the previous day in an attempt to contact local guerrilla forces for evacuation assistance. They didn't return and their fate was uncertain.

Twenty-two men owe their lives to a courageous group of U.S. Navy DE sailors who entered enemy held territory at night in unknown waters, commando fashion, to rescue their fellow countrymen. I am proud to have been a part of that rescue mission, a small military action remembered only by those of us who served on one of the "Trim and Deadly" destroyer escorts of World War II."

Frank Reynolds and the monkey on *Chaffee*.

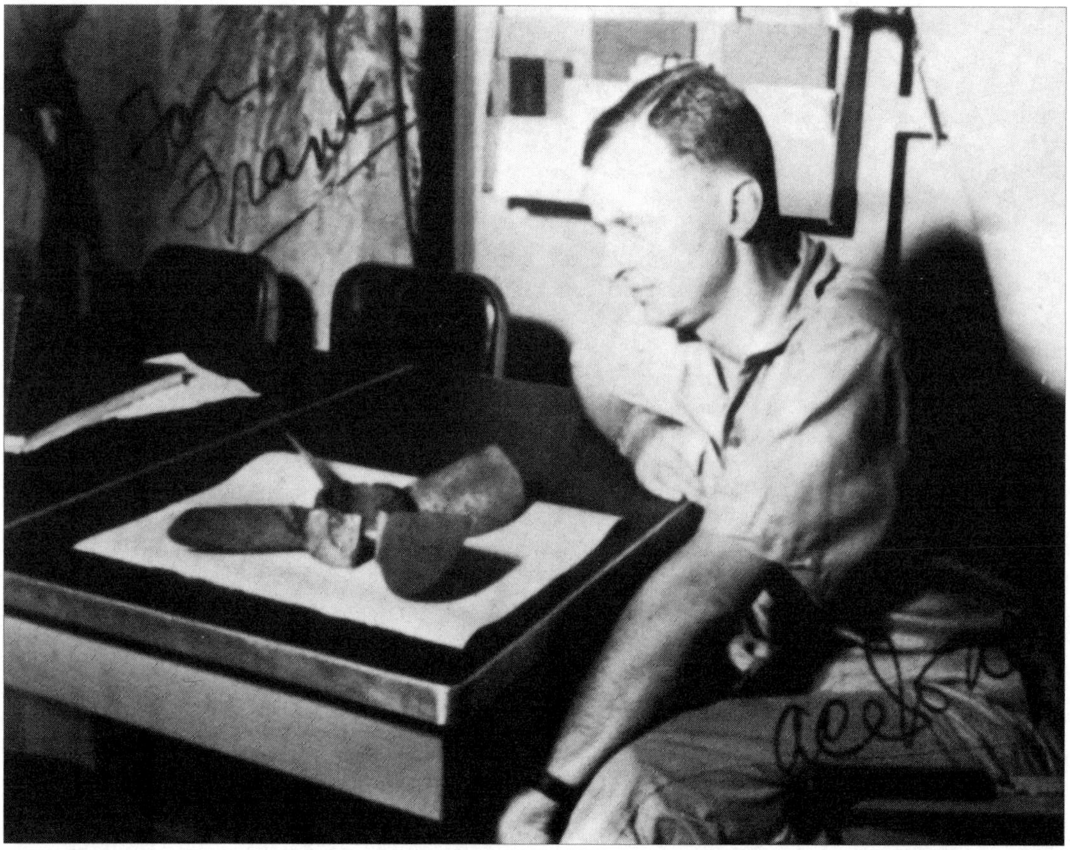

Priceless souvenir — Propeller left by torpedo as it passed through the hull on *Chaffee*.

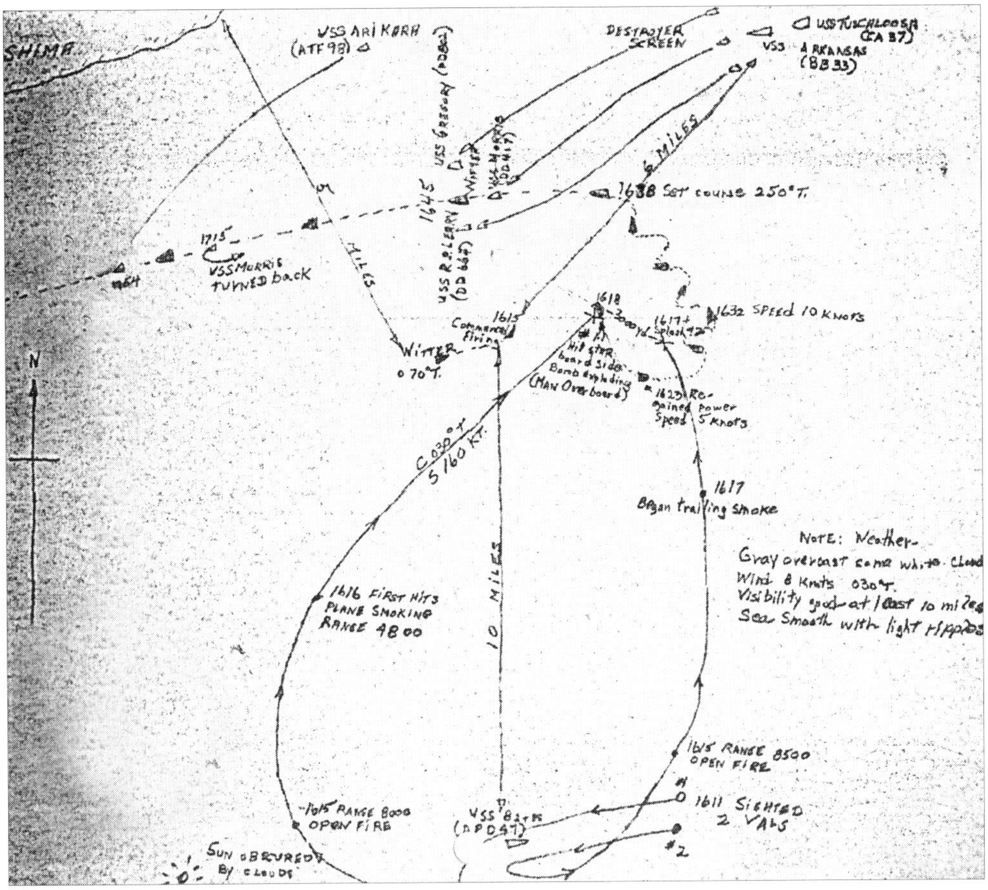

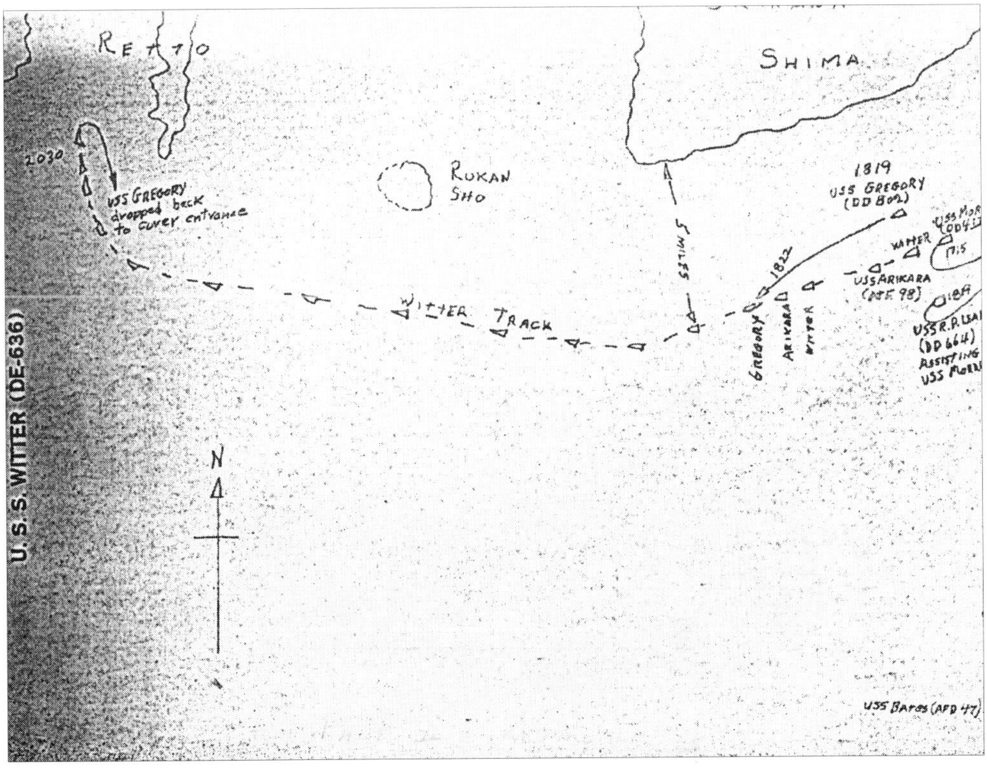

U.S.S. WITTER (DE-636)

Part 1 & 2 of action for *USS Witter (DE-636)*

Yokosuka P1Y1 ("Frances")

Nakajima C6N1, Saiun ("Myrt")

Kawanishi N1K1-J, Shiden ("George")

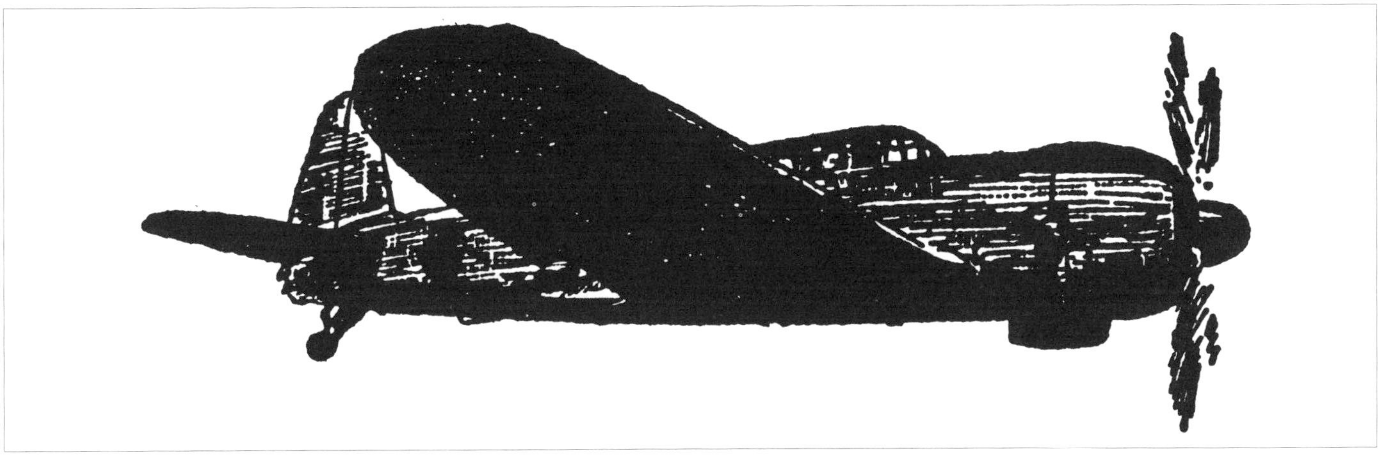

Nakajima B6N2, Tenzan ("Jill")

Mitsubishi G4M2 ("Betty") and Ohka Glide Bomb

Yokosuka D4Y2, Suisei ("Judy")

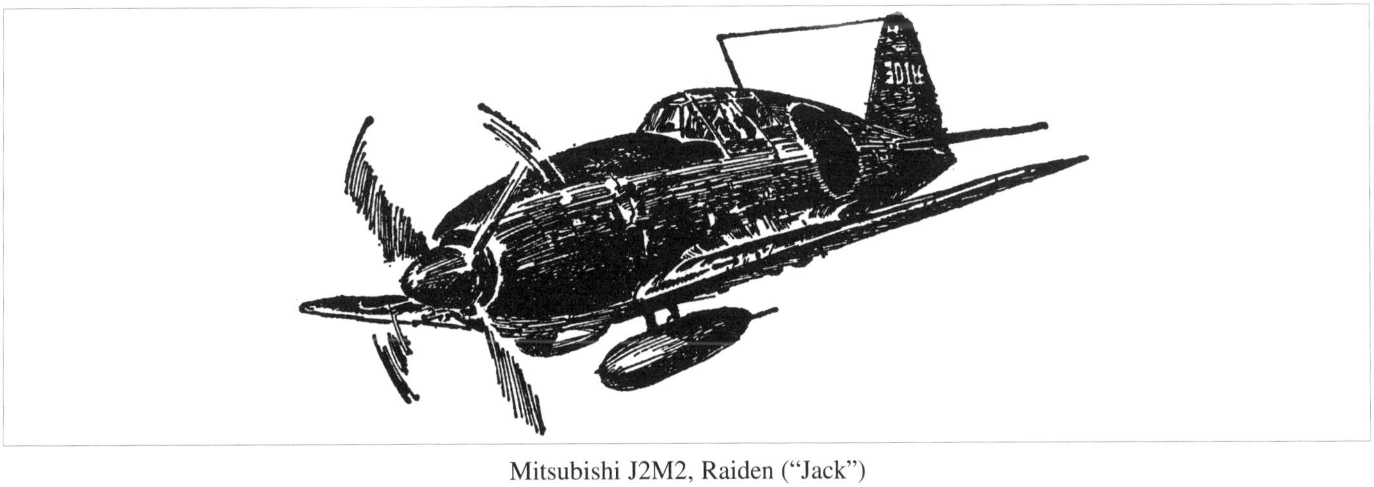

Mitsubishi J2M2, Raiden ("Jack")

Gaping hole where *kamikaze* dove into the *Bowers'* bridge structure. US Navy Photo

Lewis M. Andrews, Jr.

Chapter XIV - The Pacific Typhoons

The Savage Sea Can Kill

War at sea, as on land, is a fight between us and the other fellow. The enemy wants to kill us, so we kill him. But there is a killer who can be as dangerous as the enemy. He has claimed countless hulls and bones from the beginning of time. He is unbeatable, beautiful and horrible, the best and the worst. As many poems have been written about him as any other phenomenon of nature. He has been dreaded and he has been loved. HE IS THE SEA.

The Third Fleet was the most powerful war machine afloat that man had ever devised. Huge aircraft carriers with their squadrons of planes, flanked by mighty battleships, cruisers and destroyers swept all before them in their inexorable march to the heart of Japan. This was the Fleet that destroyed the mammoth ships of the Emperor, the son of the sun, and for a time the ruler of the Pacific and Indian Oceans. There was no force left on he face of the globe to challenge the Third Fleet, EXCEPT THE SEA!

On the forenoon watch, 17 December 1944, near the Philippines, the sea struck the Third Fleet. Before it subsided, it sank three destroyers, wrecked 200 aircraft, killed 790 officers and men and inflicted severe damage on:

4 Battleships
8 Aircraft carriers
7 Cruisers
11 Destroyers
3 Destroyer escorts
2 Oilers

The Commander-In-Chief, Pacific Fleet, Admiral Chester W. Nimitz, remarked, "It was a more crippling blow to the Third Fleet than it might be expected to suffer in a major action." The foe was a giant typhoon which inflicted more damage on the navy than any other storm since the famous hurricane at Apia, Samoa in March 1889. The Japanese, in their fondest dreams, had never wrought as much damage on our forces than did this typhoon!

The Second Battle of the Philippine Sea was largely concluded with most enemy vessels sunk, damaged or routed. . The struggle for conquest of the Philippines, however, was still being waged in bitter amphibious campaigns. The invasion of Mindoro was underway and receiving heavy air strike support from the Third Fleet. Fueling, particularly for destroyers and destroyer escorts, was always a matter of concern and priority. Admiral Halsey ordered fueling operations to begin on the morning of 17 December.

Meteorology, a very inexact science even today, was considerably less exact in 1944. Weather reports were made by search planes only in exceptional cases since they were reluctant to break radio silence. Such reports as were received were 12 hours old by the time they reached ships in the operating areas. .In this particular storm, each large aircraft carrier and the battleship *New Jersey (BB-62)* had a weatherman on board, but they failed to determine the ferocity of the impending storm. It burgeoned into a full typhoon almost unnoticed.

The night of the 17th, the refueling rendezvous was changed three times in an attempt to avoid and outguess the storm. The fourth change set a rendezvous for the morning of the 18th in the hope of finding smoother seas, but that position took many of the ships directly into the path of the storm. The wind backed and the seas rose rapidly, all evidences of a typhoon. At 1345 on the 18th, the first official reference to the storm being a typhoon was signalled by Admiral Halsey.

Destroyers and destroyer escorts had to break off fueling from battleships or carriers because of inability to hold station and the resultant snapping of hose lines. Other destroyers were unable even to commence fueling operations.

This was a cantankerous and unpredictable tempest. As the Third Fleet altered course, so did the typhoon. As its center roared in from the east, Halsey ordered a course to the northwest. The storm then changed direction, forcing the fleet to change to the southwest, only to be completely enveloped by the storm's fury. Hour after hour, the glass fell as the fleet wallowed in the vicious tempest. Admiral Halsey finally suspended fuel transfer maneuvers and placed the Fleet on a course which, it was expected, would avoid the full fury of the storm at 150 miles from the storm center. By 0700 on 18 December, the reading had dropped to 29.58 and kept falling rapidly until it reached a minimum of 27.95 at noon. A force 12 increasing north wind and turbulent sea caused considerable difficulty in steering.

Battleships acted like rafts in a white water maelstrom. Escort Carrier *Kwajalein (CVE-98)* lost its steering. Light Carriers *Cowpens (CV-25)* and *Monterey (CVL-26)* experienced gasoline fires when aircraft broke loose from their tethers on deck. The flight deck of *Hancock (CV-19)*, 57 feet above her waterline, scooped up green water! By that time, all ships except battleships had lost formation. All were laboring heavily, rolling in the troughs of the sea. Some ships reported visibility down to 3 feet as a result of heavy rain and spray. The commanding officer of the destroyer *Dewey (DD-349)* reported that the needle-like spray, driven by fierce winds, removed the paint from metal surfaces like a sand blast machine! With this type of havoc being played out on heavy warships, try to imagine the fury that was visited on destroyers and, above all, destroyer escorts.

By mid-afternoon, the storm center was only 35 miles distant, and the wind velocity was reported to be as much as 132 knots. Unfortunately, some of the destroyers had previously pumped out their water ballast, preparing to take on fuel. Consequently, they were riding high, in no condition to ride out a storm such as this. Severe damage was commonplace on destroyers such as *Alwyn (DD-355)* and *Hickox (DD-675)* which rolled 75 degrees with salt water pouring into their stacks, ventilators, intakes and the like. Imagine the terror and helplessness of the crews pinned against bulkheads and sides, all lights gone, interior communications and propulsion lost, lying broadside in the trough and at the mercy of the sea. Cables parted, rafts and small boats were torn away, antennae twisted into junk.

Three destroyers capsized and sank on the 18th. *Spence* was the first at 1100 when her rudder jammed; there were only 23 survivors. At about 1200, *Hull (DD-350)* was pinned down by the waves and rolled over; only 55 men and 7 officers, including her skipper, survived. Shortly thereafter, *Monaghan (DD-354)* disappeared; only 6 of her crew survived. . The normal complement of a destroyer was about 275-300 officers and men, about 850 for the three ships; the survival of a total of 91 highlights the immensity of the tragedy. The typhoon was aptly named – Cobra!

TASK FORCE 30.8
MELVIN R. NAWMAN

Lighting the Blow Torch with a Cigar

Melvin R. Nawman (DE-416) operated in Escort Division 72 with *Anzio (CVE-57), Mitchell (DE-417), Tabberer (DE-418)* and *Robert F. Keller (DE-419)*. This division, a hunter-killer unit of the Third Fleet, weathered the wrath of Typhoon Cobra.

The tremendous damage to vessels in Typhoon Cobra was an experience shared by *Melvin R. Nawman*. Remembering the original meaning of the word, *kamikaze*, the so-called Divine Wind that wrecked the fleets of the Kublai Khan when he attempted to invade Japan, one couldn't help but wonder if that wind were coming once more to save Japan.

Furious winds drove waves to the height of a 10 story building. Yeoman Ken Dempsey was on the bridge of the *Melvin R. Nawman*, and recalled a question he addressed to the Captain, Lieutenant Commander Fred W. Kinsley:

> "Sir, what does it take to tip this vessel over?" The Skipper said, "Ken, if you see the needle at 72 degrees and you're standing in a foot of water, start praying. That's it."
>
> "At the height of the typhoon, that needle went to 72 degrees and froze there," said Dempsey, "and we were standing in 2 feet of water. Believe me, I was praying."

He wasn't alone. Below decks, men strapped into bunks were also praying the 306 foot ship could ride out what was later declared to be the worst typhoon experienced by the U.S. Navy. Said Captain Kinsley of Marblehead, Massachusetts, one of 48 officers and enlisted men who recently gathered for a 3 day reunion:

> "I wasn't as worried as maybe I should have been. I was under the impression that destroyers or destroyer escorts would never sink purely as a result of the weather."

At one point, *Nawman* passed through the eye of the storm. The wind velocity momentarily dropped to zero. Said Kinsley:

> "But we still had mountainous waves. When the ship fell to the trough, you had the impression that you were in the Empire State Building, near the top, and the cable broke in the elevator."

The constant whiplashing of the mast caused a number of guys to snap, permitting the mast to teeter and partially tear itself from the deck plate. The mast created a dilemma because of its erratic swaying. Its fall was a certainty, but nobody could predict the direction. Whichever way it might collapse, it would be a dangerous threat to the security of the ship. Held by one remaining guy wire, the mast finally broke loose from the deck plate and dangled over the side, knocking out all communications and radar. In this precarious position, it had the potential to punch a hole in the ship.

Sid Dashevesky, Shipfitter First Class, went topside to cut the mast loose with a welder's torch. He was one of several shipmates who volunteered to go outside onto the deck to assist. Dashevesky wrote in a letter to Dempsey years later, prior to a reunion. "The wind was so fierce it kept blowing the torch out. Someone came out of the pilothouse with a lit cigar and helped to keep the torch lit."

Another seaman helped the exhausted Dashevesky, and the job was done. The loss of all electronics was somewhat balanced by the increased stability of the ship without the mast.

Nawman, out of communications for 20 hours, was on the flagship's "missing" list until she finally rendezvoused with other units of the scattered fleet. She limped back to Pearl Harbor for repairs. There were no personnel casualties.

But most of the reunion conversation was usually about the typhoon, Kinsley said. "He wasn't scared of the typhoon," Dempsey said with a laugh, "We were."

The typhoon damage was repaired, and the year 1945 brought action off the invasion beaches with the Fifth Fleet. *Melvin R. Nawman* continued to screen *Anzio* as its planes rained bombs on Japanese emplacements. At Iwo Jima, the ship was a scant 50 yards from the carrier *Bismarck Sea* when it was sunk in a *kamikaze* attack. See the chapter "*Iwo Jima to Okinawa*."

ROBERT F. KELLER

"I Knew That This Was Becoming a Struggle for Survival"

10 December 1944. *Robert F. Keller (DE-419)*, with Escort Division 72, screened the logistics ships supporting the landings on Mindoro. The Task Group then sped northwest on the 16th, straight into the teeth of a howling typhoon. On the morning of 18 December, the wind tore away anemometer vanes as the ship battled the waves astern of the carrier *Anzio (CVE-57)*. In the eerie mid-day darkness, *Keller* rose high in the air on the crest of monstrous waves, only to crash into the troughs below.

The nightmare is related by *Keller's* commanding officer, Lieutenant Commander R.J. Toner, and is Reprinted by Permission from "Proceedings," Copyright © 1976 U.S. Naval Institute.

"The harsh buzz of the sound-powered phone brought me sharply into wakefulness. I reached through the darkness toward the head of my bunk to grasp the accustomed shape of the phone from its cradle. As I answered 'Yes' into the mouthpiece, another part of my consciousness was aware of the staggering motion of the ship. I braced myself against the erratic actions of the destroyer escort which several times almost pitched me bodily from the bunk.

'This is the Officer of the Deck, Captain. The sea has been making up for the past hour or so. The wind has increased to gale force, and I'm having difficulty keeping station on the carrier. Also, the chief engineer has requested permission to commence deballasting.'

I glanced at the luminous hands of the ship's clock above the foot of my bunk. It was 0430. 'Is it light enough to make out the surface of the sea?' I asked.

'Not light enough to make out things clearly, Sir, but what I can see doesn't look good.'

'Very well, I'll be on the bridge in a few minutes. Meanwhile, tell the chief engineer not to deballast. I doubt if there is going to be much fueling today.'

The soft red light filled the sea cabin. I could feel the springs of the bunk sag deeply under me as an upward heave of the ship thrust my weight against them, then a light feeling in the pit of my stomach as the ship dropped from beneath me.

I would soon have to make a decision as to whether I should grant permission to deballast. This is done by pumping out the sea water which had been taken into the ship's fuel tanks to compensate for the weight of the fuel burned. To deballast would remove tons of water from the fuel tanks, making the ship lighter and, in effect, cause a comparative top heaviness, a dangerous condition for a ship in heavy weather. With an effort, I eased myself out of the rolling, pitching bunk to pull on my shirt and trousers.

Since there was no immediate emergency requiring my presence on the bridge, I made my way carefully into the darkened passageway, moving cautiously so as not to be thrown against jutting equipment, thence down the steep ladder leading to the wardroom, dimly lit with red battle lights. I moved slowly to the buffet, on which an electric coffee maker was bolted to the top. The coffee was swirling about in the glass container which was held firmly to the heating coils by metal bands. Pouring the coffee into a cup was quite a trick since I balanced myself against the leaping motion of the ship, holding the cup in one hand and cautiously pouring the coffee with the other, meanwhile attempting to maintain an upright position.

My mind reviewed the situation facing us as I sipped the hot, bitter coffee. An operational message received earlier had designated our Task Group amongst other units scheduled to fuel at first light. We were steaming a few thousand yards ahead of the carrier which, when fueling operations commenced, would detach specific ships from the antisubmarine screen to fuel and to rejoin the formation before other escorts were detached. *Keller's* turn would put us alongside the oiler at about 0830. Since it would require a few hours to deballast, we would have to start pumping within the next half hour if we were to be ready to commence fueling as scheduled.

I was not too concerned. *Keller* was my third combatant sea command since the war began, and the approaching heavy weather, although an unpleasant prospect, did not cause me undue concern; nor did I think it would present any unusual complications. We had fueled at sea in heavy weather several times, and the officers and men, as well as I, had profited by the experience. The ship had been secured for heavy weather before I had turned in last night. Lifelines had been rigged along the weather decks, and there was nothing to be done now but to recognize and take steps to handle each situation as it arose.

I finished the coffee and placed the cup in its hole in the fiddle board. Leaving the wardroom, I mounted the ladder leading to the pilot house which led to the open bridge. The Quartermaster of the Watch reported that the barometer was reading less than 28 inches and falling fast. About 30 inches is normal at sea level.

The 'open bridge' on a DE is just that; it is completely open to the weather. Its principal advantage is that it gives a 360 degree view of the waters about the ship. As I emerged onto the open bridge, I was immediately conscious of a stinging sensation in my nostrils, caused by the mist-like spume that was swirling about the bridge. The watch personnel were wearing handkerchiefs tied about their noses. I did the same and felt an immediate relief. I noted that the Officer of the Deck and the bridge watch were soaking wet, but the howling wind was warm and humid, and no one bothered to put on heavy weather clothing. I took a firm hold on the spray shield of the bridge and tried to sense the temper of the wind and sea.

The first light of dawn on 18 December was beginning to break in a dirty, yellowish haze, sufficient to disclose the surface of the sea only within 200 yards of the ship. As I watched, towering masses of dull, olive green sea would build up on our port quarter, overtake the ship until the fantail was awash in a swirling coil of foam that reached to the depth charge racks. The confused mass would then pass under us like an immense sea creature, the ship yawing with a drunken motion as it rushed along with the crest. Then the bow would rise sharply, and a heavy drag could be felt as though a gigantic hand had grasped the laboring ship. The vibration of the twin screws, sometimes spinning free of the sea, caused the ship to shudder as the bow fell rapidly, buried in a smother of foam. The various coachwhip antennae about the bridge were bent almost 45 degrees before the driving blast of the wind. The spindrift, cut sharply from the crests of the seas, scudded along the troughs like dust along a country road on a windy day. Then, striking the ship,it swirled about its superstructure and struck with a hissing sound against the stack abaft the open bridge.

I had seen enough. I knew that there would be no fueling operations conducted this day. I directed the Officer of the Deck to have reveille sounded and to caution all hands over the PA system not to use the weather decks, but to remain in shelter, also to inform the chief engineer to secure the fueling detail. My capable executive officer came to the bridge at this moment and I asked him to see to it that all watertight doors were closed, the ship placed in maximum watertight integrity, and the most experienced and skillful officers and men stationed in all spaces where machinery or special equipment was operating. I had to shout with full lungs to make myself heard.

Daylight, when it came, was merely a lighter, yellowish, opaque haze and, if anything, visibility had decreased. The wind had backed, that is it had shifted in a counter-clockwise direction, so that it was now coming at us with rising intensity from slightly abaft the starboard beam. For some time, a strange shrill sound had been impinging upon my consciousness. I suddenly realized that it was the shriek of the wind about the mainstays of the mast. With the shifting of the wind, a confused sea had built up, causing the ship to lurch and yaw in wild, unpredictable motions. The Officer of the Deck reported that the ship was very sluggish in answering the helm and that he was having considerable difficulty conning her. I then relieved him of control, giving direct orders to the helmsman and engine order telegraph operator.

A tactical signal received over TBS reversed the formation course by having all ships execute a simultaneous 180 degree turn. Execution of this maneuver placed the carrier ahead of us on a southwesterly course with the destroyers in an arc astern. The carrier cancelled fueling operations and ordered all ships to rig for typhoon weather; the course change just executed was to take the formation out of the dangerous semi-circle of the typhoon. I had to assist the twin rudders with full speed on the outboard engine to bring *Keller* to the new course signalled by the carrier.

The awareness of the passage of time began to recede as my attention was more and more absorbed in the conning of the ship. I had experienced hurricanes in the Caribbean in one of my previous commands and heavy gales in both the Atlantic and Pacific Oceans in the others. Yet somehow, without ever forming the thought into words, I knew that this was becoming a struggle for survival. Normally, a course to steer is given to the helmsman, and he keeps the ship on course. However, the confused sea was making it difficult for him to keep the ship anywhere near the course of our formation. Occasionally, therefore, I would have to order an extreme amount of rudder and an increase or decrease in speed of one of the engines to add to the effect of the twin rudders and to assist the ship to struggle back to the desired heading.

The executive officer was standing beside me. Cupping his hands to his mouth, he yelled into my ear in order to make himself heard. 'Captain, the bottom has fallen out of the barometer, and we've just heard a TBS transmission from the carrier to the Fleet Commander, saying that she's having difficulty maintaining her course, that some of her planes have broken loose on her hangar deck and that fires have broken out.' I nodded to let him know I understood. There was nothing we could do except remain afloat and stay in her vicinity. I cupped my hands and yelled into the exec's ear 'Is everything secure below decks?' The exec nodded, turned and disappeared into the pilot house to continue his rounds.

In periods of such intense concentration, the body and its demands recede and fuse into a mental-spiritual sensing. It extends one's reactions to the utmost limits of the ship so that her next movement becomes as responsive and anticipated as the movements of one's own limbs. In this strange orchestration, I was conscious that the wind had continued to back and to reach crescendos of violence. Immense seas now came hurtling at us from forward of our starboard beam, the wind knifing their crests in a fury of spindrift. The ship was rolling deeply, now laboring up and across a mountainous wall of ugly sea, or pitching crazily with a skidding roll toward the depth of the trough.

These thunderous seas were not in regular sequence, nor from a predictable direction. The heavy and confused seas built up by the driving blast of the winds in their earlier directions were still not overcome by the inhuman force of the typhoon now raging upon us. I used every combination of rudders and engines, yet the powerful geared turbines and the twin rudders had little effect against the titanic forces beating down upon the slender destroyer escort hull. The ship in torment lay spent, almost inert in the fury about her. I could feel my insides quiver when an unpredictable sea smashed into her and buried her under its immense weight. Then, with agonizing slowness, she sluggishly achieved a movement of her own. Suddenly, without any transition, she was racing down a tremendous incline. I yelled for full rudder in the opposite direction.

The sensation is comparable to the sudden, breath taking drop of a roller coaster. There did not seem to be any reaction to the rudders. For an interminable time, we rushed down that vast slope. I felt a brief flash of thankfulness that she had not yawed or skidded with her stern. This was a common fault with this class of ships in a following sea, as they were designed to turn quickly. Suddenly, the bottomless rush was over, a cross sea smashed into *Keller's* starboard bow and the impact could be felt through every frame of the ship. I mid-shipped rudders and waited for the next onslaught.

Looking back now, I recall an impersonal detachment from everything but sensing the ship and the force of wind and seas. I have a sailor's profound respect for the sea and I have felt her many times in my life, but this absorption was too intense to admit awareness of fear. I recall that, from time to time, someone would yell into my ear, giving me bits of information. The fire on the carrier was under control, one ship in our formation reported her lifeboat shattered, another reported damage to parts of her superstructure. Our radar indicated that *Tabberer* on our starboard bow had closed to one half her former distance. The formation of our Task Group disintegrated as each ship fought for her life. The reports I received indicated that, so far, *Keller* was unharmed, except for superficial breakage. Each time, I would acknowledge the information; then my mind and that part of my being that sensed the ship withdrew into the intimate problem of keeping her afloat.

Ordinarily so responsive to her powerful engines, *Keller* lay like a stricken creature without reaction to her rudders or radical speed changes. She was almost 'In Irons', an old expression from the days of sail, when a ship, coming about from one tack to another, failed to pay off on the new tack and lay helpless in the eye of the wind. Then gradually *Keller* would take on a life of her own, and slowly the gyro repeater would indicate that she was coming back to the course I had ordered to meet the next thrust of the sea.

Someone was pulling my arm violently and pointing toward the murk, the color of burnt amber, on our starboard bow. He was excited and yelling at the top of his lungs, but I couldn't hear him. My eyes were stinging and blurred from the driving force of the spindrift. Then suddenly I saw what caused his alarm. There, only a few hundred yards from us, pitching high over the crest of a sea with its entire forefoot uncovered, was the sharp reinforced bow of a destroyer escort. Behind her, I could make out the tophamper of the mast. The looming shape was almost upon us.

I yelled into the voice tube that led to the pilot house, 'All engines ahead flank!' Then, grasping the cradle phone of the TBS, I yelled into it the code name of *Tabberer*. Those within the radio shack, removed from the shriek of the wind, told me later that they heard my voice over the loudspeaker in strong urgent tones call *Tabberer* and say, 'My engines are ahead flank, back down full or you'll ram me!' A moment later, over the loud speaker came the calm Georgia voice of the skipper of *Tabberer*, my friend, saying 'Rogah, Ah'm backin' full'.

All watertight doors and hatches had long since been secured. Experienced personnel, including damage control parties, were manning their stations. In situations like this, where one is committed to a course of action, when all has been done that seamanship and experience indicates, everything hangs on a heartbeat. It's up to the ship and the imponderables now. *Tabberer*, every part of her visible as were the figures on her open bridge, buried her bow into an immense sea abeam of us. Then, seeming to leap clear of it, she passed 100 yards astern of *Keller* in a flurry of foam and spray; then she was lost in the murk.

Shortly after noon, the Quartermaster's log indicated a rising barometer. The wind continued to back and, although it no longer blew with its former insane fury, the ship continued to make heavy going of it; so I kept the conn. I remember eating an apple that was handed to me and thinking that the salty taste of the spray mingled well with that of the fruit. Toward late afternoon, the sky to the west cleared and the sea abated sufficiently to permit me to change course and rejoin the carrier, whose distant shape and those of other ships could be made out scattered along the horizon.

On the following day, *Tabberer* rescued several survivors. Accordingly, *Anzio*, *Keller* and two other relatively undamaged ships of *CortDiv 72*, were ordered into the area where the survivors had been picked up to conduct a thorough search.

The tremendous seas worked up by the typhoon were still running. The carrier, normally a relatively stable ship, was rolling and pitching in such a manner that it seemed to us on the hard riding destroyer escorts that flight operations would be impossible. Yet *Anzio* flew her scheduled search missions for several days.

On the second day of the search, the carrier took a green sea over her bow. The immense flood of sea water washed a seaman overboard from a relatively protected position below her flight deck. *Keller* was ordered to pick him up. I was on the bridge and immediately took the conn. I directed the Officer of the Deck to have Combat Information Center plot the position of the carrier and to give me a course to a position 500 yards astern of the carrier's present position. As I brought the ship about and headed in the general direction of where the man might be, 'Man Overboard' quarters were sounded and additional lookouts were stationed.

'There he is,' 'I see him.' Several men were pointing almost dead ahead. Now a new problem presented itself. I realized that we could not launch a boat in these seas. I directed the exec not to lower the whaleboat, but to rig as many mattresses as possible along our starboard side and to have several strong swimmers standing by with lines secured to their life jackets.

I reduced speed until we had bare steerageway, and then sighted the small figure in the water ahead of us. The helmsman in the pilot house could not see him, so he was conned toward the man's position, who sometimes dropped out of sight behind the crest of a huge sea. I had a clear view from my position on the starboard side of the bridge. I backed the engines when the man was about 50 yards to leeward and somewhat forward of our beam. *Keller* handled beautifully; the wind caused us to drift down upon the man. He caught a line heaved from our deck, fastened it about himself, and was hauled aboard without injury. I feared the injury that might have resulted had he been dashed against our bilge keel, a strip of steel about a foot wide, welded to the turn of the bilge to reduce the ship's roll.

The rescued man was cared for by the medicos. A signal to the carrier advised our recovery and that we were proceeding to rejoin the formation. I increased speed slowly as we headed almost directly into the long surging seas. After a few minutes of observing how she handled at ten knots, I was about to order an increase to twelve knots when, to my astonishment, I heard the cry 'Man Overboard'! *Keller* had taken a huge green sea over the foc'sle, which roared down the port weather deck. Then, with the roll of the ship, it had crossed to the starboard side of the fantail and washed overboard the watch at the depth charge racks.

I instinctively gave the order 'Right Full Rudder!', to throw the stern away from the man. Fortunately, he was still in sight and apparently uninjured. We executed the same procedure as for the previous recovery and had our man on board in a very short time. *Anzio* reversed the formation course so that all ships would pass close aboard *Keller*, enabling her to rejoin the formation without difficulty.

Our double rescue was a blessing in disguise, for it gave us confidence and an expertise which we were able to put to excellent use two days later. On the third day of the search, one of our lookouts sighted what appeared to be some wreckage on our starboard bow. The mid-morning was bright with heavy seas still running, but the wind somewhat abated. Through my binoculars, I was able to make out the figures of 3 or 4 men grouped together. The seas were still too heavy to risk lowering a boat. As a result of our previous experiences, mattresses were rigged over the side without an order being given as soon as 'Man Overboard' was piped.

As we approached the castaways, I was engrossed in handling the ship and couldn't pay attention to their condition other than to note their location. However, I was struck by what seemed to be an oddity; the men appeared to be wearing white gloves. As *Keller* drifted down upon the huddled group, several men volunteered to go overboard to assist the survivors who appeared to be in a weakened condition. Permission was granted, and these brave men risked circling sharks as well as the sharp edges of the bilge keel. Riflemen were standing by to shoot any sharks that got too close. The four survivors were brought aboard without injury, along with their floater net which had supported them and our rescuers.

The rescued men were very young, 17 to 19 years of age. They were weak but lucid after three days and four nights on the floater net without food or water. Several other men had been with them but, one by one, had slipped away. The evening before we sighted them, a chief petty officer, who had become delirious, had said 'Excuse me, lads, I'm going below to the chief's mess for a sandwich.' Before anyone could stop him, the Chief cleared himself from the floater net and was last seen swimming away over the crest of a wave.

The medicos later informed me that, what had appeared to be white gloves on the men's hands, was actually a condition known as 'Immersion Hands (and feet)', caused by excessive exposure in water.

The survivors reported that they had seen the rigid life rafts go end-over-end, spilling men and equipment into the raging seas. However, those lucky enough to reach the floater nets – an open weave net of lines with rubber disks secured at intervals – survived the worst of the typhoon. The floater nets were as flexible as the motion of the seas and the survivors, their feet thrust through the open weave of the nets, rode atop the waves. At times, an immense sea would crash down on them and they would emerge choking, half drowned. Despite warning, some would gulp whole mouthfuls of salt water, causing a few to become crazed.

Two days after the last rescue, one of our lookouts sighted a body floating in the now much calmer seas. We put over a boat but, as it approached the body, a shark was sighted. I gave orders over the loud speaker to the boat officer not to allow any of the men to enter the water. A line was placed about the body to tow it to the ship. A stretcher was lowered, and the body was hoisted aboard.

The body was dressed in the uniform of a chief petty officer.

None of the survivors recognized the corpse. The medicos had the painful task of taking finger prints, identifying dental work, scars and other markings. Modern destroyers no longer have sail makers, an extinct rate in the Navy. However, the boatswains mates sewed the body in a canvas shroud and weighted it with 40 millimeter rounds.

After all these years, I still recall the brilliant Pacific sunset as I walked to the fantail to read the 'Service For the Dead'. The ship was at GQ, except for a small representative group of the ship's company, drawn up on either side of the fantail near the flag-draped figure lying on the deck. The men's bodies swayed in unison with the surge and lift of the sea. All hands uncovered. Then, from the Book of Common Prayer, I read the short and beautiful words for Burial at Sea. The burial detail had lifted the body on its wooden pallet and, when I read the words 'We therefore, Oh Lord, commit the body of our shipmate unto Thy Hands and into the depths', the inboard end of the pallet was raised and the body launched into the sea, leaving the fluttering colors held by a boatswains mate. Taps were sounded, the traditional three rounds fired, then the shrill piping of the boatswain calling 'Now secure from Burial Service'.

For several days, the area in which the destroyers went down was thoroughly searched by ships and planes. Orders were finally received to secure the search and proceed to Ulithi Atoll. When we anchored in the vast lagoon, we made preparations to transfer the survivors to a hospital ship. By this time, with the resiliency of youth, all were sufficiently recovered to walk to the gangway and enter the waiting boat without assistance. Two of the men still wore bandages on their hands.

Prior to departing from Ulithi for the next phase of the Philippines campaign, I recommended decorations for the officers and men who went overside during the rescue of the survivors. For the others, I held Meritorious Mast and awarded Letters of Commendation which became a part of their service records.

Keller's crest, amongst those of other ships I have commanded, is above me in my study as I write. Two tridents, quartered on a field of red, two lamps of learning quartered on a field of blue – and beneath, *Multum in Parvo*.

TABBERER

"He Must Have Cut His Teeth on a Marlinespike"

7 December 1944. As *Tabberer (DE-418)*, commanded by Lieutenant Commander Henry L. Plage, was steaming in company with the Third Fleet fueling group to the east of the Philippines, rising wind and a choppy sea forced her to break off preparations to take on fuel. By evening, the little warship was fighting a full typhoon.

This author was fortunate in having been able to locate the reports of the captain which so vividly revealed that officer's "forehandedness," an old navy euphemism for being prepared for the worst well before the need arises. In addition, we read between the lines the words of a confident commander disseminating courage from the top down. He talks about lost steerageway and being trapped in deep troughs as survivable situations. He accepts rolls of 72 degrees from the vertical with confidence in the self-righting ability of his ship.

"0200 on 18 December. *Tabberer* was steaming in the screen of the carrier *Anzio (CVE-57)* with *Escort Division 72*. Because of the helmsman's difficulty in maintaining his heading and the proximity of vessels on the same base course as this DE, the commanding officer increased speed and turned the vessel sharply from the base course in order to get clear of other ships.

The new course put the vessel in the trough of the sea, but it was not considered dangerous since the roll was not exceeding 40 degrees. When well clear of other ships, this DE was brought back to the base course, southeast. However, the course proved to be untenable because the ship kept falling into the trough. An attempt was made to keep the vessel headed down wind but this was impossible, although various speeds up to 18 knots were used with full rudder. Ahead full on one engine while backing full with the other engine was attempted but without result. (Any destroyer or destroyer escort man knows that full ahead on one engine and the same in reverse on the other will invariably cause the ship to whip around, literally on a dime. The failure of this DE to respond accordingly highlights the fury of wind and sea.)

Seventy-five percent of fuel capacity was aboard; as much fuel oil as possible was shifted to the port tanks to balance the starboard list when it became apparent that the ship would have to ride out the storm with wind and sea on the port beam.

Visibility was about 30 feet. The ship had been riding quite well at 10 knots, rolling up to 55 degrees. In spite of various changes of wind direction and attempts by the captain to steady up on a course, the ship invariably fell back into the trough.

1315. The barometer began to rise, and other ships were picked up on radar from 2000 to 5000 yards ahead. They were identified as the destroyers *Hickox (DD-673)* , *Benham (DD-796)* and destroyer escort *Waterman (DE-740)*. Over the TBS radio, it was learned that all the DEs were in the trough, steaming at three knots and without steering control due to the wind and sea. This vessel reduced speed to three knots and remained at this speed until the storm was over in order to avoid collision with other ships ahead. The maximum roll experienced was 72 degrees to starboard, the ship recovering rapidly with no hesitation.

The lower ceramic insulator on the main port guy to the top of the mast crumbled in a quick 60 degree roll to starboard. (Lengthy wire cable on ships are usually interrupted with ceramic insulators to block or reduce the flow of a lightning strike.) The loss of this insulator gave the main guy about three inches of slack, and the mast began a slight movement back and forth. An effort was made to take up on the turnbuckle, but the men were unable to hold their positions in the furious wind. Soon after, the second insulator shattered, giving the main port guy more slack. As each insulator disintegrated, the mast swayed in an increasing arc, in turn shattering more insulators until the mast top whipped about eight feet, side to side, breaking the weld at the step (base). The severe motion put a very heavy strain on the port guys. This continued ominously until evening when the top insulator of the main port guy crunched, leaving that stay so slack that the intermediate guy took all the strain and parted immediately. This put all of the strain on the main guy attached to the top of the mast with no support halfway up the mast, as previously supplied by the intermediate guy.

1828. The mast buckled on a 50 degree roll, and the top fell over the starboard side, crushing the starboard flag bag and the number three floater net basket. The base of the mast rested at the signal bridge level, the bull horn catching it on the starboard main deck bulwark. All engines were stopped. A cutting torch and axes had been kept standing by, and the mast was soon cleared from the side. If the mast had fallen on the ship, the various radar and other antennae could have been saved. However, since the mast was dangerously banging the side of the ship, it was cut loose as soon as possible. The ship's roll was improved immediately. All power had been previously cut from all leads to the mast shortly before it fell, and no danger from live power leads was present."

After cutting away the shrouds of the mast, and free at last, *Tabberer* was able to proceed. She could not transmit but was still able to receive radio messages via the coachwhip antennae mounted on the bridge.

During the height of the storm, special watches had been set on all operating machinery, and boiler water levels had been kept at a maximum. Water entered the air vents to the engine spaces and fell on the generators and switchboards, causing a few minor electrical shorts and sparking. The affected areas were covered with canvas, and no more trouble was experienced. A canvas sleeve attached to each flooding vent led the water away from the electrical equipment. Because of the heavy rolls, lubricating oil from the turbine in the turbo-generator was thrown into the generator, threatening to oil soak the generator windings. . The oil level was lowered to a minimum safe level, and a shield was placed over the generator. The port engine began excessive vibration on three different occasions during the storm. The engine was stopped and started slowly again, eliminating the vibration, the cause of which was never determined. Other minor engineering casualties occurred but were handled as they arose.

When the mast fell, one flag bag and all radio antennae were lost except the radio direction finder antenna. The Morse code receiver was quickly hooked into the RDF antenna, and "Fox" guard (long range radio channel from Commander, Pacific Fleet) was resumed. Only eight messages were missed! The emergency TBL (voice) transmitter antenna was rigged and ready for use by midnight.

The Morse code transmitter emergency antenna was rigged and ready for use. An emergency TBS antenna was rigged atop the pilot house and, by late afternoon of 19 December, the TBS was ready for use. By the morning of 20 December, virtually all radio receivers and transmitters were usable with effective communication the same as the former permanent installation. The emergency radio measures were extremely helpful in the rescue of survivors carried out by this vessel as the storm receded.

The motor whale boat had been previously rigged in and was secured with gripes (canvas straps) plus additional 5" lines. Although the boat was lashed as securely as possible, the constant heavy roll made it work free of some of the lashings with resultant disabling damage to hull and engines.

The 5" ammunition stowage battens were carried away in the extreme rolls; the projectiles and powder cans broke out of their stowage and created a delicate situation before they could be secured. Taken all in all, this vessel was very seaworthy in inclement weather and could withstand rolls in excess of 72 degrees without danger of capsizing!

The storm eased rapidly on the evening of the 19th. *Tabberer* gained visual communication with *Dewey (DD-349)*. Both set course and speed, proceeding to the Task Force 38 rendezvous, with *Dewey* standing radar guard for the DE, giving courses and speed to make by visual signals.

2150. Chief Radioman Ralph Elden Tucker was rigging emergency antennae near the stack when he heard a shout and noticed a small light on our starboard beam. He immediately called 'Man overboard'. The ship was promptly turned toward the light and maneuvered to pick up a man in the beam of a 24 inch searchlight. The first impression was that he had fallen overboard from *Dewey*. However, when aboard, he stated that the destroyer *Hull* had capsized during the typhoon and that there were probably more men in the water in that vicinity. (Refer to the capsizing of destroyers *Hull*, *Monaghan* and *Spence* in the prelude to this chapter.)

Immediate search of the area was instigated. The first man had been recovered at 2200. One or two whistles were heard in the distance, attracting the ship in that direction. Fifteen minutes later, a second man was located and brought aboard. It was very difficult to find the swimmers with the 24 and 12 inch lights. They were in troughs much of the time and the lights would pass over their heads. Also, due to the many white caps on the water, it was difficult to distinguish one from a swimmer. In a rescue maneuver, the ship had to proceed to an upwind position, about 50 yards above the man, and then drift down to him. This did not take long since the wind was still quite strong.

At times when men were being brought aboard, the ship's roll would put the edge of her main deck under water. The task of locating survivors was facilitated by the small lights attached to their kapok jackets and by their blowing whistles and shouting. When no more men could be seen or heard in that immediate area, a systematic search was begun. The ship was stopped every 10 minutes; all lights were turned out, and all eyes searched for life jacket lights and listened for whistles or shouts. Several men were located in this manner. A whistle could be heard much farther than our lights could spot them because of the heavy seas. All ventilating blowers in the bridge structure were turned off to cut the noise level on the bridge to a minimum. The pitometer (speed) log had been damaged so that the dead reckoning tracer could not be used to control the search. The rescue operation was conducted entirely by manual dead reckoning through the night.

The destroyer *Benham (DD-796)*, which had been in company with Dewey, stayed in the area until about 2400 on 19 December and then proceeded to the rendezvous as she had not located any survivors. The emergency antennae, previously rigged for a transmitter and receiver, enabled us to contact a shore station, but the strength of the signal was weak. The frequency was changed, and a message reporting our damage and location of *Hull* survivors was given to *Benham* at 0343 for relay. No more men were located until daylight when survivors were picked up at various times through the morning. Until later in the day, there was no concentration of survivors; they were strewn about the area. Lieutenant Commander James Alexander Marks, commanding officer of *Hull*, was the 18th survivor rescued. As each man was recovered, a lookout (All off-duty crewmen were lookouts) would spot another man in the vicinity, usually up to 1500 yards away. The sea was much calmer, although still quite rough.

After the 0950 recovery, no others were seen in the general vicinity. Since several men had been recovered in this immediate area, it was decided to start another expanding box search with the present position as the center. The pitometer log had been put back in operation, and the search was conducted from the CIC with the executive officer in charge. With the sea becoming less rough, the search was planned so as to cover a visual area of 1500 yards on each side of the ship. .

1310. A message from the Third Fleet Commander directed *Tabberer* to proceed to a rendezvous with other damaged ships 90 miles south of her position, to arrive there by sunset, and then proceed to base. . It was believed that other men were in the water but so scattered that it would be very difficult to find them. Search was continued as long as possible before heading to the rendezvous at 1400.

Six minutes after the DE altered course, another man was spotted and recovered. A careful search was carried out, and the course was resumed to the rendezvous. Fourteen minutes later, still another man was sighted and picked up. The search was continued in that area although it was now impossible to make the appointed locale on time. A course was again taken toward the rendezvous, although all hands hoped more survivors would be sighted before long. Twenty minutes later, a group of two officers and five enlisted men were sighted and recovered. One of the officers was Lieutenant (junior grade) George Hand Sharp, son of Rear Admiral Alexander Sharp, Commanding Mine Craft, Pacific Fleet.

Lieutenant (jg) Sharp had lashed his group together in a circle early in the morning and had kept them together, although several had wanted to swim toward this ship which could be seen in the distance all day. He stated that he could see the DE conducting an expanding box search and would eventually get to his group. The only reason the group was spotted was because seven men together could be seen at two miles while the lookouts would never have seen a single man at that distance.

The course to the rendezvous seemed to be a profitable one, the men apparently being strung out on a line of bearing. .That course, therefore was continued. Between 1550 and 1630, another four men were recovered. Several sightings were made but all proved to be empty kapok life jackets. It was debated whether to send another report to the Commander of the Third Fleet reporting that we were still finding men and would stay in the area or proceed to the rendezvous and arrive about three hours late. The Third Fleet Commander's message saved this DE's captain from making a difficult decision. The ship was ordered to stay in the area and search until dawn the following morning.

The crew cheered when told that the search was to be continued, even though they had been through a typhoon the day before and had not slept in over 36 hours. The forty-first man was recovered at 1830. Sunset had begun, and this man fortunately had enough lung power left to make himself heard. Later that night, communication was established with the Commander Third Fleet and he was sent a report of rescue operations.

He directed this ship to remain in the area, searching throughout the night, until relieved by an escort carrier with escorts. The area was searched all night without success, although it was believed several men had been rescued during the night by destroyers of the Task Force that passed through the area.

0840. The carrier *Rudyard Bay (CVE-81)* with two escorts relieved *Tabberer*, ordered her to proceed to base and to be alert for destroyer *Spence* survivors. At 1050, a raft was sighted, and ten *Spence* survivors were taken aboard. They reported that several more men had been on the raft the evening before but swam off during the night. A retiring search was immediately started, and the *Rudyard Bay* was promptly notified. Sixteen minutes later, two more *Spence* survivors were rescued and two more within the next 20 minutes. *Rudyard Bay* with escorts now arrived on the scene, started a retiring search and ordered *Tabberer* to resume course to the base. Forty-one survivors from *Hull*, including the skipper and four other officers, plus fourteen from *Spence*, a total of fifty-five had been rescued by *Tabberer*.

Survivors heaped their praises on Captain Plage and his crew for their courage, determination and magnificent seamanship in rescuing men from the brutal sea. Captain Toner of *Robert F. Keller*, whose typhoon experience is related in the preceding narrative, recounted what the modest skipper of *Tabberer* did not enter in his reports of damage and survivor rescues:

"*Tabberer* received from Admiral Halsey 'Well done for a sturdy performance'. In inquiring about her captain, Halsey fully expected to hear that he was an old salt, possibly from the merchant marine, who had 'cut his teeth on a marlinespike'. He was amazed to learn that Plage owed his 'salty' experience to NROTC at Georgia Tech!

A few days later, as *Tabberer* proceeded through the channel into the immense lagoon where a major portion of the Third Fleet lay at anchor, the *Essex* class attack carrier flying the flag of Commander Third Fleet sent a signal to *Tabberer*, challenging her to identify herself. *Tabberer* gave the proper reply. Then came a puzzled signal from the carrier 'What type of ship are you?' Because of *Tabberer's* dismasted condition, the signal watch on the huge aircraft carrier could not identify her by sight. Weary and somewhat exasperated, Captain Plage signalled in reply, 'Destroyer escort, what type ship are you?"

After anchoring in his assigned berth, the captain laid below to the wardroom for a cup of coffee. Before the cup was finished, an excited messenger appeared at the doorway. 'Captain, Admiral Halsey's barge, flying his flag, is standing toward us!' The Skipper grabbed his cap and raced to the gangway. 'Good Lord', he thought, 'I bring in a dismasted ship, then sent that damn fool message insulting the Admiral's flagship'.

Admiral Halsey was piped aboard, and the smile on his face reassured the skipper. All hands were called to quarters, and Admiral Halsey pinned on the Legion of Merit for our captain's actions in saving the ship and rescuing survivors.

Outstanding rescue efforts during the storm also won several members of *Tabberer's* crew Navy and Marine Corps medals and the ship, the Navy Unit Commendation."

WATERMAN

"I Got Guts but I Don't Want to See 'Em"

After escorting Service Force units supporting the Leyte landings, *Waterman (DE-740)* operated between 2 November and 23 December, screening carrier forces east of the Philippines.

Sunday morning, 17 December 1944. The sea was choppy. Nothing was thought of that. Her crew had ridden the outer edge of a typhoon last trip out and thought they had seen it all. But not quite.

While operating in Destroyer Division 104, along with *CortDiv 72*, in Task Group 30.8, *Waterman* encountered the worst weather of her career, the infamous Typhoon, "Cobra." Her Commanding Officer, Lieutenant Commander J.H. Stahle, recalled:

"This day (18 December) was a never to be a forgotten one and was indelibly impressed in the minds of the crew."

0715. It was frequently necessary to use full speed to bring the ship's head back to the proper course. Fortunately, the *Waterman* had 84 percent fuel and was well ballasted with salt water. The heavy sea made it impossible to gain the new screening station. The ship rolled heavily in the trough, and steering conditions were extremely difficult. All attempts at fueling were unsuccessful and, at 0826, the formation was ordered to change course to the south, an unfeasible command in the rising force of the storm.

Waterman, like *Tabberer*, was unable to break out of the trough despite any combination of engines and rudders. It might conceivably have been possible to bring the ship off the trough by going ahead flank speed on both engines but the captain considered that the strain on the hull might be such as to cause the ship to break up. The DE rode out the storm in the trough of the sea with the engines turning over at five knots. The same problem with water entering the windward air intakes deluged the engine room spaces, in one case knocking a man down bodily from the forward main propulsion board. However, the engine room force acted quickly to divert the water into the bilges, from where it could be pumped overboard. Lieutenant Vincent P. Finigan recalled the fury:

"Dear Mr. Andrews:

I am sending you some information about the *Waterman* that I have nurtured for many years. The years during the war are the ones that I constantly reflect on and will never forget.

I can remember vividly the typhoon of December '44. It was a harrowing experience. I was Officer of The Deck when we switched controls from the flying bridge to the wheelhouse because it was so fierce in the open. The TBS announced '*Finigan* this is *Flanagan*, I am taking water down the stack and can only last ten minutes.'

I promptly called back *Flanagan* (destroyer *Hull*) and I believe I said '*Flanagan* this is *Finigan* can you hear me?' After several attempts, we got no response. The radar screen was obliterated; we could see nothing; visibility was zero. *Hull* went down and no further word was heard from her."

The winds and seas gradually hauled around to the east, placing the ship in the navigable semi-circle of the typhoon, although the center was still approaching. Most of the time, vision was obscured by flying spume and rain. The major concern was the possibility of heavy machinery or other equipment breaking loose and going through the side of the ship. At one time, there was so much water in the conning bridge that gallons of it went spilling over the leeward sponson. Damage from the storm consisted of a badly stove-in motor whaleboat but otherwise was generally light.

This vessel was extremely fortunate in surviving the typhoon without serious damage. During the height of the storm, it was encouraging to communicate with other vessels nearby by means of TBS, all of whom seemed to be suffering similar difficulties. The SL radar went out of operation frequently but was quickly repaired by the technician. Collision with another vessel was a constant worry because it was next to impossible to handle the ship. At 1800, orders were received from *ComDesDiv 104* to proceed on easy riding southerly courses to a rendezvous with the Third Fleet at 0700 the next morning.

1815. *Waterman* broke out of the trough under full speed. One man was critically injured during the storm so that courses and speeds were chosen to put the least motion on the ship, even though this meant not arriving at the designated rendezvous at the specified time.

Reprinted by Permission
Sunday Magazine Section
New York Times
April 22, 1945

"I am First Class Boatswain's Mate N.W. Tashman Jr., author of this *Times* article. I remember the fury of that horrendous Philippine Typhoon, and I wish to relate a first-hand account of the battle of the *Waterman* against an implacable enemy. It was won by brave seamen and by shipbuilders at home. Here is the story of a battle at sea off Luzon. It was not an engagement with the Japanese but a long and bitter fight against a typhoon. This ex-Bosun's mate tells what happened to *Waterman* and pays tribute to her builders.

Somewhere in this country walk our saviors. They are the creators of our hull, a hull whose perfect construction defied destruction by a force more formidable than any mortal enemy - a raging sea that slugged, hammered and lashed at our ship for 38 hours, and howling angry solid sheets of wind that tried to tear us apart.

Our men had shown fearlessness in action against the enemy, against magazine fires, burning oil, and torpedo attacks. But against this new enemy, they admitted fear. All were on edge, some were numb, others prayed. They came through and for this they give full thanks to the men who built our ship. And for that we will be ever grateful to the non-uniformed, undecorated and often unfairly belittled shipyard workers.

Up to about noon on 17 December, all further refueling operations were canceled. Scout planes returning to flat tops were having a tough time landing. Two planes still aloft were flagged off because it was impossible to land on the rolling, pitching deck of the carrier. Pilots, asking for instructions, got this, as heard on our TBS:

'Turn your plane loose and bail out. Destroyer will be standing by to pick you up.'

Back came the word from one of the pilots, 'Repeat!'

As the order was repeated word for word, the pilot said: 'That's what I thought you said the first time!'

They bailed out as ordered and were picked up shortly afterward.

Then ships by units were formed up to ride out what was figured to be just another slight interruption in the progress of the campaign against the enemy. The barometer continued to fall. The sea continued to rise, and the wind continued to gain in intensity. Now reports began to come in:

'Man overboard. Keep a sharp lookout!'

The first such report struck a fearful note. It also created a great respect for the sea and invited extra precautions.Visibility was zero which means you couldn't see 50 yards. Blasts from whistles were practically useless. The wind prevented the whistles' shrill from carrying any place but to leeward.

Men below in the engine rooms occasionally walked on the starboard side as the ship heeled over. Telephone watch standers topside anxiously asked the engineers if we were taking water through the seams. Reports were heartening. The only water below decks was coming in through ventilators! Time after time, we'd fall off the top of a mountainous wave and hit the bottom with a resounding whoomph, shaking every inch of the hull from stem to stern.

Some men on off-watch sections remained in the gun shields. They seemed to feel that, by watching the sea, they'd be able to know what was coming or at least be the first to know. Others were frightened and worried. They lay below in their sacks, lashing themselves in so as not to be thrown out. The more they saw of the typhoon, the more fearful they were that we wouldn't pull through. Men who had never been seasick were feeling badly. Forget chow!

For hours, we had proceeded unharmed through the storm. Now our life lines and stanchions were being knocked down, and some were carried away. Number three life raft was gone. Number one gun shield, bearing the brunt of each thwack of solid sea that covered our fo'c'sle, was weakening. The motor whaleboat was beginning to strain at the gripes as wind and sea took alternate turns at it.

A depth charge broke loose on the fantail. Our charges had been set on safe to allay fear of going off, but 300 pounds of TNT rolling around on the loose was dangerous. A few men detailed to it soon had the charge secured. It was not so easy. The fantail was under water, and the men had to work with safety lines.

The sea at last dealt a Sunday punch to the motor whaleboat. The waves followed through, again and again, methodically, just seeming to take time enough to draw back and put everything behind their blows. The gripes parted, and the boat crashed between the davit and the deck housing.

That done, the sea started back on the stubborn gun shield, attacking with confidence. Smack, thwack, crack, whoomph! The center shield was stove in six inches. Another hour of pounding, and one of the braces that held the shield to the deck parted. And as it gave way, it peeled up the deck with her like the cover of a tin of sardines, exposing the innards of the ship to tons of water filling the passageways below. A mattress, flat board and 5"x5" wood shoring were placed below the gap to strengthen the deck and bulkhead surrounding the gash. We still shipped water, and the watertight doors were secured for safety.

Out on gun number two, the war cruising watch was still trying to stand, keeping an eye out for men who might be washed overboard.

Our skipper had the wheel personally now, and there he stayed for the next five hours. Orders had come through from SOPAC (Southern Pacific Command), 'Every ship for herself.' A rendezvous was designated. From then on, the only ships we passed were two fleet tugs laboring along. Forty-eight hours later, we saw no ships.

Floater nets, with the help of the sea, were picked up out of their racks and draped over men and guns as if they were silk fish nets. Considering the fact that they were made of two and a half inch line and carried some fifty pounds of rations and gear to be used in case of abandon ship, the gun crew breathed easy when they checked and found no one hurt.

Then one of the loaded magazines jumped the rack in the 20mm magazine room, immediately abaft the number two-3" gun. Gunner's Mate Homer McCoy and this Boatswain's Mate juggled it as the ship lurched and bounced crazily.

The gunner was scared, and with good reason. Twenty millimeter ammunition is fitted with ordinary percussion caps, like rifle bullets. A round could go off if dropped on the steel deck. In the magazine room with hundreds of rounds, one firing could cause a sympathetic firing of all rounds, creating an horrendous explosion. This Boatswain's Mate was not so well versed in the ingredients he was juggling. Jokingly, he remarked to the gunner: 'Hang on. Ain't you got no guts?' Meekly came the answer, 'I got guts, but I don't want to see 'em'.

This 'Boats' scurried up a scuttle after getting the loose magazine back in its rack and returned with some line cut off a life ring. Records were made in knot tying as the men turned to securing the ammunition. .

Injuries were slight among the men on watch, though the Quartermaster was thrown across the wheelhouse and his back cut wide open. How he made it to sick bay or how 'Pills' ever was able to work on him no one was able to figure out. One and a half hours later, he had 18 stitches in his back.

It seemed as if the storm would never end. At 1400 of the second day, 18 December, all topside watches were secured. Men stayed together in groups down below, awaiting word to man their stations. . No one believed the enemy would be around to pay a call in that weather. Yet, this was a navy ship. She must be ready to fight, even in a typhoon.

About 1600 the same day, the captain said the worst was over, but when he said it would be at least another 24 hours before we could look for any rest from the beating, the men actually groaned. They were glad to know the worst was over, but they still feared that the ship had taken all she could take and that another 24 hours would sound her death knell.

By 0400 of the third day, we were back on watch. By noon, there was the sun. The sea was still running high. The wind was fresh and moderate. We were alone. Nothing was in sight but sky and water. We headed for our rendezvous.

After hours of steaming, we were still alone. Our TBS, sound and radar were out. Our radio couldn't transmit. Soon, 'Sparks' was reporting what little he could pick up. A station was calling us.'Report your position.'

We couldn't. We heard them call the three ill-fated ships. No answer. Hours later, reports were heard to task force commanders.'Four ships unheard from'. We were one of them.

The sea was just about normal now. Outside of the visible damage aboard ship, life was beginning to take on some of the old routine.

One thing began to concern most everyone; the injured man was running a high fever. The sulfa shot into his veins and sprinkling in the wound had not prevented infection, and 'Doc' (colloquial for Pharmacist Mate) advised transfer to a ship with better medical facilities. Hour after hour, we searched the horizon.

'Sparks' finally got the radio going. We reported to the Task Force Commander. A new rendezvous had been ordered, and we headed in that direction. It was good to see ships again. Christmas was just ahead, and it would be a merry one after all.

We were ordered to return to port for repairs and transferred our Quartermaster to an aircraft carrier that had all the facilities of a modern hospital. We were sorry to see him leave as he was placed on the stretcher and carried between ships on a breeches buoy; he was a good shipmate. That flat top sent back 300 pounds of turkey for our Christmas dinner! Nobody said anything, but the crew would gladly have eaten beans that Christmas Day. They had enough to be thankful for.

NOTE: As editor of *GO*, (A periodical founded by me after the war) the writer of this *Times* article was a member of the fleet of 300 ships deployed for the Leyte invasion and disrupted by the typhoon. I hope the story will be interesting to anyone who ventures to sea in any kind of craft. Almost, always unpredictably, the anticipation of adventure offshore constantly persists, and it's that challenge added to the solace and beauty of the sea at her kindest that takes us out there again and again."

BANGUST

From One Typhoon to Another

Robert H. Burgess, Fire Controlman on *Bangust (DE-739)*, had a rare gift of being able to record and describe cataclysmic events about him in a manner that places the reader in the midst of the cauldron.

"I was in that storm on Bangust. We were serving as escort for oil tankers with the Third Fleet which had been carrying out assaults on Japanese strongholds in the Philippine Islands. Ships were in need of refueling. Our Task Group consisted of twelve fully loaded fleet oil tankers, three fleet tugs, five destroyers, ten destroyer escorts and five escort carriers with replacement planes.

Early Sunday morning, 17 December - I recall the date since it was my son's first birthday, and I hadn't seen him for seven months - I was writing a letter home. There was a slight overcast and a rolling sea. Conditions even then were such that I noted in my letter, 'The sea has picked up considerably and, writing this at the mess table, my body is in constant motion due to the roll and pitch of the ship. Writing isn't too pleasant under present conditions'. I brought the letter to a close, planning to continue that afternoon, but it wasn't resumed until two days later!

About 1000 on the 17th, we rendezvoused with the Third Fleet, and our Task Group split into three sections, servicing the three carrier task groups comprising the Third Fleet. In this manner, all ships could receive fuel, food, planes, personnel and mail from home. Those requiring fuel maneuvered close and parallel to tankers so that hoses could be passed without strain. It was always a ticklish operation but doubly so when the ocean is abnormally rough. Lines and hoses carried away. Breeches buoys and trolleys used to transfer relief pilots, mail and supplies were useless. Planes could not take off or land on the rolling, pitching decks of the carriers.

Neither the course nor strength of the storm had been determined accurately. There had not been time to establish weather reporting stations because of the rapid westward advance of the Pacific Fleet.

I recall our 306-foot DE, small compared to the carriers, cruisers and oilers, making heavy weather of it as she dipped her bow into the sea, throwing spray over the bridge. The warm waters of the tropical Pacific raced aft along the decks, and the winds whipped the froth around the guns and deck fittings. Rolling and pitching were the constant motions of the ship as she tried to maintain her position in the screen.

Earlier in my letter, I mentioned that the seas were picking up. That was written right after Sunday noon chow, and I stayed below deck for a while after that. When I went on deck again, things were really changing fast. No one was allowed on the weather decks unless his work called for it, and even then he had to wear his life belt. A group gathered on the boat deck to take it all in and marvel. All the night long of the 17th, we pitched and rolled. The next morning, I looked out of a hatch and never had I seen such fury. The seas went up-up-up, and then we'd be on a crest and could look down-down-down.

Froth was everywhere and, when the wind picked it up, it looked like clouds of steam. It was practically impossible to sleep, stand, or sit since our bodies were in constant motion. All the time, we were trying to steady ourselves. Our meals consisted of crackers, spam and coffee because it was impossible to keep anything else on the range. Heavy rain started to fall the evening of the 17th, and the seas grew rougher and more confused. Even then, no one was aware that a typhoon was upon us, where the eye of the storm was, or how it was moving."

Storekeeper Daryl Dugan said he'd never forget:

> "Johnny Carruth and I were knocked off of our feet by a big wave and scurried to get back inside. We kept hearing of men overboard, but it seemed impossible to rescue anybody in those seas.
>
> It was a dreadful night with ships at the mercy of the storm, calling for help and running out of fuel. We were rolling so bad that all the gun watches were secured. Things were being torn from their moorings above deck. The life lines were torn down by objects striking them with terrific force. Several times, GQ was sounded as circuits shorted. Word was passed each time that it was a mistake.
>
> Sleep was impossible; you would be thrown out of your sack. The mess hall looked like a pig pen, with coffee and crackers and other food sliding and swishing all over the place. Staying on one's feet was a trick. The compartments were full of foul air from being enclosed, and the ventilation was inadequate. Lots of guys were sea sick."

Bangust Radioman John Roulet's log:

> "18 December 1944. We figure that the storm must be at its height. The winds were logged at over 100 knots. We cannot alter course because we cannot get out of the trough. Now the ship is rolling worse than ever. The wind has risen to 120 knots!
>
> This afternoon, they said that we could be out of the storm by 2200 tonight. We were able to come to a new course, so maybe things are a little better. We spotted a light in the water. Evidently, there must be survivors, but we were unable to make a contact."

The fleet became dispersed over some 2500 square miles of

ocean. By late Monday, the 18th, the wind began to moderate and the sky to brighten. The eye of the typhoon had passed. Admiral Halsey wasn't aware that any of his ships had sunk until *Tabberer* radioed that she was picking up survivors.

As a result of the typhoon, the Third Fleet could not carry out its planned attacks against Japanese airfields on Luzon and, except for those vessels assigned to the search detail, the fighting ships returned to Ulithi for repairs, rest and replenishment. Fire Controlman Burgess continued:

> "Our ship was one of those searching for survivors. We had been spared any serious damage or loss except for several floater nets being swept over the side and a depth charge, set on safe, rolling around our deck. Nonetheless, at the time of the storm, all on board the *Bangust* were aware that we were in a storm like none of us or our ship had ever weathered. We found no survivors but did encounter floating wreckage and empty life rafts. In port, we talked to crews who did pick up survivors, and they related tales of horror. That is why that holiday season, so many years ago, remains so fresh in my memory."

It remains fresh in the memory of Storekeeper Dugan as well:

> "It was still rough on the morning of 19 December but, by 0900, we opened up hatches and got out on deck to look over the damage. What a mess! The life rafts were all gone and many other items were missing or broken. Our little bookkeeping office had everything on the deck, papers, ink etc. about a foot deep. We came through the storm in very good shape compared to other ships.
>
> Ships started reporting, a process that continued for two days. We heard reports of ships being blown hundreds of miles off course. We were almost into enemy held islands in the Philippines before we turned.
>
> We were happy to be alive. We hit Ulithi on Christmas Day. It was more like Thanksgiving to us."

Radioman Roulet referred again to his log:

> "25 December, Christmas Day. We arrived in Ulithi at 1030 in the morning. *Swearer (DE-186)* came alongside. I spoke to a steward's mate from *Spence*, one of only about 25 survivors. He told us the ship was out of fuel and, about two minutes after the generators stopped, she took a roll and didn't recover. He was thrown down but managed to open a hatch and make his way out onto the starboard side of the hull. He jumped and grabbed a kapok life jacket in the water as waves washed him away from the ship.
>
> The *Spence* went down with practically all hands in about seven minutes. There were two others with him in the water, and they spent three days floating in their life jackets. He said the others kept seeing ships on the horizon. He admits that he saw a task force unit although he knew it never existed. After being passed up one night by the *Swearer (DE-186)*, they were picked up late on the afternoon of the next day. Boy, there is one guy with a lot of guts!"

Typhoon Number Two

Storekeeper Dugan:

> "It was many months after the typhoon before I could get the thought of the loss of the three destroyers and their men out of my mind. Our ship endured a second typhoon on 5-6 June 1945 off Okinawa while serving as part of a screening unit replenishing the fighting ships. Again *Bangust* came through unscathed while the cruiser *Pittsburgh (CA-72)* lost her entire bow section. As I look at those storms in retrospect, I can say they were quite an experience to have endured, but I wouldn't care to go through another."

Radioman Roulet opened his log:

> "04 June 1945. Our second typhoon. It rained last night and it is overcast. Our Task Group was fueling when we received a message ordering all fueling discontinued in preparation for typhoon weather approaching from a distance of 330 miles from our 0900 position. I sure hope it isn't bad. These merchant ships in our convoy are loaded with ammunition and are not equipped with radar. They are dangerous to be nearby during a storm.
>
> At 1800, it looked as though we would pass by the typhoon, and we resumed fueling prior to dark. However, that was wishful thinking. In fact, the storm was getting worse and wave heights were increasing. Fueling was discontinued. The merchant ships are starting to have a bad time. The Convoy Commander ordered a 90 degree turn. We finally left the merchant ships to fend for themselves. They are helpless. I'm glad I'm not in the merchant marine tonight.
>
> 05 June. Typhoon. The barometer dropped precipitously. The winds increased in intensity. We still have control though. It is impossible to sleep. Over TBS radio this morning, I heard of several men lost from various ships. One was washed over on one ship and picked up by another ship right behind almost immediately. (See the *Conklin* story later in this chapter). A CVE lost 20 planes on deck last night. The destroyer *Kalk (DD-611)* is in a bad way; no sound, no radar, no radio.
>
> *Waterman (DE-740)* can't be contacted, but one of the merchant ships is located. The Convoy Commander is locating ships and reforming the convoy. It is now 1045 and still pretty rough, but I think the worst is over. I had spam and coffee for breakfast this morning. All the topside watches except the bridge had been secured last night. The repair parties are still standing by.
>
> Boy, the guys prayed last night and every man agrees that he was pretty scared. I was. Well, this makes number two for the "B." I wonder how many she can stand. A destroyer lost it's mast. It is noon now and beginning to clear up. Task Group 30.8 is reforming. We lost one depth charge, a boat canopy, a flag bag cover, and various items, but the ship fared pretty well, all things considered."

A year prior to the December Philippine Typhoon, on 10 and 11 June 1944, *Bangust* had eliminated one submarine from the Mikado's service. See narrative *Pacific Antisubmarine Warfare*.

Lewis M. Andrews, Jr.

DONALDSON

A Tale of Two Typhoons

On 1 July 1944, while *Donaldson (DE-44)* was on patrol duty around the Marshall Islands, one of the men felt that the crew should have some religious base, and a bible class was formed. The first church service was held on the following Sunday and was piped over the public address system. About 30 men attended and started with the singing of the Navy Hymn. Through contact with the base bible class in Honolulu, *Donaldson* received religious literature, several bibles and a piano accordion. With ammunition replaced, fuel tanks bulging and the bible class well equipped, *Donaldson* was ready to depart, and the crew was ready to sing, "Praise The Lord and Pass The Ammunition."

7 September. The DE dropped anchor at Manus for rest, recreation and beer at Duffy's Tavern. However, the stay was cut short. *Donaldson* was needed to escort transports and attack cargo ships to Palau in the Carolines. The echelon was just in time to disembark badly needed reinforcements. Bible class was well into the Corinthians.

23 September. *Donaldson* joined a task group with *Lake (DE-301)*, *Crowley (DE-303)* and a destroyer heading for Hollandia, New Guinea, with the unladen troop ships. The crew of *Donaldson* never had a chance to drink even one beer in Hollandia because, just after the hook was dropped, it was raised to head for Manus. Two days later, while entering the anchorage in Manus, a tanker rammed the Australian troop ship, *HMAS Don Marquis*. *Donaldson*, being the closest to the stricken ship, was called upon to board her and render assistance.

A fire-fighting party was formed and boarded the Australian ship. From the deck of *Donaldson*, all fire hoses poured water on her. The nauseating smell of death and dying permeated the atmosphere. The boarding party opened the hatches of the troop quarters where hundreds of Australian soldiers were burned alive, a sight that would haunt dreams for many a night thereafter. About an hour after the damage control party boarded the ship, the navy sent fire fighting boats to finish the job. For her efforts, *Donaldson* received recognition for a job well done.

26 September. *Donaldson's* Task Group returned to Palau with troop reinforcements. On the prior departure, it was believed that the island was secured, but the return was greeted by intensive fighting.

16 October. The ship left Tulagi for Palau, arriving to find that our forces were still bombing and fighting. The next destination was Ulithi to pick up more K-rations, mail, fuel and a few days of liberty on Mog-Mog. Some of the drinkers traded their beer for coke, but unfortunately not by itself. Apparently, Aqua Velva (an after shave lotion) and coke made a palatably good drink. One crewman recalled:

"After drinking the mixture, the men looked like hell, but they smelled great."

3-30 October. *Donaldson* was on continuous patrol duty between Palau and Ulithi. The Japanese were still attempting to reinforce Palau. Lookouts spotted a group landing before they could open fire.

9 November. The ship pulled into Manus. The night before, an ammunition ship blew up, doing damage to quite a few ships and killing many sailors. A DE was badly hit. Bodies were floating around the anchorage. It was as bad as the *Don Marquis* disaster.

16 December. The Task Group joined another formation of tankers, carriers, destroyers and destroyer escorts. *Donaldson* drew alongside the carrier *Yorktown (CV-5)* to pass mail, and the DE crew gazed in astonishment at her gargantuan size, dwarfing their own ship.

17 December. The fleet changed course, but it was too late for *Donaldson*. The wind and the sea had already taken hold of her.

18 December was brutal for *Donaldson*. By this date, the DE was rolling so badly that the galley was secured. Battleship sailors in storms would sing out a refrain:

"Roll, roll you son-of-a-bitch, the more you roll the less you pitch,"

But the men on *Donaldson* would have traded a little more pitching for considerably less rolling. At one point, the ship rolled 78 degrees. A roll of 78 degrees without capsizing seemed like something of a miracle. One has to stop and think that 78 degrees from the vertical is only 12 degrees from the horizontal. The deck becomes the side and the side becomes the bottom, pinning terrified and helpless men. The pressure and noise became unbearable. Over the loud speaker, the captain roared:

"All hands lay over to the port side!"

Because of the noise and confusion, some of the crew thought the end had come and attempted to fight their way topside. Three of them were claimed by the sea forever.

In the meantime, the electric boards shorted and caught fire, power failed, and the lights went out. The diesels, fighting with all their strength, were running red hot. Salt water was pumped into them in an attempt to cool them down, replacing the non-existent fresh water coolant. The gyroscope went out, as did the bridge steering. The after steering watch took over by hand, cranking the steering engines as directed by telephone from the bridge. At 1230, a patch of blue sky became visible. The wind went down to 60 knots. Some of the crew felt relief. Bible class members, as well as several (previous) non-believers, started reciting Psalm 23:

"The Lord is my Shepherd..."

This lull only lasted for a short time, and then the ship was hit on the other side with even greater fury. The blow was to be the last big one. While the crew of *Donaldson* mourned the loss of some of their shipmates, the navy mourned the loss of three destroyers. By 1800, visibility increased from zero to a few hundred yards. The storm was over, and *Donaldson* had survived.

19 December. The crew worked furiously, cleaning up, checking depth charges, repairing the whaleboat, checking water tight integrity, hanging up $10,000 of invasion money to dry. *Donaldson* was missing for two days because she picked up the small minesweeper *Canary (AMC-25)* and led her to the rendezvous. On 20 December, the ship refueled at sea and received a message from the flagship that this DE had kept her station bet-

ter with her standby magnetic compass than most of the other ships did with their gyrocompasses. The next day, a crewman was transferred to the carrier *Sitkoh Bay (CVE-86)* to receive medical care for wounds received while securing a K-gun during the typhoon; the impulse charge exploded.

The flagship passed the word that the Task Group was to return to Ulithi. December 24 arrived, and *Donaldson* limped into the lagoon. She tied up alongside *Lake* and picked up all the Christmas mail. Food from home was always a delight and emphasized the ethnic diversity of the crew, bound together in their little destroyer escort. The men received Polish sausage from Chicago, cheese from Milwaukee, kosher salami from Cleveland, rye bread from New York, and various other goodies from around the states. Christmas of 1944 was one happy day. The ship was in port, the majority of the crew was alive and well, and the bible group was singing Christmas carols. That day, the crew also showed a little more respect for the "small boy" *Donaldson*. Good ship and sound, sound as a dollar!

On New Years Day, 1945, there was liberty on Mog-Mog for the starboard watch. A fight broke out on the little atoll. The crew got back to the ship without assistance from the shore patrol. However, most of them were drunk, bloody and sore but all were happy—happy that is until the captain read them off and restricted half of the watch from further liberties while in port. There was some further excitement.

12 January. A sub put a torpedo into an empty ammunition ship and escaped. From 15 through 21 January, the sea was very rough with winds reaching a velocity of 50 knots, 340 miles from southern Japan.

9 May. *Donaldson* passed within 16 miles of Okino Diato Jima, 900 miles from Tokyo. It had a pier and a good anchorage. The heavy ships shelled the beach without receiving return fire. The shelling did some damage, at least giving the Japanese something to think about. Two days later, the incredulous crew heard Tokyo Rose announce that *Donaldson* had been sunk on 9 May. It was good for a laugh.

4 June. While transferring passengers to the carrier *Hornet (CV-8)*, the ships started to receive warnings of an approaching storm. The operation was discontinued, and the crew prepared the ship for another cantankerous blow by nature. Everything was battened down. In the early afternoon, the radio shack received a message that a tropical storm was lurking in the lower latitudes, and all ships were to stand by for a severe blow. *Donaldson* was ordered to proceed at best speed on a southeasterly course to avoid the full impact of the storm. By midnight, the wind escalated to a full gale, 40 to 50 knots; the barometer fell steadily. The sky was black and ominous. .

0400 on 5 June. Winds increased to 60 knots. A half hour later, all ships were told to fend for themselves, and all pretense of holding formation was abandoned. An hour later, the storm had the *Donaldson* once more in its clutches. Wind force had passed 100 knots!

There was a weird light on the mast that lit up the antennae and guy wires from the mast to the sound hut. "Saint Elmo's Fire" meant disaster to sailors of bygone days. (This book author observed this phenomena more than once. The standing rigging and antennae lit up like neon tubes, an unwelcome sight at night in submarine infested areas.) The men in the forward crew's compartment were thrown out of their sacks by a roll of 55 degrees and prayed that the screws would keep turning and the ship would hold together. Water squirted in past the "watertight" hatches. Word was passed over the loudspeaker for all hands to remain below decks, and all open deck watches were abandoned. There was less confusion this time; the crew listened for orders and responded with alacrity.

0540. The storm was at its peak. The barometer had dropped to 28.22 and wind force was logged at 110 to 120 knots. At its worst moments, the ship rolled 68 degrees. At dawn, a life raft was sighted about 300 yards on the starboard bow with a desperate man frantically paddling in the direction of *Donaldson*. The raft had been driven by the wind onto the track of the DE. He was quickly and efficiently rescued from the clutches of certain death and was identified as having been washed off *Howard F. Clark (DE-533)*. By 0730, the worst of the storm was over. The barometer started to rise; the wind slackened, and the sea fell off. By early afternoon, the sky began to clear and the logistic group started to reform. The formation had taken another beating by Mother Nature. However, no ships foundered as in the typhoon of December 18.

No one was lost on *Donaldson*, and there were only a few minor injuries. The typhoon experience of 18 December caught the ship unprepared, but this time she was ready. Admiral Halsey's mighty Third Fleet was refueled and continued prowling the Pacific for the remnants of the Japanese fleet.

0800 on 14 June brought a landfall on San Pedro Bay, Samar. After dropping the anchor, the ship was invaded by the natives selling souvenirs. Fire Controlman First Class Zane Grimm stated that the women on this island were very beautiful.

Such being the case, during a movie on the fantail, a few crewmen tried to jump ship one night in search of a promised native party that included girls, tuba, and song. They arranged for a native boat to meet them 50 yards off the starboard bow. After 20 minutes into the movie, they jumped over and swam to the prearranged spot, but – no boat. It was too far to swim to shore so they had to swim back to the ship. By the time they came alongside, they were exhausted and called for help. The next day, they were brought before Captain Hartman and lectured on the virtue of worthy use of leisure time. The captain must have been in a sympathetic mood because their punishment was only no liberty for the remainder of the ship's stay in San Pedro Bay.

By contrast, the bible class was well into the Books of Genesis and Romans. The group gathered for Christian fellowship, testimonial service, singing of favorite hymns, and sometimes a brief, stirring gospel message. It wasn't a matter of good or bad; some of the same men in the botched shore party were in this group as well.

A considerable portion of the *Donaldson* narrative was supplied by Fire Controlman Zane Grimm, a former crew member.

CONKLIN

A Killer Typhoon at Okinawa

Having previously participated in the destruction of two enemy submarines (See chapter *Pacific Antisubmarine Warfare*), *Conklin (DE-439)* was to meet the gravest challenge to her existence, the same 5 June typhoon narrated above by

Donaldson.

By midnight, it had become clear that the Task Force had run into a typhoon, heading into the eye of the storm, with most of the ships – and the *Conklin* – in the dangerous semi – circle.

Most sailors who have gone to sea for any length of time have had the experience of waves whipping up into small mountains of gray, grisly water crashing over the forecastle and turning into white cutting streaks, washing the ship from stem to stern. They have heard the wind turn from a sigh to a moan to a scream in the rigging as the storm built to a crescendo. They have experienced that monotonous and grinding lurch in all directions that permits only standing, eating and fitful sleeping, if at all.

But sometimes the sea gets worse than that.

After midnight, the wind no longer just screamed in the rigging; it became an eerie noise, as though it was brought up from the depths. The radar was useless because the sea about the ship was higher than the antenna on the mast. The Officer of The Deck on the flying bridge had only mountains ahead of him, knowing nothing of what lay beyond. The sky was black and the sea more so. A huge mass that would surely engulf them all moved onto the DE. Somehow, it was surmounted, but only to look down into a deep, seemingly bottomless alley, with another, worse wave ahead. The impact of sea and wind was lost on nobody, and all wondered who would control *Conklin*, the crew or the sea. A time like that comes to some seafaring people.

She made one third speed into the wind. At 0410, the enemy was forgotten, and running lights were on. "God forbid," thought the captain, "that the crest of the next sea will bring down on our bow the hull of another ship I cannot see." The propellers repeatedly came out of the water, and the freed shafts vibrated the men from crown to toe.

At first, there was the annoyance of a heavy sea, the inevitable tired and wretched feeling, dizzy seasickness for many. Then there was added the impossibility of moving without holding, decks falling away from feet, bulkheads seeming to snap out to crack a skull, the knowledge of sea doings that set a destroyer man apart from others. But now there was something more, an uncontrolled swerve, an inability to head up into the sea, a feeling beyond seasickness, beyond gripe, beyond weariness, but not beyond fear.

0500. Lieutenant Peter J. Meros, Officer of The Deck on the flying bridge, looked up at the crack of doom. It would be presumptuous to guess what that young man thought when he saw this wave coming. One thing he must have known was that it was so much bigger than he and bigger than his ship that it could not be mastered and could not be undone except, albeit, by the Hand that made it. He must have known that *Conklin* would not surmount this wave like the others.

Tons of water surged clear over the bow and crashed down on the flying bridge. He was engulfed in the sea, torn loose from his ship, swept away. We do not know if he expired then and there or many moments later. Perhaps there went through his stunned brain the thought of a home somewhere, the vision of a childhood pleasure in the warm sun, a schoolteacher smilingly talked to him, something he always wanted to do crossed his mind, and then he drowned.

Conklin had rolled at least 75 degrees to starboard, and lay on her side with her bridge structure partially submerged! The superstructure doors were smashed open. The combat information center and radio shack were flooded, and all radio and radar gear were put out of commission. Water poured down the ventilation ducts into the engineering spaces and interior communications control. The board was submerged and all electric terminals, thermostats, rheostats and circuit breakers were shorted. The gyroscope stopped.

The signalman striker, on the flying bridge with Lieutenant Meros, saw the wave coming too. It was like no wave he had ever seen, almost vertical, a sheer wall of black terror hovering above his head. When he looked up at that mass of water coming down on his head, he was alone with his God. His fingers grabbed one or two fixed objects, but they were torn from his hands as he tumbled over and over in the sea. He believed he might die, but he didn't. The battle he fought in the next few hours before his rescue by another ship, was like the passage of many days. He fought to live, and he won the fight.

The telephone talker on the flying bridge literally died and lived again. Like Lieutenant Meros and the signalman striker, he saw the wall of water, this fate beyond his ability to fight. There was no place to go and no place to hide. The salt water crashed down on him, stunning him with the blow and tearing whatever he had been holding onto. At times, he was upside down, prone or standing in nothing but the black space of the sea, no top nor bottom. He didn't want to drown; he didn't want to die. He struggled for the surface, but there was none. His eyes popped. His lungs felt as though they would burst. His senses reeled. He wasn't sure if he were awake or asleep in a bad dream. Either way, he struggled with every ounce of strength to live.

He hit something solid and held on. He didn't know what it was, but he did know it was his only hope. Whatever this thing was, he would hold it to his last drop of strength. When the wave receded, he lay clutching a metal fitting, gulping in air in fitful, palpitating gasps, alive but not for the moment understanding how he got from the flying bridge to the fantail. It took him several moments to comprehend that he had been washed overboard and washed back again! The Hand that made the wave spared the life of the bridge talker.

In the crew's quarters, off duty men were hanging on to the nearest bunk or stanchion, not even able to pour or hold a mug of coffee. Some of the best sailors were seasick while others bemoaned the delights of *terra firma*. There were even a few jokes. Then the wave hit, and there were no more jokes. The side of the ship became the deck; the deck became the side. The lights went out, plunging the men into total blackness. Those who couldn't keep their grasp on what they had been holding were flung through the air, banging heads, shins, elbows, knees, lying in a heap. Water poured on them. They were disoriented. How can one be lying flat on the side? Where was the exit? With eyes bulging, neck muscles distended, they tried to claw their way to somewhere, anywhere not to be drowned.

Seaman First Class Anthony J. Monti was walking along an interior passageway, holding the guard rail tightly to keep from falling or banging his head on one thing or another. Seeing an open hatch nearby did not occur to him as anything out of the ordinary. There were hatches all over the ship, and a sailor spent a large part of his seagoing life climbing up and down hatches. When his ship whipped over on its side, he lost his grip on the guard rail and snapped through the air. Perhaps he covered his face or put his hands out in front of him, expecting to hit a bulkhead. But, in the sudden darkness, he just kept falling and falling, as in a nightmare, through the open hatch to the deck below.

And there his once strong, young body lay motionless in death on the steel plates.

Seaman First Class R.E. Smith was pitched through the same hatch at the same time and lay dazed and agonizingly clutching a broken arm.

Seaman First Class Rudolph Slavich had been standing watch on the starboard quarterdeck. He didn't have a chance and was swept into the sea as the wave rolled over *Conklin.* His dazed mind probably never did grasp the meaning of being on a deck one moment and in the sea the next. We do not know how long he fought, how hard was the struggle, what he thought of, how much of his life raced back across his mind. Did he try to swim back? Did he see the hopeless chasm between his ship and himself widening?

We really don't know any of the answers except that he belongs eternally to the sea.

Conklin stood up again. The storm abated, the winds died, and the seas gradually calmed. She was badly hurt, with extensive structural damage along her port side. Separated from the fleet by the fury of the storm and damaged beyond combat usefulness, she was ordered to proceed to the Navy Yard, Mare Island, California for repairs.

Thus ended the saga of *Conklin.* In due course, the war ended; her officers and men were demobilized and dispersed to the far corners of their country. Their ways parted and their common interests were blurred in time. But one thing was sure. The men who served on *Conklin* have carried through their careers a healthy respect for Mother Nature in general – and the sea in particular.

RESCUE AT SEA

A First Lieutenant Discovers His Own Mettle in a Typhoon

On 13 November 1943, *Dempsey (DE-26)* rescued 45 survivors of the torpedoed merchantman *San Juan* off Viti Levu, Fiji Islands. In October, she screened oilers at sea during the invasion of the Gilberts and sank a Japanese patrol craft, taking one prisoner. She continued extensive convoy duty until the end of the war.

This yarn was first published in the *Princeton Alumni Weekly* by Lieutenant Joe Sloan and was submitted to *DESA NEWS* by his friend, Harvey Phillips, in the spring of 1985. Lieutenant Sloane did not indicate the area of this salty narrative, but Majuro is a likely assumption.

"A stiff breeze shredded the low gray clouds and whipped up a sharp chop across the dreary expanse of the lagoon. Dark shapes of ships lay scattered here and there, motionless amidst the hurrying whitecaps. The island fringing the harbor flung up an occasional ragged palm, tossing its broken arms in the wind. To seaward, great sheets of spray shot up from the reefs and from the sides of a rusty freighter, stranded months before at the treacherous inlet.

My ship, *Dempsey*, tugged at her anchor chain, lying half across the wind, swinging senselessly from one position to another. We were in from 10 days at sea, and all hands were looking forward to some recreation or at least to a few nights of decent sleep. The Officer of The Deck stood in the lee of the deck house, discussing with the watch the merits of the evening movie.

I was in the chart room, working on my navigation in preparation for the day when I, a first lieutenant, would be transferred to another ship as executive officer, responsible for the ship's safe and accurate passage. I felt my inadequacy with figures all too keenly and just now found the computation of moonrise and moonset even duller than usual. My gaze kept wandering to insignificant details. The short roll of the ship and the threatening weather made me uneasy; perhaps it was the memory of the run through the edge of a typhoon a few months before.

Just then, I heard the clatter of the signal lamp outside. I closed my books and went out on the signal bridge. "Damn!," I heard the signalman exclaim. As I turned to him, he handed me the signal board. The penciled words: "STAND BY TO GET UNDERWAY IMMEDIATELY," leaped off the page.

So that was why I felt so uneasy; we were going out into that mess. I felt a sense of injustice - we were just in from a long trip and, though fueled and ready, we had a right to a little peace and quiet. I resented the brass on the beach for picking us for the assignment and wondered for the thousandth time why I had ever thought the navy was more romantic than the army. In the army, at least you didn't have to try to sleep with one leg wrapped around a stanchion. I knew that I was, and always would be, a landlubber. How could anyone love the sea when it was a gray-green tumult, shaking the vessel into a mass of complaining steel? But there it was; we were going out.

I retreated to the wardroom, where everyone was wondering what was up and giving candid opinions about the ancestry of the area escort commander who had probably picked us for this chore. The conversation was cut short by the PA speaker blaring out the captain's voice:

"Now hear this! We are getting underway immediately to proceed to the assistance of *SC 1047*, almost out of fuel and making heavy weather of it in a typhoon 90 miles to the northwest. All divisions make the necessary preparations for getting underway."

The speaker clicked off, but the words stayed on in my brain, for this was going to be my job, and doubtless far from pleasant. I realized that it would tax the skill of the most experienced, and I was anything but that. My imagination has always been vivid. In my mind's eye, I could see the little subchaser careening wildly in the storm, could almost catch the white-faced expression of her young skipper trying to guess how long it would be before help might arrive.

The problem was that I, Joe Sloane, who only a few weeks before had been a young professor at Bryn Mawr - and an art professor at that - was the rescuer for whom they waited, the focus of their agonized hope, the agent of their salvation. I found myself resenting the whole situation. Who was I to go around rescuing ships in gales? Why were the lives of a lot of men I'd never seen be put in my hands with the odds of rescue against me? I was deeply grateful for my boatswain, Larson, and his 10 years of sea experience. If he were allowed to do most of it, we would pull it off. I headed for my cabin and some rain gear.

Once *Dempsey* moved out of the harbor, the size of the sea became apparent. Green water poured up the hawse-pipes, sending the anchor detail scurrying for shelter behind the gun mount.

As we passed the stranded freighter, a particularly huge wave came crashing down on her decks. I felt the eyes of the detail on me, as if they said what was on their minds. I forced a grin and was relieved to be able to point out that the jack staff was improperly secured. In the ensuing activity, the thought of what lay ahead was forgotten.

When the course had been set, I breathed a little more easily, for it seemed to be a following sea, and the ship rode easily enough in synch with the waves. Until things changed, it might even be possible to catch a little sleep before I'd have to take over for the midwatch. I went up to the bridge and found that a message had just been received on the radio, giving *1047's* probable position and the disquieting news that it might run out of fuel before morning.

Captain Weber's face reflected the gravity of this report. There would be little chance for a small craft in that sea once she lost steerageway, broached and capsized with the probable loss of all hands. For some time, nobody broke the silence. Then I asked:

> "Well, sir, what will we do when we get there?" But even as I spoke I knew the answer.
>
> "Why, I guess we'll take her in tow, Joe. If we can, that is."

Of course, the solution was that simple. When we got to the rendezvous we would take her in tow. Just go below and learn how to do it in *Knight's Modern Seamanship*. Do it in the dark in the middle of a screaming wind and huge waves with a crew that hadn't even seen the sea 18 months before. And who was going to see to it? Why, I was, of course. I was first lieutenant, wasn't I?

To be sure, no one ever mentioned this routine in any of the schools I'd been to, but the navy tradition was that you did such things - and did them well - whether you knew much about them or not. There had been that pharmacist's mate who had removed a sailor's appendix in a submerged submarine because there wasn't anyone else around to do it. So now I was to rescue a subchaser in a typhoon because there wasn't anyone around who knew any more about it than I did. Even the redoubtable Larson had never been mixed up in anything like this. The captain must have read my mind, for he said with a grin:

> "Don't worry about it, Joe. You know you're only young once."

Later, when I consulted the chapter in *Knight's* book which dealt with rescuing vessels in storms, I read:

> "Some difficulty may be experienced in getting the line over."

"Some difficulty" indeed! *Dempsey* arrived at the anticipated rendezvous point shortly after midnight, but there was nothing in sight. Then we saw a solitary rocket climb into the scudding clouds and disappear - the subchaser was trying to help us find her. As we headed toward her, we plowed directly into the waves, and we felt the full force of the storm for the first time. . Our comparatively easy motion gave way to a series of sickening plunges into huge mountains of rushing water whose tops, higher than our bridge, were whipped off into hissing sheets of cold spume.

Looking forward, I watched each wave lift our bow until it hung out over a great chasm; then the water swept under us as *Dempsey* buried her bow in the dark mass rising to meet us. The wonderful little ship trembled, shook the water off the foredeck, and plunged ahead while the standing rigging, like taut fiddle strings, wailed an eerie accompaniment. It was a sight I can see to this day. The *1047* reported twice that her fuel could give out at any time.

As I went below, I rehearsed the plans for the hundredth time, but in that wild water with seas washing over the weather deck two feet deep and more, the chances of success seemed all too slender. It was my baby. Even though Larson would handle the lines and men, I knew just where the responsibility lay. We had worked out the whole thing together; the captain had approved it, but was my plan adequate?

I must have dozed off because, in no time at all, the messenger of the watch was shaking me and reporting that the subchaser was only two miles ahead and still underway. I staggered into my rain gear and buckled on a life jacket in the hope that, if I were washed off, I might be picked up. On deck, I found my men hard at work under Larson's sharp eye, laying out the mooring lines in long loops. He appeared calm, almost indifferent to the heaving deck and the water swirling around his legs. I noticed that the wind had dropped considerably.

I made my way to the port rail for a quick look and, as *Dempsey* heaved to the top of a wave, I could see the lights of the subchaser a short distance ahead. She had turned on every light available - even the anchor light! Presently, the big searchlight on our signal bridge pierced the blackness. I could glimpse a tiny hull slipping out of sight into the hollows beyond. As I turned away, the whole sequence ran through my mind. I envisioned the firing of the line gun, the small, white line arching through the dark, the messenger following, then the hawser, then making the line fast. But, could it be done?

Slowly, *Dempsey* drew abreast, and I could see that the SC had several men stationed in the bow to take our line. I knew they had to be there but I felt sorry for them - they were so vulnerable. The subchaser was plunging stubbornly into each wave, and the little group on her deck would disappear into the trough, only to reappear a moment later, their jackets gleaming wet in the cold glare. I half expected to see the bow rise empty after each dip, but the tiny group hung on and even managed cheerful waves with thumbs up.

Dempsey seemed big and far steadier in comparison; their deadly peril was transmitted to us all, and we were hanging on with them. I was looking at a picture - the roaring seas, the blue beam of our searchlight, the plunging hull across the water. In a movie, we might have thought it overdone. While imitated danger is exciting from the safety of a theater seat, the real thing is a whole different matter.

My talker, trying to protect his chest phone from the spray, leaned over and bellowed in my ear:

"Captain wants to know are you ready, sir!" Larson, standing beside me, grinned and nodded.

> "Tell the captain we're ready when he is!"
>
> "Captain says get the line over as soon as you can, sir!"

The position looked about as good as it was going to get, so through cupped hands I yelled "Fire!" to the gunner's mate on the deck above. A flat report from the line-throwing gun, and then a thin white line arched out toward the *1047*. The wind caught it and whipped it aft too fast; the cord fell into the sea astern.

But the second shot was perfect, landing right across the bow where those incredible figures seized it and began to haul it in rapidly. Soon, the messenger line was crossing the water, dragging the first towline after it. As I watched this hawser start across, I was almost afraid to breathe. Then I saw the water and wind make a huge bite in the line just as the loop was about to reach the chaser. A moment of awful strain and the messenger snapped, letting the hawser drift rapidly aft.

There was a long drawn "Aaaah!" from the men around me, cut by Larson's voice above the roar of the wind:

"Haul away! Get it inboard on the double!"

The danger of fouling our propellers was very real. In a moment, the men were engaged in a fierce struggle with the wet, slippery hawser which could spell disaster for everyone.

Soon, the wet length of cable was sprawled over the deck and was made ready for the next try. On order, the subchaser dropped back to the port quarter, a harder shot for the line gun, but far more easily handled once the messenger was received. Again the white line curved out into the dark and fell squarely aboard. A hush fell as the messenger and then the hawser slid out into the water. The great loop on the end could be seen snaking through the crests and finally climbing up the chaser's bow to the chock - but there it stuck. I felt the great heave of the men on that small deck, felt the missed beat in their hearts as they saw success snatched away by a piece of bad luck. Then suddenly the loop slid through, and the line was secured on the gun mount.

Half an hour later, in the growing light of dawn, I looked back at the subchaser riding easy at the end of our hawser and knew we had done a good night's work. I looked at Larson, and he looked at me. We both realized that what we had just been through would be our common property forever. I went forward, more tired than I had ever been in my life but, now that it was all over, I wouldn't have missed a minute of it. As I headed for my sack, the messenger of the watch came up with a dispatch.

"Captain thought you might like to see this, sir. It came over just after we got them in tow."

"ENGINES STOPPED FOR LACK OF FUEL TWO MINUTES AFTER HAWSER SECURED. THANKS."

USS Conklin – US Navy Photo

Silverstein (DE–534) in Typhoon Viper. Artist's Conception. Painting by Sam L. Massette © American Naval Art

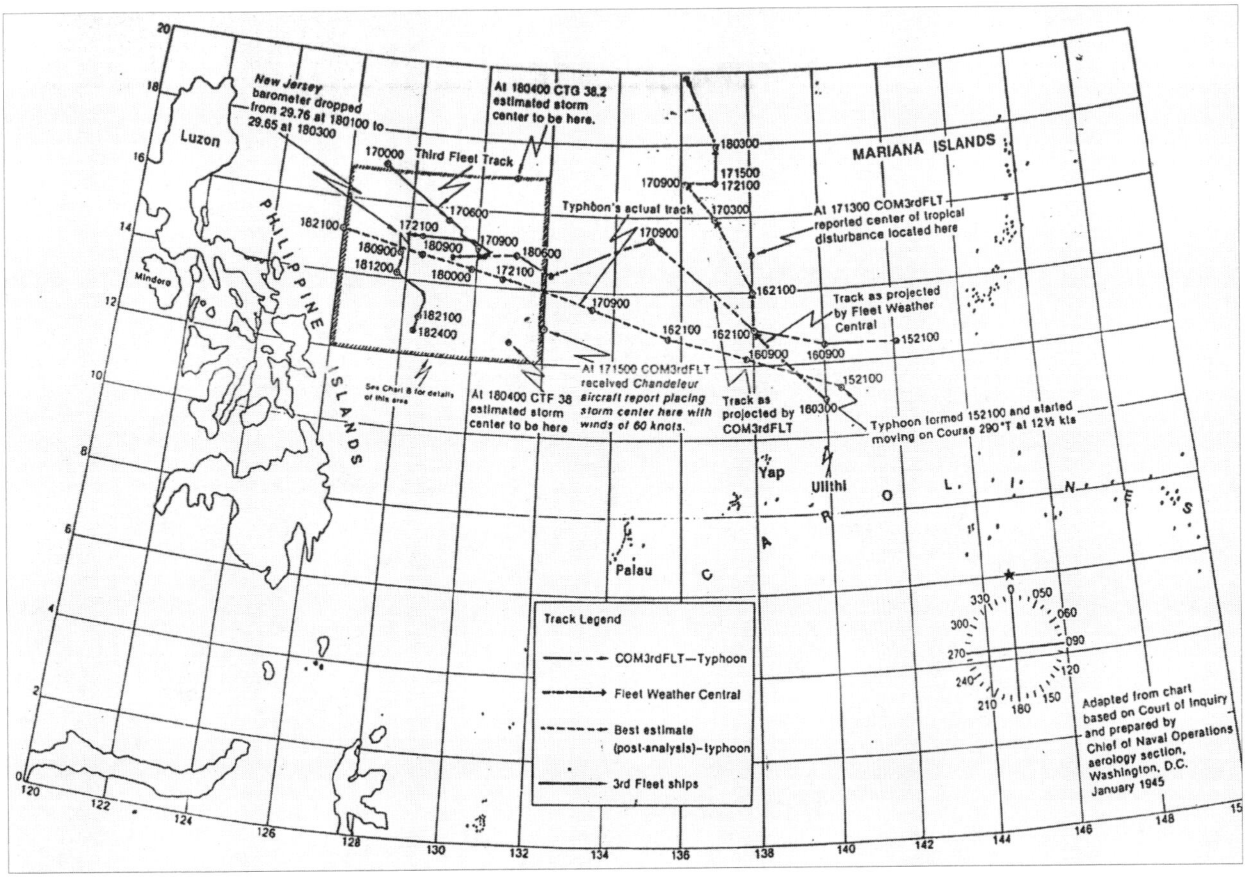

Track of typhoon, 17-18 Dec. 1944

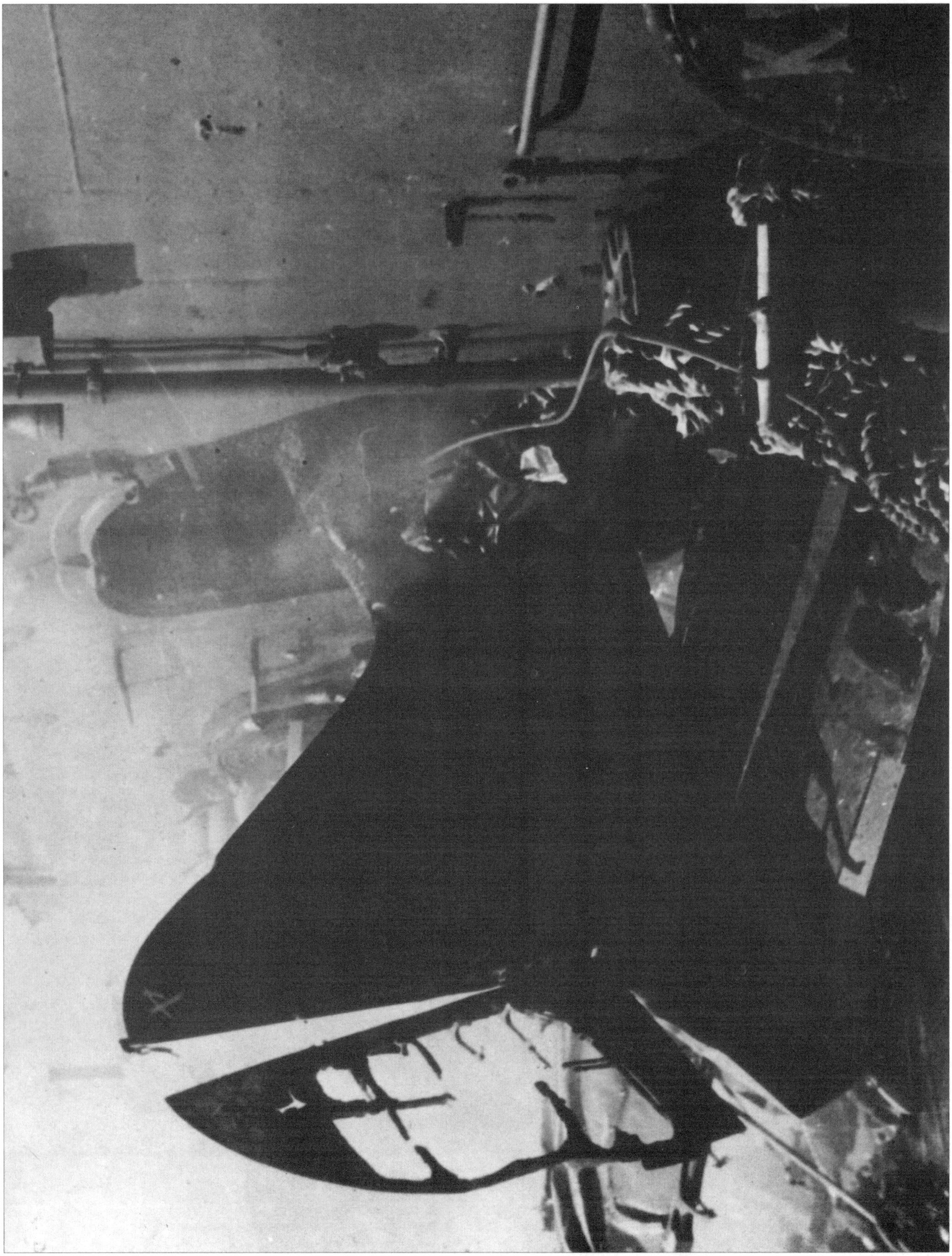

The *kamikaze* flew straight into the door on the main deck superstructure of *Rall.* US Navy Photo

Lewis M. Andrews, Jr.

Chapter XV - Iwo Jima To Okinawa – The Destroyer Escorts

The Kamikaze Crescendo

In August 1945, a confidential American appraisal of naval action against the *kamikazes* described it as "The costliest operation in the history of the American Navy." The suicide corps sank 34 ships, damaged 288 and killed 2300 men! The damage at Pearl Harbor paled by comparison, the difference being that we had a vastly greater navy in 1945 than in 1941. Most of the carnage was at Okinawa. The Japanese also paid an enormous price, over 2000 planes and pilots destroyed, some of their best young men.

The melee ceased with the collapse of Japanese resistance on Okinawa and the decision of their high command to garner *kamikaze* planes and pilots for the expected attack on Japan proper. Fortunately for both sides, the atom bomb aborted the planned assault and invasion.

To afford maximum protection to major fleet units, lighter ships were assigned picket stations in a perimeter of 30 to 100 miles from the main force. Mostly, they consisted of destroyers, destroyer escorts and fast transports. At the height of the attacks, almost any vessel with antiaircraft capability was pressed into service on the picket line. Ostensibly, the pickets would be the first to sight incoming raids. Practically, they bore the brunt of the assault and suffered greatly in casualties to men and ships. They took heavy pressure off the carriers and the forces invading Okinawa.

Winston Churchill described it as "the most intense and famous (battle) in history." Hanson W. Baldwin, in his book *Battles Lost and Won*, called it the greatest sea-air battle ever fought.

Among the dead, when the American flag finally flew over the burned and scarred island, were the commanders of both armies. Lieutenant General Simon Bolivar Buckner was fatally wounded by an enemy shell explosion near his observation post. Facing defeat, Japanese General Ushijima died in the ceremonial death of hara-kiri.

Some DEs and APDs were attacked repeatedly in a single day. Metalsmith First Class Chester Pike was on *Vammen (DE-644)*. In 1986, he wrote an article in DESA NEWS, the quarterly publication for destroyer escort veterans, recalling his memories of Okinawa. He expressed the deep emotions of many of the men who were there:

> "When our destroyer escort left Pearl Harbor at the end of February 1945, most of the crew sensed something different about this mission. We were not allowed specific information, but word did filter down from the bridge that Iwo Jima, a recent campaign on everyone's mind, had been a picnic compared to our new assignment. The Philippines was the staging area for the main invasion force. We left there on 25 March 1945 as the lead escort for a flotilla of LSTs and LCIs. Once underway, we learned we were to rendezvous off Okinawa with the largest, most powerful armada ever assembled. One April was the date set for invasion, Easter Sunday.
>
> Just before daybreak, we manned battle stations. The sun rose on a calm sea and a lovely spring morning. Soon, the higher elevations of Okinawa were in sight, and we worked our way in near the main landing beach on the west side of the island. This site had been chosen because of the shallow water and two enemy airfields nearby. A week of bombing from the air and shelling from the sea had already put these and other Japanese airfields out of operation. Boats took American soldiers in as far as they could, and the men casually waded ashore. The only battle sounds were from the big guns of the battleships and cruisers and the whine of shells overhead on their way to enemy positions inland. It seemed that nothing could be easier than this. What a shock awaited us! The Ryukyu string of islands, of which Okinawa was by far the largest, was the last bastion to defend Japanese soil. The Japanese were desperate. With little hope of winning, they gambled on a victory at Okinawa as grounds for a negotiated peace instead of unconditional surrender. Every effort was directed toward destroying or crippling the U.S. Fleet. Their strategy was to pull their land defenses inland, thus bringing the American ships close inshore where the *kamikazes* could more readily attack them. American military leaders had estimated a 30-day campaign to secure the island. It required over 2-1/2 months of savage fighting in which 110,000 Japanese and 12,000 Americans died.
>
> General Ushijima chose to defend only the southern one-sixth of the island. The Americans secured the residual area in the first few days of the campaign. The general made his main defense at the rugged, strongly fortified Shure Line. It was not until 22 June that the American High Command finally announced to the world that only mopping-up operations remained on Okinawa.
>
> Meanwhile, offshore, the *kamikazes* came by the hundreds with their bombs and only enough fuel for a one-way flight. The young, fanatical pilots believed that they would attain instant and eternal glory when they flew their planes into enemy ships.
>
> American pilots did a good job intercepting and shooting them down off the coast, but some always got through. While they still had to face naval antiaircraft fire, many *kamikazes* reached their targets. On overcast days, they would suddenly appear out of the clouds and dive on the nearest ships in sight. On sunny days, they circled high, out of antiaircraft range, until they spotted choice victims. Then, like hawks descending on a prey, they came out of the sun, crashing the decks of large or small ships alike.
>
> For one six week period, there were continuous air raids at Okinawa both day and night. The log of *Vammen* recorded battle stations manned 40 times in one four week period.
>
> Most of our duty at Okinawa was on the radar picket line. Each of 15 or 20 ships was assigned a patrol sector offshore. The ship's radar normally detected the incoming planes; then we alerted the fighters to go out after them and warned the ships of the fleet that bogies were coming in".

In a subsequent letter to this author, Chester Pike also indicated some compassion for the enemy:

> "A cloudy morning on 28 May. The Japanese launched one of their last, desperate *kamikaze* attacks. From my damage control battle station on the main deck of *Vammen*, I

could hear planes overhead but couldn't see them. Soon, one plunged into plain view, close enough that I could see the pilot and read his facial expressions.

He appeared to be very young. Only a few seconds elapsed from his appearance to his disappearance. He was clearly frightened, and I could see that he was looking around for the largest available target. Under heavy fire, he headed for another DE nearby. He quickly took a hit, nose-dived into the sea and sank immediately. We took credit for the hit."

Chester closed his earlier article:

"Okinawa was the last major battle of World War II. It and the other battles of that war are receding into the distant past. The great military and naval leaders of the era are gone. Reporters now refer to the heroic events of 1941-45 as belonging to another age. I wonder if other battle veterans of WW II experience the same deep-seated fear which I, in recent years, have come to know. I am afraid the world will forget.

World, don't forget Pearl Harbor, Corregidor, Midway, North Africa, Sicily, Normandy, Leyte Gulf, The Bulge, Iwo Jima, Okinawa. World War II was our finest hour!"

And that is precisely the reason this author undertook the daunting task of writing this book.

GENDREAU

A Gallant Ship in the Clutch of War

Gendreau (DE-639), like *Borum* in *Operation Overlord*, was unique because two of her enlisted personnel maintained meticulous diaries. The pages paint a symphony of sailors on the road to war, the brutal reality of conflict, then retreat to peace in the profound farewell address of the captain.

From opposite ends of the ship, two sources tell of *Gendreau* going into battle. One came from an office near the wardroom, a recount of the experiences of the ship from commissioning in Norfolk, Virginia, to Tokyo Bay by Yeoman John P. Cosgrove. The other was from the battle diary of Motor Machinist Mate Third Class John A. Virum. Cosgrove had the advantage of access to ship's logs and action reports whereas Virum's diary depended on daily activities as he saw them. Virum recorded personal experiences such as getting a shiner in a fight, winning a few dollars at dice, drinking too much beer, being bawled out by the skipper. On his twenty-first birthday, as a typhoon roared, a galley buddy baked him a cake.

As previously mentioned, regulations forbade keeping a camera or maintaining a diary aboard ship for security reasons. However, Virum decided he would take his chances and keep a secret diary. Fifty years after the fact, we are happy to have it and can only wish there had been more of them, regulations not withstanding. Yeoman Cosgrove had an advantage in that he was encouraged to maintain an official ship's history.

Virum was adept at keeping his diary out of sight. Amid the drama of the Okinawa invasion, he never forgot that he was simply a Minnesota civilian in a Navy uniform. Both diaries were clarified and abridged by the author as necessary but without detracting from the content. Yeoman Cosgrove recalled the beginning:

"Ours is the story of the trials and tribulations of a little destroyer escort and her valiant crew, an exciting, monotonous, dreary, interesting, lonesome and wonderful experience from Norfolk and San Francisco through thousands of miles of the big, blue, beautiful and sometimes not-so-pacific Pacific.

For the most part, the crew was green - only about 10 percent had been to sea before.

For our skipper, Lieutenant Commander A.D. Kilmartin, Naval Academy 1934, this was his first command. He came to *Gendreau* after a year's duty on the Far Eastern desk, Navy Intelligence, following a tour as naval attache in China for five years. The captain was a tall, slim, erect, mustachioed, handsome, spirited, typical naval officer with distinct diplomatic bearings in his early thirties. Very soon, the crew nicknamed him 'Navy Regs' because he lived by the book. Except for the first executive officer, Mr. Lachlan, who called him 'Al', he was 'Captain' in the full sense of the word.

17 March 1944 was a landmark day for the crew, the beginning of a new era, a distinctively different way of living, the day we had been preparing for since boot days. We now became an integral part of a living ship. The crew was a cross section of America, from the north, south, east and west. - 23 May 1944. We silently and thoughtfully slipped through the Golden Gate and waved so long to a few people high on the big red bridge. We knew we were leaving our country for a long while, and we wanted to wave to somebody. They must have known our feelings by waving back and perhaps murmuring 'God bless them'.

While in the vicinity of Hawaii on 31 July, we rescued two survivors from a plane crash. A few days later, we picked up another pilot while operating with the carrier *Ranger (CVA-61)*.

About seasickness. Sailors are not immune to it in peace or war; it is a dreadful feeling. Some people are never bothered with it, some get used to it, and others never conquer it. Many regulars are subject to it even as they near the 20 year mark. But as time slipped by, we became used to the rough seas, and seasickness was no longer an ordeal. We laughed when someone's tray spilled or when a rack of cups or bowls was torn loose from some mess cook's sweaty arms. We couldn't get sick any more - we're salty now.

We were no longer boots but fighting men. There was no fun in the mess hall now; we wanted to eat and anything that might hinder our eating would be damned. To hold a tray from sliding (and usually to the deck), one would jab a sheath knife into the wooden table, closely against the tray, so as to firmly hold it in place.

13 September was a rough day. We were a few days out of Pearl. Together with two other DEs, we were escorting three 'jeep' carriers. About halfway to Manus, we had to fuel.

We pulled alongside the carrier *Breton (CVE-23)* and started fueling. Waves drenched all of us in the fueling detail on the main deck, and it began to drizzle. We had taken a few thousand gallons of oil when suddenly the fantail began to swing out. We saw the black, snake-like fuel hose stretch out and then break sharply, spurting oil. Then, as the skipper tried to correct for the heavy swing out, our bow began to swing in. The first lieutenant, chief engineer, Chief Bos'un's Mate, Andy Anderson, Brodie, Satterfield, Carpenter and Chief Water Tender Webster were on the main deck, trying to get the tow line loose. Someone yelled 'Look out, we're going to crash', but only the chief engineer and Carpenter were able to get clear. The others hastily ran one way and then another, and finally stopped as our bow came under the towering flight deck of the carrier - a monster to us.

There was a resounding crash of tons of metal and, as the two ships rolled, much of our superstructure was crushed by the carrier's gun sponsons, causing considerable damage. Then, as suddenly as they collided, the two ships parted. Miraculously, there were no injuries. Mr. Sherfey finally succeeded in cutting the 10" towing hawser with an axe. All power was turned off on the mast; aerials had been torn loose and were dangling. Chief Ward, Jimmy Aikens, Buck Ashton, Wasniewski and Harold Osborn were on the job and worked continuously for hours with makeshift repairs and jury rigs. One of our heavy shrouds had carried away, and our 90-foot mast was wobbling. All hands pitched in, none the worse for the experience. Patched up, we continued on our way to Manus.

Five days after the collision, we stopped at Emirau, St. Matthias group, northwest of New Ireland, to fuel again. At Manus, we went alongside the destroyer tender *Piedmont (AD-17)*, undergoing repairs until 1 October. The island contained a few trees, baseball field, handball courts, swimming beach and a large sign 'Welcome to Duffy's Tavern'. Compared later on to Purvis Bay, Tulagi, Ulithi, Kerama Retto and Okinawa, it was good 'liberty'.

Our next trip took us southeast from New Guinea and New Britain to the Coral Sea and finally into the famed Iron Bottom Bay, bounded on the southwest by Guadalcanal and, on the northeast by Florida Island. We steamed past the cone-like Savo Island through the bay and into port at Purvis, our home base for the next six months.

The Purvis natives caught our attention in their narrow dugout canoes with outriggers. Frequently, multi-colored parrots perched on the graceful upswept stems and sterns. The men were very small, usually bare to the waist, and many had hair bleached to a straw-like color. We seldom saw women. When we did, it was only a glimpse of the small, large breasted females. The natives kept their women well hidden.

We were assigned to *CortDiv 73*. Of the six ships in our division, *Fieberling (DE-640)*, *William C. Cole (DE-641)*, *Paul G. Baker (DE-642)*, *Damon M. Cummings (DE-643)*, and *Vammen (DE-644)*, ours flew the pennant of Commander Paul G. Hammond, later relieved by Commander Rowland H. Groff, Naval Academy 1926, an experienced destroyer officer. It wasn't long before we were out practicing with ships of our division. We would fire at sleeves towed by planes or at a small uninhabited island (Rua Dika) for shore bombardment. On occasion, we maneuvered with PT boats.

We pulled into Espiritu Santo on the afternoon of 7 November, fueled and moored alongside *HMAS Australia*. She had been hit by a suicide plane in the Battle of Lingayen Gulf. *Kamikazes* were hush-hush because they were more effective than the navy cared to admit. We found out all about them later on.

Christmas Eve found Purvis Bay filled with troop transports stopping by for the holiday. On Christmas morning, an LCVP with an improvised band from a transport made the rounds of the smaller ships in the harbor, playing Christmas carols, but there all resemblance to the season ended. The weather was more like the Fourth of July at home.

10 January 1945. We had our first serious casualty, causing the death of one of our most popular and best liked men, Seaman First Class Jimmy Cameron. We were making practice submarine runs that day. When we fired a depth charge pattern, Jimmy was struck by one of the arbors. He died without ever knowing what had happened, and we buried him the next day on Guadalcanal.

The evening of 29 January. We were anchored at Lunga Roads off Guadalcanal. An ammunition ship, *Serpens (AK-97)* lay 2000 yards astern of us. Earlier, she had been flying code flag Baker, signal for ammunition handling. We had a movie that evening under an almost full moon. The scene could not have been more peaceful. After the movies, most of us hit the sack. A little after 2300, a deafening roar shook the ship and brought us to our feet.

The night was filled with blinding light and falling debris. Huge pieces of flaming red hot metal fell in the water on all sides. Directly astern of us, a billowing black cloud of smoke fanned outward and upward and, as it cleared, we could see nothing where the *Serpens* had been anchored. She had disappeared. The navy later revealed that she had been lost due to enemy action.

In early February at Purvis Bay, ships came pouring in; tenders, transports, floating dry docks, destroyers and smaller craft crowded the harbor. Our lazy little recreation beach became a mass of howling humanity, and a lot of us stopped going over, including the officers. We knew that something really big was up. Word also got around that we were going to be in it.

We had returned from a short escort job when our next catastrophe occurred. Port Purvis was over-crowded that afternoon when we steamed toward the entrance channel and were ordered to drop the hook outside the main harbor. We dropped the anchor once, but the skipper decided we were too near a reef. We pulled up the hook and got ready to drop it again when we backed onto another coral reef. Both propellers were badly bent and the shafts were out of line.

17-20 February saw us in dry dock while members of the repair ship *Tutuila (ARG-44)* and our ship's force worked night and day to get the ship back in shape. The word was out now. We were going to be in a big invasion and we had to be ready for sea by an early date.

Our skipper was relieved by the executive officer of *Fieberling (DE-640)*, Lieutenant Martin Victor. He was a lawyer from Syosset, New York, a graduate of both Harvard and Yale, and a Naval Reserve Officer. He had been on active duty since 1940, both in the Atlantic and Pacific, in destroyers and destroyer escorts. He had been on the destroyer *O'Brien (DD-415)* when she was sunk.

Tempest, Fire and Foe

It didn't take long for the new skipper to gain our confidence; he even knew how to interpret Navy Regs in such a way that they held enjoyment and benefit for the crew. His was the enormous task of taking over responsibility for the ship only 15 days before the initial landings on Okinawa. He took command with a firm hand and pulled us through the most grueling operation of the war.

We arrived at Ulithi on 21 March, having drilled constantly en route, preparing for the ordeal ahead. The harbor was crammed with U.S. ships and a newly arrived British task force. Like all atolls, Ulithi consisted of a large lagoon surrounded by coral reefs and islands. The anchorage was rough and exposed to heavy swells from the sea. Nearby was the strongly fortified Yap, blasted continually by our air force, but still a menace. The sight of the assembled force was so great, so powerful that nobody could doubt the invincibility of the United States Fleet and the assurance of our ultimate victory over Japan.

The next few days were frantically spent in last minute repairs, taking on stores and other activities incidental to the invasion. There was no liberty. Many of us were excited at the prospect of finally being included in the war; some were tense and became more so as departure day approached; others were non-committal, and the old-timers weren't saying very much. We were all thinking!

Palm Sunday, 25 March. We departed from Ulithi, leading a flotilla of landing craft. We had written letters home, and many wondered if they would write again. Our watch, quarter and station bills or mustering stations at GQ, fire, collision, man overboard, etc. were sharpened to a point of high efficiency. We were constantly on the lookout for submarines, aircraft, or other indications of enemy interference. The strain increased. Radio programs from Ulithi, Saipan and Guam faded out. All that remained were the propaganda broadcasts from powerful Japanese stations in Japan and China.

Several days before we reached Okinawa, we were met by our own CAP (Combat Air Patrol), and were they a welcome sight! On the eve of the landing, we sighted Okinawa in the distance, barely visible against the rays of the setting sun. In the far distance, we could hear the resounding boom of gunfire as our battlewagons pounded the shores of Okinawa.

Shortly after midnight, Easter Sunday, GQ called us to battle stations. The silence of the dim moonlit night was split by the streaming tracers of antiaircraft fire from the landing ships behind us. A bogey was coming in, about bridge height, and heading for us"!

Motor Machinist Mate John Virum remembers the action:

"The general alarm galvanized the crew of *Gendreau*. As untested warriors, adrenaline flowing, we dashed to battle stations, and the stillness of night was shattered by streaming tracers of nearby antiaircraft fire. As the *kamikaze* zoomed straight for the bridge, the DE's sights instantly locked on the raider. A burst of shell fire sliced off the invader's wing, and he splashed 50 yards off the starboard quarter!"

A wave of exhilaration swept the ship as the crew responded superbly to its first encounter. This was the decisive moment these young mariners had looked forward to for months with varying degrees of anticipation or foreboding. This was our first action against the enemy and also our first plane shot down. Later in the day, we were cited for shooting down the first plane on D-Day.

We had a battle breakfast of bacon and eggs, eating in shifts, a few at a time while the rest remained at battle stations. We were secured from GQ about 1800, but I stayed in my gun tub. This is the sixth day that I haven't had my clothes off.

After dark, we were again attacked by enemy night fighters. One plane was shot down over our fantail! The shrapnel was really flying thick. I'm so tired I can't sleep anymore. All I can say is that this was one hell of an Easter Sunday, and I thank God for bringing us through."

Back to Yeoman Cosgrove:

1 April. "It was 'April Fool', but to us it was more like the Fourth of July because about 0600 all hell broke loose. The dawn was beginning to break, and our ships had again started a shore bombardment that did not stop until Okinawa was secured three months later.

0715. We were detached from the landing ships and proceeded out to one of the screening stations near Ie Shima. Around us, transports were unloading troops, supplies and ammunition. Hundreds of small landing craft circled and then proceeded toward the beach. Above, squadrons of planes, loaded with bombs and rockets, filled the sky. The landings were successful.

After being detached from the landing ships, we were assigned with destroyers and destroyer escorts in maintaining a picket line about Okinawa, ostensibly screening against possible submarine attack. The picket line was referred to as 'Bogey Highway'. We spent more than 20 continuous days on that hectic 'highway' when the 'traffic' was heaviest. During that time, we went to battle stations sixty-seven times. Sometimes, there was action and other times we just stood by, watching, waiting, searching and praying.

'Bogey' was a colloquialism for a located suicide plane. We had our fill of these one way rammers, and while ships all around us were being hit, we got off with narrow escapes, and more than once we thought 'here's one with our name on it'. These suiciders came in assorted sizes and shapes which Radio Tokyo kept telling us were winning their war!

We will always remember the Tony which made a strafing run from port to starboard, his aim reminding us of a blind man at a turkey shoot. The starboard gunners followed him out and peppered him. We didn't down him, however, and he circled to make a suicide attempt from starboard to port, heading into our heaviest fire, barreling right for us like mad. This time, we really filled him with lead, but he kept coming. With a quick change in speed and course, we out maneuvered him, but his wheels barely missed the antennae abaft the stack. He splashed about 20 yards on our port beam! We wiped the sweat from our brows and secured from battle stations. Torpedoman Third Class George Kennedy and Fire Controlman Second Class Kenneth Ward had a piece of shrapnel land between them, and now each carries half a memento of that bogey."

Virum made a diary entry corroborating the above, but he added:

"That makes two Japanese planes shot down. I was really scared when he began strafing us. It's only a feeling you get when you see it actually happen. I haven't had any mail now for two weeks. Honey, I really miss you a lot, and I wish I was home with you now more than ever."

Back to Cosgrove:

"Along with the 'kami-crazies' was the constant threat of mines broken loose by our sweepers or laid by enemy submarines. We also had to worry about aircraft, suicide swimmers, suicide boats, suicide torpedoes, shore batteries, midget subs and obstructions to navigation. No, we didn't think about all these things at once, but we were constantly on the alert for any or all of them. The strain was debilitating, and the captain had the responsibility for everything. We were amazed to see how well he handled the ship and himself. He set an example for all of us, officers and men alike. Gradually, we became accustomed to the constant strain. Few of us slept below, but we learned when we could best take showers and shave and when it was best to sleep - or try to! We also learned to hate the sunsets and sunrises for they were mostly associated with suicide attacks, and we didn't like bright moonlit nights for the same reasons. We even 'turned-to', making the ship look just as good or better than any other DE in the forward area.

6 April. The Japs made one of their heaviest assaults on our forces. A little after sunset, a Kate bounced in on us. He dodged this way and that, and we poured lead into him until we were sure he was dead, but he kept coming. The skipper maneuvered radically, while at the same time bringing the maximum fire power to bear on the target. Just before being shot down, the pilot released what could have been either a torpedo or a bomb. It exploded upon impact with the water, The plane then nosed up, and our lead filled its 'belly' until it burst into flame, veered off and splashed about 500 yards astern!

Early the next morning, *Bowers (DE-637)* reported a plane racing in on her. Our forward main battery pumped some shells into this 'bogey', but *Bowers* got the credit, and we an 'assist'. *Bowers* later took a suicider and suffered heavy casualties." (See heroic narrative of *Bowers* in this chapter).

Virum kept score and hoped for the best:

"That makes four. We sank another mine, so that's four of them now. I pray Dear Lord to bring us through and with victory ours. I sure miss Mary's mail. All we do is eat, go to G.Q. and try to sleep a little. I send you a big kiss, honey, hope you like it."

Back to Cosgrove:

"12 April. We had another red letter night. There was no moon, and we felt a little safer covered with darkness until a plane came over and dropped a flare. That's a very peculiar, helpless feeling, and another plane got a line on us. His range kept getting closer and closer. From radar, 'bogey bearing 045, 10 miles closing!' Yet, strain as we would, we could not see him. Suddenly, the whine of his engine could be heard. Then we saw him coming out of the black, and we had time only to squirt a few rounds at him. A few seconds later, we saw a torpedo wake passing right under our bridge. We began thinking that we had a charmed life.

Friday, the thirteenth! (Who needed that date at Okinawa?) Another problem. Coxswain Joe Kreon was sick and 'Doc' Peck thought it was appendicitis. After the captain radioed for assistance, the destroyer minelayer *Harry F. Bauer (DM-26)* hove into view within a short time. A doctor examined Joe and said that an operation was necessary so we put him in the motor whaleboat and sent him over to *Bauer*. He underwent an appendectomy that afternoon and was returned to the ship about a week later, weak but better, and it wasn't long before he was 'back to battery'.

The 13th continued its gloom. We heard of the death of President Roosevelt, a distinct shock. Soon, the Jap radio was filled with news about our late Commander-in-Chief. We listened for details of the death, but radio Tokyo blared forth with wild stories, blaming the war on him, while at the same time tearing Mr. Truman apart.

We were now in our third week on the 'highway', feeling more like three years. We had little news from the States and learned that the ground fighting on 'Okie' was getting tougher. We thought more than ever about home and wondered how things were. In the silence of waiting at battle stations, we thought about everything in the past we ever did and what we would do if we ever got a future. That's what we did to forget about the present. All hands topside were bleary-eyed, watching for bogies and suicide craft on the water as well. The captain listened to reports from the CIC nerve center. The engineers were on the alert for 'bells'; the repair parties waited, wondered and grasped at every word from the bridge talker telling of topside doings; ammunition-passing parties sweated it out. Eventually, it all works itself into the tapestry of one dull pattern. Yesterday is tomorrow and when will it ever stop and, God we're so tired. We were too tired to stay awake and, upon securing from GQ, too tired to sleep. Most of us remained near our battle stations and still they came.

16 April. Now they were coming in pairs or more, and we thought that our goose was cooked for sure. About 15 minutes before sunset, two Oscars came in out of the sun. They had us spotted and circled for a split attack. Two more planes came in from the same direction, and we held our breath and heaved a sigh of relief when we saw that they were Hellcats. We opened fire but stopped when it was apparent that our planes were closing in for a kill. One plane started to dive on us with an F6F right on his tail. Had we been a little further away, the dog fight might have been exciting. As it was, we were too close. The Jap caught fire as the 'Hellcat' poured several bursts into him. Then, blazing, he struggled to crash on our ship. We opened fire and he splashed about a thousand yards astern! The other plane had

high tailed it with the other F6F hot on his tail. We never did know what happened to the second Jap, but we took our hats off to the pilot who knocked out the bogey that started to dive on us.

Throughout the campaign, we never failed to open fire on all enemy planes within range of our guns; nor did we ever open fire on a friendly. The tribute goes to our recognition experts topside, and especially to Lieutenant (jg) Kinkaid and Coxswain Don Couture, who conducted recognition classes and were on the bridge at GQ, 'hawk eyes'. In the same manner that it takes men to run a ship, it takes men to fight a ship. We found that there is more to a ship than steel. Throughout the entire campaign, the personnel performance was outstanding.

22 April. We left Okinawa in convoy with destroyers and destroyer escorts, including the famous *Laffey (DD-459)*, limping back to the states after becoming a casualty at Okinawa. The farther we got from Okinawa, the better we felt. Five days later, we arrived at Tanapag Harbor, Saipan. The evening before, we saw the B-29 bombers, the first we had ever seen, and they were a wonderful sight, like a miniature fleet of airborne battleships. Saipan looked beautiful. Movie screens were rigged on the fantails of most all the ships in the harbor; there were liberty facilities for officers and men. It wasn't over an hour after our arrival, however, that we learned that our stay was to be brief and that we would be leaving that same afternoon. It was a deep disappointment to all of us. We convoyed urgently needed troop reinforcements.

This time, we anchored at Hagushi Beach, scene of the initial landings; and it was about that time our troops were having so much trouble on the island. Because of heavy rains, there were no air attacks during the first two days and, on the third day, we joined the battleship *Tennessee (BB-43)* with another escort and left for Ulithi and availability. We hoped!

Arriving in Ulithi on 7 May, we received availability, had movies on the fantail, liberty on a small uninhabited island where we drank beer while sitting on tree stumps or went swimming. We left our weather deck hatches and doors open to give us a little more air for sleeping and, in general, relaxed for the first time since leaving Ulithi."

On a day in May, a note of poignancy was injected into Virum's life:

"I had a letter from Mary saying she got engaged to a sailor from California! I sure feel bad about it. I loved her so. I also got seven letters from Sis and also a couple from Mom and Carol S."

Virum accepted Mary's farewell with good grace. The next day he wrote to her for the last time. Back to Cosgrove:

"The morning of 8 June. We escorted a group of LCIs along the western coast and around the southern tip of Okinawa where they landed tanks and troops. That particular day was clear and sunny, and we had a ringside seat at what was happening to the southern part of Okinawa. Overhead, navy fighters and bombers were winging in with tons of explosives which they dropped on Jap positions. Some of the fighters would go down for strafing runs. Once in a while, a single burst in the air would indicate ineffective AA firing attempts by the Japs. Inside our track line, battleships were pounding away; several cruisers were letting 8" salvos go at short intervals; a number of destroyers were firing 5" batteries, all slamming away at the island. The LCIs landed that evening at Sakibaru Saki without mishap. We escorted them in a safe distance and screened while they unloaded."

John Virum gave this account of damage from enemy shore batteries:

"0751 on 9 June turned out to be the unluckiest of our unlucky days. At a range of 3500 yards, a Jap shore battery opened up on us. We were not at GQ; a number of us were still in the chow line on the starboard side. Others were in the mess hall finishing breakfast. A 6" shell scored a direct hit in our number one fire room. Three others landed astern. No one knew what had happened. On the bridge, the captain and the commodore had been supervising the formation of LCIs. Mr. Kutner was the Officer of The Deck and immediately hit the general alarm, but the alarm had been shorted and all we heard was a hum. 'Bud' Pearson, Yeoman bridge talker at the time, passed the word over the phones to go to battle stations, but the circuit had been cut and only a few stations received the word. Mr. Follin, then assistant gunnery officer, was making time to his GQ station, calling to others to do the same. But most of us didn't have to be told what to do. The place to be was at one's GQ station, and that is where each went on the double.

Steam, combined with the acrid smoke of the explosion, was pouring out of the number 1 fire room, filling the passageway and officer's quarters so that it was impossible to see. Breathing was labored.

The watch had just been relieved, and we were not sure how many men were in fire room number 1. Water Tender Second Class Jim Mannion and Fireman First Class Al Malone, both wounded by the explosion, managed to get from the lower level of the fire room back to the after battle dressing station before many of us were aware of just what had happened. They told us that two more men were on watch with them but, by that time, Water Tender Second Class William Mack had gone down in the darkness of the forward fire room to secure steam valves. He returned with Chief Water Tender 'Web' Webster from the flooded fire room. In short order, Lieutenant Sherfey's engineers rigged an emergency cable for communications, restoring power forward and shifting control to secondary aft."

Back to Cosgrove:

"Fireman First Class John Robert Moeller and Fireman Second Class Harry Earl Scott were trapped below. Lights were out, and the mess hall was filled with hot steam. We managed to get topside through the forward hatch.

Slowly, the ship gained headway on one screw and pulled away from the beach, into which she had been drifting. *Paul G. Baker (DE-642)* was nearby and offered assistance, but we were able to take care of ourselves. Damage control parties completed shoring bulkheads fore and aft of the fire room, and we proceeded at 10 knots for Kerama Retto, the 'bone yard' for ships and graveyard for sailors, where repair facilities were available.

Harry Scott was found dead under the oil and water in number 1 fire room. Jack Moeller was missing in action. Scott had not been out of the states much over a month and Moeller had been with us since commissioning. Two fine shipmates, and it is to them, Cameron and the wounded that this history is dedicated. Mannion and Malone were transferred to a larger ship for medical treatment an hour or so after we arrived at Kerama Retto. We held a military funeral for Scott and Moeller at the Armed Forces Cemetery.

The rest of the month slipped by quickly. We were subject to air raids nearly every night, but the skipper would 'button-up the ship' and seldom call us to battle stations. It was about this time that Okinawa was secured, but it made little difference to us. We still had bogey raids to contend with. One night, about sundown, two got through and crashed onto two seaplane tenders *Curtis (AV-4)* and *Kenneth Whiting (AV-14)*.

Friday 13 July. With repairs barely completed, we were underway to report to a task force operating in the East China Sea. It included battleships, cruisers, escort carriers, about 12 destroyers and several other destroyer escorts. Our little DE was going out to operate with first line ships.

We had to be on the ball all the time. The unit was covering mine sweeping operations off the coast of China. A number of times, Jap planes tried to come in on us, but they were shot down or driven off by our fighter planes before they ever came within sight. Drifting mines were our biggest worry.

Seldom, if ever, did a day go by when the ships didn't see and sink a mine. We had one very close call. One moonlit night, Seaman First Class Gerald K. Dotson, a lookout, reported a mine dead ahead. Mr. Kinkaid, Officer of The Deck, acted on instinct and swung the ship first in one direction and then in the other so that we 'crabbed' around the mine. Several men saw the mine drift by, not more than five feet from the ship.

On one trip, our task force got as close as 85 miles from Shanghai, making us a little jumpy. We picked up a pilot from the *Makin Island (CVE-93)*, whose plane had crashed about two miles from us.

We went right into one of the heaviest typhoons of the season. We slowed speed until we were barely bucking the storm. With each wave, there came the shock of the ship dropping down into nothingness and then coming up against the water with a resounding thud that shook her from stem to stern. Gigantic waves towered over us as we were tossed around like a cork.

7 August. We were still in Buckner Bay when the Okinawa (U.S.) radio was sending out the regular news broadcast. A powerful new bomb had been dropped on Hiroshima. It meant more to us than we could ever tell. Until now, we felt that the war had at least a year to run.

The morning of 10 August. We heard that Russia had declared war on Japan and, a few hours later, we heard the news of the second atomic bomb at Nagasaki. That evening, Radioman Second Class Jim Kirkpatrick, was on duty, guarding one of the voice circuits, when he heard that Japan had surrendered. He immediately informed Lieutenant Shakleford, the Officer of The Deck, and the news was soon all over the ship.

There were shouts of joy throughout the ship. Nonetheless, two enemy planes came in. One was shot down by night fighters, but the other succeeded in torpedoing a merchant ship on the other side of the island.

Sunday morning, 12 August. We received news of the allied answer to the Japanese surrender terms. That evening, a Jap plane came in and torpedoed the battleship *Pennsylvania (BB-38)*. On the 13th, a transport was hit by another torpedo plane. Yes, the war was still going on.

14 August. Hotter than hell. We were alerted to enemy air attacks throughout the day, and you could almost feel the mounting tension in the bay. We were afraid that the answer might come in the form of another Pearl Harbor, and Okinawa was the logical place to try it. In the meantime, Admiral Halsey's carrier planes resumed their bombardment of Japan, and the B-29s were again on their bombing missions. Late that afternoon, we received orders to get underway. We had just weighed anchor when the word we had been waiting to hear came. 'Radio Tokyo has announced that Japan surrenders unconditionally to the Potsdam Ultimatum'."

During this uncertain period, some of the carrier pilots with the Third Fleet reported that they still saw some enemy planes in the vicinity. Uncertain as to what action to take, hostile or passive, Admiral Halsey was asked for instructions. His famous reply: 'Shoot them down in a friendly manner!'

The resultant mood could not have been more profoundly expressed than in John Virum's last diary entry: Finally, in jubilation, he inscribed in capital letters: "JAPAN SURRENDERS. THE WAR IS OVER three years, eight months and eight days after we went to war. Whoopee".

That was it. *Gendreau* sailed to Tokyo Bay and performed some occupational duties before returning to the United States.

The captain, Lieutenant Commander Martin Victor, delivered the following farewell address two months after the end of the war:

> "For the men of *Gendreau*, returning to peaceful ways of life, the past years will fade in memory, but this story will recall valued shipmates and a life strange and uncongenial to many of us, that of the seafaring man. In regarding it in future years, let us consider the cost of failure to live in peace with the world and, in that light, judge the politicians of the day. We may take pride that we were among those who, with our own hands, defended the country in battle, but let us not for that reason ask privileges as civilians. We shall remember the sometimes irksome but always vital role of military leadership, discipline and planning, all directed toward the objective of defeating the enemy.
>
> Now, as citizens, remember the obligation to question, consider and examine both ideas and men, realizing that the objective itself is not always clear. Beware of popular leaders of the moment, being careful not to follow blindly, but to think and act in the interest of the country. Your recent life in the Pacific with its boredom, dangers and absences from the

United States will drive home what it means to be an American."

WALTER C. WANN

A Close Call

Walter C. Wann (DE-412) had a string of confrontations with the enemy from battleships to *kamikazes* well before the Okinawa campaign, starting with her assignment to "Taffy Two" during the Battle off Samar on 25 October 1944

On 10 November in Seeadler Harbor, Manus, *Wann* came close to being damaged when *Mount Hood (AE-10)* blew up in a cataclysmic blast which atomized the ammunition ship and crew. Only 2000 yards off the doomed ship's port quarter, *Wann* found herself showered by debris from the exploding ammunition ship. Fortunately she sustained only minimal damage, and none of her men were hurt.

At Lingayen Gulf, this DE was heavily engaged in driving off Japanese suicide ships which were attempting to crash major fleet units.

27 March saw *Wann* screening a transport group bound for Nansei Shoto in the Ryukyus. Approaching Okinawa with the invasion force on the morning of D-Day, 1 April, her task unit was deployed to cover the landings. This DE took an Oscar under fire, but the pilot employed evasive maneuvers and banked away from the ship.

1309 on 12 April. The Japanese launched a determined series of air strikes lasting four hours. About one hour into the engagement, after eight raids had been plotted in the CIC, attention was concentrated on a plane closing from the starboard quarter, speed 200 knots, position angle 15 degrees. Lookouts quickly identified it as a Val.

The commanding officer, Lieutenant Commander John W. Stedman Jr., promptly ordered emergency flank speed and the helm put over sharply to the right in an attempt to bring the most guns to bear. Fire was opened when the plane turned directly toward the ship in a power dive at high speed. Large sections of the wing and cowling were torn off by *Wann*'s guns, and the propeller was seen to stop, an indication that the aircraft's engine was knocked out. A stream of black smoke trailed astern of the plane. Nonetheless, it seemed beyond doubt that the plane would crash into the ship's starboard side at the waterline, an apparent dead certainty to the exposed, anxious and sweating gunners — but to a man, they stood to their guns!

However, at a range of about 450 yards, either from damage to the engine or controls or wounding of the pilot, the plane's nose came up, causing the craft to dive over the ship just aft of the stack in a steep vertical bank to the right. Its wing carried away several radio antennae, and the plane splashed a bare 20 feet off the port bow!

There followed a heavy, muffled underwater explosion, throwing a huge wave of water and gasoline over the forecastle and bridge, with plane fragments hitting the superstructure and mast. Because of the absence of shrapnel, it was considered that no bomb was carried by the aircraft (or maybe a dud), the explosion being caused by the plane's gas tanks alone. No trace of survivors or even parts of the plane, could be seen in the water where the plane crashed. Reports from Repair one indicated no immediate damage to the hull, but the severe underwater explosion had disabled the sonar gear.

1500. A second attack developed, another Val streaking in for *Wann*. Her gunners set it afire and, as it faltered, the *kamikaze* was shot out of the sky by two American fighter planes.

Wann remained on patrol off Okinawa until 14 April, when she sailed for Guam in company with the battleships *Nevada (BB-36)*, *Maryland (BB-46)*, and the cruiser *Pensacola (CA-24)*, as part of a task unit escorting a convoy of transports. Arriving at Apra Harbor, Guam, on the 19th, *Wann* effected battle damage repairs.

Returning to Okinawa on 14 May, *Wann* was assigned to various patrol stations and, although frequent enemy air attacks sent the ship to an anxious succession of alerts, she had no further encounters with enemy aircraft. On 4 July, *Wann* joined Vice Admiral Jesse B. Oldendorf's Task Force 2, providing cover for operations in the Ryukyus and for mine sweeping operations in the East China Sea.

Following the Japanese surrender, *Wann* rode out four typhoons. She steamed to Wakayama, Honshu, Japan, standing in readiness to render support for the landings there, should it be needed.

Walter C.Wann was employed in occupation duties until 4 November 1945 when, in company with *Escort Division 69*, she got underway from Yokosuka, Japan, bound to San Diego, California.

ENGLAND

As Though the Spirits of Six Submarines Crews Sought Revenge

Less than a year after *England (DE-635)* had made antisubmarine history by dispatching six submarines to the sea bed, she became embroiled in a war of another kind. See chapter *Pacific Antisubmarine Warfare*. In March, April and May of 1945, *England* was assigned a picket station in the Okinawa area at the height of the Japanese *kamikaze* offensive. Lieutenant Commander John Williamson was now in command. This DE was repeatedly attacked by enemy planes, including torpedo, bombing, strafing and suicide types, and was credited with splashing three of them. One of these planes had missed by a few yards and splashed close aboard.

Sunset on 9 May. *England* had been in a screening position five miles from Kerama Retto since 0900 the same morning. The weather was clear, and there were air alerts throughout the day. Flash red! A five-plane raid was approaching. The attackers were picked up in her air search radar as three Val dive bombers came into view at seven miles, heading for *England*. The closest was about 7000 yards. When the range closed to 6000 yards, *England* went to flank speed, began evasive maneuvers and opened up with her 3" battery. The other two aircraft were downed by American fighter planes.

The plane was taken under fire by *England* with her 3" main battery, and soon the din was joined by her 1.10" heavy machine guns. The plane grew ever bigger as the 20mm guns started firing at close range. The *kamikaze* came on like a demon from hell on the starboard quarter and heading for the bridge.

As in a flash in a bad dream, the crew could see the whir of the propeller, the dangling axle where one wheel had been shot off, the holed fuselage and wing. There were two pilots, one behind the other, and the gunners could see the forward one riddled with bullets and slumped forward. For a brief moment, it appeared that the *kamikaze* might miss the bridge, but the port wing hit the boat davit, causing the plane to careen into the superstructure deck and envelop it in a horrendous gasoline fire. The 250 pound bomb went through the wardroom and exploded over the main deck, showering it with shrapnel. The flying bridge and the signal bridge lost all communication and were surrounded with smoke and flames, threatening to entrap all personnel in the area. Captain Williamson gave the order to evacuate, more easily said than done with the roaring blaze beneath them.

Some men on the signal bridge jumped over the side, taking their wounded with them so that they would not be consumed by the flames. Others made it down by various means such as clutching a raft on the port side and clambering like monkeys to the main deck; those below played water hoses on them as they went through the fire. Most of the men on the bridge escaped by getting atop the sound shack, jumping to numbers three and four 20mm platforms, then shinnying down the number two 3" gun barrel. One way or another, most of them, including the skipper, avoided an unpleasant death.

After the crash, all controls were lost forward, but the guns aft were manned and ready to blast away at the other two planes. Under the circumstances, gun captains exhibited practiced firing discipline by not shooting because of the proximity of our own fighter planes. Within 20 seconds after the crash, repair party number two had hoses playing on the bridge structure. Within an hour, the fire was brought under control, but some flames were not extinguished until midnight.

The explosion and resultant fire were almost fatal to the ship. The casualties were severe, claiming over 30 percent of the crew three officers and 24 men killed, 10 missing and 25 wounded.

Destroyer-minesweeper *Gherardi (DMS-30)*, minesweeper *Vigilance (AM-324)* and tug *Gear (ARS-34)* came to the assistance of *England*. The swimmers with their wounded were picked up, and *Gear* took the crippled DE in tow to Kerama Retto for emergency repairs. From there, she went to Leyte for further patching. *England* was knocked out of the war and was directed to proceed to the Navy Yard in Philadelphia as best she could. This 13,000 mile journey was accomplished on canned goods, without refrigeration, and conning from secondary control aft.

Anybody watching *England* enter the harbor with her charred bridge still showing the silhouettes and Japanese flags for six submarines and three planes, her devastated forward section, the crew lining the rails at attention, Old Glory snapping jauntily from her mast, would have found it difficult to mask the lump in his throat or the catch in his voice.

She was decommissioned on 15 October 1945, but her name will never be erased from the history of naval warfare.

Tony Germanotta, staff writer of the *Ledger-Star*, filed a report on the annual reunion of *England's* personnel in Norfolk, in 1982.

"There are no more destroyer escorts. They were all scrapped or sold to foreign governments after the war. *England* was one of the most famous, earning a Presidential Unit Citation. But the thousands of men who served aboard DE's in their short heyday in World War II will not let them be forgotten. Although *England* was not sunk by the *kamikaze* attack, other DEs were not that lucky.

The *kamikaze* still dives in 'Hap' Johnson's dreams, streaming through a hail of fire to crash into his small American ship and turn it into an inferno. Lee G. Johnson, a redhead whose easy smile led to his nickname, was the only survivor from his gun squad. 'You see it when you dream', Johnson said as a gang of his old *England* shipmates gathered around solemnly. 'You see it when you wake up. You see it as long as you live. And you see the guys, the guys who died.'

'They came out of the sun, three of them', Johnson recalled of the attack. An American plane shot down one of the attackers, he said, and another was destroyed by fire from a sister ship. (This is at variance with the action report which states that both were shot down by friendly aircraft.) But one Japanese plane continued to come, despite being battered by *England's* fire.'

'It hit about 15 feet from me on the starboard side', Johnson said. My gunner was killed, my loader was killed.' Johnson was knocked over, his life vest torn to shreds. As he struggled to get up, some shipmates jumped down into the flames from the deck above.

'You want to know why I love these guys', Johnson said. 'Two or three who were also trapped with me asked if they could help me. They saw my life jacket was all ripped up so they put on a new life jacket and they threw me from the ship. I spent 14 months in the hospital with 100 shrapnel wounds. I still have one in my right lung about the size of a silver dollar.'

'It's not a thing you talk with other people about', Johnson said, as a couple of other *England* crewmen nodded. 'They don't understand. The only war stories we tell, are to each other."

O'FLAHERTY

She Held Her Own

At the end of July 1944, *O'Flaherty (DE-340)* screened the escort carrier *Santee (CVE-29)* from Eniwetok to Guam. There she witnessed her first action, operation *Forager*, the invasion and reoccupation of Guam by the mighty Pacific Fleet.

Leaving Guam, she returned to Eniwetok. At midnight on 3-4 October, O'*Flaherty* was directed to proceed on a 600 mile dash in search of the survivors of a PBM amphibious aircraft that had crashed at sea. With the aid of search planes, she located and rescued the 12 crew members approximately 48 hours later.

In January 1945, O'*Flaherty* served in the Lingayen Gulf Attack Force where she was exposed to frequent *kamikaze* raids. Following that operation, she retired to Ulithi where she was transferred to the Fifth Fleet. From 10 February through 14 March, her carriers supported the Iwo Jima invasion with air strikes and spotting for the big guns of the battleships and cruisers. Many ships suffered damage during the operation, but O'*Flaherty's* Irish luck held out.

16 March. Two days before Iwo Jima was declared secure, *O'Flaherty* departed to participate in the invasion of Okinawa. As a unit of Task Group 52.1, Destroyer Division 120, she screened

the carriers of the Amphibious Support Force.

The task units were in operating areas off Okinawa, near Miyako Shima, throughout the period covered by this action. Escort vessels were disposed in various peripheral positions to provide the best possible antisubmarine and antiaircraft protection.

Dawn on 2 April. *O'Flaherty* drew her first blood. Lookouts spotted a single enemy fighter plane, a Zeke, as it came in low in horizontal flight, distance four miles. All hands to GQ. One minute later, the plane disappeared into the clouds as the DE dropped her hook in the Kerama Retto anchorage.

0850. The Japanese aircraft was again sighted. Once more "Man your battle stations!" Four minutes later, an enemy plane was spotted flying at an altitude of 3000 feet off the starboard beam and was taken under fire by the after 40mm gun. The plane was hit and turned down in a slow dive to splash off the port quarter of an LST ammunition ship astern of this destroyer escort!

Late afternoon on 3 April. Three planes made their attacks on the ship concentration. A fourth came in low from astern. Two of them made vertical dives on *Wake Island (CVE-65)*. The first plane crashed into the port bow of the carrier at the waterline; the second was splashed close aboard her starboard bow. The third plane made an unsuccessful dive on *Capps (DD-550)*. *O'Flaherty* opened fire on the fourth enemy plane astern of *Capps* at a range of 600 yards. The DE ceased firing as the *kamikaze* turned away with three friendly fighters in pursuit.

6 April. Both fighter and bomber planes attacked ships in the harbor. However, *O'Flaherty* drove off all planes approaching her.

O'Flaherty participated in the Okinawa operation from 21 March to 22 June except for a short period in April while undergoing repairs at Guam. She then performed picket and auxiliary escort duty until the Japanese surrender.

CROUTER

An Action Packed War Cruise

Arriving in Noumea, New Caledonia, *Crouter (DE-11)* reported for duty with the South Pacific Force on 3 September 1943.

Until 1 April 1944, the ship was engaged in escort and screening duties in the Solomons, New Hebrides and Treasuries. She escorted a light cruiser bombardment force to the vicinity of Buka and Bougainville Islands. On another occasion, off Cape Torokina, *Crouter* was fired upon by a Japanese shore battery, but no damage.

15 July. She was called on to pick up the crew of a crashed Hell Diver aircraft. The operation developed into a double rescue when a PBY that had landed to pick up the survivors was itself damaged and unable to take off. *Crouter* reached the sinking PBY after dusk. Sharks were sighted under the swimmers and were driven off by small arms fire. At considerable risk to his life, Gunner's Mate Edwin J. Bernick dove into the water to aid the exhausted swimmers. The crews of both planes, 10 in all, were brought safely aboard.

Engineer Officer, Lieutenant (jg) Cykler, was the same officer who braved acute danger in attempting to salvage a furiously burning freighter at Guadalcanal while he was assistant engineer officer on *Osterhaus (DE-164)*. See chapter *Central and South Central Pacific*. His report on problems faced in rescuing the airmen:

> "The captain was having a difficult time maneuvering near the aircraft. It was late in the day, and the seas were running six to seven feet, trough to crest. Several lines from the ship to the aircraft had parted. Finally, Nat Brown and I suggested to the skipper that we launch a life raft, paddle to the disabled craft and pick up the flyers. With the OK, we launched the raft with the sea painter still attached and climbed in.
>
> At that moment, the captain ordered the ship lightly ahead, enough to overturn the raft with me pinned underneath; Nat fell free. Somebody cut the sea painter to relieve the water pressure, and we floated astern where I wiggled free of the raft. Somewhat later, Nat, the raft and I got together. It was now dark, and the flyers had been rescued. We could spot the ship using its 24" searchlights while looking for us. As we came up on the crest of a wave, I spread my handkerchief out between my two hands, and a searchlight struck the white cloth; the ship turned in our direction. We got a chewing out — so much for trying."

On 2 August, Lieutenant Charles F. Braught relieved Lieutenant Commander George W. Worth as commanding officer.

Orders were received in March to proceed to Leyte and join a task unit of the Fifth Fleet, composed of transports and destroyers, under the command of Rear Admiral J. L. Hall. This formation comprised the southern attack forces in the forthcoming operation to take Okinawa. Included in this Task Unit was the flagship of the amphibious operation with Vice Admiral Turner aboard. The echelon arrived off Okinawa on the morning of the assault, 1 April 1945. John Cykler recalls from his memoirs:

> "Invasion day. We were in column between two heavies, both of which took hits from shore batteries. While in the outer island screen, our surface radar picked up several enemy aircraft, and we soon saw one plane heading for us about 100 feet above the surface. Our newly acquired identification officer said it was one of ours. Nonetheless, the commence fire order was given, and we shot the plane down. Luckily for us, the pilot was unhurt when we fished him out of the sea; our I.D. officer knew his job only too well. The pilot had been hit by a Japanese plane, and his windshield was covered with oil, blocking his vision. He was trying to return to base and didn't see us."

This ship was assigned a screening station off Kerama Retto, retiring to seaward with the transport groups during the periods of darkness. On 6 April, returning from a convoy to Saipan, a Marine pilot, Second Lieutenant R. L. Wickser, was rescued after he crashed off the starboard bow of *Crouter* near Okinawa.

21 April. On returning to Okinawa from another convoy, *Crouter* was assigned a screening station off Ie Shima. A Japanese plane attempted to torpedo her. Lieutenant (jg) Cykler recalls how unwelcome a torpedo was to the black gang (engineers below decks), those in greatest peril:

"I was below in the main engine control with a telephone talker directly connected to the bridge talker. My talker's face turned ashen —- and then green —- as he told me the news. I told him if we couldn't feel anything in 10 to 15 seconds, we'd be safe. It was reported that the torpedo was 'porpoising'. We were lucky. It dove under the ship and came up on the port side! I assumed that its depth control malfunctioned."

The same night, an enemy plane dropped a bomb which exploded astern. The following day, groups of civilians were observed on Ie Shima waving white flags in an attempt to surrender to the DE.

A torpedo wake was seen crossing the bow on the night of 27 April. On the next night, four suicide bombers attempted a coordinated attack on four ships. One splashed, just missing *Crouter*; the second crashed in the wake of *England (DE-635)*; and the remaining two made successful crashes into a nearby escort. During this attack, the *kamikazes* employed running lights and recognition devices similar to American ships in an attempt to confuse them, but the ruse was soon detected. Later that night, another Japanese plane attempted to attack *Crouter* but was driven off by 20mm gun fire.

30 April. A twin-engine enemy bomber attempted to crash into the DE. It was repeatedly hit by most guns able to bear and passed over the forecastle in flames, splashing close aboard! Radarman Third Class John Sedory from Banning, California, remembers:

> "Our biggest battle experience was at Okinawa where we and other DEs screened for the invading Task Force. *Kamikazes*, torpedo attacks, a near hit by an enemy plane which dropped a bomb right off the fantail, shore batteries taking pot shots at us, etc., made for an interesting if not dangerous time. As one man said, 'A guy could get killed around here'. Everyone wanted action until we got more than we wanted. But my shipmates handled themselves in the true navy tradition of giving their all and their best.
>
> While I was a radarman on normal duty, I was a gunner on a 20mm at GQ. For as long as I live, I will remember tracers going into the *kamikazes* as they flew over, seemingly unaffected by the many rounds of ammunition that appeared to be penetrating the planes. On one occasion, a *kamikaze* passed over the starboard side, continued on over the port side, then made a turn to come back to get another try at crashing us. Fortunately, he hit the water before he reached the ship. This was just one of many such incidents in that battle. In spite of the Japanese being our enemies, each time I saw one of their planes splash, I thought, 'There goes a human being about to face eternity'. A sobering thought I have never forgotten."

1-6 May. *Crouter* patrolled screening stations off the southern tip of Okinawa, behind the Japanese lines and at the entrance to Chimmu Wan on the western side of Okinawa. During this time, another pilot, Lieutenant (jg), F.S. Sidall, flying a Corsair from the carrier Shangri-La (CV-38), was rescued uninjured after he made a water landing following a surprise attack on his plane by Japanese fighters.

9 May. The DE was detached and assigned to escort a convoy to Saipan. During the two periods at Okinawa, she accounted for two planes and one probable without receiving casualties to the ship or personnel.

Radarman John Sedory concluded:

> Well, that war's over, and a couple more since. Many brave men have died, giving their all to preserve the freedom we have come to enjoy in this country. I am proud to have been a very minute part of that great bunch of guys. God bless them all!"

Crouter reported to Guam on 21 May for training with submarines, remaining there until 18 September. She returned to San Pedro, California, on 5 October 1945.

WHITEHURST

An Unhappy Introduction to the Kamikazes

Barely a month after sinking the Japanese submarine *I-45* (See chapter *Pacific Antisubmarine Warfare*), *Whitehurst (DE-634)* again came to grips with the enemy on 21 November 1944 while screening a 12-ship convoy en route to Hollandia. On each of two occasions, she was attacked by a Japanese Lilly. In the first attack, the plane skimmed over the water, dropped one bomb which fell clear of the ships, caused no damage and then departed. The pilot of the second plane was less fortunate. As he started a low, gliding, bombing attack, the DE commenced fire, scored hits, and the plane caught fire. Immediately afterward, other ships of the convoy opened up, and the aircraft splashed! *Whitehurst* received the major credit.

23 March 1945. After a lengthy sojourn to Australia, a tonic for the crew, *Whitehurst* joined the armada preparing to invade Okinawa on the very doorstep of Japan. Two days later, this DE and *England (DE-635)* were among the first American ships to arrive.

6 April. While patrolling off Kerama Retto, *Whitehurst* opened fire and drove off an enemy plane that was attacking *SS Pierre*.

Evening of 11 April. *Whitehurst* cleared Kerama Retto anchorage after fueling and was assigned a perimeter station, relieving *Manlove (DE-36)*. *Miles (DE-183)* was relieved from an adjacent station, leaving *Whitehurst* to patrol both sectors. Her mission was to search the area, using underwater echo-ranging gear and radar to prevent entry of submarines, torpedo boats, *kamikazes* or other enemy forces into the Kerama Retto anchorage. Nearby stations were manned by *Vigilance (AM-324)* and *Crosley (APD-87)*.

1430. Four Vals intruded into the area at an altitude of 1500 feet. They split up to evade friendly fighters. One aircraft unsuccessfully attempted to attack *Crosley*.

Another broke away and headed for *Whitehurst* where it was promptly taken under fire by her 3" guns. It circled rapidly and commenced a 40-degree angle dive. At the same time, two other Vals attacked, one from the starboard beam and from astern. The two latter planes were shot down in flames by the DE's starboard 20mm and 1.1" guns! However, the first plane continued its dive in spite of receiving several 20mm hits that tore chunks out of the plane. The *kamikaze* crashed into the ship's forward superstructure on the port side of the pilot house, entered the combat information center and burst into flames! A small bomb jettisoned loose, went completely through the superstructure, and exploded some 50 feet off the starboard side.

Whitehurst steamed in circles out of control. The Val had demolished the CIC immediately below the flying bridge, enveloping the entire bridge structure in a roaring fire and black smoke shooting up into the sky. All hands in the CIC and the pilot house were killed instantly as well as those in the radio room just below the CIC. All the men at the forward gun mounts were either killed or severely wounded by bomb fragments.

Unharmed officers and men displayed an heroic discipline in rushing to the aid of the damage repair parties, saving the DE from total destruction. The ship was in a tight turn to the left and, when it headed into the wind, the flames and smoke cleared sufficiently to enable several flying bridge personnel, including the wounded commanding officer, Lieutenant J.C. Horton, to escape over the forward side of the bridge structure. By the time the captain made his way to secondary control, communication had been established with the engine rooms, after steering and after guns. The repair parties were already fighting the fire, and the ship was then headed across the wind to allow the flames to blow clear.

When *Vigilance* received the message that *Whitehurst* had been hit and needed assistance, she rang up full speed and raced to the burning DE. By the time she arrived, however, the *Whitehurst* crew had the fire under control. Nonetheless, the minesweeper lent invaluable medical assistance in tending to the wounded. The prompt administering of first aid and the injection of plasma saved many lives. Of the 23 wounded men treated on *Vigilance*, 21 recovered.

By mid-afternoon, the fires were almost extinguished, and four men who had been blown overboard were picked up by *Crosley*. Since all of the signal bridge personnel on *Whitehurst* had been wiped out, killed or wounded, *Vigilance* put a signalman on board the stricken ship so that she would have a communications capability. Captain Horton concluded in his action report:

> "The officers and crew reacted very well to their first battle casualties. The after gun crews stood by their guns although, at first, it may have appeared that the ship was doomed.
>
> In addition to prompt assistance from *Vigilance* and *Crosley*, first aid training by the crew proved of great value. Although one third of the complement was either killed or seriously wounded, and the leading pharmacist's mate was badly burned, all wounded were cared for quickly. It is believed those who died could not possibly have been saved."

Whitehurst limped into Kerama Retto anchorage for temporary patching to make her seaworthy. Shortly thereafter, the battle-scarred veteran departed for Pearl Harbor to receive proper battle damage repairs as well as some up-dated alterations.

This was not the end of *Whitehurst*. The DE, with turbo-electric propulsion, was converted to a floating power station. On 25 July, she headed for the Philippines. Although Japan had surrendered soon after her arrival, she stayed to supply the city of Manila with power for the next three months.

WITTER

Taking the Worst in Stride

21 March 1945. *Witter (DE-636)* stood out from Ulithi with Task Force 54, bound for the Ryukyu Islands and the last great amphibious operation of World War II. Having previously made acquaintance with the *kamikaze* corps at Leyte Gulf, the crew had no illusions as to what might lie ahead. Their attitude was best described as wary.

On the 25th, she rendezvoused with a minesweeping unit about six miles south of Okinawa and began screening it as well as the heavy units of Admiral Oldendorf's bombardment group. For the next 12 days, *Witter* continued her antisubmarine screening duties for various fleet units off Okinawa. Though subjected to intermittent air attack and a witness to several suicide attacks, she remained unscathed.

Afternoon of 6 April. Off the southeastern coast of Okinawa, she sighted two enemy aircraft, range eight miles, and approaching rapidly. The warship rang up 23 knots and began evasive maneuvers. *Witter*'s log describes a furious action:

> "1613. Plane two appeared to be diving on this ship, so left 20 degrees rudder was ordered to put it on the starboard beam and plane one on the starboard quarter.
>
> 1615. Commenced firing on both planes. It became apparent that plane one was the more persistent in his dive, so right full rudder was ordered, putting him on the starboard beam and plane two on the bow. Plane one began trailing smoke at a range of 4800 yards.
>
> 1617. Plane two was also trailing a plume of smoke. It splashed just off the starboard bow, distance 3000 yards!
>
> 1617. Left full rudder was ordered because it appeared that plane one was going to hit the ship. It was hoped this maneuver would cause him to overshoot. Numerous 3"/50 caliber bursts were seen to bracket the kamikaze, but he couldn't be stopped.
>
> 1618. The plane hit on the waterline, starboard side! Its 500 pound bomb exploded inside the starboard fire room, tearing a huge hole in the side of the hull, the blast extending inboard above the keel to the port side. The interior communication room flooded immediately, severing communications with engine room and repair parties."

Over the next 15 minutes, communications were restored to all guns, and all were ready to fire. Communications with the engine room was reestablished, and full control was again on the bridge, with steering control aft.

Communications with the repair parties was established through messengers and two stand-by circuits. Compartments flooded were the IC room (interior communications panels and controls) and adjacent storerooms; starboard fire room; starboard engine room and seven fuel tanks. One compartment was open to the sea. Casualties were six dead, six enlisted men and one officer with minor injuries.

Speed was increased to two thirds ahead on the port engine, and course was set for Kerama Retto. The bridge was advised that a man had gone overboard during the action; destroyers in the area were notified.

Morris (DD-417), *R.P. Leary (DD-664)*, and *Gregory (DD-*

802), operating with the battleship *Arkansas (BB-33)*, and the cruiser *Tuscaloosa (CA-37)*, about six miles to the north, closed this ship. Back to the log:

"1745. Enemy planes reported about 10 miles to the north, closing.

1754. Fleet Ocean Tug *Arikara (ATF-98)* closed rapidly, offering assistance. *Witter* requested her to take station ahead while informing her that no assistance would be required until inside of the nets at Kerama Retto.

1816. Enemy plane reported splashed to the north.

1819. *Morris* reported being hit by suicide plane and burning!

1819. *R.P. Leary* ordered to close *Morris* to render assistance. *Gregory* was stationed ahead of *Arikara* and *Witter*.

1825. *Bates (APD-47)* reported en route to assist Morris.

1830. *Arkansas* reported that *Tracy (DM-19)* had recovered our man from the water.

2134. Arrived at Kerama Retto, Nansei Shoto. Secured from GQ."

The Escort Division Commander (*ComCortDiv 40*), Commander F.R. Harris, was on board *Witter* during this action. His report to the Commander Fifth Fleet and Commander-in-Chief U.S. Pacific Fleet summarizes the ordeal of *Witter* and her sterling performance:

"I was on the bridge of *Witter* when the attacking planes were first sighted, and I consider that the commanding officer fought his ship well and that being hit was unavoidable. I saw numerous hits on the plane that crashed us, and I do not understand how it managed to hit the ship. My impression at the time was that the plane's controls were locked in place.

I have only the utmost admiration for the ability to control damage and to keep going displayed by the entire personnel of *Witter*. I alternated with the commanding officer in conning and in checking the damage and I was impressed by the efficiency of the damage control and engineering personnel. This ability to "carry on" was based on a solid foundation because the *Witter* had, for several months prior to the action, carried out a well organized and comprehensive program of training to prepare for all types of casualties.

I consider that the ability and energy of her commanding officer in training his crew for action and damage control resulted in saving a badly damaged ship and is deserving of commendation."

Witter remained at Kerama Retto until late June, undergoing temporary repairs and dodging sporadic air attacks by constantly shifting from anchorage to anchorage, a process which slowed repairs considerably.

Finally, on 25 June, *Witter* appeared seaworthy enough to attempt the voyage home and departed from the Ryukyu Islands. She arrived in San Diego, California on 24 July.

FOREMAN

Four Kamikazes Came into Her Life

After escorting a resupply convoy to San Pedro Bay, Luzon, in the first week of November 1944, *Foreman (DE-633)* began escorting combatant ships, auxiliaries, and merchantmen from Manus to Hollandia, Eniwetok, Majuro, and Ulithi. In late March 1945, she sailed to Ulithi to prepare for the attack on Okinawa.

She arrived off Okinawa on 25 March and spent the next five days with a fire support unit bombarding the island in anticipation of the landings on 1 April. Two days later, with her Task Force under heavy air attack, she had her first experience with the *kamikaze* corps.

27 March. The attack occurred during dawn alert while *Foreman* and *Witter (DE-636)* were screening the cruiser *Indianapolis (CA-35)*, the latter then being engaged in fire support operations five miles north of Kerama Retto. The sky was overcast. The attack commenced with two of six planes engaged in bombing shipping about 10 miles astern.

The first plane, a Val, made a long, straight suicide dive on *Foreman*, grazing the starboard bow before splashing! One man was injured, but material damage was negligible. IFF (Identification friend or foe) was received and believed to have come from the first plane. (This same observation has been noted in other *kamikaze* narratives. Apparently, the Japanese had more or less compromised the IFF. The damage was somewhat mitigated by the fact that no escort would take an IFF seriously if it came from a closing bogey.) Also, friendly aircraft tried to be careful not to get within antiaircraft range, although not always successfully).

The identity of the second plane was doubtful, a Tony or an Oscar. It was seen to splash as the column of water from the Val cleared away! A third unidentified plane, seen by only three people on the bridge, descended in a vertical dive and splashed between *Witter* and *Indianapolis*! Neither of the two ships reported having seen this aircraft before it hit the water 20 seconds after the second plane.

0100 on 3 April. Following the troop landings, *Foreman* was assigned a patrol off the entrance to the transport anchorage at Kerama Retto. While approaching the southern limit of her sector, just coming about to the reverse course, she received an urgent aircraft warning from control, "Flash Red-Control Yellow." Firing could be seen over Kerama Retto, and the radarman sang out a bogey on his scope, only three miles from the ship. CIC estimated its speed at 250 knots. The crew had already been summoned to GQ when the word was passed, "Action Port."

As the ship's turn was about half-completed, a Val was sighted two miles astern, coming out of the moon. The SA radar operator who had picked up the bogey now reported it to be on the starboard beam and closing rapidly. Action stations were shifted to starboard. The attack was so fast that, by the time a report could be made to the Officer of The Deck, the bogey was one mile on the starboard bow. It turned sharply toward the DE, making its approach from 1000 yards at 240 knots. Fire was opened immediately, but the lightning speed of action only permitted one 3" and twenty 20mm rounds to be expended. The firing time from first to last shots was five seconds. In spite of the short time frame, hits were observed. The aircraft continued to close, apparently not seriously damaged.

0120. With the ship almost through her turn, a large bomb struck the starboard bow, passed through the hull and exploded approximately 30 feet beneath the keel!

Number one fire room was flooded, and the number one boiler casing was penetrated. Steam immediately filled the entire inside of the superstructure up to the flying bridge. All light and power forward was lost, and the starboard shaft stopped. The number two main condenser lost vacuum when the gauge glass was shattered, and the port shaft was stopped to prevent a building up of pressure in the condenser. The Loran receiver was knocked to the deck; the after 3" gun was jammed in elevation; the gyros in the torpedoes were tumbled; the recoil gun cylinders on the 1.1" gun were loosened; several depth charges were thrown from racks to the deck; and a magazine was knocked from the starboard after 20mm gun.

Nonetheless, the repair parties reported the extent and nature of the damage to the commanding officer, Lieutenant Commander W.J. Carey Jr. in record time. Light and power forward were restored 14 minutes after the hit. Within 40 minutes, the main engines were on a two-motor "split plant" operation and ready for 2/3 speed. Remarkably, there were no fatalities.

Fully repaired at Ulithi between 17 April and 29 May, *Foreman* returned to a patrol off Okinawa on 3 June. Eight days later, another suicide pilot attempted a formal introduction.

Dusk on 11 June. *Foreman* was leaving her assigned anti-small craft station and was proceeding to effect a rendezvous with the destroyer minesweeper *Hambleton (DMS-20)*. The latter was leaving her station, adjacent to *Foreman*, so that both could join up for dusk alert and to lend mutual close support. Just as the junction was accomplished, *Hambleton* reported a bogey approaching, distance 19 miles.

Foreman increased her speed to 23.5 knots. Her CIC began plotting the radar bogey and making continuous reports to conn as the aircraft approached from a distance of six miles.

With the DE still turning, lookouts reported a Val crossing the bow from port to starboard. *Foreman* steadied on course. The *kamikaze*, while under fire from *Hambleton's* 5" guns, circled the formation clockwise, closing the range to about three miles on *Foreman's* starboard bow, altitude 2000 feet. Radar lost the bogey, but visual contact was maintained. *Hambleton's* guns were able to take the plane under fire much earlier than *Foreman* whose 3" main battery had a much shorter range, giving the plane an initial advantage.

When the bearing was just forward of the destroyer escort's starboard beam, the plane went into a steep dive. The DE commenced fire immediately, speed was increased to flank, and the ship's course was changed to the left to bring the plane abeam to starboard. *Foreman* opened up as the range closed until every gun on board that could be brought to bear was firing. Upon closing to 1000 yards, the pilot, apparently discouraged by the volume of fire, swerved right and turned onto *Hambleton*, attempting a suicide dive. Captain Carey opined in his action report that this attack was not pressed home with the characteristic determination of most suiciders, the Japanese pilot having changed targets in mid-air. He passed over *Hambleton's* stern and splashed on her port side! After a close-up look, the plane was recognized as a Sonia instead of a Val.

29 June, *Foreman* was assigned to escort duty with a force covering minesweeping operations in the East China Sea and flying air strikes on Japanese targets on the Chinese coast. With the end of the war, she sailed from Wakayama, Japan, with homeward bound service passengers, arriving at San Diego, California, on 17 October.

RIDDLE

Another Day in the Traumatic Days of Okinawa

Riddle (DE-185) had made the DE hall of fame by sinking Japanese submarine *I-10* with the assistance of *David W. Taylor (DD-551)* on 4 July 1944. See chapter *Pacific Antisubmarine Warfare*.

Riddle had conducted convoy and screening activities in the Central and South Pacific until early in 1945 when she joined the Iwo Jima assault in February. She was part of an antiaircraft and antisubmarine screen and escorted various fleet units in their operations throughout that bloody battle area.

18 March. *Riddle* was assigned to an escort group en route to Kerama Retto. The first day of April found the DE off Okinawa, patrolling a station with the Task Force under enemy air attack.

1840 on 2 April. While *Riddle* was screening an anchorage, a formation of transports and escorts was attacked by several enemy aircraft nearby. One suicide plane crashed into the transport *Henrico (APA-45)* and, a short time later, another *kamikaze* "made a landing" on *Dickerson (APD-21)*. Both ships were enveloped in raging fires (described in chapter *Iwo Jima to Okinawa – High Speed Transport*) Two days later, in the same sector, the body of an American sailor, Seaman R.C. Hassel, was recovered. Burial services were conducted by the captain, Lieutenant Commander Francis P. Steel.

Daybreak on 6 April. Suicide warfare came to the Fifth Fleet in all its fury. While *Riddle* was proceeding to deliver mail to *Samuel S. Miles (DE-183)*, enemy aircraft were reported in the vicinity but did not enter the sector patrolled by *Riddle*.

After fueling from the oiler *Niobrara (AO-72)* in late afternoon and proceeding to her station near Kerama Retto, enemy aircraft were again reported in the vicinity. Antiaircraft fire was seen over Kerama Retto anchorage, and a burning plane crashed in that area. Minutes later, an LST near Kerama Retto anchorage and a Victory ship in the anchorage were on fire.

1839. After two hostile planes had been shot down by friendly fighters nearby, an enemy plane was observed approaching Kerama Retto anchorage, about five miles from *Riddle*. Flying low and under heavy antiaircraft fire from ships, It splashed just short of the entrance.

1847. A suicide plane crashed into the port side of a Victory ammunition ship about three miles from *Riddle*. Her superstructure was afire, and *Riddle* proceeded to assist in recovery of survivors. However, two minesweepers, in closer position to the stricken ship, rescued the men in the water. *Gilmer (APD-11)* attempted to go alongside the burning ammunition ship but withdrew after reporting the fire beyond control and ammunition in ready boxes exploding. Actually, two Victory type ships were burning, *SS Hohes Victory* and *SS Logan Victory*.

7 April. That morning, *Riddle* recovered the body of a merchant seaman from one of the Victory ships. A few minutes later, another body was taken aboard, a Japanese aviator. Both were buried at sea. In the late evening, an enemy aircraft was reported in the vicinity and was seen to crash about seven miles away.

Lewis M. Andrews, Jr.

8 April. The first streak of light found *Riddle* still screening on station off Kerama Retto anchorage. Japanese aircraft were nearby with an air attack imminent. A half hour later, an enemy aircraft was sighted three miles from this vessel; another was shot down five miles away.

Early afternoon on 12 April. *Riddle* was patrolling off Zanpa Misaki, Okinawa Jima. Many enemy aircraft were in the vicinity, one about five miles from *Riddle*. The wind was north at 12 knots. Visibility was good, the ceiling unlimited; slight sea, moderate swell. Quartermaster First Class Robert N. Currie was eye witness to the succeeding events.

> "As senior quartermaster, my GQ station was on the bridge, overseeing the helmsman, the engine order telegraph operator and the phone talker and making notations in the quartermaster's log of the times and changes of courses, speeds, and the locations and observations of any unusual events. I was on the starboard flying-bridge when the following action took place:
>
> At 1412 hours, four F4U fighters of Combat Air Patrol (CAP) attacked enemy planes directly over our screening area. A torpedo plane came in with an F4U on its tail. Our 40mm guns opened fire on the plane. It started burning and splashed 1000 yards astern of *Riddle*! A few minutes later, another plane shot down by CAP planes splashed off our starboard quarter! *Rall (DE-304)*, in the screening station next to us, was hit by a suicide plane. I witnessed the plane diving on her and saw a huge explosion, followed by a large ball of fire. (*Rall* narrative follows this one).
>
> At about this time, the quartermaster on our helm asked me if I would relieve him for a few minutes. He had been on the wheel for a long time and wanted a few minutes rest. Permission was received from the Officer of The Deck, and the relieved helmsman went out on the starboard flying bridge that I had just vacated.
>
> A minute or two later, I received a frantic command, 'LEFT FULL RUDDER…ALL ENGINES AHEAD FULL!' At the same time, our 3" main battery, 40mm and 20mm guns opened up. The same helmsman and two signalmen came dashing through the pilot house from the starboard bridge. As they ran by me, I heard one of them yell, 'Here come the sons of bitches!' I had seen the results of *kamikaze* crashes on many of the ships we had moored to in the Kerama Retto repair facility, and it was not a pretty sight! You could smell death emanating from these ships, and now I had visions of our own bridge being blown to bits and my becoming another war statistic."

Task Force 51 was under air attack in spite of the understated signal received, "Flash Blue, Control Green." Captain Steel ordered the ship turned left and opened fire with all guns that would bear as one of the enemy started a suicide dive on this vessel from the starboard beam. It was hit repeatedly and caught fire but continued it's dive, passing over *Riddle* about amidships, just clearing the 40mm director by a few feet, then splashing a few yards off the port beam!

This was a coordinated attack, a second plane was diving from ahead immediately after the first plane splashed. The ship was still turning left at flank speed during the second suicide attempt. Guns were immediately oriented to the second plane. This aircraft, after seeing the first *kamikaze* miss, took a wide turn on the starboard bow and commenced a suicide run. It was hit many times and began to burn but continued its dive. It struck the 40mm gun and director, the after 3" gun, the port depth charge rack, the after port "K" gun loading rack and then hit the main deck on the port quarter. Part of the plane or a bomb pierced the deck plating, passed through the carpenter shop and exited the side of the ship! The remainder of the plane splashed off the port quarter. Quartermaster Currie:

> "While all this was going on, I had the helm at full left rudder and was crouching down, trying to make myself as small a target as possible. The telephone talker was doing the same thing as I remember that our eyes met for a moment during the chaos. His eyes had an empty look. I imagine mine looked about the same to him.
>
> When the second plane hit the stern, there was a sensation on the bridge of a slight rising motion somewhat like that of an elevator. And suddenly no guns firing just complete silence. We were still turning at full left rudder at a speed of about 20 knots. Within a second or two, I received an order to steady up on a course. Immediately, I realized that we had lost steering which is controlled through two electrical cables, one each port and starboard. It was routine to shift control from one cable to another every few days. But, in order to do this, a control handle in the pilot house, directly behind the helmsman, had to be turned at the same time as a similar control is turned in the after steering station. And the after steering station was right next to the carpenter's shop where the plane and bomb had struck.
>
> Now all this had happened within a few seconds of being crashed. I had no idea of where or how bad we were hit. With the permission of the OOD, I told the telephone talker to contact the after steering station. But by this time, the sound powered phones were being flooded with casualty and damage reports. Our talker, realizing the importance of having a ship capable of being steered, announced in an authoritative voice that he had a priority message and all others were to get off the line. He then quickly contacted the quartermaster stationed in the after steering compartment, and we shifted control from the port to the starboard cable. I was then able to steady up on course. This entire procedure took about 25 seconds, but I recount it because of the coolness of our quartermaster in the after steering area. The bomb had penetrated the carpenter's shop only a few inches from the steering station and had knocked out our port steering cable. The noise of the guns, the explosion, the plane smashing our deck and the destruction of the 'K' guns and depth charge racks near this quartermaster's battle station was horrendous. Yet, he stayed at his station and carried out his duties faultlessly."

Considering the severity of the attack, personnel casualties were relatively light. One man, stationed on the after 20mm gun, was missing since the attack by the first plane. Since he was not recovered by any ship in the area, he was presumed to be lost. Six men were seriously wounded, and there were some minor injuries.

Material damage was extensive and disabling to a combat

warship. In addition to the above, holes about 24" in diameter in the main deck and in the ship's side on the port quarter and several smaller holes were caused by fragments of the plane or bomb. Several frames and the two outboard deck stringers were fractured.

Riddle recovered two missing men from the water other than the one who was lost. In the late afternoon, *PCE(R)-855* arrived alongside, and a doctor with two pharmacist's mates came aboard. *Riddle* continued to Kerama Retto to transfer the wounded to a hospital ship and for repairs.

Dawn on 16 April. With the barest details attended to, the DE sortied with a task unit to Saipan. Her exit was marked by a flaming enemy aircraft splashed by CAP a few miles from *Riddle*. She took departure from Kerama Retto with Aware Saki and Tokashiki Jima Islands falling away in the distance, like a slow awakening from a nightmare. Quartermaster Currie related a happy ending to the story:

> "By 23 April, we were again ready for action and departed from Guam, escorting another convoy to Okinawa. We remained in the Okinawa area through May and most of June.
>
> Toward the end of June in Leyte Gulf, the Philippines, I received orders to return to the states for rehabilitation leave and further assignment to new destroyer construction. About six other *Riddle* crewmen received similar orders. We arrived in San Francisco in early August shortly after the first atom bomb was dropped on Japan. On my return home, I married my fiance of some two years, and we spent our honeymoon in New York City, celebrating the end of the war in Times Square."

Captain Frank Steel was commissioned as a reserve officer in the Yale University graduating class of 1933. He was this author's first commanding officer on the minesweeper *Mockingbird* in the months before the attack on Pearl Harbor. I took command when he received a new assignment to a larger vessel. Frank was an outstanding officer, and I considered him to be a lifelong friend. He received the rank of Commander before returning to inactive duty after the war. I regret that he will not be able to read this book.

RALL

The Agony and the Victory

This was the same *Rall (DE-304)* that had previously sent a Japanese sub to the bottom after it torpedoed the oiler *Mississinewa*. See chapter *Pacific Antisubmarine Warfare*. She had been in commission almost one year. Her story is typical of the mission but atypical of the enormity of the challenge that she faced. *Rall* engaged five *kamikazes* almost all at once.

After invasion rehearsals in Hawaii, preparatory to the Iwo Jima assault, she departed with an escort group, convoying garrison troops for the occupation of that island. *Rall* and other escorts then screened the assault troops back to Saipan.

She headed for the Ryukyus on 25 March 1945, screening transports carrying the 27th Army Division for the Okinawa invasion. En route, *Rall* detonated by gunfire a floating mine in the convoy path. The Task Group arrived off Okinawa on 9 April.

On the afternoon of 12 April, *Rall* was patrolling a station 15 miles northwest of Hagushi Beach, Okinawa Shima, Nansei Shoto. Her captain, Lieutenant Commander C.B. Taylor, observed that the weather was clear and fair, the sea calm, and visibility unlimited.

Ever since the invasion began on 1 April, there were numerous engagements between ships and suicide planes in the area, and Captain Taylor was on the alert. On the previous night, SOPA (Senior Officer Present Afloat) had warned all ships of an impending large scale raid the next day. So, they had a lot to think about in the balmy evening. Taylor drilled the gun crews, drilled them again and then some more. Standing on the flying bridge, he could look down and see every fault, be quick to correct it or just as lively compliment a handy gunner. The men didn't mind. They knew where they were, and there were foundering ships and dying men about them. The more the captain ran them, the more they liked it.

1325 on 12 April. From Commander of Task Force 51, "Flash Red."

"General Quarters!" Grabbing his helmet and life jacket, each rushed up or down ladders to his appointed station to the tune of the bong-bong-bong of the ship's alarm. Each knew this could be an afternoon to remember if he survived the ordeal to come. One thing was certain; if he lived, he would never forget this day. Previous calls to battle stations had been accompanied with "This is a drill." The call this day ended with "This is not a drill." One little word, "not," was enough to send the blood pounding in the temples, shorten the breath, create an urgency never before experienced.

1430. A flight of friendly Corsairs shot a Jap out of the air five miles away. A gun captain patted his gun barrel and whispered, "Don't fail me baby." No less than 14 separate air attacks had been tracked into the area in the last couple of hours as the "Divine Wind" brought death and damage to the American invasion fleet off Okinawa.

1440. Enemy planes were sighted on the starboard beam, distance five miles. They split into a number of groups, maneuvered for position, and prepared to attack *Rall*.

Plane one, a Nate, leveled off and commenced a glide toward the ship broad on the starboard beam. As it came within range, it was immediately taken under fire by all guns that could bear, including three 3" main battery guns, five 20mm and the quadruple 1.1." The deck plates rattled and tattooed the feet as eardrums rebelled against the clatter.

The Jap was hit repeatedly but he kept closing.

"Right full rudder"! yelled Taylor as he increased speed to 18 knots.

The *kamikaze* got bigger and bigger until it looked as though it would fly into a gunner's mouth. The Jap flew straight into the doorway of the central main structure in an acrid cloud of flame and smoke! The plane's engine tore away from the fuselage and kept right on going, crashing through the 1.1" clipping room.

Upon impact, the upper strake in the hull plating on the starboard side was carried away as well as the outboard main deck plate, leaving a hole some 3X4 feet. Parts of the plane, bits of metal and fabric fell into a section of the crew's living compartment. The wreckage of the fuselage, snapped wings and tail remained on the main deck outside the passageway burning furiously.

The plane had a payload, a 500 pound bomb. It penetrated the hull plating just below the main deck, starboard side. With a slightly forward motion, it slid along a bulkhead inside a compartment, four feet above the deck, and exited through the shell plating on the port side. It exploded above the water line, 14 feet from the ship. The explosion showered the entire port side with shrapnel, and *Rall*'s gunners fell over everywhere, dead and wounded. A later inventory of damage counted over 1000 holes in decks, bulkheads, framing, lockers, piping, gun tubs and everything within the area of detonation.

The skipper knew that, in spite of the fact that the ship was hurt, it wasn't going to sink, and it was still a fighting ship.

As plane one was crashing into *Rall*, plane two was roaring in on the port beam, the side that had received the most casualties from the bomb. It was taken under fire by a single port side 20mm gun, the only one that had not sustained damage, casualties or shock on that side. To their everlasting tribute, they knocked the *kamikaze* right into the sea, close aboard on the port beam!

> "Rudder amidships!"
> "Rudder amidships, aye, aye sir!"

Plane one had just crashed *Rall* and plane two had been shot down when the number two 3" gun had already taken under fire plane three, screaming in on the starboard bow. That aircraft just twisted and rolled over as though suddenly gone crazy and plunged into the water in a cloud of steam and debris!

Plane four had been diving from the starboard quarter. The after 3" gun took it under fire, sending the plane and pilot down 250 fathoms!

It was only 30 seconds after the crash of plane one, but *Taylor's* men were firing on plane five! This plane dove for the severely damaged port quarter, strafing the decks with machine guns and leaving a wake of still and rolling men on *Rall*'s deck. Its guns also succeeded in hitting the port side depth charge ready impulse locker on the fantail, blowing it up with a frightful flash of searing flame and smoke. Three men were blown over the side. Having delivered its morbid calling card, this plane flew on to find other targets, only to be shot down by ships in the task force a few miles away.

The attack ended as suddenly as it had begun. Within 30 seconds, *Rall* had been attacked by five *kamikazes*, hit by one, strafed by another, and yet she shot down three others. Withal, though badly hurt and undermanned, fighting a furious fire, *Rall* was neither incapacitated nor unable to fight!

As the guns ceased their clamor, and as the last Jap of the day flew away, a face blackened, hard breathing captain on the flying bridge had to swallow and clench fists as he looked aft. Below and about him were the men he had for so long chided, complimented, upbraided and cherished. The smoke from the burning *kamikaze* on the fantail wafted toward his face and over the side. Only 30 seconds, and a captain could see how his men would fight. The panorama that lay before him was an ugly one as he looked down at his battered deck and muttered a prayer for 21 men killed, 36 men seriously wounded, two officers seriously wounded and seven men slightly wounded.

Rall returned to Hagushi Beach to transfer her wounded and to bury her dead on Okinawa. Ordered to return to the United States for structural repairs, she arrived in Seattle on 18 May 1945.

SAMUEL S. MILES

Down to the Wire with the Kamikazes

Before this last Pacific Operation, *Samuel S. Miles (DE-183)* had already become a seasoned ship of war by shooting down two enemy planes in the Saipan operation and sinking an "I" class submarine near the Admiralties. See narrative *Pacific Antisubmarine Warfare*.

After guarding the bombardment force at Iwo Jima in February, *Miles* left for Okinawa on 21 March 1945 as part of an antisubmarine screen for battleships and cruisers of the Gunfire Support and Covering Forces. The DE continued to escort the heavy ships as they shelled Okinawa during daytime and retired at night. Several planes attacked the formation, damaging some ships, and four planes were seen to fall.

Dawn on 27 March. *Miles* was in night retirement with her Task Unit when she was attacked by a Japanese plane. The aircraft first made a bombing dive on a destroyer 8000 yards on *Miles'* starboard quarter. The bomb missed, and the *kamikaze* headed across the rear of the formation, flying low along the water between the cruiser perimeter and the destroyer screen, drawing fire from the cruisers. The plane turned toward *Miles'* side of the screen, causing cruiser fire to cease as their flak approached the DE.

Miles opened fire with all guns that could bear on her starboard side. The plane turned to cross the DE's bow as it cleared the formation, range 400 yards, altitude 100 feet. Tracers from the 20mm guns were seen to be entering the plane, and a burst from a 3" projectile near the base of the left wing ripped the wing off. *Cassin Young (DD-793)* was also firing in this area when the plane erupted in fire. Splashes from the destroyer's guns appeared on both sides of *Miles*, close aboard, but fortunately nothing hit the DE. The aircraft hit the water about 500 yards on *Miles'* port bow! The plane was identified as a twin tailed, twin engined Nell.

2 April. A bomb was dropped at *Miles* but missed.

Evening on 11 April. *Miles* went to GQ with three enemy planes nearby. One peeled off and made a suicide dive on *Manlove (DE-36)*, 4000 yards ahead of *Miles*. (*Manlove* narrative follows *Miles*.)

Another plane singled out *Miles* as its target. After making two runs at her without any offensive action, it dived on the ship from the port bow in a suicide attempt. All guns that could bear maintained a continuous fire when the plane was in range, and it burst into flames. It just missed the forecastle, killing one man on number two 3" gun with its wing as it swept across the ship and exploded in the water about 25 to 50 feet off the starboard side!

The explosion was from a bomb on impact, causing casualties and damage from shrapnel and fragments of the plane. Seaman Chuck Markham remembered that day all too well and recorded it in his diary:

> "The plane was identified as a Tony. In addition to those wounded by shrapnel two were hurt in falls. There were many holes through the hull and superstructure on the starboard side but, within an hour, all were plugged to control flooding and to keep light from shining out. The ship lost power forward on one shaft but it was restored in an hour. Other damage included severance of the degaussing cable,

loss of three radio antennae, shorting the sound gear, and perforation of the motor whaleboat."

Jack Robinson was gun captain on a 20mm machine gun cannon, generally recognized as the antiaircraft weapon of last resort if the *kamikaze* got past the 3" and the 40mm quad – which it did. He remembers the nightmare very well:

"This was a particularly bad day. We had some alerts but no action. Then, at about 1730 hours, GQ was sounded. When I got up to my gun forward, I saw a destroyer escort about 5000 yards dead ahead of us. Two Japanese planes came in very high from the port side. One of the planes went into a steep dive and crashed off the port bow of the DE ahead of us. The second plane started a dive on the same ship, but pulled out, circled, and then made a run on our ship from starboard. (At some variance from the action report.)

All starboard guns were trained and firing on this plane. It once again pulled out of its dive, and it appeared to me that he crossed our vessel about midship. It then climbed to a point where it started its dive on our port bow. It looked as if it would hit me between the eyes, and I was sure I would be dead in a few seconds. Being on the starboard side and limited by the stops on my gun, I could only train the gun dead ahead and could not fire on this plane. I knelt down as low as I could with the gun pointed straight up, put my head down as low as possible, closed my eyes, and waited. I heard the gun captain on 3" gun number two tell his crew to hit the deck! That gun had jammed and could not fire. My gun crew was down on the deck (praying, I assume). The next thing I heard was a loud roar, followed by a tremendous explosion and a painful concussion. I believe I was blacked out momentarily."

It is quite possible that Jack did just that. Try to imagine in your mind's eye an airplane literally flying into your face with the pilot intent on killing you and himself at once. As a time frame, we are talking about a handful of seconds plus a few microseconds when the overload on the brain circuits causes them to short out, to mitigate the reality of the moment and even to substitute trivia. He recalled:

"We were in a big crap game about 20 minutes before GQ was announced. I had the dice and I was rolling when the general alarm went off and we raced to our stations. We had just loaded, the gunner was firing, I saw that Jap plane coming in and I thought, 'My God I'm going to meet my Maker! There's no way I want these dice in my pocket!' So I threw the dice over the side just when the *kamikaze* hit! I then opened my eyes, and the first thing I saw was a man lying on the deck decapitated. At first, I didn't know who it was but, when I saw the hot shellman's gloves on his body, I knew it was R.C. Allen. I heard the talker on 3" gun number two call for medics and then the gun captain cancelled the request - stating medics wouldn't be able to do anything for him. I found Allen's helmet laying at my feet and mashed like a tomato can. The inside of the helmet was covered with blood, hair, and gray matter. His body was lying on the sloped deck, and the blood from the torso drained down into our gun mount. My gun shield and myself were splattered with blood and gray matter. The crew of 3" gun two moved his body to the side, covered it with the gun cover and prepared for the next attack. I heaved the helmet over the side."

Chuck Markham remembered:

"It seems no matter how grave the situation is, a little humor comes out. When the plane hit, the fuse setter on 3" gun number two was wounded and lying on the deck in our gun mount. All he was saying was 'Son-of-a-bitch - I ran the wrong way!"

1940 the same day. Another Jap plane, a Val, singled out *Miles* for attack. The plane was picked up on SL radar and tracked intermittently. It made four separate attacks on *Miles*, strafing on the first two. The third was a suicide run, from which it pulled up after missing, having come close enough to nip the commission pennant off the low stub mast aft. It then came in a fourth time but finally turned away, disappearing in the darkness. Possibly, it was damaged beyond capacity to attack again because one 3" influence (magnetic) burst and many 20mm and 40mm hits were seen tearing it up during the third and fourth runs; a piece of the plane was seen to fly off. All guns that could bear fired at this plane whenever they could see anything for a point of aim in the dark, usually the twin exhaust flames. Jack Robinson referred to this attack:

"It was now dark and another plane was in our vicinity. It made some passes, but in the darkness all you could see was the exhaust from the engine. Then it was reported as 'downed'. We were still at GQ, but relaxed a little. Some of the men were looking for fragments for souvenirs. I stepped on what I thought was one, picked it up and put it in my pocket. Then we secured from GQ. When I went to the mess hall to get a cup of coffee, I looked at my souvenir and found it to be a piece of Allen's skull. Went topside and disposed of it. Hardly anyone slept that night, and most of us stayed on deck, close to our battle stations."

2110 .*Miles* finally secured from GQ. Conduct of all hands while under attack was exemplary, and gunnery was good. She resumed patrol.

0340 on 12 April. *Miles* went to GQ with enemy aircraft in the vicinity. One Tony passed down the starboard side at 0552, distance 3000 yards. Fire was opened on this plane but without results.

PCE-853, a casualty handling vessel, came alongside shortly after noon while *Miles* was still at sea, and took aboard the wounded man and the body of the one man killed for burial ashore. The Task Group Commander ordered the DE into Kerama Retto for repairs. She was relieved by *Whitehurst (DE-634)*.

By 3 May, *Miles* was back in the Okinawa area after final repairs in Ulithi and was assigned as part of a screen for the escort carriers operating off Okinawa and Sakishima. The carriers were flying planes on bombing, observation, and combat air patrol missions.

The story of this DE could not be closed without further reference to the dice that went overboard to save Jack *Robinson*'s soul. Once the *kamikaze* action had calmed down, crew members formed up to resume the crap game that had been so rudely interrupted by the Japanese. When Jack was asked to produce the dice, he shook his head innocently:

> "Gee fellas, I just don't recall what became of them."

In July 1945, *Miles* returned to the United States, a patched up veteran, full of scars and battle stars.

MANLOVE

From Killing Submarines to Killing Kamikazes

As previously mentioned, a sense of humor is an antidote for depression or trauma, both of the latter being in abundance at Okinawa. This author asked Al Maynard, the former executive officer of *Manning*, for some of his observations:

> "I arrived in Mare Island, California, in October, 1943 to help put *Manlove (DE-36)* in commission. I was a lieutenant (jg), assigned as her gunnery officer. In the ensuing months, I became a full lieutenant and was promoted to exec. I recall passing under the Golden Gate Bridge into the broad Pacific with 165 crew members out of a total of about 200 who had never been to sea before. If you are familiar with the ground swells outside San Francisco, you can imagine the appearance of our decks with all of the landlubbers being seasick. This was more than a shakedown; it was a shakeout!
>
> Now, I skip forward to 1984 and the first *Manlove* reunion. The organizer was Nelson Davis, my gunner's mate, first class. When I called him to confirm our attendance, I just couldn't place his name after all these years, whereupon he jogged my memory."
>
> "You remember on shakedown when we were in column formation with another DE about 400 yards astern of us. Then you must remember when we accidentally released an armed depth charge that blew up just forward of that DE! Immediately, word was passed over the loud speaker: WILL THE GUNNERY OFFICER REPORT TO THE FLYING BRIDGE ON THE DOUBLE! I would be embarrassed to repeat the captain's words. In addition, some uncomplimentary salty language was blasting over the TBS from the other DE. Also, do you remember the next day on maneuvers when we laid down the smoke screen before all ships got into position and they wound up in zero visibility? THAT'S ME, SIR!"

On 24 March 1944, during her first hunter-killer assignment, *Manlove* located the Japanese transport submarine *I-32*, attempting to replenish the enemy garrison at Wotje. In the ensuing coordinated depth charge run, *Manlove* and *PC-1135*, sank the sub. See narrative *Pacific Antisubmarine Warfare*.

For several months, *Manlove* convoyed among Majuro, Kwajalein, Eniwetok and the Marshalls. On 9 March 1945, under the command of Lieutenant Commander E.P Foster Jr., she departed from Eniwetok for Saipan to join a unit of the Fifth Fleet, then assembling for the Okinawa campaign. Al Maynard recalled:

> "After participating in the Guam, Tinian and Saipan campaigns, we were anchored off Saipan when a letter from my wife informed me that her cousin, John T. Rice, was a Marine Corps Captain with a company on Saipan. He was probably the only man in the Pacific Theater who had been in Belton, South Carolina recently and had seen my first son who I had never seen. I was starved for news. John told me that my son looked like any other baby he ever saw! I was appalled at the man's ignorance to even think such a thing, let alone say it.
>
> Nonetheless, I invited him aboard ship to keep peace in the family. We had fresh provisions for the Okinawa invasion, and he had been on "C" rations. We had a great fried chicken dinner for him, and would you believe it, he didn't eat a bite. He got seasick while the ship was at anchor! Just like a marine. He went up to the area designated as the captain's quarterdeck to heave over the side. This promptly brought the captain out of his cabin."
>
> "Mister, you can't be sick up here!"
>
> "Oh yeah – you just watch – oops!"

Manlove sailed with the invasion fleet and arrived on patrol station off Okinawa on 2 April. There she assisted in repelling enemy air attacks until she had some unpleasant encounters with the *kamikazes*, one in particular.

Any day was a bad day to be the target of a suicide plane, but two days in particular, 6 and 12 April, seared *Manlove* memories. The Japanese hurled hundreds of their "Divine Wind" zealots at the American fleet as it smashed its way into their front door. Many DEs were attacked sequentially by anywhere from one to six planes bent on suicide. The stress on the crews was severe. The enemy sacrifice was futile, but our side paid a heavy price.

Mid-afternoon on 6 April. While patrolling her station, *Manlove* made contact on radar with a merged group of bogies and friendlies approaching from a distance of 18 miles. Weak IFF signals were noted from ranges of 18 down to nine miles and initially caused some confusion.

1528. Two bogies were identified as Vals, both flying approximately 30 feet off the water, closing on a course normal to the vessel's track. At the same time, four F6F Navy planes appeared on the scene and took off after one of them. The enemy plane went into a steep climb and was splashed by the American aircraft from about 900 feet!

Two minutes later. The second plane had *Manlove* in her sights and was closing that ship at 150 knots, distance 4000 yards. With lightning speed, the F6Fs peeled off from their first kill and closed the Val. The American planes were plotted in the DE's CIC as a stern chase on the Jap, still approximately 30 feet above the water. The navy planes succeeded in turning the Val's heading and splashing it, with a sigh of relief and appreciation from the *Manlove* crew! Fire was not opened by the DE because American hunters were in too close to the hunted. Captain Foster wrote in his action report, "As results indicate, they (F6Fs) did a 4.0 job."

Less than an hour later, another suicider was spotted paralleling *Manlove*'s course. As the bogey swung away, the DE opened fire with nine rounds of antiaircraft main battery projectiles to mark the plane with air bursts for ships stationed nearby. This plane was fired upon by numerous vessels, but the results were not apparent to this DE.

1824 on that fateful day of 11 April. The Officer in Tactical

Command of the area patrolled by *Manlove* set Flash Blue. Normally, this did not call for going to GQ but, for some unknown reason, an uneasiness felt on the bridge induced Captain Foster to order his ship to GQ.

No sooner had the crew manned battle stations when two aircraft were spotted at an altitude of 1200 feet on the port bow. The planes wobbled their wings, indicating some kind of signal. At first, the ship spotters were elated to think that Army Air Force P51 aircraft had arrived in the area to assist their ground forces on Okinawa as well as the navy forces offshore. However, such thoughts were promptly dispelled as one of them, a Tony, peeled off and commenced a run on *Manlove*, the latter being in a tight turn to starboard.

The after 3", 1.1" and port 20mm antiaircraft batteries opened up on this target, and it was splashed 20 feet off the port beam by a direct hit from the 3" and numerous hits from the automatic guns!

Fire was opened to starboard on the second Tony which was closing from an elevation of 1000 feet, distance 4000 yards. As soon as fire commenced, this Tony backtracked and set off to the south where it attacked the *Samuel S. Miles* (previous narrative).

The Tony splashed by *Manlove* had strafed that vessel from the after 3" gun forward to the officers' head on the port side. It was carrying two bombs, both of which the pilot intended to present to *Manlove*. It was at an altitude of only 70 feet when hit by the 3" shell which caused it to wing over and splash, exploding at the same time. Shrapnel and fragments came aboard the DE, causing the death of one man and the wounding of ten others, nine of whom required hospitalization.

The major part of the casualties were on the after 3" and 1.1" guns. The captain was proud to state that the wounded men at these guns remained at their stations, trained around on the second bogey and drove him off before being relieved. The behavior of these men was the highlight of the engagement. While pharmacist mates were giving plasma, members of the repair and ammunition parties were able to successfully bandage and treat other wounded. The training of the men to take care of their shipmates and administer first aid was truly heart warming.

Standing orders had been published for all hands who were topside but not manning guns to stay under cover during air attacks. If it were necessary to be on deck, then they should lie prone during any attack. The one man killed disobeyed these orders. Had he been either under cover or flat on the deck, he might not have been killed.

Prior to this last action, the commanding officer had set up a plan of turning away from the attack at the last minute so as to cause the plane to shear its wings in the stack and mast. It was a "best guess" plan born of imagination rather than experience because most DEs only had their *kamikaze* training on the job and with the real article. Nevertheless, word was passed to all hands as to just what to expect. Signalmen were told to clear the action side of the signal bridge, and during the action these men obeyed the orders. Later, the attacked side of the signal bridge was found punctured with numerous holes. Without saying it, this plan also merited a 4.0.

The performance of ordnance was excellent, second only to the crew. There was considerable random damage from shrapnel and strafing.

Al Maynard also remembered the screen off the west side of Okinawa, beginning at D minus 2. *Manlove* and two other DEs were ordered to maintain antisubmarine and antiaircraft screens at 2000 yard intervals. After the first *kamikaze* attack, Captain Foster called him in to say:

> "To hell with this 2000 yards! Let's see if these other two ships won't close to 200 yards when we get the first bogey warnings...then we'll triple our fire power."
>
> "I gave Foster credit for our survival. We didn't exactly follow orders to the letter, but our group accomplished our objective of destroying Japanese planes."

With a chuckle, Al Maynard related something that is funny now but not then.

> "The incident the crew enjoys reliving the most was when we were assigned the mail duty in a task force off Okinawa. We entered an anchorage, picked up the mail and proceeded to deliver it. The captain took the conn, delivering to the first six ships, then told me to take the conn so he could take a nap. Well, I didn't do badly on the first two deliveries but I was hot-dogging it a little. The Admiral was on board the battleship *Texas (BB-35)*, our next mail stop. When we came alongside, *Manlove* seemed to prefer going ahead instead of reversing. We rammed the side of the battleship, leaving our anchor and part of the chain on her deck. Well, I guess the navy would never let me hear the last of the starboard anchor, and what's left of our crew will never let me forget it.
>
> And my wife's nephew, Mr. Will Ball, former Secretary of the Navy, says the only reason that the navy never called me back from the Reserve was that they ran out of anchors."

After repairs at Guam, *Manlove* returned to patrol off Okinawa where she continued to contribute to the success of the campaign until ordered back to the United States on 5 July 1945.

SEID

They Just Kept Coming

On the night of 21 October 1943, *Seid (DE-256)* received a message from *Stoney Point*, a transport the DE was escorting, stating that she had just passed a man in the water. Upon reversing course and illuminating the area, it was discovered that the swimmer was a *Seid* crewman. Though surrounded by sharks and supported only by a life belt, he was recovered uninjured. Questioning revealed that he had fallen asleep on the fantail and fell off the ship as she rolled!

8 January 1944. While operating as an escort with the Third Fleet, *Seid* sustained severe damage to her hull and equipment during a typhoon. When repaired and once more seaworthy, she spent the remaining months of that year and into 1945 in convoy activities.

On 27 March 1945, *Seid* stood out of Saipan Harbor to escort Transport Squadron 15 to Okinawa. Upon arrival on 1 April, the DE acted as antisubmarine screen for her Task Unit as it feigned landings on the southern tip of the island. While at anchor at Kerama Retto on 6 April, the destroyer escort's crew tasted first blood with an assist in downing a *kamikaze*, recognized as a Zeke.

Lewis M. Andrews, Jr.

Previous to the action in which *Seid* opened fire, three enemy planes had been shot down, two by aircraft and one by ships in the west anchorage. Two Japanese planes had made successful suicide dives into friendly ships, one in the anchorage and one outside the southern antisubmarine net. A friendly plane was mistakenly shot down by the surrounding ships and fell 2000 yards on the port beam of *Seid*. This ship did not fire, having identified the plane in time.

1838. The CIC on *Seid* reported to the captain, Lieutenant Commander Arthur F. Craft, an enemy plane closing from the starboard quarter, distance seven miles. It was taken under fire by ships in the area as this DE's gunners reported they were on target and tracking.

1840. With the bogey at 8000 yards, number three 3" gun and the 1.10" gun commenced firing. The 3" gun fired short with eight second timed fuses. As the plane made a left bank, four second fuse bursts began to score. At 4000 yards, the intruder turned left and crossed astern of the ship. Two second bursts were then seen hitting above the wing of the *kamikaze*, and the 1.10" was scoring repeatedly. At 1500 yards, the burning plane splashed!

Seid reported that it was more endangered by the indiscriminate firing of the ships than by the plane. (This was an initial problem at Okinawa. Eager gun crews, concentrating on the target, often didn't realize they were endangering other friendly craft. As the campaign wore on, gunners learned to be more discerning.)

1325 on 12 April, the longest day the crew would ever remember, found *Seid* patrolling on her station when the first portent of what was to be rumbled from the sky. Another picket ship had previously reported bogies approaching. The DE went to battle stations and set Material Condition Able (partial GQ). About 1400, two suspicious-looking planes had been noted near the hills in Okinawa. The area condition was Flash Blue, Control Green.

1433. The gunnery officer reported four planes between his ship and the sun on the port bow; three were Navy or Marine Corsairs attempting an attack on a single VAL. The position angle was 35 degrees, range 3000 yards. The *kamikaze* made a steep dive under the Corsairs and then leveled into a power dive toward the port bow of *Seid*, the position angle dropping to 20 degrees. The DE opened fire with all forward guns, and the Corsairs flew clear.

The plane engine and controls did not seem damaged in any way as it started its run on the DE. The skipper had an unobstructed view of the entire attack from the port wing of the flying bridge. He saw numbers two and three 20mm guns firing steadily into the plane and four shells from number one 3" gun exploding near the plane early in the dive. The Val attempted to strafe, but its shots fell short. A slender stream of smoke trailed from the plane.

At 900 yards, two 3" simultaneous hits were scored, one under and forward of the left wing and one just above the right wing, forward of the canopy. At 300 yards, a direct 3" hit was scored just abaft the engine. The body of the plane and the engine ripped apart. Heavy black smoke and flame enveloped the fuselage as it splashed about 100 yards off the port bow!

The shredded remnant of the pilot fell clear but sank with the plane. The engine, after it broke loose from the fuselage, landed 50 yards from the ship and ricocheted 30 yards more before it sank. Scraps of metal fell over the forward part of the ship and the bridge, but there were no personnel or ship casualties.

Captain Craft noted that the plane had crashed about 20 seconds after the firing began. Its speed was estimated to have been in excess of 200 knots. He also noted that the visibility was excellent and the sea was smooth, offering a steady gun platform. After the enemy pilot had made his dive to elude the Corsairs, the plane was a small but steady target.

The captain further noted that the courage and skill displayed by the gun crews was outstanding. Considering the short time between sighting and opening fire, it seemed incredible that all guns opened on the target and stayed on. Number one 3" gun fired five times in 20 seconds and had another round in the gun when the plane crashed. The men on the forward guns thought the plane was going to smash into the forecastle or on one of the guns. Despite this, nobody wavered, and their last desperate rounds saved the ship from severe damage.

1906 the same day. After being warned by the ship's CIC that a bogey was near, several of the bridge personnel saw a low-flying Nell approaching with the island of Iheyo Retto in the background. Just prior to this contact, a Navy PBM had taken off in the same direction as the sighting. Its IFF momentarily confused the ship's radarmen as to enemy identification. The visual range was five miles (10,000 yards), broad off the port bow, speed 200 knots. The aircraft was 25 feet above the water and heading directly at *Seid*.

The ship was zigzagging when the skipper gave the order for right full rudder. All guns that could bear were unmasked, and the Nell was taken under fire at 6000 yards. As the plane turned sharply to the left, it was under heavy fire with several hits by the 1.10."

Its nearest approach to the ship was 3000 yards, at which time the 20mm guns found their target and the 3" guns were placing accurate flak. Meanwhile, the ship was swinging with the plane on the port beam. Appearing to be in a no-win situation, the pilot retreated beyond 5000 yards. All guns ceased firing in order to conserve ready ammunition. The ship's rudder was shifted to full left.

1910. The Nell made another left turn for a new approach, this time on the starboard bow. The plane was again taken under fire by the forward guns at 5000 yards and closing. Its altitude increased to 40 feet as all starboard guns were unmasked and on target. The plane passed along the starboard beam at 4000 yards. During this run, the *kamikaze* had been well holed and was smoking on its port side. Cease firing was ordered as the pilot again turned off to 6000 yards and beyond, from the frying pan into the fire.

When the guns stopped firing, the now very unstable Nell received one short burst from an American night fighter plane and went down in flames about 7000 yards off the DE's starboard bow! After the Nell had been splashed, *Seid* remained near it momentarily, looking for survivors. There were none.

The skipper noted in his action report that the rate of fire from all guns was highly satisfactory. Also, discipline was very good with all guns holding fire and ceasing fire when so ordered. The captain was impressed with the accuracy, indicating that good tracking had been done by the men on the directors. There were neither personnel nor ship casualties in this action.

Captain Craft went on to note that this ship had very limited combat experience. In each of the above two attacks, the enemy had attempted suicide. When the Nell came in low over the water directly toward the ship, it was assumed that it was attempting a torpedo or skip bombing attack that would be followed by a suicide attack. In both attacks, it was proven that *Seid's* gun power was sufficient to shoot down the enemy. The crew had little doubt about their ability to do it again. The next trial was not long in coming.

Late twilight. A bogey was reported by the Combat Information Center on the starboard quarter, distance of five miles and closing.

Visibility was very low. There was still some gray in the west, but picking up a plane was very difficult, even with binoculars. The guns were ordered to fire at any low altitude target approaching the ship if not identified as friendly. This bogey circled to the starboard beam, range still five miles, then started its approach. When the *kamikaze* closed to 3000 yards abaft the starboard beam, the DE's rudder was thrown hard left. The after guns opened up when the plane's exhaust became visible in the dark.

1932.3. The firing lasted only 20 seconds as the plane, a Betty, approached astern at 200 knots, passed down the port side 20 feet above the water, and disappeared from view ahead. The ship was leaving a broad phosphorescent wake, clearly visible from the air. *Seid* began to make stack smoke and to maneuver radically in an effort to conceal the ship's movements and to prevent being silhouetted against the twilight glow in the west or the Nell still burning from the previous attack.

Several bogies were on the SL radar scope at close range. The Betty that had attacked was tracked by CIC out to four miles where it remained on the starboard beam for one minute. It then commenced closing rapidly, and the ship's rudder was put full left. The plane was taken under fire on the starboard quarter at a range of 1000 yards. Flames spurting from the engine area of the fuselage were clearly visible through the nose of the plane. The aircraft was screaming through the air at a very high speed. In passing over the ship, she nearly hit the after gun director.

1935.8. The *kamikaze* cleared the ship by the scantiest of margin and then plunged into the water about 3000 yards on the port beam! The plane lingered for about 10 minutes while burning, then disappeared into the deep.

A torpedo wake passed about 10 yards off the port side as *Seid* was steadied with right full rudder. With the torpedo clear of the ship, the rudder was shifted and the DE crossed the torpedo wake.

1937.2. No sooner had the ship begun to avoid that last *kamikaze* when another bogey was reported closing fast on the port quarter, and the almost perfunctory command sounded "Commence fire!."

1937.5. "Cease fire!" The after guns aimed well. The plane passed down the starboard side below the level of the flying bridge with the port wing and the fuselage on fire. It splashed about four miles away!

1937.7. A torpedo track was sighted 15 yards off the starboard bow!

1937.9. A short burst was fired at a plane passing close aboard the starboard side from forward to aft. The prior left full rudder remained, and apparently no damage was done to the plane. However, the forward gun crews and men on the depth charge stations reported having seen a torpedo drop and pass along the starboard side.

1940. A bogey closed on the starboard beam. Firing commenced. The firing came from number one 20mm gun, the only one that could see the closing aircraft in time to shoot. The skipper shifted the rudder in violent maneuvers. This plane was so close that the only part of it seen by the flying bridge personnel was the port wing as it was rising, evidently to avoid hitting the ship.

1942. No sooner had *Seid* steadied when the fourth torpedo streaked down the starboard side of the ship, passing near the stern. This was the last attack.

The stack smoke was beginning to give fair coverage. The ship was maneuvered radically to keep it inside the smoke screen and, at the same time, to locate any hostile planes closing the ship.

Planes had dropped "window" throughout the area. ("Window" was a name coined for intense radar reflection particles or strips, like aluminum foil, which could clutter a radar screen and make it difficult to identify a target.) The SA (air search) radarmen encountered difficulty in distinguishing between planes and window, whereas the SL (surface search) radar operators had little trouble in distinguishing between the two. By 2215 the area was clear of enemy planes.

A conservative recap showed that the ship had been attacked five times in nine minutes. The stress on taut nerves certainly was enormous. The rapid sequential threats of instant death took its toll. In spite of it all, officers and men displayed a cool proficiency that merited admiration. *Seid* was credited with splashing four enemy planes while evading five torpedoes on one day.

At least three twin engine enemy bombers made the torpedo attacks. It seems possible that either the second or third attack could have been the first plane returning and that the fifth attack could have been made by the plane that made the fourth attack.

The executive officer, Lieutenant Peter R. Phillips, in charge of the CIC, had direct communication with the commanding officer at the conning station. He took a position at the SL radar and did an outstanding job giving relative bearings and ranges directly to the captain. From this information, the ship maneuvered and conn had the location and activities of the nearest bogies constantly available when an enemy commenced his attack. *Seid* had racked up a remarkable score for night gunnery based solely on time-honored visual aim. Only larger fleet units at that time had radar fire control equipment.

In all actions participated in by this ship, the excellent work of the gunnery officer, Lieutenant (jg) William U. Osborn, Jr., and his assistant, Lieutenant (jg) Lloyd Christiansen, had been apparent in the gun discipline displayed. There were no heroes. The cooperation of the entire crew was needed to bring the ship through.

On 21 May, after repairs at Apra, Guam, she reported to the Submarine Force, Pacific Fleet. *Seid* operated out of Apra Harbor as an escort and training ship for submarines for the remainder of the war.

BRIGHT

A Jury Rig and a Four Leaf Clover

Between 24 November 1944 and 30 April 1945, *Bright (DE-747)* was engaged in convoy escort operations and conducted a series of hunter-killer searches near the Hawaiian and Marshall Islands.

Harold E. Cowell Sr., Electrician's Mate Third Class,

recalled some of his harrowing days on *Bright*:

> "Saipan had been secured for some time, and Tinian was the B-29 base. It was an awe-inspiring sight to watch the "big birds" (B-29s) come home from sorties over Japan. Little more than scraps for tails held them aloft just long enough to land."

On 5 May, *Bright* sailed from Saipan with a convoy to Okinawa. En route, she had a brush with a Japanese submarine. After several hours of hedgehog and depth charge attacks, the wiley sub captain rewarded *Bright* for her efforts by launching a torpedo which passed close aboard. Cowell recalled:

> "I was at my battle station, Repair I, in the forward mess hall during our attacks on the sub. It was a very small compartment with about fifteen other men standing by. Suddenly, a message from the lookout on the flying bridge hit my ear phones:
>
> 'Repair I, standby to receive a torpedo!'
>
> A few of the men saw the sudden expression of despair on my face. My jaws moved, but no words came out as the ship swerved to port, then to starboard, then leveled off. The submarine had fired a torpedo from astern on the port side, and the damned thing was traveling directly toward our bow and Repair I. A command for left rudder had been given from the bridge, but our executive officer, Lieutenant Fletcher Seymour, immediately countermanded that order:
>
> 'Right full rudder – emergency right full rudder – NOW!'
>
> Had Lieutenant Seymour not reacted so fast, the ship would have been athwartship of the torpedo, the end for us.
>
> Upon arrival, we were immediately sent out to run the ping line (Sonar echo ranging), an antisubmarine patrol and screening station close to Okinawa. We covered a 7000 yard sector for about three days with General Quarters an hourly event."

On the evening of 12 May, the crew got a first glimpse of what might be in store for them. A flight of *kamikazes* flew into the anchorage, close enough to *Bright* to precipitate her opening fire with main and secondary batteries, but without apparent result. One plane splashed in Hagushi Anchorage and another crashed into the battleship *New Mexico (BB-40)*(described in previous narrative). The action continued with antiaircraft firing witnessed off *Bright's* bow. Three hours later, *Bright* received orders from Task Group 51.5, directing her to fuel from the oiler *Kaskaskia (AO-27)*

0152 on 13 May 1945. The wind was logged as a gentle breeze from the west, about the only observation that would be gentle that day. The sea had a light swell, visibility was good, temperature mild, a marvelous day for cruising the Western Pacific any place except Okinawa. Enemy aircraft were reported in the vicinity. "Flash red, Control green" was issued for *Bright's* area.

0935. *Bright* was steaming astern of *Kaskaskia*, awaiting her turn to fuel when enemy aircraft were sighted in the vicinity of Point Bolo. *Kaskaskia* promptly discontinued all fueling operations and increased her speed to 18 knots. Her screening vessels as well as those escorts waiting to fuel formed a circular screen around her. The all clear followed 16 minutes after the hostile aircraft had first appeared. *Bright* again started to fuel, taking only 17 minutes to fill her tanks and cast off.

1207. *Bright* received orders to relieve *Sims (APD-50)*. An hour and 18 minutes later, she arrived on station and commenced her patrol. A check of neighboring stations established *Barr (APD-39)*, and *McClelland (DE-750)*. (Narratives covering *Sims*, *Barr* and *McClelland* included in this and next chapter.)

1915. In a matter of seconds, a bogey appeared and disappeared from the radar screen as it slipped behind the land mass of Tonachi Jima. Three minutes later, CIC reported friendly aircraft showing strong, authentic IFF with another "pip" in the same vicinity showing weak IFF. Combat Air Patrol planes were seen in the direction of Tonachi Jima and the other plane, assumed for the moment to be friendly, circled in the same vicinity. At the same time, CIC reported an additional bogey at a range of eight miles. The main battery and 40mm were trained on this target on the starboard side with the 20mm battery maintaining sector lookout.

1919. A low flying plane was discovered closing this vessel's port beam rapidly and was also picked up by radar with weak IFF at a range of only three miles. The ship's guns shifted to port, and the plane was taken under fire at a range of about 3500 yards. The airplane, seen by both *Bright* and *McClelland* was showing running lights. (This was reported by several ships during the Okinawa battle. It is believed that the pilot hoped a gun would fire at him, thereby giving him a point of aim to crash his plane in the dark.) At about 750 yards, the *kamikaze* burst into flames. The port wing was seen to fall off, causing the aircraft to veer toward the fantail of *Bright*. The plane crashed directly astern of the DE, with the stub portion of its sheared port wing hitting the port depth charge racks! Electrician's Mate Cowell gave us a view from the lower deck:

> "The men were well aware that there was a war going on, but we still had not been hit by anything more than seagull droppings. At 1924 hours on the evening of Sunday 13 May, Mother's Day, a plane was sighted off our port beam. It was flying parallel to us, bobbing up and down, obscured at times by some low hills. With complete disrespect for motherhood, the pilot turned his plane toward us. An order from the bridge told the gunners to hold their fire because the plane had a friendly IFF. Accordingly, the gunners held fire, but warily. The bridge again came over the sound powered phones and repeated that the plane had a friendly IFF. Third Class Electrician's Mate Robert Flint Thomas was manning a 20mm gun on the port fantail and watched as the plane came in ever closer to the ship. He opened fire on the *kamikaze* and, at his signal, the entire ship's armament opened up in unison.
>
> Lookouts said that Thomas emptied two cans of ammo at the plane and that many of the projectiles hit. He later told me that he wouldn't have let his own brother come in that close, IFF or no. The pilot had been hit many times, but the plane kept coming in. The after 3" gun fired and blasted the air with shellbursts. The 40mm, with its staccato, ear-splitting booming hit the plane's port wing, shearing it off five feet from the fuselage. Hitting the depth charge rack with the wing stub spun the aircraft directly astern into our vulnerable after steering engine room. The plane was carrying a 500

pound bomb which exploded on impact. The blast lifted the rear of the ship higher than normal and made it ride a wave downhill."

The result was immediate loss of steering with rudders jammed hard left. It was impossible to keep the vessel from circling, regardless of any combination of engines.

Immediately upon hearing the explosion, Repair II proceeded promptly with damage control measures. Hoses streamed water on flames coming out of the after steering compartment for a short time until the source of the electrical fire was determined.

All cables to this compartment were ruptured, and electrical fires were soon put out with carbon dioxide extinguishers. At the same time that fires were being controlled, repair party personnel were delegated to cut off electrical power aft of the main board. The 40mm magazine compartment was deliberately flooded due to proximity to the fire. Additional short circuits caused an electrical fire in another compartment. Repair party men entered it with rescue breathing apparatus and doused this fire with carbon dioxide. Smoke filled all after living compartments. Cowell recalled the trials of the crew:

"Two men stood their General Quarters stations in the aft steering engine room, Motor Machinist Mate Third Class Peter D. Vercolio and Electrician's Mate Third Class Harold E. Crane. The blast tore the interior to shreds below the lower deck level. It lifted a five inch by five foot by six foot piece of steel, which held the two main steering motors and the hydraulic ram between the rudder posts. It was thrown about 15 feet forward of its original position and left resting at a precarious angle upright against the forward bulkhead.

On entering the compartment, rescue parties found a body among all the rubble, twisted but alive. It was Vercolio. He had been blasted with fragments of the bomb and other shrapnel. One of the lasting marks on his body was from the gray paint on the bulkheads which had atomized and penetrated his skin as though he had been tattooed a solid blue color; it lasted for many years. He was removed from below decks through a two foot scuttle hole by Pharmacist's Mate Third Class James W. Johnson and Watertender First Class Prentice Marshall.

Lieutenant Seymour kept the rescue party looking for Crane for half an hour until he was found under a pile of gear at water level. Chief Machinist's Mate Mack Paluch and Chief Motor Machinist's Mate Paul Potter got him out through a hole in the deck while fighting flames that were threatening to consume them.

We were lucky to have the Division medical officer on board. The two battered men were taken to the wardroom where the doctor, N.N. Paul operated all night on the two wounded men. Dr. Paul removed bomb fragments from both victims, sutured and cleansed their wounds until they were ready to be transferred to a hospital ship in the morning. Pete Vercolio had a bomb fragment that broke the bone in his thigh. Today, he has one leg shorter than the other.

Harold Crane suffered severe damage to his right arm which was in a cast above his head for two years. Doctors at various navy hospitals worked on it for many more years and finally restored it to almost full use."

1925. In the midst of this awkward situation, a bogey was discovered in the vicinity and was taken under fire by *Barr*. The plane was also briefly fired upon by *Bright's* number three 3" gun, and the aircraft splashed shortly afterward. With *McClelland* standing by to assist, TBS transmission was relayed between *Bright* and the Task Group Commander to arrange for a tow.

Furious and unrelenting antiaircraft fire in all sectors prevailed as *Bright* worked her engines unsuccessfully in an attempt to steady on a course that would enable her to fight off further attacks. Within a short time, all fires were reported under control with electrical circuits in the after part of the ship de-energized.

2045. *Wickes (DD-578)* commenced protective circling about *Bright*, pending arrival of the tug and repair ship *Gear (ARS-4)* two hours later. She proceeded under tow to the anchorage at Kerama Retto, arriving after midnight. The commanding officer, William A. McMahon, commented on the events of the day:

"Personnel performance was excellent; firing was commenced as soon as the target was distinguished. All gunners stood by their weapons, firing until after the plane crashed. The result was that the *kamikaze* was hit and in flames and was deflected from his original course aimed at the engineering spaces. The 40mm was especially effective and was responsible for the plane's loss of a wing and its swerving from the intended course.

Coordination between CIC and gun control was excellent. Whenever an aircraft came within range of the radar, CIC informed the captain and gun control. The SA and SU radars were both in excellent operating condition due to their constant adjustment and maintenance by skilled radar technicians aboard this ship."

Cowell recorded a story of outstanding crew initiative:

"The next morning, with everyone still jittery from happenings the night before, we were taken to the graveyard of broken ships at Kerama Retto. There we were at the mercy of two-man suicide subs, *Baka* manned rocket bombs and air attacks. Each night, the harbor was covered with a smoke screen.

On the second day, we heard about the time element of getting into a floating dry dock. We found out that, with our low priority, we were 245 days down the list. Then we discussed repairing the ship ourselves. The engineers, the seamen, and the officers all had different ideas as to the best solution. The captain spoke to us over the public address system. He asked that each man who had an idea on how to repair the ship to make it seaworthy should send his idea along with a detailed description to him. Then he and his committee would choose the one most likely to succeed.

For some time, I had been experimenting with a diving mask which worked very well by utilizing the ship's air supply with a valve stem from a tire, acetylene hose and three valves to reduce the 3000 pound pressure to a working pressure. The captain asked me if I would inspect the hull of the ship. I went down and checked the screws, the rudders, the seals and the hull. I spent 22 minutes in the water and found everything true and in line. There was absolutely no damage lower than two feet below the water line.

It was then decided to go ahead and try some method of installing a jury rig. Of all the ideas, Shipfitter First Class Andrew W. Gibson submitted the one that was accepted. From then on, our ship was a beehive of activity. Many men volunteered and were put to work on hundreds of jobs.

I can remember going to a disabled destroyer which was out of service for the duration. We pulled alongside in our commandeered LCVP (landing boat) with all of our equipment in its hold. While someone kept the Duty Officer occupied, the rest of us cannibalized his ship. We had acetylene torches going and took any large piece of plate that we felt would fill the gaping wound in our rear end.

The adrenaline must have been running strong as the crew worked night and day in our after engine steering room. I worked for 72 hours straight until I went temporarily blind from arc welding. Others were cutting and placing the giant pieces of this jig saw puzzle into place.

The idea that was accepted for our jury rig was basically simple, but it involved the entire ship. The two rudder posts in after steering were unharmed so, to each was hooked a l-l/8 inch wire rope, each line to the opposite side of the hull to a snatch block, then up to the main deck to another snatch block, and then forward along each side of the main deck with blocks guiding to the forecastle and hooked to a section of anchor chain around the windlass. The chain was colored about every five links with a different color. This could be seen on the bridge, from where an order would be relayed to the helmsman standing his watch at the anchor windlass control to move his chain to the left (or right) to the red link, or any other color, and then back to amidship. In foul weather, the helmsman would move below to the boatswain's locker and, with sound powered phones, would move the windlass as directed until told to stop.

To summarize, a rig was installed to use the anchor windlass instead of the demolished steering engine.

When the hull was finally patched watertight, we decided to try her out. I must say that we were surprised at this outstanding feat of seamanship accomplished by all hands. The order was given to take the ship out for a trial run. A few officers from the shore command came aboard to join us for a shakedown.

The captain ran the ship smoothly, then called for left rudder, then right rudder. All went well. Then he called for full left rudder at 15 knots. Everyone was elated as the cables held and the ship acted as it had before being hit, a real champion.

The *Bright* was designated squadron commander of a flotilla of disabled ships that were being sent south to Ulithi. At Ulithi, we were told that the shipyard could not help us. In Kwajalain, we received orders to go to Pearl Harbor. At Pearl, the base gave us a nice party but had no facilities to repair our damage. Our next orders were to report to Swan Island Shipyard in Portland, Oregon.

I have sailed a lot of seas, but there is a particular beauty to traveling up the Columbia and the Willamette rivers in a great ship, small in size but large in heart. Our arrival in Portland had been announced previously by the press. When we stood up the river, all the bridges were filled with streamers, people throwing confetti and blowing horns, both young and old. The residents of Portland were marvelous to us and made us feel as though we had won the war in the Pacific all by ourselves.

Recapping our experiences in the Western Pacific, *Bright* destroyed a floating mine close aboard. We had a close call with a torpedo. We survived the *kamikaze*. We had a one in eight chance of having a doctor on board, and we had the best in Doctor Paul. Because *Bright* had survived several times against odds, the captain dubbed us 'lucky'. He asked me to paint a large four leaf clover on the stack. With his hands, he showed me a circle of about 18 inches diagonally. I painted one on the stack for him, but it was five feet in diameter!"

FIEBERLING

Too Close for Comfort

Fieberling (DE-640) arrived at Pearl Harbor on 27 June 1944 for escort duty to Eniwetok, making three such voyages to the staging ground for the Marianas operation. She served in convoy and screening operations in the South Pacific until 17 February 1945.

After amphibious landing rehearsals at Guadalcanal, *Fieberling* entered Ulithi Harbor the third week in March to load stores and ammunition for the assault on Okinawa. She arrived off the island on 31 March, covered the landings the next day, and headed for her patrol station, nominally antisubmarine, actually antiaircraft.

1601 on 6 April. The action began when a large group of bogies swept in and attacked the northern radar pickets as Task Force 54 commenced night retirement. This vessel was still en route to her station, six miles from the center of the formation. One of the attackers, tracked in by radar, was shot down by the oncoming destroyer screen, but not before several rounds of 5" antiaircraft shells from the destroyers burst above the water, close aboard this destroyer escort. Fortunately, there were no injuries.

1625. A second raid developed. Some of the enemy planes broke off to strike Kerama Retto while two attacked the screening and picket vessels within the inner patrol screen. A general burst of fire from the formation, splashed at least one Val or Kate.

1642. The first heavy raid was made upon TF 54, four or five bogies being splashed in flames. Antiaircraft fire was also visible in the transport anchorage area off the western beaches. This DE spent the ensuing hour maneuvering to clear battleship and cruiser formations and to head for her assigned screening station. She arrived just as a number of single plane raids drew fire from distant ships on various bearings from *Fieberling*.

1746. A large two-motor plane appeared, distance nine miles, slowly circling at 2000 feet. *Fieberling's* CIC commenced tracking, and her commanding officer, Lieutenant Commander E.E. Lull, ordered a change of course and speed. The helm was put hard over to the left to unmask the battery to assist *Leutze (DD-481)* and to bring the bogey into the line of fire. After clearing nearby ships, the *kamikaze* dived to within a few feet above the water and began a long run on *Leutze*, 800 yards from *Fieberling*.

1759. The after control spotted the approach of a second low-flying bogey, also intending to crash *Leutze*. *Fieberling* took it under fire with her 3" battery at 4000 yards and locked on it with gun number three and the 40mm until the instant of crash! Her forward guns broke off as the ship swung again to port to meet the threat to their own vessel posed by the first bogey. At this point, casualties occurred in the 40mm power drive and firing cut out, a situation that would soon prove to be highly — and dangerously — embarrassing.

1806. The starboard lookouts warned that the first bogey, a Zeke with two good sized bombs under its wings, was coming in fast on *Fieberling* about 6000 yards on the beam and at an altitude of 600 feet. The DE opened fire with her 3" battery. She maintained fire until within the danger bearing of the destroyer. Several bursts were observed on or very near the plane which finally took fire and splashed close aboard its intended target! Throughout most of the run, no other ship appeared to have the plane under fire. Credit was claimed by *Fieberling* for splashing or, at the very least, damaging this bogey, probably a Betty.

By that time, the ship was dead ahead of Task Force 54 which had executed a 45 degree turn to port, thus giving the appearance of *Fieberling* being the leading escort of their screen. The bogey first turned left, as though to pass up *Fieberling* for better bait. The DE came right with full rudder at flank speed to keep the *kamikaze* abeam and opened fire with her 20mm guns when the pilot closed the range to 1200 yards. The 40mm was out and the 3" battery was delayed in disengaging from other targets.

Automatic 20mm fire was effective, however, with many hits scored as the *kamikaze* passed down the ship's starboard beam. The target faltered noticeably, side-slipping left and right. Then, apparently concluding he could do no better, the pilot banked sharply and attempted to dive into *Fieberling's* bridge. As the ship continued her right turn at maximum speed, she appeared to have thrown him off. Nonetheless, the pilot released his bombs, which crossed within eight feet of the after director and then splashed harmlessly over the side. He then winged over upside down, sharp right, broad on the starboard quarter, and struck the SA radar antenna which cut through his right wing and sent him spinning and splashing 40 yards on *Fieberling's* port bow!

1810. Another suicider, showing no quarter for *Fieberling's* disabilities, made a run on this DE, but was shot down by a cruiser while still 1200 yards away.

Being without radar and having no chance to assess further damage, the vessel proceeded at best speed to a less exposed station within the protective screen of Task Force 54 where she was engaged for the last time with a suicide plane. *Fieberling* opened fire with her 3" battery at a plane which was diving upon a destroyer. The bogey splashed under heavy fire from all nearby ships!

1835. With dark setting in and being in doubt as to the stability of the damaged mast structure, *Fieberling* proceeded to the Northern Anchorage. Early on 7 April, after effecting emergency repairs by the ship's force, the captain reported readiness for duty but without radar, 40mm battery or main radio and requested early tender availability to complete repairs. In reviewing their close call, Captain Lull summarized:

> "Although we had considerable materiel damage, there were no injuries to personnel. However, it is believed that the opportunity presented itself before the final wing-over for a large volume of accurate automatic fire on a beam target. In addition, we employed effective high speed maneuvering to take advantage of the very tight turning circle possible with a DE. Both circumstances were major contributing factors in saving the ship."

After escorting a convoy of assault ships to Saipan in April, *Fieberling* returned to Okinawa for patrol, escort and radar picket duty. She returned to Portland, Oregon for overhaul in November, then sailed from San Diego for occupation duty off the Chinese coast. Back in San Diego in August 1946, she operated along the west coast and in the Hawaiian Islands, testing experimental equipment.

FAIR

Not "Fair" to the Kamikazes

Fair (DE-35) had previously sunk Japanese submarine *I-21* (See chapter *Pacific Antisubmarine Warfare.*) Following a patrol assignment at Eniwetok in July 1944, she screened a logistics group during the assaults on Tinian and Guam. From 13 October to late March 1945, she was back at Eniwetok, escorting convoys to Ulithi, Manus, Guam, and Guadalcanal.

Guarding a convoy composed primarily of LSTs, *Fair* sortied from Ulithi on 27 March and, after the initial assault on Okinawa on 1 April, she put into Kerama Retto. On 6 April, before departing for Saipan with unladen transports, things began to happen. In the morning, *Fair* was on her screening station, just west of Tampa Misaki, Okinawa Island.

0315. Commander Task Force 51 set Flash Red, Condition Yellow with orders to ships outside of the smoke screen to fire on all planes contacted visually. *Fair* was at battle stations for the next three hours, during which time many bogies were present and numerous flares were dropped. The weather conditions were unfavorable with heavy strato-cumulus clouds at an altitude of 900 feet; the wind was northwest, force three. The reference point for bogey reports was near this ship's station, and her CIC maintained current information.

0418. Low flying aircraft were heard approaching on the DE's port bow. One was seen almost dead ahead at 1000 yards, elevation angle five degrees above the horizon. Two 20mm guns and two 3" guns opened fire promptly. However, the plane disappeared into the clouds and proceeded over the land area.

0554. An aircraft was heard approaching from the starboard quarter, and all guns adjusted to that general direction. A single plane came out of the clouds, close to the estimated bearing, distance 1800 yards, angle five degrees above the horizon. Identification of the plane was difficult due to the poor light and the short time of the action. After a few seconds of tracking, the 1.10" quad opened fire with full director control and scored multiple hits. This was followed seconds later by all three 3" and six 20mm guns. The 3" bursts were very close, two from pre-set fuze settings, one from a magnetic influence type fuze. The 20mm fire was very accurate. Two of the LCIs being escorted also opened fire with their 20mm guns.

After a few 1.10" rounds, a small fire appeared on the port side of the aircraft fuselage abaft the wing and spread slowly. Twenty seconds after firing commenced, the plane burst into flames, went into a steep dive and splashed 1800 yards off the starboard quarter!

2240 on 21 April. A twin engine aircraft passed astern from

starboard to port at a range of 1500 yards, elevation 700 feet, up moon. The *Fair* gunners opened fire with the 1.10" and 20mm guns. Although the plane was probably damaged, there was no evidence of destruction.

0405 on 26 April. During a Flash Red air alert, a Betty flew low over the entrance to Chimu Wan, 2-1/2 miles from *Fair*. The plane approached from the north, then turned 180 degrees and went back from whence it came. While visible through binoculars up moon from the DE, the gun crews were not able to get on target.

Early evening of 12 May. The next action was a surprise attack with *Fair* anchored about 2000 yards from *New Mexico (BB-40)*. Lacking a warning, the DE was not at battle stations. The first plane made a slow approach in a shallow glide, approaching from the starboard quarter of the battleship. The plane, under heavy fire, did not start to burn until it banked sharply to port and dived. *Fair* opened fire when the plane was just forward of her starboard beam. Two of her war cruising ready gun crews each fired one full 20mm magazine at the Oscar at a range of 950 yards. Both guns had tracked the plane and both appeared to be highly accurate. The gunners claimed they were on target, and it appeared to officers on the bridge that these two gun crews scored many hits. While *Fair* was firing, the plane banked sharply, burst into flames and splashed! Although this ship scored many hits and contributed to the plane's destruction, there were other ships firing, and the concentration of fire was responsible for downing the *kamikaze*.

Two minutes later, the second Oscar approached the battleship in a shallow dive dead astern, catching most of the ships present by surprise. This plane was not observed in time for *Fair* to begin tracking and only a few rounds of all calibers were fired without success. There was considerable danger of damaging other ships in the area, and the order was passed to cease fire. The *kamikaze* crashed into *New Mexico*!

Just after midnight on 13 May. *Fair* illuminated a small boat at a distance of 1500 yards, proceeding at slow speed. Several other ships anchored in the vicinity also illuminated and their combined fire sank or drove the boat away. When last seen, it was afire. Very likely, this was one of the many surface suicide boats that the Japanese used in the Philippines and Okinawa with very limited success.

The next assignment for *Fair* was an escort voyage to Saipan and Guam, returning to Okinawa on 10 June for local escort duty and patrol. She cleared Okinawa in July 1945 for Portland, Oregon and was decommissioned on 17 November 1945.

GRADY

One Less Kamikaze

With the American offensive in the Pacific entering its climactic phase, *Grady (DE-445)* departed from Pearl Harbor for Ulithi, arriving on 10 January 1945. For the next month, the ship escorted a vital tanker group engaged in refueling units of the Third Fleet, then conducting air strikes against Formosa and Japanese installations on the Chinese mainland. Her next destination was Iwo Jima to screen escort carriers engaged in air bombardment prior to the amphibious assault on 19 February.

On 3 March, she fueled in Saipan and departed for Espiritu Santo. There, the ship joined in preparations for the upcoming Okinawa invasion, the last giant step on the long sea road to Japan. *Grady* departed as one of the escorts screening the various units en route to Okinawa. The Screen Commander was in *Rall (DE-304)* (previously narrated in this chapter).

Ulithi was a mere overnight stop at anchor. Dawn saw that atoll falling away astern as the Task Group headed for Kerama Retto, arriving on 9 April and anchoring inside the harbor. In accordance with a secret dispatch from Commander Task Group 51, *Grady* effected a rendezvous with the transport screen during the attack and occupation of Tsuken Shima.

From 9 to 12 April, *Grady* patrolled in various assigned stations off Tsuken Shima and in Nakagusuku Wan, screening transport and fire support groups without significant contact with the enemy.

As the bloody fighting raged ashore, *Grady* and the other ships engaged in equally fierce radar and antisubmarine picket duty and were savagely attacked by Japanese suicide planes.

However, this first assignment as a screening vessel during the occupation of Tsuken Shima proved uneventful. The main concern was one of piloting, maintaining assigned patrols while keeping clear of reefs, unswept waters, and fire support vessels. The sound gear was an invaluable asset in locating reefs and mines. Sniping and machine gun fire from Tsuken Shima was a problem, minimized by keeping unnecessary topside personnel under cover.

On the evening of 15 April, while *Grady* was assigned a screening sector off Hagushi Beach, she took a pot shot at an enemy aircraft passing close overhead, expending a few rounds of 40mm and 5" caliber ammunition (*Grady* was one of the newer DE classes with 5" guns). The plane flew on; no hits were observed.

Mid-morning on 16 April. A plane was picked up and tracked for 50 miles by radar and received close attention from the captain, Lieutenant Commander Francis R. King, until the plane came into view low over the water, broad on the starboard beam, and heading directly at the ship. The aircraft, a Kate, was taken under fire with the after 5" gun. After three bursts placed directly in front of him, the pilot turned off, trailing smoke and heading for destroyer *Metcalf (DD-595)* in the adjacent station.

Metcalf also worked the plane over. It then passed between the two ships, heading for the transports anchored off Ie Shima, but burst into flames under fire from both vessels! The time between the first and last shots was only 50 seconds. Weeks and months of preparation and training reached their climax in seconds; we kill them or they kill us, just that simple. It was believed by the *Grady* crew that a special 5" projectile from her battery did the final damage, but the crew of *Metcalf* had other convictions. Either way, it added up to one less *kamikaze*.

At night, when enemy aircraft were in the immediate vicinity, *Grady* invariably slowed to nine knots and withheld fire. The plan was quite successful in that the ship was never attacked at night although enemy aircraft frequently passed within visual distance. Her officers believed that their unchanged Atlantic camouflage was a great asset under these conditions as the single gray Pacific color made a ship stand out except in conditions of extreme darkness. However that might be, the essential factors for escaping detection were believed to be maximum reduction of wake and minimum silhouette.

Grady operated until 26 April in various screening sectors and in Hunter-Killer Group Four. On 26 April, she was ordered into Hagushi Anchorage for radar repairs.

After one convoy in early May, *Grady* returned to the picket stations off Okinawa, occasionally providing antiaircraft fire in the transport anchorages. She continued this arduous duty until 28 June when she sailed for Leyte Gulf where she was assigned as offshore patrol vessel and escort for convoys to Okinawa. *Grady* began the long voyage home on 5 November, two months after the surrender of Japan.

PAUL G. BAKER

An Embattled Veteran Came Through

After clearing Pearl Harbor on 8 September 1944, *Paul G. Baker (DE-642)* spent the next six months convoying to ports in the South and Southwest Pacific with such unfamiliar names as Emirau Island; Manus in the Admiralties; Port Purvis, Florida Island; Bougainville, Lunga Point, and Guadalcanal in the Solomons; Treasury Islands; Sasavelle Harbor in Munda; Purvis Bay; Espiritu Santo in New Hebrides; the Russell Islands. Readers might have difficulty in locating many islands in a modern atlas because some groupings are no longer colonies and, as new countries, have changed names to correspond to their respective cultures. Names are gone, but memories linger.

Leaving the Russell Islands on 15 March 1945, *Baker* steamed via Saipan and Ulithi with a troop-laden transport for the assault on Okinawa. The task unit arrived on the day of the initial landings, 1 April, and this DE took station on the inner transport screen off Hagushi Beach. Her first taste of enemy air activity came at dusk that day when she opened fire on a plane crossing astern. She protected the transports during unloading by day and retirement by night until she departed to guard empty transports to Guam.

Arriving again off Okinawa on 18 April, *Baker* joined the dangerous but vital patrol screen which protected American forces fighting to capture the island stronghold.

22 April *Baker* was patrolling approximately five miles south of Kerama Retto anchorage. Visibility was good with 60 percent cloud coverage. The wind was force three from the southwest. Sunset was predicted in another hour and twenty minutes. The sea was calm. The warning net advised that enemy air attacks were probable.

1737. "Flash Blue, Control Green." Twelve minutes later, the minesweeper *Density (AM-218)* stated that a suicide plane had dived at her but that it had missed its target and splashed. In another two minutes, destroyer *Isherwood (DD-520)*, adjacent to *Density*, reported that she had been hit amidship by a suicide plane, causing a large fire, but was proceeding under her own power to Kerama Retto. This was not your favorite Okinawa evening news program; gunners stood by nervously as tension increased on ships in the area.

The air search radar on *Baker* was handicapped by the land blocking the anticipated bearings. Nonetheless, they were able to pick up some bogies on radar at 12 miles. Friendly planes were also in the area.

1850. The warning net at Kerama Retto announced "Flash Red, Control Yellow" and warned there were many bogies in the area. One minute later, *Baker* sighted a flight of six to seven friendly fighters at about six miles, flying in the direction of her area.

As lookouts followed the friendlies with their glasses, the attention of the captain, Lieutenant Commander W. Gordon Cornell, was drawn to a single plane emerging from the clouds five miles beyond the friendlies, elevation 6000 feet. A few seconds after breaking into the clear, it commenced erratic movements while still making good the same base course, identifying the aircraft as hostile. Suddenly, this plane, tracked in the CIC, changed course and went into a shallow glide straight for *Baker* and decreasing altitude to 2500 feet.

As it passed a mile from the minesweeper *Swallow (AM-65)*, patrolling a station 7500 yards from *Baker*, both ships opened fire. Suddenly, the plane rolled over into a straight 50 degree dive, headed for *Swallow* and crashed into the minesweeper's main deck!

Baker proceeded to her assistance at flank speed, as did the minesweepers *Gayety (AM-239)* and *Spector (AM-306)* and the Fleet Ocean Tug *Molala (ATF-106)*. Three minutes after being crashed, *Swallow* capsized and lay keel up, then disappeared under the waves.

Baker lowered her whaleboat, threw over three rubber aircraft rescue life rafts and lowered survivor and cargo nets as she approached the stricken vessel. The survivors were concentrated within an area 400 yards in diameter. She picked up nine officers and 69 men. The *Gayety* rescued 11 men, *Spector* one man, and *Molala* 15 men, a total of 105, reported to be all but one of the ship's company. Three badly burned men were given first aid treatment on *Baker*. Shortly thereafter *PCE(R)-855* came alongside to take off survivors.

The air attacks continued to be heavy and frequent for patrol vessels off Okinawa. With the exception of an unclassified sound contact and destruction of two floating mines, *Baker* continued her screening activities into the month of May without significant enemy contact.

Early hours of 4 May. Ships were bathed in bright moonlight, which escorts needed like the proverbial "hole in the head." An air alert was broadcast. Many bogies in the area were crowding the radar scope on *Baker*. An enemy plane, low on the water, commenced a run on *Baker's* port quarter. The DE immediately went to flank speed with hard left rudder. Although the plane was located from the open bridge, it was difficult to get guns on the target. *Baker* commenced fire at 2500 yards with 3" gun number three, the 1.10" gun and the after 20mm and 50 caliber machine guns. The plane continued on a closing course until within 500 yards when it rolled and turned to the left, passing up the port side of the ship at about 350 yards, then disappeared in the darkness. No hits had been observed. However, about two minutes after the plane passed, there was a heavy underwater explosion close aboard, which did no damage. It quite possibly was a torpedo or bomb released by the plane.

0900 *Baker* took an aircraft under fire with her 3" main battery, range 8000 yards, expending 39 rounds, but without results. Bombs were dropped, but there were no casualties.

0818 on 8 May *Baker* was ordered to change station to five miles south of Kerama Retto. In late afternoon, she recovered the body of a Japanese soldier with papers that were delivered to the Commander Task Force 51.5 on the Amphibious Force Flagship *Eldorado (AGC-11)*.

9 May. There were several raids from evening until 2246. A large number of planes were involved, and two nearby ships were crashed by *kamikazes*.

0800 on 11 May. The DE was ordered to change station and arrived at the new one in time to set up plots on incoming raids. Two planes approached and were splashed by a destroyer in an adjacent station.

12 May *Baker* was directed to report to the transport area. She had no sooner anchored at 1912 when, with no prior warning from control, two enemy planes appeared overhead and dove on *New Mexico (BB-40)* only 1000 yards from the DE. (Same action as in *Fair* narrative.) *Baker* opened fire with all guns that could bear. One plane was splashed, but the other crashed into the battleship. Meanwhile, all ships in the vicinity opened fire on two more planes which proved to be friendly. Fortunately, they missed.

The night of 13 May. Several suicide boats were reported to the south of the transport area but they were destroyed. Enemy aircraft approached, and *Baker* opened fire on a plane at 5000 yards, locked into visibility by shore searchlights. No hits. At 0530, *Baker* was underway to fuel, then returned to her station just before sundown, in time to go to GQ as a flight of enemy planes drew near. Two ships in stations three miles to the south of the DE were crashed by suiciders.

14-22 May. Air raids every night. GQ-GQ-GQ – Exhausted but alert. No man was under any illusion as to the danger of this mission, the bloodiest battle in the history of the United States Navy.

24 May. From 2113 until 0430 the next morning, the enemy attacked in force and relentlessly. At least two ships in the anchorage area were crashed by *kamikazes*. Early in the raid, before the smoke coverage was very effective, several ships, including *Baker*, each took a single plane under fire, but no hits were scored. One plane was picked out by searchlights and passed over *Baker*, tripping a severe response, but no results.

0800 on 25 May. Enemy planes again attacked in force. Only a few planes succeeded in reaching the anchorage. The *kamikaze* thrust appeared to be somewhat blunted. However, that was wishful thinking. The bulk of the *kamikaze* corps, several thousand pilots, were being held in reserve for an anticipated invasion of their northern islands.

1 June. In the pre-darkness, low-flying enemy planes, undetected until four miles from the anchorage, were splashed before reaching it

3-4 June, Between 0230 and 0400. Six enemy raids were in the area, one passing over the anchorage, but no attacks were attempted. Late in the morning, *Baker* was underway to her station off Ie Shima. She arrived in time to begin plotting a large number of bogies. Shortly after midday, she proceeded to her dusk antiaircraft station south of the Ie Shima anchorage. About 25 planes were splashed by the Combat Air Patrol and none reached the anchorage.

6 June. Intermittently, from late afternoon until late evening, enemy air raids came in from the north, west, southwest and southeast. However, CAP splashed almost all of them, and none reached Ie Shima.

Mid-morning on 8 June *Baker* was ordered to a new station, four miles south of Okinawa, to relieve destroyer *Gherardi (DD-637)*. Shortly before and after the noon hour, enemy planes were in the area. Commencing at sunset and lasting all night, scattered air raids came into the general area, but only one threatened *Baker*. For the day, a total of thirty-seven raids were logged.

10 June. At 0800, *Baker* was underway at flank speed to the assistance of *Gendreau (DE-639)*, hit by shore battery fire about five miles distant. On approaching the damaged ship, *Baker* was advised that, although her forward fire room was flooded, she was underway and did not need aid.

1900 on 11 June. After anchoring at Nakagusuku, bogies were reported approaching. A few minutes later, a low flying Sonia was tracked coming into the anchorage over land. All ships within range opened up with everything they had. The *kamikaze* made a dive on the dock landing ship *(LSD-6)*. Apparently, the reception was too warm because the pilot zoomed up, maneuvered radically and, from an elevation of 400 feet, headed for *Baker*. Changing his mind once more, he swerved off and singled out a liberty ship. At this stage of *Baker's* involvement at Okinawa, her gunners were a well rehearsed team; they splashed the plane about 50 feet from its intended target and 800 yards from *Baker*!

Raids from near and far continued until this DE finally departed with the blessing of all hands. On 20 June 1945, she sailed in the screen of a battleship and cruiser force to patrol southeast of Okinawa. She returned to Kerama Retto on 1 July.

In September, *Paul G. Baker* steamed to Yokosuka Naval Base, Tokyo Bay, an American navy pilgrimage. She then pointed her bow toward the United States, arriving at Astoria, Oregon, on 21 November 1945.

SEDERSTROM

A Nut Too Tough for the Kamikazes

After a number of convoys from Pearl Harbor to Ulithi, *Sederstrom (DE-31)* spent the period of November 1944 to mid-February 1945 screening auxiliaries, escort carriers, and merchant ships between Eniwetok and Ulithi. In March, she escorted reinforcements and supplies to Iwo Jima, then patrolled off that island until she was recalled to Ulithi to stage for the Okinawa campaign.

Sederstrom departed from the Western Carolines for the Ryukyus in the screen of escort carriers and arrived off the southern tip of Okinawa early on the afternoon of 24 March. For the next three weeks, she screened and provided plane guard services for the carriers as they supported the landings on Kerama Retto and Okinawa. The captain, Lieutenant Commander Farley, put his crew through battle station drills that would prove their worth very shortly. By mid-April, Japanese aerial resistance, particularly the *kamikazes*, had taken a major toll among destroyer types. Consequently, beachhead screening ships, like *Sederstrom*, were reassigned to the picket line.

22 April. *Sederstrom*'s day to remember. While patrolling off the West Coast of Okinawa just after sunset, several enemy raids were reported to be approaching. A few minutes later, the ship's SA (air search) radar picked up a group of eight bogies broad on the port bow, distance 35 miles, and closing rapidly. Radar then lost the raid because of land return from Aguna Shima behind the bogies.

1920. The raid was picked up again on both air and surface radars as the planes departed from the southern tip of Aguna

Shima. The raid split, four planes altering direction to the north, the other four on a course parallel to the track of *Sederstrom*. The skipper ordered a course change to bring all guns to bear and, at the same time, began to maneuver radically at flank speed.

1926. *Sederstrom* opened fire on four planes as they emerged from cloud cover at a range of 1500 yards, position angle 20 degrees. The flight formation was evidently surprised as all planes veered sharply when this vessel opened up. Lookouts reported that the second group of four planes was under fire from *Richard W. Suesens (DE-342)* in an adjacent station and that *Stern (DE-187)* also nearby but on the other side, had other planes under fire. (Both *Suesens* and *Stern* narratives are in this chapter.) *Sederstrom* hit the lead plane of the formation with a 3" burst, causing it to wing over sharply. The other three planes were also under fire and one, trailing smoke, disappeared from the radar screen, chalked up as a "probable."

The plane that was hit earlier came down the starboard side aft at a distance of 1000 yards, banked sharply and headed for *Sederstrom* in a steep dive from astern. It was hit again with a 3" burst. Many hits from automatic weapons were seen on the suicider's engines, now smoking and on fire. When directly overhead, the *kamikaze* headed for the bridge. Hard left rudder and a murderous barrage of antiaircraft fire caused the aircraft to roll over. With wings vertical and apparently out of control, it splashed only a few yards off the starboard bow!

Gasoline and pieces of metal showered the bridge and forecastle, but damage was minor. One man forced overboard during the action was quickly recovered. The alert gunners also scored hits on two other *kamikazes*, damaging one and probably downing the other.

In early May, *Sederstrom* escorted the battleship *Arkansas (BB-33)* out of the combat area. She then left the Ryukyus on an escort mission to Guam where Captain Farley turned over command to Lieutenant Commander B.H. Bossidy and returned to the United States for new construction.

Sederstrom resumed escort duties with aircraft carriers and merchant ships. She returned to the United States in July for repairs. However, the war ended before she could return to the combat zone.

RICHARD W. SUESENS

The Drums of War Beat Louder

Richard W. Suesens (DE-342), commanded by Lieutenant Commander R.W. Graham, was a seasoned veteran well before the hell of Okinawa. With the Seventh Fleet, she saw her first action in October 1944 in the invasion of Leyte, Philippines, screening troops and supplies to the area. She was assigned to "Taffy Two," a covering force for the landing, only a few miles from "Taffy Three," the embattled force that turned around a superior Japanese Fleet off Samar. In the invasion of Luzon, at Lingayen Gulf, she sent a *kamikaze* to its rightful place on the sea floor. See chapter *The Philippine Campaign*.

Returning to Leyte, she prepared for Operation "Iceberg," the invasion of the Ryukyus. She sailed with the Western Islands Attack Force, arriving at Kerama Retto on 26 March. *Suesens* took a screening station between Yakabi Shima and Tanoki Shima while Task Group 51.1 deployed for the landing. Several ships were under air attack, but enemy planes did not close within six miles of this Task Group; only a whisper of war.

During the night of 28-29 March, enemy aircraft scouted the formation without attacking; no longer a whisper of war; more like a distinct sound of war.

The night of 29-30 March. Several enemy planes again scouted the formation, and the attack cargo ship *Wyandot (AKA-92)* was damaged by a near miss from a single plane. While in night station, enemy planes over the formation were fired on by screening ships. A Betty passed directly above *Suesens* twice. The remainder of the night was quiet. The sound of war was closer, much closer.

The night of 2 April. Enemy planes were in the vicinity of the formation with as many as nine groups at one time. The ships were under attack several times, and one plane was shot down by the destroyer minesweeper *Fraser (DM-24)*. One bomb was dropped and a near miss was scored on one of the transports.

3 April. The convoy was under a 45 minute assault by suicide planes. The attack transports *Goodhue (APA-107)* and *Henrico (APA-45)* were hit by planes of the first wave while a third plane crashed *Dickerson (APD-21)*. (This is same action as described in a prior narrative about *Riddle*. The ordeal of *Dickerson* is narrated in the next chapter on the APDs.) The second wave attacked, and four more planes were shot down by screening ships. *Suesens* fired at one of the planes but did not score hits due to extreme range. At 2120, the night retirement was temporarily halted when *Suesens* was ordered to leave the screen to escort *Goodhue* back to Kerama Retto anchorage to discharge wounded personnel. The war drum beat became ever louder.

0600 on 3 April. The formation was surrounded by enemy aircraft and was continuously under attack. A Tony dived on *Suesens* from the starboard side, passed over the forecastle, and splashed on the port side after being hit repeatedly by 20mm and 50 caliber machine guns! *Suesens* spilled blood. Was the worst over or just begun?

17 April. *Suesens* took a screening station 15 miles west of Zamba Misaki at 0825 until ordered to relieve *Gendreau (DE-639)* 7000 yards southwest of Koba Shima. During the night, enemy planes were in the area from after sunset until 2300, and several heckler planes passed overhead within one mile.

1921. A Judy made a direct low level attack on *Suesens* but it was driven off by AA fire. The drums were beating louder. From then on, several planes passed overhead but did not attack.

1900 On 20 April, a Betty began a direct attack on *Suesens* at about masthead height. After being subjected to rapid AA fire, it turned off at about 3000 yards and retired to the southwest. From then until midnight, enemy planes were in the area continuously. Several passed very close to this DE but were not seen because of poor visibility. Window was dropped several times, and 15 flares were dropped by two planes. There were eighteen raids that day.

2042 on 21 April. A single low flying Jill circled *Suesens* twice at ranges under 4000 yards and launched a torpedo on the port beam at 500 yards. The plane was taken under heavy AA fire before the torpedo was launched, and the aircraft passed about 100 yards ahead of the ship at an altitude of 25 feet. The ship was violently maneuvered, and the torpedo passed 10 yards down the port quarter to the great relief of all hands. The drums were louder than ever. It was apparent to the crew that they were in a furious fight, and the end was nowhere in sight. Several additional heckler planes were in the area almost to midnight but none attacked this ship.

Early morning on 22 April. A horn-type contact mine was hit three times by rifle fire, but the shooting was interrupted by the arrival of enemy aircraft in the area.

1926 About six twin engine Frances planes made a furious coordinated suicide attack on *Suesens* and *Sederstrom* (same action as described in prior narrative on *Sederstrom*), and the minesweeper *Scurry (AM-304)*. Three planes attacked *Suesens* in the first wave from port and starboard, and two were shot out of the air, splashing astern! The third plane was driven off. Gunners had but a brief moment to wipe the stinging sweat from their eyes. Engineers below felt the rattle of the grates and the recoil from salvos while listening breathlessly to reports from their telephone talkers.

1929. That third plane returned with a fourth. Both were taken under fire by the *Suesens*' grim-faced gunners; one was hit by a 40mm shell and retired to starboard with a glow of fire in the fuselage. The war drums beat with a savage fury and pounding in the breasts of the crew.

1934. The fourth was hit as it dived in from starboard and splashed just off the starboard bow! In spite of the darkness, the gunners maintained a high and accurate rate of fire, positively splashing three suicide planes and damaging a fourth. Captain Graham wrote in his report that the action was so rapid that an item-by-item detailed report was impossible.

23 April. Several hecklers approached during the night, sending the ship to GQ twice during the midwatch. A dead Japanese pilot was picked up, and all useful gear was dried and set aside for intelligence. The body was then returned to the sea, weighted down with a five inch shell. The war drums were subsiding, having passed their crescendo.

26 April. At 0810, *Suesens* was underway to escort a number of transports to Ulithi. As she took her departure from Okinawa and the hills of that bloody island faded in the distance, every man had his own thoughts, stark memories for the rest of his days, and a reverent offering of gratitude for his own life.

Suesens returned to Okinawa in June, but the exhausted enemy had largely withdrawn from the area. She participated in convoys and covered minesweeping forces in the East China Sea as the blockade of the Japanese home islands tightened. She also participated in occupational duties after the Japanese surrender and before returning to the United States.

EDMONDS

Ninety Days at Okinawa

The Central Pacific, Leyte, Morotai and Lingayen Gulf. *Edmonds (DE-406)* had guns blazing in all of them. She now would face up to the most difficult and dangerous of all, Iwo Jima and Okinawa. From 10 February, when she sortied from Ulithi with a carrier group, until 27 March, *Edmonds* was part of the Iwo Jima operation.

The night of 21 February. The carrier *Bismarck Sea (CVE-95)* was sunk by huge internal explosions following a successful *kamikaze* attack. *Edmonds* and three other screening vessels were directed to assist in rescue operations. Heading his ship up-wind and then allowing it to drift slowly down toward survivor concentrations, the skipper, Lieutenant Commander John S. Burrows of Scarsdale, New York, repeatedly enabled survivors to clamber aboard with the aid of life lines, ladders, cargo and floater nets. The captain recalled:

> "For the most part, the men struggling in the water remained calm, but some were shouting continuously for help. We used the ship's loud speaker to call out words of encouragement and to direct them to life lines and nets. The ship's motor whaleboat was bringing alongside boatload after boatload of survivors. All hands on Edmonds, except those necessary for ship control, manned the rail tirelessly, pulling exhausted men aboard with the aid of all available rescue gear."

Thirty of the officers and crew of *Edmonds* voluntarily entered the water to rescue survivors. Six of them were awarded decorations by the commander of the Fifth Fleet. Proudly, the captain noted:

> "The crew really showed its stuff that night. Not a single man slept in his bunk, and few slept at all. The entire ship was turned over to the comfort and needs of the survivors. And every man who wanted it, crew and survivors alike, was served a full breakfast the following morning."

The commanding officer also commended the officers and men who remained at control stations for long hours without relief so the others could perform rescue operations and attend the injured.

Despite darkness, heavy seas, and continuing enemy air attacks, *Edmonds* rescued 378 survivors, including the captain and the executive officer. As Group Commander, she directed the search throughout the night and into the next day. All survivors were placed aboard transports anchored off Mount Surabachi, site of the famed planting of the U.S. flag by the marines a few days before. Ensign Frank P. Whitbeck of Southbury, Connecticut, recalled a few sidelights from the Iwo Jima episode:

> "After being rescued, the *Bismarck Sea* commanding officer, Captain John Lockwood Pratt had to face a decision as to whether to transfer to one of the destroyer screening vessels with much more comfortable accommodations than a DE. Captain Pratt declined the invitation, signaling back, in effect, that: 'Things are going very well where I am and I prefer to remain on *Edmonds* with my surviving crew members.' Score another one for the DE!
>
> The transfer of survivors and the communication involved in this operation gave me my one and only opportunity to code and transmit an outgoing message. Believe me, when the reply came back, 'Your message received and understood', I breathed a deep sigh of relief. This was what I had been trained for, and thank God I didn't blow it. (All major combat ships, including destroyer escorts, were restricted to highly important situations in transmitting Morse code messages because they could permit the enemy to locate ship dispositions through the use of high frequency direction finders).
>
> Once, when Edmonds' voice code name was *Errol Flynn*, we engaged in fueling at sea with a tanker code

named *Gypsy Rose Lee*, after a famous strip teaser of the time. You can imagine the conversation: 'Hello *Errol Flynn*, this is *Gypsy Rose Lee*, ready to receive you, over'. And later on, 'Hello *Gypsy Rose Lee*, this is *Errol Flynn*, first hose over'. It was hard to keep a straight face and steady voice during this exchange."

For the final great offensive campaign of the Pacific War, *Edmonds* was again screening CVEs at the outset. Underway from Leyte on 27 March, she remained in the Okinawa zone until 23 June, just short of three months, during which time the ship anchored for only an occasional 24 or 48 hour period at Kerama Retto or Okinawa.

In the first part of this campaign, *Edmonds* operated with Carrier Division 22, alternating between direct air support off Okinawa and air strikes on the Sakishima Group to the southwest. On 4 May and again on 11 May, the *Edmonds* sank by gunfire two mines menacing the path of the carrier formation. She also rescued the crew of a carrier based torpedo plane.

15 May. *Edmonds* reported to Commander Task Group 51.5 to take part in the Iheya-Aguni operation. CTG Commodore F. Moosebrugger, in the amphibious force flagship *Biscayne (AGC-18)*, assigned *Edmonds* to duty on the various screening stations outside of the transport areas.

24 May. All ships present at Hagushi Anchorage were alerted by a dispatch to expect heavy dusk air attacks. *Edmonds* and *O'Neill (DE-188)*, also narrated in this chapter, were anchored at the extreme southeast edge of the anchorage on standby anti-suicide submarine and boat duty. At 2107, with enemy bogies closing in, the DEs went to battle stations, and all ships at anchor made smoke. Due to their position and a brisk wind, both *Edmonds* and *O'Neill* had no smoke cover. Therefore, when an enemy plane appeared above at 2130, *Edmonds* got underway and opened fire with her after twin 40mm gun. The plane withdrew.

2146. A Betty appeared broad off the starboard bow, 5000 feet high, and was taken under fire. The plane passed down *Edmonds*' port side while she was effecting a sharp course change with full speed and rudder. She ceased firing one minute later as the plane was splashed by combined fire with other picket ships!

0020 on 25 May. An airplane engine could be heard closing the ship, unreported by radar due to land block. Only a general guess as to relative bearing and especially altitude could be made from the sound of its engine. One minute later, a Japanese type trainer, in an obvious attempt at suicide, appeared on *Edmonds*' starboard bow, coming down wind at about 130 knots, 40 feet off the water.

The plane, although heard, was in sight so short a time it could not be fired on. It passed directly over the number one 5" gun mount at the same height as the bridge. Although the pilot tried to correct his aim, probably having seen our mast and lowered his left wing, he was unable to crash us in the few seconds he could see the ship. He turned around our stern on a course to his port and disappeared in the smoke screen. No damage was inflicted on *Edmonds* but by a very narrow margin. It is believed that this DE materially assisted in shooting down the plane.

The night of 25 May. While off Hagushi Beach, a *kamikaze* passed some 30 feet over the bow of *Edmonds*, circled astern and crash-dived *O'Neill* in the next station after apparently riding in on that DE's fire! *Edmonds* had not opened fire initially because she could not see the plane but did begin firing shortly after *O'Neill* opened up. Lieutenant (jg) Whitbeck remembered distinctly:

> "The sound of the engine could be clearly heard from my location in CIC as the plane passed over. I was glad to hear that sound die away, but then came the explosion on *O'Neill*."

Edmonds' small boat was immediately manned with a fire and rescue party to furnish all possible assistance. Later, her CIC conned the *PCE-855* by radar and TBS through the smoke and into the vicinity of *O'Neill* so that she could render medical assistance and evacuate wounded personnel to a hospital ship in the area.

Considering the length of this operation, with no personnel going ashore for a period of over 90 days and the long hours spent at GQ, the morale of the crew was unusually high throughout the ordeal.

Again, while in Hagushi Anchorage on the night of 18 June, *Edmonds* assisted in shooting down another Jap plane, one of the few which penetrated the iron ring which had been established by the Combat Air Patrol and the picket line.

As a screening ship for amphibious landing forces, *Edmonds* also participated in the capture of Iheya Shima and Aguni Shima in the Ryukyu Group from 3 to 10 June. In the first of these operations, *Edmonds* worked with *Gainard (DD-706)*, a fighter director ship, north of Okinawa, at the time less than "a stone's throw from Tokyo." (A fighter director DD or DE was able to plot both bogies and friendlies at the same time and thereby direct our planes to an intersection with enemy aircraft. This was one of the techniques this author was involved in at the Norfolk DE training Center.)

Edmonds departed from Okinawa for Leyte as screen commander on 20 June 1945, covering the battleships commanded by Rear Admiral McCormick. She was entering Leyte Gulf on the morning of 15 August when victory in the Pacific was announced. On 8 October, while standing by for further orders at Manila, word was received that *Edmonds* was to return to Leyte and there rendezvous with the three remaining ships of *Escort Division 63* for return to the United States. *Edmonds* was going home! From an anonymous crew member:

> "For sixteen months, *Edmonds* had been operating almost continuously in every major Pacific campaign of the last year of the war. She traveled the equal of four times around the world and was underway an average of seven out of every 10 days. She inflicted damage on the enemy and saved many American lives to fight again - and live again. She came through unscathed with her bow riding high - a "small boy" who had done a man sized job".

O'NEILL

To All My Grandchildren – With Love

Occasionally, when searching for material for this book, this author acquired documents that illustrated life aboard ship as well as the dark side of war. We are indebted to Petty Officer Philip D. Farrand for excerpts from a bound book he published for his grandchildren. He wanted them to know what their grandfather did in World War II and to remember the sacrifices of those who served. Farrand was a plank owner of *O'Neill (DE-188)*. His tenure was from boot and service camps, where he became a qualified electrician, to victory and back to the U.S. He witnessed a raw crew, most of whom had never been on a ship before, turn into first class fighting men.

After shakedown, *O'Neill* was assigned to a number of convoy escort operations from US ports to the United Kingdom, Ireland, Morocco and Tunisia. In the Pacific in February 1945, *O'Neill* was assigned to Task Force 58 under Admiral Raymond Spruance.

"We arrived at Guam, a territory of the United States, seized by overwhelming Japanese forces in the opening days of the war despite heroic resistance by a handful of Marines. After its recapture, it became the central location of Pacific operations. We had liberty, and Johnnie and I went ashore to a deserted air strip that still contained some Japanese pill boxes or gun emplacements.

They were steel reinforced cement block houses, affording the men inside protection from all but direct hits while firing their machine guns. Capture of those pill boxes by infantry would have been too costly. However, small breathing apertures made them vulnerable to American tanks with their protective armor and flame throwers. They drove up to the block enclosures and shot flames right into those tiny openings, burning their occupants to death. Burial details had not yet been assigned to remove the corpses inside.

We saw a boot with a bone sticking out of it, and the stench of death was all about the pill box. We picked up some .30 caliber shell casings that were lying about. They had USA markings, apparently seized when the Japs captured the island. When I brought those shell casings aboard ship, I had to throw them away because the nauseating stench had even saturated them.

While assigned as escort to a large convoy of tankers, we came close to hitting a mine. The starboard lookout, outside the quartermaster's shack, failed to see it. We missed it by no more that 15 feet. It was a stubborn critter with numerous contact firing horns protruding from its skin. We hit it repeatedly with small caliber ammunition to no avail. Finally, our skipper advised the Commodore that it was slowly sinking, so we were ordered back to convoy.

We had a fellow aboard ship who couldn't do anything right. He had been in the deck gang and screwed up so they put him in the engine gang. The Chief motor machinist mate made him Oil King, meaning he had to clean the fuel oil. The oil goes through a centrifugal pump for cleaning before it goes into the main engines. While on watch, he let the purified oil tank run dry, and our engines quit when we were right in front of the convoy. He had been playing pinochle. We quickly circumvented the purified oil and ran regular oil into the engines to start them again. The Chief took him away from that job and put him on another which we thought was less important, watching the evaporators. All he had to do was to make fresh water and store it in the fresh water tanks. He screwed up again, left his watch to play pinochle as before. While playing, he ran salt water straight through the evaporator and into two fresh water tanks, contaminating them. As a result, we were restricted from baths and even drinking water because we had only one tank of fresh water left. We put him back into the deck gang to chip paint for the rest of his navy career.

We weren't out to sea very long when the Third Fleet under Admiral Halsey came over the horizon. It was Task Force 58 when it was under Admiral Ray Spruance, the most awesome sight I'd seen in my life. From horizon to horizon, in every direction as far as we could see, was the United States Fleet. It was a beautiful sight on a beautiful afternoon. The carriers launched their planes and the sky was full of our aircraft. It was like a great parade on July 4th.

We spent three days fueling the fleet from the tankers. There were carriers, battleships, cruisers, destroyers, tenders. We were about 100 miles off the coast of the Philippines. After refueling, elements of the fleet left to bombard Japanese emplacements on Luzon.

Back in Ulithi, we moored next to a large supply ship, and our Chief boatswain's mate noted that they were disposing of a huge Manila cargo net. In those days, fenders were made of woven Manila and were in short supply. He asked the supply ship if they would pass the net to us and they were only too glad to comply. When they dropped that cargo net on our forward deck, hundreds of cockroaches scurried out, down and into the inner compartments of the ship.

From then on, we had roaches on that ship like you wouldn't believe. When I arose in the morning, I would open my locker and there were at least six of them sitting on my towel. I had all my shaving gear in an empty wood cheese box. I would take out my razor, shave lotion, shaving soap, tip the box upside down on the deck, and stomp all the bugs with my foot. We sprayed the after sleeping compartment. All that did was chase the roaches up the degaussing cable forward. The men forward decided to spray too. That sent the roaches back aft again. We never got rid of them.

About this time, the B-29 bombers were taking off from Saipan and adjacent Tinian to bomb the Japanese home islands. Because of the lengthy round trip to Japan, an emergency airstrip was needed somewhere between. Iwo Jima was determined to be the best for that purpose, and the 4th and 5th Marine divisions would fight to take it. The Third Marine division was on Guam, resting after the battle just fought for Saipan and Tinian.

Because of the stubborn resistance on Iwo Jima, it was decided to bring the Third Division to the area and hold it in reserve. We were sent to Guam to escort the transports to a position about 90 miles south of Iwo Jima.

D-Day plus 6. The land situation deteriorated, and we had to send in the Third Division. We moved close up to the shore, so close that we could see our tanks and the enemy pill boxes. We watched a tank come down the hill and drive by a pillbox. It would go to the front of it and fire away with its flame throwers. It was a horrible sight. Then the tank would ride around the pillbox, go back up the hill and repeat the action. After two attacks, the pill box was burned to a crisp, presumably along with its occupants.

That was our first taste and sight of war. We were subsequently assigned to antisubmarine picket duty to guard one of the cruisers that was hove to and bombarding shore targets. They were reducing enemy gun emplacements and using a small Piper Cub for a spotter. The aircraft was flying around the end of the island, right over the Japanese. Whenever one of their guns fired, the pilot of the airplane would radio the gun coordinates to the cruiser which would then wipe out the emplacement. The Japs never attempted to shoot down the little aircraft. I can't understand why because it was the reason all of their artillery was being destroyed. In fact, the pilot radioed that he couldn't find any more gun positions, and he requested a ship to draw fire from the shore so that he could report their position.

Right away, our captain, Lieutenant Commander David S. Bill, volunteered the mighty *O'Neill.* It was a good thing we couldn't go very fast because the cruiser told us that we were too slow and they were going to send in a destroyer. The Japanese opened fire on it. It is customary, when firing at a ship, to fire one shell over, one shell short, and then you know the range, somewhere between the two. This would be followed by rapid fire.

However, the Japanese didn't miss on the first round, a direct hit on the fantail, right on the depth charge racks. Fortunately, the charges didn't explode. Nonetheless, the shell did a lot of damage to the stern. The cruiser opened fire with her 8" guns. She put salvo after salvo into the shore batteries. There couldn't have been a flower that wasn't blown to pieces by the time of cease fire. It was an exhilarating experience for us to watch those 8" salvos rip into the heart of the enemy.

We had severe losses. A great many occurred when the LCVPs hit the beach. The guns from Mount Surabachi on the left and from the right side of the landing area effected a cross fire right where the LCVPs landed. We had control of the air so we weren't concerned about Japanese planes. Our carriers would send waves. They would go up high and then dive and drop their bombs. We could see the bombs explode, watching the war from a ringside seat, 300 yards off shore!

We went around what was then called Sugar Loaf Hill, now better known as Mount Surabachi. Atop the hill, the famous flag fluttered in the breeze. The Japanese were in caves, beyond the reach of naval guns. It was hand to hand combat all the way up Mount Surabachi, about 2000 feet above sea level.

We stopped at Samar in the Philippines to join a convoy of transports coming from Luzon. We weren't told where we were going, except that we would be within 400 miles of the southernmost Island of Japan.

We weren't at sea very long when, one evening, we were called to GQ. It was a bright moonlight night, and a Japanese bomber flew low astern, following our brilliant phosphorescent wake. The plane followed the ship and flew right over us so low it nearly hit our mast. He didn't drop any bombs, and we didn't fire our guns. The bomber just flew away from us and another ship shot it down. The skipper, of course, was furious at our not having opened fire. The reason was that the gunnery officer didn't give the order to do so. *O'Neill* was fortunate that this buck fever lapse on its first enemy encounter didn't end in disaster.

We continued heading north until 1 April when the first troops were loaded into LCVPs and landed on Okinawa. Frogmen had previously gone into the landing area to clear any possible mines.

We were on escort duty most of the time and at GQ nearly all of the time. We seldom changed clothes; we slept in them. We didn't get showers and would wash and shave only once in a while. We would sleep a bit, then stand watch, go to General Quarters, sleep some, stand a watch, sleep a little, go to General Quarters for days on end. It was rough, but yet it was exciting. We were in the middle of the war.

Heavy surface ships bombarded the shore every night, hitting targets illuminated by star shells. The Japanese were taking a beating but they kept fighting and the suicide planes kept coming. Mostly, they flew from bases on Kyushu, the Japanese island nearest Okinawa. Planes from our carriers were intercepting and shooting them down like ducks, but the Japs seemed to have an endless supply. Those that evaded our fighters faced murderous antiaircraft fire from surface ships but a number still ran the gauntlet and scored hits.

2200 one evening. While at GQ, we heard five rapid explosions. A bomber at a very high altitude and beyond the range of our main battery dropped a stick of bombs, hoping to score a hit on us. They missed us by at least 500 yards, not very much when considering the altitude of the plane.

While on picket duty, the whaleboat was put over the side and identified a bloated Japanese body. The skipper promptly told the boat crew to sink it. It wouldn't go down of its own accord so a man struck it with an ax. The stench, even in the open sea, was so bad that we all began to feel sick. It was right at chow time, and nobody was about to eat chow with the stench of that body still permeating the air. Still, the body wouldn't sink. We got some dummy, practice hedgehogs, tied them to the body, and it sank. His papers and billfold included a photo of the man and his wife.

25 May. We were still patrolling the northern area of Okinawa when a Betty flew in and dropped its bombs on the island. It was banking to the left, directly over our picket line. It went over a ship close by and then came right over us. We opened fire, and the aircraft splashed! All hands were very excited and our skipper was elated. He called the squadron commander:

'Commander, Commander this in Bovine, Splash one Betty Bomber.' He got no response so, a few minutes later, he said: 'Commander, Commander this is Bovine, Splash one Betty Bomber.' Still no response. So he again reported: 'Commander, Commander this is Bovine, Splash one Betty Bomber.'

Finally, the radio came on and the talker asked: 'Bovine, is this the same aircraft you're reporting or have you shot down three tonight?'

Although the skipper wasn't supposed to be smoking on the flying bridge, he stuck a cigarette in his mouth, lit it and threw the lighter over the side as he would a match!

We were all proud when we were able to paint a Betty Bomber on the side of the flying bridge. On one bright moonlit evening, a bomber spotted one of our escorts close by which immediately began evasive maneuvers. Seeing open water between two sand bars, her skipper thought he could go through at full speed. Unfortunately, there was a submerged coral reef in the middle, and a shaft of antler coral hooked her bottom like a barb. Fortunately, the ship was not attacked. We were assigned patrol duty around her. Tugs were unable to budge the vessel until divers went down and dynamited the coral.

We entered Buckner Bay to anchor and do some engine maintenance. One afternoon, a number of us off watch sat on the fantail, chatting and enjoying the weather. Suddenly, we could hear the clanging of bells on other ships calling their crews to GQ. I don't know why we were not doing the same. We were about 1000 yards from the battleship *New Mexico (BB-40)*.

Two low-flying planes, about 500 feet above the water, sneaked through without being discovered until they were actually visible. They got within 2000 yards of the battleship and then climbed. All ships started firing. The sky had become covered like polka dots with black clouds of smoke from the exploding shells. It was awesome. Upon reaching the apogee of their climb, the planes pealed off and screamed down on *New Mexico*. One of them splashed between the BB and another ship. The other one hit *New Mexico* on the forward gun turret, doing very little damage. (This same action was described in prior narratives on *Fair* and *Paul G. Baker*.)

While in Buckner Bay we were alerted to the presence of suicide torpedo boats. The Island of Camereta, about 14 miles from Okinawa, was still in Japanese hands and where the suicide boats were built or stored. They had railroad type launching tracks on the beach and launched their boats, really manned torpedoes, at night. The operator would scream "Banzai" and head for the nearest enemy ship.

The situation was serious enough so that we were ordered to put to sea and search for the torpedo boats even though two of our four diesels were still off line for maintenance. We spent four hours looking for them, but to no avail. At 2200, a Betty came in using our IFF, identifying it as one of ours. It landed on the Okinawa airstrip; Japanese jumped out with hand grenades and destroyed 10 marine corsairs parked on the strip. Naturally, the marines killed the Japs, but it was another example of the length to which the enemy would go to inflict damage with total disregard for their own lives.

That evening, a suicide plane crashed into the post office, setting it afire and burning up all the mail. Near midnight, same evening, we were ordered to join other escorts in making smoke because of the bright moonlight. We set smoke pots on the fantail and covered the heavy units to protect them from incoming raids.

0025 on 25 May. An aircraft came out of the smoke screen and headed into the forward part of *O'Neill*. The plane veered off, coming down the port side of the ship, some distance astern of us. It then swung around to the left and started an approach directly toward our fantail. Receiving increasing 20mm fire as our battle stations were manned, the plane banked to the right and came down the starboard side. By that time, all of our guns were firing. The plane turned around again and approached us on the starboard side forward. Suspecting that we were underway, he aimed at the forward part of the ship to compensate. He headed right at the anchor pad, a sheet of steel about 2" thick. We weren't underway though and, if we had to be hit by a *kamikaze*, the spot he picked to fly into was the one we would also have offered him. A bit further aft, and he would probably have crashed into the wardroom. (In the previous narrative, *Edmonds* made reference to *O'Neill* being crashed.)

The wings (biplane) struck the water before the plane struck the ship, causing a tremendous spray which smothered gasoline fires almost before they started. Even so, we had the odor of gas throughout the forward compartments. All this happened in a matter of seconds, just as I was coming out of the sack. I slept in my clothes but I was trying to find my shoes right by the bottom lockers. I had one shoe on just about the time the plane hit. It threw me back and my foot flipped the shoe. In this pitch black room, I heard the skipper on the speaker system pleading: 'Shoot him down, shoot him down, shoot him down!' Right after that, we had a tremendous explosion and severe rocking of the ship. I fumbled around in the dark and found my shoe. I didn't tie it and raced up the hatch. Another fellow in the repair crew and I (Our repair crew was just beginning to form.) grabbed a fire hose about midships on the port side and, as we were running forward with the fire hose, we were conscious of a crunchiness under foot. It was shrapnel from a bomb that had exploded. We ran forward. In fact, we ran all the way to the end of that hose but it wasn't far enough. We didn't reach number one 3" gun where the action was. So we grabbed another fire hose about the same length and went forward with that, but we found it to be full of shrapnel holes. Other guys were taking care of the wounded. I was an electrician, and my job was to prevent a fire. So I went below deck under the anchor windlass. Near the chain was a severely arcing large electric panel. We sent a man back to disconnect that panel, shutting down all lights forward.

If there were going to be a fire from gas fumes, the arc that we were drawing from the box would have caused it. Therefore, we secured the board and went topside. I noticed there was something hanging to the life line on the port side. Two of us pulled it in. Much to our surprise, it was a parachute; suicide pilots didn't need them.

He also must have had sacks of rice because grains were scattered all over the deck. We were told that it was common in the Shinto religion to bring along rice on a suicide mission to feed the soul of the deceased. There were anti-personnel bombs on the aircraft. One was picked up on the starboard side and thrown overboard. Apparently, there were others because the ship was peppered with shrapnel. The pointer and trainer on number one 3" gun, Doner and Costello, were severely injured.

I went by the officers' wardroom and saw most of the injured lying on the deck. (The wardroom of a DE was used as a battle dressing and surgery area.) Some of them had marked 'M' on their foreheads; they had been given morphine. One of the big surprises of that evening was that, within 15 minutes after being hit, we had a barge alongside with two doctors aboard.

One of the sights that bothered me terribly was a friend named Loftis holding his handkerchief where most of his lower jaw had been blown away. Some had legs off and other severe injuries. Both Doner and Costello died two days later, the only deaths aboard ship from the suicide plane. It was a traumatic experience for all of us. While sitting at anchor the next day, the battleship *New York (BB-34)*, 500 yards astern of us, opened fire with heavy salvos. After having just been hit by a suicide plane, hearing this tremendous firing just scared the hell out of us. Every time she let go a blast, we would jump a couple of inches off the deck.

We had a huge clean-up the next day. About a week later, we noticed an odor coming from the torpedo tubes. Someone found a decaying piece of the hand of the pilot from the suicide plane. The gunnery officer was informed, and he told the assistant gunnery officer to get rid of it. The order was passed along to the first class gunner's mate, then to the third class and finally to the striker at the bottom of the chain, a lesson in navy protocol.

Someone I haven't mentioned is Tokyo Rose. She was an American of Nisei ancestry living in Japan at the outbreak of the war, and was recruited to give propaganda broadcasts to our ships. During the final months of the war, the Americans were getting ever closer to Japan and also within radio range of Japan's Propaganda Ministry. We tuned in the program every day, and she was on the air most of the time. She played the latest music and records from back home, a great show. Her music was the very latest. All the Glenn Miller songs were recorded. One of the things that annoyed us was that she would name ships that supposedly were hit the night before in spite of the fact that *kamikazes* never returned to report. She never did announce us so I guess she didn't care whether or not we were hit.

Information relative to the severity of the suicide planes seldom reached the United States. The press was mum. It was near the end of the war, and the U.S. government didn't want to create apprehension among the people. (Farrand is correct. The public was, and today largely still is, ignorant of the severity of *kamikaze* attacks on our forces.)

The day after the attack, we were sent to Camereta Island which had been secured by us by that time. All ships that had been hit by suicide planes were sent there for damage assessment. While there, we noticed one ship had no superstructure. It was leveled right down to the main deck after having taken four suicide planes. It looked like somebody had taken a broom and swept the superstructure right off the ship. There were 20 to 30 body bags lying on the deck.

We stayed in Wiseman's Cove for five days. We shipped off our injured and tried to find out whether or not we were seaworthy. We had to cut loose our anchors to leave Buckner Bay because the windlass was destroyed. The repair personnel ashore decided that we were to return to the Philippines to go into dry dock and determine how much subsurface damage was done. After being dry-docked, it was determined that we had damage to our bilge keel and that the only place it could be repaired was back in the states, which was not bad news for us. We were elated to hear that we were headed back to Los Angeles

We now had two aircraft painted on our bridge because we were given credit for the suicide plane. We didn't shoot it down, but we got credit for knocking it down. I guess we hit the ship against it and we got credit for it. We were a proud ship. We were saddened by the loss of two men and twenty injured who had been transferred. We had been a part of the war, had been successful in at least shooting down a bomber, and we had done several things to assist in the invasion of Okinawa. We had done our job well.

We were assigned to a crippled convoy returning to the States. We were escorted and also escorting. We had no sound gear but had antiaircraft capability. Other ships had inoperative antiaircraft batteries but had sonar. One way or another, our ships were headed back to the US on crutches.

But that didn't bother us. The sweetest music to our ears was that the war was over for us, and we were headed home"!

SWEARER

Safely Steered Through the Nightmare

Swearer (DE-186) contributed to the war effort in the Pacific by shepherding the logistics groups which fueled the Third and Fifth Fleets to and from strikes against the enemy. While so engaged, the destroyer escort participated in raids on Palau, Yap, Woleai, Truk, Satawan, and Ponape in March and April 1944. In early April, she also screened escort carriers to a resupply rendezvous with the larger carriers engaged in operations in Western New Guinea.

She participated in the capture and occupation of the Marianas from June to August, then moved south to Manus to screen escort carriers during the Western Carolines and Leyte operations. In November, the DE resumed duty with the fueling groups, weathering the 18 December typhoon Cobra off the Philippines and rescuing nine survivors from the destroyer *Spence*). (See chapter *The Pacific Typhoons*.)

From 21 January to 6 February 1945, *Swearer* convoyed cargo and troopships bound for the invasion of Iwo Jima, arriving on 19 February, the date of the assault. For five days, she patrolled the transport area and helped fight off Japanese air attacks.

On 8 March, *Swearer* was assigned to Task Group 51.1, the Western Islands (Okinawa) Attack Force under the command of Rear Admiral Kiland. She went into that campaign expecting resistance from enemy aircraft, suicide boats, and submarines. Frequent drills were conducted to insure maximum readiness for attacks from any quarter. The captain Lieutenant Commander John Trent, felt that his ship and its personnel were at a maximum point of readiness.

Between 19 and 26 March, *Swearer* screened a convoy of cargo, troop, and amphibious warfare ships to the staging area at Kerama Retto. She remained in the vicinity of Okinawa for three months, patrolling, screening, escorting, and fighting off *kamikazes* without ever being sent to a rear area for even a short break.

The morning of 26 March. *Swearer* was patrolling her station off Kerama Retto when a Val dived on a destroyer 2000 yards on her port bow. The plane missed its target by about 200 yards, but the incident served to alert all hands to the situation they were going to face for the next three months. *Swearer* was assigned to Task Unit 51.5, under Commodore Moosebrugger who commanded the entire picket operation. The main assault on the Okinawa Islands commenced.

0600 on 1 April. The enemy wasted no time in extending greetings to *Swearer* when lookouts reported a destroyer under dive bomber attack, distance five miles. As *Swearer* went to GQ, one aircraft broke off the attack on the destroyer and headed for the DE from an altitude of 3000 feet. The plane was momentarily lost in the clouds, but the SA radar was able to give bearings to the conn so that a course change could place the intruder abeam. When it broke into view, commencing a dive on this ship, it was taken under fire by all guns that could bear. The ship was turning with full right rudder during the 10 seconds of the dive. Numerous hits were scored, and parts of the plane were seen to drop off before it splashed 10 yards off the starboard quarter!

In his book, *Stand By Arnold*, the author, R.M.C. "Chesty" Arnold, takes us to the point of engagement in a manner that only somebody who experienced the moment could relate it. Chesty, still in his late teens, was a yeoman first class with a battle station on a 20mm gun.

> "As dawn broke on Easter morning 1945, our radar picked up suicide planes circling in the early mist directly above us. Suddenly, one broke out of the clouds, dead on course for my position on the port side forward. There was just enough time to comprehend the possible tragic consequences of the moment. I truly felt this was it. I had a moment of sadness. I thought of my family and could see their sorrow. Here it came, an airplane, a flying bomb steered directly at us to bring about our destruction.
>
> At the moment it appeared out of the clouds, John Hinson, our gunner was the first to see it and yelled, 'Here he comes at 300 degrees!' At the same time, he whipped the gun right on target in unbelievable speed and accuracy, opening fire at the same time. I could see his tracers pouring into the Zero as it raced into us. As I was having my morbid thoughts, he and the other gunners kept pouring ammunition into the plane.
>
> What great guys! They must have wounded or killed the pilot or damaged the plane in some way because it suddenly burst into flames and veered slightly. We could feel the heat as it just missed the ship and splashed! Our captain had called for full right rudder to change the ship's position, and we were grateful to him as well as to our gunner. They saved our lives. This was a jolting experience that I was not prepared for. This was the real thing, and we realized we were in for a long and perilous experience."

Swearer was then assigned as escort to an amphibious group of 35 landing craft to a retirement area about 150 miles south of Okinawa. On 14 April, she was recalled to the Okinawa screen. From that time until the conclusion of the operation, *Swearer* was employed in various stations and on various missions in the Okinawa area.

Chesty Arnold had some pertinent observations in his book about some of those "missions." His description of terror, allayed by a deep and abiding religious conviction, strikes a chord in many of those who still remember a time of war:

> "As the days unfolded, there were planes everywhere. There were literally hundreds of ships involved, and I witnessed many getting hit. It was unbelievable, dog fights above and *kamikazes* diving in all directions. We had been ordered to proceed to a new station to replace a destroyer which had been disabled by suicide plane crashes. A half hour into steaming to our new destination, word came over the TBS that the ship replacing us at our prior station had been smashed by an attack of several *kamikazes*!
>
> We arrived at our designation off Ie Shima that afternoon and stayed at GQ all night. The skies for miles around were brilliant with antiaircraft fire over the sea. The battle raging on Okinawa was lit up by thousands of flashes coming continually from the explosions and firings of weapons from both sides. In addition, there was the firing of flares and flame throwers ashore and the supporting bombardment by the larger ships offshore.
>
> What a spectacle! We saw explosions as *kamikazes* crashed into ships and as fires erupted from planes dropping on Ie Shima. Our radar had bogies or blips on its screen continuously. We had already seen the devastation these planes had wrought. Even now, over a span of many years, my memory conjures many experiences with great clarity.
>
> On one particular evening, there was a brilliant full moon. Our captain was maneuvering *Swearer* in a manner that would make the ship's silhouette the least likely to be detected by the enemy. The planes were in the vicinity. The situation was extremely grave. I was very much afraid. Slowly, tears of fear, frustration and hopelessness began to flow down my cheeks. At my battle station, nobody could see my moist eyes in the semi-darkness. I thought of the hereafter and remembered my conversion through Christ, and I repeated *John 3-16.*
>
> Out of the depths, the 23rd psalm crept into my memory. I recited it to myself the best I could. When I came to 'Yea, though I walk through the valley of the shadow of death, I will fear no evil, for thou art with me, thy rod and thy staff they comfort me.' I felt a calm and peace come over me and I was reassured and secure."

16 April. The next attack on this ship came at mid-morning while patrolling about five miles north of Ie Shima. The flash condition was red, and many bogies were approaching. Two planes were seen heading for *Swearer*, distance of six miles. They split, one attacking this ship and the other diving on *Bowers (DE-637)*. The plane attacking *Swearer*, a Val, was almost skimming on the water. It was taken under fire by the main battery on the starboard beam at 6000 yards. As it came within range, all guns that could bear opened up. The plane burst into flames 100 yards out. Lurching upward, out of control, it cleared the ship abaft the stack, and splashed about 40 yards off the port beam! Chesty Arnold recorded that episode:

> "We were one of the picket ships, stationed 40 miles to seaward of the inner screen as radar warning stations to report enemy planes approaching the main battle area. In the morning, other vessels reported large numbers of suicide planes en route to our area. As they came into view, they began diving at various ships. It was fortunate that we had noticed two low-flying planes over the island of Ie Shima and that we had kept our eyes on them.
>
> They picked us as their target. Again, I must say it is a frightful gut feeling to realize you have been chosen to be a target. A normal bullet can be fatal, but when you can

observe a 40 foot 'bullet' as it comes at you, the feeling is indescribable. Our guns opened up when the planes were still quite a distance out, but they continued to bear in on us, racing above the water at an altitude of 30 to 40 feet. Our gunners, sharpened from previous actions, were superb. Although our DE only had three 3" guns, one battery of 40mm guns and several 20mm guns, we were told later that the fire from our guns was like that of a destroyer."

(While it is true that the three 3" guns or two 5" guns of a DE were not to be compared to the five 5" guns of a DD, most *kamikazes* were downed by the close-in fire of 40mm and 20mm guns. It is doubtful if DDs were substantially more successful in downing attacking *kamikazes* than were the DEs. Also, DEs were more maneuverable.)

"Our gunners poured ammunition into the planes in a continuous, withering fire. Finally, one of them seemed to have had enough, because he veered and decided to attack another destroyer escort, *Bowers*, hitting dead on in her superstructure (Next narrative).

The explosion was tremendous. I still can see the fuselage and tail section of the plane as it passed overhead and which, for some reason, was not destroyed. I could see the possibly dead pilot in his attire, black robe, white scarf and his arms dangling out of the cockpit. In spite of the damage it wrought, it was hard to believe that the entire aircraft didn't disintegrate beforehand.

Our gunners kept blazing away as the remaining plane continued its attack on us. It was on a perfect collision course. At the last moment, those of us on the port side not being part of the action, jumped down onto the main deck behind the superstructure. We crouched with our fingers in our ears, awaiting the crash and explosion. It didn't come. A second later we saw the plane careen over our heads and we felt the heat as it splashed a few yards from the ship on our side! We were astounded. One moment we saw it on a collision course - the next moment the plane burst into flames, lurched up and over our superstructure and into the ocean.

Our gunners were superb. Once again, they stood by their guns with confidence and bravery. This was the continuation of an unbelievably charmed and miraculous deliverance from annihilation. Surely, God was walking with us 'through the valley of the shadow of death'. My mind's eye sees so much I can't describe."

Shortly after *Bowers* had been hit by the other *kamikaze*, it was afire throughout the bridge structure. *Swearer* immediately proceeded to go alongside, put parties aboard to fight fires and lend medical assistance. The fire was quickly brought under control, but the personnel casualties were so many, and of such a serious nature that it took almost two hours to transfer all badly wounded personnel to *Swearer*. Shortly thereafter, *Connelley (DE-306)* came alongside and transferred survivors of *Bowers* they had picked up in the water. A total of 59 wounded were ferried by us to the hospital ship *Hope (AH-8)* late that afternoon.

Logs, action reports and war diaries are necessarily terse and devoid of emotions relative to the desolation of war. Commanding officers are expected to report the facts without delving into irrelevant detail. Not being under such constraints, Chester Arnold filled in the gory realities of battle:

"Our captain immediately maneuvered us alongside the disabled *Bowers*. Coming to a complete standstill was dangerous with *kamikazes* still in the area. While underway, we had maneuverability but dead in the water we were sitting ducks. It was hell. There were dead men all over the superstructure and decks. The gunner on the number two 3" gun was broken in half, still seated at his position with his head lying backwards on the deck. The dead on the superstructure were twisted and contorted as they hung over the railings. They were swollen and looked like bronze statues you see on historic bridges.

The odor of burning flesh was horrible. We brought the dead and wounded aboard and laid them down all over our decks, wherever a place could be found for them. I was sick from what I had seen. I couldn't help it. I had to find a spot where the scene was blocked from view. The entire crew was dazed."

Many veterans, commissioned and enlisted alike, seasoned in the winter of war, have unkind memories of being taken to task for minor infractions by those still basking in the spring of war. A time like that came to Chesty Arnold:

"In the anchorage after we transferred the dead and wounded, we were tied up side by side to a group of ships, preparing to get underway to return to patrol duty. Our captain came to me with an urgent message to be delivered to the captain of a large supply ship, which was moored at the inboard end of the ships we were nested with. He said to hurry, that we were getting ready to cast off the lines.

Per standard procedure, I saluted the flag and the Officer of The Deck on each ship I crossed until I came to the large supply ship. There, being unfamiliar with the nomenclature and under pressure for extreme hurry, I went up the wrong ladder and got into officer country by mistake.

I was accosted by the captain, the officer I was actually looking for. Before I could state my business and pass on the message, he gave me a tongue lashing about navy procedure and where aboard the ship enlisted men could or could not go. My feelings were hurt to the quick and I was extremely frustrated and upset over the day's happenings. Naturally, I could do nothing but, as I looked at him, I felt quite disgusted and thought that he could have been a little more gracious under the circumstances. To me, a boot camp this close to the war we had just come from and to which we were returning the same day seemed awful strange to me."

Lest anybody have mixed feelings relative to the above incident, this author would like to draw attention to the fact that Chesty dedicated his book to his deceased commanding officer, a singular honor that most of us ex COs would have equated with honors bestowed from higher ranks. Chesty continued with the sagging verve of the crew:

"We went back to our patrol station, and everyone was visibly shaken from the day's tragic events. Our nerves were practically on the outside of our skins, and our bodies reacted to the slightest sound, particularly the intercom system.

Whenever the captain would push the button to the loud speakers, they would make a static sound. On hearing this grating noise, the men would lurch with apprehension before the announcement was made. It was an instinctive, uncontrollable movement that had become habit from bad news. Usually, it was the captain, 'Now all hands man your battle stations'. For days on end, we would go back and forth to GQ.

A few days after we had picked up the survivors from *Bowers*, we were at GQ. It was a beautiful day, but we had acquired dozens of bogies on our radar screen about 50 miles off and heading our way. Several ships were steaming in their respective stations and, as the *kamikazes* closed in, we could see Marine and Navy pilots engaging them. Corsairs, Hellcats, and P-51 Mustangs shot down 50 percent or more of the enemy, but the rest would get through the defense. It was always a thrill to see our pilots with their superior skill knocking the Japs out of the sky. This day, we saw suicide planes falling in smoke and others diving at various ships, some making hits, others missing and exploding in the water.

We were in our battle gear helmets, life preservers, etc. The situation seemed very grave as usual. There were three of us on our 20mm antiaircraft gun which fired explosive shells somewhat larger than a huge cigar and housed in a magazine almost a foot square which held perhaps 50 rounds. I was the trunion operator, you know, like cranking old Fords. A lot of people don't know what a trunion is, making me a little mysterious through the years.

Second Class Gunner's Mate Hinson, the gun captain, was the man who aimed and pulled the trigger. A real expert. Seaman First Class Carol* was the loader, and his responsibility consisted of lifting and placing the magazines on the gun.

As we prepared for action, Carol threw the magazine of shells in place on top of the gun and started to slither off into the confines of a safer area, wherever that might be. Angered, the gun captain, ordered, 'STAND BY CAROL!'. Carol whirled and, in a blaze of fury shouted 'STANDBY SHIT!'. With that, he continued his slither to wherever. Hinson and I looked at each other in stunned silence as if Carol had made a profound statement. Apparently, he wasn't worried about the consequences. He believed that self preservation took precedence over anything as insignificant as a battle station. I thought Hinson might whip his gun around and let Carol have it, but he kept his cool and concentrated on the enemy. Carol had embellished his oration with a few other choice opinions, but back then it wasn't 'chic' to leave one's battle station while an attack was threatening. In the ensuing 30 minutes, we had reason to believe that we would be attacked. Enemy planes were approaching, encountering our defense planes and attacking ships in the area. However, we weren't attacked and, in the end, the incident blew over."

21 April. *Swearer* was patrolling a station three miles north of Kerema Retto in company with the minesweeper *Steady (AM-118)*. At sunset, lookouts spotted two planes approaching out of the sun, distance 5000 yards. When the nearest one, a Hamp, had closed to 3000 yards, passing rapidly up the port side, it was taken under fire by the 40mm. The 3" ready gun opened fire belatedly as the plane circled to attack *Barry (APD-29)*. No hits were scored, and cease fire was ordered just before the *kamikaze* crashed *Barry* amidships. The other plane, an Oscar, did not close *Swearer* but dove on the landing ship, *LSM-59*, crashing her just abaft amidships. Shooting had ceased before all *Swearer's* battle stations were manned. The attackers were undetected earlier because two navy planes were closing Kerama Retto simultaneously and on the same range and bearing. Also, the attackers were low on the water and in line with the intense glare of the setting sun. (The ordeal of *Barry* is narrated in the next chapter, *Iwo Jima to Okinawa – The Fast Transports.*)

LSM-59 sank, and *Swearer* and *Steady* proceeded to pick up survivors. *Swearer* recovered 31 men who were later transferred to *PCE(R)-853* in Kerema Retto.

Although *Swearer* was only attacked once at night, near the close of the operation, enemy planes were over the ship on numerous occasions. They were not fired upon because they could only be seen when they were between the moon and the ship, a position where the attackers apparently could not see the ship. It was not believed to be wise to open fire and attract their attention.

Early evening of 13 May. *Swearer* was escorting *LSM-277* on the northeast coast of Okinawa. Several bogies were picked up on SA radar at 30 miles. An enemy float plane, a Jake, circled the ship once, dived at a 30 degree angle, and dropped one 250 pound bomb which landed 100 feet off the starboard beam without damage to the ship or personnel. Due to poor visibility in the semi-darkness, the ship's guns did not open fire until the plane had closed to 2500 yards in a dive. No hits were scored and the plane retired over Okinawa.

The destroyer escort continued to patrol Kerama Retto until 5 July. During that time, she suffered one more air attack by a torpedo bomber on 27 June. Neither plane nor ship inflicted damage upon the other.

Swearer headed for the United States on 13 July. After a stop at Pearl Harbor, she entered San Diego on 27 July for overhaul. The war ended three weeks later.

* The name has been changed for the protection of the individual.

BOWERS

An Embattled Change of Command

"Though World War II produced many heroic incidents among ships and men, the *Bowers (DE-637)* action can be placed high on the list. She was hit by a Val *kamikaze* off Okinawa which killed or wounded half of the crew and demolished her superstructure. Though a flaming holocaust, her crew rallied at the commands of her first lieutenant to smother the flames and bring the ship back to the United States."

Quoted from the Division of Naval History, Ships Histories Section, Navy Department Washington

This narrative relies largely on the report of Lieutenant T.B. Hinkle, first lieutenant and damage control officer. All logs, notebooks, track charts and other data were destroyed by fire. Within the space of a very few minutes, the third in command was to become the first in command and to prove himself worthy of the job.

The Articles for The Government of The Navy, enacted by

Congress, state that the senior officer on board shall assume command in the event of the death or incapacitation of the captain, the executive officer and so on. If this should indeed come to pass, who would the new captain be? How would he conduct himself and the ship upon assuming his new responsibilities under the direst conditions?

On 1 April 1945, *Bowers*, under the command of Lieutenant Commander C.F. Highfield, arrived in the transport area at Okinawa Shima, Nansei Shoto, as antisubmarine and radar picket vessel. Fireworks started almost immediately with numerous alerts and submarine attacks. Air raids became ever more frequent.

Mid-afternoon on 7 April. A radar contact was obtained on a plane on the port beam, distance nine miles. Within two minutes, the range narrowed to 5000 yards and, three minutes after that, was observed visually at 1700 yards and closing the port side rapidly. *Bowers* opened fire with all guns on target. The aircraft was hit repeatedly and set afire. It banked sharply to the right, lost altitude and, at two feet from the water, attempted to recover control. *Bowers*, meanwhile, was in a hard left turn to keep her guns bearing on the *kamikaze* as it struck the water and burst into flames!

Dawn on 16 April. An aircraft radar contact was recorded at six miles, then lost for a brief interval, again sighted astern at 1800 yards. All guns that could bear opened fire. The plane continued to approach in a 20 degree glide, strafing the ship until it closed to 700 yards. A hail of fire from *Bowers* slammed into the *kamikaze*, and it burst into flames, splashed off the port beam and sank with its pilot!

Remarkably, in view of the strafing, there were no personnel casualties and only minor damage to the hull. Lieutenant Hinkle did mentally record that the morning was refreshingly cool and that the sky was clear with only a few cumulus clouds, a true sailor. One hour after the first radar contact on the *kamikaze* just splashed, the captain ordered the crew to stand down from battle stations. But relaxation was only good for the next two hours.

0857. Antiaircraft fire ahead. General Quarters! The invasion of Iwo Shima had begun, and enemy aircraft were attacking all targets with everything they had.

0939. *Bowers'* air search radar picked up two unidentified pips, presumably Japanese, distance eight miles. Almost immediately afterward, the two aircraft were sighted flying very low on a course to cross the starboard bow of the DE. To feel and know the tension of the moment, remember that our forces were heavily engaged with the enemy over a wide area and that voice radio was crackling with this and that action report or order. Captain Highfield promptly gave instructions to the helm to maneuver the ship so that all port side guns would bear.

As the two *kamikaze* planes approached the port bow at a range of about 3000 yards, they separated. One ran straight at the ship and was shot down only 1000 yards away!

The other one, however, held a course parallel to but opposite to that of *Bowers* while flying down her port beam. The plane managed to keep a range of about 5000 yards from the DE as all three 3" main battery guns were firing as fast as they could. Empty shell cases bonged onto the steel plates and were kicked out of the way. The 1.1" quadruple mount joined the fray, and *Bowers* was throwing up a wall of fire at a son of Japan.

On reaching a point just abaft the beam, the pilot turned directly toward the ship. All port side 20mm guns, now in range, opened fire. Some 20mm and 1.1" shells could be seen bursting on the plane, but no parts were shot away, and she did not catch fire. Perhaps the ancestors were with this pilot. He just kept coming and strafing. Above the clatter and din, Highfield could see some of his men topple over, hit by machine gun fire, only a prelude of what was to come.

The pilot probably intended to crash the ship on that run but, in the face of vicious antiaircraft fire, he possibly became confused and missed by a scant few feet. He passed over the after 3" gun so low that, had the gun been elevated a trifle more, he would have hit it and crashed. He almost struck the water on the starboard side but regained control and commenced gaining altitude. All guns on *Bowers* continued to fire, scoring hits that miraculously did not destroy the plane. Was a divine wind blowing from the Sea of Japan?

When the pilot had attained a range of 1500 yards and an altitude of 50 feet, he began a counter-clockwise turn with the obvious intention of attacking the ship from dead ahead or on the starboard bow. The captain began to maneuver his ship to keep the VAL on the starboard beam. All guns that could bear slammed away at the kamikaze. His sweep was continuous and approaching. He came in just forward of the starboard beam, closer and closer, bigger and bigger, and crashed into the upper forward section of the flying bridge!

The steel plate was penetrated by the impact as the plane embedded itself into the Asdic hut. There was an instantaneous explosion of high octane gasoline with resultant fire enveloping the entire upper part of the bridge and pilot house. The bomb carried by the plane penetrated the forward section of the pilot house, passed through it, grazed and dented the after part of the port doorway, struck the 24" searchlight and continued another 20 feet before it exploded.

The *kamikaze* had struck!

Personnel casualties from the bomb explosion and shrapnel were heavy, 37 being killed instantly, 11 missing and 56 severely wounded. Many of the latter subsequently succumbed. Within a matter of seconds, the effective complement of *Bowers* was reduced by half. The captain was blown overboard, and the executive officer was grievously wounded. The ASW and CIC officers were killed instantly. Material damage was extreme. All radio, radar, sonar, fire control instruments and bridge steering were knocked out.

Lieutenant Hinkle was then in repair I. All repair parties, I, II, and III, had been busy passing 3" ammunition when the Jap hit. Hinkle immediately proceeded to the scene of damage and, upon coming out of the starboard forward light lock door, discovered the fire already burning furiously on the bridge and around the pilot house. He promptly gave orders to the men of repair I to rig all possible hoses and to do their best to bring the fire under control. The assistant first lieutenant, Lieutenant (jg) R.A.F. Meagher, was at the scene, directing men from repair II and III with suitable equipment to the scene of the fire. He also did an outstanding job in getting seriously wounded men to the central dressing station in the wardroom.

The topside of *Bowers* was a raging fire, soaring skyward in a vertical column.

At the outset, Hinkle found insufficient men to man the hoses. He took a hose himself up over number two 3" gun and took charge of fire fighting from that area. Within exactly one minute after he had first seen the fire, he had three hoses playing on it in steady streams. After approximately five minutes, five hoses were at work, two forward and three abaft the bridge structure. At the same time, and from the same station, he directed that all ammunition that was loose and adjacent to the fire be jettisoned.

A burning ship steaming out of control in circles had some clear thinking men aboard who wanted to live, save others, and keep their true love, their ship.

Carpenter's Mate First Class Carter, on his own initiative, turned on the sprinklers in the 20mm clip shack, located immediately under the pilot house, probably preventing an ugly explosion. He was a dynamo in getting men to move on the double.

There was a violent roar, like an explosion, and eight depth charges were seen flying through the air as the "K" gun circuit shorted on the flying bridge. But the lives of many men in the water, including the badly wounded captain, were saved because the charges had been set on safe by Torpedoman Third Class D.R. Tillotsen. Had there been any boys among the able-bodied remaining, they were now men.

It occurred to the assistant engineering officer, Ensign R.V. Beach, that *Bowers* was not under command and doing a lot of uncontrolled running about. He took the liberty of notifying Lieutenant Hinkle that, as far as he could determine, Hinkle was the senior officer aboard and that no one was at the conn. Hinkle then instructed Beach to take the conn at secondary aft (sky II), the emergency bridge station abaft the stack, and advised Beach he would stay at the scene of the fire for the time being.

Beach, a reserve engineering officer who had never stood a bridge watch, promptly installed himself at secondary aft as Officer of The Deck. He instructed the engineering officer to stop the ship. (An officer of the deck, regardless of rank or assignment, is senior to everybody on board except the captain and the executive officer until he is relieved of his watch.) He proceeded to the fantail and shouted down to the helmsman at emergency tiller aft to put the rudder amidships. He then located the electrician and directed him to rig up sound powered telephones from secondary conn to main engine control, after steering and to all other stations. Ensign Beach looked highly professional on his very first watch outside of the engine room. *Bowers* was under command.

The fight to control the fire raged on. Flames and columns of smoke soared above the mast. In the wardroom, the dressing party applied tourniquets, bandages, burn ointment, morphine, the Lord's Prayer, and tried to keep from slipping in the blood. The broken bodies lay helpless, some in excruciating agony, their lives dependent on the fire fighters — and the sweating fire fighters knew it.

Lieutenant (jg) T.E. Davies, the senior engineering officer, was in number one fire room when the plane hit. Upon hearing the explosion, he checked with both fire rooms and both engine rooms to determine if there were damage. Damage in the lower spaces proved to be minimal. The fresh water main in the forward engine room was pierced by shrapnel and had to be secured. A branch line from the fire main in the forward fire room, supplying the fire plugs on the port side, was ruptured slightly but was not secured until all fires on the ship had been extinguished. The fire main pressure was kept at 100 pounds or more at all times. The men below knew their ship had been badly hurt, that command had changed two steps down, and they gave their all.

When satisfied that his engineering plant was operating normally, Davies proceeded topside and rendered valuable assistance in seeing to it that hoses were carried up, fighting the fire from abaft the bridge, and assisting in the care of the wounded. He organized gun crews from survivors on deck who were unscathed or not too seriously wounded to be able to fight the ship.

The threat of renewed attack was ever present and, although the ability of *Bowers* to withstand another blow was considerably in doubt, she proceeded to get ready for it. Number two 3" gun and five of the 20mm guns were out of action, but all remaining guns were manned and ready with sufficient ammunition standing by.

Shortly thereafter, *Swearer (DE-186)* came alongside to assist. (It is interesting to relate this account of the *Bowers* action with the one supplied by Chesty Arnold in the previous narrative on *Swearer.*) She rigged three hoses and played them on the roaring blaze on her sister vessel. The fire was finally brought under control after a 45 minute struggle. A few of the seriously wounded were transferred to *Swearer*, but the movement of wounded was suddenly interrupted by antiaircraft fire on the port beam, about five miles off.

Swearer broke away, and *Bowers* got set for another attack. Lieutenant Hinkle relieved Ensign Beach at the conn. When the planes were gone, *Swearer* returned alongside *Bowers* and received the rest of the seriously wounded. *Connolly (DE-306)* had meanwhile picked up those who had been blown into the water, including the seriously wounded Captain Highfield, and transferred them to *Swearer*.

The next hour saw more action in the area as *Bowers* awaited a renewed onslaught. There she stood, underway with her forward area still smoldering; her remaining battle stations manned, some by men with bloody bandages; her first lieutenant in command at secondary conn and reporting to the Task Group Commander that the ship was ready and able to fight.

But the Task Group Commander thought otherwise; this valiant ship had enough of war this day. He ordered her to proceed to the nearest base where urgent repairs were effected under the duress of continuous air alerts. Under the able command of her new captain, Lieutenant Hinkle, *Bowers* returned to the United States without further incident.

MELVIN R. NAWMAN

A Weathered Veteran of Sea and Foe

Melvin R. Nawman (DE-417) had survived Typhoon Cobra in December 1944 (See chapter *Philippine Typhoons*) and now would face up to two more life-threatening situations, Iwo Jima and Okinawa.

At Iwo Jima on 21 February 1945, the crew of *Nawman* witnessed the sinking of the carrier *Bismarck Sea (CVE-95)* by a *kamikaze*. Yeoman Third Class Kenneth Dempsey had a bridge telephone station at the time and recorded the awesome and unforgettable scene:

> "Shortly after dusk, six Japanese planes came roaring in about 20 feet above the water. Four were shot down by gunfire from assembled ships, but the fifth crashed into the starboard quarter of *Bismarck Sea*, causing that ship to erupt

into a 100 foot high tower of flame.

Nawman approached to within 50 yards of the carrier's bow and turned on all her searchlights, illuminating the stricken ship and a large number of men still aboard. In spite of urging them to jump into the water, many were frozen with fear and refused to go. Only a few appeared to have on their life jackets, and several seemed to be naked or scantily clad.

Ninety minutes after the *kamikaze* struck, *Bismarck Sea* rolled over on her starboard side, for a moment exposing her keel. The bow rose about 20 feet into the air and, within a few moments, she disappeared below the surface. *Nawman* maneuvered into the center of the oil slick and took aboard seven survivors. It was a terrible nightmare, never to be forgotten."

A previous narrative in this chapter covering *Edmonds(DE-406)* was deeply involved in the *Bismarck Sea* action.

Okinawa was *Nawman's* longest combat in number of days spent fighting *kamikazes* in port and off-shore. In the late afternoon of 2 April 1945, *Nawman* left the anchorage at Kerama Retto, Okinawa, in company with the carrier *Lunga Point (CVE-94)*, *Patterson (DD-392)* and *Mitchell (DE-417)*, the latter with Commander Escort Division 72 embarked. The escorts formed their stations in the screen with *Nawman* on the starboard bow of the carrier.

1830. A bogey was reported to the Task Group Commander by the attack cargo ship *Suffolk (AKA-69)*, 40 miles from *CortDiv 72*. Nine minutes later, the same bogey, now at a distance of 27 miles and closing, was reported by *Patterson*, and all escorts went to GQ. A transport, *Henrico (APA-45)*, was on fire on *Nawman's* starboard beam. (The *Henrico* disaster would have placed *Riddle (DE-185)* and *Suesens (DE-342)* in the same neighborhood at the same time. Both are narrated in this chapter.) All antiaircraft action involving gunfire from *Nawman* took place in six minutes, beginning to end.

At the beginning of the attack, *Nawman* rang up 22 knots and was fish-tailing along the *CortDiv 72* base course in a manner designed to close *Lunga Point* to 1500 yards and to unmask her main battery. The first plane, a Frances or a Nick, was taken under fire by *Nawman's* after 40mm gun, making her the first ship to open fire on this target. Her 40mm fire appeared to be short in range. The plane went into a shallow dive on a course parallel to the DE until about 50 feet above the water. After leveling off, it opened the range to 3500 yards ahead of *Mitchell*. It then went into a steep climb to 1500 feet, turned a half circle and headed directly for *Mitchell*. *Nawman* again took the plane under fire, this time with her forward 5" gun, when the plane was broad on her starboard bow. She ceased fire when the aircraft was on her starboard beam because *Mitchell* fouled her range. The plane passed over *Mitchell* at less than masthead height. As soon as the aircraft was clear, *Nawman's* after 5" gun maintained fire it until it retired from the area.

While the after 5" gun was firing on the plane which "buzzed" *Mitchell*, a second plane, probably the same type, appeared at an altitude of 2000 feet, range 7500 yards on *Nawman's* starboard bow. This plane had been maneuvering erratically but it seemed to have picked *Nawman* for a target. Five inch fire from the forward gun and rapid fire from the forward 40mm gun drove off the plane.

1843. *Nawman's* after 5" gun took a plane under fire on her starboard quarter, the trainer and pointer having had this plane in their sights for several minutes. The range was 5000 yards with a position angle of 25 degrees. Five or more rounds produced a fire about the port wing and sent the plane twisting downward, burning intensely until it splashed in a cloud of spray!

The after 5" gun shifted to engage a plane on the port quarter, range 5500 yards, position angle 15 degrees. This gun was firing rapidly, and again the pointer and trainer felt that they were on target. In a shroud of smoke and fire, the *kamikaze* exploded in mid-air!

Personnel performance was, as usual, the key to success. No plane got closer than 5000 yards or within effective range of the automatic weapons, a credit to the efficiency of the 5" gun crews. Bronze Stars were awarded to the pointer and trainer of the after 5" gun. (The trainer controls the horizontal or azimuth motion of the gun whereas the pointer controls the vertical movement and also closes the firing key). The captain reported that, although the CIC kept an accurate picture of the situation at the height of the action, he was much too busy to make use of it, being preoccupied with station-keeping and maintaining the battery unmasked.

In the final stages of the war in the Pacific, *Nawman* spent 47 consecutive days at sea screening carrier task forces operating off the east coast of Japan. On 22 December, pressed into "Magic Carpet" duty, this doughty destroyer escort happily pointed its bow toward home, arriving in San Francisco on 15 January 1946.

GILLIGAN

Captain, There Is a Live Torpedo in the Crew's Quarters!

The vicissitudes of war were not new to *Gilligan (DE-508)*. During the campaign to secure the Marshall Islands in October 1944, she escorted vital cargoes to *Kwajalein*, bombarded Mille Atoll and Jaluit Island, and sank a small Japanese vessel

In November, she escorted merchantmen to Eniwetok and Saipan. While moored at Ulithi Lagoon on the twentieth, fleet oiler *Mississinewa (AO-59)*, loaded with 400,000 gallons of high octane aviation fuel, was torpedoed inside the lagoon with a loss of 50 officers and men. Seconds later, *Gilligan* saw a midget Japanese submarine pass close aboard. With other escort vessels, she conducted a number of depth charge attacks, possibly damaging the midget.

On 31 December, *Gilligan* departed from Manus to escort troopships to Lingayen Gulf, arriving on D-Day, 9 January 1945. While screening for an attack group of Vice Admiral Wilkinson's Task Force 79, she was crashed by a *kamikaze* and sustained severe casualties and damage. See subchapter *Return to Luzon* in chapter *The Philippine Campaign*. Retired Rear Admiral Carl E. Bull, a Lieutenant Commander in command of *Gilligan* at the time, related to this author the events surrounding his ship's activities after Lingayen Gulf.

"We were repaired at Pearl Harbor and returned to the fight in time to be at Okinawa. *Gilligan* was a fine ship. After the Lingayen combat and the blood-letting, the crew became a real fighting unit.

Now, back on the line after repairs and modifications to

make her better able to handle plane attacks, she was once more engaged in deadly combat. This time, she had three quad 40mm to replace the torpedo tubes and one quad 40mm lost when hit by the *kamikaze*. Again, *Gilligan* would be fighting for her life.

Gilligan sailed on 29 March as convoy escort and, on 17 April, closed the western beaches of Okinawa to commence antiaircraft screening around the transport anchorage. She was then assigned to a station off Okinawa, a one ship position between the multiple destroyer radar pickets to the north and the transport area to the south. Naturally after the Lingayen experience, there was a good deal of apprehension in the crew.

Minutes after relieving the station, lookouts spotted a single bogey circling the ship. The DE waited for the bogey to get in range of her 5" guns. When it did, it went into a steep dive. The first salvo hit, knocking the plane into the sea! With that success behind them and the knowledge that they could shoot them down, the crew was now ready for a far more serious engagement.

It was several weeks after the first experience and now the night of 27 May when the CIC reported numerous bogies approaching. The ship went to GQ and waited, but not for long. Apparently, the Japs had decided that a single ship was an easier target than the multiple ship radar picket group to the north. *Gilligan* was repeatedly attacked by several torpedo planes.

Using sonar gear for advanced warning, *Gilligan* threaded the torpedo tracks, hearing the sound increasing to maximum as the torpedoes passed down the sides, and then with relief, the decreasing sound as the torpedoes continued out to sea. Because of the phosphorescent water, it was possible to see the torpedo tracks as they streaked close aboard down the sides. The Japanese planes were so low as they passed over the ship that, lighted by the flare of the firing guns, it was possible to see the rivets in the skins of the planes and the pilots in the cockpits.

As one of the planes passed over the starboard quarter, there was a large splash alongside, throwing water over the fantail, followed by a plane on fire and crashing in the water! It was assumed that a wheel or landing gear had been shot off prior to the crash, causing the initial splash but, since other attacks were coming in, no more time was given to speculation. Somewhat later, the captain noticed the ship was developing a list to starboard. A call to damage control and to the engine room brought negative replies of any damage. But the list developed to about 10-15 degrees as damage control was directed to keep looking.

A short time later, the damage control officer came to the bridge and reported that the watertight door to the after crew's quarters had been opened and the space found flooded. He also reported a hole in the side of the ship at the water line, and that he would immediately try plugging it with mattresses and shores (Structural building timber used to temporarily support weakened or damaged bulkheads or close ruptures in the hull.) He was back again a few minutes later, his face pallid and his voice excited:

'Captain, there is a live torpedo in the crews quarters! What should I do'?

'Get the damn thing out!'

All crew members were at battle stations, the reason the flooded compartment had been unnoticed. Volunteers were called, and a plan formulated to slide the dud torpedo back to the entrance hole. The engineers would stop and lock the starboard shaft and, when all was ready, the skipper would put the ship into a tight right turn with the port screw to cause the ship to heel over to starboard and thus facilitate sliding out the torpedo. When all was ready, the plan was executed, and there was an unearthly silence of several seconds until all were sure that the torpedo had sunk clear of the starboard screw. There was a loud cheer, and the *Gilligan* continued with the fighting through the night. A relief ship was sent at daybreak. *Gilligan*, however, remained on station to assist her relief until the attacks broke off, then proceeded to Kerama Retto for repairs.

A sheet of steel was welded over the hole, and *Gilligan* was sent back out on the line, remaining at Okinawa for 45 days and getting credit for at least five planes shot down. (The skipper and crew claimed 10, including action at Lingayen Gulf.)

A review of the path of the torpedo showed that, after entry, it had lodged in a crew member's locker, and the detonator mechanism in the nose had buried itself in a BIBLE. When the word got around, there was no question in the minds of the crew but that Someone 'upstairs' had saved us. At that location, had the torpedo exploded, the ship would undoubtedly have broken in half and been lost. The next Sunday in Kerama Retto, before going back on the line, a church service was held. There was no chaplain available so the captain conducted the service on the fantail. Everyone was present!"

Perhaps a less involved person, someone not on board when it happened, would explain that the torpedo was dropped too close to the ship to arm itself and that was the reason for its failure to explode, but that would not have been an acceptable answer at Okinawa in 1945.

FLEMING

The Sights and Sounds of Okinawa

Only two months after sinking Japanese submarine *I-362* (See chapter *Pacific Antisubmarine Warfare*), *Fleming (DE-32)* was about to experience the greatest challenge to her existence since she was commissioned. On 13 March 1945, she arrived at Ulithi to prepare for the mammoth assault. Assigned to the screen of carrier Task Group 52.1, she headed for the invasion of the Ryukyu Islands. On 31 March, a plane from the carrier *Petrof Bay (CVE-80)* crashed on takeoff. *Fleming* rescued the pilot, Ensign Robert H. Allison.

Lieutenant James T. Krause, ship's Gunnery Officer, recalls his harrowing experiences at Okinawa:

"Okinawa, to many of us who were there, is known as the forgotten battle of World War II. Even though the loss in life was severe, most people back home knew little about it. It was understandable in a way because the war in Europe had ended with the collapse of Germany, and a Japanese surrender was expected soon.

At sea, the attacks were inflicted almost entirely by *kamikaze* suicide planes. Seven days before the invasion, our ship arrived at Okinawa with a force of 20 light aircraft carriers. Their planes pounded the island from before dawn until after dark each day.

We were released from the carrier force after the invasion started, and we began a couple of months of hell on picket duty off the coast of Okinawa. We were attacked day and night by *kamikazes*. Quite often, we would see a couple of enemy planes come over us and attack while one plane stayed high and returned to Japan. We soon learned that the high ones were on reconnaissance, recording the results of suicide attacks. After a while, the day attacks lessened because of the heavy losses the enemy sustained from American fighter planes before reaching their targets. The massive air attacks now came at dusk, intensified shortly after dark and lasting until early light.

The following is an example of a typical day beginning in the late afternoon. We would have early chow while it was still light. After eating, the exec would come over the speakers and say, 'Walk to your Battle Stations and stand easy' When dusk was upon us, he would say over the speakers, 'Raid number 15 (could be 10, 12, 20, etc.) range 75 miles, bearing 015 degrees.' Minutes later, 'Raid number 16, range 80 miles, bearing 010. Raid number 15, now range 60 miles, bearing 015.'

This would continue until we would have five or six raids stacked up. When the first group of planes was 15 to 20 miles away, the general alarm was sounded, and the ship was at full alert. Believe me, we were ready even if GQ had not sounded. A few minutes later, all hell broke loose and continued off and on until the next dawn or later. On the worst night, we had over 200 Japanese planes attacking the pickets. So many ships were hit that they were ordered to group together for mutual support.

During the operation, we were directed to escort a carrier to Guam for repairs. While there, several of us from the gunnery department acquired a number of 50 caliber machine guns, stands, and a huge amount of ammunition, over 100,000 rounds. Once aboard, the stands were welded to the deck, four on each side. The mounts were on the flying bridge, signal bridge, amidships, and aft. Over the following days, the men were drilled on mounting the guns, loading and firing. After our return to Okinawa, this additional fire power helped us splash a few suicide planes before they hit us."

17 May. At various times through the day, *Fleming* relieved the minesweeper *Staunch (AM-307)*, *Finnegan (DE-307)* and *Vammen (DE-644)*. Several times, Air Flash Red was broadcast during the night, keeping the anxious crew of *Fleming* at GQ. Just before midnight, a Val was heard close aboard without warning. It passed down the starboard side under machine gun fire, then disappeared.

20 May. While patrolling the same station, the DE went to GQ with the first evening Air Flash Red. *Thatcher (DD-514)*, in an adjacent station, was hit by a suicide plane. *Fleming* headed toward her to offer assistance until forced to maneuver for her own protection from bogies in the immediate vicinity. In late evening, three Zekes made suicide or bombing runs on *Fleming*. The DE splashed two and one turned away with neither ship damage nor personnel casualties! Yeoman Walter F. Lynch traced his memory back to those stressful days:

"I did not do anything other than manning my battle station in the radar shack (CIC). Most of what I tell you was heard over interior communications during the action.

The captain, Lieutenant Commander K.E. Burgess Jr., was on the flying bridge, maneuvering the ship to evade planes and to bring maximum fire power to bear on the targets. Lieutenant Campen, our executive officer, was in the combat information center where I was stationed. He was watching plots of enemy planes and was in direct communication by voice tube with the commanding officer.

When the planes were in their final runs, Mr. Campen said 'We did all we could do in here (CIC). Lie down on deck and cover your heads with your arms'. It was then up to the gun crews who were hammering away at the planes. I remember lying on the deck and wondering what it would feel like to die if those planes smashed into the bridge structure carrying their usual armament of 500 pound bombs.

I said a quiet prayer to myself and, in that instant, I had a vision of my mother back in Philadelphia, and she was also praying and seemed to be reassuring me that everything would be all right. If I were to have died in that instant, she would have been the last person I would have seen in this life."

26 May. Just after midnight, one Frances, after looking over *Fleming* and *Abercrombie (DE-34)* in a nearby station, decided to crash into *Abercrombie*. However, it was destroyed and splashed by gunfire from that DE (narrated in this chapter). Two hours later, *Fleming* was straddled for several minutes by friendly 5" fire, a not uncommon hazard at Okinawa. Shrapnel and spray landed aboard, but fortunately there were no casualties.

0344. A bogey circled overhead. It too was shot down by gunners on *Abercrombie* after making two passes at that vessel. Forty minutes later, *Fleming* secured from GQ after receiving an Air Flash White. It was only a four hour respite until "Air Flash Red" sent her tired crew back to battle stations. She received orders from the Task Group Commander to proceed with *Gosselin (APD-126)* to lend assistance to ships damaged in a nearby area.

0920. Arriving at the desolate scene, *Fleming's* crew beheld the landing ship *LSM-135* burning, settling and abandoned; and minesweeper *Spectacle (AM-305)* dead in the water, both ships having been hit by suicide planes. *W.C. Cole (DE-642)*, was superficially damaged by a near miss. Going alongside Fleet Ocean Tug *Tekesta (ATF-93)*, *Fleming* received 11 men from the LSM, including the executive officer and three stretcher cases. She transferred survivors in Ie Shima.

1108. *Bates (APD-47)* was hit by two suiciders (narrated in next chapter). *Fleming* proceeded to the scene in company with *Gosselin*. There they beheld the sight of *Bates*, burning fore and aft with fires spreading rapidly and engulfing the ship. *Fleming* put her whaleboat over to pick up survivors. *Gosselin* lay to off *Bates*, recovering the remainder of personnel abandoning ship. Yeoman Lynch continued:

"As far as rescue operations were concerned, we were at battle stations and I was once again in the CIC with my headphones. Some strong swimmers from the crew tied lines to themselves and swam out to assist wounded survivors to the side of *Fleming*. Some of the wounded being helped on board screamed in pain from their burns.

Fleming's wardroom was converted into an operating room for the wounded. We were fortunate to have had Doctor Bellamy, *Escort Division 31* medical officer, on board at the time. Together with the pharmacist mates and volunteers from crew members trained in first aid, he treated all of the wounded patients. Dr. Bellamy collapsed from sheer exhaustion afterward and had to be transferred to a hospital ship along with the injured he treated."

27 May. Two Flash Reds were received which foretold heavy enemy air raids throughout the night, and the *kamikazes* did not disappoint their enemies. In late evening, a Jill passed overhead. The ships were illuminated by flares dropped from a high altitude. *Fleming* reduced speed to one third to minimize wake visibility and presented her stern to the flares, much too bright for comfort. An unidentified enemy plane made a low approach on the port bow. Taken under fire, it turned away. Two minutes later, the crew felt and heard two very heavy explosions nearby, probably bombs or torpedoes exploding at the end of their runs.

On 5 July, *Fleming* was underway in company with *Sederstrom (DE-31)*, *Fair (DE-35)*, *Manlove (DE-36)* and *Swearer (DE-186)* toward Saipan and Pearl Harbor. On 20 July, she headed to Portland, Oregon, for an overhaul. The war ended before repairs could be completed.

ABERCROMBIE

In the Thick of It

Abercrombie (DE-343) was a veteran. On 25 October 1944, a few miles from the Battle off Samar, she grimly watched the column of smoke in the distance, marking the sinking of the carrier *St. Lo*. She saw the topmasts of a Japanese cruiser over the horizon, the splashing of shells from her big guns and listened to the voice radio crackling the loss of *Samuel B. Roberts*.

On 21 March 1945, she sailed north from Leyte with a group of attack transports in Task Group 51.1, part of the screen for the Western Islands Attack Group. This would be the toughest mission of her career. *Abercrombie's* unit went into action in the Ryukyus a week before the majority of the invasion force. It grew colder and rougher as the force approached the objective. However, it was a cloudless dawn over a calm sea when *Abercrombie* nosed in among the rocky, pinnacle islands of Kerema Retto. Her unit's assignment was to secure that small island group before the main assault.

There was the familiar pattern of bombardment by guns and rockets, foaming lines of landing craft moving toward a smoky beach, tracers streaming into the sky as an occasional enemy plane disputed the landings, the friendly roar of Wildcats, Hellcats and Corsairs circling overhead.

For five days, *Abercrombie* patrolled endlessly, on the alert for aircraft and submarines attempting to thwart the operation. On 1 April, attention shifted to the main objective when the landing force stormed ashore on Okinawa itself. She spent another five days guarding the supply ships against attack.

She escorted transports and LSTs as they went back to sea each night of the first two weeks to avoid counterattacks. She picked up dead enemy pilots and searched them for articles of intelligence value. She rescued four half-drowned survivors found clinging to an oil drum one midnight. She took part in antisubmarine searches, was fired at from ashore, dodged bombs, buzz bombs, and torpedoes. She escorted battleships, landing ships (LSMs), and ammunition ships. At the beginning of the month-long Okinawa operation, she made a fast round trip to Saipan, Ulithi and back to Okinawa, returning on 17 April.

The nights on the patrol line were a desperate game of blind man's bluff with the enemy. One night, Japanese planes came in over the water, circling and searching. *Abercrombie* glided quietly through the sea, her guns following the enemy's position in the darkness until it was seen. She then churned up to full speed, twisting and turning, her guns hammering and blazing as the enemy attacked. She had 16 separate encounters such as this. In one fantastic moonlit night she chewed the wing off of one suicider and riddled another as it passed overhead on its second run. Both planes fell flaming into the sea!

Abercrombie claimed certain assistance in downing another plane and in the destruction of one of the enemy's piloted rocket bombs, known as bakas. When not standing watch on a radar picket station, she conducted antisubmarine searches, rescued downed American airmen, and provided escort services to a variety of ships. She finally left the Okinawa area around the middle of June, shortly before the campaign ended. Out of all this, *Abercrombie* emerged without a scratch, a dent, or a man injured by enemy action.

After the long grind, the ship had 12 days of rest at Saipan for repairs, dry-docking and upkeep. This was performed under a sky always noisy with the comings and goings of the B-29s on their round trips to Japan.

Abercrombie arrived back at Okinawa on 4 July and joined a task force of battleships, cruisers, carriers, and destroyers operating about 100 miles to the north and east as a covering force for a large-scale minesweeping operation. The same force steamed further north to China. Its aircraft took off, heavily laden with bombs and rockets for assaults in the Shanghai area.

On 8 August, *Abercrombie* again sailed south from Okinawa. On the way down, steaming along the east coast of Samar on a moonlit mid-watch, the first news was received of the enemy's willingness to surrender. In a few days it was confirmed. On 23 August, *Abercrombie* steamed back into a different Okinawa where ships now blazed with lights and showed movies on deck.

On 24 September, *Abercrombie* arrived off Wakayama in Honshu on the approaches to Japan's Inland Sea after a two-day voyage from Okinawa with four other destroyer escorts. They were part of the fire support group for the landings, lying quietly at anchor, but present "just in case." In the daytime, small groups of her men were permitted ashore on sightseeing parties where they wandered, amazed at the sudden transition from war to peace. Throngs of Japanese civilians and soldiers, bitter enemies a few weeks ago, seen only through the sights of guns, were now at peace. At night, the shore and the ships glittered with lights as though they were in San Diego, not Wakayama.

It took time to realize it, but the war was truly over.

HALLORAN

Trial by Fire

Beginning in August 1994, *Halloran (DE-305)* convoyed fast fuel replenishment groups in the Western Pacific, supplying the fleets off Palau, Yap, and Luzon. While moored at Ulithi on 20 November, she witnessed the torpedoing of the oiler *Mississinewa (AO-59)* and searched the harbor fruitlessly for a suspected midget submarine.

Halloran was underway on 22 January 1945 with the escort screen for the amphibious task force designated to capture Iwo Jima. She served as a barrier patrol ship during the landings from 19 to 28 February.

The far-steaming DE's next assignment was with the Okinawa assault forces. *Halloran* was assigned to the screen for the floating reserve transport group which sailed from Espiritu Santo on 25 March. Drills and training, assigned by the Commander Escort Division 61, were carried out while en route. Damage control, antiaircraft gunnery, plane recognition and first aid were stressed.

It was assumed that air attack was very probable and floating mines a substantial hazard. While attached to this Task Unit, *Halloran* and five other DEs screened twenty ships, including attack transports, attack cargo ships, infantry landing ships and three oilers.

The Task Unit arrived at Okinawa on 9 April and was reassigned to Task Group 51.5, patrolling in picket stations. Once at her destination, screening stations were variously assigned on 7000 and 5000 yard sectors, forming barrier dispositions along with destroyers, destroyer escorts, destroyer mine sweepers, and high speed transports.

Mid-afternoon on 12 April. While on station on that memorable day, *Halloran* repelled three Vals and three Jills, splashing one and damaging two others. One Val came in on a suicide gliding attack and was shot down by 1.10" fire! Hits from her 20mm and bursts from 3" magnetic influence shells blasted two Jills. The crew believed it was well justified in claiming an assist on one of two Jills, both of which were also under fire by the destroyer *Zellars (DD-777)*. In two cases, *Halloran* was under direct attack!

A floating mine was exploded by 20mm gunfire. In the evening, there were torpedo attacks in the area with the ship being brightly illuminated by flares dropped from enemy planes.

20 April. There were early morning and evening prolonged raids. Just after dusk, *Halloran* opened up on a Jill, attacking with a torpedo. After launching, it passed close enough aboard to cause several hearts to skip a beat; it missed by a scant 15 feet! Bursts from 3" shell fire were spotted around another attacking plane at a range of 3000 yards. The aircraft also dropped a torpedo, headed for *Halloran*, and then retired. Rapid maneuvers served to avoid the torpedo.

21 April. There were more raids during evening hours. *Halloran* fired at an enemy plane going by at 1000 yards, but poor visibility did not permit adequate tracking. All adjacent ships in the sector had opportunities to fire on bogies which were persistent hour after hour. One torpedo was dropped, exploding harmlessly at the end of its run near a ship in an adjacent sector. Jap planes frequently dropped marker lights, evidently used in homing by subsequent raids.

22 April. In evening attacks, enemy planes sortied in force, sinking the minesweeper *Swallow (AM-65)* in an adjacent station and hitting the destroyer *Isherwood (DD-520)*, also nearby. *Halloran* picked up a casualty blown overboard from *Isherwood* and searched for others. Captain A M. Townsend, Commander Mine Squadron 3 in destroyer minelayer *Gwin (DM-33)*, took over the sector command.

23-25 April. *Halloran* took aboard the body of a Japanese aviator to investigate for possible papers.

29 April. There were strong raids in the area. A low-flying enemy plane was picked up visually, previously unreported and not showing on the radar scope. As *Halloran* gave warning to the Task Group, the aircraft circled the ship out of range and then made a suicide dive on the evacuation transport *Pinkney (APH-2)* in Kerama Retto.

21 June. A suicide plane attacked *Halloran*, but her gunners splashed it in the nick of time, a scant 75 yards from the ship! However, a bomb carried by the *kamikaze* killed three men and caused considerable damage to the hull and superstructure.

After repairs at Kerama Retto, *Halloran* patrolled off Iwo Shima from 5 to 13 July, then assumed tactical command of an escort screen for Tank Landing Ships en route to the Philippines. She departed from Luzon for the United States on 10 September 1945.

Halloran's trial by fire was finished — forever.

GRISWOLD

A Few Days with the "Suiciders"

Having dispatched Japanese submarine *I-39* to the bottom of the sea in December 1944, *Griswold (DE-7)* now had to contemplate meeting with a much greater threat from the sky. The long Pacific campaign was moving into its final phase in March 1945 as American forces invaded Okinawa, and *Griswold* soon moved up to the front.

Griswold departed from Eniwetok on 7 May. En route to the forward areas, gun crews had three periods of antiaircraft firing practice on towed sleeves as well as daily pointer and trainer drill for the main battery and tracking drill for automatic weapons. In addition to *Griswold*, the ships in the screen were minesweepers *Prevail (AM-107)* and *Zeal (AM-131)*, destroyer minelayer *Tracy (DM-19)*, and destroyer escort *Swearer (DE-186)*. The latter vessel's exploits are narrated earlier in this chapter. This composition of diverse vessels, designed for different tasks, illuminates the desperate requirement to assign virtually anything with an antiaircraft capability to the Okinawa picket line.

Upon reaching Okinawa on the morning of 27 May, the commanding officer, Lieutenant Commander Logan Cresap Jr., took *Griswold* to Hagushi Anchorage, Okinawa Jima, Nansei Shoto. Early on 28 May, prior to contact with the enemy, *Griswold* witnessed gunfire nearby from destroyers *Bradford (DD-545)* and *Claxton (DD-571)*. One enemy plane was destroyed.

The following day, *Griswold* was underway from Kerama Retto and arrived at her station to relieve *Osmond Ingram (APD-35)*. The commander of Escort Division 8, embarked in *Griswold*, assumed command of the screen on dusk antiaircraft stations. She patrolled in company with *Zeal* 1500 yards astern, 22 miles due west of Okinawa.

0211 to 0430 on 31 May. The sky was almost completely overcast with occasional rain squalls. The moon was in its third quarter phase, directly overhead, and providing occasional illumination. The sea was calm. Visibility was 2000 yards, and the ceiling about 500 feet.

0211. A bogey was picked up by air search radar on *Griswold* at a distance of 10 miles, speed 230 knots. The plane had not been contacted until it gained sufficient altitude to pass directly over the island of Tonachi Shima. "General quarters! This is not a drill! Repeat, This is not ——" At Okinawa in 1945, battle stations were invariably manned ahead of required time and without urging.

The bogey was on a course leading to Hagushi but, when astern of the formation, it altered course sharply, paralleling that of *Griswold* and *Zeal*. It zoomed into a cloud at an altitude of about 900 feet, descended to 600 feet over *Zeal*, then leveled one mile astern of the DE at 100 feet. Its twin exhausts were sighted 1500 yards on the starboard quarter as it turned to dive on *Griswold*.

0217. The pointer and trainer of number three 3" gun locked onto the Betty immediately. The gun had been previously loaded and trained on search radar bearings. It opened fire in local control at 1000 yards with a preset two-second projectile. (Shell will burst two seconds after leaving the gun muzzle.) The first shot scored a direct hit in the middle of the plane which burst into a roaring fireball. The *kamikaze* was deflected slightly away from the ship, passed down the starboard side with one engine still running, and splashed 150 feet on the starboard bow without damage to the DE!

The above deserves repeating. One round from a 3" gun ended the fight. That was the total ammunition expenditure report, one only 3" projectile!

The enemy force encountered by *Griswold* consisted of two aircraft. One was the *kamikaze* that was so readily shot down. The other closed for inspection but failed to press home an attack, reversing course at a distance of six miles, probably an observer.

1845 on 5 June. The fight came to *Griswold* once again before departing from Okinawa. This DE stood out of the south entrance of Kerama Retto to relieve the destroyer minelayer *Henry A. Wiley (DM-29)*. Twenty-four hour surface and air search by radar had commenced on *Griswold* after getting under way. All hands went to battle stations for the usual evening alert. Because of the proximity of high land to the northward, a window of opportunity existed for any aircraft approaching from that direction. The ship's air search radar was virtually useless in an arc roughly from west to northeast.

1928. SOPA at Kerama Retto ordered "Flash Red, Control Green." The cloud ceiling was about 800 feet, and the overhead was shrouded. The ship's rudder was put over to reverse course.

1932. A plane, identified as a Tony and carrying two bombs, believed to be bearing American insignia on its wings, came out of a dense cloud above the DE in a vertical dive.

The *kamikaze* overshot the ship. Had *Griswold* not commenced turning one minute before, the dive would have been accurate. The aircraft endeavored to recoup by pulling out from the vertical and turning with left rudder at the same time. The pilot exerted his best effort to crash on the inside bow of the ship as she turned. However, he failed to take into account the fact that a turning ship, particularly with its rudder hard over, becomes inclined at a considerable angle to its direction of advance. The marauder crashed 150 feet on the port bow with a terrific explosion, showering the ship with small fragments but causing neither damage nor casualties!

The fortuitous evasive maneuvers of *Griswold* undoubtedly contributed materially to the kamikaze's failure to close the ship. The air speed of the plane was believed to have approached 500 miles per hour on reaching its intended target. The entire action took place in not more than three seconds and, although all guns were loaded, none were able to get on target and fire.

Two minutes later, two other American ships were seriously damaged by *kamikazes* as Japan made her desperate but futile effort to reverse the tide of war. The battleship *Mississippi (BB-41)* and the cruiser *Louisville (CA-28)*, both on fire support stations, had been hit. The minesweeper *Requisite (AM-109)*, two screening stations from *Griswold*, reported that a Tony splashed 30 feet on her port bow.

The war ended, and she sailed triumphantly into Japanese waters, anchoring in Tokyo Bay on 10 September. *Griswold* cleared Tokyo six days later and arrived in San Pedro, California, on 8 October 1945.

JOHN C. BUTLER

A Terrible Day for Kamikazes

John C. Butler (DE-339) had been in the retiring screen in the Battle off Samar. She had expended every 5" round on board, firing at the Japanese Fleet on the never-to-be-forgotten day of 25 October 1944.

Then came the air attacks in Leyte and Lingayen Gulfs and, most recently, the furious battle of Iwo Jima.

In the latter engagement, *Butler* was one of the screening ships for an escort carrier group that set course for Iwo Jima as a part of the covering force for the amphibious landing. She remained off Iwo Jima with the carriers in support of marines who stormed that fortress island on 19 February 1945. Two days later, she helped fight off an enemy suicide plane attack and was witness to the sinking of the escort carrier *Bismarck Sea*. She became a target of a close run by an enemy torpedo bomber which narrowly missed its mark.

Butler rescued the crew of a downed friendly aircraft, transferring the survivors to the beach at Iwo Jima under the fire of Japanese shore batteries. She was not hit by the enemy gunfire and left Iwo Jima on 9 March for Ulithi in the Carolines. There, she formed a part of the escort for transport and amphibious ships bound for Okinawa. Now she had to face up to the *kamikaze* fury at Okinawa. This is a tale of veterans honed to perfection — and courage.

As the first waves of assault troops landed on 1 April 1945, *Butler* joined the screen of Rear Admiral W.D. Sample's four escort carriers, *Suwanee (CVE-27)*, *Chenango (CVE-28)*, *Santee (CVE-29)*, and *Steamer Bay (CVE-87)*. *Butler* was kept busy transferring men and material between larger ships, guarding individual escort carriers into Kerama Retto for rearming and rescuing survivors from American plane crashes in the water.

Butler was detached from the carrier screen on 15 April for repairs at Kerama Retto before taking an isolated patrol station to the north of Ie Shima. The patrol was quite routine until 20 May. Just prior to sunset on that day, radio warning from the flagship at Iwo Shima indicated the presence of enemy aircraft in the vicinity to the DE.

"Flash red, control green!" Battle stations were manned and, almost immediately, a lookout shouted, "Aircraft at three-five-zero!" (A relative bearing, 10 degrees off the port bow.)

Two single engine aircraft were sighted exactly one minute later. One started a run on shipping off the southern beach of Iwo Shima. The other went into orbit, looking very much as if its pilot would be glad to die along with *Butler*.

Pace ordered the engine room to increase to flank speed and, at the same time, directed full left rudder. Suddenly, three enemy aircraft were sighted on the starboard beam and another flight of four on the starboard quarter, four and six miles distant respectively. The four split into two groups of two each and flew off in the direction of Okinawa. The three, however, squared off for a coordinated attack on *Butler*. One circled out of the formation and orbited astern of the DE. When deep on the port quarter, he raced in toward the ship.

"Commence Fire!" The two 5" guns began slamming away at the oncoming *kamikaze*. It suddenly burst into flame and dropped into the sea!

Pace then directed the gunnery officer to shift fire to the two remaining planes on the starboard beam. The gun crews roared in exuberance as a 5" direct hit blew one plane to bits in mid-air some 4500 yards off!

The pilot of the third plane, possibly an observer, flew off in the direction of Izeru Island. While the main battery was firing away at planes no. 2 and 3, a fighter plane broke out of the blue and screamed in on the port quarter where it was promptly taken under fire by the automatic weapons, 40mm and 20mm guns. The plane took repeated hits and broke into a white hot fireball. Blazing wildly and out of control, the aircraft passed 200 yards astern, banked in a wide circle toward the starboard bow, and splashed 1000 yards from the DE!

Three down for *Butler* without a scratch! Captain Pace picked up the interior communication microphone and thanked all hands for a great job, excellent shooting, splendid teamwork. The gun crews drank it all up, but they didn't have much time to enjoy the pat on the back. Only four minutes after opening fire on the above planes, two enemy aircraft were sighted approaching from the direction of Motobu Peninsula. Once again, the familiar command from gunnery control, "All guns, Main battery, 40 millimeter, 20 millimeter. Action port. Range—. Bearing—. Commence fire!"

Pace maneuvered to place both planes on the port beam so as to give all guns that could bear as wide a field of fire as possible. One plane banked slightly and then went into a straight glide in an obvious attempt to crash the bridge. He was hit repeatedly by automatic fire. His landing gear was shot away, but he kept closing. This blazing incendiary looked sure to pile right into the bridge, and he did indeed pass so closely overhead that he knocked over and demolished both air search and surface search radar antennae. Many a throat lump was cleared and many a bead of perspiration was wiped away as the plane smashed into the sea close aboard on the starboard beam!

It takes a little imagination to think of yourself as a 20mm gunner on a wing of the flying bridge and seeing this plane coming in directly at you, getting bigger and bigger, showing more and more detail, the engine roar getting louder and louder. The veins in your neck and arms become distended. Beads of sweat pop out on your forehead. The adrenaline flows. Something within you says, "Get the hell out of here before he hits." But you don't. Discipline, common sense, and previous intensive drill put you through the motions, almost like a robot. You have the plane in your sights, and your hand closes on the firing key automatically.

The second aircraft had been maneuvering with the *Butler*, holding onto the port quarter, and began an approach almost simultaneously with the first. Hit repeatedly by automatic fire, the Jap broke off his approach at no more than 200 yards, banked sharply but failed to regain control. He crashed into the sea with a violent explosion about 500 yards on the port quarter!

Butler had killed five *kamikazes* in six minutes! The gun crews were exulting and slapping each other on the back. One thing was for sure, if *Butler* were to be sunk, it would be the most expensive sinking the Emperor would chalk up that day. But there wasn't too much time to celebrate, only three minutes.

1840. Two enemy planes were sighted approaching on the port quarter from the direction of Mobotu Peninsula.

As *Butler* opened fire with both main and automatic batteries, Pace maneuvered to put one aircraft broad on the port beam. The two planes split, the first diving for the bridge and the second remaining off the port quarter. This was the sixth attack in 10 minutes. Trainers and pointers at gun stations licked parched lips, wiped stinging sweat from their eyes and closed fingers on the firing keys.

The first plane was rocked by repeated hits from the 40mm and 20mm guns. It went out of control and roared in over the ship so low it cut the radio antenna as it passed and crashed close aboard on the starboard bow with a frightful explosion, showering the ship with water, debris, and scraps of the pilot's clothing!

The second plane had started to run on the port quarter, in coordination with the first plane but turned away at a range of 800 yards after receiving several hits from the automatic weapons. The aircraft was smoking and losing altitude. Nobody saw the conclusion of that action because, as the skipper noted in his log: "Attention was diverted to new targets." The gunnery officer ordered commence fire with the 5"main battery on two enemy aircraft approaching the starboard bow about four miles off. One minute later, however, the cease fire order was given to avoid the possibility of damaging a flight of Corsairs about to pounce on the Japs.

1845. The Task Group Commander ordered *Butler* back to Hagushi Anchorage for repair of lost radar and radio antenna.

Preparation for combat required many hours of drill, drill and more drill, more hours of target practice followed by more hours of critique. When action finally did come, it arrived like a streak of lightning and departed in the same manner. A very few minutes could decide the fate of the crew, a fighting ship and, in a more remote sense, the security of the Task Force. In the case of this DE, a whole lifetime had been lived in a space of 13 minutes. Within that time frame, *Butler* had been attacked by nine *kamikazes*. Of these, five radial type fighters (four Zekes and one Oscar) were definitely destroyed and one Zeke was damaged and quite possibly destroyed. The cost, aside from three antennae and ammunition, consisted of three enlisted casualties, all treated on board and restored to duty.

The day Admiral Blandy stepped aboard *John C. Butler* with bosun's pipe shrilling and officers and men at stiff attention, he had a dual job to perform. The Admiral talked from his heart to the ship's company that bright, sunny day. He represented on the quarterdeck the President of the United States who desired that *Butler* be awarded the Presidential Unit Citation: "For extraordinary heroism in action against powerful units of the Japanese Fleet off Samar."

Second, the Admiral had to take up the matter of 20 May 1945. He awarded one silver star and five bronze stars for valor in the air action off Iwo Shima, Okinawa.

John C. Butler continued escorting and screening of battle forces blasting at Japanese positions and amphibious assaults to the end of the war when she returned to the United States.

OBERRENDER

The Fury of the Kamikaze

On 1 August 1944, *Oberrender (DE-344)* was assigned to protect convoys plying between Pearl Harbor and Eniwetok. Later, she escorted Rear Admiral Sprague's "jeep" carriers to the Philippines for the invasion of Leyte. A brief trip to Morotai, however, caused her to miss the epic Battle off Samar. This happenstance was only her first brush with fate. The second occurred three months later.

The ship was in Seeadler Harbor, Manus, on 10 November 1944, anchored only 1100 yards from *Mount Hood (AE-11)* when that ammunition ship blew up. The force was so horrendous that flying debris and live ammunition were scattered almost over the entire anchorage. As a result, *Oberrender* sustained superstructure damage and was forced to spend the remainder of the month at Manus for repairs.

As United States forces pushed closer to the Japanese home islands, *Oberrender* moved along in the van. Through April and into May 1945, Okinawa was the focus of attention, and a third brush with fate would not pass this vessel lightly by.

The Task Group arrived in the Okinawa area on 17 April and was then dissolved. *Oberrender* reported to the Commander Task Group 51.5. Thereafter, she occupied a number of stations around the operating area with *McClelland (DE-750)*. Lieutenant Commander Samuel Spencer, commanding officer of *Oberrender*, was screen commander. On 5 May, fire was opened with her 5" battery on an enemy plane at long range but without scoring hits.

On 6 May, all ships in the Task Group were at GQ because of air alerts during the mid and morning watches and again at sundown, but no enemy planes were sighted until the evening of 9 May. That day, however, brought much to report. *Oberrender* went to battle stations as enemy planes were reported over the inter-fighter director circuit.

A plane was reported by the *Oberrender* CIC, range 34 miles, sending her to full speed. Several more reports on the plane indicated its distance reduced to 17 miles, altitude 22,000 feet. This DE was further advised over the same circuit that the combat air patrol (CAP) had been called off from pursuit of the plane because it was so high. Nonetheless, *Oberrender* remained at GQ.

Concurrently with this message, *Oberrender* recorded the plane on her air search radar on the same bearing but down to a range of only 16 miles. Very shortly, her CIC plotted it at five miles. The skipper called for flank speed. The plane was picked up visually at 9000 yards, altitude 18,000 feet, position angle 35 degrees. The atmosphere was very clear, although visibility was impeded by the sun near the horizon as the attacker approached out of the west.

About this time, *Oberrender* sighted the plane as it started a power dive at a 35 degree angle of descent. The ship was put in a hard left turn and fire was opened with both 5" guns. The 40mm guns commenced fire at a range of 4000 yards; one shell hit the plane's engine while others continually found their mark. Five 20mm guns opened fire at about 1500 yards just after a 5" inch burst had loosened the port wing, causing it to flap like a wounded duck. As the plane closed in, the ship had swung around sufficiently far in its turn to bring the *kamikaze* well back on the starboard quarter, almost dead aft.

The wing came off at about 250 yards, causing the plane to swerve to the right but not quite enough to miss the ship completely. It was on fire and smoking badly for the last 2300 yards. The 20mm guns number 25 and 27 fired to the end, scoring hits until the plane struck a glancing blow on the platform of gun 25. The port wing, which was floating clear of the plane, hit the after fire room uptake just below the stack, doing slight harm. The plane itself did little damage other than to demolish the number 25 gun bucket.

A 500 pound delayed-action bomb went through the main deck a few inches inside the starboard gunwale. The bomb went off in the forward fire room, compartment B-1, causing very heavy damage in the midships area, including the hull, deck, and superstructure. The force of the explosion lifted the deck about four feet, buckling all the deck longitudinals and forcing the superstructure upward. The hull plating and frames on the starboard side were torn loose from the deck and forced outward. There was a large hole about 10 X 25 feet in one compartment, starboard side below the water line. Examination by a diver afterward showed that the keel had been wrinkled for 25 feet under that compartment. The forward and after bulkheads of that compartment blew out, flooding two adjacent compartments. Three fuel oil tanks forward were ruptured, and another compartment was flooded with fuel oil and water. The shock of the explosion snapped all headstays and backstays on the mast, catapulting the air search radar antenna overboard. The motor whaleboat was blown into the water and sank.

To summarize, the ship was almost broken in two. The longitudinal strength of the hull was very seriously weakened in that area. All the longitudinal structural members were buckled.

Personnel casualties were very heavy. Three were killed in action. Five were missing and presumed dead since no other ships in the area reported rescuing crew members. Thirty-seven men were classified with various degrees of wounds. *PCE(R)-855* came alongside and removed twenty-two serious personnel casualties for further transfer to two hospital ships and two transports. Fifteen were retained for treatment on board.

The number of casualties was extraordinary but could have been worse were it not for her forehanded captain. His action report explains:

> "Where a large number of persons are injured at a single stroke, as was the case here, the normal pharmacist complement is unequal to the task. Moreover, the services of repair party personnel are urgently needed for damage control, fire fighting, etc. and are not available to assist the phar-

macist mates. With this possibility in mind, we previously developed a group of about six men with considerable first aid experience, gave them battle stations which were not of a vital nature and trained them to render first aid if needed. Also, we emphasized first aid for all hands in our training program. Both efforts paid dividends. The specially trained group turned to throughout the ship and was assisted by men who could be spared from other stations, leaving the repair parties substantially intact to save the ship."

The ocean going tug *Tekesta (ATG-93)* passed a towline to the incapacitated DE and towed her into Kerama Retto. In spite of the crash, the performance of ordnance equipment was good. The ship had opened fire on two occasions during the period covered by her picket station assignment, once with the 5" battery on 4 May and with all calibers on 9 May. Fire discipline and recognition were believed to have been above average.

Oberrender was beyond repair. She was decommissioned on 11 July 1945, stripped of all remaining worthwhile equipment, and her hulk was sunk by gunfire the following November.

WILLIAM C. COLE

Telling It the Way It Was

Seaman J.B. Curry on the *William C. Cole (DE-641)* had a salty and realistic recollection of his ship from the earliest days to the end:

"Life aboard *Cole* proved to be interesting and exciting. We were a young, green crew with little experience and much to learn. Our first trip outside the Golden Gate Bridge, San Francisco, was a mess. Seasick sailors, including new officers, were incapacitated. Our captain, Lieutenant Clay Harrold, questioned if there were enough able bodied sailors to get us back inside the Gate.

At Pearl Harbor, *Cole* drilled for target practice, maneuvers, etc. We made a few mistakes, such as running over our tow line when the target we were pulling flipped over, but things began to come together. Our executive officer, a stern New Englander, expected everyone to be perfect and, above all, to be busy at all times. I sometimes wondered how many tons of paint we applied. We were the freshest looking ship in the fleet."

Cole reported to the Commander Fifth Fleet on 23 February 1945. Until the first week in March, she performed screening duties off the transport staging area, Lunga Point, Guadalcanal, protecting the transports during landing exercises.

On 31 March, *Cole* and *Paul G. Baker (DE-642)* joined ships of *Escort Division 73*, guarding *Transport Squadron 18* en route to Okinawa. Although taciturn in their wardroom discussions, the officers had few illusions about the hazards of the forthcoming operation. The enlisted personnel, fed with a combination of rumor and fact, also had trepidations for the future. Seaman Curry remembers:

"Early one morning, we left the Caroline Islands on convoy duty. Our destination was a mystery at the time. Every morning, we could look out over the horizon and see that other ships had joined us. We soon learned by radio where we were headed. 'Tokyo Rose' knew our ships by name and number. She informed us that we were on a suicide mission and should turn back before it was too late. She said there would be PT boats loaded with explosives to ram us and also planes to dive on us. The scuttlebutt aboard *Cole* was too much .Are our leaders crazy? Why don't we turn around, etc.?"

The ships made their final approaches through the western islands off Okinawa and arrived at the beachhead by midday. Light enemy aircraft activity greeted the initial forces activity that would, in time, become heavy and nearly ceaseless. Curry noted:

"Landing Day on Okinawa seemed to be too easy. The marines and army had little initial resistance. They were aided by firepower from heavy ships. Of course, the lack of early engagement was part of a trap the enemy hoped to spring on our forces.

Things began to warm up, air raids every night. We prayed for darkness. There were nights when the sky was so bright with antiaircraft fire and burning of planes and ships that you could read a book topside while at GQ. We were soon on picket duty at night, watching for the PT boats that Tokyo Rose had mentioned. Everyone in the vicinity was warned to post double guards because of rumors that Jap suicide swimmers with explosives were making their way out to the ships and climbing the anchor chains."

Between 1 and 4 April, the ship went to GQ numerous times during the many air raid alerts. *Cole* assisted in downing two planes. Between 5 April and 17 May, in company with *Bunch (APD-79)*, *Richard W. Suesens (DE-342)*, *Charles Lawrence (APD-37)* and *Chase (APD-54)*, she made two round trips to Ulithi, escorting transport divisions, the battleship *West Virginia (BB-48)* and the cruiser *Tuscaloosa (CA-37)*. *Cole* headed back to Okinawa, arriving on 17 May.

While screening on station, *Cole* observed moderate enemy air action from 19 to 23 May but, on the 24th, she came under attack. Between early morning on that day until dawn on the 25th, the ship destroyed two enemy aircraft. First, an Oscar attempted a suicide run while *Cole* was off Ie Shima and crashed within a few feet of her starboard beam! The plane passed so close to the ship that one of its wingtips bent a "spoon" on a tube of the torpedo mount. The second plane, a Tony, came in from the starboard side and was taken under heavy fire from the ship's 40mm and 20mm guns. This attacker overshot the DE and splashed 100 yards beyond its target! Seaman Curry says he never could forget the action:

"We were called to battle stations early that morning. Several ships near us had already taken hits from *kamikaze* planes. By the time I reached my station on the bridge, an LST on our port side had been hit. Ammunition was exploding, a fire raged on board and in the water, requiring us to keep our distance. When I looked up into the sky, there were at least six more planes circling like buzzards as though they were trying to decide who should be next. Many of the crew from the LST were seriously injured and were afloat in their life jackets near by. From my position on the bridge, I had an uninterrupted view of the awful drama unfolding before my eyes. Captain Harrold gave orders to help get the wounded aboard *Cole*. With the fires and ammunition exploding on the LST, this was like hell on earth.

In the meantime, the *kamikazes* above us had decided on a target, us. We had one coming from forward and also one aft. I tried to keep an eye on both. When it looked like we were sure to be hit, some of our crew jumped over the side. We were a lucky ship. The plane forward missed us, and one of our gunner's mates who stuck by his gun got the one back aft. That plane exploded a few yards from us. Many fragments or pieces landed on *Cole*. When the raid was over, there was a mad rush for souvenirs. I carried one piece of aluminum for years with a stamped marking that read, 'Made by U.S. Aluminum Co'. Much of the plexiglass blown onto the deck from the plane was later used to make jewelry as Christmas presents for wives and girl friends. We are still looking for that brave little gunner's mate who saved our lives. We have had three ship reunions and would like very much to make some contact with him or his family to honor him. His name is P.E. Mullin. Everyone called him Moon Mullin (a popular comic strip at that time).

I watched the second plane explode just as it was about to hit us. I also watched the Jap pilot float slowly in the water as his chute opened; he looked like a limp rag doll. I was surprised that he had a parachute as I had always thought that *kamikazes* did not carry life-saving equipment.

There was a comical side to this event. The Jap pilot landed very near our first class signalman who had jumped over the side. Our Lieutenant J.A. McGee had a .45 sidearm and was set on making sure the pilot was dead. Our first class signalman had to yell real loud to let him know that the shots were too near him.

I left my GQ station to go below deck and help pick up wounded from the LST. The neck chain that held my dog tag broke, and I stuffed it quickly into my back pocket. That pocket got caught in a hatch latch was ripped open and my tag fell onto the deck. The person behind me thought it belonged to the injured sailor I was carrying. As we set our patients down in the after head, he placed my tag on the sailor I brought in. We rendezvoused with a hospital ship in the middle of night to transfer our wounded. The following morning, our first class yeoman made a sudden stop as he passed me in the chow line. He rushed to his office for his clip board. 'J.B. I logged you off this ship last night wounded in action.' Several attempts were made to radio the hospital ship. Captain Harrold called me to his office and told me to write letters to my wife and other kin to disregard any message they might receive because *Cole* was unable to make radio contact.

We had to be the luckiest ship in the fleet. The plane approaching us on the bow must have had our Sky Pilot in the cockpit with the *kamikaze* pilot. He had to be an expert to miss us at that point. You had to be aboard *Cole* to enjoy all the scuttlebutt after that morning. Prior to the action, a number of our crew had tried to conduct church services on the fantail. We had no chaplain. There was very poor attendance at that time, but after the battle experience we had standing room only."

On 30 May, *Cole* loaded ammunition at Kerama Retto to replenish her magazines before weighing anchor for Saipan on the next day with a convoy of merchantmen. Seaman Curry remembers a sidelight:

> "After Okinawa, we operated from Saipan, covering the sea to rescue any downed B-29 personnel flying to and from Saipan to bomb Japan. We witnessed many of them on their return, wondering how they made it back. Some planes had large holes and chunks of tail sections missing. We had been so busy that we couldn't spare the time to take on stores. Our food supply was getting very low. We were awakened early one morning to a very strange signal or whistle from the boatswain's mate. Our skipper got on the mike and yelled, 'Fish Call'. They had spotted a school of tuna. We fired a depth charge from a 'K' gun, and the surface became white with fresh fish. What a pleasure — fresh fish for several days!"

The remainder of the war was spent in convoys among various islands. Following training exercises with submarines, antiaircraft firing practices, and a six day availability, the destroyer escort patrolled off Tinian until relieved on 17 August, two days after Japan capitulated, ending the long Pacific war.

In closing this narrative, the author would like to pay a special tribute to Mr. Curry or "J.B.," as he likes to be known. Both the skipper's action report and war diary covering the Okinawa actions are missing from the files at the Navy Historical Bureau in Washington. This history would have been a grade less than scant were it not for his efforts. His final remarks:

> "*William C. Cole* had its first reunion last year in Saint Louis, Missouri, Another one is planned in February of this year (1994) in Nashville, Tennessee.
>
> We found out many things about *Cole* after 50 years. The reunion brought all sections of the ship together with interesting sea stories from each section. We were a mixed group from all parts of the U.S. There were times when our southern boys would get into heated discussions with our yankees regarding the Civil War. Even when we were at General Quarters, those with headsets would get conversations going.
>
> We were a good ship. Everyone did his job well, and I am sure that the experience of serving aboard *William C. Cole* enriched all our lives in many ways.
>
> NOTE – Mr. Andrews – I am sorry I do not type, so try and make out my handwriting. Please let me know if I can be of further assistance. Good luck on your book."

Sincerely,
J. B. Curry

WESSON

An Okinawa Day to Remember

19 February 1944. After a long passage from the Canal Zone

to Kwajalein Atoll with many stops in between, in company with *Riddle (DE-185)*, *Wesson (DE-184)* was assigned to patrol the harbor entrance. Three days later, she unexpectedly tasted her first action when she accosted and sank a Japanese cutter, killing six of the enemy and taking five prisoners. Succeeding months saw this DE in screening activities among Majuro, Eniwetok, Manus and the Palaus.

On 14 September, *Wesson* effected a rendezvous with carriers off the Palau Islands. During flight operations, she rescued three airmen whose plane had crashed upon launching. Early October saw her underway in a task unit centered around five escort carriers in the Philippine Sea. On 24 October, she witnessed American forces storming ashore on Leyte, marking the return to the Philippines.

In the first week of February 1945, *Wesson* departed from the Marianas to support the invasion of Iwo Jima. On 16 February, as the carriers began air strikes against the island, the DE operated in the screen, protecting the carriers for 10 days. After returning to Ulithi, she got underway to escort Task Force 54 to Okinawa. Arriving off Kerama Retto on 25 March, the DE took a station in the transport screen. The next day, *Wesson* and *Barton (DD-599)* helped to protect the battleships *Tennessee (BB-43)* and *Nevada (BB-36)* and the cruisers, *St. Louis (CL-49)* and *Wichita (CA-45)* while they shelled enemy emplacements on Southern Okinawa.

28 March. The formation came under attack by Japanese planes, spotted by *Wesson's* lookouts at a distance of five miles. She opened fire at the first of three raiders at 2000 yards, altitude 800 feet. Tracers were seen disappearing into the fuselage just above the wing. Flames sprouted from the aircraft, enveloping it in a ball of fire as it crashed astern of the screen! Moving pictures of this action were forwarded to Intelligence Operations by the DE's captain, Lieutenant Commander Henry Sears. Unfortunately, they never could be relocated.

30 March, *Wesson* proceeded to the west of Zampa Misaki, destroying four mines by gunfire while en route.

1 March. In the early hours, the enemy struck with a sizeable formation of planes, and the action continued incessantly until dawn. In the late afternoon, there were so many enemy planes darting in and out of clouds that the ship maneuvered continuously in tight turns of up to 180 degrees; it became virtually impossible for the skipper to submit a sketch of his track when filing his action report later on. Scattered clouds provided the *kamikazes* with extremely effective cover, preventing sufficient tracking to obtain a good director solution. Four Vals were sighted in *Wesson's* vicinity. One plane attacked her but was repulsed by repeated fire. Quoting the skipper:

> "When the plane was first picked up, radical maneuvers were initiated. At the time of firing, we were just completing a hard right turn. When the plane was taken under fire by us, it had started a dive on this ship but was turned back by close 3" proximity bursts and 40mm fire. It then attempted to crash a destroyer on our port side but missed and splashed nearby!"

7 April. *Wesson* relieved *Sterett (DD-407)* north of Ie Shima and the Motobu Peninsula and began screening landing craft *LCI-452* and *LCI-558*. At 0345, the destroyer escort fought off a small enemy air attack which lasted until dawn. Six hours later, *Wesson* opened fire on four enemy planes. From the captain's diary:

> "0917. Three planes approached undetected from behind land masses and clouds and crossed the ship's bow 3000 yards ahead, altitude 2000 feet. Shortly afterward, a single plane was sighted broad on the starboard beam at close range, racing toward *Wesson*. Three 20mm guns emptied their magazines at the plane, scoring hits on the engine and the fuselage; the tail surfaces were entirely destroyed. Nonetheless, it crashed into the ship at the torpedo tubes."

Electrician's Mate Second Class Vergle E. Williams of Silver City, North Carolina, related a nightmare come true:

> "The *Wesson* had seven battle stars, and I was on board for all of them, Okinawa being the last one. My station was in the propulsion room on the port shaft. I had just come off watch. We had been to battle stations so much that I put my hammock on the starboard side in front of the degaussing board, closer to my GQ station than my usual spot. I woke up to the sound of the 40mm and 20mm guns going off, then the GQ bell.
>
> I hit the deck running and, almost at the same time, the ship was crashed. I ran to the starboard hatch to go up to my GQ station. Standing at the bottom of the ladder with my hands on the rail, I looked up to see a bloody shipmate hanging onto the hatch cover and hollering for help! He toppled over on the cover, closing the hatch and landing on top! I could not get out!
>
> As I went by my station to go to the port side hatch, I saw my watch relief, Paul Lee, who was badly hit. The shaft had stopped; the motors were on fire! I closed down the propulsion board, unconscious reflex I guess. There was fire and water everywhere! I got to the outside hatch; it was warped shut from the crash. Paul and I were trapped! We worked on the fire and plugged what holes we could see in the ship's bottom as best we could until the water ran us back to the upper deck. We thought she was going down! We could not get out! A nauseating situation!
>
> Our engineer officer, Lieutenant M. Chetrovich managed to open the hatch and came down to check on us. That was my first sigh of relief; we could get out! The Jap had hit on the torpedo tubes over our heads. The ship had gone down until the deck was awash!
>
> I retrieved my hammock later, it had a shrapnel hole the size of a softball about where my chest had been, lucky me for jumping up so fast. I feel like I've been on credit ever since!"

Five men died instantly, one was missing, and twenty-five were wounded, two of whom died later. *Wesson* lost and regained power intermittently and was fighting a fire on the boat deck and flooding in the engineering spaces. All power was lost aft, propulsion was lost on the port shaft, and the rudder was jammed full right. *Lang (DD-399)* came alongside and supplied a submersible pump and gasoline, then took *Wesson* under tow. The tow line parted, and *Wesson* steamed to Kerama Retto on one shaft with *Lang* screening ahead.

Despite continuous enemy air attacks, the destroyer escort completed emergency repairs on 10 April. The next day, she got underway for San Francisco via Saipan. From 17 May to 25 June, she received an overhaul while her battle damage was being repaired.

The DE returned to the Philippines about the same time that Japan surrendered and conducted various occupation and post-war duties. Ordered back to the United States, she arrived at San Diego on 6 December 1945 and again transited the Panama Canal en route to Charleston, South Carolina, the end of her odyssey.

WILLMARTH

A Veteran of Many Battles

Willmarth (DE-638) sortied from Humboldt Bay, Hollandia, on 7 November 1944 to screen Task Group 78.14, comprising *HMS Ariadne*, sixteen assorted landing craft and two PCs, destination Morotai. As the convoy neared its objective in late afternoon, the DE's lookouts observed antiaircraft fire in the distance. Two bogies passed within four miles of the convoy, but *Willmarth* did not fire because she carried the only reliable air warning radar in the entire convoy. Opening fire would have exposed the small vessels to air attacks. On 11 November, the DE anchored off the southern coast of Morotai, near *Ariadne*, while the convoy proceeded elsewhere on the island to load for the impending invasion of Mapia and Asia Islands. The mission of the assault group was to establish weather and LORAN stations.

Before dawn on 13 November, *Willmarth*, in company with *Shaw (DD-373)*, *Caldwell (DD-605)* and *PC-1122* bombarded the southern part of the island prior to the landings but did not provoke return fire from the beach. After a half-hour of firing, *HMS Ariadne* signalled that "H" hour would be 0630.

Willmarth remained at her bombardment station for the rest of the morning, ceasing fire as the first assault wave splashed toward the beachhead. The accompanying landing craft laid their own barrage close to the landing area. By noon, the island was in American hands. When surrounded, the remaining garrison, only 12 to 14 Japanese soldiers, committed suicide.

Meanwhile, since she was no longer needed for bombardment, *Willmarth* patrolled the invasion beach and came across canoes full of natives. One native, speaking good English, told *Willmarth* that the remainder of the Japanese garrison, about 170 men, had waded across the reef to Bras Island the previous night, thus accounting for the sparse reception given the invasion forces.

While plans were being laid to go after this remnant on Bras Island, *Willmarth* conducted a patrol around the unloading infantry assault craft and made abortive attempts to free several LCIs, stranded on the reefs by low tides. In the late afternoon of the 15th, the DE succeeded in towing off one craft after about an hour's effort and began operations to free another. However, her efforts were thwarted by the parting of the line and the near approach of darkness.

Five craft were abandoned on the reef when the Task Group headed for Morotai. Underway again on the 18th with the Asia Island occupation force, *Willmarth* and two PCs served as escort for *Adriadne*, four LCMs, four LCIs, and four LCI(G)s (LCIs with assault weapons). Four hundred troops were embarked in the assault craft.

Three-fourths of a mile off Igi Island, *Willmarth*, *Adriadne*, and *PC-1122* conducted shore bombardment before dawn on the 19th. Troops splashed ashore from landing craft eight minutes after the bombardment ceased and met no opposition. An unfortunate result of the shore bombardment was that two natives were wounded and one killed. The Japanese had evacuated the island on the previous evening in the face of imminent invasion.

Willmarth subsequently screened the movement of the convoy to the Mapia Islands, where the landing craft loaded troops and unloaded shore personnel and supplies. When the loading was completed on 20 November, the convoy shifted to Asia Island where the destroyer escort screened the landing craft as they embarked more troops on the 21st. *Willmarth* continued screening until arriving in the southern anchorage near the navy base at Morotai at noon on 22 November where she witnessed a bold enemy night air raid on airfield installations despite antiaircraft fire and searchlights.

While the rest of the task group departed from Morotai on the 23rd, *Willmarth* remained behind as *LSM-205* and *LSM-314* loaded equipment for the Asia and Mapia Island forces. She then escorted those craft to Hollandia where they delivered their cargo. Over the next three days, *Willmarth* escorted the same two landing craft on their appointed rounds, dropping off supplies at Asia and Mapia Islands. The first arrival of the little convoy at Mapia on the 26th almost went unnoticed. *Willmarth* experienced great difficulty in contacting anyone on shore. The skipper noted, "We finally succeeded in rousing someone by blowing our siren and whistle together."

A jeep soon appeared on the beach, its occupants using the headlights to signal. Heavier swells than at Asia Island made unloading through the surf difficult. One of the LSMs was holed several times by scraping on the jagged coral heads of the reef. When unloading was completed at 1130, the diminutive convoy headed for Hollandia. *Willmarth* spent the next three months operating on local escort missions among Manus, Ulithi, Hollandia, and the Palaus.

4 March 1945. *Willmarth* reported to the Commander Fifth Fleet and got underway on the 21st to screen the sortie of the pre-invasion bombardment group, TF 54, as it headed for Okinawa.

Willmarth operated with fire support units built around the battleship *Colorado (BB-45)* in designated fire support areas off Okinawa. The destroyer escort screened *Colorado* on 26 March as the battleship delivered gunfire support for the troops ashore. Over the next two days, the DE screened other fire support units and escorted them to night retirement areas.

1 April. *Willmarth* was steaming in a circular screen around a night retirement group based on the battleship *Idaho (BB-42)* when several enemy planes flew near the convoy. Screening destroyers fired upon the intruders who probably did not come to attack the allied force but merely to keep it awake and to permit it as little rest as possible.

Willmarth was detached from this duty to provide a screen for the battleship *Arkansas (BB-33)*. The DE patrolled to seaward as the BB worked inshore to open fire on Japanese positions holding up the American advance near Naha airport. About six hours after starting the patrol, Japanese shore battery guns boomed out salvoes at *Arkansas*.

The battleship's main battery quickly trained 'round to open counter-battery fire. *Willmarth* was located one mile to seaward of the battleship. A Japanese shell hurtled over the DE's bridge, heard by all men nearby as it splashed 150 yards beyond the ship. With one boiler inoperative while repairing a leaking gasket, the DE was hampered in getting away, but she headed seaward at her best speed. Soon, another shell landed only 15 yards beyond her starboard quarter. While increasing the range, *Willmarth* turned toward each splash, "chasing salvos," thus avoiding a straddle from the Japanese guns. *Arkansas*, by this time beyond range of the Nipponese guns, ceased fire; *Willmarth* soon emerged from the enemy battery's zone of fire and proceeded to sea unscathed.

Willmarth screened a station until 6 April, when she returned to Kerama Retto with an appendicitis patient on board for medical treatment. Several bogies flew near the ship while she steamed to the fleet anchorage, and one was downed by a nearby vessel.

1525. While still three miles north of Kerama Retto, *Willmarth* spotted three Val dive bombers. One peeled off and maneuvered in an attempt to crash the ship. Bracketed by flak, the Val bore in. Heavy 3" and 1.1" fire peppered the plane as it dodged in and out of the broken clouds. Seven 3" bursts rocked the aircraft as it made its deadly approach. Lookouts noted a wisp of smoke trailing from the suicider's port wing as the pilot went into his dive. The 20mm battery opened up when the plane's range dropped to 2000 yards and, at 800 yards, the Oerlikons seemed to have their effect. Pieces of the Val's wing began flying off in the slipstream and six feet of the port wing broke away. The Val spun into the sea 20 yards off the ship's port side, slightly abaft the beam!

Willmarth entered Kerama Retto in late afternoon and, while preparing to anchor, saw *LST-447* hit by a suicide plane close by. Flames had engulfed the entire midships section of the stricken landing ship, and explosions tore holes in her side. Jagged edges in turn ripped gashes in *Willmarth's* hull at the waterline. One hole, unfortunately, opened up one of the destroyer escort's fuel tanks, and the oil leaking out made further close operations hazardous.

Willmarth stood clear while dense smoke from the burning LST further complicated fire fighting. Eventually, the destroyer escort picked up the ship's survivors and transferred them to the attack transport *Crescent City (APA-21)*. While steaming to the ship's anchorage in the harbor, she took an enemy plane under fire as it approached. Fire from all ships present in the harbor knocked it down.

Willmarth anchored and patched the hole in her side. On 10 April, the destroyer escort departed from the Okinawa area, bound for Guam in a screen for 12 transports. Boiler trouble kept *Willmarth* in Guam the entire month of May and most of June.

Underway again on 3 July, *Willmarth* stood out of Ulithi lagoon, screening the logistics force of the Third Fleet which would provide the needed supplies for Admiral William F. Halsey's fast carrier task forces as it pounded the Japanese homeland. She picked up the crew of a downed Avenger on 20 July; two swimmers from the DE helped to get the airmen on board. However, one of the crewmen subsequently died.

Willmarth was at sea when the atomic bombs were dropped upon Hiroshima and Nagasaki on 6 and 9 August respectively and when Japan surrendered on the 15th.

WILLIAM SEIVERLING

A Very Able Ship of War

On 24 November 1944, *William Seiverling (DE-441)* sailed from Pearl Harbor to Ulithi in company with a hunter-killer group built around the carrier *Tulagi (CVE-72)*. For the next three months, she operated from Ulithi with the HUK Group, keeping the sea lanes in the Central Pacific clear of Japanese submarines. On 28 December, the *Tulagi* Group departed for Luzon to support the Lingayen landings, scheduled for the second week in January 1945.

En route, enemy air attacks were frequent, but *Seiverling* didn't see action until she arrived off Lingayen Gulf. On 7 January, her guns warded off a single, apparently desultory attacker. She patrolled off Lingayen for 10 days, then headed back to Ulithi.

19 February. *Seiverling* reported to the Fifth Fleet, heading for Iwo Jima to support the battle then in progress. For about a month, she conducted antisubmarine patrols of the sea lanes between the Marianas and Iwo Jima, then returned to Ulithi.

21 March. She got underway to join the assault on Okinawa. Her first mission in support of the campaign was antisubmarine protection for escort carriers whose planes were providing close air support for the infantry. In April she began another series of antisubmarine patrols between Okinawa and Ulithi with the same *Tulagi* Hunter Killer Group.

Seiverling arrived at Kerama Retto on the morning of 20 May and, for the next eight days, was assigned to patrol duty in the various screens about Okinawa. It was during this period that the ship came under enemy air attack on four occasions.

During the next four days *Seiverling* interchanged stations variously with *Tisdale (DE-33)*, *Talbot (DD-390)*, and *Tattnall (APD-19)*. Hostile planes were in the vicinity daily and their attacks on this ship took place during the exceptionally heavy air raids suffered in that area between 24 and 26 May.

1925 on 24 May. All hands to General Quarters. Many enemy planes were nearby. Numerous attacks were visible on Ie Shima and on ships in the vicinity. All vessels in the area were at GQ continuously throughout the night as bogies were tracked on radar scopes. Several passed directly overhead but were not visible to lookouts.

0245 on 25 May. An enemy plane was tracked by both radars, heading directly at *Seiverling* and flying very low. It passed directly over her stern from port to starboard and dropped a flare, identifying itself in the bright light as a Nell. Speed was increased to flank as the skipper, Lieutenant Commander Charles F. Adams Jr., commenced radical maneuvers, and all guns that could bear opened up on the target. The flare only lasted about a minute, and so did the plane. It splashed about 2000 yards on *Seiverling*'s starboard beam!

0305. The DE remained at flank speed to avoid a second plane diving at the ship and she again opened fire on the *kamikaze*. One minute later, the pilot joined his comrade by splashing 200 yards on the starboard beam with explosions and flames!

0327. She opened fire momentarily on a plane flying parallel to her course, about 3000 yards on the starboard beam. However, no results were apparent. Twenty-six minutes later, *Seiverling* commenced fire on a plane overhead with the same negative results. The air attacks subsided about 40 minutes later. At first light, *Seiverling* resumed her regular patrol. No sooner had she settled into that comfortable routine when she was ordered to proceed at once to assume patrol of another station.

0757. Radar indicated approaching enemy planes in large raids. The weather was poor, heavily overcast and raining intermittently. *Seiverling* joined company with *Bates (APD-47)* in the same station, maintaining a distance of 1000 yards from each other for mutual support. At 0910, several planes began orbiting the ships while out of visual range, varying from 1000 to 4000 yards. The mind's eye can perceive men standing to their guns, peering intensely and anxiously into the murky sky and awaiting the sudden roar of a plane with a suicide-bent pilot literally flying into their faces.

0920. After tracking planes on the SL radar, a plane was sighted diving directly at *Seiverling*. Once again, the skipper maneuvered the ship at high speed to unmask as many guns as possible. Fire was opened immediately with almost the entire battery at a range of 2500 yards. *Bates* also fired and, after twisting and weaving, the plane, a Hamp, passed on *Seiverling*'s port side, disappeared in the mist, then circled back and splashed in flames about one mile from the DE! A second Hamp had been tracked on the SL radar for some time and came into view through the rain at about 4000 yards, a very few minutes after the first Hamp had splashed. Both ships opened fire immediately. Appearing to be undecided about his target, and in the face of heavy fire, The pilot turned away at about 1500 yards and retired after receiving some damage from gun fire.

For a brief interval, all local bogies disappeared from the radar scope, but the crew was kept at battle stations as *Seiverling* continued her patrol in company with *Bates*. Rain continued sporadically with visibility slightly improved. Enemy planes were reported to be in the vicinity. *Seiverling*'s CIC detected several nearby on her radar.

1118. Fifteen seconds after radar warning, a Val was tracked on the DE's port bow and sighted at about 4000 yards in a dive directly at *Seiverling*. The DE opened fire immediately with all available guns. Her action report states that *Bates*, for some unknown reason, failed to open fire on this plane which promptly changed course, diving directly at the APD, still 1000 yards ahead of the DE. Despite hits from *Seiverling*, the *kamikaze* made a perfect landing and crashed into the after end of the deck house of *Bates*! The after area of the ship and the boat deck were enveloped in flames, probably caused by the gasoline carried in the plane.

A minute later, a second Val appeared from the same direction and repeated the dive of the former one. Gunfire from *Seiverling* deflected the plane from herself. However, *Bates* again failed to fire until the plane was a few hundred yards from her bow, at which time about three or four bursts of 40mm were noted, too late to stop the aircraft as it struck the forward face of the bridge. The entire structure burst into a roaring inferno as on the stern. The flames spread rapidly and did not subside until the ship was burned out. *Bates* appeared to go completely out of control immediately upon the crashing of the second plane and eventually went dead in the water. The DE maneuvered to clear her and to take enemy planes under fire.(A narrative of the trials of *Bates* is related in the next chapter.)

1122. A third Val dived toward *Bates'* starboard bow and dropped a bomb close aboard, then passed over to her port side to commence a run on *Seiverling*. This DE had been firing on the plane while it was diving on *Bates* and was able to discourage the pilot with heavy gunfire in his run on *Seiverling*. At the time the bomb was dropped, *Seiverling* had opened the range to *Bates* considerably while maneuvering to unmask her guns on one beam or the other.

The last round fired in the DE's number one 5" gun caused a casualty, injuring three men slightly, temporarily damaging the rammer, and placing the gun out of action. Fortunately, this incident occurred at the end of the attacks. Had it been necessary, fire could have been maintained, albeit at a slower rate, by means of hand ramming which the gun crew was prepared to do.

1130. *Seiverling*, *Gosselin (APD-126)* and *Fleming (DE-32)* closed *Bates*. *Seiverling* screened while *Gosselin* and *Fleming* began the rescue of personnel from the water and from the bow of *Bates*. *Daily (DD-519)* also assisted with the rescue. At 1205, the area was reported clear of hostile planes. The tug *Cree (ATF-84)* arrived to take the savaged vessel in tow. Two hours later, all ships departed except *Seiverling*, *Cree* and the tow. En route to Ie Shima, *Seiverling* attempted to help extinguishing the fires on *Bates* but was unable to get alongside because of excessive yawing of the tow.

At mid-afternoon, *Seiverling* resumed her station patrol. *Herndon (APD-121)* relieved *Rednour (APD-102)* nearby and assumed command of the sector. The weather through the night of 25-26 May continued very bad, but no enemy planes appeared in the area. *Seiverling* was relieved by *Talbot (APD-7)* at 1450. Captain Adams had every reason to be proud of the performance of his ship:

> "Fire discipline was excellent. Although targets closed rapidly from initial short ranges due to poor visibility, fire was not opened until the command was given. Orders to cease fire were obeyed promptly. Communications via sound powered telephones on all gunnery circuits was good; circuit discipline was excellent."

On reaching Hagushi Anchorage, *Seiverling* joined the antiaircraft screen and patrolled until 2018 when orders were received to anchor under cover of smoke in the outer area of the anchorage. Enemy planes maintained their presence all night, and the crew remained at battle stations until 0530 on 28 May. A half hour later, one plane dived on the anchorage as the smoke was lifting but disintegrated in midair by 5" bursts from seven or eight destroyers. *Seiverling* returned to the picket line once again to relieve *Tattnall (APD-19)*. Shortly thereafter, she rejoined *Tulagi* and *Escort Division 30*.

At the end of June, *Seiverling* operated with a logistics support echelon for the Third Fleet carriers during the air strikes on the Japanese home islands. She then joined *Salamaua (CVE-96)* to conduct antisubmarine patrols with *CortDiv 30* until the end of the war. *Seiverling* arrived in Tokyo Bay on 2 September, the day Japan formally surrendered to the Allies.

STERN

We Have Met the Kamikazes. They are Ours.

After calling at Pearl Harbor and the Marshall Islands, *Stern*

(DE-187) reached Ulithi on 12 December 1944 where she was assigned to the logistics echelon of the Third Fleet. *Stern* operated with that fleet for part of December and most of January 1945, supporting operations in the liberation of Luzon. Returning to Ulithi on 8 February, she was attached to the screen of the attack transport group about to invade Iwo Jima. The task force arrived off that island early on the morning of the 19th, and the assault groups began landing under intense, hostile fire. From that morning until 1 March, the escort protected American transports off Iwo Jima.

The DE was routed to the Philippines. On arrival, she was assigned to screen the transports of the Western Islands Attack Group, and sailed for the Ryukyu Islands on 21 March.

On arrival in Kerama Retto, *Stern* performed antisubmarine duty off the islands until 5 April when she was ordered to escort a resupply convoy to Guam. From there, she sailed to Leyte to join another task unit, Okinawa-bound, and was back off Kerama Retto on 18 April. Her tour off Okinawa on picket station was unbroken until July.

13 May. After sundown, three approaching planes were picked up by air search (SA) radar from a distance of eight miles. When the range had closed to 5 1/2 miles, they appeared in the surface search (SL) radar and were tracked until the conclusion of the attack. The bearing remained steady until the planes closed to 2500 yards, the limit of visibility. No reply was received to *Stern*'s IFF challenge. At approximately 4000 yards, plane exhausts came into view; all guns commenced tracking the planes. The *Stern* gunners opened fire at 2000 yards. Immediate hits were scored on the first *kamikaze*. Smoke and flame were seen to belch from the wing and fuselage. Guns continued firing as the aircraft circled, apparently trying to make a suicide attack. Many 20mm hits were apparent from 500 down to 100 yards. In a vertical bank, the plane passed close aboard aft and splashed 50 feet from the DE on the starboard side opposite the davits! It went under without even pausing on the surface; there was no explosion. The gun crews barely had time for a breath of air before plane number two roared in from 1000 yards off the starboard bow. This suicider must have sustained earlier hits because, immediately after *Stern* opened fire, it was seen to nose down and crash into the sea! Nobody knew exactly what happened to the pilot of the third plane. He stayed on course and opened the range until he disappeared from the radar scope at a distance of 13 miles.

18 May. Planes were picked up by SA radar at a range of eight miles during the period between sunset and darkness in a hazy horizon, greatly impairing visibility. At six miles, they appeared on the SL radar scope and were tracked in on that radar until conclusion of the attack. No reply was received in response to the IFF challenge. The planes remained on a steady bearing during the entire approach, and the vessel was turned to a course to bring as many guns as possible to bear on the target. As the enemy came into visual range, at 1600 yards, firing commenced immediately.

The leading plane was hit at once. Smoke and flame poured from its engine. It turned to starboard, climbed to about 500 feet, then nosed down and splashed about 1000 yards from *Stern*!

An aircraft flying on the port wing of the first plane was also hit immediately on opening fire; flame and smoke were seen to be erupting spasmodically. Like suicider number one, it also turned to the ship's starboard side and passed 500 yards beyond the fantail, opening out to 2000 yards. It then turned and made a direct approach from the opposite side. At 500 yards, all 20mm guns able to bear were firing, and several hits were apparent. Large pieces of the plane flew off. The *kamikaze* passed astern of the DE at an altitude of 300 feet in wobble flight, then nosed over, fell off on one wing, and splashed about 75 feet from the ship's starboard side after crossing over the fantail. The plane exploded, and pieces of metal were blown across the ship and into the water!

The third plane was about 800 yards astern of the first two and turned slightly away as firing commenced. It crossed the ship's bow 500 yards ahead under fire from all guns forward. The pilot turned away from the escort and opened out to nine miles, disappearing over southern Okinawa. This plane was visible to 3" gun crews one and two, but it was impossible to train either gun fast enough to stay on the target. Hits on this plane were possible, but no damage was claimed.

The evening of 27 May. *Stern* was on station and steaming in condition I because of enemy aircraft reported in the vicinity. The moon was almost full. However, visibility was limited to about 2000 yards with a low, overcast sky.

An enemy aircraft was located on the SA radar, distance 10 miles and closing this vessel. A friendly aircraft was also recognized close behind. At 7 1/2 miles, both planes were on SL radar and tracked in the Combat Information Center. The two planes remained on a steady bearing until they closed to 2 1/2 miles, at which time the friendly aircraft was plotted as breaking off.

It was a Betty torpedo bomber, picked up visually at 2000 yards. All guns commenced firing at 1500 yards. Several 40mm hits were recorded at 1000 yards, and the *kamikaze* burst into flames about 500 yards from *Stern*. The aircraft passed over the ship just aft of the stack, below mast height, and splashed approximately 50 feet off the port side, flinging debris and bomb fragments in all directions! Material damage to the ship consisted of shrapnel holes in the superstructure on the port side which were repaired by the ship's force. There were no personnel casualties of any consequence.

On 1 July, *Stern* sailed for the west coast of the United States, via Ulithi and Pearl Harbor. After transiting the Panama Canal, she was deactivated at the Navy Base, Norfolk, Virginia.

McCLELLAND

Torpedo and Kamikaze Handled in Stride

Near the end of January 1945, *McClelland (DE-750)* screened a task group bound for Iwo Jima. She arrived off that island on 20 February, the day after the initial landings. On the 21st, The Task Group was attacked by three suicide planes; two scored hits on ships of the main body while the third was splashed. The next day, the combined fire of the group destroyed four more enemy aircraft as they went into their attack dives. *McClelland* then assumed screening and hunter-killer activities about the island.

In the last days of February, the destroyer escort steamed to Espiritu Santo to prepare for the Okinawa offensive. She arrived off the Okinawa beaches on 9 April, remaining until 8 June. During that long and bitter campaign, she took part in the capture of Isuken Shima, performed escort services among the Ryukyus, and helped to maintain the antiaircraft and antisubmarine screen.

15 April. While temporarily in the transport area at Hagushi anchorage, *McClelland* and other ships opened fire on two enemy aircraft. One plane fell in flames; the other exploded in midair a few yards before it crashed into a transport!

16 April. In a screening station near Ie Shima, *McClelland* and other vessels took a group of enemy planes under fire. Several suicide attempts were made on ships in neighboring screening stations with one destroyer escort badly hit. Friendly Corsairs shot down two Vals. One Corsair, however, was accidentally downed by fire from the ships; the pilot was rescued by *McClelland*. On the same day, the body of a Japanese suicide pilot was picked up, and his effects were forwarded to intelligence authorities.

22 April to 11 May. In one instance, *McClelland* took an enemy bomber under fire during a dusk raid. The plane retired unscathed and without pressing home the attack. Another time, during a night air raid, several enemy bombers were in the immediate vicinity. One was fired on by this ship without result.

12 May. While anchored in the transport area, this DE took enemy planes under fire during a surprise night suicide raid. One plane was shot down by the combined gunfire of many ships in the area. A second plane crashed into the midship section of a battleship anchored about 300 yards off *McClelland*!

0923. After a night of intensive air raids, enemy planes again were in the immediate area. *McClelland* and three other ships were patrolling stations west of Okinawa when an enemy plane was sighted being pursued by four Corsairs. The Japanese plane was attempting to evade a Corsair close on its tail and, at the same time, to crash into one of the ships. The suicide plane weaved from side to side, closing the group. The *kamikaze* crashed into *Roper (APD-20)*, about 2000 yards from this ship. No vessels in the vicinity opened fire on the suicider since the Corsair was too close on his tail. (The travail of *Roper* is narrated in the next chapter.)

1927. While patrolling a station west of Okinawa, antiaircraft fire was sighted astern of *McClelland*. A few seconds later, an enemy suicide plane crashed into the fantail of *Bright (DE-747)* (Narrated earlier in this chapter). *McClelland* was under attack by a Kate flying low over the water in an apparent torpedo launch approach. The plane was taken under fire and veered sharply down toward the water, temporarily out of control. It pulled out of its dive a few feet above the surface and retired without further attack. From the actions of the plane, it was probable that it was hit. *McClelland* covered *Bright*, then laboring without steering control. By 2105, the damaged DE appeared to be able to proceed to port.

2235. There were many enemy aircraft about. A series of 14 flares were seen, dropped by a plane over a nearby vessel. Antiaircraft fire from ships and shore batteries erupted at various times, and fires on six or seven ships hit in the vicinity were easily visible.

28 May. The main enemy action during this period consisted of moonlight suicide aircraft attacks on screening vessels, unusually heavy on the two days of 28 and 29 May. Visibility was excellent, and many suicide and some torpedo raids were launched.

0145 on 28 May. *McClelland*'s radar made contact on a plane, plotted by the Combat Information Center as on a collision course with this vessel. The DE opened fire and, although hits by her 20mm guns were plainly visible, the aircraft remained under control. Shortly afterward, a torpedo passed close aboard, 25 to 50 yards astern. In the original aspects of the attack, it was thought that the plane was attempting a suicide crash but, after dropping the torpedo, the aircraft retired without attempting suicide tactics.

Contact was lost at nine miles on the SA radar, and another screening vessel near that position reported that an enemy aircraft splashed in the water in that vicinity without any ships firing on it. However, it was not possible to accurately determine whether this was the plane which made a torpedo run on *McClelland*, and no claim was made by her commanding officer, Lieutenant Commander G.D. Williams.

Throughout the night, other suicide crashes were all too visible; one was nearby on *Loy (APD-56)* (also narrated in the next chapter). Since other vessels in the vicinity assisted *Loy*, *McClelland* remained on station. A float type enemy plane passed overhead without pressing an attack on this vessel. The plane was tracked and witnessed in its crash into *LCS-119*, causing large fires.

1 June. At 0733, enemy air attacks were resumed. However, no planes were seen by this vessel, most raids being reported splashed by the combat air patrol and radar pickets further away. At mid-morning, this DE was assigned to another station. During late afternoon, lookouts sighted a horned type mine; it was destroyed by rifle fire. One hour before sunset, *McClelland* took her dusk antiaircraft station three miles off Kerama Retto. The minesweeper *Prevail (AM-107)* joined for mutual support, 800 yards astern of the destroyer escort. An hour later, lookouts reported a low flying plane at two miles. Side lobes from nearby land obscured the radar scope until a check was made after visual contact. The plane did not resemble a friendly and its maneuvers aroused suspicion that it was a bogey. In a matter of seconds, the Combat Information Center confirmed the plane as enemy. The aircraft, a Zeke, maneuvered toward the ship's stern, gaining altitude. It commenced a dive from about 2000 feet. The 40mm and number three 3" gun opened fire approximately 20 seconds after GQ was sounded, and hits were scored by 40mm shells. The ship's rudder was put to full left and speed was increased when the plane was about 1000 yards astern. All guns that could bear on the target were now firing. The *kamikaze* was clearly seen to be smoking and then flaming at 500 yards. The ship had by then turned about 45 degrees, and the plane splashed a scant 25 yards off the starboard beam! The entire action from sighting to crashing was 45 seconds. This action lays considerable credit on the gun crews who had very little time to man their guns, track the target and commence firing. This vessel had experienced many dusk raids in the past. As a result, gun crews customarily congregated informally at their battle stations around sunset without call or alarm. General Quarters had graduated in men's minds from a necessary chore to urgent survival.

This author spoke with Don Thorn, at the time a seaman first class with a battle station on one of the 20mm guns that fired on the suicide plane. I asked him about his feelings when the plane was roaring in at him:

> "When I saw that suicider so close I could see the 'meat balls' on his wings, I remembered with misgivings all the times I never went to church when I should have and hummed half aloud to myself the strains of "Ave Maria" the

while shooting at the Jap!"

A ship's history published to all hands sounded the depths of emotions of the crew that faced up to the bloodiest naval battle in history:

> "During those 196 action-packed hours, many of them spent during two months on the picket line at Okinawa, *McClelland* shot down her Jap, a suicider intent on crashing us. She probably damaged another, whose torpedo passed abaft the fantail. With other ships, she fired at many other planes whose destruction was the result of team work, rather than a single ship's action. She sank her share of mines. She aided in the search for enemy submarines.
>
> The crew came to fear and dislike the full moon – first at Iwo Jima and then even more at Okinawa. In the daylight, the ship had a chance, but at night, when the planes were almost invisible, the odds were all with the *kamikazes*. Many planes were shot down, but many ships were hit.
>
> Luck stayed with *McClelland*. Again and again, ships in adjacent stations or in stations recently occupied by 'Mac', took suicide hits. They flared up in plain view, then smoldered until the damage control parties got the fires under control. It was hard to realize that men were dead and dying, that *McClelland* might be next. And sometimes it wasn't so hard to realize, when 'Mac' herself was under attack, that a few seconds might mean life or death.
>
> But 'Mac' lived through 196 hours of action, lived on to reach the goal for which she had been fighting. That goal was Tokyo.
>
> Many of *McClelland*'s tasks lay in the between-the-battle routine, the hundred and one odd jobs that had to be done if the ship were to operate effectively. Her ports of call read like the peacetime itinerary of an affluent yachtsman – Hawaii, Eniwetok, Guam, Saipan, Tulagi, Espiritu Santo, Ulithi, Leyte, Sasebo and Tokyo Bay. Her hours of liberty were few and precious. Moments of pleasure were snatched from long months of danger."

In early June, *McClelland* steamed to Saipan to join the Third Fleet's logistics task group east of Japan. She screened provision units of Task Force 38, then striking the Japanese homeland. She arrived in Japanese waters in late September, remaining in Tokyo until 12 October 1945 when she finally turned her bow in the direction of the United States.

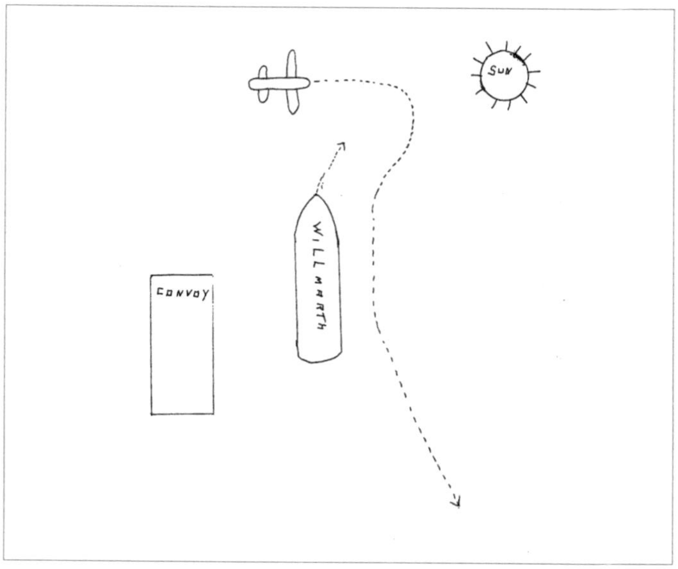

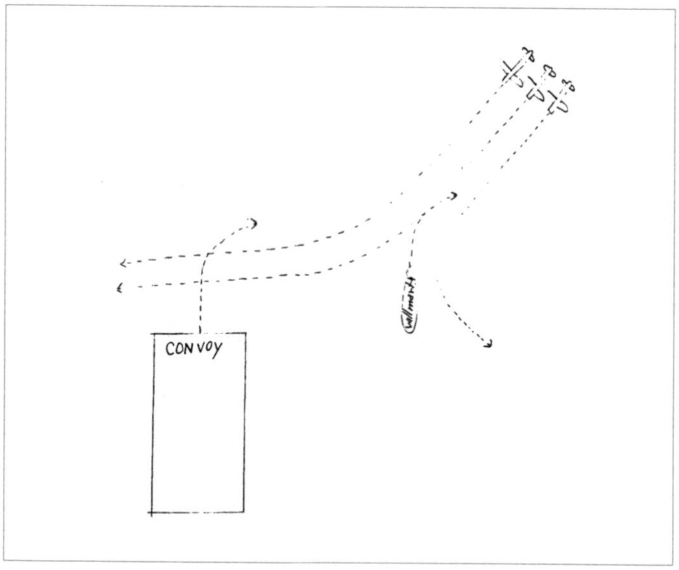

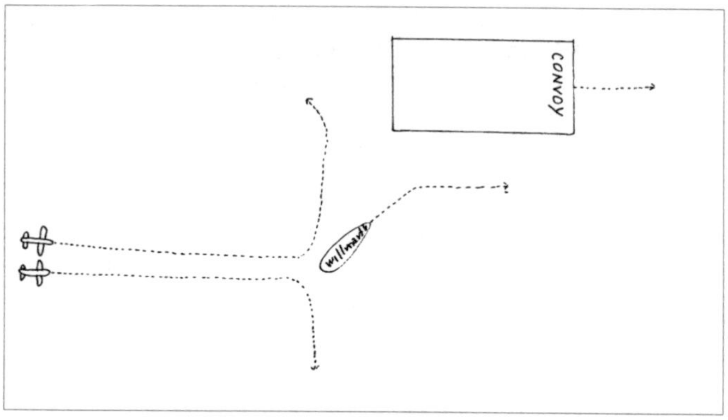

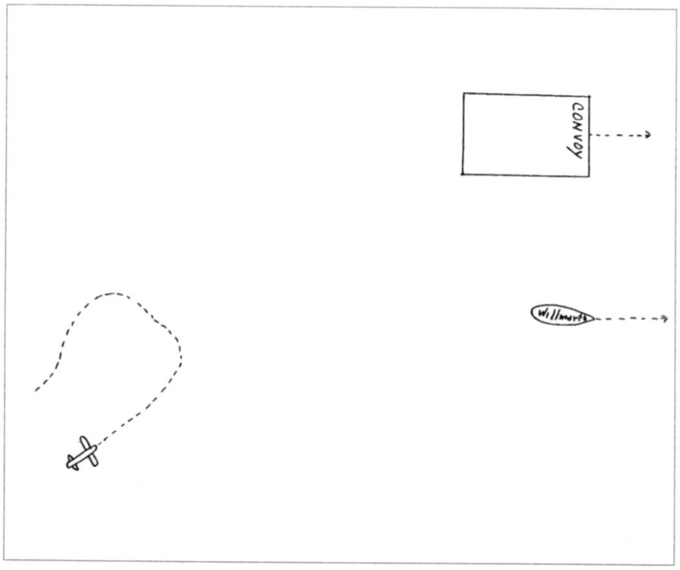

All the above drawings are from *Willmarth*, October 1944

USS John C. Butler – US Navy Photo

John C. Butler (DE–339) engaging a kamikaze off Okinawa Shima. Artist's Conception.
Painting by Sam L. Massette © American Naval Art

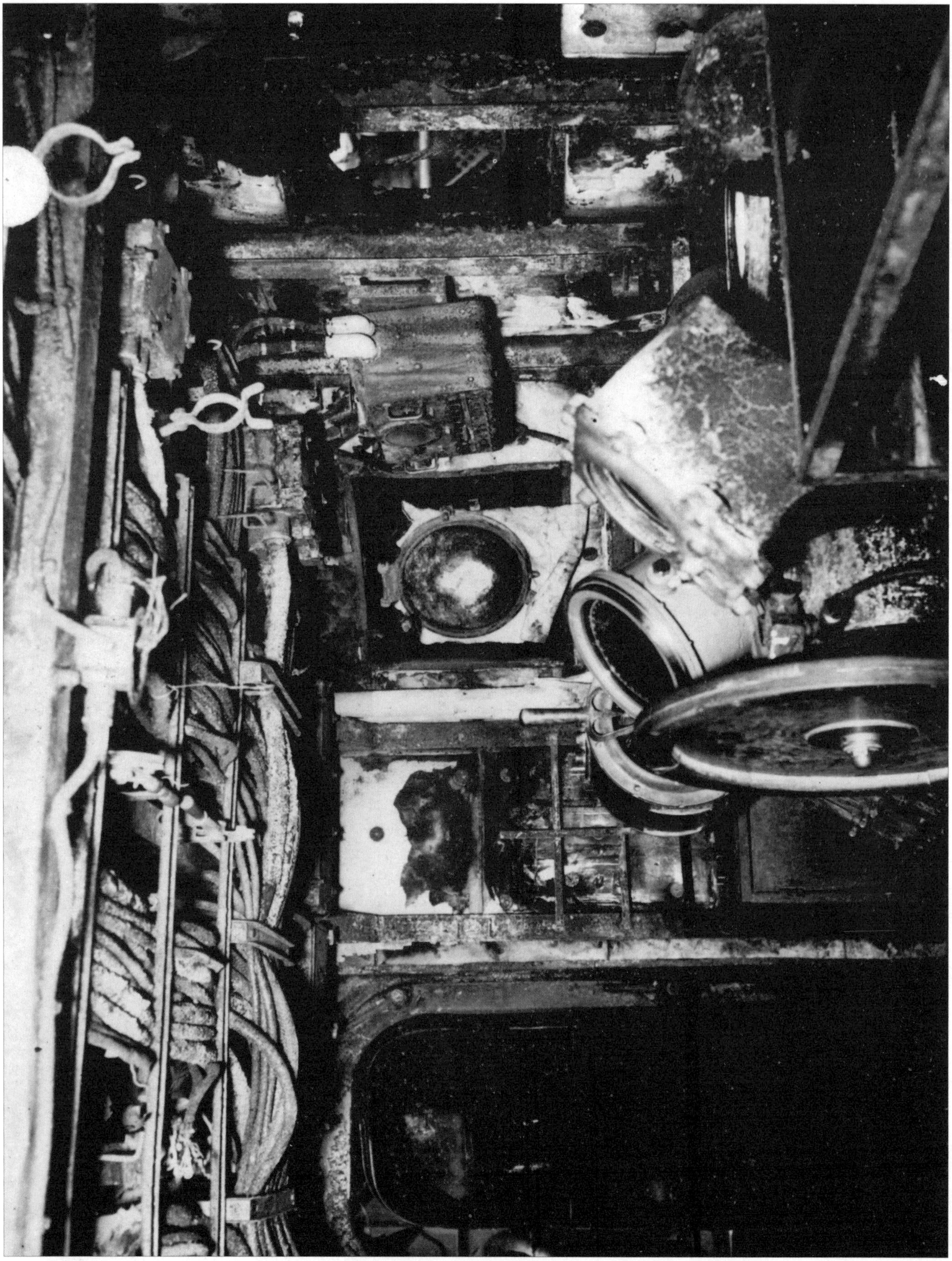

Bowers' smashed and burned out bridge interior. US Navy Photo

Bowers' wrecked radio shack. US Navy Photo

Rall shoots one into the sea. US Navy Photo

Lewis M. Andrews, Jr.

Chapter XVI - Iwo Jima To Okinawa – The High Speed Transports

Most of the high speed transports (APD) were conversions from destroyer escorts, some after extensive service and others while still on the ways. Converted APD crews were largely the same as those who had manned them as DEs. Crews from bottom up APDs were drawn from DE pools. In addition, several Wickes Class World War I design destroyers, labeled "four pipers" because of their four funnels, were also converted to APDs. They performed the same functions in the same transport divisions as the converted DEs. All APD crews received additional training for ordnance modification, handling of landing craft (LCI) and underwater demolition teams or invasion troops.

Irrespective of DE or DD antecedents, APD veterans are considered to be the equal of DE veterans in the Destroyer Escort Sailors Association. APD vessels retained most of their antisubmarine capabilities and were frequently employed as escorts when no troops or UDT teams were aboard. In prior chapters, we have seen how the APD transports functioned at Ormoc Bay, Lingayen Gulf and elsewhere. At Iwo Jima and Okinawa, they endured the same travail as befell the destroyer escorts and other categories on the picket line.

A word about underwater demolition teams (UDT). Their job was to remove underwater obstacles to amphibious landings. They also acquired pre-landing intelligence, vital to the success of island hopping campaigns. Needless to say, UDT was a very hazardous avocation. The same was true for the APD ships which often operated close to the shore and within range of enemy gun batteries.

BLESSMAN

From the Beaches of Normandy to the Sands of Iwo Jima

About six weeks after her participation in the Normandy invasion (See chapter *Operations Overlord and Neptune*), *Blessman (DE-69)* entered the Sullivan Dry Dock and Repair Corporation Yard, Brooklyn, New York, where she was converted to APD-48.

At Pearl Harbor, Underwater Demolition Team 15 reported aboard ship. *Blessman* had performed admirably less than a month before while under heavy *kamikaze* attack at Lingayen Gulf, landing her underwater demolition teams while raining covering fire on the enemy-held beach. (See chapter *The Philippine Campaign*)

3-13 February 1945. During this period at Ulithi and Saipan, this APD engaged in rehearsals for a major operation. Drills were held by the gunfire support ships where *Blessman* was frequently employed as a screening vessel for the heavier bombardment units and transports.

14-24 February. The operational period covered by *Blessman* would prove to be the most traumatic since the day of her commissioning. She was assigned to a task unit along with *Bull (APD-78)*, *Bates (APD-47)*, *Barr (APD-39)*, *Gilmer (APD-11)* and *Waters (DD-115)*. Underwater demolition teams were embarked in their respective APDs as the Task Force departed from Saipan. The next step was to be Iwo Jima, one of the best defended islands in the world!

Blessman arrived at Iwo Jima on 16 February. On the following morning, she was assigned to circle the island for close observation of the beaches. The underwater demolition teams were charged with the reconnaissance of the eastern and western beaches of the island. On D-2, this mission was successfully completed. No enemy surface ships were expected, and it was anticipated that the American carrier force would keep hostile aircraft to a minimum. Because of the heavy shore batteries known to be on Iwo Jima and the vulnerability of the APD transports with their huge quantities of explosives stowed on board, the APDs were directed to retire out of range of enemy artillery once their UDTs were back aboard. When not involved in reconnaissance operations, they were employed as part of the outer screens, covering transports and the heavy ship bombardment group.

17 February. In a pre-dawn operation, *Blessman* rendezvoused with *Gilmer* and approached the island. The Japanese believed she was preparing to land troops and took her under fire. Fortunately, the fire was erratic, and she was unharmed. Both ships lowered and sent off their boats at mid-morning as heavy ships subjected the enemy to a terrific bombardment. *Blessman* moved out to 8000 yards from the beach. At noon, she closed the beach again to pick up the returning boats, completing the assigned reconnaissance. The only ship's crew casualty was Motor Machinist Mate Frank W. Sumpter. The UDT, however, reported very heavy opposition from the beaches, although the swimmers were able to complete their job. Virtually all of the LCI boats were hit by 20mm fire. There were numerous casualties on other boats but only two in the *Blessman-Gilmer* joint operation.

Because of the severe damage to the boats, the afternoon operation had to be delayed about one and a half hours beyond the schedule. By mid-afternoon, the APD was again on station and, a few minutes later, *Blessman* called away her boats. They returned two hours later, remarkably without casualties. *Blessman* was then directed to close with the amphibious forces flagship *Estes (AGC-12)* just south of Mount Suribachi. The commanding officer of the UDT was transferred to *Gilmer* for debriefing on the reconnaissance of the western beaches.

It had been a brutal day. With her immediate task completed, *Blessman* withdrew to her night screening station to await the arrival of the marines who were to land the following morning.

18 February. *Blessman* proceeded to *Gilmer* to pick up her UDT commanding officer, along with Commander Silcock of the Royal Navy, Marine Corps Lieutenant Pottoff and UDT 14 Lieutenant Onderdonk for further transfer. That evening, *Blessman* received orders for further UDT activity. The controlling vessel was the destroyer *Paul Hamilton (DD-590)*. *Blessman* sharply increased speed to reach her assigned area. But the Japanese had other plans for this APD.

Tragedy struck quickly. A Betty bomber appeared out of the black night, coming in low over the port quarter. Just clearing the foremast, strafing as it approached, it dropped two 500 pound bombs on the speeding ship. One hit the stack, glanced off and continued overboard without exploding. The other, however, scored a direct hit in the starboard mess hall. Fire broke out immediately in that area, the galley and troop quarters on the main deck, and all power was lost. The ship was turned into a flaming inferno. The mess hall had been crowded with tired men, writing letters home. In that instant 21 men of the *Blessman's* crew and 19 men of UDT 15 stopped writing, forever. In addition, 23 were wounded, one seriously.The night was heavily overcast with occasional light rain. However, the sea was brilliantly phosphorescent, and the ship's wake at 20 knots could have been seen for a considerable distance. Just prior to the attack message from *Blessman*, a "Flash Red" - "Control Yellow" condition existed, and Japanese planes were known to be in the area. Former Radarman Joe L. Young harked back to that night at Iwo Jima, recollections of a 19 year old, as remembered 52 years later:

> "I had just been relieved from my station at 2000 before the bomb hit. I consider myself to be very lucky; God surely had something else in mind for me later on in life. On going off duty, I headed for my bunk in the mid-aft crew's quarters, below the main deck. As I passed through the mess hall, where the bomb would hit, I stopped and talked with some guys for 30 or 40 minutes before going on down to my bunk. I chatted with some bunk mates a while and was partly undressed for bed when the explosion hit.
>
> At first, I didn't think of the noise as an explosion. I was so far aft, it sounded like we had been rammed by another large ship. Immediately, everyone made for the ladder to get topside. In war zones, the large hatch was always bolted down and the little round one was left open, just big enough for one man to crawl through.
>
> This created a problem right off; one man panicked and was at the ladder trying to climb ahead of the men already in line waiting to get up. He was finally restrained, and we went up. I headed for my radar post, where I had foolishly left my life jacket. I remember climbing to the top deck where the bomb had first hit, one deck above the main deck. As I looked forward, beyond the stack, I could see a gaping hole and a spreading fire. Some of the ammunition on the small boats in their davits, just above the mess hall, had begun to explode like firecrackers."

For 100 endless minutes, the stricken ship lay dead in the water. Number 2 fire and engine rooms had to be abandoned because of acrid smoke filling the area. Flames poured fiercely from the gaping hole in the superstructure. Water poured into her riddled hull. The 500 gallon per minute handy billy was demolished by the bomb hit, and all others were rendered inoperative by the shock. Joe Young continued:

> "I made my way forward, climbing over debris to get to the bridge ladder and on into the CIC to get my life jacket. Then I began to take stock of things. There was no power except a few dim battery emergency lights; most of the light was coming from the fire. The ship was listing sharply to starboard. The fire had reached some of the larger ammunition storage rooms, and the 40mm shells were exploding from the heat. The small emergency fire equipment that was placed all around the ship apparently failed to operate."

Only bucket brigades were available to be thrown into the fight against the flames, a valiant last but obviously insufficient method for serious damage control. A message for assistance was relayed through *Barr* on the UDT channel to the Screen Commander; without power or means of pumping, the fire could not be brought under control. *Gilmer* was ordered to go to the aid of *Blessman*.

Ammunition began to explode as the fire raced toward the magazines. With enemy planes in the vicinity, this looked like the end of the *Blessman*. Joe Young recalled:

> "I went down in the forward crew's compartments to find some more emergency fire equipment. The compartments were filled with smoke and very dark except for a battery powered lantern I had with me. The ship was listing very badly by now. I lost all count of time; maybe 30 minutes had passed since the explosion. I suddenly felt a great fear that someone would close and lock the compartments, so I got out fast. When I reached topside, the word was passed for help on the fantail to get the UDT's huge store of plastic explosives overboard; the fire was spreading to that area.
>
> I went back to help bringing explosives up from below and throwing them overboard. By this time, I was sure the ship would capsize to starboard. She seemed to me to be listing about 40 degrees. Damage control tried to shore up some of the holes below the waterline but couldn't plug them all."

All topside ammunition aft was jettisoned, and attempts were made to clear ammunition from the clip shacks along with bedding from the troop quarters in order to halt the spread of the raging fire. In spite of their efforts, small arms, 20mm and 40mm ammunition began exploding. Wounded were cleared as quickly as possible from the burning areas and placed on the fantail and forecastle with the doctor rendering emergency treatment. Meanwhile, the bucket brigades had kept the fires from spreading to the boat deck, confining the flames to the enclosed spaces on the main deck.

Gilmer proceeded at full speed toward the approximate area of the distressed ship, meanwhile staying in direct communication and obtaining a more accurate position of *Blessman*. At about 2210, she picked up the stricken APD on her radar, then saw the light of her burning midship section. Just as destruction had come out of the night, now help appeared just as suddenly. *Gilmer* was a beautiful sight to the fighting hearts in *Blessman*.

Gilmer closed *Blessman* to about 300 yards and lay to while the situation was analyzed, in the meantime lowering boats and preparing to go alongside *Blessman* and fight fires. In order to accomplish the job, and because the officers of *Gilmer* were overburdened, members of the staff of the Task Group Commander on *Gilmer* were detailed to handle certain duties. Staff Commander Kauffman, assisted by staff Lieutenant (jg) R.M.S. Boyd, was placed in charge of the boats and the removal of wounded from *Blessman* to *Gilmer*.

By now, the extent of the fire and bomb damage could be estimated. The forward and after parts of the ship were divided by the fire, leaving personnel gathered fore and aft. Cherry red flames could be seen through the main deck cargo hatch which had been blown open.

As soon as the boats were lowered, *Gilmer* went along the lee side in order for her hoses to reach. The spirit of the *Blessman* crew was evident as *Gilmer* came close aboard. A group of men on the fantail were singing "Anchors Aweigh" and courageously attempting, with no hope of success, to put out the fire with a bucket brigade of helmets.

There was some wind and considerable sea; the first attempt missed but the second attempt put *Gilmer* alongside at 2300. Hoses were then worked from *Gilmer* and from the fantail of *Blessman*. *Gilmer* stayed alongside until the fires were out. The Task Force Commander advised the *Blessman's* skipper that the salvage ship *Gear (ARS-340)* was on her way. The tow was requested in order that *Gilmer* might depart to carry out her mission later that morning, 19 February, D-Day. At 0240, *Gear* arrived and received a line from *Blessman*. *Gilmer* cleared the area and proceeded to *Estes* to transfer the 30 casualties taken aboard. Joe Young remembers the night.

> "It sure was a good feeling to see another ship. In considering the possibility of going into the water, at least there was comfort in another ship near by. The old "four stacker" immediately started spraying water on the fires. Then she passed over by one of her cranes a large diesel motor and pump, mounted in a metal frame, to assist us in pumping out the sea water.
>
> If I were to single out any one person who did so much to save the ship, it would be Motor Machinist's Mate First Class Walter Nolan. He was a big man, strong, friendly, and nice to talk to. He took charge of this pump, locating it and making it work as if it were an every-day operation. His ability to get help from others and his rapport and easy communication between himself and the captain was a big factor in the ship's survival."

The conduct of the crews of both ships was exemplary and merited high praise. *Blessman* still had some 40 tons of high explosives aboard, and the crews of both ships were familiar with the hazards involved. Two of the hoses transferred from *Gilmer* to *Blessman* were not used to fight the fire but to keep down the temperature aft where the high explosives were stowed and had started to warm up alarmingly. Joe Young had some further thoughts:

> "Not long after the pump was started, the ship began to right itself. When daylight came, there was the task of retrieving the dead. Voluntary help did this, but I could not bring myself to do it and can't think of doing anything like it to this day. So I gave all the help I could in other places. I remember two marine advisors who were aboard ship and got killed. They were Sergeants, and had been together all through the Pacific, from Guadalcanal to Iwo Jima. That hit me, such a waste."

Appropriately, the *Blessman* captain caused the following to be entered in the log:

> "Without the expert and courageous help of *Gilmer*, the fire would have spread to the ship's magazine and also the troop's magazine aft. They contained some 40 tons of Tetratol, Bangalore torpedoes, Block TNT and other demolition explosives. If this had happened, the ship would have had to be abandoned because it was impossible to flood those magazines or to effectively fight any fire. The actions of the *USS Gilmer* were in accordance with the highest standards and traditions of the United States Navy."

Particular commendation and credit for saving *Blessman* and her crew went to:

> Lieutenant Commander Philip LeBoutillier, the commanding officer of *Blessman*, for his cool courage, the spirit of his crew, and his determination to save and fight his ship.
>
> Lieutenant Quant, commanding officer of *Gilmer*, for his superlative seamanship in keeping *Gilmer* alongside *Blessman* under great difficulty and constantly adjusting his position so that the hoses could be kept in the most effective positions.
>
> Lieutenant Commander D.K. O'Connor for the cool and efficient manner in which he took charge of the fire fighting and quickly brought about organization and control of the fire.
>
> Commander D. L. Kauffman and Lieutenant (jg) R.M.S. Boyd for organizing and supervising the removal of casualties under difficult and hazardous conditions.

The next morning, as the marines began their bloody but victorious battle for Iwo Jima, the men of *Blessman* held burial at sea services for those shipmates who would never sail again.

With the aid of pumps received from *Gear*, water was kept under control and reduced sufficiently so that bomb fragment holes beneath the waterline in the number one engine room could be plugged. Minimal repairs rendered the ship seaworthy.

Then began the long cruise under tow to Saipan. *Blessman's* crew lived more like soldiers than sailors. With all cooking facilities demolished, the crew built a fireplace on the fantail where they prepared all their meals every day. Joe Young remembers peeling a mountain of potatoes.

The repair officers at Saipan thought it a waste of time to restore the ruined ship. While they were writing reports, *Blessman's* crew went to work, effecting their own repairs. In a few days, they had made such rapid strides that the repair officers had to revise their estimates. Now, they decided that her spirit was invaluable. She was repaired enough to proceed to the Mare Island Navy Yard, California, to be placed in fighting trim and to return to the war.

But *Blessman* had fought her last battle. A veteran of wars with two enemies in two oceans, finally shedding her share of blood and steel, the long war ended before she could again come to grips with the foe.

DICKERSON

A Sad Ending after Twenty-Six Years

In a previous life, *Dickerson (DD-157)* was a "Four-Piper." Early in 1943, *Dickerson* escorted tanker convoys to North Africa and operated with the *Card (CVE-11)* HUK Group at Casablanca for antisubmarine operations in the Middle Atlantic. In August, she underwent conversion to a high speed transport in Charleston, South Carolina, and was reclassified *APD-21*.

As such, her first assignment was escort of convoys from

Espiritu Santo to Guadalcanal. On 30 January 1944, she landed a New Zealand reconnaissance patrol on Green Island, the Solomons, and reembarked it after two days when her boats were strafed by enemy planes. Two weeks later, she landed troops on the island to capture and occupy it.

Beginning April 1944, *Dickerson* supported landings at Seleo Island and Aitape in New Guinea. At Poi, in the Marshalls, she embarked a UDT for action at Saipan and Guam. She remained in the Marianas to supply control and fire support for her UDT until the end of July, then returned to the west coast of the United States for overhaul.

She sailed on 27 December for the invasion of Lingayen Gulf on 9 January 1945, again supporting the operations of a UDT. Shortly afterward, she joined the screen of a logistics support force for the invasion of Iwo Jima on 19 February, returning to Leyte with 58 prisoners of war. She departed again on 24 March with an amphibious convoy to capture the island of Keise Shima, on which heavy artillery would be placed for the bombardment of Okinawa.

On the night of 2 April, the *kamikazes* attacked in strength. The termination of the career of this ship was sudden, with all logs, notes and other data consumed in fire. Fifty-four officers and men, including the commanding officer, executive officer, and most senior officers were lost. The ensuing paragraphs are extracts from four separate perspectives for submission to the Navy Department.

Lieutenant (jg) James D. Ebert:

"I was Officer of The Deck during the watch preceding GQ and was at my station as gunnery officer on the flying bridge during the attack. At 1645, in company with *Herbert (APD-22)*, we proceeded to the transport area southwest of Kerama Retto and reported to the Screen Commander of a sixteen ship transport group. There were only three escorts, namely two APDs and one destroyer minelayer. The raid condition was "Flash White" for no enemy planes in the area.

1825. I was relieved for supper by Lieutenant (jg) Earl K. Corwin and had started to dine in the wardroom when the GQ alarm sounded; I returned to the flying bridge, my station. I suddenly noticed five enemy planes, identified by Lieutenant (jg) W.T. George, recognition officer, as two Nicks and three Zekes. A twin-engined Nick approached the ship just off the starboard bow and passed over us at about a 600 foot altitude, speed 350 knots. All forward guns that could be brought to bear opened fire, but no hits were recorded. The plane turned over our port quarter, circled the convoy, and approached us in a shallow glide from astern. Only the after guns, two single mount, locally controlled 40mm and two 20mm could be brought to bear, the latter for only a few bursts.

The plane hit the top of number one stack, and I was thrown to the deck by a loud blast. Upon recovering my senses, I realized the situation was grave. Two fire controlmen, Lieutenant (jg) George, and myself were apparently the only men alive forward of the galley deck house. The plane had swept the galley deck, killing two gun crews except for a few who jumped over just before the crash. The plane then smashed into the base of the bridge structure, toppling the mast toward the after end of the ship. The entire well deck and bridge structure below me were a mass of flames.

The four of us, unable to move aft, jumped from the flying bridge to the 20mm platform forward of the bridge, then jumped to the forecastle deck. There we found a scene of indescribable horror. An explosion had completely eliminated number one 3" gun, leaving a hole in the deck 23 feet wide and 14 feet long. The men serving on that 3" gun were mutilated from the devastation wrought. The chief petty officers quarters below were a mass of rubble.

I thought that a bomb from another plane was the cause rather than the suicide plane, considering the angle of its approach. (It was a second *kamikaze* that crashed into the foc's'l.) Realizing that it was impossible to escape past the bridge structure or through the hatch above the chief petty officers' quarters, we gathered at the bow. There we were joined by a badly wounded chief. It was not possible to jump overboard while the ship was making 10 knots, and there was no possibility of reaching the after end of the ship.

Ready ammunition lockers on the well deck and forecastle were exploding. The fire was directly above the forward magazine, and I expected it to detonate any minute. Darkness was setting in rapidly. I then noticed one of our boats astern and concluded that the order had been given to abandon ship. I considered this very wise and altogether proper; I would have done the same thing under the circumstances, I am sure.

At this point, *Bunch (APD-79)* closed the forward part of our ship and commenced fire-fighting measures. The ship slowed, and the five of us then jumped from the foc's'l. After a short time in the water, we were picked up and brought to Kerama Retto."

Lieutenant (jg) L.G. Howard:

"When GQ sounded, the assistant engineer officer and I ran to our rooms, donned life jackets, grabbed binoculars, and proceeded to our stations. On arriving, I made certain that all standby pumps were ready for instant use. The men were on station and were checked for helmets and life jackets. The bridge was then advised that the engineering stations were manned and ready.

Our guns opened up, and word was received that a plane was diving at us. The ship's speed remained at 10 knots, and we soon experienced a heavy jolt, accompanied by sparks and smoke pouring through a blower in the forward engine room. A pressure of 90 pounds was maintained on the fire main and, after checking on both the after engine room and fire room by phone, word was passed to the bridge that the engineering plant was undamaged. The talker was certain he received a 'Roger'. Since our first report was that the plane had crashed the fantail, we assumed the bridge had gotten the message.

After trying without success to reach the bridge again, I sent a man topside to check on the location of the hit. He promptly returned to report that a plane had hit the bridge and a fire was raging.

Going topside, I met Lieutenant (jg) A.Q. Brinkerhoff who told me that a few of us were the only surviving officers. Proceeding to the vicinity of number one stack, I saw that the fire was raging below the decks and forward of the bridge, itself a mass of flames. Due to the proximity of the fire to the forward magazine and the fact that it would soon be dark, I ordered the word passed to secure the main engines and lay aft on the fantail to abandon ship. I then returned below to assist where possible. The propellers were stopped, the fire room personnel banked the boilers, and the petty officer of the watch reported that all his men were on the fantail.

The men were instructed to remove helmets and all heavy gear and to lace up their life jackets. Upon the discovery that two men couldn't swim, I assigned two swimmers to each non-swimmer. I also cautioned the men not to drift apart. One of our boats had already begun rescue operations.

It was suggested that ten men remain aboard and assist in fighting the fire as *Bunch* was coming along our starboard side to assist us. However, I decided against it and proceeded with the original order. We were in the water approximately 20 minutes before being rescued by a boat. To the best of my knowledge, all of the men on the fantail were rescued by boats from *Bunch* and *Herbert*.

The boat I was on continued picking up other swimmers and, after half an hour, we went aboard *Bunch*. By that time, *Bunch* had placed a fire fighting crew aboard *Dickerson*. During the night, the fire was finally brought under control. Somewhat later, a tug arrived and towed *Dickerson* into Kerama Retto.

The following morning, I boarded *Dickerson* to check on damage and to salvage personal gear. The ship was listing hard to port, and the port alleyway was flooded. The after engine room was dry, and the forward engine room was mostly dry with machinery above water. The fire room was flooded with six feet of water, partly submerging both boilers. Several salvaging parties were aboard so we reported to an attack transport in Kerama Retto for further orders.

Lieutenant (jg) A.Q. Brinkerhoff, Jr.:

"Upon finishing supper, about 1825, I walked topside for some air and a cigarette before evening alert. When I went to the bridge, the area control was "Flash White, Control Yellow," indicating no enemy aircraft in the vicinity. Our speed was 10 knots.

I had been standing on the wing some five minutes, observing the ship dispositions in the convoy when two planes came in fast on the starboard bow. General quarters was immediately sounded. As I left the bridge, I noticed one of these planes diving at the convoy.

I went to my room, donned my life jacket and binoculars, and ran down the port passageway to my GQ station on the after deck house, in charge of the 40mm battery. My battle station talker had no sooner contacted control when it reported a plane coming in dead ahead. The 40mm guns swung around and were only able to expend about six rounds before the plane had passed directly over us as if he were going to bomb. No results of our firing were apparent. Our guns followed him out as he crossed our port quarter, expending perhaps ten more rounds.

The plane circled above the convoy which threw up a heavy barrage of antiaircraft fire; it then turned back in our direction. Command on the flying bridge must have also observed the plane's turn for we were immediately informed of its approach. When the distance was about 5000 yards, I ordered the 40mm guns to commence firing. The plane was in a glide headed directly at us. The 20mm guns were not able to bear because of the 40mm guns in their line of fire, but they opened up as the plane neared, although only a few rounds were expended. The 40mm guns continued to fire until the end. To a man, the gunners stood by their posts.

The plane passed about 20 feet above the after deck house with its port engine on fire. I remained in the starboard passageway some 60 seconds with my foot entangled in a lanyard from one of our depth charge cradles; I managed to extract my foot by removing my shoe. Going to the fantail, I saw about 35 men milling about. I was told that both after life rafts had been cut loose and quite a few men were in the water, having jumped or been thrown from the forward part of the ship. There was at first a great deal of confusion and noise, but this was subdued to some extent. Preparations were already underway for setting the depth charges on safe, and two men mounted the after deck house to throw the ammunition over the side.

I then went forward as far as possible to the scene of the fire. Because of the heat and flame, I was unable to get very close. The fire was coming from the entire bridge structure and seemed to be emerging from the hatches leading to the wardroom and seamen's compartment, directly under which was the forward magazine. It was impossible to flood this magazine as the valve was below those hatches. I ran aft, and the hose at the ship's office was broken out and led to the fire. Turning on the water, we had ample pressure on that line. The after hose had been broken out previously but would not reach. The leading petty officers in the after damage control party brought up two handy billies.

Going aft, I decided that the ship might be turned to keep the fire confined to the well deck. I instructed the signalman, who had charge of the operation, to switch to emergency steering at secondary control aft with the aid of one other man. With two men, I mounted the after deck house to await steering power. The word was given some 30 seconds later, and I immediately swung the wheel to port. We had made only two revolutions when something snapped, and the wheel had no effect. The cable broke, a mechanical failure.

About this time, I saw the supply officer, Ensign J. B. Collinson, on the fantail, keeping the men in order and checking on ammunition and depth charges aft. Going forward again, I could see that the fire was no more under control than previously so I instructed the boatswain's mate to lower the number three boat. I then instructed the boat coxswain and the boatswain's mate in charge to stand by astern.

I saw the engineering officer, Lieutenant (jg) Howard, emerging from the after hatch of the forward engine room and I informed him that we were, as far as I knew, the two senior surviving officers. Proceeding forward again, I believed that, if anything, the fire was gaining even though two hoses were in operation. Going aft, I instructed the signalman to contact *Bunch* and request her to bring fire fighting equipment alongside. Then, thinking of the location of the fire, I told the signalman to warn them of it's proximity to the magazine. A few moments later, we again contacted

Bunch to ask that a boat be lowered for survivors.

Going forward again, I spoke with the senior men who were fighting the fire. They informed me that, though they were not accomplishing much, they thought they might extinguish it. Going as far forward as possible, I agreed with their opinion. Going aft, I contacted the remaining officers and told them the situation, suggesting that all but 10 men abandon the ship. This was agreed upon, and the officers and men went over in an orderly fashion as instructed by Mr. Howard. With the 10 men aboard, I again started forward. (This is at variance with the testimony by Lieutenant (jg) L.S. Howard.)

Two explosions prevented me from going further forward than the ship's office. I believed this was the start of the forward magazines going up and so ordered the remaining men to clear the ship. I was positive that there were no men aboard between the galley deck house (forward side) and the after end of the ship. I then jumped over from the forward part of the after deck, hoping to reach *Bunch*. They threw me a buoy with a light as it was now quite dark. I waited until one of their boats was close enough to hail. About 30 minutes later, I boarded *Bunch* and reported to the captain, giving him as much information as I had.

I wish to commend the following named men for their outstanding examples of leadership and bravery:"

Chief Electrician's Mate Russell Samuel Beach
Boatswain's Mate First Class James Irvin McAdams
Pharmacist's Mate First Class Virgil Lee Hoff
Water Tender Second Class George Henry Lepkowski
Metalsmith First Class Nicholas Fiasconaro
Fireman First Class William Alfred King
Signalman First Class William Ernest Otto
Coxswain Virgil George Peterson

Ensign I.E. Hertle:

"I was in my room when GQ sounded and immediately ran aft, stopping at the forward engine room hatch to put on my life jacket and helmet. The guns were firing while I was on my way to the engine room and continued firing until I was below. The men were at their stations. Soon after I reached the engine room, the firing stopped.

We continued at the same speed. Then the guns commenced firing again, this time with added intensity. Shortly thereafter, I felt a crash which severely shook the ship. A few sparks that came down the air vent were the only other indication that the ship had suffered damage. The engineering plant functioned normally. I moved to the communication port between engine rooms to check damage in the forward engine room; there was very little.

The chief engineer passed the word through the communication port to put more pressure on the fire main. Next, the forward engine room asked if we had communication with the bridge. I asked the talker if he could reach that station, and he replied in the negative. All men remained below. The next order I received was to prepare to abandon ship. I repeated the order to the men and then sent a man up to loosen the after hatch in number two engine room. Then I glanced through the communication port and saw the men going up the ladder. I asked if an order had been passed to abandon ship, and the answer was affirmative. I ordered my men to leave the engine room but I stayed to watch the chief close the throttle.

Then I went back to check on the man opening the after hatch and ordered him out. All men then quickly left the compartment. After that, I went forward to the communication port again and saw the chief engineer move to the starboard throttle station. I watched for a moment and then went topside. The chief engineer and I reached the deck about the same time; he was the only other officer I saw in the area. That part of the ship was all ablaze. An order had been passed to abandon ship, and the men were concentrated on the fantail. Our supply officer and Lieutenant (jg) Brinkerhoff, were there also.

Number 3 boat had been lowered, and a man was in it trying to get it loose from the forward cable. The sea was rough, and the boat was being tossed hazardously against the ship, nearly capsizing several times. The engine was started and the boat moved away from the ship, pulling in again at the fantail for men to climb aboard. However, the danger of the rough sea throwing the boat into the propeller guards caused this procedure to be abandoned. The boat backed off to pick up men after they had jumped in the water. The chief engineer ordered everyone overboard and to swim away from the ship. I looked for a moment to see if I could be of help and then jumped over the side. I was picked up about 20 minutes later."

Bunch and *Herbert* rescued all survivors and *Bunch* succeeded in putting out the fires which had virtually demolished *Dickerson*. The smoldering hulk, beyond repair, was towed to Kerama Retto, then out to sea and sunk two days later.

One question this author finds unresolved is, when the attack threatened, why did the ship not go to fast speed and erratic steering while unmasking broadside guns These would have been standing instructions to the conn even before the captain reached the bridge. If there is an answer to that question, most likely it is lost forever in the depths where *Dickerson* sleeps.

KNUDSON

At Okinawa, Splash Beat Crash Any Time of the Day

Knudson (APD-101) did not have a DE or DD antecedent; she was an APD from the bottom up. Departing from Norfolk, Virginia, for the Pacific, she arrived at Pearl Harbor on 9 February for training with Underwater Demolition Teams. With UDT 19 embarked, she steamed to Ulithi and arrived on 12 March to prepare for operations in the Ryukyus. Nine days later, this APD headed for the assault and invasion of the Kerama Retto Group and Okinawa.

Upon arrival, she lent support to reconnaissance and demolition operations on Kuba Shima, Geruma Shima and Keise Shima, screening night retirement groups, transferring personnel and mail and patrolling in screening stations.

The first few days were preoccupied with the UDT team. The launching and recovery of boats and the loading of explosives and equipment in the boats were handled efficiently. The transportation of an Underwater Demolition Team was an entirely new experience for this vessel and most of the personnel aboard. The team was assigned to the APD from 1 March until 25 April. Its complement of 13 officers and 85 men were berthed on board for 56 days.

Relations between the ship's company and UDT personnel were very good. Nonetheless, the commanding officer, Lieutenant Commander T.K. Dunstan, was required to address a few problems arising from the lack of UDT indoctrination in shipboard routine. The majority of UDT personnel had no experience afloat except for transportation from one base to another. Training was the indicated remedy.

All UDT personnel were assigned battle stations, primarily in fire fighting parties stationed throughout the ship. A small portion of UDT personnel was also employed on supplementary gun watches during War Cruising (Condition A), and UDT officers were assigned junior officer of the deck watches.

Enemy snooper raids were frequent during night retirement but did little damage other than disturbing sleep. This problem was somewhat abated by allowing one section of the watch to sleep during times of the day when there was little or no enemy activity.

26. March. After sunrise, *Knudson* witnessed the only daylight attack in the vicinity of the ship before D-Day. The target was tracked for two miles through broken overcast before opening fire. Firing ceased at 2000 yards because of a number of mechanical gun failures and the wounding of the port side 40mm pointer by shrapnel from one of two bombs dropped close aboard; the firing pedal was thus released while the plane was passing, and the gun ceased firing.

Nonetheless, the plane was seen by the ship's observers to bank sharply after the attack, continue in flight for approximately two miles low on the water, and then splash broad off the starboard bow! Some of the gunners must have looked at one another, amazed.

Enemy air activity increased considerably after D-Day, with large attacks occurring on 6 and 12 April. The former took place in mid-afternoon, the latter shortly after dark. Many smaller attacks were made, most of them at dusk or at night. This ship was not actually attacked by aircraft after the one attack described above but was in the vicinity of numerous attacks.

From D-Day to D+7, *Knudson* patrolled an outer screening station. During that time, three enemy planes passed in close proximity without warning. They were flying low and were missed by radar. No reports from other ships had been received. From D+7 until departure from the area, this APD was patrolling an inner screening station. Although there was more air activity than before, not a single enemy plane passed near the ship without prior warning. This was fortunate because reports of vessels that were hit while patrolling outer screening stations revealed that at least some of the attacks were complete or nearly complete surprises.

During the next two weeks, *Knudson* conducted screening patrols off the western shore of Okinawa. She then sailed on 14 April on escort assignments to Guam and Ulithi, guarding the battleship *Nevada (BB-36)* and the cruiser *Portland (CA-33)* from submarine attack. Returning to Okinawa on 8 May, the APD resumed screening and helped to repel enemy air attacks until 15 June when she departed from Hagushi Anchorage for Leyte.

Knudson engaged in convoys in the Northern Philippines as well as to Okinawa. After one round trip to the west coast of the United States, The ship arrived in Tokyo Bay on 4 September. She operated out of Yokosuka Naval Base until the 20th, when she returned to the United States. She arrived at San Diego on 11 October, displaying her one Japanese flag painted on the side of the bridge.

BARBER

At Okinawa, No Smile Could Equal That of Lady Luck

As a destroyer escort *(DE-161)* in the Atlantic, *Barber* distinguished herself with the *Croatan* Hunter Killer Task Group and ran the gauntlet of German torpedo planes without harm to Casablanca convoys. (See narratives *The Hunter Killers* and *Mediterranean Convoys*.) Conversion to (APD-57) was completed on 17 January 1945.

Barber was at Ulithi on 30 April when *Hazelwood (DD-531)* limped in from Okinawa with her bridge completely demolished and being conned from Sky II, a *kamikaze* victim. This sight had a sobering effect on the *Barber's* men because, a few days later, they would be steaming to her same operation area.

At 0430 on 10 May, *Barber* dropped her hook in Hagushi Anchorage and, for the next 10 weeks, the enemy made his presence known daily. On the outer fringe of the anchorage, the guns of the "big boys" roared day and night. At dusk, Japanese planes came in with the setting sun. Smoke generators pumped out protective covering, and the general alarm rattled taut nerves day and night. Kamikazes were overhead, and tracer rounds could be seen from the dog fights. Shrapnel from nearby guns fell on the ship constantly.

0855 on 11 May. While stationed on the inner picket line, *Barber* was ordered to proceed at full speed to the assistance of *Hadley (DD-774)*. Reports had been received of 150 enemy planes headed for the anchorage, and *Hadley* and *Evans (DD-754)* were in their path on the picket station, 40 miles from the anchorage. The two destroyers together had shot down 48 enemy planes but sustained severe damage.

The ocean was calm and serene as *Barber* approached *Hadley*. There was a stillness and absence of noise with the bizarre exception of a bell concert. On approaching the stricken destroyer, the crew suddenly realized that the sound of belfry chimes came from empty brass 5" shell casings floating and gently touching each other. The ocean seemed to be full of them. Varying amounts of sea water in each casing created a range of tones. It was weird! And what a contrast to the chilling sight that loomed before their eyes.

Hadley's deck was still smoking from the crashed planes, and the ship's crew had a dazed look as it worked to keep the ship afloat. *Barber's* men were awed at the sight of dismembered bodies strewn about the deck as she took on 55 of the wounded. One 18-year-old casualty died aboard *Barber* while being treated on a mess hall table. The wounded were transferred to a nearby hospital ship.

The next morning, the APD was assigned to a picket station north of Iwo Shima to relieve *Gilligan (DE-508)*. (*Gilligan's* severe trials are detailed in the previous chapter.) The DE sent a message via blinker light as *Barber* approached:

'We have been on this station for five days and have shot down seven Jap planes. Two suicide planes dived on us and torpedoes passed close aboard!"

Some welcome! The crew expected almost anything but, despite many raids, the enemy did not come close. The Japs seldom came by day. When they did, it was around chow-time, just for aggravation. At dusk every evening, they came with robot-like punctuality. This routine, despite the constant awareness of imminent danger, tended toward a morbid monotony.

15 May. *Barber* captured four Japanese soldiers on a raft who were armed with grenades tied about their necks. Those grenades were meant for well-meaning people who might attempt to rescue their enemies. The ease with which they were subdued led some to believe that a crack might be perceived in the touted Japanese stoic countenance.

Whenever *Barber* fueled, a new picket station followed. She was a luck ship. Every picket station which she relieved or in which she was relieved was the scene of a casualty to the other ship.

17 May. While on night patrol, a single bogey almost landed on the fantail. He dropped a bomb that exploded in the water on the port side and continued through the 40mm and 20mm fire without apparent damage, as though to say, 'Sorry I missed, but good night'.

On 20 May, the Japanese launched one of the most concerted efforts of the entire Okinawa campaign. Midget subs, mines, *kamikazes* and all their available arsenal were thrown at U.S. naval forces. *Barber* spent a busy night tracking down two midget subs. In the darkness, she ran over one of them, and the metal to metal contact noise screeched from the bow to the stern, but no explosion. The evaluation was a probable kill. "Lady luck" was a mild superlative for this happenstance. (See the disaster of the *Underhill* which tried to ram a midget sub in the chapter *Pacific Antisubmarine Warfare*)

24-25 May. The crew was on battle stations for almost 24 hours without interruption. The 'night crawlers' continued to come out. On the night of the 24th, thirteen American ships were hit, each less than 20 miles away. Close to 100 raids were recorded during those two days. *Barry* (*APD-29*) had come on station with *Barber* and became a casualty (later in this chapter).

The nights were so black that lookouts couldn't see the planes but could hear them overhead. Once a ship sent her tracer rounds into the sky, the low-flying *kamikaze* would turn into the source of the fire. Antiaircraft fire in the vicinity was often followed by a fireball as a suicide plane exploded into a ship. *Barber* went through a typical exercise on the night of the 23rd; fingers were ready on the firing keys, but a nearby ship shot the plane down before it reached her.

Barber captured three more Japanese paddling around. One spoke Spanish and said he had been a taxi driver in California.

16 June. *Barber* was called in for a rest off Hagushi. The crew watched the battleships bombard the shore installations south of Naha Airport. It was about time for the air raids to begin when there was a bright burst of flame on the horizon and the sound of an explosion. *Tiggs (DD-591)* was hit, and *Barber* was ordered to proceed at best speed to the rescue. After a few minutes underway, there was a second explosion as the destroyer's magazines blew up. Darkness fell before *Barber* arrived. She placed her medical staff on one of the other ships and used her small boats and search lights the rest of the night while looking for survivors.

There was a heavy raid the next day. Word was received that Marine General Simon Bolivar Buckner, Invasion Commander, was killed on Okinawa on 19 May. On 22 June, V-E day was broadcast and, on that night, another heavy raid came from Japan to remind the ships that the Pacific War was still very much in operation. Fifty-six planes were reported shot down with no damage to the anchorage. The American flag was flying over the airfield at Naha.

24 June (eclipse of the moon). There was a heavy raid all night. Three planes were shot down over the anchorage. A bogey made a torpedo run on *Barber* and missed. *Barber* fired and missed.

The Fourth of July was much more than a day to celebrate independence. *Barber* was emancipated from the horrors of Okinawa, her men taking with them the imprint of an experience that time could never erase.

She left Okinawa for Saipan with four other escorts and thirty-two LSTs. On the day after reaching Saipan, she was sent to patrol the flight lanes used by the B-29s bombing Japan. There was an awesome sight overhead with B-29s in front, back and on all sides of the APD as far as the eye could see. On their return, they witnessed a crash and sped to the scene while another bomber circled over the site. Huge sharks were in the area, hunting in the wreckage. Small arms fire kept them at bay as the boat handlers fished up confidential papers from the wreckage. *Barber's* radio was tuned to the frequency used by the planes overhead and received a report that survivors were sighted some distance from the downed plane. She rescued all eleven of the crew and proceeded to Guam.

21 July. *Barber* escorted the carrier *Salamaun (CVE-96)* to Ulithi, then steamed to Leyte Gulf. The water in the harbor was filthy and too still. Dysentery was making its rounds on the many ships anchored in the stale water. Relief came when *Barber* and *Tatum (APD-81)* were ordered to screen the battleships *Mississippi (BB-41)* and *Texas (BB-35)*, and moved out of the port on 8 August.

History was in the making. The first atomic bomb was dropped and then Russia declared war against Japan. The second bomb was dropped and the enemy was reported to have accepted the Allied terms of surrender.

No tears were shed on *Barber*.

Most of the historic data of the APD phase of *Barber* was supplied by a plank owner who preferred to remain anonymous.

BARR

Like the Phoenix, Arisen from the Ashes

In the Atlantic, *Barr (DE-576)* had her stern blasted off by an acoustic torpedo immediately after the carrier *Block Island* was torpedoed and sunk by the same U-boat. (See chapter *The Hunter-Killers*). She was towed to the Boston Navy Yard for repairs and a complete face lift, emerging as *APD-39*.

Shortly after Christmas, 1944, Underwater Demolition Team 13 embarked with rubber life rafts, face masks, swim fins and other gear for its operations. The next month saw *Barr* on the island of Maui, Hawaii, where practice was held for nighttime demolition of obstacles that might hinder amphibious invaders and underwater reconnaissance. Personnel also spent a few days swimming on the beaches at Maui.

Early in February, *Barr* joined a task group, comprising two battleships, a communication ship and several destroyers, bound for Ulithi Atoll. This was the crew's first acquaintance with Pacific atolls. Never before had they witnessed such a massive array of ships of every type. *Barr*, *Gilmore (DE-18)*, *Bull (APD-78)*, *Bates (APD-47)*, *Blessman* (APD-48), and *Waters (DD-115)* performed a full scale demolition and reconnaissance operation at Ulithi in preparation for the severe trials to come.

The group, confident and ready, advanced on Iwo Jima on 16 February, three days before D-Day. The first task for the UDTs was to set out navigation lights near the beach for the approaching invasion forces. The teams encountered heavy fire but escaped without casualties. As *Barr* proceeded to retrieve her returning boats, she attracted a strong response from shore batteries. Her UDT lost one rubber life raft and all its gear, but nothing else of consequence was lost.

17 February. At 0830, all boats were lowered with the UDT and necessary gear. As several armed craft moved toward the beach, ready to launch a heavy attack with their rockets and 40mm guns, the Japs apparently believed this was the initial invasion force and opened fire on the landing craft with everything they had. One after another was hit and most were disabled; several sank. This was one of the point blank beatings the navy encountered at Iwo Jima. All of the APDs and UDT 13 escaped with few losses and no casualties.

On the eve of D-Day, 18 February, UDT 13 was ordered to reestablish a navigation light that was thought to be inoperable. The light was put back in operation without incident, and the team returned to *Barr*. During the same night, *Blessman*, in position next to *Barr*, took two bomb hits from an enemy aircraft with severe casualties and damage (Detailed at the beginning of this chapter).

On D-Day, *Barr* was stationed in the transport area. Occasionally, shrapnel struck the water in and about the ship. UDT 13 personnel assisted in guiding some of the marine landing forces to the beaches. *Barr* then screened the staging area with *Bates* and other ships.

About 16 days after Iwo Jima was just about secured, *Barr* returned to Guam via Saipan for three days of liberty, ball games and beer parties. In company with *Knudson*, *Barr* returned to Ulithi for rest and resupply. Her next assignment was not long in coming.

Barr got underway for Okinawa, arriving on 25 March. She commenced operations in and around Kerama Rhetto with *Bates*, *Gilmore*, *Bull* and *Knudson* and with the support of destroyers *Edwards (DD-619)*, *Porterfield (DD-682)* and *Preston (DD-95)*. *Estes (AGC-12)* was the Amphibious Force flagship of Rear Admiral W.H.P. Blandy.

The next several months were spent screening and protecting the beach areas from enemy subs and as a barrier for any enemy aircraft that might filter into the island. Just about every night and early morning, the screen encountered Japanese suicide planes as they inflicted heavy damage and casualties on the outlying ships.

Barr was then ordered to escort a group of ships back to Saipan for yard availability and liberty for the crew. Leyte was the next port for sonar repairs. Underway on 17 June to Manila, *Barr* carried a shipload of Filipino U.S. Navy personnel on leave from Task Force 38 to visit their homes which some had not seen for many years.

Upon returning to Okinawa, *Barr* was given a special assignment to carry several top Army generals and colonels from General (Vinegar Joe) Stillwell's staff on a tour of the Okinawa outer islands surrounding the main island. Typhoon warnings were beginning to make their appearance and, over the next several weeks, *Barr* encountered several of them. On 1 August, a typhoon sent all ships racing out of the harbor to the open sea for room to maneuver.

Of approximately 140 days in and around Okinawa, *Barr* spent 100 days on screening duty. After the atomic bomb was dropped, there was a lot of speculation about the next step. The crew knew that something big was in the offing because peace talks materialized soon after the second bomb was dropped. On 13 August, *Barr* and other APDs were urgently called into Buckner Bay, Okinawa, for assignment.

They were *Sims (APD-50)*, *Pavlic (APD-70)*, *Reeves (APD-52)*, *Runels (APD-85)*, and *Horace A. Bass (APD-124)*. That evening, and on through the entire night, the crew worked feverishly taking on a full supply of stores and fueling. At noon the following day, *Barr* and the other five APDs, steamed out of Buckner Bay. Three hours later, the captain announced that they were to rendezvous with the main task group en route to Japan.

Barr took aboard approximately 150 British marines from *HMS King George* and *HMS Gambia* at sea to be disembarked on the beach in Japan. Within the next couple of days, the task force came within sight of Mount Fujiyama, and the APDs took refuge in Sagami Wan Honshu, an anchorage just outside of Tokyo Bay. Several days later, the APDs entered Tokyo Bay, and *Barr* discharged the British marines onto the beach. She was then assigned to evacuating allied prisoners of war. *Barr* operated with the antiaircraft cruiser *San Juan (CL-54)*, the hospital ship *Benevolence*, *Reeves* and *Runels*. Sailing as far north as Kamaisha, *Barr* was able to evacuate approximately 1200 repatriates. Many of these men had been captured in the Philippines and had survived the Bataan Death March. A number were pilots who were shot down over Japan during air raids. Also, there were many navy men who had been taken captive during the war.

A very exciting day for *Barr* during the evacuation of POWs came on 1 September. *Barr* and *Reeves* were ordered into inner Tokyo Harbor. With many correspondents aboard, *Barr* was to pick up some civilians. The two vessels passed between two small fortified islands with huge gun emplacements. *Barr* was ordered to tie up alongside the dock. Thus, this ship, the *USS Barr (APD-39)* was the first U.S. warship, major or minor, to tie up alongside a dock in Tokyo, the goal of the U.S. Navy for nearly four years.

After completing the task of evacuating all allied prisoners of war assigned to her, *Barr* reported to her command for further assignment. Anxiety became a growing factor because the men knew that they would soon be going home — and that is exactly where they went.

HORACE A. BASS

Kamikazes and Other Matters.

Originally *DE-691, Horace A. Bass* was reclassified while under construction and emerged from the yard that built her as *APD-124*. She was under the command of Lieutenant Commander F.W. Kuhn of Palisades Park, N.J. during her entire war career.

On 23 February 1945, *Bass* made the long transit from Quincy, Massachusetts to the western Pacific in company with *Gosselin(APD-126)* and *Barr* (*APD-29*). On 2 April, she joined a task force from Ulithi, screening a convoy to Okinawa.

Storekeeper First Class Ira H. Huntley on *Bass*, manifestly was not one of the green ones. Having been in the navy since 1939, he was one of the more experienced enlisted men in *Horas A. Bass*. He reminisced on the beginning of the severe trials for his new ship:

> "I can't recall if we realized en route that we were sailing into an area where the greatest battle of the Pacific was being waged. I don't even believe we knew that we were about to join the largest fleet ever assembled in the Pacific and the final major amphibious strike of a long war. For us, it was an appointment with destiny.
>
> The initial landings had taken place five days prior to our arrival on 6 April. After seeing our charges safely into Kerema Retto, *Bass* steamed to a patrol area off Hagushi anchorage. We arrived just in time to receive the Emperor's greetings, the severest air suicide assault of the war. In a single day, the enemy lost 371 planes to the guns and fighter aircraft of the U.S. Fleet.
>
> The first salvo against the foe by *Bass* brought credit for one 'splash' when the forward gunners spotted a *kamikaze* hurtling toward the transports in the inner anchorage. A burst of 40mm shells shredded the plane before it reached its target, and it plummeted into the sea! It was a great beginning for a crew that included few veterans. The kids jumped up and down and cheered as if they were at a football game. That day marked the entry of *Bass* into the most grueling duty of the entire war. To her sailors, it meant days of patient and alert patrolling, sometimes hours of high tension during the numerous alarms."

On 10 April, *Bass* was temporarily relieved of the high tension of Okinawa to join a convoy to Guam. Returning with a new convoy to Okinawa, she sank a Japanese submarine en route. (See chapter *Pacific Antisubmarine Warfare*).

Bass remained on patrol until May when, in company with a DE, a PC and an SC, she escorted a convoy of 34 landing craft to Saipan. After a short stay, *Bass* was sent back to Okinawa where she stayed until mid-August. The constant picket line duty began once again, and air raids continued around the clock, bringing the same story of losses to light naval units and severe damage to the enemy.

The morning of 8 June. *Bass* was steaming close by the island of Iwo Shima when an alert lookout spotted four suspicious planes flying in low over the water. Before an area alarm was sounded, the ship had manned her battle stations. Suddenly, one of the planes, a Judy, left the formation and started to dive on *Bass*. Her gun crews poured fire into the plane as it made a death-dealing run, deflecting it sufficiently to bring pilot and plane to a watery grave 10 yards off the starboard quarter! No casualties. No serious damage.

The campaign was officially declared secured on 20 June, but for *Bass* and her sister ships, the fighting continued. Storekeeper Huntley remembered it all too clearly:

> "The early morning of 30 July. A day none of my shipmates will ever forget. A full moon had just emerged from behind a low cloud, casting its yellow rays over the calm waters. In another day and time, such a panorama might entrance the mind with its beauty and mystery, but not for the *Bass* men that night. We were aware that the moon was silhouetting the semi-circle of picket ships arrayed off the coast of Okinawa, from Kiese Shima to Le Shima. *Bass* was in the southern end, next to Kiese Shima. The nearest enemy plane was 60 miles away, only next door when making 300 knots.
>
> Those on watch saw the plane only when they heard its motor coughing and sputtering on the side away from the moon. It was an ancient Japanese biplane, armed with death for its pilot as well as his intended target. Before our guns could be brought to bear, the plane crashed into the superstructure, ripped off the radio antenna and part of a life raft, tumbled over the side and exploded alongside the ship! A concussion wave swept the *Bass*, and the port side midship was riddled with bomb fragments.
>
> After months of duty on the line, watching other ships on all sides being hit, the law of averages had caught up with *Bass*. One man was killed, three were seriously wounded and ten others received minor injuries."

Seaman James S. McGarity had been sleeping soundly when he heard a terrible explosion occasioned by the *kamikaze* that had crashed his ship. He bounced out of his bunk, zipped on his clothes, grabbed his life jacket and helmet and raced for his battle station. That station was the forward 40mm gun that had disposed of two prior suicide pilots. Arriving on deck, he was confronted with fire and smoke. Looking at the pile of plywood and canvas debris deposited by the plane before going over the side, he was deeply concerned because many of the men made a habit of sleeping topside to get relief from their stifling hot quarters. One was an electrician's mate, "Windy" Rinaldi. He was definitely known to have been sleeping topside in the area of impact. "Poor Windy," muttered McGarity, "He must be dead." Suddenly, some of the debris started to move. Believing it must have been the Japanese pilot, he screamed to the men nearby, "That must be the Jap pilot! Let's kill the son-of-a-bitch!" They started after a figure beginning to move in the dark but, before they reached him, they heard a voice, "No guys. It's me, Windy. Don't touch me. It's me, Windy. I'm OK, hear, Windy OK!"

Some of the larger holes in the ship's side were rapidly plugged and *Bass* put into Buckner Bay for repairs. Before they could be completed, however, she was ordered out to sea to ride out a typhoon, which she managed to do successfully even with a parade of unplugged holes in the side. While still in Buckner Bay, the captain heard some scuttlebutt to the effect that Admiral Oscar Badger was forming up a small task force to enter Tokyo Bay in the event that rumors about Japanese surrender became fact.

Lewis M. Andrews, Jr.

Bass headed north with five other APDs to join the fueling support group of the Third Fleet and to screen the oilers for the next three days. On 19 August, *Bass* was assigned to a task force in the initial occupation of the Tokyo area. The task force included the battleship *Iowa (BB-61)*, the cruiser *San Diego (CL-53)*, fast mine sweepers, transports and a screen of destroyers and high speed transports. *Bass* assembled demolition and prize crews from the heavy ships of the Third Fleet. The force steamed off Japan for over a week, awaiting conclusion of surrender terms, meanwhile skirting the edge of a typhoon.

On 27 August, the battleship *Missouri (BB-63)* led the powerful American and British Fleets past the Nipponese shore defenses into Sagami Wan. One day prior to the main body's entry, 29 August, *Bass* steamed up Tokyo Bay and dropped anchor off Yokosuka Naval Base in company with an advance force of destroyers, minesweepers and battleships. Ensign Hodges, who had been on the bridge part of the time, recalled that they were piloted through the mine fields by Japanese Lieutenant Commander Sadaoh Murosa.

The night before the official surrender on 30 August, *Bass* was ordered to put a prize crew aboard the giant Japanese battlewagon *HIJMS Nagato* whose big guns overlooked the boat lanes. (HIJMS = His Imperial Japanese Majesty's Ship.) She was considered a potential threat unless neutralized before the scheduled landings at 1000 the next day. Prior to seizing her, a salvage crew from *Bass* was to insure that a shore cable to the bow of the *Nagato* was not a remote booby trap control.

Admiral Badger had requested that the *Bass* skipper and boat officer meet with him on his flagship. Ensign Hodges, the boat officer, recalled the meeting:

> "This was my first and only contact with an admiral. We sat at the table, and Admiral Badger presented a blown up picture of the *Nagato*, showing an electric cable on the bow, apparently bringing current from the shore. He was suspicious that the cable was meant to trigger a huge explosive device. He asked if we could slip into the bay under cover of darkness and cut the cable. Captain Kuhn quickly volunteered my services! At 0430, before the invasion and occupation of Japan, seven men and myself slipped in under the *Nagato*'s bow. I had a pair of rubber gloves and an old fashioned screw type cutter. That cable was at least six inches in diameter! Fortunately, my bosun's mate reached down and pulled on the cable. The damned thing was already cut and just dangling. I breathed a sigh of relief and reported by radio to *Bass* (and the entire Fleet), 'The cable is cut!'
>
> I didn't say how or why. The message was acknowledged by Admiral Badger himself and he then ordered my men and me to go aboard *Nagato*. If all was OK, I was to hoist code flag Able (A). If there appeared to be danger, I was to hoist code flag *Baker* (B).
>
> The entire fleet had big guns trained on the *Nagato*. Had I hoisted *Baker*, I wonder if I would have been on the receiving end of our fire power. There was in my party a Lieutenant (jg) from the battleship *South Dakota (BB-57)*, along as an observer for her commanding officer. After the *Nagato* was secured, the captain was to become her ceremonial captain, receiving the Japanese Commander's sword.
>
> I had a 50 pound portable radio and I was told to talk continuously during the securing process so that listeners would know that the situation aboard *Nagato* was OK. My little party and myself lined up the over 1000 Japanese personnel on the fantail and kept them there until a marine amphibious force landed troops at a nearby seaplane ramp."

With Captain Thomas J. Flynn commanding the prize crew aboard *Bass*, she nosed her way through the breakwater to Yokosuka Ko, the great naval base, and at 0800 was alongside and in control of the last battleship left to the Imperial Japanese Navy.

The surrender of *Nagato* by the Japanese commanding officer took place at 0810. The rising sun was struck from the mainmast, and the American ensign was run up. While the prize crew stood guard over the ship, *Bass* gunners inspected the magazines and guns to insure Japanese compliance with the surrender terms. The *Bass* engineers, with the help of interpreters, lighted off the *Nagato*'s boilers and set her auxiliary power plant in operation. *Bass* stayed alongside *Nagato*, acting as barracks and headquarters ship for the prize crew until relieved of that duty on 5 September.

A great deal of suspicion pervaded the American crews who still had a Pearl Harbor view of the Japanese. Captain Flynn wanted a thorough inspection of the ship to be certain that there were no booby traps. Seaman Jim McGarity was ordered to buckle on a .45 automatic, take a *Nagato* seaman with him, carefully search a given area of the ship and report anything that looked a bit leery. They walked around, opening various hatches and storage lockers. On opening one locker, Jim was stunned to see several cases of bottles with Japanese writing on them as well as plain English which read, "Refined Japanese Saki," obviously reserved for the wardroom.

"It's a gold mine," McGarity muttered half aloud. He opened a bottle, but he was afraid to drink it lest it be poisoned. He ordered the Japanese seaman to take a swig, but the latter shook his head vigorously and repeatedly said, "No - no - no!" But McGarity was not to be put off. The Japanese sailor hesitated, then decided that this American was more of a threat than his own officers who had surrendered. He took a huge gulp, about one quarter of the bottle. After 10 minutes or so, the Japanese still looked healthy and even a bit more mellowed.

McGarity was elated. He later procured a mail sack from the duty mailman on *Bass*, returned to *Nagato*, filled the sack and managed to squirrel it past the Officer of The Deck.

In relating his tale to this author, McGarity was somewhat wistful. "I could have made a fortune, but I was only an eighteen year old and didn't know any better. I just gave it away to my shipmates."

He had to take it easy because he had the 0400-0800 deck watch. Earlier that night, three heavy imbibers of McGarity's largess took a boat without permission with the avowed intention of going to Tokyo to bring back the Emperor's white horse as a souvenir to end all souvenirs. When the three returned during McGarity's watch, they were arrested by, of all people, their perpetrator, under orders of the Officer of The Deck. McGarity took them to the sick bay for the doctor's opinion as to their state of inebriation. The doctor, a Lieutenant (jg), told a bosun's mate to hold both arms straight out and see if he could touch one index finger to the other. After three unsuccessful tries, the bosun blurted out to the doctor, "For Christ Sake, if you want to know if I'm drunk, just ask and I'll tell you, but don't make a God damned ass out of me." The doctor turned to McGarity, "Lock them up."

On 10 September, *Bass* moved into the inner harbor of Yokosuka Ke, assuming duty as barracks ship for the Port Director and his staff. She continued these duties until 15 March 1946 when she was detached and sent back to the U.S. Storekeeper Huntley was philosophic as the days of war retreated to the background of memory:

> "This is not the story of a ship that compiled a brilliant war record but rather the story of a ship that carried out its orders and did the job it was made to do, and did it well.
>
> The small units of the Fleet during those times never received much publicity but, without them, the carriers, battleships and cruisers could not have accomplished the feats for which they received so much credit. (From the rest of us small ship sailors, Amen!)

None of this class of vessel are in existence today, but *Horace A. Bass*, along with the few hundred ships like her, performed a vital role in winning the war. I served on four combat ships during my naval career that spanned a period of six years. But the best part of that career was aboard this escort type vessel. I had a great respect for the captain as a man and as a commanding officer. Concerned for the rest and health of the crew, he always gave us as much time as possible before calling us to General Quarters when an air raid appeared imminent off Okinawa or wherever it happened to come from. He was an expert at handling a ship in any kind of weather, or while refueling in a rough sea." A compliment from ranks below can often mean as much to a commanding officer as a compliment from ranks above.

TATUM

Kamikaze, a Personal Experience

Tatum (DE-789) convoyed to numerous ports in the United Kingdom and North Africa, operating deep into the Mediterranean to Alexandria, Egypt. In August 1944, she escorted landing craft from Naples to Ajaccio, Corsica, then covered them as they stormed ashore in Southern France. In late November, she returned to the United States for conversion to APD-81, commencing the second and most grueling period of her life. Quartermaster Second Class Ned W. Gowing, a plankowner, related much of what this new duty entailed:

> "After conversion to a high speed transport, we assumed that our ship would be in the invasion of Japan, scheduled for March 1946. (Very few people were then aware of the atom bomb which would end the war abruptly.) After gunnery practice in Hawaii, we finally made a landfall on Okinawa on 18 May 1945."

On arriving off Okinawa's Hagushi Beaches, *Tatum* reported for duty with the antiaircraft pickets stationed around the perimeter of the island. Gowing remembers the breath-taking details:

> "29 May. We had been at GQ most of the night. In the dark, early hours, we heard heavy antiaircraft fire directed at a plane about 500 yards on our port beam. Then we saw a terrific explosion of red flame about 50 feet off the water, the end of a *kamikaze*! At daybreak, TBS announced low-flying bogies over the anchorage, and we saw antiaircraft fire going into low stratus clouds. Then a fighter plane dived out of the murk at a steep angle 1000 yards astern, strafing several ships nested together. The plane suddenly burst into flames about 200 feet above the water and splashed close aboard a small landing craft!
>
> At 0900 hours, we proceeded to a picket station three miles north of Ie Shima, the island where Ernie Pyle had recently been killed. The area was popularly known as 'Suicide Gulch'. Arriving about noon, we commenced our patrol. As a quartermaster during GQ, my job was to keep the ship's log on the flying bridge.
>
> 9 June 1945. At 1920 hours, enemy planes were reported in the vicinity. Shore batteries on Ie Shima went into action, firing at planes out of our visual range. One of our lookouts spotted a plane 400 yards off our starboard quarter, circling around to our starboard bow. When it started in on us, we opened fire, and I dropped to the deck."

As the first intruder swooped in across her bow, *Tatum's* guns opened up and scored hits on its wing and fuselage. It banked sharply as it headed for what seemed to be an inevitable crash. About 40 feet from the APD, the plane's port wing and tail struck the water. A 500 pound bomb skipped along the surface, careened off the underside of a gun sponson, and pierced the hull and two of her longitudinal (fore and aft) bulkheads. (A 'skip' bomb was a conventional aerial bomb dropped from a plane flying so low that the bomb would hit the water flat, before its nose turned down. It would then ricochet off the water and into the side of the ship.) The dud came to rest with the nose protruding eight inches into the executive officer's stateroom. The plane also skimmed over the water into *Tatum*, dented her hull and knocked out her gyro compass, fire control director, and communications with the engine room. Gowing continued.

> "The plane was blazing in the water off our starboard quarter. *Tatum's* guns would now have to be fired by local control.
>
> Another plane was sighted off our port quarter, two miles away. All port side guns commenced firing, but another plane had slipped around to our port bow unnoticed and started his dive directly at us. It was racing in, but in time for our guns to change targets. I was sure it was heading straight for me. When I looked up, it was burning in the water, a scant 100 yards off the port beam!
>
> Meanwhile, a third plane was coming in broad on the starboard quarter, headed for the bridge at very high speed, about 200 feet above the water. I didn't hit the deck that time but just stood watching it, too paralyzed to do anything. It came in right over the mast, did a half roll, and went into the water just off the port bow, burning up instantly!"

The pilot of the fourth plane apparently had been holding back and waiting for his colleagues to open a favorable route of attack. Gowing recalled the attack as though it were only the day before:

"A lookout spotted a plane circling three miles off our port quarter, then heading for us from our starboard quarter, flying low and gathering terrific speed. It didn't seem possible it could miss. As it flew over the ship, one wing broke off. The plane banked steeply around the mast, spraying gasoline on us and splashing very close aboard the port bow! An underwater explosion rocked *Tatum* but caused no damage.

Just after the plane burned in the water, we thought we saw a ceremonial robe on the surface, but we were unable to retrieve it. A sharp lookout indicated no other planes about, and it seemed that we had splashed a complete raid. Our communications officer, Lieutenant Cohen, had been giving a running account of the action on TBS, and it was heard by most of the ships in the Okinawa area."

A couple of the crew were slightly injured but only required on-board treatment. Despite considerable damage to the APD, her crew had all essential equipment back in operation within 15 minutes. Relieved by *Walter C. Wann (DE-412)*, she headed for Hagushi. Gowing recalled:

"We limped into Naha harbor on one engine to pick up a bomb disposal officer. We then proceeded out two miles to the 100 fathom curve where the crew was ordered back to the fantail while the dud was disarmed and lowered over the side.

0900. We received a visit from Vice Admiral Hill, who commended the captain and crew. That same morning, we painted four little rising sun flags on either side of the bridge."

Tatum returned to Hagushi the following morning, then moved to Kerama Retto for temporary repairs. Permanent repairs were effected at Leyte. Thereafter, she participated in various convoys. After cessation of hostilities, she carried out POW evacuation and occupation duties among the islands and along the China coast. It was not until April 1946 when she headed back to the United States.

LOY

The Enemy Did Not Need This APD

Loy (DE-160) departed from New York on 12 November 1943 for convoy escort duty, including two round trips to Bizerte and Algiers and one from Boston to Halifax. She spent April and May 1944 with the *Core (CVE-13)* Hunter-Killer Group from the Azores to Casablanca. Between June and October 1944, she made two more Atlantic convoys prior to conversion to APD-56.

Loy stood out from New York on New Years Day 1945 and arrived in the Leyte Gulf area, Philippines, on 4 March. For the next three weeks, she held antiaircraft practice and exercises with UDT 4 and the Western Islands Attack group. She was assigned to various task formations for screening operations in preparation for Okinawa.

26 March. The group arrived at Kerama Retto before daybreak. At dawn, the commanding officer of *Loy*, Lieutenant Commander R.W. Pond Jr., was alerted to several Vals attacking the screen. A *kamikaze* made an unsuccessful attack on *Crosley (APD-87)* while another crashed *Kimberly (DD-521)*. Two others roared in on *Gilmer (APD-11)*, 1500 yards from *Loy*. The first one made a gliding attack but was driven off by gun fire. The next plane plummeted into a vertical dive out of the clouds directly on *Gilmer*, missing by a few feet. Guns on *Loy* had tracked this plane with a director solution but were unable to fire because *Gilmer* fouled her range.

During the night off Kerama Retto, several low-flying enemy aircraft passed close to *Loy*. They were tracked near *Tatum* with *Loy*'s surface radar, but the range was too great to permit her to fire. One plane was hit by a nearby ship and set afire. Another made a gliding attack in *Loy*'s direction and was fired upon. Two 5" shells burst about 25 yards ahead of this aircraft which then reversed course and landed in the water about 2000 yards from *Loy*!

27 March. During minesweeping operations, *Loy* made a reconnaissance of the Okinawa preferred beaches. She also conducted demolition activity without opposition and with excellent fire support from the big guns of Task Force 52. Several members of UDT 4 reported sporadic sniper fire when close to the beach, but fire support ships had difficulty finding suitable targets.

The evening of 28 March. Enemy planes made runs on the Kerama Retto area. Three were tracked nearby on *Loy*'s surface radar and two were sighted for short intervals. One Betty splashed near *Scribner (APD-122)* after passing *Loy* close aboard. As the plane was not under fire, the reason for the splash was ascribed to pilot error.

29 March. Several alerts were sounded after dawn with antiaircraft fire in the distance. *Bunch (APD-79)* ordered *Loy* to assist the rocket landing ship *(LSM(R)-188)*. A *kamikaze* crash killed the captain, pharmacist's mate and six others. About thirty men suffered serious injuries. Although the LSM was slowly sinking, *Loy*'s doctor and pharmacist's mate boarded her to render first aid. A repair party from the APD, equipped with gasoline handy-billies, assisted the LSM crew, enabling the battered ship to proceed to port. In the afternoon, the boats and men of UDT 4 were lowered for a successful reconnaissance of Purple and Orange beaches.

30-31 March. In the morning, UDT 4 and other UDT units made a successful pre-assault demolition of obstacles on the preferred beaches. *Loy* returned to Kerama Retto anchorage for the night.

Loy and UDT 4 personnel aided the assault by supporting control ships and the beach masters of Purple and Orange beaches. Landings were successfully completed without much opposition, and the next few days were spent aiding the beach masters to improve the beaches for landing craft.

UDT 4 members reported that the covering barrage from battleships and cruisers was the best they had ever experienced. It never landed near them nor fell short in the water, and all enemy firing was answered promptly and accurately. Single Japanese planes attacked various units operating close to *Loy* during twilight. In daylight, CAP(combat air patrols) did an excellent job, and no enemy planes were seen. However, the Okinawa campaign had just begun.

1 April. *Loy* had been anchored for the night in the Western Anchorage, Okinawa Gunto. About 0300, the APD got underway to carry out an attack order on the Okinawa preferred beaches. At dawn, she arrived off Purple Beach to deliver UDT personnel and a British Liaison Officer. A Val made a gliding attack on the bom-

bardment group, was taken under fire by several ships and appeared to be hit. It then dived at the cruiser *Biloxi (CL-80)*, 1500 yards from *Loy*.

Loy fired a few rounds of 5" ammunition, and one of her boats near *Biloxi* reported that flak from *Loy* hit the plane's tail. Heavy fire from *Biloxi* rocked the plane 250 feet above her and splashed it close aboard! Just before diving on the cruiser, the aircraft had released a bomb 200 feet from *Loy*'s landing boat, but without damage. The boat picked up a wheel from the plane for a souvenir.

After dispatching boats and UDT 4 personnel to assist the Beach Master on Purple 1 and 2 beaches, *Loy* stood clear until her services were required. The assault met little opposition, and progressed rapidly.

2 April. Just before dawn, *Loy* left her screening station to proceed to Purple Beaches. A Val came in astern and was taken under 40mm fire. The plane was shot down by ships on *Loy*'s port quarter. The APD anchored off Purple Beaches while UDT 4 personnel improved the reef for landing craft.

3 April. As the clock moved past midnight, *Loy* was patrolling off Okinawa. Enemy planes attacked in the area. Just before first light, she left her patrol station and proceeded to the Hagushi Beaches. The demolition team left the ship at noon with 10 tons of tetrytol to blow a channel in the reef off Orange 1. *Loy* remained on station until after dark. At 2005, enemy planes attacked in the area, and all ships emitted dense smoke.

4 April. The demolition team set off their explosives in the assigned areas and returned to the ship just after midnight. *Loy*'s engines were kept on line all night so as to be ready in an emergency.

6 April. At dawn, the demolition party blew off coral heads at Orange Beaches, then returned to the ship. In early afternoon, the UDT 4 commander left the ship in Hagushi Anchorage to discuss operations with Rear Admiral Blandy, Commander Task Force 52. Vals made a surprise attack on the anchorage in late afternoon.

One Val headed directly at *Loy* but was shot down by LSTs anchored just ahead of her! Another was shot down over the beaches before it could make an attack. Two F6F planes were also shot down by ships and shore batteries through failure of gunners to recognize the planes. Fire from ships in the anchorage set ablaze a landing barge loaded with oil and some other Army supplies. *Loy* had to get underway to clear the burning oil barge that was drifting toward her.

7 April. Before dawn, enemy bombers attacked the anchorage. A bomb landed in the water near *Loy* but without damage. At daybreak, she sent her demolition team into Hagushi Beaches to blow up various obstructions as assigned by the Beach Master and to blow a heavy one through the reef. In early evening, at her night screening station, enemy planes were in the area. One of the planes was splashed about a mile away by minesweepers patrolling inside of *Loy*'s station.

8 April. While *Loy* was patrolling her station at daybreak, a Val was spotted coming in low, distance five miles, off the starboard bow. The crew had just secured from routine battle stations but they were quickly manned again. The plane headed directly for *Loy*. Ship speed was increased to 22 knots, and the skipper maneuvered to keep the plane on the starboard beam. When it closed to about 6500 yards, *Loy* commenced rapid fire with her 5" gun, using magnetic proximity ammunition. She managed to get several bursts close to the aircraft but it was so low over the water the gun crew couldn't tell whether the bursts were caused by the influence of the plane or the earth's magnetic field. After the plane closed to 5000 yards, bursts were so close that the plane decided to retire.

The aircraft was kept under fire until the range opened to 7000 yards, the limit for the APD's director. All shells appeared to burst but, as the aircraft opened the range, flying just off the water, shell bursts were short. The last few were spotted over the plane. It then climbed to about 200 feet when it burst into flames, cause unknown. It may have been under fire from other ships or downed by F6F planes which came out of the clouds near the ship shortly after the splash. *Loy*'s guns might also have inflicted damage that caused the fire. The incident boosted the morale of the crew, proving that suicide planes could be driven off by alert gun crews.

12 April. At Hagushi Beaches, shortly after midnight, *Waters (APD-8)* came alongside and transferred five tons of Tetrytol to *Loy*. An hour later, enemy planes attacked shipping off the Hagushi Beaches and five suicide aircraft were shot down by American planes within sight of *Loy*. In mid-afternoon, Lieutenant Colonel C.L. Davis and a group of Army observers for the Menna Shima operation came aboard.

13 April. An hour before dawn, *Loy* got underway for the Ie Shima operations, arriving off Menna Shima where she put off two boats with tetrytol to assist marines and army personnel in improving the reef and beach for the landing of large artillery.

16 April. In the dark, early morning hours, *Loy* was underway to conduct assault operations on Ie Shima. On arriving, she lowered boats to transfer demolition personnel to beach control vessels and to assist the Beach Master. Later in the morning, *Loy*'s air search radar showed several Vals commencing suicide runs on ships in the outer screen, trying to break through and hit transports and fire support vessels off the beaches.

Several planes were downed by American fighters and vessels in the outer screen. One Val broke through the perimeter and started an approach on the transport area, gradually closing *Loy*. She was the only ship to fire on this plane, opening up at 8000 yards off the port beam with her 5" gun. Most of the shells burst near the plane and it splashed about 7000 yards off her port beam!

In the meantime, another Val came through the screen and started an attack from ahead while yet another one closed the ship on her port quarter. The 5" gun was trained and fired ahead to take the Val coming on her bow. However, several F6F friendlies came in from a high altitude and splashed this plane before it closed to 6000 yards. The plane on the port quarter turned away from *Loy* and made a diving attack on the destroyer *Barton (DD-599)*. Taken under heavy fire by many ships in the transport area, she was splashed near *Birmingham* !

Several other Vals tried to get ships in the transport area but were either shot down by CAP or by ships in the outer screen. A post war analysis of the action credited *Loy* with two suicide planes that month, one on 8 April and the other on 16 April.

Leaving Okinawa on 25 April, *Loy* arrived in Guam early in May. From 11 to 15 May she engaged in convoy escort, returning to Okinawa and the station patrols in the antiaircraft screen. On 25 May, she embarked survivors from *Barry* (*APD-29*) after that ship had been crashed by a *kamikaze* (narrated later in this chapter).

Lewis M. Andrews, Jr.

The night of 27-28 May. *Loy* was off Okinawa with *Finnegan (DE-307)* for mutual protection. The moon was full and the surface visibility was four miles. At 2231, two sets of flares were dropped by an enemy aircraft and the SL radar picked up a low flying plane approaching from the same direction.

The bogey gradually approached *Loy* at low altitude. All guns were alerted and coached onto the target. At 2000 yards, the aircraft was picked up visually, and guns opened fire. The target developed into two twin-engine Betties, making a simultaneous attack on the starboard side. The forward plane, was taken under fire by the 5" gun. On the third round, the *kamikaze* exploded in the air!

Loy opened fire on the after plane with number five 20mm and number three 40mm guns. Although hit repeatedly, that plane pressed home its attack even as it's starboard engine was set ablaze. *Loy*'s 40mm guns knocked the plane over on its port wing. The *kamikaze* executed a quick turn to the left, within 300 feet of the fantail, and tried to make a landing on the stern. It almost crashed the ship and disappeared in the gun smoke about 200 feet from the starboard side. A loud underwater explosion astern shook the ship violently! The action was so fast that the port 20mm guns were only able to fire half a magazine each before the plane splashed.

2315. A third enemy plane was picked up on the surface radar at 11 miles, gradually approaching the screen, and the ship ahead of *Loy* took it under fire. The plane circled twice and headed toward *Loy*. This aircraft was not visible due to adverse light conditions but could be followed on radar. It was recognized as a Jill as it started a dive from the direction of a dark cloud on the starboard beam. The 5" gun failed to score a hit, but the *kamikaze* was struck repeatedly by automatic guns. Although on fire, it continued toward the APD to within 75 feet from her hull when the right wing came off and the plane splashed, exploding with a violent concussion! The severed wing landed on the starboard boats and number five 20mm gun, destroying the boats and gun mounts in the area.

Fragments of the plane and bomb were driven with great force through the side of the ship. Most holes were quite small but the largest, a 5 inch diameter hole at the water line, allowed large quantities of water to flow into the after engine room.

Three men were killed outright and fifteen were injured. Fragments of hot metal or burning particles pierced two drums of gasoline and several drums of fog oil stowed on the fantail, causing an intense fire. Shrapnel did much damage to topside gear, antennae, halyards, flag bags, etc. Two pieces pierced the mast, severing the coaxial cable to the air search radar and cutting up other lines inside and outside the mast. Secondary conn aft took control.

All engines were stopped. The greatest dangers to the safety of the ship were the severe leak in the after engine room and the fire on the fantail. Damage control parties and the engine room detail plugged the leaks with available materials; wood plugs, wedges and mattresses proved to be the best stop gaps. Flooding was reduced to less than 200 gallons a minute before any machinery was extensively damaged. However, both electric motors to the main condensate pump had been sprayed with sea water; they required baking to remove the moisture.

The repair parties successfully fought the fire with fog spray and CO2. Two compartments were deliberately flooded to prevent the spread of the fire. With the leaks also brought under control, the ship got underway near midnight, steaming on boiler number one with a two motor operation. Captain Pond again ordered all engines stopped because the ship was listing to starboard. Fuel was shifted and one port side boat was swung out to help correct the starboard list. The ship then proceeded at five knots.

0038. While en route to the anchorage, a twin-engine Betty, plane number four, was picked up on the SL radar, distance three miles, headed for *Loy*. This aircraft was sighted at 2000 yards to starboard, and all guns that could bear commenced firing. The plane was hit by a 5" burst under its starboard wing, throwing it over on its port wing in a manner similar to plane number two. Although on fire, the craft pulled up and commenced a turn to the left. As the fires in the plane increased in intensity, the pilot tried to crash the ship. However, he fell short and his plane exploded in the water 1500 yards off!

0512. After arriving in the anchorage, ships were attacked by a Rufe. Several ships, including *Loy*, took the plane under fire, and it exploded in the air. This aircraft, *Loy*'s fifth, splashed about 1000 yards from the ship!

0810 A Tony made an attack on the anchorage, a gliding run out of a low cloud cover and headed directly at *Loy*. She and several other ships opened fire. This plane, an astonishing number six, was splashed about 300 yards on her port beam! All appearances indicated that *Loy* was largely responsible for destroying this plane.

By any standard, the performance of the crew of *Loy* in successfully engaging six aircraft sequentially under nerve-shattering circumstances was admirable. For the entire night, 2231 to 0810, the exhausted but valiant crew had been embattled with *kamikazes*. The skipper noted in his action report:

> "During all enemy aircraft attacks on the 27th and 28th, this vessel took six planes under fire and, without assistance from any other ship, destroyed four enemy aircraft. We also assisted in the destruction of two other enemy planes, one of which was largely destroyed by this vessel.
>
> All gunners stayed in their own arcs of fire and, during the simultaneous attack, they picked out planes coming in on their own sectors and effectively opened fire on time and when in range. All gunners stood with their guns during the attack. At no time was there any evidence of personnel flinching or shirking their duties. Officers and men exhibited an *esprit de corps* that was a credit to the navy. When plane number three dived on the ship, the gunners stood to their guns and kept firing until the plane exploded 100 feet or less from the side of the ship. Three men were killed at the 20mm guns, while they might have saved their lives by stepping back several feet. Two of those killed actually kept on firing until the plane exploded 50 feet from their gun. One gunner on a 50 caliber machine gun was blown over the side while still firing at the plane; he was rescued by *Finnegan*.
>
> The fire on the fantail gave some trouble for a few minutes. Gasoline and oil proved to be a stubborn mixture. Repair parties were delayed in fighting the gasoline fire because the quick releasing gear on the gasoline stowage racks was jammed. Repair party members took axes and went through the flames under fog spray to cut the cables holding the gasoline drums. After the gasoline was jettisoned, the oil fire was soon brought under control. Fire dam-

age to the fantail was confined to scorched paint.

After the ship was hit, morale remained high. Although the vessel was damaged, three more planes were successfully taken under fire and destroyed."

Adding the two *kamikazes* shot down in April to the six destroyed in May, the header of this narrative, "The Enemy Did Not Need This APD," requires no further definition.

REDNOUR

A Quick Acquaintance with a Kamikaze

Arriving at San Diego on 11 March 1945, *Rednour (APD-102)* engaged in training exercises before proceeding to Pearl Harbor. There, she assisted in the training of Underwater Demolition Teams through 8 April when she then steamed as a convoy escort to Ulithi.

Departing from Ulithi, she overtook a convoy to the Hagushi beaches of Okinawa, arriving on 26 April. She patrolled off Kerama Retto through the following month and assisted in the screening of inward and outward bound convoys, all the while repelling incessant air raids.

The night of 27 May. *Rednour* was patrolling 14 miles west of Zampa-Miski (Point Bolo), Okinawa, in company with *Loy* and *Eisele (DE-34)*. The sea was calm with bright moonlight and good visibility. An urgent warning sent *Rednour* to sharply increased speed to repel an air attack. Shortly before midnight, the first suicide plane to attack *Loy* was exploded in midair by her gunners, and another aircraft partially crashed her. A third plane evaded *Rednour's* gunfire, but a fourth was picked up on her air search radar, distance nine miles, and rapidly closing her starboard bow. Seven minutes later, *Rednour* opened fire on that aircraft with her 40mm and 20mm guns. The plane circled and passed out of range.

2341. A fifth *kamikaze* approached on her starboard bow. The APD opened fire with guns of every caliber as the plane passed across her bow and out of range. Four minutes later, an Oscar, probably the same plane, was sighted close aboard, approaching the starboard quarter and was immediately taken under fire. The plane was carrying a 250 pound bomb under each wing. *Rednour* was maneuvered violently to escape the plane attempting to crash the ship.

Despite the withering fire thrown up by the gunners, the *kamikaze* crashed the fantail on the starboard side, blowing a 10 foot wide hole in the main deck, wrecking and partly flooding a compartment below and starting a large fire! Three lay dead, and 13 were wounded.

The plane came in horizontally, 10 feet over the water, but the path of the bombs through the ship was vertical, detonating simultaneously on impact, a high order explosion with no fragments recovered. No gases or fumes were noted after the explosion, but several shrapnel holes were blown through the side of the hull. Two steel plates were penetrated, one with a thickness of 1/2 inch and the other 1/4 inch.

The commanding officer, Lieutenant Commander Roland H. Cramer, largely credited the forward repair party and assisting volunteers who rallied to bring the fire under control only a few minutes after the crash. One third of the 40mm batteries were disabled. The smoke generator was destroyed. Hull holes, at and above the waterline on the starboard side, caused flooding when making tight turns to starboard. Structural damage was massive above and below the main deck.

Nonetheless, the ship was not out of action. The fire was doused. Oil in the flooded compartment was covered by a blanket of foam to prevent recurrence of the fire. After driving off another suicide plane, *Rednour* entered Kerama roadstead for temporary repairs.

Departing from Okinawa on 14 June, *Rednour* steamed to California. Arriving at San Pedro on 22 July, she underwent a general overhaul, then got underway for service in the Marshall-Gilbert Islands Command with *Transport Division 104* until the Japanese surrender.

HOPPING

Her Battles Came from Air and Shore

In her Atlantic days, *Hopping (APD-51)* had been *(DE-155)*, attached to Escort Division Six with this author's *Sims*, the narrative of which is related in chapter *Convoys to The United Kingdom*. Her commanding officer, Lieutenant Commander W.J. McNulty was an highly experienced DE-APD skipper. The transport steamed to Pearl Harbor, arriving on 15 January 1945. While there, she trained with underwater demolition teams, the Navy's famed "frogmen."

Hopping participated as a unit of Underwater Demolition Group 52.13. Commander Task Unit was Captain R.D. Williams, flying his pennant on *Bunch (APD-79)*, the same control vessel as in the *Dickerson*, *Loy* and other narratives in this chapter. UDT 7, commanded by Lieutenant Commander R.F. Burke, was embarked in *Hopping*. The APD got underway to Okinawa with the Task Group on 21 March. Antiaircraft tracking exercises were conducted en route.

The group arrived in its designated area, west of Kerama Retto, before dawn on 26 March. Daybreak brought "Flash Red - Control Yellow." One minute later, an enemy aircraft was seen to burst into flames and hit the water five miles from *Hopping*, followed by another plane splashing and exploding seven miles away. Heavy antiaircraft fire from American ships was like a sign hung in the sky, "Welcome to Okinawa"!

The assault on Kerama Retto began at 0800 on 26 March. *Hopping* occupied a station in the 30-ship screen, covering the heavy fire support ships. Enemy aircraft attacked the Group just before dawn on the 28th, and a Val was sighted about three miles from the APD. It was splashed by other screening ships. Four minutes later, *Hopping* opened fire on another Val at an elevation of 3000 feet, only a mile away. It splashed close aboard *Crosley (APD-87)*!

On the night of 28 March, *Hopping* received orders to patrol a screening station six miles from the Kerama group. Coinciding with her arrival shortly before midnight, her TBS blared, "Flash Red - Control Yellow." Speed was reduced to 10 knots to minimize the phosphorescent wake. Lookouts sighted aircraft only two miles off. Twenty minutes later, they reported antiaircraft fire at a distance of six miles.

The wind was force three from the northwest with a calm sea, mild temperature and a full moon. The sky was partially overcast with visibility about five miles. Midnight heralded 29 March. So did Flash White - Control Yellow!

0108 on L-3 (three days before landing). A low-level Val screamed in out of the black, about 20 degrees abaft the starboard beam, crossing over *Hopping*'s bridge to the port side. A bomb was dropped, but later than intended. It fell across the forecastle and hit the water about 20 yards off the port bow. The plane came in for a second attack, this time on the port beam, but unaccountably flew off.

A Betty, attacked from the port quarter, crossing the ship's bow and releasing a bomb which exploded 100 yards off the starboard bow. The plane disappeared, leaving the crew waiting anxiously in the semi-darkness. It didn't take long. The same Betty attacked from dead ahead. All guns on *Hopping* that could bear blasted away at the deadly intruder. A bomb fell close aboard the port bow as the Betty, like a previous Val, splashed off the starboard beam of *Crosley*!

0345. A twin engine airplane, probably another Betty, was driven off by antiaircraft fire as it approached the starboard bow of *Hopping*. Two hours later, *Hopping* gunners sighted a Val closing rapidly. It passed down her starboard side and then flew off.

Although *Hopping* had opened an accurate and rapid fire on all four direct attacks, it was not definite that any targets were damaged by her. The Betty that was splashed was also fired on by *Crosley*.

0922. Quickly donning her other hat as a high speed transport, *Hopping* lowered away UDT 7 in four boats with inflatables aboard at 6000 yards off the beach, behind the support of battleships, light and heavy cruisers, destroyers and infantry amphibious gunboats. The mission was to conduct reconnaissance and demolition work on the Yellow (code named) sectors of the western beaches of Okinawa Jima. Two hours later, the UDT returned, having completed its mission.

0900 on L-2. UDT 7 went in under the same fire support and cleared beach obstructions from Yellow beach two. One man received minor wounds from 40mm shrapnel. The obstructions were blown up, and the UDT returned to the ship.

Pre-dawn on L-day, 1 April. Enemy aircraft attacked the fire support and transport ships off the beaches of Okinawa Jima. A plane burst into flames and hit the water six miles from *Hopping*. Five minutes later, amidst heavy antiaircraft fire, another *kamikaze* plunged into the water, this time only 1-1/2 miles from *Hopping*. A Val crossed her bow from port to starboard, dropping a bomb a mile ahead of the ship. A Val, possibly the same one, burst into flames and splashed at a distance of three miles!

7 to 10 April. *Hopping* operated with the Eastern Islands Attack Group. The Task Group Commander was Rear Admiral W.H.P. Blandy on board the Amphibious Force Flagship *Estes (AGC-12)*. UDT 7 conducted reconnaissance of the beaches off the southern coast of Tsugen Jima, Eastern Islands, during the morning of 7 April.

The morning of 9 April. The cruiser *Pensacola (CA-24)* started the day with a shore bombardment of Tsugen Jima at close range. *Hopping* proceeded into Nakagusuku Wan in order to conduct a UDT reconnaissance of the approaches to Purple and Brown (code named) beaches off the east coast of Okinawa Jima. In early afternoon, all boats returned with their mission completed.

1615. *Hopping* acted on orders from the Commander Cruiser Division 4 on *Wichita (CA-45)* to proceed out of Nakagusuku Wan and to take up a screening patrol outside the entrance to the bay off Tsugen Jima.

1700. The shore battery, located near Tsugen Jima light, opened fire on *Hopping*! The enemy fire was effective and accurate. Ranging shots were observed straddling the ship, followed by six consecutive hits on the port side. Two enemy shells failed to detonate even though they passed through several bulkheads. The shells were later concluded to be 4.7" armor piercing projectiles and 75mm shrapnel rounds. Captain McNulty responded quickly to the surprise attack.

Full speed was ordered as GQ was sounded. Because of the shell hits, however, number two fire and engine rooms were secured, and a maximum speed of 18 knots was obtained by number one fire and engine rooms. Propulsion was from the starboard screw only. The gun crews rallied quickly and methodically. *Hopping* opened fire with her 5" and 40mm guns. Using her surface search radar for opening ranges and correction by visual spotting, she fired a total of 29 antiaircraft (shrapnel) 5" rounds and 108 rounds of 40mm.

Enemy shells severed the 115 volt supply to number three 40mm mount, limiting usage of the gun to manual control. The compressor pump unit of one gun sight was punctured with several shrapnel hits which completely destroyed it. A 5" gun gas ejector part broke after firing six rounds. Nonetheless, the gun continued to fire, a courageous and hazardous thing for the gun captain to do. The breech might have "cooked off" on any successive round (as on *Samuel B. Roberts* in chapter *The Battle off Samar*).

The enemy battery ceased firing at the opening of counterfire and did not fire again. *Hopping*'s shots were rapid and accurate with the strong possibility that the enemy battery was put out of action or at least damaged. *Wichita* and *Pensacola* commenced heavy bombardment of the area shortly after *Hopping* opened fire.

Ship's company casualties were one killed and ten wounded. UDT casualties were one killed and eight wounded. Battle damage was considerable throughout the ship.

Four wounded were transferred to the cruiser *Mobile (CL-63)* and three to *Estes (AGC-12)*. While lying to and effecting transfer of the wounded, the *Hopping* crew witnessed the main assault on Tsugen Jima by the Eastern Islands Attack Group.

Hopping anchored at Kerama Retto to transfer the nine remaining wounded to the transport *Gosper (APA-170)* and to effect emergency repairs of battle damage. Burial services at sea were conducted en route for the two men killed in the action.

Hopping proceeded to Ulithi for further repairs, arriving on 23 April. Returning to Okinawa on 17 May to resume screening duties, she was soon back in the thick of the fighting as the air and land battles raged. She remained off Okinawa continuously until the island was secured, fighting off countless mass attacks by the desperate Japanese. The ship sailed on 8 August with a convoy bound for Leyte where she learned of the surrender of Japan.

DANIEL T. GRIFFIN

Sixty-One Days at Okinawa

Like *Hopping*, *Daniel T. Griffin (APD-38)* was destroyer escort *(DE-54)*, operating in Escort Division Six in the Atlantic. This author knew her commanding officer, Lieutenant Commander J.A. Eastwood, to be an highly proficient and experienced officer, and I was not at all surprised to learn about his exploits at Okinawa.

Griffin arrived at Pearl Harbor on 6 February 1945 to serve with underwater demolition teams. She then reported to the staging area at San Pedro Bay, Leyte, on 5 March for emergency repairs and training. Along with *Hopping*, *Griffin* was assigned to UDT exercises under the Commander Transport Division *(ComTransDiv)* 104 on *Bunch*. The ship's training at Leyte and en route to Okinawa emphasized antiaircraft tracking and damage control. During rehearsals, *Griffin* screened APDs carrying underwater demolition teams, again demonstrating the dual capabilities of APDs to carry troops or to screen troop carriers.

Griffin arrived at Kerama Retto on 26 March. Her deploy*ment was at variance to other APDs. She would not participate in normal UDT operations unless directed to relieve another APD with a UDT aboard. Upon reaching her objective, *Griffin's* primary mission would be to supply and support UDTs from other ships. In addition, she would take aboard the UDT from any APD that might be damaged in action and carry on the damaged ship's operations. Her secondary mission consisted of shallow water minesweeping with her four LCVPs.

Griffin's engineering plant was kept in full operation during the period and was never secured. War cruising condition was to be maintained while at anchor; the depth charge battery and sonar were manned continuously; the antiaircraft battery would be cocked during daylight hours and during good visibility at night.

2250 on 29 March. The misty night was dark and overcast with low visibility. *Griffin's* radar gained contact on a bogey roaring in on the starboard side from a distance of 11 miles, identified as a twin engine Betty. The APD executed a 90 degree emergency turn to port.

2307. The plane appeared on her port quarter and passed up very low on the port side. The ship opened fire at a range of 1500 yards. The director operators lost sight of the target after firing approximately six 5" rounds. Firing was checked and resumed three times. The last order to cease fire was issued with the plane on the port bow. Just as Captain Eastwood executed a 90 degree emergency turn to starboard to resume the base course, the Betty made a swift turn ahead and closed on the starboard bow with a steady bearing. Lookouts picked it up at 1500 yards. All guns within the firing sector opened up. The Betty closed to 800 yards, then abruptly and surprisingly broke off and retired. No damage to the plane was apparent, but it was believed that the 20mm and 40mm guns scored hits in the final action.

6 April. A new day brought excellent weather with good visibility and broken overcast at 3000 feet. It was also one of the worst days of the entire Okinawa campaign for ships on picket stations.

1331. A low-flying Francis, apparently coming from Naha Field, made a surprise approach on *Griffin*. It turned to the ship's port and passed abeam at a range of 3500 yards. Due to possible personal stress, the helmsman applied left rudder instead of right rudder as ordered, thereby fouling the bearing of the 5" gun. Also, there was an ordnance failure on the starboard after 40mm during this action, attributed to faulty loading. However, the gun was quickly cleared and resumed firing. All ships in the vicinity were shooting at this plane, but no hits were claimed. The aircraft was shot down by a friendly fighter aircraft five miles from *Griffin*.

1612. A complete surprise attack developed when two Vals broke through cloud cover astern. *Griffin's* radar had reported only friendlies in or near her station. Diving at a 60 degree angle, one plane was immediately identified and taken under fire. Full speed ahead and left full rudder were applied, placing the aircraft on the port quarter at the time of its bomb release. The bomb exploded 100 yards on the ship's starboard beam. During the plane's recovery from the dive, one 40mm round hit the starboard wing. After leveling off, the aircraft appeared to shudder as though temporarily out of control, then steadied in a shallow glide and splashed about 4000 yards on the starboard quarter without smoke or fire! The starboard lookout aft, following this plane with his binoculars, reported that no other ships were in the vicinity and saw no indications of other ships firing at the plane. It looked like a *Griffin* only splash beyond doubt.

One minute after the first attack, radar reported a Val overhead, circling to a position astern and then diving at a sharp angle. With *Griffin* still turning under left full rudder, applied in the first attack, the plane released a bomb on the ship's port quarter which exploded about 100 yards off. While recovering from its dive and passing over the stern at close to 300 feet, two 40mm shells found their mark on the port wing, causing a large section about halfway out from the fuselage to rip off. Another 40mm shell hit the tail section, destroying the port altitude control, part of the rudder, and part of the starboard altitude control. The craft continued its flight momentarily and was taken under fire by other ships in the area. While this plane was not observed by *Griffin* personnel to crash, destroyer *Gregory (DD-802)* reported that the Val she was firing at had splashed!

Of the estimated four to five planes in this raid, two had attacked *Griffin* with 500 pound bombs. The portion of the hull along the engineering spaces on the port side was slightly bowed in by the second bomb but without significant damage.

1752. Continuing a very long day, the radar gained contact on two bogies, distance 14 miles. They circled at a range of 11 miles when the bearing steadied and the planes came straight in. Captain Eastwood put *Griffin's* helm hard over to port to reverse her heading at full speed and to close *Morris (DD-417)*. This maneuver afforded both vessels mutual close fire support and placed the enemy planes on their starboard bows.

1815. The aircraft were sighted forward of the starboard beam of *Griffin* at a 3000 foot altitude, diving and heading directly for the two ships. The APD commenced firing with her 5" gun. One plane turned and made a suicide run on *Morris*. The *kamikaze* penetrated extremely heavy fire from the destroyer and crashed into her port side at the water line!

The second plane continued in a suicide attack on *Griffin*. At a range of 4000 yards, just forward of the ship's starboard bow, the plane exploded and disappeared from the surface radar screen! Lookouts reported seeing one wing and what they thought to be the tail falling to the water. A five second gasoline fire and considerable smoke on the surface of the sea was recorded.

The captain ordered full speed ahead to the assistance of *Morris* and went alongside her starboard side. *Griffin* had just commenced fighting fires when she was obliged to pull away from the destroyer at full speed to meet another bogey reported closing to six miles. This plane banked away, and *Griffin* returned alongside *Morris*.

Considerable concern was expressed over the condition of the *Morris*' magazines which had not been flooded. It was felt that fire might detonate the destroyer's magazines which, in turn, could detonate over 100 tons of tetrytol stowed throughout the APD. Fortunately, that did not occur. As night came on, *Leary (DD-664)* came alongside the port side of *Morris* and assisted in extinguishing the flames. All fires were soon brought under control.

6 April passed into history, but *Griffin* had more trials ahead.

24 April. A drifting mine was sighted and sunk by rifle fire.

28 April 1945. *Griffin* spotted a single engine enemy plane on her port bow, crossing ahead and barely skimming the surface at a radar range of 1000 yards. The aircraft circled to starboard, maintaining a constant range. While turning at full speed under right full rudder, the APD concentrated heavy fire on the aircraft. The plane broke off the attack abruptly when it had circled to a position on the starboard quarter. Although the APD's fire appeared concentrated on the plane, neither hits nor indications of damage could be claimed.

9 May. Another drifting mine was sighted and sunk.

Griffin continued screening and convoying troop redispositions until the end of the war, returning to the United States in December 1945.

BARRY

A Long Life and a Quick Death

A World War I designed *Wickes* class destroyer, *Barry* underwent a conversion to a high-speed transport at the Charleston, South Carolina Navy Yard. In January 1944, she was reclassified *APD-29* and, four months later, departed for Mers-el-Kebir, Algeria.

In August, she landed troops on the Islands of Levant and Port Cros, as well as on Southern France. Between August and December, *Barry* served on escort duty in the Western Mediterranean before returning to the United States en route to the Pacific. She arrived at Pearl Harbor on 24 March 1945. Following training in the Hawaiian Islands, she joined the screen off Okinawa on 16 May.

1600 on 23 May. *Barry* relieved *Barr (APD-39)* and commenced patrolling off Zampa Misaki. *Loy (APD-56)* was in the adjoining station, distance 7000 yards, and *Sims (APD-50)* was guarding a station 7000 yards astern. (*Barr*, *Loy* and *Sims* are narrated separately in this chapter.) As evening approached, the ships formed their dusk antiaircraft stations, moving five miles toward the Hagushi Anchorage for mutual close support. Normal stations were resumed at 1930, and enemy planes were reported in the area. *Barry* went to GQ four times during the night and the morning of the 24th.

25 May. The same routine of closed-in stations at dusk and return to normal stations at nightfall were repeated on the second day of patrol, *Barry*'s last. Two enemy planes were seen to splash at some distance shortly after midnight. Remaining inconspicuous in the screen was the main method of security from air attack. Accordingly, a speed of 12 knots was employed to decrease bow and stern wakes.

0030. A small, surface pip on the radar scope, initially at 9000 yards, was identified by radar as a low flying bogey at 3000 yards and closing rapidly. The moon was partially obstructed by clouds; surface visibility was poor.

Lookouts sighted two enemy planes flying in close formation at a 200 foot elevation, streaking in from a distance of 2200 yards. The gunners promptly commenced firing. CIC furnished guns with initial ranges and bearings to enable them to locate the target. Local gun control was necessary because of poor visibility and the expectation of attack from two sectors, requiring divided fire.

Considering the short opening range to the target and the little time for firing, the gunnery was very effective except for the number one .50 caliber ammunition feed which jammed. Intensive previous training enabled the ship to open fire quickly and in fairly large volume once the plane was sighted. It did not, however, prevent the plane from continuing on its path into the ship. The skipper, Lieutenant Commander C.F. Hand, wrote in his action report:

> "One of the planes was leading the other slightly and came in strafing from the starboard corner of the galley deck house. Hits from the 40mm were seen on the plane which banked sharply toward the bridge, now strafing an area from the flying bridge to the waterline. The strafing was very effective in wounding personnel and scattering the forward damage control party. The gunner on number three 20mm on the galley deck was wounded. Considerable materiel damage was caused to the bridge and search lights as well as injuring six members of the bridge force such as telephone talkers, helmsman and signalman. Twenty seconds after sighting the plane, it crashed and exploded at the waterline!"

The effectiveness of the bomb, as distinguished from the impact of the burning plane, was difficult to estimate. There was a blinding flash on the half deck after impact as numerous doors were knocked askew. Fixed bridge gear, such as bearing repeaters and the wind gauge, were knocked loose from their moorings by shock. Twenty-eight men, wounded by shrapnel, were in need of immediate assistance.

Four compartments were pierced; fire broke out in the radar transmitter shack, half deck, radio shack, and the bridge. Oil tanks and the forward fire main were ruptured. Fires prevented the flooding of magazines; generators went out on shock; internal and external communications were disrupted. The ship took an immediate 10 degree list to starboard, then shifted and settled on a 10 degree list to port. Again from the log:

> "Steering control was lost. All engines were ordered stopped. The second plane was under fire by the after 20mm and .50 caliber guns. This plane also passed over the after deck house at a 200 foot elevation and splashed 2,000 yards on *Barry*'s port quarter!"

The last recorded time on *Barry* was 0022 on 25 May. The signalman and quartermaster were severely injured, and many hours elapsed before the logs could again be accurately kept. However, the sequence of events is reasonably accurate.

Communication with nearby ships was hindered with radios silenced by loss of power or impact shock. Both bridge signal lights were smashed beyond use. *Barry* managed to catch the attention of a nearby APD by blinker with a battery-operated boat lantern, but usage was discontinued due to the proximity of enemy planes.

0045. Boats were launched to correct the list and to off-load the casualties. Attempts to fight the fire were unsuccessful. Explosions of magazines and oil tanks were deemed imminent. The main plant was secured, and the word was passed to abandon ship. The commanding officer ordered boats with casualties to ships at the scene. The balance of the crew was to lie off until such time as the danger of magazine and fuel explosion was unlikely; then the crew was to reboard. First to the rescue after *Barry* had been hit was the *Commander Transport Division 105*, Captain Kennaday, in *Sims*. His promptness of action was largely responsible for *Barry*'s remaining afloat. Shortly after his arrival, *Commander Destroyer Squadron 64*, in *Harry E. Hubbard (DD-748)*, arrived and took over coordination of rescue and salvage facilities.

The *Barry*'s skipper boarded *Sims* as the latter's commanding officer, Lieutenant Frank M. Donahue, closed *Barry*, playing several streams of water on her forecastle. *Sims* approached *Barry* bow to bow and put a fire fighting crew aboard with the *Sims'* first lieutenant, Lieutenant (jg) Archie Smith, in charge. (See the following narrative relative to the Sims salvage effort.) The water had risen until the forward magazine was covered, minimizing the danger of explosion. The commanding officer of *Barry* returned aboard at approximately 0200.

Five minutes later, eleven officers and twenty enlisted personnel of *Barry* returned in the boats and climbed aboard to assist in fire fighting. The wounded and the medical officer were taken aboard *PCED-855* which then evacuated the area. *Loy* commenced laying smoke around *Barry* and *Sims* as an enemy plane was driven off by fire from the guns of the screening ships. With the flames partially under control, *Sims* recalled its fire fighting party and drew aft as the salvage and repair vessel *Deliver (ARS-23)* came alongside *Barry* to continue extinguishing the flames. Fires were out by dawn, and ten men from *Roper (APD-20)* attempted lighting off the main plant. Their efforts were unsuccessful.

Deliver commenced towing *Barry* to Kerama Retto, escorted by the destroyer *Hubbard*. En route, *Hubbard* splashed an enemy bomber six miles off *Barry*'s starboard bow. Fifteen minutes later, another enemy plane was downed by *Hubbard* with four American Corsairs diving through heavy antiaircraft fire to assist. An hour later, *Hubbard*, assisted by *Barry*, splashed a third plane. Had it not been for the presence of *Hubbard*, *Barry* would probably have received additional damage from the three aircraft.

The wounded ship was anchored off the beach at Kerama Retto. *Barry* was found to be so extensively damaged that repair was not justified. She was decommissioned on 21 June and towed to sea to be used as a decoy for the *kamikazes*. While under tow, she was attacked by Japanese suicide planes and sunk along with her escort, *LSM-59*. From the Mediterranean, across the Atlantic and the broad Pacific oceans, this gallant ship finally plunged to her watery grave.

Captain Hand was grateful for the aid rendered by *Sims*:

"This command commends the quick action of the officers and men of *Sims* in their successful efforts to combat the fires aboard *Barry*. This vessel was under attack by enemy planes during the period of fire fighting and *Sims*, despite her compromised position, remained bow to bow until fires could be controlled by *Barry* personnel and until such time as *Deliver* could come alongside and continue with the fire fighting."

SIMS

She Came Through with Flying Colors

In the spring of 1944, after having been at sea for over three years, this author was transferred to Norfolk, Virginia, to help organize a training unit specializing in antisubmarine warfare and radar fighter aircraft control. My executive officer on *Sims (DE-154)*, Lieutenant Frank M. Donahue, ascended to command upon my recommendation. Lieutenant Keith M. Urmy became executive officer. On 23 September 1944, *Sims* entered the Boston Navy Yard for conversion to a high speed transport and was classified *APD-50*.

I retained a special interest in that ship, her officers and men. Since practically all DEs and APDs in the Atlantic passed through my facility before proceeding to the Pacific, I knew the destination of each. Beginning with the Philippine campaign, our operation had been kept abreast of *kamikaze* activities so that appropriate counter-measures could be included in our program. After *Sims* left Norfolk, I knew her ultimate assignment would be Okinawa.

Sims arrived in the Philippines on 21 March 1945. A week later, she stood out of Leyte Gulf, bound for Okinawa. Unfortunately, there was little to be gleaned from her action reports but this was more than made up by two "plankowner" diaries whose yellow-tinged pages meticulously maintained the life of *Sims* over 50 years ago. One diarist was Yeoman First Class O.G. "Teddy" Percer; the other was Charlie Jacobs, the ship's pharmacist's mate.

The stress upon the nerve fabric of this crew come through to the reader in following the day by day and hour by hour tension of anticipated and actual combat.

1 April (Easter Sunday), Percer: "Before daylight, two DDs fired on friendly planes but no damage. The first landing hit the beach at 0830; we can hear the guns in the distance. Received word that our landing party is already 500 yards inland. We are patrolling 15 miles from beach. Battleship *Maryland (BB-46)* is bombarding shore and just blew up an ammunition dump."

2 April, Percer: "0530 manned battle stations and witnessed a Japanese suicide plane dive into the attack cargo ship *Tyrrell (AKA-80)*. Later, we picked up an officer, Ensign Enfried H. Johnson, who was blown overboard by the explosion.

4 April, Jacobs: "An incident. Doctor Kellam operated on Couch's head at 1430 after Couch dropped a foot locker on it. Some feat!"

7 April, Jacobs: "180 plane attack at Okinawa. At least twenty ships were hit."

12 April, Jacobs: "Took up new screening position 15 miles north of the invasion beaches. High Motobu Peninsula to the east. The marines are mopping up the Japs ashore here."

13 April, Jacobs: "Twenty plus ships (cruisers, destroyers, high speed transports and others) are bombarding the large island of Ie Shima to port. Dive bombers are blasting the volcanic peak. Quite a sight! At least 111 out of 175 Jap planes were splashed in yesterday's raids, but over twenty U.S. ships were hit."

16 April, Percer: "We manned battle stations the second time this morning and, just as we were securing, a Val came up astern. I was bridge talker with the 40mm gun aft and reminded the crew to track the plane and fire when ready without orders. However, Lieutenant (jg) J.F. Collins, a staff officer with *ComTransDiv 105*, gave the order anyway. We splashed the *kamikaze* about 15 feet off the starboard bow! Coxswain J.J. Sturniolo was on the director of gun mount 43 which did the job.

A little later, while still at GQ, we spotted three Jap planes low on the horizon. We fired at the first one with our 5" gun, attracting the attention of our fighters who shot it down. We did the same for two other *kamikazes* and watched our fighters splash them. Today was our first attack. We shot down one and were partly responsible for downing three more."

Same day, Jacobs: "We fired 51 rounds from our 5" gun. At least six Japs were knocked down by the F4Us (Corsairs) near the ship."

19 April, Jacobs: "Heavy casualties ashore. Heard that Ernie Pyle was killed on Ie Shima on the 16th. No mail for the past three weeks."

21 April, Percer: "We got underway for Ulithi in the Carolines, escorting two cruisers. Tonight, after chow, some of us met in the mess hall to discuss church services to be held tomorrow and each Sunday thereafter because services will be few and far between when we return to Okinawa. Mr. Tolson and Mr. Urmy talked to us."

25 April, Jacobs: "Beer party and swim on a tiny uninhabited island. Crystal clear water. Everyone has coral cuts."

3 May, Jacobs: "*Sims* arrived in the Western Okinawa transport area in the afternoon and was assigned a patrol station at sundown. At 2005, we left our station to search for survivors of destroyer *Little (DD-803)*, sunk by suiciders. No bodies recovered."

4 May, Percer: "We sent our boats over to the destroyer *Nicholson (DD-442)* to pick up survivors she had recovered from the *Little* disaster. Included were the skipper, Commander Hall, and the exec, Lieutenant Commander Clausner. *Little* had been hit by four *kamikazes*, and most of the survivors were wounded, six seriously. I worked all night getting names, rates, and helping Dr. Kellam and Chief Pharmacist's Mate Mobley. We also received one dead man. The doctor gave blood plasma to four of the seriously burned."

Same day, Jacobs: "This was my first experience as a pharmacist's mate with the realities of war and massive casualties. The transfer of wounded from the destroyer to *Sims* in a fairly rough sea was scary. I worked on the casualties all night and into the morning. Terrible burn cases. Several non-medic crew members assisted. Before dawn, we took aboard two survivors of the landing craft *LCS-25* from *Pavlic (APD-70)* and proceeded at best speed to the transport area off Western Okinawa."

0843 on 5 May, Jacobs: "Flash Red. Battle Stations. A Tony sailed over us on a dive into the anchorage at Kerama Retto. Friendly fire from surrounding pickets burst all around us and shrapnel landed on our fantail. Fortunately, no injuries."

9 May, Jacobs: "Captain Kennaday came aboard. We are now flagship of *TransDiv 105*."

9 May, Jacobs: "The ship that took our screening position in the morning was hit, as was a ship two stations down. The Corsairs knocked down a Nip right over our heads. Some of the crew are getting jumpy, but morale is high.

1854. *Sims* fired one 5" round at an enemy plane which crashed into the bridge structure of *England (DE-635)*. Smoking heavily, *England* proceeded under her own power to the vicinity of Kerama Retto." (The same *England* that sank six Japanese submarines per chapter *Pacific Antisubmarine Warfare* and subsequently was hit by a *kamikaze*, described in the previous chapter.

13 May, Jacobs: "The APD which relieved us at Kerama was hit on her fantail by a *kamikaze*. This is the third time our relief on the picket line has been hit! At 1900, we went to the outer picket line to search for survivors of the destroyer *Bache (DD-470)*, hit by suiciders. Arriving at the stricken *Bache*, we commenced a search for any survivors. There were none."

14 May, Jacobs: "*Sims* commenced screening *Bache*, now being towed. Six hours later, arrived at Kerama Retto. Our engineering officer, Mr. Philip Moreau, examined our screws in a diving helmet. One is bent. Fired at a Jap Betty and A PBM Mariner (ours) at GQ this evening."

1930 on 18 May. Bogeys were picked up by the SA radar at five miles. The raid split at three miles, and a Tony was sighted on the port bow. *Sims* commenced fire and swung ship to port to keep the batteries unmasked as the plane commenced a suicide dive from the port quarter. Hits were observed by all guns which knocked off its port wing at 200 yards. A second bogey commenced a simultaneous suicide dive from high over the starboard quarter at the same time. All starboard guns were on target. Both planes were splashed at the same instant close aboard the port side in vicinity to the signal bridge with a violent concussion which lifted and whipped the entire ship!

Lieutenant (jg) Archie L. Smith was a "plankowner" of the *Sims* and the first lieutenant at Okinawa. Today, he is a retired and highly respected attorney living in Asheboro, North Carolina. This author asked Archie what he could recall from those hectic days:

> "Regarding the *kamikaze* attack on *Sims*, I recollect the afternoon we took two close aboard. The midship damage control party was inside under the boat deck. We thought the bridge had been hit so we pulled hoses up through the hatch and up the ladders to the bridge. When we arrived, it was evident that the open bridge had not been hit, but nobody was around! Later on, we joked that the entire flying bridge complement must have dived down the brass voice tubes when they saw the *kamikazes* screaming in.
>
> I remember that Chief Gunner's Mate Ed Horton was among those with me at the time. As you well know, being in damage control, we were always below deck during General Quarters. On this particular occasion, while we were alone in the bridge area, an enemy aircraft was spotted approaching from starboard and several thousand yards away. Then two Marine Corsairs appeared, and I was determined I would stay above deck and watch. The marines did their job and splashed the Jap plane at some distance from us. Now I can say I have actually seen some action!"

The first report of damage indicated that SA radar, sonar, master gyro, 5" director, 5" ammo hoist, forward fuel oil service line, after main turbine and TBS radio were all out of operation. The chief engineer secured the number one fire room, spun the number two main turbine which had only tripped out, and set two-motor control aft, allowing up to 18 knots. Steering by magnetic compass, Captain Donahue headed for the area inside of the destroyer screen to make a complete estimate of the damage sustained in the attack. In the meantime, the engineers were able to light off number one boiler and to resume split plant operation at 20 knots. A check with all stations indicated that there were no personnel casualties.

Sims anchored in the transport area to effect repairs. The SA radar was temporarily repaired by the ship's force. All the damage, except the fuel tank leaks, were repairable by the ship's force.

21 May, Jacobs: "*Chase* (*APD-54*) was damaged at Kerama Retto by a mine or explosive charge applied by frogman. Mail call. Thousands of letters. I got 30."

0030 on 25 May. Flash Red. Battle Stations. A bogey was heard circling overhead. The skipper changed the speed to full ahead and put on full left rudder. As the Jap commenced his dive, all 20mm guns on the port side commenced fire. In a steep dive from port to starboard, It passed near the ship's mast and splashed close aboard the starboard side, spewing flame and shrapnel! Ten men and one officer were treated for burns and lacerations but none of the injuries were serious. The damage consisted of reopening of the already damaged fuel oil tanks from the action of 18 May and dents of a superficial nature topsides and around gun shields. Charlie Jacobs had a more salty recollection of this engagement:

> "Splashed a *kamikaze* about midnight. He blew up and scattered debris and shrapnel all over the ship. Mr. Bacon and Mr. Harris were injured, as was Schneider (in the butt). Eight others had minor wounds. Never prayed like that in my life. At GQ for nearly 17 hours straight."

0049. A radio message ordered *Sims* to proceed with all dispatch to her sister ship, *Barry*, hit by a suicide plane, afire and in need of assistance. (A continuation of the prior narrative on *Barry*.) Captain Donahue made his approach on the windward side and waited for small boats to clear the side of *Barry*. All hands were abandoning that ship due to a fire in the vicinity of a magazine. *Sims* closed the burning ship and played five hoses on the fire. The results were not too effective, so she backed off and approached the leeward side of *Barry*, enabling her fire fighters to get at searing flames more directly. This helped to some extent, but a boarding of a fire fighting party was urgent. The port bow of *Sims* was placed alongside the foc'sle of the abandoned ship, and a volunteer fire and rescue party boarded the burning ship. It manned three hoses from *Sims*' fire main and a 500 gallon per minute handy billy.

The volunteer boarding party was under the immediate supervision of the same Lieutenant (jg) Archie Smith mentioned above. This author asked Archie why he volunteered for such a dangerous assignment in full knowledge that the fire could have ignited the *Barry*'s magazines, wiping out the entire party. In his own thoughtful and laconic manner, he replied:

> "Time has dulled my memory of some of the details surrounding the boarding of *Barry*. However, the seriousness and dangerous nature of the event does trickle back now and then. Perhaps the flow of adrenaline at the time prevented even a thought on the part of the volunteers to refuse the opportunity to be of help in a situation that demanded immediate attention. We were navy, and another navy ship needed help. I am positive that any man on *Sims* would have done the same thing if more men had been required.
>
> Regarding the actual fire fighting efforts, the men and the three hoses were divided among the areas where the fires seemed to be most intense. The handy-billy was operated from the weather deck where suction could be obtained for the pump. Fortunately, the amount of water was sufficient to keep the temperature down below the level which could have caused an explosion of the magazines. As pointed out in your letter, the forward magazine was eventually flooded. I remember that there was also some ready storage on the weather decks for antiaircraft ammo. These lockers got rather hot and were opened so that we could throw the ammunition overboard.
>
> Officers of the abandoned ship returned aboard and indicated they could handle the towing situation after the *Sims* fire and rescue party returned aboard their own ship. The tug that arrived on the scene took the disabled ship in tow. *Sims* screened as the tug towed, pumped, and fought smoldering fires remaining in *Barry*."

For their courage and gallantry in risking their lives to save a navy vessel from destruction, the Silver Star medal was awarded to Lieutenant Frank Donahue and Lieutenant (jg) Archie L. Smith. Navy and Marine Corps medals were awarded to the other members of the boarding party:

Lieutenant (jg) James F. Collins
Third Class Gunner's Mate Vic M. Simonian
Commissary Steward Jay B. Seuders
Third Class Motor Machinist's Mate Warren J. Lusk
First Class Machinist's Mate Robert G. Henkel
Seaman First Class Donald F. Carroll
Third Class Gunner's Mate Edward P. Carroll
Third Class Fireman Charles Richard Jr.
First Class Carpenter's Mate Joe A. Pendergraft

Over the next few days, Charlie Jacobs bemoaned the life of a pharmacist's mate:

> "Work. Finally hit the sack at 2200. Up at 2400 to give penicillin shots."
>
> "Slept late – 0900! Closed Mr. Bacon's wound – 24 sutures."
>
> "Sedatives for Mr. Bacon and Harris at 0130 and 0300."

27 May, Jacobs: "Left on six day cruise to Saipan. Sixteen ships, including a DD, 3 APDs and 2 DEs, all damaged. Motley group. Captain Donahue asked everyone to attend services to thank God for bringing us safely through the last 24 nights."

The fight did not come to *Sims* again. After the Japanese surrender, she joined the Third Fleet to pick up Allied POWs and to ferry troops to key points in Japan. On 2 December, she headed for the United States, proudly displaying four Japanese planes painted on her superstructure.

ROPER

Between a Rock and a Hard Place

The "four-piper" *Roper (DD-147)*, was active in the Atlantic from the first day of war. She made a number of transatlantic convoys before entering the Charleston Navy Yard for conversion to a high-speed transport, *(APD-20)*, in October 1943.

On 13 April 1944, she joined the Eighth Fleet at Oran, Algeria. Assigned to support the offensive in Italy, *Roper* landed units of the French Army on Pianosa on 17 June. In July, she convoyed along the western coast of the embattled Italian peninsula. As part of the "Sitka" Force, she landed troops on Levant Island in August. She returned to the United States in early December.

Roper sailed west on 29 January 1945 After reporting to the Pacific Fleet in Hawaii, she proceeded to Guam. On 1 May, she departed in convoy. Her formation was composed of five tugs and tows with a speed of five knots along a route with the unsettling designation of "Ambush." The screen was composed of the minesweeper *Prevail (AM-107)* and *Roper*. Both escorts conducted training in aircraft recognition and fired at balloon targets en route to Okinawa.

Arriving in mid-morning on 22 May, the APD was ordered to proceed to Hagushi in company with *Manlove (DE-32)* and to report to Commander Task Group 51.5. (By this time, most readers must have realized that assignment to TG 51.5 meant a station on the Okinawa picket patrol, the most dangerous job in the Pacific.) *Roper* arrived at Hagushi late in the afternoon of 23 May.

The early hours of 25 May. *Roper* was ordered to proceed to the vicinity of *Barry*. *Sims* was already alongside the burning vessel so that *Roper* joined the protective screen around the two ships. As noted in the *Barry* narrative, an attempt by men from *Roper's* engineers to light off *Barry*'s main propulsion plant was futile.

0759. *Roper* sighted three DEs and received a visual signal from *ComCortDiv 61* in *Abercrombie (DE-343)*: "You may join us. Fall in on our starboard beam." (Non-Navy readers might presume that "You may join us" left *Roper* with an option. Not so. It is a polite phrasing of an order from one officer to another his junior. Make no mistake; it was a command.)

The tactical situation on the evening of the same day: Japanese planes in force had been over the area since early evening of the day before. Several ships had been hit by *kamikazes* in Hagushi Anchorage and on the screening stations. The weather at this time was rainy, sky overcast, and the sea calm.

0915. A flight was contacted by radar at a range of 11 miles and was followed as it circled the area while hidden in the clouds. *Roper's* lookouts sighted four planes, distance four miles, altitude 800 feet and headed for the formation. They were identified by the recognition officer as a Zeke with three Corsairs on its tail.

The Zeke headed for *Roper*. The Corsairs were disposed with one pursuer directly astern and one on either side of the kamikaze, all firing and within a plane's length from the Zeke. A decision was made by *Roper's* captain, Lieutenant Commander U.B. Carter, not to fire because it appeared certain that the Corsairs would splash the Zeke and it would have been impossible to fire on the enemy without hitting our own planes. None of the other escorts opened fire for the same reason. One of the contradictory things about war, however, is that "certainties" often fail to live up to their dictionary definitions.

0921.5 Captain Carter ordered a course change in order to present a beam aspect to the aircraft. He also ordered flank speed.

0922. The Zeke crashed into *Roper's* forecastle! Its gasoline exploded, throwing up a 200 foot sheet of flame. The port wing entered the starboard side, making a hole six feet square, five feet above the water line. The aircraft motor hit the number one 3" caliber gun mount and, with the starboard wing or part of the fuselage, it glanced into the air and exploded about 30 feet over the water and 50 feet from the port side near the stern. Several fragments of the motor block inflicted small holes in the port side from stem to stern. One of them killed the first lieutenant who was crouching just forward of the after deck house, ordering his repair men to hit the deck. There was speculation that a bomb with a delayed fuze had been installed in or on the motor. The propeller chewed three holes, each about three feet long, in the forecastle deck inside the working area and forward of gun number one. The pilot's flying helmet, pieces of his leather jacket, and small pieces of his anatomy were left hanging on the same gun.

Fires were started in the chief petty officers' quarters and wardroom country. Repair parties at the scene promptly began fighting the flames. Immediately after the crash, the skipper ordered all engines stopped to avoid fanning the flames. Great quantities of smoke were coming from the holes in the forecastle deck, hatches on the well deck and from the wardroom escape scuttle on the forecastle. On orders from the captain, the forward magazines were flooded. The fire extended below the first platform deck. Unscathed men at gun stations on the forecastle jettisoned ready service ammunition.

A man wearing a rescue breathing apparatus got through the smoke to the magazine flood valve on the half deck, and a hose was dropped into the handling room from the main deck. Two hoses were played on the fire through the holes in the forecastle deck until foam apparatus was brought into play. Upon determining that no fires existed below the first platform deck, the same man with the rescue breathing apparatus went down through the chief petty officer area hatch to the lower sound room and removed demolition charges which were jettisoned.

0942. After a muster to ascertain that nobody had been knocked over the side, the APD headed to the transport area at five knots, accompanied by *Abercrombie* and two Corsairs. Half an hour later, the fires were under control and speed was increased incrementally to 15 knots.

1100. The damaged ship stood into Hagushi Anchorage under her own power. One dead and seven seriously injured were transferred to the hospital ship *Relief (AH-1)*, and *Roper* then proceeded to Kerama Retto for temporary repairs, which were completed on 30 May. The captain noted in his report:

> "The Medical Department, consisting of the medical officer, a chief pharmacist's mate and a pharmacist's mate second class, performed their duties in a rapid and efficient manner.
>
> This was the first action in which this vessel has been

involved since reporting to the Pacific Fleet. This commanding officer now believes that the only way to prevent a suicide plane crash is to splash it before it can reach the ship and that it was a mistake not to open fire regardless of the Corsairs."

Without commenting on the above, we have to agree that most of us would not want to be obliged to make such a fateful decision. To borrow a popular phrase, the skipper was truly "between a rock and a hard place."

Returned to the United States to complete repairs, *Roper* departed from the Ryukyus and reached San Pedro, California, in early July 1945. In August, she shifted to Mare Island but, with the cessation of hostilities, repair work was halted and the ship sold for scrap.

CHASE

Another Score for the Divine Wind

Between 14 September 1943 and 23 November 1944, *Chase (DE-158)* escorted six transatlantic convoys to North African ports. During her second such crossing, while approaching Bizerte on 20 April 1944, *Chase* drove off attacking enemy torpedo bombers with gunfire, then rescued swimmers from three torpedoed merchant ships. On the return passage, 5 May, *Chase* rescued 52 survivors from the torpedoed *Fechteler (DE-157)*.

After *Chase* was reclassified *APD-54*, she got underway for Pearl Harbor, arrived on the afternoon of 5 March 1945, and reported to the Amphibious Forces, Pacific Fleet.

The next day, a fire broke out on a ship in a nearby nest of LSMs (medium size landing ships). The *Chase* fire and rescue party, under the direction of Lieutenant Blake Hughes, aided the burning ship's personnel in extinguishing the flames. His men, at great risk to themselves, went below to train hoses on magazines and bulkheads, possibly preventing an ugly ammunition explosion.

Chase was underway the same day, escorting an attack transport to Ulithi, arriving on 21 March. The next six days were spent taking aboard supplies and checking equipment. On 27 March, the APD screened a task group scheduled to simulate a landing on the southeast coast of Okinawa as a diversion from the main assault. The voyage was uneventful until 1 April.

At daylight on that morning, as the diversion Task Group approached its objective, it received more attention from enemy aircraft than did the main landings. During the attack, one Japanese plane was shot down nearby, a suicide plane hit an LST and a third plane passed near *Chase* to commit suicide on the attack transport *Hinsdale (APA-120)* in the body of the Task Group. *Chase* had joined in a blaze of antiaircraft fire but without result.

On 3 April, the APD assumed a screening station two miles from Kerama Retto. Although many enemy planes were seen in the area, none came within range of her guns until late afternoon on 6 April when she shot down a Betty. Throughout the day, there were heavy enemy air attacks in the Kerama Retto area. Two ammunition ships and one LST were hit by *kamikazes* within visual range of *Chase*, one plane having flown directly over her before making its death dive.

The following day, *Chase* became an escort vessel for a convoy of battle-damaged ships to Guam. After only one night in Apra Harbor, she escorted a convoy back to Okinawa. Arriving at Nakagusuka Wan on 22 April, she was assigned to screening duty in the perimeter around Okinawa. Most of the time, enemy planes were near and, on 28 and 29 April, attacks were extremely severe.

28 April. In the early dark hours, *Chase* and an adjacent ship opened fire on an enemy plane which exploded and splashed! It was impossible to ascertain which ship shot the plane down. That night, *Chase* opened fire without result on another enemy plane passing off the port bow. The ship's personnel remained on battle stations almost the entire day. During a 24 hour period, there were over fifty separate enemy raids, each with one to eight planes. The following day, *Chase* joined a convoy, escorting landing craft to Ulithi. Arriving on 5 May, she was assigned availability for repairs, completed on 12 May.

On 14 May, *Chase* departed for Okinawa with *William C. Cole (DE-641)* as a screen for the battleship *West Virginia (BB-48)* and the cruiser *Tuscaloosa (CA-37)* and arrived off Hagushi Beach on 18 May. *Chase* was then assigned to a station five miles from Kerama Retto. Several air alerts were sounded on 18 and 19 May.

Sunset on 20 May. An enemy plane, picked up at four miles, approached at an altitude of 3500 feet. All guns in the firing sector opened up on the *kamikaze*, diving on *Chase* from ahead, angle 70 degrees. The APD maneuvered violently, and the plane missed the ship but hit the water a scant ten yards from the starboard side of the fantail! Its two bombs exploded and ripped *Chase's* hull open, flooding the engine and fire rooms. As a result, several compartments aft were flooded, the ship lost power, the steering gear jammed, and the ship developed a dangerous starboard list. Casualties were heavy, and one man was killed outright.

With her steering gear jammed at hard left, *Chase* drove off another suicide plane. Every effort was made to correct the list which threatened to capsize the ship. Because of the inadequacy of available equipment to pump out flooded compartments, the commanding officer, Lieutenant Commander, G.O. Knapp Jr., ordered all hands to go aboard the minesweeper *Impeccable (AM-320)*, which was standing by to await arrival of a rescue tug.

Navy Department

Hold For Release
Press And Radio
Until 9 A.M. (E.W.T.)
22 September 1945

USS Converse Salvages the USS Chase

"The destroyer *USS Converse (DD-509)* salvaged a ship that had been abandoned and given up as lost and helped to rescue its crew. *Converse*, a three-year veteran of Pacific warfare, was ordered to go to the assistance of *Chase* at about 1930. When *Converse* arrived on the scene, she picked up about a dozen swimmers alongside. *Impeccable* took on most of the other survivors.

Nonetheless, Captain Harry H. McIlhenny, in command of a destroyer squadron and aboard *Converse*, and the commanding officer of *Converse*, Lieutenant Commander E.H. McDowell, decided to attempt to salvage *Chase*.

The whaleboat was lowered, and a line-handling detail with a score of picked men, commanded by Lieutenant Bernard Levin, boarded the abandoned ship. They handled lines when *Converse* pulled up along the port side. Meantime, the whaleboat searched the waters for scattered survivors still adrift.

Lieutenant (jg) Joseph D. Nitzschke, the *Converse* engineering officer in charge of damage control, sent a repair party to *Chase*, headed by Machinist Mate F.T. Martin. Martin found 60 percent of the starboard side of the ship under water and six of the compartments open to the sea. Torpedoman's Mate William Brooks set the depth charges on safe.

Martin and his men brought submersible pumps, rigged up electrical power from *Converse* and set two handy billies to work. Within an hour, three pumps were emptying the after fire room and other pumps were being readied in the engine room and the living compartments.

Electrician's Mate First Class Harold Hasse, Electrician's Mate First Class Clayton H. Blankenship and Motor Machinist's Mate First Class Francis J. Bornhorst restored part of the communications.

Within two hours, Skipper McDowell was assured that the APD would not sink. By nightfall, the ship had begun to right herself. *Chase's* captain, damage control officer, first lieutenant and the damage control parties went back aboard. The pumps from *Converse* were secured when the rescue tug *Shackle (ARS-9)* took over. *Chase* was towed into Kerama Retto Harbor by *Converse*. Some of the men, hot and weary, discovered ice cream aboard and took time out for a few helpings."

Seaman Cosmo Vitale of *Chase* related a personal experience:

"After we were hit by the Jap plane, a minesweeper tied up on our port side, and word was passed over the PA system to abandon ship. Frank Scott, our barber, and myself left *Chase* and climbed down onto the tug. Going through the passageway, I saw Frank Baker in sick bay; he had been wounded. Shortly afterward, we noticed some unrecognized men in the water. After we pulled a few in, we realized they were our own people. When they had heard the word to abandon ship, some of them came on deck on the starboard side and jumped overboard, not knowing there was a tug alongside to port.

After all the swimmers who we thought were recovered, we heard yelling from out in the ocean fog. somebody was out there. I heard an order to cast off all lines. We still heard a steady, 'Help, help, help'. Without realizing what I was letting myself in for, I told a sailor aboard the tug that I was going out and to keep feeding me a line I had tied around myself. I told him that, when I jerked on the rope, to pull us in. Over I went.

The fog closing from Okinawa was very thick. The voices on the tug were growing faint. I was really alone. Then it hit me. What the hell was I doing out here? My whole life passed in front of me. I started thinking about the destroyers coming into the harbor minus smoke stacks and masts, courtesy of the *kamikazes*. I wanted to go back, but I kept on going. Then I thought about the sharks and started to cry. I sure got myself into a fine situation.

The sailor on the tug was still feeding me line, and the man in the water was still calling for help. I really wanted to tug on the line and be pulled back, but I kept on swimming. Suddenly, the fog lifted, and I could see him floating on his back. I thought it was a friend of mine named Lucersick, so I yelled over, 'Lucersick, is that you?' He said, 'No'. I told him to turn on his stomach and swim toward me. As soon as I got him, I started yelling toward the tug, 'Pull us in, I got him'.

I tugged on the line and, for a second, I thought that the other man had let the line loose, but then it started tightening up. I could feel us moving. When they pulled us over the side, I was completely out of breath. As I lay on the deck, gasping and soaking wet, one of our officers said, 'Vitale, you saved him'. The man I rescued took my hand and shook it.

I realized then that I had a fight with this sailor the first week aboard the ship, and we hadn't talked since!"

Work continued all night, and the men who remained aboard the ship received written commendations in their records. *Chase* moored alongside the destroyer *Leutze (DD-481)* and received light and power until her auxiliary plant was ready for use on 22 May. Personnel continued pumping out compartments, repairing battle damage, and carrying on maintenance work while awaiting assignment to a dry dock. It was not until 4 August when a dry dock was available. Repairs were minimal, enough to make the ship seaworthy. No effort was made to repair the engineering plant.

On 23 August, *Chase* left the Okinawa area under tow, and arrived in San Diego, on 11 October 1945, 5 weeks after the war ended.

RINGNESS

After Okinawa, a Witness to Disaster

Ringness (APD-100) was originally laid down as *DE-590* but was reclassified while still in the construction stage.

When passing Hawaii's famous Diamond Head on 1 March 1945, headed for the forward area, there were many on board who wondered when that vista would be seen again. On the 9th, the crew saw Funa-Futi, Ellice Islands - their first glimpse of the South Sea Islands which would no longer be described as being romantic.

Early on the morning of the 13th, *Ringness* passed Guadalcanal and anchored at Port Purvis, Florida Island. The layover was transitory, remembered only by the torrid climate. From there, she turned northward in company with the destroyers *Massey (DD-778)* and *Drexler (DD-741)*, escorting the carriers *Suwannee (CVE-27)* and *Chenango (CVE-28)* to Ulithi, Caroline Islands, arriving on 22 March. At Ulithi, the crew witnessed the greatest collection of naval vessels ever seen in one anchorage.

Ringness, commanded by Lieutenant Commander William C. Meyer, commenced intensive pre-invasion preparations for an assault upon heretofore secret enemy territory. Saipan was the next stop on 26 March where *Ringness* joined Task Group 51.2. The following day, she and other escorts screened transports and cargo vessels to Okinawa.

Tempest, Fire and Foe

This was a six day journey in a very small part of an invasion fleet which covered a far greater area than the island which was to be stormed. The expected enemy air assault upon the approaching force did not materialize, leaving many to wondering. Japanese strategy was to unfold later in the campaign.

The landing took place on Easter morning, 1 April. During the two days following, *Ringness* engaged in anti-suicide boat patrol along the southeast coast of Okinawa, where intelligence reports had located Japanese nests. The night of 2 April found the APD conducting an attack on an enemy midget submarine with undetermined results.

Ringness received orders to proceed in company with two other high speed transports, *Humphreys (APD-12)* and *Sims (APD-50)*, to Ulithi, arriving on 6 April. On the following day, she was once again screening a convoy back to Okinawa, .

Upon this second arrival, the ship was assigned to patrol duty, undergoing numerous air attacks as the enemy unleashed its air power. *Ringness* was unscathed, but the crew was treated to a chilling sight when a suicider passed over the bow and crashed close aboard the cruiser *St. Louis (CL-49)*. This patrol lasted four days, when the APD was again assigned to escort duty, departing from Okinawa on 16 April with another task group and arriving at Saipan five days later.

After two days in Saipan, *Ringness*, *Fieberling (DE-640)* and *Barr (APD-39)*, again sailed for Okinawa on 23 April, escorting a convoy of LSTs and LSMs. On the morning of the 27th, a torpedo fired from an enemy submarine missed *Ringness* astern and, three minutes later, another torpedo passed under her bow. The torpedo wakes precipitated GQ, and ready gun crews began firing on the partially surfaced sub which quickly submerged. The captain ordered a depth charge attack.

Twenty-four minutes after the first torpedo was fired, the submarine exploded close to the surface, hurling a giant spray of debris and water 200 feet in the air. *Ringness* believed she had made a kill. Unfortunately, under orders not to tarry, she did not attempt to recover tell-tale debris or search for a diesel oil "wellhead." The attack was classified as "results undetermined." On the same morning, she again had an excellent sonar contact and again her depth charges slid into the water, but this time with negative results.

On 30 April, *Ringness* arrived at Okinawa for the third time since the invasion began, remaining the entire month of May, a period marked by the continued attempt of the Japanese air fleet to break the ring of ships protecting the invaders.

As the attacks raged, not all vessels were as fortunate as *Ringness*. On 4 May, deck and bridge hands witnessed the death dive of a *kamikaze* onto the flight deck of the carrier *Sangamon (CVE-26)*, turning it into a roaring inferno. *Ringness* stood by the crippled vessel and aided in the rescue of personnel forced over the side by flames and explosions. She also rendered emergency medical treatment.

Sudden orders sent the APD to the famed "hot corner," radar picket station 15, which had received the shock of one of the heaviest air attacks of the period on 11 May. It is believed that a speed mark was set for APD vessels during the race to assist the destroyers *Hadley (DD-774)* and *Evans (DD-552)*. Both DDs smashed a relentless assault by an entire Japanese air armada. The smoke of battle had scarcely cleared when there commenced the grim tasks of rescue and salvage.

The job completed, *Ringness* returned to Okinawa. The enemy air assault continued unabated. Combat Information Center reported a bogey headed their way, the beginning of a tense duel. The enemy pilot, a member of the *kamikaze* corps in good standing, followed the APD's phosphorescent wake in the dark, then went into a dive. The captain immediately directed evasive maneuvers at flank speed. The plane overshot its mark and circled for another try. On the second approach, the aircraft again missed its target, splashing and exploding in the wake of its intended victim!

On the night of 31 May, *Ringness* was ordered to leave Okinawa. Early the next morning found her with her anchor at short stay off Hagushi Beach. With the area under heavy air attack, the Union Jack was hauled down as she moved out of the anchorage. A *kamikaze* provided a climax to her month long stay at Okinawa by splashing in the exact spot where she had been anchored only minutes before!

2 August. After escorting a group of carriers to Ulithi atoll, *Ringness* was en route to Leyte on a track about 200 miles south of the course of the heavy cruiser *Indianapolis (CA-35)*. She received an urgent radio dispatch to proceed at best speed to that area north of the Palau Islands to assist in the rescue of survivors reported in the water. Early on the morning of 3 August, the APD arrived in the designated area and began a search for swimmers. The *Ringness* crew had no inkling that it was proceeding to one of the worst single combatant ship disasters of the war. Lieutenant James E. Holland on *Ringness* recorded many of the sad details.

On 30 July, *Indianapolis* was steaming alone from Guam to Leyte. She had just completed a mission of historic importance, the delivery of the components of the atomic bomb on a fast run from San Francisco to Tinian.

Silhouetted by moonlight, the cruiser was a ready target for Japanese Commander Machitsura Hashimoto, captain of submarine *I-58*, lying directly in the path of *Indianapolis*. The cruiser was suddenly struck by two torpedoes. Within 12 minutes, the warship capsized and plunged beneath the waves, carrying with her approximately 400 of her crew of 1200 men. Those not trapped in the hull, jumped or were cascaded into the sea.

The commanding officer, Captain Charles B. McVay III, was tried by court-martial, an unusual proceeding for a ship sunk in action against an enemy. It remains an issue which has been much criticized to the present day, some questioning if the captain might have been made a scapegoat to cover operating deficiencies which contributed to the sinking and great loss of life.

Whereas it has always been doctrine for destroyer-type escorts with antisubmarine capability to screen capital ships, *Indianapolis* was directed to sail unescorted. Furthermore, her non-arrival in Leyte Gulf was never reported, causing the castaways to fend for themselves in the merciless sea. However, this is a book about DEs and APDs and not qualified to comment on Captain McVay except to point out that he was apparently unaware of the destruction of *Underhill (DE-682)* in the same general area only six days prior to the loss of his ship.

For over four days, the 800 survivors in diminishing numbers drifted aimlessly without food or water. The few available rafts could accommodate only a handful of lucky ones; many simply drifted in their life jackets. Still others had no life jackets and were doomed unless they could remove them from dead shipmates. The tropical sun beat down without mercy, swelling tongues and blistering skin and lips. Schools of sharks swam about in a feeding frenzy. Many became delirious and died from drinking salt water. Others swam toward imaginary rescue vessels or islands, only to disappear forever. Many were overcome by exhaustion and despair and simply gave up.

On the fourth day after the sinking, the pilot of a patrol aircraft sighted what appeared to be bobbing heads on the water. The pilot immediately dropped a life raft and a radio transmitter. All air and surface units were dispatched to the scene at once. After steaming at high speed through the night, *Ringness* joined in the rescue operation the next morning. All hands off watch became lookouts. Holland recalls being on the bridge when Captain McVay and several of his crew were hauled from a raft encircled by sharks. When he identified himself as the commanding officer of the *Indianapolis*, all were stunned to learn for the first time that the victim of the sinking was this famous battle-tested heavy cruiser.

A message was immediately dispatched by Commander William C. Meyer, commanding officer of *Ringness*, to the Commander-in-Chief Pacific Fleet:

> "Have 37 survivors aboard including Captain Charles McVay III. States he believes ship hit 0015, sank 0030. 30 July. Position on track exactly as routed by Port Director, Guam. Speed 17, not zigzagging, hit forward by what is believed to be two torpedoes or mines followed by magazine explosion."

More survivors were rescued until the APD's fuel supply became dangerously low, forcing the skipper to put into the Palau Islands for replenishment. After the transfer of survivors and refueling, *Ringness* returned to the sinking area and continued a fruitless search until ordered to return to Leyte Gulf. Rescue ships recovered 316 of the original 1199 men. The great tragedy was that 500 of those who had escaped the sinking vessel perished in the sea.

Holland recalls being amazed at the composure displayed by Captain McVay while seated in the *Ringness* wardroom on the night of the rescue. He described how he had been swept into the sea, looked up into the night and saw the propellers hovering above him as the ship made its final plunge. Certain that he would be taken under with it, he swam frantically and somehow managed to escape.

As a result of the court-martial trial at which the captain of the Japanese submarine who sank *Indianapolis* was called to testify, Captain McVay was found guilty of failure to follow a zigzag course. Retiring from the navy, he moved to Litchfield, Connecticut, where, on 6 November 1968, he died from a self-inflicted gunshot wound.

On 14 August, the President officially announced the Japanese surrender. While the *Ringness* lay quietly at anchor off Samar, peace came to the world. However, her job was far from being completed. There were countries to be occupied and people to be liberated. It became her duty to continue in the occupation to come.

REGISTER

Three Point Five Out of Four; a Highly Respectable Score

Following shakedown in the British West Indies, *Register (APD-92)* departed from the U.S. East coast and headed for Pearl Harbor, arriving on 3 April 1945. On the morning of 27 April, she sailed from Pearl Harbor as an escort in a convoy to Ulithi, Caroline Islands. As daily routine, gun crews fired on a towed sleeve or tracked friendly targets. Gunnery instruction, consisting of movies and lectures, was frequently held. Arriving in Ulithi on 13 May, she sailed in the screen of an Okinawa-bound convoy two days later.

Register anchored off the Hagushi beaches on the 19th and the next day got underway for her screening station. The ship patrolled a sector 7000 yards long in phase with vessels in adjoining sectors. Suicide raids occurred almost daily.

The commanding officer, Lieutenant Commander J.R. Cain Jr., a seasoned merchant marine officer, observed that there was no wind, the sea was smooth and visibility was five miles. Flash Red came over the TBS circuit as the first planes came into view.

1920. On *Register*, "Commence Fire!" The APD increased speed to maximum with radical course changes for evasive action. One plane was seen to dive on *Chase* (*APD-54*). A flight of about 10 Zeros, approached *Register*. Four of them roared in on her starboard side from a fast-setting sun. A great cheer from the crew marked the splash of a *kamikaze* from her 5" gun!

1925. Two more Zeros, commenced a coordinated attack, one coming from ahead, the second from astern. The plane attacking from astern splashed off the starboard beam!

The plane heading for the bow attempted to crash the bridge after dropping two bombs close aboard. *Register's* gunnery was highly effective in that a number of hits were scored but not enough to stop this plane from reaching the ship. The Zero passed down the port side and hit the king post which deflected it up and overboard on the starboard quarter! Most likely, the pilot was dead or unconscious because he failed to strafe deck personnel on his approach.

1927. Ceased firing. Three planes were downed and the fourth was believed to be damaged. As the action ceased, several combat air patrol planes came into the area. There were no further attacks by the enemy this day. In general, ordnance performed quite well except for two minor deficiencies. Captain Cain noted in his action report:

> "The enemy approached very low over the water, coming in on our starboard beam with the sun behind them. Two planes kept within range of the 5" while two others broke from the formation, one attacking from forward and one attacking from aft. These planes were not picked up by radar until they were about 5000 yards off. The attackers cleverly came over a small island near Kerama Retto which made radar detection very poor. Visual sighting picked up the planes before the radar did.
>
> Attacks were apparently directed at APDs. The destroyer just north of us and the minesweeper immediately south of us were not harassed while *Chase* was attacked and damaged at the same time we were attacked." (*Chase* narrated earlier in this chapter.)

Fortunately, no lives were lost in the crash into the king post. The commanding officer, two other officers and nine men were injured, but not seriously. All were treated and retained aboard. Battle damage was not disabling but would require extensive repair.

Relieved the following morning, *Register* proceeded to Leyte, where repairs were completed. By 29 June, she was again ready for action. Assigned to escort duty, she convoyed transports and carriers between Okinawa, Leyte and Ulithi. While returning to Leyte on a convoy, she was ordered to join in the search for survivors of the *Indianapolis (CA-35)* disaster. She rescued 12 of the cruiser's crew. After transferring them to the hospital at Peleliu, she returned to the scene but found only empty life rafts and floater nets.

At Leyte when hostilities ended in mid-August, *Register* screened battleships and cruisers of Task Group 95.7 to Okinawa, then returned to the Philippines for the month of September. In October, she escorted transports carrying occupation troops to Japan, then served as harbor entrance patrol ship at Wakayama. Finally, she headed back through the Panama Canal to Philadelphia to begin inactivation.

BATES

A Gallant Ship Meets a Fiery End

After returning to *England* from the blood-stained waters of Normandy, *Bates (DE-68)* made one more Atlantic convoy prior to being converted to *APD-47* for Pacific duty. She arrived at Pearl Harbor on 4 December 1944 and started training with underwater demolition teams. Departing from Hawaii, she arrived at Ulithi on 23 January 1945, where she continued UDT training, preparing for the invasion of Iwo Jima.

10 February. *Bates*, *Bull (APD-78)*, *Barr (APD-39)*, and *Blessman* (APD-48) arrived off Iwo Jima for pre-assault reconnaissance. Frogmen swam ashore from 500 yards out. Intense fire from the beaches devastated the landing craft supporting the swimmers. Twelve LCIs took part and all were hit, but the boat crews persisted until all the swimmers were recovered. Further reconnaissance by the UDTs was covered by gunfire support from the heavy ships. *Bates* remained offshore while her UDT cleared beach obstacles. On 4 March, she returned to Ulithi for repairs.

The APD departed from Ulithi for her last operation. On 25 March, with UDT 12 embarked, she arrived at Kerama Retto and commenced underwater reconnaissance. The UDT reconnoitered under cover of heavy gunfire from destroyers, gunboats and carrier planes. The assault on the next day was a complete surprise to the Japanese. By late afternoon on 28 March, the island group had been secured.

Bates continued to Okinawa and assumed patrol duties in the outer screen. During the first serious *kamikaze* attack on 6 April, destroyer *Morris (DD-417)* was hit by a suicide plane, and *Bates* went alongside to take on survivors. She then shifted to convoy duty as Screen Commander of two round trips with Ulithi-Okinawa convoys.

Bates again arrived at Okinawa on 21 May and reported for duty to the commander of the Transport Screen. In the evening, an enemy plane was taken under fire as it flew over her fantail at an elevation of 200 feet. It splashed 500 yards from a ship within her sector! On 23 May, *Bates* was ordered to the western end of Ie Shima.

During the night of 24-25 May, *Bates* maintained dusk patrol on her station. Somewhat later, she formed 180 degrees relative (directly astern) and 1000 yards from the destroyer minelayer *Shannon (DM-25)*. *Shannon* took enemy planes under fire by radar control about five times. One of the planes visible to *Bates* was taken under fire by both ships but without result. Except for one four hour period, the APD was at GQ from 2000 on 24 May until 0945 on 25 May, once firing on another plane near Ie Shima. In the meantime, at 0700, she was joined by *William Seiverling (DE-441)*, relieving *Shannon*.

1115. The visibility was fair with intermittent rain and the wind at force one. Flash condition - Blue, Control Green. Friendly planes had been landing and taking off during the morning on the nearby army aircraft landing strip on Ie Shima. *Bates* was at war cruising condition with one twin 40mm aft and one twin 40mm forward manned and two 20mm amidships manned. Condition Baker (B) was set (most watertight hatches and doors closed and dogged).

Three planes approached from a 500 foot elevation. At first, they appeared to be friendly. They were near the western end of Ie Shima with their wheels down as if coming in for a landing. Despite the ruse, they were quickly identified as VALS. *Seiverling* and *Bates* opened fire as the ships went to full speed.

One plane passed down the port side of *Bates*, banked over the ship, and dropped a bomb, scoring a near miss. Damage was extensive. The bomb ruptured the starboard hull in one compartment, the number one fire room and the number one engine room. The third plane crashed into the starboard side of the fantail, demolishing the starboard stern winch and rupturing a fuel tank! Almost simultaneously, the second plane crashed into the wheelhouse on the port side, spraying burning gasoline over the bridge!

The shock of these crashes resulted in considerable damage to the hull and loss of all power with no pressure on the fire mains. The fires were confined to the bridge, the wheelhouse and after crew's quarters. The leaking fuel oil, however, was ignited and spread rapidly over the water. Inasmuch as the boat davits on earlier APDs were not of the gravity type, they could not be launched without power. All life rafts, as well as fenders and whatever was buoyant, and could be lowered were cast off. As the flames and smoke moved forward, all men with the wounded were ordered to the forecastle.

Gosselin (APD-126) started an approach bow to bow but, when about 20 feet away, backed down because of the burning oil in the water. Other rescue ships were willing to help but were prevented from doing so for the same reason. In addition, about 40 tons of tetratol, carried for UDT 12, was stowed aboard and may have influenced the decisions of nearby ships not to come alongside.

1145. As the ship was in flames and enveloped with smoke from the wheelhouse to the stern, abandon ship was ordered. No wounded men were lost in the water in spite of their having to be dropped overboard and cared for by their swimming shipmates. The commanding officer of *Bates*, Lieutenant Commander H.A. Wilmerding, reported:

> "The performance of personnel was magnificent. Abandon ship was done in an orderly manner, and no

wounded were lost although they had to be helped through the water. No one was seen to jump overboard without orders to do so."

Seaman First Class Joe *Lowe* shares his experience on that fateful morning:

"I was down at sick bay getting treated for an ear infection when the general alarm for battle stations went off. I just went out the hatch and up to topside when I saw the planes. One dropped a bomb close aboard, causing severe damage. Two other planes crashed us, one in the pilot house and the other straight down into the fantail, going through the deck into the sleeping compartments below, killing people, how many I do not know.

The second one that hit the pilot house killed almost everyone in it; the plane's wings split apart and spilled its burning fuel all over the area, then fell into the water, igniting the leaking fuel. Another concern was the 20mm ammunition that was popping off all over the place.

I was never so scared in my life, having to jump into flaming water, not knowing how to swim and with a life jacket that wouldn't inflate; I didn't know it until I got into the water and it started to deflate. Luckily, my buddy was nearby; he could swim and gave me his jacket.

I remember seeing the captain and the chief boatswain's mate giving their life jackets to others, the skipper's going to his black mess cook. The man was so scared that he wouldn't jump and, when he finally did go, I saw him leap to the anchor chain and just hold on until the flames finally got to him. I never saw him again; they say he died. I got picked up in the water after being in for about 10 or 15 minutes. I was a very lucky sailor and am thankful that I am still around to remember that day."

This author was surprised and pleased to receive the following personal account from Seaman Louis R. Frost with a notation,

"Joseph Lowe sent me your letter. He said I was more qualified than him because I was on the bridge and saw it all."

On 24 May, all ships in the Okinawa area received a radio message warning them to be on alert for increasing heavy enemy air attacks as the Japanese would be marking the death of Tojo's son. The warning turned out to be correct because, when darkness fell, the planes started attacking and it lasted most of the night. Some planes were suiciders and some were medium bombers raiding Ie Shima. A ship near us was struck by a suicide plane.

The weather was drizzling rain with lots of fog banks. While patrolling, I was on watch at the port aft 40mm gun when the phone talker said the bridge wants Louis R. Frost (me) to report to the conn and take the place of one of the starboard lookouts who was sick. I went up to the bridge at about 1100. I was good at identifying planes by engine sound. Fifteen minutes had passed, and I heard plane engines. They were in a fog bank off the starboard bow. I knew they were Japs.

I immediately called to the Officer of The Deck to sound the alarm, which he did. Just then, there was a small break in the fog bank dead ahead of the ship. I saw three planes jump over from the starboard fog bank to the port side of the ship. I immediately warned the O.O.D. of the impending attack on the port side.

Only seconds had passed when the first plane came out of the fog and dived into our stern. The bomb he was carrying sent plates flying in the air. Part of the plane went through the bottom of the ship, I learned afterward. Seconds later the second plane came out of the fog and headed for the bridge.

Three of us jumped down into the wheelhouse. The two ahead of me were trying to get out the starboard door which was dogged down. The port door was open so I headed that way without knowing the plane was close to impacting. When I heard the engine noise, I figured I could not make another step so I fell on the deck by the search light and pulled my arms over my head. The plane slammed into the bridge right where I was lying, and debris fell on me plus I got saturated with gasoline. The searchlight blocked the heavy pieces of the plane from hitting me.

I immediately jumped up and started to run for the ladder on the aft side of the bridge that went down to the boat deck. Before I could reach the ladder, the gasoline exploded, setting everything on fire including me. Luckily, I was wearing foul weather gear. I then had to jump from the signal bridge down to the boat deck. I hit the radio antenna on the way down, landed unbalanced and cracked my heel. Two shipmates in the gun tub helped me tear off my burning foul weather gear.

I donned a stray kapok life jacket, but a shipmate came up to me badly wounded with shrapnel in his stomach and asked me to help him. I tried to pull his wound closed and told him to put his hands over the wounds and press in so he would not lose too much blood. I then put my life jacket on him and tied it up tight because I was afraid he would pass out in the water and drown.

All the life rafts and nets were overboard except one on top of the battery locker, so four of us decided we would put it overboard and use it. I told them to attach a line to the raft so it wouldn't drift away. Just when we were ready to go over, I heard an airplane engine and I told the men to take cover. The plane strafed across our four landing craft and dropped a bomb which missed but ruptured our port side hull. The bomb destroyed our raft so when we were ready to leave the ship we had to swim for it.

While on the hospital ship headed for the base hospital in Guam, I talked to a shipmate (Keenan) who was badly burned. He told me he was in crew's quarters aft when the first plane hit. Trying to exit the quarters, he fell through where the deck plates were missing and landed down among the oil tanks. He said he could not get out. He then tasted salt water in the oil and figured there must be a hole in the bottom. He dove down, went out through the bottom of the ship and came up on the starboard side in all the burning oil on the water.

This is how we know the first plane went clean through the ship. I have read several stories on how we were hit but they were not correct. There was no hole in the starboard side of the hull. The only plane to cross over the ship was the one strafing and he dropped his bomb on the port side. The plane that hit the bridge could not have carried a bomb or I would not be writing this."

(Readers will note sharp inconsistencies with the official version of what comprised *kamikazes* one, two and three and the account given by Seaman Frost. Since he was on the bridge at the time of attack, has taken pains to supply an action diagram, and no diagram was attached to the action report, this author will let both reports stand without comment. Considering the severe trauma of a few minutes of living hell, it is not surprising that two or more witnesses could render conflicting recollections.)

In the time available, condition affirm (closing all possible watertight hatches and doors) was set as far as possible, thereby keeping the ship afloat for over seven hours after the attack. Depth charges were set on safety by men on the fantail. In the afternoon, the sea-going tug *Cree (ATF-84)* was able to get a line aboard the tortured vessel and, though *Bates* was listing badly, towed the ship into Ie Shima anchorage where she capsized, still burning, and sank in 20 fathoms of water. Casualties were high: 23 killed and 37 wounded, 30 percent of the crew!

This was the end of a great and storied ship. Before her conversion to an APD, she was claimed by her crew to be the first ship to arrive off the French coast in the Normandy invasion. She screened the capital ships as they bombarded German installations, lent covering fire for commandos, and dodged dive bombers and heavy artillery shells. As an APD, the ship and her UDT teams were in constant danger as her sister ship, *Blessman*, was blasted at Iwo Jima (narrated in this chapter). Now, at Okinawa, the last battle of a terrible war, she went down with her colors still flying.

TATTNALL

An Old but Gallant Fighting Ship

Tattnall (DD-125) was another Wickes class four pipe destroyer commissioned shortly after the conclusion of World War I. The entry of the United States into World War II saw her escorting Caribbean convoys, frequently through the Windward Passage between Cuba and Haiti, one of the most dangerous areas during the height of the U-boat blitz. (This author recalls the months after the attack on Pearl Harbor when a Caribbean convoy consisted of six subchasers, such as my *SC-532*, and a four piper flagship. That was all we had!)

Following reclassification as *APD-19* and training on the East Coast, *Tattnall* became flagship of Transport Division 13. In the Mediterranean, the division feigned a successful landing north of Rome to draw off German reinforcements as the main body of troops broke through enemy lines at Monte Casino. *TransDiv 13* also captured several fortified islands to clear the way for Allied landings on Southern France.

After some needed yard availability in the U.S., *Tattnall* headed for the western Pacific via a string of islands, arriving at Okinawa on 10 April 1945. She remained in the Ryukyus until the end of the month, standing guard on various screening stations. This ship fired at enemy planes several times in the days preceding the night of 29-30 April when she first drew Japanese blood.

Late evening of 29 April. While en route to her assigned station, bogies were reported by area control to be in her vicinity in the inner screen off Hagushi Beach. The moon was bright with very good visibility. However, no enemy approached closer than five miles from the ship. Shortly after the crew stood down from GQ, the warnings started again with bogies about 65 miles away, closing and sending the crew back to battle stations.

0213 on 30 April. A Betty was sighted on the port quarter, range 4000 yards. The APD went to full speed and opened up with her 3" and 40mm guns, but no hits were claimed. Within two minutes after firing, the Betty dropped out of sight.

0220. A Betty, possibly the same one, was again located by lookouts, approaching just forward of the starboard beam. The commanding officer, Lieutenant Commander B.A. Habich, again ordered full speed with full left rudder to bring the aircraft abeam to starboard. As the 40mm guns commenced fire, the plane turned sharply to reverse its course and proceeded to the outer screen from whence it came.

0229. A Betty again approached from the outer screen, most likely the one that appeared briefly twice before. *Tattnall's* gunners opened fire and scored several hits, setting the plane's port motor ablaze. The entire aircraft was soon enveloped in flames and splashed 2000 yards on the starboard side with a violent explosion, leaving a large area of burning gasoline on the surface of the water!

0233. At the instant of crashing, radar reported that it was tracking another plane coming from the same direction, distance five miles and making a sharp turn toward *Tattnall*. The skipper again ordered full rudder, placing the plane on the starboard quarter, 4000 yards distant, position angle 20 degrees. Hits were seen as the plane raced along the starboard side only 50 yards off, attempting to turn into the hull at midships. However, it splashed about 15 yards abreast of number one 3" gun, showering the forward part of the ship with wreckage, gasoline and water!

There were no personnel casualties, but flying metal tore a hole in the main deck forward, lodged in the steering cables and momentarily caused loss of steering control. Orders were promptly issued to all gun stations not to fire until the gasoline was washed off the decks.

0245. No sooner had the APD resumed her patrolling course and speed, when radar reported an enemy plane just forward of the starboard beam, distance eight miles and heading for *Tattnall*. Again, the APD went to flank speed and commenced evasive maneuvers. Three minutes later, a twin engine plane dead ahead passed down the starboard side at a range of about 1000 yards. The plane was not taken under fire because of the lingering presence of gasoline on the decks. For reasons known only to the *kamikaze* pilot, no attack was made.

The following day, *Tattnall* departed from Okinawa to convoy a number of ships to the Marianas, arriving at Saipan on 3 May and returning to Okinawa on the morning of the 19th. Assigned to a sector in the outer screen, her position was approximately 15 miles southwest of Zanpa Misaki, Okinawa. After being on station for about six hours, her crew quickly responded to the alarm when another ship reported a raid.

Just before sunset, *Tattnall* lookouts sighted a low-flying enemy plane on the port bow, distance four miles, appearing to be heading for a ship 7000 yards astern. She opened fire with her 40mm at too great a distance to do damage but to attract attention of other ships in the danger zone. The plane started a steep climb as it passed astern of *Thatcher (DD-514)*, did a wing-over and dived into the destroyer, crashing her abaft the bridge!

Enemy planes continued in the area and, in early evening, CIC reported a low-flying bogey at 10 miles. Visibility was good, but low cumulus clouds served to hide the air target. The plane was plotted on radar at a speed of 150 knots, altitude 200 feet, and drew antiaircraft fire as it passed over each ship in the screen. *Tattnall* increased speed to flank with full right rudder. The maneuver to avoid the plane was to present the stern, bringing the maximum 40mm guns to bear, but the ship's large turning circle and sluggish maneuvering qualities prevented accomplishment of the tactic (DEs or APDs derived from DEs were much more maneuverable than the four pipers). "Commence fire" produced only one 20mm firing on the plane, heading on a collision course with the port beam. There were no hits.

The aircraft, a single-engine, two-float Paul, dropped one 250 pound bomb about 50 feet off the port beam. The aircraft then climbed sharply and disappeared from radar at about 10 miles. Shrapnel hit the ship's mast, severing a cable to the surface radar and putting it out of action. It also pinched a cable running to the air search antenna, but it remained in operation. Again, no casualties.

On 25 May, *Tattnall* was at GQ for 18 hours without a break, the same day her sister ships, *Barry* and *Roper*, were crashed by *kamikazes* as previously narrated in this chapter.

Tattnall conducted a number of convoys and post-war occupation duties before returning to the United States, arriving in San Francisco on 30 October 1945.

PAVLIC

Telling It the Way It Was

Throughout this book, the author has generally avoided data relative to routine duties. However, three chronicles from meticulous and scintillating diarists warranted enlarged treatment. The first is the diary of *Borum (DE-790)* in chapter *Operations Neptune/Overlord/Channel Islands* by Quartermaster Frederic Shelby Brooks. The second is a description of the trials of *Gendreau (DE-639)* by Yeoman John P. Cosgrove and Motor Machinist Mate John A. Virum in chapter *Iwo Jima to Okinawa – The Destroyer Escorts*. The third is an APD history drawn from *Assignment Okinawa, The War Cruise of The USS Pavlic (APD-70)*, by Lieutenant (jg) Jack F. Boland. None of these ships was the most outstanding DE or APD in terms of accomplishment although all served extremely well. Rather, they had diarists who bequeathed to us shipboard life in a war, memory of which is slowly slipping away.

In all cases, the description of the birth of a fighting ship with expected foul-ups by green crews and intensive training to create an effective fighting team replicates the early life of virtually all DEs and APDs. For *Pavlic*, It was the spring of war with excitement and haunting anticipation. As mile by mile, the ship approached the forward combat areas, one could almost hear a distant drumbeat, becoming louder until the crew is enveloped by the winter of war. The drumbeat then becomes ear splitting with clashes of cymbals as *kamikazes* scream through walls of fire to crash into ships. It does not end abruptly; it slowly recedes into the background as the end of war approaches. The boys are long gone; all who emerge are men with memories they carry to the ends of their days.

The *Pavlic* history is necessarily abridged. Modifications have been made wherein technical clarification or interaction with other ships are required.

Pavlic, originally designated *DE-699*, was reclassified *APD-70* on the ways, and commissioned at Orange, Texas.

Crew members arrived at Orange from various bases on the East Coast. From Norfolk, there came the largest contingent in the care of Lieutenant Hal Walker, recently transferred from escort duty in the North Atlantic. From Fort Pierce Amphibious Training Center, arrived the 16 members of the Boat (B) Division, Ensign Mel Taylor in charge. Several officers came from the Sub Chaser Training Center (SCTC) in Miami. Lieutenant Keeley was returning from leave following a tour as skipper of a subchaser in the Solomons. Lieutenant Commander George Stembridge came as executive officer from the cruiser *Brooklyn*, George Taylor as engineering officer from a destroyer, and Dick Gibbs as gunnery officer from armed guard duty on a merchantman in the North Atlantic. Five highly capable chief petty officers arrived, giving credence to the saying that "The chiefs run the navy."

Pre-commissioning work kept all hands busy. From bow to stern, everything from the anchor chain to electric motors to blowers, condensers, evaporators and battle lanterns had to be installed and tested. Crates of parts, cabinets, and paper had to be loaded. Training exercises, from the firing range to antisubmarine attack simulators, were scheduled. Finally, the great tangle of power cords and hoses on the dock disappeared. On the afternoon of 29 December 1944, with a few wives and many girl friends in attendance, *Pavlic* was commissioned as a U.S. Navy fighting ship. One hitch in the proceedings occurred when a seagull left his mark on the executive officer's cap. Captain (Lieutenant Commander) C.V. Allen, managing to ignore the bird's handiwork, ordered Stembridge to set the watch. *Pavlic* was assigned to *Transport Division 105*, Pacific Fleet.

For 18 days, the crew got their first taste of watch-standing and work parties, while identifying with the ship. On 8 January, with all hands at their first "Special Sea Detail" posts, Captain Allen gave the order to "single up all lines, let go forward, let go aft, starboard engine back one-third." *Pavlic* pulled into the Sabine River and headed for her first of many ports of call.

As soon as the ship entered the Gulf of Mexico, the captain ordered the Bo'sun's Mate of the Watch to sound "General Quarters - all hands man your battle stations! This is a drill." How often the crew would hear this call without the final disclaimer - that it was only a drill!

The response was somewhat better organized than a kindergarten fire drill on the first day of school. However, the reports finally did reach the bridge, and the exec announced, "Captain, all stations manned and ready." Allen was not impressed. We did it again and again. We test fired all guns. Allen ordered the engines to flank speed, then emergency back full with the ship shuddering in protest.

After two full days of strenuous activity, *Pavlic* sailed for Galveston. Again, more drills: "Fire in the aft crew's compartment - this is a drill." This repair party exercise did rather well. First Lieutenant Keeley even got a grudging compliment from the skipper.

After three days at Galveston filled with work parties, local bars, and, for some of the more adventurous, the Jack Tar Motel, *Pavlic* headed for its shakedown cruise in Bermuda.

It was early morning on a cold 29 January when we sighted land. As we sailed up the channel, everyone off duty was topside, admiring the pastel cottages and homes along the shore. However, our two weeks there would prove to be days and nights of hard work and constant battering by high seas with one brief evening of liberty in Hamilton.

Shakedown consisted primarily of practicing antisubmarine techniques. We were working with *Yokes (APD-69)*, three destroyers and a captured Italian submarine, manned by her original crew. Each day at dawn, the small flotilla of new ships got underway from the Hamilton anchorage to rendezvous with the sub. Once the antisubmarine screen was formed to seek and "sink" the sub, the waves were so high that the other ships of the screen were visible only when *Pavlic* was at the crest of a wave. Once the sub was detected by sonar, each ship would make its run and drop a yellow dye marker to simulate a depth charge. The seas were so rough that it was often impossible to tell where the marker was or if a "kill" was confirmed. Seasickness was common. Each day ended well after dark when *Pavlic* returned to the harbor.

After two weeks, the APD was ordered to Norfolk for final refitting. Liberty was given to those of the crew who lived in the eastern states. Shipyard workers kept busy with last-minute alterations. Ashore, downtown Norfolk offered movie theaters. Judy Garland in "Me and My Gal" was playing at one. Numerous bars, jammed with sailors were the only other attraction.

After two forgettable weeks, *Pavlic* got underway for San Diego via the Panama Canal. As *Pavlic* headed into the South Atlantic, the wind and waves diminished. Joe Pirochta and Paul Kluzek, known for their susceptibility to seasickness, could almost enjoy the trip.

The coastlines of Florida, Cuba, Puerto Rico and Haiti came and went as *Pavlic* approached the Panama Canal at Colon. Captain Allen had never before traversed the Canal and was unsure of the protocols. He sought the advice of Lieutenant Keeley, who had previously skippered a subchaser through the Canal. When asked about the uniform to be worn, Keeley suggested clean dungarees. Allen, however, played it safe and ordered the crew to man the ship's rail in dress blues.

As a net tender opened the nets for *Pavlic*, one of their sailors shouted to *Pavlic's* bridge: "Hey, anybody want to buy a pea coat (A sailor's cold weather coat)? Officers manning the rail thought the remark worthy of Jack Benny and struggled to maintain their dignity. Their unsuccessful efforts brought glares from Allen and Stembridge.

With only one night at Colon, the port and starboard watches were each given two hours of liberty. The Port Director ordered us to provide shore patrol personnel, so four junior ensigns strapped on their brassards and wandered through the downtown area. Bars were everywhere, full of sailors and "Blue Moon" girls, women who sipped non-alcoholic drinks at the expense of unwary sailors.

Pavlic entered the fresh water of Gatun Lake, pausing just long enough for the crew to take a short swim off the fantail and to pump fresh water through her fire system pipes. *Pavlic* dropped the hook for the night off Balboa.

Tradition places the captain at the head of a long table to starboard while the wardroom mess officer, a monthly job rotated among the junior officers, sat at the other end to port with the remaining officers seated in between according to rank. One night, we were experiencing a heavy ground swell as we took our assigned seats. I was the monthly mess officer. Bowls of soup were the first course. As mine was placed in front of me, the ship suddenly took a starboard roll. To my horror, my bowl of hot soup slid the entire length of the table, emptying itself on the captain's lap. Even Stembridge had to struggle to maintain his composure as he promptly relieved me of my duties as wardroom mess officer.

After a week of painting the ship in camouflage colors and loading ammunition, *Pavlic* pointed her bow westward to Pearl Harbor. Captain Allen could not resist telling lengthy and repetitious tales in the wardroom about his previous command *Brooks (APD-10)*, a converted four piper. Unintentionally, Allen had portrayed *Brooks* as the best ship in the Pacific. Many officers hoped that *Pavlic's* path would cross that of *Brooks*. This would indeed happen.

Drills continued without let-up; the clanging of the General Quarters alarm was now met with rapid manning of battle stations. Scuttlebutt about the suicide plane and its deadly effectiveness against vessels in the combat areas circulated. Reports on the bloody fighting at Iwo Jima were heard on the radio. "Rum and Coca-Cola," was a reminder of Panama and the Blue Mooners "working for the Yankee dollar."

In the afternoon of 21 March, those off watch came topside as we made a landfall on Diamond Head. Lieutenant Keeley pointed out the Royal Hawaiian Hotel on the famous Waikiki Beach. Here it was - the Pearl Harbor of "the day that will live in infamy," now teeming with ships, activity, and an energy totally focused on the war.

Pavlic got her berthing orders to tie up outboard of *Brooks*! As *Pavlic* picked her way past Hickham Field and Hospital Point, eyes strained to see the storied old four piper. Finally, there she was off the port bow, looking like a derelict. Her fantail was covered with debris, and one of her stacks was askew.

Captain Allen uttered not a word. It was so bad it ceased to be funny. Then we reached the obvious explanation; this ship had been a victim of a suicide plane. "So, this is what *Pavlic* could look forward to," thought most of the crew secretly. All references to *Brooks*, from the captain on down, ceased on that day.

Three weeks at Pearl were a combination of intensive training and liberty parties for all hands. Daylight hours were devoted to exercises with other APDs. We fired at target sleeves towed by aircraft. Gun crews on the 40mm and 20mm guns got in plenty of practice, eliciting only one complaint from a pilot that the tracers were coming uncomfortably close to his aircraft. The crew of the 5" gun practiced shooting at "sleds" towed by other ships. On 28 March, with an Underwater Demolition Team embarked, *Pavlic* proceeded to Maui to observe destruction of underwater obstacles by the UDT.

A big treat was an invitation by the UDT to take a few crewmen ashore on Maui to let them set off a few explosives. This gave them a sense of the dangers faced by the UDT and a healthy respect for the teams.

No layover in Honolulu would be complete without visiting the famed Royal Hawaiian Hotel, which the navy had commandeered for use as an officers' R and R (Rest and Recreation) location for submarines returning from patrol. Her pink art-deco design remains to this day a symbol of the Pacific islands of childhood fantasies. On 1 April, the air waves were filled with the landings at Okinawa, but seemed remote as one gazed across the now peaceful harbor.

Word circulated that the Japanese were launching heavy *kamikaze* attacks against the fleet supporting the Okinawa invasion. There were devastating losses amongst destroyers and other small ships, as well as carriers. We received confidential communications detailing how to combat this unprecedented form of warfare. On 10 April, we saw sailing into the harbor the battered, listing hulk that only a few days earlier had been a magnificent new *Essex* class carrier, *Franklin (CV-13)*. She had been crashed and ravaged by fires and explosions.

Radarman John Foute recalls an evening when, along with three other APDs, *Pavlic* was ordered to participate in a night firing exercise. At dusk, Captain Allen ordered Foute, on duty in CIC, to activate both radars. The surface gear would not respond. Allen was notified and was highly displeased. Technicians were summoned. After two hours of trying everything in the book, the gear still refused to cooperate.

Foute suddenly recalled that he had not oiled both antennae, located at the top of the mast, since San Diego. Grabbing an oil can in the darkness, he climbed up the mast. As a precaution against being knocked off, he threw a control switch on the mast, then oiled the antenna. Suddenly, he found himself gasping for air because the engine room watch was blowing tubes before getting underway (An expulsion by steam of residue in the boiler tubes).

Forgetting about the control switch, Foute raced down the ladder. He ran to CIC to tell the radarmen that he had solved their problem, only to find them both exhausted and frustrated. Then he recalled that he had forgotten to throw that dammed switch, requiring another trip up the swaying top. In his own words:

> "Upon leaving the radio shack, I made my way in pitch blackness to the bridge and slipped by the Officer of The Deck. Finding the ladder, I climbed to the top. Driven by inspiration to stay out of trouble, I found that little switch and returned to the bridge, slipping passed those on duty. The antenna worked."

There was one caper that three young officers managed to pull off. It was dark, and the crew, including Captain Allen and the exec, were seated on the fantail, watching a movie. I had the watch and was on the bridge. We had posted armed sentries fore and aft to guard against enemy suicide swimmers. Suddenly, the bow sentry called up to me: "Sir, I hear something, somebody's trying to climb aboard!"

I ran to the bow; the sentry had his rifle pointing at the water below. A boat was alongside with somebody attempting to climb up a line dangling over the rail. Abruptly, the climber plunged into the water; the line he was climbing was not secured. Then a voice from the boat: "Hey, Jack - don't shoot - it's just us."

"Us" were Lieutenant Keeley, Ensign MacMillan and Ensign Mel Taylor. They missed the last liberty boat from the dock but, emboldened by a few beers, they spotted a sporty little Chris Craft tied up, a quick solution to returning to the ship. Taylor, our boat officer, took the helm and found *Pavlic* in the dark. With the captain and exec still at the movie, nobody would ever know; Boland (me) had the watch and wouldn't turn them in. MacMillan would go up first and was the one I saw falling into the water right near the boat's propellers. I was able to muster a couple more guys, and we hauled up the three in complete silence.

The unmanned boat drifted off into the night. Within 10 minutes, a destroyer alerted all ships in the anchorage that she had a suspicious looking craft in sight. A few ships went to GQ. Finally, word was passed that the craft had been identified as the Admiral's stolen barge. It was not until the day in Tokyo Bay when Allen was being relieved by Keeley as skipper, that Keeley felt it would be safe to tell Allen about that evening.

Thursday, 12 April. For better or worse - and the old hands assured everybody it was to be for the worse - *Pavlic* departed from Pearl at dawn on Friday the thirteenth. Could there be a more ominous omen?

On this same day, the Japanese launched a heavy attack with nearly 200 *kamikazes*. Rumors of frightening scenes filtered through the crew's mess and the wardroom, including a new terror weapon, a manned rocket-driven glide bomb called *Baka* with speeds up to 500 miles per hour. We heard that *Hopping (APD-51)*, had been hit by a shore battery and suffered many casualties (narrated earlier in this chapter).

At last, *Pavlic's* bow was headed toward the South Pacific, to Guadalcanal, Tarawa, Suva, New Georgia - names already inscribed in the annals of World War II. Ulithi Atoll was to be our next stop. It was not only the main anchorage for the Fifth Fleet but the staging area for the Okinawa campaign. So, it was to be Okinawa after all.

On our second day out, hard off the starboard bow, Kwajalein atoll became visible. Still considered to be hostile territory, we set condition one and kept a sharp lookout for the enemy. Only a few months before, Admiral Spruance's Fifth Fleet had launched a massive assault to take the Marshall Island group.

On 25 April, *Pavlic* dropped her hook in the magnificent harbor at Ulithi. Small boats plied the harbor with liberty or work parties and mail runs. Mog Mog Island had a recreational area like none other in the Pacific. Hundreds of sailors could roam the beach or find a comfortable spot in the sand to drink beer. Each liberty party was responsible for bringing its own cases of beer and for insuring that no one drank too much. The officers had three clubs, one for flag officers, one for commanders and captains and one for lower ranks.

Everybody got to spend an hour or two away from the confines of the ship at the recreational area. There was touch football, softball and the chance to walk on dry land for a bit or a swim in the lagoon.

On the 27th, *Pavlic* and two other APDs, escorted nine liberty ships to Okinawa. Daily dispatches listed the suicide crashes. Even the few among the crew who had seen earlier action seemed apprehensive about our immediate future. The formation had not traveled five miles when the *Pavlic* sound operator suddenly announced, "Bridge, sonar contact, bearing 130 degrees, 2500 yards!"

Allen immediately ordered GQ, alerted the convoy and changed course to intercept. The pinging and return echo grew louder as we closed in, but the target barely moved. Allen asked the sonar operator if he believed it was a sub. "Hard to say, Sir." A large fish or a thermal gradient seemed a better possibility. Allen made up his mind, "stand by to drop depth charges." *Pavlic* headed toward the target and dropped seven charges, shallow setting. We waited anxiously. Nothing happened; the silence became embarrassing. It turned out that the first class gunner's mate in charge failed to set the charges. Our first shot at the enemy was a dud.

Late in the afternoon of 3 May, the convoy terminated in Okinawa. Heavy fighting was much in evidence ashore as we entered Nagasuku Wan (Buckner Bay). On proceeding to our assigned berth, we crossed the bow of the battleship *New Mexico (BB-40)*, anchored about 150 yards from a troopship, from which replacements for the 25th Army Division were disembarking. Suddenly, a burst of 40mm fire erupted aboard *New Mexico*. The guns were trained directly at the troopship and a dozen or so shells exploded among the soldiers. A sailor had accidentally tripped the firing mechanism on one of the Quad-40 mounts, resulting in six dead and 20 wounded.

I had the deck. Ten minutes later, the command ship, *Delegate*, ordered us to get underway to rescue survivors at "Roger Peter 10." I asked the quartermaster, "Where in hell is Roger Peter 10?" I called Captain Allen to the bridge, and we broke out the charts. Roger Peter meant radar picket station, and number 10 was a station north of Okinawa, not far from the southernmost Japanese island of Kyushu. Our course would take us through an area marked "mine fields." Captain Allen ordered the helmsman to steer this course and the rest of us to keep our mouths shut about the mine fields.

We reached RP10 at 2230. It was foggy, and we couldn't see a thing. We turned on the ship's searchlight. Nothing. Engines stopped, dead in the water, listening. Suddenly, the bow lookout cried out - thinks he heard a voice off to starboard. All eyes strained to see through the fog. "Light in the water," someone shouted. We lowered an LCVP and picked up two swimmers, survivors of *LCS-25*. As our boat came back alongside, one of the survivors hollered up to us: "Put out that searchlight, you dumb sons-of-bitches!" We did.

We had barely recovered the boat when *Delegate* announced, "Flash Red, three raids, 50 miles, closing." Sure enough, raid one showed up on our radar, heading directly for us. *Pavlic* was a sitting duck, but the Japanese pilots never saw us. Luck was with us.

Our two passengers told us that their LCS had been on station with the destroyer *Little (DD-803)* and other small craft. At sundown, a raid of about 10 planes caught them by surprise, coming in low, just off the water. Two Betty bombers released *Baka* bombs that flew at very high speeds at the column. One hit *Little* amidships, inflicting a mortal wound. The amphibious ships *LCS-25* and *LSM-195* were hit, and several crew members were blown overboard. One LCS survived and picked up some men from the water. Casualties were high.

We cruised the area until dawn. Wreckage and dozens of sharks were everywhere. We tried to close our minds as to what all those fins meant. We found no more swimmers.

We had proceeded but a short distance, however, when one of the lookouts spotted a body in the water, a hundred yards to starboard. Ralph Barnard, boat crew member, recalls approaching the body in his LCVP with Ensign Taylor. Sharks were everywhere and it was evident they had already won the race. Several attempts to lift the body onto the boat failed - the sharks were too close. So, Taylor snagged the torso with a boat hook and towed it to *Pavlic*.

Yokes, our sistership from Orange, Texas, joined us on the return trip, as well as a destroyer and several LCIs, all carrying survivors from the previous evening. *Delegate* broadcast, "Condition Red," sending all ships to GQ. The raid passed us by. Having seen so intimately the damage inflicted the previous evening, our crew was quite tense until orders to "secure from GQ" were passed.

Captain Allen called for burial at sea services for the sailor the boat crew had retrieved. I recall that his name was George and that he was married and the father of two children. With *Yokes* standing by for protection, the service commenced. Instantly, we had a "Flash Red" condition, bogies closing at five miles. Both ships went to flank speed, but our luck held. At sundown, we completed the service with "Doc" Putzel presiding. The war was becoming all too real.

For the next several days, *Pavlic* was assigned to a station north of Okinawa, known as "suicide alley." Within a three day period, thirteen "Flash Red" conditions were ordered by *Delegate*, mostly in the early morning, early evening or late at night. Obviously, the enemy was taking advantage of the prevailing poor visibility. The mid-watch could count on a few harassing planes to prevent ship crews from getting any sleep.

9 May. While fueling, we could see our aircraft making bombing runs on Ie Shima, just off the Okinawa coast. We were to learn later of correspondent Ernie Pyle's death by sniper fire on that sand spit. Fueling completed, we joined up with *Oberrender (DE-344)* and the destroyer *Farenholt (DD-491)*.

Right on schedule after evening chow, *Delegate* warned "Condition Red" with bogies at 15 miles and heading for us. The ships went to flank speed while training all guns in the anticipated direction of the danger. Two specks appeared high in the sky as *Oberrender* and *Farenholt* opened fire. One plane broke off its descent. The other, ignoring a hail of fire, headed at *Oberrender* and crashed her amidships (narrated in previous chapter). The plane carried a 500 pound bomb which exploded in the DE's engine room, bursting steam pipes and scalding to death anyone who survived the explosion. *Pavlic* and *Farenholt* immediately went to her aid to help put out fires. Our boat went alongside, and several of our crew went below decks, looking for dead and wounded. Eight of the DE's men died - five in the engine room where the bomb had exploded. Over fifty men were wounded, of whom *Pavlic* took three to a transport which was serving as a makeshift hospital and morgue.

The men who went below decks on *Oberrender* had horrifying stories to tell about what they had found. For at least a week afterward, Lieutenant George Taylor and Ensign J.G. Harris, the engineering officers, manned GQ stations with their sidearms at the ready as a means of reminding some of the black gang that, bad as it was, this was their battle station.

Under the Geneva Convention, hospital ships were clearly marked, lit up at night and were never escorted by a combat vessel. Nonetheless, a suicide plane had crashed a hospital ship stationed in the anchorage to receive casualties from ashore as well as from the Fifth Fleet.

10 May. *Pavlic* was assigned to escort *Relief (AH-1)* to Guam with hundreds of wounded aboard. This was, of course, a violation of the Geneva Accord, but there was no alternative. We rendezvoused with the hospital ship at dawn and fell in astern to give us some chance of not being silhouetted by her bright lights. The trip, while eerie, proved uneventful. On her return to Okinawa, *Pavlic* was permitted to drop anchor, the first time since leaving Ulithi.

It had been a quiet day, but evening was fast approaching. In the wardroom, what was to become a tradition over the next several months, a game of "hearts" was in progress with life jackets and helmets at the ready. Sure enough, at 1910, "Flash Red - bogies 20 miles, closing." Ray Wildes recalls running to his battle station:

> "The sky was full of flak. *Pavlic's* 5" opened up at five planes circling menacingly. One plane went into a dive on *New Mexico*, which only a few days before had tragically fired on a troop transport. *New Mexico's* 40mm were right on. The plane burst into flames and splashed! A second one tried his luck. No better! Then a third. This one hit near the bridge, killing over a hundred of the crew and ending the BB's career as a ship of the line!"

(In the heat of battle, it is often difficult to determine results. Actually, a plane flew into the battleship and another hit her with a bomb, starting a fire. Fifty-nine were killed and 119 were wounded.)

This had been my 26th birthday, and I couldn't help wondering if I would make it to the next one.

The next day was Sunday, and the area was quiet enough to allow a church service on the fantail. Our good Doctor Putzel, who would go on to a distinguished career in medicine after the war, did the honors. "Doc" was just out of medical school and quiet, even retiring, but well-liked by everyone aboard. Again, at 1850, the nightly attack came. This time, *Bache (DD-470)* was hit.

On Monday, we were assigned to patrol a short distance offshore from the anchorage and to act as a screen for a large group of LSTs arriving from Ulithi, loaded with men and tanks. Shortly after noon, we were surprised and greatly cheered by the arrival of a group of nine veteran Fletcher class destroyers. The best damned destroyer men in the Pacific were here to help. As they passed close aboard at full speed in precise formation, we could see the insignia on their stacks; Captain Burke's Little Beaver squadron was joining the fight. (Arleigh Burke, nicknamed "Thirty knot Burke," became an Admiral in post war years and Chief of Naval Operations.)

For all the experience and battle skills acquired in months of fighting the Japanese fleet, six of these sleek warships were destined to be damaged or sunk before a month was up. Their skippers were to learn the difficulty of defending against an enemy bent on suicide.

The next day, one of the Little Beavers, *Thatcher (DD-514)*, was assigned to a picket station with *Pavlic* and another destroyer, *Boyd (DD-544)*. Previously, a launch had come alongside with a second doctor for us. The value of APDs as rescue ships was becoming apparent, and a second doctor was a necessity to treat the large number of casualties we were receiving aboard.

20 May. It took only one day for our new young doctor to earn his keep. The evening before, one of *Pavlic's* nearby division mates, *Sims (APD-50)*, had taken a suicider aboard and suffered severe casualties. (Previously narrated. Actually, the suicider crashed close aboard, inflicting a few treatable casualties.)

Thatcher, *Pavlic*, and *Boyd* were patrolling in column around the perimeter of the picket station. Evening approached and, like clockwork, the "Flash Red - many bogies - closing" warning came from Academy, code name for command ship. All ships went to GQ and flank speed. Suddenly, three black specs appeared in the darkening sky. *Thatcher* opened fire at long range, but the bogies continued to close. Other ships nearby opened fire. One plane went into a dive, aiming at another destroyer - two planes remained. Both were now 1000 yards off and the three ships were firing furiously. One plane veered away, disappearing into the smoke. On came the third, heading right into *Thatcher's* starboard gun mounts! The DD was instantly engulfed in flames, lost power, and lay dead in the water! (The same *Thatcher* as in prior narrative on *Tattnall*.)

Pavlic and *Boyd* hastened to her sides, *Pavlic* to her starboard with fire hoses and rescue gear broken out and two boats ready for lowering to pick up anyone blown overboard. A tense half hour ensued. All three ships, lit up by *Thatcher's* fire, were sitting ducks for other Jap pilots. Thatcher's casualties were passed over the rails to *Pavlic*, and *Pavlic's* boats found a couple of men in the water.

Without warning, *Boyd*, on *Thatcher's* port quarter, opened up with her port guns, and tracers lanced into the evening sky. Then we saw two approaching shapes, dimly lit, at low altitude. *Boyd* cut her lines, put on flank speed and brought her maximum fire power to bear. The Jap pilots flew off.

Meanwhile, *Pavlic* had continued to fight the fire and evacuate casualties. Herman Everett of *Pavlic* relates his memory of that evening. He was in one of the boats that had been launched:

> "One man was lowered from *Thatcher's* bridge area onto our boat in a metal wire stretcher with a strap across his chest. We circled the ship to return to *Pavlic's* starboard fantail. Rogers and I lifted the stretcher with a line tied to it. The men on the fantail were holding the line. The stretcher was resting on the top rail of the boat. Suddenly, the ship moved a few feet. It pulled the stretcher out of our hands. The man had a heart beat and a pulse - I knew because I checked - although he was not conscious. He and the stretcher went into the water. I still cannot get this out of mind. But now I've heard that someone jumped in to save him. I would be much relieved if this were so."

There is evidence now that this was indeed the case. Joe Pirochta says that a crew member named Panger was the rescuer. Panger, himself, was hospitalized the next day for symptoms of battle fatigue.

It was a bad evening. *Register (APD-92)* and *Chase (APD-54)* had been hit (previously narrated). *Pavlic* brought *Thatcher's* casualties to the anchorage the next morning.

On the 24th, *Pavlic* needed to replenish her food supplies and put into Kerama Retto alongside an attack cargo ship. There were no mutterings among the work parties this time. There would have been considerable worries had the crew known what the enemy had in store for the next few days.

That evening, the Japanese made a suicide attack on Yontan airfield - paratroopers descended on the field and raced around throwing phosphorous bombs at parked planes before they were cut down. Simultaneously, 182 *kamikazes* were launched against the picket line. *Bates (APD-47)* was sunk while *Roper (APD-20)* was badly damaged (both previously narrated), as were three destroyers and two DEs.

25 May. Flash Red was in effect almost all day. There seemed to be no end to the raids approaching from the north. Japanese records show that at least 493 of their planes attacked

the Fleet on 24-25 May. Six picket ships took hits, and an LSM was sunk.

26 May. Captain V.M. Kennaday, *ComTransDiv 105*, came aboard and hoisted his pennant. He wanted to see for himself just how tough things could be out on the picket line.

27 May. His timing was excellent. Things were quiet during daylight hours as the Japanese took time out to regroup from their severe losses of pilots and planes. Their records indicate that we had been targeted by *Kikusui* number seven meaning a massive suicide attack.

Just after midnight, *Pavlic's* sonar picked up a solid contact. Captain Allen was notified and he immediately took over the conn. I was on watch in the CIC with Radarman John A. Foute Jr. and Radarman Ben H. Pace on the air search radar. The pinging grew louder, and there was no question that this was a submarine. Captain Kennaday appeared in the doorway to observe the action.

Since we had been at GQ for so long, and only recently set the 2400 to 0400 watch, the skipper decided to give the crew a break and mustered only the depth charge detail to augment the regular watch. In CIC, we relayed range and bearing data to the bridge. Helmsman Clint Tew swung *Pavlic* toward the target. Range closed to 500 yards, then to 100 yards. "Drop depth charges," ordered the skipper, and four charges rolled off the fantail. Moments of silence passed, followed by four explosions.

In CIC, our job was to try to re-establish contact with the target and then give the target data to the nearest ship so it could attack. I made an "X" on the board. From *Foute*- "Destroyer, bearing 320 relative, range 2000, course 140 degrees. I marked another "X" - "Ask the destroyer if they have contact," suggested Captain Kennaday. "Negative," was the reply.

I did some quick calculations. "Tell the destroyer to come to course 060 degrees," I hollered, "range 1800 yards from her." "Roger" from the destroyer. Another reading from Foute. I plotted it immediately, and my heart sank. I had given a reciprocal bearing, from the sub to the destroyer instead of vice versa. Captain Kennaday saw the error but he was most gracious. I never forgot what he said. "Forget it. We'll get him next time." He must also have said something to Allen on the bridge because Allen never mentioned the incident.

We stayed at GQ all night. We could not know it at the time, but the Japanese were launching *Kikusui* eight the night of 27-28 May and it would last until 30 May. Before it was over, two Fletcher class destroyers would be sunk, *Drexler (DD-741)* and *Braine (DD-630)*. Another was damaged, and two DEs and two APDs were also damaged. *Pavlic* would have a role in assisting two of these vessels.

0503 on 28 May. The Japanese sub was within *Pavlic's* sonar range again. We had secured from GQ at about 0400. As the loudspeaker announced a sub contact, a bleary-eyed crew donned life preservers and helmets and trudged to their battle stations. The sonar contact was solid. Depth charges were armed, attack speed, 15 knots, was signaled to the engine room and *Pavlic* made her run. We had only four depth charges left which were enough for one try. But, we also had an advantage. This time, I was not in CIC but Joe McGarvey and Bill Kennedy were; there were no errors.

Andrew Quinn was on duty in the pilot house and Jack Wilferd was on the signal bridge. They recall the excitement of displaying the "sub attack" flag, warning ships to stay clear. *Rednour (APD-102)* was astern as *Pavlic* charged down the sonar bearing. Again, ear splitting explosions lifting *Pavlic's* screws out of the water, shattering light bulbs and drinking glasses in the aft compartments.

After the turbulence settled, sonar picked up a blurred noise. We circled back and entered a big pool of black oil with no further sonar contact. We learned after the war that the Japanese did indeed lose a sub that day in that location, attempting to evacuate several high ranking army officers from Okinawa. (No mention is made in the *Dictionary of American Naval Fighting Ships* relative to *Pavlic* sinking a submarine, the reason this author did not include and expand on this episode in chapter *Pacific Antisubmarine Warfare*.)

The attacks started as usual at 1800 hours. "Flash Red, 2 bogies, closing." Lee, our bridge spotter, picked them up on our starboard quarter. Bogeys were reported on other stations with an occasional TBS message from a picket ship announcing, "Splash one bogey."

2130. Things seemed quieter, so *Pavlic* secured from GQ. 2135 - Back at GQ as three fires lit up the sky - score three for the bad guys. Suddenly, from *Pavlic's* starboard quarter, a suicider came into view, low in the sky, heading directly for us. Taylor recalls his 40mm swinging into action. Paul Kluzek and Earl Kralovec opened fire with their 20mm weapons. Tracers danced into the night air - a ball of fire exploded, tumbling into the sea about 400 yards away!

An hour passed. Another plane came in from starboard, this time closer to *Rednour*. Her 40mm fire lit up the sky. Her doctor, whose battle station was in the wardroom, stepped through the door to see the action. As he did so, the plane slammed aboard, killing him instantly and a number of the crew as well (previously narrated).

Rednour was able to control the fire herself, but she had no doctor for her many casualties. *Pavlic* put a boat over (mine) with Simon Levy as coxswain. We went alongside *Rednour's* port quarter and our doc climbed aboard. Before we could cast off the boat, however, *Rednour's* screws churned and almost pulled the boat under. Only skillful work with our bow hook saved us.

Our trip back to *Pavlic* was adventurous. *Pavlic* had to keep way on because she couldn't risk sitting dead in the water. We were not half way back when *Pavlic* went to full speed, and the 5" gun crew, with Dean Koppenhaver and Sam Robinson passing the shells, took a bogey under fire. *Pavlic* disappeared into the dark and then circled back. The boat crew got safely aboard.

Minutes later, three bogies were spotted off the port bow. This time it was the twin 40mm guns on the port side that got in a few licks. Tom Cook, our youngest crew member (fifteen when he enlisted by misrepresenting his age) recalls that his gun jammed. Jim Bancroft, manning the port 20mm guns, remembers two of the planes banking away, but the third, a Betty, turned and headed straight for the bridge. The captain shouted, "Hit the deck." Henry Grimmer, also on the guns, apparently didn't hear the order. With gun captain Pirochta's help, he continued pouring lead at the plane. Suddenly it plunged into the water, a mere 50 yards from the bow! Grimmer and Pirochta became the most popular guys aboard.

Pavlic's incredible luck still held. An hour later, two more attacks came, one turning away and one falling victim to *Clemson (APD-31)*, which had replaced the damaged *Rednour*.

Dawn on the 29th. There was heavy fighting to the north. *Pavlic* was ordered to the area. A destroyer, *Drexler (DD-741)*, had been sunk and survivors were in the water. As we arrived, there was oil and wreckage everywhere. Mel Taylor and his boat crew fought off sharks to pick two men out of the water. An LCI, laden with survivors, many injured, came alongside to pass them over our fantail.

Drexler had taken two hits by bomb-laden Bettys. She sank in two minutes with a heavy loss of life. Barnard recalls one survivor telling how he was ordered by a chief to come below to secure a valve. Rather than obey, the sailor jumped overboard. *Pavlic* transported 134 survivors back to Buckner Bay. The chief was not among them.

We dropped anchor as all four LCVPs hurried the survivors to hospital ships. The crew used the few hours of respite to clean up living quarters and replenish ammunition. *Delegate* passed the word to expect heavy suicide attacks at any time. In the afternoon, a raid broke through the Combat Air Patrol, and an enemy pilot crashed into *Barber (APD-57)* (previously narrated).

1800. *Pavlic* returned to her station. "Flash Red - many bogies, 100 miles, closing." Moments later, "Many bogies - designated raid 2 - 75 miles, closing." Captain Allen had decided we would go to GQ only when enemy planes were within five miles; otherwise, we would be at GQ endlessly. Darkness settled in. Both raids were now within 20 miles, then 10. Tracers lit up the sky as other ships took them on. Then a bright flash and another and another, as planes crashed aboard picket ships. I recall 10 hits within a 15 minute period.

Then, the inevitable call to *Pavlic* to proceed to a destroyer badly damaged. Again, flank speed as our little ship raced to the scene. There she was, her decks almost submerged, listing heavily to port with smoke pouring from her superstructure. It was *Shubrick (DD-639)*, looking as if she'd sink at any moment. Allen decided to chance it, tie up to her and get her survivors off as quickly as possible. Dead and injured were gathered on her fantail. As some of her crew grabbed our lines, others were ready with stretchers.

Within 10 minutes, *Pavlic's* decks were a ghastly sight. Bodies lay everywhere, placed as gently as we could. Our after damage control party had been designated to board the stricken destroyer to retrieve survivors which meant I was there with a walkie-talkie to *Pavlic's* bridge. We had ninety percent of the survivors transferred when the bridge demanded to know if we could cast off - bogies reported close by. I remember asking for a couple of minutes so I could find a *Shubrick* officer to ask if we had everybody. I then reported "all clear." Those were tense moments with the real possibility that *Shubrick* would suddenly sink or a Japanese pilot would spot us.

As *Pavlic* headed to Buckner Bay, a working party was organized to remove the bodies from the fantail to the cargo hold. Joe Pirochta was a member of this group:

> "Two of the bodies were chiefs burnt beyond recognition and curled in a fetal position. Two others were blown to bits. One of the fellows had his stomach thrown on top of him; the blood ran down the stretcher all over my hands. The other fellow's head was blown off, and we stuffed old rags into him to stop the blood from running all over the decks. When we got to Buckner Bay, we took all of the bodies to a large transport, where the dead were piled up three high. A chaplain had funeral services, and all were buried at sea. People just can't realize how terribly our boys died out there. I'll never forget it as long as I live."

This was the end of *Kikusui* number eight. In addition to *Drexler*, *Braine (DD-630)*, had been sunk. *Shubrick* did not sink, but was out of the war. Two APDs had been hit in addition to *Rednour*, *Tatum (APD-81)* and *Loy (APD-56)* (all previously narrated) along with a large attack transport in Buckner Bay. Two destroyer minesweepers were hit as well as three merchantmen in the anchorage.

After our 72 hours of no sleep, the attacks petered out, and we were allowed to stay at anchor for a few days in Buckner Bay. The evening raids continued, but they were single plane attacks for the most part. One pilot succeeded in hitting the battleship *Pennsylvania (BB-38)*, anchored right near us, causing heavy casualties.

For those final days of May, no one was able to change clothes or to be free of his life jacket. Helmets were either on or close at hand. Having witnessed the damage a *kamikaze* could inflict, nobody needed any urging about safety precautions. The men whose battle stations kept them topside, where they could see and respond to approaching danger, had tough assignments. Those below deck also didn't have an easy time. Men like Bill Bass, Arlyn Brockmeyer, Peterson and Ray Wildes, had to perform their duties knowing that they were surrounded by pipes loaded with superheated steam under great pressure.

Another group to go through uncertain moments of battle, relying upon the accuracy of their gunners, were the damage control parties which included Barton, Damrell, Massey, Howerbamp, Hetzel, and Tommie. Quint Weaver had the choice assignment in after steering control; his job would start only if the bridge had been hit and the steering knocked out. After a month or so, Quartermaster Third Class Martin Miller was awarded this choice duty.

In the course of five short weeks, the crew had been transformed from a group of young, undertrained but willing novices to a cohesive, can-do team who knew they could entrust their lives to each other. There was no longer a job we couldn't do well- from convoying to attacking submarines, from fueling at sea to rendering assistance to less fortunate ships under the most difficult circumstances.

Our Division Commander, Captain Kennaday, wrote to us upon leaving *Pavlic* at the end of May:

To the officers and men of the *USS PAVLIC*

> "I want you to know what I think of your performance of duty during the past three days.
>
> While that duty was not more than any of us might expect to have been required in time of war, the manner in which you all performed it excited my highest admiration. You were brave, efficient, hard-working, cheerful, thoughtful, and compassionate in a way that warmed my heart and made me proud to be one of you. The hours were long and the risks we knew not how great, which made the mental as well as the physical strain heavy. It was hard, important work, well performed in every respect.
>
> Well done - keep it up."

J. M. Kennaday
Captain, U.S. Navy,
Commander Transport Division 105

Tempest, Fire and Foe

The month of June provided its own unique challenges. The Japanese no longer had enough planes for the massive *Kikusui* attacks we had been experiencing, but launched two smaller ones instead, the last on 7 June. However, nightly raids continued to hit the picket ships. We would lose *Barry* (*APD-29*) (previously narrated), and two destroyers, *Porter (DD-356)* and *Twiggs (DD-591)*.

The big event of early June was a typhoon. *Pavlic* had been resting in Buckner Bay and was on stand-by rescue duty. Admiral Halsey ordered the Third Fleet away from Okinawa on what he thought was a safe course. As it turned out, a second typhoon developed directly in the path of Halsey's Fleet. By the night of 5 June, *Pavlic* found herself in mountainous waves, winds shrieking in excess of 100 knots, and in real danger of capsizing. One roll measured 49 degrees on the inclinometer. The ship seemed to hesitate longer than she should before coming upright. We were thinking about the extra weight of the LCVP's and whether they would tip us over. (Some DEs rolled much more than that in typhoons but they were better balanced than APDs with all their topside weight; the fear was well founded. See chapter *The Pacific Typhoons* for a detailed description of this typhoon.)

21 June. Japanese resistance on Okinawa collapsed after a series of futile *banzai* attacks, followed by an orgy of suicide. The former crack Imperial 32nd Division had deteriorated into a handful of demoralized officers coming forward with white flags while stumbling over their own dead. They were followed by dazed infantrymen, almost more dead than alive.

Although Okinawa was declared secured by the marines and army ashore, there were many Japanese pilots who didn't agree. On the 25th, a flight of bogies came within a mile of us as we were on patrol close to Ie Shima. We were at GQ and had the planes in visual contact when suddenly the sky around them erupted with air bursts. When the smoke cleared, the planes were gone, victims of a shore battery on Ie Shima.

On the evening of 2 July, while patrolling just off Ie Shima, a full moon silhouetted the ship and illuminated our wake. Keeley had the bridge and I was in CIC. A bogey was in the area. Had it been a month ago, we'd have gone to GQ immediately, even though the general condition, "Flash Red," had not been ordered.

Keeley went to the voice tube, "Jack, are you watching the bogey?" I assured him we were, and that he was one of ours. Our planes were equipped with an IFF relay box that would respond to a radio challenge, indicating he was friendly. What I didn't know was that the enemy had captured a box and equipped their planes with similar ones. Minutes passed. The plane began to circle overhead.

> Keeley: "Jack, you sure that's not a Jap?"
>
> Me: "Relax. IFF says he's friendly - maybe he's having some fun."
>
> A minute went by. From the voice tube: "Hey Jack, here comes the friendly - Oh no, he's got a torpedo," he yelled as he sounded GQ.
>
> I jumped up and banged on the skipper's sea cabin next door to the CIC where Allen was asleep. "Wake up, Captain," I shouted. "We're under torpedo attack."

The sound of machine gun fire directly above my head drowned out Allen's response. Bill Graves, Gunner's Mate First Class, manned the 50 caliber machine gun. Earl Hetzel was also on gun watch. While the bogey had been circling, Graves called to the bridge and requested permission to open fire. He was told to hold it, the plane was ours.

> "Ours hell," said Graves. "If that guy comes around again, I'm going to fire at him."
>
> "You know where you'll be if you fire without orders," warned Hetzel.
>
> At that point, Graves heard Keeley shout, "Here he comes"!

Graves' machine gun shattered the silence. (Needless to say, no reprimand was ever given to Graves. No commendation either.) Ignoring Graves' effort, the Japanese pilot bore in on our port side. Everyone topside braced for the seemingly inevitable crash. Suddenly, however, the plane pulled up, skimming *Pavlic's* mast. It wasn't a suicide plane this time. A torpedo bomber had us in his sights!

> "Torpedo in the water," came the cry from the bridge, "Coming from port side, midship"!

I braced for the explosion, thinking about all the guys below decks and what a terrible tragedy was about to happen there. Moments ticked by. Then a miracle. From the starboard lookout, "Torpedo wake going away. He missed! he missed!"

The pilot dropped his "fish" too close to us and it was still diving, going directly under the ship, when it should have leveled off.

4 July was memorable for a another reason. We were north of Okinawa, not far from Kyushu. The sky was full of bombers, all headed for Tokyo. It had to be one of the greatest displays of massed air power ever, and it gave us a sense that we would win after all.

Evening of 22 July. Air attacks still occurred, though less frequently. More often than not, the planes aloft were Corsairs, not Vals, Kates or Bettys. *Pavlic* was patrolling a mile off the Buckner Bay anchorage. No bogies about, condition Flash Green. Without warning, skimming over the waves and headed right at *Pavlic*, was another Japanese torpedo bomber. Before the watch could react, it dropped its "fish" and flew over the bridge. Unbelievably, this torpedo also passed harmlessly under the ship. Unfortunately, it headed directly into the anchorage crowded with transports. An explosion lit up the night, followed by calls for assistance from a ship that had been making ready to unload its cargo of soldiers.

On the night of the 28th, we witnessed a bizarre incident in the Okinawa Campaign while on "suicide alley." Less than a mile away, was the destroyer *Callaghan (DD-792)*. She had been at Okinawa for the entire campaign, 117 days. Twelve suicide planes were painted on her bow; eleven downed by gunfire, one by crashing. With her was the destroyer *Cassin Young (DD-793)*. Early in the evening, *Delegate* had radioed *Callaghan*, that she was to be relieved shortly after midnight to proceed to San Diego for overhaul. *Pavlic* and other ships in the area sent her "Well done" and "Best of Luck" messages. For her, the war would be over.

But not quite. An hour before her scheduled departure, her Officer of The Deck reported a bogey at 10 miles, closing. The bogey closed on *Callaghan*. She opened fire. We saw the tracers and then an air explosion. "Splash one bogey," her OOD announced. But, instantly, another explosion. A second suicide plane had trailed behind the first one so that *Callaghan's* radar showed only one blip. The second plane had a 250 pound bomb aboard. It crashed *Callaghan* and started a fire! Her damage control parties raced to the affected area, arriving just as the ammo exploded, killing most of them. *Callaghan* was mortally wounded and took down with her the dreams of home, the last ship to be sunk by a *kamikaze*.

Cassin Young rendered assistance and picked up survivors. As she was proceeding back to the anchorage, however, a plane appeared in the sky, showing "friendly" on the IFF system. The destroyer held her fire, until it was too late. This "friendly" dove into her starboard quarter, killing over 60 of her crew and ending the war for her also. It could have been *Pavlic* ordered on that rescue mission.

As it turned out, this was to be the last organized suicide raid of the war. Only an occasional single plane would appear in the skies after the end of July. In all, the navy had lost nearly 10,000 sailors and as many more injured, not to mention 368 ships damaged, and 30 sunk by the "Divine Wind" off Okinawa. It was the costliest campaign in the annals of the U.S. Navy.

The next evening, our old friend *Rednour*, took another suicide plane hit (previously narrated). This time she was severely damaged and all of us aboard *Pavlic* were sorry to learn that she would no longer man the picket stations with us.

Typhoon warnings were broadcast again. On 1 August, *Pavlic* was on station when orders came to depart immediately to escort an attack transport and a merchant ship away from Okinawa to avoid the oncoming storm. For the next two days, sleep again became impossible as the ship battled against waves driven by winds of 90 knots.

On returning to Okinawa, we were given the rest of the day off. The captain allowed liberty to the men off watch. Each was issued two cans of beer and our boats brought them to a nearby beach. For most, it was the first time we'd set foot on land for 93 days!

It was becoming apparent that the enemy air squadrons were ready to concede Okinawa. We figured that they would now try to conserve remaining "assets" for what we all knew was still ahead of us - the invasion of the home islands. None of us looked forward to the prospect of another Okinawa or worse.

Then, a miracle occurred. From the Armed Forces radio, we heard reports about something called an "atom bomb" and a city called Hiroshima. Although we had no idea of what this was, it sure sounded good. The word was that we had some sort of super weapon, and surely the Japanese would not let their country be totally destroyed.

10 August. We were patrolling off Hagushi anchorage. It was a warm evening, and many of the crew not on watch were topside trying to avoid the intolerable heat below decks. The radio shack watch was startled. There was a message to all ships of the fleet and all units ashore that the enemy was willing to discuss surrender.

There was much unwarranted hoopla with weapons fired without permission, killing 15 men and drawing official censure. *Pavlic* did not participate in the firing.

Reality set in within an hour. A bogey was picked up on radar on a course directly to us. Unless our radar wasn't working properly, this guy was closing at 450 mph, an unheard of speed. The plane became visible and indeed it was moving. He ignored us and slammed into a transport in the anchorage. We later learned that the Japanese had a couple of experimental planes with jet-assisted engines they were developing. This must have been one of them.

The rumors of surrender turned out to be true. On the 14th, *Pavlic* received orders releasing her from picket duty and to join the Third Fleet now assembling in the waters off of Tokyo Bay.

RYUKYU GLORY WON BY LITTLE WARSHIPS

Picket Line Guarding Fleet off Okinawa
Balked Enemy Air Force in Blazing War.

By W.H. LAWRENCE

Aboard a Flagship, in the East China
Sea off Okinawa June 26 (Delayed)

> "The Navy threw a 'picket line' across 'Bogey Highway' to keep Japanese ship breakers out of the Okinawa transport area. These picket ships - none larger than destroyers - fought and won the longest and hardest battle in the history of naval warfare. They suffered the greatest losses in men and ships ever sustained by the United States Navy, but they fulfilled their mission of keeping the bulk of enemy aircraft out of the transport area where vital supplies for the troops were being unloaded. It is no exaggeration to say that these little ships, which seldom have the chance for the glory given to the aircraft carriers and the battleships, performed a major role in our great victory on Okinawa.
>
> This thrilling story, which can be told for the first time now that the Okinawa campaign is won, constitutes an epic that will live forever in the annals of the navy. It is the story of tough little ships and brave men whose extraordinary gunnery took care of the best the Japanese air force could throw at our Okinawa operation.
>
> They were at General Quarters hundreds of times during the 82 days of the land fighting on Okinawa. These air alerts lasted from a few minutes to several hours at all times of the night and day as the Japanese sent one to 400 aircraft in a single attack.
>
> Commanded by Commodore Frederick Moosbrugger, these picket ships stood guard as much as 60 miles away from the Hagushi anchorage. They were the sentinels to fight approaching Japanese planes, surface craft or submarines.
>
> To form the picket line, the navy stationed destroyers, destroyer escorts and high speed transports in great arcs before the approaches to the Hagushi anchorages. These pickets moved back and forth 24 hours a day. The enemy chose to fight the main battle along the picket line. One out of every three ships that served on the outer picket line was sunk or damaged in this fierce vendetta with the *kamikazes*."

Along with our Division Mates - *Barr*, *Sims*, *Bass (APD-124)* and *Wantuck (APD-125)*, we joined Task Force 31 on 16 August. Standing topside, you could look to the horizon in any direction and see nothing but warships. On the 20th, the British Fleet appeared, and *Pavlic* took aboard about 200 Royal Marine landing force troops. Mount Fujiyama loomed nearby, and one could see why it deserved to be known as the most beautiful mountain in the world.

The ceremony would be held aboard *Missouri (BB-63)* on 2 September 1945 with General MacArthur presiding. There were some problems. How could we safely get the Missouri into Tokyo Bay, which was guarded by four forts with 18" guns, capable of sinking a battleship? How about suicide swimmers, underwater obstacles, and mines?

The versatile APDs had a job. Instead of going for POWs, *Pavlic* was assigned to Fort number four, to see to it that its big guns were immobilized. *Sims*, *Barr* and *Runels* (APD-85) got the other forts. On 30 August, three days before the surrender, the little ships steamed into Tokyo Bay. The boats were lowered, and our landing party was dispatched to Fort number four

The Japanese defenders surrendered peacefully. The Emperor had spoken and, like it or not, these Japanese marines were ready to quit. As Ensign George Miller and the landing party hauled down the Rising Sun flag and raised the American flag over the fort, it occurred to us that this might be the first American flag raised in Japan by the occupation forces.

The landing party returned with prisoners, whose faces showed that they fully expected to be executed on the spot. They couldn't believe that they would be offered cigarettes and food and that the stories they heard about their enemy were largely untrue.

Pavlic proceeded up Tokyo Bay towards the big naval shipyard at Yokosuka. The long channel was alive with white bed sheets as the civilian population tried to ensure that we knew they had surrendered, and "please don't fire at us." It was indeed a moving sight. These were the enemy - a nation which had never lost a war, a people who had come to think of themselves as invincible, now enduring this final humiliation. I have never forgotten that day.

We disembarked the Royal Marines. They were immediately replaced with 200 L Company, Fourth U.S. Marines. We then headed for Tateyama Wan, a Japanese naval air base some 20 miles south of Yokosuka. With us were *Sims*, and *Stockham (DD-683)*. We put the marines ashore at Tateyama. They were prepared to accept the surrender of the Japanese garrison, a hundred or so soldiers. About an hour later, the Marine Captain called us on his radio:

> "*Pavlic*, we've got a problem here. Please pass the word that we need reinforcements immediately. I've got a Jap general with me, and he wants to surrender a whole army division to us - there must be 10,000 Japs here."

We relayed his message to the troop transports, anchored about 10 miles away. Some army general came on the radio and told us to tell the marines to accept the surrender, to have the Japs stockpile their arms, that reinforcements would be on the way and, meanwhile, you marines and sailors are *not*, repeat *not* to take any "souvenirs" (meaning Japanese rifles).

By now, the entire Third Fleet had steamed into Tokyo Bay. Our marine contingent was replaced by army troops the following day. We were ordered back to Yokosuka, passing *Missouri* and the last remaining Japanese capital ship - *HIJMS Nagato*, heavily damaged, but still afloat. We were assigned anchorage fronting the former residence of the senior Japanese commander at Yokosuka, now flying the U.S. flag.

The enemy had laid down his arms. Yet, it was still a dicey situation. We could go ashore only in pairs, and it was prudent to wear a weapon conspicuously displayed. Standing watch, we quickly learned that suicide swimmers were still anxious to slip aboard and cut the throat of any unwary watch stander. As one destroyer escort was to learn the hard way, there were still mines in the area.

However, the war was over. For us, there was no doubt about the wisdom of Truman's decision to drop the atomic bombs. we now knew that we would not be part of the invasion forces already being prepared for the assault on the home islands. We knew that our chances of surviving that operation were slim. *Pavlic's* luck could not be expected to last forever. But now, we were to be spared this fate. And all of us can recall the sheer joy of knowing that we were going to live, that we were going home.

We were, with few exceptions, not career military people. Captain Allen was one exception. To his credit, he succeeded in earning his fourth stripe in years to come, eventually retiring as a Captain and commander of a destroyer division in the Pacific. He and Keeley did remain friends over the years, and he died in the late 1980s. Being skipper of a fighting ship in those days was not an easy job and, although he was not liked by some of his officers and crew, he was respected as a man who knew his job and did it well. (This author recalls an observation by Admiral Lord Nelson: "The captain of a ship walks the bridge alone and friendless and is contemptuous of snide remarks out of earshot by officers unburdened by the weight of responsibility.)

Now, over fifty years later, this final bloody battle of World War II is a receding memory, even to those of us who were there. While American losses at sea were the heaviest in history, the Japanese sacrificed 7500 pilots and planes in *kamikaze* missions.

U.S. Navy Captain (later Admiral) Frederick Moosbrugger was the man in charge of the radar picket ships throughout the entire campaign. His action report includes the following and it seems to say it all:

> "The performance of radar picket ships was superb throughout the Okinawa campaign. Acts of heroism and unselfishness, fighting spirit, coolness under fire, and unswerving determination, endurance, and qualities of leadership and loyalty exceeded all previous conceptions. set for the U.S. Navy.
>
> Never in the annals of our glorious naval history have forces done so much with so little against such odds for so long a period. Radar picket duty in this operation might well be a symbol of supreme achievement in our naval traditions."

Reprinted by permission
THE NEW YORK TIMES
Friday, 29 June 1945

Bates (APD-47) after attack by three *kamikazes* just before she capsized and sank. Courtesy crewman Louis R. Frost.

Blessman bomb damage. Photo submitted by Philip Leboutillier, former commanding officer.

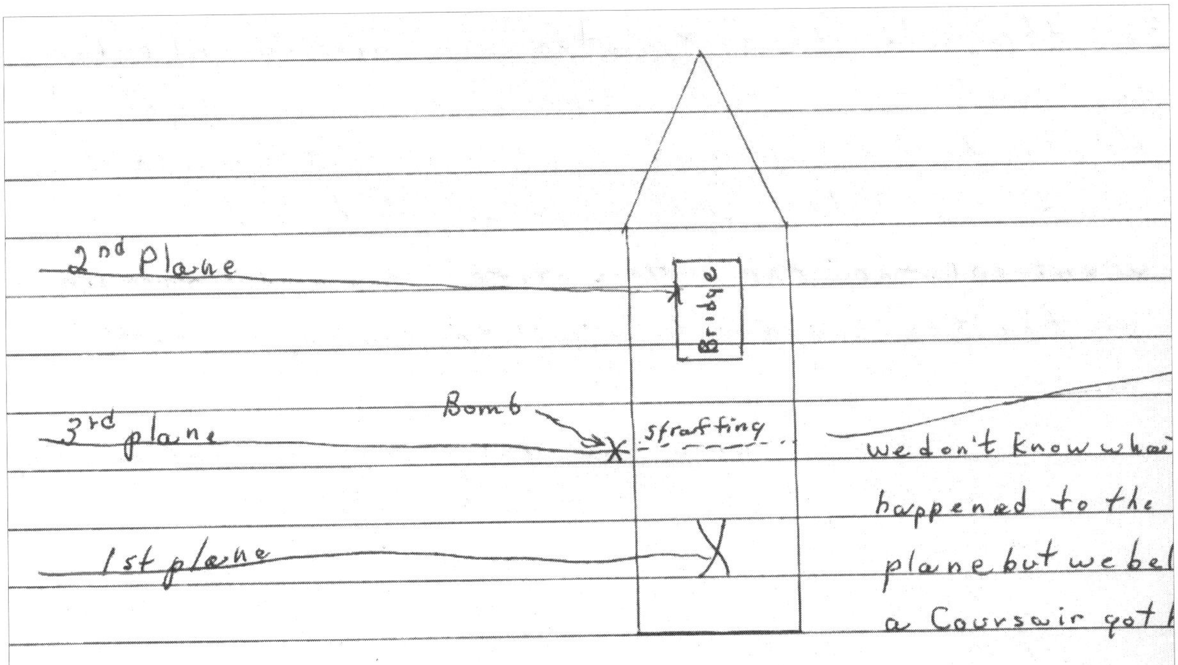

Diagram of *kamikaze* attack on *Bates*. Drawing by crewman Louis R. Frost.

Jubilation aboard the *USS Wileman (DE-220)* at news war ended. US Navy Photo

Chapter XVII - The Divine Wind In Retrospective

Although destroyer escorts and high speed transports were not the only vessels that engaged Japanese suicide planes, their presence was considerable and constitutes the two longest chapters in this book – and the bloodiest. Who were these men who willingly took their own lives in droves so that they could destroy their enemy and their ships? What was their mind-set, alien to most occidentals?

Reprinted from the book *The Divine Wind*.
by permission of the publisher

"The *kamikaze* or 'Divine Wind' program was started in October, 1944, by Admiral Onishi, the Commander Japanese Naval Forces in the Philippines. The Second Battle of The Philippine Sea ended the Japanese Navy as an effective fighting force. When the Japanese Fleet returned to Japan, the main strength of its aircraft carriers and cruiser squadrons had been wiped out, and its only remaining battleships were *Yamato*, *Nagato*, and *Haruna*. As a result, the Japanese Navy turned to *kamikaze* tactics.

When the Americans landed on Okinawa, the Japanese sent the remnants of their Second Fleet to the Ryukyus with orders to beach themselves off the coast and fire every gun of every ship until the last shell had been expended or the last ship destroyed. On 7 April, the day before they would reach Okinawa, they were intercepted by 300 U.S. carrier planes. All the Japanese ships, except a few destroyers, were sunk or were dead in the water. This greatest of suicide actions had cost the Japanese the *Yamato*, a light cruiser, and four destroyers, plus the lives of over 2500 men.

The U.S. Navy reported that the Okinawa campaign caused about 10,000 American casualties, mostly a result of attacks by suicide planes, compared to 3,385 American casualties at Pearl Harbor. Here is an excerpt from a letter written by a *kamikaze* pilot to his parents just before leaving on a suicide mission:

Dear Parents:

'Please congratulate me. I have been given a splendid opportunity to die. This is my last day. The destiny of our homeland hinges on the decisive battle in the seas to the south, where I shall fall like a blossom from a radiant cherry tree. I shall be a shield for his Majesty and die along with my squadron leader and other friends. I wish that I could be born seven times, each time to smite the enemy. How I appreciate this chance to die like a man! I am grateful from the depths of my heart to the parents who have reared me with their constant prayers and tender love. I am grateful as well to my squadron leader and superior officers who have looked after me as if I were their own son and given me such careful training. We are 16 warriors manning the bombers. May our death be as sudden and clean as the shattering of crystal…'

In his book, *Reflections Upon Our National Character*, a Japanese author wrote the following:

"It is often said that the Japanese excel in loyalty and courage. To the Japanese, death holds no terror. Their brave conduct on the field of battle serves as evidence of this attitude. It is a point of strength. But it is also a point of weakness, for the Japanese are prone to make light of their lives and be too ready to die. Courage is all too often a matter of impulse rather than a matter of mature deliberation. On the other hand, occidentals place high value on the life of the individual. They do not die so readily and, therefore, they cannot comprehend the psychology of *kamikaze* pilots. It is not a question of bravery, since occidentals display great bravery in many ways. But when they embark upon a hazardous undertaking, it is done with the utmost of individual enterprise and intellect. That approach should serve as a lesson for us."

The following is a quotation by Vice Admiral C.R. Brown's foreword in the book *The Divine Wind*:

"Among those of us who were in the Philippines and at Okinawa, I doubt if there is anyone who can depict with complete clarity our mixed emotions as we watched a man about to die, a man determined to die in order that he might destroy us in the process. There was a hypnotic fascination to a sight so alien to our western philosophy. We watched each plunging *kamikaze* with the detached horror of one witnessing a terrible spectacle, rather than as the intended victim. We forgot self for the moment as we groped hopelessly for the thoughts of that other man up there. And dominating it all was a strange mixture of respect and pity, respect for any person who offers the supreme sacrifice to the things he stands for, and pity for the utter frustration which was epitomized by the suicidal act. For whatever the gesture meant to that central actor out there in space, and however painful might be the consequences to ourselves, no one of us questioned the final outcome of the war. This 'Divine Wind,' the *kamikaze*, this Special Attack Corps, was just another form of *banzai* charge made by men experiencing the bitterness of defeat and unwilling to accept that reality."

This book author has noted that some writers have linked the *kamikaze* mentality to the predominant Japanese Shinto religion. This may be a factor but not necessarily a determinant. A surprising revelation is that Christian Japanese pilots also joined the *kamikaze* corps. Although there was probably peer pressure, pilots were not forced into compliance. Indeed, many did decline, and there is no evidence to indicate that they were punished or ostracized. They simply remained in conventional combat units.

The end of Admiral Onishi, who organized the *kamikaze* corps, tells much about the Japanese national character. When the Emperor ordered the armed forces to surrender, the Admiral considered himself to be a failure for not having been able to turn the tide with his suicide pilots. He retired to his quarters where he proceeded with the nationally accepted purge of disgrace, *Hara-Kiri*, suicide by disembowelment. However, he botched the procedure and attempted to finish himself off by cutting his own throat. He didn't do a very good job there either and bled profusely. An aide offered to shoot him through the head, but he declined because that would interfere with honorable suicide. He permitted himself to bleed to death!

The Monterey Herald
Dateline: April 29, 1990

The Quest of The Thunder Gods

At 0530 hours on 12 January 1945, thirteen men on *Gilligan (DE-508)*, a destroyer escort patrolling the Lingayen Gulf in the Philippines, were blasted into the sea after a hit by a *kamikaze* suicide bomber. Twelve men died. But the thirteenth, Navy Lieutenant William K. Stewart, was pulled out of the shark-infested waters after about 45 minutes, seriously wounded, but alive.

On 21 March 1990, Stewart had lunch in Tokyo at the annual reunion of the 'Thunder Gods Association' — the name by which the suicide corps was (and is) known in Japan.

Stewart, now a retired attorney and longtime resident of Carmel Highlands, California, was invited to Tokyo by Hatsuho Naito, a distinguished naval historian.

It was the first time the Thunder Gods had ever had an American veteran at one of their meetings — much less one of their targets. They were anxious to meet Stewart, and he returned their curiosity.

His interest in the *kamikazes* dated back to his moment of terror in 1945. For even when Stewart was in the water, surrounded by the wreckage of the bomber, he recalled wondering about the Japanese pilot who had given his life for his country. What made him do it? What sort of man — or boy — could be so driven as to sacrifice his life for his Emperor, his country, or whatever?

It took many years, but Stewart was to get some — but not all — of the answers. They came when he was an honored guest of the Japanese pilots association at the pristine and colorful Yasakuni Shrine in Tokyo. His invitation stemmed from a letter he wrote to Naito after reading the English translation of his book, 'The Thunder Gods'.

There are about 200 remaining members of the Thunder Gods, survivors of the original corps estimated to have numbered about 10,000. Almost to a man, the *kamikaze* pilots believe that their membership in the suicide corps was, and still is, 'the most profound experience of their lives', said Stewart.

Stewart said that they also know that their being alive today is a matter of pure chance. A fair percentage of them were senior pilots, who were acting as *kamikaze* instructors, and who were being held in reserve for the very last-ditch defense of the main Japanese islands.

Others were still in training at war's end and a few had taken off on suicide missions but failed to find a target or were forced to return to base due to mechanical difficulties.

To return to Stewart's personal experience, it came when the largest amphibious invasion fleet of the Pacific Theater entered Lingayen Gulf in January of 1945.

The *Gilligan* crew was aware that, three months earlier in the Leyte invasion, the Japanese had started using suicide planes as a desperate measure to stop the American reconquest of the Pacific Islands. The increasing number of battered ships returning to base bolstered, all too vividly, the scary stories of the Japanese planes diving on the exposed vessels of the American task force.

The first suicide attacks at Lingayen took place the day of the invasion. Everyday they came, flying from Formosa (now Taiwan) on their one-way mission of flight and death. Since the *kamikazes* concentrated on the picket screen, *Gilligan* knew her turn was coming even before the attack took place. In Stewart's words:

> 'I was in command of the after battery on *Gilligan*. We tracked the Japanese plane with radar well before it came into view, flying at full power just a few feet above the water. As it emerged from the mist, we opened fire with the quad 40mm guns.'

The Betty was Japan's largest military plane, a two-motored look-alike of the American B-25. The 40mm explosive shells plowed into the plane but were not enough to stop the momentum of the aircraft. With its wing on fire (and the pilot probably dead at the controls), the plane swept across the gun deck of the destroyer escort, cascading the guns, crew and the torpedo tubes into the sea. The bombs of the attacker failed to detonate, but its exploding gasoline lit up the sky.

Stewart knew he was badly injured, for he could feel the femur bone of his left leg sticking out at right angles, and he was conscious of blood in the water.

He was picked up by a destroyer during a lull in the battle and then transferred back to *Gilligan*. A young doctor on the ship got into an argument with *Gilligan's* captain. The doctor said Stewart's leg had to be amputated immediately. But the captain, asserting his command responsibility, directed that nothing be done until he could be treated properly.

Stewart credits the captain with a courageous decision that saved his leg and possibly his life.

Stewart later learned that there were two main groups of *kamikaze* pilots. The first group (which started at Leyte in October of 1944 and continued through the Lingayen invasion) used conventional Japanese military aircraft for their missions. Later, the Japanese developed the *Ohka*, a flying rocket-powered bomb carried under the belly of the Betty bomber and launched in mid-air.

Last month's reunion of the pilots was at Yasakuni, a Shinto shrine adjacent to the Imperial Palace in Tokyo, closely associated with the Japanese Imperial family and by extension with the military element in Japan.

'The meeting was no American veterans' party of antics and booze. It was an intensely religious ceremony conducted with solemnity, dignity and not a little pathos', Stewart said.

After removing their shoes, the participants entered the first hall for a preliminary greeting and prayer. The group progressed to the second large room, knelt in even rows on the *tatami* mats and were blessed by two priests. Then, in reverential silence, the veterans filed into the third and most important place of worship where two lesser priests were joined by the head prelate.

After a short homily, the acolytes brought to the altar for his blessing the 'divine fish and the divine vegetables', all submitted for the peace and the repose of the souls of the pilots who had given their lives, Stewart said.

Silently, the entire audience rose from their knees and passed back to the entry where each person ritually washed his hands and invoked the blessings of the gods. He noted that few, if any, of the men he later talked to believed in the Shinto religion or in the efficacy of the rites performed.

What they did believe in, Stewart said, was the obligation of keeping alive the memories of their dead comrades and reminding themselves that, by the grace of the gods, they were alive.

Next, the group paraded across the grounds to a military museum where Stewart had his first view of the *Ohka* suicide flying bomb: 'It is a stubby vehicle, not more than 12-feet long, with an exploding cherry blossom painted on its nose. It certainly looks like what it was designed for — a one-way trip to death.'

After the religious ceremony, the ice broke. For the first time, the solemn air of the proceedings was supplanted by a feeling of congeniality as the men assembled in a dining hall on the museum's top floor. It was a rather Spartan box lunch, presided over by Ashino Yukino, the association's president.

After many speeches, many introductions, Stewart was startled to recognize his name mentioned — and before he had time to think, he was pushed onto the podium: 'I think it was as much to allow the guests a better look at this odd visitor as much as to hear what I had to say.'

Stewart suspected that his short talk was embellished by the translator, for it seemed to be received favorably. At that point, he took the opportunity of presenting to the group an old photo of his ship, the *Gilligan* — their erstwhile target which they had failed to sink. 'Not surprisingly, the photo was much more interesting to the pilots than my translated remarks.'

He also thought it noteworthy that the caste system prevailed at the reunion: All pilots wore gold name tags; the mechanics and maintenance crew members had purple tags, and the others (Stewart included) wore white tags.

The meeting was concluded by yet another high-ranking Shinto priest in full ceremonial garb, delivering what Stewart deduced was 'a cross between a sermon and a football rally pep talk'. The priest, a retired naval officer who had 'turned religious' spoke of the need for the young people to be patriotic without being chauvinistic. His exhortations, Stewart observed, were accepted by the group with a certain air of skepticism.

The formal ceremonies had begun about 11 a.m. and concluded by 2 p.m. It was then that 'real party' began and Stewart got some answers to the questions he had pondered for years.

Mr. Oshinaka, one of the senior pilots (now a successful import-export trader in foodstuffs) invited a select group of about 30 ex-pilots for 'real food and serious drinking'.

Yoko Narahashi, a translator provided by Naito was the go-between for the give-and-take between Stewart and his former enemies. Mr. Narahashi, a film producer who is currently making a documentary on the *kamikaze* phenomenon, proved to be more knowledgeable about the suicide program than many of the Thunder Gods themselves, Stewart said. In an atmosphere of camaraderie, assisted by much saki, Stewart repeated his question to 'those old men — my contemporaries'.

'Why did they volunteer to kill themselves?'

As the party wore on, a consensus seemed to emerge: The reason was not (as the American fighting men had been led to believe) a fanatical devotion to the Emperor. It was simply a comprehension that, since Japan was about to lose the war, they might as well die in the most effective way. That is, to kill and destroy as many enemy men and ships as possible.

Oshia Fujiama, a retired business executive, (who now spends most of his time playing golf) put it simply. He said that he knew, as early as the Leyte invasion in October of 1944, that the war was lost. He also figured that, as a fighter pilot, he was going to die — suddenly and cleanly. But instead, he was placed in command of an *Ohka* unit and had the heart-breaking task of deciding, at the time of each mission, which of his young pilots would fly to their death knowing that, finally, he would be following them.

Some of the pilots conceded that their motive was to avoid capture by the Americans who might seek revenge for the brutality suffered by American captives.

Stewart also conversed with a pilot, who had been, like himself, engaged in the battle at Lingayen Gulf. Both men confessed to being scared out of their wits at the time.

Only half-joking, Stewart reminded his hosts that, in view of the tremendous world-wide commercial success of Japan, they had actually won the war. The Japanese veterans smilingly conceded their economic achievements. At the same time, they said that they regarded the war as a tragic mistake by both sides, but a mistake that was clearly initiated by Japan.

The Thunder Gods, as a group, know war, they told Stewart, and they are determined that Japan will never fight again.

THE ATOM BOMBS

The dropping of two atom bombs on Japan was both an historical event and a deliverance for thousands of service men. The two chapters covering the Okinawa campaign suggest prayerful gratitude by all hands in that another blood bath in the planned storming of the Japanese home islands was cancelled. In the last narrative covering *Pavlic*, Lieutenant Boland said it all in very few words:

"We were not going to die after all. We were going home."

In recent years, a vociferous minority has sought to second-guess President Truman for permitting the use of such a devastating weapon. Even the prestigious Smithsonian Institute placed a placard next to the *Enola Gay*, the plane that dropped the bomb on Hiroshima, derisive of that plane's mission as well as the war effort in general. An outraged public and Congress forced its removal. I think it fair to suggest that few, if any, castigators were in Okinawa in 1945.

The toll of 160,000 lives in Hiroshima and Nagasaki was a big number standing by itself. However, it was a trifle when compared to the military and civilian casualties already suffered by Japan and the millions more certain to follow an invasion (70,000 were killed in Tokyo in one conventional air raid only weeks before the dropping of the first atom bomb). The homeless were already in the millions, facing a winter of freezing, pestilence and starvation. The atom bomb achieved what other bombs failed to do. It cracked the mind-set of the Emperor and his entourage; the unthinkable became the thinkable — surrender.

Before the atom bomb was dropped, my time on the "beach" was drawing to a close. A friend in the Bureau of Naval Personnel told me on the side that I should expect to receive orders to a new DE command within a week or so. The pride I felt in being assigned to a new *Butler* class DE with 5" guns was tempered by the knowledge that Honshu was not going to be an improvement over Okinawa; it could possibly be worse. The Japanese were known to have squirreled away a few thousand *kamikaze* pilots for the occasion.

The atom bombs fell, followed by peace. If such orders had been processed for me, I never got them. Instead, I received the last orders I ever would receive from the navy since the day five years and one month before when I first set foot on the deck of the battleship New York as an apprentice seaman, striking for midshipman. I was ordered to inactive duty.

USS Sims flying bridge – US Navy Photo

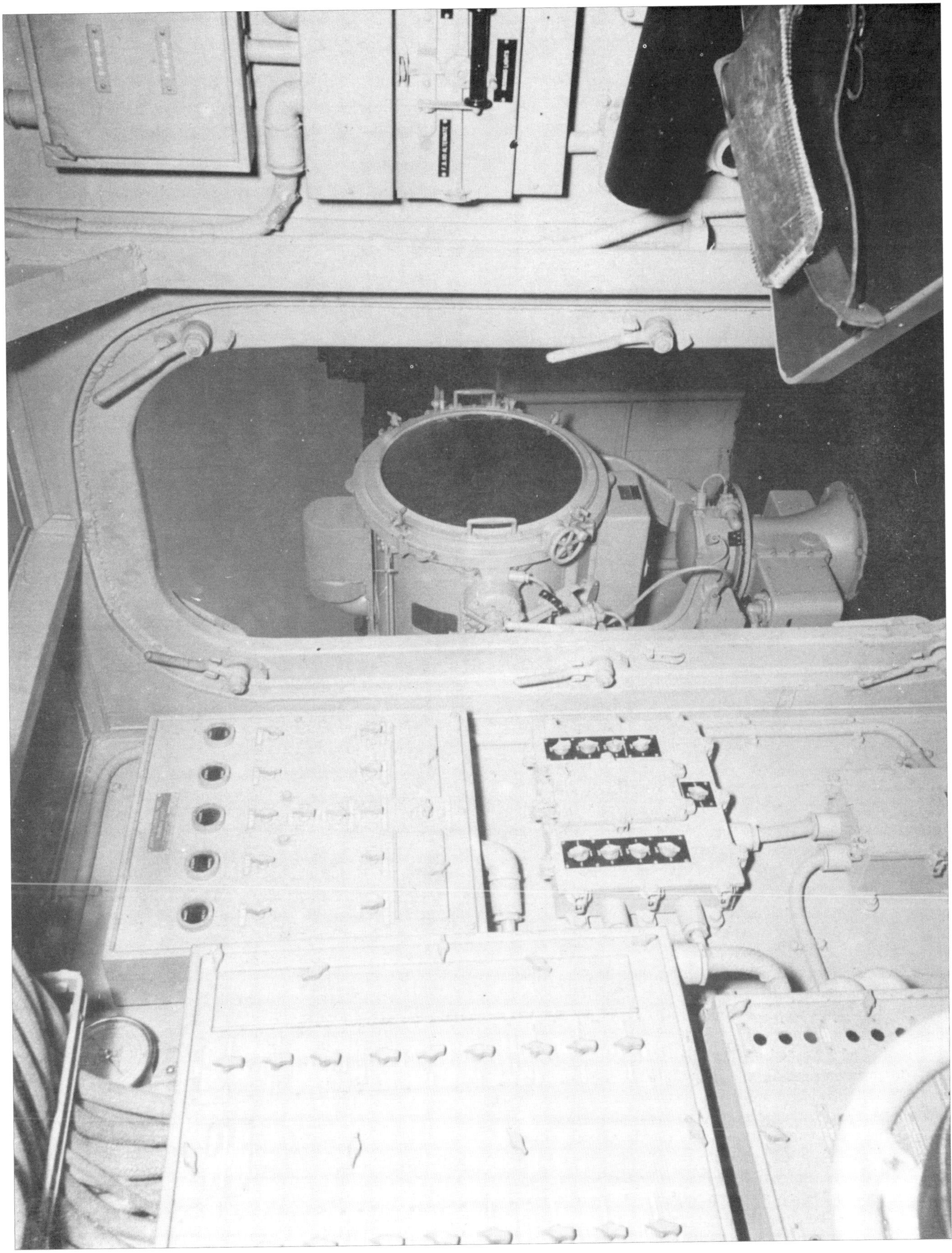

USS Sims signal bridge – US Navy Photo

Chapter XVIII-Over The Horizon

It is a rare person who can appreciate the enormity of events in his own time. We are so preoccupied with daily activities that we move through historical events of the greatest magnitude without realizing that we often are important actors on the world stage.

So it was with the conclusion of World War II. In particular, those of us who did not plan to make the navy our careers chafed at the bit to return to pre-war freedoms, our ambitions, our loved ones. We couldn't wait to hang up the uniforms, don the civvies, forget how to salute, at last free of restrictive regulations. We rushed pell-mell back to civilian life. How wonderful!

However, as the years went by, we began to sense a little something missing from our lives, an intangible that material reward could not replace. Perhaps, with some discomfort, we realized that a value was slipping from our lives that transcended the structured life of the navy, a growing void that subsequent years could not replace. It appeared under many labels: Honor, duty, loyalty, valor, patriotism, comradeship, unselfishness, a will to conquer the wicked oppressors of the world.

The older we got, the more we subconsciously yearned to relive a time of greatness, to renew contacts with men who were more than friends; they were comrades-in-arms. It didn't take many years after the war for the Destroyer Escort Sailors Association to come into being as well as a smaller Destroyer Escort Commanding Officers Association. Slowly at first, ship reunions materialized, then mushroomed into annual events.

In corresponding with destroyer escort veterans for book input, I found the foregoing to be a common bond, irrespective of prior rate or rank and regardless of material success in civilian life. As for myself, I believe that my five years in the navy were the best of my life, the most informative, educational and uplifting experience I ever had. Life has been good to me, and I have no right to complain, but I do indeed associate myself with the words of wisdom offered by my very good friend, Al Chester.

Captain Alvin P. Chester was a World War II DE and APD skipper with experiences described in narratives *Ormoc Bay* and *Mopping Up* in *The Philippine Campaign*. He is also a retired and an uncommonly successful shipping magnate.

Nonetheless, he writes in the last chapter of his book, *A Sailor's Odyssey*:

> "Throughout history, the overall effect of greed on people as a whole has varied. Sometimes, decency prevailed, and greed was not the driving force in a specific area. I had the good fortune to experience a time when I shared the company of individuals who subordinated their own interests to comrades and their ship.
>
> In writing *A Sailor's Odyssey*, it soon became apparent I was describing a special time. Although my odyssey ended in 1945 and there followed many active and financially rewarding years, something about my odyssey overshadowed all the years which followed. During the twilight of my life, I find myself drawn back to the past in much the same way as I had been drawn to the future in my youth. I am not alone. Increasing numbers of my generation make annual pilgrimages to relive this short period with those they shared it with - in memory of those now ghosts of the past.
>
> We were not knights in shining armor, nor did all of us reap any special awards or recognition. Whether the captain or lowest rating in these unusual ships - the destroyer escorts - we shared the hardships. Regardless of rank or rate, our survival was linked in a unity of purpose and survival. Although I have strong feelings for every ship in which I served and for my shipmates, something special about the intimate piece of steel called a destroyer escort still captures me. So small, so trim but deadly, it sailed in many seas. It was an experience few had in the past or will have in the future. For this ethereal adventure, I am most grateful. I realize now that it was the climax of my life."

Over fifty years after leaving that U-boat killer, remembered as *Bronstein (DE-189)*, her First Class Soundman, Clinton L. Gantt, remembers the "Good Old Days":

> "When I think of the 'Good Old Days', I always wander back to the Navy. We were young and didn't know any different. We were just doing what we were told and trained to do. No second thoughts that we were right. We were on a good ship with a great crew, just like family. We each had a job. We were trained in that job. At the time, that is what we had to do.
>
> So we had a home with a family. Good chow. The best medical attention and care when needed. We saw a lot of the world that we just may not have seen as civilians. A good clean place to sleep with all the amenities we needed. On top of all this, we were being paid and had money to spend, places to go, things to do and met a lot of fine people. Where else would you have the opportunity to do all that?
>
> This, among other things is why I consider days in the navy as the 'Good Old Days."

Scott (DE-214), like a great many other destroyer escorts, was consigned to Green Cove Springs, Florida, deactivated and decommissioned. There she sat unattended, awaiting the call of the scrap metal company, hardly a just reward for guarding sixteen convoys to Europe and back without losing a ship. William Rumens was a crew member who expressed the parting sorrow of his shipmates:

"The saddest sight I ever saw,
Is a decommissioned man-o'-war,
A vessel once so full of pride
But now so helpless in the tide.
A ship whose life has become complete,
But now is absent from the fleet,
A ship that once knew the touch of spray,
As thru the storm it fought its way,
A ship that now is drab and drear
As it lies alone at a worn out pier.
A ship for which men moan and sigh
A ship with no flag flowin' on high
A ship whose decks have turned to rust,
No longer know the seaman's touch.
A ship that quickly goes to rot

As against the docks it chafes and rocks;
A ship that groans in the dead of the night
Like a man condemned to a deathly plight;
And thus I say that the saddest sight
Is a ship deprived of its former might".

Raymond Doolan, Signalman Third Class and plankowner on *Charles J. Kimmel (DE-584)* tells of his feelings the day his ship ceased to exist:

The Last Goodbye

"Feel no remorse about our ship. She had her sad and happy days on the oceans and seas of the world. We shared her bad times, the hurricanes and typhoons, and we fought her enemies coming from foreign lands under the sea and in the air. She was a ship of combat, born in war, and now destined to die in a time of peace. But these past happenings never put her down.

She was once our home and school, a gallant protector of our seagoing family. Her guns are silent now and her war years are finished. We all survived the ordeals thrust upon her by endless patrols and battle missions in campaigns of long ago. Now she moves silently outbound under cable tow. No longer the escort leader with sister ships in the screen, protecting convoys of ships destined for zones of combat. Her orders are final. For this is the last outbound voyage. The wind and sea gently ride along with her, and we remember in the calm of the morning mist how her colors once looked two-blocked at the fore. Perhaps she too can hear voices from the past... a faraway command by her captain 'All ahead full, come right to zero-nine zero'... or... 'God bless this ship and all who sail in her,' by the mother of her namesake at our commissioning. Surely, we remember voices of her long departed crew, sea bags in hand, 'Permission to leave the ship sir,' in her final port of call. These were the sounds of the sailors who once shared her sea life.

Now she moves forward, slowly rising and falling on the deep Pacific swell. The cable tow is hauled in by her lonely companion – a small navy tug in the final escort to nowhere. Her greatest times are past, but yet she remains proudly undefeated. she was never sold for scrap or traded away to a foreign shore. They kept her afloat for this last voyage as a target ship for the new navy and its modern combat frigates. The *C.J.K.* will now serve a final purpose for the ships who were designed to follow her.

She waits for the fire salvos. The signal is given, and the deadly inbound missiles of the frigates that track her smash into her topside. She accepts this final end, this last naval goodbye, knowing no enemy ever touched her or those who sailed in her. This is the warriors' way to die! She slowly rolls on her side. The explosive fires leap and cover her bridge and torpedo deck. Her 5" turret forward tears itself from its mount of twisted steel. Smoke rises from her broken hull compartments, and then her smashed stern explodes as a second salvo screams into her. Tons of water enter as she slips beneath the waves. The bow slowly rises vertically for the descent into oblivion. The morning sunlight reflects on the gray hull number...584...is seen – but only for a quick moment. Then she is gone...forever...in 400 fathoms.

Old friend DE-584! You know our final salute is for you...and also for us. We would like to think that there will never be another ship or crew like we once were. You will always be in our thoughts. Thank you...goodbye brave destroyer escort...Farewell!"

June 15, 1957 news item:

"The Destroyer Escort *USS C.J. Kimmel (DE-584)* was stricken from the naval decommissioned list and towed 35 miles west of Oceanside, California. She was sunk as a target test vessel by U.S. Navy frigates, utilizing ship to ship guided missile weapon systems. The test was a success."

One of the most fitting and moving tributes this author ever read was written by Jim Vick, a crew member of the *John C. Butler (DE-339)*, veteran of The Battle off Samar, the Philippine campaign and Okinawa. It was published in the July-August 1988 issue of *DESA News*, the quarterly publication of the Destroyer Escort Sailors Association. Jim was not quite so philosophical or forgiving for the demise of his ship as was the above author of *C.J. Kimmel*, but we can readily relate to his sorrow:

Hi Chet:

"I just want to say that I give God the praise for healing an old man (He had been ill). I just want to say that the same God was still with us in all our battles.

Getting back to the *Butler*, there was no one that loved her more than I. They couldn't sink her in battle; they had to bring her in after she returned (to the U.S.) and was at rest in the harbor, then took her out and made a target of her! When I heard she was sunk as a target, to me she died and a part of me died with her. The ocean is big, looks like they could have found a place to have tied her up without sending her to Davey Jones' Locker.

I'll appreciate anything that comes out on the *Butler*. That would be something to look forward to. I have a display of the picture of the *Butler*, medals, citations, etc., in my bedroom that I go in and look at very often. I was on the 20mm on the port side, right across from the 40mm you were on."

Jim

I think it was remarkable that the Destroyer Escort Sailors Association was able to repatriate to the United States the *USS Slater (DE-766)* from Greece. That vessel had been given to the Greek Navy shortly after the war. Because of tight budget constraints, the U.S. Navy couldn't consider offering the funds to bring her home. The Greek government gave it to the Association without charge, but the towing fees of several hundred thousand dollars were defrayed entirely by destroyer escort veterans who dug into their own pockets for the money! The DE arrived in September 1993 and is now a DE museum in the Hudson River at Albany, New York. Hopefully, she will be there for generations to admire and to remember.

The only regret this author has in the enormous task of researching, compiling, editing and writing this book is that I didn't do it several years earlier, before the "Taps" roster began to lengthen so ominously. I would have liked for many more of our shipmates to have had the opportunity to read about DEs other than their own.

Now, as I enter my eighties, I find myself pausing to remember bright young faces in my platoon in midshipman school, many of whom elected to join the Far East Fleet in the Philippines after being commissioned as ensigns. What a lark! They crossed to the west coast in drawing room compartments, went to Manila first class on an American President Line ship and looked forward to liberties in storied ports like Shanghai, Hong-Kong, Singapore, Bangkok. In the thunder of sudden war, their fleet was all but wiped out, taking many of my friends with it. A few others, sick and emaciated, stumbled from Japanese POW camps as the war drew to a close.

I remember our First Class Machinist Mate, killed in an accident on the dock near the minesweeper *Mockingbird*, my first command, before the war even started. I recall the smiling and confident Lieutenant Commander Ken Hartley, my skipper on the corvette *Might* and subsequently killed on the *DE Brough*. I occasionally think about Lieutenant Bob Newcomb who I relieved as executive officer on the DE *Sims* and who subsequently went down with the *DE Underhill*. I often think about all the young men who went down to the sea in small ships to fight for their country in World War II, particularly those who did not return or were so damaged in mind or body that they could not enjoy the sweet fruits of victory.

I would like to believe that, somewhere OVER THE HORIZON, the one we all must cross, never to return, we will see our shipmates and navy friends again, en route to our separate destinations. We will see them in the flower of our youth, laughing and telling great yarns, as the sunlight sparkles on the sea and the whispering bow wave parts to let us through. I would like to take my final evening star sights, not to locate a point on this planet, but among the stars themselves.

Your Shipmate,

Lew Andrews

Last lights on *Silverpalm*

Chapter XIX - Destroyer Escorts of WWII

An astonishing 563 destroyer escorts were launched by American yards in less than three years; 78 were transferred to the Royal Navy, eight to the Brazilian Navy, and six to the Free French Navy.

The remaining 375 destroyer escorts and 94 modified to high speed transports were assigned to American Fleets and Task Groups. They were manned by men recently drawn from civilian life, some of whom had never seen salt water before. Their officers were mostly reserves, previously ordered to active duty. These crews went down to the sea to fight a highly proficient, experienced and tenacious enemy. They were sent forth to screen major war vessels, to convoy troops and materiel through all the oceans of the world, to face submarine and air attacks, to duel with shore batteries while assaulting beachheads, to brave hurricanes and typhoons. They were even called upon to attack an overwhelmingly superior enemy force of battleships and cruisers, helping to turn a potential disaster into a great victory.

BUILDING YARD	ABB.
Bethlehem Steel, Hingham MA	Beth-Hing
Bethlehem Quincy, MA	Beth-Quin
Bethlehem San Francisco	Beth SF
Boston Navy Yard	Boston
Brown Shipbuilding, Houston, TX	Brown
Tampa Shipbuilding, Tampa, FL	Tampa
Western Pipe And Steel,San Pedro CA	PipeWest
Consolidated, Orange TX	Consol
Charleston Navy Yard	Charleston
BUILDING OR MODIFYING YARD	
Defoe, Bay City	Defoe
Dravo, Pittsburgh, PA	Dravo
Federal Shipbuilding, Newark, NJ	Fed Ship
Mare Island Navy Yard	Mare Is.
Norfolk Navy Yard	Norfolk
Philadelphia Navy Yard	Phila
Puget Sound Navy Yard	Pug Sound

DE Radar Picket Ship	DER
Anti-Submarine Warfare	ASW
Coast Guard	CG
Fast Troop Transport	APD
Naval Reserve Force	NRF
Miscellaneous Vessel	MV

EVARTS CLASS — GENERAL MOTORS TANDEM DIESEL (GMT)

These were the first Destroyer Escorts to be built, a total of 97, with 32 consigned to the Royal Navy. Their hulls were somewhat shorter than subsequent DE classes because they did not have torpedo tubes. They were not considered to be as flexible in deployment as other classes and were scrapped after the cessation of hostilities. Several of this class distinguished themselves in anti-submarine warfare and convoys to the United Kingdom, the Mediterranean and in the Pacific.

Destroyer Escorts 5-50, 256-265, 301-307, 527-530.

MAJOR CHARACTERISTICS

Length Overall	289'-5"
Extreme Beam	35'-1"
Mean Draft	11'-10"
Displacement	1,436 Tons
Machinery, Diesel	Gen. Motors
Designed Shaft Horsepower	6,000
Trial (Flank) Speed	21.5 Knots
Fuel Capacity	198 Tons
Designed Complement	Off: 6, Enl: 150
Average Complement	Off: 9, Enl: 185

ARMAMENT

Main:	(3) 3"/50 Caliber Guns
Secondary:	(1) Twin 40mm or 1.1" Quad Guns
	(9) 20mm Guns
ASW:	(2) Depth Charge Racks
	(8) "K" Gun Projectors
	(1) Hedgehog
Torpedoes:	None

Lewis M. Andrews, Jr.

EVARTS CLASS

SHIP	NUMBER	YARD	COMPLETED	DECOM	MODIFIED	DISPOSAL
EVARTS	**DE–5**	**Boston**	**15/04/43**	**02/10/45**		**Scrapped 07/46**

Flagship Escort Division 5. Numerous convoys to North Africa and Sicily. Heavily engaged with enemy torpedo planes en route Bizerte 11 May 1944. Went to assistance of *Block Island* and *Barr* hunter-killers after latter were torpedoed late May 1944. See chapters *Convoys to Mediterranean* and *The Hunter-Killers*. One battle star.

WYFFELS	**DE–6**	**Boston**	**21/4/43**	**25/09/45**		**China**

Twenty-one successful convoys to North Africa, many in horrendous seas requiring shepherding of separated merchantmen. May 1944, in convoy UGS-40, numerous enemy aircraft taken under fire. Credited one assist in downed Junkers. See narrative *Mediterranean Convoys*. One battle star.

GRISWALD	**DE–7**	**Boston**	**28/04/43**	**19/11/45**		**Scraped 01/47**

Escorted South Pacific convoys July 1943 to April 1944. Four hour attack on Jap sub 12 September produced probable but uncredited kill. In Pacific, Ssank Jap sub *I-39* on 24 December 1944. Splashed two *kamikazes* at Okinawa 31 May and 5 June 1945. Ended war triumphantly in Tokyo Bay. See chapters *Pacific Antisubmarine Warfare* and *Iwo Jima to Okinawa*. Three battle stars.

STEELE	**DE–8**	**Boston**	**04/05/43**	**28/11/45**		**Scraped 01/47**

From 9 February to 12 May 1944, conducted escort/screening operations to the Marshall, Gilbert, Marcus and Wake Islands with Task Force 58. In June, joined *Hoggatt Bay* Hunter-Killer Group in Carolines and Philippines. Screened 3rd Fleet Strikes against Leyte, and Formosa. Two battle stars.

CARLSON	**DE–9**	**Boston**	**10/05/43**	**0/12/45**		**Scraped 12/46**

About 11 months from July 1943, escorted convoys to Guadalcanal and Solomons. October 1944 to March 1945, escorted in Eniwetok, Ulithi, Leyte, Iwo Jima, Saipan, Okinawa areas. Participated in assault on Okinawa and repelled *kamikaze* attacks. Close call with air launched torpedo. Two battle stars.

BEBAS	**DE-10**	**Boston**	**15/05/43**	**18/10/45**		**Scrapped 02/47**

September 1943 to April 1944, patrolled among Espiritu Santo, Guadalcanal and New Caledonia. May 1944, convoyed among Majuro Atoll, Eniwetok and Marshalls. September to December with hunter-killer group in Southwest Pacific. December 1944 to April 1945, patrolled off Palau, Ulithi and Eniwetok. May and June on Okinawa picket patrol. July and August, screened 3rd Fleet in Jap home island raids. Three battle stars.

CROUTER	**DE-11**	**Boston**	**25/05/43**	**30/11/45**		**Scrapped 12/46**

From 24 July 1943 to 31 March 1944, escorted convoys and attack groups in Efate, Espirutu Santo, New Hebrides, Viti Levu, Fijis and Port Purvis. Convoyed attack forces to Okinawa. Splashed two *kamikazes* on picket station. See chapter *Iwo Jima to Okinawa*. One battle star.

BRENNAN	**DE-13**	**Mare Is.**	**20/01/43**	**09/10/45**		**Scrapped 08/46**

The first DE placed in commission. Operated as a school ship for the Sub Chaser Training Center in Miami throughout entire war.

DOHERTY	**DE-14**	**Mare Is.**	**06/02/43**	**14/12/45**		**Scrapped 12/46**

Escorted convoys west coast U.S. to Hawaii and Alaska, also plane guard for Army Air Force strikes over Kuriles 23 April 1943 through 28 September 1944. Arrived at Guam 16 February 1945 and conducted escort operations from there to Okinawa for balance of war.

AUSTIN	**DE-15**	**Mare Is.**	**13/02/43**	**21/12/45**		**Scrapped 02/47**

Over one year from September 1943, plied cold Alaskan waters as weather ship and aircraft homing signal. April 1944, assigned to Commander Forward Areas for ASW and air/sea rescue. Convoyed to Western Carolines, Guam, Saipan, Iwo Jima, Eniwetok and Okinawa. Conducted searches for post-war enemy hold outs.

E.G. CHASE	**DE-16**	**Mare Is.**	**20/03/43**	**16/10/45**		**Scrapped 04/47**

Sailed from New York on 19 September 1944 to escort an ill conceived and ill timed convoy to the U.K. Tugs and barges, unfit for North Atlantic weather, wallowed in mountainous seas with attendant losses of ships and men. See chapter *Convoys to the U.K.*

EVARTS CLASS

SHIP	NUMBER	YARD	COMPLETED	DECOM	MODIFIED	DISPOSAL
E.C. DALY	**DE-17**	**Mare Is.**	**03/04/43**	**20/12/45**		**Scrapped 02/47**

In Pearl Harbor on 28 May 1943, piped aboard Admirals C.W. Nimitz and R.A. Spruance, their first visit to a DE. August to November, escorted in Ellice Islands, once rescuing crew of downed patrol bomber. Aleutian waters November to January 1945. Air/sea rescue from Saipan to Iwo Jima to war's end.

GILMORE	**DE-18**	**Mare Is.**	**17/04/43**	**29/12/45**		**Scrapped 03/47**

Numerous escort assignments with convoys and USC&GS survey ships to and from Aleutians with Escort Division 14 from June 1943 to January 1945. Sank Jap sub *I-180* 26 April 1944. Participated in recapture Attu and Kiska. Numerous convoys and rescue missions Western Pacific 1945. See chapter *Pacific ASW*. One battle star.

B.R. HASTINGS	**DE-19**	**Mare Is.**	**01/05/43**	**25/10/45**		**Scrapped 03/47**

12-20 November, preliminary bombardment Tarawa. Balance 1943, escorted convoys. Supported Kwajelein occupation February 1944. 30 March to 1 April, supported raids on Palau, Yap, Ulithi, Woleai. Convoy, plane guard and hunter-killer duty to end of war. 15 June sank Jap sub *RO-44*. See chapter *Pacific ASW*. Four battle stars.

LeHARDY	**DE-20**	**Mare Is.**	**15/05/43**	**25/10/45**		**Scrapped 01/47**

Convoyed to Tarawa in November 1943 and joined screening operations with 5th Fleet invasion of Gilbert Islands. January and February 1944, ASW operations for invasion of Marshall Islands. Screened for capture of Eniwetok and to end of war. Joined in Wake Island recapture ceremonies. Two battle stars.

H.C. THOMAS	**DE-21**	**Mare Is.**	**31/05/43**	**26/10/45**		**Scrapped 02/47**

November and December 1943, performed convoy and ASW patrol vicinity Gilbert Islands. In 1944, convoyed cargo and transports to various invasion areas, including Marshall, Palau and Admiralty Islands. On 21 November, rescued seven of crew from downed PBM plane. Convoyed to war's end. Two battle stars.

WILEMAN.	**DE-22**	**Mare Is.**	**11/06/43**	**16/11/45**		**Scrapped 02/47**

In 1943, escorted to South Pacific ports. Aided repelling of attacks by three Bettys on 24 November while convoying troops to Gilberts. In January 1944, screened operation "Flintlock," recapture of Marianas. In June, screened attack on Saipan. Numerous convoys to end of war. Four battle stars.

C.R. GREER	**DE-23**	**Mare Is.**	**25/06/43**	**02/11/45**		**Scrapped 03/47**

September 1943 to October 1944, convoyed to Ellice, Gilbert and Marshall Islands. Screened attack forces Ulithi to Eniwetok and Guam to February 1945, repelling one air attack. June 1945 to war's end, in various convoys and recapture ceremonies on Wake Island. Two battle stars.

WHITMAN	**DE-24**	**Mare Is.**	**03/07/43**	**16/11/45**		**Scrapped 02/47**

In September 1943, commenced screening actions in South and Central Pacific. In January 1944, participated in invasion of Marshalls, followed by the Marianas in June. Numerous convoy and ASW operations to end of war. Four battle stars.

WINTLE	**DE-25**	**Mare Is.**	**10/07/43**	**14/11/45**		**Scrapped 08/47**

In 1943, convoyed to South Pacific and screened "Galvanic," recapture of Gilberts. 3 January 1944, accidentally rammed and damaged by *Dempsey (DE 26)* while refuelling. Star shell illumination to support troops at Peleliu. Helped repel air attack on Saipan Christmas Eve. Dueled with Wotje shore battery 2 April 1945. Numerous ASW screening actions to end of war. Three battle stars.

DEMPSEY	**DE-26**	**Mare Is.**	**27/07/43**	**22/11/45**		**Scrapped 05/47**

Starting 23 September 1943, screened various Pacific convoys from bases to forward areas, including rescue of 45 survivors from torpedoed merchantman. Sank Japanese patrol craft near Peleliu on 28 October 1944, taking one prisoner. Continued convoy duty to end of war. Three battle stars.

DUFFY	**DE-27**	**Mare Is.**	**05/08/43**	**09/11/45**		**Scrapped 08/47**

Screened carriers in Marshall Island strikes late 1943. Escorted transports to invasions of Ellice Islands, Marianas and Leyte in 1944 where she downed a bomber. In 1945, covered air strikes, engaged shore batteries, conducted psychological warfare vs. by-passed Jap garrisons. See chapter *The Philippine Campaign* Two battle stars.

EVARTS CLASS

SHIP	NUMBER	YARD	COMPLETED	DECOM	MODIFIED	DISPOSAL
EMERY	**DE-28**	**Mare Is.**	**14/08/43**	**15/11/45.**		**Scrapped 08/47**

Late 1943, screened tankers for attack on Gilberts. Early 1944, participated in assault on Marshalls. In 1945, escorted combatants and auxiliaries to Bougainville and various Southwest Pacific ports. To end of war, screened and escorted to Guam, Iwo Jima, Saipan and other locations. Four battle stars.

STADTFELD	**DE-29**	**Mare Is.**	**26/08/43**	**19/11/45**		**Scrapped 07/47**

Screened Task Unit in reconquest Marshalls January 1944. From 12 February to 6 July, escorted invasion units to Admiralty, Russell, New Hebrides, Solomons, Iwo Jima, Eniwetok. Returned to U.S. on 20 July 1945. Four battle stars.

MARTIN	**DE-30**	**Mare Is.**	**04/09/43**	**15/11/45**		**Scrapped 07/47**

In January 1944, joined Task Group for initial Marshall operations. Convoyed merchantmen until October to escort fuelers for strikes on Formosa, Luzon and Okinawa. In December 1944, screened LSTs for Leyte mop-up operations. To war's end, convoyed to Western Pacific ports.

SEDERSTROM	**DE-31**	**Mare Is.**	**11/09/43**	**10/11/45**		**Scrapped 02/48**

Escorted 24 December 1943 to 10 March 1944 to Gilberts, Funa Futi, Samoa, Wallace and Gilbert Islands, Marshalls and Kwajelein. Screened attack groups to Saipan, Tinian, Philippines, Iwo Jima. Splashed one *kamikaze* off Okinawa on 22 April 1945. Resumed escort operations until 5 July. See chapter *Iwo Jima to Okinawa*. Five battle stars.

FLEMING	**DE-32.**	**Mare Is.**	**18/09/43**	**10/11/45**		**Scrapped 03/48**

June to August 1944, convoyed in Central and South Pacific. October 1944 to end of year, convoyed to Eniwetok and Ulithi, preparing for Iwo Jima and Okinawa operations. Just after midnight on 14 January 1945, sank Jap sub *I-362*. March to May, screened carriers for Okinawa assault. On 20 May, splashed two *kamikazes*. On 25 May, rescued survivors of *LSM-135* and *Bates (APD-47)*. See chapters *Pacific ASW* and *Iwo Jima to Okinawa*. Four battle stars.

TISDALE	**DE-33**	**Mare Is.**	**11/10/43**	**12/10/45**		**Scrapped 03/48**

At end of 1943, convoyed to Ellice Islands and joined "Flintlock," Marshalls invasion. May and June, covered storming of the Marianas. Rendered ASW coverage in Battle of The Philippine Sea and fired star shells to interdict Japanese reinforcement of Saipan. In July, supported troops with harassing and illuminating fire at Saipan. Supported "Iceberg," Okinawa carrier operations in March 1945. Convoyed to end of war. Four battle stars.

EISELE	**DE-34**	**Mare Is.**	**18/10/43**	**16/11/45**		**Scrapped 02/48**

In 1944, patrolled off Tarawa, escorted to Guam, Eniwetok, Marianas, Palau, Carolines, Philippines while still enemy held. March 1945, sortied Ulithi with Okinawa assault forces and remained on picket station with CVEs while fighting off massive *kamikaze* attacks. Two battle stars.

FAIR	**DE-35**	**Mare Is.**	**25/10/43**	**17/11/45**		**US Army, sold 1949**

On ASW patrol near Tarawa on 4 February 1944 with *Charrette (DD 581)*, sank Jap sub *I-21*. Convoyed to South and Central Pacific ports, invasions of Saipan, and Tinian, March to June. Splashed a *kamikaze* at Okinawa on 6 April 1945.In May, repeatedly engaged suicide planes and boats. See chapters *Pacific ASW* and *Iwo Jima to Okinawa*. Five battle stars.

MANLOVE	**DE-36**	**Mare Is.**	**08/11/43**	**16/11/45**		**Scrapped 03/48**

February and March 1944, engaged in hunter-killer operations. On first assignment, 24 March, with *PC 1135*, sank Jap sub *I-32*. Numerous convoys throughout Central and South Pacific for about a year. Arrived on picket station, Okinawa, April 1945. On 11 April, damaged by *kamikaze*. See chapters *Pacific ASW* and *Iwo Jima to Okinawa*. Five battle stars

GRIENER	**DE-37**	**Pug Sound**	**18/08/43**	**19/11/45**		**Scrapped 03/47**

Spent most of 1944 escorting in Gilberts-Marshalls area. Rescued crew of 13 from downed PBM plane on 26 January 1944. Shelled Kusaie Island battery on 1 June. Spent remainder of war escorting and plane guarding. Three battle stars.

WYMAN	**DE-38**	**Pug Sound**	**01/09/43**	**21/12/45**		**Scrapped 06/47**

In June 1944, assigned ASW operations with TG 122, based on *Hoggatt Bay (CVE-75)* in the Marshalls. On 18 July, developed radar and then sound contact leading to attacks and destruction of enemy submarine *RO-48*, previously located and attacked by *Lake (DE-301)*. On 28 July, in cooperation with *Reynolds (DE-42)*, engaged and destroyed Jap sub *I-55*. August to March 1945, reassigned to South Pacific convoys. Convoyed to end of war. See chapter *Pacific ASW*. Six battle stars.

EVARTS CLASS

SHIP	NUMBER	YARD	COMPLETED	DECOM	MODIFIED	DISPOSAL

LOVERING DE-39 Pug Sound 17/09/43 16/10/45 Scrapped 01/47

Escorted to Gilbert Islands December 1943. Numerous convoys to Marshalls and Eniwetok through September 1944, then to Saipan, Guam and Marianas until March 1945. Operated with 3rd and 5th fleets in capture of Iwo Jima and Ryukyus. Three battle stars.

SANDERS DE-40 Pug Sound 01/10/43 12/12/45 Scrapped 06/47

January through July 1944, escorted convoys to Gilbert and Marshall Islands, including bombardment Kusaie Islands. Guarded logistics support to fast carrier operations in Western Pacific November through March 1945. Four battle stars.

BRACKETT DE-41 Pug Sound 18/10/43 23/11/45 Scrapped 06/47

December 1943 to June 1944, convoyed among Marshalls, Gilberts, Carolines, Admiralties and Marianas. Supported occupation of Majuro Atoll 29 January to 7 February and capture of Saipan 28-29 July. Screened 5th and 3rd Fleet raids against Okinawa 26 March to June 1945. Three battle stars.

REYNOLDS DE-42 Pug Sound 01/11/43 05/12/45 Scrapped 05/47

January and February 1944, convoyed Majuro to Kwajalein March to May, with Commander Submarine Force, and operated with Hunter Killer Group. On 28 July, assisted *Wyman (DE 38)* with sinking of Jap sub *I-55* Detached in August to provide forward area escort to end of war. See chapter *Pacific ASW*. Eight battle stars.

MITCHELL DE-43 Phila 17/11/43 29/12/45 Scrapped 01/47

Sailed for Pacific war zone June 1944, screening convoys to the Admiralties. Guarded harbor entrances and destroyed floating mines. Sustained damage in collision with whale on 3 December. Performed patrol missions in attack on Iwo Jima February 1945 and on Balikpapan in July. Nine battle stars.

ANDRES DE-45 Phila 15/03/43 18/10/45 Scrapped 02/46

On night of 4 May 1943, made dramatic rescue off Cape Charles of 28 merchant seamen and three navy armed guard from torpedoed *Oneida*. Operated as school ship at SCTC until November 1944 when assigned to *CortDiv 80* and several convoys to Gibraltar.

DECKER DE-47 Phila 04/12/43 22/10/45 China lost 11/54

July 1943, convoyed East Coast US to Gulf of Mexico. August 1943 to April 1945, escorted nine convoys to Casablanca, Bizerte, Tunisia, Palermo, and Oran. On 11 May 1944, with UGS-40, aided in repelling massive torpedo and bombing attacks. See chapter *Mediterranean Convoys.* One battle star.

DOBLER DE-48 Phila 17/05/43 02/10/45 Scrapped 07/46

July 1943 convoyed East Coast US to Gulf of Mexico. August 1943 to June 1945, escorted 11 convoys to Bizerte, Oran and Palermo from Boston, New York and Norfolk. On 11 May 1944 with UGS-40, aided in driving off massive torpedo and bombing attacks without damage to convoy. See chapter *Mediterranean Convoys.* One battle star.

DONEFF DE-49 Phila 10/06/43 02/12/45 Scrapped 01/47

From September 1943 to January 1945, operated in Alaskan waters, convoying, air/sea rescue and reconnaissance from Attu to Kuriles. March to August, patrolled and convoyed Guam to Saipan and Okinawa. With *Mayrant (DD 402)*, received surrender Japanese garrison on Marcus Island.

ENGSTROM DE-50 Phila 21/06/43 19/12/45 Scrapped 01/47

Over a year from August 1943, operated in Alaskan waters. Fought howling, icy gales, escorted combatants and auxiliaries, acted as radar picket for air operations. During 1945, escorted to Eniwetok, Saipan, Guam, and Iwo Jima. Saw action at Okinawa.

SEID DE-256 Boston 11/06/43 07/12/45 Scrapped 02/47

8 August to December 1944, escorted convoys in Carolines with 3rd Fleet and TF 57. Christmas 1944, covered invasion of Fais Island. Arrived Okinawa with invasion squadron on 1 April 1945 and assigned to picket stations. 12 April, splashed four *kamikazes* while evading five aerial torpedoes. See chapter *Iwo Jima to Okinawa.* Two battle stars.

SMARTT DE-257 Boston 18/06/43 05/10/45 Scrapped 08/46

Three round trip convoys New York to Casablanca 25 October 1943 to 20 April 1944. With UGS 40 on 11 May, scored hits on first wave of three JU-88s. Splashed one in second wave attack. Splashed 1 and damaged another in third wave. Six more round trips 4 July 1944 to 14 June 1945. See chapter *Mediterranean Convoys.* One battle star.

EVARTS CLASS

SHIP	NUMBER	YARD	COMPLETED	DECOM	MODIFIED	DISPOSAL
W.S. BROWN	**DE-258**	**Boston**	**25/06/43**	**04/10/45**		**Scrapped 08/46**

Numerous convoys east coast US to North Africa. At sunset 11 May 1944, UGS-40 attacked by flight of Junkers 88s, Heinkel 111s and Dornier 217s. This DE drove off at least six, splashed one, splashed another along with *Dobler (DE- 48)*, damaged at least one other. See chapter *Mediterranean Convoys.* One battle star.

WC MILLER	**DE-259**	**Boston**	**02/07/43**	**17/12/45**		**Scrapped 05/47**

Early in 1943, screened Operation "Galvanic," recapture of Gilbert Islands. At Tarawa, patrolled area "Longsuit". Spent 1944 screening assault operations on Kwajalein, Majuro, Eniwetok, Tinian and Saipan. On 14 July, sank Jap sub *I-6* after six hours of attacking. See chapter *Pacific ASW.* Seven battle stars.

CABANA	**DE-260**	**Boston**	**09/07/43**	**09/01/46**		**Scrapped 06/47**

Supported strikes on Ellice and Gilbert Islands and screened attacks on Kwajelein and Marshall Islands October 1943 through February 1944. Screened invasions of Marshalls, Saipan, Tinian, Guam, Palau Islands and Iwo Jima. Supported Third Fleet attacks on Japanese home islands in 1945. Seven battle stars.

DIONNE	**DE-261**	**Boston**	**16/07/43**	**18/01/46**		**Scrapped 07/47**

In June 1944, screened invasion of Marianas. Rescued seven Japanese prisoners. Screened *California* while she bombarded Saipan. Provided fire support for Guam landings on 21 July and bombarded Tinian on 24 July. Patrol and escort duty September to January 1945. Covered Iwo Jima landings February to March. Screened 3rd Fleet strikes on Japan to end of war. Six battle stars.

CANFIELD	**DE-262**	**Boston**	**22/07/43**	**21/12/45**		**Scrapped 07/47**

Screened Marshall Island strikes 13 October to 17 November 1943. Convoys to Marianas, Eniwetok, Ulithi and Philippines. March 1944, participated in assault and capture of Northern Iwo Jima. Conducted numerous subsequent convoys, culminating in Tokyo Bay. Four battle stars.

DEEDE	**DE-263**	**Boston**	**29/07/43**	**09/01/46**		**Scrapped 07/47**

Early 1944, convoyed Majuro to Eniwetok. Escorted oilers to Philippines in closing days of that battle. Joined Task Force 58 in raids on Bonins June through September. February to April 1945, escorted Marines in assault on Iwo Jima. Screened bombardment force on Japanese home islands. Six battle stars.

ELDEN	**DE-264**	**Boston**	**04/08/43**	**18/01/46**		**Scrapped 07/47**

Early 1944, escorted oilers in occupation of Marshalls. June 1944, heavy action in Marianas. Thwarted enemy moves on Saipan and sank several barges. Delivered harassing fire on Tinian. Screened oilers in invasions of Palaus and Leyte. Screened carrier raids on Japan. Six battle stars.

CLOUES	**DE-265**	**Boston**	**10/08/43**	**26/11/45**		**Scrapped 06/47**

Arrived Gilberts 11 March 1944 to cover landings at Bikini, Enyu, and Rongelap. Between 2 and 27 May, conducted reconnaissance of Japanese held islands with native scouts. Okinawa picket screen 22 March to 28 April 1945. In July, supported amphibious operations vs Balikpapan. Three battle stars.

LAKE	**DE-301**	**Mare Is.**	**05/02/44**	**03/12/46**		**Scrapped 01/47**

From July to September 1944, conducted escort and ASW operations in the Marshalls. For the next two months, escorted transports to invasions of Palaus and Pelelius, followed by the Bonins and Iwo Jima. In August 1945, guarded oilers off Japanese coast. Two battle stars.

LYMAN	**DE-302**	**Mare Is.**	**19/02/44**	**05/12/46**		**Scrapped 01/47**

From 20 August 1944 and for next 13 months, convoyed and screened invasions of Palau and Peleliu. In October, escorted 1st Marine Division to Russell Islands. In December, screened invasion of Lingayen Gulf. Covered Iwo Jima replenishment group in February 1945. March to June, involved in fierce struggle at Okinawa. Rolled 65 degrees and was damaged in Philippine typhoon on 5 June. Triumphantly ended war in Tokyo Bay. See chapter *The Pacific Typhoons.* Five battle stars.

CROWLEY	**DE-303**	**Mare Is.**	**25/03/45**	**03/12/45**		**Scrapped 01/47**

September to November 1944, escorted to Guadalcanal, Manus, Palau, New Guinea and Solomons. Rescued survivors from torpedoed merchantman *Don Marquis.* Until February 1944, escorted oilers for carriers striking Luzon, Formosa and China coast. In March, escorted to Okinawa. July to end of war, supported 3rd and 5th fleets raiding Japan home islands. Five battle stars.

EVARTS CLASS

SHIP	NUMBER	YARD	COMPLETED	DECOM	MODIFIED	DISPOSAL
RALL	**DE-304**	**Mare Is.**	**08/04/44**	**11/12/45**		**Scrapped 04/47**

September 1944, convoyed to Ulithi and the Palaus. In November, escorted assault ships at Leyte. On 20 November, sank midget submarine in Ulithi Lagoon. December to March 1945, convoyed to Admiralty Islands and assault on Iwo Jima. Escorted army troops to Okinawa. On picket station at Okinawa on 12 April, sustained furious *kamikaze* attacks, splashed several and was hit. See *The Midgets* in chapter *Pacific Antisubmarine Warfare* and *Iwo Jima to Okinawa.* Three battle stars.

HALLORAN	**DE-305**	**Mare Is.**	**27/05/44**	**02/11/45**		**Scrapped 04/47**

August to December 1944, escorted oilers from Manus and Ulithi to Palau, Yap and Luzon. In January 1945, escorted amphibians for capture of Iwo Jima. Screened forces to Saipan, Tulagi and Espiritu Santo until March. In April, convoyed to Okinawa and joined barrier patrol. On 12 April, repelled six *kamikazes*, splashing one and damaging two. On 20 April, narrowly missed aerial torpedo. On 30 May, splashed *kamikaze close aboard*, sustaining losses and damage. Philippine convoys to war's end. See chapter *Iwo Jima to Okinawa*. Three battle stars.

CONNOLLY	**DE-306**	**Mare Is.**	**08/07/44**	**22/11/45**		**Scrapped 06/46**

From 22 January 1944 to 1 March 1945, screened and provided fire support to landings at Iwo Jima. April through June 1945, convoyed to Espiritu Santo and Okinawa, covering LST landings at Nansei Shoto. Continued escort work in Philippines to end of war. Two battle stars.

FINNEGAN	**DE-307**	**Mare Is.**	**19/08/44**	**27/11/45**		**Scrapped 06/46**

Screened and conducted ASW exercises September 1944 to January 1945. In February, screened transports to attack on Iwo Jima. On 26 February, sank Jap sub *I-370* in 4 hour attack. In March, convoyed to Okinawa and joined ASW patrol. On 28 May, fired on *kamikaze.* Philippine escort assignments to end of war. See chapter *Pacific ASW.* Three battle stars.

O'TOOLE	**DE-527**	**Boston**	**22/01/44**	**18/10/45**		**Scrapped 03/46**

School ship at SCTC, Miami, until September 1944. September to December, coastal US and transatlantic convoys. Liaison ship between CTG 275 and hard pressed Convoy NY 119 September to October. Subsequent convoys to Reykjavik and North Africa. See chapter *Convoys to the UK.*

J.J. POWERS	**DE-528**	**Boston**	**29/04/44**	**16/10/45**		**Scrapped 02/46**

May to September 1944 , convoyed troops and materiel to the UK. Departed New York on 19 September with convoy NY 119 and rescued four crewmen from army tug *ST-719* on 26 September. Three additional round trip convoys to Casablanca to end of Atlantic war. See chapter *Convoys to the UK.*

MASON	**DE-529**	**Boston**	**20/03/44**	**12/10/45**		**Scrapped 04/47**

First American DE to be manned with predominantly black crew. June to August, convoyed to the UK. On 20 September, 1944, sailed from New York with Convoy NY 119 and into the teeth of a furious storm which caused serious damage to this DE. Operated in North African convoys to end of war. See chapter *Convoys to the UK.*

J.M. BERMINGHAM	**DE-530**	**Boston**	**08/04/44**	**12/10/45**		**Scrapped 03/46**

June to August 1944, convoyed to the UK. On 19 September, departed New York with ill-fated Convoy 119 to the UK. After arriving Plymouth on 20 October, returned to sea to search for straggling barges. Three more round trip convoys to Oran to end of Atlantic war. See chapter *Convoys to the UK.*

Lewis M. Andrews, Jr.

BUCKLEY CLASS — TURBO ELECTRIC (TE) 3" GUNS

One hundred and two *Buckley* class DE's were constructed for the US Navy during World War II. Forty-six more went to American allies under Lend-Lease. Another eight were cancelled before completion as the war began to wind down. They were of the Long Hull design (306'), as were all classes subsequent to the *Evarts* design. They needed the extra length for their torpedoes and turbo-electric plants which delivered 12,000 shaft horsepower, double that of the *Evarts* diesel powered DEs. Many in this class made the DE hall of fame. To name a few: *England* sank six Japanese submarines, *Underhill* was lost in action, and *Donnell* was crippled. Others sank U-boats and fought off *kamikazes*.

These ships were each designed with a triple torpedo tube mount, not supplied to the *Evarts* Class, located about amidships on the first superstructure deck. A number of armament changes were made at a later date. A decision was made in the latter part of 1944 to replace the 3" main battery with two 5" destroyer type mounts. However, the number of ships to be converted was reduced. Only 11 were converted before the end of the war (*Rudderow* class).

The requirement for increased antiaircraft defense against Japanese *kamikazes* created secondary battery changes. Four of this class had installed four Bofors 40mm guns, replacing the torpedo tubes and mounted in the same location, approximately amidships. Additional ships had this modification made, many in Pearl Harbor before heading for *kamikaze* active areas. Two more 20mm Oelikons were added to the stern, increasing that total to fifteen, more or less. 50 and 30 caliber machine guns were frequently added where available.

Because of the need for fast transport of small troop contingents to the myriad of Pacific Islands, the spring of 1944 saw 50 DEs approved by the Bureau of Ships for conversion to APDs. In addition, four were converted to generator power plants with heavy duty cable shore connection reels. These ships were used to supply power in a number of emergency situations; Cherbourg, Manila and Guam among them.

Destroyer Escorts 53-54, 56-57, 59-60, 62-63, 65-66, 68-70, 153-161, 198-223, 575-578, 633-644, 665-667, 675-683, 693-705, 789-800.

MAJOR CHARACTERISTICS

Length Overall	306'- 0"
Extreme Beam	36'- 9"
Mean Draft	13'- 6"
Displacement	1,400 Tons
Designed Shaft Horsepower	12,000
Trial (Flank) Speed	24 Knots
Boilers	Fairbanks Morse
Machinery	General Electric
Designed Complement	Off: 6, Enl: 180
Average Complement	Off: 11, Enl: 204

ARMAMENT

Main:	(3) 3"/50 Caliber Guns
Secondary:	(1) Twin 40mm or 1.1" Quad Guns
	(9) 20mm Guns
ASW:	(2) Depth Charge Racks
	(8) Depth Charge "K" Guns
	(1) Hedgehog
Torpedoes:	(1) Triple Mount

BUCKLEY CLASS

SHIP	NUMBER	YARD	COMPLETED	DECOM	MODIFIED	DISPOSAL
BUCKLEY	**DE-51**	**Beth Hing**	**30/04/43**	**03/07/46**	**DER**	**sold, 1969**

Training ship on Atlantic Seaboard June 1943 to April 1944 when she joined *Block Island* Hunter-Killers. On 6 May, engaged *U-66* in epic battle that included hand-to-hand combat. While in convoy 19 April, joined *Reuben James (DE-153)* in sinking *U-879.* Navy Unit Commendation. See chapters *The Hunter-Killers* and *Twilight of the U-boats*. Three battle stars.

SHIP	NUMBER	YARD	COMPLETED	DECOM	MODIFIED	DISPOSAL
C. LAWRENCE	**DE-53**	**Beth Hing**	**31/05/43**	**21/9/46**	**APD-37 (10/44)**	**Scrapped 09/64**

October 1943 to September 1944, eight convoys of high speed tankers, freighters and transports, New York to Londonderry, Northern Ireland. Hove to for 20 hours in "Christmas Hurricane" of 1943. Converted to APD October 1944. Arrived Ulithi March 1944 to join Northern Attack Force Screen for Okinawa assault. Repelled numerous *kamikaze* attacks. See chapter *Convoys to the UK.* One battle star.

SHIP	NUMBER	YARD	COMPLETED	DECOM	MODIFIED	DISPOSAL
D.T. GRIFFIN	**DE-54**	**Beth Hing**	**09/06/43**	**30/05/46**	**APD-38 (10/44)**	**Scrapped 10/44**

August to September 1943, convoy to *Casablanca.* October to September 1944, eight convoys New York to Londonderry, including "Christmas Hurricane" 1943. As APD, sailed to Okinawa invasion. Screened ships sweeping mines at Kerama Retto, delivered explosives to Okinawa beaches. On 6 April, repelled several *kamikazes*, splashing at least two. Went to aid *Morris (DD-417)*, disabled by suicide attacks. Balance of war in convoy and redeployment of troops. See chapters *Convoys to the U K and Iwo Jima to Okinawa.* One battle star.

SHIP	NUMBER	YARD	COMPLETED	DECOM	MODIFIED	DISPOSAL
DONNELL	**DE-56**	**Beth Hing**	**26/06/43**	**23/10/45**	**IX 182 (07/44)**	**sold 04/46**

August 1943 to May 1944, four convoys to Londonderry, Northern Ireland, including "Christmas Hurricane" 1943. On fifth trip, 3 May, torpedoed while depth charging U-boat, sustaining 29 killed and 25 wounded. Towed to Scotland. In August, towed to Cherbourg to supply emergency electric power to war damaged city. See chapter *Convoys to the UK.*

SHIP	NUMBER	YARD	COMPLETED	DECOM	MODIFIED	DISPOSAL
FOGG	**DE-57**	**Beth Hing**	**07/07/43**	**27/10/47**	**DER**	**sold 01/66**

October 1943, convoyed in Caribbean and to Algiers. December to August 1944, six convoys to Londonderry. September 1944, escorted to Plymouth and Cherbourg. Homeward bound from *England* on 20 December, torpedoed while searching for U-boat that had previously torpedoed an *LST*, 4 killed and 2 wounded. Towed to Boston Navy Yard. See chapter *Convoys to the UK.*

SHIP	NUMBER	YARD	COMPLETED	DECOM	MODIFIED	DISPOSAL
FOSS	**DE-59**	**Beth Hing**	**23/07/43**	**30/10/57**		**Target 11/65**

September to December 1943, convoyed to Caribbean and North Africa. December 1943 to October 1944, seven convoys to Londonderry. Thereafter served as operational development activity vessel in antisubmarine warfare.

SHIP	NUMBER	YARD	COMPLETED	DECOM	MODIFIED	DISPOSAL
GANTNER	**DE-60**	**Beth Hing**	**23/07/43**	**02/08/49**	**APD-42 (02/45)**	**China 02/66**

December 1943 to October 1944, completed eight convoys to Londonderry. November to February 1945, served as SCTC school ship. After conversion, reported to 5th Amphibious Force, Pacific Fleet on 28 June. Entered Tokyo Bay in September after Japanese surrender.

SHIP	NUMBER	YARD	COMPLETED	DECOM	MODIFIED	DISPOSAL
G. W. INGRAM	**DE-62**	**Beth-Hing**	**11/08/43**	**15/01/47**	**APD-43 (02/45)**	**sold 01/67**

October to November 1943, round trip to North Africa via West Indies. Five more trips to North Africa from Boston or New York November to July 1944. In December, convoyed to *England* and return, escorting slow invasion craft damaged in Normandy invasion. Was attacked by *U-870* which sank *LST 359* and damaged *Fogg (DE 57).* After conversion, sailed to Eniwetok and Okinawa, arriving just after Japanese surrender. See *chapter Convoys to the UK.*

SHIP	NUMBER	YARD	COMPLETED	DECOM	MODIFIED	DISPOSAL
IRA JEFFREY	**DE-63**	**Beth Hing**	**15/08/43**	**18/06/46**	**APD-44 (02/45)**	**Sunk 07/62**

November 1943 to December 1944, seven troop convoys to Northern Ireland or England. Attacked by U-boat which sank an *LST* and damaged *Fogg (DE-57). Jeffrey* assisted and escorted damaged DE through heavy seas to the Azores. After conversion, arrived in forward Pacific areas just after Japan surrendered.

SHIP	NUMBER	YARD	COMPLETED	DECOM	MODIFIED	DISPOSAL
LEE FOX	**DE-65**	**Beth Hing**	**30/08/43**	**13/05/46**	**APD-45 (02/45)**	**Scrapped 01/66**

This DE's introduction to the North Atlantic was traumatic. Almost capsized in a hurricane on 17 October 1943 which also started an engine room fire. In a storm off Cape Cod on 11 December, a projectile explosion on the forecastle caused fire and damage. 18 Atlantic crossings to Londonderry between November 1943 and January 1945. Two merchant vessels torpedoed and sunk on last convoy. As APD, arrived in Philippines at war's end.

Lewis M. Andrews, Jr.

BUCKLEY CLASS

SHIP	NUMBER	YARD	COMPLETED	DECOM	MODIFIED	DISPOSAL
AMESBURY	**DE-66**	**Beth Hing**	**31/08/43**	**03/07/46**	**APD-46 (02/45)**	**Scrapped 1960**

As *ComCortDiv 19*, made several convoys to UK. On 1 June 1944, with TG 1247, joined attack on Normandy beaches, screening heavy bombardment group. Participated in numerous antiaircraft and antisubmarine actions. On 11 June, went to aid of mined *LST-496*, removing crew and troops before it capsized. As APD, sailed for Pacific, arriving in forward area at war's end. See chapter *Operations Overlord/Neptune.* One battle star.

BATES	**DE-68**	**Beth Hing**	**12/09/43**		**APD-47(07/44)**	**Sunk 25/05/45**

Engaged in UK convoys until 31 May 1944 when assigned to Normandy Invasion. On 8 June, rescued 163 from mined *Meredith* (DD-726). Transferred to Pacific after conversion and operated with UDTs at Iwo Jima. On 6 April 1945, rescued 23 from Morris (DD-417), hit by *kamikaze* at Okinawa. On 25 May, engaged three *kamikazes* resulting in loss of ship. See chapters *Operations Overlord/Neptune* and *Iwo Jima to Okinawa*. Three battle stars.

BLESSMAN	**DE-69**	**Beth Hing**	**19/09/43**	**15/01/47**	**APD-48 (07/44)**	**Chile 11/66**

Several NY to Londonderry convoys. Screened heavy bombardment units in attack on Normandy beaches. Assisted mined transports *Susan B Anthony* and *Francis C Harrington*, transferring wounded to hospital ship. As APD, assisted destruction two *kamikazes* at Lingayen Gulf and operated underwater demolition teams there and at Iwo Jima where she was hit by a 500 lb aerial bomb with heavy casualties. See chapters *Operations Overlord/Neptune, The Philippine Campaign, and Iwo Jima to Okinawa*. Three battle stars.

J.E. CAMPBELL	**DE-70**	**Beth Hing**	**23/09/43**	**15/11/46**	**APD-49 (07/44)**	**Chile 11/66**

October to December 1943, one convoy to Londonderry. December to October 1944, three convoys to French North Africa. After conversion, convoyed in rear as well as forward Pacific areas to end of war. One battle star.

REUBEN JAMES	**DE-153**	**Norfolk**	**01/04/43**	**11/10/47**	**DER-45**	**target 68-71**

July to November 1944, convoyed to Mediterranean. On first voyage, splashed one out of nine attacking German bombers. Hunter-Killer operations in North Atlantic November to April 1945. See chapter *Convoys to the Mediterranean.* One battle star.

SIMS	**DE-154**	**Norfolk**	**24/04/43**	**24/04/46**	**APD-50 (09/44)**	**Scrapped 04/61**

From spring of 1943 to summer of 1944, made eight convoys to Londonderry with *CortDiv 6*. Weathered the Christmas 1943 hurricane. Sister DE *Donnell* torpedoed on one crossing. On another convoy, an Esso tanker, *Seakay*, torpedoed and lost. Sims made embarrassing attack, followed by "unwinding spring" search but without result. As APD, downed four *kamikazes* at Okinawa, the last one close aboard, causing some damage and a few injuries. Rescue party saved *Barry* when set afire and abandoned after *kamikaze* attack. See chapters *Convoys to the UK* and *Iwo Jima to Okinawa*. Deployed occupation troops at end of war. Two battle stars.

HOPPING	**DE-155**	**Norfolk**	**21/05/43**	**05/05/47**	**APD-51 (09/44)**	**Scrapped 08/66**

From September 1943 for one year, engaged in nine convoys to Londonderry. Took sister ship *Donnell (DE-56)* in tow after she was torpedoed until it could be turned over to a seagoing tug. As APD, splashed several *kamikazes* on 28-29 March at Okinawa. On 9 May, silenced enemy shore battery in Buckner Bay but received several hits. Fought off many *kamikaze* attacks. See chapters *Convoys to the UK* and *Iwo Jima to Okinawa*. One battle star.

REEVES	**DE-156**	**Norfolk**	**09/06/43**	**30/07/46**	**APD-52 (09/44)**	**Ecuador 06/60**

August to September 1943, a slow convoy from Norfolk to North Africa. For a full year from October, operated in convoys to the United Kingdom. Rescued 84 seamen from torpedoed tanker *Seakay* on 18 March 1944. On 3 May, covered torpedo-damaged *Donnell (DE 56)* in tow and received aboard her seriously wounded. In March 1945, as an APD, she began 109 harrowing days off Okinawa. At end of hostilities, assisted in repatriation of American POWs. See chapter *Convoys to the UK* and *Iwo Jima to Okinawa.* One battle star.

FECHTELER	**DE-157**	**Norfolk**	**01/07/43**			**Lost 04/05/44**

September- December 1943, two convoys to Caribbean and North Africa. February 1944, convoyed to Azores and Londonderry. April 1944, convoyed Hampton Roads to Bizerte, undergoing two days of air assault. On return, 5 May, torpedoed and sunk in Western Mediterranean, 29 killed and 26 wounded. Survivors rescued by *Lansing (DE-159)* and *Chase (DE-158)*. See chapter *Convoys to the Mediterranean.* One battle star.

BUCKLEY CLASS

SHIP	NUMBER	YARD	COMPLETED	DECOM	MODIFIED	DISPOSAL

CHASE DE-158 Norfolk 18/07/43 15/01/46 APD-54 (11/44) Scrapped 11/46

Six transatlantic convoys East Coast US to North Africa September 1943 to summer 1944. On 20 April, drove off attacking torpedo planes and rescued swimmers from torpedoed merchantmen. On 5 May, rescued 52 survivors from torpedoed *Fechteler (DE-157).* After APD conversion, joined Okinawa operation. AA fire drove off several *kamikazes.* She splashed one on 20 May but sustained severe damage. See chapter *Iwo Jima to Okinawa.* Two battle stars.

LANING DE-159 Norfolk 01/08/43 13/09/57 APD-55 (11/44) Scrapped –

November 1943 to January 1944, two convoys to North Africa via West Indies. April to October, three additional runs to Mediterranean. On last one, fought off five JU 88 attackers and had near torpedo miss. On the return, encountered *U-967* which torpedoed *Menges (DE-320)* and *Fechteler (DE-157).* Rescued 125 survivors and dropped them off in Gibraltar. As APD, arrived at Okinawa shortly after war's end. See chapter *Convoys to the Mediterranean.* One battle star.

LOY DE-160 Norfolk 12/09/43 21/02/47 APD-56 (11/44) Scrapped 08/66

November 1943 to January 1944, escorted three convoys to North Africa via Netherlands West Indies. April and May, two round trips to Casablanca. June to October, two convoys to the UK. As an APD, was heavily engaged with *kamikazes* March 1945 to end of Okinawa campaign. On 29 March, supplied medical and repair help to amphibious ship *LSM (R)-188* hit by *kamikaze.* In support UDT operations, splashed one suicider on 8 April and another on the 16th. On 25 May, took aboard survivors of *Barry (APD-29)*, a *kamikaze* victim. Two days later, splashed three *kamikazes* in two attacks, but sustained 18 casualties and some damage on third raid. Following day, splashed another close aboard. See chapter *Iwo Jima to Okinawa.* One battle star.

BARBER DE-161 Norfolk 10/10/43 22/05/46 APD-57 (11/44) Scrapped —

December 1943 to October 1944, escorted convoys to North Africa. On 26 April 1944, with three other DEs, sank *U-488.* After APD conversion, proceeded to the Pacific where she engaged largely in convoy to the end of the war. See chapter *The Hunter-Killers.* Three battle stars.

LOVELACE DE-198 Norfolk 07/11/43 22/05/46 Target 04/68

19 April 1943, departed Solomons to screen debarking second wave of relief troops in New Guinea battle zone. In July, bombarded shore targets at Toem. Arrived Leyte Gulf on 25 October to protect 7th Fleet replenishment units. Splashed an enemy plane on the 26th. Six days later, en route Kossol Straits, her screen beat off massive suicide plane attacks. On 21 November, credited with assist in downing enemy bomber in convoy. Continued escorting Philippines to Okinawa to end of war. See chapter *The Philippine Campaign.* Three battle stars.

MANNING DE-199 Charleston 01/10/43 15/01/47 Scrapped 08/68

In January 1944, sailed to South Pacific to convoy in the Solomons area. In March, escorted fleet oilers to a rendezvous to fuel 3rd Fleet heavies for attack on Carolines. In April, transferred to *CortDiv 37* to operate in 7th fleet along with *Lovelace.* Screened to Humboldt Bay, Cape Cretin and Aitape in May as fleet advanced westward. In October, screened convoys to invade Philippines. On 24 to 28 October, heavy *kamikaze* attacks. Splashed a bomber on 24th. On 23 November near Leyte, scored hits on dive bomber during large scale attack. In Mindanao Sea on 2 January 1945, again repelled massive attack. From March 1945 to war's end, operated ASW patrols in South China Sea. See chapter *The Philippine Campaign.* Four Battle Stars.

NEUENDORF DE-200 Charleston 18/10/43 15/05/46 Scrapped 11/67

Arrived Noumea 28 January 1944. Through March, convoyed in Solomon and Hebrides Islands area. April-November, reported to 7th Fleet and convoyed materiel and troops to Hollandia, Aitape, Tenahmerah Bay, Wakde, Manus and Biak. Bombarded enemy shore installations in Maffin Bay. In January 1945, operated in Philippines, guarded mine sweeping force and joined *Manning (DE-199)* in ASW operations. In April, designated flagship for Commander Local Naval Defense Forces Iloilo and Panay to war's end. Three battle stars.

J.E. CRAIG DE-201 Charleston 01/11/43 02/07/46 Target 02/69

Escorted from Espiritu Santo to Guadalcanal and Raboul. Bombarded enemy troops on Wakde-Sarmi on 27 May 1944. In June and July, supported landing operations at Biak Island with prolonged shelling. Resumed screening western Pacific operations to end of November. On 23 November, attacked by five torpedo planes in Leyte Gulf; dodged all and splashed one Jill. On 4 January 1945, went to assistance *Ommaney Bay (CVE-79)* after she was crashed by a *kamikaze.* Weathered severe typhoon on 1 and 2 September. See chapter *The Philippine Campaign.* Four battle stars.

Lewis M. Andrews, Jr.

BUCKLEY CLASS

SHIP	NUMBER	YARD	COMPLETED	DECOM	MODIFIED	DISPOSAL

EICHENBERGER DE-202 Charleston 19/11/43 14/05/46 Scrapped 1972
January to April 1944, convoyed to Espiritu Santo, Milne Bay and New Guinea. May and June, saw action covering landings at Biak, Humboldt Bay and Wakde. October and November, convoyed to Palaus, Hollandia and Leyte. Assisted damaged *Ommaney Bay (CVE-79)* after she was bombed and lost three men killed in rescue party. February 1945, supported Mindoro landings. Remainder of war in Philippines and Okinawa. Four battle stars.

THOMASON DE-203 Charleston 10/12/43 19/12/45 Collision (07/45) Scrapped 1947
May-August 1944, joined 7th Fleet at New Guinea. On 13 May, coordinated with army AA units in repelling air attack. On 19 May, shelled enemy emplacements at Sarmi. Again shelled Sarmi on 6 November with *Neuendorf (DE-200)* and army air spotters; set fire to installations. On 28 December, sortied for Luzon with San Fabian Attack Force. 781 While on ASW patrol with *Neuendorf* on 7 February 1945, gained contact on Jap sub *RO-55* and sank it with hedgehogs. ASW patrols and convoy escort to end of war. See chapters *Pacific ASW* and *The Philippine Campaign.* Three battle stars.

NEWMAN DE-205 Charleston 26/11/43 18/02/46 *APD-59* Scrapped 08/66
Six North Atlantic convoys February-June 1944. As APD, flagship TransDiv 103 to Hollandia, arriving in November. In December, embarked troops of the 24th Division for invasion of Mindoro. On 11 January 1945, landed 158th Regimental Combat Team (RCT) at Lingayan, adding own gunfire support to the heavies. Several amphibious operations followed through July: San Felipe, Luzon; Grand Island, Subic Bay; Puerta Princessa, Palawan; Zamboanga; Cebu; Morotai; Borneo. Five battle stars.

LIDDLE DE-206 Charleston 06/12/43 18/03/67 *APD-60* (07/44) Scrapped 06/67
February to June 1944, made three round trips to Wales, Gibraltar and Tunisia. After APD conversion, sailed to Leyte and reported to 7th Fleet. Embarked 141 troops in flanking diversion in Leyte Gulf area on 6 December. At Ormoc Bay on the 7th, attacked sequentially by 6 *kamikazes.* She shot down five but was crashed by the sixth, killing 38 officers and men. Returned from repair yard in February 1945 and participated in several troop landings to end of war. See chapter *The Philippine Campaign.* One battle star.

KEPHART DE-207 Charleston 07/01/44 21/06/46 APD-61(07/44) Korea 05/67
Splashed two planes at Ormoc Bay on 7 December 1944 after landing troops. On 11 January 1945, landed Leyte reinforcements under heavy air attack. Until April, disembarked troops throughout Philippines. In May and June, landed Australian troops in Borneo. Screened operations in South China Sea to end of war. See chapter *The Philippine Campaign.* Five battle stars.

COFER DE-208 Charleston 19/01/44 28/06/46 *APD-62* (07/44) Scrapped —
March to June 1944, two convoys to Bizerte. After APD conversion, arrived Hollandia for 7th Fleet duty. November and December, ferried resupply troops to Leyte and Ormoc Bay, fighting off furious air attacks. On 7 December, while under attack, went to aid of *kamikaze*-damaged *Liddle (APD-60).* Landed troops on Mindoro under severe attack on 15 December. January to April 1945, continued landing troops in Philippines, firing on shore batteries. April to June, minesweeper flagship. Silenced shore batteries that sank *YMS-481*, rescuing 19 survivors. On 8 June, rescued 59 survivors of minesweeper *Salute (AM-294)*, including 42 injured. On 18 June, rescued 23 survivors of *YMS-50.* See chapter *The Philippine Campaign.* Eight battle stars. Recommend *Odyssey of A Sailor* by her CO, Alvin P Chester.

LLOYD DE-209 Charleston 11/02/44 18/02/58 *APD-63* (07/44) Scrapped 06/66
Began with a convoy to North Africa in May 1944. Three months after APD conversion, headed for Pacific, arriving in Hollandia, New Guinea in November as flagship of Transport Division 103. Transported troops for next five months to islands in the Philippine Archipelago, including Ormoc May, Mindoro, and Lingayen Gulf. On 4 January 1945, knocked out a shore battery after disembarking troops. Proceeded to Leyte, splashing three aircraft en route. In February, joined in assaults on San Felipe and Subic Bay. Sortied Mindoro on 8 March to seize Zamboanga. May-July, landed troops on Brunei and Balikpapan, Borneo. See chapter *The Philippine Campaign.* Four battle stars.

OTTER DE-210 Charleston 21/02/44 01/ /47 Target 07/70
From February 1944 almost to end of year, convoyed to Mediterranean. In December, joined three DEs as a hunter-killer group without aircraft. On 16 January, group sank *U-248.* In April 1945, picked up survivors of *Frederick C. Davis (DE-136)*, torpedoed by *U-546.* Started to refit for Pacific War when Japan capitulated. See chapter *Twilight of the U-boats.*

J.C. HUBBARD DE-211 Charleston 06/03/44 15/03/46 APD-53 (06/45) Scrapped 05/66
June-December 1944, three Mediterranean convoys. December 26 sailed with *CortDiv 62* and sophisticated new electronic gear to locate weather-reporting U-boats. Lead to sinking of *U-248* on 16 January 1945. Joined in attacking *U-546*, the sinker of *Frederick C. Davis (DE-136).* See chapter *Twilight of the U-boats.* Two battle stars.

BUCKLEY CLASS

SHIP	NUMBER	YARD	COMPLETED	DECOM	MODIFIED	DISPOSAL

HAYTER	**DE-212**	**Charleston**	**16/03/44**	**19/03/46**	**APD-80 (06/45)**	**Scrapped 01/67**

June through November 1944, three escorts to the UK and the Mediterranean. On 2 January 1945, joined *CortDiv 62* to locate weather-reporting submarines. Assisted in locating *U-248*, made contact and depth charged that U-boat until sunk. Had started joint U-boat attack with *Frederick C. Davis (DE-136)* when latter was sunk. Recovered 65 survivors and 12 dead, rendered medical assistance. See chapter *Twilight of the U-boats.*

W.T. POWELL	**DE-213**	**Charleston**	**28/03/44**	**17/01/58**	**DER-45**	**Scrapped 10/66**

After various assignments in the Caribbean, she convoyed UGS-48 to North Africa on 10 July 1944. Nearing the coast on 1 August, several German planes attacked, but "friendlies" in the area assisted in intercepting the bogies. The escorts laid a highly effective smoke screen, and did not sustain casualties. She escorted two more GUS/UGS convoys before being transferred to a hunter-killer group 28 November to 24 December. Continued convoy and ASW operations to end of war.

SCOTT	**DE-214**	**Phila**	**20/07/43**	**03/03/47**		**Scrapped 01/67**

October 1943 to October 1944, 16 convoys to Londonderry. November 1944 went to assistance of *Frament (DE-677)* after collision with Italian submarine. Various training duties at Key West and Guantanamo to end of war.

BURKE	**DE-215**	**Phila**	**20/08/43**	**22/06/49**	**APD-65 (01/45)**	**Scrapped —**

From November 1943 to January 1945, nine convoys to North Africa and Europe. After conversion, joined the Pacific Fleet, working with UDTs, picketing at Iwo Jima and convoy escort. One battle star.

ENRIGHT	**DE-216**	**Phila**	**21/09/43**	**21/06/46**	**APD-66 (01/45)**	**Scrapped —**

Early in 1944, made six North Atlantic convoys. On 16 April, a collision with a merchantman in convoy inflicted severe damage. Converted to an APD, sailed to Okinawa in time to take part in screening operations. Carried mail among Southern Philippines and to Brunei Bay, Borneo. One battle star.

COOLBAUGH	**DE-217**	**Phila**	**15/10/43**	**21/02/59**		**Scrapped 1973**

Began Pacific duty February 1944, escorting in the Solomons, screening the invasion of Emirau in April, and trips to Manus and Eniwetok. Joined the 7th Fleet in October to guard carriers as they covered the Leyte landings. In November, continued cover for carriers in Leyte operation. In January and February 1945, screened transports to Lingayen Gulf invasion. In March, embarked troops relieved from original assault forces on Iwo Jima. Escort services to end of war. Three battle stars.

DARBY	**DE-218**	**Phila**	**15/11/43**	**1952**	**NRF 59-62**	**Target 05/70**

January to July 1944, screened to Bora Bora in the Society Islands, Espiritu Santo, New Hebrides, Solomons and screened Emirau Landings on 10 April. Convoyed Guadalcanal, Eniwetok, New Hebrides, Manus, Majuro to October. Ponape hunter-killer group and shore bombardment on Tanga. January 1945, escorted invasion troops to Luzon. Numerous convoy assignments to end of war. Two battle stars.

J.D. BLACKWOOD	**DE-219**	**Phila**	**15/12/43**	**01/08/58**	**NRF 58-70**	**Target 07/70**

February-March 1944, served as training ship and coastal escort in the Caribbean. Sailed to the Pacific in late March. Until the end of the war, operated as escort ship for convoys bringing vital supplies from rear to forward combat areas.

F.M. ROBINSON	**DE-220**	**Phila**	**15/01/44**	**20/06/60**		**Scrapped 08/72**

On 2 May 1944, joined *Bogue (CVE-9)* Hunter-Killer Group. Off Cape Verde Islands on 13 May, sank the Japanese submarine *RO-501*, the former German *U-1224*. Presidential Unit Citation awarded to Group. From 2 August, convoyed five round trips to North Africa. On fourth convoy, put a repair party on torpedoed merchantman to save it from sinking. Served as school ship at Miami Naval Training Center to end of war. See chapter *The Hunter-Killers.* One battle star.

SOLAR	**DE-221**	**Phila**	**15/02/44**	**21/5/46**		**Scuttled 06/46**

April to October 1944, escorted convoys to Casablanca. December to January 1945 took part in various training duties.In February, resumed Mediterranean convoys. Various training assignments to end of war.

FOWLER	**DE-222**	**Phila**	**15/03/44**	**28/06/46**		**Scrapped 1967**

May 1944 to May 1945, Six convoys East Coast US to North Africa. On fifth, 27 February 1945, two merchantmen torpedoed but brought to port. On 28 February, with French escort, sank *U-869.* Sundry duties to end of war. See chapter *Convoys to the Mediterranean.* One battle star.

Lewis M. Andrews, Jr.

BUCKLEY CLASS

SHIP	NUMBER	YARD	COMPLETED	DECOM	MODIFIED	DISPOSAL
SPANGENBERG	**DE-223**	**Phila**	**15/04/44**	**18/10/47**	**DER-45**	**Scrapped 10/66**

Spent most of the war as a school ship for officers at various points on the East Coast. In July 1943, joined *Escort Division 66* for convoy to North Africa with UGS-48. On 1 August, formation attacked by about 20 enemy bombers; damage averted by excellent smoke screening by escorts. In September, as *CortDiv 66*, escorted UGS-55 to North Africa. Attacked a sub near Argentia during February 1944 but without result.

SHIP	NUMBER	YARD	COMPLETED	DECOM	MODIFIED	DISPOSAL
AHRENS	**DE-575**	**Beth Hing**	**12/02/44**	**24/06/46**		**Scrapped 06/67**

On 22 April 1944, joined the *Block Island* Hunter-Killer group. On 29 May, a U-boat torpedoed both the carrier and *Barr (DE-576). Ahrens* rescued 673 survivors within 45 minutes and at same time directed *Eugene V Elmore* in locating and sinking *U-549*, the sub that had torpedoed the two ships. In July, returned to North Atlantic convoys. In December, sailed to Pacific to join 7th Fleet where she engaged in numerous convoy and screening operations to the end of the war. See chapter *The Hunter-Killers.* Two battle stars.

SHIP	NUMBER	YARD	COMPLETED	DECOM	MODIFIED	DISPOSAL
BARR	**DE-576**	**Beth Hing**	**15/02/44**	**12/07/46**	**APD-39 (07/44)**	**Scrapped 1960**

Operated with *Block Island* Hunter-Killer Force. Disabled by acoustic torpedo from *U-549.* As APD, operated underwater demolition teams which were badly mauled at Iwo Jima. Launched UDTs at Okinawa and screened in picket line without casualty. Ended war in Tokyo Bay. See chapter *The Hunter-Killers.* Three battle stars.

SHIP	NUMBER	YARD	COMPLETED	DECOM	MODIFIED	DISPOSAL
A.J. LUKE	**DE-577**	**Beth Hing**	**19/02/44**	**18/10/47**	**DER-45**	**Target 10/70**

On 13 July 1944, made her first of two convoys to Bizerte. On 21 March, convoyed to the UK, calling at several ports. Converted to DER at end of war.

SHIP	NUMBER	YARD	COMPLETED	DECOM	MODIFIED	DISPOSAL
R.I. PAINE	**DE-578**	**Beth Hing**	**26/02/44**	**21/11/47**	**DER-45**	**Sold 1968**

April-May 1944 convoyed to Casablanca and patrolled in Mediterranean. Joined *Block Island* Hunter-Killer Group late May and engaged in rescue operations when the carrier and *Barr (DE-576)* were torpedoed. Rejoined North African convoys and ASW patrols to end of European war. See chapter *The Hunter-Killers.* One battle star.

SHIP	NUMBER	YARD	COMPLETED	DECOM	MODIFIED	DISPOSAL
FOREMAN	**DE-633**	**Beth SF**	**22/10/43**	**28/06/46**		**Scrapped 06/65**

Arrived Ellice Islands January 1944 to conduct escort and ASW patrols in the Solomons and Western New Guinea. In October, convoyed hospital transports. Various escort duties from November to March 1945, arriving at Okinawa on the 25th. Two days later, while guarding bombardment group, splashed a *kamikaze* close aboard but without casualties. On 3 April, took a direct bomb hit causing considerable damage but no loss of life. Returned to the fight on 3 June and assisted in splashing a *kamikaze* 8 days later. On 29 June, covered mine sweeping and air strikes on Chinese coast. Escort duty to end of war. See chapter *Iwo Jima to Okinawa.* Five battle stars.

SHIP	NUMBER	YARD	COMPLETED	DECOM	MODIFIED	DISPOSAL
WHITEHURST	**DE-634**	**Beth SF**	**19/11/65**	**25/07/65**	**NRF**	**Target 07/69**

February to May 1944, convoyed extensively in forward Pacific areas. Took part in invasions of Wakde Island, Humboldt Bay, Bosnic and Biak. Came under shore battery fire at Biak but was undamaged. Drove off attack by two planes near Leyte on 27 October. On 29 October, responded to distress call from torpedoed-*Eversole (DE-404).* Found sinking DE and sank her attacker, sub *I-45.* A month later, while in convoy, downed an attacking Lilly. Drove off a *kamikaze* at Kerama Retto and another while on picket station on 6 April 1945. In early afternoon of 12 April at Okinawa, again drove off a *kamikaze.* Same day, attacked by three suiciders at once; two were splashed, but the third crashed the DE, inflicting enormous damage and casualties. After emergency repairs, headed back to the US. See chapters *Pacific ASW, The Philippine Campaign* and *Iwo Jima to Okinawa.* Six battle stars.

SHIP	NUMBER	YARD	COMPLETED	DECOM	MODIFIED	DISPOSAL
ENGLAND	**DE-635**	**Beth SF**	**10/12/43**	**15/10/45**		**Scrapped 1945**

One of the most heralded DEs in WW II. Over a period of eight days from 18 May 1944 and again on 31 May, she sank six Japanese submarines without air or substantial surface assistance; an all time record. For the balance of the year, escorted in the Solomons and to the Treasury Islands, Australia, Hollandia and Leyte. Early in 1945, escorted to Philippines, Iwo Jima, Ulithi, and Okinawa. On 9 May 1945, attacked by three *kamikazes*, of which two were splashed by our aircraft, but one of which crashed *England* just below the bridge 37 men were killed outright and 25 were wounded. Material damage was heavy, effectively ending *England's* war service. See chapters *Pacific ASW* and *Iwo Jima to Okinawa.* Presidential Unit Citation and 10 battle stars.

BUCKLEY CLASS

SHIP	NUMBER	YARD	COMPLETED	DECOM	MODIFIED	DISPOSAL
WITTER	**DE-636**	**Beth SF**	**29/12/43**	**29/10/45**		**Scrapped 12/46**

Departed Southern Solomons on 25 April 1944 to engage in extensive supply and ASW operations in the New Guinea area for operations at Cape Cretin, Cape Sudest and Wakde-Sarmi. In July, proceeded to Northern Solomons and the Treasuries, conducting ASW and AA patrols. As part of 7th Fleet, arrived Leyte Gulf shortly after initial landings. Enemy air attacks abounded. The DE splashed an attacking torpedo bomber on 24 October. November-March 1945, engaged in extensive escort operations in South and Central Pacific. On 21 March, headed for the Ryukyus. Unscathed after 12 days of patrol, that fateful day of 6 April dawned. Attacked by two *kamikazes*, she splashed one. The other crashed into the ship, causing extensive damage and casualties. See chapters *The Philippine campaign* and *Iwo Jima to Okinawa.* Two battle stars.

BOWERS	**DE-637**	**Beth SF**	**27/01/44**	**18/12/58**	**APD-40 (06/45)**	**Philippines 04/61**

Assigned to Pacific Fleet 6 April 1944. Numerous escort operations in the Solomons, invasions of Leyte, and the Southwest Pacific. Joined picket operations at Okinawa March-April 1945. On 17 April, splashed two *kamikazes*, then received direct hit causing serious damage and casualties. After conversion, operated in training groups to end of war. See chapter *Iwo Jima to Okinawa.* Four battle stars.

WILLMARTH	**DE-638**	**Beth SF**	**13/03/44**	**26/04/46**		**Scrapped 07/68**

June-October 1944, escorted convoys in the Solomons, Admiralties, Treasuries, Emirau, Bougainville and Dutch New Guinea with *CortDiv 40*. Attached to 7th Fleet, she sailed on 20 October for liberation of Philippines. On the night of 25th, oiler *Ashtabula (AO-51)* was torpedoed. At 0458 next morning *Willmarth* assisted splashing an attacking Jill. She downed another at 1420 the same day. On 15 November, bombarded enemy installations on Pegun Island prior to invasion of US troops. On the 19th, bombarded Igi Island. This DE, continued escort, troop movements and patrol duties until assigned to Okinawa. At 1525 on 6 May, splashed one Val north of Kerama Retto and explosions from a crashed *LST* damaged her hull. Screened Third Fleet as it pounded Japanese home islands. See chapters *The Philippine Campaign* and *Iwo Jima to Okinawa.* Four battle stars.

GENDREAU	**DE-639**	**Beth SF**	**17/03/44**	**13/03/48**		**Scrapped 1973**

June - October 1944, engaged in escort of convoys and landing craft for operations covering Russell Islands to New Georgia. In late March 1945, sailed for the Ryukyus, screening landing craft for invasion of Okinawa. Transferred to the picket line, she was heavily engaged with *kamikazes* and torpedo bombers, splashing several in month of April. On 10 June, was hit and damaged by shore battery. A few days later, she rolled more than 60 degrees in an Okinawa typhoon and received some damage. See chapters *Iwo Jima to Okinawa* and *The Pacific Typhoons.* Battle star information not available.

FIEBERLING	**DE-640**	**Beth SF**	**11/04/44**	**13/03/48**		**Scrapped 1972**

June 1944-February 1945, escorted for the Marianas operation, also to Manus and Purvis Bay. Arrived at Okinawa on 31 March to cover landing of assault troops and then conducted ASW patrols. On 6 April, damaged by a near *kamikaze* miss. After diversionary convoy, returned to Okinawa on 28 June. Escorted from Okinawa to Guam and Saipan to end of war. See chapter *Iwo Jima to Okinawa.* One battle star.

W.C. COLE	**DE-641**	**Beth SF**	**12/05/44**	**03/02/47**		**Scrapped 1969**

August 1944, proceeded to Pacific forward areas. With exception of some availability, engaged in almost ceaseless screening and convoy operations for heavy units, oilers, and freighters. On 24 and 25 May 1945, on Okinawa picket station, attacked by two *kamikazes* and splashed both after one very close call and with only minor damage. Resumed intensive escort operations until end of war. See chapter *Iwo Jima to Okinawa.* One battle star.

P.G. BAKER	**DE-642**	**Beth SF**	**25/05/44**	**03/02/47**		**Scrapped 1969**

In October 1944, went to Solomons to conduct convoy assignments, ie Bougainville, Guadalcanal, Munda, New Hebrides, Russell Islands.Heavily engaged at Okinawa. First action on 1 April 1945 while guarding off-loading transports. On 22 April, *kamikazes* attacked formation, crashing nearby *Isherwood (DD-520)* and *Swallow (AM-65).* On 12 May, two "suiciders" headed for *New Mexico (BB-40)*; *Baker* splashed one but the other crashed the BB. Opening fire again on 24th, *Baker* splashed another on 11 June, preventing a crash on a merchant vessel. Screened warships and convoyed merchantmen to end of war. See chapter *Iwo Jima to Okinawa.* One battle star.

D.M. CUMMINGS	**DE-643**	**Beth SF**	**29/06/43**	**03/02/47**		**Target 1969**

September to November 1944, convoyed to Eniwetok, Port Purvis, Florida Island, Solomons and Ellice Islands until January 1945. March to April, convoyed *LST*s to Okinawa invasion. Continued escorting to end of war. One battle star.

BUCKLEY CLASS

SHIP	NUMBER	YARD	COMPLETED	DECOM	MODIFIED	DISPOSAL
VAMMEN	**DE-644**	**Beth SF**	**27/07/44**	**01/08/62**	**NRF 60-69**	**Target 07/69**

January-March 1944, convoyed and screened in forward combat areas. At Okinawa 1-8 April, no attacks recorded. On 28 May, credited with an assist in downing a Tony. Convoyed and conducted ASW patrols Okinawa to Philippines to Ulithi to end of war. One battle star.

JENKS	**DE-665**	**Dravo**	**19/01/44**	**26/06/46**		**Scrapped 09/68**

January-April 1944, engaged in transatlantic convoys. In May, joined Guadalcanal Hunter-Killer Group. Took part in capture of *U-505*, recovered some prisoners, and her small boat seized valuable documents on the submarine. In late June, operated in training exercises, then made four convoys to the Mediterranean. See chapter *The Hunter-Killers.* Two battle stars.

DURIK	**DE-666**	**Dravo**	**23/03/44**	**15/06/46**		**Scrapped 01/67**

Two convoys, East Coast US to Casablanca and to Bizerte and Palermo, May to November 1944. School ship in Norfolk November to January 1945. Two more voyages to Oran, January to May 1945. In June, resumed school ship duties.

WISEMAN	**DE-667**	**Dravo**	**04/04/44**	**16/05/59**	**NRF 59-68**	**Scrapped 1973**

Arriving in the Philippines on 3 March 1945, this turbo-electric powered DE of the *Buckley* class, provided an unusual service to war-ravaged Manila. Tied to a dock, she supplied 5,806,000 kilowatt hours over five and a half months. Her evaporators supplied 150,000 gallons of fresh water to army installations and small craft in the vicinity. She also used her radio equipment to handle harbor radio traffic. From there, she went to Guam to supply similar services before returning to the US. *Donnell (DE-56)*, torpedoed in the author's *CortDiv 6*, supplied the same service at Cherbourg as described in chapter *Convoys to the UK.*

WEBER	**DE-675**	**Beth Quin**	**30/06/43**	**15/01/47**	**APD-75 (01/45)**	**Target 07/62**

Late 1943 and most of 1944, convoyed to Londonderry, Cherbourg and Bizerte without sighting the enemy. Required some hull repair after collision with a Portuguese fishing boat. Converted to an APD mid-March 1945, proceeded to Pacific to engage in escort and screening operations for heavy fleet units at Okinawa. War ended while training in Leyte for invasion of Japanese home islands. One battle star.

SCHMITT	**DE-676**	**Beth Quin**	**24/07/43**	**28/06/49**	**APD-76 (01/45)**	**Taiwan 02/67**

October 1943 to September 1944, 16 Atlantic voyages to Londonderry without incident. October to December, joined a convoy from Norfolk to various North African ports. As an APD, arrived off Balikpapan, Borneo to screen bombardment by heavy units in June. Her underwater demolition teams conducted night operations and this DE lead the first 17 waves of landing craft to the beach. One battle star.

FRAMENT	**DE-677**	**Beth Quin**	**15/08/43**	**30/05/46**	**APD-77 (01/45)**	**Scrapped —**

Autumn of 1943-December 1944, made six convoys from New York and Boston to the UK, Cherbourg and Gibraltar. After APD conversion, sailed to forward combat areas in the Pacific for convoy duties. On 10 June, rescued entire crew of *William D Porter (DD-579)*, hit by a *kamikaze* at Okinawa. Escorted mine sweeping and occupation duties after surrender of Japan. One battle star.

HARMON	**DE-678**	**Beth Quin**	**31/08/43**	**25/03/47**		**Scrapped 01/67**

December 1943-September 1944, conducted screening activities with Third Fleet. From November 1944 to February 1945, covered transports in Lingayen Gulf. Escorted men and supplies to Iwo Jima in March. Three battle stars.

GREENWOOD	**DE-679**	**Beth Quin**	**25/09/43**	**01/08/62**	**NRF 62-67**	**Scrapped 02/7**

Sailed to South Pacific in November 1943. Conducted extensive convoys to New Hebrides, and Australia. In December 1944, departed New Guinea to take part in operations at Leyte Gulf and then Iwo Jima.

LOESER	**DE-680**	**Beth Quin**	**10/10/43**	**22/09/68**	**NRF**	**Scrapped 09/68**

Arrived Funafuti on 16 January to commence escort operations to *Solomons* and New Hebrides. On 25 November, arrived at Manus for duty with Amphibious Group 3. 11 January until early February, escort and ASW patrols vicinity of Lingayen Gulf. Sortied Ulithi for invasion of Iwo Jima on 5 March. Shortly thereafter and to war's end, conducted training exercises in Hawaii. Two battle stars.

GILLETTE	**DE-681**	**Beth Quin**	**27/10/43**	**12/ /46**		**Scrapped 01/73**

Various Caribbean operations from January to June 1944. July to February 1945, took part in convoys to the UK and the Mediterranean. Then assigned as a training ship until April when she sailed to the Philippines. Conducted screening operations in that area and Okinawa to end of war.

BUCKLEY CLASS

SHIP	NUMBER	YARD	COMPLETED	DECOM	MODIFIED	DISPOSAL
UNDERHILL	**DE-682**	**Beth Quin**	**15/01/43**			**Lost 24/07/45**

1944 saw this vessel in convoy escort duties to North Africa and England. Early in 1945, she headed to the Pacific to screen convoys in the Ryukyus. On 24 July 1945, she rammed what she thought to be a conventional submarine but which was a suicide vehicle. Resultant explosion destroyed the DE and caused large loss of life, including commanding officer, Lieutenant Commander Robert M Newcomb. See chapter *Pacific ASW.*

H.R. KENYON	**DE-683**	**Beth Quin**	**30/11/43**	**03/02/47**		**Scrapped 12/69**

Made five North Atlantic crossings from July 1944 to August 1945. Sailed to Leyte to take part in operations and convoy screens from there to New Guinea and Okinawa.

BULL	**DE-693**	**Defoe**	**12/08/43**	**05/06/47**	**APD-78 (07/44)**	**Scrapped —**

October 1943 to July 1944, six convoys to Londonderry, Northern Ireland. After conversion, operated with UDTs in the Pacific, also furnishing fire support and screening at Lingayen Gulf in January 1945, Iwo Jima February-March, and Okinawa March-July. Performed occupation duties after end of war. Three battle stars.

BUNCH	**DE-694**	**Defoe**	**21/08/43**	**31/05/46**	**APD-79 (07/44)**	**Scrapped —**

Six convoys to the UK, November 1943 to December 1944. After conversion, operated with UDTs and fire support groups at Okinawa. On 4 April 1945, rescued 61 from *Dickerson (APD-21)*, sunk by *kamikaze.* Divided time between picket operations and convoy until July when she returned to the US. Two battle stars.

RICH	**DE-695**	**Defoe**	**01/10/43**			**Lostmine 08/06/4**

On 5 June 1944, sailed to the French coast with ships of "Operation Neptune" to screen heavy bombarding units at Utah Beach. On 8 June, was ordered to assist *Glennon (DD-840)* which had struck a mine. Immediately afterward, *Rich* struck three mines in succession which destroyed the DE with heavy casualties and loss of life. See chapter *Operations Overlord/Neptune.* One battle star.

SPANGLER	**DE-696**	**Defoe**	**31/10/43**	**08/10/58**	**NRF**	**Scrapped 11/69**

January 1943, as flagship of *Cortdiv 39,* escorted to Espiritu Santo, Guadalcanal, Purvis Bay, Bougainville, Majuro, Emirau, Rendova and Manus. In late May 1944, left Tulagi with load of hedgehogs for the famed *England (DE-635)*, *Raby (DE-698)* and *George (DE-697)* and joined in sortie from Manus to locate enemy subs, ultimately sunk by *England.* Remainder of war spent in South and West Pacific convoys. Two battle stars.

GEORGE	**DE-697**	**Defoe**	**20/11/43**	**08/10/58**	**NRF**	**Scrapped 06/69**

From winter to spring of 1944, escorted convoys in South Pacific. Operated in same hunter-killer group with the famed *England (DE-635.)* October until February 1945, resumed ASW patrols and convoy escort to New Guinea, Manus, Guam, Saipan, Philippines and Iwo Jima. Convoyed to Okinawa until surrender of Japan.

RABY	**DE-698**	**Defoe**	**07/12/43**	**22/12/53**	**NRF**	**Scrapped 06/68**

Beginning March 1943, escorted fast convoys from Guadalcanal to Manus. For a short period, engaged in hunter-killer activities in Solomons. Accompanied slaughter of six Japanese subs by *England (DE-635).* Spent remainder of war in convoy escort duties in south and west Pacific. Three battle stars.

MARSH	**DE-699**	**Defoe**	**12/01/44**	**16/08/58**	**NRF 58-69**	**Scrapped —**

On 25 March 1944, departed in convoy to the UK. Beginning 23 May, made three convoys to the Mediterranean. 9 July to mid-August, convoyed to various Mediterranean ports. On 14 August, sortied Naples for operation "Anvil," the invasion of Southern France. For next month, supplied shore bombardment and escorting as required. Reassigned to the Pacific, she arrived at Eniwetok on 20 December. Until May 1945, escorted in forward areas. Then assigned to pacification of by-passed islands in the Marianas, utilizing propaganda broadcasts or shelling, depending on cooperation of isolated garrisons. In August, resumed escort duties to end of war. One battle star.

CURRIER	**DE-700**	**Defoe**	**01/02/44**	**04/04/60**		**Target 07/67**

Her war began with a transatlantic convoy to Casablanca May and June 1944. In July, escorted convoys between Mediterranean ports. In August, along with 28 other escorts, convoyed 112 landing craft LCIs with US 45th Infantry to invade Southern France. In September, she became ComCortDiv of the "Naples Shuttle," supplying materiel to the troops. In December, arrived in forward Pacific area, convoying between ports. On 26 August, joined with *Osmus (DE-701)* to accept surrender of garrison on Rota. Two battle stars.

Lewis M. Andrews, Jr.

BUCKLEY CLASS

SHIP	NUMBER	YARD	COMPLETED	DECOM	MODIFIED	DISPOSAL

OSMUS DE-701 Defoe 17/08/43 15/03/47 Scrapped 12/72

As part of *CortDiv 39*, arrived in Solomons-New Hebrides area late 1943. In January 1945, shifted escort operations to Western Carolines, Admiralties and the Palaus. For balance of war, escorted vessels among Marianas and to Okinawa. One battle star.

E.V. JOHNSON DE-702 Defoe 18/03/44 18/06/46 Sold 09/68

Completed three escort of convoys to North Africa May to November 1944. Reassigned to the Pacific, convoyed to advance bases, including Okinawa. On 4 August 1944, engaged a submarine for three hours, sustaining damage but also possibly destroying or damaging the submarine.

HOLTON DE-703 Defoe 01/05/44 31/05/46 Scrapped 11/71

On 14 October 1944, freighter and tanker collided in convoy causing huge conflagration. Rescued crews and extinguished roaring fires throughout the night with own hoses and repair party. February 1945, sailed to Manus and convoyed in Philippine area to end of war.

CRONIN DE-704 Defoe 05/05/44 31/05/46 Scrapped 1970

July-November 1944, made two convoys to North Africa. On the second, rescued 24 survivors of the stricken *George W Mcknight.* Rerouted to the Pacific, she arrived in Manus January 1945. Assigned to the Philippine Sea Frontier, she escorted to the end of the war.

FRYBARGER DE-705 Defoe 18/05/44 09/12/54 Scrapped 12/72

She began her war assignments with two convoys to Bizerte July-November 1944. After receiving additional AA equipment, she arrived at Manus in January 1945. Until 30 August, convoyed to Lingayen Gulf, Manila and Zamboanga in the Philippines; Hollandia, Borneo; and Okinawa.

TATUM DE-789 Consol 22/11/43 15/11/46 APD-81 (12/44) Scrapped 05/61

March-August 1944, four Atlantic convoys, the first to the UK, the rest to and in vicinity of North Africa. In August, screened amphibious landings on south coast of France. After APD conversion, proceeded to Pacific forward areas, arriving Okinawa May 1945. On 29 May, attacked sequentially by four *kamikazes* and splashed all four. Sustained some damage, but was spared worse by a dud bomb in the wardroom. See chapter *Iwo Jima to Okinawa.* Two battle stars.

BORUM DE-790 Consol 30/11/43 15/06/46 Scrapped 04/67

Spent entire war in Atlantic. Early in 1944, underwent training for amphibious warfare. Assigned to "Operation Neptune," crossed the English Channel to screen bombardment forces on 6 June 1944. Remained in area to harass enemy occupation forces on Channel Islands and to engage E-boats. Hit by enemy shore batteries but suffered only light damage and casualties. Returned to the US too late to go to the Pacific. See chapter *Operations Overlord/Neptune.* A truly outstanding war diary. One battle star.

MALOY DE-791 Consol 13/12/43 28/05/65 Sold 03/66

Spent entire war in Atlantic. In March 1944, arrived in the UK for training in amphibious warfare. On D-Day, 6 June, crossed the Channel with attack forces. Screened the heavy units as they reduced enemy fortifications. Remained in the area raiding enemy shipping and dueling with German forts on the captured Channel Islands. Returned to the US too late for the Pacific War. See chapter *Operations Overlord/Neptune.* One battle star.

HAINES DE-792 Consol 2712/43 29/04/46 APD-84 (12/44) Scrapped 05/61

Mediterranean convoys to Casablanca and Alexandria June 1944. Took part in invasion of Southern France and Corsica until November. Headed for Pacific after conversion to APD only to learn of end of war when she reached Pearl Harbor. One battle star.

RUNELS DE-793 Consol 03/01/44 10/02/47 APD-85 (12/45) Scrapped 1962

March to May 1944, one convoy to the UK. Late May and June, convoy to *Casablanca.* In July, patrol operations along North African coast. Late July, assignment shifted to Naples area for Operation "Dragoon," invasion of Southern France. Convoyed troops and supplies from Mers-el-Kebir to French coast and guarded *LST*s bringing supplies from Corsica to Marseille. As APD, convoyed in Marianas and Okinawa from early July 1945 to end of war.

HOLLIS DE-794 Consol 24/01/44 16/10/56 APD-86 (12/44) Scrapped —

In spring of 1944, worked in research group to develop acoustic torpedo counter measures. End of May, sailed to Casablanca in carrier screen. August to December, convoyed vital supplies to Southern France theater. After APD conversion, became UDT flagship, but war ended by the time she reached Guam.

BUCKLEY CLASS

SHIP	NUMBER	YARD	COMPLETED	DECOM	MODIFIED	DISPOSAL
GUNASON	**DE-795**	**Consol**	**01/02/44**	**13/03/48**		**Target 07/74**

April-June 1944, convoyed to various ports in the Caribbean. July until January 1945, made three convoys to the Mediterranean and the UK. Spent Christmas-New Years aiding slow tow convoy that had been attacked by U-boats. Transferred to Pacific, took part in convoy escort in forward areas until surrender of Japan.

SHIP	NUMBER	YARD	COMPLETED	DECOM	MODIFIED	DISPOSAL
MAJOR	**DE-796**	**Consol**	**12/02/44**	**13/03/48**		**Sold 11/73**

From 4 July 1944 to 29 December, made several convoys to North Africa and to the UK. Transferred to the Pacific, she arrived Manus on 1 April 1945. Escorted convoys in forward areas.

SHIP	NUMBER	YARD	COMPLETED	DECOM	MODIFIED	DISPOSAL
WEEDEN	**DE-797**	**Consol**	**19/02/44**	**26/02/58**	**NRF 56-50**	**Sold 10/69**

March-December 1944, three convoys to the UK and North Africa. Departed for Pacific forward areas end of January 1945. Escorted to Hollandia, Ulithi, Leyte, Manila, Subic Bay, Zamboanga, Iloilo and Okinawa to end of war.

SHIP	NUMBER	YARD	COMPLETED	DECOM	MODIFIED	DISPOSAL
VARIAN	**DE-798**	**Consol**	**29/02/44**	**15/03/46**		**Sold 01/74**

Convoyed in Mediterranean bound convoys June to November 1944. On 26 December joined with *Hayter (DE-212)*, *Otter (DE-210)*, and *Harry E Hubbard (DE-748)* in hunter-killer group that sank *U-248* on 16 January 1945. On 24 April, joined with 10 other DEs to sink *U-546* which had torpedoed *Frederick C. Davis (DE-136)*. Operated in escort and training missions to end of war. See chapter *Twilight of the U-boats*. Two battle stars.

SHIP	NUMBER	YARD	COMPLETED	DECOM	MODIFIED	DISPOSAL
SCROGGINS	**DE-799**	**Consol**	**30/03/44**	**28/02/47**		**Sold 04/67**

June to November 1944, three convoys to Bizerte. Spent remainder of war on patrol and hunter-killer sweeps at Halifax, NS, and eastern US ports. In May and June, guarded *Guadalcanal (CVE 60)* as she trained pilots off Norfolk, Va.

SHIP	NUMBER	YARD	COMPLETED	DECOM	MODIFIED	DISPOSAL
J.W. WILKE	**DE-800**	**Consol**	**07/03/44**	**24/05/60**		**Sold 02/74**

After commissioning in March 1944, spent several months in convoy from US ports to Bizerte, the UK and France. December 1944 to May 1945, operated in a hunter-killer group in the Newfoundland-Nova Scotia area. Spent remainder of war as a student training ship at the Sub Chaser Training Center in Miami.

RUDDEROW CLASS — TURBO ELECTRIC DRIVE (TEV) 5" GUNS

The *Rudderow* class had turbo electric drives similar to the *Buckley* Class but differed from the latter in main armament with two 5"/38 caliber destroyer-type guns in movable mounts, one each fore and aft. The bridge was lower than those in the *Buckley* class, but the LOA was the same, ie 306'. Original plans called for 72 ships to be modified from the *Buckley* class before completion. However, 50 were transferred to the urgent APD program instead, leaving only 22 to be commissioned as DEs.

The Naval Reserve Fleet operated and maintained this class until the 1960s when most were disposed of, one going to Taiwan and another to Korea.

Most of this class saw heavy action in the Philippine liberation campaign, operating with the 7th Fleet.

Destroyer Escorts 224-225, 230-231, 579-589, 706-709.

MAJOR CHARACTERISTICS

Length Overall	306'-0"
Extreme Beam	36'-11"
Mean Draft	13'-09"
Standard Displacement	1,450 Tons
Designed Shaft Horsepower	12,000
Trial (Flank) Speed	24 Knots
Machinery	General Electric
Boilers (2) Manufacturers	BW, CE, FW
Fuel Capacity	340 Tons
Designed Complement	Off: 6, Enl: 180
Average Complement	Off: 12, Enl: 208

ARMAMENT

Main:	(2) 5"/38 cal Guns
Secondary:	(2) Twin 40mm Guns
	(10) 20mm Guns
ASW:	(1) Hedgehog
	(2) Depth Charge Racks
	(8) "K" Gun Projectors
Torpedoes:	(1) Triple Mount

RUDDEROW CLASS

SHIP	NUMBER	YARD	COMPLETED	DECOM	MODIFIED	DISPOSAL
RUDDEROW	**DE-224**	**Phila**	**15/05/44**	**15/01/46**		**Sold 06/68**

October 1944, steamed to New Guinea to join 7th Fleet. After some local escort, arrived in Luzon in January 1945. In January and February, escorted to landings in Lingayen Gulf and Subic Bay. Late February, assisted torpedoed destroyer *Renshaw (DD-499)* in Mindanao Sea. In March, escorted in operation "Victor IV" to occupy Zamboanga. Returning to Leyte, engaged in numerous convoy and screening operations to unload supplies and disembark troops in the area to end of war. Two battle stars.

DAY	**DE-225**	**Phila**	**10/01/44**	**15/05/46**		**Target 03/69**

Arrived New Guinea area November 1944 and convoyed locally until January 1945. Convoyed to Lingayen Gulf, fighting off three air attacks, thence to aid of Philippine guerrillas on Luzon. February and March, convoyed Manila, Subic and San Pedro Bays. Supported landings at Legaspi in April. Command ship for minesweepers in South China Sea in May. Joined Borneo invasion in June. Remained in Philippine area to end of war. Two battle stars.

CHAFFEE	**DE-230**	**Charleston**	**09/05/44**	**15/04/46**		**Sold 06/48**

January 1945, escorted attack forces to San Fabian, Lingayen area. On 23 January, lady luck smiled when a dud aerial torpedo penetrated the bow. April to June, convoyed and guarded landings in Southern Philippines. June and July, escorted reinforcements to Balikpapan, Borneo. For remainder of war, convoyed among Borneo, Philippines and Okinawa. Two battle stars.

HODGES	**DE-231**	**Charleston**	**27/05/44**	**22/06/46**		**Sold 1973**

January 1945, joined attack forces at Lingayen Gulf. Early on 9 January, attacked by *kamikaze*. The pilot misjudged target angle and crashed close aboard after knocking over foremast and various antennaes. No personnel casualties. In March, engaged in Philippine patrol and escort operations. On 11 April, bombarded enemy emplacements in Legaspi area. Patrol, escort and training duties to war's end. One battle star.

RILEY	**DE-579**	**Beth Hing**	**13/03/44**	**15/01/47**		**Taiwan 07/68**

In June 1944 with convoy UGS 46, fought off German aerial attack on 10 July before reaching Bizerte. Second convoy to North Africa in August. Underway for Pacific in October, arriving at Humboldt Bay on 11 December. The same month, began convoys to Leyte and the Lingayen assault area with TG 78.9. On 29 January, with operation "Mark VII" to Zimbales Province. Patrolled off Bataan and participated in numerous Philippine and East Indian convoys and landings. Two battle stars.

L.L.B. KNOX	**DE-580**	**Beth Hing**	**22/03/44**	**15/06/46**		**Sold 01/72**

June 1944, made two convoys to Bizerte. In November, sailed to the Pacific with *CortDiv 67.* December through June 1945, engaged in ASW, convoy and escort duties. While convoying in support of Lingayen Gulf landings, assisted in fighting off numerous suicide attacks. Joined in campaign to retake Southern Philippine Islands. Three battle stars.

McNULTY	**DE-581**	**Beth Hing**	**31/03/44**	**02/06/46**		**Sold 01/72**

In July 1944, on first convoy, helped repel an air attack while en route Bizerte. After second convoy to Tunisia, sailed to Pacific in November with *CortDiv 67.* Less than a day after arriving Hollandia, departed for Leyte with TG 789 with second supply group on 3 January 1945. On 12 January, several *kamikaze* attacks damaged two merchantmen and killed 100 soldiers. Continued escort duty to Lingayen Gulf and Leyte. With San Narcisso Attack Force in western Pacific to end of war. Two battle stars.

METIVIER	**DE-582**	**Beth Hing**	**07/04/44**	**01/06/46**		**Sold 05/69**

June to October 1944, in two convoys to North Africa. In Pacific, assigned to 7th Fleet. Steamed to Hollandia in November to engage in eight months of escort duty, including Lingayen Gulf landings, Subic Bay, and invasion of Okinawa on 4 May. At war's end, convoyed to Korea before heading back to San Diego. Three battle stars.

G.A. JOHNSON	**DE-583**	**Beth Hing**	**15/04/44**	**31/05/46**		**Sold 09/66**

June to October 1944, participated in two Mediterranean convoys and assisted in repelling an air attack on one of them. Headed for New Guinea in November and departed with cargo convoy for Lingayen Gulf in January 1945. On 12 January, the convoy was attacked by four *kamikazes*, but all ships came through unscathed. Continued with convoy escort to end of war. Subsequently, aided in reestablishing local control in Korea and China.

C.J. KIMMEL	**DE-584**	**Beth Hing**	**20/04/44**	**15/01/47**		**Target 11/69**

August 1944, convoyed to Oran and Naples, supporting invasion of Southern France. November 1944, sailed to Pacific to convoy troops from Hollandia to Leyte. In December and January 1945, joined San Fabian Attack Force to Lingayen Gulf, undergoing three successive days of enemy air assault. Balance of war in Southern Philippines attacking isolated Japanese garrisons. At Auqui Island, made daring rescue of 22 survivors of downed air transport while under enemy guns. One battle star.

RUDDEROW CLASS

SHIP	NUMBER	YARD	COMPLETED	DECOM	MODIFIED	DISPOSAL
D.A. JOY	**DE-585**	**Beth Hing**	**28/04/44**	**65 NRF**		**Sold 03/66**

August and September 1944, convoyed to Bizerte. Sailed to Hollandia to guard troop landings on Leyte in November. Escort and patrol duty in Philippines, covering several troop landings at Lingayen Gulf, Mangarin Bay and Mindoro. Escorted in Manila Bay area to end of war. Two battle stars.

SHIP	NUMBER	YARD	COMPLETED	DECOM	MODIFIED	DISPOSAL
LOUGH	**DE-586**	**Beth Hing**	**02/05/44**	**24/06/46**		**Sold 1969**

In June 1944, engaged in coastal convoys before escorting a convoy to Bizerte. Headed to the Pacific, arriving at Espiritu Santo to join the Third Fleet on 1 November. Convoyed in southwest Pacific and witnessed disastrous explosion of ammunition ship *Mount Hood (AE-11)* at Manus on 20 November. While protecting landing of 11th Airborne Division on Nasugbo on 31 January, engaged at least 20 suicide boats, sank several and rescued *PC-1129* survivors. Regrettably, two nights later, sank two friendly PTs that failed to correctly identify themselves. See narrative *The Philippine Campaign.* Three battle stars.

SHIP	NUMBER	YARD	COMPLETED	DECOM	MODIFIED	DISPOSAL
T.F. NICKEL	**DE-587**	**Beth Hing**	**09/06/44**	**22/02/58**		**Sold 12/72**

June to July 1944, convoyed to Bizerte with UGS 50. On return, headed for Pacific with *CortDiv 71.* At Espiritu Santo on 1 November, took dangerous aerial torpedo cargo to Seeadler Harbor on 7 November. Several area convoys to end of December. On 28 December, sailed with TG 78.1 and the San Fabian attack force, the 43d Infantry Division, in initial assault on Luzon. On 10 January, rescued five from transport *DuPage (AP-86)*, hit by *kamikaze.* Lengthy escort assignments including Subic Bay, Okinawa, and San Pedro. One battle star.

SHIP	NUMBER	YARD	COMPLETED	DECOM	MODIFIED	DISPOSAL
PEIFFER	**DE-588**	**Beth Hing**	**15/06/44**	**01/06/46**	**NRF**	**Target 05/67**

In company with *CortDiv 71*, arrived in Manus on 7 November 1944. After a convoy from Hollandia to Leyte, joined TG 78.5 on 28 December for invasion of Luzon. On 30 December, screened "Blue Beach" attack group to San Fabian assault area. Escorted various amphibious landings in the Philippines to the end of the war. One battle star.

SHIP	NUMBER	YARD	COMPLETED	DECOM	MODIFIED	DISPOSAL
TINSMAN	**DE-589**	**Beth Hing**	**26/06/44**	**11/05/46**	**NRF**	**Sold 05/72**

Reached Hollandia on 2 December 1944 and turned around to convoy to Leyte and subsequent area convoys. On 12 January 1945, her slow moving tows to Lingayen Gulf attacked by four *kamikazes*, two of which were splashed by other escorts. The next day, *Tinsman* knocked a raider out of the air. On 27 January, sailed with Amphibious Group 8 and the 11th Airborne Division to take Nasugbu Bay. That night, group was attacked by swarms of suicide "Q" boats. Aided DE *Lough* in sinking six. Numerous area convoys to end of war. See narrative *The Philippine Campaign.* Two battle stars.

SHIP	NUMBER	YARD	COMPLETED	DECOM	MODIFIED	DISPOSAL
DE LONG	**DE-684**	**Beth Quin**	**31/12/43**	**08/08/69**		**Target 02/70**

Arrived at Miami 10 March 1944 for training duty off Florida until the end of the war.

SHIP	NUMBER	YARD	COMPLETED	DECOM	MODIFIED	DISPOSAL
COATES	**DE-685**	**Beth Quin**	**24/01/44**	**30/01/70**		**Target 09/71**

Served as school ship for student officers and nucleus crews at Miami from April 1944 to September 1945.

SHIP	NUMBER	YARD	COMPLETED	DECOM	MODIFIED	DISPOSAL
E.E. ELMORE	**DE-686**	**Beth Quin**	**04/02/44**	**31/05/46**		**Sold 05/69**

April 1944, joined *Block Island* HUK. Returning from Casablanca on 29 May, *Block Island* and DE *Barr* torpedoed. Directed by OTC in *Ahrens*, *Elmore* sank *U-549.* Towed *Barr* until relieved by tug. Joined 7th Fleet in Hollandia in December and escorted reinforcements to Lingayen Gulf in January 1945. Provided AA cover for two days of intensive attacks. Operating from San Pedro, escorted several assaults in Philippines and Okinawa to end of war. See narrative *The Hunter-Killers.* Four battle stars.

SHIP	NUMBER	YARD	COMPLETED	DECOM	MODIFIED	DISPOSAL
HOLT	**DE-706**	**Defoe**	**09/06/44**	**02/07/46**		**Korea 06/63**

Steamed to New Guinea and arrived in November 1944. Joined 7th Fleet and departed on 28 November to screen carrier forces in Leyte Gulf. Sortied in December to escort forces to Mindoro. On 14 December, helped to shoot down several enemy aircraft attempting to interrupt the invasion. Returned to screening duty to San Pedro and Lingayen Gulf where she downed an attacking *kamikaze* close aboard on 23 January 1945. Convoyed and screened Subic Bay to Luzon and the Legaspi landings, then to the Borneo invasion. See narrative *The Philippine Campaign.* Two battle stars.

SHIP	NUMBER	YARD	COMPLETED	DECOM	MODIFIED	DISPOSAL
JOBB	**DE-707**	**Defoe**	**04/07/44**	**13/05/46**		**Sold 11/69**

Arrived in New Guinea to join 7th Fleet on 21 November 1944. Promptly assigned to a convoy to Leyte and then with a slow convoy to Mindoro. In the latter operation, beginning 13 December, experienced continual air raids and downed at least two aircraft without damage to convoy. Convoy escort duty briefly interrupted by striking a reef. In June 1945, screened landings in Borneo and other areas to end of war. See narrative *The Philippine Campaign.* Three battle stars.

RUDDEROW CLASS

SHIP	NUMBER	YARD	COMPLETED	DECOM	MODIFIED	DISPOSAL
PARLE	**DE-708**	**Defoe**	**29/07/44**	**07/62**	**NRF**	**Target 10/70**

Together with *CortDiv 60*, reported to 7th Fleet in January 1945. Assigned to Philippine Sea Frontier and carried out numerous operations among Kossol Roads, Leyte, Lingayen Gulf, Subic Bay, New Guinea, Okinawa, Ulithi and Hollandia.

SHIP	NUMBER	YARD	COMPLETED	DECOM	MODIFIED	DISPOSAL
BRAY	**DE-709**	**Defoe**	**04/09/44**	**10/05/46**	**APD-139 (07/45)**	**Target 03/63**

Assigned to *CortDiv12*, Atlantic Fleet and, during late 1944, participated in antisubmarine operations off Long Island. In 1945, trained with American submarine crews in Norfolk and New London. In March, went to aid of minesweeper *Heroic (AMc-84)*, saving her from sinking.

CANNON CLASS — DIESEL ELECTRIC (DET)

Outwardly, this class resembled the *Buckleys* except for a slightly shorter hull. The main difference lay in its diesel electric power plant and attendant lower shaft horse power and speed. The *Evarts* class was diesel direct drive whereas *Cannon* class ships used diesel power to create electricity to drive the vessels. Sixty-six of this class were commissioned in the US Navy. Six others were transferred to the Free French Navy.

Bronstein (DE 189), was one of the most famous of this class, and her commanding officer, Lieutenant Sheldon Kinney, was awarded the Navy Cross for spectacular operations against U-boats while with the *Block Island* hunter-killer group. A number of this class had additional antiaircraft batteries installed in lieu of torpedo tubes. As with the *Evarts* class, the navy looked on these ships as temporary expedients to meet the U-boat menace rather than as permanent construction.

Destroyer Escorts 112-113, 162-197, 739-750, 763-771

MAJOR CHARACTERISTICS

Length Overall	306'- 8"
Extreme Beam	36'- 8"
Mean Draft	11'- 8"
Standard Displacement	1,525 Tons
Designed Shaft Horsepower	6,000
Trial (Flank) Speed	21 Knots
Engines	General Motors
Fuel Capacity	305 Tons
Designed Complement	Off: 6, Enl: 180
Average Complement	Off: 11, Enl: 185

ARMAMENT

Main:	(3) 3"50 Caliber Guns
Secondary:	(1) Twin 40mm Guns
	(8) 20mm Guns
ASW:	(2) Depth Charge Racks
	(8) Depth Charge "K" Guns
	(1) Hedgehog
Torpedoes:	(1) Triple Tube

CANNON CLASS

SHIP	NUMBER	YARD	COMPLETED	DECOM	MODIFIED	DISPOSAL
CANNON	**DE-99**	**Dravo**	**26/09/43**	**19/12/44**		**Brazil 12/44**

November 1943 to December 1944, convoyed from Trinidad to Recife, Brazil, interrupted by one voyage from Brazil to Gibraltar with tankers and fuel for Mediterranean operations. Transferred to Brazil in December 1944.

SHIP	NUMBER	YARD	COMPLETED	DECOM	MODIFIED	DISPOSAL
CHRISTOPHER	**DE-100**	**Dravo**	**23/10/43**	**19/12/44**		**Brazil 12/44**

Commissioned October 1943 and decommissioned December 1944 at Natal, Brazil when transferred to Brazilian Navy.

SHIP	NUMBER	YARD	COMPLETED	DECOM	MODIFIED	DISPOSAL
ALGER	**DE-101**	**Dravo**	**12/11/43**	**10/03/45**		**Brazil 03/45**

From January 1944 to March 1945, convoyed Trinidad to Recife in Brazil when it was transferred to the Brazilian Navy.

SHIP	NUMBER	YARD	COMPLETED	DECOM	MODIFIED	DISPOSAL
THOMAS	**DE-102**	**Dravo**	**21/11/43**	**13/03/47**		**China 10/48**

In February 1944, joined *Block Island* Hunter-Killer Group and contributed to destruction of *U-79.* In April, assigned to Mediterranean convoys. In June, reassigned to *Card* Hunter-Killer Group. On 5 July, together with *Baker*, sank *U-233.* In March 1945, participated with other DEs in the sinking of *U-548.* See chapter *The Hunter-Killers.* Four battle stars.

SHIP	NUMBER	YARD	COMPLETED	DECOM	MODIFIED	DISPOSAL
BOSTWICK	**DE-103**	**Dravo**	**01/12/43**	**30/04/46**		**China 12/48**

In February 1944, assigned to the famous *Block Island* Hunter-Killer group. On 1 March, joined *Bronstein* and *Thomas* in sinking *U-709.* In April 1945, patrolled in the Northeast Atlantic attached to *Card* HUK and, on the 30th, assisted *Thomas*, *Coffman* and *Natchez* in sinking *U-48.* See chapters *The Hunter-Killers* and *Twilight of the U-boats.* Three battle stars.

SHIP	NUMBER	YARD	COMPLETED	DECOM	MODIFIED	DISPOSAL
BREEMAN	**DE-104**	**Dravo**	**12/12/43**	**26/04/46**		**China 10/48**

February 1944, attached to *Block Island* Hunter-Killer Group and participated in sinking *U-801* near Cape Verde Islands. In March 1945, joined *Bronstein* in picking up gold belonging to National Bank of Poland at Dakar, French West Africa, and transporting it to New York. Spent remainder of war in hunter-killer operations. See chapters *The Hunter-Killers* and *The Saga of the Polish Gold.* One battle star.

SHIP	NUMBER	YARD	COMPLETED	DECOM	MODIFIED	DISPOSAL
BURROWS	**DE-105**	**Dravo**	**19/12/43**	**14/06/46**		**Holland 06/50**

February 1944 to May 1945, seven convoys to the UK and one to Bizerte. In June, headed for the Pacific, arriving at Eniwetok Atoll, Marshall Islands on 13 August. Conducted antisubmarine sweeps to end of war. Operated between the Philippines and Okinawa and supported occupation of Japan.

SHIP	NUMBER	YARD	COMPLETED	DECOM	MODIFIED	DISPOSAL
CARTER	**DE-112**	**Dravo**	**03/05/44**	**10/04/46**		**China 12/48**

July 1944 to January 1945, convoyed to Bizerte and Oran in North Africa. On 22 April, in mountainous North Atlantic seas, this DE and *Neal A Scott (DE-769)* sank *U-518* in joint hedgehog attacks. After German surrender, captured *U-234* attempting to flee to a neutral country with a German Major General, Japanese officials and important cargo. See chapter *Twilight of the U-boats.* One battle star.

SHIP	NUMBER	YARD	COMPLETED	DECOM	MODIFIED	DISPOSAL
C.L. EVANS	**DE-113**	**Dravo**	**25/06/44**	**29/05/47**		**France 03/52**

October 1944 to May 1945, made five round trips to Glasgow, Southhampton, Plymouth and Le Havre. Training and plane guard duty to end of war.

SHIP	NUMBER	YARD	COMPLETED	DECOM	MODIFIED	DISPOSAL
LEVY	**DE-162**	**Fed Ship**	**13/05/43**	**04/04/47**		**Scrapped —**

For eight8 months following August 1943, screened oilers in Central and South Pacific operations. In early 1944, operated in screens for oilers in Hollandia, Truk, Satawan and Ponape. June to August, screened oilers for Admiral Mitscher's carriers in assault on Philippines. In early 1945, blockaded and bombarded by-passed garrisons. In August and September, accepted surrender of Mille and Jaluit Atolls. Five battle stars.

SHIP	NUMBER	YARD	COMPLETED	DECOM	MODIFIED	DISPOSAL
McCONNELL	**DE-163**	**Fed Ship**	**28/05/43**	**29/06/46**		**Scrapped 10/72**

September and October 1943, convoyed to Samoa, New Caledonia, New Hebrides and Guadalcanal. Until June 1944, operated from same area in convoys to Solomons. Participated in recapture of Guam July to August 1944. In logistics group TG 308, screened oilers carrying fuel for fast carrier attack forces in forays from Formosa to Mindanao. Performed patrol and bombardment missions against by-passed islands in the Marshalls to end of war. Three battle stars.

CANNON CLASS

SHIP	NUMBER	YARD	COMPLETED	DECOM	MODIFIED	DISPOSAL

OSTERHAUS DE-164 Fed Ship 12/06/43 29/06/46 Scrapped 11/72
Departing New Hebrides October 1943, made repeated convoys to Solomons advanced bases. On 11 October, with *Bebas (DE-10)*, quelled flames and rescued personnel from two2 torpedoed merchantmen. In succeeding months, escorted troops and supplies to Guadalcanal, Fijis and Marianas. July to November, covered recapture of Guam and gave logistics support to fast carriers in Philippine campaign. Spent remainder of war in convoys from Ulithi to advanced combat areas. Three battle stars.

PARKS DE-165 Fed Ship 23/06/43 03/46 Scrapped 07/72
Spent first half of 1944 convoying to Kossol Roads, Leyte, Lingayen, Subic, New Guinea, Okinawa, Ulithi and Hollandia. Engaged with frequent sound contacts but with negative results. Assigned to numerous post-war operations. Four battle stars.

BARON DE-166 Fed Ship 05/07/43 26/06/46 Uruguay 05/52
October 1943 to August 1944, escorted convoys among South Central Pacific Islands. Screen and fire support ship April to July 1944 in Hollandia landings, Truk-Satawan-Ponape raids and recapture of Guam. For remainder of war, engaged in hunter-killer, air-sea rescue, patrol, and escort duties.

ACREE DE-167 Fed Ship 19/07/43 01/04/46 Scrapped 07/72
October to June 1944, engaged in numerous convoys to the Societies, New Caledonia, Hebrides, Fijis, *Guadalcanal*, Noumea, and the Russell Islands. With TG 53.19 in Marianas invasion, supplied illuminating and harassing fire on Tinian. Continued escort and training operations to end of war. Five battle stars.

AMICK DE-168 Fed Ship 26/07/43 16/05/47 Japan 06/55
With *CortDiv 15*, made nine round trips to North Africa and Mediterranean between November 1943 and May 1945. One convoy attacked by German aircraft but no casualties. Barely arrived in Western Pacific when war ended.

ATHERTON DE-169 Fed Ship 29/08/43 10/12/45 Japan 06/55
Operating under Task Force 62, made several convoys to Casablanca, Bizerte and Oran. On 9 May 1945, between Boston and New York, together with *Moberly (PF-63)*, attacked and sank *U-853*. Arrived in Western Pacific in August 1945 to take part in picket stations and convoys to end of war. See chapter *Twilight of The U-boats*. One battle star.

BOOTH DE-170 Fed Ship 19/09/43 04/04/46 Philip 12/67
January 1 1944 to May 1945, eight convoys to the Mediterranean. Transferred to Pacific and escorted numerous convoys to various islands. At war's end, aided in accepting Japanese surrenders and evacuations from by-passed islands.

CARROLL DE-171 Fed Ship 24/10/43 19/06/46 Scrapped 12/66
Between January 1944 and May 1945, eight voyages to Gibraltar, Casablanca, Bizerte and Algiers. She arrived in Western Pacific at end of war. Searched for by-passed Japanese garrisons, accepted surrenders, supplied and supervised Japanese evacuations.

COONER DE-172 Fed Ship 21/08/43 25/06/46 Scrapped 07/72
November 1943 to May 1945, nine convoys to North Africa. Arrived in Hawaii at about time Japan surrendered. Post-war activities included guarding troops returning to the USA.

ELDRIDGE DE-173 Fed Ship 28/08/43 17/06/46 Greece 01/51
Between January and May 1944, made nine round trips to Casablanca, Bizerte and Oran to safely deliver convoys of men and materiel. Departed for the Pacific in May 1945. En route Saipan, contacted and attacked underwater object without results. Participated in Saipan-Ulithi-Okinawa convoys to end of war.

MARTS DE-174 Fed Ship 03/09/43 20/03/45 Brazil 03/45
From November 1943 to August 1944, convoyed and escorted in southern waters, including Trinidad, Recife, Bahia and Gibraltar. August - November, assigned to *CortDiv 24* as part of HUK operations with carrier *Tripoli*. Trained Brazilian seamen in vessel operations and turned the ship over to the Brazilian Navy in March 1945.

PENNEWILL DE-175 Fed Ship 15/09/43 01/08/44 Brazil 08/44
After shakedown in Caribbean, operated in convoys from Trinidad to Recife, Brazil, December 1943 to April 1944. From May to July 1944, engaged in sundry convoy and patrol duties in Caribbean and South Atlantic operations. On 28 July, was decommissioned and turned over to Brazilian Navy.

CANNON CLASS

SHIP	NUMBER	YARD	COMPLETED	DECOM	MODIFIED	DISPOSAL
MICKA	**DE-176**	**Fed Ship**	**23/09/43**	**12/06/46**		**Scrapped 06/67**

September 1943 to November 1944, escorted convoys from New York to Recife, Brazil, then attached to 4th Fleet for Mid-Atlantic hunter-killer operations. Detached in March 1945 for training exercises on Atlantic Coast and one convoy to Oran. Directed to the Pacific, she arrived at Pearl Harbor one day after Japan surrendered.

REYBOLD	**DE-177**	**Fed Ship**	**29/09/43**	**15/08/44**		**Brazil 08/44**

Sailed south in January 1944 to join 4th Fleet in South Atlantic antisubmarine warfare. Until July, convoyed from Recife to Trinidad, also Brazil to Gibraltar. At end of July, transferred to Brazilian Navy.

HERZOG	**DE-178**	**Fed Ship**	**06/10/43**	**01/08/44**		**Brazil 08/44**

After convoying in the Caribbean in late 1943 and early 1944, joined TG 416 in South Atlantic. On 15 June rescued German prisoners after their U-boat was sunk by aircraft. Turned over to Brazilian Navy on 1 August 1944 under terms of Lend-Lease agreement.

McANN	**DE-179**	**Fed Ship**	**11/10/43**	**15/08/44**		**Brazil 08/44**

February 1944, convoyed Caribbean to Recife, Brazil. En route, rescued 10 survivors of downed B-17. In July,ended convoy duty and joined screen of cruiser *Memphis* hunter-killer group searching for U-boats. Steamed to Natal in August to decommission and transfer ship to Brazilian Navy.

TRUMPETER	**DE-180**	**Fed Ship**	**16/10/43**	**05/12/47**		**Target 1973**

In February 1944, headed for Brazil with TG 272. In Rio de Janeiro in March, joined 4th Fleet and TG41.6 with its flag in carrier *Solomons.* For next five months, conducted ASW sweeps of South Atlantic. In September and October, convoyed Brazilian Expeditionary Force to Italian Front. Returned to New York in March 1945 and convoyed to Mediterranean at end of Atlantic war. Headed for Pacific in July, but war ended before she could reach combat area.

STRAUB	**DE-181**	**Fed Ship**	**25/10/43**	**17/10/47**		**Sold 08/73**

Departed New York December 1943 for Mediterranean convoy and ASW activities with carrier *Mission Bay.* In February 1944, sailed for Rio de Janeiro with carriers *Mission Bay* and *Wake Island.* In March, joined TG 41.6, led by carrier *Solomons.* In June, carrier planes sank a U-boat, and survivors were rescued by *Straub.* In August, patrolled out of Recife. Rejoined Mediterranean convoys at end of Atlantic war. Transferred to Pacific, but war with Japan ended before reaching combat area.

GUSTAFSON	**DE-182**	**Fed Ship**	**01/11/43**	**26/06/46**		**Holland 10/50**

On 20 February 1944, joined 4th Fleet based in Recife, Brazil. Convoyed Trinidad to Cape Horn to Cape of Good Hope and back. On 23 April, made unsuccessful attack on *U-860.* In company with other escorts, while on training exercises in Casco Bay, Maine, helped to sink *U-857* on 5 April 1945. In May, participated in convoys to Oran. Sailed for Hawaii when Japan surrendered in August. See chapter *Twilight of the U-boats.* One battle star.

S.S. MILES	**DE-183**	**Fed Ship**	**04/11/43**	**28/03/46**		**France 08/50**

In February 1944, convoyed in Marshalls vicinity. Guarded fleet oilers in strikes against Carolines and Hollandia area. During capture of Saipan and Tinian, splashed two enemy planes. Late 1944 and early 1945, supported Philippines recapture. Near Palau on 3 October, sank *I-177.* After guarding the invasion forces at Iwo Jima in February, screened the bombardment group at Okinawa and splashed a plane on 27 March. On 11 April, a *kamikaze* near miss killed one crew member and inflicted damage. After additional screening, sailed to US in July. See chapters *Pacific ASW* and *Iwo Jima to Okinawa.* Eight battle stars.

WESSON	**DE-184**	**Fed Ship**	**11/11/43**	**25/07/46**		**Italy 01/51**

Arriving at Roi, Kwajalein Atoll in February 1944, engaged a Japanese cutter, killing six and taking five prisoners. From that time forward, conducted convoying, screening and plane guard operations for Task Force 38. On 26 March 1945, attacked a submarine without conclusive evidence of a kill. On 27 March at Okinawa, splashed a *kamikaze* in furious attack. On 7 April, amid countless attacks, hit by *kamikaze* on torpedo mount, killing five, wounding 25 and one missing. Furious attacks continued to 14 April. Returned to US for deactivation December 1945. See chapter *Iwo Jima to Okinawa.* Seven battle stars.

CANNON CLASS

SHIP	NUMBER	YARD	COMPLETED	DECOM	MODIFIED	DISPOSAL
RIDDLE	**DE-185**	**Fed Ship**	**17/11/43**	**08/06/46**		**France 08/50**

February 1944, escorted to Marshalls and conducted ASW patrols in Roi-Kwajalein-Majuro-Manus areas until end September. On 4 July, along with DD *David W Taylor*, sank submarine *I-10*. October to January 1945, convoyed to Philippines invasion, then operated in the Admiralty, Western Carolines, Leyte and Marianas areas. In Okinawa on 12 April, attacked by two *kamikazes*, shot one down and was crashed by the other. One dead, several wounded and severe damage. Various duties without further incident to end of war. See chapters *Pacific Antisubmarine Warfare* and *Iwo Jima to Okinawa*. Twelve battle stars.

SHIP	NUMBER	YARD	COMPLETED	DECOM	MODIFIED	DISPOSAL
SWEARER	**DE-186**	**Fed Ship**	**24/11/43**	**27/08/47**		**France 08/50**

Arrived Eniwetok March 1944. Screened logistics in raids on Palau, Yap, Woleai, Truk, Satawan and Ponape through April. June to August, joined in Marianas capture, then Western Carolines and Leyte operations. In November, supported carrier strikes on Luzon, Formosa, China Coast, Nansei Shoto. In February 1945, convoyed to Iwo Jima invasion and fought off air attacks. Three grueling months on Okinawa picket station, splashing two *kamikazes*. Returned to US in July. See chapter *Iwo Jima to Okinawa*. Nine battle stars.

SHIP	NUMBER	YARD	COMPLETED	DECOM	MODIFIED	DISPOSAL
STERN	**DE-187**	**Fed Ship**	**01/12/43**	**26/04/46**		**Holland 05/51**

February through May 1944, made several convoys to the UK and North Africa. On arriving in the Pacific, assigned to Logistics Group 308 with Third Fleet December through January 1945. Supported invasions of Luzon and Iwo Jima through March. In April, convoyed to Okinawa. During that bloody battle, she downed five *kamikazes* without damage to herself. Returned to the US in July. See chapter *Iwo Jima to Okinawa*. Three battle stars.

SHIP	NUMBER	YARD	COMPLETED	DECOM	MODIFIED	DISPOSAL
O'NEILL	**DE-188**	**Fed Ship**	**06/12/43**	**02/05/46**		**Holland 10/50**

January to October 1944, sailed in Atlantic convoys, US ports to the UK, Morocco, Tunisia and Algiers. Then headed for Pacific and the Third Fleet, culminating in capture of Luzon. In February, assigned to Fifth Fleet and invasion of Iwo Jima. In April, assigned to Okinawa picket line, downed a bomber on 25 May and was hit next day by a *kamikaze*. The cost was two killed and 17 wounded. See chapter *Iwo Jima to Okinawa*. Three battle stars.

SHIP	NUMBER	YARD	COMPLETED	DECOM	MODIFIED	DISPOSAL
BRONSTEIN	**DE-189**	**Fed Ship**	**13/12/43**	**05/11/45**		**Uruguay 05/52**

In February 1944, attached to *Block Island* Hunter-Killer Group. On 1 March, together with *Thomas* and *Bostwick*, sank *U-709*. Later same day, she sank *U-603*. On 16 March, together with destroyer *Corry*, sank *U-801*. In company with *Breeman*, rescued the gold belonging to the National Bank of Poland at Dakar, French West Africa and brought it to New York. Remained in hunter-killer operations to end of war. See chapters *The Hunter-Killers* and *Saga of the Polish Gold*. Four battle stars.

SHIP	NUMBER	YARD	COMPLETED	DECOM	MODIFIED	DISPOSAL
BAKER	**DE-190**	**Fed Ship**	**23/12/43**	**04/05/46**		**France 03/52**

Two convoys to the Mediterranean February to May 1944. Subsequently attached to various hunter-killer groups. While operating with *Card* in TG 2210 on 5 July, forced *U-233* to surface after depth charge attacks, then engaged with shellfire. Sub crew abandoned before being rammed by *Thomas*. Took 31 survivors prisoner. Operated as plane guard for carrier to end of war. See chapter *The Hunter-Killers*. One battle star.

SHIP	NUMBER	YARD	COMPLETED	DECOM	MODIFIED	DISPOSAL
COFFMAN	**DE-191**	**Fed Ship**	**27/12/43**	**30/04/46**		**Sold 1973**

One convoy to Bizerte April-May 1944. In February 1945, joined in North Atlantic Barrier sweep. In April, joined with *Thomas*, *Bostwick* and PF *Natchez* in sinking *U-548*. See chapter *Twilight of the U-boats*. One battle star.

SHIP	NUMBER	YARD	COMPLETED	DECOM	MODIFIED	DISPOSAL
EISNER	**DE-192**	**Fed Ship**	**01/01/43**	**05/07/46**		**Holland 03/50**

In February 1944, became flagship of *CortDiv 55*. Made two Mediterranean convoys and five to the United Kingdom and France, guarding lifelines of war. Left for Pacific in June 1945 for screening and convoy duty to end of war.

SHIP	NUMBER	YARD	COMPLETED	DECOM	MODIFIED	DISPOSAL
GARFIELD THOMAS	**DE-193**	**Fed Ship**	**24/01/44**	**27/03/47**		**Greece 01/51**

March to September 1944, made three convoys New York to Bizerte. October to May 1945, five convoys to the United Kingdom. Arrived in Pearl Harbor in July and convoyed to forward combat areas until end of war.

SHIP	NUMBER	YARD	COMPLETED	DECOM	MODIFIED	DISPOSAL
WINGFIELD	**DE-194**	**Fed Ship**	**28/01/44**	**26/08/47**		**France 10/50**

May 1944 to May 1945, convoyed to North Africa and several ports in the UK. In July 1945, transferred to Pacific, but war ended before she could contact enemy. Spent next few months taking surrender of Japanese garrisons on isolated islands.

SHIP	NUMBER	YARD	COMPLETED	DECOM	MODIFIED	DISPOSAL
THORNHILL	**DE-195**	**Fed Ship**	**01/02/44**	**17/06/47**		**Italy 01/51**

May to September 1944, convoyed to North Africa. During next eight months, convoyed to England and France. In June 1945, headed for the Pacific and arrived day after Japan surrendered.

CANNON CLASS

SHIP	NUMBER	YARD	COMPLETED	DECOM	MODIFIED	DISPOSAL
RINEHART	**DE-196**	**Fed Ship**	**12/02/44**	**17/07/46**		**Holland 06/50**

May 1944 to May 1945, convoyed to Bizerte, Liverpool, Plymouth, Le Havre, Southhampton and Gourock in Scotland. Transferred to Pacific, arrived at Eniwetok shortly after Japanese surrender.

ROCHE	**DE-197**	**Fed Ship**	**21/02/44**	**22/09/45**		**MinedScuttled 03/46**

May to June 1944, convoyed to Bizerte. July to October, made another convoy to Bizerte and one to Plymouth. Throughout winter and spring 1944-1945, made five more convoys to the UK. On one convoy, rescued 11 men from a merchant ship after collision with another. In May, transferred to Pacific and arrived after Japanese surrender. Struck mine and scuttled in March 1946.

BANGUST	**DE-739**	**West Pipe**	**30/10/43**	**17/11/46**		**Peru 02/52**

February 1944 to August 1945, escorted and screened in various campaigns, including Kwajalein, Majuro, Palau, Yap, Ulithi-Wolesai, Saipan, Guam, Tinian, Battle of the Philippine Sea, Leyte. Escorted Third Fleet logistics in raids on Formosa, Nansei Shoto and Iwo Jima. Screened Fifth and Third Fleet raids on Japan. On 11 June 1945, sank Japanese submarine *R-42*. See chapter *Pacific Antisubmarine Warfare.* Eleven battle stars.

WATERMAN	**DE-740**	**West Pipe**	**30/11/43**	**31/5/46**		**Peru 10/49**

Escorted and screened heavy ships in the battles for the Marianas, Kwajalein, Majuro, Tarawa, and Makin in the Marshalls and Gilberts. Supported the invasion of the Western Carolines. Escorted service vessels that were bombing and destroying Japanese on Leyte. Caught in infamous 17 to 19 December typhoon, suffering considerable damage. Spent rest of war in convoy duty. See chapter *Pacific Typhoons.* Eight battle stars.

WEAVER	**DE-741**	**West Pipe**	**31/12/43**	**03/07/47**		**Peru 10/49**

Arrived Majuro the latter part of March 1944 to commence logistics service with Third and Fifth Fleets. Operating from Majuro, she guarded oilers supplying the fast carriers. Assignments took her to Truk, Satawan and Ponape in April and May. In the summer months, supplied carrier fuel for invasions of Western Carolines and Palaus. Weathered Typhoon Cobra. In last year of war, guarded fuel supplies for the assaults on Luzon, Iwo Jima, Okinawa and Japanese home islands. At end of war, joined in Japanese surrender ceremonies and occupation operations. See chapter *Pacific Typhoons.* Nine battle stars.

HILBERT	**DE-742**	**West Pipe**	**04/02/44**	**19/06/46**		**Sold 10/73**

On 2 May 1944, sailed to Kwajalein to join 5th Fleet for capture of Saipan and Tinian. Screened carriers in Admiral Marc Mitscher's command in Battle of Philippine Sea, followed by screening actions at Iwo Jima, Okinawa and Japanese home islands. After Japanese surrender, returned to USA in December 1945. Eight battle stars.

LAMONS	**DE-743**	**West Pipe**	**29/02/44**	**14/06/46**		**Sold 10/73**

June 1944, sailed in logistics screen supporting Saipan invasion. Continued screening for Pelelieu assault. Sailed with TG 30.8 for invasion of Leyte in October and spent next three months screening fleet oilers in Philippine campaign. In February 1945, guarded oilers in assault on Iwo Jima. In March, convoyed oilers to Okinawa and spent succeeding two months on picket duty without mishap. Next joined logistics screen for fast carrier raids on Japanese home islands. Nine battle stars.

KYNE	**DE-744**	**West Pipe**	**04/04/44**	**17/06/46**	**NRF**	**Sold 11/73**

Underway 12 August 1944 to screen supply task force for capture of Palau Islands. Sortied on 15 September to screen transports to Pelelieu and as convoy for wounded marines to rear base. To end of the year, screened logistics for Task Force 38. Participated in Luzon landings January 1945 and screened operations for assault on Iwo Jima. Continued screen and patrol operations in Okinawa campaign. Supplied logistic support for assault on Borneo and for Third Fleet attacks on Japan proper in July. Accompanied fleet into Yokahama Bay for Japanese surrender. Returned to the USA in November 1944. Six battle stars.

SNYDER	**DE-745**	**West Pipe**	**05/05/44**	**05/05/60**	**NRF 46-60**	**Scrapped 08/72**

October 1944, escorted to Eniwetok, Manus, Saipan and Kwajalein. Joined HUK (TG 123) in February 1945 and, with a few exceptions, continued until May. Then escorted to Okinawa and screened three damaged destroyers to Iwo Shima. Screened escort carriers supporting army operations on Okinawa. In July and August, performed ASW operations near Guam until war ended.

HEMMINGER	**DE-746**	**West Pipe**	**30/05/44**	**17/06/46**	**NRF 46-50**	**Thailand 07/59**

Arrived Pearl Harbor in August 1944. Participated in training exercises and hunter-killer convoys to Eniwetok. In April 1945, escorted convoys to Okinawa and screened carriers neutralizing Sakishima Gunto. Supported ground forces on Okinawa and carriers attacking Kyushu.

CANNON CLASS

SHIP	NUMBER	YARD	COMPLETED	DECOM	MODIFIED	DISPOSAL

BRIGHT | **DE-747** | **West Pipe** | **30/06/44** | **19/04/46** | | **France 11/50**

24 November 1944 to April 1945, operated with a hunter-killer group, TG 123, between Hawaiian and Marshall Islands. Assigned to picket duty at Okinawa, she sustained a *kamikaze* crash close aboard her stern, wounding two men and demolishing after portion of the ship. Shortly after, returned to the US. See chapter *Iwo Jima to Okinawa.* One battle star.

TILLS | **DE-748** | **West Pipe** | **08/08/44** | **21/06/46** | **NRF 46-58** | **Target 04/69**

From February 1944, conducted extensive convoy operations among Hawaii, the Marshalls and Eniwetok. In May 1945, convoyed extensively from Ulithi to Okinawa during period of fierce enemy resistance. Screened fast carriers for strikes on Japanese home islands until end of war.

ROBERTS | **DE-749** | **West Pipe** | **02/09/44** | **03/03/46** | **NRF 46-50** | **Target 1968**

In November 1944, joined HUK with CVE *Corregidor.* January and February 1945, operated in the Marshalls. In March, group searched in vain for Lt. General M.F. Harmon USA whose plane was lost. In April and May, convoyed to and from the Okinawa battle area. In June, escorted to Guam and conducted patrols into July. Continued escort assignments to end of war and shortly thereafter. Returned to the US in October. One battle star.

McCLELLAND | **DE-750** | **West Pipe** | **19/09/44** | **15/05/46** | **NRF 47-59** | **Sold 1973**

January 1945, sailed in logistics screen for assault on Iwo Jima, fighting off numerous air bombing and *kamikaze* attacks. Arrived in Okinawa in April and participated in convoys to islands in the Ryukyus. Also assigned to picket line where she splashed a *kamikaze* on 1 June. Assigned to TG 308, she screened oilers refueling the fast carriers that were attacking Japanese home islands. See chapter *Iwo Jima to Okinawa.* Three battle stars.

CATES | **DE-763** | **Tampa** | **15/12/43** | **28/03/47** | | **France 11/50**

February to May 1944, two convoys to North Ireland. Took part in various training duties and two additional transatlantic convoys before reassignment to the Western Pacific. Arrived at about time Japan surrendered.

GANDY | **DE-764** | **Tampa** | **07/02/44** | **17/06/46** | | **Italy 01/51**

On second day of first voyage to the UK in April 1945, joined *Joyce* and *Peterson* in hunt for U-boat that had torpedoed *Pan Pennsylvania.* Rammed *U-550* after sub was depth charged to surface by *Joyce.* Sub sank. Four *Gandy* men injured. Five more transatlantic convoys May 1944 to May 1945. Sailed for Pacific and reached forward areas at time of Japanese surrender. See chapter *Convoys to the United Kingdom.* One battle star.

E.K. OLSEN | **DE-765** | **Tampa** | **10/04/44** | **17/06/46** | **NRF 46-50** | **Sold 10/73**

August 1944 to May 1945, six convoys to the UK. On fifth voyage rescued two men and escorted damaged French cruiser and merchantman to Azores after collision. After transfer to Pacific, escorted ships to Manila and Yokohama before returning to USA.

SLATER | **DE-766** | **Tampa** | **01/05/44** | **26/09/47** | | **Greece 03/51**

In remaining months of 1944 to May 1945, made five convoys to the UK. In June 1945, transferred to Pacific and arrived at Eniwetok about the same time Japan surrendered. After several years in the Greek Navy, was maintained in floating, but not operating, condition. The Destroyer Escort Sailors Association was anxious to obtain a WW II DE for posterity The Greek government returned it to DESA without charge, and expenses to tow it to the US along with maintenance were paid for by private subscription from DE veterans. Permanently docked in Hudson River at Albany, N. Y. as a DE museum. In early September 1993, she arrived at the Intrepid Maritime museum on the West Side of Manhattan, New York, and will remain there for future generations to see the part played by their forebears in WW II.

OSWALD | **DE-767** | **Tampa** | **12/06/44** | **30/04/46** | | **Scrapped 08/72**

August 1944 through May 1945, made 11 convoys across the North Atlantic with loss of only one merchant vessel, *SS Jacksonville.* Participated in unsuccessful search for attacker. Following end of war with Germany, operated in various training exercises.

EBERT | **DE-768** | **Tampa** | **12/07/44** | **14/06/46** | | **Greece 03/51**

Guarded several convoys across the North Atlantic October 1944 to May 1945. After German surrender, sailed to Pacific in June 1945. Escorted occupation troops to Japan before returning to United States.

CANNON CLASS

SHIP	NUMBER	YARD	COMPLETED	DECOM	MODIFIED	DISPOSAL
N.A. SCOTT	**DE-769**	**Tampa**	**31/07/44**	**30/04/46**		**Sold 1968**

December 1944, escorted convoy UGS-63 to Oran. On return trip with GUS-63 in January 1945, convoy attacked by U-boat, and *Scott* took over ASW search. Her hedgehog attacks were rewarded with undersea explosions. However, British escorts relieved her as *Scott* returned to convoy station. On 22 April, operating with *Carter (DE-112),* sank *U-518* while on North Atlantic Barrier Patrol. Upon German surrender, escorted surrendering U-boats to US ports. See chapter "Twilight of the U-boats". One battle star.

SHIP	NUMBER	YARD	COMPLETED	DECOM	MODIFIED	DISPOSAL
MUIR	**DE-770**	**Tampa**	**30/08/44**	**09/47**		**Korea 02/56**

Starting December 1944, convoyed from US ports to Mediterranean and also participated in hunter-killer group in barrier patrol. After German collapse, accepted U-boat surrenders, including *U-234* with high ranking *Luftwaffe* officers and civilian technicians. Participated in training exercises to end of war.

SHIP	NUMBER	YARD	COMPLETED	DECOM	MODIFIED	DISPOSAL
SUTTON	**DE-771**	**Tampa**	**12/12/44**	**19/03/48**		**Korea 02/56**

A late arrival from the shipyard, she was assigned to *CortDiv 79* and sailed to Argentia, Newfoundland, in early March 1945. As part of the Barrier patrol, she made ASW sweeps until German surrender in May. She participated in taking surrendered U-boats to ports in the US. One sub, *U-234*, yielded, among her prisoners, General der Flieger Ulrich Kessler of the *Luftwaffe.* After some further duties on the East and Gulf Coasts, she was placed in reserve.

EDSALL CLASS — FAIRBANKS MORSE DIESELS (FMR)

This class produced a total of 85 destroyer escorts. In outward appearance, *Edsall* class ships were similar to the *Buckley* class. The hull differed from the *Evarts* diesels ships essentially in its length; it was of the long hull design, 306 feet. Although originally scheduled to have two 5"/38 caliber main armament, all but one had the more traditional three 3"/38 caliber guns in circular shields.

They were powered by Fairbanks Morse diesel engines (FMR). There were many DEs of note in this class such as *Pillsbury (DE-133)* and *Chatelain (DE-149)* which aided in capturing *U-505*. Several were heavily engaged in Mediterranean convoys. There were several disasters too, including *Leopold (DE-319)*, *Holder (DE-401) Menges (DE-320)*, *Frederick C. Davis (DE-136)* and *Fessenden (DE-142)*. Most of this class were in transatlantic convoys, but many also served in hunter-killer (HUK) task groups, the U-boat killers. Thirty *Edsalls* were manned by Coast Guard crews.

At a later date, additional 20mm antiaircraft guns were mounted in the stern area. The triple torpedo tubes on ships listed below as standard armament were ultimately replaced by director controlled 40mm antiaircraft guns.

Destroyer Escorts 238-255, 316-338, 382-401.

MAJOR CHARACTERISTICS

Length Overall	306'
Length at Waterline	300'- 0"
Extreme Beam	36'-10"
Mean Draft	12' - 03"
Displacement	1490 Tons
Shaft Horsepower	6,000
War Endurance	5,100 mi/12 Knots
Trial (flank) speed	21 Knots
Fuel Capacity	310 Tons
Average Complement	Off: 11, Enl: 202 men

ARMAMENT

Main:	(3) 3"50 Caliber Guns
Secondary:	(1) Twin 40mm Guns
	(8) 20mm Guns
ASW:	(2) Depth Charge Racks
	(8) "K" Gun Projector
	(1) Hedgehog
Torpedoes:	(1) Triple Tube

EDSALL CLASS

<table>
<tr><th>SHIP</th><th>NUMBER</th><th>YARD</th><th>COMPLETED</th><th>DECOM</th><th>MODIFIED</th><th>DISPOSAL</th></tr>
<tr><td>EDSALL</td><td>DE-129</td><td>Consol</td><td>10/04/43</td><td>11/06/46</td><td></td><td>Sold 06/68</td></tr>
<tr><td colspan="7">Started career as training ship at SCTC Miami. March 1944 to June 1945, participated in several convoys to the UK and Mediterranean as well as training exercises. On sixth convoy, went to rescue and extinguished fires on two tankers that collided.</td></tr>
<tr><td>JACOB JONES</td><td>DE-130</td><td>Consol</td><td>29/04/43</td><td>26/07/46</td><td></td><td>Sold 07/71</td></tr>
<tr><td colspan="7">July to December 1943, operated in Mediterranean convoys. January 1944 to June 1945, screened convoys to the United Kingdom. Up to the time of the German surrender, had totalled 20 Atlantic crossings, including numerous ASW patrols and one attack on a suspected U-boat. In August 1945, she sailed for the Pacific area as the Japanese were preparing to surrender.</td></tr>
<tr><td>HAMMANN</td><td>DE-131</td><td>Consol</td><td>17/05/43</td><td>25/10/45</td><td></td><td>Sold 10/72</td></tr>
<tr><td colspan="7">July 1943 to March 1944, participated in convoys to North Africa, during which time she made several submarine attacks on enemy submarines but could not record kills. March to November 1944, traversed the North Atlantic in convoys to the United Kingdom. On one crossing, rescued 70 survivors from torpedoed merchant ship Lone Jack. Sailed for the Pacific July 1945, but Japan surrendered before she could reach forward combat areas.</td></tr>
<tr><td>R.E. PEARY</td><td>DE-132</td><td>Consol</td><td>31/05/43</td><td>13/06/47</td><td></td><td>Sold 09/67</td></tr>
<tr><td colspan="7">From March 1944 to June 1945, escorted ten convoys to the UK and one to France in July. While returning to New York in March 1945, two merchant vessels collided, and Peary escorted one to harbor. The war in the Pacific ended while en route, and she was redirected to the East Coast of US.</td></tr>
<tr><td>PILLSBURY</td><td>DE-133</td><td>Consol</td><td>07/06/43</td><td>20/06/60</td><td>DER</td><td>Sold 07/65</td></tr>
<tr><td colspan="7">After four convoys to Casablanca, joined Guadalcanal (CVE-60) HUK in North Atlantic. On 8 April 1944, in company with Flaherty (DE-135), sank U-515 after successful hedgehog attack and lively surface engagement. On 4 June, near Cape Verde Islands, gained sound contact on U-505. Together with Chatelain (DE-149), and Jenks, brought the sub to the surface with depth charge attacks. Withering fire disposed of sub gun crews, and she was captured along with prisoners - an intelligence bonanza. On 24 April 1945, Pillsbury sank U-546. Presidential Unit Citation. See chapter The Hunter-Killers. Five battle stars.</td></tr>
<tr><td>POPE</td><td>DE-134</td><td>Consol</td><td>25/06/43</td><td>17/05/46</td><td></td><td>Sold 01/71</td></tr>
<tr><td colspan="7">After three convoys to the Mediterranean, attached to Guadalcanal (CVE-60) HUK. Assisted in sinking of U-515 and capture of U-505 in April 1944. Continued with HUK operations to end of war in Atlantic, too late to go to the Pacific. Presidential Unit Citation. See chapter The Hunter-Killers. Three battle stars.</td></tr>
<tr><td>FLAHERTY</td><td>DE-135</td><td>Consol</td><td>26/06/43</td><td>17/06/46</td><td></td><td>Sold 11/66</td></tr>
<tr><td colspan="7">September 1943 to February 1944, three convoys to Casablanca. In March, joined Guadalcanal (CVE-60) HUK. On 9 April, received part credit for sinking of U-515. On 4 June, screened carrier while other escorts captured U-505. In April 1945, sailed to Argentia, Newfoundland, to join barrier patrol. After torpedoing of Frederick C. Davis (DE-136), recovered survivors and joined other DEs in sinking of U-546. Rescued five prisoners, including captain. Presidential Unit Citation. See narratives The Hunter Killers and Twilight of the U-boats. Four battle stars.</td></tr>
<tr><td>FREDERICK C. DAVIS</td><td>DE-136</td><td>Consol</td><td>14/07/43</td><td></td><td></td><td>Torpedoed</td></tr>
<tr><td colspan="7">October to December 1943, convoyed to North Africa under severe air attack. Also participated in sinking of U-73. In January 1944, escorted troops and materiel to the Anzio landings. Patrolled area for six months, fighting off air raids and jamming radio controlled air launched missiles. Frequently came under shore bombardment. In June and July, rendered same services in invasion of southern France. While on barrier patrol in North Atlantic, torpedoed with heavy loss of life while attacking U-546. Navy Unit Commendation. See chapters Convoys to the Mediterranean and Twilight of the U-boats. Four battle stars.</td></tr>
<tr><td>H.C. JONES</td><td>DE-137</td><td>Consol</td><td>21/07/43</td><td>02/05/47</td><td></td><td>Sold 07/72</td></tr>
<tr><td colspan="7">Departed USA for her first Mediterranean convoy October 1943. On 6 November, downed an attacking enemy plane. On 26 November, downed enemy fighter plane and studied tactics of glider bomb launchings. Jones and Frederick C. Davis (DE-136) were subsequently fitted with powerful electronic jamming sets. As a result, in January 1944 off the Anzio beachhead, and again in operation "Anvil" off the French Mediterranean coast in August, they decoyed most glider bombs in their vicinity and also furnished other units with early attack warnings, for which she received Navy Unit Commendation. Participated in North Atlantic barrier patrol January 1944 to German surrender. Sailed for Pacific June 1945, but Japan surrendered when she reached Pearl Harbor. See chapter Convoys to the Mediterranean. Three battle stars.</td></tr>
</table>

Lewis M. Andrews, Jr.

EDSALL CLASS

SHIP	NUMBER	YARD	COMPLETED	DECOM	MODIFIED	DISPOSAL
D.L. HOWARD	**DE-138**	**Consol**	**29/07/43**	**17/06/46**		**Sold 10/72**

October 1943 to March 1944, three convoys to Casablanca. Operated with HUK *Core (CVE-13*, *Wake Island (CVE-65*, *Mission Bay (CVE-59)* to end of the Atlantic war. Arriving in Pacific at end of war with Japan, engaged in occupation of various islands before returning to USA.

SHIP	NUMBER	YARD	COMPLETED	DECOM	MODIFIED	DISPOSAL
FARQUHAR	**DE-139**	**Consol**	**05/08/43**	**14/06/46**		**Sold 10/72**

October 1943 marked beginning of three convoys to Casablanca. In April 1944, sailed again to the Mediterranean as part of hunter-killer group organized around the carrier *Card (CVE-11)*. In June 1944, attached to *Wake Island (CVE-65)*. On 9 June 1944, rushed to aid of torpedoed DE *Fiske (DE-143)* and recovered 186 survivors. In September, began convoy duty with carrier *Wake Island (CVE-65)* in South Atlantic. On 6 May 1945, obtained contact on U-boat and, with other escorts, sank last U-boat of war, *U-881*. Arrived at Pearl Harbor in time for Japanese surrender. See chapter *Twilight of the U-boats*. One battle star.

SHIP	NUMBER	YARD	COMPLETED	DECOM	MODIFIED	DISPOSAL
J.R.Y. BLAKELY	**DE-140**	**Consol**	**16/08/43**	**14/06/46**		**Sold 01/71**

October 1943-March 1944, three convoys to Mediterranean. Assigned to *Core (CVE-13)* HUK until May 1944. In June, joined *Wake Island (CVE-65)* HUK. After wide ranging search, task force located and destroyed *U-804*. Made several depth charge attacks on a sub after torpedoing of *Fiske (DE-143)*. In September, attached to *Mission Bay (CVE-59)* HUK where she took part in her first successful sinking, the *U-1062*. With the *Tripoli (CVE-64)* HUK patrolled South Atlantic until November 1944. Early in 1945, rejoined *Mission Bay* group in Barrier Patrol until German surrender. Sailed to Pacific only to join in victory celebrations in Pearl Harbor. See chapter *The Hunter-Killers*. One battle star.

SHIP	NUMBER	YARD	COMPLETED	DECOM	MODIFIED	DISPOSAL
HILL	**DE-141**	**Consol**	**16/08/43**	**07/06/46**		**Sold 10/72**

After training period, made five Atlantic crossings to Mediterranean, guarding supplies for the Italian and Southern French offensives. Early in 1945, joined *Mission Bay (CVE-59)* in mid-Atlantic Barrier Patrol convoy sweeps and plane guard. In July, sailed to Pearl Harbor only to learn of Japanese capitulation before arrival. Directed to return to mainland US.

SHIP	NUMBER	YARD	COMPLETED	DECOM	MODIFIED	DISPOSAL
FESSENDEN	**DE-142**	**Consol**	**25/08/43**	**30/06/60**	**DER-142**	**Target 12/67**

November 1943 - March 1944, escorted two convoys to Casablanca. On 20 April, her third such crossing, convoy heavily attacked by large German aircraft formation, sinking one DD and two DEs. In Gibraltar convoy in June, escorted two surrendered Italian submarines. Subsequently, joined *Mission Bay (CVE-59)* HUK. On 3 September 1944, with two other DEs, sank *U-1062* near Cape Verde Islands. Patrolled South Atlantic until November when she participated in training until February 1945. Joined in Barrier Patrol to end of Atlantic war. Sailed to Pacific but too late for action. Accepted surrender of Wotje garrison and evacuated Japanese personnel. See chapters *Convoys to the Mediterranean* and *The Hunter-Killers*. Two battle stars.

SHIP	NUMBER	YARD	COMPLETED	DECOM	MODIFIED	DISPOSAL
FISKE	**DE-143**	**Consol**	**25/08/43**			**Sunk 02/08/44**

December 1943 to May 1944, convoyed to the Mediterranean On third such run, convoy attacked by German bombers, but *Fiske* was unscathed. Subsequently, joined *Wake Island (CVE-65)* HUK. On 2 August 1944, this DE and *Douglas L Howard (DE-138)* located and attacked *U-804*. *Fiske* was torpedoed, broke in half and sank. Thirty killed and fifty seriously wounded. Survivors rescued by *Farquhar (DE-139)*. See chapter *The Hunter Killers*. Two battle stars

SHIP	NUMBER	YARD	COMPLETED	DECOM	MODIFIED	DISPOSAL
FROST	**DE-144**	**Consol**	**30/08/43**	**18/06/46**		**Sold 12/66**

After one North African convoy November-December 1943, joined *Croatan (CVE-25)* HUK. On 26 April 1944, joined other escorts in sinking *U-488*. While guarding a convoy to Casablanca on 11 June, made initial contact and attack on *U-490*; escorts blasted it to the surface and sank it with gunfire, *Frost* taking 13 prisoners. On 3 July, she thwarted a torpedo attack on her own ship and sank *U-154*. In September, rescued survivors of capsized *Warrington (DD-383)*. On nights of 15-16 April 1945, together with *Stanton (DE-247)*, sank *U-880* and *U-1235*. See chapters *The Hunter Killers* and *Twilight of the U-boats*. Presidential Unit citation and seven battle stars.

SHIP	NUMBER	YARD	COMPLETED	DECOM	MODIFIED	DISPOSAL
HUSE	**DE-145**	**Consol**	**30/08/43**	**06/65**	**NRF**	**Sold 06/74**

Two convoys to Casablanca interspersed with training November 1943-February 1944. In March, transferred to *Croatan (CVE-25)* HUK. On 7 April, escorts blasted *U-856* to surface, then sunk by *Huse* and *Champlin (DD-601)* gunfire. On 26 April, escorts sank *U-488*. After a severe beating with depth charges and hedgehogs, *U-490* was caught on surface and sunk by gunfire on 11-12 June. On three occasions, *Huse* recovered downed pilots from carrier. Sailed for Pearl Harbor only to learn of war's end on radio. See chapters *The Hunter-Killers* and *Twilight of the U-boats*. Five battle stars.

EDSALL CLASS

SHIP	NUMBER	YARD	COMPLETED	DECOM	MODIFIED	DISPOSAL
INCH	**DE-146**	**Consol**	**08/09/43**	**17/05/46**		**Sold 10/72**

Early in 1945, joined *Croatan (CVE-25)* HUK. Took part in several U-boat attacks. On 11-12 June, joined *Huse (DE-145)* and *Frost (DE-243)* in sinking *U-490* with gunfire after dumping 40 depth charges on her; took 60 enemy POWs. On 3 July, took part in sinking *U-154.* Sailed to Hawaii in August 1945, but Japan surrendered before she was sent to forward areas. See chapter *The Hunter-Killers.* Four battle stars.

BLAIR	**DE-147**	**Consol**	**13/09/43**	**28/06/46**	**DER-147 (12/57)**	**Sold 12/72**

Starting November 1943, spent the next 20 months in transatlantic convoys, including Casablanca, the United Kingdom and the European continent. Also attached to a hunter-killer group. The war terminated while en route to the Pacific.

BROUGH	**DE-148**	**Consol**	**18/09/43**	**22/03/46**		**Sold 10/66**

Made 24 round trips across the Atlantic, escorting allied shipping to European ports. Shortly after commissioning and shakedown in Bermuda, ran into fierce storm that killed her commanding officer, LCDR Kenneth J Hartley, while he was supervising damage control on the open deck.

CHATELAIN	**DE-149**	**Consol**	**22/09/43**	**14/06/46**		**Sold 08/73**

Atlantic convoys November 1943 to March 1944. Subsequently assigned to *Guadalcanal (CVE-6)* HUK. Joined in the sinking of two U-boats and capture of a third. First was *U-515* while en route Casablanca to US on 9 April 1944. The captured sub was *U-505*, in one of the most dramatic events of the Atlantic war, earning the Presidential Unit Citation for entire group. *Chatelain* was first to gain contact and blast the U-boat to the surface. The third was *U-546*, the sub that sank *Frederick C. Davis (DE-136).* See chapter *The Hunter Killers.* Five battle stars.

NEUNZER	**DE-150**	**Consol**	**27/09/43**	**01/47**		**Sold 07/72**

Beginning January 1944, made four convoys to Mediterranean. In unusual experience during second convoy homeward bound, fueled two surrendered Italian submarines underway. Detached and assigned to *Guadalcanal (CVE-60)* HUK until November. Went through punishing storm. After torpedoing of *Frederick C. Davis (DE-136)* on 24 April 1945, joined six other DEs to hunt down and sink the attacker, *U-546.* Made last convoy of the Atlantic war. See chapter *Twilight of the U-boats.* One battle star.

POOLE	**DE-151**	**Consol**	**29/09/43**	**01/47**		**Sold 01/71**

After one convoy to Casablanca, arriving January 1944, shifted to North Atlantic convoys for next 15 months, escorting high speed tankers and transports to the UK and the European continent. In June 1945, acting as *ComCortDiv 22*, sailed to Honolulu and conducted patrols for balance of war.

PETERSON	**DE-152**	**Consol**	**29/09/43**		**ASW**	**Sold 08/73**

Early December 1943, first convoy to Casablanca, then shifted to North European operations. *Leopold (DE-319)* torpedoed in convoy 1 March 1944. On 16 April, joined *Gandy (DE-764)* and *Joyce (DE-317)* to rescue survivors of *Pan Pennsylvania* and to sink *U-550* in blistering fire fight with depth charges, main batteries and ramming. Continued convoys to April 1945 and headed for Pacific in June with *CortDiv 22.* The war ended shortly thereafter. See chapter *Convoys to the United Kingdom.* One battle star.

STEWART	**DE-238**	**Brown**	**31/05/43**	**27/03/46**		**Memorial**

June 1943 to February 1944, carried out various training assignments. After one convoy to Argentia, Newfoundland, returned to training assignments in the Caribbean. Also part of HUK sweeps in Caribbean and East Coast. June to January 1945, made three more convoys to the UK. Reached Pearl Harbor at time of Japanese surrender and returned to East Coast of US.

STURTEVANT	**DE-239**	**Brown**	**16/06/43**	**31/10/56**	**DER (10/56)**	**Scrapped 09/73**

On 24 September 1944, she got underway for what would be 21 months of transatlantic convoy. The first three were to Casablanca and Gibraltar The next five were to Londonderry, Northern Ireland. She rounded out her Atlantic experience with two convoys each to Liverpool and Cardiff and one to Southampton. In June 1945, set out for the broad Pacific, but that war ended before she could get beyond Hawaii.

MOORE	**DE-240**	**Brown**	**01/07/43**	**30/06/47**		**Target 04/74**

September 1943 to year end, two convoys to North Africa. In March 1944, after extensive training exercises, joined *Tripoli (CVE-64)* HUK for South Atlantic operations. For balance of European war, served with *Core (CVE-13)* HUK along East Coast US in ASW sweeps. In June, sailed with other DEs as *ComCortDiv 7* to the Pacific. Ten days after arrival in Hawaii, came news of Japan's surrender.

EDSALL CLASS

SHIP	NUMBER	YARD	COMPLETED	DECOM	MODIFIED	DISPOSAL
KEITH	DE-241	Brown	19/07/43	20/07/46		Scrapped 11/72

Following extensive East Coast US convoys, joined *Tripoli (CVE-64)* HUK in North and South Atlantic sweeps, Brazil to Newfoundland. In July, assigned to HUK operations with *Core (CVE-13)*. On 30 August, she launched hedgehog attacks without result. On 23-24 April 1945, escorts contacted U-boat that had torpedoed *Frederick C. Davis (DE-136)*, blasted it to surface and sank it with gunfire. Finding herself in Hawaii at end of hostilities, joined in escort, mopping up operations and plane guard duty. See chapter *Twilight of the U-boats*. One battle star.

SHIP	NUMBER	YARD	COMPLETED	DECOM	MODIFIED	DISPOSAL
TOMICH	DE-242	Brown	27/07/43	20/09/46		Scrapped 11/72

December 1943 to March 1944, three convoys to North Africa, the third being UGS/GUS 36 in which she was engaged with enemy aircraft. She also attacked a U-boat without apparent success. May to October, continued convoys to North Africa. In November, underwent HUK training. The balance of the year and into the spring of 1945, engaged in ASW patrols along the Atlantic Coast and with the Barrier Patrol. With the collapse of German resistance, she was transferred to the Pacific, but that war ended before she could get into action.

SHIP	NUMBER	YARD	COMPLETED	DECOM	MODIFIED	DISPOSAL
J.R. WARD	DE-243	Brown	05/07/43	13/06/46		Sold 07/71

Starting September 1943, made three convoys to the Mediterranean. In March 1944, attached to *Tripoli (CVE-64)* HUK. Patrolled waters from Cape Verde Islands to Brazil without luck. In August, assigned to *Core (CVE-13)* HUK. Made a few futile attacks. Same group sailed again into severe North Atlantic weather in January 1945, returning in May. En route to Hawaii, received news that war had ended.

SHIP	NUMBER	YARD	COMPLETED	DECOM	MODIFIED	DISPOSAL
OTTERSTETTER	DE-244	Brown	06/08/43	20/06/60		Target 08/74

November 1943-February 1944, made two convoys to Casablanca. Starting in May, completed three voyages to Argentia, Newfoundland and the UK. In July, she sailed to the Pacific, but the war ended before she could reach the forward areas. Carried out numerous occupation duties in Japan, Korea and China.

SHIP	NUMBER	YARD	COMPLETED	DECOM	MODIFIED	DISPOSAL
SLOAT	DE-245	Brown	16/08/43	06/08/47		Sold 01/71

October 1943 to May 1944, operated in North African convoys. While with UGS-36, convoy attacked by several enemy aircraft; two shot down and two damaged by the convoy. In spring of 1944, joined *Tripoli* HUK group from Newfoundland area to the Caribbean. In October 1944, engaged in Atlantic coast sweeps. In July 1945, ordered to Pacific She had just begun logistic operations in Western Pacific when war ended. One battle star.

SHIP	NUMBER	YARD	COMPLETED	DECOM	MODIFIED	DISPOSAL
SNOWDEN	DE-246	Brown	23/08/43	06/08/47		Sold 01/71

December 1943 marked her first North Africa convoy. On 24 March 1944, attached to HUK TG 21.15. On 28 March, *Snowden (DE-246)*, *Frost (DE-144)*, *Barber (DE-161)* sank *U-488*. On 12 June, supported *Frost (DE-144)* and *Inch (DE-146)* as they sank *U-490* and again as the same two sank *U-154* on 3 July. *Snowden* recovered prisoners and debris. With TG 22.5 on 22 August, covered *Croatan CVE-14)* while *Stanton (DE-247)* and *Frost* sank *U-1235* on 15 April 1945. Sailed for Pearl Harbor in August, but war ended before arrival. See chapter *The Hunter Killers*. Three battle stars.

SHIP	NUMBER	YARD	COMPLETED	DECOM	MODIFIED	DISPOSAL
STANTON	DE-247	Brown	07/08/43	02/06/47		Sold 12/70

November 1943 to April 1944, made four North Africa convoys. Was with UGS-37 on 11 April when convoy was attacked by 24 aircraft. Stick of bombs dropped close aboard. In November, joined *Croatan (CVE-14)* HUK. On 15 April 1945, gained sound contact and, together with *Frost (DE-144)*, attacked repeatedly hour after hour until *U-1235* was destroyed. On 16 April, accompanied by *Frost* and *Huse*, blasted *U-880* to the bottom. With Atlantic war ended in May, headed for Pacific, but the war ended before she reached the combat area. See chapter *The Hunter Killers*. Three battle stars.

SHIP	NUMBER	YARD	COMPLETED	DECOM	MODIFIED	DISPOSAL
SWASEY	DE-248	Brown	31/08/43	15/03/46		Scrapped 11/72

November 1943 to March 1944, four convoys to North Africa. The fourth was UGS-37 with her 60 merchant ships, a prime enemy target. An hour before midnight on 11 April, attacked by 24 *Luftwaffe* aircraft. Close call with aerial torpedo. Splashed one bomber and had second near hit by torpedo. Sailed for North Atlantic on 4 June with *Croatan (CVE-25)* HUK TG 22.5. On 15 September, together with *Frost (DE-144)*, searched for survivors of DD *Warrington*, capsized in Caribbean storm. On 25 March, joined Barrier Patrol where her group sank two U-boats. Arrived at Pearl Harbor too late for combat. See chapter *The Hunter Killers*. One battle star

EDSALL CLASS

SHIP	NUMBER	YARD	COMPLETED	DECOM	MODIFIED	DISPOSAL
MARCHAND	**DE-249**	**Brown**	**08/09/43**	**25/04/47**		**Scrapped 01/71**

As *ComCortDiv 20*, made her first convoy to Mediterranean December 1944. Second convoy to Northern Ireland ran into furious gale on 25 February 1945. At 2200, two merchant ships collided and caught fire. As this DE went to assistance of one of the ships, she too sustained collision damage. Nonetheless, she rescued 28 survivors while *Ricketts (DE-254)* saved 38 others. Despite heroic efforts, one merchant ship went down. She made nine more convoys to Northern Ireland to end of Atlantic war. Like so many others, arrived in Pacific too late for enemy action. See chapter *Convoys to the United Kingdom.*

SHIP	NUMBER	YARD	COMPLETED	DECOM	MODIFIED	DISPOSAL
HURDT	**DE-250**	**Brown**	**30/08/43**	**01/05/46**		**Mexico 10/73**

Departed on first convoy to Casablanca December 1943. This DE made 11 more convoys to the UK through the worst weather the North Atlantic had to offer until released in June 1945 after Germany surrendered. Arrived in Pearl Harbor only weeks before the Japanese capitulation. Was assigned to various occupation duties.

SHIP	NUMBER	YARD	COMPLETED	DECOM	MODIFIED	DISPOSAL
CAMP	**DE-251**	**Brown**	**16/09/43**	**13/02/51**	**DER (12/55)**	**Vietnam**

After duty as school ship, began convoy escort duties to Casablanca, various ports in the United Kingdom, guarding troops and mountains of equipment for the assault on the European continent. Battled huge seas and sustained severe damage in collision with merchant ship. Sent to Pacific in July 1945 to serve in various occupation tasks.

SHIP	NUMBER	YARD	COMPLETED	DECOM	MODIFIED	DISPOSAL
HOWARD D. CROW	**DE-252**	**Brown**	**27/09/43**	**22/05/46**		**Scrapped 09/68**

December 1943 to May 1945, 11 arduous convoys to Casablanca and to the UK. After German surrender and extensive training in the Caribbean, sailed to Pearl Harbor, arriving on 25 July. Engaged in weather reporting duty until end of war.

SHIP	NUMBER	YARD	COMPLETED	DECOM	MODIFIED	DISPOSAL
PETTIT	**DE-253**	**Brown**	**23/09/43**	**06/05/46**		**Target 09/74**

January 1944, completed first transatlantic convoy to *Casablanca*. February 1944 to June 1945, numerous convoys to the UK and France. Transferred to the Pacific, she arrived at Pearl Harbor on 25 July. In Marshall Islands, searched for possible allied survivors to end of war and a few months beyond.

SHIP	NUMBER	YARD	COMPLETED	DECOM	MODIFIED	DISPOSAL
RICKETTS	**DE-254**	**Brown**	**05/10/43**	**17/04/46**		**Scrapped 11/72**

First and only convoy to *Casablanca*, completed January 1944. Beginning February, made 12 transatlantic convoys to the UK and France. On first convoy, this vessel and *Marchand (DE-249)* were distinguished for rescuing personnel and conducting damage control in heavy seas on two collided merchant tankers. Decorations awarded three officers and six enlisted personnel. Arriving in Pacific August 1945, engaged in accepting surrender of isolated Japanese garrisons. See chapter *Convoys to the United Kingdom.*

SHIP	NUMBER	YARD	COMPLETED	DECOM	MODIFIED	DISPOSAL
SELLSTROM	**DE-255**	**Brown**	**12/10/43**	**06/60**	**DER (10/56)**	**Scrapped 04/67**

January-February 1944, she made her first convoy to Casablanca. In March-April, her second convoy to the Mediterranean, UGS-36, was enlivened by an enemy night air attack, burning one merchant ship. May-July saw her completing two more convoys to same area. From August to May 1945, made six convoys to the UK. Transferred to the Pacific in July, conducted convoys in the Alaska area to the end of the war. See chapter *Convoys to the United Kingdom.* One battle star.

SHIP	NUMBER	YARD	COMPLETED	DECOM	MODIFIED	DISPOSAL
HARVESON	**DE-316**	**Consol**	**12/10/43**	**30/06/60**	**DER (02/51)**	**Scrapped 12/66**

Off to unfortunate start with severe damage in collision 15 December 1943. Beginning February 1944, for next 15 months, attached to convoys to the UK. Ordered to the Pacific, arrived in Pearl Harbor at war's end. For next several months, supported occupation landings in Japan.

SHIP	NUMBER	YARD	COMPLETED	DECOM	MODIFIED	DISPOSAL
JOYCE	**DE-317**	**Consol**	**30/09/43**	**17/06/60**	**DER (10/51)**	**Scrapped 12/72**

First convoy was to North Africa December 1943. Second convoy to Londonderry in March was marked by loss of *Leopold (DE-319)* to a U-boat torpedo. *Joyce* recovered 28 survivors while fending off the sub. In next convoy the following April, rescued 31 survivors from torpedoed *Pan-Pennsylvania*, then located and depth charged the sub. Forced to surface, *U-550* was shelled and sunk with assistance of *Gandy (DE-764)* and *Peterson (DE-152). Joyce* took 13 prisoners, including sub captain. Eight more convoys until German surrender May 1945. Arriving in Pearl Harbor in July, conducted convoys to end of war. See chapter *Convoys to the United Kingdom.* One battle star.

SHIP	NUMBER	YARD	COMPLETED	DECOM	MODIFIED	DISPOSAL
KIRKPATRICK	**DE-318**	**Consol**	**23/10/43**	**24/06/60**	**DER (10/51)**	**Scrapped 08/74**

January 1944 to May 1945, one convoy to the Mediterranean and ten to the UK. After bombardment exercises in the Caribbean, transferred to Pacific. Arrived in Hawaii on 11 July and conducted ASW training to end of war.

EDSALL CLASS

SHIP	NUMBER	YARD	COMPLETED	DECOM	MODIFIED	DISPOSAL
LEOPOLD	**DE-319**	**Consol**	**18/10/43**			**Torpedoed**

After first convoy to Casablanca in January 1944, departed New York with convoy en route to the UK. While investigating submarine contact eve of 19 March, struck by acoustic torpedo from *U-255* which broke her back and sent her to the bottom. 171 officers and men lost in explosion and drowning. Only 28 survivors. See chapter *Convoys to the UK.* One battle star.

MENGES	**DE-320**	**Consol**	**26/10/43**	**01/47**		**Scrapped 01/71**

On first Mediterranean convoy, night of 20 April 1944, convoy attacked by 30 enemy torpedo bombers. Splashed one plane and rescued 137 survivors of *Lansdale (DD-426)* and two German pilots. On 3 May, torpedoed by *U-371*, demolishing her stern, killing 31 and wounding 25. Towed to NYC, forward section welded to after section of *Holder (DE-401)*, torpedoed in prior convoy. On 18 March 1945, assisted *Lowe (DE-325)* in sinking *U-866*. Ended war service as training ship at Coast Guard Academy. See chapters *Convoys to the Mediterranean* and *Twilight of the U-boats.* Two battle stars.

MOSLEY	**DE-321**	**Consol**	**30/10/43**	**15/03/46**		**Scrapped 01/71**

On second convoy to Mediterranean, off Algeria night of 20 April 1944, convoy attacked by three waves of bombers. First blew up troop transport, killing 580. Next wave hit two more merchantmen and sank *Lansdale (DD-426). Mosley* downed one JU-88 and damaged another. On return voyage, *Menges (DE-320)* hit by acoustic torpedo from *U-371*, sunk next day by escorts. *Fechteler (DE-157)* fatally hit by torpedo from *U-967.* After convoying eight more months, joined DE HUK and assisted in sinking *U-866* 18 March 1945. On Barrier Patrol with *Mission Bay (CVE-59)* HUK, assisted two DEs in sinking *U-518* on 22 April. Remained on Barrier Patrol to end of war. See chapters *Convoys to the Mediterranean* and *Twilight of the U-boats.* Two battle stars.

NEWELL	**DE-322**	**Consol**	**30/10/43**	**21/09/68**	**CG (07/51)**	**Scrapped 12/71**

After safely escorting her first convoy to Casablanca, joined screen of UGS/GUS-38 to take part in 20 April 1944 action off Algiers with three waves of 30 aircraft. At 2104, three planes roared in between this DE and *Lansdale (DD-426).* Her 20mm and 40mm guns ripped one plane, causing it to explode. For next 15 minutes, her guns blanketed attackers, forcing them to turn away from the convoy. When *Lansdale* went down, many crew members went over the side to rescue exhausted swimmers. She made two more convoys to Bizerte, then spent remainder of war in training exercises and carrier plane guard duty. See chapter *Convoys to the Mediterranean.* One battle star.

PRIDE	**DE-323**	**Consol**	**13/11/43**	**26/04/46**	**CG (07/51)**	**Scrapped 01/71**

After shakedown, spent twelve months escorting six convoys to Mediterranean. Heavily involved in UGS/GUS-38 action with German aircraft off coast of Algiers on 20 April 1944. Five ships went to the bottom, including a transport with over 500 men and the *Lansdale (DD-426).* On return voyage, assisted three other escorts in sinking *U-371*, taking 49 prisoners. On 1 March 1945, with three other escorts, sank *U-866.* After two more UK convoys, conducted ASW exercises to end of war. See chapters *Convoys to the Mediterranean* and *Twilight of the U-boats.* Three battle stars.

FALGOUT	**DE-324**	**Consol**	**15/11/43**	**18/04/47**	**CG (08/51)**	**Target 06/75**

On 4 December, rescued 11 survivors from torpedoed tanker. Eight convoys to North Africa February 1944 to June 1945. On 20 April 1944, heavily attacked by German aircraft, blowing up an ammunition ship, sinking a destroyer, damaging other merchant ships. On home voyage, 3 May, a DE was torpedoed and avenged by other DEs sinking the U-boat. On 5 May, another DE torpedoed and sunk. Spent remainder of war in training exercises One battle star. See chapter *Convoys to the Mediterranean.*

LOWE	**DE-325**	**Consol**	**22/11/43**	**20/09/68**	**CG (07/51)**	**Scrapped 09/68**

After one successful North African convoy in February-March 1944, assigned to UGS/GUS-38. In antiaircraft action night of 20 April, her guns helped to drive off attackers. Outmaneuvered two torpedoes heading for her starboard side with hard right turn, passing them to port and starboard. Racked up 12 Atlantic crossings until assigned to four ship HUK. On 18 March 1945, credited with destruction of *U-866.* After rescuing crew of foundered schooner, spent remainder of war in training exercises. See chapters *Convoys to the Mediterranean* and *Twilight of the U-boats.* Two battle stars.

T.J. GARY	**DE-326**	**Consol**	**27/11/43**	**22/10/73**	**DER**	**Tunisia 10/73**

March 1944 started string of transatlantic convoys, culminating in German surrender May 1945, a total of eight round trips to the Mediterranean and the UK without the loss of a single ship. In December 1944, went to aid of Coast Guard *PF-19*, badly damaged in collision with merchant ship. Arrived Pearl Harbor in July and screened convoys to end of war.

BRISTER	**DE-327**	**Consol**	**30/11/43**	**04/10/46**	**DER**	**Taiwan 11/71**

June 1944 to June 1945, made two transatlantic convoys to Italy and five to the United Kingdom. Transferred to the Pacific, she arrived in Pearl Harbor at war's end.

EDSALL CLASS

SHIP	NUMBER	YARD	COMPLETED	DECOM	MODIFIED	DISPOSAL

FINCH **DE-328** **Consol** **13/12/43** **04/10/46** **CG (08/51)** **Scrapped 02/74**
March-May 1944, two convoys to Casablanca. In July, screened shipping for assault on southern France. September 1944 to May 1945, five convoys to the United Kingdom. In July, arrived in Pearl Harbor and joined carrier task force to end of war. Carried out occupation duties, including evacuation of allied POWs from Korea.

KRETCHMER **DE-329** **Consol** **12/13/43** **01/10/73** **CG (06/51)** **Scrapped 05/74**
After few months in convoy and training exercises in Caribbean, made two convoys beginning June 1944 to Naples with supplies for assault on Southern France. September to April 1945, five convoys to the UK. Following German surrender, transferred to Pacific, arriving in Pearl Harbor early July. Screened convoys to end of war, occupation and repatriation of Allied POWs.

O'REILLY **DE-330** **Consol** **28/12/43** **15/06/46** **Scrapped 04/72**
March-September 1944, made three convoys to North African ports. She then switched over to the UK convoys, screening five round trips. On her second crossing, near Plymouth, England, 18 November, she attacked a sub but without evidence of damage. Ordered to the Pacific in April 1945, she spent several weeks at training, and the war ended before she reached forward areas.

KOINER **DE-331** **Consol** **27/12/43** **1968** **CG (06/51)** **Scrapped 09/69**
From February 1944, made four convoys from Curacao to North Africa and Naples. September 1944 to May 1945, guarded five convoys to UK. Arriving in Pearl Harbor in June, operated with *Corregidor (CVS-58)* HUK to end of war. Returned home via Indian Ocean and Mediterranean, completing her circumnavigation.

PRICE **DE-332** **Consol** **12/01/44** **30/06/60** **DER** **Uncertain**
On first convoy to Mediterranean, attacked by German bombers in force on 11 April 1944. Credited with downing one plane. Escorted torpedo damaged *Holder (DE-401)* into Algiers. Two more convoys followed to North Africa. September-May 1944, reassigned to North Atlantic convoys. Rerouted to Pearl Harbor in July and assigned to Pacific convoys to end of war. See chapter *Convoys to the Mediterranean.* One battle star.

STRICKLAND **DE-333** **Consol** **10/01/44** **15/06/46** **DER** **Scrapped 10/72**
Sailed in convoy UGS-37 to Mediterranean; attacked by German bombers on 11 April 1944 off Algeria. In furious action, shot down a bomber on strafing run. Sister DE torpedoed and badly damaged. Continued Bizerte run for next five months. In October, transferred to North Atlantic convoys until May 1945 when reassigned to Hawaii. War ended shortly thereafter. See chapter *Convoys to the Mediterranean.* One battle star.

FORSTER **DE-334** **Consol** **25/01/44** **15/06/46** **CG (06/51)** **Vietnam 09/71**
First convoy to Bizerte, Tunisia, March-April 1944, convoy UGS/GUS 37, saw furious action. On 11 April, she shot down one or more planes from German attack formation. Took off wounded and provided cover for torpedoed *Holder (DE-41)*. For one year from May 1944, made six convoys to the UK, France and Bizerte and also served as school ship. Sailed to Pacific, but war ended before reaching forward areas. See chapter *Convoys to the Mediterranean.* One battle star.

DANIEL **DE-335** **Consol** **24/01/44** **12/04/46** **Scrapped 01/71**
March to May 1944, served as school ship in Norfolk, Va. June to June 1945, two convoys to Naples, Italy, and five to the UK and France. Sailed to Pacific, but hostilities ended shortly after her arrival.

R.O. HALE **DE-336** **Consol** **03/02/44** **15/07/63** **DER** **Scrapped 08/74**
After serving as training ship, entered transatlantic convoy service July 1944. First two were to Italy, then five more to the UK and France. After German surrender, underwent training exercises and proceeded to Pacific. However, war ended before she could leave west coast of US.

D.W. PETERSON **DE-337** **Consol** **17/02/44** **27/03/46** **Scrapped 01/71**
July 1944 to June 1945, made seven Atlantic convoys to the Mediterranean, the UK and France. In August, underway to Pearl Harbor but proceeded no further because of the Japanese surrender. Returned to the US.

MARTIN H RAY **DE-338** **Consol** **28/02/44** **03/46** **Scrapped**
June 1944, marked beginning fourteen trans-Atlantic convoys to Italy, France and the UK without loss. Depth charged several contacts but without visual evidence of destruction. Arrived Pearl Harbor only days before Japanese surrender.

EDSALL CLASS

SHIP	NUMBER	YARD	COMPLETED	DECOM	MODIFIED	DISPOSAL
RAMSDEN	**DE-382**	**Consol**	**19/10/43**	**23/06/60**	**CG (06/54)**	**Uncertain**

Made first convoy to Casablanca January 1944. Second convoy to Bizerte, UGS-36, heavily engaged with German aircraft on 1 April. In 15 minute battle, one merchantman damaged, five planes shot down, one by this DE. After one more convoy to Bizerte, shifted to North Atlantic, seven convoys to the UK and France. After German surrender, assigned to Aleutians as plane guard to end of war. See chapter *Convoys to the Mediterranean.* One battle star.

MILLS	**DE-383**	**Consol**	**12/10/43**	**27/10/70**	**DER NRF**	**No record**

January 1944 was start for nine transatlantic convoys to Mediterranean, Northern Ireland, England, France. On second voyage to North Africa 1 April 1944, off Algiers, convoy attacked by German torpedo bombers. Liberty ship hit and set afire. Rescued survivors in water, and boarding party extinguished flames on ship so it could be towed to harbor. Arrived Adak, Alaska, July 1945 and served as plane guard and escort to end of war. See chapter *Convoys to the Mediterranean.* One battle star.

RHODES	**DE-384**	**Consol**	**25/10/43**	**10/07/63**	**DER**	**Scrapped**

After first serving as training ship, made first Mediterranean convoy January 1944. Two days out of Bizerte on second convoy, UGS-36, attacked by large number of *Luftwaffe* bombers and torpedo planes. One merchantman damaged and five aircraft splashed by escorts. In July, shifted to North Atlantic, six convoys to UK and France. In June 1945, reported to Alaskan Sea Frontier and screened strikes in Sea of Okhotsk and bombardment of Kuriles before end of war. See chapter *Convoys to the Mediterranean.* One battle star.

RICHEY	**DE-385**	**Consol**	**30/10/43**	**01/47**	**CG (06/54)**	**Target 07/69**

January to July 1944, escorted convoys to Casablanca, Oran, Bizerte. September-October convoyed to Belfast and Londonderry. January to May 1945, convoyed to ports in England and France. In April convoy, rescued 32 men from two tankers that had collided and burned. In July, transferred to North Pacific Fleet, Adak, Alaska.

SAVAGE	**DE-386**	**Consol**	**29/10/43**	**17/10/69**	**DER**	**Unknown**

Beginning January 1944 with *CortDiv 23*, until early 1945, convoyed to Mediterranean, African and European ports. On 1 January, helped fight off *Luftwaffe* attack on convoy UGS-36, sustaining one minor crew casualty. Transferred to Alaskan and Siberian waters June 1945, escorted tankers in train of TG 92, then bombarding Kuriles Islands. See chapter *Convoys to the Mediterranean.* One battle star.

VANCE	**DE-387**	**Consol**	**01/11/43**	**10/10/69**	**CG (05/51)**	**Target**

In February 1944, began a series of eight convoys to the Mediterranean. On more than one occasion, she held the "whip" position, shepherding recalcitrant merchantmen. On 14 October, a U-boat torpedoed two merchant vessels; *Vance* attempted unsuccessfully to ram and launch depth charge attack. After 11 May 1945, placed prize crews on surrendering submarines. Arrived in Pacific too late to engage the Japanese enemy.

LANSING	**DE-388**	**Consol**	**10/11/43**	**21/05/65**	**DER**	**Scrapped 02/74**

February 1944 began her first of eight Atlantic convoys to North African ports. On second convoy, one merchantman damaged by torpedo from U-boat. Routed to Pearl Harbor, war ended before arrival.

DURANT	**DE-389**	**Consol**	**16/11/43**	**27/02/46**	**CG (05/51)**	**Scrapped 04/74**

February 1944 to June 1945, eight voyages to North Africa Division accepted surrender of *U-873* as Germany asked for peace. Sailed for Pacific but that war ended before she reached forward areas.

CALCATERRA	**DE-390**	**Consol**	**17/11/43**	**02/07/73**	**DER**	**Sold 05/74**

February 1944 to June 1945, assigned to the Mediterranean convoys. Covered the transport of men and supplies to the Italian and French fighting fronts. Attacked two submarines and engaged enemy aircraft in various convoys while guarding the merchant vessels. Transferred to Pacific, war ended before she reached Pearl Harbor.

CHAMBERS	**DE-391**	**Consol**	**22/11/43**	**20/06/60**	**DER**	**Sold 1974**

Began the first of eight convoys to North African ports from New York and Norfolk February 1944. Braved mountainous seas and U-boats to bring her charges to port without loss. Sailed from New York to the Pacific in July 1945 only to have the war end before she could reach combat areas.

MERRILL	**DE-392**	**Consol**	**27/11/43**	**12/09/47**	**DER**	**Sold 1974**

February 1944 began a series of fifteen convoys between US and the Mediterranean. En route to Pearl Harbor in August 1945, received news of enemy capitulation and returned to US west coast shortly thereafter.

EDSALL CLASS

<table>
<tr><th>SHIP</th><th>NUMBER</th><th>YARD</th><th>COMPLETED</th><th>DECOM</th><th>MODIFIED</th><th>DISPOSAL</th></tr>
<tr><td>HAVERFIELD</td><td>DE-393</td><td>Consol</td><td>29/11/43</td><td>30/06/71</td><td></td><td>Sold 12/71</td></tr>
<tr><td colspan="7">Began HUK operations with Bogue (CVE-9) February 1944. Task Group had considerable success, sinking U-575 on 23 March, Japanese RO-501 (ex U-1224) on 13 May. Recovered one pilot from ill-fated Block Island. Operated in Barrier Patrol spring of 1945. Was in Pearl Harbor when war ended. See chapter The Hunter-Killers and Twilight of the U-boats. One battle star.</td></tr>
<tr><td>SWENNING</td><td>DE-394</td><td>Consol</td><td>01/12/43</td><td>25/09/47</td><td></td><td>Scrapped 07/72</td></tr>
<tr><td colspan="7">After Mediterranean convoy February 1944, joined Bogue (CVE-9) HUK. On 13 March, other escorts sank U-575 as Swenning remained in carrier screen. In June, rescued eight from crew of downed RAF bomber. After several months on Barrier Patrol, sailed to Hawaii, but war ended a few days after arrival.</td></tr>
<tr><td>WILLIS</td><td>DE-395</td><td>Consol</td><td>10/12/43</td><td>12/09/47</td><td></td><td>Scrapped 07/72</td></tr>
<tr><td colspan="7">February 1944, joined Bogue (CVE-9) HUK. Their search for U-boats took them around the far reaches of the Atlantic Two of the group escorts and aircraft scored their first kill on 13 March. On 2 June, another sub was sunk by Bogue aircraft, the Japanese I-52 (former U-boat). Attacked but did not sink a contact on 2 August and again on 14 September. Weathered the furious storm of mid-December, described in author's Sims. Continued ASW patrols with Barrier Sweep to end of war. Transferred to Pacific, but Japanese surrendered before she could see action. See chapter The Hunter-Killers. One battle star.</td></tr>
<tr><td>JANSSEN</td><td>DE-396</td><td>Consol</td><td>18/12/43</td><td>12/04/46</td><td></td><td>Scrapped 07/72</td></tr>
<tr><td colspan="7">Joined Bogue (CVE-9) February 1944. Took part in emergency patrol off Maine in September. In March 1945, assigned to Barrier Patrol and conducted several U-boat attacks. Made contact on U-546, sub that had sunk Frederick C. Davis (DE-136), expended 40 depth charges and, with other escorts, sank the sub. See chapter Twilight of the U-boats. One battle star.</td></tr>
<tr><td>WILHOITE</td><td>DE-397</td><td>Consol</td><td>16/12/43</td><td>02/07/69</td><td>DER</td><td>Scrapped 07/72</td></tr>
<tr><td colspan="7">On second convoy to North Africa, UGS/GUS 40, starting April 1944 and culminating in Mid-May, saw considerable action with enemy aircraft. On 13 May, attacked by a Junkers, damaging it and forcing it to drop its torpedo prematurely. About 17 enemy planes downed by convoy gunners and friendly aircraft without loss or damage to convoy. Ordered to area where Block Island and Barr were torpedoed while Ahrens and Eugene E Elmore were sinking a U-boat. Took Barr in tow to Casablanca. Continued to end of Atlantic war as part of Barrier patrol. Subsequently sailed to Pacific, but Japanese surrendered while Wilhoite was still training in Hawaii. See chapter Convoys to the Mediterranean. Presidential Unit Citation, Navy Unit Commendation, one battle star.</td></tr>
<tr><td>COCKRILL</td><td>DE-398</td><td>Consol</td><td>24/12/43</td><td>21/06/46</td><td></td><td>Target 1973</td></tr>
<tr><td colspan="7">February to December 1944, participated in Mediterranean convoys, training and Atlantic coastal convoys. Subsequently took part as unit with Bogue (CVE-9) HUK. In April 1945, patrolled with mid-Atlantic Barrier and took part in sinking U-546, the sub that had sunk Frederick Davis. Sailed to Pacific too late to take part in that war but operated in support of occupation.</td></tr>
<tr><td>STOCKDALE</td><td>DE-399</td><td>Consol</td><td>31/12/43</td><td>18/04/47</td><td></td><td>Target 1972</td></tr>
<tr><td colspan="7">On first convoy to North Africa in convoy UGS-37, formation attacked by Luftwaffe aircraft off Algeria on 11 April 1944. Holder (DE-401) damaged by torpedo. Two more Mediterranean convoys before reassigned to North Atlantic for five convoys to UK. Transferred to Pacific, arrived Pearl Harbor July 1945, a few weeks before war ended. See chapter Convoys to the Mediterranean. One battle star.</td></tr>
<tr><td>HISSEM</td><td>DE-400</td><td>Consol</td><td>13/01/44</td><td>15/05/70</td><td>DER</td><td>Target 1975</td></tr>
<tr><td colspan="7">Convoy UGS-37 was first convoy, a baptism of fire. Thirty-five Luftwaffe bombers attacked convoy night of 11-12 April 1944. This DE splashed one and damaged another Holder (DE-401) torpedoed. Made a total of seven convoys across North Atlantic from June 1944 to collapse of Third Reich, May 1945. Arrived in Pearl Harbor July 1945, and war ended following month. See chapter Convoys to the Mediterranean. One battle star.</td></tr>
<tr><td>HOLDER</td><td>DE-401</td><td>Consol</td><td>18/01/44</td><td></td><td></td><td>Torpedoed</td></tr>
<tr><td colspan="7">Departed 24 March 1944 with convoy UGS-37. Just before midnight on 11 April, convoy attacked by German planes. While firing and making smoke, she was torpedoed by an enemy plane. Continued fighting while damage control parties kept her afloat. Towed to New York, damaged forward section cut away and after section welded to forward section of Menges (DE-320), hit by acoustic torpedo in convoy UGS-38. Menges' was surviving name. See chapter Convoys to the Mediterranean. One battle star.</td></tr>
</table>

JOHN C. BUTLER CLASS — WESTINGHOUSE GEARED TURBINES (WGT)

This class undoubtedly was the best of the lot. Turbo geared, it was the fastest and most nearly conformed to fleet specifications. The armament was about the same as the *Rudderow* class as was its exterior profile and low bridge structure Although many more were authorized, only 83 were completed before war's end. There were a number of armament variations installed on different vessels of this class. A few had two 40mm twins in lieu of torpedo tubes. As described in the narrative of the Battle off Samar, it was fortunate that those embattled DEs had their torpedo tubes.

Many heroic deeds were performed by DEs in this class such as *Samuel B Roberts*, *Dennis*, *Raymond* and *John C. Butler* at the Battle off Samar; *Tabberer* in Typhoon Cobra; and many others in Lingayen Gulf and Okinawa.

Destroyer Escorts 339-372, 402-424, 438-450, 508-510, 531-540.

MAJOR CHARACTERISTICS

Length Overall	306"
Length at Waterline	300'
Beam	36'-10"
Mean Draft	9'
Displacement	1,600 Tons
Shaft Horsepower	12,000
War Endurance	4,650 mi/12 Knots
Trial (Flank) Speed	24 Knots
Fuel Capacity	350 Tons
Complement	Off: 15, Enl: 203 men

ARMAMENT

Main:	(2) 5'/38 Cal Guns
Secondary:	(2) Twin 40mm Guns
	(10) 20mm Guns
ASW:	(1) Hedgehog
	(2) Depth Charge Racks
	(8) "K" Gun Projectors

JOHN C. BUTLER CLASS

SHIP	NUMBER	YARD	COMPLETED	DECOM	MODIFIED	DISPOSAL
JOHN C. BUTLER	DE-339	Consol	31/03/44	18/12/57		Target 06/70

One of the most embattled of all DEs. Screened carriers in invasion of Morotai and Peleliu September 1944. The October invasion of Leyte precipitated Second Battle of the Philippine Sea, and this DE was one of a force of four DEs and three DDs, escorting several CVEs, that suddenly found itself in battle with an overwhelmingly superior force of enemy capital ships, from which it emerged remarkably unscathed. In January, sailed with attack force to Lingayan Gulf, splashing several *kamikazes.* In February, fought off severe air attacks in assault on Iwo Jima. In picket line at Okinawa, shot down five *kamikazes*, sustaining only minor damage. Spent rest of war on convoy duty. See chapters *The Philippine Campaign* and *Iwo Jima to Okinawa.* Five battle stars.

SHIP	NUMBER	YARD	COMPLETED	DECOM	MODIFIED	DISPOSAL
O'FLAHERTY	DE-340	Consol	08/04/44	01/47		Scrapped 12/72

July 1944 escorted Majuro, Eniwetok-Tarawa areas. Screened carriers in Guam invasion. In July, 600 mile dash to rescue twelve flyers from downed PBM aircraft. In October, assigned *CortDiv 64* HUK and worked successively with three carriers. Operated in Lingayen Gulf January 1945. Shifted to 5th Fleet in February to screen assault on Iwo Jima. In March, began ninety day stint at Okinawa. On 2 April, splashed a kamikaze. Operated out of Guam to end of war. See chapter *Iwo Jima to Okinawa.* Four battle stars.

SHIP	NUMBER	YARD	COMPLETED	DECOM	MODIFIED	DISPOSAL
RAYMOND	DE-341	Consol	15/04/44	22/09/58	NRF	Scrapped —

Arrived at Manus August 1944 to escort carriers staging assault on Morotai. In October, supported air operations at Leyte. On 25 October, participated in Battle off Samar, damaging Japanese cruiser with gunfire and rescuing survivors of *St Lo (CVE-63).* January 1945, escorted carriers to Saipan and Tinian. In February, screened Task Unit assaulting Iwo Jima. Performed ASW and convoy screening duties at Okinawa March to mid-May splashing five enemy planes. For remainder of war, convoyed from Western Carolines to Ryukyus. See chapters *The Philippine Campaign* and *Iwo Jima to Okinawa.* Five battle stars.

SHIP	NUMBER	YARD	COMPLETED	DECOM	MODIFIED	DISPOSAL
R.W. SUESENS	DE-342	Consol	26/04/44	15/01/47		Scrapped 03/72

Collided with minesweeper Valor (AMC-108) in Buzzard's Bay June 1944, an unfortunate beginning of illustrious career. In September, joined 7th Fleet. Screened carriers attacking Leyte, also performed plane guard duties as part of "Taffy 2". On 25 October, screened carriers flying planes to support embattled "Taffy" 3 off Samar, only 12 miles away, until Japanese Fleet retired. January 1945, headed with attack force to Lingayen Gulf. On 12 January, after rescuing *Gilligan (DE-508)* survivors, splashed *kamikaze* close aboard, injuring 11 of crew. In February, screened resupply runs to Nasugbu. In March-April, joined picket forces on Okinawa, splashing four planes and assisting destruction two others. May-June, resumed picketing at Ulithi and Okinawa July-August, covered minesweeping operations in South China Sea. See chapters *The Philippine Campaign* and *Iwo Jima to Okinawa.* Five battle stars.

SHIP	NUMBER	YARD	COMPLETED	DECOM	MODIFIED	DISPOSAL
ABERCROMBIE	DE-343	Consol	01/05/44	15/06/46		Target 01/68

July-August 1944, training and convoying in Caribbean, then off to Hawaii, arriving late August. In October, screened escort carrier group for attack on Leyte, return to Philippines. In December, screened amphibious attack on Luzon, then directed troop landings in Lingayan Gulf and again at Mindoro. In March 1945, screened attack force headed for Okinawa, then covered landings. In picket line for two months from April, engaged 16 *kamikazes*, claiming two splashes and two assists. Took up occupational duties at war's end. See chapter *Iwo Jima to Okinawa.* Four battle stars.

SHIP	NUMBER	YARD	COMPLETED	DECOM	MODIFIED	DISPOSAL
OBERRENDER	DE-344	Consol	11/05/44	11/07/45		Target 06/11/45

Convoyed to Eniwetok in August, the Marshalls in September 1944. Following months, escorted Admiral Sprague's CVEs to Leyte via Morotai, just missing Leyte Gulf Battle. Damaged by proximity to explosion of ammunition ship *Mount Hood (AE-11)* on 10 November. December-March 1945, escort and patrol duties in Dutch East Indies and Philippines. On 9 May at Okinawa, crashed by *kamikaze*, twenty-four killed, wounded, missing. Beyond repair, sunk in target practice. See chapter *Iwo Jima to Okinawa.* Three battle stars.

SHIP	NUMBER	YARD	COMPLETED	DECOM	MODIFIED	DISPOSAL
R. BRAZIER	DE-345	Consol	18/05/44	16/09/46		Target 01/69

August 1944, schoolship and ordnance testing. Convoy to Italy in September. December-January 1945, escorted tankers to Leyte. February-March patrolled Hollandia to Philippines. May to August, screened attack and supply vessels in recapture of Mindanao. One battle star.

SHIP	NUMBER	YARD	COMPLETED	DECOM	MODIFIED	DISPOSAL
E.A. HOWARD	DE-346	Consol	25/05/44	25/09/46		Scrapped 1973

After one Mediterranean convoy, transferred to Pacific, arriving Leyte January 1945. Convoyed almost continuously among Palaus, San Pedro Bay, New Guinea and Leyte. In April, escorted troops and supplies in Davao Gulf, bombarded Samal Island and others In June, escorted MTBs to Balikpapan, screened minesweepers and covered landings to end of July. Remained in Far East on occupation duties. One battle star.

Lewis M. Andrews, Jr.

JOHN C. BUTLER CLASS

SHIP	NUMBER	YARD	COMPLETED	DECOM	MODIFIED	DISPOSAL
J. RUTHERFORD	DE-347	Consol	31/05/44	21/06/46		Target 12/68

December 1944, arrived in Bora Bora via Galapagos and Society Islands. January-February 1945, nine voyages Hollandia to Leyte, and Lingayen in March, supporting recapture of Philippines. May-June, convoyed *LSTs* to Manila, rescuing distressed freighter en route. In July, escorted amphibians to reinforce Balikpapan invasion. Patrolled San Bernadino Strait to war's end. One battle star.

SHIP	NUMBER	YARD	COMPLETED	DECOM	MODIFIED	DISPOSAL
KEY	DE-348	Consol	05/06/44	09/07/46		Scrapped 03/72

After convoy to Naples, Italy in autumn 1944, joined 7th Fleet, arriving at Hollandia, New Guinea, in December. In January-February 1945, made five runs to Leyte and conducted ASW patrols in South China Sea. March-May, operated in Southern Philippines, screening ships Leyte to Mindanao, Jolo, Sulu and Legaspi to Luzon. Bombarded and destroyed Japanese PT base. Sailed to Dutch East Indies in June to cover invasion force at Balikpapan and conduct ASW patrols. Operated in Leyte Gulf to end of war. One battle star.

SHIP	NUMBER	YARD	COMPLETED	DECOM	MODIFIED	DISPOSAL
GENTRY	DE-349	Consol	14/06/44	02/07/46		Scrapped 01/72

October-December 1944, two convoys to Marseilles and Oran. Transferred to Pacific, arrived Manus February 1945. Next four months, convoyed New Guinea to Philippines and throughout Philippine Archipelago, Palaus and Western Carolines. In July, escort and picket assignment to end of war.

SHIP	NUMBER	YARD	COMPLETED	DECOM	MODIFIED	DISPOSAL
TRAW	DE-350	Consol	20/06/44	07/06/46		Target 08/68

August 1944 to January 1945, operated variously as training, convoying or patrol ship. Her convoys were to the Mediterranean and largely uneventful, except for some periods of heavy weather. Reassigned to Pacific, arrived Seeadler in February. March-April, convoyed between New Guinea and Philippines. May to end of war, convoyed in Philippine area and Okinawa.

SHIP	NUMBER	YARD	COMPLETED	DECOM	MODIFIED	DISPOSAL
M.J. MANUEL	DE-351	Consol	30/06/44	30/10/57		Target 08/68

October 1944, escorted first convoy to Marseilles, followed by two more to France and North Africa in November and December. Transferred to Pacific, arrived Manus, Admiralties, February 1945. March-July, convoyed among Leyte, New Guinea, the Palaus, Ulithi, Manila, Subic Bay and Lingayen Gulf. Late July, escorted to Okinawa. Philippine patrol duties to end of war.

SHIP	NUMBER	YARD	COMPLETED	DECOM	MODIFIED	DISPOSAL
NAIFEH	DE-352	Consol	04/07/44	17/06/60	NRF	Target 07/66

After two convoys to Europe and North Africa, arrived Manus on January 1945. Primarily in convoys to end of war, escorting to New Guinea, Ulithi, Palau, Guam, Manila, and Okinawa. Also, assigned on occasion to weather, search and rescue and mail. Once flew three star flag of ComPhilSea.

SHIP	NUMBER	YARD	COMPLETED	DECOM	MODIFIED	DISPOSAL
D.C. BARNES	DE-353	Consol	13/07/44	15/01/47		Scrapped 09/73

School ship for officers Norfolk, Va. September-October 1944. Arrived Hollandia in November and escorted convoys from there to San Pedro, Leyte. Took part in assault and occupation of Borneo June-July 1945. Remained in Far East to support occupation and liberation of various areas before returning to the US in April 1946.

SHIP	NUMBER	YARD	COMPLETED	DECOM	MODIFIED	DISPOSAL
K.M. WILLETT	DE-354	Consol	19/07/44	26/02/59	NRF	Target 03/74

Arrived Hollandia, New Guinea, on November 1944 for duty with 7th Fleet. Made seven escort trips to Leyte December-January 1945. On 25 January, splashed enemy torpedo plane attempting attack on merchantman. February to June assigned to ASW patrols from Mindoro to Luzon. In June, escorted convoys from Leyte to Ulithi and Okinawa. In July, convoyed amphibious craft to Ryukyus, weathering a typhoon 30th-31st.

SHIP	NUMBER	YARD	COMPLETED	DECOM	MODIFIED	DISPOSAL
JACCARD	DE-355	Consol	26/07/44	30/09/46		Target 10/68

Arrived Hollandia November 1944. In December, experienced first air attack at Leyte. Escorted eleven convoys until joining a HUK group in March 1945. From May to end of war, resumed escort duty and antisubmarine patrols in Philippines. One battle star.

SHIP	NUMBER	YARD	COMPLETED	DECOM	MODIFIED	DISPOSAL
L.E. ACREE	DE-356	Consol	01/08/44	10/10/46		Sold 06/73

November 1944, arrived Hollandia via Societies and New Hebrides to join 7th Fleet. Numerous convoys among Leyte, Palaus and Hollandia. January-March 1945, screened troop and supply convoys to reinforce Luzon invasions. April-July, conducted ASW patrols in South China Sea, also training activities with fleet submarines. July to end of war, escorted convoys to Okinawa.

SHIP	NUMBER	YARD	COMPLETED	DECOM	MODIFIED	DISPOSAL
G.E. DAVIS	DE-357	Consol	11/08/44	11/11/54	NRF 51-54	Sold 01/74

Arrived New Guinea February 1944. Next three months, served in SW Pacific on convoys and antisubmarine patrol. Conducted patrols Mindoro and Luzon areas. In June, escorted to Leyte Gulf. In July, convoyed Philippines to Okinawa to end of war.

JOHN C. BUTLER CLASS

SHIP	NUMBER	YARD	COMPLETED	DECOM	MODIFIED	DISPOSAL
MACK	**DE-358**	**Consol**	**16/08/44**	**11/12/46**		**Sold 06/73**

Attached to 7th Fleet, convoyed Hollandia to New Guinea, Kossol Roads, Palaus and Leyte to March 1945. Damaged screws on uncharted shoal in Mangarin Bay. Repaired in June, returned to escort duty. In July, reported to Subic Bay Port Director. After Japanese surrender, assigned to air-sea rescue.

WOODSON	**DE-359**	**Consol**	**28/08/44**	**11/08/62**	**NRF 57-62**	**Sold 08/66**

September 1944, aided rescue survivors of capsized *Warrington (DD-383)* in Caribbean. Heading for Pacific, arrived Hollandia, New Guinea in January 1945. Operated Hollandia-Leyte convoys through March. In April-May, escorted within Philippines. End of May, escorted and trained with US submarines to end of war.

J. HUTCHINS	**DE-360**	**Consol**	**28/08/44**	**25/02/58**	**NRF 46-58**	**Sold 02/74**

Arrived Hollandia January 1945. For next several months, escorted resupply convoys to Leyte and Lingayen. In May, joined HUK group and trained with American and British submarines. In encounter en route Luzon to Okinawa on 9 August, sank two Japanese midget subs and probably damaged a third with gunfire and depth charges — all within a few hours. See chapter *Pacific ASW.* Navy Unit Commendation. Number of battle stars unclear from records.

WALTON	**DE-361**	**Consol**	**04/09/44**	**31/05/46**		**Target 08/69**

Arrived at Bora Bora, Society Islands, December 1944. January 1945, convoyed Hollandia to Leyte. February-May, convoyed Hollandia to Lingayen Gulf and Leyte to the Palaus; also patrolled at Leyte Gulf. In May, visited Manila, Leyte and Hollandia, then engaged in ASW sweeps on the west coast of Luzon followed by training with British and US submarines, then sweeps between Leyte and Okinawa. At Subic Bay when hostilities ceased.

ROLF	**DE-362**	**Consol**	**07/09/44**	**03/06/46**		**Sold 09/73**

Sailed from San Diego for Southwest Pacific on December 1944. After escorting from New Guinea to Leyte, operated under Philippine sea frontier. May to August 1945, operated with a HUK. Just prior to Japanese surrender, participated in search for midget subs.

PRATT	**DE-363**	**Consol**	**18/09/44**	**14/05/46**		**Scrapped 01/73**

Arrived Manus, Admiralties January 1945. CortDiv for New Guinea-Philippines convoys until May. That month to August, trained and escorted US and British submarines in Subic Bay and Northwest Luzon coast. Joined Korean occupation force at end of war.

ROMBACH	**DE-364**	**Consol**	**20/09/44**	**09/01/58**	**NRF 46-58**	**Sold 12/72**

Arrived Manus January 1945. January-March, convoyed Hollandia to Leyte. In May, served with Local Naval Defense Force among various Philippine Islands. Until end of war, operated in HUK group patrolling Leyte-Okinawa and North Luzon routes.

McGINTY	**DE-365**	**Consol**	**25/09/44**	**19/09/59**	**NRF 59-61**	**Sold 10/69**

Arrived Eniwetok January 1945. Next three months, escorted Eniwetok to Guam and Ulithi. Served as patrol ship at Ulithi and on additional convoys to Palaus and Okinawa in June-July. After war, screened minesweepers and aided evacuation of POWs.

A.C. COCKRELL	**DE-366**	**Consol**	**07/10/44**	**02/07/46**		**Target 09/69**

January 1945, arrived in forward Pacific area and screened convoys among Eniwetok, Guam, Saipan and Kossol Roads. In February, rescued crew of downed flying boat. Another air personnel rescue in March. In final month of war, patrolled isolated or by-passed Japanese garrisons. Joined with others in racing to rescue of *Indianapolis* crew.

FRENCH	**DE-367**	**Consol**	**09/10/44**	**29/05/46**		**Sold 09/73**

January-April 1945, engaged in convoys in forward areas. In May, assigned to air-sea rescue and local area screening. In June, bombarded Malakal and Arakabesan Islands. In July, took charge of rescue operations grounded army freighter in Palaus. In August, joined in search for *Indianapolis* survivors.

C.J. DOYLE	**DE-368**	**Consol**	**16/10/44**	**02/07/46**		**Target 1968**

Arrived Eniwetok March 1945. Engaged in local convoy escort, rescuing downed aviators. Bombarded by-passed Japanese garrison on Koror Island. In August, raced to rescue *Indianapolis* crew, the first to radio cruiser's loss. Rescued 93 survivors and gave last rites to 21. Last to leave the scene. Performed occupation duties after end of war.

JOHN C. BUTLER CLASS

SHIP	NUMBER	YARD	COMPLETED	DECOM	MODIFIED	DISPOSAL

T. PARKER DE-369 Consol 25/10/44 01/09/67 NRF Sold 07/68

Arrived Pearl Harbor January 1944. March-April, convoyed marine replacements for casualties on Iwo Jima and screened operating ships in that area. In May, joined ASW patrol in vicinity Peleliu. In June, shelled enemy installations at Koror Naval Base. Conducted convoys to Okinawa until war's end. One battle star.

J.L. WILLIAMSON DE-370 Consol 31/10/44 14/06/46 Sold 1970

Arrived Pearl Harbor January 1945. February-March, escorted supplies to assault on Iwo Jima and remained four days on ASW patrol. Arrived Majuro in March to spend three weeks inducing Japanese holdouts to surrender, employing psychology and shelling. Fired on shore batteries at Mili, Alu and other islands, taking scores of prisoners. In April, conducted ASW patrols at Ulithi. In July, convoyed to Eniwetok and Okinawa until end of war.

PRESLEY DE-371 Consol 07/11/44 20/06/46 Sold 1968

Arrived at Noumea in March 1945. Engaged in convoy operations among Leyte, Manus, Saipan and Ulithi until end of war. Performed post-war occupation duties.

WILLIAMS DE-372 Consol 11/11/44 04/06/46 Target 06/68

Information not readily available.

R.S. BULL DE-402 Consol 26/02/44 03/46 Target 06/69

Arrived Eniwetok June 1944 and escorted until August. Joined Task Force to support landings on Morotai in September and screened carriers as they attacked Leyte in October. During Battle off Samar, rescued 24 from *Suwanee (CVE-27)*, hit by a *kamikaze*. On 29 October, rescued 139 from *Eversole (DE-404)*, torpedoed and sunk by enemy sub. In January, screened carrier in Lingayen landings. Following month, screened carriers to Iwo Jima. April-June, escorted carriers with planes flying sorties against Okinawa. Operating under Philippine Sea Frontier, escorted among islands to war's end. See chapter *The Philippine Campaign*. Five battle stars.

R.M. ROWELL DE-403 Consol 09/03/44 02/07/46 Sold 1968

Arrived Pearl Harbor July 1944 and screened carriers to Solomons. In September, covered landings on Morotai. On 3 October, rescued survivors of *Shelton (DE-407)*, torpedoed by enemy sub. Later same day, mistakenly sank sub that proved to be *Seawolf (SS-197)*. Next covered carriers bombing Leyte landings. Attached to "Taffy One," witnessed first *kamikaze* attack of war and supplied medical aid to *Suwanee (CVE-27)*. Operated AA and ASW patrols, covering Lingayen landings in January. In February, guarded transports to Iwo Jima. March to war's end, convoyed within Philippines. See chapter *The Philippine Campaign*. Six battle stars.

EVERSOLE DE-404 Consol 21/03/44 Torpedoed

Arrived in Hawaii June 1944. Assigned to escort and antisubmarine duty in Manus-Eniwetok area. In August, she screened carriers to attack on Morotai, then in October, to the assault on Leyte. On 28 October, gained contact on submarine; hit by two torpedoes while going in on the attack. Sinking ship abandoned. Tremendous explosion killed or wounded most survivors in water. Two DEs rushed to rescue, one recovering survivors, the other sinking attacker, *I-45*. See chapter *The Philippine Campaign*. Two battle stars.

DENNIS DE-405 Consol 20/03/44 31/05/46 Sold 1973

On 12 October 1944, screened escort carriers in Leyte assault. On 25 October, took part in what is believed to have been the most dramatic destroyer escort action of the war, the Battle off Samar. Four DEs, three DDs and six "jeep" carriers stumbled into action with vastly superior enemy force of capital ships. Their stout defense convinced the enemy to withdraw. Rescued 434 survivors of *St Lo (CVE-63)*. At Okinawa on 4 May 1945, rescued 88 from *Sangamon (CVE-26)*. June to end of war, supported air strikes and screened convoys. See chapter *The Philippine Campaign*. Presidential Unit Citation. Four battle stars.

EDMONDS DE-406 Consol 03/04/44 31/05/46 Scrapped 15/05/72

Arrived Pearl Harbor June 1944. In August, reported to 7th Fleet and embarked *ComCortDiv 63*. Screened carriers attacking Morotai and Leyte. In December and January 1945, escorted carriers at Lingayan Gulf. With 5th Fleet, guarded carriers at Iwo Jima in February. Recovered 378 crew, including captain, from *Bismarck Sea (CVE-95)*; thirty heroic crew members went over the side in darkness and heavy seas to rescue men in water. Screened carriers to Okinawa in April before assigned to dangerous picket duty. Convoyed in forward areas to war's end. See chapter *Iwo Jima to Okinawa*. Five battle stars.

JOHN C. BUTLER CLASS

SHIP	NUMBER	YARD	COMPLETED	DECOM	MODIFIED	DISPOSAL
SHELTON	**DE-407**	**Consol**	**04/04/44**			**Torpedoed**

In July 1944, convoyed from Pearl Harbor to forward areas. In September, assigned to Morotai Attack Force. On 3 October, torpedoed by Japanese submarine *RO-41. Richard M Rowell (DE-403)* came alongside to evacuate crew when Commander Task Group ordered ship abandoned and to be sunk by gunfire. See chapter *The Philippine Campaign.* One battle star.

SHIP	NUMBER	YARD	COMPLETED	DECOM	MODIFIED	DISPOSAL
STRAUS	**DE-408**	**Consol**	**06/04/44**	**15/01/47**		**Target 1967**

On 24 June 1944 in Caribbean, attacked sound contact, observed oil and bubbles, but not conclusive. Arrived forward Pacific areas on 1 August; assigned to convoy screen and ASW patrol. Joined TF 38 in September. Rescued some Japanese from a raft. In October, convoyed among West Carolines, Palau, Peleliu and Anguar. Destroyed enemy swimmer group. March to end of war, convoyed to Okinawa. Three battle stars.

SHIP	NUMBER	YARD	COMPLETED	DECOM	MODIFIED	DISPOSAL
L.A. PRADE	**DE-409**	**Consol**	**20/04/44**	**11/05/46**		**Scrapped 01/72**

In September 1944, departed Pearl Harbor for Eniwetok. After escorting and patroling Eniwetok and Ulithi areas, sailed with HUK to Palaus to support their capture. In November, aided distressed seaplane. November 1944-March 1945, escorted to Leyte, Manus and Ulithi. Joined in attack on midget sub. March-June, escorted convoys to Okinawa. Escort and patrol operations to end of war. One battle star.

SHIP	NUMBER	YARD	COMPLETED	DECOM	MODIFIED	DISPOSAL
JACK MILLER	**DE-410**	**Consol**	**13/04/44**	**01/06/46**		**Sold 06/68**

Arrived Pearl Harbor July 1945 After intensive training, sailed in convoy escort to end of war. Engaged in numerous post-war occupational duties.

SHIP	NUMBER	YARD	COMPLETED	DECOM	MODIFIED	DISPOSAL
STAFFORD	**DE-411**	**Consol**	**19/04/44**	**16/05/46**		**Scrapped 03/72**

After various training assignments in Atlantic, headed for Pacific, arriving at Pearl Harbor July 1944. Served in convoys and HUK groups to November, then reported to 3d Fleet in December. In January 1945, sailed with TF 77, the Lingayen Attack Force. Intensive air attacks almost from beginning. While screening *Ommaney Bay (CVE-79* with two other DEs, splashed a *kamikaze* and was crashed by another in turn. Returned to US for repairs, reassigned to Okinawa in June. On 27 July, evaded air-dropped torpedo. Remained on picket and ASW patrol to end of war. See chapter *The Philippine Campaign.* Two battle stars.

SHIP	NUMBER	YARD	COMPLETED	DECOM	MODIFIED	DISPOSAL
W.C. WANN	**DE-412**	**Consol**	**02/05/44**	**31/05/46**		**Sold 06/68**

Arrived in Hawaii September 1944. In October, joined "Taffy Two" to cover Leyte landings. Weathered severe storm same month. On the 25th, screened carriers as planes raced to assistance of embattled ships off Samar. Heavy caliber shells landed close aboard. In November, endangered but not damaged by *Mount Hood (AE-10)* explosion. On 7 January, drove off two attacking aircraft at Mindoro while en route Lingayen Gulf as landing ship controller. Considerable AA action until departure. Arrived Okinawa screening station on 1 April. Withstood severe attacks and splashed one *kamikaze.* Departed Okinawa in June and assigned minesweeping operations in South China Sea till end of war. See chapter *Iwo Jima to Okinawa.* Four battle stars.

SHIP	NUMBER	YARD	COMPLETED	DECOM	MODIFIED	DISPOSAL
SAMUEL B. ROBERTS	**DE-413**	**Consol**	**28/04/44**			**Sunk 25/10/44**

Perhaps most renowned DE of WW II. Arrived Pearl Harbor August 1944. In October, assigned to 7th Fleet and proceeded toward Leyte in screen of Air Support Group off Samar. In total surprise, Task Group encountered powerful Japanese Fleet. Battleships and cruisers against DDs and DEs. In daring torpedo attack, probably scored one torpedo hit on cruiser and at least 40 hits from 5" battery on another cruiser. Battered by heavy caliber shells, she went down, leaving 120 survivors clinging to rafts 50 hours before rescue. See chapter *The Philippine Campaign.* Presidential Unit Citation. One battle star.

SHIP	NUMBER	YARD	COMPLETED	DECOM	MODIFIED	DISPOSAL
LeRAY WILSON	**DE-414**	**Consol**	**10/05/44**	**30/01/59**		**Scrapped 05/72**

Arrived Manus, Admiralties, and departed 12 October 1944 for Leyte invasion, escorting fabled "Taffy 2" carriers. Screened Admiral Stump's CVEs as they covered troop landings. December-January 1945, sailed with invasion force to Lingayen Gulf. On 10 January, splashed a *kamikaze* close aboard, but wing hit ship, killing six and wounding seven. After repairs, escorted convoys to Okinawa and joined picket operation. On 26 May, attacked midget sub. Two days later, splashed a *kamikaze.* To end of war, screened oilers and other logistics vessels in train of Halsey's carriers, blasting the Japanese homeland. See chapters. *The Philippine Campaign* and *Iwo Jima to Okinawa.* Four battle stars.

JOHN C. BUTLER CLASS

SHIP	NUMBER	YARD	COMPLETED	DECOM	MODIFIED	DISPOSAL
L.C. TAYLOR	**DE-415**	**Consol**	**13/05/44**	**23/04/46**		**Sold 1973**

Sailing from Pearl Harbor on 16 October 1944 with *Anzio (CVE-57)* HUK, contacted Japanese submarine after 14 hour search. Coordinated attack with two aircraft sank *I-41*. Weathered infamous Typhoon Cobra December 17-19. In January, sailed with 3d Fleet to cover Lingayen landings. February-March at Iwo Jima, guarded CVEs as they softened land resistance. Escorted attack ships to Okinawa. Accompanied Mitscher's carriers as they bombed Japan. Night of 15-16 July, sank Jap sub *I-13*. Continued 3d Fleet operations until Japanese surrender. See chapter *Pacific Antisubmarine Warfare*. Seven battle stars.

M.R. NAWMAN	**DE-416**	**Consol**	**16/05/44**	**30/08/60**	**NRF**	**Scrapped 07/72**

October 1945, escorted among Eniwetok, Marshalls, Ulithi, West Carolines. Weathered Typhoon Cobra off Philippines in December. February 1945, screened *Anzio (CVE-57)* as her planes bombed Iwo Jima. In March, redeployed to Okinawa where her gunners splashed two *kamikazes* in April. Until end of war, escorted in vicinity of Guam. See chapters *The Pacific Typhoons* and *Iwo Jima to Okinawa*. Four battle stars.

O. MITCHELL	**DE-417**	**Consol**	**14/06/44**	**24/04/46**		**Scrapped 03/72**

Arrived Ulithi November 1944. Conducted ASW sweeps ahead of TF 38 carriers as they headed for Mindoro. In January 1945, screening and plane guard duties for carriers in Formosa strikes and Lingayen landings. In February, screened carriers as they bombarded Iwo Jima targets. Continued screening carrier bombing at Okinawa March-June. To end of war, operated with carriers off Japanese coast. Five battle stars.

TABBERER	**DE-418**	**Consol**	**23/05/44**	**05/60**	**NRF**	**Scrapped 07/72**

October 1944, sortied Pearl Harbor with *Anzio (CVE-57)* HUK. Next two months, conducted ASW sweeps for 3d Fleet and covered TF 38 Luzon strikes, supporting Mindoro invasion. During 17-19 December, faced full force of Typhoon Cobra; on occasion, rolled to 72 degrees from vertical. In midst of maelstrom, courageously maneuvered to recover swimmers from three capsized DDs. In February, screened TF-38 in strikes on Iwo Jima; stayed in area to help repel air attacks. Operated 52 days at Okinawa without being attacked. Reassigned to *Anzio* HUK, operating ASW sweeps to end of war. See chapter *The Pacific Typhoons*. Four battle stars.

R.F. KELLER	**DE-419**	**Consol**	**17/06/44**	**21/09/59**	**NRF**	**Sold 1973**

Arrived at Pearl Harbor October 1944 and was assigned screen for 3d Fleet carriers until February 1945. Weathered vicious Typhoon Cobra 17-19 December, rescuing four crewmen from capsized *Hull (DD-350)*. Joined HUK in Philippine Sea and adjacent waters. In February, screened carriers at Iwo Jima. In March, acted as ASW and AA screen to and from Okinawa. In July, assisted *Lawrence C Taylor (DE-415)* in sinking Japanese sub *I-13*. See chapter *The Pacific Typhoons* and *Pacific Antisubmarine Warfare*. Battle stars not recorded.

L.E. THOMAS	**DE-420**	**Consol**	**19/06/44**	**03/05/46**		**Sold 09/73**

After one trip to Italy in September 1944, sailed to Manus, Admiralties, arriving in December. January-February 1945, escorted among Leyte, Manus and Hollandia. In March, patrolled Sulu sea lanes from Mindoro to Luzon. April-June, operated with Davao Gulf Resupply Echelon and Davao Gulf Attack Unit. Conducted bombardment missions. Covered Borneo and outer island landings to end of war. One battle star.

C.T. O'BRIEN	**DE-421**	**Consol**	**03/07/44**	**21/02/59**	**NRF**	**Sold 03/74**

August 1944 to April 1945, screened convoys among bases in forward areas. In May, covered landings at Davao with shore bombardment. Landed troops in Balut, Philippines in July. In August, screened convoys and aided redeployment of troops before returning to US.

D.A. MUNRO	**DE-422**	**Consol**	**11/07/44**	**24/06/60**		**Target**

October-December 1944, engaged in various Atlantic screening activities. January-May 1945, convoyed and supported naval and amphibious operations in the East Indies and the Philippines. May-July served in Borneo assault, escorting convoys and bombarding enemy emplacements. Operated in antisubmarine patrols to end of war. Three battle stars.

DUFILHO	**DE-423**	**Consol**	**21/07/44**	**14/05/46**		**Sold 1973**

After Caribbean tour and one Casablanca escort convoy, sailed to Pacific, arriving in forward area on February 1945. Operated in Philippine amphibious operations. At Leyte in December, possibly downed enemy plane. Engaged in shore bombardment and psychological warfare against by-passed Japanese-held islands to end of war. One battle star.

JOHN C. BUTLER CLASS

SHIP	NUMBER	YARD	COMPLETED	DECOM	MODIFIED	DISPOSAL

HAAS DE-424 Consol 02/08/44 31/05/46 Sold 12/73
Arrived Manus January 1945. Promptly entered operations among Japanese holdout islands. Provided fire support and shore bombardment to cover various landings in Philippines and East Indies. Returned to escorting in July. In August, just before Japanese capitulation, served as a dispatch ship with forces off China coast. Battle stars unclear from records.

CORBESIER DE-438 Fed Ship 31/03/44 02/07/46 Sold 12/73
October to December 1944, screened convoys in forward areas: Luzon, Saipan, Kossol Roads and Manus. On 23 January 1945, in consort with *Conklin (DE-439)* and *Raby (DE-698)*, sank Japanese submarine *I-48* off Yap. Supported fast carrier strike forces in Okinawa campaign and operated in picket line in June. Performed occupation duties after war's end. See chapter *Pacific Antisubmarine Warfare.* Two battle stars.

CONKLIN DE-439 Fed Ship 21/04/44 17/01/46 Sold 05/72
July to November, performed convoy and plane guard duty in forward Pacific areas. On 19 November, together with *McCoy Reynolds (DE-440)*, sent Japanese submarine *I-77* to bottom. In January 1945, as OTC with *Corbesier (DE-438)* and *Raby (DE-698)*), sank *I-48.* February to June 1945, screened logistics of TF 58 in Okinawa operation. On 5 June, heavily damaged in Okinawa typhoon; one killed, many injured, two washed overboard with only one rescued. Returned to US for repairs same month. See chapters *Pacific Antisubmarine Warfare* and *The Pacific Typhoons.* Three battle stars.

McCOY REYNOLDS DE-440 Fed Ship 02/05/44 07/02/57 Portugal Scrapped 1968
September 1944, escorted to Palaus and screened ships shelling Peleliu. On 25-26 same month, engaged submarine several hours with eleven depth charge and hedgehog attacks, finally sinking *RO-47.* October-November, escorted troopships and oilers refueling carriers bombing Luzon. On 19 November, with *Conklin (DE-439)*, sank Jap sub *I-37* after eight attacks. March to May 1945, escorted to Okinawa and aided stricken *Bunker Hill (CVE-17).* Weathered Okinawa typhoon on 5 June. ASW and AA patrols at Okinawa to war's end. See chapter *Pacific Antisubmarine Warfare.* Four battle stars.

W. SEIVERLING DE-441 Fed Ship 01/06/44 21/03/47 Scrapped 09/73
Arrived at Oahu September 1944. After intensive training, sortied with *Tulagi (CVE-72)* HUK. In January 1945, Task Group headed for Lingayen in support of TF 77. In February, screened 5th Fleet units to assault on Iwo Jima and swept approaches to battle area. In April, screened carriers pounding enemy at Okinawa. In May, assigned to picket duty and withstood numerous attacks. Splashed three *kamikazes.* June to end of war, guarded logistics and replenishment operations with 3d Fleet bombing Japanese home islands. See chapter *Iwo Jima to Okinawa.* Four battle stars.

U.M. MOORE DE-442 Fed Ship 18/07/44 22/05/46 Target 07/66
After refueling in Pearl Harbor end October 1944, joined *Corregidor (CVE-58)* HUK. Then with *Tulagi (CVE-72)* Group, swept Marianas-Palau area. January 1945, underway for assault on Lugayen Gulf. Was close aboard *Ommaney Bay (CVE-79)* when carrier was hit by *kamikaze*; she picked up four survivors. On 5 January, splashed an Oscar. Took off 57 crew from crashed *Stafford (DE-411).* Together with *Halligan (DE-584)*, splashed a Val on 6th. Splashed another by herself on 7th. Sank Jap sub *RO-115* night of 31 January-1 February. Screened carriers attacking Iwo Jima. Beginning March, 78 grueling days at Okinawa. June-July, screened 3d Fleet as it bombarded Japanese home islands. See chapters *Pacific Antisubmarine Warfare* and *The Philippine Campaign.* Five battle stars.

K.C. CAMPBELL DE-443 Fed Ship 31/07/44 31/05/46 Sold 11/73
Arriving Pearl Harbor October 1944, was assigned HUK with *Corregidor (CVE-58)* and patrol of Marianas and Western Carolines. Sortied in January 1945 with Lingayen invasion forces. In February, escorted carriers in Iwo Jima beaches. March-May, covered carrier strikes on enemy forces on Okinawa. In June, screened logistics group supporting carrier bombardment of Japanese home islands. ASW patrols in August to end of war. Four battle stars.

GOSS DE-444 Fed Ship 15/06/44 10/10/58 NRF Scrapped —
I On December, 1944, joined *Tulagi (CVE-72)* HUK. Sortied Kossol Roads for Lingayen Gulf January 1945. On the 5th, downed two *kamikazes* in fierce raid that hit several ships in Task Force. Continued to screen carrier group at Lingayen until 20th. February to June, operated with 5th Fleet, covering carriers in Iwo Jima assault. In early July joined TF 38 screen as capital ships and aircraft hit Japanese home islands. In late July, returned to HUK operations to end of war. See chapter *The Philippine Campaign.* Four battle stars.

JOHN C. BUTLER CLASS

<table>
<tr><th>SHIP</th><th>NUMBER</th><th>YARD</th><th>COMPLETED</th><th>DECOM</th><th>MODIFIED</th><th>DISPOSAL</th></tr>
<tr><td>GRADY</td><td>DE-445</td><td>Fed Ship</td><td>11/09/44</td><td>18/12/57</td><td>NRF</td><td>Scrapped —</td></tr>
<tr><td colspan="7">Arrived forward Pacific areas on December 1944. In January, served with logistics group of 3d Fleet. Screened escort carriers in pre-invasion bombardment of Iwo Jima. Got underway in March for invasion beaches of Okinawa. Together with Metcalf (DD-595), downed a kamikaze on picket station 16 April. Continued in that operation with one interruption to end of June. Then assigned to off-shore patrol in Philippines to end of war. See chapter Iwo Jima to Okinawa. Three battle stars.</td></tr>
<tr><td>C.E. BRANNON</td><td>DE-446</td><td>Fed Ship</td><td>01/11/44</td><td>18/06/60</td><td>NRF</td><td>Sold 10/69</td></tr>
<tr><td colspan="7">Arrived Manus March 1945 and operated in inter-island convoys. In May, convoyed assault forces to Tarakan, Borneo and covered troop advance with highly effective gunfire. Rendered similar support at Brunei Bay on 10 June. Continued convoys in last days of war and thereafter off China coast. One battle star.</td></tr>
<tr><td>A.T. HARRIS</td><td>DE-447</td><td>Fed Ship</td><td>29/11/44</td><td>27/07/46</td><td>NRF</td><td>Target 04/69</td></tr>
<tr><td colspan="7">Arrived in forward Pacific areas February 1945 and screened convoys and amphibious operations for next three months. Joined in feint at Morotai and covered landings at Zamboanga, Santa Cruz, Davao in Philippines and Brunei on Borneo. Convoyed to end of war. Two battle stars.</td></tr>
<tr><td>CROSS</td><td>DE-448</td><td>Fed Ship</td><td>08/01/45</td><td>02/01/58</td><td>NRF</td><td>Sold 03/68</td></tr>
<tr><td colspan="7">May to September, escorted convoys Ulithi to Okinawa. Shortly thereafter, returned to the US. One battle star.</td></tr>
<tr><td>HANNA</td><td>DE-449</td><td>Fed Ship</td><td>27/01/45</td><td>11/12/59</td><td>NRF</td><td>Sold 12/73</td></tr>
<tr><td colspan="7">Sailing from San Diego, arrived in Hawaii early May 1945. After intensive training, sailed to Eniwetok in June to join Marshall-Gilberts Surface Patrol and Escort Group until after Japanese surrender. Served in various occupation duties.</td></tr>
<tr><td>J.E. CONNOLLY</td><td>DE-450</td><td>Fed Ship</td><td>28/02/45</td><td>20/06/46</td><td></td><td>Target 02/72</td></tr>
<tr><td colspan="7">Arrived in Pearl Harbor for intensive training June 1945. Sailed to Eniwetok to assume escort duties in July. Screened logistic support units of 3d Fleet during final strikes on Japanese mainland. Assigned to occupation duties. One battle star.</td></tr>
<tr><td>GILLIGAN</td><td>DE-508</td><td>Fed Ship</td><td>12/05/44</td><td>31/03/59</td><td>NRF</td><td>Scrapped 03/72</td></tr>
<tr><td colspan="7">Arrived forward Pacific areas November 1944. On 17th, possibly damaged midget sub after torpedoing Mississinewa (AO-59). Escorted troop ships to Lingayan Gulf December-January 1945. On 12 January, crashed by a kamikaze, inflicting serious damage, raging fires, 12 dead and 12 wounded. Repaired in March, sailed to Okinawa and picket station. Splashed at least five planes and possibly damaged a submarine. On 27 May, Japanese torpedo bomber scored direct hit, but fortunately it was a dud. Spent remainder of war in convoy escort in Philippines and East Indies. See chapters The Philippine Campaign and Iwo Jima to Okinawa. Number of battle stars unclear from records.</td></tr>
<tr><td>FORMOE</td><td>DE-509</td><td>Fed Ship</td><td>05/10/44</td><td>07/02/57</td><td></td><td>Portugal -5/46</td></tr>
<tr><td colspan="7">Arrived Manus January 1945 in time for Lingayen Gulf assault. Subsequently, guarded minesweeping operations and convoyed to Leyte until March. Assigned to picket line in invasion of Panay. In May, sailed to Borneo with OTC embarked for landing operations. Repelled air attacks and engaged in four bombardment operations. June to end of war, escorted among Philippine and East Indian islands. Two battle stars.</td></tr>
<tr><td>HEYLIGER</td><td>DE-510</td><td>Fed Ship</td><td>24/03/45</td><td>20/06/46</td><td></td><td>Target 1969</td></tr>
<tr><td colspan="7">Arrived in Pearl Harbor from San Diego in June 1945. Departed for Guam after six weeks of training in Hawaii, arriving after Japanese surrender. Performed post-war duties in finding allied survivors as well as isolated Japanese soldiers.</td></tr>
<tr><td>E.H. ALLEN</td><td>DE-531</td><td>Boston</td><td>16/12/43</td><td>09/01/58</td><td></td><td>Sold 02/74</td></tr>
<tr><td colspan="7">This destroyer escort served the entire war as a schoolship for precommissioning escort vessels in Miami and Norfolk.</td></tr>
<tr><td>TWEEDY</td><td>DE-532</td><td>Boston</td><td>12/02/44</td><td>06/69</td><td>NRF</td><td>Target 05/70</td></tr>
<tr><td colspan="7">April 1944-April 1945, indoctrination cruises for officers and nucleus crews. Rescued six downed aviators. While preparing to join CortDiv 63, war ended.</td></tr>
</table>

JOHN C. BUTLER CLASS

SHIP	NUMBER	YARD	COMPLETED	DECOM	MODIFIED	DISPOSAL
H.F. CLARK	**DE-533**	**Boston**	**25/05/44**	**15/07/46**		**Sold 09/73**

After training in Hawaii, arrived at Manus December 1944 in time to join screen of carriers sailing to invasion of Lingayan Gulf. Arriving 3 January, experienced frequent *kamikaze* attacks. Next day, was attacked directly and splashed several enemy aircraft. Screened carriers and rescued downed U,S aviators during landing operations. In February, screened logistics and replenishment groups in attack on Iwo Jima. During Okinawa operation, screened convoys from Ulithi and refueling ships until June. Continued screening logistics and carriers striking Japanese home islands to end of war. See chapter *The Philippine Campaign.* Battle stars unclear from records.

SHIP	NUMBER	YARD	COMPLETED	DECOM	MODIFIED	DISPOSAL
SILVERSTEIN	**DE-534**	**Boston**	**14/07/44**	**30/01/59**		**Sold 12/73**

Arrived at Guam January 1944. In February, joined 5th Fleet logistics support for attack on Iwo Jima. Same month, sank vessel and captured six enemy soldiers. Assisted torpedoed *Patuxent (AO-44)* In March, convoyed to Okinawa. In July, released from 3d Fleet and returned to convoy duty to war's end. Two battle stars.

SHIP	NUMBER	YARD	COMPLETED	DECOM	MODIFIED	DISPOSAL
LEWIS	**DE-535**	**Boston**	**05/09/44**	**27/05/60**		**Target 03/66**

Arrived in Pearl Harbor on December 1944. Assigned to TF 38 and 3d Fleet. January 1945, conducted ASW operations. In February, assigned 5th Fleet for attack on Iwo Jima. Operated in Okinawa for duration of campaign. On 5 June, encountered Typhoon "Viper," sustaining some damage. Screened 3rd Fleet attacks on Japan, China mainland and Formosa. See chapter *Pacific Typhoons.* Three battle stars.

SHIP	NUMBER	YARD	COMPLETED	DECOM	MODIFIED	DISPOSAL
BIVEN	**DE-536**	**Boston**	**31/10/44**	**15/01/47**		**Target 07/69**

Arrived in Manus on March 1945. Spent entire time in convoy escort from Kossol Roads and Palau Islands to Leyte and from the Philippines to Okinawa later on. Patrolled Philippine Islands and made one trip to Hong Kong.

SHIP	NUMBER	YARD	COMPLETED	DECOM	MODIFIED	DISPOSAL
RIZZI	**DE-537**	**Boston**	**26/06/45**	**28/02/58**		**Scrapped 1974**

Completed shakedown day after cessation of World War II hostilities.

SHIP	NUMBER	YARD	COMPLETED	DECOM	MODIFIED	DISPOSAL
OSBERG	**DE-538**	**Boston**	**10/12/45**	**09/57**		**Scrapped 03/74**

Information not readily available.

SHIP	NUMBER	YARD	COMPLETED	DECOM	MODIFIED	DISPOSAL
WAGNER	**DE-539**	**Boston**	**22/11/45**	**03/60**		**Target 11/74**

Construction incomplete at end of war.

SHIP	NUMBER	YARD	COMPLETED	DECOM	MODIFIED	DISPOSAL
VANDIVIER	**DE-540**	**Boston**	**11/10/45**	**06/60**	**DER**	**Target 11/74**

War ended before ship completed. Converted to DER for post-war activities.

Appendix A – Destroyer Escort Losses

ATLANTIC

NAME	CAUSE	DATE
Fechteler	Submarine	5 May '44
Fiske	Submarine	2 Aug. '44
Frederick C. Davis	Submarine	24 Apr. '45
Holder	Air Attack	11 Apr. '44
Leopold	Submarine	9 Mar. '44
Rich	Mine	8 June '44

PACIFIC

NAME	CAUSE	DATE
Eversole	Submarine	29 Oct. '44
Oberrender	Air Attack	9 May '45
Samuel B. Roberts	Surface Action	25 Oct. '44
Shelton	Submarine	3 Oct. '44
Underhill	Submarine	24 July '45

Appendix B – Presidential Unit Citations

England (DE–635)	May 19-31, 1944 (Pacific)	Lt. Cdr. W. B. Pendleton
Bronstein (DE–189)	February 29-March 1, 1944 (Atlantic)	Cdr. S. H. Kinney
Task Group 22.11	February 26-April 19, 1944 (Atlantic)	Capt. J. B. Dunn
Bogue (CVE–9)		Capt. J. B. Dunn
Haverfield (DE–393) (F)		Cdr. T. S. Lank, ComCortDiv 51 Lt. Cdr. J. A. Mathews, U.S.N.R.
Swenning (DE–394)		Lt. R. E. Peek, U.S.N.R.
Willis (DE–395)		Lt. Cdr. G. R. Atterbury, U.S.N.R.
Hobson (DD–464) (until March 25)		Lt. Cdr. K. Loveland
Janssen (DE–396) (until April 7)		Lt. Cdr. H. E. Cross, U.S.N.R.
VC Squadron Ninety Five		Lt. Cdr. J. F. Adams, U.S.N.R.
Task Group 22.2	May 4-July 3, 1944 (Atlantic)	Captain. A. B. Vosseller
Bogue (CVE–9)		Captain. A. B. Vosseller
Haverfield (DE–393) (F)		Cdr. T. S. Lank, ComCortDiv 51 Lt. Cdr. J. A. Mathews, U.S.N.R.
Swenning (DE–394)		Lt. R. E. Peek, U.S.N.R.
Willis (DE–395)		Lt. Cdr. G. R. Atterbury, U.S.N.R.
Janssen (DE–396)		Lt. Cdr. H. E. Cross, U.S.N.R.
F. M. Robinson (DE–220)		Lt. Cdr. J. E. Johansen, U.S.N.R.
Task Group 22.3	June 4, 1944 (French West Africa)	Capt. D. V. Gallery, Jr.
Guadalcanal (CVE–60)		Capt. D. V. Gallery, Jr.
Pillsbury (DE–393) (F)		Cdr. F. S. Hall, ComCortDiv 4 Lt. Cdr. G. W. Casselman, U.S.N.R.
Pope (DE–134)		Lt. Cdr. E. H. Headland
Flaherty (DE–135)		Lt. Cdr. M. Johnston, Jr.
Chatelain (DE–149)		Lt. Cdr. D. S. Knox, U.S.N.R.
Jenks (DE–665)		Lt. Cdr. J. F. Way
VC Squadron 8		Lt. N. D. Hodson
Task Unit 77.4.3	October 25, 1944 (Samar, Philippines)	R. Adm. C. A. F. Sprague
Samuel B. Roberts (DE–413)		Lt. Cdr. R. W. Copeland, U.S.N.R.
Raymond (DE–341)		Lt. Cdr. A. F. Beyer, Jr., U.S.N.R.
Dennis (DE–405)		Lt. Cdr. S. Hansen, U.S.N.R.
John C. Butler (DE–339)		Lt. Cdr. J. E. Pace

Appendix C – Navy Unit Commendations

UNIT	DATE AND PLACE OF ACTION	COMMANDING OFFICER
Buckley (DE–51)	May 5-6, 1944 (Mediterranean)	Lt. Cdr. B. M. Abel, U.S.N.R.
John C. Butler (DE–339)	May 20, 1945 (Okinawa)	Lt. Cdr. J. E. Pace
F. C. Davis (DE–136)	Jan. 22-Feb. 23, 1944 (Anzio Campaign)	Lt. Cdr. R. C. Robbins, Jr., U.S.N.R.
Johnnie Hutchins (DE–360)	August 9, 1945 (Pacific)	Lt. Cdr. H. M. Godsey, U.S.N.R.
Herbert C. Jones (DE–137)	Jan. 23-Feb. 16, 1944 (Anzio Campaign)	Lt. Cdr R. A. Soule III, U.S.N.R.
Rall (DE–304)	April 12, 1945 (Okinawa)	Lt. Cdr. C. B. Taylor, U.S.N.R.
Richard W. Suesens (DE –42)	Oct. 20-Nov. 29, 1944 (Leyte Operation) Jan. 9, 1945 (Lingayen Gulf Landing) Jan. 31-Feb. 1, 1945 (Manila Bay-Bicol Operation) Mar. 26-April 4, 1945 } (Okinawa) April 15-April 22, 1945 }	Lt. Cdr. R. W. Graham, U.S.N.R.
Tabberer (DE–418)	Dec. 18, 1944 (Western Pacific)	Lt. Cdr. H. L. Plage, U.S.N.R.

Appendix D – Division Commanders

ATLANTIC FLEET

July 15, 1943... September 2, 1945

ComCortDiv 1 - Lt. Cdr. E. W. Yancey
ComCortDiv 2 -
Cdr. H. H. Connelley
Cdr. H. W. Howe
Cdr. R. P. Walker
ComCortDiv 3 -
Lt. Cdr. N. Adair, Jr.
Cdr. C. W. Musgrave
ComCortDiv 4 - Cdr. F. S. Hall
ComCortDiv 5 -
Cdr. C. M. E. Hoffman
Cdr. R. A. Fitch, U.S.N.R.
ComCortDiv 6 -
Capt. H. T. Read
Cdr. H. T. Chase
ComCortDiv 7 - Cdr. T. K.Dunstan, U.S.N.R.
ComCortDiv 9 -
Cdr. J. H. Forshew, U.S.N.R.
Cdr. E. W. Yancey
ComCortDiv 12 -
Cdr. H. T. Chase
Cdr. E. R. Perry
Cdr. A. B. Adams, Jr.
ComCortDiv 13 -
Cdr. F. D. Giambattista
ComCortDiv 15 -
Cdr. F. C. B. McCune
ComCortDiv 17 -
Cdr. R. N. Norgaard
Cdr. A. Wildner
ComCortDiv 18 - Cdr. S. C. Small
ComCortDiv 19 - Cdr. H. W. Howe
ComCortDiv 20 -
Cdr. J. Rountree, U.S.C.G.
Cdr. P. B. Mavor, U.S.C.G.
Lt. Cdr. W. B. Ellis, U.S.C.G.
ComCortDiv 21 -
Cdr. L. M. Markham, Jr.
Cdr. A. B. Adams, Jr.
Cdr. E. H. Headland, Jr.
ComCortDiv 22 -
Cdr W. W. Kenner, U.S.C.G.
Cdr. R. J. Roberts, U.S.C.G.
ComCortDiv 23 -
Cdr. E. J. Roland, U.S.C.G.
Cdr. F. P. Vetterick, U.S.C.G.
Cdr. J. H. Forney, U.S.C.G.
ComCortDiv 24 -
Cdr. C. T. S. Gladden, U.S.N. (ret.)
Cdr. C. G. McKinney, U.S.N.R.
ComCortDiv 35 -
Cdr. J. R. Litchfield, U.S.N.R.
ComCortDiv 45 -
Cdr. E. J. Roland, U.S.C.G.
Cdr. H. A. Loughlin, U.S.C.G.
Cdr. C. C. Knapp, U.S.C.G.
ComCortDiv 46 -
Capt. R. E. Wood, U.S.C.G.
Cdr. R. H. French, U.S.C.G.
ComCortDiv 48 -
Cdr. G. A. Parkinson, U.S.N.R.
ComCortDiv 51 - Cdr. T. S. Lank
ComCortDiv 52 - Cdr. C. R. Simmers
ComCortDiv 54 - Cdr. M. E. Dennett
ComCortDiv 55 -
Cdr. R. P. Walker
Cdr. W. A. Session, U.S.N.R.
ComCortDiv 56 -
Cdr. W. A. P. Martin, Jr.
Cdr. W. L. Harmon
ComCortDiv 57 -
Cdr. W. H. Kirvan
Cdr. T. G. Murrell, U.S.N.R.
ComCortDiv 58 - Cdr. E. E. Garcia
ComCortDiv 59 -
Cdr. A. W. Slayden
Cdr. L. S. Bailey, U.S.N.R.
ComCortDiv 60 - Cdr. H. Mullins, Jr.
ComCortDiv 62 - Cdr. J. F. Bowling, Jr.
ComCortDiv 66 -
Cdr. G. F. Adams, U.S.N.R.
Cdr. H. H. Connelley

Lt. Cdr. V. A. Isaacs, U.S.N.R.
ComCortDiv 67 - Cdr. F. G. Gould
ComCortDiv 71 - Cdr. E. W. Yancey
ComCortDiv 74 -
Cdr. C. F. Hooper, U.S.N.R.
ComCortDiv 76 - Cdr. C. M. Lyons, Jr.
ComCortDiv 77 -
Cdr. H. G. White, U.S.N.R.
ComCortDiv 78 -
Lt. Cdr. D. B. Poupeney, U.S.N.R.
ComCortDiv 79 -
Cdr. M. H. Harris, U.S.N.R.
ComCortDiv 80 - A. L. Lind, U.S.N.R.
ComCortDiv 85 -
Cdr. R. B. Randolph, U.S.N.R.

PACIFIC FLEET

July 20, 1943... October 1, 1945

ComCortDiv 7 -
Cdr. T. K. Dunstan, U.S.N.R.
ComCortDiv 8 -
Cdr. T. F. Fowler
Cdr. C. S. Kirkpatrick, U.S.N.R.
ComCortDiv 9 -
Cdr. E. W. Yancey
Cdr. E. C. Powell, U.S.N.R.
ComCortDiv 10 -
Cdr. J. L. Melgaard
Lt. Cdr. P. V. Walker, U.S.N.R.
Cdr. G. B. Coale, U.S.N.R.
Cdr. C. B. Henriques, U.S.N.R.
Cdr. W. H. Harrison, U.S.N.R.
ComCortDiv 11 -
Cdr. F. W. Schmidt
Lt. Cdr. H. E. Cross, U.S.N.R.
Cdr. H. E. Cross, U.S.N.R.
ComCortDiv 14 -
Cdr. L. F. Sugnet
Cdr. W. B. Pendleton
Cdr. R. McAfee, U.S.N.R.
ComCortDiv 15 -
Lt. Cdr. T. L. Bergen, U.S.N.R.
ComCortDiv 16 -
Cdr. F. L. Tedder
Cdr. J. B. Cleland, U.S.N.R.
Cdr. L. C. Mabley, U.S.N.R.
ComCortDiv 20 -
Lt. Cdr. W. B. Ellis, U.S.C.G.
ComCortDiv 22 -
Cdr. L. M. Thayer, U.S.C.G.
Lt. Cdr. V. E. Bakanas, U.S.C.G.
ComCortDiv 23 -
Lt. Cdr. J. H. Forney, U.S.C.G.
ComCortDiv 24 -
Cdr. C. G. McKinney, U.S.N.R.
ComCortDiv 26 -
Cdr. T. C. Thomas
Cdr. G. F. Davis, U.S.N.R.
Cdr. G. F. Adams, U.S.N.R.
ComCortDiv 27 -
Cdr. W. L. David, U.S.C.G.
ComCortDiv 28 - Cdr. W. S. Howard, Jr.
ComCortDiv 31 -
Cdr. J. D. McKinney
Lt. Cdr. J. G. Urquhart, Jr.
Cdr. C. A. Kunz, U.S.N.R.
ComCortDiv 32 -
Cdr. R. H. Groff, U.S.N.R.
Cdr. C. K. Hutchison
ComCortDiv 35 -
Capt. J. R. Litchfield, U.S.N.R.
Cdr. W. C. Hughes, U.S.N.R.
ComCortDiv 36 -
Cdr. R. D. Williams
Cdr. C. A. Kunz, U.S.N.R.
Cdr. R. D. Williams
Cdr. R. D. DeKay, U.S.N.R.
Cdr. R. H. Wanless, U.S.N.R.
ComCortDiv 37 -
Lt. Cdr. M. W. Firth
Cdr. W. H. Putnam, U.S.N.R.
ComCortDiv 39 -
Cdr. H. Hains
Cdr. R. R. Jackson, U.S.N.R.
Lt. Cdr. E. L. Holtz, U.S.N.R.
ComCortDiv 40 -
Cdr. L. M. Markham, Jr.
Cdr. C. A. Thorwall, U.S.N.R.
Cdr. F. W. Hawes
ComCortDiv 44 -
Cdr. E. C. Woodward
Lt. Cdr. W. B. Hinds, U.S.N.R.
ComCortDiv 47 - Cdr. W. L. Harmon
ComCortDiv 49 -
Lt. Cdr. R. E. Lockwood
Cdr. J. G. Urquhart, Jr.
Cdr. J. W. Golinkin, U.S.N.R.
ComCortDiv 51 - Cdr. T. S. Lank
ComCortDiv 53 -
Cdr. J. M. Fox, Jr., U.S.N.R.
ComCortDiv 55 -
Cdr. W. A. Sessions, U.S.N.R.
ComCortDiv 56 -
Cdr. W. D. Day, U.S.N.R.
ComCortDiv 57 -
Cdr. T. G. Murrell, U.S.N.R.
Cdr. D. H. Johnson, U.S.N.R.
ComCortDiv 58 - Cdr. E. E. Garcia
ComCortDiv 60 -
Cdr. E. E. Lull, U.S.N.R.
ComCortDiv 61 -
Cdr. H. Reich, U.S.N.R.
ComCortDiv 63 - Lt. Cdr. J. W. Bewick
ComCortDiv 64 -
Lt. Cdr. H. H. Love, U.S.N.R.
Cdr. H. H. Love, U.S.N.R.
Cdr. R. D. White, U.S.N.R.
ComCortDiv 65 -
Cdr. D. C. Brown, U.S.N.R.
ComCortDiv 67 - Cdr. F. G. Gould
ComCortDiv 69 -
Cdr. T. C. Phifer
Cdr. G. R. Keating, U.S.N.R.
ComCortDiv 70 -
Cdr. E. E. Pare
Cdr. R. Cullinan, Jr. (ret.)
ComCortDiv 71 -
Cdr. W. C. F. Robards
ComCortDiv 72 -
Cdr. H. H. Connelley
Cdr. A. Jackson, Jr., U.S.N.R.
ComCortDiv 73 -
Cdr. W. N. Putnam, U.S.N.R.
Cdr. P. L. Hammond, U.S.N.R.
Cdr. R. H. Groff, U.S.N.R.
ComCortDiv 74 -
Cdr. C. F. Hooper, U.S.N.R.
ComCortDiv 76 -
Cdr. L. M. King, U.S.N.R.
ComCortDiv 77 -
Cdr. H. G. White, U.S.N.R.
ComCortDiv 78 -
Lt. Cdr. D. B. Poupeney, *U.S.N.R.*
ComCortDiv 82 -
Cdr. W. C. Jennings, U.S.N.R.
ComCortDiv 85 - Cdr. R. B. Randolph, U.S.N.R.
ComCortDiv 86 - Cdr. J. F. Way
ComCortDiv 87 -
Cdr. W. C. P. Bellinger, Jr.
ComCortDiv 89 -
Cdr. R. J. Toner, U.S.N.R.

Appendix E – Conversions

DESTROYERS CONVERTED INTO DESTROYER - TRANSPORTS

MANLEY (APD–1)
LITTLE (APD–4)
GREGORY (APD–3)
STRINGHAM (APD–6)
COLHOUN (APD–2)
MCKEAN (APD–5)
SCHLEY (APD–14)
RATHBURNE (APD–25)
TALBOT (APD–7)
WATERS (APD–8)
DENT (APD–9)
TATTNALL (APD–19)
KILTY (APD–15)
WARD (APD–16)
ROPER (APD–20)
DICKERSON (APD–21)
HERBERT (APD–22)
CROSBY (APD–17)
CLEMSON (APD–31)
GOLDSBOROUGH (APD –32)
GEORGE E. BADGER (APD–33)
GILMER (APD–11)
KANE (APD–18)
HUMPHREYS (APD–12)
MCFARLAND (APD–26)
OVERTON (APD–23)
SANDS (APD–13)
WILLIAMSON (APD–27)
BARRY (APD–29)
BELKNAP (APD–34)
OSMOND INGRAM (APD–35)
GREENE (APD–36)
HULBERT (APD–28)
NOA (APD–24)

DESTROYER ESCORTS CONVERTED INTO DE - TRANSPORTS

CHARLES LAWRENCE (APD–37)
DANIEL T. GRIFFIN (APD–38)
GANTNER (APD–42)
GEORGE W. INGRAM (APD–43)
IRA JEFFERY (APD–44)
LEE FOX (APD–45)
AMESBURY (APD–46)
BATES (APD–47)
BLESSMAN (APD–48)
JOSEPH E. CAMPBELL (APD–49)
SIMS (APD–50)
HOPPING (APD–51)
REEVES (APD–52)
CHASE (APD–54)
LANING (APD–55)
LOY (APD–56)
BARBER (APD–57)
NEWMAN (APD–59)
LIDDLE (APD–60)
KEPHART (APD–61)
COFER (APD–62)
LLOYD (APD–63)
JOSEPH C. HUBBARD (APD–53)
HAYTER (APD–80)
SCOTT (APD–64)
BURKE (APD–65)
ENRIGHT (APD–66)
CROSLEY (APD–87)
CREAD (APD–88)
RUCHAMKIN (APD–89)
KIRWIN (APD–90)
KINZER (APD–91)
REGISTER (APD–92)
BROCK (APD–93)
JOHN Q. ROBERTS (APD–94)
WILLIAM M. HOBBY (APD–95)
RAY K. EDWARDS (APD–96)
ARTHUR J. BRISTOL (APD–97)
TRUXTUN (APD–98)
UPHAM (APD–99)
BARR (APD–39)
RINGNESS (APD–100)
KNUDSON (APD–101)
REDNOUR (APD–102)
TOLLBERG (APD–103)
WILLIAM J. PATTISON (APD–104)
MYERS (APD–105)
WALTER B. COBB (APD–106)
EARLE B. HALL (APD–107)
HARRY L. CORL (APD–108)
BELET (APD–109)
JULIUS A. RAVEN (APD–110)
WALSH (APD–111)
HUNTER MARSHALL (APD–112)
EARHART (APD–113)
WALTER S. GORKA (APD–114)
ROGERS BLOOD (APD–115)
FRANCOVITCH (APD–116)
ENGLAND (APD–41)
WITTER (APD–58)
BOWERS (APD–40)
JENKS (APD–67)
DURIK (APD–68)
YOKES (APD–69)
PAVLIC (APD–70)
ODUM (APD–71)
JACK C. ROBINSON (APD–72)
BASSETT (APD–73)
JOHN P. GRAY (APD–74)
JOSEPH M. AUMAN (APD–117)
WEBER (APD–75)
SCHMITT (APD–76)
FRAMENT (APD–77)
KLINE (APD–120)
RAYMON HERNDON (APD–121)
SCRIBNER (APD–122)
DIACHENKO (APD–123)
HORACE A. BASS (APD–124)
WANTUCK (APD–125)
BULL (APD–78)
BUNCH (APD–79)
BRAY (APD–139)
GOSSELIN (APD–126)
BEGOR (APD–127)
CAVALLARO (APD–128)
DONALD W. WOLF (APD–129)
COOK (APD–130)
WALTER X. YOUNG (APD–131)
BALDUCK (APD–132)
BURDO (APD–133)
KLEINSMITH (APD–134)
WEISS (APD–135)
CARPELLOTTI (APD–136)
DON. O. WOODS (APD–118)
BEVERLY W. REID (APD–119)
TATUM (APD–81)
BORUM (APD–82)
MALOY (APD–83)
HAINES (APD–84)
RUNELS (APD–85)
HOLLIS (APD–86)

Appendix F – Destroyer Tenders

October 1, 1941… October 1, 1945

MELVILLE
DOBBIN
WHITNEY
BLACK HAWK
ALTAIR
DENEBOLA
DIXIE
PRAIRIE
CASCADE
PIEDMONT
SIERRA
YOSEMITE
HAMUL
MARKAB
ALCOR

Appendix G – Destroyer Escorts Built For United Kingdom and Free French Fleets

UNITED KINGDOM

DESTROYER ESCORT	DATE TRANSFERRED	DESTROYER ESCORT	DATE TRANSFERRED	DESTROYER ESCORT	DATE TRANSFERRED
BAYNTUN (BDE–1)	*FEB. 13, 1943*	*DAKINS (DE–85)*	*NOV. 23, 1943*	*KEMPTHORNE (DE–279)*	*OCT. 31, 1943*
BAZELY (BDE–2)	*FEB. 18, 1943*	*DEANE (DE–86)*	*NOV. 26, 1943*	*KINGSMILL (DE–280)*	*NOV. 6, 1943*
BERRY (BDE–3)	*MAR. 15, 1943*	*EKINS (DE–87)*	*NOV. 29, 1943*	*LAWFORD (DE–516)*	*NOV. 3, 1943*
BLACKWOOD (BDE–4)	*MAR. 27, 1943*	*FITZROY (DE–88)*	*OCT. 16, 1943*	*LOUIS (DE–517)*	*NOV. 18, 1943*
BURGES (BDE–12)	*JUNE 2, 1943*	*REDMILL (DE–89)*	*NOV. 30, 1943*	*LAWSON (DE–518)*	*NOV. 25, 1943*
DRURY (BDE–46)	*APRIL 12,*	*RETALICK (DE–90)*	*DEC. 8, 1943*	*PAISLEY (DE–519)*	*NOV. 29, 1943*
1943		*HALSTEAD (DE–91)*	*NOV. 3, 1943*	*LORING (DE–520)*	*DEC. 5, 1943*
BENTINCK (DE–52)	*MAY 19 1943*	*RIOU (DE–92)*	*DEC. 14, 1943*	*HOSTE (DE–521)*	*DEC. 14, 1943*
BYARD (DE–55)	*JUNE 18, 1943*	*RUTHERFORD (DE–93)*	*DEC. 16, 1943*	*MOORSOM (DE–522)*	*DEC. 20, 1943*
CALDER (DE–58)	*JULY 15, 1943*	*COSBY (DE–94)*	*DEC. 20, 1943*	*MANNERS (DE–523)*	*DEC. 27, 1943*
DUCKWORTH (DE–61)	*AUG. 4, 1943*	*ROWLEY (DE–95)*	*DEC. 22, 1943*	*MOUNSEY (DE–524)*	*DEC. 31, 1943*
DUFF (DE–64)	*AUG. 23, 1943*	*RUPERT (DE–96)*	*DEC. 24, 1943*	*INGLIS (DE–525)*	*JAN. 12, 1944*
ESSINGTON (DE–67)	*SEPT. 7, 1943*	*STOCKHAM (DE–97)*	*DEC. 28, 1943*	*INMAN (DE–526)*	*JAN. 24, 1944*
AFFLECK (DE–71)	*SEPT. 29, 1943*	*SEYMOUR (DE–98)*	*DEC. 23, 1943*	*SPRAGGE (DE–563)*	*JAN. 14, 1944*
AYLMER (DE–72)	*SEPT. 30, 1943*	*CAPEL (DE–266)*	*AUG. 24, 1943*	*STAYNER (DE–564)*	*DEC. 30, 1943*
BALFOUR (DE–73)	*OCT. 7, 1943*	*COOKE (DE–267)*	*AUG. 30, 1943*	*THORNBOROUGH (DE–565)*	
BENTLEY (DE–74)	*OCT. 13, 1943*	*DACRES (DE–268)*	*AUG. 31, 1943*		*DEC. 31, 1943*
BRICKERTON (DE–75)	*OCT. 17, 1943*	*DOMETT (DE–269)*	*SEPT. 10, 1943*	*TROLLOPE (DE–566)*	*JAN. 10, 1944*
BLIGH (DE–76)	*OCT. 22, 1943*	*FOLEY (DE–270)*	*SEPT. 16, 1943*	*TYLER (DE–567)*	*JAN. 14, 1944*
BRAITHWAITE (DE–77)	*NOV. 13, 1943*	*GARLIES (DE–271)*	*SEPT. 20, 1943*	*TORRINGTON*	*JAN. 18, 1944*
BULLEN (DE–78)	*OCT. 25, 1943*	*GOULD (DE–272)*	*SEPT. 25, 1943*	*NARBROUGH (DE–569)*	*JAN. 21, 1944*
BYRON (DE–79)	*OCT. 30, 1943*	*GRINDALL (DE–273)*	*SEPT. 30, 1943*	*WALDEGRAVE (DE–570)*	*JAN. 25. 1944*
CONN (DE–80)	*OCT. 31, 1943*	*GARDINER (DE–274)*	*SEPT. 30, 1943*	*WHITAKER (DE–571)*	*JAN. 28. 1944*
COTTON (DE–81)	*NOV. 8, 1943*	*GOODALL (DE–275)*	*OCT. 11, 1943*	*HOLMES (DE–572)*	*JAN. 31, 1944*
CRANSTOUN (DE–82)	*NOV. 13, 1943*	*GOODSON (DE–276)*	*OCT. 16, 1943*	*HARGOOD (DE–573)*	*FEB. 7, 1944*
CUBITT (DE–83)	*NOV. 17, 1943*	*GORE (DE–277)*	*OCT. 22, 1943*	*HOTHAM (DE–574)*	*FEB. 8, 1944*
CURZON (DE–84)	*NOV. 20, 1943*	*KEATS (DE–278)*	*OCT. 28, 1943*		

FREE FRENCH

DESTROYER ESCORT	DATE TRANSFERRED	DESTROYER ESCORT	DATE TRANSFERRED
SENEGALAIS (DE–106)	*JAN. 2, 1944*	*MAROCAIN (DE–109)*	*FEB. 29, 1944*
ALGERIEN (DE–107)	*JAN. 23, 1944*	*HOVA (DE–110)*	*MAR. 18, 1944*
TUNISIEN (DE–108)	*FEB. 11, 1944*	*SOMALI (DE–111)*	*APRIL 9, 1944*

Reprinted, by permission, from Theodore Roscoe, *United States Destroyer Operations in World War II* (Annapolis, Md.: Naval Institute Press, 1953).

Appendix H – Abbreviations

AA — Antiaircraft
AD — Destroyer tender
AE — Ammunition ship
AFD — Floating dock
AH — Hospital ship
AKA — Attack cargo ship
AK — Cargo ship
AMc — Coastal minesweeper
AM — Minesweeper
ANL — Net laying ship
AO — Oiler, tanker
APA — Attack transport
APD — High speed transport, DE & DD hulls
AP — Transport
AR — Repair ship
ASW — Antisubmarine warfare
ATF — Fleet ocean tug
AT — Ocean tug
BB — Battleship
BDE — British destroyer escort
C.O. — Commanding Officer
CA — Heavy cruiser
CGC — Coast Guard Cutter
CIC — Combat Information Center
CinCLant FLT — Commander in Chief, Atlantic Fleet
CinCPac FLT — Commander in Chief, Pacific Fleet
CL — Light cruiser
CNO — Chief of Naval Operations
ComCortDiv — Commander Escort Division
ComCortRon — Commander Escort Squadron
ComDesDiv — Commander Destroyer Division
ComTransDiv — Commander Transport Division
Corsair — Marine Corps fighter aircraft
CortDiv — DE Escort Division
CortRon — DE Escort Squadron
CTF — Commander Task Force
CTG — Commander Task Group
CTU — Commander Task Unit
CV — Aircraft carrier
CVE — Escort carrier
DD — Destroyer
DE — Destroyer escort
DER — Radar picket escort ship
DesDiv — Destroyer Division
DesRon — Destroyer Squadron
DM — Destroyer minelayer
DMS — Destroyer minesweeper
GUS — Convoy U.S. to Mediterranean
HE — Heinkel fighter–bomber, German
HIJMS — His Imperial Japanese Majesty Ship
HMS — His or Her Majesty Ship (UK)
HMAS — His or Her Majesty Australian Ship
HMCS — His or Her Majesty Canadian Ship
HMNZS — His or Her Majesty New Zealand Ship
HUK — Hunter/Killer ASW
I — Japanese submarine
JU — Junkers fighter–bomber, German
K–Gun — Depth charge projector
LCI(L) — Landing craft, tank
LCI(M) — Landing craft, infantry, motor
LCI(R) — Landing craft, infantry, rocket
LCPL — Landing craft, personnel, large
LCRL — Landing craft, inflatable
LCSR — Landing craft, swimmer, recon
LCM — Merchandized landing craft
LST — Landing ship tank
LCVP — Landing craft personnel
LSD — Dock landing ship
P38, P40 — Army Air Force fighters
PBY — Amphibious Patrol Bomber
PC — Large subchaser (173')
PT — Motor torpedo boat
RAF — Royal Air Force
RO — Japanese submarine
SC — Subchaser (110')
SOPA — Senior officer present afloat
SacLant — Supreme Allied Commander Atlantic
Seabee - Construction Battalion
Sky II — Secondary control or bridge
TBS — Ship to ship radio
TF — Task Force
TG — Task Group
TU — Task unit
TransDiv — APD Transport Divison
UDT —Underwater demolition team
U — German submarine
UGS — Convoy Mediterranean to U.S.
VC — Aircraft squadron
YMS — Auxiliary minesweeper
YT — Harbor tug
Y- Gun — Depth charge projector

Appendix I – Publications Acknowledged

The author wants to acknowledge the following publications used in the preparation of this book.

Anderson, Peter. "Against All Odds." *The Boston Globe Magazine* (January 27, 1985).

Arnold, David. "The Final Hours of the U-853." *The Boston Globe*. Reprinted with permission.

Arnold, R.M.C. "Chesty". *Standby Arnold.*

Boland, Jack F. Ltjg. *Assignment Okinawa, The War Cruise of the USS Pavlic (APD-70)*. 1993.

Brust, Richard, Jr. "U-505 the Boarding Action." *DESA* (July – August 1983).

Carter, Glen. "Storm Shattered Convoy 119." *The Seattle Times*. Reprinted with permission.

Day, J. Edward. *An Unlikely Sailor.* West Virginia: McClain Printing Co.

Farago, Ladislas. "The Tenth Fleet. The 'Fleet' In Being." *DESA* (July – August 1983).

Lawrence, W.H. "Ryukyu Glory Won by Little Warships." *The New York Times* (June 29, 1945). Reprinted with permission.

Mio, Lou. "Ship Stories…" *The Plain Dealer* (December 13, 1989).

Norfolk Star Ledger, *Hit by Kamikaze*

O'Keefe, Joe. "Pre–World War II Home Front Jitters." *The Washington Times*. Reprinted with permission.

Pineau, Roger. *The Divine Wind.* Maryland: Naval Institute Press, 1953. Courtesy of Mrs. Roger Pineau.

Porter, Silvia. "The Great Nazi Gold Rush." *Colliers Magazine* (September 15, 1945).

"Pt. Judith Service Recalls Lives Lost at Close of WW II." *The Providence Journal Bulletin* (November 13, 1990). Reprinted with permission.

Roscoe, Theodore. *United States Destroyer Operations in World War II.* Maryland: Naval Institute Press, 1953. Reprinted with permission.

"Sharks Prove Jap Sub Hurt." *The Sunday Oregonian* (September 23, 1945).

Tashman, N.W., Jr. "Typhoon: The Ordeal of a Ship." *The New York Times* (April 22, 1945). Reprinted with permission.

"The Allies Turned the Corner 50 Years Ago." *St. Louis Post Dispatch.* Copyright © 1993. Reprinted with permission.

"The Guest of the Thunder Gods." *The Herald* (April 29, 1990). Monterey, California. Reprinted with permission.

Toner, R.J. Captain USN. "Typhoon – December – 1944." *Proceedings of the U.S. Naval Institute* (1976).

"When Death Lurked Beneath The Waves." *The Philadelphia Inquirer*. Reprinted with permission.

Appendix J – Shipmates

The following is a list of destroyer escort veterans of World War II who supplied this author with recollections, diaries or ship histories, including commanding officers whose action reports or war diaries were often basic to the narratives. The ship or activity covered is also indicated.

ABEL, BRENT *Buckley*
ADAMS, PAUL *Underhill*
ALBRECHT, RICHARD *Gustafson*
ALLEN, ELMO *Edgar G. Chase*
ARNOLD, R.M.C. (Chesty) *Swearer*
BAKER, F.J.T. *Carter*
BAKETAL, S.T. *Ramsden*
BARNARD, H.A. JR. *Rowell*
BENCHLEY, NATHANIEL *Underhill*
BERGEN, JOSEPH *Hayter*
BLACK, EDWARD *Rich*
BLUE, VICTOR *Holt*
BLUST, RICHARD JR. *U-505*
BOLAND *Pavlic*
BOSSIDY, B.H. *Sederstrom*
BRAUGHT, CHARLES F. *Crouter*
BREMER, T.G. *Evarts*
BRINKERHOFF, A.Q. JR. *Dickerson*
BRODIE, GEORGE W. *Fiske*
BROOKS, F.S., Jr. *Borum*
BROOKS, H.F. *Blessman*
BROUSSEAU, H.G. *Samuel S. Miles*
BULL, CARL E. *Gilligan*
BURDETT, L.C. JR. *Walter C. Brown*
BURGESS, K.F. JR. *Fleming*
BURGESS, ROBERT W. *Bangust*
BURROWS, J.S. JR. *Edmonds*
BUTLER, E.F. *Dobler*
BYRD, JOHN A. *Johnnie Hutchins*
CAIN, J.R. Jr. *Register*
CANULLA, FRANCIS *Mosely*
CAREY, W.J. JR. *Foreman*
CARINCI, JOSEPH *Hissem*
CARSON, M.V. *Leray Wilson*
CARTER, V.B. *Roper*
CASUCCI, C.C. *Farquhar*
CATON, C.E. *Goldsborough*
CHESTER, ALVIN P. *Cofer*
CLARK, WILLIAM P. *Fleming/Stern*
COAKLEY, ROLLINS W. *Savage*
CODY, H.S. *Decker*
COLE, PAUL E. *Huse*
COOK, JOHN Lawrence C. *Taylor*
CORNELL, W. GORDON *Paul G. Baker*
COSGROVE, JOHN P. *Gendreau*
COSMO, VITALE *Chase*
COWHERD, GRANT *Reuben James*
CRAFT, ARTHUR F. *Seid*
CRAIG, K. *Croatan* HUK
CRAIG, VOLNEY H. *Stafford*
CRAME, RAYMOND L. *Amesbury*
CRAMER, ROLAND H. *Riddle*
CRAMER, ROLAND H. *Rednour*
CRESAP, LOGAN JR. *Griswold*
CROCKER, D.S. *Fair*
CROCKER, J.C. *Coffman*
CRUTCHFIELD, A.R. *Buckley*
CULLINAN, RALPH JR. *Lawrence C. Taylor*
CURRY, J.B. *William C. Cole*
CYKLER, JOHN F. *Osterhaus*
CYKLER, JOHN F. *Crouter*
DAVIDSON, J.R. *Bostwick*
DAVIS, HANK *Bangust*
DAY, J. EDWARD *Fowler*
DE GIACOMO, HARVEY *Lloyd*
DEMPSEY, KENNETH *Melvin R. Nawman*
DI MILLA, SALVATORE J. *Escort Division 12*
DIGAETANO, FRANK A. *Haverfield*
DISHAROON, C.R. *Shelton*
DOHR, JOHN *Convoy GUS 38*
DOOLAN, RAYMOND *Charles J. Kimmel*
DOWDELL, JAMES S. *Shelton*
DUGAN, DARYL *Bangust*
DUHAIME, EDWARD J. *Holton*
DUNSTAN, D.K. *Knudson*
DUVALL, W.H. *Fechteler*
EBERT, JAMES D. *Dickerson*
EDWARDS, HOWARD D. *Baker*
EGIDI, LOUIS *Liddle*
EICHENBERG, GEORGE *Amesbury*
EMRICK, MICHAEL P. *Bates*
ESHEIM, ROBERT *Bangust*
FARAGO, LADISLAS *Tenth Fleet*
FARRAND, PHILIP D. *O'Neill*
FELDMAN, HERBERT *Lowe*
FIESEL, WILLIAM C. *Borum*
FINIGAN, VINCENT P. *Waterman*
FOREST, EDGAR H. *Johnny Hutchins*
FORREST, EDGAR H. *Lloyd*
FOSTER, E.P. JR. *Manlove*
FRANCIS, D.F. *William C. Miller*
FRASER, MALCOLM B. *Francis M. Robinson*
FROST, LEWIS R. *Bates*
FURNER, RICHARD A. *Menges*
GALLAGHER, DAN *Eversole*
GAMMELCARR, PETER N. *Lloyd*
GANTT, CLINTON L. JR. *Bronstein*
GIAMBATISTA, F.D. *Frost*

Lewis M. Andrews, Jr.

GILL, C.B. *Fechteler*
GLADSON, DON *Gustafson*
GLEIS, S.N. *Wyffels*
GODSEY, H.M. *Johnnie Hutchins*
GOWING, NED W. *Tatum*
GRAHAM, JAMES W. *Mason*
GRASEK, LOU *Seakay*
GREY, J.R. *Lawrence C. Taylor*
GRIGGS, WILLIAM L. *Kephart*
GRIMM, ZINN *Donaldson*
HALE, NORMAN *Donnell*
HAND, C.F. *Barry*
HANNA, RICHARD L. *Lough*
HARTMAN, F.C. *Elden*
HAY, S.M. *Peterson*
HELMINGER, JOSEPH *Joyce*
HEMENWAY, ROBERT D. *Lloyd*
HENRIQUES, CHARLES B. *Oberrender*
HERBIG *Buckley*
HERRMANN, GEORGE III *Witter*
HERTLE, I.E. *Dickerson*
HICKOX, PAUL M. *Thomas F. Nickel*
HIGGINS, J.W. JR. *Price*
HODGES, ALLEN *Horace A. Bass*
HOFMAN, H. *Finnegan*
HOLDEN, P.D. *Neal A. Scott*
HOLLAND, JAMES *Ringness*
HOWARD, L.G. *Dickerson*
HUEY, FREDERICK *Hayter*
HUGHES, J.N. *Barry*
HULL, E.E. Earl V. *Johnson*
HUNTINGDON, D. *Raymond*
HUNTLEY, IRA *Horace A. Bass*
IRVINE, J.M. *Kephart*
JACOBS, CHARLES *Sims*
JENCKES, W.D. *Gilmore*
JENKINS, CHARLES W. *Stafford*
JENSEN, CARL *Lough*
MATHEWS, JERRY A. *Haverfield*
JOHANSEN, J.E. *Francis M. Robinson*
JOLY, ALPHONSE *Amesbury*
JONES, HERBERT M. *Jobb*
JONES, WILLIAM A. *Gustafson*
JORDY, J.J. *Earl V. Johnson*
KARTHAS, NICHOLAS G. *Huse*
KEALLY, "BO" *Johnnie Hutchins*
KELLOGG, D.M. *Thomas*
KELLOGG, F.D. *Maloy*
KEYES, EDWARD J. *Hayter*
KIDD, THOMAS L. *Kenneth M. Willett*
KILEY, JOHN C. JR. *Stanton*
KING, FRANCIS R. *Grady*
KINNEY, SHELDON H. *Bronstein*
KINSLEY, F.W. *Lawrence C.Taylor*
KINSLEY, F.W. *Melvin R. Nawman*
KIRKPATRICK, C.S. *Goss*
KOSSOFF, JEAN *Rich*
KRAUSE, JAMES T. *Fleming*
LABEDIS, JOSEPH C. *Stanton*
LAMPE, JOHN *Reuben James*
LANIER, WILLIA M.D. *England*
LAPHAM, HAROLD A. *Bangust*
LAWSON, GEORGE T. JR. *Ulvert M. Moore*
Le BOUTILLIER, PHILIP JR. *Blessman*
LIGHT, LYLE A. *Leray Wilson*
LOVE, H.H. *Barr*
LOWE, ALLEN E. *John J. Powers*
LOWE, JOSEPH *Bates*
LOWE, W.W. *Hissem*
LYNCH, WALTER F. *Fleming*
MABLEY, L.C. *Hubbard*
MAHONEY, JOSEPH *Maloy*
MAKI, EDWARD K. *Holder*
MARKHAM, CHARLES *Samuel S. Miles*
MAYNARD, AL *Manlove*
McCABE, F.M. *Menges*
McCLEES, H.C. *Cofer*
McGARITY, JAMES (MOE) *Horace A. Bass*
McGIBBON, E.L. *Conklin*
McGRAW, DONALD C. Jr. *McClelland*
McLENDON, ROY L. JR. *Ringness*
McMAHON WILLIAM A. *Bright*
McNULTY, WILLARD J. *Hopping*
McQUILKEN, MILFORD *Richard W. Suesens*
MEEHAN, W.J. *Goldsborough*
MENDEZ, J.D. *Amesbury*
MEYER, ROBERT *W.C. Miller*
MILLER, D.C. *Howard F. Clark*
MILLER, J.M. *Breeman*
MONTAGUE, ROBERT W. *Loy*
MORGAN, WILLIAM *Holt*
MORRIS, S.F. *Fowler*
MORRIS, WILLIAM T. JR. *Wilhoite*
MYHRE, L.A. *Varian*
NORTHCUTT, JAMES W. *Haverfield*
NOSCH, VINCENT *Buckley*
NOVOTNY, RICHARD *Leopold*
O'KEEFE, JOSEPH D. *Borum*
O'KEEFE, JOSEPH JR. *Gendreau*
PALMER, WALTER *Ramsden*
PARKER, E.P. *Wyman*
PAYNTER, R.B. *Gendreau*
PERCER, O.G. "TEDDY" *Sims*
PHIPPS, SHIRLEY *Kenneth M. Willett*
PICKELS, WAYNE *U-505*
PLACZEC, WILLIAM F. *Herbert C. Jones*
POMA, NICHOLAS *Lawrence C. Taylor*
PORTER, SYLVIA *Polish Gold*
POWERS, WILLIAM *Ulvert M. Moore*
READ, K.E. *Tinsman*

REITH, HERBERT *Menges/Holder/Joyce*
REYNOLDS, FRANK J. *Chaffee*
ROBERGE, WALTER L. *Swearer*
ROBERTS, LEONARD J. *Haverfield*
ROBERTSON, JOHN *Samuel S. Miles*
ROHNKE, O.C. *Savage*
ROOSEVELT, F.D. JR. *Ulvert M. Moore*
ROTH, E.B. *Wilhoite*
ROULET, JOHN *Bangust*
RUMENS, WILLIAM *Scott*
SALOMAN, G. LEWIS *Shelton*
SANDERS, HANK *Chase*
SANKER, WALTER Z. *Amesbury*
SAPP, MITCHELL E. *Fessenden/Farquhar*
SCARBOROUGH, GEORGE *Snowden*
SCHMIDT, EJLIF *Shelton*
SCHOENROCK, O.A. "ROCKY" *Inch*
SCHRADER *CortDiv 12*
SCHREIBER, ALFRED *Ricketts*
SEARS, HENRY *Wesson*
SEDORY, JOHN *Crouter*
SELLERS, GEORGE W. *Joyce*
SENOFF, DAN *Earl V. Johnson*
SESSIONS, W.A. *Gandy*
SHAMBROOM, WILLIAM D. *Blessman/Strickland*
SHOVAN, JOHN *Otter*
SILEO, RAY *Reeves/Seakay (tanker)*
SIMON, GEORGE W. *Mosley*
SLOCUM, WILLARD W. *Maloy*
SMITH, ARCHIBALD F. *Sims*
SMITH, PAUL H. *Lough*
SPENCER, SAMUEL *Oberrender*
SPINNER, LEN *Marchand*
STAFFORD, J.H. *Natchez*
STAHLE, J.H. *Waterman*
STEDMAN, JOHN W. JR. *Walter C. Wann*
STEEL, FRANCIS P. *Riddle*
STEINBERG, HARRY *Underhill*
STEWART, WILLIAM K. *Gilligan*
STOCKTON, JAMES E. *Earl V. Johnson*
STOREY, FREDERICK G. *Charles J.Kimmel*
STREET, GORDON *Donnell*
SULLIVAN, E.D. *Neal A. Scott*
SULLIVAN, RAY *Rowell*
SVITAK, FLORIAN R. *Moore*
SWEITZER, ROBERT C. *Keith*
TASHMAN, N.W. JR. *Waterman*
TAYLOR, C.B. *Rall*
TAYLOR, WILLIAM R. *Lloyd*
THORN, DONALD *McClelland*
TURNER, BLANEY C. *Lough*
VICK, JAMES John C. *Butler*
VILLANELLA, JOSEPH T. *Chatelain*
VIRUM, JOHN A. *Gendreau*
WALDRON, RICHARD *Sims*
WELCOME, LEIGH H. *Cofer*
WEPMAN, E.R. *Smartt*
WHITBECK, F.P. *Edmonds*
WHITELY, ROBERT Q. *Wilhoite*
WILBER, ARTHUR B. *Amesbury*
WILLIAMS, G.D. *McClelland*
WILLIAMS, VERGLE E. JR. *Wesson*
WILLIAMSON, JOHN A. *England*
WILMERDING, HENRY A. JR. *Bates*
WORTH, GEORGE W. *Crouter*
YOUNG, JOSEPH L. *Blessman*
YOUNG, WARREN *Leopold*

Index

Page numbers followed by *i* refer to illustrations.